▶ **Human Social Behavior**
Concepts and
Principles
of Sociology

# Human Social Behavior

## Concepts and
## Principles
## of Sociology

Gordon J. DiRenzo

University of Delaware

HOLT, RINEHART AND WINSTON   FORT WORTH   CHICAGO
SAN FRANCISCO  PHILADELPHIA  MONTREAL  TORONTO  LONDON  SYDNEY
TOKYO   MEXICO CITY   RIO DE JANEIRO  MADRID

**Publisher:** Ted Buchholz
**Acquisitions Editor:** Chris Klein
**Project Management:** Editing, Design & Production
**Production Manager:** Kenneth A. Dunaway
**Art & Design Supervision:** Editing, Design & Production
**Text Designer:** Donald W. Shenkle
**Cover Design:** Hannus Design Associates
**Cover Photograph:** Greg Pease

*Address for editorial correspondence:*
Holt, Rinehart and Winston, Inc., 301 Commerce Street, Suite 3700, Fort Worth, Texas 76102

*Address for orders:*
Holt, Rinehart and Winston, Inc., 6277 Sea Harbor Drive, Orlando, Florida 32887.
1-800-782-4479, or 1-800-433-0001 (in Florida)

Printed in the United States of America

0   1   2   3   049   9   8   7   6   5   4   3   2   1

ISBN 0-03-032447-5

**Library of Congress Cataloging-in-Publication Data**

DiRenzo, Gordon J.
   Human social behavior: concepts and principles of sociology/
  Gordon J. DiRenzo.—1st ed.
     p.   cm.
   Includes bibliographical references.
   ISBN 0-03-032447-5
   1. Sociology.    I. Title.
  HM51.D54    1990
   301—dc20                     90-30904
                                                   CIP

For My Children

**Maria Giulia**
**Chiara Veronica**
**Marco Santo**

with whom I share,
and from whom I learn,
the complexities, challenges, and joys of
human social life

# About the Author

**Gordon J. DiRenzo, Ph.D.,** is Professor of Sociology at the University of Delaware in Newark, Delaware. He is certified as a social psychologist and sociologist by the American Sociological Association, and serves as a consultant to a variety of agencies and organizations.

Professor DiRenzo received his undergraduate and graduate degrees from the University of Notre Dame, and also undertook graduate and postdoctoral studies at Harvard University, Columbia University, and the University of Colorado. His fields of specialized interest and research are social psychology, personality psychology, social psychiatry, personality and social systems, political psychology, and the epistemology of the behavioral sciences.

Dr. DiRenzo has been a member of the faculty of several colleges and universities, including Indiana University, Fairfield University, the University of Portland (Oregon), the State University of New York (Stony Brook and Cortland), the University of Notre Dame, and Brooklyn College of the City University of New York. He is also an affiliate member of the medical staff of the Medical Center of Delaware and Saint Francis Hospital (Wilmington) in their respective Departments of Psychiatry.

Professor DiRenzo is the author or co-author of numerous articles and other books in the fields of sociology and psychology, including *Personality and Society* (Ginn Press); *We the People: American Character and Social Change* (Greenwood Press); *Personality and Politics* (Doubleday); *Concepts, Theory, and Explanation in the Behavioral Sciences* (Random House); and *Personality, Power, and Politics* (University of Notre Dame Press).

Dr. DiRenzo has studied, lectured, and traveled extensively in foreign countries. He has served as Senior Fulbright-Hays Professor at both the University of Rome and the University of Bologna in Italy. He is listed in several biographical references, including *Who's Who in America, Who's Who in American Education, American Men and Women of Science, Contemporary Authors,* and *Who's Who in the World.*

# Brief Table of Contents

▼

# Complete Table of Contents ▼

xii

PART TWO  **The Social Individual**  83

xv

▼

# PART FIVE Social Dynamics 517

▼

xix

# Lists of Boxes, Tables, and Figures ▼

## TABLES

▼

xxiii

▼ FIGURES

xxiv

▼

xxv

# Acknowledgments

One of the most pleasant tasks in the writing of this text is to offer an expression of gratitude to the people who have played a role in its production. They are many, and the importance of their contribution far exceeds the all-too-brief recognition that I am able to make here.

Particular thanks, however, go to Inez Cook, Carol Andersen, Judy Watson, Anna Wu, and Tracy Brogdon who prepared various segments of the manuscripts for this project; Karen Page, Christine Steele, and Tricia Falcone who provided assistance in bibliographical searches; Kurt Cylke who drafted the chapter summaries; Dana Zeidler who assisted in the preparation of the glossary; Michael Klausner with whom many discussions were held about the nature and content of an introductory text, and who had drafted preliminary materials for selected chapters of an earlier project of this type; Elsa Peterson for assistance in the selection of photographs; Martha Cameron who contributed to the copyediting process; and Lizette Starr, Sally Rooney, Rene Pelham, and James Wright, who assisted in the preparation of the ancillary materials.

The text has benefited from the evaluation and constructive criticism offered by several colleagues who reviewed the manuscript at various stages of its development and made many valuable suggestions for its improvement. It is a pleasure to acknowledge in particular the following among these scholars: Eugene Fappiano, Southern Connecticut State University; Barbara Illardi, University of Rochester; Samuel Z. Klausner, University of Pennsylvania; Richard Lamanna, University of Notre Dame; Lauren Langman, Loyola University (Chicago); Lloyd Leuptow, University of Akron; Stephen Spitzer, University of Minnesota; and Joseph Ventimiglia, Memphis State University.

My students at the University of Delaware, with whom the book was pretested over several semesters, offered many helpful suggestions on content and design.

All of the fine people at Holt, Rinehart and Winston deserve my appreciation for the keen interest and highly professional skills that they have contributed to this project. Among these many individuals I offer a special word of gratitude to Christopher P. Kline, Acquisitions Editor, for his foresight, cooperation, and patience at each stage; and to Stacy S. Emerick, Editorial Assistant, for her good cheer and efficiency in every respect. All of the staff at Editing, Design & Production in Philadelphia have my thanks for their efforts in the production process.

My greatest debt, as always, is owed to my wife and children whose interest and patience have provided the indispensable motivation for executing a project that has required a long period of sacrifice and tolerance on their part. To them, and for them, I dedicate this labor of love.

GORDON J. DIRENZO
NOVEMBER 1989

# Note to the Student

This textbook has been produced primarily for you. Efforts have been focused on writing with a style that challenges your intellect, stimulates your curiosity, and rewards your attention. The fundamental objective here has been to provide you with a fund of sociological knowledge that will survive beyond the final examination at the end of the semester and endure for the better part of a lifetime.

A number of study aids are provided in the text in an effort to facilitate the mastery of its content. You are strongly urged to make good use of these features, which are briefly described here.

1. *Prologues.* Each part of the text, as well as each chapter within the part, begins with a brief prologue that offers a very general description of what is to follow. These prologues are written with continuity in order to underscore the logical order and sequence of the various subdivisions of the text, and thereby to make for a cohesive and synthetic presentation.
2. *Outlines.* At the beginning of each chapter, the reader will find a detailed outline that is intended to provide an overview of the contents of the chapter and to highlight major topics and subtopics. These outlines can serve also as a very useful tool for reviewing the material.
3. *Key Concepts.* Within each chapter, key concepts are placed in bold-face type and defined as they initially appear. All of these concepts appear again in list form at the end

of the respective chapter. Such a listing is provided as another tool which should be used for reviewing the principal contents of each chapter.

4. *Boxed Readings.* Numerous topics have been selected for special treatment and presented in a series of boxes throughout the text. These many boxes, for the most part, elaborate on a number of controversial issues, either in contemporary society or in the field of sociology today. A few of these boxes are in the form of excerpts from books and newspapers which provide examples and descriptions of topics that are discussed.
5. *Graphics.* A large number of different kinds of graphic material—tables, figures, photographs, and cartoons—have been incorporated into the text. Each graphic has been carefully selected and designed either to illustrate one or more key concepts or to provide supplementary material for a more concrete understanding of a particular topic.
6. *Glossary.* At the end of the textbook, there is a glossary that contains over 500 entries of key concepts and their definitions. It contains definitions for all of the key concepts indicated in the text as well as a number of other basic terms in the field of sociology. This glossary, in addition to being a valuable aid for study, is designed to help the student to build a strong sociological vocabulary.
7. *Chapter Summaries.* Each chapter concludes with a summary statement that capsulates and highlights the major points and issues of each chapter.

▼   8. *Bibliography*. Nearly 1100 articles and books are included in the bibliography that can be found at the end of the text. These references, with complete bibliographical information, comprise a convenient resource for both classical and contemporary materials in the field of sociology and related disciplines.

These many study aids have been incorporated to make the use of this text, along with the study of sociology, an efficient, effective, and pleasant activity. My hope is that you will relate to this text in a highly individual fashion, so that not only will you discover sociology to be an informative and exciting discipline, but one in which you also can find a significantly personal meaning.

# Note to the Instructor ▼

This text is designed to provide a comprehensive and contemporary understanding of the field of sociology. Such a goal is not only ambitious and demanding, but also one that requires a somewhat distinctive perspective.

The majority of introductory texts in the field of sociology are hybrids of descriptions of American society and analyses of social problems. This text does not adopt such an approach. It is intended to be a scientific text on human social behavior which, while universal in perspective and cross-cultural in presentation, is exemplified chiefly through the structure and dynamics of the American society.

## Content and Organization

Treatment of the fundamental knowledge of sociology offered herein is rigorous, extensive, and timely. Much more coverage is given to individual topics than is usually the case in introductory texts. Particularly thorough treatments are provided on the topics of socialization and personality. The latter topic, moreover, is treated in several of the substantive chapters in conjunction with the analyses of various types of social structure and human social behavior.

Classic and contemporary literature in the field of sociology and related disciplines is judiciously balanced and cohesively integrated. A special effort, moreover, has been made to provide the latest empirical findings and up-to-date documentation from resources in the various fields of the social sciences.

The comprehensive treatment of topics and the methods of presentation permit the instructor to be selective of material in terms of personal interests and special requirements. Partly because of its extensive coverage as well as its pedagogical format, this text does not require auxiliary materials, such as a reader or study guide. Of course, the instructor may choose to complement the text with microcomputer software and audiovisual materials.

This text consists of fourteen chapters that are organized into five parts. These divisions are intentionally designed, and ones which will lend themselves, realistically and ideally, to the structure of the academic calendar.

Part One provides an introduction to the field of sociology—its development, current orientations, and methodology. Part Two focuses on the nature and development of the social individual, with chapters on culture, socialization and social learning, and personality and the self. Part Three explores the nature of social organization and discusses the basic principles of social structure and three types of social systems, moving from the macro-level of analysis to that of micro-analysis. Individual chapters are devoted to society, including social institutions, demography and ecology, complex organizations and bureaucracies, and social groups. Part Four focuses on social differences with chapters on social stratification and minority-majority relations. Part Five on social

▼

dynamics deals with collective behavior, deviant behavior, and social change and explores the nature, directions, and implications of social change.

## Ancillary Materials

**xxxii**

A set of ancillary materials, prepared by the author, is available to accompany this text.

1. *Instructor's Manual.* A concise *Instructor's Manual* contains the following elements for each chapter: introductory statement, outline, list of key concepts, summary, and discussion questions. For each of the five parts of the text there is a prologue statement that is intended to provide a measure of continuity and synthesis for the fourteen chapters and the many topics that they treat. Included in the *Instructor's Manual* as well is a glossary which, containing more than 500 entries, is somewhat of a minidictionary in itself.
2. *Test Banks.* An extensive file of test questions that are directly related to our text contains 2200 items. Four types of questions have been prepared for each chapter: multiple-choice, complete-the-blank, true-false, and essay. The *Test Bank* is offered by the publisher in both print and software formats. The latter, known as *ExaMaster*™, is supplied on diskette for use with IBM, Apple II, and MacIntosh microcomputers.

    *ExaMaster*™, a highly simplified, versatile, and powerful computer program, combines the additional capabilities of randomly generating tests within parameters specified by the instructor or of permitting instructors to create and/or to edit their own tests. Another significant feature of this program is that users can modify or supplement the *Test Bank*, or add graphics and statistical or mathematical notation of their choice.

The publisher also provides a customized test construction service, known as *Request Test*™, for instructors using *Human Social Behavior.* Exams can be generated within forty-eight hours and dispatched either by mail or FAX.

3. *Lecture Tools.* A set of color transparency masters, for use in the classroom with overhead projectors, is available from the publisher. Included in these generic materials are many tables and figures that have been drawn from *Human Social Behavior.* Another lecture aid, provided in the *Instructor's Manual* and the *Test Bank*, consists of a series of essay questions for each chapter which can be used for class discussions and review sessions.
4. *Microcomputer Tools.* A number of software packages of a generic nature are compatible with *Human Social Behavior.* These tools, which can be used in lieu of workbooks and study guides, provide interactive programs that can be utilized for classroom demonstrations of hypothesis testing and to provide "hands-on" experience for sociological analysis. These materials and their sources are described more fully in the *Instructor's Manual.*

## Pedagogical Features

Several pedagogical aids which have been incorporated into the text for the benefit of the student should be equally profitable for the instructor. These features are described briefly in the preceding *Note to the Student.*

A textbook is never finished. Knowledge accumulates continuously—and, in this day and age, more and more rapidly. Even as this is being written, some of the knowledge presented in the following pages is becoming obsolete. There exists, thus, the perpetual need for revision. Such is no less the case with the volume in hand. This book, along with its ancillary materials, represents only the latest stage of a long-evolving text with a rather unique focus: a psychosocial perspective that attempts to provide an analysis of human social behavior as the product of the dynamic interrelationship between social systems and personality systems. Its development, in large part because of its unique focus, has been a very lengthy process, and one that continues with refinement on a daily basis. The book will have achieved its fundamental objectives, nonetheless, if the student and the instructor come away from reading and using this textbook with the high level of challenge and excitement with which its writing and production were undertaken.

▼

**xxxiii**

# Preface

▼

The purpose of this text is to acquaint the student with the nature, objectives, concepts, theoretical approaches, research methods, empirical findings, and principles of the field of sociology which is concerned with human social behavior.

Sociology, however much and rightly called the science of human groups or society, is essentially about the behavior of people. Franklin H. Giddings, an early American sociologist, described the field as one concerned with "the subject matter of the psychology of society, otherwise called sociology." Our text is written in this perspective of "psychosociology" which attempts to understand human behavior as the interactive product of both social forces and psychological forces.

Human behavior is unlike any other phenomena studied by science. There is a subjective dimension to the human being that is both a very unique and a very vital part of human nature and which, accordingly, cannot be ignored in the study of human social behavior. A complete, indeed even an adequate, explanation of social phenomena needs to include an understanding of those subjective dimensions existing within the people who are the agents of social phenomena. Such a sociopsychological perspective, we believe, makes for a more comprehensive and a more valid presentation of sociology.

One of the fundamental questions of sociology has been the nature of the relationship between the individual and society. In his seminal writings for what was to become the science of sociology, its founder, Auguste Comte (1798–1857), was concerned with the problem of how the individual is both the product and the producer of society. Sociology, as the study of human social behavior, must concern itself of necessity with the nature and dynamics of the individuals who are the agents of social behavior. As another sociologist, Charles H. Cooley (1864–1929), has written, "A separate individual is an abstraction unknown to experience and so likewise is society when regarded as something apart from individuals." Sociology for too long, however, and yet today in many quarters, has concentrated exclusively on explaining the nature, structures, and dynamics of society. While presupposing the existence of individuals for both the functions and the explanations of society, too little attention has been given to the individual who is the agent of society.

## A Personality and Social Systems Approach

This text incorporates a "personality and social systems" approach, which is not one that proposes an alternative way of analyzing human social behavior. Rather, such an approach is one that supplements the traditional, and more strictly, sociological approach with another, yet essential, dimension. It offers a more complete and comprehensive explanation of human social behavior—the fundamental subject matter of sociology.

▼

Actions of individuals in any situation are always personal, however much they reflect the determining influence of the social environment. That environment, in turn, can be reflected in individual actions only to the extent that it is mediated through the individual's psychological system or personality, which itself is essentially a social product. Accordingly, personality in many respects has a central place in sociological analysis. Any sociological explanation that does not make explicit use of personality theory and data is either impossible or severely limited. A proper understanding of any social situation and its probable consequences, therefore, assumes a knowledge not only of the relevant facts about the social situation, but also of the relevant facts of the personalities operating within that social situation.

Personality has been traditionally treated in the field of sociology—when treated at all— almost exclusively as a dependent variable. Such an approach is a partial and distorted one. Personality needs to be seen as both an independent and a dependent variable—as agent and as effect: how personality as both producer and product affects the structure, function, and processes of society and its various social systems.

Sociological analysis, therefore, in its attempt to understand the structure and function of social interaction and social organization often requires the use of specific theories of personality as well as general psychological theories. Such an approach does not constitute the reduction of one field to the other. Rather, it represents the integration and coordination of the two for the fundamental purpose of yielding a more complete and comprehensive explanation of both social and individual behavior.

Among the principal concerns in this regard are the analysis and understanding of 1) how social systems influence personality, 2) how personality and social systems combine to determine social behavior, and 3) how the congruence between personal needs or abilities and structural requirements affects both individual and social function. While the intent, thus, is to depict the mutuality of relationships between social and personality systems, much of the research data deals primarily with the effects of sociocultural systems on personality. Social systems in this respect are viewed primarily as independent variables and the personality systems as the dependent ones. Personality, however, is not simply a secondary, derivative, and noncausal variable. Accordingly, a special effort is made to discuss research that shows how personality systems as independent variables may affect the structure, processes, and function of social systems. The relationships are examined in a variety of contexts.

# Interdisciplinary Orientations

In order to explain human social behavior, one needs to deal with four elements, or—as I prefer to call them—systems: cultural systems, biological systems, personal systems, and social systems. All uniquely human activity takes place by means of the interaction of each of these interdependent systems. Human action, of course, can be explained partially in terms of any one or two of these systems. A comprehensive explanation, however, requires the relatively simultaneous analysis and synthesis of all relevant systems.

The longstanding concern of sociologists for disciplinary purity has led many of them to adopt a too narrow focus and to be reluctant to consider or to utilize the contributions of related disciplines. This sociologism is an unrealistic approach to the complex phenomenon of human social behavior. In addition to integrating and applying the major theoretical perspectives that characterize contemporary sociology, this text incorporates much theory and research from allied disciplines. The concern with personality, of course, makes it necessary to consider many relevant aspects and perspectives of psychology in general, and personality theory in particular. Yet, at the same time, the contributions that anthropology and biology, as well as other fields, have made to the understanding of particular dimensions of human social behavior are cited throughout.

## Theoretical Perspectives

In this text, not a single theoretical orientation has been adopted to the exclusion of others, the position being that all of the major theoretical approaches contribute to the understanding of social phenomena. No one of them alone is adequate to deal with all of the kinds of questions that may be asked about a given social event, situation, or process. Many of the theoretical approaches, certainly the major ones, that exist in the field of sociology today are considerably compatible. They all share fundamental similarities and complement each other in several respects. Each approach will be introduced wherever appropriate for the analysis and understanding of a particular topic, concept, or principle. Our theoretical perspectives, therefore, are eclectic and pragmatic. They remain both open and essentially interdisciplinary. To the extent that our approach is guided by any theoretical orientation, our book tends toward a structural-functional and social systems perspective for which there has been a resurgence of interest throughout the sociological world during the past decade.

The concept of system is herein considered to be an analytical tool that is of fundamental help in organizing diverse aspects of the empirical world. This use of the concept should imply neither an ideologically conservative bias nor a rejection of other perspectives. The emphasis rather is on an effective synthesis of all theoretical orientations. Correspondingly, the concept of system does not emphasize structure at the expense of process. Throughout the book attempts are made to deal with questions of structure *and* process as well as stability *and* change.

## Concepts, Theory, and Empirical Research

The text focuses on concepts, principles, and theories which constitute the fundamental elements of sociological analysis and rules where appropriate on empirical evidence that these sociological orientations have uncovered in the quest for understanding how and why human social life is as it is. This book thus, for the most part, is not issue oriented or problem oriented in terms of contemporary social concerns. However, attention is drawn to controversial issues within the context of scientific analysis. Similarly, cross-cultural comparisons and contrasts are liberally presented whenever appropriate.

The concern for what human social life should be, could be, or ought to be, are secondary issues that—however important—cannot be confronted until the nature and dynamics of social reality themselves are first understood. It is the purpose of sociology, we believe, to accomplish this task. The applications of sociological knowledge involve another set of questions and considerations which sociologists alone are not competent to address.

## Objectives

Efforts have been directed at presenting the fund of sociological knowledge in clear and comprehensive terms, while retaining a sense of scientific sophistication and academic dignity.

▼ Our basic objectives are to train the student to think sociologically and, in this respect, to impart a long-enduring perspective for the analysis and understanding of social phenomena. To this end, it is hoped that this text will prove challenging and provocative—one requiring intellectual effort rather than one that is simple yet tiring. The emphasis has been on a presentation that is readable and interesting—one that will engage and challenge the student, provoke rather than bore, reward rather than offend. To achieve these goals, in whatever measure, will have justified an arduous, yet pleasant, undertaking.

# ONE ▼ ▼ ▼ ▼ Sociology: Science and Method

▼

What is sociology, and what do sociologists do? These two questions serve respectively as the focus of the first two chapters of this text. In Chapter 1 we discuss the origin, history, and contemporary nature of sociology, as well as a number of related issues, such as the value of sociology and its specialized vocabulary.

Chapter 2 deals with the way in which sociologists undertake their enterprise. The emphasis in this respect is placed on a comprehensive discussion of scientific knowledge, the nature of the scientific method, and related issues pertaining to the discipline of sociology.

These two chapters are intended to provide a basic understanding of the science and art of sociological analysis. Together they should serve as a meaningful context for discussing the principles of sociology and its general fund of knowledge which are presented throughout successive chapters. ▲

▶ Chapter 1 **SOCIOLOGY: THE SCIENCE OF HUMAN SOCIAL BEHAVIOR**
▶ Chapter 2 **METHODS OF SOCIOLOGICAL RESEARCH AND ANALYSIS**

# 1     Sociology: The Science of Human Social Behavior

People are in many ways unique beings. One distinctive aspect of our human nature is our awareness of our existence and environment. The Greek philosopher Plato wrote in his *Apology* that "the unexamined life is not worth living." Yet, after millions of years of existence, understanding ourselves is still the biggest problem and greatest challenge for human inquiry. In this chapter we introduce and discuss some of the ways in which the science of sociology contributes to the search for answers to the nature and meaning of human life. Our treatment explores the history and nature of sociology, in particular, the field as it is today—its broad scope, orientations, objectives, values, and relationship to other fields. ▲

## Outline

4

▶ One of the most basic, and intriguing, questions that any reflecting being can ask is simply "Who am I?" Other related questions are "Where did I come from?" and "Where am I going?" Many fields of study attempt to answer these seemingly simple, but really complex, concerns about the nature and functions of life. Sociology is one of these fields. Sociology, however, provides only some of the answers to these questions—but answers that are not provided, and cannot be provided, by any other field of study.

# Nature and Definition of Sociology

**Sociology** is the science of human social behavior. Like some, but not all, other species, human beings are social animals. Such a basic aspect of human nature means that the existence and the function of human beings require collective and collaborative activity. In the immortal words of the British poet, John Donne (1624), "No man is an island, entire of itself; every man is a piece of the continent, a part of the main." Hence, in a very fundamental sense, there is no such thing as nonsocial or asocial human behavior.

Human attributes neither originate nor mature outside a social context. Virtually all that a human being does, especially that which is uniquely human, is social—either in the sense that it is done by interaction with other people or in the sense that it was made possible as a consequence of such interaction. Similarly, many of the most perplexing questions, and certainly the most distressing problems, that we encounter in life are those that relate to our dealings with other people. Our social interactions, moreover, extend beyond personal interactions. Social relationships include all actions that take into account other people—whether or not those people are physically present. Right now, you the reader are engaged in a social relationship with the author of this book. Hence, many of our seemingly personal actions are actually social ones.

Social life, to a great extent, is so common and so habitual that much of it constitutes an unconscious set of activities that are usually taken for granted. Yet, only in a relatively recent period of human history has there been any systematic effort to explore and understand human social life. Such is the basic objective of sociology.

## THE VALUE OF SOCIOLOGY

People travel to wonder at the height of mountains, at the huge waves of the sea, at the long courses of rivers, at the vast compass of the ocean, at the circular motion of the stars; and they pass by themselves without wondering.

St. Augustine,
*The Confessions*, 399 A.D.

## MISCONCEPTIONS ABOUT SOCIOLOGY

Sociology has been defined in a variety of ways, and, as with many other things in the human intellectual sphere, there are several misconceptions about the nature of sociology. Perhaps, in some respects, it is easier to say what sociology is not.

1. Sociology is not **socialism,** which is a political and economic philosophy that advocates the vesting of social control and ownership of the means of production in the community or society as a whole. Such a doctrine is the antithesis of capitalism which represents free enterprise and private ownership.

2. Sociology is not **social work,** which is a field of endeavor concerned with providing assistance and therapy to individuals who find themselves in undesirable or unfortunate social circumstances, or who are adversely affected by societal problems. One such,

5

▼

rather common, example is providing aid and counsel to people who experience poverty.

3. Sociology is not **social engineering,** which is a broad but rather ill-defined field concerned with the reconstruction, modification, and/or improvement of society and the social environment. Efforts to eliminate poverty through social planning and economic reform involve various aspects of social engineering.

6

Sociology is simply a science in search of answers to questions within its domain—the social behavior of human beings. In the words of one of its distinguished thinkers, sociology studies the social bond; it investigates the forces that enable human beings to stick together in the "social molecules" in which they are found from the very moment of their conception to that of their death (Nisbet, 1970). Sociology, as the scientific study of human social behavior, is concerned with the structure and function of society. The fundamental objective of sociology, then, is simply to understand and to explain the character of the social nature and existence of human beings. Quite fundamentally, sociology seeks to answer the question: "Why do people act the way that they do?" and, more personally, "Why do I do what I do?" The domain of sociology, however, lies not so much in the dynamics of the individual as in the broader, common, and collective patterns of social behavior.

One of the basic premises of sociology is that we are able to understand ourselves by understanding the society in which we live. C. Wright Mills (1959), one of the more colorful figures in American sociology, called this ability "the sociological imagination," by which he meant the analysis of human social behavior in terms of the broader social context of groups, organizations, and societies. To understand this social world, and our place within it, is to understand ourselves—at least in terms of human social nature and its dynamics.

## HUMAN VERSUS NONHUMAN SOCIAL BEHAVIOR

Sociology is the study of *human* social behavior because its practitioners are not essentially interested in the behavior of other social animals and beings, such as chimpanzees, baboons, fish, bees, ants, or slime molds—except perhaps insofar as such knowledge contributes to the understanding of our own social behavior.

Initially, sociology held the mistaken belief that human beings were the only social animals on the face of the earth. In relatively recent years, however, we have come to know that there are many, many more social beings. There are, in fact, approximately 1 million known living species and tens of thousands of these are social to some extent. (It is estimated that there may be as many as two to three million unknown species, and that a great number of these may have a social nature of one form or another.) This situation has given impetus, especially in recent years, to the development of a new field of biology, known as **sociobiology,** which is concerned primarily with the social behavior of nonhuman species (see Chapter 3). This field has its parallel in the rather recent development of **biosociology,** a branch of sociology that is concerned with explaining the biological dimensions of human social behavior, and which, to this end, explores the social activity of nonhuman beings as well. See Lopreato (1984), Shepher (1983), Barash (1982), or Van Den Berghe (1978) for detailed treatments of this question. Yet, although during the past 10 to 20 years there has been more and more concern on the part of some sociologists with the social behavior of many other creatures, it is fair to say that the primary concern in sociology overwhelmingly remains that of the social behavior of human beings.

## Historical Perspectives

The history of a field also tells much about its nature and scope. With this in mind, let us

TABLE 1-1. Significant Milestones in the History of Sociology ▼

## I. The Ancients Study Man in Society

557–479 B.C.    Confucius, *Great Learning*
427–347 B.C.    Plato, *The Republic*
348–322 B.C.    Aristotle, *Politics*
106–43 B.C.     Cicero, *De Republica*
121–180 A.D.    Marcus Aurelius, *Meditations*

## II. Philosophers Explore the Social Nature of Man

1377    Ibn-Khaldun, *Muqaddimah*
1516    Thomas More, *Utopia*
1624    Francis Bacon, *New Atlantis*
1651    Thomas Hobbes, *The Leviathan*
1690    John Locke, *Two Treatises of Government*
1726    Jonathan Swift, *Gulliver's Travels*
1748    Charles Montesquieu, *The Spirit of the Laws*
1762    Jean Jacques Rousseau, *The Social Contract*

## III. The Age of Enlightenment: Sociology Envisioned

1807    Henri de Saint-Simon, *Introduction to the Scientific Work of the Nineteenth Century*
1830    Auguste Comte, *Course of Positive Philosophy*
1835    Adolphe Quételet, *An Essay on Social Physics*
1876    Herbert Spencer, *Principles of Sociology*

## IV. Sociology in Europe

1848    Karl Marx, *The Communist Manifesto*
1897    Emile Durkheim, *Suicide: A Study on Sociology*

1905    Max Weber, *The Protestant Ethic and the Spirit of Capitalism*
1908    Georg Simmel, *Soziologie*

## V. Sociological Beginnings in America

1883    Lester F. Ward, *Dynamic Sociology*
1896    Franklin H. Giddings, *Principles of Sociology*
1896    William G. Sumner, *Folkways*
1902    Charles H. Cooley, *Human Nature and the Social Order*
1905    Albion W. Small, *General Sociology*
1908    Ellsworth A. Ross, *Social Psychology*
1912    Charles A. Ellwood, *Sociology in Its Psychological Aspects*
1918    William I. Thomas, *The Polish Peasant in Europe and America*
1921    Robert E. Park, *Introduction to the Science of Sociology*
1934    George H. Mead, *Mind, Self, and Society*

## VI. Modern Sociology

1947    Pitirim A. Sorokin, *Society, Culture, and Personality*
1950    George A. Homans, *The Human Group*
1951    Talcott Parsons, *The Social System*
1957    Robert K. Merton, *Social Theory and Social Structure*
1956    C. Wright Mills, *The Power Elite*
1959    Erving Goffman, *The Presentation of Self in Everyday Life*
1967    Harold Garfinkel, *Studies in Ethnomethodology*
1969    Herbert Blumer, *Symbolic Interactionism: Perspective and Method*

7

▼ look briefly at the historical development of sociology.

## EARLY SOCIAL THOUGHT

The concern with human social life is perhaps as old as humankind. Recorded speculation about human social life goes back thousands of years. We can trace intellectual inquiry on the origin, nature, and functions of society to many ancient civilizations and thinkers: the Chinese philosopher, Confucius (577–479 B.C.); Greek thinkers, such as Plato (427–347 B.C.) and Aristotle (348–322 B.C.); or the early Roman thinkers, such as Cicero (106–43 B.C.) and Marcus Aurelius (121–180 A.D.).

So extensive are the contributions to social thought throughout recorded history that justice cannot be done to their number and value in this much too brief description. However, a few major observations should serve to put our discussion in a proper intellectual context.

All of the social thought that occurred up to about the middle of the nineteenth century can be labeled as **social philosophy**—knowledge about social behavior that is derived principally from the methods of inductive and deductive reasoning. Moreover, even this thought was largely concerned not so much with explaining the actual nature of human social relationships as with ascertaining what the nature of these relationships ought to be. Much of this early thought, therefore, had a moralistic and even utopian character, such as that exemplified in the quasi-literary works of Thomas More's *Utopia* (1516), Francis Bacon's *New Atlantis* (1624), and Jonathan Swift's *Gulliver's Travels* (1726).

Sociology, however, is concerned with what society *is*—and what the individual's relationship to it is—not what they *ought* to be. Its essential focus is that of explaining the actual relationship of social order and stability to social conflict and change. Questions of this particular kind began to receive systematic attention only during the seventeenth and eighteenth centuries—a period that has come to be known as the Age of Reason. It was the English political philosopher, Thomas Hobbes (1588–1679), who originally posed what has become the classical question for sociology: How is society possible? Two principal theses were originally advanced on this question: (1) the social contract and (2) social evolution.

Hobbes, in his *Leviathan* (1651), developed the notion of a **social contract theory** of the origins of society. This thesis asserted that individuals, originally existing in a "state of nature," had voluntarily surrendered their independent rights and personal freedom in order to form an absolute government for their own mutual harmony and collective protection against a social order motivated at every turn by self-interest and characterized by perpetual conflict and the inevitable war of all against all. Society, in the social contract perspective, was not a natural phenomenon, but rather a human contrivance to serve mutually desired ends.

Similar statements, although with substantial variations on the notion of a social contract, were provided by other thinkers of the seventeenth and eighteenth centuries. Chief among these were John Locke (1632–1704), another British philosopher, who wrote rather persuasively that government should depend upon the consent of the governed; the French philosopher, Jean Jacques Rousseau (1712–1778); as well as some of the prominent intellectuals in the new American colonies. Many of these themes were subsequently expressed in the American Declaration of Independence.

An example of the competitive thesis was offered by another French philosopher, Charles Montesquieu (1689–1755), in his *The Spirit of the Laws* (1748). Montesquieu affirmed the existence of social laws that were similar to those established in the natural sciences. The law of progress, or the necessary development of human societies toward higher and better stages, was accorded the dominant position among these social laws of nature. Such a thesis serves as the basis of **social evolution**—a doctrine upon which much of sociology has been built, and which today commands considerable allegiance among sociologists and other social scientists.

Up to the beginning of the nineteenth century, the explanations of human society and social life consisted, for the most part, of philosophical speculation. Some social thinkers eventually became intrigued with the possibility of the development of a new epistemology—a new way of knowing—with the development and expansion of the methods of science which rely on the sensible, or empirical, observation of reality. There seemed to be no *a priori* reason why the scientific approach could not be applied to social behavior, especially since there was widespread belief that the social behavior of human beings manifests regular and recurrent patterns that could provide the foundation for the development of a basic system of generalized principles. Accordingly, several prominent social thinkers of this period—known as the Age of Enlightenment—began to take steps toward the development and actualization of a *science* of society. One French philosopher of the time, Henri de Saint-Simon (1760–1825) wrote of *la science politique*, and in so doing laid the foundation for many of the ideas later developed and elaborated by the acknowledged founding fathers of sociology.

Much of this interest in applying the methods and principles of science to the study of society may have been as much a reflection of the social climate, as of the intellectual environment, of the times. It was in a milieu of tumultuous social change and extensive social turmoil, along with the felt need for social reform and societal reconstruction, that sociology had its formal origins and early beginnings. Western Europe during the late eighteenth and early nineteenth centuries was characterized by widespread social disorganization and unrest—a combination of economic and political revolution and technological change. Chief among these events were the industrial revolution, which developed in England and spread to other nations, and the political turmoil of the French Revolution, which began in 1789 and had widespread effects in other lands, perhaps most significantly so in colonial North America.

Out of this social and intellectual history has emerged modern-day sociology—a field of inquiry only about 150 years old and, hence, one that is relatively young when compared to many of the more established fields in the physical and natural sciences. Yet, as one contemporary sociologist (Merton 1963:249) has paraphrased the Italian genius, Galileo Galilei, "Sociology is a very new science of a very ancient subject."

## THE FOUNDING FATHERS

The Persian historian-philosopher, Ibn Khaldun (1332–1406), might have been the first to suggest that the understanding of society could be achieved most effectively by systematically observing the uniformities in social phenomena and thereby discovering their underlying natural laws.* It was in the tradition of Western civilization, however, that the field of sociology unfolded. Contemporary sociology throughout the world is the nearly exclusive product of this tradition.

---

* While nearly all of our philosophical and social thought is the product of Western civilization, many of the same kinds of questions occupied the reflections of thinkers in Eastern cultures. One of the most remarkable attempts to develop a "science" of society was made by Ibn Khaldun. Several centuries before the development of the scientific method in the West he theorized that human behavior was governed by natural laws that eventually could be discovered through the systematic observation of uniformities in social phenomena. In his most famous work, *Muqaddimah* ("Prologomena") written in 1377, Ibn Khaldun presented his conception of history as an evolutionary process and his use of historical data as a means to explain the ways in which society had changed and progressed from one stage to another. These very notions, as we shall see, came to play a central role in the writings of early sociologists.

9

**Auguste Comte** (*left*), **Herbert Spencer** (*middle*), and **Karl Marx** (*right*). (*Left,* Culver Pictures; *middle,* Culver Pictures; *right,* The Bettmann Archive)

AUGUSTE COMTE. The formal establishment of sociology as a modern science is attributed to Auguste Comte (1798–1857), who was greatly impressed by the progress being made in such sciences as physics and chemistry. He reasoned that the method of these disciplines—the scientific method—should be applicable to the study of society. Comte developed a **positivistic philosophy,** one that advocated the use of systematic observation and experimentation, to understand natural phenomena and to serve as the basis of social progress.* He believed, moreover, that positivism could yield the knowledge that was necessary for both the construction and reconstruction of society on a rational basis. Comte, somewhat activistically motivated in trying to improve the human condition, was preoccupied with building a magnificent society for the French people, "la belle France," as he called it, in the wake of the political and economic revolutions that France had witnessed only a few decades earlier.

Comte's genius, however (and here is where he distinguished himself from his intellectual predecessors, as well as from many social activists of our day) was to assert that in order to build a magnificent French society, it was

* To stress its scientific nature and to distinguish it from traditional philosophy.

first necessary to know what it is that constitutes society—its nature, structure, and dynamics. He envisioned a field of study which he called *social physics*, modeled specifically upon the empirical methods and scientific procedures of the discipline of physics.

Comte soon realized, however, that the label "social physics" had already been used by the Belgian statistician Adolphe Quételet (1796–1874) in his work *On Man and the Development of Human Faculties: An Essay on Social Physics* (1835), itself a very influential contribution to the emergence of the social sciences. Whereupon Comte coined the name "sociology" (*sociologie*) for his new discipline, and described it as the "queen of the sciences" as a reflection of its position at the apex of his hierarchy of sciences based upon increasing intellectual complexity. Sociology, for Comte, was the culmination of all knowledge!

Comte remained primarily a theorist rather than a researcher. His principal concern was outlining the nature and scope of a science of sociology rather than "doing" sociology. His theories are elaborated in two multivolumed works: *Course of Positive Philosophy* (1830) and *System of Positive Politics* (1854). In these works, and within the philosophical perspectives of positivism and logical empiricism, Comte outlined the organic view of society—

one which resembled the characteristics of a living organism: Society has a structure, its parts function interdependently, and it evolves by means of natural laws through a series of fixed stages from simple to more complex forms. Comte divided his new science of sociology into two segments: social statics, concerned with the organization and stability of society; and social dynamics, concerned with the forces of social change. This analytical distinction, in various forms, is still used widely today as a fundamental division of the field of sociology. These essentials of Comte's sociology remained the focus of speculation and elaboration for many years as his writings spread throughout Europe.

HERBERT SPENCER.   Another prominent figure, chiefly responsible for the elaboration and diffusion of sociology during its infant years, was the English philosopher and naturalist Herbert Spencer (1820–1903). He produced a series of volumes on the "principles" of various fields of knowledge. In his three-volume work entitled *Principles of Sociology* (1876–1896), as well as in earlier writings, Spencer provided a highly systematic theory of the structure and function of society.

The intellectual climate of Spencer's day was captivated by the writings of Charles Darwin (1859) and the theory of biological evolution. Spencer is responsible for applying this thought to human social life and initiating the doctrine of **"social Darwinism,"** which was instrumental in shaping much of the early sociology. The implicit analogy between society and the biological organism had been made in more rudimentary form by Comte; and, indeed, it had a much older history in ancient philosophy. It was Spencer, however, who elaborated this thesis as the core of his sociology.

Society, according to Spencer's theory, functions in terms of its own *natural* laws. His doctrine of social evolution—that all societies change from simple to complex forms—maintains that society develops through natural

processes and by these means (natural selection) we would witness the "survival of the fittest" societies.*

It does no good, therefore, to try to create or alter societies, which can only develop and act according to their fundamental nature. Indeed, any attempt to interfere with these natural laws through social planning would be detrimental to the natural course of social progress that is inherent in society. Hence, for Spencer, whatever constitutes society at any given time is identical to what society ought to be, and vice versa.

Spencer's evolutionist conception of society was a most influential one. It was disseminated in the United States chiefly by William G. Sumner (1840–1910), an early American anthropologist, and provided justification for such social institutions as racial segregation. Spencer's conception of society, moreover, encouraged the development of the doctrine of **laissez faire,** which opposed all forms of government control of socioeconomic life and facilitated the development of capitalism.† While evolutionist conceptions of society and social dynamics are still somewhat in vogue in many academic circles, most social theorists today reject the strongly conservative bias in Spencer's formulation, especially because social Darwinism can be taken as a justification for the status quo and precludes any human efforts directed at social change.

KARL MARX.   Decidedly antithetical to the Spencerian position, Karl Marx (1818–1883), the German-born social philosopher, maintained that revolution, not evolution, was the basic dynamic of human society and the only

▼

**11**

---

* The phrase "survival of the fittest" was later used by Darwin (1859). Spencer, incidentally, was the eldest of nine children, and the only one to survive beyond childhood.

† John D. Rockefeller, the American oil tycoon, is alleged to have observed: "The growth of a large business is merely a survival of the fittest . . . This is not an evil tendency in business. It is merely the working out of a law of nature" (quoted by Lewontin, Rose, and Kamin, 1984:26).

▼ realistic means by which social reform and social progress could be attained. Every society, he argued, contains the "seeds of its own destruction" and is essentially not an orderly and self-regulating entity. Marx felt that the task of social scientists consisted in an active pursuit to change society and not merely to study it.

Marx's work, along with that of his colleague Friedrich Engels (1820–1895), is the philosophical basis of communism and was for a long time considered primarily as a contribution to the fields of political science and economics. For these reasons, Marx was not accepted as a "sociologist" by his contemporaries. Indeed, he was greatly, but not totally, ignored by the sociological communities of Europe and America for nearly a century. Only during the past few decades have sociologists increasingly acknowledged the relevance of Marx's work to the broader questions of the structure and function of society and, more particularly, the relationship of the individual to the social order.

Marx was one of the first proponents of a "conflict theory" of social dynamics and social change. The principal elements of his interpretation of society are presented in *The Communist Manifesto*, written with Engels in 1848, and further elaborated in *Das Kapital* (1867).

Marx was strongly influenced by the German philosopher, Georg Hegel (1770–1831), and especially by Hegel's approach to logical reasoning known as the **dialectic process:** an idea (thesis) generates its opposite (antithesis), with the ensuing conflict resulting in a reconciliation (synthesis) that in turn becomes a new thesis. Marx accepted this Hegelian view of social change, except that for him it was material conditions rather than ideas that constitute the fundamental element of the dialectic process. Thus, his theory of society is essentially one of **dialectical materialism.** Society, catalyzed by social conflict, progresses via fixed stages—slavery, feudalism, capitalism, and socialism—to an eventual perfect state of communism.

Marx's theory of society, increasingly popular today, is basically one of economic deter-

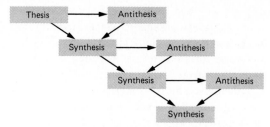

FIGURE 1-1 The Dialectical Process of Social Dynamics. The dialectical model of society affirms that the fundamental dynamics of social interaction reside in a perpetual cycle of conflict and its resolution.

minism: The structure of society and social change are determined by the nature of the relationship between people and the prevailing mode of economic production. Central to this relationship are the dynamics of alienation. One class of individuals is exploited by another class. The subordinate class feels alienated (powerless and socially isolated); this alienation in turn leads to social revolution.

Marx emphasized that the basis for social change was the inevitable conflict and constant struggle for power between economic classes. Thus, the history of humankind is a history of perennial contests between the ruling and exploiting class on the one hand and the oppressed and exploited class on the other hand. Under capitalism these two classes are referred to, respectively, as the bourgeoisie and the proletariat. Marx saw the development of society culminating in a communist utopia that would be free of conflict because conflict, he argued, was not intrinsic to society. His views have had a profound influence on modern history, and they serve today as the political and economic basis of many socialist societies throughout the world which together comprise nearly half of the world's population. Curiously, though, many of these societies, the Soviet Union in particular, seem determined to establish communism without first experiencing capitalism— an essential stage in the evolutionary process of Marx's dialectic.

The three different formulations on the nature of society that distinguished the first generation of sociologists had a common objective: progress. Each conceived of progress as taking place via a different vehicle: Comte via science, Spencer via evolution, and Marx via revolution. To a great extent, these competing perspectives of social dynamics still underscore much of the sociological enterprise today.

# Development of Modern Sociology

The development of sociology as a truly empirical science, rather than as a primarily theoretical one, was the work of the second generation of European sociologists and—by the end of the nineteenth century—the first generation of American sociologists. The common task for these individuals was to explain society as it actually *is*, not as it was thought to be or ought to be, and to develop methods and techniques for accomplishing this goal.

## EUROPEAN FORERUNNERS

A host of individuals in Europe contributed to the refinement and growth of sociology during what has come to be known as the "classical era." The following are widely considered to be first and foremost among the principal figures of this period.

**EMILE DURKHEIM.** Sociologists owe their distinctive identity as scientists primarily to the French sociologist, Emile Durkheim (1858–1917). Durkheim was among the first to clearly demonstrate the empirical viability of the new science of sociology. As social theorist and social researcher, he studied different kinds of behavior and made contributions to many fields. A dominant theme in many of his investigations centered on the dynamics and forms of the integration of society—what today is referred to as "social cohesion"—that complex of forces that functionally unites society and makes for its efficient operation. Durkheim, in this respect, presented an essentially evolutionist theory of society and spoke of "mechanical solidarity" versus "organic solidarity" as the two principal types of society based on the varying dynamics of social cohesion. The former rests on social similarities and relatively simple social organization among people, while the latter is rooted in social differences and complex forms of social organization.

Durkheim earned his place in the annals of sociology principally through his highly influential treatise *The Rules of Sociological Method* (1895) and his highly innovative analysis of suicide—the first major scientific study of a social

**13**

**Emile Durkheim** (*left*), **Max Weber** (*middle*), and **Georg Simmel** (*right*). (*Left,* The Bettmann Archive; *middle,* German Information Center, *right,* Bildarchiv Preussicher Kulturbesitz)

▼

**14**

problem (*Suicide*, 1897). In this latter work, Durkheim very effectively brought together empirical data and theoretical interpretation to provide a uniquely sociological explanation for varying rates of suicide in different societies and in different social segments of populations, such as those based on marital status and religious affiliation.

Durkheim argued that society had a reality of its own that could not be reduced to other kinds of phenomena. The basic units of analysis for sociology consisted of what he called "social facts," which referred to such things as laws, customs, values, institutions, organizations, and social processes such as cohesion. Social facts, as realities in themselves, are external to the individuals over whom they exert control, and these can be understood only in terms of other social facts. Suicide was one such social fact which Durkheim convincingly investigated, and one which we shall explore in more detail in subsequent chapters. Other social facts include such phenomena as power structures and social stratification. In no way, argued Durkheim, could social facts be reduced to, or explained by, biological or psychological phenomena. Such analyses essentially would reduce social phenomena to individual phenomena. His insistence on this fundamental rule of the sociological method gave sociology an exclusive and indisputable field of investigation.

Durkheim's formulation of sociological analysis, and his development of research methods, including the effective use of descriptive statistics, remain classical contributions to the field of sociology which continue to serve as basic models for much sociological research today.

MAX WEBER.   Another prominent figure in the early history of sociology whose work continues to have a major impact today was Max Weber (1864–1920), a German sociologist. Like Durkheim, Weber made significant contributions in the areas of both theory and research methods. Weber's influence in sociology, however, has occurred primarily during the past 30

to 40 years, owing to the long-time unavailability of English translations of his work.

Weber (pronounced Vay-ber) argued that sociologists should not only study "social facts" through objective and quantitative methods, but also understand "social action" by means of qualitative analysis that sought to uncover the subjective dimensions and personal meanings (beliefs, values, motives, and attitudes) of human social behavior. This search for empathy or "sympathetic understanding" of the mind of social actors was described in what Weber called the method of **Verstehen.** Concurrent with this methodological concern, Weber advocated a "value-free sociology" in which sociologists assume a neutral stance and withhold their personal value judgments, both in doing behavioral research and in the resolution of social problems.

In terms of theory, Weber concerned himself with such questions as the origin and development of political, legal, economic, and religious institutions. Much of his intellectual effort consisted of a refutation of Marx's thinking, particularly in arguing that not all social change is due to economic structures but that the contrary could be true as well. His best-known work is *The Protestant Ethic and the Spirit of Capitalism* (1905), which has had a major impact in all of the social sciences. In this work, Weber attempted to document the focal role that the Protestant Reformation played in the industrial revolution by providing a religious ideology that justified and encouraged economic success through rational means, discipline, and hard work. Other principal concerns centered on the nature and role of authority and bureaucratic organization, as well as the role of beliefs and values in influencing behavior. In an essentially evolutionist perspective, Weber saw society as moving progressively toward an organization of increasing rationality—one based on the legality of rules, rather than on traditional beliefs, such as religion.

Weber's work has influenced a number of current theoretical orientations in the field of sociology and continues to serve in great measure as a basis of much sociological activity today.

GEORG SIMMEL. Unlike other European sociologists who were interested primarily in the broad analysis of society, Georg Simmel (1858–1918), another illustrious German scholar, influenced the development of sociology by initiating an interest in the study of small units of social behavior, a concern that has become the basis of social psychology which, as we shall soon see, is one of the core fields of sociology today.

Simmel regarded the dynamics of interpersonal relationships and small-group interaction as the foundation on which more complex social phenomena are based. Society, in his view, was an intricate web of group affiliations—not an organization or reality unto itself. Accordingly, Simmel concentrated his analysis on the elementary forms and invariable processes of social interaction, such as cooperation, conflict, amalgamation, submission, and domination, by which social behavior takes place among people, and studied such phenomena as the influence of numbers of people on small groups and social behavior. He also formulated concepts of "social nearness" and "social distance" that are akin to many of the fundamental processes and principles of social dynamics. These contributions provided one of the principal models of what is now known as formal analysis, or formal sociology, which focuses on the recurring modes of social interaction. Simmel's work was especially influential in the United States, to which we now turn our attention.

## SOCIOLOGY IN AMERICA

Sociology was becoming well-established in the United States by the turn of the century. American scholars, while pursuing the paths laid out by the pioneers of the discipline, nevertheless began to make their own distinctive imprints on sociology as they developed specialized interests in certain areas of our new science, as well as to make application of it to selected social issues and problems of the day. Sociology in America developed with a strong empirical orientation, and, hence, was more scientifically precise than European sociology, which even as recently as the 1960s remained predominantly theoretical in nature.

AN "AMERICAN SCIENCE." So much in fact did sociology develop in the United States, at least in its empirical dimensions, that it came to be known as an "American science."* This development undoubtedly was accelerated by the expectation that many Americans had for this new science in bringing about a widely desired social reform, since the United States was also experiencing many of the social and economic problems that come with the industrial and demographic expansion of society. Reformist orientations did indeed characterize much of early American sociology, and such perspectives, occasionally and unavoidably mixed with social philosophy, no doubt accounted for much of the popularity of sociology in America. Perhaps the major figure in these early beginnings of American sociology was Lester F. Ward (1841–1913), who was strikingly influenced by the writings of both Comte and Spencer, and the fundamental importance which they attached to evolution. Ward reaffirmed the essential tenets of Comte's sociology in the pursuit of social reform through sociological knowledge and social progress through social action. Like Comte, sociology was the science of sciences for Ward.

By about 1925, the science of sociology was no longer only an expectation, but a reality that had assumed its place among the various fields of study. Courses in sociology were being of-

▼

**15**

---

* Sociology failed to expand significantly in Europe during the first half of the twentieth century, marked by two world wars, in a large part because it was repressed by totalitarian and dictatorial governments, especially in Germany and the Soviet Union.

▼ fered in many colleges and universities, professional associations had been formed, sociological journals began to appear, and the scientific enterprises of both empirical research and theory construction were well underway, despite the fact that the welcome mat was not yet outside the gate of some of the older and more conservative American colleges and universities.*

**16** THE CHICAGO SCHOOL. The unofficial "capital" of American sociology was located at the University of Chicago. The department of sociology at Chicago, the first in the country, was established in 1892 and reigned undisputed from 1915 to 1940. Its founder, Albion W. Small (1854–1926), was also responsible for the establishment of the American Sociological Society.

The "Chicago School" of American sociology (see Bulmer, 1984), as it became known, concentrated its activities, particularly with an emphasis on social problems and research "in the field," on studies in social disorganization, social deviance, urban phenomena, and human ecology. Extensive community studies were conducted under the skillful direction of Robert E. Park (1864–1944) and Ernest W. Burgess (1886–1966). Among the other principal fields of focal interest at Chicago were those of social interaction and personality, which we shall discuss subsequently in more detail. These latter areas were of principal concern at the University of Michigan as well, which rivaled Chicago as the chief center of American sociology during this early period.

At mid-century a new wave of purely abstract and theoretical concerns developed within the circles of American sociology. Two major figures spearheaded these efforts: Pitirim A. Sorokin (1889–1968), who established the department of sociology at Harvard University, and his colleague and rival, Talcott Parsons (1902–1979). Both of these men attempted independently to create a general theory for sociology—one comparable to Einstein's classic contribution to physics—that would embrace many different types of social phenomena and all of the dynamics of society. Sorokin's approach was principally historical (see Chapter 14), while Parsons combined the various theoretical approaches of several earlier sociologists, especially Emile Durkheim, Vilfredo Pareto, and Max Weber. Equally prominent during this recent period were the students of these sociological theorists who contributed to the modern development of the structural-functional approach to sociological analysis which we shall discuss subsequently.

Today nearly 250 eminent institutions offer graduate programs in sociology. However, sociology is no longer confined to universities and academic settings. More and more it is also becoming an applied discipline, expanding considerably beyond academic circles into several sectors of the workaday world. Sociology has now taken its rightful place in the realm of scientific enterprise and human intellectual effort. Nonetheless, one must not lose sight of the comparative infancy of sociology in assessing its fund of knowledge, extensive though it may be.

## Sociology Today

Sociology, as we see, is really a twentieth-century science. It came of age during the past 60 years, and most especially during the period since World War II. Previous to that time, the field of sociology experienced considerable retardation by being banned in Nazi Germany and fascist Italy. Sociology in China is being revived only now after a generation of being

---

* Harvard University, for example, did not establish a department of sociology until 1930. Quickly thereafter, however, it became one of the most distinguished centers of sociological learning and research. Other renowned institutions, such as Johns Hopkins University—as with Oxford and Cambridge in England—did not offer curricula in sociology until as late as the 1950s and the 1960s.

suppressed by the communist regime. And in the Soviet Union only in the late 1980s has sociology not consistent with Marxist-Leninist ideology been allowed to function.

The growth and complexity of sociology can be measured in many ways. At the turn of the century, for example, there were only a handful of sociologists in the United States and perhaps only a few hundred by 1925, while today there are approximately 20,000. Similar indications of phenomenal growth can be ascertained from the number of courses offered in virtually all colleges and universities—and, indeed, nowadays, even increasingly so in high schools. Sociology, moreover, is no longer an exclusively American science. The discipline has spread to every part of the world (see Mohan & Martindale, 1975), as reflected, for example, in the development and composition of the International Sociological Association, and it has taken on many different interests and orientations. To explore the many facets and accomplishments of sociology, particularly in the past half-century, is the pleasant and exciting task before us.

## SUBFIELDS OF THE DISCIPLINE

Nearly every aspect of society and human social life has received the analytical attention of sociologists. This has resulted in a complex body of knowledge that in turn has given rise to a number of subfields within sociology, as well as the specialization of activity and expertise on the part of sociologists. Many of these areas, which seem to increase nearly every year, are simply labeled the "sociology of" such and such, for example, sociology of complex organizations.

Other subfields have traditionally carried somewhat different labels, but are, nonetheless, well-established divisions of sociology, and, hence, have the same distinguishing character-

istics in terms of their goals and functions: for example, social gerontology or criminology. For a more comprehensive list of subfields in sociology, see Table 1-2.

Each of these subfields of sociology is concerned fundamentally with the nature and dynamics of the phenomena comprised within the more limited sphere of respective kinds of social behavior and the related aspects of society. The more specific concerns of many of these fields will be described in our discussions throughout the subsequent chapters of this text. One other general description of the field, however, is appropriate at this time.

## MAJOR ANALYTICAL DIVISIONS

Sociology, like some other disciplines in the social sciences, is frequently divided for analytical and theoretical purposes into micro- and macrodimensions. This distinction is helpful in terms of the extent to which sociological explanations may be generalized or extended to include, or to exclude, certain categories of social behavior. Each of these dimensions, or levels of analysis, is distinguished further by the different theoretical approaches and methods of investigation that they employ.

MICROSOCIOLOGY. **Microsociology** is concerned with the analysis of the elementary forms and processes of social behavior. Activity here concentrates on social interaction—that behavior which takes place, relatively informally, in one-to-one and small-group contexts, such as the family or the classroom.

MACROSOCIOLOGY. **Macrosociology,** also known as *systematic sociology*, studies society as a whole, and thus is concerned with broad-scale or grand-scale analysis. Concerns at this level include the relatively formal structures and social dynamics that are more typical of com-

▼

17

▼ TABLE 1-2. Subfields of Sociology

| | |
|---|---|
| Adolescence | Occupations/professions |
| Art | Penology/corrections |
| Biosociology | Personality |
| Childhood | Politics |
| Clinical sociology | Population/demography |
| Collective behavior | Poverty |
| Community | Public opinion |
| Complex organizations | Race and ethnicity |
| Crime/criminology | Religion |
| Death | Rural-urban sociology |
| Delinquency | Science/knowledge/technology |
| Development/modernization | Sex roles |
| Economics | Small groups |
| Emotions | Social change |
| Education | Social control |
| Family/marriage | Social deviance |
| Human ecology | Social disorganization |
| Language/linguistics | Social gerontology |
| Law | Socialization |
| Leisure/sports/recreation | Social movements |
| Literature | Social organization |
| Mass communications | Social policy |
| Mathematical sociology | Social psychiatry |
| Medicine/health | Social psychology |
| Military | Stratification/mobility |
| Minority relations | War |
| Music | Work/industry |

plex organizations, such as bureaucracies, institutions, communities, culture, social movements, and social change.

Microsociology and macrosociology overlap somewhat in scope and concerns, just as their respective phenomena interpenetrate the reality of social behavior. Just as macrosociology is the context for the other, so, too, the social interactional concerns of microsociology have no ultimate meaning except in terms of the total context of social dynamics.

# Social Psychology: A Core Subfield of Sociology

One field of sociology deserves special discussion, partly because of its intimate relationship to the development and contemporary function of sociology and, more importantly perhaps, because of the particular perspective and emphasis that we have adopted for this text. This is the core field of **social psychology,** sometimes called psychosociology.

**Everyday Activity.** Social behavior that takes place in face-to-face interaction or in the context of small groups comprises the focus of microsociological analysis. The encounters of everyday life, including those of the campus scene, make up a large share of this type of social analysis. (© Susan Lapides 1984/Design Conceptions)

**Grand-Scale Action.** Analyses at the macrosociological level concentrate on social behavior that occurs on a broad scale, invariably involving formal structures and processes. International relations, such as those that are the core of the United Nations, exemplify such concerns. (J. P. Laffont/SYGMA)

▼

**20**

Some would argue that sociology is fundamentally social psychology. Of the great number of subareas that comprise sociology today, the field of social psychology (in terms of the number of sociologists who have adopted it as an area of specialized interests, and, hence, in terms of the amount of research activity) is one of the most extensive and most dynamic of all. Moreover, nearly all of the substantive areas of the field, such as socialization, social deviance, and collective behavior, are heavily socio-psychological in their theoretical orientations. Such a situation reflects the fundamental assumption shared by many sociologists that a comprehensive understanding of human social behavior requires an assessment of the subjective or psychological input of its agents as well as an analysis of the objective conditions of its social environment or context.

Social psychology, in addition to having justifiable claims to its own existence as an independent discipline, is a subfield of psychology as well. Yet, while treated as a relatively new subfield of both sociology and psychology, social psychology is actually just as old, or just as young, as its two parental areas. The sociological history of social psychology can be traced to Auguste Comte. Notwithstanding his claims that sociology is the queen of the sciences, Comte actually spoke of "la morale positive" (positive morality) as occupying the very pinnacle of his hierarchy of sciences. *La morale positive* was concerned with explaining how human beings were simultaneously the product and the producer of society.* Such a question is fundamentally in search of the nature and function of social interaction—a concern that, with all of its ramifications, would clearly constitute today much of the domain of social psychology. Indeed, it can be argued that much of the same was true of the works of several of the other classical figures in sociology: for example,

Durkheim's concern with social cohesion, Weber's exploration of *Verstehen*, and even Marx's interest in alienation (see House, 1981). Hence, in many respects sociology really originated as social psychology.

Psychology, for its part, is usually considered to have had its scientific beginnings with the work of Wilhelm Wundt (1832–1920), a German psychologist who developed the first formal psychological laboratory at the University of Leipzig in 1879. Wundt formulated an area of study known as *Die Volkerpsychologie*, traditionally translated as "folk psychology," which dealt substantially with the phenomena of social interaction. Hence, psychology, contrary to popular beliefs or assumptions, did not originate with clinical concerns or the broad subfield of what today is known as "abnormal psychology." On the contrary, psychology had its beginnings in a search for explaining the nature of intimate processes of social interaction.

Despite these parallel beginnings, the two social psychologies developed along somewhat different, yet decidedly overlapping, paths. Social psychology, as a branch of sociology, is concerned with the psychological dimensions of collective behavior. Included in this field are the study of such behavioral phenomena as crowds, fads, mobs, panic, fashions, and social movements. This branch of social psychology is often referred to as psychosociology. As a subfield of psychology, social psychology is concerned with the explanation of the dynamics of individual behavior in terms of its social dimensions, such as the social context in which it may occur. This variety of social psychology includes such concerns as the social aspects of motivation, cognition, emotion, and perception.

Social psychology, as a subfield of both sociology and psychology, has a common subject matter: human social behavior. Yet, each branch or variety is distinguished by the focus and perspectives of its particular concerns. Social psychology, however, basically stresses neither the behavior of the individual, nor the

---

* In his *System of Positive Politics* (1854), Comte states his intention to publish *Le Systeme de Morale Positive*, a project he was unable to complete before his death.

dynamics of society as such, but rather the *interactive* behavior that takes place between the *socius* and the *psyche* in either a singular or collective context. Understood in this respect, social psychology or psychosociology encompasses both the microtheoretical perspective and the macrotheoretical perspective, and, as such, can quite properly be perceived to be the core of sociology.

## PIONEERS IN SOCIAL PSYCHOLOGY

Much of the early efforts at sociological research consisted of contributions that were undertaken within the perspectives of "social psychology." This situation was exemplified in Europe by the work of two French sociologists, Gabriel Tarde (1843–1904), who offered a psychosociological explanation of the basic elements of social behavior in his work on the *Laws of Imitation* (1890), and Gustav LeBon (1841–1930), who, during the same period (1895), studied the phenomenon of crowding. Sociopsychological orientations, however, were much more fundamental and extensive in the development of American sociology. One illustrious pioneer, Franklin H. Giddings (1855–1931) of Columbia University, spoke of

"the subject matter of the psychology of society, otherwise called sociology" (1896). Such a conception of the field has not only been a pervasive one, but one that has in great part charted the formulation of much sociological theory and explanation. Charles A. Ellwood (1873–1946), often acknowledged to be the principal founder of psychological sociology, is credited with being the first to have effectively demonstrated the combination of sociological and psychological principles in his *Sociology in Its Psychological Aspects* (1912).

The two foremost exponents, and most frequent contributors to psychosociology, were Charles H. Cooley (1864–1929) and William I. Thomas (1863–1947). Cooley formulated principles for the formation of the self and explored the nature and role of primary groups in social behavior. Thomas developed the situational approach which emphasizes the subjective meanings of human behavior and stresses the fundamental importance of the study of personality in social behavior. Other principal pioneers were: Albion W. Small (1854–1926), who focused his work on an analysis of the process of human association; Ellsworth A. Ross (1866–1951), who reworked the contributions of Georg Simmel, Gustav LeBon, and other European sociologists; and George H. Mead

▼

21

**Charles H. Cooley** (*left*), **George H. Mead** (*middle*), and **William I. Thomas** (*right*). (*Left*, American Sociological Association; *middle*, University of Chicago Archives; *right*, American Sociological Association)

▼ (1863–1931), the distinguished American philosopher, who extended Cooley's work on self-information and whose contributions in this respect constitute the principal basis of symbolic interactionism—a theoretical orientation of primary significance in sociology today.

## APPLICATIONS OF SOCIAL PSYCHOLOGY

22

Contemporary sociology draws heavily from the subfield of social psychology, especially in terms of the processes of social learning, psychological development, and the study of personality (see Turner, 1988). There is perhaps very little sociological analysis that is actually done without at least an implicit use of theories of personality formation and function. As Cooley (1902) stated, the "individual" and/or "society," when considered in terms of the other, are "mere abstractions." This position essentially states the central thesis and concern of our approach to sociology in this text: the inseparability and reciprocal or complementary nature of society and the individual. It is most crucial that we underscore this theme at the outset of our consideration.

Often, we both give and get the sociological impression that human social life contains no people, that it can be explained without any explicit consideration of people. Unfortunately, the valuable works of many sociologists, even the widely acclaimed and classic contributions of Durkheim and Weber, often reflect this defect. Yet, as William I. Thomas (1918) stated in an appropriate response to the highly prevalent, and strictly or traditionally sociological, thesis advocated by Durkheim: "The cause of social or individual phenomena is never another social or individual phenomenon alone, but always a combination of a social and an individual [personality or psychological] phenomenon."

A typically and traditionally sociological explanation for something like juvenile delinquency or crime would begin by specifying the amount, or rate, of such a behavior on the part of a particular society, or on the part of a particular segment or population of that society. It would then attempt to use sociological structures and dynamics to explain this particular kind of behavior.* More frequently than not, however, it is found that such behavior does not occur at all times under the particular set of sociological circumstances that is specified. There is only a given probability. Combining a "psychological" explanation with the "sociological" one—a more complex analysis that permits the assessment of the behavior in question on the part of individuals manifesting certain kinds of psychological dynamics or personality characteristics—may make it possible to show that only particular kinds of people in particular kinds of social situations perform the specific behavior in question. Such an approach that accounts for more of the variance of the behavior in question provides a more precise and a more complete explanation.

There are spheres of sociology, of course, that do not deal with personality or psychological analysis, and need not do so. Certain areas of demography and human ecology are cases in point. Additionally, specific theoretical approaches, such as role theory and conflict theory, can be developed and pursued independently of psychological considerations. Yet, no science of human social behavior or society can be considered complete unless it explains the behavioral nature of those individuals who comprise it and sustain it. And, by the same token, no science of individual behavior, such as psychology, can be complete until it explains the nature of the phenomena by which individuals are made into functional and sustaining members of society, which constitutes the context of any uniquely human behavior.

Hence, in order to understand the nature of human social behavior as well as the structure

---

* This type of purely sociological approach is often called a "State-Rate" explanation. See Chapter 13 for an elaboration.

and function of society, we often need to understand the psychological nature and function of the individuals who are responsible for that behavior and who are the agents of society. Sociology, without such considerations of personality and other psychological dynamics, is a distortion of social reality. Neither can we ignore the relevant contributions of the several other fields of the social and behavioral sciences to which we now turn our attention.

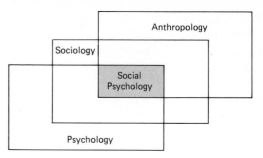

FIGURE 1-2    The Behavioral Sciences in Perspective.

**23**

# Sociology's Place in the Social Sciences

Sociology is only one among several academic disciplines that have taken the social behavior of human beings as their subject matter. These fields are known collectively as the social sciences—in contrast to the natural and physical sciences, such as biology, chemistry, and physics.

## THE BEHAVIORAL SCIENCES

Some of the social sciences comprise a subcategory frequently referred to as the behavioral sciences. This distinction is a somewhat elusive one although it is convenient for many people to think of the social sciences, in very broad and generic terms, as those disciplines that are concerned with human phenomena: their origin, nature, dynamics, and history. The behavioral sciences, as a distinctive subcategory, are those disciplines that have a specific focus on the actual behavior of human beings—whether as individuals or as members of society. These disciplines usually include sociology, psychology, and anthropology. The *inter*relationship of these fields, particularly with regard to social psychology which is the focus of our approach in this text, is depicted in Figure 1-2. Distinctions among the disciplines can be understood more clearly, however, in terms of their specific foci.

## MATERIAL AND FORMAL OBJECTS

Each of the social sciences has a common subject matter but a different focus. While all of the social sciences share the same *material* object in studying human social behavior in one form or another, each discipline has a different *formal* object in that each studies a particular aspect or dimension of social behavior. Such are the basic distinctions among such specific social sciences as economics, political science, and geography. The different disciplines may be seen as asking different questions about social phenomena, as well as providing different answers. All of these efforts are complementary to each other in that, together, the various contributions provide a more complete explanation and understanding of social reality and human behavior.

## GENERALIZING AND SPECIALIZING SCIENCES

All sciences seek to discover universal principles to explain the behavior of the phenomena in question. We need to distinguish, however, between synthesizing, or generalizing, sciences on the one hand, and analytical, or specializing, sciences on the other. The *generalizing* social sciences are those which concern themselves with social behavior in more abstract aspects,

▼

such as in terms of the basic or underlying processes and elements that are common to any social behavior. The *specializing* social sciences are those which study social behavior in the concrete forms in which it occurs, such as economic, political, or religious activity.

The behavioral sciences—sociology, psychology, and anthropology—are usually thought of as generalizing sciences. One cannot speak of nonsociological behavior, or even of nonanthropological or nonpsychological behavior, although it is quite possible to speak of noneconomic or nonpolitical behavior. All human behavior is essentially comprised of psychological, sociological, and anthropological dimensions.

Sociology, however, has a dual character and a role as both a specializing and a generalizing science. Comte conceived of sociology as a generalizing science, as is reflected in his according it the supreme position as "queen of the sciences." He argued that if there are *n* sciences, each one concerned with only parts or pieces of behavioral and social reality, then there is need for an *n* + 1 science to synthesize, to unify and to integrate, the individual sciences. Sociology, as the generalizing science, is the *n* + 1 discipline of the social sciences which is concerned with the totality of social life. The relationship of sociology to the other social sciences may be described partly in this way. Sociology, however, is both a specializing as well as a generalizing social science. Its concerns in the former dimension are reflected in the many subfields of sociology which already have been mentioned. Sociology, then, is one among several disciplines, as well as the pivotal discipline, of the social sciences.

## INDIVIDUAL DISCIPLINES

Sociology, as the basic discipline among the social sciences, necessarily draws on all of the separate social sciences. To describe, if only in brief terms, the nature of some of the other social sciences, and to show, thereby, their sim-

ilarities and differences, should be useful in providing a more complete description of the nature of sociology. We shall distinguish in this respect generalizing sciences and specializing sciences.

**Anthropology,** a generalizing science, is literally "the science of man," and focuses its attention on variations in the human experience. Up to very recent times, anthropology concentrated on the study of primitive and nonliterate societies, but today this discipline has widened its scope to include modern civilizations. Anthropology has two principal divisions: **Physical anthropology,** akin to biology and physiology, draws on the methods of archaeology. It is concerned with the evolution and development of the human species. **Cultural anthropology,** clearly resembling sociology, is concerned with the development and social organization of human societies, and the sociocultural life of human beings.

**Psychology,** a generalizing science, is concerned with the individual behavior of the human being, especially mental phenomena, including such dynamics as sensation, perception, cognition, motivation, and affect. It seeks to explain the behavior of individuals, as individuals or single actors, in both social as well as nonsocial contexts.

**Economics,** a specializing science, is concerned with behavior in the marketplace—those aspects of human social life that involve the production, distribution, and consumption of material goods and services.

**Political science,** a specializing science, is concerned with the theories and systems of government and their attendant political behavior—including questions of law, authority, power, public order, and social organization.

**Geography,** a specializing science, is concerned with the relationship of people and social dynamics to their physical environment (land, sea, and sky).

Nearly all sociologists are in agreement that it is impossible to be fully competent without an adequate knowledge of the other social sciences. Compounding the sociological approach with the particular perspectives and contributions of the other social sciences makes it possible to yield a more complex explanation and understanding of human social behavior. We shall draw on some of the perspectives and data of several of the other social sciences in our detailed discussions of particular topics in the subsequent chapters.

## DISCIPLINES AS ARBITRARY AND ARTIFICIAL DISTINCTIONS

There are no absolute demarcations for the scope and limits of each of the several social sciences. The boundaries of the various sciences, of whatever kind, are to a great extent an arbitrary matter. What is included or excluded in any one of the various fields is purely a conventional decision, one which is both time-bound and culture-bound. What we, as Americans, label as sociology does not necessarily find a perfect counterpart in the intellectual and scientific circles of many other societies. The same is true of nearly all other fields of inquiry.

The time-bound character of the distinction between the various fields is seen in that the scope and limits of each field has been undergoing constant change since their formal beginnings. Social sciences, like all fields of knowledge, are dynamic enterprises, continually changing and developing. The demarcations between these fields and the distinctions in terms of subject matter are more apparent than real. With the constant accumulation of information and empirical data, the complementary integration of the conceptual and theoretical perspectives of the separate fields of knowledge becomes all the more necessary. Hence, given the increasing concern for multi-

disciplinary perspectives which are found in all areas of intellectual and scientific inquiry today, the arbitrariness of disciplinary boundaries is becoming more and more evident.

All of these situations underscore the basic artificiality that characterizes any attempt, however necessary from a practical point of view, to distinguish separate fields of study, be they social sciences, physical sciences, or other academic disciplines. The individual sciences metaphorically constitute a chain of knowledge, the separate links of which overlap or intertwine with each other as a conceptual reflection of the phenomena being explained. If we assume, as indeed do the majority of scientists and other intellectuals, that all reality is one, then to divide the study of this one reality into a number of disciplines is a totally false reflection of the phenomenon that we are seeking to explain. Yet, the finite intellectual capacity of the human being requires the fragmentation of reality for effective investigation and comprehension. What must not be forgotten is the ultimate need to go back, pick up the many pieces of intellectual analysis, and fit them together so that they reflect the actual reality that we are trying to explain. Such a task is a proper and obligatory one for sociology as the generalizing and synthesizing discipline of the social sciences.

## AN OPEN AND INTERDISCIPLINARY APPROACH

Recognizing the very complex nature of the phenomena we seek to explain, it should be clear that no one field of study has a monopoly on answering the social dimensions of our fundamental question: "Who am I?" An approach which recognizes the value and the need of an interdisciplinary perspective is the kind that we feel is necessary for any proper understanding of human social behavior. Such an approach, while presenting challenges from a procedural point of view, has the virtue of providing a more

▼

**25**

▼

comprehensive, and, hence, more valid, explanation of human social behavior. It does so by preventing, or at least forestalling, theoretical closure—that is, the exclusion of essential dimensions and variables of human behavior. Factors that affect the phenomena under investigation are often arbitrarily and conventionally ignored by the specialized foci of the individual disciplines—a procedure which, accordingly, results in serious distortions in the explanation and understanding of the subject matter before us.

26

## Theoretical Perspectives in Sociology

Sociological analysis can be undertaken within a number of theoretical perspectives. Orientations are neither right nor wrong. They are merely ways of looking at phenomena. Just as a glass or cup, for example, may be considered half-full or half-empty, so, too, may sociological phenomena be approached from different conceptual and theoretical perspectives.

Each theoretical orientation begins with a different set of assumptions, each has a different focus of analysis, and each asks essentially different questions. The ultimate value of any orientation as a sociological tool, however, is in terms of its utility—how well it contributes to, and facilitates, the sociological task of explaining human social behavior. Each perspective, therefore, has its own advantages and its own limitations. For the majority of sociologists today, moreover, there is seldom complete allegiance to any one perspective. More frequently than not, sociologists prefer to combine the perspectives of one or more orientations and proceed with an eclectic approach that utilizes whichever orientation appears to be the most productive in a given theoretical situation.

Hundreds of sociological theories have been formulated to explain various kinds of social behavior. Most of these efforts, however, can be seen as applications or variations of a few major theoretical approaches. The principal theoretical approaches that are prevalent in sociology today may be conveniently categorized in terms of those that are strictly sociological in character, and those which are primarily psychosociological (see Table 1-3). The former tend to have a more macrosociological perspective, while the latter emphasize a primarily microsociological orientation. Each of these approaches represents a somewhat different model of human social behavior. Models are preconceptions, working or *a priori* assumptions, about the nature of the phenomena to be explained. They serve as general representations describing in broad terms the assumed nature of the relevant phenomena and the way it is assumed that they may occur. The following are brief descriptions of the principal theoretical orientations that are utilized in the field of sociology today.

## MACROSOCIOLOGICAL THEORIES

STRUCTURAL-FUNCTIONAL ANALYSIS. **Structural-functional analysis,** one of the dominant and most prevalent theoretical orientations in sociology today, assumes that order, regularity, and balance are the principal forces of social activity and that, hence, they should constitute the basic foci of sociological investigations. This perspective was initially introduced into sociology by several of the founding fathers of the discipline, and particularly by Comte, Spencer, and Durkheim.

Structural-functional analysis, often known as *functionalism* or *functional theory*, postulates a parallel in the essential nature of society and a biological organism. The structural-functional orientation conceives of society as a system or complex organization composed of many interrelated parts or structures that function together in a highly orderly and efficient

TABLE 1-3. Major Theoretical Approaches in Sociology ▼

| | Structural-Functional Analysis | Conflict Theory | Symbolic Interaction | Social Exchange Theory |
|---|---|---|---|---|
| Level of analysis | Macrosociological | Macrosociological | Microsociological | Microsociological |
| Nature of society | A social system consisting of interdependent units | A social order characterized by competing groups and classes, each pursuing its own interests | A social reality continuously created through social interaction | A social reality continuously created through social interaction |
| Basis of social interaction | Consensus deriving from shared beliefs and values | Conflict and coercion | Shared symbols and meanings | Social reciprocity |
| Focus of analysis | Social order and the perpetuation of society | Competition for control of limited resources | Individuals as social actors | Elementary forms of social behavior |

fashion. Society is assumed to be composed of many component parts, or structures, all working in an interdependent fashion and contributing to the total function of the social system. The family group, for example, constitutes a structure that performs a number of functions for society, as do various social mechanisms, such as laws in regulating order.

Structural-functional analysis focuses its attention on the contribution that each part, or structure, makes to the total function of the system and the way the various structures work together in that regard. The analytical task is to explain the organization and function of each of the many interrelated parts and thereby to yield a composite understanding of the nature of society. It also includes a corresponding emphasis on the structural-functional requisites of society. The structural-functional perspective utilizes, either simply or in combination, evolutionary or organismic models of society.

Stability, equilibrium, and harmonious function are inherent in the social system, and its orderly, highly efficient function is maintained by a set of shared values and beliefs—basic consensus—among its constituents. Interference in the established and ongoing process of society results in social change.

Principal examples of structural-functional analysis in sociology today are the quite sophisticated and highly comprehensive "general theory of action" developed by Talcott Parsons (1951), as well as the conceptual formulations for more empirically testable theories of the "middle range" elaborated by Robert Merton (1968). Both of these theoretical contributions have been a major influence in contemporary sociology.

Critics argue that the structural-functional approach, especially with its focal concern on social equilibrium or balance, has a conservative or repressive set of implications: It allegedly

**Pitirim Sorokin** (*left*), **Talcott Parsons** (*middle*), and **Robert Merton** (*right*). (*Left,* Harvard University; *middle,* Harvard University; *right,* Columbia University)

overestimates the amount of consensus in society, and studies society as it is rather than as it might be or ought to be (Mills, 1959; Gouldner, 1970; Abrahamson, 1978). In short, the structural-functional approach is seen as maintaining the status quo, and thereby precluding social change (which is seen as disruptive or dysfunctional). Such a view is not totally justified insofar as the dynamics of change are not necessarily incompatible with, nor precluded by a focus on order and equilibrium. Organisms also undergo change throughout their life course, yet they are viewed as continuously maintaining a basic state of functional equilibrium. Social change, moreover, may itself contribute to social order and equilibrium.

CONFLICT THEORY. A theoretical orientation that has received much attention in sociology in more recent years is that based on the processes, forms, and consequences of conflict in human behavior. **Conflict theory,** completely antithetical to structural-functional analysis, focuses on the elements of change and revolution. It has its main roots in the contributions of Karl Marx and Friedrich Engels (1848), as well as those of other European sociologists including Ludwig Glumplowicz

(1899) and Georg Simmel (1908), who explored the positive contributions of conflict as a unifying force in social behavior and one with potential for contribution to the survival of societies.

The conflict orientation assumes that the fundamental dynamics and conditions of human life are dissension and competition rather than consensus and integration. Conflict is a continuing and inevitable dimension of social life, and all societies are in a constant state of change. Conflict theorists maintain that societies continuously experience an inevitable competition for scarce resources, especially power, wealth, and prestige. Exploitation of certain segments of society is the inescapable outcome of the dynamics of inequitable distribution. Poverty and racial discrimination would be offered as two rather prevalent manifestations of these dynamics. While conflict necessarily involves tension and hostility, it need not result in violence.

Harmonious equilibrium, argue conflict theorists, is an illusion. Social order is essentially a product of coercion and restraint, not consensus or shared values. The "establishment"— that segment of society that controls its resources and means of production—constrains and exploits the subordinate strata in terms of its own interests.

The fundamental social process, according to conflict theory, is an endlessly competitive struggle for social advantages between various social segments of society (for example, socio-economic classes, racial and ethnic categories, and even the sexes), and not a continuous or steady effort at maintaining harmony or equilibrium. Society, then, is perceived to be inherently unstable, and in a perpetual state of change.

Thus, conflict theory is concerned chiefly with the dynamics of change as the principal focus of sociological analysis—the development and transformation of social institutions, forms of social organization, and patterns of behavior. Social change, in this perspective, stems fundamentally from what is assumed to be the inevitable conflict that is found between the inescapability of dominant and subordinate strata in society, which is manifested in terms of the inequitable distribution of power, wealth, and other human resources.

Conflict theory was revised and introduced into modern sociology by the late C. Wright Mills who, working in the tradition of Marx, argued in his well-known book, *The Power Elite* (1956), that American society is dominated and controlled by corporate, political, and military leaders. The majority of conflict theorists, who, on the whole, tend to assume an activistic or reformist posture toward society, today eagerly subscribe to the basic premises presented by Marx and Mills. Other contemporary formulators of conflict theory are Ralf Dahrendorf, the German sociologist-economist (1959), who advocates a "dialectical conflict theory," in which both consensus and conflict are seen as central features of social life; and Lewis Coser (1956), who has elaborated the perspectives of Simmel and propounds a "conflict functionalism." Coser, for example, argues that conflict increases cohesion and solidarity in social organization; and, moreover, that conflict can draw attention to structural problems within a social system, thus contributing to its survival and function. Each of these somewhat oppos-

ing theories attempts to combine the principles of consensus and conflict which are seen as central features of social life and inherently complementary.

Advocates of conflict theory are strong critics of equilibrium models of society. They contend that structural-functionalism is inherently conservative and works against social change by directing attention to the stability and/or maintenance of social systems. While conflict theorists focus nearly exclusively on basic dimensions of society that functionalists may ignore, they tend to overlook the aspects of order and stability.

## MICROSOCIOLOGICAL THEORIES

SYMBOLIC INTERACTION.  A uniquely sociological or psychosocial perspective that has become an increasingly popular orientation, especially in America, focuses on individuals as social actors rather than on the systems in which social action occurs. It seeks, thereby, to explain more about the actual processes of human social behavior (and their meaning for participants) rather than about the structure and function of society or the social system in which they take place.

**Symbolic interaction** theory maintains that the individual and one's interpersonal relationships are the most important aspects of society, and, more particularly, that this interaction is mediated by shared symbols, such as language, beliefs, and values that derive from the societal formation and participation of the individual or social person. People do not respond to stimuli in themselves; rather, they respond to the meanings that they impute to these stimuli. A traffic light, for example, has only an arbitrary and conventional meaning, as do human gestures or the words and sounds of any language. Hence, for social interactionists, people live in a symbolic as well as in a physical world. To

▼

29

▼ understand the formation and manipulation of symbols is the basic goal of the symbolic interaction approach.

The emphasis in this perspective, however, is on the specific interaction that occurs between people, and more particularly on the meanings that social behavior has for the individual actors. Central to this position is the application of what Charles H. Cooley (1902) called "sympathetic introspection," or the emphatic understanding of one's behavior. Any valid comprehension of human behavior often requires an understanding of how actors perceive reality—how, in the words of William I. Thomas (1928), they form a "definition of the situation." For, as Thomas contended, "If men define situations as real, they are real in their consequences." Hence, for the symbolic interactionists, behavior can be understood only when it is studied in its whole context—not only the situation as it exists in its objective forms, but also in its subjective dimensions as it seems to exist to the actor himself.

Symbolic interaction derives chiefly from the psychosociological work of George H. Mead (1934), and particularly from his concerns with the formation of the social self, about which we shall have more to say in Chapter 5. Other historical figures who indirectly contributed to this perspective were Max Weber, Georg Simmel, and, of course, Cooley and Thomas. Among the chief protagonists of the different varieties of symbolic interaction that are prevalent today are Herbert Blumer (1969), who first used the term "symbolic interaction," Erving Goffman (1959), Manford Kuhn (1964), and Sheldon Stryker (1980).

Goffman, relying on theatrical principles, formulated a variation on the symbolic interactionist perspective known as **dramaturgy** which focuses on impression management and the roles that individuals play in order to create and control particular reactions among others. His approach in effect accepts the Shakespearean position that "All the world's a stage, and all the men and women merely players."* Goffman has effectively applied the dramaturgical approach to the study of how people cope with the stigma of mental illness and physical and social handicaps.

Another variation of symbolic interaction is **labeling theory** which has been applied primarily in the field of deviant behavior (see Chapter 13). This perspective concentrates on the significance that names (for example, criminal, homosexual, deviant, schizophrenic, psychotic) given to specific kinds of behavior and their agents have for the very production of the behavior itself. Becker (1963), for example, has applied this particular perspective to an analysis of marijuana users.

A third form of symbolic interaction that has been developed in more recent years is that of **ethnomethodology** (Sharrock and Andersen, 1986; Garfinkel, 1967). This perspective, incorporating fundamental elements of phenomenology which maintains that all reality is subjective reality, places a much greater emphasis on the subjective dimensions of human behavior. It seeks to understand the unspecified, implicit, and unconsciously used guidelines, "folk rules," or "ethnomethods" by which people construct social reality, and thereby achieve definitions of situations and use them in the process of social interaction in order to create and sustain an orderly social life. Typical ethnomethodological concerns would be an understanding of why strangers in elevators avoid eye contact and what happens when one stands too close to another person while engaged in conversation. Many of its advocates allege that ethnomethodology, while accepting many of the core elements, and having much in common with the symbolic interaction approach, is nonetheless sufficiently different to be considered an independent theoretical orientation (Stryker, 1980).

---

* *As You Like It*, Act II, Scene 7.

30

C. **Wright Mills** (*left*), **Erving Goffman** (*middle*), and **George C. Homans** (*right*). (*Left,* Columbia University; *middle,* American Sociological Association; *right,* American Sociological Association)

Critics argue that symbolic interaction is by and large limited in its application to the analysis of small segments of social behavior, or what more technically comprises the microlevel of social behavior, such as that between individuals and within groups. In these respects, the many varieties of symbolic interaction have provided a wealth of insights into the basic aspects of social interaction. Its utility for macrosociological analysis, whatever it may be, is largely undeveloped.

SOCIAL EXCHANGE THEORY. **Social exchange theory** focuses on the elementary forms of social behavior, including the goals and motives of participants in social interaction. It is based fundamentally on the principles of behavioristic psychology, and draws heavily in particular on the work of B. F. Skinner (1953), the Harvard scientist who has elaborated his own version known as operant reinforcement theory (see Chapter 4). Intellectual roots of social exchange theory can also be found in the concepts and principles of utilitarianism that derive from classical economics.

Social exchange theory basically extends the psychological principles of stimulus and response, with the significant difference that it incorporates an emphasis on the element of rationality in human behavior. It assumes that people are more likely to perform behavior for which they receive positive rewards (or have received positive rewards in the past), and, correspondingly, are not likely to perform behavior for which they receive negative rewards (or have received negative rewards in the past). The economic dimension of social exchange theory consists in its emphasis on the costs and profits (material or psychic) that are involved in the social behavior. People, in short, act to maximize their rewards and to minimize their costs.

Accordingly, patterns of social interaction are maintained only insofar as they are found to be rewarding or to yield a net profit, in such terms as happiness, security, and any other form of motive gratification. Costly patterns of behavior (for example, anxiety, boredom, anger) do not pay off. Social relations terminate when the interaction is no longer seen by one or other partners as a fair exchange—when one is giving more and getting less. A marital divorce, for example, would be explained in these terms.

One of the key concepts of social exchange theory is *reciprocity* which refers to the "give-and-take" phenomenon that is alleged to be the basic dimension of social behavior. For instance, when you give someone a gift or do a favor for someone, you usually expect that per-

▼

**32**

son to reciprocate the courtesy. People often make campaign contributions to political candidates in the expectation that they can be exchanged at a later date for "political favors" from the elected officials. Plea bargaining between defense and prosecuting attorneys is another form of behavioral exchange. Similarly, one may conform to the wishes of another in terms of certain behavioral norms, such as manners or dress styles, in return for that person's friendship. Social behavior in the perspective of exchange theory is essentially a trade off of one kind of behavior for another. Such reciprocity is assumed to be indispensable for sustained social interaction, which in turn is the fundamental ingredient or process of any form of social organization.

Social exchange theory, in great part, has developed basically as an alternative to structural-functional analysis. The two chief protagonists of this perspective are George C. Homans (1950, 1974), who has developed an exchange theory that is essentially behavioristic, and Peter Blau (1964), who has formulated a version that seeks to incorporate the fundamental principles of the structural-functional perspective, primarily for application on the macrolevel of sociological analysis. Both versions of social exchange theory have captured considerable attention throughout the field of sociology.*

## THEORETICAL CONVERGENCE

These different theoretical orientations that characterize sociology today are themselves the rightfully expected products of a maturing and self-correcting science of society and human social behavior. While somewhat contradictory, competitive, and even seemingly antagonistic, they are not necessarily incompatible, especially since each focuses on different aspects of social behavior and social organization. There is reason to expect that in due time these various

* See Burgess and Bushell (1969) for representative presentations of this theoretical orientation.

approaches, no doubt among others yet to be formulated, will be synthesized and unified into an eclectic orientation—perhaps into *the* sociological approach. Indeed, these theoretical orientations already borrow from each other and combine one or more of their competitive, yet complementary, perspectives. Several sociologists (Coser, 1956; van den Berghe, 1963; Smelser, 1968a; Gouldner, 1970) have spoken of the "functions" of social conflict, and others (Merton, 1956) have introduced the concepts of "strain" and "tension" into functionalist theory. Each orientation, moreover, rests on a common core of concepts and principles, and utilizes similar methods of analysis. Each orientation also shares an awareness of the complexity of the phenomena that it seeks to explain. Theorists are increasingly of the opinion that conflict and consensus, order and change, are different yet integrated dynamics of all social life.

The competition inherent in these approaches, therefore, is to a great extent one of emphasis rather than one of seeking exclusivity in sociological explanation. Sociologists are more and more recognizing the convergence that can be found in these principal theories (see, for example, Wiley, 1987; Eisenstadt and Helle, 1985). Hence, it is the concepts of interaction and synthesis, rather than separation and contradiction, which have become more popular and acceptable in evaluating the merits of the major theoretical perspectives in sociology today. Such an orientation has created new developments in the field of theoretical sociology, and strengthened social theory in general.

It is sufficient for the present to realize that none of these orientations or approaches is necessarily right or wrong. Each is an assumption in the form of a model or working conception of the nature of the phenomena under investigation. Each of them has contributed to the fund of sociological knowledge, and collectively they provide a stronger, more complete, and comprehensive approach that minimizes the risk of distortion and error in sociological explanation. We shall have more to say in subsequent chapters about the complexities and implications of these different perspectives and approaches as we apply them appropriately to the analysis of particular dimensions of society and social behavior.

# The Value of Sociology

Sociology deals with phenomena with which people inevitably have had some firsthand and frequent experience, and about which they possess some knowledge. Most people, to be sure, know something about the nature and function of their society, for not only are they part of it, but a minimal amount of knowledge is needed to function in it. However, for nearly all people, such knowledge is limited to their own particular experiences which, regardless of how much they may have in common with those of other people, are nonetheless quite personalized. Common experience in a lifetime of eating, for example, does not make one a dietitian or a physiologist. Nor does a lifetime of breathing and seeing make one a lung specialist or an ophthalmologist. Similarly, a lifetime of social interaction does not make one a sociologist.

## COMMON SENSE AND THE OBVIOUS

Since everyone engages in social activity in nearly every moment of life, it is quite understandable that people often come to believe that there is little of value or of surprise in the study of sociology. Indeed, the professional sociologist often is seen only as one who painfully elaborates the obvious, and, more frequently than not, with complicated and unnecessary jargon. Such a naive criticism of sociology, still rather prevalent today, is a heavily loaded accusation. First of all, it implies that the subject matter of sociology—human social behavior—can be understood by means of common sense

alone. It further implies that an otherwise simple explanation is needlessly complicated by means of an artificially contrived vocabulary.

While one may often know *what* people do and even *how* they do it, and, accordingly, on occasion might be able to predict their behavior, most of the time the lay person cannot explain *why* people behave as they do. The answer to this question is a sociological and scientific one. Indeed, it may be obvious that people behave as they do because it is human nature to do so. But to say that human nature causes behavior is really no explanation at all. We still need to know the nature of human nature, and how and why it functions as it does. Common-sense and/or simplistic answers may be neither sufficient nor valid for this explanatory task.

One of the persistently haunting dilemmas about common-sense explanations is that they are so full of contradictions. Consider, for example, the apparent contradictions in the common-sense "explanations" or understandings of human behavior that are clearly manifested in the several sets of aphorisms that are given in Table 1-4.

Within the perspectives of science, there is always a need to verify the obvious. The same principle is no less true for sociology, or any of the other social or behavioral sciences. Indeed, if the nature of social reality were self-evident, then there would be no disagreements among people about social life—either what it is or what it ought to be. Such a situation, as we all know, is hardly true. What everyone knows, through common sense, the obvious, is not known with certitude until it is proven to be so. The obvious "truth" in this respect often turns out to be false. There are no obvious answers in science. Even knowing "in general" or "on the average" or "usually" is insufficient for the ideal goals of precision and certitude that characterize scientific knowledge. We need to know when, and under which conditions, and why, phenomena occur as they do. Every assumption and principle, insofar as it is possible,

▼   TABLE 1-4.  Apparent Contradictions in Common Sense

| | | |
|---|---|---|
| Absence makes the heart grow fonder. | vs. | Out of sight, out of mind. |
| Look before you leap. | vs. | He who hesitates is lost. |
| Money answereth all things. | vs. | You cannot buy happiness. |
| Birds of a feather flock together. | vs. | Opposites attract. |
| No two people are alike. | vs. | Politicians are all alike. |
| A good beginning makes a good ending. | vs. | If you start with a bang, you'll end with a bust. |
| Two heads are better than one. | vs. | If you want a thing done well, do it yourself. |
| Patience is a virtue. | vs. | Patience is the virtue of asses. |
| Familiarity breeds contempt. | vs. | To know her is to love her. |
| Old age is an incurable disease. | vs. | You're as young as you feel. |
| Women are unpredictable. | vs. | Isn't that just like a woman. |
| Abundance, like want, ruins many. | vs. | You can't have too much of a good thing. |
| Above all, to thine own self be true. | vs. | When in Rome, do as the Romans do. |
| Better safe than sorry. | vs. | Nothing ventured, nothing gained. |
| Haste makes waste. | vs. | Strike while the iron is hot. |
| Most people are essentially honest. | vs. | Every man has his price. |
| It follows as night follows day. | vs. | You never can tell. |
| History never repeats itself. | vs. | There is nothing new under the sun. |
| Never too old to learn. | vs. | You can't teach an old dog new tricks. |
| Antiquity surrenders, defeated by new things. | vs. | The earliest, oldest, and longest has still the mastery over us. |

Source: *Sociology,* George A. Lundberg et al. New York: Harper & Row, 1968, p. 33.

is proven in science. Nothing can be taken for granted, at least, not ideally.

Perhaps it would be sufficient for our purposes to demonstrate the importance of this position in sociology with a description of a few common-sense "truths" about human nature and social behavior which have been found to be false through sociological research. Consider one well-known sociological study conducted for the Research Bureau of the U.S. Army during World War II (Stouffer, 1949). The following propositions about the adjustment of servicemen to military life were investigated:

1. Better-educated men are more likely to suffer psychological breakdown in military service than those with less education.

2. Southern soldiers are better equipped to survive the rigors of tropical climates than northern soldiers.

3. Black soldiers are less ambitious for promotion than Whites.

4. Soldiers from rural backgrounds manifest higher morale than those with urban backgrounds.

5. Southern Blacks prefer southern to northern White officers.

6. Soldiers were more eager to be returned home while the fighting is still going on than after the enemy has surrendered and hostilities have ceased.

One might argue that so obviously correct were/are these propositions that it was a waste of resources to spend time, money, and energy in order to determine whether they indeed are true or false. Why not take these widely accepted beliefs for granted, as self-evident or common-sense truths, and move on to more sophisticated questions? The simple answer is that Stouffer's research revealed all of the above propositions to be false: Poorly educated soldiers showed more psychoneurotic symptoms than those with high levels of education; Southerners showed no greater ability than Northerners to adjust to tropical climates; Blacks were more eager than Whites for promotion; soldiers with urban backgrounds showed higher morale than those with rural backgrounds; southern Blacks preferred northern White officers; and soldiers were less eager to be returned home during fighting than after surrender.

It is quite curious to realize, as Lazarsfeld (1949) points out, that had we mentioned the actual results of the investigation first, the reader most likely would have labeled these statements as obviously true too. More recent research, on militancy among Black Americans and other minorities, has shown similar contradictions of the common-sense approach. For example, the common-sense view might hold that militancy is likely to be more common among individuals who are the most deprived socio-economically, are the least well-educated, and hold the least prestigious occupations (for example, manual laborers, janitors, and trash collectors). On the contrary, sociological research shows that militancy among Black Americans and other minorities has increased as their standard of living has risen: Militancy is more likely to be found among the less deprived and more educated individuals, as well as those with more prestigious occupations and higher incomes (Marx, 1969).

Since every kind of human reaction is conceivable under a given set of circumstances, it is of crucial importance to know which reactions *actually* occur, or at least occur most frequently, and under which particular conditions. Sociology, as science, is concerned with what is actually true and not with what is conceivable true. Perhaps these brief illustrations are sufficient to redress the naive criticisms about the value of sociology. It should be additionally helpful to comment briefly on the nature of sociological problems which often are confused with social problems.

## SOCIOLOGICAL PROBLEMS VERSUS SOCIAL PROBLEMS

The theoretical problems and scientific questions of sociology are not to be confused with **social problems.** The latter include such things as crime, poverty, population dynamics, mental illness, and so forth—all of which are social conditions thought to be undesirable or problematic by the people in a particular society. Such concerns belong to the domain of social engineering which, as we saw earlier, is concerned with the improvement and reconstruction of society.

**Sociological problems,** on the other hand, are represented by issues that are concerned with the explanation of the nature and function of human social phenomena apart from any *a priori* judgment on the worth or desirability of the behavior in question. Sociological problems therefore involve the explanation of the nature and dynamics of social behavior and not the development of strategy and techniques for the control or change of social phenomena.

The problems of sociology are essentially those that are related to breaking the behavior code or explaining what Nisbet (1970) has called the "social bond." Just as biologists have concerned themselves with breaking the genetic code in order to unlock the mystery of biological life, and just as chemists and physicists occupy themselves with explaining the bond or unification of chemical and physical elements, so, too, do sociologists, along with other social

▼

**35**

**36**

**Social Issues versus Scientific Questions.** Poverty and overpopulation, as found in the Barrio of Caracas, Venezuela, represent *social problems*—conditions judged to be undesirable by the members of a society. Corresponding *sociological problems* are presented in regard to the theoretical explanation of such situations. (Mark Antman/Image Works)

and behavioral scientists, seek fundamentally to unravel the mysteries of the nature, structure, function, dynamics, and change of human social behavior and society.

Social problems involve questions of social policy which determines the way society should function, and which kinds of social behavior are preferred or desired. Social policy, at least in a democracy, is the responsibility of the citizens and their elected officials or the public administrators—not the scientists. Sociologists, however, can, do, and should take a key role in specifying the implications and consequences of alternative types of social policy. Such a contribution is but one aspect of the practical value of sociology. The practical application of sociological knowledge, however,

as well as that of the other social sciences, to the solutions to problems in society ("social problems" as well as "societal problems") is an undertaking quite different from the analysis and assessment of social behavior and the structure and function of society. It is these latter undertakings that primarily represent the intellectual and scientific value of sociology.

# The Language of Sociology

The first step in understanding sociology, as in any other scientific discipline, is the mastery of its basic vocabulary. A large portion of this text will be devoted to an exposition and definition of sociological concepts. What we present in this text are the fundamental or core concepts that are considered to be indispensable for an understanding of the field on the part of the novice. It essentially may seem, on the one hand, that we will be using familiar terms in strange or unfamiliar ways; and, on the other hand, that we are using esoteric terms for relatively common and familiar phenomena. Neither situation may in fact be correct. It is important, therefore, that the student grasp these fundamental terms of sociology, and perceive them as technical or scientific terms—however much one may be in the habit of using many of the same words in a more popular and everyday vocabulary—and, similarly, however new or strange many of these terms may appear to be.

Sociologists, for these reasons, are often criticized for their jargon, or "sociologese." A selected sampling: anomie, dysfunction, mores, dyad, latent pattern maintenance, reference group, symbolate, ethnocentrism, and hypergamy. "Why not talk in plain language?" ask the critics. Strangely, such complaints and requests are seldom made about the physical and natural scientists who similarly employ a technical vocabulary, and ones that are far more unintelligible to the outsider. Criticism of this kind is but another manifestation of the naive expectation about the sufficiency of common-sense knowledge for social behavior: Why make things so terribly and unnecessarily complicated?

While some of the criticism of the technical language of sociology is perhaps justified, much of it reflects a misunderstanding about the nature and methods of science in general, and those of sociology in particular. Every field of science necessarily develops its own technical vocabulary as part of the search for precision in its explanatory task, and as part of its discovery of the phenomena of reality.

The specialized vocabulary of any discipline, moreover, is necessarily unintelligible to the outsider. Scientific concepts are the result of certain intellectual experiences. Accordingly, it is frequently difficult for laymen to comprehend concepts without the experiences out of which they have emerged. To translate, for example, the meaning of *Gemeinschaft* and *Gesellschaft*, two central sociological concepts that have retained their originally German labels, in any accurate way necessitates a paragraph or two and not merely a corresponding English word. Sociological concepts, like all technical terms, are the shorthand of the discipline. They facilitate communication both in an economical and in an intellectually precise manner.

Neologistic activities and the development of technical vocabularies constitute very essential dynamics of science. Searching for and discovering new phenomena—new bits of reality—require the formation of new concepts and the creation of new labels or words for them. Such an activity is a basic and integral part of all sciences. It occurs in sociology for the very same reason it occurs in chemistry and physics. What is fundamentally different, in these respects, about such things as atoms, neutrons, apogee, perigee, micromicrocuries versus anomia, anomie, status crystallization, hypergamy, and enculturation? Perhaps the difference is only the specific words and the concepts that they represent. (Compare the concept of "stress" in physics with that of "strain" in sociology and "anxiety" in psychology.) Conceptual analysis and clarification is one inherent and persisting feature of any scientific enterprise. All fields are in need of continually testing and refining their conceptual tools.

The criticism of jargonizing is naive for yet another fundamental reason. Among other things, it presupposes that we already know all that there is to know about human social behavior.* There is, according to this argument, nothing new in the realm of social reality to be

▼

---

* Such an argument rests on a misunderstanding which Alfred N. Whitehead (1938) in his *Modes of Thought* called "the fallacy of the perfect vocabulary."

▼

encountered or to be discovered. To accuse social scientists of needlessly creating or inventing jargon implies that there are no new behavioral phenomena which are, or can be, discovered. Why assume that the social and behavioral sciences have discovered all of the phenomena in their fields, but that the physical and natural sciences have not yet accomplished this basic task—despite their much longer history and more extensive resources? For example, in 1952, the Periodic Table of Elements showed about 96 chemically distinct atoms—totally unique bits of physical phenomena. At the present time, there are 107 chemically distinct atoms. Within the short span of less than 40 years, scientists have named several new elements. These bits of reality either always existed and we simply did not know it, or they have newly come into being. Should not sociologists and other behavioral scientists do the same when they discover new elements of behavioral phenomena?

One of the language problems peculiar to sociology, as well as to the other social and behavioral sciences, is that many of the words used to represent its concepts have meanings in other frames of reference—some technical, some not. Many sociological terms are taken from our common and everyday vocabulary, and, therefore, have nontechnical meanings as well. Basic examples would include "role," "culture," "group," "power," "function," and "norm." This situation compounds the problems for the student not only because of the nontechnical and nonscientific denotations that these words have, but also because of the connotations that the popular usage of these words have acquired. By way of contrast, the vast majority of words in the physical and natural sciences (for example, neutron and proton) usually have only one technical or scientific meaning.

Unlike some of the other scientific disciplines that have escaped the liabilities of the languages of everyday discourse, either by coining totally new terms as necessary, or by utilizing mathematical terminology, sociology by and large has developed a vocabulary based on terms of popular usage. Similarly, many sociological terms also have different conceptual and technical meanings in other fields of science. For example, "culture" as a focal term in sociology also has technical meaning in biology, as do other sociological terms such as "mass" and "density" in physics. Further difficulties are created, unfortunately, in that the same sociological term may be given various conceptual meanings by different sociologists. Correspondingly, the same phenomena may be labeled differently by various sociologists. Such practices are permitted in the absence of any standard vocabulary for the field. All of these situations have compounded the problems of scientific communications for both the professional sociologist as well as the novice student.

The primary issue here, however, is not so much linguistic as it is one regarding the validity of sociological and scientific concepts. Words or labels attached to phenomena are arbitrary. But concepts, or the metaphysical referents of words, are not necessarily arbitrary. Words are only symbols for concepts as well as for the phenomena which are represented by the concept. "Tree" could quite easily be used to represent dog, and "dog" could quite easily be used to represent tree. This arbitrary use of symbols can be seen in that different languages have different words for the same phenomenon. Hence, the more crucial considerations in the vocabulary of sociology are those represented by the validity and utility of the conceptual apparatus. Concepts, unlike words, are not arbitrary. Concepts are either true or false and, hence, represent a crucial consideration for sociology, as for any other science. We shall devote more attention to these questions in Chapter 2. Let us realize for the moment that the development of an adequate and precise vocabulary for sociology, one that is consistent with the requirements and characteristics of scientific knowledge, is an exacting and often exasperating task. Such a situation is all the more true of sociology, which must deal with phenomena which are as highly complex as human social behavior.

# Summary

Sociology is the science of human social behavior. It is not to be confused with socialism, social work, or social engineering. The foundations of modern sociological thought were laid in Europe during the nineteenth century. Auguste Comte, credited with the formal establishment of sociology as a discipline, was impressed by the progress being made in such sciences as physics and chemistry. He argued that the method of these disciplines—the scientific method—could be applicable to the study of society and social phenomena. Another principal figure, chiefly responsible for the elaboration and diffusion of sociology during its infant years, was Herbert Spencer, who provided a highly systematic theory of the structure and function of society. Spencer is responsible for initiating the doctrine of "social Darwinism" which was instrumental in shaping much of the early sociology, as well as that of the present day. Decidedly antithetical to the Spencerian position, Karl Marx, the German-born social philosopher, maintained that revolution, not evolution, was the basic dynamic of human society. Marx saw the task of social scientists consisting of an active pursuit to change society and not merely to study it.

A host of second-generation sociologists in Europe contributed to the refinement and growth of sociology during what has come to be known as the "classical era." Emile Durkheim was among the first to demonstrate clearly the empirical viability of the new science of sociology. His formulation of sociological analysis and his development of research methods, including the effective use of descriptive statistics, remain classic contributions to the field of sociology and continue to serve as basic models for much sociological research today. Georg Simmel influenced the development of sociology by initiating an interest in the study of small groups and the basic forms of social behavior, concerns that have become the bases of social psychology. Another prominent figure in the early history of sociology whose work continues to have a major impact today is Max Weber. Like Durkheim, Weber made significant contributions in the area of both theory and research methods. Sociology, however, is really a twentieth-century science. It came of age during the past 60 years, and most especially during the period since World War II. Sociology, as both a generalizing and specializing science, consists today of a number of subfields, each concerned with a facet of society and human social life.

The field of social psychology, concerned with the psychological dimensions of human social behavior, deserves special attention. Social psychology is a branch not only of sociology, but of psychology as well. As a branch of sociology, this field is concerned with the psychological dimensions of collective behavior. As a branch of psychology, the focus is on the dynamics of individual behavior in terms of its social dimensions. In order to understand the nature of human social behavior, as well as the structure and function of society, we often need to understand the psychological nature and function of individuals, who are agents of society. Sociology without considerations of personality and other psychological dimensions is a distortion of social reality.

Sociology is generally divided into two analytical categories, micro- and macrosociology. Microsociology is concerned with the analysis of the elementary forms and processes of social behavior. Macrosociology focuses on society as a whole and is concerned with social analysis on a broad scale. Each of these divisions is distinguished further by the different theoretical approaches and methods of investigation that they employ.

39

▼

▼      Sociological inquiry can be undertaken from a variety of theoretical perspectives or conceptual orientations. The major macrosociological theories are structural functionalism and conflict theory. Structural functionalism, often called functionalism, assumes that order, regularity, and balance are the principal forces of social activity. These forces should constitute the basic foci of sociological inquiry within this perspective. Conflict theory is based on the processes and forms of conflict in human behavior. This perspective focuses on the elements of change and revolution. The major theoretical approaches of microsociology are symbolic interaction and social exchange theories. Symbolic interactionism takes the approach that the individual and one's interpersonal relationships are the most important aspects of society. Social exchange theories focus on the elementary forms of social behavior, including the goals and motives of participants in social interaction. While somewhat contradictory, competitive, and even seemingly antagonistic, these four theoretical approaches are not necessarily incompatible. Each focuses on a different aspect of social behavior or social interaction and, therefore, they may be complementary in many cases.

     The value of sociological knowledge is reflected in the errors and contradictions of "common-sense" observations that often are made about human social behavior. Similarly, it is important to distinguish sociological problems (scientific questions) from social problems that involve value judgments.

     Sociology, as with any science, has a technical vocabulary which in many instances cannot be distinguished from that used in other disciplines or contexts. Much more significant, however, is the validity of the concepts that this technical vocabulary represents.

# Key Concepts

anthropology
biosociology
conflict theory
cultural anthropology
dialectic process
dialectical materialism
dramaturgy
economics
ethnomethodology
geography
labeling theory
laissez faire
macrosociology
microsociology
physical anthropology
political science
positivistic philosophy
psychology
social contract theory
social Darwinism
social engineering
social evolution
social exchange theory
social philosophy
social psychology
social problem
social work
socialism
sociobiology
sociology
sociological problem
structural-functional analysis
symbolic interaction
*Verstehen*

# 2 ▼ Methods of Sociological Research and Analysis

More perceptive, perhaps cynical, students invariably contest any assertion of sociological principle with one seemingly simple question: "How do you know that?" To understand how a field of study acquires its knowledge is to understand the very nature of that field in yet another dimension—its capabilities and its limits. Moreover, there tends to be a parallel between the growth of a discipline and the development of its research technology. In this chapter, then, we look at the principal techniques and tools used in sociological research. Additionally, we explore the limits of science in the study of social behavior and the social responsibility of scientists, with particular emphasis on sociologists. ▲

## Outline

42

▶ Sociological knowledge has experienced a tremendous growth in recent years. Much of this is due to the extensive development of research methods and techniques in sociology and allied social and behavioral sciences. It is necessary to have some understanding of the nature of these research methods, the various techniques and procedures, in order to evaluate the knowledge which they help produce. *How we know* has significant implications for *what we know!*

# Approaches to Sociological Knowledge

Sociology can be pursued via the scientific method or the humanistic method. The scientific orientation is the dominant one today; however, many people in the field approach the subject matter of sociology in the tradition of the humanities. Examples of the humanities are the fields of art, literature, philosophy, and history. No one, of course, can say absolutely what sociology should or should not be; and, correspondingly, no one can say which methodological perspective is the correct one. Moreover, despite their own individual preferences, the overwhelming majority of sociologists feel that sociology should be allied with both the sciences and the humanities. Such a situation is a distinct advantage for sociology. Most sociologists, in fact, usually draw eclectically from the several perspectives that characterize the field of sociology today.

The **humanistic method** relies primarily on subjective analysis, including such processes as intuition, speculation, impression, insight, and common sense.* While subjective analysis may be the typical and distinctive perspective of the humanist or the artist, just the opposite is true

---

* For a description of the humanistic approach to sociology, see Alfred McClung Lee (1973) or Peter T. Berger (1963).

of the scientist. Scientists employ objective analysis in their work, which is performed in a highly systematic fashion; they seek to establish facts and demand empirical proof as the basis of their knowledge. Subjective analysis, of course, is not irrelevant in science. On the contrary, intuition and common sense play a fundamental role in the formulation of hunches and hypotheses, which are the starting points of scientific research. Moreover, subjective analysis in one form or another is often incorporated into the scientific method.

The **scientific method** in sociology is concerned with an objective discovery of laws or general principles of human social behavior. The humanistic orientation seeks chiefly to describe behavioral phenomena. More basically, however, and at the risk of oversimplification, it may be said that each of these two major modes of investigation involves an essentially different **epistemology**—that is, a set of principles by which we come to know or to understand the phenomena in question.

All knowledge inevitably involves an epistemological foundation. The place of epistemology in science, however, is neither well understood nor easily accepted. All too often, epistemology, or the philosophy of science, is divorced from the field of scientific methodology, from which it is essentially inseparable. Yet, as Einstein (1949) observed, science without epistemology is a muddled undertaking.

Epistemology constitutes the cognitive map of the scientist. It is concerned with such things as the definition of the universe or field of discourse, the establishment of appropriate boundaries, the assessment of the nature and validity of assumptions and postulations that are inherent in all kinds of explanations, the limits of methods and techniques or tools, the adequacy and implications of conceptual language, the tenets of the philosophical doctrines which may serve as the basis of theoretical explanation, as well as the intellectual fads and vogues of the times that comprise the context

▼

43

▼

in which the scientist works. So much of sociology has grown out of philosophy. We need to be mindful, therefore, of the philosophical orientations that are inherent in particular sociological theories in order to assess their assumptions, objectives, and limits.*

Let us illustrate the importance of epistemology with a brief consideration of the role of assumptions in the intellectual and scientific enterprise. Assumptions are simply untested assertions. In some areas of study, and with the use of some methods—for example, philosophy and the principles of logic—it is frequently alleged that the question of assumptions does not apply. Rather, one begins not with assumptions but with self-evident truths. A self-evident truth is defined as an assertion, the validity of which is so obvious that it could not be otherwise. An example frequently implied in much philosophical speculation is the first principle of logic—the principle of noncontradiction.

The *principle of noncontradiction* states that a thing cannot both be and not be at the same time in the same respects. It is impossible, for instance, for a door to be both open and closed at the same time. Such a statement is said to be self-evident because it is impossible to conceive of it as not being true. Logical people would clearly accept the principle of noncontradiction in this argument. Yet, in the scientific mode of inquiry, whatever has not been empirically validated—that is confirmed or proved to be true by knowledge derived through any of the senses—remains an assumption, an empirically unproven or unverified assertion.

The significance of this statement is that knowledge is only as valid as the assumptions upon which it is based. So long as the assumptions remain, there remains a question of the validity of this knowledge. Accordingly, one ideal of the scientific orientation is to minimize,

indeed to eliminate, all assumptions upon which its knowledge is derived.

The nature and number of assumptions varies from discipline to discipline, as well as in terms of the particular phenomena under investigation. There is, however, a common set of fundamental assumptions that are shared by all scientific disciplines: for example, that reality exists and that this reality is knowable.* Each science, moreover, has its own characteristic set of assumptions. The following are examples of specific assumptions that usually undergird sociology as a science, but that are not postulated at all times in the humanistic approach:

1. Human behavior is explainable.
2. Human behavior is generalizable.
3. Human behavior is predictable.

Many scholars dispute one or all of these assumptions. For example, some argue that human behavior is so individualized and unique that any attempt to generalize about it, or to develop a science for it, is doomed to failure. Others defend the position that the human capacity for free will precludes scientific predictions, or at least works against them.

So far, none of our discussion is meant to say that one method of inquiry is superior to the other. Rather, these two methods—the humanistic and the scientific—are obviously different, and their differences make for very significant consequences. Each method imposes limits on the kinds of data that can be analyzed by the investigator and further limits what can or cannot be done with the derived data and knowledge. Of course, it should be clear that the majority of sociologists, ourselves included, have exercised a personal judgment or preference to the effect that scientifically derived knowledge is superior to that obtained through other methods. Science is considered to be su-

44

---

* For more on this question see the contemporary works of Robert Nisbet, especially *The Sociological Tradition.*

* All attempts to prove the existence of reality have failed, as anyone familiar with the philosophical works of David Hume, Immanuel Kant, René Déscartes, and others knows.

perior because it yields more certain knowledge, knowledge that can be verified objectively. All scientific knowledge, of course, is subject to revision. Even "objectively verified" knowledge may be true for today, but perhaps not for tomorrow. Similarly, "erroneous" perceptions or understandings may be the product of imprecise tools and techniques that traditionally improve over time as technological advancements occur.

# What Is Science?

Our discussion so far begs the question, What is science? More specifically, Is sociology a science? There is much controversy surrounding both of these questions.

The word "science" can be defined in various ways. Historically, it meant any type of knowledge or study; today, however, it has a more restricted designation. Accordingly, the answer to our second question is correspondingly arbitrary. These questions, however, are crucial ones that cannot be ignored in the interests of a proper understanding of sociological knowledge and the methods by which it is derived.

"Science" is, nonetheless, a highly value-laden term. Western society holds scientists as people of knowledge in high regard in contrast to saints, holy men and women, prophets, humanists, and artists. Indeed, the value of science in our own society has resulted in a bandwagon effect, whereby nearly every discipline seeks to identify itself as a science in the hope of reaping prestige and preferential treatment. Anything "scientific" carries an aura of keen fascination and respect. But there is nothing magical about science. As the distinguished philosopher, Bertrand Russell, stated: "*Science* is only the name for a particular system of knowledge, awareness or understanding, acquired by particular methods; it must come to terms with the other systems acquired by other methods—ascetic, historical, intuitive and subconscious, imaginative and visionary."

What, then, is this particular system of knowledge, acquired by particular methods? Two principal sets of criteria have traditionally been used to distinguish science from other kinds of knowledge: (1) the characteristics or qualities of the knowledge that constitutes the substance of a particular discipline and (2) the particular set of methods, including procedures and techniques, that are used to acquire any systematic knowledge of the universe or reality.

All scientific disciplines meet one or the other of these sets of criteria, always in varying degree, and most of them meet both—as does sociology. By either criterion, however, scientific knowledge is always a matter of degree, as is reflected in the present gap between the precision of our understanding of physical phenomena, such as protons and neutrons, and our understanding of behavioral phenomena, such as attitudes and values.

## CHARACTERISTICS OF SCIENTIFIC KNOWLEDGE

Scientific knowledge may be characterized by other attributes but the distinguishing qualities are universality, causality, and certitude. Some disciplines may possess some or all of these characteristics to a much greater degree than others. Similarly, these characteristics may be true for one or more of the nonscientific or humanistic disciplines.

UNIVERSALITY.   There is no science of the particular. Science seeks to explain all phenomena of the same type and, hence, is universal in the application of its knowledge. It is not essentially concerned with single or particular instances of a given type of phenomena, as is the case in the humanities and the arts. Accordingly, sociology is not limited in its concerns, for example, with the social behavior of Americans or that of the 1980s. Rather, sociology is concerned with explaining social behavior

▼ wherever and whenever it occurs and whoever may be responsible for it. Discrete and concrete events, of course, provide the particular objects of investigations and analysis; the specific objective of science, however, is the search for universal or standard forms and repetitive patterns that can be stated as generalizations.

Science is a nomothetic activity: It seeks general principles or laws of the phenomena that it studies. A large number of such principles comprises the fund of scientific knowledge in sociology. For example, the relationship between organizational morale and productivity is a curvilinear one, rather than a unilinear one, as is popularly thought to be the case. Most generalizations in sociology, however, are stated as probabilistic relationships between variables, that is, as statements that specify the tendency for two or more variables to be related in one way or another. In sociology, as in other social and behavioral sciences, it appears that **scientific laws**—statements of invariant relationship between phenomena—may not be as extensive as they are in the natural and physical sciences. There is optimism on the part of a great number of sociologists that one day laws governing human social behavior will be uncovered. Although we must be content, at least for the moment, with a lesser degree of precision in principles or "law-like" statements, this situation does not invalidate the fundamental quality of universalistic or generalized explanation.

All scientific propositions, moreover, may be nothing more than probability statements. Such a situation appears to be emerging in the physical sciences as more and more knowledge is accumulated in these fields. In physics, for instance, the Heisenberg principle of uncertainty (1953) states that it is impossible to specify with absolute certainty both the position and the momentum of a particle of matter (or electrons around an atom) at any given moment because an increase in the precision of one measurement reduces the precision of the other. A situation of this kind not only adds further recognition to the complexity of behavioral phenomena but also serves to demonstrate the essential oneness of all phenomena, at least in terms of its essential characteristics from the perspective of scientific explanation (DiRenzo, 1987).

CAUSALITY. Science seeks to determine the causes of the phenomena that it studies. A **cause** may be defined as a necessary and sufficient condition for the occurrence of a given phenomenon. There are different types of causes that can be distinguished in this respect: final, formal, efficient, and material. We need not describe in detail here the nature of these various types of causes, except to say that in all cases the search for causes is essentially an attempt to answer the not-so-simple question, Why do phenomena occur as they do? The search for causes, therefore, is a much more complex undertaking than merely describing what occurs and how it occurs. However necessary elaborate descriptions are for an understanding of the phenomena in question, they do not constitute *explanations* of them. Moreover, in many fields, such as the humanities, the question of cause does not apply. It is meaningless to seek the cause of linguistics or art in the same sense as the cause of deviant or conformist behavior.

CERTITUDE. Science can, and does, seek to determine whether its knowledge of a particular phenomenon is true or false. It is concerned with determining truth insofar as this is possible. But such a question has no meaning or applicability in several of the nonscientific disciplines. To ask whether literature or music is true or false, right or wrong, has absolutely no meaning. A piece of art either is or is not art. To ask whether it has certitude is absurd. The question of certitude, however, is inescapably essential to scientific knowledge.

Scientific knowledge may be distinguished by other characteristics. Three qualities, however, distinguish scientific knowledge from any other variety. They are also the necessary conditions for doing so.

# METHODS OF SCIENCE

Another principal criterion for distinguishing science from nonscience is method—the procedures and techniques by which phenomena are observed and knowledge is accumulated.

The scientific method is equated to the empirical method. The **empirical method** consists fundamentally of the controlled sensory observation of reality. The data, and the purported truth, of scientific knowledge can be seen, heard, tasted, smelled, and felt. Not only can the truth or falsity of scientific knowledge be determined, but in many fields its validity can be demonstrated in an empirical, that is, sensibly observable, manner.* One need not accept the truth of scientific knowledge in these instances on the strength of self-evident postulations or logical principles which either do not require or cannot be given sensory verification.

Some would argue that those disciplines that are not empirically derived, but rather logically deduced, such as philosophy or mathematics, are not sciences.† Such an argument rests upon the exclusive employment of one criterion of science at the expense of others. Nonetheless, the scientific, that is, empirical, method is not

used in the humanities, though several of these disciplines could be considered scientific in terms of other criteria.

Science is unified in terms of its method. The fundamental procedures of the scientific method, sometimes called the logic of science, are the same for all sciences, natural as well as social. The specific nature of the different phenomena that are the concern of each science imposes various limitations and certain requirements that may demand modification in the scientific method for each field, but the general canons of logical inquiry remain the same in all scientific disciplines. There are no differences in the *logic* or *structure* of the scientific method as utilized in either the social or the natural sciences. There are differences in the *content* or *techniques* of the scientific method as it is applied in the individual disciplines. Many sciences, given the varying nature of their particular subject matter, have their own research tools and techniques. For example, chemistry uses test tubes and litmus paper, physics uses micrometers and atom smashers, sociology uses questionnaires and interview schedules, and psychology uses personality tests and polygraphs. The different categories of science, therefore, are distinguished not by the general methodology of basic procedures common to them, but rather by the specific procedures and techniques that are employed in this process.

However valid these distinctions may be, and however necessary they may be to serve the needs and limitations of human inquiry, the basic dichotomy of the social and physical sciences has been the source of much confusion and meaningless questions about intellectual sophistication and superiority. There certainly are differences, very real ones, in the comparative success that the different fields of science have had in explaining reality. Science, however, whether measured in terms of qualitative or quantitative criteria, turns out to be only an ideal against which any individual discipline

**47**

---

* Some theories of behavior (for example, psychoanalysis to a large extent) cannot for the most part be empirically validated. Hence, while they appear to be logically true, it seems impossible to determine whether these theoretical formulations are indeed really true—at least with the present state of research technology. Such theories may be scientific in character, but not in terms of the methods by which they are derived.

† Others contend that mathematics is a metascience—more in the nature of a scientific language or tool of all sciences rather than a separate science with its own substantive concerns.

▼

makes an approximation. In other words, we may question the effectiveness of the behavioral disciplines, or any other field of study, as nomothetic or generalizing sciences, but the basic orientation and mode of analysis remains essentially scientific.

## APPLICATIONS OF SCIENCE: PREDICTION AND CONTROL

48

We need to distinguish between the essential qualities and methods of scientific knowledge and its applications, real or potential. Given the characteristics of scientific knowledge (universality, causality, certitude), scientists often apply this knowledge to predict the occurrence of relevant phenomena. Ideally, knowing the causes and conditions of human social behavior, sociologists can predict the occurrence of such phenomena. Indeed, the accurate prediction of phenomena is itself empirical confirmation of the validity or certitude of that body of scientific knowledge (see DiRenzo, 1966*b*).

Prediction in the field of sociology, while not characterized by complete precision, is quite common in terms of such things as success or failure in marriage, population dynamics, and crime rates. A quite impressive example of prediction and control in sociology can be offered from the field of deviant behavior. Two criminologists, Sheldon and Eleanor T. Glueck, formerly at the Harvard Law School, developed a prediction index for juvenile delinquency based on the measurement of a set of social factors: (1) supervision of the child (by mother), (2) discipline of the child (by father), and (3) cohesiveness of the family. This predictability index was prepared on the basis of a rather comprehensive and comparative study of 500 boys adjudicated as delinquent and 500 boys who were listed as nondelinquent (Glueck & Glueck, 1950).

An intriguing application of this procedure was made in 1954 on a sample of 301 6-year-old boys selected among those entering school for the first time in the city of New York. The objective was to predict the probability of delinquency during the next 10 years. The Gluecks' predictability index was found to be amazingly accurate. Delinquency adjudication, which was forecast for 33 boys, turned out to be 85 percent correct; potential nondelinquency forecast for 243 boys turned out to be 95 percent accurate; and a set of 25 boys who were given a 50 percent chance of being found delinquent revealed that 9 were adjudicated delinquent and 16 were not. This impressive prediction of human behavior is all the more amazing when one realizes that it was projected over a period of 10 years, regardless of potential, and indeed actual, change in the three variables that were the basis of the prediction during the 10-year interval.

The control dimension potentially implied here is that the predictability tables provided guidelines for attacking the problem of delinquency at an age when it is believed the intervention of remedial measures has a high probability of success. For this purpose, "A Manual of Procedures for Application of the Glueck Prediction Table" (Craig & Glick, 1976) was developed and has been used extensively by the New York City Youth Board and other social agencies.

Control involves human intervention in order to alter the natural course of events. First of all, simply on the basis of scientific knowledge, control may not be possible. To be able to explain why phenomena occur does not imply, therefore, that one is able to control or manipulate those phenomena. For example, to be able to explain the weather, as meteorologists can do with a fairly strong measure of success, does not mean, therefore, that meteorologists automatically know how to control the weather so that we can have rain or sunshine as we like. Similarly, astronomy can explain the nature and function of the stars to a great extent, but it is unable, given the present state of our technology, to manipulate and control them. Prediction and control are not so much qualities of scientific knowledge itself as they are applied functions of science. These activities amount to engineering which, as such, requires a totally different set of skills. Engineering, or control, involves doing or making things, and this is quite another activity from science's essential concern with discovery, however much the latter may be required for the former.

The primary goal of science is explanation. Prediction and control may be seen, among others, as secondary goals of scientific knowledge. The degree to which these applied functions are realized varies with the individual disciplines of science, based on the nature of subject matter, history, technology, and resources. Moreover, some sciences do not permit the applications of prediction and control, at least, not at the present. Such fields include philosophy, theology, mathematics, and astronomy.

Questions about prediction and control lead easily to another concern about science: its application and the solution of problems.

## "PURE" VERSUS "APPLIED" SCIENCE: A FALSE DICHOTOMY

Distinctions that are often drawn between "pure" and "applied" science constitute a false dichotomy. First of all, as we have seen, there is no such thing as a "pure" science, if by that term we mean a totally empirically derived and/ or confirmed knowledge—or even a body of data that completely or ideally manifests the qualitative characteristics attributed to scientific knowledge.

A more proper distinction is that between pure and applied *research:* Is the objective of scientific investigation to contribute to a particular fund of knowledge or to the solution of a particular problem? The epistemological ori-

entation and the methods of procedure remain essentially scientific in both types of research situations.

Scientific research may be used as a means of solving problems and achieving particular goals. Applications of scientific knowledge, however, do not constitute science. Rather, such endeavors would be known more properly as technology or as art. Applied sociology is manifested in such forms and endeavors as social engineering (for example, urban planning), social work, and sociological practice. The application of sociological knowledge and methods in these respects is directed at the solution of practical problems. In these endeavors there is a focus on *doing* or *making* as the fundamental objectives of the sociological enterprise rather than on *discovering* or *finding*, that is, explaining reality.

This distinction between pure and applied research is an important one for sociology. Sociology emerged in part out of the desire to reform and improve society. Such a goal in itself is a legitimate one, but once sociology moved into the category of science, it had to relinquish any attempts at social reform or social action in the judgment of many of its followers. Yet, in recent years there has been a reemergence of sociological activism, particularly as government and private foundations have provided financial support for "scientific" intervention into social and societal phenomena. A rapidly expanding parallel to these developments is that of the clinical practice of sociology,* which has similar orientations or applications in terms of client-practitioner relationships and the treatment of personal problems of a sociological nature. All applications of sociological activity involve **value judgments,** which are decisions about the desirability or preference of

▼

49

* The field of clinical sociology, as a vehicle for effecting social change, involves such tasks as social policy analysis, counseling, sociotherapy, organization and/or community development, and conflict resolution (Fritz, 1985).

**Applied Sociology.** One application of sociological knowledge and methods of social research involves urban planning and other forms of social engineering that are concerned with the design or modification of social environments. (© Joel Gordon 1983)

phenomena and events, and, as such, belong to the area that has come to be known as the policy sciences (a loose use of the term "science"). It is important, therefore, to distinguish between the scientific functions of sociology as a method of knowing and its practical concerns and applications in the resolution of social and behavioral problems.

## Sociology as Science

The scientific methodology of sociology is fundamentally no different from that of the natural and physical sciences. Neither is the nature of the knowledge so derived from this methodology. A number of arguments, however, are frequently advanced against the possibility of a science of sociology. The principal objections to a science of sociology are discussed below.

The contents of this book are directed at dispelling these objections. The reader is advised to hold his or her judgment in abeyance until the conclusion of this volume.

## HUMAN BEHAVIOR IS A MYSTERY

Accordingly, it cannot be explained, at least not in any completely satisfactory way. To take all the "mystery" out of human behavior is the very goal of sociology and the other behavioral sciences. The fundamental objective of these disciplines, as mentioned in the preceding chapter, is to break the "behavior code" in order to explain the principles of human behavior, just as biologists have broken the "genetic code" to reveal the principles of human life. The fact that so much of the "mystery" of human behavior has already been unraveled seems to be sufficient reason for assuming that much more can be learned. Moreover, whether human behavior is scientifically explainable can only be determined by making such an attempt in order to determine how successful the effort can be.

## HUMAN BEHAVIOR IS RATIONAL

However true, there is no *a priori* reason why a science of rational behavior should be any more difficult or impossible than one of nonrational phenomena. Not all human behavior, moreover, is rational. A science of rational behavior may be a more difficult and arduous task than a science of nonrational behavior, but it need not necessarily be an impossibility. Not all theoretical approaches in the social and behavioral sciences assume rationality to be an essential characteristic of human behavior. Several humanistic approaches (for example, phenomenology and existentialism) exemplify this position. Moreover, other approaches, such as behaviorism (see Chapter 4), argue that rational behavior is far more susceptible to scientific and theoretical analysis than is nonrational or irrational behavior (see Hitt, 1969). In any event, this question again cannot be satisfactorily resolved unless the effort at scientific exploration is made.

## HUMAN BEHAVIOR IS TOO INDIVIDUALISTIC

With an apparently infinite variety of people, what is constant about human behavior that would potentially make for a fund of scientific knowledge about it? Human behavior, even on the part of given individuals, is said to be highly changeable from one situation to another. Such gross variability would not permit generalities or predictions of human behavior. Therefore, goes the argument, only the study of unique elements or variables can comprise the study of sociology and/or of human behavior in general. However, the same is true of genes, atoms, and chemicals; therefore, the same objection should be true of the natural and physical sciences. But sociology does not study the unique or infinitely variable. Like all sciences, it studies the repetitive and patterned, even invariant, features of its phenomena.

Moreover, people are not infinitely flexible or individualistic—or, at least, we can assume that to be the case. And as with physical or natural phenomena, it is the constants, or universal elements, that make possible a science of human behavior. For sociology, it is the essentials, not the accidentals, of social life that comprise the indispensable elements for a science of human social behavior.

## HUMAN BEHAVIOR IS TOO COMPLEX

So subtle and so elusive are the intricacies of human behavior that they preclude any significant understanding—whether by scientific methods or other means. Such a view is not only pessimistic; it is fatalistic! The basis of the argument is quite correct: There are a large number of determinative factors that account for the intricate complexity of human behavioral phenomena. That human behavior is highly complex, however, does not necessarily make it impossible to explain. Such difficulties can be seen as methodological problems and need not mean that any scientific attempt to understand human behavior is doomed to failure.

To counter arguments of this kind, one need only bear in mind the prediction and control possibilities that have been achieved thus far in the field of sociology. However limited such accomplishments may be in a comparative perspective, they can be seen in large part as a function of time and the status of the discipline at the moment, for all of the reasons already mentioned.

▼ ## HUMAN BEHAVIOR INVOLVES FREE WILL

Human beings, goes the argument here, can upset and/or distort predictions because they are free moral agents. Of course they are free moral agents, and of course they can invalidate predictions. Efforts of this kind, however, presuppose a conscious intent directed at that very end—a calculated and premeditated action. Such is not the case in the overwhelming amount of human behavior, however much the contrary could be true. Moreover, it is on this very basis of freedom that the predictions of sociology and other behavioral sciences are made.

The assumptions of free will and individual choice are among the variables that enter into scientific calculation, explanation, and prediction of human behavior. Nonetheless, the freedom of human beings depends, in part, on the stability and predictability of conditions to achieve desired ends. If prediction were not possible for human social behavior, social life would not be possible. Even the simplest of acts, such as walking down the street or driving a car without getting killed, presupposes a high degree of probability. It is the predictable uniformity or stability in patterns of behavior and social interaction that provides the basis of nearly all social life. In point of fact, however, the assumption of free will, or its opposite, has no effect on the observation and explanation of human behavior. The same results are obtained no matter which particular assumption is made. The matter of free will becomes a problem or consideration only in regard to whether individuals should be held responsible for their behavior, such as in instances of criminal or delinquent activity.

Of course, freedom of action that is present in human behavior makes scientific prediction less accurate than in some other scientific fields, but it does not render prediction impossible. That the quality of prediction in sociology is not as precise as it is in the physical sciences cannot be denied. This imprecision, however, is not so much the fault of the sociological methods as of the phenomena that are studied. Moreover, as we mentioned earlier, the superior degree of precision that has long been characteristic of some of the natural and physical sciences is now being challenged. Probabilistic rather than absolutist predictions and explanations may be the only eventual kind of certainty to expect from all fields of science.

## HUMAN BEHAVIOR REQUIRES SUBJECTIVE ANALYSIS

The biases of the researcher, it is argued, will always enter into scientific analysis and render it nonobjective and contrary to the ideal character of science. Admittedly, this objection would appear to have some merit on its surface. Sociologists, nonetheless, view this objection as only another of the methodological problems that are particular to their field of inquiry. Such obstacles have, to a great extent, been resolved already by the development of tools and techniques which either eliminate or minimize the nonobjective dimension of research on human behavior. Moreover, it is possible to conduct subjective analyses of human behavior within the orientation of the scientific method. Symbolic interaction is an example of such an approach.

Objections of this kind do not in themselves invalidate or preclude the application of basic tenets of the scientific method in the study of human behavior. These very objections exemplify the complications of the scientific process for the disciplines of human behavior, and sociology in particular. Fortunately, they do not render impossible a science of sociology. Such objections are essentially methodological problems that require a particular resolution on the part of sociology as well as the other social and behavioral sciences. Whether a science of sociology is possible can only be determined by undertaking the necessary effort and engaging in scientific activity.

# Behavioral Science versus Physical Science

There are several factors that account for the differential progress of the behavioral and physical sciences. First, there is the relatively late development of the social and behavioral sciences. Sociology, as a formal and systematic discipline, is only about 160 years old.

Second, there is the question of the complexity of subject matter. As complicated and impenetrable as the phenomena of the physical and natural sciences may seem, analysis in the behavioral sciences is conducted under incomparably more frustrating conditions. It is much more difficult to explain social or behavioral phenomena such as anomie or alienation, conflict or cooperation, suicide or delinquency than physical or biological phenomena such as gravity or reproduction. $H_2O$ is always $H_2O$. One suicide or act of delinquency, however, is not completely like any other. Many problems in the behavioral sciences, moreover, can only be studied in their true setting, and not in the somewhat artificial and simplified confines of a laboratory.

Third, research in the social and behavioral sciences is hampered nowadays by considerations of law and ethics which do not present themselves as frequently or as extensively in many of the natural and physical sciences. The latter sciences, for example, usually destroy, or are permitted to destroy, the phenomena that they investigate, while such is not the case in the social and behavioral sciences. In addition to challenging the methodological creativity of the social and behavioral scientists, such situations often preclude the pursuit and analysis of highly significant questions that work against scientific progress, at least temporarily.

Fourth, there is a question of social values, with its attendant considerations of social recognition and prestige, which is reflected in the wishes of people who prefer one kind of knowledge at the expense of another. The allocation of resources and rewards is made in a corresponding fashion.

Fifth, there is the question of investments in the two broad areas of intellectual activity, the sciences and the humanities, as well as the individual disciplines. For example, each year the U.S. government appropriates billions of dollars for scientific research, but these assets are disproportionately allocated to the natural and physical sciences. Actual funding for basic research in the social and behavioral sciences for 1988 constituted less than 4 percent, versus 49 percent for the natural and physical sciences, of total appropriations for the National Science Foundation. Provisions of this budget for sociology ($3,800,000) were 13 percent of appropriations for the social and economic sciences, and only .002 percent of the total budget. Appropriations for applied research were not essentially any different.* Notwithstanding the real difference in the true cost of research activity in the various fields of investigation, the significant disparity in the allocation of resources manifests, in large part, a differential judgment of worth attached to both scientific knowledge and humanistic knowledge, as well as to the social and behavioral disciplines more specifically.

Lastly, there is the issue of human apprehension. Many people with some insight into the nature of the behavioral sciences are afraid that human freedom may eventually be annihilated, or, at least, greatly diminished, as human behavior becomes increasingly predictable and subject to control. Such a threat—no less true in the natural and physical sciences, especially now that scientists have the right to patent synthesized forms of life—is indeed a very real one. For example, there have been

53

* Source: *Budget Summary, Fiscal Year 1989*. National Science Foundation Washington, D. C.

▼ recent instances in which social scientists and methods of social research have been used, with apparent success, to select juries favorable to the defendants. Yet, these fears involve considerable misunderstanding on the part of the general public about the nature and purposes of scientific research.

These kinds of complications notwithstanding, there is growing support for social science research. This is due, in large part, to the fact that problems in the physical sciences increasingly involve human dimensions in one way or another. Space exploration, for example, was not possible until a number of problems of a

54

sociological and psychological nature, such as the effects of social isolation, had been resolved. Such a situation cannot fail to demonstrate the essential unity of knowledge in the behavioral and physical sciences.

## Major Steps in the Scientific Method: The Case of Sociology

Scientific research is a very complex process. As the sketch on this page suggests, it could be described as a twisting, winding, rocky,

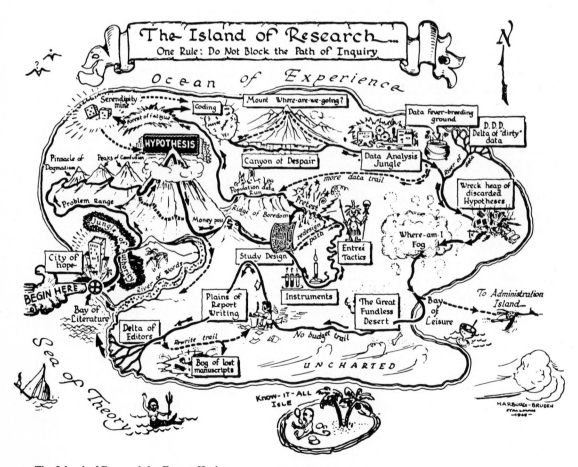

The Island of Research by Ernest Harburg.

bumpy, frequently detoured road. Traversing this course is much like trying to find the correct path through a maze, with all of its dead ends, roadblocks, and inevitable frustrations. At the same time, this activity is a fascinating and entertaining one. Here we can describe in only general terms the process and method of scientific research. Our discussion will concentrate on the fundamental logic and procedures of scientific research. We are not concerned here with the many specific techniques of scientific research; such a treatment would require an entire text in itself.

There are six basic steps in the process of scientific research. These steps are roughly successive ones, although, as the accompanying illustration shows, the research process is more typically a back-and-forth procedure rather than a simply progressive one. Backtracking and crisscrossing are very much a part of the typical progression through the empirical process of scientific research.

## FORMULATION OF HYPOTHESES

The first step is the formulation of a research **hypothesis,** which is a statement of assumed relationship between two or more phenomena (*relational hypothesis*) or simply of the occurrence of phenomena with no attempt to state a particular relationship (*descriptive hypothesis*). Hypotheses represent propositions that are basically questions in search of an answer. The function of an hypothesis is to give focus to research by generating questions that lead to scientific propositions which can be put to a test in order to determine their validity. Here is an example: The size of families is inversely related to the educational level of the parents, such that the higher the level of education, the smaller the family. It remains to be determined through empirical research whether this hypothesis is true, and, if so, under which kinds of qualifying

conditions. The research task is to determine whether the hypothesis can be confirmed—that is, whether there is empirical evidence to substantiate the hypothesis. Of course, as with nearly all hypotheses, this statement implies only a **probabilistic relationship,** not an absolute one. Hence, the objective of the research process is to specify the nature of that probability as precisely as possible.

Hypotheses often derive from hunches, intuitions, common sense, and personal experiences that one may have about the nature and function of particular phenomena. Such situations are very important instances of the role that subjectivity plays in the scientific method. In more objective and ideal perspectives, however, hypotheses, in the form of inductive or deductive relationships, derive from theories—to which hypotheses themselves, upon empirical confirmation, ultimately contribute. This is an example of the circular nature of the research process, and that of the relationship between hypotheses and theory in particular.

## RESEARCH DESIGN

Depending upon the nature of the problem and the availability of resources, scientists may select or construct their research design from a variety of research strategies. Variations in procedures and techniques often stem from different theoretical approaches. Some orientations lend themselves more effectively to qualitative research; others are more suitable for quantitative research. Much depends, too, on whether the research is to be exploratory or explanatory. **Exploratory research** is a preliminary, and basically descriptive, type of research that seeks to refine the various elements of the research problem and research design. **Explanatory research,** either descriptive or experimental in nature, is a much more sophisticated undertaking that seeks to provide substantive answers to the research problem.

▼

55

▼ Ideally, all **research designs** begin and end the same way—with theory. A **theory** may be defined as a set of logically interrelated concepts of empirical reference that purport to explain reality or phenomena. Theory states a logical relationship between observable facts. When facts are conceptually ordered, assembled into propositions, and placed in their logical relationship to each other, they constitute a theory. Theory, however, has a dual function: (1) to generate hypotheses, which serve to initiate the research process; and (2) to provide explanations at the culmination of the research process. Theory, hence, is both the alpha and the omega of the research process; that is, it functions as both the starting point and the end point of the research process.

**56**

## SAMPLING

Data collection usually involves the process of sampling—itself a highly complex set of operations. **Sampling** consists fundamentally of a set of procedures by which a portion of a given population is selected as representative of that population. Since it is usually impossible, and even unnecessary, to study the entire population of people whose behavior is the subject of a particular research problem, the researcher needs only to assemble a relatively small collection, or *sample*, of individuals who are considered to be typical of those in the population under study.

Sampling contrasts to the **case-study technique**, which is an in-depth assessment of one or a small number of individuals considered to be typical or representative of a much larger collectivity about which we wish to inquire.

UNIVERSE AND SAMPLE. Two central concepts in sampling are universe and sample. The **universe** (or population) is the set of individuals to be studied (for example, college students), while the **sample** consists of the set of

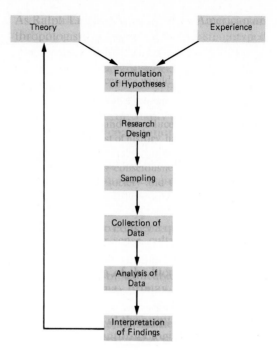

FIGURE 2-1  Major Steps in the Research Process.

particular individuals who are selected (for example, the students at a particular college or in a particular class) to represent the universe for the purposes of the research in question.

SAMPLING DESIGNS. Sampling designs and techniques are numerous, and some are more appropriate than others for specific purposes. The principal types of sampling used in sociology include the following:

**Random sampling** affords an equiprobability of selection to each individual in the universe (population). A procedure such as drawing names out of a hat, or selecting every fifth or sixth name in a telephone directory, would constitute a random sample.

**Stratified sampling** utilizes the principles of random selection within the various subcategories of a particular universe. Such categories might be those based on age, sex, race, or socioeconomic variables. Proportional distributions of the categories selected in the stratified sample reflect those in the universe.

**Quota sampling** essentially establishes a fixed number of individuals with particular characteristics without imposing any controls on their selection.

**Area sampling** selects individuals from particular physical or geographical areas, such as a neighborhood or census tract.

**Availability sampling,** also known as convenience sampling, simply utilizes whichever individuals are available in a particular place at a given time.

**ADEQUACY AND REPRESENTATIVE- NESS.** Two fundamental characteristics that are imperative in all kinds and instances of sampling are *adequacy* and *representativeness*.

An **adequate sample** is one that is of an appropriate and sufficient size to permit the kind of analysis and projections that the researcher wants to perform. Adequacy refers fundamentally to the complexity and diversity of the phenomena under investigation. As a general rule, a greater number of controls are required in social science research than in the physical sciences. This situation is due to the greater complexity and variability of human behavior. The more complex the universe and the dimensions under study, the more complex and larger the corresponding sample must be. For example, in order to sample a barrel of wine, 1 or 2 ounces would be sufficient, assuming the wine is thoroughly mixed. Given the homogeneous nature of the contents of the barrel, one drop of wine is like any other. A barrel of people, however, is not homogeneous. Each individual has a very great number of differences, many of which may be significant in terms of the behavior being studied. Accordingly, the selection of any one

or two individuals, or even a small number, could present a variety of highly significant biases. This problem of potential distortion can usually be counteracted by the selection of a relatively large number of people. On the other hand, it inevitably surprises one to learn that public opinion polls conducted throughout our country of over 250 million people frequently involve adequate samples of less than 1500 individuals.

Social scientists also need to ensure that research subjects constitute a **representative sample** of the people about whom they wish to generalize. A sample that is typical of one segment of a universe, but not of the entire universe, is said to be unrepresentative. An unrepresentative sample, however adequate, poses an even more serious threat to the validity claims of any research. Sociologists employ various kinds of statistical tools and measurements to determine the adequacy and representativeness of a sample.

## COLLECTION OF DATA

The next step of the scientific method involves a series of activities concerned with accumulating evidence—the individual bits of information that are necessary to put the hypotheses to an empirical test in a manner consistent with the research design. These elements of empirical observation constitute the *facts* of scientific research.

Data collection may take many forms, depending upon the nature and objectives of the research design or problem: surveys, field research, content analysis, experimentation, laboratory research, and computer simulation. All of them, in one way or another, are concerned with sociometrics, or the empirical measurement of relevant phenomena.

**OBSERVATION.** Observation is the most primitive, as well as the most sophisticated, of

**58**

**Collecting Data.** Observation of social behavior is the fundamental process in sociological research. Use of the two-way mirror for this purpose combines nonparticipant observation and laboratory research. (© Susan Lapides 1984/Design Conceptions)

research techniques. **Observation** fundamentally involves the use of one's senses to record information: Seeing, feeling, tasting, touching, and smelling are the basic vehicles of observation. There are, however, many different kinds of scientific observation and, correspondingly, many different types of tools for it.

**Simple observation** is a casual and informal type of observation that involves no standardization of observational techniques and no control over the pertinent variables in the research situation. Any conscious effort in paying attention to, and recording, social behavior constitutes an act of simple observation.

**Systematic observation** is a formal and more precise type of observation that places rigorous controls on both the observer and the observed phenomenon, usually involving various types of instruments and highly refined procedures.

Two subtypes of simple and systematic observation are participant and nonparticipant observation.

**Participant observation** involves a situation in which the observer plays an active role in the behavior under study. The expectation is that a greater depth of experience can be obtained from such personal experience in the natural setting.

Driving a taxicab or acting as a sheriff's deputy, for a period of time, can provide the opportunity to collect data, as well as to have subjective experiences, for analyzing the social behavior of people in a number of respective dimensions. Of course, research projects incorporating such techniques and procedures would be more sophisticated than our very brief description suggests. A well-known example of participant observation is William F. Whyte's classic study, *Street Corner Society* (1943), an assessment of the behavior of teenage boys in an ethnic ghetto of Boston. Whyte himself was trustfully admitted to the gang that he observed over a prolonged period of time and participated fully in its many activities.

More recent examples of this kind of observational and research technique are found in Herbert Gans' *The Urban Villagers* (1982), a broad analysis of the emergence of a close-knit community among strangers in middle-class America; and in *Tally's Corner* (1967), a study by Elliot Liebow of social life in a Black neighborhood of Washington, D.C.

**Nonparticipant observation** involves the contrary situation in which the observer takes a totally passive and noninvolved part in the behavior that he or she observes. Examples would be scientific observation made through one-way glass or, more informally, as a spectator at an athletic event. Criminal, delinquent, or other deviant forms of behavior obviously require nonparticipant observation. Among many well-known examples are Erving Goffman's *Asylums* (1961*a*), a year-long study of social interaction in a mental hospital; Lewis Yablonsky's *The Hippie Trip* (1968), a description of the nonconventional lifestyle of particular segments of young people in our society during an earlier period; and Gary Fine's *With the Boys* (1987), a three-year assessment of children in five Little League baseball teams, learning to play, work together, and generally be "men" through participation in organized sports. Sociologists have developed a number of **unobtrusive measures** for nonparticipant observation which consists of techniques that are disguised or in other ways do not intrude on the behavior under study (see Webb, 1981).

EXPERIMENTATION. Another form of data collection that is used in sociology, although it is popularly thought of as confined to the natural and physical sciences, is experimentation.

**Experimentation,** itself a form of observation, essentially involves the manipulation of social phenomena or social situations in order to measure their effect in selected respects. This type of data collection permits control over one or more elements under investigation. It is, obviously, not suitable for some types of sociological study, such as the analysis of riots or panic behavior.

There are three principal elements, or variables, in experimental analysis. A **variable** is any phenomenon or condition whose properties or values may vary rather than being immutably fixed. Age, sex, and religion are common examples of social variables.

The **dependent variable,** the phenomenon being studied, is determined by, or dependent upon, other variables. In a cause-and-effect relationship, the effect is the dependent variable. The dependent variable in sociology is usually a form of human action, such as an attitude or a behavior.

The **independent variable** represents the causal factor in a cause-and-effect relationship. The independent variable, under some circumstances, constitutes the experimental variable. In some experimental situations, however, the independent "variable" is considered the given, constant, or invariant factor for the analytical problem at hand. It determines or influences the dependent variable, perhaps only under certain conditions, such as in conjunction with another variable or set of variables.

The **intervening variable** is a test factor or experimental element that is introduced into the experiment in order to determine its ability to produce a dependent variable as a consequence of its interaction with the independent factor. Under such circumstances, the intervening variable would constitute the causal variable.

Experimentation usually involves exposing subjects to an experimental element (intervening variable) in order to determine what effects (dependent variable) this experimental variable

59

▼ has, if any, on the behavior of another (independent variable). Suppose, for example, we wish to know whether watching selected programs on television leads to the production of criminal or delinquent behavior (dependent variable). We can expose a sample of people with particular characteristics (independent variable) to a predetermined number of selected programs for a predetermined length of time at predetermined intervals (intervening variable). Another sample of similar people—selected in terms of whichever factors we wish to control or hold constant, such as age, sex, educational level, religious background, and so forth— would not be exposed to the television programs, and preferably would be deprived of any exposure to television for the predetermined time period. After the designated period of time has elapsed, we can determine whether the rate of criminal or delinquent behavior (dependent variable) in the two samples differs. If so, it may then be possible, on the basis of these procedures and findings, to make an estimation or projection of the extent to which television exposure is thought to contribute to the production of crime and delinquency.

Experimental research makes use of a number of different forms of research design suitable for different purposes and with different sources. All of these designs are variations on the classical model of the "before-and-after" technique which involves measures of an experimental population and a control population both before and after the introduction of an experimental, or intervening, variable. There is, in all cases, an application of logical rules, or what have come to be known as the classical canons of experimental research design.* Figure 2-2 illustrates the classical design of exper-

60

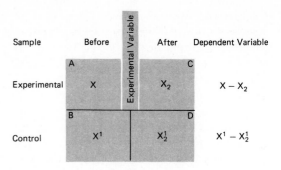

FIGURE 2-2   Classical Research Design.

imental research. There are several variations on the classical before-and-after experiment, including the elimination of either the before or the after segment, the utilization of experimental segments without the control counterparts, or the use of only the after experimental block (ex post facto analysis).

Observation and experimentation may be conducted in either the natural setting, known as field research, or in the contrived setting of the laboratory.

FIELD RESEARCH.   **Field research** of whatever type is conducted in the true context of the behavior under study. Examples of observational research in this mode would be the comparisons of public and private education or coeducation and sex-segregated education. Experimental research in the field setting is illustrated in the well-known investigation by Muzafer Sherif (1961) of group dynamics and intergroup relations in the Robbers Cave study, which involved competition and cooperation among different groups of boys (see Chapter 9), as well as the extensive work on prosocial (altruistic or helping) behavior that has been conducted by several scientists in the past two decades (for example, Schwartz & Gottlieb, 1980; Latane & Darley, 1970).

* Formulated by John Stuart Mill (1843), these are known as the method of agreement, the method of difference, the method of concomitant variation, and the method of residues.

FRANK AND ERNEST                                            by Bob Thaves ▼

DON'T THINK OF US AS BUMS, SIR — THINK OF US AS THE CONTROL GROUP FOR THE AFFLUENT SOCIETY.

THAVES 3-16

61

Reprinted by permission of NEA, Inc.

LABORATORY RESEARCH. **Laboratory research** consists of observation and/or experimentation that is conducted in the somewhat artificial confines of a laboratory. Research on the formation and dynamics of social groups assembled within a laboratory and observed through one-way glass is an example of this type. Another type of experimental research, not often considered as such, would be simulation through the use of computers or other electronic and mechanical devices. In these forms of research, the behavior under investigation is reproduced in another medium in order to permit various kinds of control or manipulation that the research may not be able to perform in a natural setting.

An example of experimental research on human social behavior performed in a laboratory setting is the controversial study of authority and obedience conducted by Stanley Milgram (1974), in which subjects were ordered to administer "electric shocks" of increasing voltage to people who repeatedly performed improperly on memory tests. Another example of laboratory experimentation is the fascinating work by Philip Zimbardo (1973) on interaction between "inmates" and "prison guards" in a simulated prison (see Chapters 6 and 13).

SURVEY RESEARCH. The methods and techniques of data collection par excellence for the sociologist are those embodied in public opinion polls and survey research. **Survey research** and opinion polling are concerned fundamentally with measuring the behavior of people in terms of the systematic analysis of such things as attitudes, values, opinions, beliefs, and customary practices. These techniques perhaps comprise the single most important invention of the social sciences during the past century (Converse, 1987).

Survey research is either of the **cross-sectional** or **longitudinal** variety. The latter type includes repeated collections of data and analyses over a given period of time in order to observe and to control for stable effects and long-term consequences of related elements. Cross-sectional research, on the other hand, consists of a one-time observation, collection of data, and analyses at a given point in time. Most survey research is of this type, which, of course, is more economical and gives quicker results, despite the uncertainty that may surround their durability.

The principal tools used in survey research are the interview and the questionnaire. An **interview** consists of a purposive, often highly

▼

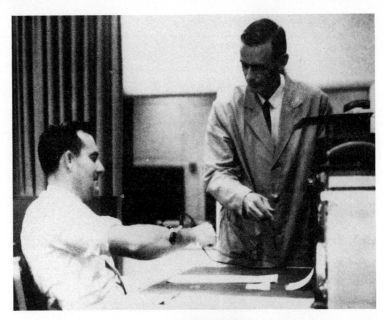

**Human Experiments.** An impressive and controversial study of experimental research in the laboratory setting is Stanley Milgram's analysis of the dynamics of authority and obedience in which subjects were ordered to administer "electric shocks" of increasing voltage to individuals who repeatedly performed improperly on memory tests. Subjects (*upper*) assumed that they were administering shocks to other "subjects." The latter were actually members of the research staff who were strapped to electrical connections in another room (*lower*). (Copyright 1965 by Stanley Milgram. From the film *Obedience,* distributed by the New York University Film Division and the Pennsylvania State University, PCR.)

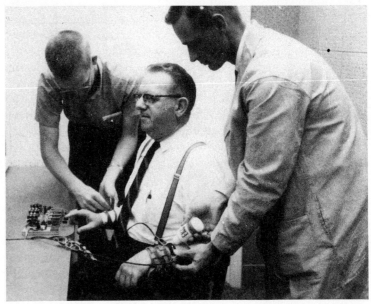

structured, conversation aimed at revealing one's attitudes, opinions, values, beliefs, and modes of behavior relevant to a particular topic. There are many different forms of the interview. The specific tool that is usually used for maintaining control and systematization of the questions that are posed in a highly skillful manner is known as the **interview schedule.** Sometimes, instead of an interview schedule, the interviewer may use a less structured **interview**

**Social Surveys.** The principal type of data collection used by sociologists is that of survey research, most commonly in the forms of interviewing and polling. Expert skills are required for these techniques, which on the surface might appear to be rather simple tasks. (Mark Antman/ Stock, Boston)

**guide,** which consists of a simple enumeration of topics to be covered in a less formalized or structured interview, rather than a set of specific questions.

The **questionnaire,** well-known for its use in public opinion polls, is an instrument for securing the answer to questions or items that is self-administered by the respondent. Its basic structure and format are otherwise similar to that of the interview schedule.

Questions that comprise these instruments consist of both highly structured and unstructured, or open-ended, items. The instruments themselves often consist of projective or disguised measures, such as personality inventories, in addition to a number of straightforward questions.

The construction of questionnaires and interview schedules, as with all other tools of social research, requires highly skilled training in order to be used meaningfully and effectively. The development and use of these instruments are such highly cultivated arts that we must caution the student lest our necessarily brief treatment convey false impressions of simplicity or facility.

DOCUMENTATION. Another source of data that the sociologist frequently utilizes consists of documents. These materials comprise such "precoded" or previously collected information as personal and public records that often provide the only source, or the only available source, for certain kinds of data.

Personal documents—or **biograms,** as they are technically called—describe events in which one personally participates and include such things as diaries, autobiographies, and letters. One technique that is particularly appropriate for data of this kind is that known as theme or **content analysis.** Public documents include written reports, newspapers, books, magazines, pamphlets, journals, and official statistics, such as census data. Particularly useful here are various kinds of data that more recently have come to be known as **social indicators:** figures and rates for such things as population, housing, marriage, divorce, death, illness, income,

▼ expenditures, work, unemployment, social security, welfare, social mobility, use of leisure time, and social participation of various kinds. The federal government, through the Department of Commerce, now publishes an annual volume entitled *Social Indicators* that contains many data of these kinds. Much information of this type is now systematically stored in data banks for eventual use by social scientists.

64

PERSONALITY INVENTORIES. Much of the information that comprises sociological data is derived from the measurement of personality variables. The study of attitudes, values, beliefs, opinions, motivations, and self-concepts, as well as subjective states such as alienation and anomia, essentially involve assessments of personality dynamics and psychological phenomena. There are a great variety of instruments for these purposes, known generically as **personality inventories.** Included among these instruments are many types of **projective tests,** such as sentence completions, which are constructed in such a manner that the specific objective of their measurement is disguised from the manifest level, with the expectation that the respondents will unknowingly project psychological phenomena into their responses. For a more detailed discussion of personality inventories, see Chapter 5.

Other methods of data collection, too technical for elaboration here, include self-rating scales, sociometric devices, indicators, and indices.* We shall have occasion to discuss some of these techniques in more detail throughout the subsequent chapters of this book. Suffice it to say, for our purposes, there is a rather large, and constantly expanding, body of research tools and techniques for data collection in the field of sociology. Each one has its strengths, weaknesses, and limitations that determine its

* See Miller (1983) for a comprehensive inventory of research techniques.

TABLE 2-1. Forms of Data Collection

| | |
|---|---|
| Observation | Simple vs. systematic, participant vs. nonparticipant |
| Experimentation | Laboratory, field |
| Survey research | Cross-sectional or longitudinal, interview, questionnaire, poll |
| Documentation | Biogram, case study, context analysis |
| Personality inventory | Projective test, self-rating scale, objective test |

appropriateness for particular kinds of research problems.

## ANALYSIS OF DATA

Facts, however valid and reliable, do not speak for themselves. Accumulated data need to be interpreted in order to have explanatory meaning. Specifically, there is the need to discern the independent-dependent, cause-and-effect, relationship within the observed phenomena. Many different steps comprise this phase of the research process.

VALIDITY AND RELIABILITY. First, it is necessary to determine the accuracy of the data, that is, to test it for validity and reliability. **Validity** refers to the correspondence between that which a scientific investigation or research instrument purports to measure and that which it actually measures. For example, does a personality test that is designed to measure racial prejudice actually measure racial prejudice; or, does it really measure political attitudes, which are not the intent of the instrument? Similarly, are the findings that are derived in a specific investigation actually true? Do people mean what they say? Do the attitudes and values that are measured by a given questionnaire or interview schedule truly correspond to the way people act, which, after all, is really the subject of the research?

**Reliability** refers to the degree to which a scientific investigation or research tool is influenced by irrelevant and extraneous factors. Suppose that, in conducting a survey on attitudes toward war or poverty, one gets different answers to the same set of questions asked of the same people on each of several different days. Such inconsistent data would be considered unreliable because they are seemingly influenced and biased by an unknown factor, such as the events of the particular day on which the survey was conducted or, perhaps, the person of the researcher.

Reliability is determined by replication—a repeat of the same study, or versions of it, one or more times in order to ascertain whether consistent or substantially similar results can be obtained each time. Investigations and instruments lacking validity may be highly reliable; but unreliable investigations cannot be valid ones.

The student needs to keep these two criteria of validity and reliability foremost in mind when assessing a set of research findings and the particular method by which they were derived. Ample material in the remaining pages of this volume will provide sufficient opportunity for practicing this critical and scientific skill.

QUANTITATIVE AND QUALITATIVE ANALYSIS.   All data analysis fundamentally consists of data reduction, which includes a complex set of processes by which the data are reduced to a more manageable form. Basically, in sociological research, we are measuring qualitative phenomena which need to be quantified in one way or another in order to be amenable to scientific treatment. There are two basic modes of data reduction and data analysis: quantitative analysis and qualitative analysis.

**Quantitative analysis** consists of techniques for the reduction of the data through such meth-ods as categorization and classification. These processes are known more technically as **coding.** Quantitative analysis also involves the manipulation of data through statistical analysis and tabular presentation.

**Qualitative analysis** consists of the logical ordering of the data; it includes such processes as conceptual specification and theoretical interpretation. Among the more sophisticated techniques of qualitative analysis are model construction and mathematical formularization.

Quantitative analysis, often coupled with qualitative analysis, yields **empirical generalizations,** which are simply descriptive, but factual, statements concerning the phenomena under analysis. The following would be examples of empirical generalizations: (1) rural families are larger than urban ones; (2) deliquent gangs are found more commonly in slum areas than in middle-class neighborhoods; (3) suicide shows a curvilinear relationship with social cohesion.

STATISTICAL ANALYSIS. **Statistical analysis** consists of various techniques for reducing quantitative data in order to represent them in a more orderly and meaningful way. Statistical analysis is itself a highly complicated mathematical process. There are two basic types of statistical analysis, each of which makes a fundamentally different contribution to the research process.

**Descriptive statistics,** consisting of methods for organizing and summarizing data, usually serve to describe quantitative data in the form of statistical tables. These statistics take the form of such things as enumerations, frequency distributions, percentage distributions, measures of central tendency, measures of dispersion, percentile ranks, correlations, ratios, proportions, and so on. Ample analysis of descriptive statistics will be provided throughout the many discussions of this book.

**Inferential statistics,** based on the mathematical theories of probability, are concerned

65

*Extension of Descriptive*

▼

## BOX 2-1. Descriptive Statistics

Among the descriptive statistics that are most frequently used in sociology, and ones that you will find to be cited extensively in this text, are measures of central tendency and correlation.

### MEASURES OF CENTRAL TENDENCY

A *measure of central tendency* is a statistic that summarizes a set of measurements. Such measurements are more commonly known as an average. There are three principal types of averages: mean, median, and mode.

A *mean* is an average that is derived arithmetically. Summing a set of scores and then dividing by the number of scores yields a mean. Example: $5 + 3 + 3 + 6 + 8 + 9 + 15 = 49 \div 7 = 7$.

A *median* is a positional average that is derived by locating the middle score in a set of figures that are arranged in either increasing or decreasing order. Example: In the same set of scores used above, the median would be 6.

A *mode* is a descriptive average which is represented by that score (or scores) that occurs more frequently than any other score in an array or distribution of scores. Example: In the same set of scores above, the mode would be 3.

Note the variation in the value of the different measures of central tendency. Each measure has its own purpose and applications in giving meaning to data. It is important, however, to know precisely which measure one has used when speaking of "the average"!

### MEASURES OF CORRELATION

A *measure of correlation* is a statistic that indicates the degree to which two variables covary (that is, vary together) in a consistent and significant fashion. Correlations may be either positive or negative.

In a *positive correlation*, the value of both variables is said to move in the same direction. That is, as the value of one variable increases or decreases, the value of the second variable correspondingly increases or decreases. In a *negative correlation*, the values of the two variables are said to move inversely. That is, as the value of one variable increases, the value of the other decreases.

There are several measures of correlation. The measure that is most commonly used in sociology is that known as *Pearson's r*, also called the *coefficient of correlation*. This measure consists of a number that varies from $-1$ to $+1$. An $r$ of $+1$ represents a perfectly positive correlation, while an $r$ of $-1$ indicates a perfectly negative correlation. An $r$ of 0 is equivalent to zero correlation between the variables. Data seldom reveal perfect correlations.

It is important to understand that correlations do not establish a cause-and-effect relationship between the variables in question. A correlation might be spurious, in which case it is purely coincidental; or, more likely, it could be an indication that both variables are affected by yet another, unknown, variable. Correlations, nonetheless, are usually suggestive of an interactive relationship between variables. ▲

with the causal association between independent and dependent variables. Inferential statistics serve to determine the significance—the probability of the validity—of a set of data or descriptive statistics in order to make predictions or inferences about the larger populations to which one may wish to generalize from the research sample. Inferential statistics, thus, are essentially mathematical calculations that determine the probability that the findings or data based on a particular sample in a sociological study will be equally as true for other populations of people. Examples of inferential statistics will be presented as appropriate in subsequent chapters.

Scientific inquiry does not end with the mere categorization and classification of data, and their statistical descriptions, nor with statements of empirical generalization—however elegant or sophisticated all of these may be. Once the data have been analyzed in these essentially mechanical dimensions, the next step is to interpret them. This crucial step involves asking the fundamental question, What do the observed results mean? Here, at long last, comes the stage of theory construction and scientific explanation.

## THE CONSTRUCTION OF THEORY

So far in our discussion of the scientific method, we have spoken of only **descriptive analysis,** which assesses social reality in terms of providing answers to the question, What? More theoretically significant is **explanatory analysis,** which seeks to provide answers to the question, Why? Explanatory analysis presupposes descriptive analysis, but now the elaborately described data need to be interpreted in terms of conceptual and theoretical frames of reference. What do the data mean? *Why* do they occur as they do? Unless and until we answer *why* phenomena occur, and how they occur as they do, we do not have scientific explanation.

**DESCRIPTIVE VERSUS THEORETICAL EXPLANATION.** One kind of descriptive explanation, frequently confused with theoretical explanation, is that provided by models. Contrary to popular beliefs, models are not explanations of anything. **Models** simply consist of various ways of reproducing the phenomenon or behavior which is to be explained, in some other form or medium, in order that this explanation may be facilitated. For example, the flight of an airplane is in many respects a mechanical model, or reproduction, of the flight of a bird. The invention or production of an airplane, however, does not explain how the bird flies or what makes it fly. Observing and studying the behavior of an airplane may provide some insight or information that could serve as a basis for developing a theory or explanation about the principles of aerodynamics that explain the flight of both the bird and the airplane.

Models may either be conceptual or mechanical. The former, such as mathematical models, are symbolic representations of sociological entities, while the latter are in one way or another physical reproductions. One type of mechanical model is that provided by the computer. When a scientist is able to program an electronic computer to reproduce behavior, such as by having it play a game of chess, the dynamics or actions of the computer do not *explain why* people play chess or interact the way that they do. On the other hand, the computer model may *describe how* they interact in this process, and such information may assist the scientist in developing a theory or scientific explanation about why the interaction in this activity occurs as it does. Various models are similarly used in sociology to generate explanations and to facilitate the construction of theories of human social behavior.

Explanatory analysis culminates ideally in the development of theory. **Theory,** as indicated above, may be defined as a set of logically interrelated concepts of empirical reference that purport to explain phenomena. No theory,

▼

**67**

▼ however, is ever absolute. All theoretical explanations remain subject to potential revision on the basis of newly discovered facts. A case in point are the currently revised theories about the formation of the earth and other planets as a result of data collected from the exploration of outer space.

The same is true of **scientific laws,** which are defined as empirically established statements of invariant relationship between phenomena. However, scientific laws, like theories, are subject to revision. For example, for 200 years Newton's law of motion was thought to describe with complete precision the trajectories of every sort of moving body. Einstein's theory of relativity for predicting the motion of particles has shown that Newton's laws are less than all-encompassing. Scientific laws, nonetheless, constitute the zenith of scientific explanation.

Are there scientific laws in sociology? The answer, we think, is yes; but, sociologists have been reluctant to speak in such terms. They prefer, more frequently than not, to talk of "principles" or "lawlike" statements of explanation. An example of a law, or general principle of human behavior, is that automatically, inevitably, and invariably, a group structure emerges in any human situation involving the repeated interaction of two or more people over a given period of time. Another example is the universal dynamic of stratification or social ranking that inevitably characterizes the interaction of all people and the structural organization of all groups and societies. Nonetheless, while sociology can sometimes say, "If A, then B absolutely," more often it is, "If A, then B a given percent of the time." Some sociologists (Lazarsfeld, 1966) have maintained that sociology, and the other social sciences, may have to content themselves with producing statements of probability rather than with discovering absolute laws. However, since the same situation seems to be true for the physical sciences, perhaps in the immediate future we can

68

expect sociologists, as well as other social and behavioral scientists, to speak more enthusiastically about "probabilistic laws" of human behavior (DiRenzo, 1987).

LATENT AND MANIFEST PROPERTY SPACES. All scientific analysis may be said to take place within a given property space or segment of reality. It is convenient for analytical purposes to make a distinction between two types of property space: latent and manifest.

**Latent property space** refers to the hidden, nonphysical reality that is the true locus of sociological explanations. Such sociological phenomena as groups, society, social class, attitudes, and personality are latent phenomena: They cannot be observed directly. In the physical sciences, such phenomena as radiation and gravity are elements that also reside in a latent property space: that is, they cannot be manifestly observed.

It is the latent phenomena of human behavior that sociology seeks to explain. However, the empirical data with which sociologists must work—for example, concrete actions or behavior—are located in what is known as the **manifest property space:** the physical and accessible phenomena that are the focus of direct observation. So, we observe and record data in the manifest property space not to explain them, but rather to explain relevant phenomena in the latent property space. The descriptions and measurements of the manifest property space are the basis of explanations in the latent property space.

The manifest property space is only the route to the latent property space. What we do in the observation and study of the manifest property space, however, is crucial for how well and how accurately we are able to explain the latent property space. An analogy is a situation in which a person goes to a physician and gets treated for headache but dies of a brain tumor. Logical induction and deduction, on the basis of empirical evidence, play key roles in the highly crucial step in bridging the two types of property space. What we do empirically in the manifest property space must theoretically reflect the latent property space as accurately as possible. This requirement is especially true in the fundamental and ultimate consideration of concept formation, which we shall discuss in more detail in the subsequent section.

## Concepts: The Building Blocks of Scientific Theory

▼

Scientific theory consists of a set of logically interrelated concepts of empirical reference that purport to explain reality. Concepts, then, are not only the indispensable vehicles of thought

## BOX 2-2. Sociological Research: A Specimen

### PERSONALITY TYPES AMONG PROFESSIONAL POLITICIANS

Can professional politicians be distinguished by distinct types of personality? And, if so, what significance does such a situation have for the way that political roles are performed and/or the way political organizations, such as parties and parliaments, function?

These are intriguing questions, which have been asked by sociologists, political scientists, psychologists, and other social and behavioral scientists. Gathering the data required to answer such questions, however, has not been an easy undertaking—especially given the nature of the subjects involved and the methodological techniques that would be required. One attempt, with interesting results, was conducted by the author (DiRenzo, 1967a).

### SELECTIVE HYPOTHESES

Hypotheses were derived from informal observation and surveys of the literature.
1. Professional politicians are typically characterized by dogmatic types of personality with an authoritarian orientation toward power.
2. Professional politicians can be distinguished from nonpoliticians in terms of significantly greater degrees of dogmatism (authoritarianism).

### RESEARCH DESIGN

Exploratory study using the "after only" model of research design: cross-sectional survey research, including personality assessment, of an experimental sample of professional politicians, combined with a control sample of nonpoliticians.

### SAMPLING

Subjects constituted the male membership of the Chamber of Deputies of the Italian parliament. A stratified random sample was established for each of the major political parties of the Chamber. All of the members of the smaller political

*(Continued)*

▼ BOX 2-2   *(Continued).*

parties were included in the sample, and a 20 percent selection of the larger parties was drawn by means of a table of random numbers. The final number of subjects in the sample was 129, which constitutes about 22 percent of the Chamber membership.

CONTROL SAMPLE

A quota/availability sample of 500 nonpoliticians was drawn from metropolitan Rome. Subjects were nonrigorously matched by social backgrounds with the political sample in order to approximate the proportional distributions of these factors in the political sample.

COLLECTION OF DATA

Survey research techniques. An interview schedule was used for the political sample, and a questionnaire for the control sample. Both instruments incorporated a personality inventory designed to measure the hypothetical types, along with numerous questions on social and political issues.

FINDINGS

Both hypotheses were supported. Seventy-six percent of the political sample was shown to have dogmatic-authoritarian personalities. The difference in the mean score of dogmatism for the two samples was as predicted, and this difference was found to be statistically significant on the basis of various formulae of inferential statistics. Quantitative analysis of the findings suggests that the results are not due to chance factors, such as sampling error, but rather reveal a genuine relationship between the variables under study.

ANALYSIS OF THE DATA

A number of hypothetical questions were explored in terms of the theoretical significance of these data. Foremost in this regard was an assessment of how the presence of a typical personality among professional politicians might influence the way that they exercise their political roles, and the consequences in turn that this situation may have for political systems. Among the questions explored was the following: Can the formation of political alliances and coalitions between and among political parties be predicted in terms of similarities and differences in the typical kind of personality that are found among members of different political parties? The data in this study suggest that such is indeed the case. Answering questions such as this provides another dimension for the theoretical explanation of political dynamics in society. ▲

Gordon J. DiRenzo, *Personality, Power, and Politics.* Notre Dame, Ind.: University of Notre Dame Press, 1967.

but also the fundamental elements of the scientific method (see DiRenzo, 1966a). They play a key role in the very basic processes of observation that constitute the essential elements of the scientific method. Which phenomena are observed, and how they are observed, depends to a great extent on the nature of the concepts that are employed.

In a certain sense, all concepts are constructions of the mind and represent abstractions formed essentially by generalizing from particular cases. As such, **concepts** are rational-symbolic representations of universal application which comprehend the characteristics of a particular class or category of phenomena. Different types of concepts, however, have different functions. There are two basic kinds of concept that are important in our discussion of the scientific process: real concepts and nominal concepts.

**Real concepts** correspond to real phenomena or ontological reality. They are, therefore, necessarily true or false. Real concepts, or, more accurately, the definition of real concepts, are statements of the essential characteristics and/or substance of a given phenomenon.* They are, therefore, genuine and valid propositions. Real concepts do not merely have meanings; they *are* meanings. Real concepts are found or discovered—in reality; they are not simply created or invented by the scientists.

**Nominal concepts** do not necessarily have any correspondence in reality. They are not necessarily, therefore, either true or false. Their meanings are conventional and arbitrary, without any particular claims to truth. Nominal concepts merely represent an agreement or resolution concerning the use of verbal symbols (Cohen & Nagel, 1934). These concepts, often called mental constructs, are created or invented rather than found or discovered. Nominal concepts quite frequently are referred to, perhaps more properly, as conceptions.

* Concepts and definitions are used synonymously here.

An example of a nominal concept would be "social cohesion," while "social cohesiveness" would constitute the corresponding real concept. Other respective examples would be "intelligence quotient" (IQ) and "intelligence." One particular type of nominal concept frequently used in sociology is that known as the **operational definition.** Such a concept is one that consists essentially of the procedures or operations which one undertakes in order to measure a given phenomenon. "Intelligence quotient," for example, might be defined operationally as merely the result of calculating the combined scores that one obtains on a variety of tests that measure different kinds of verbal and performance abilities.

From these definitions and examples, one should be able to realize that a phenomenon may have several corresponding nominal concepts or conceptions, but only one real concept or definition. A phenomenon is what it actually is, not what it is perceived or conceived to be. Reality and perception, of course, are intimately and significantly related.

Scientific analysis usually begins with nominal concepts or conceptions of relevant phenomena (for example, social cohesion) which, however fuzzy or imprecise, give a label to a class of events on the basis of those properties that appear to distinguish all members of that particular class. Theory construction concludes, ideally, with real concepts. The development of these precise and real concepts involves a process described by Lazarsfeld (1966) as the "transmigration of concepts." This rather complex process consists, essentially, of the specification of conceptually relevant dimensions of a given phenomenon and the selection of empirical indicators for the measurements that are undertaken to establish or to verify the validity of theoretical concepts.

One such example can be illustrated by the concept of "religiosity." How does one go about selecting the empirical indicators for this concept? Assessing "religiosity" might involve the

▼

**71**

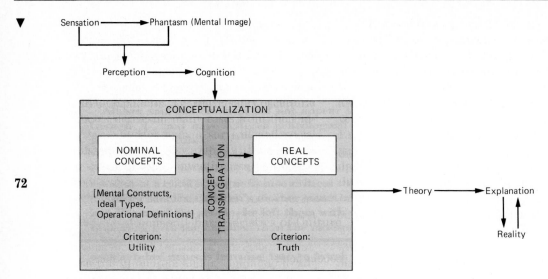

FIGURE 2-3  Processes of Concept Formation in Scientific Explanation.

measurement of such variables as the frequency of church attendance, personal prayer, and/or the intensity of participation in religious activities.

Real and nominal concepts, therefore, have quite different functions in the scientific process. Nominal concepts are tools. Their significance is measured in terms of their *methodological utility* for creating theory and building scientific explanation. Real concepts are measured in terms of their *truth* or *validity*. Nominal concepts are often the basis of purely logical systems of explanation. Real concepts, on the other hand, correspond to metaphysical reality. This distinction is important in that many kinds of logical systems (for example, Euclidean geometry with such concepts as "plane," "line," and "point") can be developed that have no necessary correspondence with the real world or real phenomena. Such is the meaning of Einstein's famous dictum: "Insofar as mathematics is about reality, it is not certain; and insofar as it is certain, it is not about reality."* Hence science, if it seeks to explain reality—if it seeks

* Quoted in Kaufman (1944).

certitude—must therefore correspond to metaphysical or ontological reality, and not merely logical reality.

Real concepts, therefore, have ontological, and not merely logical, significance. They have empirical and not merely rational consequences. One of the major sources of erroneous thinking, and a prime weakness in the construction of theory, is represented by faulty concepts. Oftentimes, nominal concepts are equated to reality, and therefore treated and regarded as real. This error is known as the process of reification—treating "phenomena" as though they were real when, indeed, they are not.

The distinction between types of concepts becomes critical in the development of theory. The more a theory consists of nominal concepts, the more likely that it has no claims to truth. The more a theory resembles a set of real concepts, the more likely it can be recognized as a valid contribution to scientific knowledge. What is intended, for example, by such terms as "anomie," "alienation," "personality," "crime," and "deviance"? To what phenomena, or kinds of phenomena, do these concepts refer? Are their referents real concepts, or simply mental constructs of the researcher? Concepts must ultimately have explanatory power and not merely descriptive power. If science seeks to explain the real, objective world, then there must be an affinity between concepts and reality. Accordingly, concepts of scientific explanation, and therefore of sociological theory, need to be real, not nominal, ones.

| Reality | De Facto | De Jure |
|---|---|---|
| Empirical | Realm of Science | Realm of Social Policy |
| Non-Empirical | Realm of Philosophy | Realm of Law and Ethics |

FIGURE 2-4  Realms of Analysis.

## The Limits of Science

Science has limits as well as strengths. One limitation is that science can deal only with phenomena that are empirical—phenomena that are observable, directly or indirectly, through the senses. The scientific method, therefore, cannot be used to determine whether God or souls exist or to explain their nature. Another limitation is that science cannot speak to questions regarding what or how reality ought to be. Science, by the nature of its method, is only concerned, and can only be concerned, with reality that is—what actually exists. Other dimensions of the limitations of science include questions about the ethics of scientific research and the social responsibilities of scientists. Let us pursue each of these issues in more detail.

### DE JURE VERSUS DE FACTO ANALYSIS

The realm of scientific analysis, as depicted in Figure 2-4, is that of *de facto* reality: reality which exists and which can be empirically observed or sensibly apprehended. Science is not concerned with *de jure* reality: reality that should or could exist. Such considerations for sociology would include the question of utopian societies that has attracted much attention in recent years.* The scientific method, insofar as

* See, for example, B. F. Skinner's *Walden Two* and *Beyond Freedom and Dignity.*

73

it is empirical, cannot explore reality that is not sensibly apprehensible. Neither is it concerned with that which cannot be determined to be or not to be ontologically true.

Science can tell us what the state of affairs is—what the nature, structure, and function of phenomena are. This kind of explanation constitutes de facto (what is) analysis. Whether such a state of affairs should exist, whether it is desirable or not, and whether the consequences of a particular set of phenomena (with a given nature, structure, and set of functions) are desirable, are questions involving de jure (what ought to be) analysis. Such questions may indeed be resolvable, but not by means of the scientific method.

Sociology, as science, attempts to describe and to explain the *facts* of social reality. The subject matter of sociology exists in the real, empirical order. It is concerned with the nature and function of society as it *is*, not as it *ought to be*. Sociology does not concern itself with de jure reality. For example, the explanation of the causes, dynamics, and consequences of poverty is a scientific and sociological question. The elimination of poverty is not a scientific or sociological question. Such a matter involves a host of moral, legal, political, and other social questions that need to be addressed in these terms, and which can be resolved only in these terms. Questions of this kind involve what, of late, have come to be known as "policy sciences"—a term which is itself a misnomer. Sociology, of course, can tell us *how* to achieve a

▼

particularly desired end, but not which end to achieve or to seek.

Sociology, therefore, does not moralize, or make judgments of value, or advocate any particular kind of social order. Sociology, as science, may be able to tell us how to resolve a problem, or how to create a particular kind of social situation or behavior (that may be desired), but it cannot tell us whether the problem—if indeed it is a problem (which itself is subjectively determined)—*should* be resolved or *how* it should be resolved. Whether the use of marijuana, for example, should be legalized or criminalized is not a question that can be resolved scientifically. Sociology, however, can demonstrate differential results in personal and social behavior from one action or the other. The different consequences, nonetheless, still leave us with having to decide which set is desirable or undesirable, good or bad—questions which again are not scientific ones. Not too long ago, the Hawaii State Legislature appropriated $25,000 for a study to determine what would happen to the state if peace were to break out. Such a question is a scientific one. Among the issues of interest were such concerns as the economic consequences of unemployment that most likely would result from the evacuation or curtailment of military forces. Science could not determine, however, whether there should be peace or war—only the consequences of either possibility.

We need to clearly distinguish between the description and analysis of objectively observable phenomena, and the evaluation of those phenomena. The latter process is frequently substituted for the former one. A chemist, for example, describes and explains the composition of water as $H_2O$. It would sound absurd were he to advocate that water should be $H_3O$ because he thinks it is preferable to $H_2O$, or else because $H_3O$ is better water! $H_3O$ is simply not water. It is something else. Only $H_2O$ is water! What should be done with water, the applications of $H_2O$, is another question, but

even that consideration is beyond the scope of science. There is no way to determine, empirically, the truth or falsity of any assertion appropriate or relevant to questions of this kind. Such statements are known as value judgments—expressions of desirability or preference. One person's taste, from a scientific perspective at least, is no better or worse than that of another. It is just different.

Sociological knowledge, as with any scientific knowledge, may be used for what are considered to be good or evil ends. Just as nuclear energy can be used to generate electricity or build bombs, so, too, sociological knowledge can be used to improve society via the solution of social problems or via the destruction of society. Breaking the code of human behavior can be used to control the behavior of people or facilitate their happiness. It is impossible to demonstrate, empirically, that humanity is worth saving or that it ought to be relegated to the category of extinct species. Hence social reality, and not social ideals, is the proper domain of the social scientists. Its analysis and explanation constitute the proper pursuit of the sociologist as scientist.

## IS THERE A VALUE-FREE SOCIOLOGY?

Science deals with facts—empirically verified assertions about real phenomena. Facts refer to the way things are. Values are not facts in this sense. They refer to the way things ought to be. Values are judgments of worth or desirability that are placed upon an object. As such, values are not subject to scientific or empirical verification. Value judgments are neither true nor false. They do not involve questions of certitude—only matters of preference, taste, desire, wish, belief, or goals. Are there values, nonetheless, in science, and more especially in sociology? The only value in sociology, as in all science, is that of truth. But, alas, the matter is more complicated than this simple statement may make it appear to be.

Science itself is a value. Even different areas of science are, to different people, more valuable than others. Contrast, for example, the dominant American value placed on the physical sciences as opposed to the social sciences. What is more valuable or desirable: knowledge about atoms or attitudes, physical space or human behavior? Such questions are not ones that science can resolve. The value of science and the values in science, however, are two totally different issues that pose totally different questions.

## SCIENTIFIC OBJECTIVITY: MYTH VERSUS REALITY

One of the characteristics of scientific knowledge and the scientific method, at least ideally, is their objectivity. Science, as an objective, seeks to demonstrate or explain, not to judge or establish preferences, not to determine the good or evil of phenomena. Is this myth or reality? The argument for us is that sociologists, as well as other social and behavioral scientists are engaged in an activity in which they themselves participate. The observer and the observed, in a certain sense, are one and the same. Such a situation contrasts with other scientific fields, such as physics and astronomy, whose objectivity is not challenged—at least not to the same extent. The question, then, is this: Can the social and behavioral scientists disengage their own personal values and biases from the method and findings of their analysis, and thereby conduct their research in such a manner that, if valid, it can be replicated or verified by other scientists using the same or similar methods?

Sociology, as a science, is ideally value-free, neutral, and objective; and, in this sense, it does not, because it cannot, evaluate or moralize. There is no such thing, for example, as Catholic, Jewish, Protestant, Moslem, or Hindu sociol-

ogy—insofar as it is a science—any more than there is a Catholic, Jewish, Protestant, Moslem, or Hindu mathematics or chemistry. If truth is assumed to be one, then logically there cannot be several, obviously contradictory, sciences or claims to that oneness of truth.

However much advocated as an ideal, the actual practice of objectivity is no easy matter in the social sciences. Indeed, many sociologists argue that objectivity is never attainable in the field of social research. Some would argue that the *facts* of science are myths; however necessary, they always contain something of the analyst. Facts, they argue, are not encountered; they are created. We believe that this position is a grossly exaggerated one. It reflects an incomplete understanding of what is meant by objectivity, neutrality, and value-free science—the differences between the ideals and the realities of the scientific enterprise.

Objectivity may be difficult to achieve in sociology and the other social and behavioral sciences, but such a goal is not an impossible one. Gunnar Myrdal's classic study (1962) of *An American Dilemma* about our nation's creed and ideals as expressed in the Constitution, and the institutionalized discrimination and segregation of Blacks, superbly demonstrates that it is possible not only to keep cultural, social, and even one's personal values from interfering with sociological research—either in the description or analyses of conflicting values systems—but also to use social and cultural values as a basis to provide an objective assessment of social behavior and social problems. Values themselves, therefore, can be the objectives and data of sociological investigation. Values, as we shall see in more detail in subsequent chapters, are major determinants of human behavior, and therefore, are major areas of study for social science and sociology in particular. There is a highly crucial difference, however, between the acceptance and the espousal of values on the one hand and the scientific study of them on the other.

75

▼

Sociology, as a science, may attempt to explain behavior that has been socially defined as evil or undesirable (for example, crime); but, to explain the nature of such behavior does not require that this behavior be defined or judged as either good or bad. Moreover, such sociological explanations—whose validity can be empirically determined—would be the same, no matter which way the behavior in question is defined. Ethical neutrality, under these circumstances, is considered to be the proper posture for the social scientist.

The values of sociologists and other social scientists do not alter the social phenomena that they observe any more than the values of the physical scientist alter physical phenomena. Whether one judges, for example, prostitution or drug usage positively or negatively will in no way alter the nature of that behavior; and, hence, the same empirical findings should be forthcoming from the scientist who holds either value. Values, however, may alter observations and perceptions of their respective phenomena, but such problems of values as potential biases are true of all sciences, although, granted, perhaps more so for the social and behavioral sciences.

The social sciences, however, have no monopoly on the psychology of selective perception. This situation, as a human dynamic, is true of scholars and scientists in all fields. Human values, and other forms of subjectivity, are present in all sciences—even the physical sciences. The mere selection of a particular set of phenomena for investigation is itself a value judgment: that it is good and important to make such a study. Yet, while the type of research that is done and the kinds of questions which are asked may imply values or value judgments, it does not necessarily follow that the data and their interpretation must be influenced by them.

Scientific objectivity in the analysis of people, society, and human behavior requires a genuine understanding of one's own values, beliefs, preconceptions, and motivations, which may be utilized in making scientific observations and

analyses. Awareness of such potential sources of bias makes it possible to control the role that they play in the research process. Yet, much more significant in the quest for scientific objectivity is that it is ensured through the common practice of the replication of research on the part of other scientists as well as the many other dimensions of scholarship. Professional and public scrutiny—review and criticism—also contribute to keeping sociology and the other social sciences objective. It is this collective and collaborative characteristic of schol-

**Value Neutrality.** Sociologists, as scientists, strive for objectivity in social research. Whether one judges the illegal use of drugs as positive or negative does not modify the behavioral dynamics that are involved, nor the nature of the empirical findings that can be derived through scientific investigation. (Allen Tannenbaum/SYGMA)

76

arly investigation that works against subjective biases and distortions, however real or unintentional. This question of values, then, is essentially a methodological problem that need not be any more insurmountable than the many others that have been discussed in this chapter.

## ETHICS OF SCIENTIFIC RESEARCH

Another limitation of science, one which, undoubtedly, nearly everyone will agree is a positive factor, is that represented by laws and codes of ethics that seek to protect both the rights of individuals who become subjects of research and the integrity and obligations of the researcher-scientist. This situation is as true of sociology as it is of all other professional fields—indeed, perhaps even more so, given the human nature of sociological data (Reynolds, 1982). Nonetheless, safeguards to protect human subjects from personal harm are today a concern in all fields. Several unfortunate incidents, involving unintended physical and psychological damage in the fields of biology, chemistry, psychology, as well as sociology, have brought these questions to the fore in recent years.*

In 1975, the federal government established a commission to oversee research involving human subjects. This commission produced a set of guidelines that is intended to regulate all research in this respect. Central to these procedures is the principle of **informed consent,** which essentially preserves the voluntary permission of participating subjects in a context of complete knowledge of the nature and risks of the research. Universities and other agencies conducting research with federal funds must abide by these guidelines; and, through the use of local review boards, it has become a fairly

common practice to extend these regulations to all kinds of research regardless of auspices.

Invasion of privacy has become a particular concern in the social sciences. Much controversy in this regard has centered around well-known cases of social research in which deception was utilized to obtain data that many people might consider to be highly personal and confidential—data which, if it had fallen into the wrong hands, could have left subjects open to blackmail and extortion.

One such case involved a series of projects on the jury process in which professors at the University of Chicago School of Law, with the official consent of a federal judge, made a number of secret tape recordings of jury deliberations in several civil cases (Vaughn, 1967). Another much more controversial case involved a sociologist, who, in a variation of participant observation, conducted a study of homosexual behavior in public restrooms—known as "tearooms" in appropriate circles (Humphreys, 1975). He agreed to serve as a lookout ("watch queen") for police and other intruders in order to note the license plate number of gays who frequented the tearooms. This information made it possible to obtain home addresses of people involved who, a year later, comprised a sample for a survey on homosexual behavior. Neither the method of their selection, nor the actual purpose of the study, was made known to the research subjects.

All data and records in these studies were kept strictly confidential, and, indeed, elaborate codes were used to ensure their anonymity. Still, there are allegations that the legal sanctity of the jury room and the constitutional privacy of individuals were knowingly compromised—all the more so through deception, or what some consider to be unredeeming dishonesty. Yet, many scientific procedures that may be judged unethical by some people are nonetheless not illegal—and, indeed, may be considered justifiable under certain circumstances in terms of the principle of the public's, and therefore the scientist's, "right to know." Some would argue

**77**

* For a discussion of these issues, see Rivlin and Timpane (1975) and Sjöberg (1967).

▼

that the pivotal issue in resolving the morality of these kinds of questions involves weighing the scientist's, and by extension the public's, right to know, versus the rights and privacy of the individual subject. Deception is one, quite common, technique that may be considered justifiable in certain circumstances, given the fact that subjects, knowingly or unwittingly, often alter their behavior when aware that they are being studied.* The crux of these matters is to guard the rights of both the subject and the researcher, while simultaneously preserving the freedom of public and scientific inquiry.

Toward these ends, the American Sociological Association, like many other professional associations, has adopted its own code of ethics and has established appropriate committees to oversee its enforcement among its members. Codes of professional ethics serve to protect not only the rights of individuals but also the integrity of scientists. They provide, quite specifically, another mechanism for ensuring scientific objectivity. Such mechanisms, of course, are necessary in a civilized and moralistic society. At the same time, however, these codes of ethics represent indispensable principles that often preclude the pursuit and analysis of a number of highly significant questions in the study of human behavior—all of which work against scientific progress. Such a situation presents a substantial challenge to the methodological creativity of social and behavioral scientists.

## SOCIAL RESPONSIBILITIES OF SOCIOLOGISTS

From its early beginnings, sociology has evolved into a highly complex enterprise. The field has come to mean different things to different people. Sociologists, in today's society, perform many roles. Foremost among them are

those of scientist, researcher, educator, consultant, practitioner, clinician, technician, engineer, and even critic. This multifarious situation frequently leads to a discussion about the social responsibilities of sociologists. Should sociologists, for example, concern themselves with social reform and/or the betterment of society?

Issues of this kind are perhaps not as troublesome or problematic for all sociologists as much as they are for those who adopt the scientific orientation. Such is the case, however, for the overwhelming majority of sociologists today. Those sociologists who adopt the humanistic mode of sociological activity are committed, explicitly or implicity, to promoting social criticism and/or to effecting social change. The same is obviously true for sociologists who are engaged in applied research or various kinds of sociological practice. Relevant questions of social responsibility, nonetheless, have become very controversial nowadays for all scholars, regardless of their methodological orientation or specific objectives.

Sociology, of course, formally began as part of a movement for social reform. It also began as a scientific enterprise. Yet, despite what may seem to be a return to its early concerns, the majority of sociologists today argue that it is more important for social scientists to understand social problems than to solve them. Many argue that the foremost task of the sociologist, at least as scientist, is to analyze, not to judge; to examine, not to advocate; to teach, not to preach; to explore, not to implore; to understand, not to activate; to explain, not to change. It is not so much that judging, advocating, preaching, imploring, activating, and changing are not the proper tasks or responsibilities of the sociologist that makes these activities illegitimate, as much as it is the fact that such activities go beyond the scientific method, and, hence, violate its fundamental tenets. Such a situation would present sociologists as scien-

78

* This phenomenon, known as the Hawthorne effect, is discussed in Chapter 7.

tists with the dilemma of being untrue to their objective, and less than honest with themselves and their fellow people.

Sociologists who are openly engaged in applied research, even those who may adopt the scientific orientation, as well as those in other activities which involve a preselected goal, do not necessarily experience these same constraints. One exception, however, is that of the sociologists engaged in the role of educator. Advocates of the scientific posture show substantial agreement in this regard with the assertion of Max Weber (1949:41):

> An unprecedented situation exists when a large number of officially accredited prophets (professors) do not do their preaching on the streets, or in churches or other public places or in sectarian conventicles, but rather feel themselves competent to enunciate their evaluations on ultimate questions "in the name of science" in governmentally privileged lecture halls in which they are neither controlled, checked by discussion, nor subject to contradiction. I take the view that a "lecture" should be different from a "speech."

Hence, goes the argument, the goal of sociology is the acquisition of knowledge about human social behavior, not the utilization of that knowledge. Just as physicists do not build bridges, physiologists do not treat sick people, and chemists do not fill prescriptions, so, too, sociologists do not determine questions of public policy, advocate social legislation, and engage in social engineering, whatever form it may take. In short, sociologists as scientists must be scholars not activists.

Some people argue that sociologists have an obligation to advocate what should be the nature and function, course and direction, of society because of their professional knowledge and expertise. However, ascribing primacy or superiority to the dictates or wishes of the sociologists, as to anyone else, is hard to square in a society where such relevant decisions are ideally arrived at in a democratic fashion—

professional competence and authority aside. The authority of the sociologist, moreover, is limited, as with that of any other scientist, to what is (the de facto realm of analysis) and the consequence of what may be—not what should be. Advocacy and criticism, however, are not the same thing. Sociologists of today overwhelmingly maintain that they, like any other member of society, have the right to criticize society. The vast majority, moreover, also maintain that serving as a critic of society is part of the modern role of the sociologist.

As a citizen, of course, the sociologist is free to express his or her values, to advocate whatever he or she likes, and to exercise freedom of choice among societal alternatives. Some sociologists, however, are of the opinion that, from an ethical point of view, social scientists should exercise a restrained or diminished freedom in their role as citizen lest their personal choices and actions, however much based on professional knowledge, be perceived as authoritative or expert, and intellectually superior to those of other members of society. Such an uncontrolled bias, it is argued, would be an unethical influence on social behavior. Hence, these issues of the role of the sociologist raise questions not so much about civil rights or professional competency as they do about professional ethics that again involve value judgments for which there are no empirical confirmations or disconfirmations, and, hence, which are neither scientifically derived nor scientifically supported. One partial resolution to this dilemma is a sociologically educated and competent citizenry—an objective to which this volume is directed.

## Summary

Sociological analysis uses two principal approaches: the scientific method and the humanistic method. The humanistic method relies primarily on subjective analysis, including such

79

▼

processes as intuition, speculation, impression, insight, and common sense. The scientific method, on the other hand, employs objective and empirical analysis. The distinguishing principle between scientific and nonscientific analysis is the highly systematic method by which phenomena are observed and knowledge is accumulated. Among the distinctive characteristics of scientific knowledge are the following qualities: universality, causality, and certitude. Applications of scientific knowledge include prediction and control.

The scientific method as used in sociology is fundamentally no different than that which is used in the natural and physical sciences. Despite these similarities, many objections to a science of sociology have been put forth. The basic arguments, which tend to focus on the nature of human behavior are: human behavior is rational, human behavior is too individualistic, human behavior is too complex, human behavior involves free will, and human behavior requires subjective analysis. Objections of this kind, however, do not invalidate or preclude the application of the basic tenets of the scientific method to human behavior. They merely exemplify the complications of the scientific process in its application to human behavior.

The major steps in the scientific method are: the formulation of hypotheses, development of a research design, sampling, collection of data, analysis of data, and interpretation of findings. A research hypothesis is usually a statement of assumed relationship between two or more phenomena. Sampling consists fundamentally of a set of procedures by which a portion of a given population is selected for study and treated as representative of that population. Among the principal types of sampling used in sociology singly or in combination are: random, stratified, quota, area, and availability sampling. An adequate sample is one that is of an appropriate and sufficient size to permit the kind of analyses and projections that the researcher desires to perform. The social scientist also needs to en-

sure that research subjects constitute a representative sample of the people about whom he or she wishes to generalize.

Among the principal types of data collection used by the social scientist are survey research, field research, laboratory research, documentation, experimentation, and computer simulation. Each of these methods, in one way or another, is concerned with sociometrics, or the empirical measurement of relevant phenomena.

Specific tools and techniques employed by sociologists in the process of data collection include participant and nonparticipant observation, content analysis, interview schedules, questionnaires, biograms, and personality inventories. Foremost among the methodological concerns in data collection are reliability and validity.

Data analysis assumes two principal forms: quantitative analysis and qualitative analysis. Together these modes of analysis are directed at the formulation and confirmation of empirical generalizations. Relevant in these respects are the employment of descriptive and inferential statistics.

Empirical research culminates in the construction of theory which purports to explain how and why phenomena occur. The methodological process takes place on the manifest level; the true locus of sociological explanation, however, resides in the latent property space.

All knowledge is organized around concepts which comprise the irreducible elements in the process of theoretical explanation. There are two basic types of concepts: real and nominal concepts. Real concepts correspond to ontological reality and are judged by their claims to truth. Nominal concepts, such as operational definitions, do not have any necessary correspondence to reality and are judged in terms of their utility. The distinction between these types of concepts is of fundamental importance in the construction of theory. The more a theory consists of nominal concepts, the more likely it has no claims to truth.

80

The realm of science is that of de facto empirical reality: reality which in fact exists and which can be sensibly or empirically observed. Science is not concerned with de jure reality—reality that ought to exist or should/could exist; nor with the realm of nonempirical reality—that which cannot be apprehended through the senses. The goal of sociology as a science is the acquisition of knowledge about human social behavior, and not the modification or manipulation of that behavior. Sociological research, as with that in any other field, is undertaken with the highest standards of professional ethics and social responsibility.

# Key Concepts

adequate sample
biogram
case-study technique
cause
coding
concept
content analysis
cross-sectional research
dependent variable
descriptive analysis
descriptive statistics
empirical generalization
empirical method
epistemology
experimentation
explanatory analysis
explanatory research
exploratory research
field research
humanistic method
hypothesis
independent variable
inferential statistics

informed consent
intervening variable
interview
interview guide
interview schedule
laboratory research
latent property space
longitudinal research
manifest property space
model
nominal concept
nonparticipant observation
observation
operational definition
participant observation
personality inventory
probabilistic relationship
projective test
qualitative analysis
quantitative analysis
questionnaire
real concept
reliability
representative sample
research design
sample
sampling
scientific law
scientific method
simple observation
social indicator
statistical analysis
survey research
systematic observation
theory
universe
unobtrusive measures
validity
value judgment
variable

▼

81

# TWO ▼ The Social Individual

Human beings are not born human—at least not fully human. The qualities and attributes that constitute human nature and that distinguish humans from other beings are not present at birth—except in a potential way, and not even then necessarily.

Here in Part 2 we are concerned with the processes of humanization—the social procedures and dynamics by which human organisms become human beings. These considerations begin the substantive portion of our text. Each of the chapters that follow is devoted to one of the central and fundamental elements of human social behavior: culture, social learning, and personality.

In Chapter 3 we discuss culture—the unique attribute of mankind—which constitutes the mechanism by which human beings relate to their physical and social environments. This consideration is followed by a discussion in Chapter 4 on social learning—the processes by which culture is transmitted from one person to another—and the dynamics of its acquisition. Chapter 5 deals with personality, which represents one of the fundamental end products of social and cultural learning. Personality, as one of the focal dimensions of this text, will play a fundamental role in several of the successive chapters of our volume, and we shall refer to selective aspects of this phenomenon throughout the text.

Together the three focal concepts of Part 2—culture, social learning, and personality—constitute the basic and indispensable components of social interaction in its distinctly human forms. These considerations will provide the conceptual tools that are indispensable for any adequate analysis of human social behavior. ▲

▶ Chapter 3 **CULTURE**
▶ Chapter 4 **SOCIALIZATION AND SOCIAL LEARNING**
▶ Chapter 5 **PERSONALITY AND THE SELF**

# 3 ▼ Culture

All human behavior is, in some sense, biologically or physiologically based, but only a small part of it is biologically or physiologically determined. The greatest portion of human behavior, especially that which is distinctly human, is essentially the product of culture. To understand human social behavior to even the slightest degree is impossible without an understanding of culture and an appreciation of its role in the formation of behavior. Hence, it is not only fitting but imperative that we begin the substantive portion of this volume with an extensive treatment of culture.

Everything that we shall talk about in this book is influenced, directly or indirectly, by culture: social learning, personality, social organization, stratification, minorities, collective behavior, social movements, deviance, and social change. It is culture that, in large part, accounts for the recurrent patterns of social behavior and societal regularity that provide the basis for a science of sociology.

Culture is both a product and a producer of human beings. Here, however, we shall consider only the nature and function of culture, and examine how it emerges as that part of the human environment that is made by people. The role of culture as a producer of human nature will be discussed in the next chapter. ▲

## Outline

▶That there are uniquely human attributes or characteristics has been a popular consideration over the years. A number of activities clearly distinguish human beings from lower animals and other beings: use of the opposable thumb, wearing clothes, smoking, laughing, smiling, and crying. Apart from such kinds of behavior, which tend to be in the nature of accidental properties, the search for uniquely human attributes has focused on characteristics that are inherent, fundamental, or essential.

Scientific contributions in this regard have been wanting. Until fairly recently, it was widely thought that human beings were uniquely social. More recent research in several fields, notably biology and entomology, has shown quite conclusively that there are thousands of social species. While there are significant differences in the nature and degree of the sociability of these various species, their large numbers demonstrate that social life and societal organization are not distinctively human.

There is, however, one uniquely human attribute: No other species has been found to possess culture. Human beings and human society cannot exist without culture, and culture exists only within human beings and human society. Thus, when we say that human beings are social, we refer to "animal" qualities and processes that are shared with other beings; but when we say that human beings are cultural, we refer to uniquely human attributes.

# Nature and Definition of Culture

Culture is a highly abstract and complex phenomenon that is somewhat difficult to explain. The original and classic definition of culture was offered many years ago by Edward Tylor (1871:1), a well-known British anthropologist: "Culture is that complex whole which includes knowledge, belief, art, morals, law, custom and any other capabilities and habits acquired by man as a member of society." **Culture,** then, refers to the entirety of knowledge and habitual patterns of behavior that are shared and perpetuated by the members of a particular society or group.

Culture in a sense represents the "total way of life" of a people—the way that they think and act (Kluckhohn, 1949). It is a design for living that is developed and utilized by a particular society or group. Forms of government, laws, religions, systems of education, etiquette, holy days and holidays, codes of morality, dietary customs, dress styles and norms, marriage and family relationships, business organizations, and commercial procedures are all embodiments and manifestations of culture.

Some people believe in Christianity, others in Buddhism; some eat two meals a day, others three; some live in democracies, others in monarchies; some work in capitalistic economies, others in communistic ones; some eat octopus, rattlesnake, or dog meat, while others eat lobster and beef; some greet each other by shaking hands or kissing, others by bowing; and so forth. These examples are expressions of the diversity of culture. Sleeping for 8 consecutive hours at night is another expression of culture. Working 6, or, more likely, 5 days, with rest on Sunday, not Saturday, is a cultural practice. Vacations in the summer and engagements before marriage express cultural lifestyles. The list of such examples is nearly endless, since practically all that we do, especially all that which is uniquely human, is touched in one way or another by culture.

Even our biological and physiological functions are influenced, indeed often determined, by culture. Among these aspects of human behavior are such things as motor gestures, sexual arousal, tolerance to physical pain, and conditions affecting nausea—all of which vary markedly among different cultures. For example, a food prohibition, such as against eating horsemeat, could be so well internalized (so strongly adopted) that one's digestive system

87

▼ would revolt automatically at the slightest violation of this practice. Similarly, note the involuntary physiological responses to embarrassment such as blushing and stammering. Culture controls many such biological and physiological functions to the extent that it specifies the "proper" occasions or situations (birth, death) for the expression of appropriate sentiments (fear, anger, happiness, sadness, embarrassment) and emotions (smiling, crying).

88 People do many things because it is apparently "natural," such as marrying for love, having babies, and working for money. Nonetheless, much of what we attribute to human "nature" is really culture specific. Culture is so common and so fundamental a phenomenon (for human existence) that it is taken for granted. Yet, culture is just as necessary for *human* survival as air is for biological survival— and equally as transparent. We can see its expressions and its effects, but not culture itself.

As Ralph Linton, a distinguished American anthropologist, remarked:

> It has been said that the last thing which a dweller in the deep sea would be likely to discover would be water. He would become conscious of its existence only if some accident brought him to the surface and introduced him to air. Man, throughout most of history, has been only vaguely conscious of the existence of culture and has owed even this consciousness to contrasts between his own society and those of some other with which he happened to be brought into contact (1945:195).

In the popular sense, culture refers to intellectual cultivation, scholarly sophistication, and appreciation of the literary and fine arts, which qualities may or may not characterize a particular set of people. Certainly, such is not the case of many of the primitive peoples about whom cultural anthropologists have provided

## BOX 3-1. Lost Tribe of the Tasaday

In most areas of the earth, the Stone Age came to an end thousands of years ago, but not in the remote mountain forests of the Philippine island of Mindanao, 650 miles south of Manila. There, scientists recently discovered a lost tribe of Stone Age human beings whose way of life has remained unchanged for aeons. Excited by their unique opportunity, Philippine anthropologists last week prepared for an expedition into the jungle to live with the tribesmen and investigate their customs before the primitive culture is contaminated or obliterated by encroaching civilization.

The existence of the Tasaday, as the tribesmen call themselves, came to light after a trapper named Dafal reported that he had encountered a mysterious people on his hunting trips into the hinterland. Philippine officials checked out the rumor via helicopter and found a group of short, brown-skinned tribesmen wearing only loincloths.

### JUNGLE HABITAT

Making contact with the Tasaday, the government agents soon determined that the tribe had been isolated for at least 700 years and perhaps for 2,000, and had no knowledge of agriculture. The Tasaday are unfamiliar with rice, taro, salt and sugar, have never eaten corn and, according to authorities, may be "the only people in the world today who do not know or use tobacco."

▼

The tribesmen also have no metal technology, no domestic animals and no permanent dwellings. Though situated on an island, they live in a mountainous, thickly wooded area of rain forest, have never seen the sea and have no word for it in their strange Malayo-Polynesian language.

The Tasaday have survived in their primitive state chiefly by gathering rather than growing food, by utilizing stones as scrapers, choppers and pounders, and by fashioning containers, knives and other implements out of bamboo. Their chief food is *natak*, the pith of wild palms. They also eat wild yams, rattan and bamboo shoots, small fish, crabs and tadpoles that they catch with their hands. Through contact with Dafal, the Tasaday have learned to trap birds in a sticky substance; civet cats, rats, monkeys and pigs are taken in primitive traps. Fires are still set by rubbing pieces of wood together, and meat either roasted over an open flame or boiled in bamboo cooking tubes.

Numbering only about a hundred, the Tasaday live in families, consisting of mother, father, unmarried children and sometimes an orphan or childless widow. Though polygamy and polyandry are customary among other food-gathering peoples with small populations, the Tasaday shun both. Their marriages are arranged by parents, but in at least one case, when women were scarce a father captured a bride for his son from a neighboring Tasaday group. The Tasaday mother delivers her own child, and the father buries the umbilical cord. Outside the family, there is no formal community organization and no single leader, but several families cooperate in food-foraging, making decisions together and depending for advice on the most experienced among them.

89

## EPIDEMIC SMALLPOX

That advice, the Tasaday believe, is based on knowledge that is transmitted by their ancestors. In their dreams, the tribesmen may see the *sugoy*, their deceased "soul-relatives," who live in fine dwellings among the treetops, as well as *Salungal*, "the owner of the mountains," who tells them where to search for palm pith and game animals.

The Tasaday are a timid people, wary of strangers and so afraid of the *fugu*, or epidemics like smallpox, that have ravaged the area in the past that they are reported to abandon sick people to die alone and unaided. Their precarious existence permits few to reach old age and they seem to find little joy in life. Yet the Tasaday like to stand in the rain and let the water course down their bodies. And they enjoy the music of the kúbing, a kind of jew's-harp made from bamboo and carried from place to place in a bamboo box.

To retain the "lost" tribe as a link with man's distant past, the Philippine government may designate the Tasaday forest home—estimated to be twelve square miles—as a preserve that will be off limits to loggers, ranchers, miners and other invaders. But even well-intentioned visitors from the 20th century may undermine any future anthropological studies of the tribe; gifts of a bow and arrow, a metal bolo knife and sugar from Dafal and the investigating scientists are already moving the Tasaday out of the Stone Age. ▲

Source: "Lost Tribe of the Tasaday," *Time,* 98:58–60, 1971. Copyright 1971 Time Inc. Reprinted by permission.

▼ extensive ethnographic studies. Yet, primitive peoples, being human, possess culture as it is understood in a sociological or anthropological sense. They too share a distinctive way of life. One such example is provided by the Tasaday of the Philippines.*

Culture, then, is a key concept in sociology. Indeed, culture is an indispensable concept in all of the social and behavioral sciences. No aspect of human social behavior escapes the influence of culture. To examine the importance of the scientific concept of culture, we need to seek answers to two basic questions: What is the function of culture, and what are its distinguishing characteristics? Answers to these questions will give us a more comprehensive understanding of the nature of culture.

**90**

## FUNCTIONS OF CULTURE

One requirement of all living organisms is the need to adapt to their environment. Culture serves as the adaptation tool, or mechanism, of human beings. The principal function of culture, in this respect, is to mediate between the needs of individuals and their physical and social environments. Culture, therefore, plays an indispensable role in the quest for human survival. Nonhuman animals have instincts or other inherited capabilities which facilitate their adaptation to the physical environment, and, for those animals who are social, these genetic characteristics facilitate their adaptation to the social environment as well. Compare, for example, the technical similarity of anthills or bird nests to houses or igloos. The former are the product of innate instinct, while the latter derive from culture and learned behavior.

Instincts are neither learned nor acquired. An **instinct** refers to constant and complicated behavior, either inherited or genetically trans-

mitted, that is universal to a species, directed toward a specific goal, and unchangeable by the individual organism. Examples of instinct are the nest-building activities of birds, their seasonal migrations, the long-distance travel of salmon to spawning waters, the dam construction of beavers, and the mating behavior of many animals. Animals are not aware of what they do instinctively. Such behavior is performed automatically, without any ability on the part of the animal to intervene.

Human beings, however, do not possess instincts, or any other type of inherited patterns of behavior except automatic responses or reflexes, such as grasping, sucking, blinking, and knee-jerking. These types of behavior, which themselves constitute highly complicated dynamics and have a universal character, differ from instincts primarily because they are not directed toward a specific goal and are elicited by stimuli outside the organism, unlike instincts. Human beings, however, do have inherited organic needs or hungers, often called biological drives, that require satisfaction, which is itself culturally specified or determined to a considerable extent.

Even our basic biological drives are influenced by culture, as evidenced in the learned gratification of the hunger drive, thirst drive, and even the sex drive. Unlike the case with instincts, then, human intervention can play a significant role in biological drives. Not all potential nourishment, for example, is defined as appropriate food—just as not all individuals are defined as appropriate sexual partners. Culture can even override biological necessities, as in situations where individuals elect to fast unto death or prefer suicide to dishonor or embarrassment. Much of this kind of behavior involves the dynamics of social perception, which, as we shall explore in more detail in a subsequent section, is essentially cultural.

Culture represents the social heritage of mankind. Every generation passes on its design for living. Each individual does not have to reinvent or design anew solutions to the innumer-

---

* Allegations have been made during the past few years that the Tasaday tribe, or at least certain aspects of its culture, may be an anthropological hoax (see Kronholz, 1985). Nance (1988) provides a counterargument based on renewed investigations during the past few years. In the absence of conclusive evidence, however, the claim remains controversial.

# BOX 3-2. Sociobiology: Nature versus Nurture ▼

Whether heredity or environment is the crucial element in human social behavior was a question of serious debate among scientists for years. Few argue the point today. Scientists nowadays are of the opinion that human development is neither entirely genetically determined nor entirely environmentally determined, and that social behavior is the product of the complex and inseparable interaction of constitutional and environmental factors. They disagree, however, about the extent of the respective contribution of these two sets of influence.

Novel versions of the nature-versus-nurture argument, moreover, have come to the fore in recent years. Much of this situation is associated with the development of the new field of *sociobiology*, which is concerned with the systematic study of the biological basis of all social behavior. While work in this discipline involves primarily the contributions of biologists, the new field does have its counterpart among sociologists in the subspecialty that is coming to be known as biosociology (see, for example, Lopreato, 1984; Shepher, 1983; Barash, 1982; van den Berghe, 1978).

Sociobiologists maintain that much social behavior is established genetically and that it derives essentially from the process of evolution. Fundamental to sociobiological theory is the Darwinian principle of natural selection and the "survival of the fittest" (those individuals best adapted to their environment will be most likely to survive and to reproduce). Through the evolutionary process, argue sociobiologists, the most functional and the most adaptive behavior has survived in the present species of human beings.

Among these kinds of behavior are territoriality, the formation of social hierarchies (inequalities in social prestige and power), religious practices, ethics, morals, aggression, altruism (concern for the welfare of others), maternal disposition in women, selfishness, self-sacrifice, differences in gender roles, homosexuality, and xenophobia (fear of strangers).

While sociobiologists do not advocate a biological determinism, and hence do not deny the influence of the social environment, their central theme is one of genetic constraints on human behavior. Hence, sociobiologists speak of capacities or predispositions to behave in certain ways. They readily admit that society and culture are also strongly instrumental in human social behavior; genes only set limits for social behavior. As one sociobiologist has written: "The genes hold culture on a leash. The leash is very long, but inevitably values will be constrained in accordance with their effects on the human gene pool" (Wilson, 1978).

Sociobiologists, therefore, acknowledge that the environment—social as well as physical—exercises a basic role in the formation of human behavior. The interaction of these different sets of variables, however, is directed at a fundamental adaptation—not so much for the individual as for the human species as a whole. It is an adaptation that enhances the perpetuation of one's genetic constitution such that genes for adaptive behavior will reoccur with increasing frequency in each new generation. This adaptation is expressed in the general proposition that genes influence culture which in turn influences genes: ". . . culture is generated and shaped by biological imperatives while biological traits are simultaneously altered by genetic evolution in response to cultural innovation" (Lumsden & Wilson, 1983:19).

*(Continued)*

91

▼    ## BOX 3-2 *(Continued).*

Chief among the more influential sociobiologists is Edward O. Wilson (1975, 1978) of Harvard University. Wilson argues that altruism—whereby individuals kill or endanger themselves in order to protect other members of the species— exists in both the animal and the insect kingdom (for example, baboons that confront leopards and certain death, or bees that kill intruders of the hive). Human beings, who die as heroes for others in battle or as martyrs for worthy causes (for example, immolation) allegedly manifest this biological dynamic. Altruism operates even more intensely among individuals who are genetically related, such as in the case of family members and relatives. For example, a woman who sacrifices her life in order to save her brother's children from a fiery death would be considered as acting not only altruistically but also in a genetically selfish way, in order to perpetuate the family genes. Other forms of social behavior, argue sociobiologists, are similarly directed at the survival and the perpetuation of one's genetic heritage. Included here would be competitiveness, sexual jealousy, and promiscuity, particularly inasmuch as these types of behavior are found extensively among males.

Sociobiologists have raised a number of highly controversial questions. Critics point out that altruistic behavior is not limited to genetically related individuals. Many people with very little genetic relationship behave altruistically toward each other. Such situations would suggest that altruism is more likely to be the product of social learning (culture). Moreover, numerous opponents (for example, see Montagu, 1980) argue that sociobiology pays too little attention, sometimes intentionally, to the many cultural differences in human behavior. Similarly, the extensive variability of human behavior among individuals within the same culture presents difficulties for sociobiologists. So, too, do the quite obvious facts of sociocultural change and the highly pervasive forms of social deviance in which people act in ways contrary to their allegedly genetic tendencies.

Many social scientists view the implications of sociobiological theories as highly dangerous and fear that they could be used, as with social Darwinism, as justifications for such undesirable practices as racism, sexism, and other forms of oppression and discrimination. Sociobiologists counter that the effort to provide the biological basis for human social behavior will enlarge rather than restrain human freedom. Similarly, others see the sociobiological perspective as shedding new light on existing theory and data, as well as generating important new hypotheses on human development (MacDonald, 1987).

Sociobiology remains a highly controversial and internally turbulent field (see Lowontin et al., 1984; Caplan, 1979). As with all controversies in the realm of science, the challenges of sociobiology, along with those of biosociology, will need to be resolved through the presentation of empirical evidence in the context of open-minded inquiry. ▲

able requirements and problems of human adaptation to the physical and social environments. All creative and technological developments, such as the wheel, fire, forms of government, languages, automobiles and airplanes, systems of law, sciences, and the arts, constitute cumulative phenomena. Each generation improves on preceding ones and seeks to perfect its social and cultural heritage. Culture, therefore, ensures human survival—both for the individual and for the species.

# CHARACTERISTICS OF CULTURE

A number of the chief characteristics of culture both describe and define this phenomenon. Some of these characteristics are discussed in this section.

CULTURE IS SYMBOLIC. Perhaps the most essential characteristic of culture is its symbolic nature. Culture is not human behavior. It is neither people nor their actions, but another distinct, though intangible, order of phenomena. In the words of Leslie A. White, one of America's most distinguished anthropologists, "culture is that class of phenomena, dependent upon symboling, which is considered and interpreted in an extrasomatic context" (1966:107).

Culture itself, then, consists of what White called "symbolates." Objects in this class or category are dependent upon, and require for their existence, the act of symboling. As an isolate is the product of isolating, a **symbolate** is the product of the act of symboling. Culture, thus, is made up of things and events that depend upon the ability to *create* symbols—a uniquely human phenomenon.

A **symbol** consists of any object or activity that stands for something else. While culture is symbolic, and therefore nonphysical, it is no less real in a metaphysical or ontological sense. Symbols or symbolates, such as values and beliefs, are things—real things. Through symboling people have created a new environment. Says White: "Only man has the ability to 'symbol'—that is, to originate, determine, and bestow freely and arbitrarily, meanings about things and events in the external world. These

meanings cannot be grasped and appreciated with the senses. Holy water, or articulate speech, are good examples. Symboling is trafficking in non-sensory meanings" (1966:106).

The symbolic nature of culture is perhaps exemplified best in human language, which, as a system of symbols, can be considered to be the fundamental symbolate. Language is the chief carrier of culture.

CULTURE IS IDEATIONAL. Culture is symbolic in an ideational sense. That is to say, culture consists essentially and exclusively of ideas—mental phenomena—rather than physical and concrete or material things. Culture inheres in the ideas and concepts that symbolize the patterns of knowledge, beliefs, values, and norms which a people utilize.

Given its symbolic and ideational nature, culture excludes physical phenomena. But culture is symbolized in, expressed through, and manifested in material objects. The specific elements of what, on occasion, is called **material culture**—carts or airplanes; igloos, huts or houses; spoons or chopsticks; abacuses or calculators—are known as artifacts.

An **artifact,** unlike culture, is a concrete, physical object that is an expression of culture. Artifacts are cultural, but not culture: They constitute representations of culture, but not culture itself. In a sense, culture is *in* the artifacts because they are manifestations of culture. A white wedding dress or a stone sculpture, for example, are material and physical expressions of the beliefs, values, and products of a given people. Whereas culture is created, artifacts are invented. Without culture, there can be no artifacts. Thus, artifacts may be said to be the cultural signature of human beings.

Anthropologists are able to learn much about the culture of a people through their artifacts, since they are physical representations or graphic expressions of that culture. Artifacts such as pottery and stone tools also reveal much about cultural processes—such as borrowing,

**93**

▼

diffusion, growth, and change. Culture itself, then, like society, cannot be observed directly. It must be studied indirectly by considering its concrete manifestations in the forms of physical objects and human behavior.

CULTURE IS LEARNED. Only those things that can be learned are cultural. Culture is learned or acquired through the process of social interaction, through being transmitted from one person to another. Culture, thus, needs to be distinguished from behavior that emerges directly from one's biological nature, such as reflexes and basic drives. Much behavior that appears to be biological, especially because it is universal, is really cultural. For example, expressions of pleasure and pain, hate and love, joy and sadness derive from culture. The capacity for these kinds of behavior is biological and innate; their actualization and content is cultural and learned. For instance, many Asians learn to rest comfortably by squatting or sitting on the floor; Westerners are more comfortable sitting on chairs or standing. The discomfort that the foreigner in either case would experience is learned, for the most part.

Practically all that one learns in life, especially that knowledge accumulated in the very early years of schooling, consists of culture. Often culture is referred to as the social heritage, or legacy, of a given people—that which is passed on from generation to generation. Processes involved in the transmission of culture or cultural knowledge from one generation to another are identified generically by the term **culturation.** We shall describe the learned character of culture in greater detail in Chapter 4.

CULTURE IS SHARED. While we can refer to an individual's culture, it is more technically correct to say that an individual *shares* in the culture of a particular people. Culture refers to the mutual, or shared, symbols and meanings of the way of life of a people. It refers to patterns of behavior that are common to a particular category of people, rather than to individual or idiosyncratic forms of behavior. Culture, thus, is a shared, rather than a personal, lifestyle. Hence, culture not only influences one's behavior, but also one's expectations of others' behavior.

Culture, in the words of Ruth Benedict (1961), is that which "binds people together." The patterned predictability of human social behavior, social organization, is rooted in the cultural prescriptions of a people. It is the shared understandings of culture that make possible social communication and social relationships, which, in turn, are the basis of society and social life, rather than mere and meaningless interaction among people. This situation of shared cultural expectation is the basis for the predictability and the continuity of human social activity. As a consequence of shared culture, one person's behavior elicits predictable responses from other individuals. Social relationships, and consequently society, exist exclusively and entirely in the probability that there will be an anticipated course of action. Culture, shared between and among individuals, is the basis of this probability and anticipation. Culture actually serves as the medium of interaction and communication, and, as such, makes its own relative stability and continuity.

CULTURE IS NORMATIVE. Culture does not represent the actual behavior of people. Rather, it is limited, in this respect, to socially expected or acceptable behavior—that is, normative behavior. Culture provides the rules and norms, or standards, that are the basis of shared social behavior. Rules of etiquette are one example. Culture, as such, expresses the desires, wishes, and preferences of a people. Social scientists, in this respect, often distinguish between *real* culture (actual practices of a people), and *ideal* culture (that expressed in their values and norms). This distinction is actually somewhat of a contradiction, but it can be helpful if properly understood.

94

Cultural prescriptions are often not followed by people, nor does society always conform perfectly to its cultural ideals. Americans, for example, believe all people are created equal, and deserve to have political and legal equality. Yet, many people systematically experience social discrimination. One reason for this disparate situation is that human social behavior is a product of several other types of phenomena—psychological, social, and biological—besides culture. Moreover, culture as a dynamic phenomenon is constantly undergoing change in one way or another, such as through growth and borrowing. In either case, the discrepancy between ideal and real culture can be a source of strain and conflict that may have very significant consequences for society and its members. Accordingly, we shall have more to say in subsequent chapters about both the normative aspects of culture and the processes of cultural change.

## Cultural Systems

Culture, like any other phenomenon, has its own dynamics, principles, and laws. People, of course, are necessary to serve culture as its producers and carriers; but, once produced, culture takes on its own nature and dynamics apart from people, and it must be so analyzed. The continuity of culture from one generation to another is but one testimonial to its transcendence of people. Some people find this view and procedure reductionistic or otherwise objectionable. An analogy, however, may be helpful here. Breathing is necessary in mathematical calculations, as in all other human activities; but mathematics can be analyzed without giving direct attention to breathing or to its human agents. Perhaps a more pertinent analogy would be economics. Economic behavior, while presupposing people of whom it is a product, has its own dynamics, principles, and laws that can be explained and predicted quite apart from

a direct concern with people. Such analytical distinctions, so long as they remain in proper perspective, provide the basis for a more refined and vivid understanding of the nature and function of culture.

The social scientist frequently treats culture as a system. To do so, however, the scientist must assume that it has a systematic nature. Such a proposition, as we saw in the preceding chapter, cannot be empirically verified. However, without this assumption—that is, if it is assumed that cultural phenomena are found randomly or chaotically—the possibility of any scientific assessment of culture is precluded.

The nature of social, and hence cultural, systems will be examined in considerable detail in Chapter 6. It suffices here to say that the concept of system implies the notions of differentiation and unity. Any system, be it cultural or social, solar or biological, is basically a number of related parts that are so integrated and independent that they function together as a unit. There is, moreover, the inherent conception that the whole is greater than the sum of its parts. A cultural system, like any system, can be analyzed fundamentally in terms of two basic dimensions: content and structure.

## CONTENT OF CULTURE

The *content* of a culture refers to the parts or elements that comprise a culture. These are often the specific things that we have in mind when we speak of culture: what people know, what they believe, what they value, and what they accept as norms of behavior. Social scientists distinguish a number of different categories or elements of culture in these respects. We shall describe the principal components of culture in the sections that follow.

KNOWLEDGE.   Culture fundamentally consists of knowledge—knowledge about what is and what ought to be. A very wide variety and

95

▼ complexity of phenomena, however, can be encompassed by ideas and human understanding. Accordingly, we can distinguish three types of cultural knowledge for analytical purposes: cognitive, evaluative, and normative. While these distinctions may be quite helpful in an analytical sense, they are often arbitrary, blurred, or simply conventional. The three types frequently overlap, as in the case when people value their norms and beliefs, or express their

**96** beliefs as values or norms.

*Cognitive knowledge* consists essentially of what a people know or believe about the world, nature, themselves, and other reality. Science and religion are two principal types of cognitive knowledge. Myths, proverbs, folklore, legend, and other things of this kind also constitute forms of cognitive knowledge. Technology, or technical knowledge about how to do things, such as flying an airplane or cooking food, is another part of this category of cognitive knowledge. Art and athletics—their styles, forms, and rules—are part of cognitive knowledge as well.

VALUES.   A second principal component of culture consists of values, or *evaluative knowledge*. Simply put, a **value** can be defined as a conception that people have about what is good, important, or desirable. The things (ideas, objects, situations, and so on) that people determine should be appreciated are the things that are highly valued. Values tend to serve as the standard, or frame of reference, against which many choices in life are made, and against which many things in life are measured in order to determine their importance or utility.

Time itself is a precious value for Americans, who, unlike many other people of the world, seem to conceive of it as being in short supply. This value orientation is reflected in such typical American clichés as "time is money" and "time is running out." Contrast this conception and value to that which is characteristic of many other societies in which time is perceived to be unlimited, and where, hence, there is a prevalent attitude and mentality that "*mañana* (tomorrow) is soon enough" for nearly all activities.

Another example of values as symbols or expressions of cultural preferences and desirabilities can be seen in the emphasis that Americans place on slimness as a manifestation of physical beauty in women—quite apart from any concern with its relationship to health. Compare this idea to the conceptions of beauty among the peoples of Polynesia, where stoutness has been revered as the indispensable mark of royal personages (see Box 3-3).

Anthropologists distinguish between the dominant and variant values of a culture (Kluckhohn, 1953). A **dominant value** is one that is shared by the bulk or greatest number of people. A **variant value** is an alternative conception of the same phenomenon. While most Americans may value the future, there are many who feel that the past or the present is more important. The former view represents the dominant value, while the latter constitute variant values regarding the phenomena of time.* America's prevalent future orientation is reflected in the emphasis that it places first and foremost on "the youth of tomorrow." This contrasts to those societies that manifest a dominant orientation toward the past in terms of such practices as ancestor worship, prestige accorded to the elderly, and active resistance to social change.

Social scientists frequently refer to the **core cultural values** of a people as those that form the foundation upon which their way of life is built. While core values do change, they remain relatively constant and intense over long periods of time and, hence, serve as distinctive characteristics of different cultures. Robin Williams (1970) has conducted extensive work on value orientations in the United States during the past few decades. His latest list of core values

---

* See Williams (1970) for the description of a set of criteria for determining dominant values.

# BOX 3-3. Beauty among the Peoples of Polynesia ▼

Bengt Danielson (1956), the anthropologist of the famous *Kon-Tiki* voyage, and other observers of life in the South Pacific, have noted the following about the understanding of beauty among the peoples of Polynesia:

The Polynesians differed considerably from us not only in the importance which they attached to physical beauty but also in their idea of what constituted beauty. To be regarded as perfect, a Polynesian man or woman must first of all be stout— the stouter the better. . . . "The perfect woman must be fat—that is the most imperative. . . . She must have no waist, and if Nature has cursed her with that defect she must disguise it with draperies, or submit to be 'miscalled' in the streets of Nukualofa; her bust and hips and thighs must be colossal. The woman who possesses all these perfections will be esteemed chieflike and elegant" (Thompson, 1902). . . . It was very common for the children in prominent noble families to be sent on a combined fattening and bleaching expedition. On Pukapuka in the Cook group they were shut into a house. . . . "The secluded children were made to lie on the leaves, their bodies and heads completely covered with mats. They might eat, lie or sleep in any position provided they kept well covered. They were given especially fattening foods in large quantities" (Beaglehole, 1938). . . . When the beauty treatment was finished the young people were paraded through their native village or were exhibited at a festival. Many eye witnesses certify that the desired result was really reached. On Mangareva the flower-decked beauties were supported by their relatives because . . . they could not walk without stumbling or collapsing under their own weight. "These fattened people were called *hakarau*. There were seven or eight of them at every feast, but the fattest one was always the last to be exhibited. As they appeared before the crowd anxious to see them, the people shouted with sheer admiration, and the one who aroused the most admiration was considered the champion" (Buck, 1938). . . . A modern beauty queen would clearly not have a chance. ▲

for the American culture includes (1) equality, (2) freedom, (3) democracy, (4) achievement or success, (5) work, (6) progress, and (7) individualism. A complete list, with fuller descriptions, of these values is presented in Table 3-1.

Spindler and Spindler (1983), more recently, have provided an assessment of the American core value system that includes such things as equality, honesty, work, action, individualism, achievement, and sociability. They describe these values not only as being peculiarly American, but also as ones that have been constant and classic for our society. The similarity in the two analyses is indicative of both the strength and pervasiveness of these values in the Amer-

ican culture. Together they provide a rather full, though not exhaustive, description of core values in the American culture. Other social scientists have described essentially similar sets of core values which are often referred to as the "American creed" (Myrdal, 1962).

The American core values, of course, are not dominant in all cultures of the world, not even among all segments of the American people. One such example is that of the Kwakiutl Indians, a tribe found in the state of Washington. The Kwakiutl are a fiercely competitive people who exemplify this core value in their cultural ritual of the potlatch—a public and festive ceremony designed to achieve social standing and

▼ TABLE 3-1. Major Value Orientations in American Society

98

1. *Achievement and success:* personal achievement, especially wealth, power, or fame

2. *Activity and work:* emphasis on haste and bustle, strenuous competition, ceaseless activity, and busyness

3. *Moral orientation:* thinking in terms of right or wrong, good or bad, ethical or unethical

4. *Humanitarian mores:* disinterested concern and helpfulness, personal kindness, philanthropy

5. *Efficiency and practicality:* emphasis on adaptability, expediency, and getting things done

6. *Progress:* emphasis on the future, and receptivity to change

7. *Material comfort:* emphasis on a high standard of living

8. *Equality:* emphasis on the equality of opportunity

9. *Freedom:* freedom from government control and freedom to handle one's own affairs

10. *External conformity:* adherence to similarity and uniformity in beliefs, values, and lifestyles

11. *Science and secular rationality:* interest in an ordered universe and in controlling nature by means of rationality and scientific methods

12. *Nationalism or patroitism:* cultural ethnocentrism, loyalty and allegiance to national symbols and slogans, pride in one's country

13. *Democracy:* advocacy of majority rule, representative government, and rejection of monarchical or aristocratic principles

14. *Individual personality:* emphasis on the unique development of each personality, independence, and self-respect

15. *Racism and related group-superiority norms:* ascription of value and prestige to individuals on the basis of race or particularistic group membership

Source: Robin M. Williams, Jr., *American Society: A Sociological Interpretation*, 3d ed. New York: Alfred A. Knopf, 1970, pp. 452–502. Reprinted by permission of the author.

prestige by demonstrating nonreciprocative generosity or by conferring social indebtedness upon one's neighbors (Honigman, 1963).

Throughout the pages of this book we shall have ample opportunity to examine the dominant and variant values of the American culture in more detail.

NORMS. The third principal category of culture consists of what may be called *normative knowledge.* This type refers to beliefs and understandings about how people should or should not behave in particular situations. A **norm** is a rule of behavior that specifies the

kinds of action which are prescribed (expected or required) as well as the kinds which are proscribed (forbidden) among a particular people. In many cases, norms are derived from values and religious beliefs. Others emerge from trial-and-error experience in the day-to-day interaction of people. In either case, norms are considered essential to social life. More than any other component of culture, norms make for shared expectations and human predictability. Social behavior in largely new or unfamiliar situations would otherwise be problematic and grossly devoid of order.

Norms, of course, are directed essentially at social control, which is achieved through the

**Cultural Patterns.** Norms of clothing and modesty are among the many aspects of living that are culturally determined. Here one can contrast the traditional dress of a Colorado Indian family in Ecuador with that of a diversity of people in Afghanistan. Differences such as these demonstrate how cultural universals can be manifested in a host of variations and at the same time fulfill a number of different functions, such as providing bodily adornment and indications of social position. (*Left,* Peter Menzel/Stock, Boston; *right,* Rick Smolan/ Contact)

application of **sanctions**—actions that reward conformity and punish nonconformity. Violations of norms typically result in *negative sanction*, or punishment of one type or another. Correspondingly, fulfilling or abiding by norms often results in *positive sanction*, or rewards of various kind, such as social approval, praise, or acceptance.

There are different categories of norms based on their social importance. More important norms are more forcibly sanctioned in appropriate ways. Let us describe the principal types of norms and sanctions, while bearing in mind that the distinctions are primarily a matter of degree rather than kind.

**Folkways** are norms that are reinforced by a mild degree of sanction. A folkway usually refers to "ought to" behavior that is considered customary or traditional. Such norms involve relatively trivial conventions of behavior, concerning such things as manners and etiquette. Examples are saying thank you to people when appropriate, shaking hands with the right hand, standing up when introduced, wearing a tie at certain social functions, using utensils to eat certain foods, not coughing in someone's face, not smoking in a nonsmoking area, or not belching at meals. These are customary, normal, typical, and habitual ways of doing things—or not doing things—which a society finds appropriate or functional. Folkways in many cases originate by chance, or are often established as common practice because of frequent repetition, and, hence, become simply customary. Violators of folkways may be considered crude or boorish, even uncouth or ill-mannered, but not evil or sinful. Hence violations of these norms usually involve only relatively mild and informal sanctions, such as gossip, ridicule, and social avoidance.

▼ **Mores*** are norms that are reinforced by strong sanctions. Mores refer to "must" behavior that is considered basic and important to the social life of a people. These norms, which have ethical or moralistic implications, are frequently formalized as part of the enacted laws of a society. Marital fidelity, honesty in examinations, avoiding plagiarism, and not appearing nude in public are examples. Violations of these mores may not always be crimes, but

**100** they constitute behavior which is considered to be highly deviant. Accordingly, these violations are usually sanctioned in relatively severe and formal ways. Such punishments include fines, imprisonment, whipping, torture, mutilation, and even death.

**Taboos,** part of the mores of a society, refer exclusively to proscribed or prohibited behavior. Violations of taboos are considered to be particularly grave forms of social deviance. Marriage between Blacks and Whites in South Africa is a taboo. Among the Amish people, a religious community found in certain regions of the United States, the use of automobiles and electricity are taboos. A universal example of a taboo is the incest regulation, which forbids marriage and/or sexual relations between specified members of a family or kinship group. Another universal taboo would appear to include any form of dishonesty, such as cheating or lying.

The demarcation between folkways and mores is neither absolute nor permanent. As a part of culture, norms are dynamic phenomena. They are constantly, although usually slowly, undergoing change, especially in terms of their importance and formality in various respects. Norms that were once mores—for example, women getting married in white dresses or washing clothes on Monday—are now considered folkways or simply customary usages in the American society. Correspondingly, current folkways—such as not smoking in designated nonsmoking areas—may one day soon become mores. And many informal norms, such as the expectation of honesty in various situations, have been codified into law or written regulations. Social norms, in these respects, reveal their relationship to, and dependence upon, cultural values.

## STRUCTURE OF CULTURE

The structure of culture refers to the organizing principles and relationships among the component parts. As such, the structure of culture is comprised of elements similar to those that comprise the structure of any system: size (number of cultural elements), complexity (the variety of cultural elements), degree of integration (amount of cohesion), and so on. Additionally, there are a number of other elements usually considered in terms of the structure of a particular culture. We shall discuss here some of the distinctive elements of cultural structure.

CULTURE TRAITS. A **culture trait** consists of one of the smallest possible units or simplest elements of culture. Analytical distinctions among cultural traits can be made in terms of the various kinds of culture content: (1) cognitive traits, (2) evaluative traits, and (3) normative traits. Artifacts may also be described as material traits of culture.

A wedding ring or a bridal gown are examples of cultural traits. Again, however, it is not the physical object that actually constitutes the culture trait; rather it is that which the physical object symbolizes or represents that constitutes the culture trait. The simple belief that God exists would be a cognitive trait. A specific value, like cleanliness, or a particular norm, such as standing when introduced or obedience to parents, are other genuine examples respectively of evaluative and normative traits of culture.

---

* This is the plural form of the Latin word *mos*, which is seldom referred to in sociological usage.

CULTURE COMPLEXES. A **culture complex** refers to a relatively large division of the structure of culture. It consists of all of those cultural traits that are in any sense related to one another and thus can comprise a cluster of interrelated or interconnected traits. Hence, a marriage complex or wedding complex would refer collectively to all those cultural elements or traits that are related to the marriage process or wedding ceremony. In addition to the rings and gown, these complexes would include all that culture represented by the bachelor's party, the bridal showers, the bridesmaids, the wedding vows, the reception, the wedding cake, the honeymoon, and so forth.

Similarly, football can be considered a culture complex consisting of all that culture represented by pep rallies, cheerleaders, victory dances, marching bands, field rules, uniforms, referees, scouts, coaches, pennants, and so on. Another example is the culture complex of holidays, such as that of Christmas: caroling, cards, trees, presents, parties, Santa Claus, family dinner, and the numerous other festivities.

CULTURAL INSTITUTIONS. A **cultural institution** consists of all those culture complexes that are thought of as being functionally related to any basic social need of human beings or to a functional need of society. A primary example is the institution of the family, which relates to the fundamental need in society of

101

**Cultural Complexes.** Among the more important of the cultural complexes found in the American society is that of Thanksgiving—a holiday that symbolizes contemporary beliefs and values as well as historical tradition. (© Joel Gordon 1983)

▼ regulating the reproduction and rearing of children. This institution in the American culture includes the romantic love complex, the dating and courtship complex, the child-rearing complex, kinship relationships, income production, and many other such elements that can be identified as culture complexes.

There are several different types of institutions in any culture. The actual number depends on the complexity of the particular culture. A few institutions, however, are basic, and they have been found in every known culture. These universal institutions are those of the family (and kinship), government, education, religion, and economics. We shall have much more to say about these basic institutions and others in subsequent chapters, especially Chapter 7.

## CULTURAL INTEGRATION

The culture of a people is not a simple conglomeration of traits or a random collection of complexes and institutions. Cultures, while differing in their internal consistency, tend to develop into systems with varying degrees of coherence and integration. Such, indeed, is required for any culture to survive. The different parts of a culture fit together into an integrated system in which each element or trait is functionally interrelated, as are the various complexes and institutions that may be distinguished.

**Cultural integration** is reflected in themes, motifs, and patterns which represent dominant variables that cut across, or run through the various elements of culture. For example, some societies emphasize competition and power; others, cooperation and peace. Such dominant or core values frequently characterize the many different dimensions or components of a culture and, as such, represent distinctive cultural themes.

One of the more well-known analyses of cultural themes is that of Ruth Benedict (1961), who classified American Indian cultures as either "Apollonian" or "Dionysian." The former, represented by the Zuñi Indians, emphasized peaceful themes (sobriety, love, humility, peace, and cooperation); while the latter, represented by the Plains Indians, emphasized militaristic ones (aggression, conflict, war, and competition). We can characterize modern cultures in similar respects. For example, we think of the Iranian or Israeli cultures as being religious, but the Soviet or Chinese cultures as primarily economic and political in nature.

Often such cultural themes or motifs are referred to collectively as the *ethos* of a society—that set of guiding principles that gives a people a distinctive character in both a sociological and a psychological sense. Sometimes this phenomenon is referred to as the **cultural ethic.** The Puritan ethic that stresses moral virtue and normative strictness, as well as the Protestant ethic that emphasizes individualism, rationality, frugality, and hard work, have been characteristic of American society and typical of its people at various times in their history. Free enterprise and personal virtues still constitute dominant themes in American culture.

Cultural integration is significant in a number of respects. One is that any addition or change in an element of culture—regardless of how small or seemingly insignificant—is likely to bring about other changes throughout the cultural system. Hence, the concept of cultural integration permits us to understand, at least in part, why new elements and cultural innovations are accepted or rejected—or, more likely, modified in such a way as to "fit" into a culture. This common practice is what is often implied, for example, by the "Americanizing" or the "Italianizing" of a particular trait or complex. It is necessary in these respects to understand the meaning, function, and consequences of any cultural element in the context of the system of which it is a part, however minor or major that may be.

Cultural integration, of course, is never complete, but always relative. In general, the simpler and more homogeneous the components of a culture are, the greater the degree of cultural integration. Modern cultures are usually characterized by considerable differentiation, and this seems to work toward fragmentation and against integration. Integration, nevertheless, is always present in sufficient degree to permit a culture to function with relative unity and stability.

# Cultural Variability

Culture is a highly diversified phenomenon. Its diversity can be seen quite simply and quite strikingly in a simple contrast of the lifestyles of Western and Eastern societies. All human beings and all societies face the same fundamental problems in terms of survival and adaptation to the physical and social environment. The solution to these problems, however, can be quite varied (see Box 3-4). Let us consider this variability of culture in more detail.

## UNIVERSALS, ALTERNATIVES, AND SPECIALTIES

Cultures have many common elements, despite their many differences, and usually quite distinctive features. Social scientists distinguish, in these respects, the categories of cultural universals, cultural alternatives, and cultural specialties. Cultural traits and cultural complexes, for example, may be described and classified in terms of the degree to which they are shared by all peoples or only by particular societies, as well as the extent to which they are utilized in any given culture.

CULTURAL UNIVERSALS. A **cultural universal** consists of an element of culture that is common to all peoples everywhere. The universals of culture seem to derive from the fact that all societies must perform the same essential functions in order to survive, that is, to

## BOX 3-4. Human Relations Area Files ▼

One of the unique tools for cultural research that demonstrates cultural variability consists of the Human Relations Area Files (HRAF), which are a detailed record of many known cultures of human history—both contemporary and extinct. These files were originally compiled in 1949 by the anthropologist George P. Murdock and housed at Yale University in Connecticut. Today, many other universities have copies of these files and keep them current.

The HRAF contain 800 categories of information on over 400 different societies and provide an enormous amount of data on the contents and structure of all known cultures. More particularly, these files permit cross-cultural analysis, which makes it possible to determine the extent of similarities and differences in hundreds of cultures. If one were interested, for example, in the practice of polygamy (marriage permitting more than one spouse), it could be determined from the HRAF not only which cultures permit this form of marriage but also how prevalent and common it is or has been. The HRAF have been of inestimable value in permitting anthropologists and other social scientists to determine the extent of universal and alternative forms of behavior in human culture. ▲

maintain social life as well as to meet the physical and psychological needs of their members. Table 3-2 contains a partial list of cultural universals compiled by Murdock (1945) and arranged in alphabetical fashion in order to emphasize their variety.

These universal elements of cultures are, of course, quite general in character. They exist universally in their form or essential nature; however, the specific nature or contents of each

▼
universal element varies from one culture to another. Norms of marriage and incest regulations, as well as forms of dancing and funeral rites, are often highly diversified in various cultures; yet all cultures contain these kinds of behavioral patterns. The universality of cultural elements derives in many cases from their indispensability for human survival and social order; their specific variability derives from the creativity and inventiveness of human responses.

104

CULTURAL ALTERNATIVES. A **cultural alternative** is an element of culture that offers people within a particular culture a choice of mechanisms in meeting personal and social needs or wishes. These cultural elements are available to all members of a particular society, yet in practice are adopted by only some people. Examples are different types of schooling (private versus public schools), different styles of dress, and different religions. Cultural alternatives represent different solutions or reactions

TABLE 3-2. Common Characteristics of Culture

| | | |
|---|---|---|
| Age grading | Food taboos | Mourning |
| Athletic sports | Funeral rites | Music |
| Bodily adornment | Games | Mythology |
| Calendar | Gestures | Numerals |
| Cleanliness training | Gift giving | Obstetrics |
| Community organization | Government | Penal sanctions |
| Cooking | Greetings | Personal names |
| Cooperative labor | Hair styles | Population policy |
| Cosmology | Hospitality | Postnatal care |
| Courtship | Housing | Pregnancy usages |
| Dancing | Hygiene | Property rights |
| Decorative art | Incest taboos | Propitiation of |
| Divination | Inheritance rules | supernatural beings |
| Division of labor | Joking | Puberty customs |
| Dream interpretation | Kin groups | Religious ritual |
| Education | Kinship nomenclature | Residence rules |
| Eschatology | Language | Sexual restrictions |
| Ethics | Law | Soul concepts |
| Ethnobotany | Luck, superstitions | Status differentiation |
| Etiquette | Magic | Surgery |
| Faith healing | Marriage | Tool making |
| Family | Mealtimes | Trade |
| Feasting | Medicine | Visiting |
| Fire making | Modesty concerning | Weaning |
| Folklore | natural functions | Weather control |

**Source: George P. Murdock, "The Common Denominator in Cultures," in Ralph Linton (ed.), _The Science of Man in the World Crisis_. New York: Columbia University Press, 1945, pp. 123–125. Copyright © 1945 Columbia University Press. Used by permission.**

"Pop, can I have the elephant tonight?"

Drawing by Carl Rose; © 1941, 1969 The New Yorker Magazine, Inc.

to the same functional problem or situation, as exemplified in the cliché that there is "more than one way to skin a cat." Complex cultures tend to provide a greater variety of cultural alternatives than is the case in relatively primitive cultures.

CULTURAL SPECIALTIES. A **cultural specialty** consists of an element of culture that is shared by people of certain social categories, but not by the total population of a particular society. Hence, cultural specialties are appropriate only for certain individuals or groups by virtue of the social characteristics they possess. Cultural elements that can be specified in terms of age, sex, or particular roles, such as occupational ones, are a few examples. The use of dresses among women and beards among men are two concrete examples of cultural specialties based on sex roles.

## HOMOGENEITY VERSUS HETEROGENEITY: INTRACULTURAL VARIATION

▼

An important dimension of a culture is its internal consistency, the nature and extent of its cultural homogeneity and heterogeneity. How uniformly does a culture apply to all people in the society? Some societies, for example, are able to maintain two or more distinctive cultures as the major components of one grand culture. Canada, with its origins in the cultures of France and England, as reflected in its official bilingualism, is an example of this kind of cultural accommodation. Switzerland is another country maintaining different cultures: French, German, and Italian. There are similar examples in other societies around the world today.

105

In general, the smaller the unit of people, the more uniform the culture. Simpler cultures, sometimes called primitive cultures, are extremely uniform or homogeneous; there is very little variation in the culture among the people. Larger, more complex, units of people tend to have cultures that are highly diversified or heterogeneous. In such cultures there are various subcultures which are characteristic of certain groups or segments of the society.

SUBCULTURES. A **subculture** is a culture that is wholly contained within a larger culture. Subcultures are considered a part of the larger culture, or a culture within a culture. Subcultures, representing the distinctive lifestyles of a particular group or segment within a society, have the same characteristics as a culture and are distinguished fundamentally by being part of a larger one. Subcultures are oftentimes manifested in specialized modes of speech, jargon, and accent; dress; foods; religious practices; political beliefs; and other values and patterns of behavior that are not normally characteristic of the society as a whole. In one sense, subcultures can be considered as variations on a theme. They represent alternative lifestyles.

▼

**Subcultures.** Mennonites, a branch of the Amish community found in certain parts of the United States, perpetuate a distinctive way of life that permits neither assimilation into, nor diffusion of, the dominant culture—not even the adoption of its modern technology, including automobiles and electricity. (Jean-Claude Lejeune/ Stock, Boston)

Subcultures basically develop among a segment of people within a given society who share a variant pattern of values. Nudist colonies and various residential communes dramatically exemplify this kind of situation. The greater the sources of social differentiation in a society, the greater is the number of subcultures. Modern, industrialized, and complex societies are usually characterized by many subcultures. They may be of several varieties: regional, ethnic, racial, religious, occupational, age, gender, political, economic, and so forth.

American culture is characterized by an enormous diversity of subcultures of all types. Thernstrom (1980) has identified 125 ethnic subcultures in the United States (for example, Italian-American, Chicano, Puerto Rican) which derive, for the most part, from the many different nationalities of the immigrants who have formed the basis of our nation's development. There are also racial subcultures, chief among

which is the Black-American subculture. Melton (1987) lists 1200 religious subcultures in the American society. In addition, there are many occupational subcultures, such as those developed among the military, university professors, musicians, and athletes in certain sports.

The Amish, a religious sect, represent a well-known subculture in this country. They actively try to maintain their distinctive way of life by not permitting assimilation or diffusion into the dominant culture. The Amish have a highly integrated subculture that includes distinctive modes of dress, language, food, transportation, schooling, agriculture, and work (Hostetler, 1980). Norms of behavior, as well as economic and social activities, are rigidly prescribed and proscribed among the Amish people.

Adolescent subculture is also important in this country. It is usually manifested in distinctive styles of dress, jargon, norms, values, and conduct. These can be so at odds with the corresponding elements in the parental culture that frequently there seems to exist a generation gap, which is itself a sociological phenomenon of considerable interest and crucial importance. During the 1960s the youth culture in the United States was characterized by distinctive patterns of sex, drug use, music, language, dress, and political values. Many of its effects remain today and even permeate the basic culture of our society (see Frith, 1982).

One can even identify subcultures within subcultures. Hasidic Jews, a Yiddish-speaking fundamentalist sect within Judaism, represent a religious subculture within a religious subculture. Apart from their fundamentalist beliefs, Hasidic Jews also have distinctive styles of dress and grooming.

Regardless of their particular type, members of groups within subcultures share characteristic ways of thinking and acting and usually manifest a highly cohesive sense of social and psychological solidarity. Such dynamics are very significant for sociological and anthropological analyses. The same is true of countercultures which, however, have quite a different significance, sociologically, for the total culture and society.

COUNTERCULTURES. A **counterculture** is a subculture that is characterized by a lifestyle that is not only significantly different from but, more importantly, in conflict with the dominant culture. Countercultures usually develop among people who, for whatever reason, are physically isolated or socially alienated from the dominant culture. Such people need to find support for their failure or unwillingness to follow the dominant patterns (Yinger, 1982).

Thus, while countercultures have all of the characteristics of a subculture, they are distinguished fundamentally by the essential element of deviant behavior in that they comprise a lifestyle that is proscribed by the wider society. Examples of countercultures are delinquent gangs or underworld crime organizations, such as the Mafia or Cosa Nostra. Adolescent subcultures may sometimes be thought of as countercultures because their unique lifestyles so frequently involve an open rejection of the dominant culture. Similar examples of countercultures are represented by nudist colonies, communes, and revolutionary movements.

Countercultures, by challenging and rejecting the dominant culture, generate strain and social conflict. This lack of cultural integration can present serious problems for the functioning of society. Often countercultures are a source of cultural and social change.

# Cultural Relativism and Ethnocentrism

Another dimension of the concept of cultural variability is that of **cultural relativism.** This doctrine maintains that in order to understand or to evaluate cultural and social facts meaningfully, we must perceive them in terms of the particular culture and society of which they are a part.

Belching during or after meals, for example, can be an act of rudeness or courtesy—depending on the culture. To Americans it is rude; but in Arab cultures and among some South Sea Island tribes, belching at the end of a meal is considered to be a form of politeness as well as an expression of appreciation for fine food. Europeans and Americans use various forms of kissing in order to express love and affection—even diplomatic greetings in some cases; yet, among many other peoples, especially Asians, kissing is completely absent—indeed, it is considered revolting.*

Hindus taboo eating beef. Jews and Muslims taboo eating pork. Most Christians make both

---

* Kissing customs vary widely among cultures in which it is practiced. Many European peoples kiss on both cheeks when greeting; the Finnish Lapps kiss the mouth and the nose simultaneously; and the Kwakiutl Indians of the American Northwest kiss by sucking the lips and tongue.

▼

108

beef and pork a part of their normal diet and find these meats delicious and nourishing. Millions of people eat grasshoppers, lizards, termites, and ants, but such "food" is considered to be absolutely disgusting by millions of other people, who, nonetheless, find oysters, clams, and shrimp—with intestinal tract intact—to be great delicacies! Similarly, among the Nuba, a primitive African people of the Sudan, milk is considered palatable only when sour; and, in short supply, it is reserved exclusively for old men and the tribe's wrestling champions. Most other cultures use milk more commonly as baby food, so long as it is sweet.

Americans set aside an hour for lunch, perhaps spending less than half of it in consuming their meal, while Italians allow three hours for a lunch break and spend at least one-third of that time in a state of repose. Eskimos who put aged parents on ice floes set out to sea in order to die are expressing values of parental honor that derive from their beliefs about the hereafter. Male Jews wear hats during religious services; male Christians do not. Spitting to many Western people is regarded as crude and disgusting. Among the Masai of East Central Africa, however, spitting is considered to be an act of respect and friendship.

Which culture is correct? Is there a universal standard against which to judge the validity of cultural values and norms? Perhaps theologically or philosophically there is. However, from an anthropological and sociological perspective, the answer to this question is no. Social scientists often contend that the mores determine what is right or wrong. To a great extent this is, of course, true. Many people would argue, on the contrary, that there is a universal standard for the evaluation of cultural behavior—such as a golden rule or a natural law. There may indeed be a natural law that pertains to the propriety of behavior for all people at all times in all places. The absolute specification of such a universal prescription, however, is difficult to determine. Even morality is, to a

considerable degree and in many respects, relative to a particular religion and, therefore, to the culture of which it is a part. Hence, the

## BOX 3-5. The Polite Art of Spitting

**Spitting is regarded as a gesture of friendship and respect among the Masai tribe in East Central Africa.**

**Newborn babies are spit upon by relatives and friends in order to wish the child a happy life.**

**Masai people also spit at each other as a form of greeting, just as we say "Hello" and "Goodbye."**

**Similarly, whenever they wish to confirm or seal a business deal, the Masai people spit at each other, much as we would shake hands in such situations.**

**And, nobody is repulsed by these practices! On the contrary, any self-respecting member of the Masai tribe would be offended not to be spit upon in the appropriate circumstances.** ▲

evaluation of many aspects or elements of culture can be undertaken only in a context of cultural relativity.

Similarly, there is no way to determine scientifically that one culture is superior or inferior to another. Cultural differences may indeed make a difference, and social scientists may be able to show empirically the various consequences of cultural differences; but they cannot demonstrate that one set of differences or consequences is better or worse, more or less desirable, than another. Once values and objectives are specified, however, it may indeed be possible to speak of "cultural superiority." Empirical evaluation, in such cases, may be able to specify which cultural mechanisms are more or less effective in achieving the stated values and objectives.

## ETHNOCENTRISM

The lack of appreciation for cultural relativity often produces ethnocentrism. **Ethnocentrism** is an attitude of superiority regarding one's own culture or subculture. It includes the belief that one's cultural knowledge, beliefs, values, norms, and other cultural practices comprise the only correct way of life. People, for example, often perceive their religion as "the only true religion," or their nation as the "chosen people of God." Ethnocentrism also consists in using one's own culture as a standard, or frame of reference, with which to judge all others. The position that the "best ways are one's own ways" is the essence of ethnocentrism. This evaluation may be a conscious act, but generally it is not. Ethnocentrism is similar to egocentrism, except that rather than referring to an individual's self-centeredness, it refers to culture-centeredness or ethos-centeredness— being centered in one's own way of life.

All peoples are basically ethnocentric. Often ethnocentrism is manifested in the form of a strong sense of patriotism or nationalism. In proper measure, such attitudes are functional in that they serve to reinforce and to maintain the culture, thus making for integration and stability which any society must have in proper measure. In the extreme, however, ethnocentrism can be a barrier to intercultural contact and international understanding and cooperation. It has accounted, at least in part, for the occasional failure of programs of cultural exchange and international assistance directed at these ends, such as those conducted by the United Nations.

Several years ago, an American Peace Corps worker in Nigeria unintentionally caused strained diplomatic relationships between the United States and Nigeria by writing a postcard to an American friend which gave her naive impressions of the cultural mannerisms of some of the Nigerian people. She stated, for instance, that she was shocked to see people "go to the bathroom in the street." The card was found by a few young Nigerians whose political sympathy was not with the United States and its physical presence in their country in the form of the Peace Corps. An ensuing outrage among certain segments of the Nigerian society nearly brought an end to this otherwise quite successful effort at intercultural cooperation.

Perhaps this incident of cultural shock reflects cultural ignorance more than ethnocentrism, for much ethnocentrism is the result of cultural isolation. Ethnocentrics are sometimes said to be wearing "cultural blinders" in that they cannot see beyond their own culture. Public urination is not very uncommon behavior—not even in technologically advanced countries where people are less puritanical than Americans and place a neutral value on essential human behavior such as elimination. Hence, ethnocentrism, in many respects, can be seen as resulting from a lack of both understanding and intellectual appreciation for culture relativism, which maintains that no culture is superior to any other and that all cultures must be analyzed in objective terms. Cultural relativism, thus, is the antidote for ethnocentrism.

▼

## BOX 3-6. The One Hundred Percent American

There can be no question about the average American's Americanism or his desire to preserve this or his precious heritage at all costs. Nevertheless, some insidious foreign ideas have already wormed their way into his civilization without his realizing what was going on. Thus dawn finds the unsuspecting patriot garbed in pajamas, a garment of East Indian origin; and lying in a bed built on a pattern which originated in either Persia or Asia Minor. He is muffled to the ears in un-American materials; cotton, first domesticated in India; linen, domesticated in the Near East; wool from an animal native to Asia Minor; or silk whose uses were first discovered by the Chinese. All these substances have been transformed into cloth by a method invented in Southwestern Asia. If the weather is cold enough he may even be sleeping under an eiderdown quilt invented in Scandinavia.

On awakening he glances at the clock, a medieval European invention, uses one potent Latin word in abbreviated form, rises in haste, and goes to the bathroom. Here, if he stops to think about it, he must feel himself in the presence of a great American institution; he will have heard stories of both the quality and frequency of foreign plumbing and will know that in no other country does the average man perform his ablutions in the midst of such splendor. But the invidious foreign influence pursues him even here. Glass was invented by the ancient Egyptians, the use of glazed tiles for floors and walls in the Near East, porcelain in China, and the art of enameling on metal by Mediterranean artisans of the Bronze Age. Even his bathtub and toilet are but slightly modified copies of Roman originals. The only purely American contribution to the ensemble is the steam radiator.

In this bathroom the American washes with soap invented by the ancient Gauls. Next he cleans his teeth, a subversive European practice which did not invade America until the latter part of the eighteenth century. He then shaves, a masochistic rite first developed by the heathen priests of ancient Egypt and Sumer. The process is made less of a penance by the fact that his razor is of steel, an iron-carbon alloy discovered in either India or Turkestan. Lastly, he dries himself on a Turkish towel.

Returning to the bedroom, the unconscious victim of un-American practices removes his clothes from a chair, invented in the Near East, and proceeds to dress. He puts on close-fitting tailored garments whose form derives from the skin clothing of the ancient nomads of the Asiatic steppes and fastens them with buttons whose prototypes appeared in Europe at the close of the Stone Age. This costume is appropriate enough for outdoor exercise in a cold climate, but is quite unsuited to American summers, steam-heated houses, and Pullmans. Nevertheless, foreign ideas and habits hold the unfortunate man in thrall even when common sense tells him that the authentically American costume of gee string and moccasins would be far more comfortable. He puts on his feet stiff coverings made from hide prepared by a process invented in ancient Egypt and cut to a pattern which can be traced back to ancient Greece, and makes sure they are properly polished, also a Greek idea. Lastly, he ties about his neck a strip of bright-colored cloth which is a vestigial survival of the shoulder shawls worn by seventeenth-century Croats. He gives himself a final appraisal in the mirror, an old Mediterranean invention, and goes downstairs.

He places upon his head a molded piece of felt, invented by the nomads of Eastern Asia, and, if it looks like rain, puts on outer shoes of rubber, discovered by the ancient Mexicans, and takes an umbrella, invented in India. He then sprints for his train—the train, not sprinting, an English invention. At the station he pauses for a moment to buy a newspaper, paying for it with coins invented in ancient Lydia. Once on board he settles back to inhale the fumes of a cigarette invented in Mexico, or a cigar invented in Brazil. Meanwhile, he reads the news of the day, imprinted in characters invented by the ancient Semites by a process invented in Germany upon a material invented in China. As he scans the latest editorial pointing out the dire results to our institutions of accepting foreign ideas, he will not fail to thank a Hebrew God in an Indo-European language that he is a one hundred percent (decimal system invented by the Greeks) American (from Amerigo Vespucci, Italian geographer). ▲

Ralph Linton, "One Hundred Percent American," *The American Mercury,* vol. 40, April 1937, pp. 427–429.

## CULTURAL DIFFUSION AND CULTURAL BORROWING

Another dimension of cultural relativism, and the caveat that it implies for ethnocentrism, is found in the origins of culture. Like nearly all cultures, American culture is the result of cultural diffusion. That such is the case is poignantly described by the anthropologist, Ralph Linton (1937), in his often quoted and still timely essay on the fallacy of "The One Hundred Percent American" (see Box 3-6). "American" culture, in turn, has spread to every part of the contemporary world, and today it is shared in part by nearly all societies—some more so than others, but most especially by those in the western hemisphere. Murdock (1934) estimated that 90 percent of the contents of every culture is acquired from other societies.

Cultural diffusion is effected by a number of factors. One of these is the extent and kind of contact that occurs between peoples with different cultures. Cultural borrowing, in any event, is selective, and, in this respect, is controlled to a great extent by the principles and dynamics of cultural integration.

# Origins and Determinants of Culture

What accounts for the diversity and variability of culture? What determines the specific contents of a particular culture? Why are some cultures more complex, or seemingly more advanced and more highly developed, than others? Why have some cultures succeeded in developing the sophisticated technology for such things as computers, lasers, space missiles, and nuclear bombs? Why are some societies relatively successful in preventing deviant behavior, providing marital and family stability, ensuring a continuation of economic development, or securing stable and peaceful governments, while others fail dismally in these respects?

These are complex questions which can be answered here only in part. Some things, however, are certain. The sources and determinants of culture are many. Moreover, these determinants operate in a concerted and dependent fashion. The intent of these two statements is to set aside the contentions of monistic or single-cause explanations that are often advanced

▼ to account for cultures and much other human phenomena. Let us discuss two of the more common examples of this type of simplistic thinking.

## BIOLOGICAL DETERMINISM

To say that culture is determined by biological factors implies that a culture is the result of the particular genetics or racial composition of a given people. Yet, the Human Relations Area Files reveal that there is much cultural variation among people of the same or similar racial backgrounds. Conversely, similar types of culture are found among people with different racial or genetic backgrounds. Culture is simply not directly associated with race or other biological attributes.

Arguments to the contrary are also the basis for claims of racial superiority, which is often offered as an explanation for cultural progress and superiority. Yet, the empirical studies that are available show that human intelligence is distributed uniformly among the many genetic populations—all peoples and races of the world.* Extensive efforts to demonstrate the genetic superiority of any one racial population over another have so far failed, so that the present working assumption is that, as far as our capacity to learn, maintain, transmit, and transform culture is concerned, different categories or classifications of human beings must be regarded as equally competent (Mead, 1958). Advanced civilizations are, therefore, not unique productions of any particular racial category, as the recent history of mankind might suggest. Highly complex cultures and advanced civilizations have been found among many different races and genetic populations. One of mankind's most advanced cultures was that of the T'ang Dynasty of ancient China (618–907 A.D.). Another is that of the classical period (300–900 A.D.) of the Maya Indians of North and Central America.

Race is frequently seen as deterministic of culture because often peoples with racially distinctive characteristics possess highly similar cultures. The cultures of the many Black societies of Africa are cases in point. Other examples would be the Chinese and the Japanese cultures. And, more generally, there is the highly common situation of speaking categorically of Western cultures as opposed to Eastern cultures. While such a procedure recognizes the many similarities among cultures, it all too simplistically overlooks their many subtle differences and highly distinctive features. Here is a case of how a somewhat accurately perceived correlation of phenomena can lead to an erroneous cause-and-effect conclusion—and one that can have enormous consequences for social understanding and interaction.

## ECOLOGICAL DETERMINISM

Another kind of single-cause explanation for cultural variation involves arguments based on geographical and meteorological considerations. One such idea is that the composition of the terrain and its climate are the principal determinants of a culture. Surely, physical environmental factors such as land and weather have much to do with conditioning a culture and perhaps setting limits for cultural development (see Harris, 1985, 1979; Hardesty, 1977; Bennett, 1976), but such factors alone do not determine a culture.

A people's efforts to survive may be constrained by its geographical location. Often these "resources" are effectively utilized, as in the case of Eskimos who build houses of ice, and Africans or Filipinos who set them on stilts over water. Ecological considerations require human adaptation, but they do not absolutely determine how people must adapt, or the particular type of cultural responses or features that will develop. Many Eskimo peoples may

---

112

* Contrary arguments and evidence are occasionally advanced on this point. For current allegations of this kind, see Jensen (1981).

live in igloos, but all do not; the Chukchee Eskimos of Siberia use tents instead (Bogoras, 1975). This latter arrangement, incidentally, has many disadvantages, including the daily chore of removing snow from the outside of the tent in order to avoid the hazards of collapse.

The physical environment may be one reason there are no major civilizations in the Arctic regions or in the torrid tropics—not yet, at any rate. But there are societies, and therefore cultures, in these areas, and each of them has many of the cultural elements of the highly advanced civilizations—from computers to Coca-Cola!

The tiny band of Eskimos who live on the rock-bound Little Diomede Island off the coast of Alaska still wear clothes made of seal skin; their houses are built of walrus hides; and the bulk of their food comes from the icy waters of the Bering Strait—just as it has for centuries. But these Eskimos have one modern cultural resource their ancestors never imagined: Everyone is a stockholder in a multimillion-dollar corporation. The Bering Strait Native Corporation is one of thirteen regional corporations that is owned and operated by the Eskimos, Aleuts, and Indians of Alaska. Here is one of the cultural developments in the Arctic region that has been brought about by the construction of the Alaskan pipeline. It represents elements of a highly advanced civilization that was not precluded by the geographical environment—indeed, in a very fundamental way, it was made possible by it. Examples such as this, however, are often used to document another variation of ecological determinism.

Many people think that the advanced state of American culture is due to its natural resources: oil, coal, iron, aluminum, gold, and rich farmland. Yet, countries that are chiefly mountainous and devoid of natural resources, such as Switzerland, have developed highly advanced and rich cultures. Another case is Japan which has very little mineral wealth, yet ranks among the most highly industrialized and technologically advanced societies of the modern world. Such examples need not be limited to the modern era. The ancient Egyptians developed one of history's most advanced civilizations in a vast region of desert, nonarable land. The Romans provided a similar example of these circumstances. And, conversely, there are a number of societies and countries that are rich in natural resources, particularly valuable coal and oil, which have not achieved—or, at least, only recently are beginning to develop—advanced industrialized cultures. Many societies of the Middle East provide examples of this situation.

Another geographical argument is that contemporary major civilizations are concentrated in the temperate zones, which are supposedly conducive to intellectual stimulation. However true this may be at the present, historical analysis indicates there have been many exceptions to these geographical patterns. The Mayan and Aztec civilizations of subtropical Mexico were culturally more advanced than the nomadic tribes of American Indians, who inhabited the more temperate regions of North America during the same period. Moreover, the Middle Eastern "cradle of civilization" that existed 2 to 3 thousand years ago—Egypt, Rome, and Greece—was localized in largely arid and desert regions that hardly had a temperate climate.

Highly diversified cultures are found in areas that have similar geographical environments, and, conversely, similar cultures are found in highly diversified physical and geographical environments. Peoples living in essentially the same climate can have widely different cultures. In the southwestern United States, for example, the Hopi and Navaho Indians have lived for centuries in the same locality but have quite different cultures. The Hopi are agriculturalists and harvest crops, while the Navaho are nomads and graze sheep. Significant differences also exist in terms of religious and family life, as well as architectural styles. The Hopi live in adobe houses, some multifamily units of which

▼

**113**

▼

could be classified as high-rises, while the Navaho live in single-family (single-room) dwellings that resemble igloos, except that they are made of tree branches. Thus, however much the climate and other features of the physical environment may influence cultural development, they do not determine that a particular kind of culture will develop or must develop in a specific geographical area.

114

While environmental factors may be highly influential in the development and composition of a particular culture, perhaps even going so far as to set limits, it now appears quite clear that environmental barriers can be conquered. Developments in the fields of communication and transportation have served in recent years to diffuse the many cultures of the world in all directions. There is probably not a spot on the earth where American culture, in one form or another, has not invited itself to join other cultures—from the North Pole to the South Pole, from the East to the West. Now it is even spreading—at least in its material manifestations—to other planets of the universe as our exploration of outer space continues!

## SINGLE CAUSALITY VERSUS MULTIPLE DETERMINANTS

No aspect of human social life can be reduced to biological or geographical explanations. Single-cause theories of cultural origins falter in their inadequate consideration of the range of human cultures in different times and in different places. They are, at best, partial explanations. They describe only some of the factors that may have a partial bearing on the development of a particular culture. And, in a given case, one factor may indeed be considerably more influential than others. These factors certainly explain much of the diversity of human cultures and the variability in the solutions of societies to their functional problems. Some single-cause explanations work better than oth-

ers, but such a situation is a relative matter which can only be considered in a specific cultural context.

A number of processes form the basic dynamics of cultural development and change. One such process that has been of long-standing interest to anthropologists and archaeologists is that of **cultural diffusion**—the dynamics by which elements of one culture are transmitted and spread to other cultures. A host of factors operate in this very complex process alone. Not all cultural elements either diffuse or diffuse at the same rate. Cultural borrowing, therefore, is itself but one of the many factors that enters into the determination of culture, especially in this very modern age with the highly sophisticated technology for instantaneous communication and phenomenally rapid transportation—all of which both facilitate and intensify social and cultural interaction. We shall have more to say in Chapter 14 about the process of cultural development and change.

# Language: The Fundamental Symbolate

The chief embodiment of culture, as well as its principal vehicle, is language. Language, in brief, functions as the fundamental symbolate. All of the characteristics of culture—symbolic, ideational, learned, shared, and normative—pertain essentially to language. Similarly, the core function of culture as mediator between individuals and their social and physical environments is achieved most fundamentally through the mechanism of language. Language not only permits the development and elaboration of culture but also promotes its transmission and perpetuation. Language, as we shall see in the next chapter, is indispensable for human development. Without language, people cannot develop fully human nature—the chief attribute of which is conceptual or symbolic thought.

**Language** consists of a system of signs with particular but arbitrary meanings attached to them, along with conventional rules governing the use of these symbols. These signs are usually oral or written, but they may also be tactile or visual signs, such as those used by the visually impaired and hearing impaired. In all respects, language is essentially symbolic—and, as such, is an exclusive capacity of human beings. The unique ability of human beings to create symbols is impossible without language. Hence, one can see quite clearly that language, culture, and symbolic ability are essentially conceptual analogues of each other.

Language has many functions—some intended, some not. One unintended function is that it promotes social cohesiveness, as is indicated in the often-heard expression that someone "speaks my language." Let us look, however, at the social significance of language, as well as its cultural character, in two very fundamental and important respects—communication and perception.

## COMMUNICATION

One obvious function of language is communication. Not all communication, however, involves language. Communication may be accomplished by a number of different means and with different degrees of sophistication. **Communication** is simply the transference of messages (meanings or intentions) from one individual to another. It is an activity found in many species of animals. To a limited degree, other species are able to communicate through a variety of mechanisms: sounds (grunts, growls, hoots, purrs), motions (gestures, facial expressions such as teeth-baring and staring, pecking), positions, and chemical emissions. But these actions do not constitute language because, in virtually all cases, they represent instinctive or innate capacities and other physiological processes rather than truly acquired or learned abil-

ities. Moreover, the meanings of these physical *signs* are, therefore, absolute or fixed, rather than arbitrary or conventional as is the case in language. Language, however, is a system of symbolic communication which essentially involves conceptual thought. There is no evidence that language or symbolic communication is found in other species—at least not to any significant degree. Only human beings communicate with language.

Symbolic communication, then, is a unique attribute and capacity of human beings. The literature on this question, however, has become quite controversial in recent years, especially with the contention that symbolic thought has been demonstrated in some other species, particularly chimpanzees and gorillas. The expectation also exists that future research may uncover a more extensive capacity for such intellectual functions among other animals. While such an eventuality, of course, may indeed come true, certain cautions need to be entered for the moment. One is to specify the terms and meanings that surround this controversy.

That other species can use and manipulate symbols taught to them is not disputed. Considerable research (Premack & Premack, 1983; Hill, 1978; Mounin, 1976) clearly and adequately demonstrates this point. Chimpanzees and gorillas, for example, have been taught to use the rudiments of symbolic language in the form of the American Sign Language—the gestural language of the deaf—as well as other special languages, such as those used in computer programming. Some chimpanzees reportedly have demonstrated the ability to manipulate as many as 400 symbols with this gestural language. However, none appears to have shown even a superficial ability to form meaningful sentences. The ability to handle syntax is totally nonexistent. Thus, while apes may be able to acquire a very simple vocabulary, there is no evidence that they have an ability to form sentences, especially to alter the order

**Symbolic Thought.** Chimpanzees and gorillas have been taught simple vocabularies in various sign languages, but there is no evidence that they have any ability for true language, which involves abstract thought and the manipulation of conceptual symbols. (Animals Animals ©)

of signs to produce different sentences (deLuce and Wilder, 1983; Slobin, 1979).

The use of any learned gestural language on the part of any animals has been confined to artificial situations. With only one quite limited exception, the language has been used nearly exclusively between human beings and chimps, not for chimp-to-chimp communication (Cunningham, 1985). Apparently, these animals are unable to teach this knowledge or to pass it on from one animal to another. At least, they do not do so to any significant degree. More recent research maintains that other species are doing nothing more than manifesting a form of stimulus-response conditioning or training. Terrace (1979) claims that, in a 6-year study, a chim-

panzee under his training rarely initiated conversation: Nearly 90 percent of the chimp's signs were responses to the teacher's signs, and about one-half of the signs showed overlap—that is, containing part, or all, of what the teacher had just signed.

However much superficial language may be found among other animals, it is light years away from that which characterizes the human being. No evidence, moreover, has been put forth to show that any other species creates its own symbols. Animals which lack the ability to create symbols possess neither language nor culture. Nonetheless, research on teaching symbolic language to animals is all quite recent—only about 20 years old. How far it will go is difficult to say with certainty. Some researchers, however, have given up these efforts with the contention that, judging from available evidence, there is no hope of any significant success. The issue is likely to remain controversial for the immediate future.

## SOCIAL PERCEPTION

Language, in addition to serving as the vehicle of symbolic communication, performs a number of other sociopsychological functions. Foremost among these is its service as the cognitive mediator between individuals and their social or physical environment. Language, and therefore culture, permits us to interpret, and to give understanding to, reality and our experiences within it. Our sensations of reality—what we can see, hear, smell, taste, and feel—have no meaning in themselves. These stimuli need to be interpreted in some way in order to be meaningful for us. Language permits us to make this interpretation—to change sensations into perceptions and thereby give understanding, however true or false, to reality.

Language serves as an intervening variable in all stimulus-response (S-R) situations of human cognitive activity. It permits action by providing definitions or labels for stimuli. Without definitions, there are no reactions, and, therefore, no behavior. People cannot respond to stimuli until the stimuli have been defined. What, for example, do you think of "totosicles"? Unless you know what these are, or know something about them, you cannot express a liking or disliking—an attraction or repulsion—for them. All of our apprehension of reality assumes the following pattern of dynamics: First we look, then we name, and only then do we see.

The same sociopsychological dynamic is basic to all human interaction. When we encounter human beings, we do not see blobs of chemical cells. Rather we "see" a man or woman, a boy or a girl, an old man or an old woman, a professor or a policeman, and so on.

There is a story about three baseball umpires exchanging views on judging balls and strikes that describes the phenomenon of social perception and language. One umpire indicated that he calls pitches as he sees them; another that he calls them as they are. The third umpire took the position that "they ain't nothing until I call 'em!" The point is that we respond differently to the same object or situation depending upon which definition is given or which label is applied, correctly or not.

People then respond to their perception and definition of things—never to things in themselves. Our definitions are ultimately supplied by our language, and hence, to some extent all definitions are cultural. Moreover, since we live in different cultures, or subcultures, with different languages, we live in different perceptual and cognitive worlds in a certain sense.

Does time, for example, move quickly or slowly? Perceptual and cultural contrasts of time may be found among Spanish-speaking peoples, whose language talks of clocks and watches as "walking" rather than "running." One might "miss" the bus or train in English, and, therefore, as the active agent, be responsible for the consequences. In Italian, on the other hand, it is the bus or train that "leaves you at the station" and makes you the passive and blameless recipient of misfortune. Similarly, in other languages, objects lose themselves, automobiles wreck themselves, and dishes break themselves by falling away from people.

All languages simply do not reflect the same reality in the same manner. Language, then, in large part shapes our perceptions and molds our thoughts.* The modern elaboration of this position was first expressed in the somewhat controversial thesis of Edward Sapir and Benjamin Whorf, noted cultural anthropologists and linguists. The Sapir-Whorf thesis, sometimes called the **linguistic relativity hypothesis,**

▼

**117**

* For a discussion of how language affects our thought processes, see Ross (1957).

▼

maintains that reality is known through the particular language that people use, and hence through one's culture.* Whorf argued that people differentially conceive of such factors as time, space, and matter, depending on the way that their languages categorize these phenomena (see Carroll, 1956). People must necessarily perceive and understand reality through the grammatical forms and linguistic categories of their particular languages. If we speak, or simply think, in one language, we think one way; if we think in a different language, we think in a different way. In a certain sense, therefore, we live in a world of words and grammar. As Sapir (1929:209) remarked, "The worlds in which different societies live are distinct worlds, not merely the same world with different labels attached." Accordingly, insofar as language is the fundamental symbolate, different cultures may be said to "think" differently. One need not have a profound imagination to understand the consequences of this situation for social interaction.

Languages differentially sensitize people to certain perceptions and blind them to others. The very composition and structure of a particular language can force the speaker to make distinctions that are not made in another language. Such is especially true in the case of vocabularies which themselves vary enormously in size for each language. The Eskimo language, for example, has as many as twenty words for snow (for different kinds or situations thereof, such as "falling snow," "swirling snow," or "frozen snow"), while the Aztec language utilized only one word for snow, frost, ice, and cold—all of which were presumably perceived as essentially the same phenomenon (see Williams and Major, 1984).

Especially demonstrable of this linguistic phenomenon is the color spectrum. The human eye can make several million color discrimi-

nations, yet most languages recognize just a handful of different colors. Among some tribes of American Indians, for example, only the primary colors (red, yellow, blue) are found in their respective languages. Many languages recognize only two colors. The Jalé of New Guinea, for example, divide the spectrum into *hui* and *ziza*, representing the warm and the cold colors, respectively. Similarly, the Dani of New Guinea speak of only two colors: "light-warm" and "dark-cool" (Rosch, 1974). Other cultures, such as the Arawak of Surinam, the Toda of India, and the Baganda of Uganda, recognize only three colors (Berlin and Kay, 1969). Contrast these several examples with the English language, which has a large number of words for distinctive colors—from aquamarine to zaffer. All people see the same color spectrum, but they subdivide it in the many different ways that their language tools permit.

As these examples show, languages permit, as well as preclude, perceptual discriminations and distinctive perceptions of reality. This is not to say that specific discriminations could not be made by the speakers of a particular language, but rather that in the normal course of cognitive processes, they are not. All people, within the limits of their own intellectual capacities, are capable of making similar perceptions. Their particular language, however, more commonly predisposes them to make specific interpretations of reality rather than others.

Oftentimes we hear translators, or foreigners, say that it is difficult, if not impossible, to express an idea in a particular language because there is no word for it. Perhaps the sociological concepts of *Gemeinschaft* and *Gesellschaft*, mentioned in Chapter 2, would be suitable examples. This situation, however, is not characteristic of only technical terms. Many examples could be given for everyday phenomena. Only in relatively recent years, for instance, under the heavy influence of Western civilizations, did the Japanese introduce the word *kissu* into their language in order to accommodate a

---

* The linguistic relativity hypothesis, although not developed as such, may be seen as an expression of the theory of symbolic interactionism, which contends that human behavior is mediated by means of symbols, many of which are cultural.

practice which did not exist in their culture. Similarly, the Tasaday tribe of the Philippines supposedly has no word to express the concept of hostility (Nance, 1988). The fact that no word exists for this phenomenon in the Tasaday language means that hostility is not an active or significant part of the cultural lifestyle of these people as well as of their cognitive functions. A similar situation exists among the Toda of India, who have no word for adultery which is an allegedly universal practice among these people. These kinds of situations often present very difficult problems for intercultural communication.

The linguistic-relativity thesis applies to the grammatical structure of language as well as to its vocabulary. The Hopi language, for example, has no tenses and no nouns for times, days, or years (Honigman, 1963). Therefore, the Hopi think in terms of perpetual movement or continuous becoming. There is no consciousness of time in the Hopi culture, and it obviously has no value to these people.

Variations in forms of address provide other interesting examples in this regard. In the Italian language, for example, there are three forms for the second person; and in the French, German, and Spanish languages there are two forms. This linguistic situation is even more pronounced in some Eastern cultures. The Thai language allegedly has fifteen to twenty forms for the second person. Accordingly, when one

## BOX 3-7. An Illustration of the Linguistic Relativity Hypothesis

**The use of one of the particular forms of "you" in Italian influences the perceptions and behavior of people. Indeed, it can be used to control the behavior of another, such as by increasing or decreasing social distance. When strangers begin to address youngsters with the formal form, these young people know that socially they are being perceived as adults. Similarly, when adults start to address each other with the informal or familiar form, they know that their relationships have become more personal and intimate. As the table below shows, English, with only one grammatical form for "you," does not permit these differences in perception and behavior.**

| ENGLISH | ITALIAN | | | |
|---|---|---|---|---|
| | Singular | Plural | Grammatical Form | Relationship |
| YOU | 1. *Tu* | *Voi* | Second Person | Informal (family, friends, children) |
| (Singular and plural usage for all | 2. *Voi** | *Voi* | Second Person | Familiar (neighbors, adults) |
| persons regardless of age or relationship) | 3. *Lei* | *Loro* | Third Person | Formal (strangers, professional associates) |

**\* Used more commonly in regional dialects, especially in southern Italy.** ▲

▼ speaks to another person in these languages, one's social interaction is directed in part by the linguistic distinctions—usually related to the formalities of social and psychological distance—that are implicit in the respective forms of address. None of these kinds of distinctions exist in the one form of the second person, singular or plural, that is used in the English language: *you.*

**120** The linguistic-relativity hypothesis is not accepted by all scholars (see, for example, Clark and Clark, 1977; and Slobin, 1979). Indeed, it remains nearly as controversial today as it was when first introduced by Sapir and Whorf. Many social and behavioral scientists argue that the basic categories of thought and language are universal for all humanity. They maintain that any concept can be expressed in any human language—granted that it may be easier in some languages than others. The Sapir-Whorf thesis, however, does not assert that people using a particular language *cannot* make particular discriminations or perceptions; rather, it states that in the normal course of cognitive functions involving the use of a particular language, they *do not* do so. Linguistic patterns, then, do not inevitably limit sensory perceptions and thought; but rather, together with other cultural patterns, they direct perception into certain habitual channels that serve to make salient for the individual certain phenomena in his world of experience.

Not all of the principles enmeshed in the linguistic-relativity hypothesis have stood up under empirical investigation. The basic thesis is, nonetheless, fairly sound (see Kay and Kempton, 1984). Some evidence for its substantiation is offered by the prevalent criticisms of sexist language. The concern for the use of such chauvinistic words as "chairman" or "policeman" or "sportsman," which allegedly convey and perpetuate the perception of these positions as exclusively or predominantly—indeed, even, naturally—male, are but a few simple examples.

Research indeed shows that the generic use of the word "man" does perpetuate stereotyped images of men dominating the social world (Schneider and Hacker, 1973; Farb, 1973). For this reason, there is much social pressure nowadays to use neutral terms such as "person" whenever possible, or, at any rate, to avoid language with sexist connotations. The same type of sociopsychological dynamic applies to the social connotations that words have acquired because of the history of their particular usage, cultural and otherwise. For example, the relatively recent substitution of "Black" for "Negro" is intended to convey a quite different, and allegedly positive, perception of people, just as in the case of "status offender" versus "juvenile delinquent," and of "educable" or "mild retardate" versus "moron." The reality remains the same in such cases as these. The perception of it, however, is intended to be quite different—essentially a positive one for the enhancement of social interaction. Language, then, as with all other aspects of cultures, is a forceful and inevitable dynamic in nearly all aspects of human behavior.

# Summary

Culture refers to the entirety of knowledge and habitual patterns of behavior that are shared and perpetuated by the members of a particular society or group. It represents in an ideal sense the total way of life of a people—the way they think and the way they act. No aspect of human social behavior escapes the influence of culture. Culture serves as the adaptation tool of humanity. Its principal function is to mediate between the needs of individuals and their physical or social environment. Culture, therefore, in the absence of instincts or other innate mechanisms of adaptation, ensures human survival—both for the individual and for the species.

The most essential characteristic of culture is its symbolic nature. Culture consists exclusively of ideas—mental phenomena—rather than physical or material things. Culture, thus, represents a category of phenomena that may be called symbolates—those which for their existence are dependent upon the act of symboling. Culture is learned or acquired through the process of social interaction. While learned, it is not necessarily an individual possession. Individuals share the patterns of knowledge, beliefs, values, and norms that comprise culture. Culture, moreover, does not represent the actual behavior of people; rather, it is limited to the socially expected or accepted behavior—that is, normative behavior.

A cultural system, like any other system, may be analyzed in terms of two basic dimensions: content and structure. The content of a culture refers to the parts or elements that comprise it. The principal components of culture include (1) knowledge about what a people know or believe about the world, nature, and reality; (2) values or conceptions of what is good, important, and desirable; and (3) norms or rules of behavior that specify the kinds of actions which are prescribed or proscribed among a particular people. The structure of culture refers to the organizing principles and relationships among the component parts. Among the chief structural elements of culture are (1) culture traits, which are the simplest elements of culture; (2) culture complexes, which are composed of a cluster of interrelated or interconnected traits; and (3) cultural institutions, which are composed of all those culture complexes that are thought of as being functionally related to any basic social need of human beings or to a functional need of society.

Cultures, while differing in their internal consistency, tend to develop into systems with varying degrees of coherence and integration. Cultural integration is reflected in themes, motifs, and patterns that represent dominant variables that cut across the various elements of culture.

Culture, as it exists among different peoples,

is a highly diversified phenomenon. All human beings and all societies face the same fundamental problems in terms of survival and adaptation to physical and social environments. The solutions to these problems, however, can be quite varied. Despite their many differences, and sometimes even distinctive features, all cultures have many elements in common. Social scientists distinguish, in this respect, the categories of cultural universals, alternatives, and specialties.

In many complex cultures there are a variety of subcultures. Subcultures basically develop among a segment of people within a given society who have a variant pattern of values and lifestyle. A counterculture represents a subculture that is characterized by a lifestyle that is not only significantly different from but, more importantly, in conflict with the dominant culture.

Cultural relativism is the doctrine which maintains that in order to evaluate cultural and social facts meaningfully, they must be understood in terms of the particular culture of which they are a part. Ethnocentrism, a lack of appreciation for cultural relativity, is an attitude of superiority regarding one's own culture or subculture.

The sources of culture are both multiple and varied. No elements, biological and ecological ones in particular, are deterministic. Cultural diffusion, the spread of culture from one society to another, is effected by a number of factors, including the kind and extent of contact that occurs between different peoples. Cultural borrowing in any event is selective, and in this respect is controlled to a great extent by the principles and dynamics of cultural integration.

The chief embodiment of culture, as well as its principal vehicle, is language, which serves as the fundamental symbolate. Language not only permits the development and elaboration of culture, but also promotes its perpetuation and transmission. Language, moreover, is indispensable for human development; and also

▼ functions as a means of communication and cognitive mediator that allows us to interpret and give understanding to reality and our experience within it. Language, as with all other aspects of culture, is a forceful and inevitable dynamic in nearly all aspects of human behavior.

# Key Concepts

122

artifact
communication
core cultural value
counterculture
cultural alternative
cultural diffusion
cultural ethic
cultural institution
cultural integration
cultural relativism
cultural specialty
cultural universal

culturation
culture
culture complex
culture trait
dominant value
ethnocentrism
ethos
folkway
instinct
language
linguistic relativity hypothesis
material culture
mores
norm
sanction
sociobiology
subculture
symbol
symbolate
taboo
value
variant value

# 4    Socialization and Social Learning

One of the most significant differences between humans and other beings is that practically all human behavior, and especially that which is uniquely human, is learned. Much of the behavior of nonhumans, particularly that of societies at the lower end of the evolutionary scale, is the result of instincts or other types of built-in biological mechanisms. All human learning, however, stems basically from culture. How, then, do we acquire culture?

The acquisition of culture, or social learning, is a highly complex process. It needs to be viewed from two fundamental perspectives: the individual acquisition of culture and the social transmission of culture. These perspectives are, respectively, the subjective and the objective dimensions of social learning and social development, more commonly called socialization—the process by which the individual is linked to society.

Sociologists by and large concentrate on the objective and collective dimensions of socialization—the nature and function of social learning in terms of its significance for society—and leave to the psychologists the subjective and personal dimensions—what happens "inside" the learner or socializee during the process of socialization. However, to understand either dimension adequately, a comprehensive explanation of the complex process of socialization is required. Hence, in our psychosocial approach to the study of human social behavior, we shall explore both of these dimensions. Our attention in this chapter is devoted to the objective dimensions while the emphasis in the next chapter will be on the subjective dimensions. ▲

# Outline

▶ Socialization is the process by which the individual is linked to society. Human biology, as we saw in the preceding chapter, is not sufficient for social life. While other species possess instincts or innate physiological mechanisms for social behavior, human social dynamics, as well as many aspects of our biological development, rely on social learning and the various processes whereby sociocultural knowledge is transmitted to, and acquired by, the human organism. These processes are known quite commonly as socialization.

# Nature of Socialization

Socialization is a complex phenomenon which consists of a number of distinct, although not necessarily separate, processes.* The principal subprocesses are the following: maturation, culturation, socialization, and personality development.

## MATURATION

**Maturation** refers to the physiological and biological development of the human organism. It is an innate and relatively automatic process—under nonfrustrating or nonhindered conditions—of moving through the life cycle from conception to death. Maturation provides the physiological and biological basis of socialization and human social development. Where there are defects or impediments in the maturation process, socialization is correspondingly precluded. Severe mental retardation would be an example of such a situation.

---

* Some social scientists (Zigler and Child, 1982; Hamblin, 1971; Wrong, 1961) have developed the practice of using the term *humanization* as a generic label for the several processes of social learning and development.

## CULTURATION ▼

**Culturation** is principally an anthropological conception of socialization. It has as its formal object the highly variable content of social learning—the particular body of cultural knowledge that is transmitted to and acquired by the individual. Culturation is a process that is external to the organism, and one that is undertaken upon the initiative of the socializers or agents of social learning. Hence, unlike maturation, culturation is neither automatic nor inevitable.

There are two analytically significant varieties of culturation: enculturation and acculturation. **Enculturation** refers to the culturation of the neonate (newborn) or culture-free organism. Here, the socializee, at least in the very early years, is in a relatively passive state of reception. Enculturation usually takes place within just one culture. **Acculturation** is simply the transmission and acquisition of a secondary culture after human development has been completed. Acculturation, however, refers more properly to learning across widely different cultures rather than learning from one subculture to another within the same society. Adult immigrants to foreign countries inevitably experience acculturation as they learn "the total way of life" of their newly adopted society. The experience of a second or multiple culturation is, in fact, relatively rare.

This distinction between enculturation and acculturation is important primarily because of the different sets of social and psychological dynamics that are involved. In the process of enculturation, the individual socializee is virtually passive, undergoing development of essential human nature; while in acculturation, not only has human development occurred, but the process is not a chiefly passive one for the socializee. The teaching and learning process is a much more interactional situation, and the socializee plays a highly selective and significant role. Moreover, it is enculturation that, as a

**Culturation.** A birthday celebration in an Indian-American family provides the immigrant parents and grandparents with an opportunity to engage in the process of acculturation, while the little girl—an American native—experiences enculturation. (Peter Menzel/Stock, Boston)

universal phenomenon, has the greater significance for the social development of human beings.

## SOCIALIZATION

**Socialization,** considered as a distinctive subprocess, refers more properly to the purely processual and structural dimensions of social learning and human development. As such, it is not concerned so much with the individual contents and differences of culturation as with the universal elements of the process of social learning that pertain to the development and actualization of uniquely human attributes.

Socialization, in these conceptual distinctions, is concerned fundamentally with the process by which human organisms are transformed into functionally human persons. One such concern of socialization is the issue of essentially human needs (such as that of social recognition or that of a satisfying self-concept), which are thought to be neither the product of, nor essentially related to, the particular contents of culturation.* Other concerns include such elements as the issues, objectives, stages, mechanisms, agents, and structures of social learning and social development. Socialization in these various respects focuses principally on the *structure* and process of social learning, whereas culturation focuses principally on

---

* See Chapter 5 for an elaboration of the concept of basic human needs.

the *contents* of social learning and as such is concerned in large part with the richly varied cultural nature of human beings. Like culturation, socialization is external to the organism; hence, it is an elective process on the part of the socializers, rather than an automatic development.

## PERSONALITY DEVELOPMENT

**Personality development** consists of the inner psychological formation of the individual in terms of unique or individuating qualities and attributes. Personality development, by and large, is a latent process and an end product or by-product of socialization and enculturation. Hence, it, too, is neither automatic nor inevitable. The conscious efforts of the socializing agents in social development are focused on culturation—the transmission of the "way of life" of the respective society. Many other things—however unintended or unrecognized they may be—nonetheless take place during that process. Chief among these latent developments is the formation of personality, including the emergence of one's self-concept.

Each of these subprocesses is, erroneously, often equated or confused, with the others—and each usually serves as the principal focus of attention for one of the respective disciplines concerned with social learning and human development. For example, biologists refer to human development as maturation; psychologists, as personality development; sociologists, as socialization; and anthropologists, as culturation. Each of these conceptual distinctions, however, really refer to only certain aspects of the complex process of human development (DiRenzo, 1977*d*). A proper and adequate understanding of socialization requires that we understand the distinctions of the various subprocesses—however purely analytical they may be—of the complex phenomenon of human development.

That these various processes are distinct is evident in their relatively automatic or necessarily elective nature. The separateness of these subprocesses, or some of them at least, can be demonstrated on the same grounds. Socialization, however, is not possible without culturation, and neither can occur without maturation. The converse is not true, on the other hand, as has been demonstrated in studies of social isolation and social deprivation in which maturation may take place without culturation or socialization. Another aspect of the distinctiveness and separateness of these processes is found in their duration. Some of these processes (for example, maturation and enculturation) are lifelong; while others (for example, socialization and personality development) are only temporary or relatively short-lived processes.

To deal with such a complex set of processes requires a rather lengthy and involved discussion. We shall concentrate our emphasis in this chapter on social development in terms of culturation and socialization. Personality development and the formation of the self—themselves very complex processes—will be discussed at length in the next chapter.

# Functions of Socialization

Socialization, generically, has several purposes. These goals are conventionally classified into objective functions—those that primarily serve the purposes of society—and subjective functions—those that primarily serve the individual (DiRenzo, 1990). This distinction, of course, is not an absolute one, given the interdependent nature of the individual and the society. As one of America's pioneer social psychologists, Charles H. Cooley (1902:84), succinctly remarked: "A separate individual is an abstraction unknown to experience—and so likewise is society when regarded as something apart from individuals." Both society and the individual, therefore, are functionally dependent on socialization. Socialization is the means by which society and the individual are linked to

▼

each other. The respective set of functions which socialization serves in this respect may be labeled for our purposes as culturation and humanization. Let us explore each of them in more detail.

## SOCIALIZATION AS CULTURATION

There are three principal functions that socialization serves in the interest of society: (1) transmission of culture, providing individuals with the fund of knowledge (beliefs, values, patterns of behavior, emotional responses, skills, etc.) which is necessary for contributing to the goals and functions of society; (2) continuity of the structure and processes of society; and (3) social control of normative patterns of behavior. These basic functions are distinct, but they are not necessarily separate from each other.

One of the fundamental questions of sociology, as we indicated earlier, is simply, What makes society possible? Why do we find that social life everywhere is characterized by relative order rather than chaos? From the point of view of society, socialization is the mechanism by which society and its culture are maintained. Socialization as culturation is concerned with the transmission of social and cultural knowledge that permits individuals to learn and perform social roles which are necessary for the function and maintenance of society.

Socialization as culturation focuses on the functional needs of society. As such, socialization provides for the many patterns of behavior that are essential for the maintenance and continuity of society and social life. Without socialization, society would not exist. If society is to endure beyond the life span of its members, it must develop ways to ensure that its systems of beliefs, knowledge, values, and norms—in short, its culture—will be effectively transmitted to the offspring of its adult members. For any society to continue as an ongoing system, it must be sure that certain key functions

will be performed. Culture provides the knowledge necessary for the performance of these functions.

Socialization involves not only the transmission of beliefs, knowledge, values, norms, and skills to each new generation but also entails the process of motivating individuals to perform important societal functions. The development of adequate motivation on the part of individuals to perform socially important tasks cannot be taken for granted. Unless individuals are sufficiently motivated to engage in activities that are essential to the maintenance of the society, the society will cease to exist as such. Individuals have to learn to want to do what is necessary to be done. Acquiring practical knowledge and abiding by norms, however costly in physical and psychological terms, are fundamental examples. The motivation to perform essential functions is developed through the socialization process.

Socialization, as culturation, is also inextricably linked to the processes and mechanisms of social control—the maintenance of the established or desirable social order, which in turn contributes to the continuity of culture and society. The violation of societal norms—social deviance—can sometimes be explained by ineffective or inappropriate socialization. We shall explore this issue in more detail in Chapter 13.

Socialization, as culturation, is a lifelong process. The individual is always, and necessarily, learning new things (for example, appropriate age and sex behavior) at every stage of the life cycle. Hence, socialization as culturation is considered primarily a functional requisite of society and its various social systems; and the particular concerns in this respect center on how and what must be transmitted to and acquired by the individual, in terms of social learning, in order to permit him or her to assume, as effectively as possible, the social statuses that he or she will occupy as a member of society and its subunits.

128

# SOCIALIZATION AS HUMANIZATION

Human beings are not born human. Characteristics that we view as uniquely and distinctively human, such as the capacity to experience guilt or shame; to experience the emotions of love, loyalty, anger, and despair; to think symbolically; the ability to develop a self-concept; and to communicate by using language are all developed gradually within a matrix of social interaction. It is through the process of socialization that biologically human infants become transformed into fully functional human beings.

Uniquely human qualities that distinguish the human being from other species all need to be acquired and developed over a relatively long period of time through social interaction and social learning. At birth, the human infant is devoid of culture, and therefore devoid of such specifically human attributes as rational thought, conscience, self-conceptions, values, morality, language—or symbolic knowledge of any kind. Nor does the human infant have any conception of itself—either as a distinct or specific entity—as a biologically or genetically

given quality. All such characteristics are the products of social learning.

Human beings are normally born with the potential and capacity to grow and to mature—which, in biological respects, is relatively automatic and inevitable. The capacities to think symbolically, to distinguish right from wrong, to entertain ideas about oneself, to judge relative worth, to speak, to express emotions of anger, fear, love, and hate, are the products of social learning and uniquely human attributes (see Table 4-1). But the actualization of these potentials requires social learning. In this sense, therefore, one needs to speak of human nature as emergent, as socially emergent, rather than as a physically or biologically given attribute. Apart from society and social life, there is no such thing as truly human nature. As Cooley (1902) has stated, "Man does not have it at birth; he cannot acquire it except through fellowship, and it decays in isolation." The newborn infant represents a set of human potentialities that may be realized only through the process of social interaction and social learning. The qualities that are most distinctively human emerge only as a result of social interaction and social

TABLE 4-1. Some Uniquely Human Attributes

| Products of heredity | Products of socialization |
|---|---|
| Physical appearance | Symbolic thought* |
| Intelligence (mental capacity) | Conscience (morality) |
| Temperament (mood dispositions) | Valuing |
| Emotional tears (crying) | Personality |
| Laughing | Self-concept |
| Opposability of thumbs | Culture |
| Far-sightedness | Language |
| Bipedalism | Speech |
| Sexual activity continuous | Emotions |
| through menstrual cycle | Incest taboo |

* Thinking per se is not uniquely human: trial-and-error, problem-solving, and conditioning are all found in lower animals.

▼ learning. The potential for human development is present in every genetically and biologically normal individual; but the realization of this potential occurs only through social interaction—chiefly and crucially in the early years of life.

Socialization as humanization is not a lifelong process. Pragmatically, we believe, there is a point in the life cycle at which an essentially human nature can be said to materialize for all intents and purposes. That is to say, uniquely and distinctively human attributes, such as symbolic thought and conscience, are sufficiently developed to permit the adequate and effective functioning of the human being on both the personal and the social levels.

This functional development is, of course, a matter of degree in each individual case. It depends on both one's potentiality and one's social experiences. In the typical or normal situation, however, it occurs relatively early—usually around 7 or 8 years, although social development is still quite incomplete in many respects throughout the period of childhood and adolescence.

Socialization as humanization cannot occur without socialization as culturation. Accordingly, while the process of human development is fundamentally a universal one, all people are to an extent molded .to the form and content of their respective culture. It is this malleability that permits both cultural and personal diversity.

# Maturation: The Biological Basis of Socialization

Socialization, whether in terms of culturation or humanization, presupposes maturation or biological development. Human infants are born less mature than any other animal. Such a situation is of fundamental importance in the social development of the human being. It is impossible to socialize an individual until appropriate and corresponding biological development has occurred. Walking and talking, as well as thinking and valuing, like all other human behavior, presuppose physiological and biological development.

Oftentimes ineffective socialization results from attempting to teach specific behavior or actualize particular potentials before the organism has sufficiently matured for it to be able to develop the particular behavior. One such example is the common practice of trying to teach children to walk before their bone structure has matured sufficiently to support their weight. Another somewhat more prevalent example of inappropriate socialization concerns attempts to toilet train children before necessary muscular development for sphincter control has taken place. Both of these kinds of behavior, while fundamentally biological, are also social and cultural to a considerable extent. How we walk (our pace and gait), as well as the specific attitudes and even posture for excretory functions, are to a certain extent cultural and social in nature. Cultural and social learning, especially in the young, is accordingly limited in its initiation by the development and maturational schedule of the biological organism. Even the onset of puberty in girls—a developmental process that is essentially biological—appears to be much influenced by environmental factors. The average age for menarche (first menstruation) has been declining at the rate of about 4 months per decade throughout most of this country. This development has been attributed to a variety of sociocultural factors, including improvements in nutrition, health care, and medical treatment.

Human infants possess three natural attributes that make them especially amenable to culturation and socialization. These characteristics are (1) plasticity—the capacity to learn alternative patterns of action; (2) sensitivity—the capacity to be concerned with, and react to, others; and (3) dependency. The helplessness of the infant, and its complete dependency on others for the most elementary gratification of needs, is perhaps unparalleled in the animal kingdom. The human baby, for example, cannot even get up its own gas without the assistance of others. Despite the limitations that are set by the nature of the organism, however, human biology is exceptionally malleable in contrast to that of other species. As we saw in the preceding chapter, many of the specific ways in which particular physiological needs are satisfied and biological potentials fulfilled are determined by cultural specifications.

In addition to the attributes mentioned above, humans are born with certain types of biological structures and characteristics that further serve to facilitate the socialization process. Humans are born with a brain that is larger than that of the gorilla and one which has a highly developed neocortex that is specialized for dealing with abstract thought and other types of symbolic processes. Our brain enables us to store and retrieve a wide range of symbols that refer to a diverse set of things, events, and ideas. In addition, we are equipped with a vocal mechanism that enables us to utter a wide range of sounds, thus facilitating linguistic development. Prehensile fingers with an opposable thumb permit humans to manipulate a much larger variety of objects than other animals can. These are some of the biological characteristics that help to facilitate the socialization process.

The nature and extent of socialization is dependent upon the nature and extent of maturation. Effective socialization requires a healthy human infant. If the infant is born with serious biological deficits, the socialization process may be hampered or even rendered impossible. For example, language acquisition and other aspects of socialization are dependent on the infant's capacity to remember. Yet, if certain areas of the brain are deficient or damaged, the memory could be precluded from developing. Other types of biological deficits may hamper social-

ization but not preclude it. Children who are born with hearing problems, for instance, do not learn to speak in the same manner that normal infants do because they are not able to hear utterances. However, through the use of special methods, deaf children can eventually learn to communicate and even speak.

Socialization, in short, depends on the socializability of the individual. Socialization, either as culturation or humanization, is impossible for individuals who suffer from extreme maturational arrest or defects. One such example would be individuals with severe and permanent mental retardation. Another instance would be individuals who suffer from total or severe impairment of their senses, hearing and sight in particular. The degree to which such individuals can be socialized, whether in terms of culturation or humanization, is related directly to the severity of their maturational arrest or defect. For individuals with only minimal maturation of the brain and cerebral-spinal system, or those who are totally deprived of the ability to see and to hear, socialization is usually impossible for all intents and purposes. These kinds of situations represent instances in which there may be a genuine desire to provide socialization, but inadequate maturation renders it impossible. A similar situation occurs whenever there are no maturational impediments present, yet socialization is not provided. This latter situation involves the matter of social deprivation to which we now turn our attention.

# Early Social Deprivation

What happens to human infants who, for whatever reasons, do not experience socialization? Without social contact—indeed without adequate amounts of social contact and the proper kinds of social direction—human babies do not thrive. They experience growth failure in terms of maturation, as well as on the level of socialization. Most importantly, they simply do

131

▼ not develop uniquely or distinctively human qualities—at least not to any functionally significant degree.

Many tales exist of **feral people**—children who allegedly have been reared by animals and act very much like them (Malson, 1982; Shattuck, 1980; Craig, 1978; McLean, 1978). Such tales of feral people are quite fascinating, but none has been authenticated. One can find accounts of a fish girl of Holland, a swan girl of Bolivia, a bear boy of Lithuania, a chicken boy of Ireland, a badger boy of Winnipeg, a sheep boy of Ireland, baboon boys of South Africa, and a very large number of wolf children, the most notable of whom are probably Amala and Kamala of Midnapore (see Evans, 1946; Singh

132

& Zingg, 1942). Some of these tales are fabrications, others proven hoaxes, and the rest probably cases of socially unwanted children, perhaps mentally retarded or otherwise maturationally defective individuals who were abandoned by their parents.

Bruno Bettelheim (1959:467) suggests that the reported behavior of feral children is produced not when animals behave like human parents, but vice versa: "The conclusion tentatively forced upon us is that there are no feral children, there are some very rare examples of feral mothers, of human beings who become feral to one of their children." Accordingly, the data regarding feral children are highly speculative and insufficient to be of much value for

**Feral Children.** Fictional accounts of feral children, such as that of Greystoke, or Tarzan, have sparked many imaginations—and long intrigued social scientists. While accounts of children reared by animals have been numerous throughout history, none has been authenticated. (© Walt Disney Productions)

social science. There is no creditable case of a person successfully reared from infancy without human influence.*

There are, however, several moderately well documented cases of social isolates—persons who had very limited social contact for an extended period of time—which dramatically illustrate much of what is known about the relationship between the individual and society, and the extent to which the person is a product of society.

## EXAMPLES OF SOCIAL ISOLATION

Many cases of early social deprivation, with varying degrees of accuracy in reporting, could be cited. Sociologists invariably discuss two highly interesting, and relatively modern, cases of children who had been virtually deprived of sustained contact and early social interaction with others from birth until they were discovered by the authorities. Each of these cases, discovered within months of each other during the 1930s in different states, has been personally observed and reported upon by a contemporary American sociologist, Kingsley Davis (1947). Let us briefly discuss these two cases of extreme social isolation.

ANNA OF PENNSYLVANIA.  Anna was an out-of-wedlock child whose birth and presence violently displeased her grandfather with

* The effects of social isolation, however, have apparently been known for centuries—but perhaps not fully appreciated. Emperor Frederick II presumably conducted an experiment during the thirteenth century in order to determine the kind and manner of speech that children would have if they spoke to no one during childhood. He bade foster mothers and nurses to suckle, bathe, and wash the children, but in no way to prattle to them, for he wanted to learn whether they would speak the Hebrew language, which was the oldest, or Greek, or Latin, or Arabic, or perhaps even the language of their parents, of whom they had been born. But he labored in vain because the children all died. Apparently they could not live without the petting and the joyful faces and loving words of their foster mothers (Ross and McLaughlin, 1949:366–367).

whom she and her mother made their home. From birth she was confined to a small, attic-type room on the second floor and did not experience any significant amount of social stimulation. In fact, it appeared that she was seldom moved from one position to another. She was given just enough attention to sustain her physically; otherwise she was ignored by her mother. She had no toys or friendly attention and was almost always alone. She was fed only cow's milk and appeared undernourished and extremely emaciated, with a bloated abdomen. When Anna was discovered by the authorities, they determined her chronological age to be 6, but her mental and social age was much lower. She was not able to talk, walk, sit up, or manifest behavior that would reflect even a modicum of intelligence. She appeared to be totally deaf and possibly blind as well and showed only perfunctory or antagonistic interaction with others. Her usual disposition was one of immobility, indifference, and a complete absence of expression. Anna was placed in an institution for retarded children in order to receive specialized training.

Approximately 4 years later, at the time of her premature death, Anna could behave in a manner typical of a child 2 to 3 years old. She was toilet-trained. She was able to wash herself, brush her teeth, and use eating utensils, although she used a spoon exclusively. In addition, she had learned to walk, identify colors, and construct things with blocks. Anna was able to interact with humans in a relatively effective manner. Most important was the fact that she had learned to speak. While it has been suggested that her extreme immaturity could be blamed, to an extent, on inherited factors (her mother was mentally retarded), the fact that she had begun to develop human attributes and behavior when exposed to social stimuli indicates the crucial importance of social-environmental factors for the emergence of social characteristics. It is impossible to know the degree of social development that may have been

▼

▼

possible in her case had she not died so prematurely. What is clear, however, is that Anna never would have reached the level of human development that she did had she remained in social isolation.

ISABELLE OF OHIO.    The case of Isabelle is quite similar. She, too, was born out-of-wedlock and kept confined for the same reason. From the age of 2, Isabelle knew only the isolation of a dark room which she shared with her deaf-mute mother. They communicated by gestures. When Isabelle was discovered at the chronological age of $6\frac{1}{2}$ she reacted in fear and hostility toward strangers and uttered only strange, meaningless sounds. Her behavior was typical of that of a 6-month-old infant and she revealed the I.Q. of a child of 19 months—a fact that erroneously led to her being designated as mentally retarded. She, too, was unable to walk; her legs were so bowed that the soles of her feet came together when she was in a standing position.

Isabelle (unlike Anna) was given a specialized training program designed to help her develop intellectual and social skills. Her slow progress at first suggested that the task was hopeless, but gradually she began to respond. She improved quite rapidly and, in a relatively short time, learned how to read, write, and count. At the age of $8\frac{1}{2}$, Isabelle's intellectual skills were similar to those of other children of the same age. Thus, as a result of her specialized training with intense social interaction, Isabelle was able to realize her intellectual potential. Isabelle eventually entered school where she took part in all activities as relatively normally as other children. While a number of factors may explain Isabelle's greater success, as compared to Anna, her case is another clear example of the effects of social isolation: limited maturation may occur, yet nothing else significant in terms of human development takes place.

Anna and Isabelle demonstrate how little purely biological resources alone contribute to the development of a completely human person. Isabelle's case shows that isolation up to the age of 6, with little cultural learning and a failure to acquire speech, does not preclude the subsequent development and acquisition of these abilities. Yet, what is not known is the maximum age at which one could remain isolated and still retain a potential capacity for complete and normal socialization.

## UNSOCIALIZED VERSUS UNSOCIALIZABLE INDIVIDUALS

The two cases described above represent instances in which socialization, either as culturation or humanization, was precluded not necessarily because of any biological defect or maturational impediment, but rather because of the lack of an active or adequate response by the socializing agents to the dependent and helpless child.

The same result—the lack of human development—can occur in situations in which there is an active response by society and its agents, yet the individual is incapable of undergoing the socialization experience because of biological defects or maturation impediments. Extreme mental retardation would be a case in point. Total lack of the external senses would be another such case.

This latter situation was approximated by the well-known case of Helen Keller (1954). Ms. Keller did not experience total sensory deprivation. She was able to smell, taste, and touch. Yet, her situation of total deprivation of sight and hearing, as well as being mute, leaves little to the imagination of how socialization would have been impossible for her, had not her teacher worked the "miracle" of establishing intellectual contact and communication through the sense of touch. Tactile sensation in this case served as the extremely unusual basis for actualizing the capacity of symbolic thought and the development of all the human attributes

134

which that makes possible. Aside from her sensory deficiencies, biological development or maturation was occurring in this young child, but without the development of any uniquely human attributes.

Helen Keller is a truly extraordinary example of resourceful triumph over severe physical impairments. Unless and until the transition from a nonsymboling to a symboling existence had been accomplished, this remarkable woman would have been an otherwise physically well developed and maturated, but cultureless, individual, devoid of any distinctively human abilities. Examples such as these demonstrate quite clearly that human nature is an emergent process.

▼

135

## BOX 4-1. Boy, 6, Like an Animal after Life in Dark Room

LAS VEGAS, Nev.—The frail 6-year-old, locked up in a dark room for most of his life with five baby brothers and sisters, now scurries about his playroom, squealing and wailing while reaching for the hugs he craves.

The boy—identified by officials only as "C"—has the mental and emotional development of a 10-month-old, juvenile officials say, the result of a lifetime of incarceration in a rundown home.

The director of a juvenile home calls it the worst case of child neglect she has ever seen.

"C," a tiny 45 pounds and about 3 feet tall, can't talk now, two months after he and his siblings were freed from seclusion. And officials say "C" may never recover from the neglect.

The others, 4-year-old twin girls, a twin brother and sister 8 months old, and a 3-year-old girl, have fared better, and they are in foster homes. The older twins are speaking short sentences.

But "C" can only say "hi" and "bye" so far, and not always that much. What he wants is to be constantly held or hugged, and he runs from one adult to another, arms outstretched for the affection he apparently missed.

When he is picked up, he shrieks and screams with delight, but the sounds are more like those of an animal than those of a little boy.

"C" lives at Child Haven, the juvenile home where he and his brothers and sisters were taken two months ago after a police officer found "C" wandering on a Las Vegas street.

The officer was alarmed because the boy couldn't talk, and took him to Child Haven. His mother was found, and turned in two children, then three more.

"The prognosis is very poor," for "C" ever learning to talk or communicate properly, said Nancy Williams, Child Haven's director. "He needed that brain stimulus in his early years. The chances of recovery are very, very poor."

"When they first arrived here they would stand in a group and make noises to each other," Nedra Scott, supervisor of "C's" cottage, recalled Friday. "The way they looked at each other, it was obvious they were communicating in some fashion."

Brian Albiser, deputy director of Clark County juvenile services, said the 6-year-old was very protective of his brothers and sisters.

▼

The children's 25-year-old mother, who Albiser described as "very limited" mentally and emotionally, visits them occasionally.

Albiser said officials are looking for the children's 30-year-old father, who was supposed to have cared for the youngsters while the mother worked at odd jobs.

Juvenile officials say the children apparently were locked in a darkened room and bowls of food were slipped to them.

Albiser said the children did not appear to have suffered physical abuse, although "C" may have suffered neurological damage from being denied environmental stimulation.

Some doctors say children deprived of contact with adults in their first three years face severe mental, language and personality retardation. Muscle development of a child's tongue is also critical to speaking, Albiser said.

136

Albiser said the children's mother sometimes left them with other people, adding, "Some of the people she left them with were not a helluva lot more capable of dealing with the children than the mother."

Meanwhile, the small boy with the flashing grin, the fiery brown eyes and the outstretched arms is learning how to brush his teeth, to undress, to use eating utensils and to point to things he wants.

Giant strides, says Mrs. Williams, for a boy who snarled and recoiled when approached by adults just 60 days ago. ▲

*The Evening Journal,* Wilmington, Delaware, April 24, 1982. Reprinted with permission of the Associated Press.

## EMPIRICAL FINDINGS ON SOCIAL DEPRIVATION

The cases of social isolation discussed above represent examples of ex post facto analysis. They were not consciously designed experiments by social scientists to determine the effects of early social deprivation. Few of us, even behavioral scientists, encounter these kinds of situations of severe estrangement from social activity, so the lesson is hard to come by in terms of either personal experience or scientific research. Moreover, for ethical and moral reasons, it is impossible, to experiment with human beings in such a way that most likely would cause permanent or severe damage. Social deprivation, however, is not without empirical documentation. Several studies have demonstrated the crucial importance of early social experience for the sociopsychological development, as well as the physical development, of the human being.

In a classical study, Rene Spitz (1945) observed two sets of babies during their first year of life. One set was being cared for in a foundling home where very little environmental and social stimulation was provided. Toys and other play objects were scarce, and bedsheets were hung over the cribs, causing the babies' field of vision to be obstructed. There was only one caretaker for every eight babies, and, consequently, little time and social contact was given to any one child. In addition, babies would lie in the same position for long periods without being picked up, cuddled, or provided with other forms of tactile stimulation. The infants in this group, however, were given excellent physical care with good nutrition and proper sanitation.

The other set of children was cared for by their mothers in a nursery attached to a penal institution for delinquent girls. Conditions were much less sterile. Children here, however, had access to many toys, an unobstructed view of the surrounding area, and much tactile stimulation. These infants spent considerable time with their mothers and other caretakers.

Spitz found that despite the fact that the physical conditions in the foundling home were superior to those in the prison nursery, the infants in the prison nursery manifested much better social and psychological health. Even the physical health of these infants was superior. They weighed more, were taller, and had lower mortality rates. The foundling-home children, in contrast, developed more slowly and showed severe mental and motor retardation. They were much more vulnerable to illness than were the nursery infants, and displayed a variety of psychogenic disorders. Indeed, 37 percent of the foundling-home children died within the first two years of their stay there, whereas none of the children in the nursery home died.

Spitz's findings have been challenged on methodological grounds (for example, the two sets of children came from different countries), but ample evidence from other studies supports the general thesis that human deprivation and inadequate social experience, especially after 6 months of age, is detrimental for the normal development of the human being—both in terms of physical and biological maturation, as well as socialization. As one psychoanalyst has put it, "Babies who aren't loved, don't live."* See Table 4-2 for a follow-up study by Spitz (1946).

Goldfarb (1945), in a similar study, but one with much more methodological sophistication, compared two sets of children for social and emotional development when they were between the ages of 10 and 14. One set had been reared in a foundling home for 3 years prior to being assigned to a foster home. The other set had been reared by foster parents exclusively. The children who were reared in the foundling home were found to be socially and psychologically immature. They had difficulty controlling their impulses and exhibited much anxiety. In addition, their linguistic and intel-

* Sandor Ferenzi quoted in Linton (1945:12).

TABLE 4-2. Developmental Levels of Child Development in Spitz's Foundling-Home Research at Age 2 to 4 (n = 21) ▼

| Locomotion | |
|---|---|
| Incapable of locomotion | 5 |
| Able to sit up alone but not walk | 3 |
| Walk with assistance | 8 |
| Walk without assistance | 5 |
| Eating | |
| Unable to feed self with a spoon | 12 |
| Able to feed self with a spoon | 9 |
| Dressing | |
| Unable to dress alone | 20 |
| Able to dress alone | 1 |
| Speech | |
| Cannot talk at all | 6 |
| Two-word vocabulary | 5 |
| Three- to five-word vocabulary | 8 |
| Twelve-word vocabulary | 1 |
| Talking in sentences | 1 |

Source: Rene A. Spitz, "Hospitalism: A Follow-up Report," *The Psychoanalytic Study of the Child,* International Universities Press, Inc., 1946, vol. 2, 113–117.

137

lectual skills were impaired. The children reared in the foster home did not show these or other types of deficiencies. Goldfarb attributed the intellectual and psychological deficits shown by the foundling-home children to a lack of proper social interaction with concerned caretakers during the first 3 years of their life. Similar findings have been reported much more recently by Provence and Lipton (1962), White (1967), Bowlby (1969), Curtiss (1977), and Pines (1981).

These studies demonstrate that even physiological and biological maturation is in many respects highly dependent on social stimulation. Without social contact—indeed, without adequate amounts of social contact and the proper kinds of social interaction—human babies do

▼ not thrive. They experience growth failure in terms of maturation, as well as on the level of socialization. Most importantly, they simply do not develop uniquely or distinctly human qualities—at least not to any functionally significant degree.

The reversibility of the developmental defects of social deprivation is a controversial question. While many deficits may be reversed, such is not the case in all respects. Kingsley Davis (1947) long ago raised the question of critical periods in regard to social stimulation and human development, and argued that after 15

**138**

years, perhaps even 10, of extreme social deprivation and social isolation, it was doubtful that distinctively human attributes could ever develop.

## CRITICAL PERIODS

**Critical periods** refer to learning that requires exposure to certain cues during a specific time period in the maturational cycle (Bornstein, 1987; Scott, 1978). The behavior in question may not be learnable after the critical period—not even with intensive instruction (see Box

## BOX 4-2. Critical Periods in Language Development

Some empirical evidence of a critical period in language development comes from children who have been victims of social deprivation. Attempts to teach language to these children have resulted in complete failure (Lenneberg, 1984). One such case is particularly interesting and illustrative of the contention that critical cues for language acquisition include an environment of normal social interaction with adults.

Genie, who was 13 when discovered in California in 1970, apparently had spent most of her life harnessed naked to a potty chair in a small room. Sometimes at night, whenever she was remembered, Genie was put into a homemade straitjacket. Genie's father, who severely beat her on numerous occasions, hated noise. There was no radio or television in her house, and people spoke in hushed tones. She heard very few other types of sound, mostly her father's growling in anger like a mad dog, and was beaten whenever she herself made any noise. Genie had not been spoken to since the age of 20 months (Pines, 1981). Despite malnourishment and physical confinement, Genie was alert and curious and eagerly sought human contact.

Psychologists and linguists tried to teach Genie language for several years after her discovery (Curtiss, 1977; Fromkin et al., 1974), but she showed no proficiency beyond that typical of a 4-year-old. While Genie learned some of the basics of language, using many words and combining them into simple phrases, she was unable to form complex sentences.

Genie apparently had been a normal baby at birth. She did learn to eat, walk, and take care of herself. Experts feel, however, that the crucial factors in Genie's lack of language development were social deprivation and the relatively late age at which language learning began (Gleitman & Gleitman, 1981). Genie eventually was placed in an institution with no further significant efforts at socialization.

▲

4-2). Some physicians further maintain that children who are deprived of contact with adults in the first three years of life face severe mental, language, speech, and personality retardation. Other evidence has been amassed to substantiate the position that critical periods also exist in regard to the effective learning of a second language—a process that is somewhat more difficult (including the problem of accents) when a child enters the teen years. Still another contention of critical periods in the human being, unconfirmed by empirical evidence, involves the alleged need of the newborn to have physical contact (bonding) with the mother shortly after birth in order to have the optimal chances for physical and emotional development (Klaus & Kennell, 1982).

# Theoretical Approaches to Socialization

More than anything else, socialization involves learning. **Learning** may be defined as the process by which behavior, or the potential for behavior, is modified as the result of experience (Mussen et al., 1984). Not all learning, however, constitutes socialization.* What is learned, of

---

* Lower animals are not socialized, as defined above, but ample research shows they do learn. And apparently they learn in some of the same ways that human beings do—although not as fast and not as much. Imitation, trial-and-error, and conditioning are three types of social learning that are characteristic of some lower animals. One example of learning via imitation is provided by certain species of monkeys who clean food (potatoes) by washing it in order to permit the attached sand to float off. Learning by trial-and-error on the part of chimps and monkeys has been demonstrated repeatedly in practical "inventions" (combining different elements into a new one), such as making a ladder out of wooden boxes to permit reaching food located in high places. Trained animals, such as household pets, that perform a variety of actions on command are commonplace examples of conditioning. Only human beings, however, have the ability to learn by means of symbols—arbitrary meanings attached to visual, oral, or tactile signs; and, hence, only they have the ability to think symbolically by means of abstract concepts. This capacity represents an innate potentiality that becomes actualized only through the process of socialization.

course, consists of highly varied knowledge. Socialization, as we shall see in more detail, involves learning such diverse things as a value system, the norms of a group, and the skills needed to perform an occupational role. While the content and context of social learning varies from society to society, the learning processes that make socialization possible are everywhere the same. Thus, whether an individual speaks English or Russian depends upon his or her culture; however, the mechanisms involved in language acquisition are applicable to everyone regardless of the particular culture.

Psychologists and social psychologists have developed several theories of learning in order to explain how knowledge is applied and behavior is modified. Many of these theories are significant for socialization—both as culturation and as humanization. We shall examine three of these theories: classical conditioning, operant reinforcement, and social learning theory. The latter theory is an example of cognitive learning, while the other two represent the principal types of associative learning which fundamentally considers all behavior to be environmentally controlled.

## CLASSICAL CONDITIONING THEORY

**Classical conditioning** refers to the process whereby an initially neutral stimulus, by being associated with a stimulus that produces a specific response, also becomes capable of producing that response. The basic principle of classical (respondent) conditioning was discovered, quite accidentally, by a Russian physiologist, Ivan Pavlov (1927), while he was doing research on the digestive system of dogs. Pavlov observed that dogs would salivate not only when food was in their mouths but also when they saw food, the feeding dish, and even Pavlov himself. The observation of this phenomenon led Pavlov to devise experiments in which he would present a neutral stimulus to the dogs

▼

*"Pavlov . . . . . . . Pavlov . . . . . . . that name rings a bell."*

Copyright Ralph L. Zamorano, 1989.

140

(the sound of a buzzer, the flash of a light) just before feeding occurred. After a series of such trials, the dogs would salivate whenever they saw or heard the previously neutral stimulus. Similar instances occur for nearly everyone when, for example, they become conditioned to experience hunger at the sound of whistles or bells that signal customary meal times.

Classical conditioning is one way in which individuals are thought to learn fears, attitudes, and a variety of behavior. One of the earliest applications of classical conditioning to human beings was made by Watson and Raynor (1920) in the establishment of a phobia. In a famous experiment, Albert, a 9-month-old infant, was shown a white rat, a white rabbit, a dog, a monkey, a Santa Claus mask, and other objects. He was not fearful of any of them. Albert did

express a fear response, however, by crying when he suddenly heard a loud noise that the experimenters made by hitting a steel bar with a hammer. The investigators then paired the fear-producing noise with a neutral stimulus in the form of a white rat. After a series of such pairings, Albert exhibited fear as soon as he saw the little white rat. By associating an unconditioned stimulus (noise) with an initially neutral stimulus (the white rat), the infant learned to fear the rat as well as other objects that looked like it.

It is important to understand that classical conditioning involves not the learning of new responses or behavior, but rather the connection of existing responses to new stimuli. Accordingly, since classical conditioning involves responses that are involuntary, this type of learning ordinarily can be used effectively on unconscious or resistant subjects.

## OPERANT REINFORCEMENT THEORY

**Operant reinforcement** (instrumental conditioning) has as its basic principle the idea that behavior which is rewarded tends to be learned and repeated, while actions that are followed by punishment are not likely to occur again. In other words, the probability of a given behavior occurring is, to a great extent, dependent upon the consequence the behavior had for the individual in the past. Rewarded responses become conditioned habits, while unrewarded or punished responses become extinguished forms of behavior.

B. F. Skinner (1976), the distinguished formulator of operant reinforcement theory, contends that much, if not all, behavior can be explained in terms of the reinforcement history of the individual. For example, a student who enjoys the classes of a particular professor (positively reinforced) is apt to take other courses offered by that professor. A person who is reinforced with a paycheck every week is likely to continue to work, and a child who is rewarded for washing the dishes is more apt to repeat that behavior than if there were no reward. Similarly, in terms of negative reinforcement, one who experiences relief of pain from taking aspirin is likely to continue using, perhaps even increase, the medication.

Most parents have utilized the principles of operant reinforcement at one time or another in the course of rearing their children. Every time a parent gives a child a piece of candy, an increase in allowance, permission to stay up late, a word of praise, or a warm smile, because the child behaved in a way that pleased the parent, the principles of operant reinforcement are being used. By the same token, whenever the parent spanks the child, withholds allowance, or temporarily withdraws expressions of affection, because the child has behaved in ways that displeased the parent, the basic tenets of operant reinforcement are being applied.

As could be discerned from these examples, the rewards or punishments that are used could be tangible ones such as a piece of candy or a slap across the face, or intangible ones like a smile or a nasty look. For this type of learning mechanism to be maximally effective, however, the reward or punishment for a given behavior should follow the behavior as quickly as possible (Atkinson et al., 1983). In this way, the child will be able to associate, or to make the connection between, the behavior and its consequence. The mother who says to a misbehaving child, "Wait until your father comes home, and I'll tell him what you did," is not using operant conditioning theory to its maximum advantage, since too much time will have elapsed between the occurrence of undesirable behavior and its negative consequence (assuming the father does indeed punish the child upon arrival home).

In many cases parents may inadvertently reward undesirable behavior. For instance, the child who screams and goes into a temper tantrum because he has not gotten his way usually receives some form of attention from the parents. The attention in and of itself may be perceived by the child as rewarding, thus increasing the likelihood of a temper tantrum occurring in the future. Although there is some controversy on the issue, most experts advise the use of reinforcement (positive or negative) to encourage desirable behavior rather than the administration of punishment in order to eliminate unwanted conduct. The use of punishment, especially in the form of physical violence, is usually accompanied by several undesirable side effects, such as aggression, fear, and anxiety.

## SOCIAL LEARNING THEORY

**Social learning theory** represents approaches to socialization and individual development that stress the processes of observation, modeling, imitation, internalization, and cognition or internal thought processes. The major differences from the previously discussed theories are the absence of external reinforcement as an essential element and the stronger stress on cognitive processes as well as social interaction.

One variation of social learning theory, known as observational learning, is that formulated by Albert Bandura (1977) and his colleagues. Bandura maintains that observational learning, resting heavily on both cognitive dynamics and social interaction, involves four processes:

1. *Attention:* attending to and accurately perceiving the modeled behavior.
2. *Retention:* symbolically processing the modeled behavior in memory through visual imagery and verbal coding.
3. *Reproduction:* accurately reproducing and rehearsing the modeled behavior.
4. *Motivation:* reinforcing the modeled behavior to encourage repetition. Reinforcement, although not a necessary component, may be internal (self-reinforcement) or external.

▼ Observation is fairly simple to understand. Learning through this process may involve such things as reading books, listening to lectures, or watching television. Modeling, however, consists of a more complex set of behavior. Through **modeling** one picks up cues from a significant person (model) in the environment, and attempts to imitate the relevant actions of that individual. Learning, thus, in both these respects is essentially a vicarious experience.

**142** One of the most important processes of socialization is **internalization**—taking on the beliefs, values, and norms of society as one's own. Through internalization, the social world becomes incorporated into the individual. The significance of socialization as an internalization process is expressed by Berger: "Society, then, is not only 'out there,' but is also 'in here,' part of our innermost being. Society not only controls our movements, but shapes our identity, our thoughts and our emotions. The structures of society become the structures of our own consciousness. Society does not stop at the surface of our skin. Society penetrates us as much as it envelops us" (1963:121). Becoming

ego-involved serves as a particularly strong mechanism of social control which is very functional from the point of view of society.

During the early stage of socialization, externally applied rewards and punishments are most influential in affecting behavior. However, as children begin to internalize values, rules, and behavioral expectations—to adopt them as their own—they find that it is self-rewarding to act in accordance with them. Children experience positive feelings if they behave in accordance with those standards and negative feelings if they do not. Thus, in time, children behave according to certain rules and norms not so much to avoid punishment from adults as to gain self-approval and avoid self-punishment. The child becomes, as it were, his or her own disciplinarian.

The internalization of societal values and norms is a matter of degree and depends on the existence of specific conditions that facilitate this process. For normative internalization to occur, it is important that the child identify with someone (for example, parents) who stands for the values and norms that are to be internalized.

**Social Models.** Socialization in the perspective of social learning theory focuses on the processes of identification, imitation, and internalization. These techniques are particularly significant for anticipatory socialization or the learning of behavior that one is expected to employ later in the life cycle. (Erika Stone ©)

**Identification** (modeling) refers to the process that leads the child to think, to feel, and to behave as though the characteristics of another person—usually a parent in the case of a young child—belong to him or her (Mussen et al., 1984). The child absorbs some of the person's motives, values, and other attributes. The identification process is an important mechanism by which the child internalizes norms and notions of right and wrong because responses acquired by identification seem to be emitted spontaneously, without any specific training or direct rewards for imitation, and they are generally relatively stable and enduring rather than transient. These conditions will tend to facilitate the identification process since the parent serves as a model for the child. This point is supported by a study which showed that children who were physically punished by their parents were more inclined to engage in physical violence outside of the home than were other groups of children who had been much less severely punished for misbehaving (Sears et al., 1953).

Observational mechanisms of learning are especially useful in helping to explain how children acquire certain attitudes, beliefs, and behavior that parents view as undesirable and do not want their children to learn. For example, parents may directly tell their children to be honest; however, the children, by observing their parents' behavior, may infer that they really are dishonest and behave accordingly. Parents who preach one thing to their children but behave in a contrary manner should not be surprised to learn that it is their deeds, not their words, which have the greater influence on their children.

None of these theoretical approaches for learning, of course, should be seen as mutually exclusive or incompatible with one another. The individual theories, in fact, complement rather than contradict each other in many respects. Research evidence suggests that all of the various mechanisms of learning are intimately involved in the highly complex and intricate processes of socialization.

▼

**143**

## BOX 4-3. Associative and Cognitive Learning versus Imprinting

**All human socialization involves associative and cognitive learning, which are relatively slow processes seemingly devoid of any critical periods and ones that emphasize the recency effect. Associative and cognitive learning theories, of whatever variety, consider the individual to be highly malleable; and, moreover, they share the fundamental thesis that whatever is learned can be unlearned. *Imprinting,* on the other hand, is a genetically based process of learning through imitation (see Horn, 1985). This form of learning is characterized by the primacy effect, critical periods, and irreversibility. Not all species imprint, and the range of imprinting varies with the particular species. Imprinting is developed most clearly in birds that are able to swim or to walk immediately after birth. Ducks and geese, for example, imprint almost everything. So far as can be determined, no imprinting occurs in the human being. Research on human beings, nonetheless, is a very difficult and hazardous process, especially because it necessarily would involve experimentation during the very first months, perhaps even days, of life. Hence, this question of imprinted learning and behavior in the human species remains quite controversial. ▲**

▼ Let us now illustrate the application of these theories to some of the pivotal areas of socialization. We shall consider in particular cognitive development, moral formation, and the acquisition of sex-roles.

# Foundations of Socialization

*Class Notes*

144 Among the most fundamental of learning experiences in the social development of the human being are cognitive and moral development—both of which are tied to maturation (Kuhn et al., 1977). Two principal theories explain the processes of intellectual and moral formation.*

## COGNITIVE DEVELOPMENT

Intellectual development is the basis of all socialization. The child is not born with the ability to reason, calculate, manipulate abstract concepts, or make use of such notions as speed, weight, causality, and quantity. Rather, these intellectual skills evolve as the child matures biologically and, at the same time, interacts with the social environment.

Learning to reason is undoubtedly the most remarkable achievement of human development. It is intriguing because anyone who has attempted to reason with a 2- or 3-year-old child has undoubtedly experienced both failure and frustration. Yet, after 10 or 12 years, the

* Developmental theories, in contrast to personality theories, are frequently difficult to distinguish. Hence, to some extent, our considerations here are arbitrary. Social theories that focus more directly on the development of human qualities (and the transmission of culture), such as cognitive ability and morality, will be discussed here. Those behavioral theories that focus more directly on psychological or personality development will be discussed in the next chapter. Such a distinction is in many respects only one of emphasis—given the complexity and unity of the processes of social development, but nonetheless a necessary one for the purposes of analytical clarity.

same child undoubtedly will manifest a distinct ability to comprehend highly abstract concepts, such as love, peace, beauty, space, and time. How does this seemingly magical transformation occur?

Jean Piaget, the distinguished Swiss psychologist, has been the principal formulator of cognitive-developmental theory. Piaget (1950, 1969) was one of the first to recognize that cognitive development is a social as well as a maturational process, and that one learns from the world by actively interacting with it. As Tuddenham (1966:212) has observed, "Piaget contrasts his emphasis upon the active interplay of organism and environment both with the environmentalist view in which experience or conditioning is impressed upon a passive organism, and with the naturalist view that intellectual capacities exist preformed and merely unfold in the course of development." Piaget sought to show, via a series of ingenious and extensive observational experiments with children, how the cognitive system and intellectual skills of the individual emerge over time and how they influence the perception of reality.

Basic to Piaget's theory are the concepts of assimilation and accommodation. *Assimilation* refers to the process by which the child incorporates new learning and aspects of the environment into his or her preexisting cognitive system, thereby modifying it. *Accommodation,* a process that is complementary to assimilation, denotes the way in which a child reorganizes his or her cognitive system in order to grasp the meanings of new environmental stimuli by experiencing and relating them to what he or she already knows. Cognitive development occurs because the existing cognitive organization and abilities of the child are constantly undergoing change as the individual is exposed to novel experiences. As the child attempts to assimilate these new stimuli, the existing cognitive structures undergo modification, extension, and development. As the child's cognitive capacities develop, he or she perceives reality in new ways. The infant perceives reality in a different manner than a 4-year-old, and the 4-year-old child will perceive its social and physical environment quite differently when he or she is 8 years old. This situation is so because as children's cognitive organization and skills develop, they are better equipped to interpret their environment.

Anyone who observes the social and psychological formation of the human being is undoubtedly struck by the "imperceptibility" that characterizes this development. Central to Piaget's theory of cognitive development, however, is the notion that intellectual growth occurs through a sequence of stages. This conception of cognitive stages embodies the following premises:

1. Each stage of cognitive development is qualitatively different from the others. These variations represent very marked differences in the thought processes and problem-solving abilities of children at different ages.
2. The stages are irreversible in sequence and are cumulative. The later stages cannot emerge until the child has experienced earlier ones. Advanced stages incorporate aspects of, and build upon, the lower stages.
3. Differences in cognitive stages refer to differences in thought organization and intellectual function. The way a child answers a question, performs a task, or solves a problem, is dependent on the stage which he or she has achieved.
4. The rate of advancement from lower to higher stages may be affected by cultural, social, and other environmental variables; however, the sequence of cognitive development is not altered.
5. Most significant from the sociological perspective is that these stages are the products of *interactional* experiences between the child and his or her world.

Piaget postulated four stages of cognitive development which may be described as follows:

1. *Sensorimotor stage.* The first stage lasts from birth to about 2 years of age. Infants and young children are preoccupied with motor activities and their five senses. Children acquire in this initial stage what Piaget has termed *motor intelligence*—an understanding of reality and themselves in physical terms.

    In the early part of the sensorimotor stage, the infant's attention and actions are focused on its body. The infant does not realize that external objects exist independently of its perception of them. While observing a 4-month-old boy, Piaget noticed that if the toy with which he was playing rolled out of sight, but was still within his reach, he did not make an attempt to retrieve it. After about 8 months, however, babies attain the principle of *object permanence*—infants come to understand that objects, including humans, are known to exist regardless of whether they can be seen at a given time. Correspondingly, children at this stage begin to distinguish between their own body and the physical environment.

2. *Preoperational stage.* Early childhood, from about 2 to 7 years, marks the second stage, which is distinguished by language acquisition. Language, of course, facilitates communication and thereby opens up to the child a rich and varied environment which will serve as the basis for cognitive development.

    During the early part of the preoperational stage, the child begins to use words to refer to objects, events, and situations. The thoughts and speech of the child are egocentric at this time. The child is unable to realize that other views of reality exist. He can only perceive things from his own perspective. This egocentrism is manifested behaviorally when, for instance, the child is asked to indicate how an object or scene would look to someone else viewing it from a different angle. Most commonly the child

145

▼

*egocentric reality*

**146**

*Law of mass conservation. lemonade glasses*

will draw a picture of the object or scene from his own perspective. Or, in another manifestation of this dynamic, if a little girl who has a sister is asked, "How many sisters do you have?" the most likely answer will be, "One"; however, when asked, "How many sisters does your sister have?" the child is likely to say, "None." This thinking shows the child's inability to take the role of her sister, to perceive herself as her sister would perceive her. As a child becomes increasingly involved in social interaction, however, the egocentrism is lost and gives way to the realization that reality can be seen from a variety of perspectives.

Toward the end of the preoperational stage, the child develops the cognitive growth needed to understand the law of conservation: that the mass or quantity of a substance remains the same even though its shape or appearance may change. In a famous experiment, Piaget poured an equal quantity of lemonade into two tall, thin, identical glasses while children aged 5, 6, and 7 years observed him do it. They all agreed that both glasses held the same amount of lemonade. Then Piaget poured the lemonade from one of the tall, thin glasses into a short, broad glass. The 5-year-old child claimed that there was more lemonade in the tall, thin glass than the short, broad one. The 6-year-old child was uncertain but eventually agreed with the 5-year-old. The 7-year-old child stated that both glasses contained the same amount of liquid. The 5- and 6-year-old children were only able to center their attention on one dimension of the glass—its height—and so thought that the tall, thin glasses held more liquid than the short, broad ones. The 7-year-old, however, had become able to center his thoughts; he could take both height and width into consideration simultaneously. As a result, the child had mastered the principle of conservation.

3. *Concrete operations stage.* Reasoning matures most strikingly between the ages of 7 and 11. It is during this period that the child begins to develop the capacity to think logically and to perceive cause-and-effect relationships. The nature of numerals can be understood. Thinking at this stage is essentially in terms of specific objects and situations. The child is able to think about concrete or material aspects of his or her environment much like adults do. Children at this stage can also distinguish between internal phenomena, such as feelings and attitudes. Thinking in terms of abstractions, however, is not possible; and the ability to imagine a range of possibilities is also lacking. For the most part, children in this stage can only deal with that which is real, tangible, concrete, and specific. Even self-conceptions are primarily in terms of physical appearance and ability.

4. *Formal operations stage.* The final stage of cognitive development starts at about 11 years of age (or the beginning of adolescence) and is marked by the child's increasing ability to think in terms of abstract concepts (for example, democracy or capitalism) and hypothetical situations. Children become capable of reaching broad conclusions from observing specifics and applying general principles to concrete problems. Individuals at this stage develop the capacity to manipulate abstract symbols and to reason in a systematically logical fashion. They also begin to think in terms of probability—the possibility of what may be rather than being limited to what is—a capacity that is most likely responsible for adolescent idealism. And, finally, adolescents display a renewed egocentrism, one that is characterized by self-consciousness, self-criticism, and self-admiration.

It should be stressed that while these descriptions of the four stages of cognitive development may give the impression that the

TABLE 4-3. Stages of Cognitive and Moral Development ▼

| Stage | Age | Focus |
|---|---|---|
| Cognitive development | | |
| Sensorimotor | 0–2 | Motor activities |
| Preoperational | 2–7 | Language acquisition |
| Concrete operations | 7–11 | Cause-effect relationships |
| Formal operations | 11 on | Abstract thought |
| Moral development | | |
| Preconventional | Variable* | Hedonistic morality (avoid physical punishment) |
| Conventional | Variable* | Societal norms and rules |
| Postconventional | Variable* | Individual conscience |

**\* No specific stages because of wide variation in age at which people pass from one level to the next.**

stages are clear-cut, and that the child is either in one stage or another, this is not the case. The stages overlap each other, and in many instances it is difficult to tell which stage a child is in at a given time. Children do not lose their initial egocentrism all at once, nor do they master the rules of conservation in a day. There is also much variation among children as to when they complete one stage and progress to another one. The sequence of stages, however, remains the same for everyone. A child, for instance, would not be at all likely to show behavior that was indicative of the formal operations stage unless he or she had completed the concrete operational one.

Piaget recognized, moreover, that many individuals never get beyond the concrete operations stage, and therefore never develop the ability to think abstractly. Indeed, empirical studies suggest that as many as one-half of Americans never develop a capacity for formal reasoning (Kohlberg and Gilligan, 1971). One can easily imagine how much greater these numbers must be in less developed societies that offer a sociocultural environment which is far

less intellectually stimulating for human development.*

## MORAL DEVELOPMENT

A crucial function of socialization, especially from the point of view of society, is the development of individual standards of morality. Morality is another uniquely human attribute, and one that comes only through social learning. Newborns do not have a sense of right or wrong; they are not born knowing which kinds of behavior society considers desirable or deviant. How then do we develop a conscience and acquire a set of moral standards by which to judge our own behavior?

The mechanisms that are involved in the child's acquisition of moral principles, such as honesty, equality, and reciprocity, are the same

* Unless one's environment encourages the use of abstract thought and hypothetical reasoning, the individual may never reach the formal operations stage. Many adults are capable of using formal operational thought only in their own areas of expertise and experience.

▼

148

ones that operate in the learning of other types of knowledge. Particular attention in this regard, however, has focused on the principles of cognitive development which emphasize the part that the child's cognitive state has upon its moral judgment and behavior.

Piaget (1932) contended that children typically pass through two phases of morality. The first of these, known as the "morality of constraint," or "heteronomy," consists of ideas that appear to have been imposed from outside by authorities. The second phase is called the "morality of cooperation," or "autonomy." Piaget contended that the latter phase usually follows the former, but that the two phases can exist simultaneously and that the same child will sometimes judge one way, sometimes another.

Piaget noted that young children who cannot take the perspective of others, or focus on more than one dimension of something at a time, are at the stage of *moral realism*. They stress the observable, material, or realistic aspects of things. In making moral judgments, these children are able only to take into account the amount of observable harm or damage done; they do not place any significance on the intentions or motives of individuals. So, for example, if a child is told that John spilled orange juice on his mother's dress while serving breakfast, and that Peter splashed orange juice on his mother's dress while he was angry at her for not letting him go to the movies, the child would claim that both John and Peter were equally guilty. No significance would be given to the different *intentions* that each child had. At about the age of 10 to 12, however, children become capable of *moral relativism*. They are able to consider several aspects of a situation simultaneously and also have learned that people have different viewpoints. As a result, they take into account motives and intentions when making moral judgments.

Many studies have been conducted in recent years in an attempt to elaborate and refine Piaget's theory of moral development. Foremost among those engaged in these activities

has been the American psychologist, Lawrence Kohlberg of Harvard University, who significantly expanded and modified Piaget's initiatives.

Kohlberg (1987, 1969) was interested mainly in the ways that people of different ages justify or rationalize their moral decisions. His method of analysis is to present to people hypothetical stories which illustrate a moral dilemma. The main characteristic of these dilemmas is that acts of obedience to laws, rules, or commands of authority conflict with the needs or well-being of other people. Children are asked, for example, if the subject of the story should behave in a manner contrary to the law but one that serves the needs of a particular individual. After they answer, the investigator asks the subjects a series of questions designed to ferret out the type of justification they used in order to reach their decision. The following dilemma is representative of the kind of problem that Kohlberg (1981) used in his research:

> A man's wife is dying from a serious disease. There is only one type of drug that can save her life, but it costs $1,000 for a bottle. The husband of the dying wife begs the druggist to allow him to pay for the drug in installments of $100.00 every month. The druggist says that the husband must pay for the drug in full or he would not sell it to him. The husband waits until the druggist closes his store and then breaks into the store and steals the drug. Was the husband justified in stealing the drug? How would you have acted in this situation? Why?

Kohlberg has analyzed the types of justifications that people of different ages give in support of their decision. He concluded that people go through three main levels of moral development, each having two substages.

1. *The preconventional level.* Our moral judgments in the initial stage of development are based on a strong desire to avoid punishment and to please those who have power over us and are the source of our rewards. Conduct is judged as being right or wrong on the basis

of the perceived physical consequences of the behavior for the individual. Kohlberg called this self-centered period one of hedonistic morality—one which is based on avoiding pain and seeking rewards.

2. *The conventional level.* Here moral development is marked by the individual judging behavior in terms of the norms and rules that prevail in the society. Behavior that is in accord with the rules of society is judged as right, and conduct that conflicts with societal norms is considered wrong. Standards that govern action and that require obedience are seen as coming from those in positions of power. Respect for authority and an overriding concern for social order characterize this level. This law-and-order orientation is one that consists of respect for norms in and of themselves, and not because of any escape from pain or personal gain that may be involved.

3. *The postconventional level.* Moral decisions in the final stage of development are guided by a set of standards that have been formulated by the individual and that may not be the same as those established by society. Adherence to one's conscience, even if it entails violating a particular societal law, is of major concern at this level. The standards that the individual has arrived at are in the form of hard, abstract, and general principles which then are applied to the solution of specific moral dilemmas. Examples of such principles would be respect for the dignity of every individual, equality before the law, and the sanctity of human life.

According to Kohlberg (1969), the stages of moral growth are universal and not dependent on culture. Every individual goes through them, and does so one at a time in an invariant sequence. Not all individuals, however, necessarily progress to the most advanced stage, which presupposes the ability to think abstractly. Progression to higher stages depends, in part, on the opportunities that people have to interact with individuals who are at the next stage of moral development. Interaction with such individuals serves to have the person reevaluate and reorganize his or her own moral principles. There is much overlap among the stages, and a given individual is apt to exhibit behavior that is indicative of contiguous stages.

Cross-cultural studies by Kohlberg (1981) support his claim that the sequence of the stages is universal. Children in Taiwan, Malaysia, Mexico, Turkey, and the United States have all shown the same sequence of moral growth. Cultural factors, however, may influence the *rate* of progression through the stages and the level that is ultimately obtained. For this reason, as well as for deviations that stem from psychopersonal experiences, Kohlberg did not specify age ranges for each of the stages that he described.

# Sex-Role Socialization

Sex is a primary factor in determining how people are socialized—current emphasis on sex equality notwithstanding. In the vast number of societies throughout the world, and to a very great extent in our own society, boys and girls are treated quite differently in the processes of socialization and enculturation (see Williams & Best, 1982). As Ralph Linton observed, ". . . the division of the society's members into age-sex categories is perhaps the feature of greatest importance for establishing the participation of the individual in the culture. In practically all societies the great majority of activities and occupations are ascribed to the members of one or a very small number of age-sex categories and prohibited to members of others" (1945:63–64).

**Sex-role socialization** refers to the process by which children learn the behavior and personal characteristics (for example, attitudes, emotional dispositions, skills) that are deemed appropriate or preferred for males and females of their respective culture. The content or specific nature of gender roles varies from one society

▼ to another, but in all societies children learn what they are expected to be like, and how they are expected to behave, depending on their biological sex or gender identity. Results of an interesting cross-cultural study of sex stereotypes are presented in Table 4-4.

In our culture sex-role expectations are reflected in the clichés that "little boys don't cry" and "little girls are made of sugar and spice"

as well as in the common references to men's "work" and women's "activities." The behavioral differences that exist, and are expected, between males and females are enormous—and they apply to nearly every facet of social life.

Differences in sex-role socialization reflect differences in the adult-role expectations of males and females. Such differences are commonly manifested in household tasks—washing cars,

150

TABLE 4-4. A Cross-Cultural Study of Sex Stereotypes*

Male-associated items

| | | |
|---|---|---|
| Active (23) | Egotistical (21) | Progressive (23) |
| Adventurous (25) | Energetic (22) | Rational (20) |
| Aggressive (24) | Enterprising (24) | Realistic (20) |
| Ambitious (22) | Forceful (25) | Reckless (20) |
| Arrogant (20) | Hardheaded (21) | Robust (24) |
| Assertive (20) | Hardhearted (21) | Rude (23) |
| Autocratic (24) | Humorous (19) | Self-confident (21) |
| Clear-thinking (21) | Independent (25) | Serious (20) |
| Coarse (21) | Initiative (21) | Severe (23) |
| Courageous (23) | Inventive (22) | Stern (24) |
| Cruel (21) | Lazy (21) | Stolid (20) |
| Daring (24) | Logical (22) | Unemotional (23) |
| Determined (21) | Loud (21) | Wise (23) |
| Disorderly (21) | Masculine (25) | |
| Dominant (25) | Opportunistic (20) | |

Female-associated items

| | | |
|---|---|---|
| Affected (20) | Emotional (23) | Sexy (22) |
| Affectionate (24) | Fearful (23) | Softhearted (23) |
| Attractive (23) | Feminine (24) | Submissive (25) |
| Charming (20) | Gentle (21) | Superstitious (25) |
| Curious (21) | Mild (21) | Talkative (20) |
| Dependent (23) | Sensitive (24) | Weak (23) |
| Dreamy (24) | Sentimental (25) | |

* Items associated with males or with females in at least 20 of 25 countries (number of countries shown in parenthesis).
Source: John E Williams and Deborah L. Best, *Measuring Sex Stereotypes: A Thirty-Nation Study.* Beverly Hills, Calif.: Sage Publications, 1982, p. 77.

shoveling walks, and cutting grass versus washing dishes, dusting, and making beds. Even social obligations differ on the basis of sex. Such is particularly the case in terms of military service, an issue that has become quite controversial in our society in recent years. Public opinion polls reveal that the majority of the American people expect men to perform compulsory military or nonmilitary service for their country. Both men and women, however, oppose any form of obligatory service for women (see Table 4-5). Even more revealing is the fact that, in American society, while women are found in increasing numbers in the military, they are prohibited by law from combat duty. Such is also the case in nearly all other societies (Collins, 1975).

TABLE 4-5. Public Opinion on Social Differentiation by Sex

|  | Favor | Oppose | No Opinion |
| --- | --- | --- | --- |

*Question:* "Would you favor or oppose requiring all young men to give 1 year of service to the nation—either in the military forces, or in nonmilitary work here or abroad, such as VISTA, the Peace Corps, or in a local community or city service program?"

|  | Favor | Oppose | No Opinion |
| --- | --- | --- | --- |
| Males | 57% | 38% | 5% |
| Females | 54% | 40% | 6% |
| Total | 55% | 39% | 6% |

*Question:* "Would you favor or oppose such a program for young women?"

|  | Favor | Oppose | No Opinion |
| --- | --- | --- | --- |
| Males | 44% | 50% | 6% |
| Females | 44% | 50% | 6% |
| Total | 44% | 50% | 6% |

**Source: The American Institute of Public Opinion Report no. 286, Questions 8A and 8B, December 1987.**

Sex-role socialization commences practically as soon as the sex of the child is determined. In the prototypical case, the parents and the other adult caretakers of the infant have more or less fully internalized their culture's ideas as to which attributes and behavior are "normal" (appropriate or desirable) for males and females. These ideas are expressed in the different ways in which parents and other adults respond to boys and girls. These differences in behavioral response are many, including the most obvious variations in names, as well as those in dress, play toys, games, furniture styles, and even the traditional colors of blue for boys and pink for girls. The same is true in terms of the differential manner or style of social interaction.

**Sex-typed behavior** consists of behavior that is rewarded or punished depending upon gender assignment. Male sex-typed behavior is that which is positively sanctioned for males and negatively sanctioned for females, and vice versa for female sex-typed behavior. Boys being encouraged to play contact sports and girls being encouraged to develop artistic talent are examples of sex-typed behavior. Boys are permitted to play with guns but not with dolls, while just the opposite activities are encouraged for girls. The same differential pattern has begun to show itself in regard to involvement with computers. Computer games, like computer camps and video games, are primarily used by and oriented toward boys (Wilder et al., 1985). It is fairly easy, moreover, for anyone to recognize and to describe both the unfeminine behavior of the "tomboy" and the unmasculine actions of the "sissy."

Parents usually have sex-typed expectations of children and treat them accordingly. Daughters, for example, tend to be perceived as more fragile than sons, and hence are handled quite differently. Male infants receive more physical contact, in such forms as being held or caressed, during the first 6 months, and less nonphysical stimulation such as being spoken to and observed, than do female infants (Lewis, 1972).

**151**

▼ After the first 6 months, however, it appears that female infants receive an increasing amount of physical stimulation. Significant too is the finding that fathers of boys describe their babies as larger and more active than fathers of girls (Rubin et al., 1974).

Whether such sex differences do in fact exist, parents apparently believe that they exist, and these beliefs lead them to treat boys and girls differently. Beliefs are quite widespread, for example, that girls are more obedient and easier to rear, while boys tend to be mean and unruly. Indeed, evidence on the differential treatment of boys and girls is unequivocal. Such differential treatment is behaviorally significant in that the actions of parents tend to bring forth more motor types of behavior in boys than in girls (Maccoby and Jacklin, 1974).

Children begin to show the effects of sex-role socialization very early. One study found that 2-year-olds chose sex-typed toys when given free rein in a natural setting (Fagot and Patterson, 1969). By the age of 5, children have internalized the sex-role stereotypes of their culture to a considerable extent.

## SEX-ASSOCIATED AND SEX-LINKED BEHAVIOR

Everyone surely has observed a large number of behavioral differences between men and women. A long-standing controversy, and one that has especially come to the fore in recent years, centers on whether these differences are learned or inherited—whether they are sociological or biological. This question involves the respective distinction between **sex-associated** and **sex-linked behavior.**

The only behavior that is unequivocally sex-linked are those actions of a purely functional nature: impregnation, menstruation, gestation, and lactation. Controversy remains about nearly all other behavioral differences between the sexes. Do women naturally exhibit more emotion than men? Are males, by nature, the more aggressive and dominant sex? Are women, by nature, dependent and passive? Do men naturally excel at certain tasks by virtue of their biological makeup? In short, how much of the social behavior that distinguishes men and women is due to differences in sex hormones, and how much is learned? What are the unfounded stereotypes? What are the myths? What are the facts?

Comprehensive surveys of the literature on sex differences by Maccoby and Jacklin (1980, 1974) have been able to establish that only a very few of the stereotypical conceptions about men and women are accurate. Males are more aggressive, both verbally and physically; males excel in visual-spatial ability (for example, block design, identifying same figure from different angles) and mathematical ability; females have a greater verbal ability. While these and other studies (for example, McManus and Mascie-Taylor, 1983; Newcombe et al., 1983) were able to dispel many cultural myths regarding sex differences, an equal number of questions in this regard remain unanswered (see Table 4-6). Moreover, the fact that some sex differences (for example, male superiority in mathematics) do not appear until children are about 11 or older, leaves unanswered the question of whether these differences are learned or genetically determined. Is anatomy destiny, or are the nonphysical differences that we see in the sexes the result of the cultural expectations and processes of sex-role socialization? This is a complex question, which we will explore in Chapter 5 in more detail.

## BIOLOGICAL VERSUS SOCIOLOGICAL BASES OF SEX ROLES

In addition to differences in reproductive organs, there are certain specific physical and biological differences between the sexes. Men tend to have more physical strength and a greater number of blood cells; women tend to have

TABLE 4-6. Male and Female Differences* ▼

Myths

Girls are more social than boys.

Girls are more suggestible than boys.

Girls have lower self-esteem than boys.

Girls lack motivation to achieve.

Girls are better at rote learning and simple repetitive tasks. Boys are better at high-level tasks that require them to inhibit previously learned responses.

Boys are more analytic than girls.

Girls are more affected by heredity, boys by environment.

Girls are auditory, boys visual.

Differences

Males are more aggressive than females.

Girls have greater verbal ability than boys.

Boys excel in visual-spatial ability.

Boys excel in mathematical ability.

Open questions

Are there differences in tactile sensitivity?

Are there differences in fear, timidity, and anxiety?

Is one sex more active than the other?

Is one sex more competitive than the other?

Is one sex more dominant than the other?

Is one sex more compliant than the other?

Are nurturance and maternal behavior more typical of one sex?

Are females more passive than males?

**\* Conclusions drawn by Eleanor E. Maccoby and Carol N. Jacklin in their comprehensive study, *The Psychology of Sex Differences*. Stanford, Calif.: Stanford University Press, 1974, pp. 349–355.**

more body fat and better overall health. Men alone have an Adam's apple—a genetically male, sex-linked characteristic. It is exceedingly difficult, nonetheless, to determine in a definitive way the extent to which the differences in behavior that seem to exist between the sexes are biological or sociological. Such is the case for at least two reasons. First of all, it is impossible to completely separate the effects of biological variables from the effects of environmental factors. Babies must be cared for and cannot be reared in isolation from adults whose differential expectations about male and female behavior may bring about that very behavior. Secondly, biological and environmental variables interact with each other in complex ways. Let us look at some of the evidence which suggests that *both* biological and sociological factors operate in bringing about differences in the behavior and identity of males and females.

▼

**BIOLOGICAL FACTORS.** Research on monkeys and other animals suggests that testosterone, a chemical hormone produced in the testes of males, and progesterone and estrogen, hormones produced in the ovaries of the female, bring about differences in behavior both between and within the sexes. When female monkey fetuses were injected with male hormones, after birth they behaved in an aggressive manner and displayed male sexual conduct (Young et al, 1964). Correspondingly, male human babies who had been exposed to abnormal amounts of female hormones prior to birth were less aggressive than babies who were not so exposed (Money and Tucker, 1975).

**154**

Kagan has noted that young girls are more likely than young boys to stay near their mothers when they are bored or fearful. Moreover, boys—more so than girls—tend to define their bodies as play objects as evidenced by their propensity to climb into large boxes and roll in them. Commenting on these behavioral differences, Kagan (1971:23) observes:

> It may be more than coincidence that the rhesus monkey and baboon, who are not taught sex-role standards, show sex differences resembling those observed in this study with children. Infant female monkeys stay close to their mothers but not infant male monkeys. Moreover, display of threatening gestures and body contact play is more frequent among male and female monkeys, whereas passive withdrawal to stress is more common among females.

Kagan cautiously concludes that, "These similarities force us to consider the possibility that some of the psychological differences between men and women may not be the product of experience alone but derivative of subtle biological differences between the sexes" (1971:23).

**SOCIOLOGICAL FACTORS.** Perhaps the strongest evidence indicating the crucial part that learning and environmental factors have in fostering psychological and behavioral differences between the sexes comes from studies of **hermaphrodites**—individuals who possess the genitals of both sexes. Evidence has shown that hermaphrodites can easily assume different gender-identities through appropriate rearing. Money and Ehrhardt (1972) have studied several cases of children reared as though they were of the opposite sex. These studies strongly argue that people are born psychosexually neutral. Regardless of chromosomal, gonadal, and hormonal attributes of a particular sex, individuals may develop identities and behavior of either sex, under appropriate social influences; moreover, sex of rearing—as opposed to biological sex—appears to be more important in determining one's gender role and identity. Furthermore, the first 2 to 3 years of life are critical. Children who are raised as girls from infancy onward view themselves as females and act as females, regardless of their chromosomal sex, whereas children raised as boys act as males. Consequently, sex reassignment (changing the sex of rearing to correspond with chromosomal sex) may be made with relative ease up to 18 to 36 months of age. If sex reassignment occurs much later, however, severe disturbances may result, and the child may never establish a secure gender identity.

Money and Ehrhardt (1972) report on a particularly interesting case of psychosexual neutrality. Genetically identical and biologically normal twin boys were circumcised at 7 months of age. One twin's penis was damaged beyond repair during the operation, and it was suggested that a vagina could easily be constructed for the boy. His parents consented, and the operation was successfully carried out when the boy was 21 months old. Following surgery, the boy was reared as a girl, taking on a female gender identification (in terms of such things as clothes, grooming, and preferences for toys) and a female sex role. Soon the child learned many sex-associated attitudes and patterns of behavior, such as aspiring to motherhood and sitting to urinate. Within a year or two, people could easily determine which of the identical twins was the female. Hormone therapy with estrogen was used at puberty to maximize female characteristics. These twins remain genetically identical, yet since late childhood they have behaved respectively very much like a traditional boy and girl. This case clearly shows that biology alone does not determine the course of sex typing; assigned sex and sex-role socialization can overcome genetic and biological dispositions.

Other evidence supporting the sociological position comes from cross-cultural studies. If the attributes and behavior that seem to differentiate the sexes are biologically determined (sex-linked), then we would expect to find much similarity among the characteristics and behavior of males and females in different cultures. This does not appear to be the case, however.

## BOX 4-4. Remaining Male or Becoming Female

**Research shows that when a child is socialized into a gender role that is opposite of his or her sex, the child will take on the dispositions and behavior that are associated with the gender role into which he or she has been socialized. A most interesting case of gender-sex determination involved the separation of a set of Siamese twins in 1984 at Children's Hospital in Philadelphia. The twin boys were joined at the pelvis; they shared a liver, urinary tract, and one leg. Surgeons kept one twin male, while the other was fitted with a vagina. Although normal in every other way, the "female" twin lacks ovaries and will be unable to conceive children. The other twin should be capable of fathering offspring. Perhaps not so surprisingly, the determination of which twin would remain male was made on the basis of observed personality. It was the "more dominant and aggressive, although physically smaller" one in whom biological sex was preserved. Was this decision made on the basis of sex-associated or sex-linked characteristics? ▲**

What seems to occur is that cultural sex-role standards and expectations lead to different child-rearing practices for boys and girls, which then bring about the very differences that were expected to distinguish the two sexes in the first place.

In a classic study, *Sex and Temperament in Three Primitive Societies*, Margaret Mead (1980), the distinguished anthropologist, studied the sex-role expectations of three New Guinea tribes: the Arapesh, the Mundugumor, and the Tchambuli. Among the Arapesh, both sexes displayed behavior that many of us might label as feminine. Males as well as females were expected to be peaceful, gentle, passive, warm, and nurturant; and both sexes participated in child care. On the other hand, the Mundugumor, a nearby tribe, expected both sexes to be competitive, aggressive, and quick to display violent actions. Among the Mundugumor, a cannibalistic and head-hunting tribe, women had negative views about child-rearing and tended to be harsh and cruel toward their children, who were expected to fend for themselves almost as soon as they could walk. These women clearly devalued children and disliked pregnancy and breast-feeding. The Tchambuli people had notions of appropriate sex behavior that were the mirror-image of the sex-role stereotypes in our own culture. Women, for instance, were expected to be dominant, assertive, and active breadwinners; while males were expected to be nurturant, gentle, and passive. Tchambuli women controlled economic production and took initiative in courtship and mating, while Tchambuli men were preoccupied with self-adornment and other such behavior that we might expect of women. Behavior that has been widely taken to be typically male in American society—for example, the male as breadwinner—would be considered appropriate only for females among the Tchambuli. Mead also found that differences of attributes and behavior *within* one sex were greater than differences *between* the sexes. These findings may be considered atypical when taken in

▼

155

**Androgynous Behavior.** Sex-role behavior is quite variable in different societies. Child care on the part of fathers among the Tilefolmin people of New Guinea shows that parental behavior is learned and can be attached to either the mother role or the father role. (Photo by E. T. Gilliard, Courtesy Department of Library Services, American Museum of Natural History)

a vast cross-cultural perspective. Mead's study, nonetheless, has provided strong evidence for the importance of learning processes and sociocultural variables as determinants of psychological and behavioral differences in the sexes.*

Overall, the evidence strongly supports the view that while biological variables play a part in determining some of the nonphysical differences that characterize the sexes, learning and sociocultural experiences can probably account

for more of the variance that exists between males and females. Hence, within certain limits, sex roles can be whatever society wants them to be. The evidence is very coercive that gender role and gender identity are primarily the products of social and cultural experiences.

## MECHANISMS OF SEX-ROLE SOCIALIZATION

The learning mechanisms involved in sex-role socialization are the same ones that operate in the child's acquisition of other aspects of culture. Parents and other adults usually reward children when they behave in ways that are congruent with parental conceptions of appro-

---

* The validity of Mead's research has been questioned during the past decade—nearly 50 years since it was conducted. Evidence to this effect, however, is inconclusive; and, therefore, the claims remain controversial (see Freeman, 1983).

priate sex-role behavior. Similarly, conduct that is deemed inappropriate for members of the child's sex are either ignored, or more often punished. Brooks and Lewis (1973) conducted a study of the child-rearing practices of 380 parents of 5-year-old boys and girls. They found that parents made direct use of rewards and punishments to teach their children sex-typed behavior. Of particular interest is the finding that aggression was the area of child behavior where the greatest sex differences were most expected by parents. Boys were allowed more aggression in their dealings with other children in the neighborhood and were more frequently encouraged to fight back. On the other hand, girls were punished for exhibiting aggression but praised and otherwise rewarded for being obedient and nice.

Children also internalize sex-role behavior through observational learning. As children watch television, look at or read books, and observe parental interaction, they are acquiring and internalizing society's notions of what constitutes proper behavior for males and females. Until recently, the majority of preschool television shows and books portrayed males and females in stereotypical fashion. Females appeared rarely or not at all in most children's television shows. Moreover, most of these programs depicted males as being active, assertive, and dominant, while females were portrayed as though their main mission in life was to follow orders given by males. Females were also characterized as not being able to have any effect on their environment; unlike the males, they were not able "to make things happen" (Sternglanz and Serbin, 1974).

Children's preschool books are another important source of sex-role socialization. Weitzman et al. (1972) found that one-third of the preschool books that were given awards by the American Library Association had no female characters, and that invariably boys were depicted as being active persons who were able to deal effectively with problems that arose in fun-filled activities; whereas girls were shown as passive beings whose primary role was to assist their mothers. Similar depictions have been found in television programs (Tavris and Offir, 1984; McArthur, 1982; Sternglanz and Serbin, 1974).

Kohlberg (1966) offered a cognitive developmental theory of sex-role socialization which is quite different from the traditional learning theories. Social learning theory holds the following sequence. "I want rewards; I am rewarded for doing boy things; therefore I want to be a boy." Kohlberg claimed that the sequence is, "I am a boy; therefore I want to do boy things; therefore the opportunity to do boy things (and to gain approval by doing this) is rewarding." He argued that children first label themselves as being either male or female by observing the physical and behavioral similarities between themselves and same-sex adults and then become motivated to identify with and imitate people who are the same sex as themselves.

Sex-role socialization is as much a complex process as is any other aspect of social and cultural learning. Accordingly, any complete theory of sex-role socialization will have to incorporate selected aspects of all relevant theories. Mussen (1969:727) echoes this point of view in stating that

> It may be hypothesized that normally, for most children, learning, identification and cognitive organization all contribute to the development and growth of sex-typing and sex-role acquisition. It seems most likely that learning [reinforcement and imitation] is of paramount importance in the very early phases of sex-development but identification and cognitive growth play vital facilitating roles later on.

## CHANGING SEX ROLES

Sex roles, as we have seen, can be whatever a society wants them to be. Our society, along with many others in the modern and industrial

157

▼ world, has undergone dramatic modifications in sex roles during the past decade—and it is difficult to predict with any certainty which direction they may assume in the future. While the roles played by men and women are still noticeably different, there has been a significant convergence in this respect. Given the "liberation" of women and the "feminization" of men, we can expect profound changes in the processes of socialization-enculturation and psychosexual development. These androgynous (non-sex-typed) aspects of social learning can themselves be expected to produce significant modifications in the culture of future society and the lifestyles of future generations.* Sex-based differences in socialization, however, are still very pervasive in all societies of the world. As sex-associated differences in socialization diminish, sex differences in behavior will eventually decrease too.

**158**

Is an androgynous society possible? No society has ever institutionalized androgynous sex roles—social behavior that is not sex-specific in any form. In no society, as we have mentioned, has the role of hunter or warrior been exercised by females—not even in modern societies where military service for women may be allowed or required. Nevertheless, many scholars believe that an androgynous society is possible, and indeed extensive efforts are currently being made toward such a goal in several societies. Several attempts of this kind, however, have failed. The question, thus, remains quite controversial.

# Agencies of Socialization

**Agencies of socialization** refer to those individuals, groups, and organizations that have either a primary responsibility or a particularly strong influence in the socialization and enculturation processes. In small primitive societies, agencies of socialization are limited, both in number and in kind. There are many such agencies, however, in complex modern societies, where socialization is a major undertaking and a prolonged process that is shared by a wide variety of agencies and takes many diverse forms.

Some of the universal agencies of socialization, such as the family and the school, are mandated by society to socialize children. In these instances, the socialization effects which these agencies exert on the child are intentional and direct. Other agencies, such as peer groups and the mass media, have not been specifically designed by society to perform socialization functions. Nevertheless, these agencies have powerful effects on the social and cultural development of the individual—however unintended and indirect they may be.

## THE FAMILY

The family, and its extended kinship, is the prime and ubiquitous agency of socialization. Much of this supremacy stems from the fact that the family not only has the initial interaction with the helpless child—and one which is nearly exclusive for a relatively long time—but also because these situations occur at a time when the child is most malleable.

The child's initial contacts with society are through his or her parents. The child takes on the parents' socioeconomic status, religion, and ethnic affiliation. All of these subcultural elements influence the way the child is reared, the kinds of outside contact he or she has with other agents, and the quality and quantity of the resources at his or her disposal—as well as what the child will be taught. As a result of his or her interaction with the family, the child learns how to interact with others, becomes sensitive to the feelings of others, and begins to realize that his or her behavior has consequences. In short, the child becomes aware of social reality

---

* Some research, although widely criticized, supports the thesis that individuals who are psychologically androgynous are more flexible and well-adjusted and have higher levels of self-esteem and achievement (Bem, 1974).

and begins to develop social skills through the intimate social interaction that characterizes the family group.

The structure of the nuclear family (parents and children) has many distinct features that facilitate its socialization functions. The family constitutes a relatively homogeneous system. Johnson (1960:122) observes that "this simplification makes it possible for the child to attend to relatively few things at a time. Thus, he has a better opportunity to make the necessary discriminations, to cope with his negative reactions due to frustration, to establish new learning more firmly, to integrate new learning with old, and to reorganize his inner world slowly." The family, being a miniature social system in its own right, enables the child to become gradually acquainted with role systems, group structures, and the basic elements of social interaction. Such knowledge and experience prepare the child for future interactions in more complex social systems.

Much of what the child learns from his or her parents and siblings is not the result of intended or deliberate socialization practices. A great deal of information is acquired and internalized via observational learning rather than through intended and direct tutoring. The parents serve as major role models for the child. Moreover, any particular interactional episode that occurs between parent and child may have several unintended and unanticipated outcomes. Therefore, how the child interprets a given statement or action is of paramount importance to the socialization process.

Sibling interaction furnishes many experiences that may serve as the foundation for social, intellectual, and physical actions outside of the family. Siblings, of course, provide playmates for each other. More importantly, however, siblings learn from each other. Older siblings are active teachers and models to their younger sisters or brothers. A child who has an older sibling becomes knowledgeable about the positions that he or she will occupy in the near future. Such **anticipatory socialization**—learning about and rehearsing the social roles corresponding to positions that one will occupy in the future—can serve to ease the transition into new positions.

The family represents society in microcosm. As a group, the family provides all the essential elements for social interaction. Family interaction that responds to the child's needs—physical as well as psychological—establishes a relationship that is of fundamental importance for the cultural, social, and psychological development of the child.

## THE SCHOOL

Schools nowadays play an ever-increasing role in socialization, as is reflected in the expansion of education at both ends of the process—from nurseries and day-care centers to colleges and professional schools. Of course, the impact of the school as a socializing agent depends on the type of society in question. In technologically advanced countries, formal education lasts for about 12 years for nearly everyone—and as many as 23 years for people who wish to be professionally trained.

The primary function of the school is to transmit to children the culture's store of accumulated knowledge, including basic skills such as reading and writing, as well as history, literature, the arts, and the sciences. Schools also transmit important cultural and social values: patriotism, competition, achievement, equality, and so forth. The school, along with the family, also functions to motivate students to prepare themselves for adult roles.

There are significant differences, however, between the school and the family as agencies of socialization. Perhaps the most important difference is that for the first time the child will be under the supervision of people who are not related through kinship. The school has the effect of diminishing the child's dependency upon the family as well as providing a setting

**159**

▼ for the development of nonkin relationships and loyalties. Through the school children begin to establish connections to the larger society and realize that the family does not comprise the whole social world. Unlike the family, where interaction between the child and parents is personal and informal, interaction that occurs within the school environment between the child and teachers is relatively formal and impersonal.

**160** As the child becomes part of the classroom social system, he or she begins to learn the nature of roles and relationships that are not founded primarily upon kinship, emotional warmth, and personal criteria. In contrast to the family, where the child is judged in terms of a variety of personal criteria, the school evaluates the child mainly on the basis of academic achievement. Teachers evaluate pupils in terms of general standards that are meant to apply to everyone. As difficult as this process is—for student and teacher—it provides a fundamental lesson for the individuals, no matter what their future role is in any essentially competitive society. Moreover, evaluations of the child made by the school not only affect its self-concept but also serve as a selection process for future statuses, and, hence, more specific types of socialization, such as occupational and professional education. Such evaluations often are made very early in the educational process in the form of tracking (assigning children to different learning groups based on ability and/or performance levels). Talent and gifted programs or remedial groups are examples of tracking.

The school also performs several unintended, often unrecognized, socialization functions in fulfilling what at times is referred to as "the hidden curriculum." These functions help the child to develop a variety of interpersonal skills that are essential for effective social interaction. By providing a context for competition and comparison, the school teaches the child the importance of following rules and regulations and getting along with other people. For ex-

ample, children learn to be patient, to wait until it is their turn to speak or otherwise participate in group dynamics, to be punctual, to appreciate fair play, and to be obedient and honest. They learn to focus their attention on the teacher and not to be distracted by peripheral stimuli, and they learn to adjust their wishes and interests to the time schedule of the school (Elkin and Handel, 1984). The mastery of the school's "hidden curriculum" by the child is considered crucial if the child is to participate successfully in more complex and demanding roles and social systems later on in life.

## THE PEER SET

**Peers** are people who are roughly the same age. Schoolmates and fellow participants in such parallel activities as sports and scouting are principal examples of childhood peers. Unlike the family and the school, the socialization effects of the peer set are usually nondeliberate or unintended. The peer set performs a number of socialization functions that are different from those of the family and the school. Peer sets are important in defining appropriate behavior, setting standards, and providing goals. Through informal sanctions, peers can enforce conformity to established or desired norms, especially those appropriate to the age cohort. Peer sets exert an especially crucial influence in the adolescent period. Unlike the child's relationships to parents and teachers, which are characterized by status-power differences, one's relationship with peers, at least initially, is on an equal status-power basis.

The youngster's involvement in a peer group may serve to loosen the bonds that he or she has established with his or her family, and to develop a stronger sense of independence (Elkin and Handel, 1984). The peer group allows a child to try out and develop interpersonal skills. The peer group also provides a context within which the child can learn how to be a leader as well as a follower, how to cope with hostility

**Adolescent Peerage.** One of the strongest influences in the process of socialization is that deriving from one's adolescent peers who, in sharing similar interests and concerns, more frequently than not constitute the most "significant others" in the social lives of children and young adults. (© Arvind Garg/Photo Researchers)

from age-mates, and how to make compromises. Hence, peer socialization is particularly instrumental in terms of the many techniques and dynamics of social interaction.

Peer groups also evolve a distinct subculture that involves values and norms that are different from (in some cases in conflict with) those of the broader culture. The child feels much pressure to conform to those particular norms and expectations because the peer group is the source of many potential satisfactions. When children start school, they quickly discover that many of their satisfactions are dependent on establishing themselves as members of a peer group. Their opportunities for companionship and their chance of being asked to play favored roles—or even to participate in various play activities—vary with a degree of acceptance by the group. It is therefore not surprising to find that most children of school age are intensely

motivated to gain peer group acceptance.

Peer groups usually develop values, norms, and practices that are different from those of adults. Such inconsistencies, often referred to as a "generation gap," present a host of sociological and psychological problems for both socializees and socializers. Ambiguity sets in, and both become uncertain about what should be learned, creating a feeling of being ill-prepared for adult roles. This situation, too, is a learning experience. Whether the "generation gap" occurs, however, seems to be dependent on the particular society. Bronfenbrenner (1970), in his comparative study of Soviet and American child-rearing practices, describes how peer relations in the Soviet Union are used to reinforce, rather than to oppose, adult standards and norms. For example, children are socialized to value group rather than individual competition. They are made to feel responsible

▼ for the progress that their collective unit makes and to bear the guilt and shame if the group does poorly. Soviet children are less apt to say they will misbehave if they know that their peers will be made aware of their responses. In comparison, American children are more likely to say that they will engage in deviant behavior if they know beforehand that their age-mates will learn of their responses.

162

## THE MASS MEDIA

The **mass media** refer to a variety of modes of communication in which there is no personal interaction between the senders and the recipients of the messages. Examples include newspapers, magazines, books, movies, radio, and television. The socialization effects of the media, in most cases, are unintended and indirect—and often unknown. Nonetheless, the contribution of the media to the socialization process nowadays is powerful and significant.

The media portray many aspects of social life and society to children. Through the process of observational learning the child acquires notions of what the society values, the kinds of occupational roles that exist, lifestyles other than the ones he or she personally experiences, and a host of skills from how to kiss a woman to how to murder someone. These lessons may serve simultaneously to reinforce, as well as to weaken, the socialization of the family and the school.

Television is only one element of the mass media; yet, there is good reason to believe that this commonly available medium (98 percent of American homes) exerts the most powerful effects of all in the socialization of the child. First, studies indicate that children spend an inordinate amount of time watching television, even though reports in this respect are not consistent. Many studies report that children between the ages of 5 and 16 spend almost as much time watching television each day as they do attending school. A 1980 Nielsen survey found that children between 2 and 5 years old spent an average of 4 hours per day watching television, while those between 6 and 11 were in front of television sets for 3.6 hours per day. More recent studies of children in grades 4 to 6 show that White children watch television for an average of 29.6 hours per week, and Black children 44.9—with significant variations and a negative correlation on the basis of social class (Tangey and Feshbach, 1988).

These situations are due, undoubtedly, to the fact that children enjoy watching television. It is plausible to assume that most parents encourage television watching (or at least do not discourage it) because it functions as a mechanical babysitter. During the time that the child's eyes are glued to the television screen, it is not "getting in the way." Secondly, most parents themselves watch a good deal of television (7.1 hours per day), thus children are deprived of substitute activities that their parents could initiate.

There has been much concern over the years about the effects of television on the child's social development and behavior. Time spent in front of the television screen is time not spent engaging in other activities that could be beneficial to children. The development of social, creative, and motor skills, which occur when the child interacts with others, plays games, draws, takes trips, or plays an instrument, is likely to be impeded if the child spends too much time sitting in front of a television. Television viewing, unlike reading and most other activities, is basically a passive activity. It does not require significant involvement, concentration, or alertness, nor does it serve to exercise the child's intellectual or creative capacities. Some contend that children who are reared on a steady diet of television do not develop a mental set that will help them to do well in school. Such children may have a low attention span as well as a low threshold for boredom, since they are accustomed to being able to change their stimulus (in the form of programs) whenever they become bored. Such is not the case, however, in a classroom setting. Moreover, it is plausible to reason that after becoming acclimated to visual, action-oriented stimuli, children are likely to find a teacher's lecture or the printed page bland and boring. In any event, research does support the position that the heavy viewing of television during the preschool years can put a child at risk for problem behavior by early elementary school age (Singer and Singer, 1981).

The second major concern is with the content of television programs. To be sure, there is much educational value to television, especially in programming made exclusively for children (see Ball and Bogatz, 1970; Liebert and Poulos, 1972). *Romper Room, Mister Roger's Neighborhood, The Electric Company*, and *Sesame Street* undoubtedly are among everybody's favorites. Many television shows, however,

project distorted and sometimes downright erroneous descriptions of one or several dimensions of the social world. Occupational roles, for example, may be presented in a distorted manner designed to emphasize the adventurous, exciting features of an occupation while neglecting to depict the less-attractive aspects. Television programs may also teach prejudice to children. Many times this occurs in a subtle way. Blacks, Chicanos, or women, for instance, may be portrayed in menial roles, or as followers instead of leaders. Such portrayals serve to perpetuate prejudice and discrimination. Television shows, and especially commercials, may socialize children into believing that popularity, social desirability, and recognition are dependent upon wearing the right clothes, driving the latest model car, or smoking the "correct" brand of cigarettes.

▼

**163**

**Media Messages.** Television has enormous benefits as an educational medium. Social scientists, nonetheless, long have been concerned about the kind of values and lessons that children may learn from injudicious programming and unmonitored viewing. (© Arthur Tress/Magnum)

▼

In terms of program content, the greatest concern has been with the effects of television violence on children's attitudes and actions. It is estimated that a typical child may see as many as 20,000 murders on television by the time he or she reaches 16! Literally hundreds of studies have been carried out to test the proposition that exposure to television violence increases the likelihood of viewers committing violence themselves. In general the results overwhelmingly support the proposition.* For example, between 1959 and 1971 Belson (1978) conducted a longitudinal study of the viewing habits of 1,565 boys aged 12 to 17 years. The study showed that those who were exposed to the largest number of violent episodes were most likely to act out aggressively.

The psychologist who conducted the study suggests that viewing violent programs results in the constant reduction of those inhibitions of constraints that the socializing agencies in a community had built up in boys against their being violent. This erosion of constraints against aggression, he argues, occurs subconsciously—the boys are not aware that it is occurring. Of course, not every child exposed to television aggression will engage in violent behavior. The child's previous experiences, state of mind, and psychological predisposition will also influence whether he or she will behave in a violent fashion. In general, however, the weight of existing evidence favors the view that exposure to scenes of violence does increase the tendency of observers to behave in a similar aggressive manner.

## CONSISTENCY OF SOCIALIZATION

Socialization is affected by the consistency of the socialization experience, in content, in techniques, and in the many different socializing agents. Consistency over time, or the lack thereof, on the part of the same socializing agents is also of crucial significance. Most references in the literature concern the issue of discipline: whether, for example, the same kind of behavior is sometimes rewarded and sometimes punished. Since inconsistency is confusing to the individual, any form of socialization under such circumstances is less likely to be effective or readily accomplished.

Consistency in socialization is rather difficult in modern society because, unlike primitive societies, status transition tends to be characterized by considerable ambiguity. For example, in the United States the legal age for consuming alcohol and negotiating contracts varies from state to state. Other difficulties are presented by discontinuities in status transition wherein learning experiences of one age status are not appropriate for a successive status. Hence, the individual has to unlearn old patterns of behavior before learning new behavior. Perhaps the most significant example is that of sex education wherein stories of the stork delivering babies are replaced with adult versions of "the birds and the bees."

Status transition in primitive societies, on the other hand, tends to be characterized by neither ambiguity nor discontinuity. Here status-occupants, as well as others, have a clear understanding of what is expected of them. Much of this clarity is due to the effective employment of **rites of passage**—public ceremonies that formally mark an individual's transition from one status to another. Such things as circumcision, tattooing, or scarification may be performed as rites of passage; and these, oftentimes quite elaborate, events provide public testimony that the individuals involved have been so effectively socialized that they are now ready to assume the rights and obligations of their new social positions.

Religious ceremonies in modern societies, such as confirmation and bar mitzvah, have

* See *Television and Behavior: Ten Years of Scientific Progress and Implications for the Eighties*, Washington, D.C., National Institute of Mental Health Report, 1982.

**Rites of Passage.** Hebrew law sets the age of responsibility and religious duty at thirteen. The transition to adulthood is marked by the Bar Mitzvah (boys) and Bat Mitzvah (girls) ceremonies, which include the privilege of reading the Torah in the synagogue. (© Cornell Capa/Magnum)

similar status-transition functions, but their effectiveness is limited to the religious community. Some social scientists today argue that consistency in socialization within a pluralistic and changing society is not only impossible but ineffective (see Gergen, 1977). Inconsistency, they maintain, enhances the adaptability that an individual needs in an ever-expanding and complex society.

## SOCIALIZATION AND SOCIAL CHANGE

It is difficult to deny that a host of changes are appearing in the structure of socialization and in the content of human development. For one thing, socialization functions are more and more being assumed by secondary social institutions. In part, this situation is due to the sharp increase in the scale of the problem in the socialization of children and youth in modern and highly technological society.

The dominance and priority of the family in the socialization process are being challenged by other agencies—some competing and some substitutive in nature. Such is true in the case of the mass media, television in particular. Television, even in the case of many educational programs, takes up a great deal of a child's waking hours that otherwise might be spent in the active company of family members. Other competition comes from the many facilities, such as day-care centers and nurseries that fulfill many socialization functions for the ever-increasing number of working mothers. It is

▼

estimated, for example, that as much as 40 percent of the children under the age of 6 with working mothers are cared for during the working day in out-of-the-home facilities. This decline in the domestic responsibilities of the family, as well as the expanding rates of family instability, particularly in the form of divorce, has been seen (with alarm) by some social scientists as constituting a deterioration of the appropriate social context for the social and psychological development of children—with the eventual consequence of increased alienation and psychological dysfunction (see Suransky, 1982; Bronfenbrenner, 1974). Research suggests, nonetheless, that children receiving high-quality day-care are not significantly different from home-reared children in terms of intellectual, emotional, and social functions (see Cochran and Gunnarson, 1985; Stith & Davis, 1984; Belsky and Steinberg, 1978). Few day-care centers, however, provide the level of resources or attention that meets the standards of high-quality care.

## Socialization through the Life Cycle

Socialization has been associated traditionally with the early- and middle-childhood stages of the life cycle. Socialization as culturation, however, occurs throughout the life course, from birth to death (Clausen, 1986; Elder, 1985). Merely absorbing information about society and its cultural fund of knowledge on a day-to-day basis represents a continuous socialization experience. More specifically, new socialization problems arise as the individual moves through the various social stages of the life cycle. As a person goes through life he or she is continually entering new social positions which require learning of their corresponding roles. Every time a person joins an organization, has a change in marital status, switches jobs or retires from one—in short, any time a person experiences a significant change in social life—

the need for socialization exists. Moreover, the processes of social change may so transform society that new socialization becomes a continual requirement. Parents today, for example, need to learn new values and attitudes about a host of central issues in the socialization process of young people, such as those discussed above, that pertain to changing sex roles.

Through socialization we learn behavior that is appropriate to our sex, age, and social position. When changes occur, as they inevitably do, then the need for socialization continues. Hence, socialization as culturation is a lifelong process, and today one can speak even of socialization for death—the final stage in the life cycle that everyone achieves (see, for example, Despelder & Strickland, 1983; Marshall, 1975). Moreover, there are various adjustments and new patterns of behavior in all areas of social life which are required of everyone by the changing dynamics and evolution of society.

In this section we shall examine the nature of socialization that occurs during the adolescent and adult stages of the life cycle. Each of these periods may be distinguished by (1) a focal issue, (2) an objective (what needs to be done from the point of view of society), (3) a task (what must be done from the point of view of the individual), and (4) the specific agencies that have the principal responsibility for socialization. Let us discuss first some of the general ways in which these stages of socialization differ from early or initial socialization in the case of the child.

### CHILDHOOD VERSUS ADULT SOCIALIZATION

One of the main differences that distinguishes socialization in childhood from adult socialization is the degree of control individuals have over their own socialization. There is a gradual change from a passive socialization process to a relatively active one as the individual moves through the life cycle. During the early stage of the life course individuals have little control over their socialization because of the extensive dependence on adults. Parents, teachers, and other adults channel children into activities that they believe will be in their children's best interests. Adult socialization, in contrast, is characterized by active participation on the part of the socializee and an increased amount of control over one's own socialization. Socializees decide in great measure both who will socialize them, and the content of that socialization.

For example, individuals decide for themselves whether they should get married, who they should marry, which career they would like to pursue, whether they should join the Armed Forces, and where they should live. Each of these experiences plays a most significant role in adult socialization.

The content of adult socialization also tends to be more specific than that of childhood socialization. The principal aim of childhood socialization is to teach children general patterns of acceptable conduct, societal values, and language skills, as well as the ability to defer gratification and to control impulses. Adults, however, are taught more specific material, such as the skills for performing an occupational role and the behavioral requisites for a number of other specific statuses. Moreover, in contrast to childhood socialization wherein the person is learning new information and skills, much of adult socialization involves learning how to synthesize or to recombine previously learned responses. Adults also learn how to coordinate and integrate the conflicting demands of the roles that they acquire as they move through the life cycle. For example, being simultaneously a father, a husband, and a son is much more difficult than simply being a son.

Adult socialization not only involves learning new patterns of behavior and synthesizing previously required responses, but also entails unlearning material that was appropriate at one time but is no longer. Children, for example, are often told mythical stories about Santa Claus and tooth fairies. Lastly, of importance, there is the status-power differential existing between children and the agencies of socialization. This difference is significantly reduced in adulthood socialization.

The differences and disjunctures between childhood and adult socialization may become even more significant in the years ahead. Some social scientists are suggesting that in highly sophisticated and modernized societies, such as the United States, children are maturing—biologically and sociologically—at an increasingly rapid pace. The projections in this respect are that childhood and adolescence may become shorter periods in the life cycle, such that one enters adulthood at a much earlier age (Winn, 1983; Elkind, 1984; Suransky, 1982). One practice of relevance is the increasingly younger age at which children begin formal schooling, along with an overall acceleration of the learning experience. First grade at the age of 5, preceded by mandatory kindergarten, are very concrete examples of this trend. Another practice of relevance is the lowering of the age of majority and legal responsibility in most social situations to 18. Even the age of criminal responsibility, particularly for capital offenses, has witnessed a decline in recent years. Some people see such trends as causing more cognitive ambiguity and resulting in a much more problematic situation for both the socializee and the socializing agents.

## ADOLESCENT SOCIALIZATION

Perhaps the most difficult role transition that the individual has to make is that from middle childhood to adolescence. This period, at least in Western societies, is usually stressful and anxiety-producing for the individual.* The central

* Many primitive societies, moreover, are not characterized by an adolescent phase between childhood and adulthood. With such clarity and open recognition of status transition, both socializees and socializers in primitive societies experience little ambiguity or anxiety about their social expectations.

▼

**168**

feature of adolescent socialization, from a structural perspective, is the gradual replacement of the family and adult kin by other agents and agencies. Problems of physical management become secondary or nonexistent. Important now are such things as acquiring values; learning skills, such as occupational ones; managing heterosexual relations; and developing competencies for adult statuses, such as marriage and parenthood. The objectives here are to move the adolescent as effectively as possible toward the eventual assumption of adult roles by getting the individual to give up early gratifications and to train for new obligations.

While there are continuities that characterize social transition from middle childhood to adolescence, there are also significant discontinuities that require adjustment and adaptation on the part of the individual. Adolescents are experiencing many ambivalent feelings. On the one hand, they are under pressure from peer groups to declare independence from their family and kin, and thereby to become totally autonomous. On the other hand, they still lack the personal, psychological, and economic resources that would enable them to successfully take on adult roles. Rebellious action, conformity to the latest fad in clothes, music, and folk heroes may be seen as symbolic of the adolescent desire to break off familial ties.

Another source of the "stress and strain" that seems to characterize the adolescent stage of the life cycle, again in the Western world at least, is sexual maturation. (Involved here are both the physical changes of secondary sex development and the emerging attitudes and feelings of one's sexuality.) Despite the sexual maturity of the adolescent, society usually prohibits, or at least discourages, premarital sexual experiences. Thus, adolescents must learn how to cope with their newly emerging sexual drive in ways that are sanctioned by the society. This difficult problem is exacerbated all the more by the ever-increasing glamorization of sex in the mass media.

The conflicts that mark the adolescent stage of life are also in large part the result of incompatible expectations that the principal agencies of socialization (the family, the school, and the peer group) may have for the adolescent. Difficulties in allocating time and resources among these three social settings must be resolved by the adolescent. Another source of difficulty stems from the disruption—or, at the very least, the alterations—of previous social relationships that result as the individual exits the middle childhood role and enters the adolescent one. Alterations in the type of relationship that adolescents have with their parents as well as with their peers create strains which require modifications in outlook. Another source of stress that is particularly prevalent during this period consists of the discrepancies that adolescents perceive between their conceptions and expectations of the adult world and that world as it really exists. This confrontation is certainly not limited to adolescence but it is likely to be more problematic and troublesome at this point in the life cycle than in either childhood or adulthood. Such a situation is so because the inexperience of the young child does not permit him or her to distinguish very clearly between the expectations or desires and the realities of adulthood. There is a tendency to view the world in terms of what one would wish it to be rather than the way it really is.

ADOLESCENT-PARENTAL RELATIONSHIPS. Adolescence is a period in which the parent-child relationship undergoes particularly significant changes. These changes are a result of both increased maturity on the part of the adolescents and features of their social environment outside of the family. One sociologist has described the changes as a shift ". . . from power to companionship and from instruction to advising" (Campbell, 1969:829). This shift is so subtle that the participants usually do not realize that it is occurring. Such changes take place, in part, because the power

their offspring must be prepared for the independence and responsibility of adulthood.

*"Son, you're all grown up now. You owe me two hundred and fourteen thousand dollars."*

Drawing by Weber; © 1983 The New Yorker Magazine, Inc.

differential between them is beginning to narrow: Adolescents are acquiring some resources that until now were the exclusive possession of their parents. Adolescents may have a job, enabling them to be less dependent on parents for financial help; in addition, by this time they have well-established friendships which are sources of emotional and social satisfaction. Parents may still use power in a primitive fashion, but doing so is apt to estrange their child and increase the time that the child spends with peers engaging in behavior which may be disapproved of by parents (Clausen, 1968). The parent-child relationship is facilitated when the parents loosen their control and recognize that

▼

### ADOLESCENT-PEER RELATIONSHIPS.
Peer group relations and pressures are most significant and intense during adolescence. In *The Adolescent Society*, James Coleman (1961) argued that adolescents develop their own subculture, which consists of values and norms that in many instances are incompatible with those of the adult world. This subculture emerges because adolescents spend much time in schools, which are age-segregated institutions that facilitate intense interaction among young people. As a consequence, adolescents develop their own set of values and priorities. Athletics and popularity are valued more than scholarship and academic performance. Emphasis is given also to social activities and other types of pleasure-seeking pursuits. This situation, argues Campbell (1975:40), is very powerful evidence that "only a youth culture of considerable strength could sustain anti-educational values in the very setting of an institution established to serve educational purposes." Adolescent life in large part revolves around a "fun culture," in which music, especially loud and quick-tempoed, as well as alcohol, drugs, and sex play a major role. Research shows that 35 to 50 percent of teenagers have engaged in sexual intercourse by the age of 16, and about 75 percent commonly use alcohol or drugs (see Jones et al., 1988).

Gordon (1957) found that the "dominant motivation" of the adolescents whom he studied was "to meet the expectations of the [adolescent] culture." If adolescents do not adhere to the expectations of their peer group, they are apt to experience social rejection. Acceptance by their peer group, coupled with independence from adult society, tends to become a valued objective for adolescents. It is expected to result in psychological and other types of satisfactions.

**169**

▼  ADULT SOCIALIZATION

Socialization does not come to an end when the individual emerges from adolescence. Just as the life cycle continues, so too does the need for further culturation. As individuals enter and exit different positions, there is a need to learn the normative expectations associated with their new positions, especially those of spouse, parent, and in-law. In some cases, there is much continuity among the norms and behavioral expectations associated with different positions that the person occupies at various stages of the life cycle. Role transitions in these instances are relatively easy and continuous. In other cases, however, there are incompatible expectations linked to a given sequence of positions.

The need for adult socialization is especially the case in the complex and rapidly changing societies of modern times. Advances in technology, for example, affect the occupational structure of society, making some jobs obsolete and creating new ones. This situation brings a corresponding need for continual socialization. Urbanization and industrialization both require and make possible much geographic mobility. As a consequnce, adults are likely to move to localities which are very different from those in which they have spent their childhood. Movement from a rural to an urban locale, for example, would require that the individual learn how to adjust to more formal relationships, cultural diversity, and unfamiliar viewpoints. Furthermore, the need for adult socialization becomes especially evident when individuals are subjected to role changes that are both unexpected and undesired, for example, divorce, widowhood, and involuntary job changes. In addition, the content of such basic roles as man and woman, husband and wife, may change so significantly over a period of time as to necessitate a certain amount of new socialization. And, finally, as the individual moves toward the later stages of the life cycle,

one must be socialized into such roles as grandparent, retiree, and senior citizen—situations that are becoming common experiences for more and more people each day.

With the transition to adult socialization comes a quite significant shift in agents of socialization. The informality of kin, peers, and teachers is replaced to a large extent by the formality of organizational agencies. Socialization becomes a more impersonal experience—undertaken in great part by professional agencies through such mechanisms as orientations and training programs. There remains, nonetheless, much that the individual must learn by personal experience—a situation that often brings its own brand of stresses and strains to the drama of human life.

One of the frequent experiences of adult socialization, often beginning in adolescence, is that of "reality shock." Persons come to learn—usually at the cost of considerable psychological pain—that their conceptions and expectations of the world do not conform to reality. For instance, the child or adolescent is taught to be submissive, dependent, and asexual, while the adult role requires that a person be dominant, assertive, and sexually active. Such sharp discontinuities in behavioral expectations necessitate additional socialization.

OCCUPATIONAL SOCIALIZATION. One of the most significant aspects of adult socialization consists of the individual being enculturated into an occupational role. Unlike homogeneous societies, where children become acquainted with the occupational structure at an early age because the work is relatively visible and simple, there is a much greater division of labor in modern industrial societies. Children do not see their parents at work, and often have no clear idea of what they do. Argyle (1972) notes that in contrast to preindustrial societies, three problems characterize industrial society in socializing their members into occupational roles: (1) the large number of occupations that a person has to choose from (over 20,000); (2) problems that members of the society have in getting to know the nature of these jobs, including the skills that are needed to adequately perform them; and (3) the lack of continuity that exists between schoolwork and later work.

Socialization into an occupational role not only entails the learning of specific skills, but also involves learning the subculture of the respective occupation. After working in an occupation for a moderate period, the person begins to acquire the work culture and worldview of that occupation. These subcultures vary considerably for different occupations. Teachers develop different lifestyles from salespeople or construction workers. Moreover, continual change in these lifestyles makes occupational socialization an ongoing process of adult life.

Depending on the type of occupation, the manner by which the novice learns his or her occupational role varies. Many corporations have formal orientation or training programs in which employees are taught how to perform their required duties. Many of the programs also aim to instill within the person the philosophy which characterizes the organization as well as a feeling of pride in being associated with the company. In other occupations, however, formal training sessions may not be the major source of occupational socialization. Indeed, studies show that in certain occupations individuals learn their occupational role almost exclusively from coworkers.

In a study of the occupational socialization of steelworkers, Haas (1974) found that not only do novices learn specific skills from veterans, but also they learn such characteristics as trustworthiness, self-control, and the importance of behaving in accordance with the norms of their work group. Veteran construction workers use a variety of ploys designed to determine whether the recruit is trustworthy and dependable in dangerous situations. Verbal harassment and binging (punching the person on the arm) are two major methods used to test the novice.

Certain conditions and procedures facilitate occupational socialization. Such techniques include isolation, the use of distinctive uniforms, and exposure to stressful experiences. All three of these techniques are used by military organizations for the orientation and training of new recruits. They have the effect of developing within the person a feeling that he or she is part of a special elite group. These techniques are particularly useful in instilling motivation, commitment, and loyalty in the person.

The occupational role tends to be internalized—to become a significant part of the individual's personal identity. Work, especially in our modern society, constitutes an important dimension of a person's life. "Thus, a man's work," as Everett C. Hughes (1951:28) once stated, "is one of the things by which he is judged, and certainly one of the more significant things by which he judges himself." Such a situation is especially likely to be the case if the person is learning a profession.

MIDDLE ADULTHOOD.   During the middle-adulthood stage of the life cycle, one's life is substantially organized around familial and occupational roles. It is at this time, often the prime of one's life, that individuals are thought to experience a "midlife crisis," or major transition. The inevitability and universality of this experience is an issue of considerable controversy.

Daniel Levinson (1986, 1977a), a social psychologist at Yale University who has spent several years studying this question, observes that: "By about forty, a man has had a chance to build a life, to pursue his goals, and to realize the fruits of his youthful labors. It is now developmentally necessary to review his progress.

▼

**171**

▼ He must deal with the disparity between what he is and what he had dreams to become" (1977a:166).

Middle adulthood, thus, is a time of crucial self-appraisal. Concerns about one's success, or lack thereof, in terms of familial roles and occupational pursuits, as well as a host of other objectives of personal meaning, enter focally into this self-appraisal. The realization of one's own mortality intensifies this process of self-assessment. The individual may feel that "time is running out and that he may soon die, or worse, have a life without meaning for self or others" (Levinson, 1977a:176). The midlife transition may be rather mild or it may involve considerable turmoil, stress, and disruption. In the latter case, it is truly a midlife crisis; in both cases, it is a socializing experience of prime significance. Figure 4-1 depicts the ages and stages which Levinson identified as eras in the life cycle of the typical male.

The middle-adulthood stage is also a period when the individual is getting socialized for future roles. One sociologist (Deutcher, 1962:522) observes that situations usually arise in middle adulthood that "provide an opportunity to an-

**172**

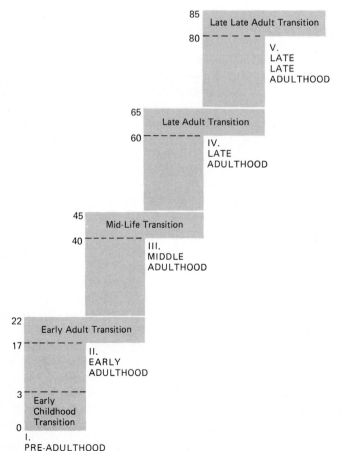

FIGURE 4-1 Eras in the Male Life Cycle. Source: Daniel J. Levinson. "The Changing Character of Middle Adulthood in American Society." In Gordon J. DiRenzo, ed. *We the People: American Character and Social Change.* Westport, Conn.: Greenwood Press, 1977, p. 153.

ticipate postparental roles, not by taking the role of the other in the usual sense, but by experiencing analogous situations which are quasi-postparental and which enable the parents to play at anticipated roles." Temporary departures of children for college, military service, or travel, and such experiences as instances in which the parents have to be away from home for extended periods of time, are cases that can prepare the individual for the eventual experience of the empty-nest syndrome.

## SOCIALIZATION IN THE LATER YEARS

One learns to be an elderly person just as one learns to become an adolescent or an adult. Only in recent years, however, have social scientists been devoting more and more attention to the socialization problems of the later years of life. One reason for this newly found interest has been the rapid increase in the number and percentage of "senior citizens" which has been occasioned by a drop in the birth rate and the expansion of life-expectancy.

Three principal types of socialization in the later years of life involve preparation for retirement, the inevitability of death, and perhaps widowhood. However strange it may seem, learning to die has become especially more common with the legalization of euthanasia in some societies. Of these three major concerns, nonetheless, most progress has been made in terms of retirement—a phenomenon occurring at younger and younger ages. Such a situation is made increasingly possible by the economic affluence of the American population and its growing emphasis on a leisure-oriented society (see Chapter 14). Yet, compared to others, the roles of the retiree and the elderly person are still poorly defined in many societies.

Several theories have been developed to describe and to explain the major types of changes that occur in the later stages of the life cycle. Let us discuss two of these theories.

DISENGAGEMENT THEORY.   The tenets of **disengagement theory** consider the later stages of the life cycle as being the reverse of the early and middle stages in terms of the tasks and objectives of socialization. This period is seen as one in which the individual gradually, yet steadily, withdraws from the statuses that had been occupied during the middle stages of life (Cumming and Henry, 1961). According to disengagement theory, individuals become less socially active as well. One's ties and relationships to others and to society weaken and are eventually severed.

Disengagement theory has been subjected to much criticism because in many cases the evidence does not support it. Atchley (1988) argues that disengagement is neither a universal nor an inevitable response to aging. The problem with any theory of aging is that extreme variability characterizes the aging process. Some people may experience acute physical and psychological deficits at 60, and others not until 90. Examinations of individual cases indicate that there is great variability in both physical status and role performance in the later years.

The same point helps us to understand the contradictory evidence that exists about the effects of retirement on the individual. Until recently, many social scientists assumed that because work is a central part of a person's life and gave one a sense of self-worth and identity, entry into the retirement role would have negative effects upon psychological and social well-being. In addition, it was thought that the retirement role is associated with illness and death in the mind of most people, making it even more undesirable and anxiety-producing. Relevant research by Atchley (1988), however, found that only 15 percent of people near retirement age or already retired who were questioned about their views on retirement had such extremely negative conceptions of the retirement role. Among those who did perceive retirement in an undesirable light, it was more likely the case that the experience had been made mandatory, rather than because of any negative feelings

▼

## BOX 4-5. Socialization for Death

People can prepare for death—and increasing numbers of them do, particularly if they are suffering from a recognized terminal illness. In pioneering research to assess how people face impending death, the psychiatrist Elizabeth Kübler-Ross (1981), has found that for many people dying is a developmental process with five successive stages: denial, anger, bargaining, depression, and resignation. Interestingly enough, it appears that these same stages, in somewhat modified form, constitute precisely the sociopsychological process that one goes through when confronting many other crises in the life cycle, such as a divorce or a major tragedy.

One's first reaction to impending death is denial ("There must be a mistake!"). Anger next sets in ("Why me?"). Then, one tries to bargain (often with God) for a way out, by such things as offering to reform one's life or to dedicate one's final days to humanitarian service. This stage is followed by an episode of depression. The final stage (which not everyone reaches) consists of resignation, or acceptance, to the reality and certainty of death.

Socialization for death not only has been rather successful, but also is becoming more common, especially in retirement communities and nursing homes, where one can find social support among both staff and peers (Marshall, 1980). Sharing in the dying experience of others, such as attendance at funerals and memorial services, is one effective mechanism in the anticipatory socialization for death.

▲

174

about it as such. Thus, whether occupants perceive the retirement role with enjoyment or displeasure is dependent upon a set of factors which vary with different people. The work role does not have the same value for all people. For some it is a central identity and preoccupation; for others, only an economic means and necessity.

ACTIVITY THEORY.   According to **activity theory,** elderly people have the same social and psychological needs as middle-aged people, and higher levels of well-being and life satisfaction are functions of activity and social engagement (Atchley and Miller, 1983). Decreases in activities that do occur result primarily from the unwelcomed withdrawal of society from the aging person. There is evidence that the majority of older individuals who are in good health continue to engage in a variety of activities (Neugarten, 1973). Even more relevant, to-

day's generation of older people are in better health, and have a much longer lifespan, than previous generations. The degree of disengagement that does take place is mostly determined by past behavioral patterns, psychological characteristics, and socioeconomic status rather than by anything intrinsic to the aging process itself.

Some sociologists have maintained that people are not actively socialized into the latest stage of the life course because the norms and expectations that society has for older people are unclear, weak, or even contradictory (Rosow, 1974). In addition, it is argued that the status of the aged involves essentially a "roleless role"—one that is devoid of any significant content. American society, for example, is one that glamorizes youth and devalues old age. As a consequence, many people do not look forward to their later years—despite how "golden" they may be made to appear with the promise of receiving "senior citizenship." Nowadays, diverse agencies in our society are responding more positively to this situation with a variety of preparations and attractions for the later years of life—in short, they seek to provide adequate and effective anticipatory socialization for the "golden years" of senior citizenship.

## RESOCIALIZATION AND TOTAL INSTITUTIONS

Oftentimes role transitions and socialization are so extreme and so extensive that they require the unlearning of existing long-held, beliefs, values, and norms, and substitution with new ones acquired in a new social context. Such a situation is often called **resocialization.** The experience is similar to that of childhood socialization, but usually a much more difficult

one. This type of learning is especially experienced by individuals who for whatever reasons find themselves in what are called total institutions.

**Total institutions** refer to social entities that are relatively isolated from all other segments of society and which as such constitute an all-encompassing environment for the fulfillment of the needs of its members. Prisons, monastic communities, mental institutions, military organizations, and boarding schools are examples of total institutions. A total institution has nearly all of the structural and functional characteristics of the total society and, as such, constitutes a miniature society within a society. Radical change in lifestyle is usually experienced by individuals who undergo socialization in total institutions. All outside ties are severed or curtailed, and the individual's needs are met

**175**

**Boys Into Men.** Boot camp, or basic training, in the Marine Corps, wherein one loses a sense of personal identity through regimented dress and grooming and experiences a relatively complete isolation from all other segments of society, is representative of a total institution that controls nearly every aspect of daily life. (David Wells/Image Works)

▼

completely by the total institutions. Virtually everything that one does is subject to the control of others and of the institution. In some total institutions, particularly military ones, attempts may even be made to remove one's identity by abandoning the use of personal names and any other distinctive features, such as clothing and grooming.

Brainwashing is an extreme form of resocialization that is often attempted with prisoners in times of war. Criminal rehabilitation (delinquent reformation) and military training are more common examples, as are religious and ideological conversions. In all instances, the individual is indoctrinated into the expected role behavior. Self-determination is discouraged; complete and unchallenged obedience is expected in every respect.

One of the more controversial examples of resocialization and total institutions of late is that of the "Moonies"—people who join the Unification Church (see Barker, 1986). Membership here requires a radical transformation, not only in one's beliefs and values, but in lifestyle as well (for example, dress and grooming). These efforts at indoctrination (segregation, isolation, and brainwashing) are so successful, over the short-term that parents often hire private detectives to kidnap their children from the Church in order to submit them to "deprogramming," which itself is another form of resocialization. The long-term effects of the resocialization are questionable; the average recruit remains only 2 years (Long and Hadden, 1983). People who leave total institutions often return to their previous values and patterns of behavior—a situation that is amply reflected in the very high rates of criminal recidivism (see Chapter 13).

## Summary

Socialization is the process by which the individual is linked to society. Human social dy-

namics, as well as many aspects of biological development, rely on social learning and the various processes whereby sociocultural knowledge is transmitted to, and acquired by, the human organism. These processes are known generically as socialization.

Socialization actually has two quite different meanings. One meaning refers to the transmission and acquisition of culture on the part of members of a particular society. The other meaning refers to the intricate, and highly intriguing, process by which individuals develop uniquely human attributes and a fully human nature. The principal subprocesses are maturation, culturation, socialization, and personality development. The goals of socialization are conventionally classified into objective functions—those that primarily serve the purpose of society: (1) transmission of culture, (2) continuity of society, (3) social control; and those that serve the individual in terms of humanization. These basic functions, while distinctive ones, are not necessarily separate from each other.

Socialization, whether in terms of culturation or humanization, presupposes maturation or biological development. Socialization, moreover, depends on the socializability of the individual. It is impossible to socialize individuals who suffer from extreme maturational defects. Without adequate amounts of social contact and the proper kinds of social direction, human babies experience growth failure, both in terms of maturation and socialization. Most importantly, they do not develop uniquely and distinctly human qualities—at least not to any functionally significant degree.

Socialization fundamentally involves learning more than anything else. Learning is the process by which behavior, or the potentiality for behavior, is modified as the result of experience. Three principal theories of learning are classical conditioning, operant reinforcement, and social learning theory. Cognitive and moral development are the foundations of socialization. Chief formulations in these respects are respectively those of Piaget and Kohlberg.

Sex-role socialization refers to the process by which children learn the behavior and personal characteristics (attitudes, emotional dispositions, and skills—known as sex-typed behavior) that are deemed appropriate or preferred for males and females by their respective culture.

Agencies of socialization refer to those individuals, groups, and organizations that have either a primary responsibility or a particularly strong influence in the socialization process. Chief among these are the family, the school, peer groups, and the mass media. Socialization as culturation, however, occurs throughout the life cycle, from birth to death. One of the main distinctions between childhood and adult socialization is the degree of control individuals have over their own socialization. There is a gradual change from a virtually passive role to a relatively active one as the individual moves through the life cycle. This transition is particularly acute during the period of adolescent socialization.

Several theories explain the types of changes that occur in the later stages of the life cycle. Disengagement theory considers the later stages of the life cycle as being the reverse of the early and middle stages in terms of the tasks and objectives of socialization. Activity theory considers elderly people to have the same social and psychological needs as middle-aged people.

Resocialization, similar to initial socialization, occurs in situations where role transitions and social learning are so extreme and so extensive that they require the unlearning of existing beliefs, values, and norms, and the substitution of them with new ones acquired in another social context. Such a situation often is experienced by individuals who find themselves in total institutions, which are segments of societies that are relatively isolated from all other sectors, and which as such constitute an all-encompassing environment for the fulfillment of individual needs. ▼

# Key Concepts

**177**

acculturation
activity theory
agency of socialization
anticipatory socialization
classical conditioning
critical period
culturation
disengagement theory
enculturation
feral people
hermaphrodite
identification
imprinting
internalization
learning
mass media
maturation
modeling
operant reinforcement
peer
personality development
resocialization
rite of passage
sex-associated behavior
sex-linked behavior
sex-role socialization
sex-typed behavior
socialization
social learning theory
total institution

# Personality and the Self

**All people are in some respects like all others.**
**All people are in some respects like some others.**
**All people are in some respects like no others.**

The previous chapter was concerned with examining the ways in which every person in one sense is like all other people (same biological nature) and in other respects like some other people (similar cultural and social experiences). Here in this chapter we complete our analysis of human social development by exploring the way in which everyone is unique—personality.

Particularly important in the sociological study of personality is the structure and dynamics of the self system which virtually plays a central role in social interaction of every kind. A major question in this regard nowadays focuses on the rather common development of an increasingly complex and diversified self in the modern society.

Our intent in this chapter is to emphasize not only the social dimensions of personality, but also, more importantly, to show the relevance of personality for social behavior. People engage in social interaction not just on the basis of culture and their social positions, but also in terms of their psychological structure and personality characteristics. Accordingly, throughout the remaining chapters of this volume, we shall consider a number of different kinds of correlation between personality and social behavior—for example, social organization, social groups, social roles, social mobility, minority-majority dynamics, collective behavior, social deviance, and social change—which demonstrate the role of personality as an independent variable in the social process. ▲

# Outline

NATURE OF PERSONALITY
  Personality Defined
  Personality and Socialization
FOUNDATIONS OF PERSONALITY:
    NATURE AND NURTURE
  Biological Foundations
    Physical Attributes

Endocrine System
Intellectual Capacities and Potentialities
Sociocultural Influences on Personality
  Family
  School
  Peer Groups
Uniqueness of Personality

▼ ► Social behavior is a product of the complex interplay of a number of dynamics—personal as well as social and cultural. Personality is a central, and indeed indispensable, element in this respect. The study of social behavior without the consideration of personality can yield only an incomplete and distorted explanation of social behavior. Conversely, the same difficulty presents itself when one attempts to explain individual behavior through personality and psychological dynamics without the consideration of the social nature of the individual and the sociocultural contexts from which all essential human behavior comes.

180

Often the study of personality is identified exclusively with the field of psychology. This conception, unfortunately, is an erroneous one. Personality has had, and continues to have, a central place in sociological analysis, as it does in each of the other behavioral sciences. Sociologists, for their part, have contributed much to the empirical study of personality and its theoretical formulations. It should be recognized, for example, that the bulk of the data that sociologists, and many other social scientists, employ in their analyses of human social behavior is personality data. Collecting information about people's attitudes, values, opinions, beliefs, motivations, and self-concepts— however much they may be shared with other people—fundamentally involves measuring aspects and components of personality.

Personality serves as the vehicle of psychosocial interaction on the individual level. To whatever extent sociocultural phenomena are responsible for human behavior, it is by means of personality. It is in this sense an intervening variable; but since this interactional process is circular rather than unilinear, the role of personality in social behavior must be seen in both dependent and independent perspectives. We must be concerned not only with the social dimensions of personality but also, and perhaps more importantly from a sociological perspective, with the relevance of personality for the explanation of social behavior (see Turner, 1988). We shall describe the dynamics of personality in both dependent and independent perspectives in more detail throughout this and other chapters. Let us look first at the nature of this phenomenon.

# Nature of Personality

Personality is a word that can be found in nearly everyone's active vocabulary where it inevitably takes on a plethora of meanings. Moreover, the term personality has been used within the behavioral sciences to refer to a description of personal characteristics, mental processes, internal psychological states, a collection of psychological traits, behavior typical of an individual, and the totality of one's social roles, among a host of other, even more ambiguous or elusive, phenomena (see Ventimiglia & DiRenzo, 1982). All of these situations compound the problems of definition and understanding. Personality, nonetheless, is not a mere mental construct that serves as a convenient term or catchall category for reference to a number of psychological processes or attributes. Again, the word personality is arbitrary, but the conceptual referents are not and these need to be specified as succinctly as possible. What, then, is personality?

## PERSONALITY DEFINED

**Personality** is the acquired, unique, relatively enduring yet dynamic system of predispositions to behavior which is localized within the individual. This definition is actually quite complex. Let us provide some further description of the individual elements.

1. Personality is *acquired*, through social interaction. Biological foundations notwithstanding, personality itself is neither innate nor inherent in the individual. Some people,

the unsocializable, may not acquire personality. Personality, then, is present neither at conception nor at birth. What is present are certain potentialities of a biological and psychological nature which serve, in part, as the foundations upon which personality develops.

2. Personality is *unique*. No two personalities, however similar, are identical. People may have similar biological, cultural, and social backgrounds, but their personal situation and experiences are never completely shared by others. Personality is also unique in another sense. It is distinctively human. While some of the animal species possess certain types of psychological attributes, none may be said to have personality as such.

3. Personality, once formed, tends to be *relatively enduring* or nonchanging. It is the more or less stable elements of the individual, not the transitory ones, to which personality refers. Personality can and does change, but only in certain respects and under very unusual conditions, which we shall explain subsequently.

4. Personality is *dynamic*. Personality is a distinct order of phenomena that has its own principles and processes which (as forms of psychological energy) play an active or causative role in the production of human behavior; it is not a simply static or passive phenomenon. Hence, personality is neither a mere reflection of, nor a microcosm of, either society or culture.

5. Personality is a *system* rather than a simple collection or conglomeration of individual parts or units. Hence, we can speak analytically of personality in much the same way as we do of any other kind of system—in terms of such basic components as structure and content, as well as the many respective elements of each, and various subsystems.*

* See Chapter 6 for a more elaborate discussion of the nature of systems.

These components are explained below in more detail.

6. Personality is a system of *predispositions* to behavior. It is not the actual or concrete behavior of the individual. Personality is that which predisposes one to behavior in a particular way. One's actual behavior, however, is a conjoint product of personality interacting with other elements, such as the social and cultural phenomena of the context in which behavior occurs. Hence, while personality is not behavior, personality is revealed in, and expressed through, behavior.

7. Personality is localized *within the individual*. Personality is an internal, or psychological, phenomenon. Personality is revealed in, and expressed in, external behavior; its locus and boundaries, however, are within the biopsychological organism.

It should be clear from this definition and description that—contrary to popular misconceptions—everyone (every "normal" individual) has a personality. This fact should be reassuring to the many people who have admired others who they thought had personality—lots of it, and especially those who supposedly had personality plus! Personality is not, as these erroneous implications would have it, a quantitative variable. Rather, it is a qualitative one. Everybody has personality—and the individual differences are in terms of the *kind* rather than the *amount* of personality.

## PERSONALITY AND SOCIALIZATION

To understand fully the nature of personality, it is necessary to understand the rather subtle distinctions among the several processes of human development which we discussed in the preceding chapter. Personality development and socialization are frequently considered to be one and the same. In fact, they are distinct,

▼

182

though not totally separate, processes. The acquisition of personality is an inextricable part of the complexity of social processes in human development. Insofar as the social development of the individual may be impossible because of biological defects or impediments, such as severe mental retardation, then personality, like all uniquely human attributes, is unable to develop. Similarly, individuals who are victims of social isolation do not develop personality. Personality development, therefore, cannot be divorced, except analytically, from the processes of socialization and enculturation. Yet, while personality development cannot take place apart from social learning, socialization and enculturation continue long after personality development has terminated.

Personality, for the most part, is a latent product of socialization and enculturation. It need not be, but in practice such is the case for the overwhelming number of people in the world at large. Unlike much of socialization and enculturation, personality development is, by and large, a nonconscious affair for both the individual and the agents of socialization. Only in a small minority of cases is there a conscious effort to develop personality, or a particular type of personality. So oblivious are most people to personality development that many of its outcomes are often unintended, especially where there are psychological problems or dysfunctions, which occur to a far greater extent than many people realize. The conscious intent and effort in the processes of socialization and enculturation are on learning social roles and norms, especially those that are functionally associated with childrearing, such as toilet training and sex roles. The psychological results or residue of this experience—a relatively unique experience of a specific set of social interactions—constitute personality. Personality, then, in one respect, is that psychological system with which one winds up after having gone through early socialization and enculturation.

# Foundations of Personality: Nature and Nurture

Personality development is rooted in two distinct sets of elements that are universally shared by all people—biological foundations and sociocultural experiences—especially those of infancy and early childhood. Neither of these kinds of elements, however, constitutes personality in itself. Rather, both contribute in different ways to the development and formation of personality.

Until quite recently, there has been a long-standing controversy about whether personality was exclusively, or even principally, the product of heredity ("nature") or of learning ("nurture"). This question, which seems to beg an absolute answer, is now considered to be rather meaningless. Although the controversy is not over—nor should it be, in the interest of scientific inquiry—the argument now focuses on the relative influence of each set of factors. Personality, therefore, is seen as the conjoint product of the interaction of both sets of factors—but in quite different respects in each case. Let us look at each of these distinct sets of personality foundations.

## BIOLOGICAL FOUNDATIONS

Whether inherited at conception or acquired either before or during the birth process, all of the elements of the biological organism that affect its interaction (type and extent) with the sociocultural environment play a role in the kind of personality that one develops. Foremost in this regard, of course, is the genetic system—concretely manifested in the many organic and physiological components that one inherits. Human beings inherit genes that determine such biological qualities as sex; physical appearance (facial features, physique, height, hair

*"We don't know whether it's his creative impulse or his destructive urge."*

Adapted from *Child Development* by William E. Martin and Celia B. Stendler, copyright 1953 by Harcourt Brace Jovanovich, Inc., and renewed 1981 by William E. Martin and Willard Spalding, used with permission of the publisher.

color and texture, eye color, and skin color); metabolic rate (energy level); the endocrine system that controls the dynamic balance of the physiological process of the body, including the rate of physical and sexual development; and to some extent, intellectual capacities and aptitudes.

Personality, however, is not inherited. The role of genetic and biological elements in personality development is only an influential, and not a deterministic, one. This principle is a fundamentally crucial one, for here rests the nexus of the entire nature-nurture controversy. There

is not a one-to-one correspondence between a particular type of biological system and a particular type of personality—as some early theories had advocated. One's biological heritage serves, so to speak, as an independent variable in the way that one will participate in social life. Personality itself, however, is the result of the highly variable interplay of the biological foundation with one's sociocultural experiences.

Biological and physiological factors, therefore, play a significant, but nonetheless indirect, role in the formation of personality. It is for this reason that biological and physiological elements are said to constitute the foundations of personality—but not personality itself. To illustrate the highly variable interplay of biological factors with sociocultural experiences in the development of personality, we need only contrast ethnic and racial Americans with people in their continent of origin: Asians with Asian Americans; Europeans with European Americans; Africans with African Americans, and so on. Even more significant contrasts of this type—to show that social experiences have much to do with the variability of personality—can be found in the personality of monozygotic (identical) twins that are reared apart from each other in social environments that are totally different. It may be possible one day to reproduce genetically identical people through the biological process of cloning. But producing identical personalities—psychologically identical people—would seem to be a far more difficult task.

Let us look more closely at the interpenetration of biological and social-cultural dynamics with three particular sets of biological foundations: physical attributes, the endocrine system, and intellectual capacities.

PHYSICAL ATTRIBUTES. Evidence exists that there are some *sex-linked* personality qualities—those that are innate in the particular sex of the organism. Natural hormonal

▼

**184**

differences between males and females, in the normal course of maturation and personality development, may inescapably account for certain kinds of personality differences. Aggression seems to be one of the most significant of such psychological attributes. Extensive surveys of the literature found that males are more aggressive, both physically and emotionally, than females, and this difference appears quite early, before the age of three usually (Maccoby & Jacklin, 1980, 1974). It is attributed to biological and physiological differences between the sexes.

More significant, however, are *sex-associated* dimensions of personality formation. Sex-associated elements refer to behavioral dispositions that are learned or acquired in the process of social development. Sex, as we saw in Chapter 4, is a primary factor in determining how people are socialized—current emphasis on sex equality notwithstanding. In the vast number of societies throughout the word, and to a very great extent in our own society, boys and girls are treated quite differently in the process of socialization and enculturation. There are "implicit theories" about the kind of personality boys and men should have vis-à-vis girls and women (Bernard, 1981).

At least until recently, it has been thought that males in American society, should be independent, assertive, self-reliant, achievement-oriented, analytical, decisive, and strong. Women should be feminine, dependent, quiet, shy, emotional, cute, and ladylike. Stereotypes are widely held by men and women, and much effort is underway to change many of these personality dispositions by way of assertiveness training. Accordingly, to the extent that individuals are socialized differentially on the basis of sex, we can expect to have sex-typed psychological qualities and personalities. Dramatic changes in personality formation are likely to result from the modification of sex roles that is currently underway in many societies.

Physique is yet another aspect of the sex-associated dimension of personality development. In our society, for example, as we saw in Chapter 3, strong value is placed on slimness and height. Obesity (for women) and small stature (for men) are not among physical qualities that are preferred by most people; and, hence, people with these characteristics encounter a different set of social and psychological responses, than do those with the opposite kinds of characteristics. A particular physique, as in the case of a particular sex, invariably means that an individual may have a particular set of social experiences than might otherwise be the case. These interactional differences play a significant role in personality development, but not in a predetermined or absolutistic way.

It is not so much the kind of anatomy or physique that shapes personality; rather, its evaluation by other people, as well as by the individual, determines the nature of the social interaction, which is the direct basis of personality formation.* The type of body one has, its size and strength, influences the kind of social roles one is likely to play. One can readily see this influence on the adult level in terms of such occupations as the jockey or the basketball player, the runner or the football player. Social experiences which indirectly rely on different body types provide significantly differential contexts in which personality development occurs. A girl who inherits a markedly masculine physique will tend to develop different behavioral and psychological characteristics than one who inherits a markedly feminine physique. Biological factors of these kinds play an influential role in personality development, but not in any deterministic or absolutist way. They influence only the manner by which individuals with certain biological characteristics are apt to interact with others in the course of socialization and other experiences of social life.

---

* This position was advocated in the now widely discredited constitutional theories of personality. For a discussion of these theories, see the section on personality typologies in this chapter.

**Crucial Residues.** Personality formation is typically a latent product of the myriad kinds of social experiences that one has during the preadolescent period of the life cycle. Being tall or short, fat or thin, homely or attractive, are among the physical attributes that influence the nature and variety of one's interactional experiences.

ENDOCRINE SYSTEM. The **endocrine system** consists of a series of ductless glands which produce hormones that enter the blood stream to play a fundamental role in regulating the rhythm and intensity of the physiological processes of the organism. The endocrine glands have a vital influence in such things as physical growth and sexual differentiation, the metabolic system, the central and autonomic nervous system, and a host of other bodily functions and processes.

Much is unknown about the many specific functions of the endocrine glands, but what is understood leaves no doubt that their complex activities can be basic to personality develop-

ment. Let us take one example, the thyroid. This endocrinal gland is responsible, in great part, for the functional levels of energy and temperament (one's generalized mode of response— lively or dull, rapid or slow) that are characteristic of an individual. Individuals that typically possess either an abnormally hyperactive (overactive) or hypoactive (underactive) thyroid can be expected to interact in quite a differential manner with a relatively constant sociocultural environment.* The thyroid gland itself does not cause an individual to develop one particular type of personality or another, but its typical function (under or over the "normal" level) will influence the nature and the amount of physical and social interaction that one will have with the sociocultural environment.

Parents and others treat active babies and children differently than inactive ones. Personality results from this interaction, and both have a foundation in the endocrine system. Correspondingly, temperamental variations based upon endocrines can affect the way individuals respond to their social world and their personal experiences within it. The social roles that one selects, and how one performs them, are also influenced by these types of biological disposition. Responses of a phlegmatic individual to a dynamic and rapidly changing society are likely to be quite different from those of a lively, active person.

INTELLECTUAL CAPACITIES AND POTENTIALITIES. Another major category of biologically given factors that indirectly shape the formation of personality is that of intellectual capacities for comprehension, reasoning, and judgment. One usually thinks principally of intelligence in this regard. Intelligence is described consensually among psychologists in

▼

185

---

* The specific influence of these abnormalities on personality development, which usually are reversible through medical treatment, varies to a large extent according to when they occur in the life cycle.

▼

terms of adaptive and goal-directed behavior (Sternberg & Salter, 1982). It may be defined as the ability to respond to new or largely unfamiliar situations—the ability to cope with one's environment and with the problems of life.

There is little doubt in scientific circles that genetic inheritance, specifically in terms of the structure and function of the central nervous system (brain, spinal column, and associated neurons), plays a fundamental role in the level of one's intelligence. The extent of this influence, however, is still highly controversial. Jensen (1981; 1969) estimates that 80 percent of intelligence is due to biological and genetic factors. Others (for example, Jencks, 1972) argue that as little as 50 percent of measurable intelligence is the result of heredity.

Measures of intelligence among immediate family members tend to correlate at about the .50 level, which is a fairly high correlation. Identical twins tend to correlate much more (.90) with each other than do nonidentical twins (.60), even when they are reared in separate environments (.72). Identical twins, however, do not correlate perfectly with each other. Accordingly, it appears from these kinds of data (Bouchard & McGue, 1981) that a certain degree of intelligence may be acquired. Some psychologists, however, argue that there are several kinds of intelligence (see Guilford & Hoepfner, 1971). Often distinctions are made between natural (innate) intelligence and social (acquired) intelligence. Others maintain that inherited levels of intelligence can be modified, primarily through increased education and enriched environments, principally early in life (see Baron, 1985; Palmer, 1976; Lazar, 1977).

However controversial or correct these questions may be, they are not refuted here. A point we do wish to make, nonetheless, is that individuals are born with a given capacity and potential for intellectual development and function, but that the specific level that one attains is determined by environmental experience.

Be it endowed or acquired, there is no direct relationship between the level of one's intelligence and one's personality. Intelligence serves essentially as a foundation for personality development, and thus only indirectly influences personality. Intelligence, like other intellectual functions, plays only an indirect, yet significant, role in the kind of personality that one develops because it influences the kinds of experiences, social and intellectual, that one has—including, in great part, the quality of social interaction with other people. Individuals with one particular level of intelligence are more likely to have a different set of sociocultural experiences than individuals with quite a different level of intelligence. The opportunity to attend college or practice a profession is decided fundamentally in terms of intellectual ability. It is social experiences of these kinds, made possible by differences in intellectual abilities, that directly influence the development of personality.

Biological foundations, as described in each of the three examples that we have selected, are not themselves determinants of personality. There is not a specific relationship between a particular set of biological elements and a particular kind of personality. Biological factors, however, as foundations upon which personality develops, along with other variables, do set limitations within which personality development occurs. One's biological characteristics, whether genetic or not, influence the manner in which people are likely to respond to the individual and the opportunities that one is likely to have for socially valued achievements. It is out of these situations and experiences that personality itself develops.

## SOCIOCULTURAL INFLUENCES ON PERSONALITY

Social experiences provide the other major foundation for personality formation. The nature, quality, and quantity of social experiences, including in very great part the personality of the people involved, constitutes the principal basis for the formation of personality. Chiefly responsible for personality in this respect, especially during the very early formative years, are the sociopsychological experiences that derive from social relations in the contexts of the family, school groups, and peer relationships. Let us look more closely at these major influences in terms of particular contributions which they make specifically to personality development.

FAMILY.   The influences of the family in personality development consist of a cryptic mix of psychosocial influences that derive, both directly and indirectly, from such factors as family size and composition (age, sex, birth order), sibling interaction, parental occupations, emotional climates (happiness or conflict), mode of authority (democratic versus authoritarian), area of residence, and a host of many other similar social and psychological factors that characterize the particular lifestyle of an individual family.

Equally important is the family subculture (ethnic or racial background, socioeconomic status, religious and political beliefs, friendships, voluntary interests, and hobbies) which provides the sociocultural context in which a great deal of social interaction repeatedly occurs, and which, as such, provides a crucial foundation for determining the directions in which personality development will occur.

Social interaction within the family is of paramount importance in the development of personality. The family, as we saw in Chapter 4, is the primary agent of socialization. Consequently, it plays a primary role in personality

▼

**187**

**Family Dynamics.** Among the principal types of social interaction that play a central role in personality development are those found in the family setting. Chiefly significant in this respect are the many elements that derive from the family subculture and the dynamics of parent-child and sibling relationships. (Erika Stone ©)

▼

188

formation. Social relations within the typical family are the most frequent, the most intimate, and the most intense. This situation is true most especially in the early years of life, which constitute the crucial period during which the basic structures, and indeed most of the content, of personality are formed. Chiefly significant are the dynamics of the parent-child and sibling relationships. Such fundamental dynamics as acceptance or rejection and over- or under-protection play a crucial role here.

Specific types of familial environments have been found to be important determinants of whether children develop a positive or negative image of themselves. Coopersmith (1967) found that children with high self-esteem have parents who have a positive self-image. Parents of children with positive self-esteem not only had high expectations for their children but were also good role models for them and provided much encouragement. The mothers were accepting of their children and expressed this feeling in concrete, specific ways through affection and emotional support. The parents established and enforced behavioral rules fairly and consistently, treating their children with respect and without coercive methods. This situation contrasts with parents of low self-esteem children. Mothers of low self-esteem children were apt to be inattentive, neglectful, harsh, and authoritarian in dealing with them.

SCHOOL. School experiences constitute another segment of the more important spheres of influence in the formation of personality. Schooling comprises a major portion of one's social activities during the first few years of life and, hence, includes the crucial period of psychological development. The influences of education come not only in the transmission of knowledge but also through the particular experiences of teacher-student interaction and peer relations.

Within the school setting the child is constantly being evaluated—both by teachers and by other children. These evaluations influence the ways in which the child views himself or herself. If children are continually judged in a negative manner, they may develop a negative self-image, which will affect their behavior in an undesirable manner.

Children, more frequently than not, are labeled "bright" or "dull." Such labels not only affect their self-concept and motivational levels but also influence the manner in which they are treated by teachers and other students. Also relevant are the dynamics of the "halo effect," by which one positive or negative quality correspondingly presumes another positive or negative quality. Children who are evaluated as physically attractive or well-behaved, for example, are perceived to be more intelligent. Just the opposite is the case for children who are perceived to be physically unattractive and disobedient.

Rosenthal and Jacobson (1968) speak of a "teacher-expectancy effect," by which they refer to the impact that teachers' expectations about a student's performance may have on the student's actual performance. Studies show, for example, that teachers wait longer for a response from children who are judged to be intelligent and high achievers, and who are more likely to be given a second chance (see Dusek, 1985; Crano & Mellon, 1978; and Good & Brophy, 1973). Similarly, high achievers are rewarded with more praise, while low achievers are likely to receive more criticism.

Quite important in the educational context are such fundamental variables as pedagogical philosophy—the way the educational process is conducted, as well as its content. Physical facilities and resources, along with extracurricular and cocurricular activities, also comprise important elements for significant social experiences in the sphere of education. All of these elements provide another interactional context out of which personality emerges as a consequence of one's particular experiences.

**Classroom Influences.** School activities, particularly in the early years of life, provide one of the major contexts for the interactional dynamics out of which personality emerges as a consequence of one's particular social experiences. (Karen Rosenthal/Stock, Boston)

PEER GROUPS. Next to the family and the school, one's peer groups usually comprise the single most important influence in personality development. Indeed, for some individuals, especially during the adolescent years, peer pressure outweighs that of the family as an element of social influence. School companions, neighborhood playmates, and voluntary associates such as Boy Scouts, Girl Scouts, and Little Leaguers, as well as the more impersonal cohorts (age-mates) found in the mass media, not only compete with the familial agents of socialization and personality development but often outdo and undo the influence of family members.

The number and composition of peer groups are important structural variables for the nature and quality of their social interaction, as is their emotional climate and lifestyle. These variables aside, the single most important influence of peer groups in personality formation comes by way of interaction with the personalities of those individuals that comprise them. The ways in which peers respond to an individual will affect that individual's self-image. If one's peers continuously criticize and scorn, one may begin to think of oneself in negative terms. On the other hand, if a person perceives peer group members as holding positive conceptions of him or her, the individual is likely to view himself or herself in those terms.

Peer groups exert an important influence on the individual because they are a source of

▼

**190**

significant reward or reinforcement. Children generally desire affection, praise, and encouragement from members of their peer groups. As a result, their actions will be influenced by the rewards and punishments that they receive or think they will receive from peers. While peer groups can be a source of much gratification for the child, they can also be the cause of psychic distress and hurt, since fear of being ridiculed or rejected by one's peers can be a traumatic experience for the young person. These, too, are important learning experiences in the socialization process—however painful they undoubtedly are.

Correspondingly, peer groups may also provide a child with emotional warmth and understanding. Peer groups may perform a psychotherapeutic function by helping children to see that others of one's age and status have the same types of problems and conflicts that one may be experiencing. Peers also serve as role models whose conduct children may imitate. The tendency to emulate peer group members is particularly strong in children who have an acute need for affection and approval.

All in all, then, sociocultural backgrounds and experiences provide the interactional contexts out of which personality emerges as a latent—unintended and unrecognized—function. We are who we are—in terms of personality and psychological composition—in large part as a consequence of a particular set of social experiences that we had during the formative years of physical maturation and socialization.

unique set of social experiences. Nobody has exactly the same set—not even identical twins who may have been reared as similarly as humanly possible. Such individuals may have highly similar experiences—as many other people do, especially members of the same family—but their experiences are never really identical.

Comparable social experiences inevitably differ in a host of subtle, yet crucial, respects for each individual involved. Siblings, for example, never have the same parents in a psychological and sociological sense. Parents, like family structure and relationships, are significantly different with the addition (or departure) of each child. The mere fact of being older and functioning in and through a different age-status is itself exemplary of this principle. Moreover, there is never perfect consistency in socialization among the many different socializing agents. Differences in the personalities of the socializing agents themselves account for considerable variation in the socialization experience. The meaning and significance of any experience, moreover, depend, in part, on one's previous experiences and the existing personality structure. Similar social experiences, therefore, have a highly personalized meaning for each individual when they are integrated with the existing personality. Not to be overlooked are the innumerable chance factors or idiosyncratic experiences that occur in everyone's daily life. These, too, especially in the formative years of early childhood, may play a significant role in the complex and infinitely varied process of personality development.

## UNIQUENESS OF PERSONALITY

Our discussion thus far has described the common experiences that people have as they move through the life cycle, especially during the early formative years of physical maturation and socialization. Each individual, however, has a

# The Personality System

One of the prominent themes in most of the explicit definitions of personality is the conception of this phenomenon as a system. Personality is widely understood to be an inclusive, comprehensive organization that consists of individual parts, elements, units, subsystems, and processes that are interrelated and unified into a whole, with the organismic implication that the whole is quite different from the sum of its parts. Yet, while there is widespread agreement about the systemic nature of personality, there is much less consensus about the specific composition of this system. Chief concerns in this respect focus on two questions: What are the kinds of elements that comprise the personality system; in short, what is the specific content of this system? And how is this content organized? Let us discuss these questions.

## CONTENT AND STRUCTURE

Like any other kind of system, personality systems may be analyzed in terms of two fundamental dimensions: content and structure.* **Personality content** refers to the specific elements or units that comprise the personality system: beliefs, ideologies, motivations, values, attitudes, emotions, psychological traits, cognitions, self-concepts, and so forth. Many of these kinds of elements, sufficiently complex in themselves, constitute subsystems of the personality. **Personality structure** refers to the coordinated arrangement and dynamic relationships among the components of personality content. Personality structure consists of such specific dimensions or variables as complexity (number and variety of elements), integration, isolation, congruity, cohesion, consonance, unity, and hierarchy. It is the interaction of personality content and personality structure that yields personality function, which ultimately accounts for one's psychological predispositions to behavior.†

It is the dimension of personality structure which, as the fundamental property of organization in the personality system, accounts for the greater part of the individuality and uniqueness of personality. The same content elements, of whatever kind, function differently in personalities that are organized or structured differently. A differential synthesis of similar elements creates a new compound of substantially different functional significance. This principle is a crucial one for understanding the interaction of personality and social systems—an issue about which we have much to say in subsequent chapters.

▼

**191**

## SUBSYSTEMS

Personality, like all systems, consists of, and functions by means of, a number of subsystems.* These subunits, having all of the characteristics of any system, may also be assessed in terms of both content and structure. Chief among the analytically distinctive, yet functionally interpenetrating and interdependent, subsystems of personality are the following: cognitive, affective, motivational, and self. Each of these focal subsystems is distinguished in the individual personality by its respective contents as well as its typical mode (manner or pattern) of function. Let us briefly describe the first three of these subsystems in order to provide a more complete explanation of the personality system. The self system, which cuts across or interpenetrates each of the other subsystems in a quite fundamental manner, will be explored in considerable detail in the next section of this chapter.

THE COGNITIVE SYSTEM. The **cognitive system** consists of such elements as beliefs, ideologies, values, attitudes, opinions, and other conceptual variables that characterize the

---

* See Chapter 6 for a more detailed description of the content and structure of systems.

† This qualification of "psychological" is intended to exclude behavior at the chemical and biological levels, such as reflexes, which are beyond the voluntary control of the actor.

* Any system—plurality of parts—that is thought of as functionally independent, yet belonging to a larger system, is considered a subsystem.

▼

content and processes of one's thought and intellectual functions. Among these kinds of elements would be included the dynamics of comprehension, imagination, perception, judgment, memory, and conscience.

Current research on personality places a heavy emphasis on cognitive processes. Various studies now indicate that cognitive styles (the way people think rather than their actual thoughts) are related quite fundamentally to basic dimensions and structures of personality. We shall have more to say about cognitive systems in a subsequent section on personality typologies.

THE AFFECTIVE SYSTEM.  The **affective system** refers to the emotional dimensions of the personality, and the patterns or modes of their arousal and discharge. One may distinguish analytically between emotions and temperament within the affective system.

**Temperament,** which is essentially physiological, perhaps even largely genetic in nature, consists of the major affective dispositions and typical moods of the individual. An emotion, on the other hand, consists of feelings or affects that are essentially social and cultural in their development and expression (see Chapters 3 and 4). While the process of their emergence seems to be standard and universal, the contents of emotions are culturally variable and strongly influenced by social factors (Kagan, 1984; Gordon, 1981).

THE MOTIVATIONAL SYSTEM.  The **motivational system** comprises those aspects of personality that are responsible for the initiation and maintenance of behavior. Personalities are distinguished by two basic features of the motivational system: the intensity or strength (valence) of individual motives, and the hierarchy of the total constellation of motives, including the implicit centrality of particular motives.

A **motive** may be defined as the mobilization of energy within the individual, and the selec-

tion of a goal for its dissipation. Motivation is a condition within the organism that impels behavior in order to obtain or to avoid certain end-states of the organism. Motives are customarily distinguished as being either biogenic or sociogenic.

**Biogenic motives** refer to innate, physiological drives, such as hunger, air, elimination, shelter, and sleep and are considered to be imperative—that is, their gratification, at least to a minimal degree, is essential and indispensable for the survival of the organism. **Sociogenic motives** usually refer to socially and culturally acquired wants, such as the desire for a college degree or a million dollars, and usually are not considered to be either universal or indispensable.

While these principal types of motives are generally recognized, there is considerable controversy about the classification of a number of specific kinds of motivation. One such example is the sex drive, which, while innate and universal on the one hand, is not widely considered to be imperative or essential for the homeostatic (balanced) or optimal functioning and survival of the organism. On the other hand, many aspects of sexual gratification are socially learned. A more significant controversy, however, concerns a set of sociological and psychological motives that may be referred to as **basic human needs.** Included in this category are such motives as social response, social recognition, social acceptance, social security, cognitive clarity, autonomy, self-esteem, and freedom from alienation, boredom, and sensory deprivation.

Motives in this category are described as *inherently* human needs, referring to the contention that, while universal in every human being, they are neither innate nor present at birth, but rather acquired in the humanizing processes of socialization and enculturation. Moreover, despite their sociopsychological nature, their gratification—at least to a minimal degree—is considered imperative for the psychological homeostasis and *human* function of the individual.

192

**Inherent Motivation.** Basic human needs for social recognition and achievement are found in all people. The self-fulfilling prophecy often helps one to attain that which might seem to be an impossible goal. (Alan Carey/Image Works)

spoke of "four basic wishes" of all people (Thomas & Znaniecki, 1918). Although Thomas revised his list of "wishes" throughout his lifetime, the final set (Thomas, 1923) consisted of the following: social recognition, social response, new experience, and security. Thomas' work needs to be seen as a pioneering effort which, as such, lacks comprehensiveness and conclusiveness; however, it was clear that by these "wishes" he referred essentially to what today are called "basic human needs" or "immanent human requirements." Research on this question has been rekindled in more recent years (Etzioni, 1977), and we shall have more to say about it in subsequent chapters.

**193**

## CONTINUITY VERSUS CHANGE IN PERSONALITY

A most controversial question in the study of personality concerns its stability and consistency. Does personality, once formed, undergo change? The answer to this question is a seemingly equivocal "yes" and "no," which is not meant to be either ambiguous or complex. Rather, it is intended only to suggest that any adequate and accurate response needs to be qualified because of the complex and systemic nature of personality.

Personality, once formed, is not a static phenomenon. Not only is it capable of producing change; under certain conditions it undergoes change. In the normal course of events, however, personality tends to resist change; its dynamics are such as to reinforce the existing personality, both in terms of content and structure. It is the stability of personality which, in part, makes for the predictability of both individual and social behavior. Important distinctions, however, need to be made in these respects.

Personality contents (attitudes, values, motives, beliefs, self-concepts) can, and do, change rather easily—and with some regularity throughout the course of life. What one believes

Several behavioral scientists (for example, Marris, 1974; Berger et al., 1973; Shibutani, 1961) have spoken in this respect of "immanent human requirements" that cannot be ignored except at the risk of doing basic or functional harm to the individual.

One of the seminal contributions to this question was the work of William I. Thomas, who

▼

or values as an adult may be significantly different from one's beliefs and values as an adolescent. Personality structure, however, does not change as readily, and in fact is quite resistant to change (Block, 1981). It is this dimension that accounts for both the relative stability and the distinctive individuality of personality.

Personality tends to reinforce and to conserve itself through selective exposure to content variables. Personality, within the dynamics of seeking a functionally congruent or compatible interaction with the social environment, tends to expose itself to people, situations, and things that work to reinforce both the existing contents and structure of personality.

People tend to interact selectively with the social world (for example, define situations, perceive social reality), and to engage in social experiences (for example, assume statuses and roles, select friends and occupations) that are likely to fulfill their existing needs and that are consistent or compatible with their existing beliefs, values, motives, and self-concepts. When people are exposed for very prolonged periods to situations that are dynamically incongruent with their personality, they experience severe stress, which under prolonged periods or conditions can became extremely psychologically dysfunctional and incapacitating.

We speak here, of course, of the "normal" course of personality interaction. Such a situation does not ignore the possibility of substantial changes that can be effected by conscious intent, such as by means of psychotherapy, behavior modification, religious conversion, and brainwashing—as well as unintentional changes that may result from severely traumatic events, such as experiencing a permanent disability or the brutal murder of a family member. All in all, however, only a minority of people undergo personality change in either of these respects.

Apart from these general principles, change in personality is very much an individual mat-

ter, depending in great part on the specific kind of personality structure that is involved. Some types of personality structure are highly susceptible, even oriented to change; other types are basically resistant to change, and indeed actively work against psychological, as well as social, change. We shall elaborate on these aspects and dynamics of personality in our discussion of social change in Chapter 14.

Many theories of personality have emphasized the primal importance of early childhood in the development of personality. Such theories assert that, for all intents and purposes, personality becomes established and permanently fixed by the age of 6 to 8 years, and sometimes as early as 2 years. Even extreme positions on this question are taken by some personality theorists, especially psychoanalysts who substantially adhere to the teachings of Sigmund Freud. Whatever the controversy in this regard, a postadolescent personality is generally thought of as showing only insignificant changes, and primarily those which are contentual in nature. Moreover, given the dynamics of psychological reinforcement, personality is thought to become all the more resistant to change as one grows older.

Of late, however, the "permanency" of personality development during childhood is being challenged more and more. There is much more emphasis being placed on personality development and psychological change in adolescence and later periods of life. These arguments against the lasting effects of early socialization assume a relatively infinite malleability in human psychological characteristics, and they contend that highly significant shifts in values, motives, beliefs, and other personality attributes can occur at virtually any point in the life cycle (see, for example, Gergen, 1977). Considerable research is being undertaken nowadays on life-span development (see Brim & Kagan, 1980; Baltes & Brim, 1979). Levinson (1977a, 1977b), for example, seeking to develop a sociopsychological theory of adult development, describes a relatively universal and age-linked set of genotypic segments of the life cycle (see Chapter 4). These stages are thought to follow an invariant developmental sequence and to be marked by a number of significant changes in personality. Nonetheless, the implicit reference in much of this question of adult personality change is, again, to certain parts or aspects of personality—primarily the content—and not to the totality or distinctive aspects of the personality system itself. "Adult socialization" or "adult development" would be more appropriate labels for much of this phenomenon. Widespread theoretical interest in adult development is reflected as well in the extensive emergence in recent years of therapeutic innovations, such as behavior modification, sensitivity groups, new forms of psychotherapy, and the like.

## PERSONALITY TYPOLOGIES

Despite the individuality and extensive variety of personality, it is possible to distinguish kinds or types of personality. Doing so makes it possible to talk more meaningfully about personality in its relationship to human social behavior.

Numerous attempts have been made to formulate personality typologies. Such efforts even predate the modern sciences of human behavior by several centuries. The Greek physician, Hippocrates (460–360 B.C.) attempted to relate personality to physiological functions—specifically, to the allegedly dominant type of body fluid that characterizes an individual. On this basis, he developed a classification of personality consisting of the following types: sanguine or optimistic (blood), choleric or irritable (yellow bile), melancholic or gloomy (black bile), and phlegmatic or listless (phlegm).

More modern typologies of personality based on bodily structure and anatomical qualities are those developed by Ernest Kretschmer (1925), William H. Sheldon (1942), and Hans J. Eysenck (1967). These efforts have come to be known collectively as constitutional or morphological theories of personality. Each fundamentally asserts a direct relationship between a particular type of anatomical structure and a given type of personality. (See Chapter 13 on deviant behavior for an application of these theories.) Nowadays, the relationship between anatomy and personality is considered to be essentially an indirect one and, hence, one with a variety of effects and concrete manifestations. Accordingly, constitutional theories are held in appreciable disrepute today.

Personality typologies based on psychological attributes have had a better reception from behavioral scientists. References, for example, abound in the literature to "oral" and "anal" personalities, based on the stages of personality development and dynamics developed by Sigmund Freud (1938); introverted and extroverted personalities, deriving from the conceptual scheme of Carl Jung (1938); and a number of different types based on the many kinds of psychological complexes expounded in the work of Alfred Adler (1929).

One of the first typologies of personality to emerge from the field of sociology was offered by William I. Thomas and Florian Znaniecki (1918), who maintained that social disorganization produced different modes or styles of psychological adaptation. They spoke of three types of personality: (1) the philistine, who rigidly overconforms in an attempt to assuage inner anxieties; (2) the bohemian, who does the opposite and is truly disorganized or carefree; and (3) the creative, who is flexible and organized. Each of these types, moreover, was distinctively characterized by the dominance of one of the four "basic wishes" of which Thomas spoke in describing the universality of socially acquired motivation.

These many examples of personality types are based on specific traits or other contentual aspects of personality. Much more recently the

195

▼ field of personality has witnessed the development of structural typologies of personality—those based on organizational characteristics. Such types of personality are formulated in terms of distinctive psychological syndromes—whole clusters of interdependent personality elements—rather than on the basis of discrete psychological characteristics. The more successful of these personality typologies are those based on the cognitive structures of personality. Extensive research (see DiRenzo, 1967a, 1967b) has shown that a variety of specific ideologies, values, and attitudes are intimately related to particular psychological syndromes or types of personality structure.

**196**

THE AUTHORITARIAN PERSONALITY. Principal examples of personality typologies are those based on the dynamics of **authoritarianism**—a personality syndrome that focuses on the elements of power and authority as its central dynamics. Authoritarianism is one of the most widely used personality variables of the past half-century. The first systematic attempts to formulate a conception of authoritarianism were made in the 1930s by two German psychologists, Erich Fromm (1936) and Wilhelm Reich (1946), who worked independently, but with a common interest, in developing a psychoanalytical social psychology. Fromm (1941) in his well-received book, *Escape from Freedom*, delimited the "authoritarian character" in particular reference to the emergence and spread of Nazism. The empirical study of authoritarianism as a personality syndrome (see Chapter 11), however, was accomplished during the 1940s by a team of social and clinical psychologists at the University of California at Berkeley. Their work, *The Authoritarian Personality* (Adorno et al., 1950), and its famous F scale, have generated one of the most extensively used typologies of personality structure: the authoritarian personality versus the democratic personality. Several synonyms, with varying conceptual and theoretical foundations, include such labels as the intolerant, stereopathic, and dogmatic personality, and their antitheses.

THE DOGMATIC PERSONALITY. Emerging out of the tradition of *The Authoritarian Personality*, but utilizing a different theoretical orientation, is the work of Milton Rokeach (1960) on the concept and dynamics of **dogmatism,** and its empirical measure, the Dogmatism, or D, Scale (see Box 5-1). Rokeach has offered these contributions as alternative approaches to authoritarianism. They have received a substantial amount of attention and appreciation in studies concerned with relating personality to social behavior. Rokeach's formulations involve the openness and closedness of belief systems and deal primarily with modes of cognitive functioning, rather than with the unconscious dynamics and processes of psychoanalytic theory.

THE MYERS-BRIGGS TYPE INDICATOR. Another example of personality typology that has attracted much attention in recent years is the Myers-Briggs Type Indicator (MBTI) developed by Isabel Briggs Myers (1985, 1987) and Katherine C. Briggs. The MBTI is based on the personality theories of Carl Jung (1938), who maintained that much apparently random variation in human behavior is actually quite orderly and consistent. This order and consistency is due to basic differences in the way that people prefer to use their powers of perception and judgment, as well as to fundamental orientations in lifestyle. All people use the same perceptive processes (sensing and intuition), the same judgment processes (thinking and feeling), and the same attitudes (introversion or extraversion, judgment or perception). Every individual, however, has a preferred orientation in each of the four paired-sets of dynamics, and that orientation is said to constitute one's dominant function. (See Box 5-2). The antithetical orientation comprises an

# BOX 5-1. The Dogmatism Scale ▼

The full version of the Dogmatism Scale consists of forty items. Several other forms have been developed. Here is an abbreviated version, constructed by Rolf Schulze (1961) and known as the D-10 Scale, which shows a coefficient of correlation of .76 with the parent scale. This form is the basis of several studies of dogmatism and personality which will be discussed in subsequent chapters.

1. The worst crime a person can commit is to attack publicly the people who believe in the same thing he or she does.
2. It is often desirable to reserve judgment about what's going on until one has a chance to hear the opinions of those one respects.
3. Fundamentally, the world we live in is a pretty lonely place.
4. In the history of mankind there have probably been just a handful of really great thinkers.
5. In the long run the best way to live is to pick friends and associates whose tastes and beliefs are the same as one's own.
6. Most people just don't know what's good for them.
7. Once I get wound up in a heated discussion I just can't stop.
8. In this complicated world of ours the only way we can know what is going on is to rely upon leaders or experts who can be trusted.
9. A person who thinks primarily of his or her own happiness is beneath contempt.
10. While I don't like to admit this even to myself, I sometimes have the ambition to become a great person like Einstein, or Beethoven, or Shakespeare.

Agreement with the above items is indicative of a dogmatic perspective. Individuals scoring highly positively on the Dogmatism Scale are most likely to possess a personality structure that is characterized by cognitive rigidity and the intolerance of individuals with opposing belief systems. A more complete description of the dogmatic personality is offered in Chapter 11. ▲

auxiliary function that the person may also use, but not with equal liking or skill. An individual's composite of his or her dominant functions yields one of sixteen possible personality types, such as an ENTP or an ISFJ.

Personality typologies have facilitated much of the theoretical effort to integrate sociological and psychological dynamics in the interests of constructing a more comprehensive understanding of human social behavior. Throughout this book we shall have numerous occasions to refer to types of personality, particularly in reference to the typologies discussed above, in terms of their functional association with different kinds of social behavior, social organization, and various aspects of society.

## The Self System

One of the most focal parts of the personality is the self system, often referred to as the "self concept" or more simply as the "self." The **self system** consists of that segment of one's personality that is made up of the total constellation and configuration of cognitions, affects,

▼ BOX 5-2. Myers-Briggs Type Indicator

Preferences for four psychological functions are scored by means of a 166-item self-report questionnaire in order to arrive at an individual's personality type. Indicator questions deal with the way an individual prefers to use his or her perception and judgment; that is, the way one likes to look at things and how one likes to go about deciding issues. ▲

198

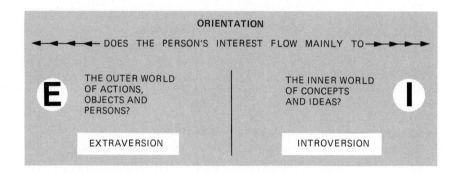

ORIENTATION

◄—◄—◄— DOES THE PERSON'S INTEREST FLOW MAINLY TO —►►►►

**E** THE OUTER WORLD OF ACTIONS, OBJECTS AND PERSONS?

EXTRAVERSION

THE INNER WORLD OF CONCEPTS AND IDEAS? **I**

INTROVERSION

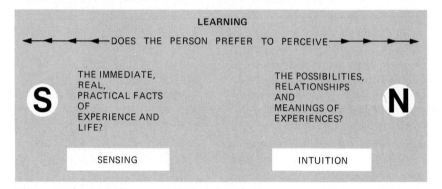

LEARNING

◄—◄—◄— DOES THE PERSON PREFER TO PERCEIVE —►►►►

**S** THE IMMEDIATE, REAL, PRACTICAL FACTS OF EXPERIENCE AND LIFE?

SENSING

THE POSSIBILITIES, RELATIONSHIPS AND MEANINGS OF EXPERIENCES? **N**

INTUITION

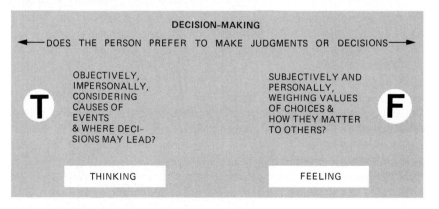

DECISION-MAKING

◄—DOES THE PERSON PREFER TO MAKE JUDGMENTS OR DECISIONS—►

**T** OBJECTIVELY, IMPERSONALLY, CONSIDERING CAUSES OF EVENTS & WHERE DECISIONS MAY LEAD?

THINKING

SUBJECTIVELY AND PERSONALLY, WEIGHING VALUES OF CHOICES & HOW THEY MATTER TO OTHERS? **F**

FEELING

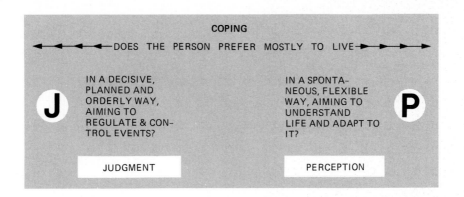

Source: From "Understanding the Type Table," published by the Center for Applications of Psychological Type, Gainesville, Florida. See also Isabel Myers Briggs, *Manual of the Myers-Briggs Type Indicator*. Palo Alto, California: Consulting Psychologists Press, 1985.

and motivations—beliefs, feelings, and motives—that pertain directly to the individual as an object.

Sociologists who concern themselves with personality have devoted the overwhelming bulk of their attention to the self system. So central is the self system to personality development and function that many sociologists are in the habit of equating one to the other. Such synonymous usage, unfortunately, involves an erroneous conception of both personality and the self system. There is no personality without a self system; and, correspondingly, there is no self system without personality. Yet, however inseparable, these two phenomena are quite distinct and many functions of personality do not involve the self. Without an appreciation of this fact, it is difficult to understand either.

## DEVELOPMENT OF SELF

It is perhaps by now implicitly redundant to point out that only human beings have a self system. Only humans can be objects to themselves—reflect on the self, describe the self, evaluate the self, and praise or reprimand the self accordingly. Other animals, of course, have simple awareness or consciousness, but they are not able to contemplate themselves. Human beings are the only animals with self-consciousness or self-awareness, which is that conscious experience of being a distinct entity, and one separate from all other people and things.*

The fundamental reason for this situation is that self-consciousness is both a state and a process that require conceptual thought. The absence of this ability in newborns means that they have no self-consciousness. It is several months, in fact, before the child develops any awareness of itself, and begins to distinguish between self and nonself. Self-consciousness and symbolic ability develop in tandem. The self, like any other aspect of personality, is a social product.

Whatever we know about ourselves, and everything we know about ourselves (for example, whether we are tall or short, slender or stout, outgoing or introverted, gregarious or aggressive, brilliant or dull), is knowledge that has been acquired through the processes of social interaction. Without people we would not psychologically know ourselves. The greater one's social isolation, in terms of the number

* Some evidence has been advanced that self-awareness may be present to some degree in higher apes, such as the chimpanzee (Gallup, 1979).

▼ and kinds of social interaction, the less clear one's self-identity is apt to be. People who lead relatively isolated lives (for example, prisoners and hermits) often experience a loss of self-identity. Considerable emotional stress and psychological dysfunction often accompany this loss, indicating the functional relationship of the self system to the personality as a whole.

## 200 CLASSICAL FORMULATIONS

Modern concern with the social and psychological nature of the self grew out of the philosophical doctrines of phenomenology. The first theoretical treatment of the self was offered by the distinguished psychologist, William James (1890), who wrote about "self-consciousness" nearly a century ago. Some of his views have become the basis for the development of modern conceptions of the self.

The principal formulations of the self that are current today, however, derive more substantially from the work of American scientists who pioneered the field of social psychology during the early part of the century, particularly in terms of the sociological orientation that has come to be known as symbolic interactionism. Two major formulations embody the classical views that have continued to serve as the foundation for all contemporary work on the self. Both emphasize the essentially social nature of the self and the basic influence of childhood in this formation. These contributions represent the conceptual and theoretical formulations of the sociologist, Charles H. Cooley, and the philosopher, George H. Mead. A consideration of the contributions of both of these individuals is indispensable for an adequate understanding of the nature and dynamics of the self system as well as human social behavior more generally.

CHARLES H. COOLEY: THE LOOKING-GLASS SELF. Cooley was influenced by so-ciological pioneers with psychological orientations, such as Gabriel Tarde (1890), Gustav LeBon (1896), and Franklin H. Giddings (1896), as well as William James (1890). Many of his conceptual and theoretical formulations derive from his very keen and perceptive observations of his own children, especially their social and psychological development within the context of the family group.

Cooley's principal contribution to the understanding of the development of the self system was in terms of his formulation of the conception of the "looking-glass self." Individuals know themselves, contended Cooley, only by means of a social mirror—as reflections of how others see and evaluate the person. According to Cooley (1902), there are three elements in the formation of the self:

1. The imagination of one's appearance to another person.
2. The imagination of the other's judgment of that appearance.
3. A self-attitude, such as pride or shame, deriving from the two previous steps.

Cooley believed that social interaction, which is most important for the formation of the self, occurred in what he called "primary groups"—small, intimate, personal associations that are usually exemplified by the family.*

Cooley's conception of the self is really a *perceived* self. Rosenberg (1973) argues that this reflected self is only one aspect of the self system, but, nonetheless, a very important one. Much behavior of people is determined not by who they actually are, but rather by who they think they are—as well as by who they would like to be. This perceptual formulation does not contend that one's conception of the self is necessarily correct. Indeed, it is quite common for individuals to have an objectively false self-con-

---

* Primary groups will be discussed in more detail in Chapter 9.

cept. The more significant issue here is that one's personality and one's behavior is determined substantially by the nature and extent of one's perceived self—regardless of its veracity or falsity. Such a situation is the basis of the well-known complexes of inferiority and superiority that many people experience. People who systematically misperceive or distort the self as positive suffer from superiority attitudes or from a "superiority complex." Conversely, those who systematically misperceive or distort the self as negative are said to be characterized by an "inferiority complex." Perception, therefore, is the crucial point in the formation of the self.

Basic to Cooley's formulation is the assumption that the individual is motivated to seek a satisfying self-concept—a situation which seems to be related to the basic psychological needs of social acceptance and social response. The individual, in this respect, is motivated to conform to the wishes of others by the presentation of that kind of behavior (or self) which is thought to be desired. Edwards (1959) demonstrated a very high correlation (.87) between traits judged socially desirable and those attributed to oneself. Accordingly, many social scientists are of the opinion that a major determinant of human behavior consists of the fundamental drives to achieve, maintain, and enhance a satisfying self-concept. Such is the case in great part because achieving self-esteem is conducive to psychological comfort or the freedom from anxiety. Hence, as Rosenberg (1979) states, it may be postulated as a cultural universal that people prefer to think well of themselves.

Cooley's formulation of the self, while substantially correct in terms of the developmental process, seems to imply that it is a continuous process of formation and change—with every "other" (individual or group) encountered. What is lacking in Cooley's construct is a formulation of the relatively enduring or permanent aspects of the self.

**GEORGE H. MEAD: THE "I" AND THE "ME."** Mead, a social philosopher and social psychologist, explicitly extended Cooley's conceptual and theoretical work on the self with a more complex and sophisticated formulation. His contributions (Mead, 1934) have come to serve as the foundation of the theoretical orientation known as symbolic interactionism—often taken to be a rather uniquely sociological variety of psychological and personality theory (see Chapter 1).

Mead's conception of the self is that of a social process which involves two analytically distinguishable elements: the "I" and the "me." The distinctive feature of the self in Mead's formulation is that it is reflexive, which means that it can serve as both an object and a subject. How is this possible—how does one get outside one's self?

The "I" represents the spontaneous and functioning part of the self—the locus of creativity and the propulsion of human action. Herein reside the impulsive forces and undirected tendencies of the individual—the initial, active, unique, motivating, spontaneous, and unorganized aspects of human experience. This part of the self is the first to develop.

The "me" represents that part of the self which reflects upon and evaluates the individual. It constitutes the specifically social (or socialized) component of the self—the internalized, and consciously recognized, demands and expectations of society. It functions as a censor or controller of the "I" in terms of approving or disapproving of the intentions of the "I." The "me" represents, in this respect, the conforming, passive, and predictable parts of the self.

Basic dynamics of the self-concept in Mead's formulation involve a conversation, which he called "minding," between the "I" and the "me." Such a conversation is exemplified in the following thought that necessarily takes grammatical license: "I would like to run across campus in the nude, but it is not (consistent

▼

**202**

with) *me*." "It's not me" because others have told me that "it's not me." They would be shocked, surprised, and incredulous to hear that I did such a thing. And who are *they?* They are the faceless collectivity of individuals whom Mead labeled the "generalized other." His term is intended to designate the rather anonymous public with which one interacts. The **generalized other** does not consist of physically or concretely real groups. Rather, it consists of a composite representation, within the individual, built up in the course of association and interaction with others. It is a composite representation that an individual holds relative to the images and perceptions that it is thought society, or people in general, have about oneself. It serves as a generalized frame of reference from which one perceives and evaluates oneself and one's behavior. The individual regulates his or her behavior in terms of the generalized other, by what he or she imagines others might do or say "if they knew" or "when they find out."

Other scholars, who have elaborated on Mead's formulation, have introduced the concept of the **significant other** (Kuhn, 1964).\* This term refers to those not-so-anonymous individuals whose judgment and social approval are highly valued and actively sought by the individual—often to the exclusion of others. Usually, significant others consist of family members, relatives, admired teachers, neighbors, and peers or age-cohorts. Mead (1934:68) wrote: "We are more or less unconsciously seeing ourselves as others see us." Morris Rosenberg (1979:97), one of the contemporary authorities on Meadian theory, has refined this position to the following more precise, and accurate in detail, statement: "We are more or less unconsciously seeing ourselves as *we think* others *who are important to us and whose opinion we trust* see us."† Research (Rosenberg, 1979)

"It's you...it's definitely you!"

Reprinted by permission of USF, Inc.

has shown, however, that *putative* significant others (those commonly regarded as such, or reputed to be) are not necessarily the real significant others. Significant others, whoever they may be, are a major source of influence and control on one's behavior.

The development of the self, according to Mead, takes place through the process by which one repeatedly "takes the role of the other," and reacts thereby to oneself as one imagines that others do or would. There are three distinct and sequential stages in this development according to Mead:

1. *Imitation or "preparatory" stage* (1 to 3 years): There is no self-consciousness in the child at birth. Infants have no conception of the world as being separate or distinct from themselves. For several months the child is unable to distinguish between self and nonself, such as himself and his bottle or crib. Along about the age of 1, the child begins to imitate whatever behavior he or she observes in others. Toward the age of 2, the

---

\* Originally used by Harry Stack Sullivan (1953).

† The reason for the "more or less" is that we cannot read other people's minds in a totally accurate manner.

child begins to use words like "me" and "mine" and "I." This behavior marks the beginning of the formation of the self-concept. Yet, during this period, there still is no real or significant conception of the self as a separate being, just as there is no understanding of the behavior that is being imitated. Such understanding is dependent on the acquisition of language, which occurs in the second stage.

2. *Role-taking or "play" stage* (3 to 4 years): Language is essential for the development of the self which can arise only within a context of communication. The requisite conversation is that between the "I" and the "me." By about the age of 3, the child has developed a rather functional vocabulary. The significant formation of the "me" begins to occur during this stage, which is marked by conscious role taking and manifested by the child's "playing at" the various roles that have been observed. This stage then is distinguished by creative play as shown in the child's imaginatively adopting social roles that one does not have, but about which one has some knowledge. Most typical examples here are the roles of father or mother. Role taking enables one to develop an awareness of, and to share the perspectives of, others, and consequently to define one's behavior in terms of the expectations of others.

3. *Role-playing or "game" stage* (5 to 6 years): The child in this stage takes on a distinct awareness of self and significance for role-taking. As opposed to the fantasy of the role-taking in the previous stage, here there is true role enactment and purposeful behavior. This stage witnesses the simultaneous performance of a number of actual roles and an understanding of the relationship they have to each other. Here begins the formation of the generalized other through awareness of the feelings, values, and expectations of others. This stage is also known as the "game stage" because here, as in games, roles

are played by rules and are dependent upon what everyone else does or must do. Consequently, since roles have meaning in terms of others, they need coordination for their proper enactment. As Mead put it, "What goes on in the games goes on in the life of a child all the time. He is continually taking the attitudes of those about him especially the roles of those who in some sense control him and on whom he depends" (1934:160).

## CONTEMPORARY PERSPECTIVES ON THE SELF

The self is far more complex than Cooley or Mead had envisioned. Much modern research has provided ample evidence of this situation. Rosenberg (1982, 1979), for example, has delineated three principal components of the self-concept: the *extant self* (what the individual actually perceives and feels when he or she engages in self-reflection); the *idealized self* (what the individual would like to perceive when he or she reflects upon the self); and the presenting or *social self* (the person one seeks to have appear, and strives to implant, in the mind of others). Each of these components, of unequal importance to the individual, is itself a highly complex phenomenon with several different dimensions.

One of the current issues that has received renewed attention of late concerns the compositional or structural nature of the self: Is it a singular or multifaceted phenomenon? One of the first comments on this point dates back to William James, who stated, nearly a century ago, that a person "has as many different social selves as there are distinct groups of people about whose opinion he cares . . . [and] shows a different side of himself to each of these different groups" (1890:293).

This view is reaffirmed yet today by many theorists (see Elster, 1988). The implication one

▼

## BOX 5-3. Assessing the Self

Many methods are used to assess various aspects of the self system. One clever and well-known technique that has been used successfully to measure the cognitive content of the self is the nonprojective "Who Am I?" test developed by Kuhn and McPartland (1954). In this totally unstructured instrument the individual is asked simply to provide, with very little reflection, twenty answers to the single question, Who Am I? Try it before reading further!

The responses to this test fall into two principal categories: *social identifications,* in which the individual sees himself or herself as an occupant of a role or as a member of a group, such as daughter, father, Boy Scout, homemaker, nurse, and so on; and *psychological identifications,* which consist of mentions or descriptions of personality traits or characteristics, such as happy, quiet, friendly, lonely, intelligent, and so forth.

Over the past three decades different results have been obtained in the widespread administration of this test. When the instrument first was used among college students in the late 1950s, social conceptions were by far the larger category of self-images offered by respondents. In more recent usage, however, data show a reversal in the principal kinds of self-images. Among college students again the major and substantially stronger type of self-images are now psychological identifications (Snow & Phillips, 1982; Zurcher, 1977). The reasons for this shift in the primary locus or frame of reference for the self remain unclear. ▲

usually derives from the formulations of Cooley and Mead, however, and certainly one to which many of their followers pay allegiance, is that there is a single, unitary self. Such a perspective of the self is being increasingly challenged nowadays with the contention that the "true" self is composed of multiple identities (see Gergen, 1977; Zurcher, 1977; Stryker, 1977) which are related to, and dependent upon, situation, circumstance, and environment. Many theorists maintain that several times each day we find ourselves donning different masks because of the complexity that is characteristic of contemporary society. Modern social life with its typical expansion in roles and relationships brings an inescapable need to adapt the self accordingly.

Others (DeVos, 1977; DiRenzo, 1977*a*) have argued that there are a number of conceptual,

as well as functional, problems in the pluralistic self-concept. Chief among the latter are questions of integration and consistency. To speak of a plurality of selves is to suggest to some a situation similar to a multiple personality, which constitutes a pathological type (a dissociative reaction that essentially involves a lack of functional integration). Gergen (1977), on the contrary, contends that self-consistency is an erroneous cultural perspective and, thus, argues for the normality of multiple self-identities in an increasingly complex and pluralistic society. There is no doubt that the self system has become a more complex phenomenon for many people in today's world. It would be more accurate to speak of "multiple identities" and "multiple role conceptions" than of multiple *selves.* This conceptual distinction between a singular self and multiple identities seems to

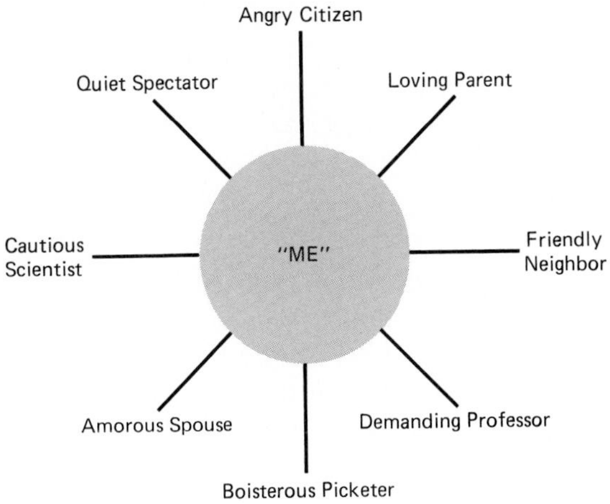

Angry Citizen

Quiet Spectator          Loving Parent

Cautious          "ME"          Friendly
Scientist                        Neighbor

Amorous Spouse          Demanding Professor

Boisterous Picketer

FIGURE 5-1    The Modern Self and Its Multiple Iden-          **205**
tity. The typical self-system in modern and heterogeneous societies today consists of pluralistic and
complex identities that often result in situations of
internal conflict and identity crises.

resolve, as well as to respecify, the problem of the compositional nature of the phenomenon in question. There still is much concern, nonetheless, for discovering the real self (see Chapter 14).

## BEHAVIORAL SIGNIFICANCE OF THE SELF

The self, like other systems of personality, is a dynamic phenomenon. It is, in a sense, in a continuous process of formation through the life cycle. This situation does not mean that the self is constantly changing. Rather, it means that individuals are constantly looking in the societal mirror and making appropriate modifications as necessary in terms of the formulations and principles discussed above.

One major dimension of this constant change in the formation of the self is in terms of "impression management," or the control of one's identities. Erving Goffman in the formulation of the "dramaturgical approach" to social interaction (see Chapter 1) refers to the various kinds of behavior intended to control one's image as "facework." In his well-known book on *The Presentation of Self in Everyday*

*Life* (1959) and other publications (for example, *Interaction Ritual*, 1967; *Relations in Public*, 1971), Goffman attempts to show how the daily interactions of people—even the most mundane interactions—are influenced by a person's sensitivity to the impressions that their actions make in the minds of other people. More significantly, Goffman describes how these reactions are manipulated (in a process of "impression management") in order to achieve, and to maintain, a positive and satisfying self. Students who change their wardrobe and grooming styles at job recruitment time manifest a poignant understanding of the dynamics and significance of a proper presentation of self.

Much behavior makes sense only in reference to the dynamics of the self. Chiefly instrumental in these respects is the *perceived self*—one's image of how others view and evaluate the individual. The perceived self is an effective predictor of human behavior. People, more often than not, act in terms of who or what they *think* they are, rather than in terms of who or what they *actually* are. Research efforts on the relationship of the perceived self versus the *accorded* self (the actual judgment of others) have shown that it is the former which has a

▼

206

far greater influence in shaping our self image. What is more significant, perhaps, is that these perceptions are usually inaccurate (Miyamoto & Dornbusch, 1956). One example of the behavioral significance of these principles is the phenomenon of the **self-fulfilling prophecy,** which contends that individuals act in such a way that they actually come to authenticate the conceptions and images of the self that are thought to be true. If we believe that we are unpopular, even though this is not the case, we will act as though we are unpopular, and indeed will become unpopular. W. I. Thomas (Thomas & Thomas, 1928:572) expressed this principle in his well-known axiom: "If men define situations as real, they are real in their consequences." The self plays a central role in dynamics of this kind.

# Theories of Personality

Quite a significant number of theories (see Ewen, 1988) have been developed to explain the specific processes and dynamics of personality development and function.* Nearly all current theories are potentially useful for the analysis and explanation of personality development and dynamics. Several of these theories have much in common with each other, and in some respects they can be thought of as mere variations on a theme. These many theories, however, may be conveniently reduced for our purposes to a few major types: psychodynamic theories, trait theories, and humanistic theories

* Often each of the many theories in the field of psychology is treated as a personality theory. It is necessary, however, to distinguish between special-domain theories (those that pertain to specific kinds of psychological dynamics, such as cognition and motivation) and holistic theories (those that pertain comprehensively to the entirety of the psychological system or personality). Social learning theories, such as those dealing with cognitive and moral development, which were discussed in the preceding chapter, are examples of special-domain theories. Here we shall confine our discussion to holistic theories. These can be reduced to a few major types.

(see Table 5-1). Let us discuss some of the specific theories of each type that are among the more popular ones today, especially as they are found in the field of sociology.

## PSYCHODYNAMIC THEORIES

No discussion of personality theory can begin without mention of Sigmund Freud (1856–1939), the Austrian physician and psychiatrist who singlehandedly formulated the most comprehensive and most influential of all theories of personality—psychoanalysis. Freud's contributions dominated the field of personality and psychological thought for nearly half a century, and today they remain a major influence in the many fields of the behavioral sciences.

Psychoanalysis, however, is only one—albeit the major one—of a category of personality theories that today are referred to more conveniently as **psychodynamic theories.** Such theories are distinguished by their nearly exclusive focus on unconscious dynamics, as well as the early social and psychological experiences of the individual. Psychodynamic theories, moreover, have been particularly influential in the field of sociology because of the new perspectives that they offered on the relationship between the individual and society.

We shall confine ourselves first to a description of classical psychoanalysis—the basic conceptual and theoretical formulations of Freud himself—and then proceed to a discussion of other psychoanalytic and psychodynamic formulations.

PSYCHOANALYSIS. Sigmund Freud's theory of personality—**psychoanalysis**—has an elegant appeal in that it explains highly complex phenomena with only a few simple principles (Freud, 1938). It is, moreover, the only truly comprehensive theory of personality, in that it explains the nature and structure of

TABLE 5-1. Theories of Personality and the Self ▼

| Theory | Formulator | Focus |
|---|---|---|
| Psychodynamic | | |
|   Psychoanalysis | Sigmund Freud | Interacting components and psychosexual stages |
|   Ego psychology | Erik H. Erikson | Psychosocial stages and life crises |
| Self | | |
|   Looking-glass self | Charles H. Cooley | Perceived self |
|   Symbolic interaction | George H. Mead | Reflexive self |
| Trait | | |
|   Idiographic | Gordon W. Allport | Individual phenomena |
|   Factor-analytic | Raymond B. Cattell | Basic traits |
| Humanistic | | |
|   Phenomenology | Ronald D. Laing | Subjective experience |
|   Existentialism | Rollo R. May | Meaning and purpose of behavior |

personality—its development, dynamics, functions, and dysfunctions—and also serves as the basis of a distinctive therapeutic method. Most of the other theories of personality speak to only one or two of these elements.

The organization of personality in the Freudian formulation consists of three major components or subsystems: id, ego, and superego.

The **id,** the unconscious dimension of personality, represents the pleasure principle. It consists of the totality of organic demands. The infant at birth is an exclusively id organism who has only one drive or motive for doing anything—physical pleasure. This basic source of psychological energy comes from the **libido**— the reservoir of unconscious biological and psychological drives—that consists of essentially sexual and aggressive drives that Freud inaccurately called instincts.

As the more primitive part of personality, the id contains all that which is inherited or biologically given in the psychological constitution of the individual. Its chief dynamic is the hedonistic impulse to seek pleasure and to avoid pain through immediate gratification. Freud described the id as a "seething cauldron of energy" that—completely indifferent to and recognizing no moral considerations—drives one to a physically or sensually pleasurable gratification. This part of personality is totally repressed and inaccessible except through dream analysis and unconscious behavior, such as slips of the tongue and mental blocks.

The **ego,** a partly unconscious dimension of personality, is reality-oriented. It represents the external world to the personality. The ego, which develops through the processes of social learning, provides the directive functions for libidinal energy and the relational parts of the personality. The ego has two principal functions. One is to control the impulses of the id and to satisfy its demands in socially acceptable ways. The function of the ego in this respect can be recognized when the child's hunger comes to be satisfied on a feeding schedule or when the physical pleasure of elimination is

▼

controlled by toilet training. The other principal function of the ego is to mediate the constant state of conflict that exists between the id and the third component of personality—the superego.

The **superego,** representing the moral component of the personality, serves as a behavioral censor or mechanism of social control. It, too, develops in the process of social learning, and typically is established by the age of 5 or 6. One of the chief mechanisms, in this respect, is that of **identification,** in which the norms and values of society become incorporated or internalized, again largely unconsciously, within the individual; and, structurally, can be seen as a split-off of the ego. The superego, when operating at the conscious level, constitutes the conscience—the complex of social ideals and cultural values.

The principal functions of the superego are to inhibit the unacceptable impulses of the id and to persuade the ego to act in accord with moralistic goals, rather than merely realistic ones. Freud's own analogy envisioned the relationship between id and superego as that between a horse and its rider, who seeks to hold in check the superior strength of its charge (Freud, 1923). Energy comes from the horse but is directed by the rider. It is these ever-present conflicts between id and superego which lead to personality dysfunction when inadequately resolved.

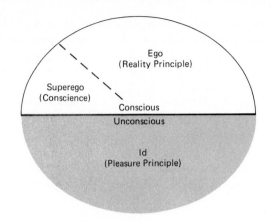

FIGURE 5-2 Freudian Personality Structure.

Personality development in the Freudian scheme is confined principally to the preadolescent years of life and involves movement through a fixed and universal process that consists of five stages: oral, anal, phallic, latency, and genital (see Table 5-2). Each of these stages is distinguished by the primary locus and focus of libidinal energy, as well as by a particular developmental task. The inevitable conflicts between the structural components of personality are present in all five of the psychosexual stages.

The nature of one's personality, and specifically the quality of one's mental health, is related directly to the manner in which one proceeds through the five stages of development: whether one successfully resolves the

TABLE 5-2.  Freudian Stages of Personality Development

| Stage | Age | Locus of Sensual Gratification |
|-------|-----|-------------------------------|
| 1. Oral | 0 to 2 years | Mouth |
| 2. Anal | 2 to 4 years | Excretory functions |
| 3. Phallic | 4 to 6 years | Sex organs |
| 4. Latency | 6 to 12 years | Relative dormancy of sexual dynamics |
| 5. Genital | Adolescence | Secondary sex development |

implicit developmental tasks or experiences fixation or regression at any one of the stages. The most crucial of these developmental tasks involves the well-known Oedipus complex (called the Electra complex in girls) that characterizes the phallic stage. This conflict consists essentially of a sexual desire for the parent of the opposite sex. The child desires to become the exclusive object of affection of the parent of the opposite sex and is jealous of the same-sex parent. Its resolution, under the perceived threat or reality of castration, involves an unconscious repression of the desire, along with an independently functional identification with the parent of the same sex, which results in a vicarious gratification. According to the principles of classical psychoanalysis, personality development is essentially complete by the end of this stage—or in about 6 years.

Central to Freud's theory is the concept of the **dynamic unconscious.** This doctrine is not exclusively Freudian; it was Freud, however, who refined and perfected its theoretical formulation. The dynamic unconscious involves a number of mental mechanisms whose function is to resolve psychological conflict. Among these mechanisms, which operate below the level of conscious awareness, are such dynamics as repression, regression, rationalization, projection, displacement, and reaction formation. The Oedipus complex, for example, is resolvable through the psychological mechanisms of repression and identification, as discussed above.

Psychoanalytic theory, for a long time, has been widely criticized as empirically unverifiable. Nowadays, however, this contention seems to be softened somewhat in the belief that with newly developed methods of research, many of Freud's hypotheses are more amenable to empirical analysis than had been supposed (see Fisher & Greenberg, 1977). Psychoanalytic theory, nonetheless, still remains in very good standing in many quarters of the behavioral

sciences, including much of sociology. In particular, there has been widespread acceptance of the doctrine of the unconscious and the focus on childhood as crucial to adult development. Whatever merits Freud's theory may have in terms of validity, none can dispute its unparalleled significance as a classic contribution that has influenced theoretical development in all of the behavioral sciences—not the least of which has been sociology.

Much of the respectability of psychoanalytic theory in sociology is due to the fact that it came on the scene during the 1920s and 1930s, a time when American sociology was undergoing a significant development in the dimensions of psychosociology. Particularly relevant, in this regard, was the crucial importance that Freud placed on social interaction during childhood, and the facility with which the basic principles of developmental stages could be related to social and cultural learning. Equally important is the fact that psychoanalysis stands alone from the point of view of ideal theory. Psychoanalysis is comprehensive and has conceptual closure, while nearly all of the other personality theories that have been developed concentrate on only some of the processes and dynamics of personality.

Psychoanalytic theory was conceived to have universal application. It applied to all people at all times, regardless of personal, social, or cultural circumstances. Several of Freud's followers, however, became disenchanted with what they considered to be his myopic view of the social and cultural dimensions of personality development and function. These individuals attempted to revise psychoanalytic theory in terms of the concepts and principles of the social sciences. Central to these revisions as well was a shift away from the inner psychological world, especially the dynamics of the unconscious, and the contention that major changes in personality can occur throughout the life cycle.

**209**

▼

**210**

Among the more well-known of the psychoanalysts who were responsible for these developments and reformulations, recasting psychoanalytic theory into a broader and more significant sociopsychological context, were Alfred Adler (1929), Karen Horney (1937), Carl Jung (1938), Henry A. Murray (1938), Erich Fromm (1941), Harry Stack Sullivan (1953), and Erik Erikson (1964), whose works we shall discuss elsewhere. The sociopsychological modifications and contributions of these neo-Freudians further facilitated the acceptance of psychoanalytic theory in the field of sociology and the other social and behavioral sciences. Today, the influence of psychoanalysis is both profound and far-reaching. More especially, the importance of psychoanalysis is reflected in the fact that it has been so thoroughly assimilated into many other theories and many other fields that its influence often is not discernible. Such is the case particularly in sociology where psychoanalytic theory, introduced largely by Talcott Parsons (see Lackey, 1987; Black, 1961) has been instrumental in the formulation of theories of socialization and social learning.

EGO PSYCHOLOGY. One brand of psychodynamic theory that is quite popular in sociology today is that formulated by Erik Erikson (1982, 1964) and known as **ego psychology.** He extended Freud's stages of personality development into broader psychosocial dimensions that encompass the entire life cycle, while at the same time deemphasizing the sexual component that played such a central role in classical psychoanalysis.

Unlike Freud, Erikson argues that personality is being shaped continually at different stages of life by the important "decisions" that one makes about alternative orientations to the world; that one's relatives, peers, and acquaintances are of primary influence in this development; and that personality development can occur at any point in one's life. He speaks of human development in terms of "Eight Stages of Man," another scheme to which many sociologists respond favorably because it, too, can be related easily to the processes of social learning and the significant periods of social development.

In each stage, which represents a specific crisis initiated by both psychological changes and new social environments to which the individual must adapt, there is potential for positive or negative development. No crisis is ever permanently resolved. While adjustment at one stage of development affects orientation in the next, the concerns of any given stage are present throughout life and continually reoccur. Each crisis, therefore, distinguishes a particular stage by its prominence rather than its exclusivity.

The eight stages of human development and their corresponding crises, which Erikson identifies (see Table 5-3), may be described briefly as follows:

1. *Infancy* (0 to 1 year): *Basic trust versus basic mistrust.* This initial stage corresponds to the oral stage of classical psychoanalytic theory. The degree to which the child develops a sense of trust or mistrust toward the adult environment depends, in great part, upon the quality of loving care and attention one receives.
2. *Early Childhood* (2 to 3 years): *Autonomy versus doubt and shame.* The second stage, comparable to the anal stage, is concerned with the emergence of relative autonomy and independence through the development of new motor and mental abilities; walking, climbing, pushing, pulling, opening, closing, and so forth, as opposed to feelings of shame stemming from failure and reprimand.
3. *Play Age* (4 to 5 years): *Initiative versus guilt.* The child's initiatives at play, motor activities, and intellectual curiosity during this stage may result in feelings of either pride or shame.
4. *Latency Age* (6 to 12 years): *Industry versus inferiority.* Expanded initiatives in activities

TABLE 5-3. Erikson's Eight Stages of the Life Cycle    ▼

| Stage | Psychosocial Crisis | Predominant Social Setting |
|---|---|---|
| 1. Infancy | Trust vs. mistrust | Family |
| 2. Early childhood | Autonomy vs. doubt and shame | Family |
| 3. Play age | Initiative vs. guilt | Family |
| 4. Latency age | Industry vs. inferiority | School |
| 5. Adolescence | Identity vs. role confusion | Peer group |
| 6. Young adulthood | Intimacy vs. isolation | Couple |
| 7. Adulthood | Generativity vs. stagnation | New family; work |
| 8. Old age | Integrity vs. despair | Retirement |

Source: Erik H. Erikson, *The Life Cycle Completed: A Review*. New York: W. W. Norton, 1982.

of doing, making, and learning during late childhood may experience encouragement or stifling with the respective development of psychological qualities of industriousness or inferiority.

5. *Adolescence* (13 to 18 years): *Identity versus identity confusion.* This crucial stage, which marks the transition from childhood to adulthood, is distinguished by a preoccupation with questions of identity: the ability to develop a sense of personal or ego identity, or to experience development stagnation in a situation of increasing role complexity and confusion.

6. *Young Adulthood: Intimacy versus isolation.* The concerns of this stage center around the ability to share with, and to care about, other people.

7. *Adulthood: Generativity versus stagnation.* The central question in this stage relates to either the end or the continuation of one's growth and development. Such concerns of continued growth and development center on feelings of making a contribution either to a new generation or to society. Here it is a question of the "need to be needed" versus personal needs and comforts.

8. *Old Age: Integrity versus despair.* This final stage of "development" is concerned with one's ability to look back on life with satisfaction and pride in contrast to a futile desire to begin life anew.

One of the more sociologically significant, and quite controversial, aspects of Erikson's theory focuses on the adolescent stage and the concern for what he has described as the "identity crisis." The fundamental question here, as in successive stages, is how one is allowed to interact with others: having the opportunity to build a positive and satisfying self, or being stuck with a crisis of self-identity and its accompanying stress and anxiety. Such a problem is alleged to be a far more difficult one in the highly complex societies of today's modern world.

Erikson has developed an attractive theory of human development that combines psychoanalytical principles with those of the social formation of the self, relying principally on the work of Cooley and Mead in these latter respects. By integrating psychological and sociological perspectives, his theory seeks to explain how the individual, at various stages of life, must continually establish new orientations toward the social world as well as toward the growth of the inner self.

▼ ## TRAIT THEORIES

**Trait theories,** much less elaborate in many respects than other theories, view personality as a complex and differentiated structure of psychological characteristics. Each seeks to explain personality in terms of the many psychological traits or predispositions to behavior that comprise or describe a particular personality. Traits, most importantly, are viewed not only as structural elements of personality but also as a source of fundamental motivation. There are several varieties of trait theory.

A **personality trait** may be defined as a relatively enduring psychological characteristic that has a fairly generalized effect on behavior in diverse settings. Traits are psychological qualities or attributes that an individual acquires as residual effects of social interaction—usually in consequence of repeated attempts to satisfy motivational needs—that become embodied in characteristic ways of reaction to stimuli (people, places, and things).

Allport and Odbert (1936) pointed out over 50 years ago that there were about 17,000 relevant terms that could be used to describe individual psychological differences. A much greater number could be found today; however, recent catalogs of personality measures identify only about 3,000 to 4,000 different personality traits that have appeared in the relevant literature. Examples of personality traits are such psychological qualities as introversion, aggression, achievement motivation, sociability, dominance, and submission. Traits, therefore, are viewed as dynamic phenomena; they are able to govern the reception of stimuli and to direct behavior. More significantly, traits are relatively consistent and stable dispositions to respond in distinctive ways.

Traits differ in the degree of their pervasiveness, consistency, and patterning or internal structure. One category of personality traits is known as "interpersonal response traits." Such traits consist of dispositions to respond in characteristic ways to people. Among the principal examples of these are the following subtypes: role dispositions (ascendance, dominance, social initiative, and independence); sociometric dispositions (accepting of others, sociability, friendliness, and sympathy); expressive dispositions (competitiveness, aggressiveness, self-consciousness, and exhibitionism).

Among the more well-known trait theories are those formulated by Gordon W. Allport and Raymond B. Cattell. These scholars respectively developed idiographic theory and factor-analytic theory.

IDIOGRAPHIC THEORY. Perhaps the most influential trait theorist has been Gordon W. Allport, former professor of psychology at Harvard University, who gave us the very term "personality trait." Allport (1937) stressed the individuality dimension of personality. He argued for the importance of **idiographic theory**— an approach that studies unique and individual phenomena. Yet, at the same time, Allport advocated nomothetic—generalizing and universalizing—perspectives of scientific analysis. This seeming dilemma between the study of the individual and the need for scientific laws was resolved, in part, by Allport's contention that individuality is a primary law of behavior.

Allport stressed the role of conscious motivation and advocated the importance of the qualitative study of the individual case. He argued that a science or generalized explanation of personality was not possible because of the uniqueness of each personality. Each individual, in Allport's view, has a personal organization of interdependent traits that are arranged in a hierarchy, the chief elements of which are cardinal or master traits (focal and pervasive); central traits (less focal, but yet generalized); and secondary traits (more specialized).

Allport suggests that there are between five and ten central traits which typically describe an individual's personality. The same trait, or set of traits, may be a property of different people, but it exists and functions differently within different personalities. Traits, moreover, are functionally autonomous in that it is common for a behavior to become an end in itself rather than simply the consequence of the stimulus which originally evoked it. The only effective way to study personality, and to be able to predict behavior, is to understand the entirety and complexity of the organization of personality traits peculiar to the individual.

FACTOR-ANALYTIC THEORY. The most extensive studies of personality traits have been conducted by Raymond B. Cattell, emeritus professor of psychology at the University of Illinois. In striking contrast to Allport, Cattell is quantitatively oriented in his study of personality. He has focused on the development of statistical techniques to measure commonalities of traits in the personality system, on the assumption that there are natural, unitary structures that are the substance of everyone's personality.

Cattell's work is known as **factor theory.** This label derives from the position that his contributions have focused on the formulation of the statistical techniques of **factor analysis** as a method of identifying specific traits and determining the trait structure of particular personalities. These techniques are based on the degree of correlation between numerous variables, and the manner and extent to which the variables group together to form factors or traits.

Cattell (1979) has identified sixteen factors that he believes are the basic traits underlying personality. Each factor is given two names in order to represent the continuous nature of the trait. Among these basic factors in the personality are the following: tough-mindedness versus tender-mindedness; concrete thinking versus abstract thinking; assertiveness versus dominance; expediency versus conscientiousness; self-assurance versus apprehensiveness; trust versus suspicion; and group-orientation versus self-sufficiency.

For Cattell and other factor analysts, personality is a profile of factors. A factor in this view, however, is not a mere conglomeration of traits or simply a measuring device for their description and assessment. In Cattell's words (1956:98), a factor

> is a statement about a functionally unitary, constitutionally or sociologically determined pattern within personality.... When the natural history of a factor is known, that is, when one knows how far it is determined by heredity, what its curve of growth is through childhood or of decline in later life, how it is affected by various learning situations or by physiological changes, etc., the ability to understand and to predict is greatly increased.

There is a lack of agreement among trait theorists regarding the number of basic traits—from five to twenty—that characterize the personality. Two dimensions, however, are found in nearly all factor-analytic studies: introversion–extraversion, regarding one's basic orientation toward the outside world; and stability–instability, which is a dimension of emotionality. One of the more important criticisms of the personality trait theories is the contention that behavior may vary widely from one situation to another. Indeed, personality tests designed to measure personality traits have not been as predictive as many theorists would like (Atkinson et al., 1983). Trait theories, nonetheless, are much in vogue today in many applied fields, such as personnel assessment, marital and family counseling, and clinical psychology. Extensive research efforts continually seek to discover significant patterns of relationship between personality traits and various aspects of social behavior.

## HUMANISTIC THEORIES

A more recent variety of approaches to personality is that which has become known as humanistic theory. Again, this is a category that consists of several different theories that share a set of fundamental tenets, but at the same

213

▼

**214**

time one that represents quite complex and somewhat disunified perspectives on the psychological nature of human beings. Chief among the unifying principles of humanistic theory is the position that its several formulations are reactions to what are taken to be major deficiencies in the "scientific" and more popular theories of personality and human behavior. The fundamental postulate of humanistic theories, is the contention that "scientific" theories—the laboratory and experimental approaches—overlook the holistic or integrative nature of personality. More important is the claim that these theories ignore the essence of *human* nature—rationality and free will.

Foremost among these alleged deficiencies of the "scientific theories" is their deterministic nature and the denial of human freedom and personal worth. Such is allegedly true in the case of psychoanalysis, with its stress on heredity and the ascription of unconscious motivation; and in the case of behaviorism (see Chapter 4) with the principle of environmental contingency. Accordingly, rather than merely assuming a competitive posture with scientific theories, humanistic theories are offered as challenging alternatives to the more popular theories of psychoanalysis and behaviorism. Humanistic theories, for example, stress the value of introspective analysis and subjective methods of data collection, as well as focusing on "human *process*" rather than on "human *nature*" (Lamberth & Rappaport, 1978), **Humanistic theories** are essentially and profoundly holistic: the whole person (mind and body) must be understood before the explanation of any parts can make sense. Individuality is stressed: the individual person is unique, both genetically, and, more especially, in terms of subjective experiences and personal worth. Rationality, like subjectivity and self-awareness, therefore, is a cardinal tenet of humanistic theories.

Much of the substance of humanistic theories consists of a core of parental philosophy. There are two principal varieties of humanistic theory: phenomenology and existentialism. These two varieties are closely related, however; each approach is seen as fundamentally seeking to reunite the long-separated perspectives and traditions of philosophy and psychology.

**Phenomenology** focuses on consciousness and the individual's unique perception of reality; hence, it is concerned with the study of subjective experiences of reality. Behavior in this view is caused by the perceptual field of the individual, and all reality is nothing more than a subjective interpretation of events.

**Existentialism** is somewhat more difficult to define, but like phenomenology is concerned with self-awareness, conscious events, and the individual's unique experiences, as well as with the meaning and purpose of one's existence. The need for such meaning, in the existentialist perspective, is the primary force that shapes personality and behavior. Fulfilling this need is important for the healthy personality. Existentialism accordingly focuses on the here-and-now and living in the present; and as a therapy it seeks to find meaning in and for one's existence in present feelings and choices rather than in influences of the past. These theories adopt both phenomenological and humanistic perspectives.

In addition to their European philosophical roots, humanistic theories can be traced to the works of several American psychologists, including William James (1980) and Gordon Allport (1937), and to Kurt Lewin (1935), who developed Gestalt psychology or field theory, which maintains that behavior cannot be adequately understood without a knowledge and consideration of the entire context or the field of forces within which it occurs.

One of the principal examples of humanistic theory is self theory, developed by Carl R. Rogers (1951). This formulation is not to be confused with the symbolic-interactionist theories of the self already discussed in a preceding section. From his clinical experience as a physician,

Rogers has developed a theory of personality, and a corresponding therapy (client-centered therapy), that represents a synthesis of the efforts of several other humanistic psychologists and focuses essentially on the dynamics of self-actualization.

Self-actualization, Rogers maintains, is the basic motivating force in the human organism. All needs, whether biogenic or sociogenic, are subservient to the motivation of the organism to maintain and to enhance itself. Rogers emphasizes "the phenomenal self"—all those parts of the perceptual and phenomenal field that one experiences as part of the self—as the core of personality organization. His approach stresses the need for congruence among three aspects of the self: the real self, the perceived self, and the ideal self. Here is one example of how the self, as only one subsystem, is equated with the entirety of personality for all intents and purposes.

Other principal varieties of humanistic theory in the existential dimension are those of Abram H. Maslow (1954), focusing on individual needs, particularly self-actualization, and their hierarchical organization; Sidney M. Jourard (1971), stressing active involvement in psychological growth; and Rollo R. May (1983), emphasizing meaning, free will, and self-perpetuation. George A. Kelly (1955) and R. D. Laing (1969) have developed humanistic theories, more phenomenological in nature, which emphasize one's ability to assess and to adjust to personal experience, including in particular the tragic and irrational episodes of life. A similar contribution is that of Albert Ellis (1974) who has developed rational-emotive therapy, which focuses on one's perception of reality and emphasizes the cognitive restructuring of the personality system.

Existentialism and phenomenology share a common theme in seeking to assess one's subjective experiences by focusing on how the individual perceives and interprets events. Unlike other theories of personality, however, they are not concerned with predicting behavior, and often their focus is more therapeutic than explanatory. The major criticism of humanistic theories is that, as with psychoanalysis, it is difficult to evaluate their concepts and propositions.

## ECLECTIC PERSPECTIVES

The various theories of personality are actually somewhat in competition with each other. Insofar as they contradict one another, the student frequently is puzzled about which is the correct or valid theory. The answer, here, is that given a lack of conclusive evidence, this question cannot be definitively answered. No theory has been proven completely true; and, moreover, no simple theory is sufficient to explain personality in all of its complexity. There are valid elements in all of these theories. To this extent, especially when put into a conjoint perspective, each theory is useful in our attempt to understand the nature and function of personality. Each of the various theories provides part of the mosaic for the complex explanation of human development and function. Further research is needed to provide the kind of conceptual and theoretical precision that ideally characterizes the endeavors of science. Meanwhile, with the extensive knowledge and many formulations that are currently available, most of the behavioral scientists take an eclectic approach to personality. Such an orientation pragmatically selects from each theory those elements and aspects that yield results, either empirically or conceptually.

# Sociocultural Dimensions of Personality

Personality, as we have seen, is essentially the product of social interaction within specific sociocultural contexts. Hence, individuals who

▼

# BOX 5-4. Measuring Personality

Many methods have been devised to assess personality. Literally hundreds of different measures of personality exist (see, for example, Mitchell, 1985). These various instruments can be classified into three principal types: observational methods, personality inventories, and projective techniques.

Observational methods (see Chapter 2) can be used in a natural or realistic setting (for example, watching children at school or workers in a factory), in an experimental setting (artificial or test situation) in which relevant stimuli are controlled by the experimenter, in the context of an interview, or on the basis of life history documents (for example, work records, test scores, and diaries). Observational methods usually use rating scales of one kind or another. A rating scale is a device for recording one's judgment about a particular aspect of an individual's personality. Sometimes an adjective checklist may be used for this purpose; but, more frequently, finer discriminations are made by assigning a numerical score, usually on a 5-point or a 7-point scale. Observational methods, while widely used, are characterized by a high degree of subjectivity that leaves serious reservations about their validity and suitability for predicting behavior.

Personality inventories, relying on an individual's self-observations, are essentially questionnaires in which a person reports his or her reactions to different situations and various kinds of stimuli. These instruments, usually consisting of a large number of questions or items, may be designed to measure a single dimension of personality (for example, introversion) or several dimensions simultaneously, such as traits or factors that can produce a personality profile. Personality inventories constitute the most extensively used type of measurement for personality assessment. Among the more well-known, and most frequently used, examples of personality inventories are the Minnesota Multiphasic Personality Inventory (MMPI), the California Personality Inventory (CPI), and the Sixteen Personality Factor Questionnaire (16PF). Personality inventories strive for objectivity and have the advantage of being fairly easy to score, either by hand or computer. Many personality inventories are constructed in such a way as to disguise their objective, and thus to eliminate—or, at least, to minimize—any intentional or unintentional distortion by the respondent. The Dogmatism Scale is one example of such a personality inventory.

Projective techniques represent a category of instruments that are designed primarily to reach the deeper and subtler dimensions of personality, including the level of the unconscious. Such instruments present an ambiguous and loosely structured stimulus to which the individual is expected to respond in an imaginative and freely associated way. The ambiguity or lack of structure in these instruments ideally encourages the subject to project deep-lying dynamics of the personality in his or her responses, which is less likely with more direct methods. Among the more popular of the projective techniques are the Rorschach Inkblot Test and the Thematic Apperception Test (TAT). The Rorschach consists of a series of ten cards, each displaying a rather complex inkblot-type design. The subject is directed to describe what he or she sees in each design. Responses are scored in terms of various criteria of analysis. Subjects for the TAT are shown a series of as many as twenty ambiguous pictures of persons and scenes, and are

216

asked to make up a story about each one. In assessment, the scorer looks for recurrent themes that may reveal one's needs, motives, values, and characteristic ways of handling interpersonal relationships. Other projective methods make use of draw-a-picture and sentence-completion techniques.

The construction and administration of any instrument for the measurement of personality is a highly sophisticated skill (see, for example, Anastasi, 1988). Among the principal problems, as in all research instruments, is the need to insure reliability, validity, and predictability (see Chapter 2). While all instruments vary in the degree to which they meet these criteria, no single instrument is considered to be a definitive measure of personality. The typical procedure, nowadays, is to use an approach in which several instruments, or a battery of tests, are administered in order to insure a maximally accurate assessment of any personality. ▲

are products of the same social experiences can be expected to be similar to each other in many psychological respects. Members of particular societies have much in common, psychologically, by virtue of sharing the same, or highly similar, types of social and cultural learning: child rearing, schooling, institutions, values, ideology, roles, and a host of other sociocultural experiences.

People from different societies often are recognized by having distinctive or distinguishing characteristics. Even people from different regions of our own country—for example, New Englanders, Southerners, Midwesterners—are frequently distinguished in terms of various dimensions or aspects of personality. The same situation is true of individuals who share other kinds of subcultures—racial, ethnic, religious, socioeconomic, occupational, and so forth. Our question, then, is simply this: Do different cultures produce distinctive types of personalities?

To the extent that the social and cultural experiences that result in personality formation are the same—or, more properly, highly similar—for different people, we can expect a corresponding homogeneity or similarity in their personalities. One concern in this respect has come to be known as cohort (people of roughly the same age) or generational differences in

sociopsychological development. Elder (1974), for example, has documented the psychological and personality development of a particular category of American people who grew up during the Depression (the late 1920s and the early 1930s). One of the chief findings in Elder's study is the influence of economic hardship in the development of the centrality of the family and in an enduring importance of children among men and women who, as children themselves, lived through this unparalleled period of American history. Similar examples of cohort or generational differences in psychosocial development would be those that characterize the "Baby-Boomers" (Americans born between 1945 and 1965) from whose ranks came the cultural "Hippies" of the 1960s, the political radicals of the 1970s, and the "Yuppies" of the 1980s.

Urie Bronfenbrenner (1970) has examined the contributions made to personality development by the emerging patterns of socialization and family dynamics in modern Western society during the past few decades. His studies reveal significant differences, between American society and the contemporary scene in the Soviet Union. Bronfenbrenner finds, for example, that a collective-centered versus a family-centered system of socialization produces

**Generation Character.** Significant variations in personality can be observed among people reared in social eras that differ greatly in terms of economic and political climates. Individuals who experienced the proverty and frugality of the Great Depression during the 1930s, or the tragedy and hardship of World War II in the 1940s, reveal significant differences in modal personality from those reared in the more affluent and tranquil periods of the 1950s and the 1960s. Today's Baby Boomers and Yuppies are examples of generational cohorts with distinctive sets of values and motives in their personalities. (*Left,* Photo Researchers; *right,* The Bettmann Archive)

individuals who are more conforming and less rebellious, aggressive, or delinquent. Americans, moreover, are far more competitive.

Another cross-cultural longitudinal study (Holtzmann et al., 1975) of personality development among school children has proposed six major hypotheses concerning personality differences between Americans and Mexicans: Americans tend to cope with problems in a more active way; Americans tend to be more dynamic, technological, and external; American cognitive structure tends to be more complex and differentiated; Mexicans tend to be family-centered while Americans are individual-centered; Mexicans tend to be cooperative and Americans tend to be competitive; and Mexi-

cans tend to have a more fatalistic outlook on life.

It is in these sociocultural dimensions of personality that it can be said that "every man is in certain respects like some other men" (Kluckhohn & Murray, 1948). Of course, the more simple the culture, the more homogeneous the personalities of its members. Correspondingly, the more complex and the more heterogeneous the culture, the greater is the number of different types of people in the society.

Social scientists have used several terms to describe these basically cultural similarities in personality. Among the principal terms are the following: national character, basic personality structure, social character, and modal personality. Each of these terms has a conceptual referent and dynamic focus that are quite distinct, but often they are used interchangeably to refer simply to the common or typical manifestation of personality in a particular society or population. Let us discuss these conceptions in more detail.

## PERSONALITY AND CULTURE

Many of the psychological effects of similar and diverse experiences of social learning and development have been shown in the works of cultural anthropologists. Chief among these efforts have been the classic works of those American anthropologists who pioneered the field of culture-and-personality studies. Ruth Benedict (1934) marked the formal beginnings of this field with her *Patterns of Culture*, which offered a psychological typology of American Indian tribes.

Among the tribes that Benedict studied were the Dobuans and the Zuñi, who provide contrasting examples of cultural and personality differences. Benedict described Dobuans as highly anxious people. Fear and suspicion dominate every aspect of their life. These people perceive the world as controlled by magic in every respect. Nothing occurs through natural causes; all phenomena are under the influence of witchcraft and sorcery. Included under this all-encompassing control are such things as illness, accidents, crop failure, death, and sexual attraction. Even children are seen as a curse and burden, and for these reasons are often unwanted. The Dobuans live in an atmosphere of constant ill will and treachery. It should not be surprising, therefore, to learn that these people are usually suspicious, distrustful, jealous, secretive, deceitful, and downright hostile individuals who openly appear quite dour and humorless. One needs to remember, nonetheless, that these personality characteristics are not consciously learned; rather, they are the understandable consequences of the kind of culturalization experienced by the Dobuans. Hence, the Dobuans are not paranoid personalities; their psychological dispositions are quite normal and rational.

The typical personality of the Zuñi of New Mexico is in stark contrast to that of the Dobuans. Benedict describes the Zuñi as quite placid people characterized by kindness, cooperation, sobriety, and a lack of individualism. As opposed to the Dobuans, the Zuñi do not see magical forces as malevolent. They do not believe in violence or immoderate behavior, nor are they aggressive or power-seeking individuals. The Zuñi are also characterized by the absence of an obsession with sin and, hence, manifest a distinct freedom from guilt. Children are warmly welcomed and treated with love and tender care. They are never punished or disciplined. One would expect that such cultural themes would produce a consistent and compatible personality among the Zuñi people, who are correspondingly a confident, trusting, secure, and serene people with a yielding disposition.

Margaret Mead, another pioneer in the field of culture-and-personality studies, conducted extensive field research in the South Pacific on social and psychological development among the peoples of Samoa and New Guinea (Mead, 1928, 1930). She was able to show quite emphatically in these studies that the stresses and strains that Americans and Westerners associate with the period of adolescence, and ones that can have significant consequences for personality, are not universal. In fact, they were reported to be startlingly absent among people in the South Pacific, in whose cultures a transitional stage of adolescence between childhood and adulthood does not even exist. Out of Mead's classic work in these studies came the concept of "national character." She proposed this concept as an analytical tool to describe those aspects of personality that are common to the individuals who live in a politically distinct nation, even though they may represent a

▼

**219**

▼ cluster of cultures. Several conceptual refinements have been made on this idea during the past half-century.

Abram Kardiner (1939), a psychoanalyst interested in studies of personality and culture, developed the term "basic personality structure" to refer to similarities in the core of personality that derive primarily from sharing in the common or fundamental aspects of culture, such as childrearing and schooling. This conceptual distinction allowed for the assessment of both sociocultural similarities as well as individual elements in personality. Kardiner's specifications, including collaborative efforts with Franz Boas, one of America's prominent anthropologists, advanced much of the work in the field of culture-and-personality studies.

**220**

Cora DuBois (1944), another anthropologist, in a study of the Alorese, who inhabit a small island in Indonesia; used the statistically derived term "modal personality"* to refer to the central tendency of personality within a given society or culture. The Alorese were found to be products of a very aggressive, even cruel, type of socialization. Child neglect and lack of discipline were typical, rather than exceptional, among these people, whose religion and folklore were characterized by distrust and uncertainty among its principal themes. The Alorese were described as a very negative people in whom inferiority and the lack of enterprise were dominant characteristics of personality. Kardiner (1945) described the social character of the Alorese as "anxious, suspicious, distrustful, lacking confidence, with no interest in the outer world," and he attributed these characteristics to the traumatic experiences of childhood in which teasing and humiliation were very common experiences, along with the lack of parental involvement.

During the past 50 years or so, the literature of the social sciences has accumulated a vast number of studies that have attempted to document and to describe distinctive patterns of national character in various societies of the world.* In the 1940s, many American anthropologists studied the relationship between culture and personality in various European and Asian nations (see for example, Benedict's study of the Japanese national character: *The Chrysanthemum and the Sword*) in the belief that such understandings would contribute to victory for the United States in World War II. Our own American society is no exception and also has received a fair amount of attention in this regard. In one study of American national character, *And Keep Your Powder Dry*, Margaret Mead (1943) focused on the idea of our country as a land of unlimited opportunity, in which much emphasis is placed on the "moral responsibility to succeed" and that this ideology is reflected in such characteristic motives as self-actualization and achievement. The social psychologist David McClelland (1976) has devoted an academic lifetime to the cross-cultural study of the achievement motive (nAch). His work indeed shows dramatic differences in the level of nAch in various societies, with Americans being among those people with the highest levels. The dynamic influence of this socially acquired motive is illustrated by McClelland in his contention that our highly advanced level of economy, with its capitalistic spirit, is both product and producer of the achievement motive. Other representative examples of works on the American national character are those by Gorer (1948), Riesman (1950), Potter (1954), DiRenzo (1977a), and Bellah et al. (1985). Some of these works will be discussed in subsequent chapters.

We speak of national character nowadays in terms of the concept of **national modal char-**

---

* The term *mode* in statistics is used as a descriptive average and refers specifically to that number or variable which occurs most frequently in a given array of items. For example, in the following series of numbers, 8 is the mode or modal event: 1, 2, 7, 8, 8, 8, 9, 10, 12, 14, 14.

* See Duijker and Frijda (1960) who offer ample evidence in an exhaustive, although now dated, survey of distinctive patterns of national character in several countries and societies.

acter, which, as defined authoritatively by Inkeles and Levinson (1969:427), refers to the "relatively enduring personality characteristics and patterns that are modal among the adult members of society." This concept refers to the stable, general dispositions or modes of psychological function that may assume a variety of concrete behavioral forms. We shall explore the question of national modal character more fully in subsequent chapters, particularly in Chapters 7 and 14.

## MODAL PERSONALITY

The concept of **modal personality,** descending from the anthropological studies of "national modal character," refers to the central tendency of personality typology within a given society or segments thereof. This concept rests on the postulate that within a given sociocultural milieu there may be a range of diverse personality types, but that one, two, three, or possibly even a few more would be found so extensively as to constitute the typical, characteristic, or dominant psychological expression for that particular population.

Personality is a property of the individual, and, in this sense, may be used justifiably, by those so inclined, as a psychological variable. Modal personality, however, is a property of the collectivity; and, hence, as an element of social organization is essentially a sociological variable (DiRenzo, 1974a). It is, moreover, a variable of much significance in sociological analysis; and one that has been grossly neglected in its respect as an independent variable.

Personality is both a social product and a social force. Throughout most of this chapter we have discussed personality primarily as a social product—that is, as a dependent variable. Personality, however, can also assume the status and functions of an independent variable—one which affects and effects social action. Hence, we need to focus our attention on the dynamic dimensions of personality in order to

explain much social behavior. What we may ask, for example, is the functional significance of the presence of distinctive types of personalities for the dynamics of society and other types of social organizations?

Personality, thus, is not only the product of sociocultural processes and systems but one of their producers as well. Scholars interested in this question assume that society, in turn, is affected by the particular types of personality or modes of psychological character that are present therein. There is probably no realm of social action in which personality does not play an instrumental role—both on the collective as well as the individual level. The concept of modal personality is a focal consideration in these respects.

In subsequent chapters, we shall relate personality, particularly in terms of the concept and dynamics of modal personality, to many elements of sociocultural organization: society, complex organizations, groups, roles, social institutions, bureaucracy, occupations, minorities, social stratification, social deviance, collective behavior, social movements, and social change.

## Summary

Personality is a central and indispensable element in social behavior. To whatever extent sociocultural phenomena are responsible for human behavior, it is by means of personality.

Personality is the acquired, unique, relatively enduring, yet dynamic system of stable predispositions to behavior that is contained within the individual. Personality, as a latent function of socialization and enculturation, emerges by and large as an unconscious phenomenon for both the individual and the agents of socialization.

Personality development is rooted in two distinct sets of elements: biological foundations and sociocultural experiences. Neither of these kinds of elements constitutes personality in

221

▼

222

itself. Rather both contribute to the development and formation of personality. Personality, therefore, is seen as the conjoint product of the interaction of nature and nurture.

Sex-linked dimensions of personality formation are those that are innate in the particular organism and include the endocrine system and intellectual capacities. Sex-associated personality qualities refer to behavioral dispositions specific to a particular gender that are learned or acquired in the process of social development.

The nature, quality, and quantity of social experiences, including in very large part the personality of the people involved, constitute the principal basis for the formation of personality. Chiefly responsible for personality in this respect, especially during the very early formative years, are the sociopsychological experiences that derive from social relations in the contexts of the family, school, and peer groups.

Personality, like any other system, may be analyzed in terms of two fundamental dimensions: content and structure. Personality content refers to the specific elements or units that comprise the personality system: beliefs, motivations, values, attitudes, ideologies, emotions, psychological traits, cognitions, and self-concepts. Personality structure refers to the coordinated arrangement and dynamic relationships among the components of personality content.

Chief among the analytically distinctive, yet functionally interpenetrating and interdependent, subsystems of personality are: the cognitive system, the affective system, the motivational system, and the self system.

Despite the individuality and extensive varieties of personality, it is possible to distinguish distinctive types of personality. Personality typologies have facilitated much of the theoretical effort to integrate sociological and psychological dynamics in the interest of a more comprehensive understanding of human social behavior. Of particular significance in this re-

spect are the typologies of personality based on the psychodynamics of authoritarianism and dogmatism.

One of the most focal segments of personality is the self system, which consists of the total constellation of cognitions, effects, and motivations that pertain directly to the individual as an object. Among the principal conceptions of the self that are current today are the formulations of Charles H. Cooley (the looking-glass self) and George H. Mead (the "I" and the "me").

The several theoretical systems that have been developed to explain the specific processes and dynamics of personality development and function may be reduced to a few major types: psychodynamic theories, trait theories, and humanistic theories.

Sigmund Freud formulated the most comprehensive of all theories of personality—psychoanalysis. Erik Erickson extended Freud's theory into broader psychosocial dimensions that encompass the entire life cycle. Trait theories view personality as a complex and differentiated structure of psychological characteristics. One of the most influential trait theorists, Gordon Allport, stressed the individuality dimension of personality. Raymond Cattell, another pioneering formulator of trait theory, developed factor theory. Humanistic theories include those of both an existentialistic and/or phenomenological nature and adopt an integrative conception of personality that stresses rationality and free will. Each of these theories provides a part of the mosaic for the complex explanation of psychological development and function.

Personality is not only the product of sociocultural processes and systems but one of their producers as well. Of relevance in these respects are the concepts of basic personality structure and national modal character. An important concept in the study of personality for sociological analysis is modal personality. This concept rests on the postulate that within a given society or segment thereof there may be a range of diverse personality types, but that one type, or only a few types, would be found so extensively as to constitute the typical, characteristic, or dominant psychological expression for that particular population. Personality is a property of the individual and may be used justifiably as a psychological variable. Modal personality, however, is a property of the collectivity; and, hence, as an element of social organization, is essentially a sociological variable.

# Key Concepts

affective system
authoritarianism
basic human need
biogenic motive
cognitive system
dogmatism
dynamic unconscious
ego
ego psychology
emotion
endocrine system
existentialism

factor analysis
factor-analytic theory
generalized other
humanistic theory
id
identification
idiographic theory
libido
modal personality
motivational system
motive
national modal character
personality
personality content
personality structure
personality trait
phenomenology
psychoanalysis
psychodynamic theory
self-fulfilling prophecy
self system
significant other
sociogenic motive
superego
temperament
trait theory

▼

**223**

# THREE ▼ The Social Order

One unmistakable characteristic of human social life is its planned and orderly nature. This distinct feature is known as social organization. Imagine how chaotic and problematic social life would be without organization! Each interaction with another person would involve a new behavioral invention. Social organization, on the other hand, allows daily life to be undertaken with a very high degree of efficiency. So common is social organization that we tend to notice it only when it is absent. Just think how exasperated we can become with inefficiency in our daily dealings with schools, stores, governments, and a host of other social agencies—as well as simply other individuals!

In this section we explore the how and why of orderly social life. We are concerned in Chapter 6 with the general principles of social organization that are fundamental to the many different kinds of social systems, regardless of their nature or social organization. Chapter 7 explores the nature of society as the all-encompassing mode of social organization, while Chapter 8 is devoted to a consideration of the structure and processes of formal or complex organizations, such as bureaucracies. Lastly, in Chapter 9, we deal with the nature and dynamics of social groups that permeate nearly all facets of human life. ▲

# 6    Social Organization

One of the classic questions of sociology, orginally posed by Thomas Hobbes, the English philosopher, in his *Leviathan* (1651), is simply this: How is society or orderly social life possible? Why is it that human interaction is not a perpetually chaotic situation? Why is it that all people are not in a constant state of conflict or warfare? Intriguing answers have been offered to these questions. Among them are those of the social contract thinkers, who maintained that social organization emerges as a consequence of man seeking to escape from a natural state of conflict, and those of the social evolutionists, who maintained that social organization has its basis in the existence of natural laws. Neither of these positions, of course, is essentially correct. As we have shown in preceding chapters, people are social by nature—but it is human learning and not human biology that accounts for the social life of human beings.

How then does social organization emerge? How is it possible for strangers to engage in cooperative interaction with one another? How are individuals able to fit their lines of personal conduct together so that patterned, productive, and predictable actions occur? How are the idiosyncratic actions of individuals transformed into ordered and relatively stable patterns of interaction? These are some of the questions that we shall consider in this chapter as we look at social organization as both process and entity. Our concerns here will focus on some of the general principles of social organization, as well as on the general relationship of personality to social organization. ▲

## Outline

▶ A fundamental feature of human social life is that the actions of individuals are relatively patterned, recurrent, and predictable. Imagine, for a moment, the amazing flow of social interaction that occurs as a daily phenomenon on the part of millions of people in any city or metropolitan area. Large numbers of individuals, many of whom are strangers to each other, are able to interact for the purpose of obtaining a wide variety of goals. Every day, billions of times every day, smooth and productive interactions occur among salespeople and customers, physicians and patients, and students and teachers. People who have never met before will exhibit similar and complementary behavior in a wide variety of social settings. Human social life, in short, is characterized by a great deal of organization. So common is social organization that we tend to notice it only when it is absent—despite the fact that social organization among human beings is learned and not the product of any innate capabilities, as is the case with other species. Exploring the nature and principles of social organization will tell us much about the character of human activity and the many forms that it assumes.

# The Nature of Social Organization

The concept of social organization refers to the network of relatively stable, structured, and recurrent patterns of behavior that occur among people. It denotes actions that are coordinated and interdependent as opposed to those that are random and isolated. The notion of social organization also implies that the regularized and recurrent patterns of action are relatively resistant to change. There will be a tendency for the action patterns to persist. Such a situation does not mean that altered patterns of action cannot or do not emerge; it simply means that there is a higher probability that they will continue rather than change sharply.

The concept of social organization enables sociologists to understand, and even to predict, certain types of behavior without requiring any knowledge of the particular characteristics of the individuals enacting the behavior. If the norms that constitute the organization of a particular group or other subunits are known, then much of the behavior of the people belonging to those subunits can be understood without any other knowledge of the individuals. It is relatively easy, for instance, to predict the behavior of people attending a funeral, students attending classes, cooks and waiters working in a restaurant, or workers interacting in a factory, without being aware of, for instance, the psychological or biological characteristics they possess. Of course, this knowledge is only partial, but still quite satisfactory for predicting behavior in the many situations of social interaction that occur nearly continuously in everyone's daily life.

## EMERGENCE OF SOCIAL ORGANIZATION

Social organization is made possible by the inherent state of "mutual dependency" or "interdependence" which—as we saw in Chapter 4 in our discussion of social deprivation—characterizes human nature. As such, social organization is both an emergent process and a product of social interaction. Social organization emerges either as the aggregate result of the diverse acts of individuals, each pursuing his or her own ends, or it may result from the joint endeavors of individuals pursuing commonly accepted ends. This distinction is sometimes made technically in speaking of "crescive" and "enacted" social organization (see Blau, 1968).

**Crescive social organization** develops spontaneously as a product of relationships that reoccur among people over prolonged periods of time, and as the modes and forms of their

▼

**229**

▼

social interactions become habitual and relatively stable. This form of social organization is exemplified by a friendship group or a gang.

**Enacted social organization** emerges as the result of deliberately and formally planned action, as in the case of a community hospital or the United Nations. These distinctions are typically analytical, since both types of social organization usually converge in the emergence of their actual dynamics. Either type of social organization, however, can be distinguished in a number of respects, since not all social interaction possesses the same kind or degree of social structure.

**230**

## RELATIONSHIPS BETWEEN SOCIAL ORGANIZATION AND CULTURE

Culture essentially distinguishes the social organization of human beings from that of other creatures. Social animals and insects, like baboons and bees, have forms of social organization (for example, division of labor, mutual independence, interaction, and predictable patterns of behavior), but they do not have culture. Culture is learned. The patterns of recurrent behavior that social insects and animals manifest, however, are the result of a form of inborn genetic programming. Such patterns of behavior are not subject to change and have remained the same for thousands of years. The structured lines of action that are characteristic of human societies, in contrast, are the product of social learning and are subject to varying degrees of change. This distinction gives humans a great advantage over other social species because human behavioral patterns can change in response to environmental changes. Such changes enable humans to adapt effectively to different types of environments.

Culture refers to an interrelated complex of knowledge, beliefs, values, norms, and other types of information that are distinctive of a given people. While fundamental in any attempt to understand human behavior, culture does not denote relationships that exist among people. Rather, culture can best be viewed as an ideal or blueprint that provides guidelines for behavior. Culture, then, furnishes the informational elements that make social organization and orderly action possible. No form of social organization would be possible without the members of a society having first internalized—to some extent, at least—the normative or expected patterns that make social organization possible.

It is necessary to make a distinction between two different, but related, aspects of social organization: the normative and the behavioral. The normative aspect refers to the norms that indicate how people are expected to act in various situations. For example, norms that constitute the social organization of the classroom specify the type of attire students should wear, what they should do when they want to make a comment or ask a question, and how they should conduct themselves during an examination. The behavioral aspect of social organization consists in the actual behavior of the students in the classroom. The classroom conduct of the students will never correspond perfectly to the idealized pattern of behavior that is represented by the normative dimensions of social structure. Some students will not adhere to the school's dress code in every detail, others may shout out a question or comment instead of waiting to be called on by the teacher, still others may let their eyes wander to the neighbor's paper during the course of an exam. In general, however, the behavioral dimension of social organization corresponds closely enough to the normative pattern so that the behavior of students and teachers is relatively stable, orderly, and predictable.

The relation between the normative and the behavioral aspects of social organization has been described well by one sociologist when he states that "the blueprint for action provided by culture has been translated into concrete social relations, and in the process the character of the expected behavior has changed somewhat." He goes on to note that "nevertheless, the expected behavior patterns are still there in acceptable though altered forms. That behavior which has not been accepted is also present, but in the form of disorganization" (Bertrand, 1971:8). In our classroom example, social disorganization would occur if a significant number of students behaved in ways that are completely incompatible with the norms that indicate proper classroom behavior. For instance, if students came to class wearing bathing suits, or always spoke while the instructor was speaking, or repeatedly looked at each other's exams, there would be a state of social disorganization in the classroom.

## NECESSITY OF SOCIAL ORGANIZATION

Social organization enables people to perform a wide range of tasks and to achieve many diverse goals with a maximum degree of efficiency. Just think for a moment how inefficient (and problematic) it would be if everyone had to deliberate for long periods of time in order to know how to behave with salespeople, teachers, employers, physicians, landlords, and others with whom we must interact. Quite to the contrary, the majority of human interactions are performed in an orderly and highly routine fashion. Before coming to class, students know that they will be expected to seat themselves, to pay attention to the instructor, to refrain from talking among themselves, to take notes, to ask questions, and to leave when the class period is over. Similarly, instructors expect students to behave in such a manner and would become very upset if they did not. Instructors also realize that their students, as well as the administration, will expect them to give a lecture or to lead a discussion, to require that students read certain books, to construct ex-

aminations, and to give each student a grade for the course. If students and instructors did not share similar understandings of their own and each other's behavior, the goal of the school—the education of students—would be difficult to attain. Most of the class period would be devoted to determining how everyone should behave. Thus, because the school class has an established social organization consisting of a set of social positions and interrelated norms which people have learned through the socialization process, class time can be used purely for its intended educational purposes.

Some people tend to perceive social organization as something that inhibits an individual's freedom and creativity. They compare human beings with puppets on a string that are constantly being manipulated. In the case of real puppets, the manipulation is being done by a human being. In the case of human beings, the manipulation is being done by cultural and social forces over which individuals allegedly have no control. Worse still, it is argued, human beings do not even realize how often their behavior is determined by social organization, culture, and other related forces.

Such a view of social organization is based on erroneous conceptions of social organization. The concept of social organization does not imply that human action is rigidly determined by cultural and social forces. Nor does it mean that a particular pattern of social organization, once established, is impervious to alteration or even to complete dissolution. Rather, social organization should be seen as merely furnishing general guidelines for action. It does not *determine* people's behavior. All actual behavior involves varying amounts of creativity on the part of the actor. Furthermore, the notion of social organization is not incompatible with a conception of people as creative and innovative beings. Human beings, of course, are very much affected by social organization (which they create), but they also interpret, modify, and replace particular modes or forms

▼

▼ of social organization. Moreover, such a deterministic view overlooks the fact that social organization saves much time, and allows individuals to use the time saved to engage more effectively in creative work. Thus, in a very important sense, social organization gives people more, rather than less, control over their lives; and they become free to engage in pursuits that interest them and provide them with satisfaction.

**232**     One of the first steps toward the explanation of social organization consists of the establishment of a common set of conceptual tools to demonstrate the elements of social organization. Once formulated, these concepts may be used to analyze a variety of different types of social organization. Fundamental, in this regard, has been the concept of social system. In order to grasp the significance of this basic concept, however, it is first necessary to explore the nature of the concept of system—the basic concept for nearly all sophisticated theories in any field of scientific explanation.

## The Concept of System

The concept of system has proven to be an extremely valuable analytical tool for many different disciplines. Such fields as physics, chemistry, biology, economics, engineering, and psychology all use the concept of system. What has become known as "general system theory" (see Bertalanffy, 1968; Berrien, 1968) provides a common conceptual and theoretical framework that can be used to integrate the different sciences. The principles of system theory are used quite extensively in the field of sociology, and have been incorporated into many of its major theoretical approaches.

A **system** is simply a plurality of parts that function as a unit, with the implication that the whole is, in a certain sense, more than the mere sum of its parts. Any system, then, implies the notions of differentiation, interdependence, and unity.

Two or more elements (parts or processes) interacting with each other in a patterned or structured and recurrent fashion constitute a system. The elements are interdependent with one another such that a change in one of the units is apt to affect one or more of the other units as well as the system as a whole. Any system is goal-directed, usually in terms of attaining long-range objectives.

Systems function by means of energy, matter, or information absorbed from their environment. Correspondingly, in the course of functioning, certain outputs and wastes are expelled from a system into its environment, which includes other systems or features of the physical environment within which the system is situated. Outputs of one system, consisting of products, services, or behavior, may become inputs of another (see Figure 6-1).

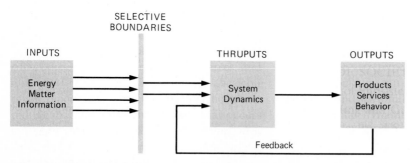

FIGURE 6-1   System Dynamics.

These same principles apply to subsystems which are simply functional or structural subunits of any system, but which retain all the characteristics of a system. Subsystems, then, are only "sub" by being thought of as a part of a larger system; otherwise, they too constitute, and can be treated as, systems. However, the greater the number of specialized subsystems, usually the more dependent is a subsystem on the superordinate system.

System analysis, which is essentially quite abstract in nature, is concerned basically with what goes into a system (inputs), what happens when it gets there (thruputs), and what comes out of the system (outputs). The notion of system, of course, as used in science, is an assumption that the phenomena in question are, indeed, organized and integrated. They may, in truth, exist chaotically. Without such an assumption, however, theoretical or scientific explanations would not be possible. Only mere descriptions could be offered. Let us now discuss several of the essential characteristics that comprise a system.

## STRUCTURE AND CONTENT OF SYSTEMS

All systems consist of two fundamental aspects: content and structure. **Systemic content** denotes the specific units or elements which constitute a system and which account for its "material" composition. The content of a biological system includes tissue, bones, muscles, organs, and several other elements. **Systemic structure** of a system refers to the coordinated arrangement or relationships that exist among the components of a system.

Systemic structure refers to the integrative dimension that unites all content elements into more or less organized and interactive patterns of relationship. Structure refers more specifically to the quality of this unification: the degree of complexity and cohesiveness in the system. Systemic structure includes such analytical dimensions or elements as stratification, centralization or isolation, integration or diffusion, complexity or simplicity, and homogeneity or heterogeneity.

The distinction between these two fundamental components—systemic content and systemic structure—has been described and illustrated by DiRenzo (1974a: 17) in his analogy of a timepiece:

> The gears, jewels, and hands constitute content elements; the coordination and organization of these parts constitute structure. The interconnection of the parts and structure, when provided with energy (a tensioned spring), produces the movement or action of the watch or clock; but its more or less efficient function, that is, the degree to which it keeps fast, slow, or accurate time, stems from the quality of the interconnections, that is, from the "goodness of fit" among the individual elements and between the two systemic components.

It is the patterned relationships that exist among the units of a system that make it a system. What makes a timepiece a timepiece, an automobile an automobile, or a human organism a human organism is the way its parts are related to one another. If you disassemble a wristwatch and place the stem, jewels, springs, handpieces, and other components on a table, you would no longer have a wristwatch, but merely a mass of individual parts. With a physical phenomenon, such as a timepiece, this point is rather clear. Less obvious is the systemic nature of social phenomena, such as that represented by society and groups.

## OPEN AND CLOSED SYSTEMS

Systems can be conceptualized as being either open or closed (Scott, 1987). An **open system** is one that engages in active interchange (input-output relations) with other systems or with aspects of its environment. (The dependence of the organism on its physical environment for nutrition and respiration is illustrative of an

233

▼

open system.) A **closed system,** on the other hand, does not have connection to its environment, nor does it engage in exchange relations with it.

The boundaries of open systems are permeable, which allows them both to influence and be influenced by their environments (see Figure 6-2). Open systems may be said to interpenetrate one another. Depending on its specific nature, an open system may exchange such things as information, energy, products, or services with other systems that are adjacent to it or with another aspect of its environment.

The distinction between open and closed systems is a matter of degree, and one that is made primarily in terms of self-sufficiency. The biological system is a relatively closed system, despite its dependence on the environment for food and oxygen. A social system, on the other hand, is usually an inherently open system—one engaged in a process of active interchange (input-output relations) with its environment, as well as one characterized by active interchanges among its internal units or subsystems.

234

## SYSTEM BOUNDARIES

All systems, by definition, have some sort of boundaries which separate them from other systems as well as from other features of their environment. If systems did not have boundaries, it would not be possible to distinguish one system from another. The boundaries of open systems are permeable, enabling them to exchange things with their environment.

Systems have a tendency to keep their boundaries intact, although under certain conditions the boundaries may break up and the system may become part of a larger one. As a consequence, the system will lose its identity and its distinctiveness. An example of this situation can be had when two classes are combined into one. Each of them, as a result of the amalgamation, loses its distinctive identity. The same thing occurs when one corporation takes over, or merges with, another.

The boundaries of a system also function to regulate the rate of inputs going into the system and the outputs exiting the system. If too many

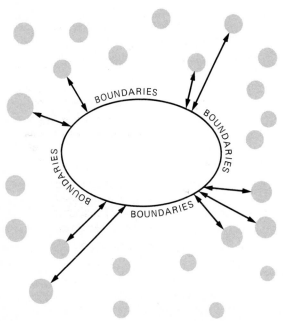

FIGURE 6-2 A System and Its Environment. An open system maintains active relationships with other systems in its environment.

inputs are allowed to enter the system, the system may not be able to process them and may thereby become overwhelmed. If too few inputs enter the system, it would not have the "raw materials" it needs to function adequately.

# DYNAMIC EQUILIBRIUM

Units that comprise a system have a tendency to maintain the relationship that they have with one another. This feature of systems is called **dynamic equilibrium.** The concept of dynamic equilibrium does not mean that a system stands still or that nothing happens within it. On the contrary, in order to maintain itself as an ongoing concern, a system is continuously engaged in activities that are aimed at keeping it in a steadily operating state. These activities involve processes and exchanges that occur both within the system and between the system and its environment. Dynamic equilibrium, then, essentially involves maintaining a functional balance between inputs and outputs.

An example can be had in viewing the human body as a complex biological system. Normal temperature of 98.6°F must be maintained if the body is to function effectively. When the environmental temperature is 100°F or more, the sweat glands of the body will be activated, and, as the sweat evaporates, the body will be cooled. In addition, other processes become triggered which have the consequence of cooling the body. Blood vessels that lie close to the skin become dilated so that the blood can give off its heat; people become thirsty and drink more liquids to replace the fluids that are lost via evaporation. Correspondingly, when the environmental temperature drops significantly, other processes and mechanisms become triggered which serve to conserve the body's heat. Blood vessels constrict and shivering occurs, both of which have the effect of conserving or increasing body temperature. Thus, in order to maintain itself in a functionally balanced and steadily operating state, dynamic processes and mechanisms must be continuously at work within the system.

There is nothing about the concept of a system or dynamic equilibrium which implies that any given system must be, or always will be, totally successful in maintaining itself in a steady state. Whether a system is able to maintain itself as an ongoing concern is an empirical question. Environmental strain is particularly problematic. Hence, if a person were to be marooned in a snowstorm for a long period of time without sufficient shelter and clothes, any attempt of the body to maintain itself in a state of equilibrium within such an environment may prove to be so inadequate that death results. Human interactional systems, however, may dissolve without the people who comprise them experiencing a physical death. What dissolves is the pattern of ongoing, structured relations that occur among the individuals. This is exactly what happens when a wife and husband separate or divorce, or when a corporation goes bankrupt.

Not only may social systems, cease to exist; they may also experience considerable change while continuing to operate. Change, thus, can occur within the process of dynamic equilibrium. Such a situation is reflected in the aging process of organic systems. Hence, it is important to understand that dynamic equilibrium does not preclude change. Moreover, change, as we shall see, may be required by dynamic equilibrium.

# REGULATORY MECHANISMS

In order for a system both to maintain itself in a balanced state and to know whether it is achieving its goals, it must be continuously fed back information from its constituent parts as well as from the environment. **Feedback** consists of that part of the informational output being produced by a system which is sent back into the system in order to motivate and to guide its component parts and processes. Units of a system that are in contact with other units

235

▼

**Functional Balance.** Social systems, like biological and physiological systems, require inputs which, when processed, serve to maintain the system in a state of dynamic equilibrium. (Lorraine Rorke/Image Works)

and with the environment of the system feed back or relay data about the state and efficiency of the system to other units. These feedback or **regulatory mechanisms** enable the system to know whether it is on the right course, whether its units are working effectively, or whether corrections should be made in its activities. Unless a system obtains adequate feedback enabling it to know whether its activities are having the desired effect, it may fail to achieve its goals or, even worse, cease to exist as an ongoing system.

The human biological system has numerous feedback mechanisms which serve to regulate bodily processes and functions. Among these are the pulse rate, blood pressure, and a host of other physiological reactions. With respect to human social interaction systems, such as a school class, feedback mechanisms are also present. It is important that the teacher receive feedback from students so that he or she will

know whether they understand the lectures. If the teacher perceives students making uncomplimentary facial expressions, squirming in their seats, looking at their wristwatches, or talking among themselves, he had better make changes in his style if he wishes to capture their attention and interest. On the other hand, if students ask questions, make comments, and maintain visual contact with the teacher, he should maintain his style since such behavior constitutes positive feedback, indicating that the system is functioning properly and adequately.

## FUNCTIONAL DIFFERENTIATION

Units that comprise a system are characterized by **functional differentiation.** This situation means that each unit performs specialized tasks.

There is, so to speak, a division of labor among the units. In biological and mechanical systems in particular, the structure of each unit is such that it enables the unit to perform a specialized function. For example, the heart, being muscle, is able to pump blood throughout the body. Similarly, the kidneys are structured so as to be capable of filtering out toxins. With regard to human social systems of interaction, individuals who are members of groups or organizations usually have specialized tasks that they perform. Every social system, thus, is characterized by a division of labor (see Alexander & Colomy, 1990).

Up to this point we have been discussing the essential features that comprise any type of system. All of this discussion, as such, has been preliminary for our major concern—social systems. Let us look now at how these various characteristics and essential features of systems apply, more particularly, to social systems.

## Social Systems

Social systems have all of the fundamental characteristics of any system and are distinguished by the properties of the particular phenomenon to which they relate—social interaction. All social systems are systems of interaction. Their chief input is information; their chief output is behavior.

A **social system** refers to the total configuration of established patterns of social activity which are proper to a given number of people functioning interdependently as a unit. Two or more individuals who, guided by shared norms or expectations, interact in patterned or structured ways in pursuit of a common goal constitute a social system. The analytical focus, of course, is on the recurrent patterns of behavior that occur among the individuals and not the individuals themselves. Accordingly, the primary units of any social system are not people but, rather, the interrelated set of social positions and social roles that structure their actions.

Social systems can involve any number of individuals. Two people interacting over a period of time who share certain norms, expectations, and goals constitute a social system. By the same token, American society or Chinese society, each with hundreds of millions of people, can also be viewed as a social system. In between these extremes are such entities as groups, communities, and complex organizations or bureaucracies, which can also be viewed as social systems. Examples of particular types of social systems would be two marriage

237

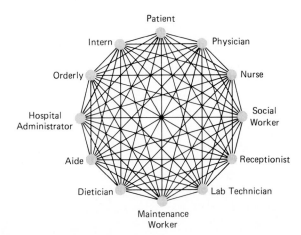

FIGURE 6-3 The Hospital as a Social System. A social system consists of a plurality of individuals, interacting in their reciprocal status-role distinctions, in pursuit of a common goal.

▼ partners, a school class, a factory, a neighborhood, a major industrial corporation, a city, the nation of India, and even the United Nations. Each of these social entities can be conceptualized as a social system because they essentially involve a plurality of individuals interacting in a patterned manner in terms of shared norms, understandings, and goals. Of course, the degree to which all of the individuals involved share these elements may vary considerably.

238

Social systems, then, come in all shapes and sizes. The smallest social system, consisting of two people, is known technically as a *dyad*. One with three people is a *triad*. Otherwise a social system with a small number of people is called a *group*. Social systems much larger in size are known as *formal or complex organizations*. The largest social system is that of *society*. Each of these forms of social organization, as depicted in Figure 6-4, can be thought of as being embedded, or nesting, within the progressively larger and more complex type of social system.

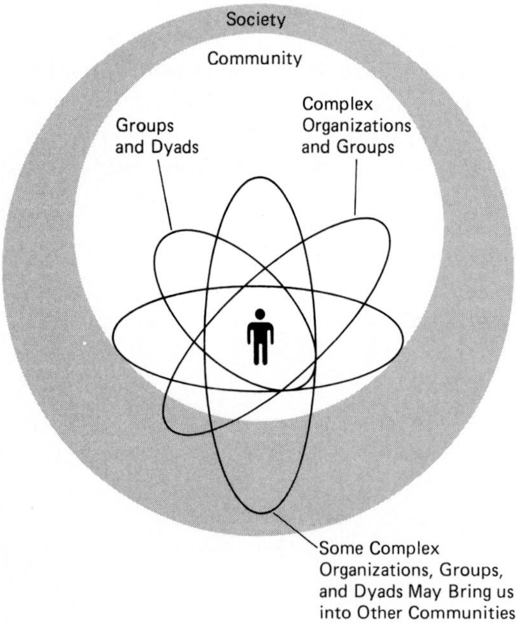

Social dynamics are quite different in each of these forms of social organization. An adequate understanding of all of these different kinds of social systems is indispensable for comprehending the highly complex nature of human social behavior. Apart from their size, social systems differ in terms of their objectives, degrees of self-sufficiency, kinds of relationships, the complexity of social organization, and a number of other dimensions. In this chapter we shall look at the common features and basic principles of all kinds of social systems—from intimate dyads to intricate societies. Subsequent chapters in this section will be devoted to an elaboration of the specific features and particular dynamics of each of the principal types of social systems.

A social system, consistent with any type of system, has two fundamental dimensions: social content and social structure. **Social content,** analogous to culture, consists of the established beliefs, knowledge, values, norms, and roles that comprise the elements of social organization. **Social structure** consists of the integral arrangement or configuration, within a social system, of all interrelationships involving the various elements of social content.

## STRUCTURAL-FUNCTIONAL ANALYSIS

All elements and processes of any system have consequences for the system. Similarly, all phenomena that comprise any given social system have consequences for that system. Such is the case, for instance, when one speaks of the consequences of an ideology, or a set of values, or the goals of a society, or the effects of laws on a corporation or community.

The essence of the structural-functional analysis of social systems is to determine the effects or consequences that a particular organizational element or mechanism (for example, po-

FIGURE 6-4 The Social Individual Imbedded Within the Nest of Social Systems.

TABLE 6-1. Classification of Consequences of Social Mechanisms ▼

| | Consequences That Foster Goal Attainment | Consequences That Impede Goal Attainment |
|---|---|---|
| Intended or recognized consequences | Manifest functions | Manifest dysfunctions |
| Unintended or unrecognized consequences | Latent functions | Latent dysfunctions |

sition, norm, belief, value, process, policy, or action) has on the functioning of the system. To assess the consequences of a given mechanism is to identify its relation to other elements of the system, and, more specifically, to determine the actual contributions that it makes to the system as concerns the attainment of its goals or its ability to cope with one or more of its four functional requisites. Consequences of any given social mechanism can be specified in terms of being positive or negative—in more technical terminology, as functional or dysfunctional (see Table 6-1).

FUNCTIONS AND DYSFUNCTIONS. **Functions,** sometimes referred to as eufunctions, consist of mechanisms that have the effect of promoting the operation and survival of the social system. The incest taboo would be said to be functional, or eufunctional, insofar as this norm works to maintain the integrity and cohesion of the family, as well as promoting societal integration. **Dysfunctions** refer to social mechanisms that produce consequences which have the effect of impeding the functioning of the system and the attainment of its goals. Values such as are found in countercultures, which work against the dominant or core culture of a society, may be said to be dysfunctional in that they inhibit integration and may, indeed, promote social deviance. One such example is reflected by those individuals whose primary value and objective is to "beat the system."

No mechanism is clearly functional or dysfunctional. Invariably, any element of a system simultaneously produces both functional and dysfunctional consequences. The important question for functional analysis, therefore, is to determine which type of consequence outweighs the other. It is in this respect that the functional value of a given mechanism can be determined.

MANIFEST AND LATENT FUNCTIONS. In functional analysis it is necessary to distinguish between the intended purposes and the actual consequences of social mechanisms. Purpose and consequence do not always coincide. Whatever is intended is often not achieved—or only partially achieved. Unintended results are frequently obtained; and some of these may be functional, others dysfunctional. That such is the case can be seen in a situation in which laws that are intended to regulate and control prostitution may actually cause this practice to become more widespread, with a potential increase of other types of associated crimes. Such distinctions between purposes and consequences of social mechanisms are made by speaking of functions and dysfunctions as being either manifest or latent.

**Manifest functions** comprise those consequences of social mechanisms that are intended and recognized by participants in the system. Manifest functions are identical to the purpose or objectives of social mechanisms. The intended purpose or manifest function of granting tenure (lifetime job security) to teachers and professors is to ensure their right to academic freedom without fear of reprisal. **Latent**

239

▼

**240**

**functions,** on the other hand, refer to those consequences that are neither intended nor recognized. A law that is designed to regulate prostitution by requiring prostitutes to be licensed may have the initially unintended and unrecognized effect of realizing a considerable sum of money through the mandatory fees that are collected. Such revenue, however relatively insignificant, would certainly be a positive contribution in meeting the administrative cost of managing and operating a local government. Hence, it would constitute a latent function.

*Manifest dysfunctions,* while obviously not intended, are clearly recognized and anticipated by the participants in a social system, and usually tolerated only insofar as the corresponding manifest functions of a given mechanism sufficiently outweigh their negative consequences. Everyone in the academic world recognizes that academic tenure also has the unintended consequence that some people, enjoying economic security, may cease to be academically dynamic or productive in any significant sense. Such a consequence constitutes a manifest dysfunction. The most troublesome type of social consequences consist of *latent dysfunctions.* Herein resides the most significantly potential contribution of functional analysis. Latent dysfunctions refer to negative consequences that are neither intended nor recognized by the participants in the social system. Again, it is conceivable that a law to control certain types of crime might actually bring about an increase in other forms of deviant behavior. Latent dysfunctions can work so extensively, and ever so silently, that they overwhelm whatever functions—both manifest or latent—that a particular social mechanism may yield.

STRUCTURAL ALTERNATIVES AND FUNCTIONAL EQUIVALENTS. These distinctions between functions and dysfunctions, as well as those between manifest and latent consequences, permit us to understand the significance of structural alternatives and functional equivalents. **Structural alternatives** refer to different mechanisms that have the same purpose and, thus, are intended to achieve the same objective. Prostitution, for example, can be regulated in a number of different ways. Confining prostitutes to specified areas of a city— the so-called Napoleon plan, as tried years ago in France—may be considered an alternative mechanism to that of simple licensing. The two mechanisms, however, are not necessarily **functional equivalents.** Each mechanism produces a totally different set of functions and dysfunctions, at both the manifest and latent levels. Hence, given the totality of its consequences, the net effect of one mechanism may be more or less functional than another.

The academic year of colleges and universities can be organized either in terms of semesters, trimesters, or quarterly periods, among other possibilities. Each of these mechanisms or structural arrangements is not necessarily functionally equivalent to the others. While each mechanism may be comparable in terms of manifest functions, their latent consequences, both functional and dysfunctional, could easily make one superior or inferior to the other in terms of the intended purpose of the system and other positive contributions to it. Similarly, a society may institute a monarchy or a republic, among other possibilities, as its form of government. While these different governmental forms may be considered as structural alternatives, they are not necessarily functional equivalents. We shall say more about this question of structural alternatives in Chapter 7 when discussing variations in societal institutions.

## FUNCTIONAL REQUISITES

For any social system to exist as an ongoing concern it must deal with certain functional requisites. **Functional requisites** consist of those essential conditions which concern the structures and processes for developing and maintaining dynamic equilibrium. These conditions, as described by Parsons (1951), constitute four basic needs of any social system: adaptation (to the external environment); goal attainment; integration (of various parts of the system); and latent pattern maintenance (dealing with conformity to and deviation from established standards). Together this set of needs is referred to as the **AGIL paradigm** (see Table 6-2). (AGIL is an acronym for *a*daption; *g*oal attainment, *i*ntegration, and *l*atent pattern maintenance and is pronouned "agile.")

*Adaptation*, an externally instrumental task, refers to the functional requisite of a social system to relate effectively to its external environment. Social systems normally do not and cannot exist in isolation. They engage, rather, in a variety of transactions with other social systems, many of which provide resources which enable the system to function in the attainment of its goals. A university, for example, purchases many items essential for its existence from corporations: books, furniture, writing supplies, research equipment, and so forth. It may receive a contract from a governmental agency to do research and, if it is state-funded, has to deal with the state legislature. The corporations it does business with, the governmental agency that it does research for, and the state legislature from which it obtains funds can be seen as other social systems which, in part, constitute the environment of the university.

In order to continue to function adequately, social systems must be able to adapt to changes which occur in its environment. If a company

TABLE 6-2. Functional Requisites of Social Systems

| Locus | Instrumental | Expressive |
|-------|-------------|------------|
| External | Adaptation | Goal attainment |
| Internal | Integration | Latent pattern maintenance |

from which the university purchases research equipment is on strike, it must either find another supplier that can fill its needs or else make do with its existing supplies. Similarly, if the state legislature votes to cut the amount of money it allocates to the university, the university must make the necessary changes which will enable it to function with less money. Social systems that have a good adaptive capacity are able to cope with both internal and external threats to their existence. Change, thus, is a necessary dynamic of social systems.

*Goal attainment*, an externally expressive task, refers to the functional requisite of achieving the intended goal of a system. All social systems exist in order to attain a particular goal or set of goals. It is the collective goal of the social system, and not the personal goals for which its members may participate, that is the focus here. The organization of all necessary activities, and the design of suitable mechanisms so that its members can work together to achieve the collective aims, comprise the functional requisite of goal attainment. The university, for example, exists in order to transmit the store of cultural knowledge to students, to train people for certain professions, to provide scholars with resources to pursue research, and to make contributions to the community within which it is located. Not all of these goals can be given equal priority because the resources needed to attain them are limited. Thus, some universities give priority to research while others emphasize the goal of teaching.

Other social systems such as corporations, prisons, and hospitals also have specific goals which provide the rationale for their existence. The goal of corporations is to produce goods or provide services at a profit; prisons have the goal of both separating certain people from society and rehabilitating them; hospitals are concerned with making sick people well.

The relationships that exist among members of a social system, as well as the activities that they engage in, are structured so as to enable

▼

**241**

▼

**Organizational Objectives.** That social systems exist to achieve certain goals, and thereby fulfill a functional requisite, can be seen readily in the collective objective of any sports team to win its contests. (Parisport/SYGMA)

the system to attain their collective goal. The structured relationships among members and the activities they perform are geared to enable the system to attain its ends. In many cases, however, relationships and activities may emerge which do not help the system attain its goal. Indeed, they may even have the effect of impeding goal attainment. Why and how this occurs will be discussed in subsequent chapters.

*Integration*, an internally instrumental task, refers to the functional requisite of coordinating and linking the units of the system with one another so that the system operates harmoniously. Social systems that have many specialized units face a greater integrative problem than those that have fewer specialized units. The social system of a university, for example, has a greater integration problem than the social system of an elementary school. There are specialized schools, academic departments, li-

braries, research institutes, and many other groups within a university. All of them must coordinate their policies and actions so that the university as a whole can operate effectively and be successful in attaining its goal. One function of a university administration, in addition to setting broad policies and seeing that they are carried out, is to coordinate the many specialized units that comprise the university.

Integration, as the bottom line, also relates to the functional need for cohesion and solidarity among the members of a social system. No social system is ever perfectly integrated. There are always strains, conflicts, disagreements, and frictions that interfere with the smooth functioning of any system. These occur, in part, because the socialization of individuals into the normative patterns of the social system is never complete. Sometimes, for instance, the personal goals of individuals will be incompatible with those of the social system. In addition, the personality predispositions and needs of some members of the social system may be in conflict with the demands of their roles.

Specialized units usually exist within social systems to deal with integrative problems. Universities, for example, have academic review boards whose purpose is to resolve conflicts that may develop between students and faculty. If a student were to accuse a professor of administering a low grade because the professor is prejudiced against students of a particular race or religion, the academic review board would hear both sides and try to resolve the conflict. Similarly, deans of colleges help to settle disputes that may arise both among faculty or between faculty and department chairpersons.

On the societal level, the judicial system can be viewed as a unit whose primary function is to resolve many types of problems and disputes that develop. Courts deal with a wide range of conflicts—from disagreements arising between two individuals to disputes involving corporations and governments. Without a judicial system, it is, indeed, difficult to imagine how any degree of stability or cohesiveness could be maintained within a complex society.

The integrative units and mechanisms of a social system could never prevent or completely resolve all of the problems and conflicts that emerge within social systems. They can be viewed as being successful, however, to the extent that they are able to keep conflicts from totally or significantly disrupting the operation of the social system.

*Latent pattern maintenance*, an internally expressive task, refers to the functional requisite of having the members of a social system learn and behave in accordance with the values and norms that constitute the system. Members must acquire, and preferably internalize, the values, norms, expectations, and other cultural elements of the social system. This goal is achieved through various types of socialization processes. Societies, for example, have specialized agencies, such as the family and the school, whose primary function is to transmit to newcomers the values, norms, and other shared understandings that comprise the society's culture. Smaller-scale social systems such as armies, schools, and corporations must also convey to their members particular sets of values, rules, and ways of looking at the world if they are to operate effectively. Armies try to indoctrinate recruits into a set of beliefs and norms which, if internalized, will turn the recruit into an effective soldier. Similarly, freshman college students are subjected to orientation sessions whose purpose is to teach them what their professors will expect of them and how they should conduct themselves as students. By the same token, new employees are processed through training programs which convey the company's philosophy, policies, and expectations.

The purpose of all of these practices is to have the individual members learn, adapt, and behave in accordance with the normative structure of the social system. The ideal objective is to have the values and goals of the social system become those of the individuals involved. All social systems, in this respect, make use of various mechanisms for developing and maintaining loyalty. Equally relevant to fulfilling the requisite of latent pattern maintenance are the development and utilization of various mechanisms of social control that deal with individuals and behavior that deviate from the expected standards.

These four functional requisites can never be permanently or completely fulfilled; rather, they are dealt with continuously to varying degrees of success. Failure to deal with them to a certain minimal extent will result in the dissolution of the system—the system will not be able to maintain its distinct identity and to operate as an ongoing concern. Moreover, the four functional requisites only speak to *what* must be done. *How* it is done is another question. The manner in which the needs are met involves considerable diversity, and this characteristic is

▼ reflected in the extensive variability of culture (see Chapter 3), which constitutes the composite response or solution to these functional needs in the case of society, as one type of social organization.

# Elements of Social Organization

**244** The basic elements of social organization consist of social positions, which may be described as locations in social space. These elements constitute the fundamental building blocks of all types and levels of social organization.

## SOCIAL POSITION: STATUS AND ROLE

Social positions, the most irreducible units of social organization, consist of two analytical aspects: social status and social role. These two elements refer, respectively, to the static and dynamic dimensions of social organization.

SOCIAL STATUS. A **social status** is a specific, socially designated or identifiable position within a system of social relationships. Examples of statuses would be the social positions of professor, student, salesperson, President of the United States, mother, son, senior citizen, detective, and even that of a sick person.

Sociologists distinguish between ascribed and achieved statuses. An **ascribed status** is a social position that is accorded an individual through no efforts on his or her own part; it is usually the result of birth, inheritance, or circumstances beyond one's control. The status of female, or Black, or prince, or senior citizen are examples of ascribed statuses. An **achieved status** refers to a social position that one holds by virtue of his or her own choice or efforts. Simple examples are those of physician, football player, husband, and actress.

Statuses within any social organization are invariably arranged in a **status hierarchy** on the basis of prestige and power, as can be simply illustrated in the organizational chart of any corporation. This structural aspect of social organization is of considerable importance in that it constitutes the ordering of social interaction and provides the basis of various kinds of social dynamics within all social organizations. We shall devote our exclusive attention to social stratification in Chapter 10.

SOCIAL ROLE. A **social role** refers to a set of interrelated norms which indicate how individuals occupying a particular position—in a given social organization—are expected to act. Roles, as the dynamic component of social position, refer to the behavior, prescribed and proscribed, that is ideally expected of an individual while occupying a given social status or social position. A social role, then, is a set of behavioral norms or expectations associated with a given status. The role norms attached to a status also specify the rights and obligations or duties incumbent upon people occupying a particular status. Thus, an individual with the status of professor has the right to require students to attend class, to do assignments, and to take examinations. Correspondingly, a professor is obligated, and legitimately expected, to prepare lectures, to meet classes, to answer student questions, and to provide final grades.

As these examples attempt to show, social status and social role are correlative or reciprocal concepts. Every status implies a role; and, similarly, there can be no role without a corresponding status. So interrelated are status and role that these concepts are often used interchangeably—although technically this is incorrect. It is helpful to distinguish between these two aspects of a social position by keeping in mind that people occupy statuses but play roles.

RECIPROCITY OF STATUSES AND ROLES. No status exists independent of other statuses. By the same token, it is impossible to define roles as a set of expectations—

rights and obligations—without reference to another role or set of roles. There cannot be the role of a parent without that of a child, or of an employee without an employer. In this respect, roles or, more technically, social positions consist of a series of rights and obligations; they represent certain reciprocal relationships among individuals. This situation calls for a definition of rights and obligations. A right is a privilege that one can expect from another, who has a corresponding duty to permit the right to be fulfilled. One person's right is another person's obligation and vice versa. There are no rights without corresponding obligations; there are no obligations without corresponding rights.

ROLE BEHAVIOR.    It is important to make a distinction between the idealized conception of a role and an actual role performance. The concept of role refers to how a majority of people believe or expect that a status should be activated. As such, a role consists of normative prescriptions and proscriptions—what a status occupant must and must not do. **Role behavior,** on the other hand, denotes the actual behavior of a person enacting a particular role. Roles are normative and universal, while role behavior is concrete and personal. There is never a perfect match of the two. For a multiplicity of reasons role behavior invariably differs from the idealized expectations that people have as to how a given role should be enacted.

Role expectations seldom specify in great detail precisely how a particular role should be enacted. Rather, role expectations indicate an acceptable range of behavior for occupants of a given status. The actual behavior of all status occupants, therefore, is likely to vary in one respect or another as each individual interprets and performs the corresponding role, and insofar as the role permits idiosyncratic action. A professor, for example, has much leeway in performing his or her role. The norms associated with this position do not specify how one should dress, which books (if any) one should

"Can I call you back? Jim and I are struggling with our roles."

Drawing by Koren; © 1983 The New Yorker Magazine, Inc.

require students to purchase and to read, whether one should use a lecture or discussion format when conducting a class, and so forth. The role expectations linked to the position of a soldier, on the other hand, are quite specific and detailed. The occupant of the status of soldier has little leeway in determining how he should enact the corresponding role. A soldier must dress, speak, and behave in a strictly prescribed manner.

Not all behavior for a given role, moreover, is specified. Much must be made up as we go along, particularly as one encounters novel contexts, be they social or physical, for role enactment. Such a situation accounts for a great deal of variation in role behavior.

It is through the concept of role behavior that organizational analysis permits an assessment of the contribution that the personality of a status occupant plays in social behavior. Individuals who occupy the same social status, and who may be required to enact the same role, have a variety of personality characteristics, abilities, skills, and behavioral dispositions. All of these variables influence both how people interpret their roles and how they perform them. Personality, thus, is a focal factor in un-

▼

derstanding role behavior, which in turn provides a more thorough explanation of the structure and dynamics of social organization. We shall have more to say on this point in a subsequent section of this chapter.

ROLE DEVIATION. **Role deviation,** another related concept, refers to concrete actions, or role behavior, that are inconsistent with the prescriptions and proscriptions of a role. Role behavior that does not fulfill the normative expectations, or which violates normative proscriptions, constitutes role deviation. Both situations have significant consequences for the functioning of social systems. A student who cheats on examinations or commits plagiarism while performing assignments would be engaging in role deviation, as would a professor who shows prejudice and discrimination toward a student by assigning unearned grades or using double standards in evaluating academic performance. Chapter 13 is devoted exclusively to an analysis of deviant behavior.

## STATUS SETS AND ROLE SETS

All statuses and roles, by virtue of being social, are also reciprocal in another sense. They are necessarily related to other statuses and roles. There can be no status of a physician without that of a patient, no status of a daughter without that of a mother, no status of an attorney without that of a client, and no status of a teacher without that of a student, and so forth. These mutual relationships can be understood more fully in terms of two basic concepts: status set and role set.

STATUS SET. Everyone has several social statuses. The common ones usually include those based on age, sex, marital position, education, occupation, religion, and racial or ethnic background. The number of potential statuses, however, that a person can occupy is virtually without limit. Individuals living in a modern, complex society occupy not one but many statuses. For example, an individual occupying the status of professor may also occupy such statuses as father or mother, husband or wife, captain of the volunteer fire company, Little League baseball coach, and so forth. The complex totality of statuses that an individual occupies at a given time is called a **status set** (see Figure 6-5).

ROLE SET. Each status has associated with it not one but several roles. Each role associated with a status indicates how the occupant of a status is expected to behave toward those individuals who occupy related statuses. The concept of **role set** refers to the totality of status-role relationships that a person has with other people occupying statuses that are related to a given status. For example, the status of professor necessitates that a person holding that status interact and have role relationships with people occupying such related statuses as student, administrator, bookstore manager, secretary, and librarian. Figure 6-6 illustrates the concept of role set.

An individual occupying a particular social position will not behave the same way for each role partner. Moreover, each role partner will have somewhat different expectations as to how one should act in the given role. Students, for instance, may expect professors to devote most of their time to preparing lectures, teaching, and holding office hours. College administrators may expect their professors to allocate a great deal of time to various committees that are established to govern the university, while co-workers may expect their professional colleagues to spend the bulk of their time in pursuit of scholarly research.

## SOCIOLOGICAL AMBIVALENCE

A common and inescapable fact of social life is what has come to be known as **sociological ambivalence.** This phenomenon refers to an incom-

246

▼

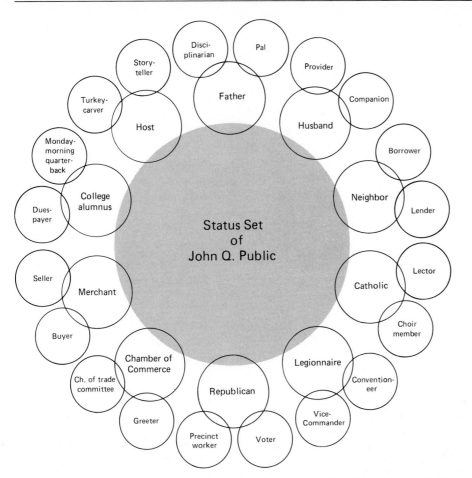

FIGURE 6-5 Status Set. A status consists of the totality of social positions that an individual occupies at a given time. Source: Adapted from George A. Lundberg et al., *Sociology*. New York: Harper and Row, 1968, p. 147.

patibility in the normative expectations of a single status or set of statuses (Merton, 1976).

Every individual at one time or another experiences difficulties in fulfilling role obligations. Such situations are particularly true given the complexity of the kind of social organization that characterizes social life in this day and age. One can hardly occupy a large number of statuses, indeed even a single status, without sooner or later experiencing inherent conflict or incompatibility in terms of role expectations.

It is important, however, to distinguish the sources of conflict and tension. There are in this regard three principal types of sociological ambivalence: role conflict, role strain, and status conflict.

ROLE CONFLICT.   The varied expectations that different role partners have for one's behavior may create role conflict for the occupant of a particular status. Tension and strain are most likely to occur when the members of an

▼

248

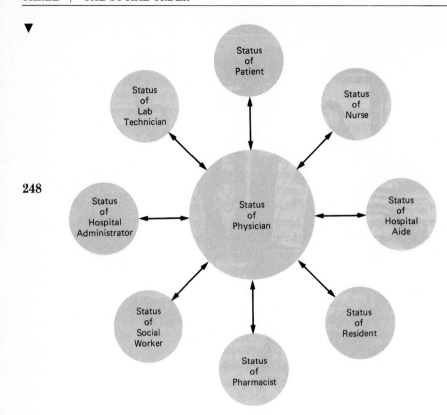

FIGURE 6-6 Role Set. Social statuses do not exist in isolation from each other. Each status has a complementary status or a number of associated statuses. The concept of role set refers to the totality of role relationships that one has while occupying a given status.

individual's role set have expectations for one's behavior that are incompatible with each other. So, for example, a professor may experience role conflict if students and their parents expect him to devote most of his time to teaching and interacting with students, while the head of his department and his colleagues expect him to make significant contributions to his discipline. Another example would be that of a person who occupies the status of supervisor in a factory. Her boss expects her to demand the most from the workers she oversees, expecting that they work at top efficiency throughout the day. The workers, however, may expect her to be sympathetic to their problems, refrain from putting pressure on them, and allow them to "goof off" at times. **Role conflict,** then, is produced when one's role partners have incompatible conceptions of how one should enact a role.

ROLE STRAIN. Related somewhat to role conflict is the dynamic of **role strain,** which refers to situations in which one experiences difficulty in coping with the various demands of a particular role. Role strain, often resulting in role deviation, is the product of the diversity of requirements that exist within a given role. Hence, rather than a difference in conflicting expectations on the part of role partners, role strain involves incompatible or inconsistent tasks that are required in a particular role. A parent who is expected to be both a just disciplinarian and a compassionate friend frequently experiences role strain that may lead to role deviation in one form or another.

STATUS CONFLICT. Tension may also arise when there is a conflict between the requirements associated with the different statuses a person holds, that is, within one status set. This situation is referred to as **status conflict.** Let us take the case of a person holding the statuses of mother and department store executive. If her child becomes ill, should she stay home to take care of the child—as expected of a mother, or should she go to work in order to negotiate an important transaction—as expected by her company? Should a person who occupies the statuses of police officer and brother arrest his brother for the commission of a traffic violation, or refrain from doing so and show only compassion or partiality toward a relative in trouble? Such conflicts between social statuses that demand contradictory behavior on the part of people occupying them can be the source of much psychological discomfort and usually result in some degree of role deviation no matter which way they are resolved.

RESOLUTION.   A number of techniques are employed in the resolution of sociological ambivalence, including many that occur on the unconscious level. Among them are the following: rationalization (defining the situation in such a way as to eliminate the conflict); avoidance behavior (simply not fulfilling either role); role segmentation—insulation of behavior played in one role from that of another (for example, underworld criminals who are upright spouses, parents, and faithful churchgoers at the same time); erection of a hierarchy of statuses, based on functional or personal need, or in terms of the degree of sanction (positive or negative support); and status abandonment, by which one simply resigns from one or all of the statuses involved. Employment of these mechanisms may not always be possible for an individual, and such a situation can produce serious problems. Difficulty or inability to cope with sociological ambivalence often is expressed through psychosomatic or physical illness, alcohol or drug abuse, and even mental illness (see Kaplan, 1983).

# Power and Authority ▼

One of the basic dynamics of human social interaction, and thus one that is found inherently in all forms of social organization, is power. **Power** represents the ability to control, or to affect the actions of another—even without one's consent. It may assume three principal forms: influence, coercion, and authority. These forms of power, in turn, may be designated as legitimate or illegitimate.

**249**

**Influence** is the power to persuade or to induce another individual to act in a certain way. Such is the case in the efforts of newspaper editors and television commentators in the formation of public opinion on a given issue. Influence may be legitimate or illegitimate, depending on the form that it assumes.

**Coercion** represents a type of power whose legitimacy is not recognized by those over whom it is exercised. More often than not coercion involves the application of force—physical or otherwise. Blackmail is a form of coercive power.

**Authority** constitutes legitimate power. Hence, authority represents power that is normally accepted and respected by those over whom it is exercised. It is sanctioned or mandated and, as such, authority is an integral part of social roles. Even more fundamentally, authority can be conceived as an essential component of the rights and obligations that inhere in a given social position. One who holds authority, therefore, has the right to exercise power; correspondingly, those over whom power is exercised have the duty to respect and to obey it.

The distinctions of legitimate and illegitimate power are crucial to a comprehensive understanding of the structure and function of any social system, and the human dynamics within them. Of particular importance in this respect are the different sources of authority and how they in turn affect the function of any social organization (see Box 6-1).

▼

## BOX 6-1. Sources of Authority

Authority is indispensable in any type of social system. An important question, thus, in the explanation of social organization concerns the sources of authority. Or, put in other terms, how is power legitimized?

Max Weber (1947) in his classic volume on *The Theory of Social and Economic Organization* distinguished three distinct types of authority in terms of their sources.

1. *Traditional authority* rests on ancient custom or long-standing practices and the widely shared belief that the legitimacy of those exercising power is natural and inevitable. Such is the case in the authority held by tribal chiefs, popes, and hereditary monarchs. The right of such individuals to demand obedience is not only seen as proper, but invariably unquestioned as well. Traditional authority is usually all-inclusive, at least within a particular domain, such as in the political or religious realm.

2. *Rational-legal authority* derives from a belief in the legitimacy of law and the right of people to exercise power under the rules and regulations of an organization. Such authority is based on a formally defined set of rights and obligations; accordingly, it resides in a particular social position. Rational-legal authority is exemplified in the legitimate power exercised by police officers and presidents. The limits of the rights and obligations of these positions are quite clearly specified and usually restricted to time and place.

3. *Charismatic authority* is rooted in the personal qualities of those who hold it. Such authority involves an attraction and devotion to the character and/or heroism of a particular person, and upon the willingness of others to obey. Charismatic authority, thus, is excerised by individuals who may be said to possess charisma, or a "magnetic personality," and who, because of extraordinary personal qualities (for example, rhetorical skills, unique vision, inspirational qualities, and deeds), are able to elicit obedience and allegiance. Charismatic authority often emerges during periods of crisis and instability. Occasionally a political or religious leader is imbued with charismatic authority. Examples of such individuals in recent years include Adoph Hitler, Fidel Castro, Mahatma Gandhi, Martin Luther King, Jr., and the Ayatollah Khomeini.

Charismatic authority often makes for a potential source of disruption to social organization that is based on traditional or rational-legal authority. Moreover, charismatic authority, unlike the other two types, is an inherently unstable form of authority in that it is not likely to endure when other individuals assume the social position in question. Weber spoke of the "routinization of charisma," by which the qualities of charismatic authority evolve into either the traditional or rational-legal variety, and as such become transferred from the individual person to the social organization.

The three types of authority are distinctive, but not pure. Often they occur in combinations of one kind or another. While the primary basis of the authority of the President of the United States is of the rational-legal variety, by now it can be said perhaps to be traditional as well in many respects. And, of course, many presidents, such as Lincoln, Roosevelt, and Kennedy, also held a certain

degree of charismatic authority. Under such circumstances, the total legitimacy
of one's authority is significantly enhanced—and represents a situation that
can have both dysfunctional as well as functional consequences for any social
system. ▲

# Personality and Social Systems

Much can be understood about the structure
and function of social systems only through an
understanding of the psychological character
of the people who participate in them. Sociological analysis, thus, often requires the use of
personality theory, and the systematic knowledge of the distinctive personality characteristics of participants in social systems. Such
information makes it possible to provide more
comprehensive explanations of the structure
and function of social systems. In terms of systemic analysis, personality and social system
each constitutes part of the environment of the
other. Once created, the products or consequences of one system flow back into the other
from which they came, reinforcing and modifying it anew. There is, in fact, a symbiotic, or
mutually dependent, relationship between personality and social organization. And, more
significant, it is personality systems that fundamentally provide energetic input for social
systems.

We shall focus our discussion in this chapter
on the general relationship of personality and
social systems—reserving for subsequent chapters the relationship of personality to more specific types of social organizations, such as
societies, bureaucracies, and groups.

## GENERAL PRINCIPLES

Social positions—status and role—comprise
one of the major linkages between personality
and social systems. Recruitment into social positions, and the quality of performances of social
roles within them, are partly a function of the
personality of individuals who occupy social
positions. Such dynamics on a sufficiently large
scale, or in a systemic fashion, can comprise a
crucial factor in the function of social systems.

One dimension of these principles was mentioned earlier: Not all status occupants perform
roles in an identical manner. Roles usually
speak to *what* must be done or not done; they
seldom specify *how* a status must be enacted.
The way roles are created and the way they are
enacted, particularly in one fashion rather than
in another, is partly a function of personality.
Personality variables, thus, constitute one of the
most significant sets of factors that are responsible for differential role performance.

Ralph Linton (1945) spoke in this regard
about "status personality" to distinguish those
aspects of personality that are associated with
a particular social position. Individuals seem
to change, or to be different people, in various
social positions, because they frequently manifest different aspects of their personality. In a
well-known experiment of role playing, Philip
Zimbardo (1972) demonstrated this principle
quite dramatically. He established a mock
prison complete with simulated cell blocks, uni-
formed guards, and a social organization typical of a penitentiary. Student volunteers were
randomly assigned to enact the roles of prisoners and guards. The "guards" were free to
devise their own methods of social control.
When the "prisoners" became rebellious, the
"guards" reacted in a highly brutal and abusive
manner—so much so that the experiment had
to be suspended for fear that physical or psychological harm would come to both "prisoners" and "guards." Similarly, Kohn and

**251**

▼

Schooler (1982), on the basis of longitudinal studies of American men and work experiences, have shown that occupational roles can produce personality changes in real long-term situations. People in highly structured jobs become less flexible and less self-directed, while individuals in less structured jobs tend to become more flexible and self-directed. These researchers argue, however, that the interaction between personality and social roles are actually reciprocal: Position affects personality, and personality affects position (role performance)—although the specific dynamics involved in these situations are quite complex.

## PERSONALITY AND ROLE RECRUITMENT

Considerable empirical evidence supports the thesis that people are differentially attracted to social positions on the basis of personality. In their extensive research, Kohn and Schooler (1982) have found, for example, that people with more flexible and self-directed personalities are more likely to obtain jobs that have little supervision and offer more opportunity for individual initiative. Conversely, individuals who are less flexible and less self-directed are more likely to be attracted to occupations that are characterized by more structure and more supervision. Such situations give rise to the presence of modal types of personality that distinctively characterize various kinds of social position.

Certain personality types tend to be attracted and/or recruited to particular social positions in a differential, rather than in a random or unsystematic, fashion, and seemingly so disproportionately as to constitute modal personality types for these social positions. Thus, while many types of personality may be found in particular social positions, one or two—perhaps as many as five or six—are found so predominantly or extensively that they may be said to typify or characterize the position in question.

A study of professional politicians, representing several major parties in the Italian Chamber of Deputies, showed that parliamentarians were distinctively characterized by an authoritarian or dogmatic and highly power-oriented personality in a ratio of 3 to 1 (DiRenzo, 1967a). Moreover, this distinctively modal profile contrasted quite significantly with control samples of nonpoliticians.

Hermann (1980), utilizing a content analysis of speeches and interviews, has attempted an assessment of the personality of members of the Soviet Politburo. Her fascinating study reveals interesting psychological profiles that suggest personality differences among individuals fulfilling different political roles within the Soviet Politburo; unfortunately, the findings are only suggestive due to the lack of comparable data for citizen samples from the Soviet Union, as well as political or nonpolitical samples in other countries.

Another study (DiRenzo, 1974b) found that college students can be distinguished on the basis of modal types of personality in terms of their principal areas of academic study. Students majoring in liberal arts and the behavioral sciences showed a distribution of dogmatic and nondogmatic personality in a respective ratio of 1 to 2. Business administration students (those majoring in marketing, accounting, finance, and business administration) were rather evenly divided in terms of the two types of personality. Majors in the physical and natural sciences, however, were modally characterized by the dogmatic personality in a ratio of 3 to 1 (see Table 6-3). Most striking in these findings is the polarity, or antithetical pattern, of modal types in the frequency distribution between the behavioral sciences majors and the liberal arts majors on the one hand, and the physical and natural sciences majors on the other—all of whom showed marked differences from those in business administration. These findings suggest that not only are individuals attracted to particular academic pursuits, but that such

TABLE 6-3.  Personality and Academic Curricula*  ▼

| | Nondogmatic Personality | Dogmatic Personality | Total |
|---|---|---|---|
| Behavioral sciences | 34 (67%) | 17 (33%) | 51 |
| Liberal arts | 57 (61%) | 36 (39%) | 93 |
| Business administration | 15 (56%) | 12 (44%) | 27 |
| Physical sciences | 8 (30%) | 19 (70%) | 27 |
| Total | 114 (58%) | 84 (43%) | 198 |

* $X^2 = 10.94$; df = 3; p < .02
Source: Gordon J. DiRenzo, "Congruences in Personality Structure and Academic Curricula as Determinants of Occupational Careers." *Psychological Reports,* 1974, 34:1295–1298. Reprinted with permission of author and publisher.

may be one basis for differential personality recruitment into specific occupations, especially insofar as undergraduate studies essentially constitute occupational and professional training.

Indeed, this position is supported by another set of data on the relationship between personality and specialization in family medicine. Again, the data show that family medicine attracts particular types of personality. Utilizing the Myers-Briggs Type Indicator (see Chapter 5), which permits individuals to be classified into one of sixteen major types of personality, in terms of characteristic or preferred modes of perception, judgment, and action (introversion versus extraversion), Quenk and Heffron (1975) found that family practitioners tend to be significantly different in personality from the general population of physicians. Family practitioners were more typical of the "sensing and judging" type. They tend to be practical, realistic, present-oriented, and organized; they are able to deal effectively with factual information and make decisions quickly; and they prefer to see immediate results of their action. Family practitioners in the somewhat different categories of "sensing and feeling" personalities tended to be the happiest in their work, to see more patients each day, and to be more active in community projects and civil affairs. "Thinking" practitioners, introverted and intuitive types of personality, tend very strongly to choose careers in neurology, psychology, pathology, and research. Harris and Ebbert (1985), in parallel research using the MBTI, compared rural physicians and family medicine residents, and found similarly distinctive differences in the modal personality for both categories.

All of these studies support the view that "certain personality types tend to be attracted and/or recruited to particular occupations in a differential, rather than in a random or unsystematic, fashion, and seemingly so disproportionately as to constitute modal personality types for these occupations" (DiRenzo, 1967a). Personality may be an individual attribute, but modal personality is an attribute of the social system. Accordingly, just as personality has crucial significance for the behavior of individuals, so may modal personalities have functional significance for social systems.

## PERSONALITY AND ROLE PERFORMANCE

No matter what it is that accounts for modal patterns of personality that characterize social

▼

## BOX 6-2. Inferential Statistics

Table 6-3 offers an opportunity to exemplify the nature of inferential statistics and their utility in the research process of sociology. The numerical and percentage distributions of personality types for the different kinds of academic curricula given in this table represent descriptive statistics. These figures provide the basis for the mathematical calculations that comprise the inferential statistics which are used to determine the statistical significance of the observed results.

The mathematical symbols ($X^2 = 10.94$; df = 3, p < .02) shown in the table footnote represent a summation of the calculations of the inferential statistics which were used to determine the probability that such findings are merely spurious or chance results, due perhaps to sampling error, or rather whether they represent a genuine relationship between the variables under study.

The statistical significance of these findings (shown by p < .02) can be interpreted in the following way. The probability that these findings are due to chance alone is 2 in 100. In other words, were such a study to be replicated 100 times, results such as these—due to mere chance—could be expected only twice. Could the researcher be so unlucky that this study represents one of those two times?

Given such a low probability of a chance event, the researcher concludes that the observed results are authentic—and not influenced by extraneous and uncontrolled factors, such as sampling bias. The results in this study, thus, are assumed to indicate a genuine relationship between the variables under investigation, and as such confirm the hypotheses of the study. Accordingly, the researcher projects these findings, and the theoretical relationships involved, onto larger, yet similar, populations of people. ▲

---

positions—differential recruitment or postoccupancy learning—modal personalities have sociological relevance only insofar as they do indeed affect individual role performances, and thereby the function of social systems. Studies that report on modal personality and role performance are not as prevalent as those which deal directly with recruitment. The relatively few pieces of research available, however, offer ample support for the thesis that modal types of personality have a marked influence on role performance and the function of social systems. Let us describe some selected samples of this kind of research.

In a study of nurse's aides in three mental hospitals, Gilbert and Levinson (1950) measured both role performance and personality.

For the former dimension, the subjects were classified as "custodial" or "humanistic" in terms of their treatment of patients. Aides were considered "custodial" in behavior if they made numerous threats to patients and placed prime emphasis on keeping the wards quiet. They were classified as "humanistic" if they were more friendly and respectful toward patients and assumed the role of "social" therapist. These modes of treatment are respective facets of the authoritarian and egalitarian personalities.

"Custodial" aides were more typically authoritarian in personality type, while the nonauthoritarian personality was modally characteristic of the "humanistic" aides. The rank order correlation between the custodial mode of treatment and scores on authoritarianism and personality was .75, suggesting an extremely strong influence of personality on behavioral performance in the role of nurse's aide.

A study of state legislators in Michigan and Indiana assessed the relationship of personality to role conception and role performance as measured in terms of career orientation and role orientation. Personality was measured in terms of the authoritarian and dogmatic syndrome—and the other dimensions in terms of the subject's personal reports on career orientation and role orientation (DiRenzo, 1977c).

Legislators possessing a dogmatic personality maintained a positive orientation toward a political career in a ratio of 2 to 1, while nondogmatic personalities were about equally divided—indeed, slightly negative, in their orientation toward a political career. Additionally, the dogmatic syndrome was found to be significantly stronger among those politicians who were positively oriented than those who were negatively oriented. As for role orientation, findings show that legislators who perceive themselves as either "professional" or "semi-professional" politicians were more typically dogmatic personalities (both numerically and in strength of the syndrome) than those who held a "nonprofessional" role orientation. Only 35 percent of the legislators with dogmatic personalities considered themselves to be "nonprofessional" politicians as opposed to 54 percent of the nondogmatic personalities.

Similar variations in the performance of legislative roles have been shown in terms of personality differences and political ideology by a number of studies. Tetlock (1984), for example, working with interview data gathered from 89 members of the British House of Commons, explored the interrelationships between political ideology and cognitive style, that is, the characteristic way of organizing and processing information. His results show that moderate Socialists have more complex cognitive styles (for example, assess policy issues in multidimensional terms) than moderate Conservatives,

who, in turn, have more complex cognitive styles than either extreme Conservatives or extreme Socialists. (Cognitive complexity, as a fundamental dimension of personality structure, is associated with open-mindedness and the nondogmatic personality.)

The relationship of personality to role performance has been assessed in the academic setting as well. Stern, Stein, and Bloom (1956) studied the performance of two samples of freshman students (61 students each), who were measured and classified in terms of stereopathy—a psychological dimension that is conceptually and dynamically similar to that of authoritarianism and dogmatism. The stereopathic personality is one who accepts authority as absolute, is submissive to it, and inclines toward rigid orderliness and conformity. Stereopathic personalities are essentially close-minded individuals who manifest a significant intolerance of ambiguity.

Instruction at the college under study utilized an approach that could be characterized as intellectually open, tolerant, and flexible. In short, the college emphasized qualities which were characteristic of nonstereopaths and relatively lacking in the stereopathic personality. The significance of such a pedagogical approach seemed to be reflected in the fact that the stereopaths received lower grades than the nonstereopaths. At the end of the first year, 3 percent of the stereopaths had withdrawn from the college, whereas only 1 percent of the nonstereopaths had done so. Intelligence showed no significant difference in this finding. The compliance of withdrawing stereopathic students strongly suggested that their action resulted from a lack of compatibility between their personalities and the pedagogical style of their college. They complained especially about the apparent lack of discipline and the refusal of instructors to give the "right" answers. Such an outcome was much as predicted, given the distinctive personality attributes of the stereopathic students and the distinctive qualities

▼

**255**

▼

256

of instruction at the college. Satisfactory role performance is a much more difficult accomplishment for a stereopathic student in an intellectually flexible and ambiguous learning environment.

Each of these studies demonstrates that personality differences are associated not only with particular social roles but also, and more importantly, with role performance. Such a situation can be crucially relevant to the structure and function of social systems.

## CONGRUENCE: FUNCTIONAL INTERACTIONS

Certain theoretical conclusions have been drawn on the basis of these kinds of findings regarding modal personality and role performance that characterize social positions. The most plausible and widely accepted explanation of these situations is that there is a congruent relationship between personality and social position which is functional for both the personal system and the social system involved.

A lack of substantial congruence between personality and social organization produces a state of tension that has dysfunctional consequences for both the individual and the social order. Several sociological studies have documented the deleterious consequences that such a stressful situation may have for the psychological functions of individuals in terms of decreased physical and mental health, deviant personal and social behavior, and even suicide as well. Coburn (1975), for example, has reported recently on the effects of occupational incongruence (overly simple or overly complex work) on psychological and physical well-being. One's health deteriorates in both dimensions. Such consequences, however, are not simply effects on individuals when they are experienced by large numbers of people. Outcomes of this kind constitute social or societal problems that bring an entirely new set of dysfunctional consequences for the social systems directly involved.

States of functional congruence can be brought about by either the independent action of both individuals and social organizations, or as consequence of their mutual interaction. What such a situation means is that individuals, insofar as they are free to do so, are most likely to select or create those social positions and social organizations that have a high or reasonable potential to fulfill their psychological needs.

To an important extent people may be attracted to specific organizational roles because they believe that the demands of the role are congruent with their personality disposition. For example, the role of librarian demands order, attention to detail, a desire to help others, neatness, and a subdued approach to people. Individuals possessing an extroverted, assertive personality and who tend to be undisciplined and impatient are not likely to be attracted to the role of librarian. On the other hand, individuals possessing personality traits that are congruent with the requirements of the librarian role are apt to be attracted to the occupation.

Certain dynamics of individual behavior within educational systems and processes, such as success and failure (degree thereof) in academic performance, can be understood most thoroughly in terms of total personality functioning, and the nature of the congruent relationship within given processes and systems, rather than as simple questions of attitudes and motivations. Some people, for example, may have a strong need to conform to social norms and to submit to authority; others may have an equally strong psychological need for personal autonomy.

Both kinds of individuals will seek out social positions that permit their respective kind of behavior. DiRenzo (1974b) suggests that much

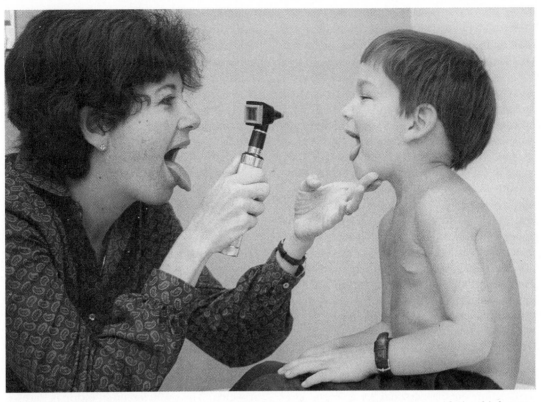

**Role Compatibility.** Success or failure in occupational roles often depends on the congruent relationship between one's personality and the demands of the role. Such a situation is functional for both the personality system and the social system involved. (Elizabeth Crews/Stock, Boston)

of the change-of-majors phenomenon that many college students experience is a consequence of lack of functional congruence between the structural dimensions of specific academic disciplines and the functional requirements of the personalities involved.

Variations that exist in the personalities of individuals may either reinforce a social organization or disrupt it. All social systems must face the problem of assuring that the needs of the system are compatible with the psychological needs of its constituent personalities. Every social system, however, functionally requires that its agents, or status occupants, possess cer-

tain psychological characteristics.* Most basic among the essential psychological characteristics is a general readiness to conform to a set of social norms. However, social systems that have a distinctive character (ideology, values, goals, means) will require personalities with a correspondingly distinctive structure. A simple illustration can be made by contrasting militaristic and religious organizations. The former are quite likely to demand or encourage, and

---

\* This principle, in one sense, can be seen as part of the AGIL paradigm, fitting in specifically at the level of latent pattern maintenance.

▼ necessarily so, obedience to authority, orderliness, and physical aggression; the latter will most likely emphasize submission to authority, nonassertiveness, introspection, and intuitive judgement. In both cases many other types of personality variables (for example, complexity of cognitive system) are free to vary.

258 In order for any social system to function well, and as intended, its members must possess the kind of personality that makes them want to act in the way that they have to act as members of the social system (Fromm, 1944). The individual must *want* to do what *needs* to be done. Hence, competence and intelligence for the respective task of a social position may be insufficient for optimal role performance and organizational function. Correspondingly, it can be said that no social system can neglect the personal needs or psychological maladjustment of its members. Low commitment or integration is a functional threat to any system. Individuals who find themselves in a social system with which they are not psychologically congruent may experience dissatisfaction and dysfunction on the personal level. Social systems, if only for their own effectiveness, must also be responsive to the psychological functions and needs of their agents. Accordingly, social organizations, insofar as they are able to do so, will attract and/or mold those individuals who have a high or reasonable potential of fulfilling its functional needs.

Inkeles and Levinson (1969) have delineated four kinds of situations of functional interaction between personality and social systems: ideal congruence; unstable congruence (incongruous fit between personality and social systems); institutionally generated incongruence (changes within social systems disrupt an existing state of relative congruence); and characterologically induced noncongruence (changes within existing personnel and/or introduction of inappropriate individuals that disrupt an existing state of relative congruence).

Changes within either the personality or the social system are apt to disrupt the "fitness" or "dependency" that exists, that is, the symbiotic relationship, between the two systems. A substantial change in one will mean a substantial change in the other. Similarly, to perpetuate one system is to perpetuate the other. Stability and change in social organization is, to an extent, a function of the respective congruity or incongruity that social systems share with the personality systems involved therein. The greater the congruity—the more perfect the "fit"—the more stable the organization and the more minimal the change (DiRenzo, 1967a).

## CONSEQUENCES OF PERSONAL INCONGRUENCE

Social systems, by and large, seem to get the "right" types of personality—personality types that they need or want. What happens, however, when individuals for whatever reasons occupy social positions that are not congruent with their personality and psycological needs or wants? The problematic situation is that social systems may recruit—actively or passively—personalities that, by and large, do not or cannot function effectively within particular social systems. Any situation that brings about incongruence or noncongruence is apt to result in dysfunctional consequences, and/or change, for either the personality or the social organization, or even for both systems.

There are many instances where an individual's personality predispositions may be incompatible with the requirements of a particular role. A person who is psychologically predisposed to be introverted, shy, and quiet, or who generally prefers to be alone, would not do well performing roles that require extroverted, outgoing, and sociable activity, such as the roles of teacher, actor, or salesperson. Similarly, individuals with a nondogmatic or nonauthoritarian personality would not do well in a role that is essentially authoritarian or militaristic, such as that of soldier or police officer. In cases of this type there would not be a good fit or correspondence between the personality tendencies of the person having to perform the roles. What, then, are the possible consequences in social positions for which there exists a conflict between the demands of a particular role and the psychodynamics of the personalities of those having to enact the role? There are, at least, four potential outcomes.

STATUS ABANDONMENT.   The simplest solution for personality incongruity is perhaps status abandonment. In this case the individual simply decides to leave the social position and find one that is compatible with his or her personality. The shy, introverted, quiet person would try to find an occupation that does not require him to engage in much interaction with others. Such an individual would seek out the occupational role that requires him to work with things instead of people.

PSYCHOLOGICAL ADAPTATION.   Disparity between the needs of one's personality and the demands of one's role may activate psychological coping mechanisms that serve to reduce the stress experienced by the person. These coping mechanisms are especially apt to develop when the person is not able to leave the role and seek out one that is better suited to his or her personality. An example of coping strategy would be the emergence of what Goffman (1961b) has termed **role-distancing behavior.** This is a type of behavior that indicates to the individual and to others that one does not take one's role seriously, that one does not embrace it wholeheartedly, and that there exists a psychological "distance" between one's personality or "true self" and the particular role. Individuals in these types of circumstances manifest an apathetic conformity and usually meet only the minimal requirements of role performance. Such people get little satisfaction from their work, and they may even try to sabotage the organization. For example, students who are not really interested in obtaining an education or concerned with learning may perform activities in the classroom that reflect the gap betwen the role of student and their real interest. Such people may chat with their friends, fail to take notes, stare out of the window, or read a newspaper while the instructor is lecturing. Such behavior indicates that a distance exists between the required activities of the role and the actual role behavior of the individual.

PERSONALITY MODIFICATION.   There is some evidence to suggest that someone who initially lacks certain personality attributes that would aid in the performance of a given role may develop the necessary attributes over a period of time. Thus, it is possible that a basically introverted person, one who is timid and retiring, may develop an extroverted and assertive psychological nature as a result of having to perform roles that require those characteristics, such as that of a salesperson. Some social scientists claim that changes in personality that occur as a result of occupying a particular position are superficial and temporary— a result of the person attempting to adapt temporarily to the demands of the role. According to this view, when the person is not performing the particular role, he or she will revert back to the "true" personality. The salesperson, in our example, may be introverted, timid, and reserved when the role of salesperson is not being enacted. Such a situation is, in effect, a manifestation of Linton's concept of status personality, described earlier.

There is evidence indicating that people's attitudes may change so that they are compatible with the roles that they perform. One researcher found that when shop stewards were made

▼

259

▼

**Organizational Training.** In order to enhance the compatibility between personality and social roles, corporations and other social organizations often conduct "training sessions" for their personnel. Teaching teamwork and interactional skills is one of the focal issues in these efforts aimed at behavior modification. (© Susan Lapides 1986/Design Conceptions)

supervisors, their initial pro-union attitudes changed to pro-management attitudes. When they went back to the role of worker because of a slowdown in production, they changed their attitudes back to the pro-union ones they originally had. Those individuals who did not become workers again, but continued in the role of supervisor, developed a greater pro-management attitude on a variety of issues (Lieberman, 1950). This study shows that people's attitudes on issues relevant to the positon they occupy may change as they change positions.*

* This situation also exemplifies the principles of cognitive dissonance whereby behavior that is not congruent with beliefs or attitudes causes psychological stress, which in turn produces an impetus for consistency.

It is also possible that if a person performs a particular role for a long time, deep-seated changes will occur within his or her personality system. Yinger makes the point that "we need to distinguish between differences in behavior which occur when one enters a new position and the possible effects of one position which become embedded in the personality system and thus influence all role performances" (1965:113). As an example, he observes that if, as a result of a man becoming a father, "he becomes somewhat more future-oriented, more family-oriented, more tender, more irritable, or whatever, *and these inclinations affect his behavior in other positions as well*, the position father had had general as well as specific personality consequences."

ROLE MODIFICATION. Another response to incongruence between personality and role requirements involves role redefinition: The role is redefined in such a way that its demands become compatible with the individual's personality. The individual must convince his or her role partners to accept the redefinition, that is, demonstrate how the new conception of the role will result in benefits to all concerned. For example, the introverted, reserved salesperson must persuade both superiors and colleagues that a relaxed, soft-sell approach (the type that is congruent with one's personality) will result in as many sales as the aggressive, hard-sell approach of an extroverted personality. Similarly, the introverted, reserved police officer must convince both supervisors and fellow officers that a low-key, somewhat passive orientation can be more effective in many problem situations than a dominant, high-powered one. Hence, we can see that innovations which often emerge in a social organization are the result of individuals with "new" or different personalities getting into strategic positions.

# Summary

Social organization refers to the networks of relatively stable, structured, and recurrent patterns of behavior that develop among people. This concept denoted actions that are coordinated and interdependent as opposed to those that are random and isolated.

Social organization is made possible by the inherent state of mutual dependency or interdependency that characterizes human nature. Social organization emerges either as the aggregate result of the diverse acts of individuals, each pursuing his or her own ends, or from the joint endeavors of individuals pursuing commonly accepted ends. Sociologists speak respectively in this regard of crescive and enacted social organization.

The principles of system theory are used quite extensively in the analysis of social organizations. A system is a plurality of parts that function as a unit, with the implication that the whole is, in a certain sense, greater than the sum of the individual parts. System analysis is concerned essentially with what goes into a system (inputs), what happens when it gets there (thruputs), and what comes out of the system (outputs). System theory incorporates the elements of differentiation, interdependence, unity, and goal attainment.

All systems consist of two fundamental dimensions: content and structure. The content of a system denotes the specific units or elements which constitute it; the structure of a system refers to the coordinated arrangements or relationships that exist among the components. Systems are conceptualized as being open or closed, the distinction being primarily a matter of degree, which is made in terms of self-sufficiency. The boundaries of a system separate it from its environment and other systems and also serve to regulate its inputs and outputs.

Dynamic equilibrium, which does not preclude change, refers to the tendency of a system to maintain the relationships that exist among the units that comprise it. This operation requires continuous feedback from both the constitutent parts of a system and its environment.

Social systems have all the characteristics of any system, and they are distinguished only by the particular phenomena (social interaction) to which they relate. Their chief input is information; their chief output is behavior. Social systems come in all shapes and sizes. The smallest social system is the dyad. Social systems with a small number of people are known as groups. Those with larger memberships are called complex organizations. Societies are the largest and most complex forms of social systems.

All elements and processes of a system have consequences for the system. Consequences of any given social mechanism are specified as being positive (functional) and/or negative (dysfunctional). Further distinctions are made by

▼

**261**

▼ speaking of functions and dysfunctions as being either manifest (intended and recognized) or latent (unintended and unrecognized). These distinctions are fundamental for an understanding of structural alternatives and functional equivalents. The functional requisites, or basic needs, of any social system are often formulated as the AGIL paradigm: adaptation, goal attainment, integration, and latent pattern maintenance.

**262** The basic elements of social organization consist of social positions, which may be described as locations in social space. Social positions, the most irreducible units of social organization, consist of two analytical aspects: social status and social role. A social status is a designated position, either achieved or ascribed, within a system of social relationships. A social role refers to a set of norms that prescribe and proscribe behavior expected on the part of the status occupants. Role behavior consists of the actual and concrete behavior on the part of a status occupant.

Social status and social role, as respectively static and dynamic dimensions of social organization, are correlative or reciprocal concepts. A status set consists of the totality of statuses that an individual occupies at a given time. Role set refers to the entirety of status-role relationships that a person has with other people who occupy statuses that are related to a given status. Sociological ambivalence is a common and inescapable phenomenon of social life. This dynamic refers to an incompatibility in the normative expectations of a single status or set of statuses and appears in the forms of role conflict, role strain, and status conflict. These situations invariably lead to role deviation.

An inherent element in all forms of social organization is power—the ability to control or to affect the actions of another. Power may be designated as legitimate or illegitimate, and as such assumes three forms: influence, coercion, and authority. The sources of authority, or legitimate power, are rooted in tradition, law, or charisma.

Personality provides energic input for social organization. Personality systems and social systems each constitute a part of the environment of the other. There is, in fact, a symbiotic, or mutually dependent, relationship between personality and social systems. This principle of congruence is fundamental in terms of role recruitment and role performance.

All of the elements and principles of social organization that we have discussed in this chapter are fundamental to all types of social systems, which can vary substantially in size, form, complexity, and objectives. Among the most important types of social systems are societies, complex organizations, bureaucracies, and small groups. Social dynamics are quite different in each of these forms of social organization. An adequate understanding of all of them is indispensable for comprehending the highly complex nature of human social behavior. We shall elaborate on these various types of social organization, discussing their specific structures and functions, in the three successive chapters.

# Key Concepts

achieved status
AGIL paradigm
ascribed status
authority
charismatic authority
closed system
coercion
crescive social organization
dynamic equilibrium
dysfunction
enacted social organization
feedback
function
functional differentiation
functional equivalent
functional requisite
influence

latent function
manifest function
open system
power
rational-legal authority
regulatory mechanism
role behavior
role conflict
role deviation
role-distancing behavior
role set
role strain
social content

social role ▼
social status
social structure
social system
sociological ambivalence
status conflict
status hierarchy
status set
structural alternative
system
systemic content
systemic structure
traditional authority

**263**

# 7 ▼ Society

In the last chapter we looked at many of the basic principles of social organization and social interaction. Sociology, as the science of human social behavior, is concerned in the last analysis with society—the all-embracing system of human social interaction. Such concerns constitute the special domain of macrosociology—the study of large-scale social systems and social interaction.

In this chapter we shall examine the fundamental structure of society, including a consideration of the different types of society in terms of their forms of social organization and modes of subsistence. A major focus of our concerns will be on social institutions which comprise the largest principal subsystems of any society. We shall explore in particular the basic institution of the family which plays a central role in every society, and which in many respects can be seen as a microcosm of society. Other major social institutions to be discussed include those of education, politics, economics, and religion.

Many of the forms and dynamics of society are based on the character of the physical environment in which it is located, as well as the nature of its population. We shall examine in these respects the ecological and demographic foundations of society and the role which such factors play in social relations. Finally, we shall explore the relationship of personality to society and discuss the significance that modal patterns of personality have for societal function. ▲

## Outline

▼

▶ Social organization is characteristic of many species of animals. Society, as a form of social organization, however, is found only among human beings. "Society," as Émile Durkheim remarked, "exists and lives only in and through individuals." Societies represent one particular type of social system, with certain characteristics and distinctive forms. Chief among these features is that society is the paramount system of social interaction—the all-inclusive and comprehensive social system. We are concerned here with the unique features of society and the diversity of its forms.

**266**

# Nature of Society

Society is the most complex form of social organization. It is the one, moreover, with which all human beings necessarily have a great deal of experience. Not only is one's entire life spent within society, but the individual in terms of his or her whole social and psychological being is the product of social interaction—all of which inescapably occurs within the context of society. Societies, as distinctive forms of social organization, however, are distinguished not so much by complexity as they are by the fact that they encompass all the necessary aspects of social life.

**Society** may be defined as a relatively independent and self-sufficient social system, usually represented by a relatively large number of people occupying a given territory, and interacting in terms of a commonly shared culture. Society, then, represents a distinctive kind of social system. It is one within which people can live a total common life, in contrast to social groups and complex organizations, which may be found within society but which have a specific purpose or limited objective.

*Society* is used to refer to small and primitive forms of social organization, such as tribes or bands, as well as large and complex ones, such as nations, like the United States.* Hence, society, as a social system, is distinguished by its ideal ability, regardless of its size or population, to provide totally for the functional needs of the individual.

Societies, like all human social systems, are the creation of people, and are maintained by them; but people themselves—even collectivities of them—do not constitute societies. Society is essentially an ordered or organized set of relationships maintained by common adherence to culturally specified rules, roles, and goals. Hence, the concept of society, like that of any social system, refers to the network or organization—the system of action and interaction—that characterizes a set of people rather than to the people themselves.

## CHARACTERISTICS OF SOCIETY

All societies have certain distinguishing characteristics: independence, self-sufficiency, mass population, territoriality, and common culture.

INDEPENDENCE. Societies are distinguished by functional autonomy; they are not a part or subunit of any other social system. Ideally, societies are perfectly self-contained; in practice, however, any society may operate in the forms and interests of mutual exchange. Societal independence is most evident in small, isolated societies, especially those of the past. Nowadays, as societies become larger and more complex, and with the extensive development of technology in the fields of transportation and communication, societies are becoming more interactive and cooperative in the interests of mutual efficiency.

SELF-SUFFICIENCY. A society is a social system through which people live a total life.

---

* See Lenski (1972) for a list of societies in the world.

It differs from a social group or a complex organization which are limited to a specific objective, such as a college fraternity, the local PTA, or the American Sociological Association. The sole objective of society is human existence itself. The self-sufficiency of society refers to the organization of action and interaction that comprises it. Societies may not be self-sufficient in terms of physical or material resources, but they are self-sufficient in terms of the necessities of social organization, and hence the personal and social needs of their members.

MASS POPULATION. Societies vary in size from a few hundred to hundreds of millions of people. Hence, the characteristic of mass population is a relative one in terms of the nature of the particular society and its subsystems. Societies constitute the largest and most complex forms of social organization with which people can be identified.

TERRITORIALITY. All social action takes place in a spatial context. Societies, however, are uniquely distinguished from other forms of social systems by the claim to a definite physical location which constitutes the principal geographical sphere in which its operations normally occur. (Nomadic tribes are somewhat of an exception to this principle.) Societies themselves can interact, as when they engage in international exchange, and such action can even take place in the land of a third society, or within a social system such as the United Nations, but this activity is rather limited and exceptional.

COMMON CULTURE. Society is essentially a cultural system. There can be no society without culture. Nor can there be a culture without society. These concepts, as we saw in Chapter 3, are correlative. Society and culture constitute, so to speak, two sides of the same coin; one is implied in the other. Culture, as we shall see below, comprises the content dimen-

sion of society. It represents the ideal pattern of organized living (beliefs, values, norms) that is distinctive of a given people. However complex or heterogeneous the culture of any society may be, every segment of society—and all the people in it—share a fundamental or common culture to a certain extent, particularly in terms of basic goals and values, as well as the norms established for their attainment.

Societies predate and postdate individuals. People come and go, but society endures, as it has since the beginning of humanity. It is the system of action that constitutes society which perpetuates itself, and not the people who are its members at any given time. If there were no people, however, there would be no society. Society exists only for and through people. So intimate is the relationship between society and the individual that one could argue that they too are correlative concepts.

## MODELS OF SOCIETY

Sociologists use several models of society to assist in their analysis and understanding. These models are the basis of, or implicit in, the various theoretical perspectives that are found in sociological analysis. No one model is sufficient in itself for a complete understanding of the complex dynamics of society. Each tends to stress certain aspects of society, sometimes at the expense of others. Most sociologists, however, are eclectic: they simultaneously use all or several of the available models to help them reach as complete and accurate an understanding of the nature and function of society as possible. Let us briefly describe the principal types of societal models that are used in sociology today.*

▼

**267**

---

* These models are discussed in more detail in Chapter 14. See also their theoretical foundations, presented in Chapter 1.

▼ EVOLUTIONISTIC. Evolutionary models are predicated on the assumption that all societies automatically and inevitably go through specified stages of development from simple to ever more complex forms, and that their structure and dynamics at any given point can be understood in terms of this process. Implicit in the evolutionary model is the notion of social progress—movement of civilization toward something bigger and better. In this view, change is seen as positive and beneficial. There are many variations of evolutionary models of society. The most common ones are those that conceive of the evolutionary process as unilinear, multilinear, or cyclical (see Chapter 14).

ORGANISMIC. Organismic models analogize societal organization to the structure and function of biological organisms and have as their fundamental concept that of homeostasis. Chief among these are structural-functional models and equilibrium models. The latter are particularly distinguished by an emphasis on order, balance, and processual regularity as the focal characteristics of society. Organismic models are reflected in the sociological works of Auguste Comte (1855), Emile Durkheim (1895), Max Weber (1922), and Talcott Parsons (1937).

CONFLICT. Conflict models are premised on the position that conflict, instability, and change, rather than order or equilibrium, are the distinguishing features of societal organization. Every society is seen as being in a continuous process of conflict and change. All the elements of society contribute to this dynamism. Conflict models may or may not incorporate an evolutionary perspective. Examples of conflict models can be found in the works of Marx and Engels (1848), C. W. Mills (1956), and Ralf Dahrendorf (1959).

Oftentimes these three models are presented as competing explanations for the nature and function of society. First of all, as we saw in Chapter 2, models are not explanations of anything. Rather, they are merely conceptual tools that are used in the attempt to understand the structure and dynamics of phenomena. Models, thus, can be judged only in terms of their usefulness in this respect, not in terms of their validity or any claims to truth. Moreover, and more importantly, it is possible to formulate a complex model in which the essential features of two or more are combined. For example, organismic models can be conceived in terms of either conflict or equilibrium, all of which may or may not be cast in the context of an evolutionary perspective. To the extent that models are useful in sociological and scientific explanations, more complex ones are apt to be the more fruitful ones. Our analysis of society in this chapter and the remaining ones will incorporate such a perspective.

## CONTENT AND STRUCTURE OF SOCIETY

Society, as with any other type of social system, may be analytically divided into content and structure. *Societal content* consists essentially of the culture of a society, which we discussed at length in Chapter 3. Chiefly included here are the principal beliefs, ideologies, values, and norms of society. *Societal structure*, on the other hand, refers to the integrative dimension that unites all the subsystems (communities, complex organizations, bureaucracies, associations, groups, triads, dyads) into more or less organized and interactive patterns of relationships. We can think of each of these components of societal organization as subsystems that are respectively embraced or enveloped within the other. Societal structure also refers to the quality of this unification: the degree of complexity and cohesiveness of the societal organization.

## STRUCTURAL AND FUNCTIONAL REQUISITES

Every social system has functional requirements—those tasks that need to be done if the system is to fulfill its purpose. Some functional requisites are common to all types of social systems. Others pertain to particular kinds of social systems. In Chapter 6 we discussed the concept of functional requisites in abstract terms by means of Parsons' AGIL paradigm. Here we can consider the concrete manifestations of the AGIL paradigm as it applies to society. Society, as one particular type of social system—one having its own particular objectives and characteristics—has its own functional requisites, and corresponding structures that are designed to meet the strategically required tasks for its function.

Aberle and his colleagues (1950) have offered the following list of functional requirements for any society:

1. Provision for an adequate relationship with the environment.
2. Sexual recruitment.
3. Role differentiation and role assignment.
4. Means of communication.
5. Shared cognitive orientations.
6. Shared articulated goals.
7. Normative regulation of means to goals.
8. Regulation of affective expression.
9. Socialization.
10. Effective control of disruptive forms of behavior.

This list of functional requisites is not exhaustive. We could add others which have been suggested by more definitive social research in recent years. Some of these others will become apparent as we continue on in subsequent chapters. Moreover, in the course of time, functional requisites may change as any society invariably does in a number of different ways. Suffice for our purpose here to illustrate the nature and purpose of functional requisites as they apply to any society.

The extent to which a society functions (that is, fulfills its purpose) is a direct result of the extent to which its functional requisites are met. This relationship is not necessarily a unilinear one. Research has shown that the association between societal mechanisms and societal function is curvilineal. The important objective then is one of optimal fulfillment of functional need rather than maximal effectiveness. The art of sociological analysis consists in perfecting the ability to determine the optimal level of interrelationship between structure (means) and function (requisites).

*Functional requisites* speak to *what* must be done in a society. *How* functional requisites are fulfilled or accomplished is another, but highly relevant, matter. Sociologists often speak in this regard of *structural requisites* that are the societal mechanisms by which functional requisites are fulfilled. Social institutions represent one major type of societal mechanism for responding to functional needs. We shall have much more to say subsequently about social institutions.

# Types of Societies

Human beings constitute a single species of social animals, but they have developed a wide variety of societies. This situation stems fundamentally from the fact that social organization for human beings is not genetically determined, as is the case with other social species. Human social organization is the product of human creation and invention.

Societies can be classified in a number of different ways. For purposes of sociological analysis, societies are usually classified according to either their chief mode of subsistence or basic technology (methods and instruments, such as tools and other devices, by which people

▼ TABLE 7-1. Modes of Subsistence

| | Hunting and Gathering | Horticultural | Agricultural | Industrial |
|---|---|---|---|---|
| Technology | Primitive (spears, bows, arrows) | Hand tools (hoe) | Mechanical means of cultivation (plow) | Massive mechanization and automation |
| Economy | Bare subsistence, no surplus | Simple crop cultivation and stock raising | Food production | Manufacturing |
| Settlements | None, nomadic | Small, temporary villages | Large, permanent | Massive, permanent, predominantly urban |
| Division of Labor | Minimal, based on age and sex | Simple | Specialized | High level of differentiation and specialization |
| Social Organization | Mostly limited to family | Development of social institutions | Emergence of complex organization and bureaucracy | Highly complex |

270

seek to control their physical environment) or their basic pattern of social organization. There is usually a correlation between these two dimensions. Indeed, in some respects these two dimensions are inextricably tied to each other, in that one is an outgrowth of the other. Consequently, a better understanding of the nature of society and its dynamics can be obtained if we analyze types of societies from both perspectives.

## MODES OF SUBSISTENCE

The mode of subsistence of a society refers to the way in which it provides its members with basic biological needs, such as food, shelter, and clothing. There are four such types, each of which shows a progressive development in technology, economy, and population (see Table 7-1).

HUNTING AND GATHERING SOCIETIES. A **hunting and gathering society** is the earliest and most primitive societal form. The dominant occupation of these societies is the search for food. People in these types of societies spend the greatest portion of their time hunting wild game and gathering food wherever it grows naturally. Such societies usually, and of necessity, have a small, frequently nomadic population (generally less than 100 people) with an uncomplicated and highly primitive technology, consisting of no more than spears, bows and arrows, and simple tools of bones and stones. Some of these societies, however, are quite large, occasionally numbering several thousands of people.

**FRANK AND ERNEST ©by Bob Thaves**

Reprinted by permission of NEA, Inc.

Social organization in the hunting and gathering society is quite simple, limited for the most part to the family unit. There is the most minimal development of a division of labor or role specialization (usually on the basis of age and sex), coupled with an emphasis on kin relationships. These societies are invariably distinguished by a highly homogeneous culture.

While quite prevalent 8,000 to 10,000 years ago, there are only a few examples of hunting and gathering societies still in existence today. Examples are found among some Eskimo tribes; the Bushmen of southwest Africa, such as the nomadic pigmy tribes in the Ituri Forest; the !Kung San on the fringe of the Kalahari Desert in Botswana in Southern Africa; and the "Stone Age" civilizations that can be found in isolated regions of Brazil (for example, the Txicao people of the Mato Grosso) and the Philippines (for example, the Tasaday people, discovered in 1971 in the remote mountain forests of the Island of Mindanao).

These contemporary forms of nearly extinct hunting and gathering societies are highly instrumental in understanding much of the sociological nature and function of more modern societies—as well as providing valuable insight into the social life of prehistoric peoples from which the more contemporary forms of society have evolved.

HORTICULTURAL SOCIETIES.    A **horticultural society** is distinguished by people who are food producers rather than food gatherers and hunters. These societies are characterized by settled, however temporary, communities that are engaged in the cultivation of grain crops, such as wheat and rice, as the chief means of subsistence. Cultivation, nonetheless, is on a very small scale, since it is undertaken only by the limited means of hand tools, particularly the hoe. The emphasis in these societies is on the constant search for fertile soil.

The division of labor in horticultural societies remains quite simple, but social organization on the whole tends to be somewhat more complex, especially in terms of extended kinship relations, which serve as the basis for many aspects of societal function, such as political administration. Horticultural societies also tend to be rather small, consisting usually of less than a few hundred people. These societies probably originated about 9,000 to 10,000 years ago (Lenski & Lenski, 1987). They served as the basis for the development of permanent settlements and villages and facilitated the expansion of technology, thereby providing the basis for the development of trade and commerce.

Among the more illustrious examples of horticultural societies are the civilizations of the Incas and Mayans of Mexico; and they were

▼

**Societal Subsistence.** Use of the hoe and other hand tools to plant corn in the *altiplano* of Bolivia demonstrates the typical mode of subsistence in agricultural societies. Limited economies of this kind are correspondingly associated with relatively simple forms of societal organization. (Jeff Rotman/Peter Arnold, Inc., 1983)

exemplified in this country's history by several American Indian tribes, such as the Cherokee, Navaho, and Zuñi. Today, simple horticultural societies are found in only three parts of the world: the remote interior of the Amazon River basins; certain islands of the Pacific, especially New Guinea; and parts of southeast Asia (Lenski, 1987).

AGRICULTURAL SOCIETIES. An **agricultural society** is distinguished by a relatively advanced technology—the use of mechanical means of cultivation. Such societies, marking a major turning point in societal evolution, emerged about 5,000 years ago with the invention of the animal-drawn plow. This fundamental invention did away with the need for frequent searches for fertile soil that are the constant preoccupation of horticultural societies. The plow, along with the development of

other aspects of agrarian technology, permitted a more extensive and thorough cultivation of soil, and thereby made possible the reuse of land by repeated renewal of organic nutrients. Such methods provided subsistence for greater numbers of people and brought the dawn of modern civilization. Relatively advanced technology resulted in more extensive occupational specialization, although Sjoberg (1960) estimates that no agrarian society has had fewer than 90 percent of its members engaged in farming. Barter and trade gave way to economies based on money. All in all, these innovations resulted in the emergence of various forms of social organization that are characterized by considerable complexity and bureaucracy.

Variations of agrarian societies—those exhibiting similar types of social organization by relying on other economic activities as physical modes of subsistence—are fishing, maritime, and pastoral societies. One of the first agrarian societies was that of ancient Egypt. Today, agricultural societies are found extensively in Africa, South America, and Asia. Contemporary examples of predominantly agricultural societies are those of Pakistan, China, Colombia, Egypt, Nigeria, India, Indonesia, Mexico, and Peru.

INDUSTRIAL SOCIETIES. An **industrial society,** the most modern type, is characterized by a technology that is distinguished by massive mechanization and automation, as well as enormous populations, often involving millions of people. The industrial revolution, along with the factory system of production, had its origin about 250 years ago in Europe, more specifically in England, from which it has spread to nearly every corner of the earth. Several societies in the world today are either industrialized or in the process of emerging to this level of civilization. Nearly all of the remaining ones, the vast majority, are merely in the process of seeking this level of development. Even agricultural communities and enterprises are giving way to "factories in the fields." Correspondingly, the percentage of people engaged in agricultural activities has steadily dwindled as societies become more and more mechanized. In the United States, the most advanced of industrialized societies, the number of farms has dropped from 8 million in 1920 to fewer than 2 million in 1986; and, correspondingly, the average farm size has increased from 150 acres in

▼

**273**

**Industrialized Society.** A new mode of economy is not all that the industrial revolution brought to the world. With it also came an unrelenting urbanization, the inevitability of mass transportation, and the rather recent emergence of the megalopolis. (© Joseph S. Rychetnik/Photo Researchers)

▼ 1920 to about 400 in 1986. Farm population during the same period dropped from 30.1 percent of the population to about 2.5 percent. Statistics such as these invariably indicate that, among other things, industrial societies have a surplus supply of food.

Industrial societies are invariably quite large and have a highly complex social structure. All of the characteristics of bureaucratic organization reach unparalleled proportions in the emergence of industrial societies. The United States, Canada, Japan, and several of the Western European countries are examples of industrialized societies.

The trend in sociocultural development from small, simple societies to large, complex ones has culminated in industrial societies. Some social scientists, see the continuation of this sociocultural evolution. Many observers have spoken of the postindustrial society under one label or another: "advanced industrial," "superindustrial," "modern society," "mass society," "information society," and "technocratic society." We shall have more to say about these social trends in Chapter 14.

## MODES OF SOCIAL ORGANIZATION

The more common way of classifying societies, one used increasingly in sociology because of its relevance to a number of theoretical perspectives found in the discipline today, is in terms of their mode of social organization. In this respect, the employment of ideal-type conceptions of society has been most useful. The **ideal type** is a mental construct or nominal type of concept (see Chapter 2) that portrays the principal characteristics of a phenomenon in its pure form (Weber, 1949). The term has nothing to do with judgments of desirability.

Ideal-type formulations, juxtaposed in antithetical perspectives, offer models that permit the measurement of any given society—from a simple, primitive village to a highly industrialized society—along the implicit continuum in order to determine whether it approximates one pole rather than the other in terms of the respective set of characteristics. This mode of analysis, along with an underlying assumption of social evolution, permits a contrast of the basic characteristics and dynamics of two radically different types of society.

Several typologies, all basically sharing fundamentally similar conceptions, have been devised for this purpose. The more well-known ideal-type dichotomies include:

1. *Militant* versus *industrial* society (Spencer, 1862);
2. *Status* versus *contract* society (Maine, 1861);
3. *Mechanical* versus *organic* society (Durkheim, 1893);
4. *Gemeinschaft* versus *Gesellschaft* (Töennies, 1887);
5. *Primary-group* versus *secondary-group* society (Cooley, 1902);
6. *Folk* versus *urban* society (Redfield, 1947);
7. *Communal* versus *associational* society (Weber, 1947);
8. *Sensate* versus *ideational* society (Sorokin, 1937–1941);
9. *Familistic* versus *contractual* society (Sorokin, 1937–1941); and
10. *Traditional* versus *other-directed* society (Riesman, 1950).

While the paired conceptions of these respective typologies have different foci and frames of reference (the sacred-secular dichotomy, for example, points primarily to religious or ideological orientations; and the folk-urban consists predominantly of anthropological perspectives), fundamentally they all refer to similar dimensions and characteristics of societal organization that, ideally, characterize the dichotomous and implicitly antithetical forms of society. Perhaps the most popular typology is that offered by Ferdinand Töennies (1887), a German sociologist, who differentiated between *Gemeinschaft* and *Gesellschaft*. These German

274

terms do not translate readily into English, but the words "community" and "society" are used, respectively, to designate the corresponding conceptual distinctions which nevertheless require more explicit definition and description. Perhaps the intended conceptual distinctions can best be understood by speaking respectively of *communal* and *associational* societies—terms that have become fairly standard in sociological usage during the past few decades.

A **communal society** (for example, the "mechanical," "sacred," or "folk") is one which tends to be relatively small in size, primary group–based, informal, and generally simple and homogeneous in social organization, with a minimal division of labor and role specialization, a high degree of social cohesion and integration, and total personal involvement and commitment. Social relations in communal societies are characteristically intimate, personal, intrinsic in value, and long-lasting. An **associational society** (such as the "organic," "secular," and "urban") tends to manifest the antithetical characteristics: relatively large, secondary group–based, formal, bureaucratic, and generally complex and heterogeneous in social organization, with extensive division of labor and role specialization, a low degree of social cohesion and integration, and partial personal involvement and commitment. Associational societies are marked by social relationships that are typically impersonal, superficial, segmental, instrumental, and short-lived. Additional characteristics that describe the organization of these antithetical types of society are given in Table 7-2.

Communal and associational societies, or *Gemeinschaft* and *Gesellschaft,* are ideal-type conceptions. No society is all one or the other. Any actual society represents only an approximation of one conceptual type or the other. All modern, industrialized societies as well as a good number of the larger agricultural ones, such as India and Greece—are examples of *Gesellschaft* societies. Of course, within such societies, there may be elements and segments of *Gemeinschaft*. Such would be the case in most family units, as well as in small and isolated communities. Examples of *Gemeinschaft* on the macro level—the total societal level—are, however, increasingly difficult to come by nowadays. Hunting-gathering and horticultural societies would be cases in point. The historical trend toward increasingly complex forms of societal organization is unmistakable. It represents one of the most important developments in human history.

# Social Institutions

Society as a complex system consists of several subsystems. The principal, and largest, types of these subunits are called social institutions. The study of social institutions has been one of the major tasks of the field of sociology. Most of the sociological research today, as well as the bulk of courses in our colleges and universities, are concerned with one or more aspects of social institutions. So enormous, in fact, is the fund of knowledge in these areas of social organization that we cannot possibly do them justice here. Comprehensive treatments of social institutions in the American society alone would exceed the limited space at our disposal in this single chapter. We shall concern ourselves with only the basic concepts and principles of institutional structure and function.

## NATURE AND DEFINITION

A **social institution** refers to all of the patterns of behavior, formal or informal, that are firmly or ideally established for the purposes of meeting a functional need or goal of society. For example, every society is characterized by a host of activities that relate to its perpetuation, and these are generally fulfilled through a number of personal and collective activities, including such practices as dating, engagement, courtship, marriage, kinship, and childrearing. All of the beliefs, knowledge, values, attitudes, social positions, roles, norms, patterns of behavior, and

275

▼ TABLE 7-2. Modes of Societal Organization

| *Gemeinschaft* (Communal Society) | *Gesellschaft* (Associational Society) |
| --- | --- |
| Traditional | Modern |
| Preindustrial | Industrial |
| Small population | Large population |
| Simple division of labor | Complex division of labor |
| Minimal role specialization | Extensive role specialization |
| Primary-group based and centered | Secondary-group based and centered |
| High cohesion and integration | Loose cohesion and integration |
| Focal unit: family and/or kinship | Multiple institutional focus |
| Primary social relationships: | Secondary social relationships: |
|   Informal |   Formal |
|   Folkways |   Mores |
|   Custom |   Law |
|   Emotional involvement |   Unemotional involvement |
|   Total personality involvement |   Segmental personality involvement |
|   Personal involvement |   Impersonal involvement |
|   Permanent and long-lasting |   Transient or transitory |
|   Intrinsic value |   Instrumental value |
| Relatively homogeneous culture | Relatively heterogeneous culture |
| Unambiguous behavioral expectations | Ambiguous behavioral expectations |
| Informal regulation of social norms | Formal regulation of social norms |
| Simple social organization | Complex social organization |
| Small group structure | Bureaucratic structure |

other cultural elements that relate to family life or its activities are part of the institution of the family. Social institutions, thus represent enduring social structures that provide ready-made solutions to the basic requirements of human living.

We have already spoken about social institutions in our discussion of culture in Chapter 3. Social institutions, however, need to be analyzed not only as elements of culture but also as elements of social structure. Institutions in a structural perspective refer to groups and organizations that have exclusive or primary responsibility for meeting the specific functional needs of society. These groups or organizations correspond to specific institutions. For example: the family group and the familial institution; the school and the educational institution; the church and the religious institution; government and the political institution; the business corporation and the economic institution. The correspondence is not exclusive; however, it is convenient, on one level of analysis, to speak in these distinctive terms. Social institutions, nonetheless, are highly interrelated and influenced by each other. Their interplay is both extensive and, necessarily, continuous. Such is the case in part because several of the various

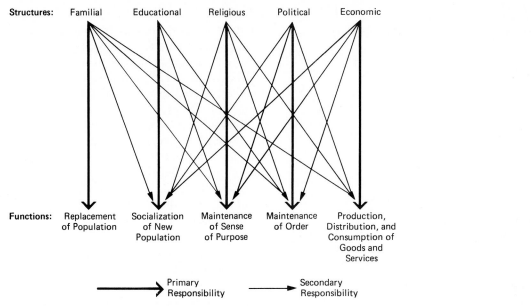

**Structures:** Familial  Educational  Religious  Political  Economic

**Functions:** Replacement of Population  Socialization of New Population  Maintenance of Sense of Purpose  Maintenance of Order  Production, Distribution, and Consumption of Goods and Services

→ Primary Responsibility     → Secondary Responsibility

FIGURE 7-1 Interrelationships of Institutional Structures and Institutional Functions.

institutional groups often contribute to the same functional problems. Figure 7-1 illustrates these interrelationships between institutional structures and institutional functions.

## DEVELOPMENT OF SOCIAL INSTITUTIONS

Social institutions develop as a response to the functional needs of society and its members. All societies, if they are to survive, must deal with certain basic problems. For example, no society can escape attention to the problem of member replacement. Every society must regulate sexual behavior and insure that the offspring of its members are properly cared for and socialized. Each society must see to it that the children learn the basic skills that are needed for them to become productive members of the society. Similarly, procedures must be developed to determine who its leaders will be and how it will protect itself from threats made by other so-

cieties. Every society must also insure that necessary goods and services are produced and distributed in an efficient manner. Mechanisms must be developed to meet these and other functional requirements if societies are to endure over time.

The initial processes of the *institutionalization* of normative behavior is for the most part a casual and informal one. Behavior tends to become routinized, as expressed in sayings such as "that's the way we do things" or "it's customary to do things this way." Efficient solutions (patterns of behavior) to regularly occurring functional problems that become preferred, repetitious, habitual, and routine (folkways) may in time acquire more and more sanction and become standardized as the highly valued and highly expected ways (mores) of doing things in a particular society. Institutionalized practices are enforced by formal or informal methods according to their functional importance and the nature and structure of the society.

## ▼ VARIETY AND COMPLEXITY OF SOCIAL INSTITUTIONS

The number of institutions, as well as their individual complexity and the extent of their specialization, varies from society to society but in general shows a positive correlation with the complexity of society. Societies with large populations and highly developed cultures have many institutions, while the most simple societies have only a basic set of institutions that, in one form or another, are found universally in all societies. Our own society has a large number of institutions that are not found in more simple ones: for example, science, recreation, medicine, sports, and the military.

Modern industrialized societies may have a relatively great number of institutions, and hence, on the whole, a very complex social organization; but in terms of some specific institutions, primitive societies often have social institutions that are far more complex. This situation is especially true of the familial institution; kinship structures and relationships can be extremely complicated. For these reasons, among others, it is important to attend to the analysis of the structure as well as the content of social institutions.

## BASIC AND UNIVERSAL INSTITUTIONS

There are several basic social institutions that are found in all societies. These institutions can be described as societal universals. From a functional point of view, they are indispensable for any society. These universal institutions are the family, education, polity (government), economy (economics), and religion.

Each of the basic institutions relates fundamentally to one or more of the functional requisites of all social systems which were discussed in the previous chapter, as well as more concretely to the functional requisites of society that were discussed in the preceding sections of

this chapter. Every institution has specific and, for the most part, distinctive functions. However, given the complex and systemic nature of society, institutional functions are multiple and overlap in the sense that these multiple functions are shared in varying degree by the different institutions.

We shall explore these universal institutions in only brief outline, with an emphasis on their fundamental components. However, one institution, the family, is such a central institution in all societies that a more comprehensive treatment of it is in order here. Our description of the institution of the family, moreover, is intended to serve as an analytical model of the structure and function of other institutions and their relationship to society.

# The Family as Core Institution

The family is one of the most highly varied units of societal organization. This is all the more true given the many changes that have affected the family in modern societies during the past decade or two. Our discussion, however, will be more traditional and somewhat anthropological in nature, so that the student may appreciate the universal nature and variety of familial institutions. Some of our discussion may seem exotic, or even idealistic, but such a situation should serve to underscore the diversity of social institutions.

## TYPES OF FAMILY ORGANIZATION

Everybody—well, nearly everybody—belongs to two families: the *family of orientation*, which is the one into which we are born or adopted, and the *family of procreation*, which is the one we produce—biologically and/or socially. Each of these families may be characterized by different kinds of social organization.

278

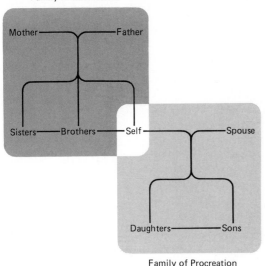

Family of Orientation

Mother——Father

Sisters——Brothers——Self——Spouse

Daughters——Sons

Family of Procreation

FIGURE 7-2  Principal Modes of the Family.

The most common type of family organization, especially in modern industrial societies, is the **nuclear** or **conjugal family,** which consists of a husband and wife and their children within one household. Some societies have institutionalized the **extended** or **consanguineal family,** which consists of the nuclear family and other relatives. An extended or consanguineal family structure serves as the basis of highly complex kinship systems, which are found quite commonly in nonindustrialized societies. Beyond these fundamental structures, however, there is a great deal of variety in the family institution.

## MARRIAGE

**Marriage** is the process by which families are formed. It is itself a complex institution but is usually considered part of the familial institution. Much of the variation of the family institution is found in marriage. There are a great number of structural alternatives that, of course, are not necessarily functional equivalents. Let us consider some of the many bases

of structural variations in marital behavior that are representative of the family institution.

NORMS OF SPOUSE SELECTION: EXOGAMY VERSUS ENDOGAMY. **Exogamous** marital structures require that individuals select a marital partner from outside a designated group, usually a kin group. Correspondingly, **endogamous** marital rules permit marriage only between individuals who are members of the same group, be it a kin, tribe, community, village, or society. Laws that forbid marriage between individuals of different races are examples of endogamy, while the incest regulation is an example of exogamy.

**279**

NORMS OF MARITAL GROUP STRUCTURE: MONOGAMY VERSUS POLYGAMY. **Monogamy** is the more well-known form of marriage; it permits only one spouse for each partner at a time. **Polygamy,** on the other hand, provides for multiple spouses for one partner. There are two specific forms of polygamy: polyandry and polygyny. **Polyandry,** in which the female may have several husbands simultaneously, is a very rare form of marriage (found today in some parts of Tibet). **Polygyny,** a much more widespread form of polygamy, but one used only by a minority of people in a particular society, permits the male to have more than one wife at the same time. **Group marriage,** also quite rare, refers to a practice by which two or more men are all married simultaneously to each of two or more women.

NORMS OF DESCENT: MATRILINEAGE VERSUS PATRILINEAGE. Descent or family lineage is traced only via the father's family or kin in **patrilineal** societies, while only via the mother's in **matrilineal** institutions. This latter arrangement is the practice among the Navaho and Hopi Indians. Some societies are **bilineal,** in that official or formal lines of descent are maintained through both parents. Only about 30 percent of known societies employ this

▼

**Marital Institutions.** While a majority of societies in the world allow polygamy, usually only the wealthy can afford this marital form. This Bakhtiari chief in Iran proudly displays his three wives and several children. (© Tony Howarth/Daily Telegraph Magazine 1980)

method. Descent in most societies is traced officially in a unilineal fashion, and only either the father's ancestry or the mother's ancestry is considered significant or official.

NORMS OF AUTHORITY: PATRIARCHY VERSUS MATRIARCHY. **Patriarchy** is a marital and family form in which primary authority is vested in the husband or father; while in a **matriarchy** it is the wife or mother who serves as the principal authority figure. Modern societies found today in highly democratic societies are emphasizing an egalitarian or democratic authority structure in which both spouses exercise authority generally and in relatively equal measure.

NORMS OF RESIDENCE: MATRILOCALITY VERSUS PATRILOCALITY. When a newly created family establishes its residence in the household or locale of the wife, with her kin group, it is known as a **matrilocal** family. **Patrilocal** families are established similarly in terms of the husband. **Neolocal** residence, a system by which newlyweds establish a new and independent residence, is the common form in Western societies today.

Each marital structure has a number of secondary variations. However, these various structures do not necessarily correspond to each other. For example, families may be matrilineal but patrilocal or matrilocal but patrilineal.

# FAMILY FUNCTIONS

There are certain commonly recognized universal functions of the family.

SEXUAL REGULATION. While sexual activity is in itself a personal matter, it usually involves other people and hence becomes a social activity and societal concern. Sexual relations, in many societies, are not permitted during certain times, such as during menstruation, pregnancy, religious festivals, or periods of mourning. Similarly, certain forms of sexual behavior may be approved in some societies, while not in others.

Sexual activity, like all other social action, needs to be organized and regulated for the purpose of harmonious and efficient societal function—all the more so because of the highly potent nature of the sexual drive. Universally, the expression of sexual activity has been assigned and confined, at least ideally, to the marital state; and, for the most part, it has been defined normatively in reference to the nuclear family, as is reflected in references to "extramarital" or "premarital" sexual conduct. Premarital sexual relations, however, appear to be allowed or tolerated in a clear majority of societies, although extramarital relations are almost universally forbidden (Murdock, 1949).

Norms regulating sexual behavior, even among marital partners, are much more extensive in primitive societies than in modern ones. All societies, however, incorporate an **incest taboo,** which clearly demonstrates the role of the family in sexual regulation (Murdock, 1949). The incest taboo prohibits sexual relations and/or marriage with *any* member of the nuclear family and with *some* members of extended families. The specificity of extended relatives varies from society to society.

The incest taboo is a truly socially derived regulation. Its universality may tend to suggest a biological or physiological basis; yet if this were the case, then there would be no need for social regulation to enforce it. Moreover, the biological dysfunctions of interbreeding (miscegenation) in human beings are unknown to primitive societies. The small size of their populations, coupled with a short life span, make it highly unlikely that genetic defects that take three to four generations to become manifest would have been observed. Murdock (1949), furthermore, has pointed out that people in some primitive societies are not aware of the connection between pregnancy and sexual intercourse.

Several functions, all social, are fulfilled by the incest regulation. Each of them, however, is directed at maintaining and strengthening the integrity of the family, as well as avoiding dysfunctional and disruptive behavior throughout the society. The objectives of the incest taboo are to preclude sexual rivalries and other hostilities among family members, preclude confusion regarding role relationships among family members, and provide for friendships and alliances between other families in order to reduce social conflict and increase social cohesion.

The regulation of sexual behavior is related, quite fundamentally, to another basic function of society—reproduction and member replacement.

REPRODUCTION OF CHILDREN. No society can survive without people. Reproduction is the principal, but not the only, means by which people are recruited into society. Immigration and conquests or capture are other means. Societies that do not utilize biological reproduction, however, have invariably passed out of existence. Such was the case with the communal society of the Shakers, as well as other religious communities, such as the Oneida and the Amana, during the present century. People in these communities lived a totally celibate life together. Their children consisted of

▼ orphans whom they reared, a practice eventually forbidden by law in some states.

Biological reproduction, although not indispensably rooted in the family, has been mandated in all societies to the family. It is an activity that requires control and regulation, and one which is inseparably associated with the societal functions of sexual regulation that are, for all the reasons given above, usually confined to the family.

**282** The reproductive functions of the family are not exclusively biological. Just as society needs people, so too do people need society. Human beings need a relatively prolonged period of caring and learning in order to become functionally autonomous as well as socially viable. No other being is helpless for as long as the human infant. The human needs for protection and assistance in both their physical and psychological dimensions can be met most effectively, and often only, by the family.

SOCIALIZATION. The family is the primary agent of socialization—both in terms of time and content. Of course, social learning functions in the modern society are shared by several other institutions. Chief among these other institutions are the educational and the religious. Yet, long before the child encounters other societal groups in any formal way, much social learning and human development has already taken place. Socialization begins at the moment of birth—perhaps even before in certain respects. Moreover, much of the type of learning that the child needs can be performed only, or at least most effectively, in a primary group, such as the family. The social nature and psychological qualities of the family as a primary group (see Chapter 9) provide that kind of social interaction which is the indispensable context for the crucial socialization and psychological development of the individual.

Socialization within the family is at once very complex and very subtle. Much socialization that takes place within the family occurs latently and unconsciously—however necessary and natural it may be. One such aspect of social learning performed by the family is in terms of the role models that are provided by the parents and older siblings. Day-care centers and other such forms of modern baby-sitting which are so prevalent in industrial societies are simply part-time extensions of the family rather than replacements for it. Certain aspects of socialization can be fulfilled only by the family group. Only the family, for instance, can transmit its own subculture in terms of such specific dimensions as ethnicity or racial backgrounds, religion, and socioeconomic class.

AFFECTION AND EMOTIONAL SUPPORT. Human beings have basic psychological needs that must be fulfilled in much the same way as biological ones. Among such needs are those for social response, social acceptance, social recognition, affection, and security. Several studies (Pines, 1981; Evans, 1972; Spitz, 1945) have shown that individuals who do not receive adequate gratification of these needs do not function well on both the psychological and physical levels. Severe deprivation of psychological needs can lead to serious psychological dysfunction, which in turn, on an adequate scale, can have significant consequences for the function of society.

Although not alone, the family group is best able to fulfill these needs, not only because of its involvement and attachments with individuals in the biological, psychological, and sociological dimensions but also because of its organizational structure as a primary group in which social and psychological gratifications can be accomplished more effectively.

Social cohesion and solidarity is perhaps nowhere stronger than in the family. Members of any family share an identification—a "consciousness of kind" or a "we-feeling"—with each other that has both sociological and biological roots. That "blood is thicker than water" can be seen in the way individual problems, crises, misfortune, and shame—as well as success, honor, acclaim, and achievement—are often assumed by, and conferred upon, one's family.

People feel a special sense of obligation to family members and kinfolk, especially when they are in need. Parents invariably support and defend their children—right or wrong— just as spouses invariably stand by each other. Such a familial "love is blind" principle has significant positive functions not only for the individual but for society as well.

ECONOMIC FUNCTIONS. In the past, the family was the basic, and often the exclusive, economic unit. This situation is still true of contemporary primitive societies—but not for modern industrial society. Yet, while its economic functions have been greatly given over to other institutions, a number of economic activities do remain in the family group.

The indispensable functions that are performed by the householders—such as meal preparation, cleaning, house maintenance, and child care—are in themselves economic activities that either a family can provide for itself or can purchase from others with the economic means (money or goods) earned by the family breadwinners.

Every modern family must have a breadwinner (or, more commonly nowadays, two) who by taking employment outside the family earns the capital by which economic activities for its subsistence are performed at the family level.* Consumption of goods and services is very much an economic function—and one no less important than production. Indeed, the major economic function of the family in modern societies is increasingly becoming that of consumption rather than production. Hence, while the style and means of the economic activities

of the family have changed, the basic function is still there.

SOCIAL PLACEMENT AND STATUS ASCRIPTION. One of the critical problems of human existence, as we have suggested in previous chapters, is finding answers to the question, Who am I? It is the family that initially provides a number of answers to this question through its status-giving functions of social placement and status ascription.

Social positions, as we shall see in Chapter 10, can be either achieved by one's own accomplishments, or ascribed by others on the basis of social criteria and relationships. Most ascription of social statuses or positions takes place in the family. Sex, age, birth order, ethnicity, racial background, social class, religion, regional affiliation, and nationality are all statuses that are conferred upon an individual by virtue of his or her family of origin. Some statuses, of course, such as social class or religion, may change through personal achievements; others, however, are permanent. One's life chances in the social mobility of society are rooted or set in the family of origin, but not definitively determined. Nonetheless, given the importance of status in structuring one's social relationships and social experiences, as well as one's personality and sense of self, it is inevitable that the family contributes most importantly, and uniquely so, to these functions.

# Educational Institutions

Educational institutions are concerned with the transmission of knowledge to individuals in order to permit them to function effectively in the social positions that they will assume in society. Education, then, in a sociological sense is essentially the transmission of culture from one generation to another.

Formal educational institutions are not needed in primitive societies. Here, and as is

* More than 50 percent of married women are now employed outside the home. This figure contrasts significantly to that of 24 percent in 1940.

▼ still the case in some respects in modern societies today, education is a function of the family. In complex societies, however, the fund of knowledge is enormously complex and associated with a high degree of technological development. Such a situation necessitates formal systems of education, which require longer and longer periods of time to transmit the rapidly expanding fund of basic knowledge. Hence, today, college education or its equivalent is becoming more and more common in modern industrial societies, not only because it is readily available but also because it is necessary for survival in many respects—as much on the part of the individual as on the part of society.

284

There are many segments to the educational system of modern societies. Many of these parts constitute institutions in themselves. Consider some of the following elements that comprise modern educational institutions: colleges and universities, private research institutes, publishing houses, libraries, scholarly journals, professional associations, accrediting boards, nursery schools, kindergartens, educational television, museums, teachers' unions, newspapers and magazines, community orchestras, and continuing educational programs. Even science and the arts, thought in some quarters to be emerging as independent and even fundamental institutions in modern societies, may be considered part of the educational institution, which in this respect takes on a relatively new function: the generation of knowledge and new technology.

Once again, the structure, and to a considerable degree the content, of educational institutions is highly varied. In the United States, for example, education at the elementary and secondary levels is administered by about 19,000 local districts, while higher education is

**Fundamental Learning.** One of the universal, and hence basic, institutions in any society is that of education. Primitive societies, such as here in Ethiopia, usually provide education in only the fundamental skills that are strategically required for social interaction and societal function. (© Image Bank)

left to private and state-administered organizations. In most European countries, on the other hand, education at all levels is administered by the national government, usually through the ministry of education. The American and Canadian university systems are based to a great extent on the British university system, which in turn shares much of the system of higher education that is found in continental Europe—and which in many respects dates from the Middle Ages.

Major developments in educational institutions throughout the world include the following three processes:

1. *Democratization:* the extension of all levels and types of educational opportunities to all members of society;
2. *Bureaucratization:* the creation of formal systems of enormous size and organizational complexity, with an emphasis on standardization and professionalization (see Chapter 8 for an elaboration on the social organization of bureaucracies); and
3. *Centralization:* an increasing control and regulation of schools by central authorities.

While these processes are worldwide trends, it is important to note that the American educational system remains comparatively decentralized with its historical emphasis on "community control," as well as its vast networks of private education at all levels.

# Political Institutions

Every society requires management. Such is the basic function of political institutions, or the **polity.** Political institutions are concerned fundamentally with the allocation and implementation of authority—the establishment and maintenance of order, and the control of disorder or deviation. Among these tasks are those of ensuring justice, protecting property, pro-

moting the individual and common welfare, and defending society from outside forces.

Political institutions have evolved, throughout history, in one central respect from the rule of tribal chiefs and pharaohs, to the power of kings and queens, to the authority invested in prime ministers and presidents. In a very basic sense, however, the fundamental structures and governmental modes of political institutions have remained unchanged. There are two basic and antithetical forms of government in contemporary societies, each of which has many ideological and methodological variations: democracy and autocracy.

Essentially, a **democracy** is a form of government in which ultimate authority derives from the consent of the governed and in which citizens have the right to participate in decision making. As described so eloquently by Abraham Lincoln, a democracy consists in government "of the people, by the people, and for the people." One can distinguish two principal forms of democracy: direct or participatory and representative. In a participatory democracy, as one can find in the town meetings of New England and the civic associations of neighborhoods throughout the United States, members of society participate personally and directly in the decision-making process; whereas, in representative democracy, found in larger political entities such as in a republic, citizens delegate their authority to others who make decisions for them.

In an **autocracy,** political power is exercised supremely by a single individual, such as a tribal chief, emperor, monarch, or dictator. Such rulers have absolute control. Truly autocratic governments, with the exception of numerous dictatorships, are becoming rare in today's societies. Modern versions, however, are those known more technically as authoritarian systems which may take the form of an **oligarchy** that consists of rule by a small number of people (or of an aristocracy or elite class). One common example is that of the military junta, such as is

▼

# BOX 7-1. Who Really Rules America?

Despite variations in the forms of government and political ideologies that are found in different societies, the basic social process and dynamics of political institutions consist in the accumulation, distribution, and exercise of power—the ability to control the behavior of people. Power is not only a scarce resource in any society, but also is inevitably distributed in an uneven manner throughout its various sectors. What, then, is the power structure of American society? Sociologists offer three competing views on this question.

1. The *ruling class* perspective, essentially Marxian, maintains that a small, economically dominant, class controls the means of production, and, correspondingly, for all intents and purposes, it has effective control of the entire society. This powerful, and allegedly ruling, class consists of the entrepreneurs.

2. The *power elite* view, formulated by C. Wright Mills (1956) argues that political power is in the hands of a ruling class that is drawn from several sectors of society, rather than only the economic sphere. Chief among these power brokers are the political, military, and business leaders of society, whom Mills saw as forming a highly cohesive and interlocking elite. Such individuals not only share similar values and beliefs, and often know each other personally, but also work closely with each other in trying to shape the policies and goals of society. Domhoff (1983) contends that the power elite consists of less than 0.5 percent of the American population, or about 1 in every 200 people. Hence, the power structure of modern, advanced societies is essentially a form of oligarchy. In the power elite perspective, democracy, wherever it supposedly exists, is but a facade and sham.

3. The *pluralist model* envisions the power elite as consisting of a variety of interest groups that compete with each other in the political and economic sectors of society. Such a perspective maintains fundamentally that the power structure is a democratic one. Yet, basic to the pluralist perspective is the contention that, while different segments within society all have power, they are not equal in the amount of power which they hold and are able to utilize. Moreover, since power is not dispersed evenly throughout society, in its many sectors and among many interest groups, no one segment ever accumulates total power (Dahl, 1981). Political and government decisions, therefore, are a product of the competition and conflict among the many different interest or power sectors in society.

Empirical studies can be marshalled to support each of these views (for example, Useem, 1984; Domhoff, 1983; Dahl, 1961; Hunter, 1953). No one perspective need be absolutely correct, since the actual power structure may vary not only from society to society, but even within particular regions and sectors of a given society. Moreover, the same seems to be true of social and political issues. Accordingly, the three positions might best be viewed as complementary, each providing an explanation for part of the power structure and political dynamics of modern and highly complex societies. As for the actual power structure in the United States, the question is far from resolved, and it will continue to be both a highly controversial subject and one for continuing sociological research. ▲

found today in Chile under the leadership of General Pinochet. Political rulers in an authoritarian structure tolerate little or no public opposition. While in principle they assume absolute control, in practice their concerns are usually limited to the political sphere. Such is not the case, however, in totalitarian societies.

**Totalitarianism** is an authoritarian form of government in which the rulers absolutely recognize no limits to their authority, and attempt to regulate virtually every aspect of social life. No opposition of any kind is tolerated. Totalitarian states frequently root their justification in a very strong sense of nationalism.

Friedrich and Brzezinski (1965) have identified six fundamental characteristics of a totalitarian political structure:

1. Large-scale use of ideology.
2. One-party governance.
3. Control of economy.
4. Control of media and censorship.
5. Control of weapons.
6. Use of terrorism.

A modern variety of totalitarianism is that of **fascism,** which ideologically allocates supreme authority to the state. Nazism, Peronism, and Francoism are all examples of fascism that existed in Germany, Argentina, and Spain during this century. Other principal examples are the nations of the former Communist bloc of Eastern Europe. Today, totalitarian societies can be found in the Soviet Union Albania, North Korea, Cuba, and China. Totalitarian societies, much in evidence in the world today, tend to be immune to revolution—although often they experience defeat at the hands of an external ememy.

Among the subsystems of modern political institutions are the following: police systems, military systems, electoral systems, political parties, welfare systems, judicial systems, penal systems, local, county, state, and national governments, legislatures, administrations and cabinets, town meetings, and taxation bureaus. As

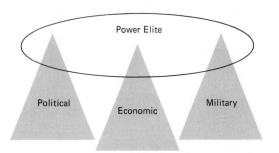

FIGURE 7-3 Mills' Three Pyramids of Power. The "Power Elite" in Mills' conception consists of three sectors: political, economic, and military.

**287**

one can readily see, many of these substructures are in themselves social institutions.

The political institution is the most inclusive and pervasive of all in its sphere of function. The authority of government spreads to every aspect of society and includes all of its members in one form or another.

# Economic Institutions

Our discussion on modes of subsistence provided some description of the nature of economic institutions or the economy. The **economy** is concerned with the production, distribution, and consumption of goods and services. Economic institutions are not only basic and universal in all societies, but they comprise one of the more focal. Such a situation is reflected in the fact that the greatest part of the human day is devoted to economic activities—even that of householders and breadwinners.

In the more primitive societies, the economic sphere of life is quite simple, and it is incorporated, as with most other societal activities, into the family. Again, as with other basic institutions, the economy today is a far more complex and sophisticated system of social organization. Earlier forms of economic activity such as trade, barter, and exchange have given way to more complex systems based on money, credit, investment, and so forth.

▼

288

Many of the modern dimensions of economic institutions are found in social organizations such as stock markets, money and banking systems, corporations, labor unions, transportation systems, communication systems, advertising firms, factories, and retail stores. All modern mechanisms, many of which are institutions in themselves, that relate to the production, distribution, and consumption of material goods and services comprise the economic institution. Common examples in the workaday world include collective bargaining and labor arbitration.

The basic elements of any economy are rooted in land (including natural resources), labor (including skills), capital (wealth and other resources), and technology. Economic institutions vary in terms of the access that societies have to these fundamental components, as well as the manner in which they are utilized and the relationship which they share among themselves.

There are three major types of economic institutions prevalent in societies of the world today: capitalism, communism, and socialism. The fundamental difference between these economic systems is the manner and the degree in which the government is involved in them, particularly with regard to the ownership of property and the means of production.

**Capitalism,** rooted in the principle of the private ownership of property, is based on a comparatively free and individualistic enterprise— open and highly unregulated competition in the marketplace. Wages and prices in a capitalistic economy are subject to the dynamics of supply and demand. The United States, Canada, England, West Germany, Italy, and Japan are examples of capitalist economies.

**Communism** is a closed and highly controlled economic system based on collective activity and the mutual ownership of wealth and other means of production. There is no private property. Its fundamentally Marxist principle is "from each according to his abilities, to each according to his needs." China and the Soviet Union are commonly offered as the principal examples of communist economies in the world today, but no society has developed as yet a totally communistic economy. The closest approximation to a true type of communism would be the kibbutzim of Israel.

**Socialism** is an economic system that is somewhat of a balance between communism and capitalism. It combines private and collective ownership of the economic means and ends of production in the interests of protecting the welfare of all members of society with minimal standards for the basic necessities of life. Private property exists in a socialistic economy, but the state assumes the ownership of all strategic industries and services (for example, railroads, airlines, mines, banks, radio, television, electrical energy, medical services, education). Finland is an example of a socialistic economy.

These three economies are ideal systems. There are no pure types to be found in the world today, and none has ever existed. Every major economy in the world today is a mixed economy—one particularly containing elements of both capitalism and socialism in varying proportions.

Even the economy of the United States, which often is taken as the example par excellence of capitalism, is a highly modified version in which there is considerable government regulation of many industrial and commercial activities, and even ownership in some cases (for example, Amtrak). Similarly, capitalistic activity is not uncommon in many communistic societies where, nonetheless, key industries are state-owned. Communism as practiced in Cuba and Yugoslavia is quite different in each concrete case, although both societies are founded on Marxist ideology which stipulates the essentials of communistic structure for the various realms of social organization.

One type of mixed economy that is rather popular today is democratic socialism, also known as the "welfare state." **Democratic so-**

**cialism** represents an economic and political system that seeks to ensure personal freedom in a context of social equality achieved through a centrally planned and closely controlled economy. Such economic systems are characterized by high taxation, designed to prevent excessive profits and wealth; and extensive welfare services (for example, health care, financial security, education, housing), designed to ensure the well-being of all members of society (see Ashford, 1988). Sweden and Austria are examples of societies operating under the structure of democratic socialism.

Whatever the form of its organization, the economy in every society today is concerned with the same objective: to increase the gross national product (GNP) by means of the production, distribution, and consumption of goods or services. One of the basic concerns of sociologists and economists is the relative efficiency of the three types of economy. That is

to say, are they functional equivalents or merely structural alternatives?

Research throughout the past century has provided overwhelming evidence that the socialistic/communistic economies are less productive than the capitalistic ones (Berger, 1986). While the standards of living have been increased and the extremes of poverty decreased in socialistic and communistic economies, the total wealth and per capita income of communistic/socialistic economies is generally far below that of capitalistic countries (see Figure 7-4). Similarly, the capitalistic philosophy of private ownership has been used to explain the differential productivity in the Soviet Union and China between privately owned lands and the larger state-owned farms. Private farms constitute less than 3 percent of the arable land in the Soviet Union, yet they produce 50 percent of the nation's meat, milk, and vegetables and about 80 percent of its eggs and potatoes. In

**289**

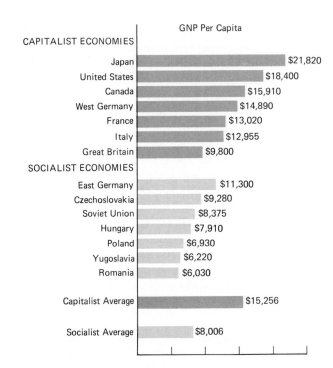

FIGURE 7-4 Capitalistic and Socialistic Economies Compared. The total wealth of capitalistic economies far exceeds that of socialistic economies. One measure of the difference is the value of the gross national product, for each person (GNP per capita) in various countries. Source: *The World Factbook: 1988* Washington, D.C.: U.S. Government Printing Office, 1988.

▼ China, private farms make up only 5 percent of its cultivated land, but they produce more than 25 percent of its noncereal crops (Hollander, 1982). Thus, capitalistic economies, would seem to be more efficient at producing wealth, while the socialistic economies seem to be more efficient in its distribution.

# Religious Institutions

290 Religious institutions include all of those elements of society and culture that are concerned with the relationship of people to the unknown and uncontrolled phenomena in their world of experience. Every religion focuses on the sacred and the supernatural as opposed to the mundane or profane phenomena of life. "Religion," as Yinger (1970:10) states, "is an attempt to explain what cannot otherwise be explained; to achieve power, all other things having failed us; to establish poise and serenity in the face of evil and suffering that other efforts have failed to eliminate." One such manifestation of religion can be had in the practice of sending nude women to till soil in the fields of India's Uttah Pradesh state at night by farmers seeking relief from drought and believing this to be the only way to appease the rain god, Varuma (*The New York Times*, 1978).

Religion is a societal response to the search for answers to the fundamental questions and issues of human existence: the meaning and purpose of life, death, suffering (anxiety, frustrations, and tragedy), the origin of humanity, the nature of our destiny, and what our behavior ought to be (morality). Every religion provides answers to the ultimate questions of personal and social existence: Who am I? Where am I going? and How do I get there? Among the Tasaday of the Philippines, these ultimate questions are answered by beliefs in the *sugoy*, their deceased "soul relatives," as well as by *Salungal*, "the owner" of the mountain on which is located the rainforest that these people inhabit. All kinds of objects, however, have served as the focus of religion: animals, trees, ancestors, gods, spirits, planets, and persons.

Perhaps one more commonly thinks of religion in the sense of an organized church or ideology, such as Roman Catholicism, the Church of England, or Episcopalianism, Judaism, or Islam. In a sociological perspective, however, religion assumes many forms: animism, spiritism, deism, theism, supernaturalism, fetishism, totemism, sorcery, occultism, magic, idealism, witchcraft, superstition, and astrology, among others. While many of these various religious systems can be distinguished in different ways, such as in terms of the use of manipulation rather than supplication, they all have much in common in terms of their societal and individual functions, as well as in terms of the basics of social organization. Among the chief elements of religious institutions are such things as doctrine (beliefs), rituals (forms of worship, such as prayer and singing), ceremonial pageantry, codes of behavior (ethics, morality, and commandments), and symbols (cross, totem pole).

Religious institutions manifest more variety than any other type of institution—and, unlike other institutions, they are also quite diversified and heterogeneous in the concrete case. Some societies have a singular religious system. Such is usually the case in small, simple societies, although there are some modern, complex societies of which this situation is virtually true, such as in Italy, Spain, and England. More complex societies, especially those that permit religious freedom, may have many different religious systems. There are, for example, over 200 distinct religions that maintain a formal existence in the United States and Canada.* The actual number is probably much greater, perhaps over a couple of thousand, when one considers the many essentially unknown religions whose organization is limited to the local

---

* See C. H. Jacquet, *Yearbook of American and Canadian Churches, 1987.*

or neighborhood level, such as the numerous storefront churches that can be found in the center cities of the United States. This tremendous number of religious organizations is itself a testimony to the pervasiveness and universality of religion. Not only does religious commitment remain strong today (Greeley, 1989), but new types and manifestations (for example, spiritualism, occultism, astrology) are replacing formal religions. Such a phenomenon whereby new religions appear constantly occurs in all societies (Stark & Bainbridge, 1985).

Christianity, with over 1 billion followers, is the largest single category of religion in the world today, and the special form that has the largest following is that of Roman Catholicism, accounting for nearly two-thirds of all Christians. Other major faiths in the world, in order of size, include Islam, Hinduism, Buddhism, Judaism, Sikhism, Shamanism, Confucianism,

291

## BOX 7-2. Civil Religion in America

Sociologically speaking, the definition of religion includes what Bellah (1967) has described as *civil religion*—a set of theistic beliefs, values, symbols, and practices that provide a type of ideological cohesion for a particular society. Perhaps in no other society today is civil religion more prominent than in the United States.

Civil religion may be described as a secular, nonsectarian religion that unites all believers around a core set of sacred beliefs, symbols, and rituals—and which as such serves as a very vital part of the American creed and cultural ethos.

There are varieties of civil religion throughout the world, but essentially all involve a linking of politics and religion (Bellah & Hammond, 1981). Such is no less the case in the United States. While there is a constitutional separation of church and state in the United States that prohibits the establishment of any particular religion as the official creed of the nation, there are nonetheless a number of fundamental religious principles (for example, belief in God or a supernatural being) which are widely shared throughout American society and which serve to unite believers of all faiths in a common and secularized ideology. This civil religion, moreover, is an important dimension of American political life.

Manifestations of civil religion in American society include the national motto of "In God We Trust," the pledge of allegiance to the flag that contains the phrase "One nation under God," the unofficial national anthem, "God Bless America," as well as "America the Beautiful," which also invokes the name of God. Other manifestations can be found in the widespread use of invocation and benediction that are an integral part of public ceremonies, especially political ones and including in particular presidential inaugurations; references to God in oaths to public office and courtroom procedures; national holidays such as Thanksgiving and Memorial Day; and the practice of providing paid chaplains for both houses of Congress.

Civil religion, therefore, does not consist of any particular religious creed, but rather of only a fundamental and general religious belief. Indeed, for many Americans religion consists of only a simple belief in God or the Golden Rule. Civil religion, in its many manifestations, is often seen as contributing in no small part to sustaining the legitimacy and efficacy of our political systems. ▲

▼ Baha'i Faith, Jainism, and Shintoism (see Table 7-3).

Sociologists classify religious institutions in terms of a number of structural characteristics: size, formal organization, complexity, cohesion, and exclusivity. The principal categories that comprise a continuous typology based on these and other variables are those of ecclesia, denomination, sect, and cult (see Table 7-4).

An **ecclesia** tends to be a large, formally organized, and highly complex religion with an explicit creed, liturgy, and ordained ministry. Such religions include all, or nearly all, of the members of a society and are usually recognized by the respective political state as the official

TABLE 7-3. Estimated Populations of Major Religions in the World

| Religion | Number of Members | Percent* |
|---|---|---|
| Total Christianity | 1,669,520,400 | 32.9 |
|    Roman Catholicism | 951,843,360 | 18.8 |
|    Protestantism | 407,821,920 | 8.0 |
|    Orthodox Faiths | 161,774,350 | 3.2 |
| Islam | 880,555,210 | 17.4 |
| Hinduism | 663,495,450 | 13.1 |
| Buddhism | 311,836,170 | 6.1 |
| Judaism | 18,169,340 | 0.3 |
| Sikhism | 17,187,390 | 0.3 |
| Shamanism | 12,381,640 | 0.2 |
| Confucianism | 6,188,160 | 0.1 |
| Baha'i Faith | 4,691,890 | 0.1 |
| Jainism | 3,555,690 | 0.1 |
| Shintoism | 3,379,030 | 0.1 |
| Total | 3,590,960,370 | 70.8 |

**\* Of total estimate of world population.**
**Source: Adapted with permission from the *1989 Encyclopaedia Britannica Book of the Year*, copyright 1989, Encyclopaedia Britannica, Inc., Chicago, Illinois, p. 299.**

religion. Examples would be the Anglican Church in England, the Lutheran Church in Sweden, the Roman Catholic Church in Italy and Spain, and Islam in Iran and Saudi Arabia.

A **denomination** is a religion that is independent of the state and usually one among many in a given society. Denominations, usually quite large in membership, also tend to be formally organized with an explicit creed, liturgy, and ordained ministry. They are by and large tolerant of other religions. The Methodist and the Baptist churches in the United States would be examples of denominations.

A **sect** usually represents a splinter group or dissenting version of a denomination, such as the Jehovah's Witnesses, the Amish, and the Mennonites. The Hasidic Jews, found extensively in New York City, constitute a Yiddish-speaking sect within Judaism. Sects tend to be fundamentalist, dogmatic, and orthodox, believing in the strict and literal interpretation of their scriptures and exhibiting intolerance toward other religions. They tend to be very cohesive, highly normative, and often set apart by special dietary and dress codes. These numbers are far greater than one might suspect. Stark and Bainbridge (1981) have identified 417 indigenous sects in the United States alone.

A **cult,** at the opposite end of the continuum of social organization, is a quite small, highly informal group of individuals without a coherent body of beliefs, liturgy, or trained ministry. The cohesion of cults by and large consists in the felt need of its members for a religious experience. Rituals tend to emphasize emotionality and spontaneity. Beliefs may be more in the nature of a philosophy or code of ethics than a religion. Cult leadership is often centered around a particular individual with charismatic qualities. Accordingly, they tend to be short-lived. Examples would be the Hare Krishna movement, the Unification Church ("Moonies"), and many of the various "Jesus movements" that have been evident in our society in recent years. Cults are interesting sociologically

TABLE 7-4. Types of Religious Institutions

| Characteristic | Ecclesia | Denomination | Sect | Cult |
|---|---|---|---|---|
| Size | Large | Moderate | Small | Small |
| Relationship with secular world | Affirms prevailing culture and social arrangements | Supports current culture and social arrangements | Renounces or opposes prevailing culture and social arrangements | Although critical of society focuses on evil within each person |
| Relationship with other religious groups | Claims lone legitimacy | Accepts pluralistic legitimacy | Rejects as corrupted | Accepts or rejects |
| Religious services | Very formal with minimal congregational participation | Formal with limited congregational participation | Informal and emotional with high degree of congregational participation | Very informal and emotional with continuous participation of adherents |
| Clergy | Specialized, professional, full-time | Specialized, professional, full-time | Unspecialized, little formal training, part-time | Charismatic, founder-leader has little or no formal training |
| Doctrines | Specific dogma, creed | Liberal interpretation of scriptures | Literal interpretation of scriptures | New and independent tradition with a rather secularized view of the divine |
| Social class of members | All social classes | Middle and upper | Mainly lower | Mainly lower |
| Sources of members | Born into the faith; seeks universal membership | Often requires later validation of membership acquired from parents | Voluntary confessional membership | Often lacks formal membership |
| Emphasis | Religious education and transmission of religion to the children of members | Religious education and transmission of religious values to youth | Evangelism and adult membership | Living one's life in accordance with basic tenets |
| Financial holdings | Most extensive | Quite extensive | Limited | None or very limited |
| Life expectancy | Extensive | Extensive | Fairly short | Brief |

Source: Partial adaptation from Glenn M. Vernon, *Sociology of Religion*. New York: McGraw-Hill, 1962, p. 174.

▼

in one specific way: All religions originate as cult movements—and such was no less the case with many of today's prominent ecclesias and denominations.

Religion, whatever its nature and form, plays a crucial role in any society. One powerful aspect of this fundamental influence comes through the ideology and values that it provides. The Protestant ethic, a religious ideology that stressed hard work and frugality as a means of salvation, is thought to have accounted for much of the economic development of England, the United States, and other industrialized countries in Western Europe. This religious spirit remains quite strong, and gives direction to the development of many societies yet today. Certain Eastern religions, such as Taoism and Buddhism, that lack these values are seen as barriers to industrial development and modernization (Weber, 1958). These particular religions, always in the interest of eternal salvation, are thought to orient people to past rather than to future accomplishments—to a withdrawal from the world, rather than a mastery of it, as formulated in the Protestant ethic.

Religious institutions, as core institutions, are very strong influences in the lives of the faithful and the believers because of their sacred and supernatural character. Religion provides a strong force in the latent realm for social cohesion and social control. Much personal and social behavior in nearly all aspects of life shows some kind of correlation with religion—political, educational, economic, and most especially familial. A plethora of sociological studies reveals variations in many types of social behavior—political beliefs, voluntary associations, family size, and education—based on religion. Religion, moreover, is usually intimately related to the major events of life, such as status transitions exemplified by birth, marriage, and death. Most people in our society and others, regardless of their personal religiosity, are "hatched, matched, and dispatched" in a religion and church of their choice.

# Changing and Enduring Social Institutions

Institutions are highly stable and change-resistant entities. Such a situation is reflected in Table 7-5, which offers a profile of the principal traits of the major institutions in American society that have endured for several decades. Yet, they do change in many respects, as can be seen in some of the modifications that have occurred within the family in recent years. One significant change is the sheer multiplicity of institutions that have developed in recent decades throughout all modern societies. Increases in the size of societal populations, modifications of ecological relationships, growth in technology, mass productivity, and the expanding complexity of organizational structure, combined with a host of other yet related factors, have all made for an age of increasing specialization and a diversity of social institutions.

There is, nonetheless, a fundamental permanence in all social institutions. Their structures may change, and their functions may be redistributed, but the basic functions remain—given their requisite nature for both societal, and therefore human, survival. Accordingly, change itself need not be problematic. The significant question concerns the capability of new institutional forms to fulfill their basic and necessary functions (see Skolnick & Curie, 1985). Or, put in other terms, can changing social institutions guarantee the survival of society—and that of its individual members as well? We shall have much more to say about these questions of institutional and social change in the concluding chapter of this volume.

# Ecological Foundations of Society

**Human ecology** is a branch of sociological study concerned with the relations between people and their physical environment (see Hawley,

294

TABLE 7-5.  A Partial List of the Traits of Major American Social Institutions

| Familial | Religious | Political | Economic | Educational |
|---|---|---|---|---|
| *Attitudes and behavior patterns* | | | | |
| Affection | Reverence | Loyalty | Efficiency | Love of knowledge |
| Loyalty | Loyalty | Obedience | Thrift | Class attendance |
| Responsibility | Worship | Subordination | Shrewdness | Studying |
| Respect | Generosity | Cooperation | Profit making | "Cramming" |
| *Symbolic culture traits* | | | | |
| Marriage ring | Cross | Flag | Trademark | School colors |
| Wedding veil | Ikon | Seal | Patent sign | Mascot |
| Coat of arms | Shrine | Mascot | Slogan | School song |
| "Our song" | Hymn | Anthem | Singing commercial | Seal |
| *Utilitarian culture traits* | | | | |
| House | Church building | Public buildings | Shop, factory | Classrooms |
| Apartment | Church equipment | Public works | Store, office | Library |
| Furnishings | Literature | Armament | Office equipment | Stadium |
| Car | Liturgical supplies | Blanks and forms | Blanks and forms | Books |
| *Code of oral or written specifications* | | | | |
| Marriage license | Creed | Charter | Contracts | Accreditation |
| Will | Church law | Constitution | Licenses | Rules |
| Genealogy | Sacred books | Treaties | Franchises | Curricula |
| Marriage law | Taboos | Laws | Articles of incorporation | Grades |
| *Ideologies* | | | | |
| Romantic love | Thomism | Nationalism | Laissez faire | Academic freedom |
| Open family | Liberalism | States' rights | Managerial responsibility | Progressive education |
| Familism | Fundamentalism | Democracy | Free enterprise | Three "r's" |
| Individualism | Moral majority | Republicanism | Rights of labor | Classicism |

Note: This outline, more than a half-century old, is reproduced with very little change. It suggests, among other things, that in the process of social change there is much permanence in social institutions.
Source: Adapted from "Nucleated Social Institutions" in F. Stuart Chapin, *Contemporary American Institutions*. New York: Harper and Row, Publishers, Inc., 1935, p. 16.

▼

296

1986). Ecology today focuses more and more on the concept of the **ecosystem**—a self-sustaining system of mutual interdependence (symbiotic dependency) between human societies and the physical environment. Such a concern is similar to that of photosynthesis as the basis of the generation and perpetuation of physical life.

Much of the work in the area of human ecology has diffused into a number of subfields, such as social geography, urban-rural sociology, and demography. We shall look briefly at each of these various aspects of human ecology in order to provide a more comprehensive understanding of the structure and function of society.

## DEFINITION AND CHARACTERISTICS

All human activity, the exploration of outer space notwithstanding, is confined to the **biosphere**—that locus or environment of soil, water, and air which is located at or near the surface of the earth, where organic life exists.

The ecological foundations or substructure of a society refer to all of those conditions and elements in the physical environment in which society is located (the biosphere) that in one way or another influence both the nature of its culture and social organization as well as the various social relations and interactions that take place within it.

Many of the differences among societies, such as the nature of their subsistence and the composition of their culture, are rooted in such ecological factors as the physical geography—the composition of the land in terms of mountains, lakes, rivers, etc.; material resources; and climate. Other geographical factors in the ecology of a society also serve to establish the nature and the extent of social interaction that occurs within its structural confines.

Ecological influences on society are most extensive in terms of the effects of the physical environment on its economic activity. A good,

though somewhat overworked, example of social ecology can be found in the societies of the Eskimo peoples. Prevalent natural resources, like fish and seals—and even snow—play a focal role in all of the Eskimo societies, not only in the economic institution but also in the religious and familial institutions.

One can readily imagine the ecological influence of the Arctic regions on the cultures and structures of Arctic societies. It is impossible to grow crops, or indeed even to domesticate animals to any extensive degree. Consequently, agricultural-pastoral societies are virtually nonexistent in this part of the world. Hunting and gathering—principally of sea mammals, fish, and seals—are typically the chief modes of subsistence, with corresponding modes of social organization for the peoples of the Arctic.

Much of this situation, however, has changed in recent years through the importation of modern technology and culture into the Arctic region. The discovery and extraction of oil and natural gas in northern Alaska has begun to revolutionize this part of the world. All of the characteristics of industrial society may soon be found in the heretofore wastelands and wildernesses of the world. Yet, here again, it is the type of natural resources as an ecological feature of the area that in great part will determine the content of the culture and the structure of societies that develop.

The physical environment of Arctic societies, of course, plays an extreme role in their culture and mode of social organization. Such a situation, nonetheless, illustrates most clearly the important influence that the ecology has, both directly and indirectly, in creating a foundation for the structure and function of a given society. Another, less extreme, influence of ecology in modern societies can be had in the effect that transient and seasonal populations have on the structure and dynamics of societies and communities that wholly or in part rely on tourism as a chief mode of subsistence. The temporary migration of people to warmer regions of a society (for example, Florida and California in the United States) or of the world (for example, the Caribbean and Mediterranean areas) constitutes an ecological function that can have, and in many nations does have, highly significant consequences for the social order. Not only does social interaction tend to be more frequent in the warmer seasons and in warmer climates, but the increase in societal and community population makes for a more intense form of social interaction that often requires modification, however temporary, in the structures of social organization.

The ecological dimensions of society and social behavior are often demonstrated in reference to the contrasting effects that can be found in the rural-urban continuum. Social ecologists, however, have expended a great deal more effort in studying the ecology of urban communities than rural ones—partly because of the great complexity of relevant forces which the former provide, and partly because the forces of social change are in this direction. Let us look at some of these activities.

## PATTERNS OF URBAN ECOLOGY

Of special significance in the assessment of the ecological foundations of urban society is the concept of natural areas. A **natural area** is a geographical sector or urban **community** that is clearly distinguished by a specific kind of activity or use such as industry, commerce, transportation, or housing.* Financial and theater districts are examples of natural areas, as are ghettos or "racial islands."†

---

* Although we often use the word "community" to refer to segments of a population, such as the "academic community" or the "scientific community," the sociological meaning of community has an essentially ecological reference. A community may be defined as a subunit of society that operates within a limited geographical area, such as a village, town, city, or suburb, and within which a comprehensive social life is enacted.

† Ghettos are areas of the community in which people of a certain social category (racial, ethnic, religious, or socioeconomic) tend to live, either voluntarily or involuntarily.

Most cities manifest these specialized areas of concentration for specific social use (Hawley, 1986). Ecological areas of the city differ according to subculture, lifestyle, and a host of other patterns of social behavior.

Natural areas are thought to be the result of unplanned or spontaneous development that emerges as a result of competition for the use of valuable land space. Chief among the various social processes responsible for this development are those of ecological invasion and ecological segregation. **Ecological invasion** refers to the entrance or encroachment of a particular social category or activity into a specified ecological area; while **ecological segregation** refers to the voluntary or compulsory process by which natural areas come to be differentiated and maintained. Natural areas, and the processes from which they emerge, make for social cohesion on the part of the in-groups, as well as social conflict in terms of social isolation from the out-groups.

The emergence and development of natural areas is not considered to be a haphazard or random affair; there do appear to be some basic patterns by which these natural areas emerge. What occurs in effect is a design without designing. Urban ecologists have developed a number of models and hypotheses to describe the process by which urban spatial patterns emerge. Let us discuss the more well-known of these ecological models for the purpose of illustrating some of the salient principles of the ecological foundations of societies.

CONCENTRIC ZONE THEORY. Ernest W. Burgess (1925), one of the pioneers in social ecology, advanced the hypothesis that the impersonal process of land-use competition led to the development of a series of *concentric zones* that diffused or radiated from the center of a city. According to this theory, each of these zones is distinguished by different social activities or populations. The pattern is uniform for all cities, even though the individual zones are not always symmetrical and are often modified

▼

by typological features of the physical environment, such as lakes and rivers. Chicago, which served as Burgess' model and prototype, is a very good example of these influences, even though its location on the shores of Lake Michigan renders only a series of half-circles. These zones, beginning from the inner city, as shown in Figure 7-5 are the following: a) central business district; b) zone of transition, consisting of factories, slums, and racial/ethnic ghettos; c) workingmen's housing; d) residential zone; and e) commuter zone.

SECTOR THEORY.   Homer Hoyt (1939) developed a variation of the concentric-zone formulation by describing the ecology of cities in terms of distinctive *sectors*. Hoyt's ecological scheme is often referred to as the star-shaped city because, when put to paper or to a map, its outlines frequently resemble that of a star. This scheme perceives the spatial organization

of cities and the direction of their growth as determined by transportation routes, such as highways, railways, and waterways. In this model, for example, the central business district is divided into several pie-shaped sectors for different activities, and the various sectors expand outwardly until the pattern is interrupted by a physical barrier such as a river (see Figure 7-5). Indianapolis is a good example of the sector model. Other suitable examples would be San Francisco, Minneapolis, and Richmond, Virginia.

MULTIPLE NUCLEI THEORY.   A third model of urban ecology was developed by Chauncey D. Harris and Edward L. Ullman (1945), who contend that cities are organized around a number of focal areas or *nuclei*—each with distinct functions, such as industry, commerce, residence, and each representing in itself a miniature community that may assume either

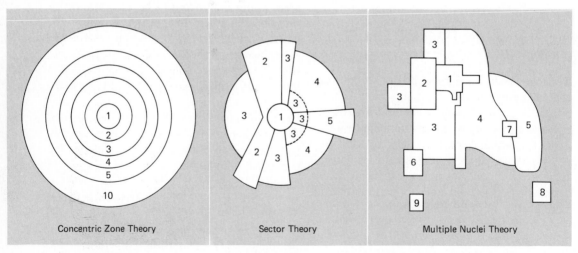

| | | |
|---|---|---|
| Concentric Zone Theory | Sector Theory | Multiple Nuclei Theory |

Key:  1. Central Business District    5. High-class Residential    9. Industrial Suburb
        2. Wholesale Light Manufacturing    6. Heavy Manufacturing    10. Commuters' Zone
        3. Low-class Residential    7. Outlying Business District
        4. Medium-class Residential    8. Residential Suburb

FIGURE 7-5   Models of Urban Ecology. Source: Chauncey D. Harris and Edward L. Ullman, "The Nature of the American City" in vol. 242 of the *Annals of the American Academy of Political and Social Science*. Homer Hoyt, The Structure and Growth of Residential Neighborhoods in American Cities. Washington, D.C.: Federal Housing Administration, 1939.

the concentric or sector pattern. Together these communities comprise a city—a social system consisting of multiple nuclei—with several areas devoted to the same activity, such as business and residential districts (see Figure 7-5). Boston and Philadelphia are offered as good examples of the multiple nuclei model.

Each of these formulations, revealing several similar elements, shows that there are patterns or natural designs to the development of societies. None of these ecological models, however, has proven to be entirely satisfactory. No one model generates a perfect explanation that accounts for all of the complex dynamics of the growth and development of urban communities. Each ecological formulation is modified in a concrete situation by a host of factors. Burgess' conception, for example, fits many American cities, but not all, and seems to have no application to European ones.* Some new cities in the western United States even tend to show a reversal of the Burgess pattern. One factor that may account for this shortcoming is the period during which a particular city developed. Burgess' scheme seems to be more typical of a city that developed in the eighteenth and nineteenth centuries (for example, New York and Baltimore). Modern urban development, on the other hand, tends to favor multiple nuclei rather than concentric zones.

The different approaches, however, are not entirely incompatible. Each of these models has some value in understanding the ecological structure of a society. Viewing them in a complementary perspective, to whatever degree is possible, provides a fuller account of the complexities of urban ecological structure. One consideration, nonetheless, must be reserved. The elements that go into the ecological process are themselves constantly changing; and, accordingly, new models and theories need to be developed in order to explain the ecological structure of a society for today and tomorrow. Multiple shopping centers, the rebirth of cities, condominium housing, new architectural styles, fluctuation in family size, innovations in personal lifestyles, rapid and private modes of transportation, among a host of other social changes—each for its own reasons and each in its own ways—have changed the specific relationship of people to their physical environment and spatial distribution. The general principle, however, remains: Whatever spatial distributions exist and whatever the ecological patterns, these in turn dictate a certain type of societal organization.

## CHANGING PATTERNS AND MODELS

The multiple-nuclei structure, in many respects, seems to be increasingly characteristic of American cities—as well as those in many other countries—as our population increasingly decentralizes with the aid of private transportation that is becoming increasingly available to all people. Shopping centers, cinemas, theaters, restaurants, and even commercial and industrial enterprises are becoming an omnipresent characteristic of the geographic and social map of American communities—all made possible by the mechanization and mobility of the population, as well as its rush to the spatial enticements of the suburbs. Such a trend is not so much a new one as it is the exacerbation of one that has been going on in the United States since the early days of the present century.

The 1970 census showed for the first time that more Americans live in suburbs of major cities than in the cities proper. Figures in the

---

* One caution that needs to be made is that the single-family detached house as a prevalent mode of residence in urban settings is quite uniquely American. Condominium-type dwellings are a far more common pattern throughout the urbanized areas of the world. Even the Anasazi, the early Pueblo Indians, lived in condominium-style dwellings, remnants of which can be seen yet today in the Chaco Canyon of New Mexico. This uniquely American residential style and the strong value attached to it in no small way accounts for the continually expanding patterns of suburban development.

299

300

1980 census revealed, much to the alarm and chagrin of city officials in various parts of the country, that our major metropolitan and urban areas experienced population decreases of as much as 20 percent over the previous decade. This dramatic change, however, may be coming to an end, or diminishing somewhat at least, with the redevelopment and revitalization of many American cities. Since the mid-1970s there appears to be a slight reversal of the urban exodus. Growing numbers of people who are choosing to remain in the cities have been joined by many economically and otherwise disenchanted suburbanites—as many as 2 million yearly (Smith, 1982). This process has come to be known as **urban gentrification.** The predominantly poor urban areas are being invaded and renovated by the "gentry" from outside. Among the better-known of the dilapidated

slums that have been transformed into enclaves of style and elegance are Queen's Village and Society Hill in Philadelphia, South End in Boston, New Town in Chicago, and Capitol Hill in Washington, D.C. It is too soon to tell how extensive or enduring this new ecological pattern will be.

Urban ecologists today are developing new models to reflect more accurately these many kinds of changes in the ecological foundations of society. One concept that has received extensive use in the United States, both practically and theoretically, is that of the **metropolitan statistical area** (MSA), which is defined officially as any county or cluster of counties containing a city of at least 50,000 people. Each of the MSAs, of which at the time of the 1980 census there were 318 in the country, usually include many different types of communities: the prin-

**Biospheric Ecology.** The development of nuclear power plants, and the potential danger they pose, have brought a modern dimension to the ecological relationship between communities and their physical environments. (Lionel J.-M. Delevingne/Stock, Boston)

cipal urban areas, the suburbs, satellite cities, and the in-between "rural" areas—all of which are considered to be in a particular type of symbiotic relationship or dependency on the focal city. About three-fourths of the American population presently live within metropolitan statistical areas.

Another new type of model, not totally ecological in nature, is that known as the political economy paradigm, which has taken many forms. An example of this model is that developed by Gordon (1977), who links the development of cities to the stage and dominant mode of economic production that they experience during a period of major growth. Gordon describes three types of contemporary cities— commercial, industrial, and corporate—of which New York, Houston, and Denver are respective examples.

Some historically commercial cities (for example, Boston, Philadelphia, and Baltimore), as well as industrial ones (for example, Chicago), may be moving into the corporate stage; while others (for example, Houston, Denver) are emerging initially as that type. The ecological dimension of the political-economic model lies in the contention that it is complementary to the ecological models. For example, the dynamics of ecological succession and transportation technology depend on the political economy characteristics of cities. Another particularly ecological dimension focuses on how and why these kinds of cities develop in certain geographical (that is, ecological) areas of a society (for example, North, South, Midwest) rather than others (see Perry & Watkins, 1978).

Geographical features and the principles of economic competition for land use are not the only formative factors in human ecology and the spatial organization of societies. Psychological, sociological, and cultural factors also need to be considered in the construction of more comprehensive models that would accurately reflect the structure and organization of people in population and ecological space.

Natural forces may also be giving way more and more to technology and engineering. Transportation and communication, along with a host of other technological and cultural changes, are altering the basic ecological patterns and natural areas of American cities. It is difficult to know what the future holds, especially when one considers the emphasis that is being placed on urban renewal not only for commercial purposes but also for residential and recreational activities. Much more controversial these days is the practice of zoning and urban planning—widely used procedures by which the local government designates certain areas of a community for specific types of activities and construction (for example, single-family or multiple-family housing, commerce and transportation, light manufacturing or heavy industry, etc.).

Entire communities are now being planned, much like Washington, D.C. was originally, even though on a much smaller scale. Similarly, urban renewal and redevelopment is to a considerable degree the product of highly sophisticated social engineering. These situations, however, do not annihilate ecological dynamics, for even planned cities and urban renewal are both based on physical ecology in the first place and then modified by the inevitability of *human* ecology—quite apart from its physical dimensions. Let us look at some of these nonphysical dimensions of human ecology.

## HUMAN ECOLOGY AND SOCIAL RELATIONS

Social relations are in part a function of the spatial or geographic distributions of a society or population. Physical proximity tends to increase the opportunities and probability for social interaction, while physical segregation (isolation and remoteness) has the contrary effect. Physical barriers—natural as well as manufactured—promote social isolation. Railroads, highways, and other artifacts of the

▼ ecological structure, as well as those of the geographical environment, often serve at one and the same time as barriers or facilitators of human interaction—both in terms of frequency and kind. An example of this phenomenon is reflected in the well-known expression about people who "live on the other side of the tracks."

302 Studies of human ecology show that people of different race, nationality, income, age, and even occupation tend to cluster together in geographical patterns. It is this usually voluntary, sometimes compulsory, phenomenon of ecological segregation that in part results in ethnic, racial, and socioeconomic ghettos. Although not required to, millions of immigrants to the United States settled in the same neighborhoods and geographical areas, and many still do. Some of these dynamics were also the function of prejudice and discrimination—social processes that have not totally disappeared from the American society (see Chapter 11). Yet, whatever the causes, it is these dynamics that resulted in America's Chinatowns, Little Italys, Harlems, Barrios, and Germantowns, as well as its Society Hills, Nob Hills, and Beacon Hills.

Spatial and social realms of interaction are for the most part fairly coextensive. **Propinquity** refers to the sociological phenomenon by which people in close physical contact tend to develop social contacts that frequently lead to lasting and intimate relationships. A generation or two ago a large percentage of married partners in the United States had lived within the same neighborhood. One study that involved an examination of 5,000 marriage license applications in the city of Philadelphia revealed that one-third of the couples lived within five blocks of each other (Rubin, 1973). Propinquity as a social force is diminishing somewhat in modern societies as ecological barriers are increasingly surpassed in various ways. Rapid transportation and increased physical mobility have had a significant effect on this particular social dynamic. It is estimated, for example, that about 20 percent of the American people change their residence every year. The general principle of

the relationship between physical and social proximity, nonetheless, remains quite true in many other respects.

Spatial proximity leads to social proximity and the development of distinctive patterns and structures of social interaction. Of particular importance, spatial and social proximity are more likely than not to result in the development of a "consciousness of kind" or a "we-feeling" among individuals. Such a social and psychological identity is manifested in a sharing of common attitudes and values that identify and bind the community. Durkheim (1964), for example, spoke of "moral density" among a population, which referred to the cohesion and integration that results from the frequency of interaction that tends to ensue from propinquity or common habitat, as well as in terms of similarity in social backgrounds. As a general principle, the more heterogeneous a society or community in terms of the social differences (race, religion, ethnicity) of its population, the less the moral integration. Also, the greater the physical mobility, the less the social intimacy. Homogeneity (of communities and neighborhoods) on the basis of race, ethnicity, and religion, however, has given way by and large to homogeneity based more exclusively on socioeconomic background. These dynamics are themselves consequences of ecological factors.

Socially homogeneous areas tend also to be psychologically homogeneous. Social scientists have argued that the unique physical and social environment of urban areas is directly responsible for distinctive values, attitudes, and patterns of behavior among urban dwellers. To whatever extent distinctive social characteristics are found among racial and ethnic ghettos, they can be traced in part to the corresponding ecological processes as basic foundations. They are not simply the result of racial and ethnic or other social differences but to ecological processes as well. Georg Simmel (1908) long ago described the "urban personality" as one characterized by increased rationality and detachment from people and events. Such a personality, argued Simmel, was highly functional and adaptive for urban life, although it was responsible as well for conflict and social disorganization in such a setting. These psychological and social identities that have a foundation in ecological relationships have profound significance for the individual and one's development of self and personality.*

Among the ecological concerns that are prevalent today are questions about the depletion of natural resources and environmental pollution. Much controversy centers around the consequences that situations of these kinds have for restructuring society in terms of such things as quality of life, family size, lifestyles, standards of living, and material culture—all of which involve the likely modification of such fundamental elements of society as values and goals. In fact, highly alarming questions have been raised about the future existence of human society. Yet, however controversial such questions may be, what seems certain is that the structure and function of societies will depend in part, as they essentially do, on whatever may be their ecological foundations.

# Demographic Foundations of Society

Another element that strongly influences the structure and function of society is its population. To state the obvious, there can be no society without people. Less obvious, however, is the fact that the type of society which exists, and the way in which it functions, including the nature of the social relations and interaction therein, are similarly dependent on people—their numbers and their characteristics. The **demographic foundations** or substructure of society refer to all of those elements of its population—size, composition, and mobility—

which determine or influence its nature, structure, function, and dynamics.

Population, like other variables that are of central concern in sociological analysis, is both a dependent and an independent variable. Accordingly, demographic phenomena fall between social antecedents and social consequences—both influencing and influenced by the social order. Our concerns in this section are limited to only the second of these considerations, in which demographic phenomena are treated as independent variables while societal dynamics and social behavior are seen as dependent variables. We want to look briefly at how the structure and function of society are conditioned by demographic phenomena.

One technique that makes it helpful for us to understand the demographic foundation of society is the **population pyramid.** Figure 7-6 consists of a population pyramid showing the composition of the population of the United States by age and sex for the year 1980. This illustration can be used as a reference for much of the discussion that follows. (Figure 7-7 shows the age-sex pyramids of Mexico, the United States, and West Germany.) The shape of each pyramid is affected by differences in fertility, mortality, and migration—demographic dynamics that vary significantly in each of these societies and many others as well.

## POPULATION SIZE

One major issue that in recent years has concerned—indeed alarmed—many people is simply the sheer size of the population of our society as well as that of much of the rest of the world. The current population of the United States is in excess of 245 million people, with a projected peak of 309 million by the middle of the next century. Estimates of the world's population exceed 5 billion people—one-fifth of whom live in China alone. Chiefly significant in this demographic concern is the comparison of the exponential growth rate of the population

---

* See Claude Fisher, *The Urban Experience*, for a discussion of the urban experience and its effects on personality and behavior. Extensive treatments on personality and the environment can be found also in Craik and McKechnie (1977).

**303**

▼

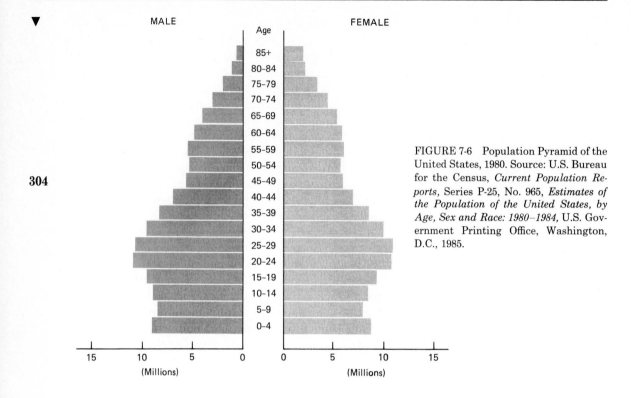

FIGURE 7-6  Population Pyramid of the United States, 1980. Source: U.S. Bureau for the Census, *Current Population Reports*, Series P-25, No. 965, *Estimates of the Population of the United States, by Age, Sex and Race: 1980–1984*, U.S. Government Printing Office, Washington, D.C., 1985.

with the production of natural resources which, despite tremendously impressive technological innovations, does not reveal a commensurate pattern of growth. Expectations that we shall soon exhaust our physical resources for such needs as food and energy have led during the past two decades to the establishment of various kinds of conservation programs, as well as the emergence of social movements for "zero population growth" (Ehrlich, 1968).

**Zero population growth** advocates a no-growth population—the simple reproduction of existing numbers. Such a policy, already operative in several societies, calls for a population replacement rate of 2.11 (fractions account for people who do not have children). In 1974 the replacement rate for the United States reached 1.9 and has remained steady, so these attempts at population control appear, on the whole, to have been quite effective in this country at

least.* Such a situation is all the more apparent when one realizes that in 1950 there were 3.3 children for every woman in the American population. Some demographers, however, perceive this situation as a temporary one and have made projections for slight increases in population during the rest of this century. Even so, the average size of the American household in 1987 was 2.66—a record low.

Zero population growth, nonetheless, may be seen as a confirmation of the hypothesis of **demographic transition.** This hypothesis, formulated originally by Warren Thompson (1929),

---

* While zero population growth may be an effective means to control population growth, what is not known are the nature and extent of its consequences. Research in China suggests that children without siblings are more uncooperative, less altruistic, and more egocentric than those without siblings (Hall, 1987). Such a situation, clearly illustrating the significance of the demographic substructure of society, is seen in some quarters as a threat to the socialistic state.

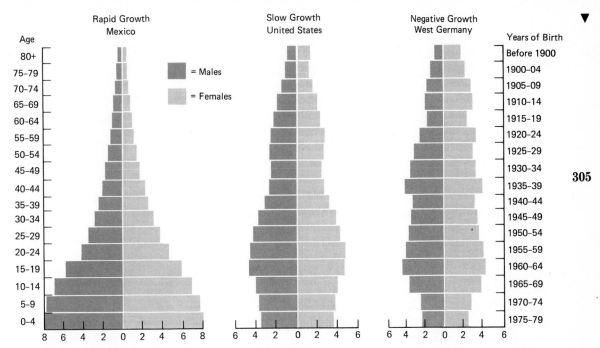

FIGURE 7-7 Population Pyramids for Societies with Different Growth Potential. Age and Sex in Percentage. Source: *World Population: Fundamentals of Growth,* Population Reference Bureau, Inc., Washington, D.C. 1987.

305

explains the process by which a population becomes stabilized as a society moves from an agrarian type to a completely industrialized one. There are three stages in the process of demographic transition by which high death rates and high birth rates gradually reverse themselves to a pattern of low death rates and low birth rates (see Figure 7-8).

Stage 1. A relatively stable demographic pattern of high birth rates and high death rates (especially among children) is found in all traditional societies.

Stage 2. A transitional pattern of rapid growth in which low death rates and high birth rates occur in the early stages of industrialization, resulting primarily from significant advances in food production and public health.

Stage 3. A new stable pattern of low death rates and low birth rates becomes typical of advanced industrial societies.

While this pattern indeed has been typical of Western societies, the hypothesis of demographic transition remains unconfirmed in non-Western nations, which—with the exception of Japan—have not developed industrialized societies.* The majority of developing nations, which are characterized by significantly different social and cultural patterns, are presently in stage 2 and are thus characterized by rapidly increasing population (for example, Afghanistan, Bangladesh, Iran, and Mexico). Only the future will determine the universal validity of demographic transition. Its confirmation would provide a very useful means for highly reliable demographic projections in the coming century. Much depends on population composition, and not all societies are the same in this respect.

Too few people can be as problematic as too

* One principal factor responsible for this transition is the changing value of large families as economic assets in agrarian society to economic liabilities in highly industrialized society.

▼

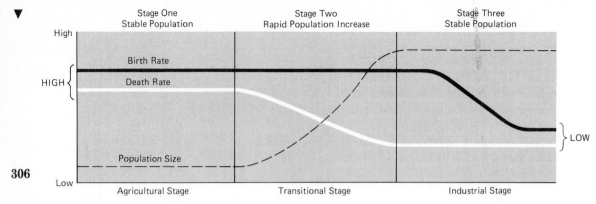

FIGURE 7-8   The Demographic Transition.

many. Not all societies, of course, share the concerns of the zero population growth movement, which fundamentally involves value judgments about a number of implicit causes and effects of demographic patterns. Many societies (for example, Singapore, Argentina, France, Romania, and the Soviet Union) want to increase their population, and some even offer a premium as an inducement to their members to have large families. Such a pronatalist proposal has been made quite seriously even in the United States. American demographer Charles Westoff (1978), former director of the U.S. Commission on Population and America's Future, who advocated a stable population in 1970, now maintains that a stable population (perhaps of 250 million people) a half-century or so from now would be politically disadvantageous. He, too, proposes a baby bonus to encourage more childbearing.

Many countries believe that relatively large populations are necessary for both political and economic objectives. Argentina, as a case in point, outlawed the use of contraceptives in 1974 in order to double its population as quickly as possible in the interests of economic development. Other countries seem to recognize the need for a minimal population, or one of critical size, in order to maintain a particular kind of society. East Germany literally constructed and maintained walls around the country until late 1989 in order to prevent people from fleeing its totalitarian regime.

Some types of societies and communities require large populations, while just the opposite is true of others. We have seen that such is the case in our discussion of *Gemeinschaft* and *Gesellschaft* societies that differ essentially in terms of the nature of social organization. Communal societies, for example, function effectively only with very small populations. The same situation is obviously true in terms of the societal mode of subsistence. Industrial societies, for example, are invariably and necessarily very large ones; correspondingly, nomadic societies are quite small. Hence, a given population size is both a requirement and a consequence of certain types of society.

A related question is that numbers affect the cost of administrative services, as well as tax rates in turn, in a quite disproportionate way. The population density of the borough of Manhattan in New York City is about 64,000 people per square mile, while that of the state of Wyoming is 4.9. However, there are certain fixed costs in both areas. Quality of function, as well as type of structure, are dimensions of society which are related directly to the absolute size of a population. Optimal size may become a crucial consideration in the future in the interests of responding to the total needs of people, physical as well as social and psychological.

One issue that needs to be explored more thoroughly is whether individuals are able to function, both sociologically and psychologically, at a normal or optimal level, regardless of population size. Crowded conditions among animals are known to lead to increased levels of aggression, abnormal behavior, physical disorders, infant neglect, and high mortality rates (Freedman, 1975). Correlational studies seemed to support the possibility that population density might have similar effects on human beings. Early studies in various American cities found an overall positive relationship between density and juvenile delinquency, mental illness, and other pathologies. These correlations, however, disappear when controls for socioeconomic variables are instituted. Moreover, there seems to be little, if any, support for the commonly stated myth that urban life is alienating. People who live in large cities report being just as happy as those who live in suburbs, small towns, and rural areas (Fischer, 1984; Shaver & Freedman, 1976). Density per se, then, appears not to be the cause of social and personal pathologies.

In his book on *Crowding and Behavior*, Freedman (1975) makes the case that physical crowding—as opposed to psychological crowding, which is essentially subjective—is not detrimental to the individual in any way. In fact, it is neither positive nor negative, but rather quite neutral in and of itself. Psychological crowding, on the other hand, is a much more complex phenomenon. Among the many factors included here are one's accustomed level of density, cultural background, and subjective state, as well as such things as the temperature and noise level. Significant relationships have been shown between variations in one's perceived "personal space" and different kinds of pathology.

Population may be significant in yet another way. Etzioni (1968a) raises the question of whether societies of different size and demographic composition are equally capable of meeting basic human needs for such things as social response, social recognition, and emotional security. He has spoken in this regard of "unresponsive" social systems or societies, which, because of their structure, are unable to meet the needs of their members in an adequate manner (see Chapter 14). The consequences of such a situation of psychological frustration are thought to be reflected in personally and socially deviant behavior that, in turn, can produce significant problems for society, such as in the form of massive social problems, like crime, mental illness, drug and alcohol addiction, and even suicide, as well as social conflict in various forms, including racial and ethnic prejudice.

## POPULATION COMPOSITION

Absolute size is not the only significant issue in regard to population. Internal composition is also quite important in a number of respects. Populations may be divided into various classifications: biological (age and sex), ethnic (racial and ethnic), geographic (regional, rural-urban), socioeconomic (occupation, income, and social class), and cultural (education, religion, and marital status). We shall discuss some of these categories for a more thorough understanding of the demographic substructure of society.

Not only are certain numbers of people crucial for society, but more especially it is the case that certain kinds of people—in terms of social, physical, and psychological characteristics—are necessary for the effective functioning of society in general, as well as for particular types of society. Of particular significance, in this regard, is the composition of a societal population in terms of age and sex.

SEX. One significant dimension of population composition is the simple matter of the **sex ratio,** which refers to the number of males per 100 females in a given population unit. Gen-

**307**

▼

## BOX 7-3. Zero Population Growth and Malthusian Theory Revisited

The first major theory of population growth was developed by Thomas R. Malthus (1766–1834), a minister who, in his *Essay on the Principle of Population* (1798), argued that the world's population would increase geometrically (2, 4, 8, 16. . .) by doubling every 25 years. The implicit concern in the Malthusian view was that the food supply, for a host of reasons, would increase much more slowly at an arithmetic rate (2, 3, 4, 5. . .), and thus would not be sufficient for the much more rapidly expanding population. The ecosystem, in short, would not have the carrying capacity to sustain the population of the world.

The feared consequences of this situation were famine and crowding, which would result in extensive suffering, disease, war, and an increase in the death rate. Malthus viewed these undesirable consequences, however, as natural and positive checks on overpopulation. Subsequently, he advocated various types of human intervention, such as late marriage and financial incentives, as other forms of population control. Birth control and abortion were rejected on religious grounds.

Malthus, of course, had not foreseen the far-reaching development of agriculture and the effects of the industrial revolution. These events significantly altered not only food production, but also lifestyles and family dynamics. The same was true of the eventual adoption of the practices of birth control and abortion.

For all of these reasons, Malthus' views were widely ignored in the early part of this century, when large families and heavy immigration were popular. More recently, though, in the past 20 years especially, Malthusian theory has received renewed attention, and once again has become quite controversial—particularly in highly industrialized and relatively less populated countries, where the concerns now are not so much for food as they are for clean air, fresh water, and ample sources of energy (see Coleman & Schofield, 1988). Such concerns have been particularly strong when one considers that the population of the world is expected to double its current size to 10 billion people by the year 2050 (World Bank, 1984).

Some people, particularly exponents of zero population growth, maintain that the empirical verification of the Malthusian theory may only have been postponed for a century or so, and that its predictions will be seen soon in the form of a crisis in the ecosystem, with polluted air and water leading to a massive loss of oxygen, energy, and food supplies (see, for example, Milbrath, 1984). Others advance the controversial argument that natural resources are virtually inexhaustible in that human technology will unfailingly discover substitutes or new ways of exploiting the existing resources (see, for example, Simon, 1981). ▲

erally, the proportion of males and females born in a given society is nearly equal. Females, however, show a slight dominance in an approximate ratio of 105:100. (This imbalance is due, in great part, to the generally higher mortality rates for males at birth and in later years.) The sex ratio of any particular society, or segment of it, however, can be significantly altered by such things as differential rates of mortality and migration, as well as social catastrophes such as war. Such a situation was dramatically revealed in Germany and the Soviet Union after World War II, when about one-third of the males were killed in battle. For example, the population of the city of Berlin in 1946, showing the effects of two major wars on its male population, had a sex ratio of only 68 (Thompson & Lewis, 1965). The societal consequences of this situation, in terms of its familial and economic institutions, were most serious; and, of course, what has never been totally assessed are the consequences which these social situations in turn had on the psychological development and function of the individual.

The overall sex ratio for the United States in recent years has been about 95:100. Sex ratios in the United States, however, have varied significantly over the years—due in part to the predominantly male immigration during the period 1880–1910. Some regions of the United States, however, have an imbalance of females. The Middle Atlantic region—New Jersey, New York, and Pennsylvania—has the lowest sex ratio (92.2), while the Mountain States have the highest (98.1). Sex ratios in Alaska and Hawaii recently stood at 132 and 121 respectively. These figures partly reflect urban-rural differentials. Rural areas, generally, tend to have higher ratios because of greater female migration to urban areas. Cities and communities that have specialized industries or occupations also manifest atypical sex ratios. For example, Washington, D.C., with its concentration of clerical workers in governmental services, had a sex ratio of 86 in 1960. Often it is the case

that societal mechanisms, such as the institutional form of marriage, are a consequence of the sex ratio that characterizes a particular society. Abram Kardiner (1939), for example, described how polyandry was permitted in Marquesan society because of the disproportionate number of males. Cross-cultural and historical analysis shows that a disproportionate sex ratio affects the sex-role behavior that characterizes a particular society (Guttentag & Secord, 1983). Other dynamics can be similarly affected. Sociologists speculate, for example, that if society became disproportionately male, crime would increase and the shortage of female partners would create more prostitution and homosexuality.

Often preference for a particular sex and sex selection can also result in imbalances within a population. Many parents in various countries terminate their childbearing only after the birth of a son. Throughout much of India today, amniocentesis is employed simply for determining the sex of a fetus. Female fetuses in this practice are frequently subjected to abortion. In other countries, such as China, female infanticide is a rather common, though illegal, practice.* In some rural areas in China the sex ratio is as high as 5:1. A recent study reveals a ratio of 117 last-born males to 100 last-born females—compared to the normal ratio of 102 males to 100 females. One can only speculate on the potential effects that a combination of genetic engineering, amniocentesis, and abortion may have on sex selection and the eventual sex ratios in the populations of many societies during the years ahead. One study of first-time expectant women in the United States found that 63 percent desired a boy (Pebley & Westoff, 1982). This 2:1 preference ratio is low compared to some other nations, particularly the nonindustrialized ones (see Box 7-4).

▼

**309**

* Among the primary reasons for these practices is the continuity of family name and old-age insurance (parental care and economic support by children), which is more likely assumed by the male offspring.

▼

## BOX 7-4. Cross-Cultural Differences in Sex Preference for Children

Inkeles and Smith (1974) conducted a study in which they asked the question: "When a family has several children, both sons and daughters equally, and a new child is coming, is it preferable that the new child be a boy, either one, or a girl?" People in many societies expressed a strong preference for male children. In Nigeria the preference was as high as 34:1, while in Bangladesh the preference was 46:1. ▲

310

| | Boys | Girls | Either | Boy-Girl Ratio |
|---|---|---|---|---|
| Argentina | 33% | 3% | 63% | 11:1 |
| Chile | 56 | 5 | 39 | 11:1 |
| India | 78 | 5 | 17 | 16:1 |
| Bangladesh | 91 | 2 | 8 | 46:1 |
| Israel* | 44 | 4 | 52 | 11:1 |
| Nigeria | 67 | 2 | 31 | 34:1 |

* Sample included only non-European Israelis.
Source: Alex Inkeles and David H. Smith, *Becoming Modern: Individual Change in Six Developing Countries.* Cambridge, Mass.: Harvard University Press, 1974.

AGE.   The composition and distribution of a population in terms of age is another factor that influences the structure and dynamics of a society in a number of significant ways. The function and maintenance of society requires the differential allocation of people to various segments of society. This situation is most especially true in terms of role allocation and occupational distribution which, to a considerable degree, is based on age—however directly or indirectly the case may be. Currently, the median age in the United States is 32.1. This figure is relatively high compared to other countries, and even our own past. The median is projected to be over 36 by the year 2020, and about 42 by 2050. Our "aging" population is one of the most significant demographic factors in American society, and one of considerable sociological significance.

Population pyramids provide a structural profile of age distribution; however, the functional significance of age composition is not as apparent. Of particular significance in this regard is that there are two principal "age" categories latent in a population: *producers* and *dependents.* The latter category includes children under 15 and adults over 64. These individuals, for all intents and purposes, are supported—both economically and in many other ways—by the producing or economically and otherwise actively engaged individuals in the population. This situation becomes crucial in terms of the dependency ratio. The **dependency ratio** is the combined number or percentage of dependents in a population divided by the number or percentage of producers (the number of dependents for every 100 producers). Low dependency ratios tend to be more functional for society in a number of different ways, chiefly economical; correspondingly, high ratios have significance in other respects, such as in the nature and quality of the culture and social activities that result from such phenomena as a "youth-oriented" versus a "senior citizen–oriented" society.

The proportion of Americans who are elderly has tripled since 1900, and one of the fastest growing segments of the population is that over age 85. In 1900, only 1 American in 25 was over 65. Today the figure is 1 in 8; and by the middle of the next century, it is expected to be 1 in 4.

The dependency ratio for a particular society may vary enormously in terms of different social categories, such as racial, ethnic, rural-urban, and regional distinctions. The same is true at the local level. Some American cities, such as Miami Beach and St. Petersburg in Florida, as well as others in the southwest (California, Arizona, and New Mexico), have an atypically large percentage of senior citizens who have taken up retirement residence in these areas. In Miami Beach, for example, 52 percent of the residents are over 65 (1980 census figures). Often such a situation results in the development of a subculture that is oriented to the interests of the elder members of society, as opposed to the youth culture that predominates in other communities.

Table 7-6 shows the composition of the United States population in terms of producers and dependents during the past century. Since 1880, the dependency ratio has declined appreciably from .71 to .57 in 1990, which is a projected figure. (Note that the category of

TABLE 7-6.  Age Distribution in the U.S. Population, 1880–2000

| Year | Dependent Children 14 years and under (%) | Active Population 15–64 (%) | Dependent Aged 65 years and over (%) |
|------|-------------------------------------------|----------------------------|--------------------------------------|
| 1880  | 38.1 | 58.5 | 3.4 |
| 1890  | 35.5 | 60.4 | 3.9 |
| 1900  | 34.4 | 61.3 | 4.1 |
| 1910  | 32.1 | 63.4 | 4.3 |
| 1920  | 31.7 | 63.4 | 4.7 |
| 1930  | 29.3 | 65.1 | 5.4 |
| 1940  | 25.0 | 68.1 | 6.8 |
| 1950  | 26.8 | 65.3 | 8.2 |
| 1960  | 31.0 | 59.8 | 9.2 |
| 1970  | 28.2 | 61.9 | 9.8 |
| 1980  | 24.9 | 64.5 | 10.5 |
| 1990* | 25.0 | 63.8 | 11.2 |
| 2000* | 22.6 | 66.4 | 11.0 |

* Estimated figures.
Sources: Conrad Taeuber and Irene Taeuber, *The Changing Population of the United States*. New York: Wiley, 1958; U.S. Bureau of the Census, *Current Population Reports,* series P-25, Nov. 1971, Sept. 1972, Dec. 1972, and May 1988.

▼ dependent children has varied over the years and now has 18 as an upper limit.) Either figure is decidedly low when compared to the dependency ratio of many other societies which is almost double that of the United States. Some countries in South America are cases in point. Recent trends, however, indicate that the dependency ratio will increase steadily for the rest of this century, owing principally to a combination of the decreasing birth rate and increasing life expectancy. In 1900, each 100 persons of working age helped support 7 elderly. In 1985 there were 19 elderly per 100 of working age, and by 2050 the ratio is estimated to be 38 elderly per 100 workers.

312

An even more startling situation that has caused considerable apprehension at all levels and in all sectors of our society is the dramatic change in the ratio of contributors to benefactors in the Social Security program. The percentage of beneficiaries has increased from .003 of contributors in 1940 to .31 in 1978. The ratio of contributors to beneficiaries was 159:1 in 1940; today it is 3:1, with the projection of a 2:1 ratio by 2030 (see Figure 7-9). This tenuous situation takes on an even more dramatic impact when one considers that the Social Security program is only one of several such mechanisms of social assistance administered by the federal government.* The viability of this operation, and many other programs of social assistance in our society, rests upon the dependency ratio. An optimal figure for this statistic has not been determined because it is constantly changing as a function of a complexity of factors in the structure and function of society. Accordingly, of crucial significance is the question of a minimal and optimal ratio of producers to dependents.

## POPULATION AND PATTERNS OF SOCIAL INTERACTION

Demographic phenomena, such as population size and composition, also affect the nature and extent of interaction within society. Changes in population size, for example, invariably result in changes in the structure of social relationships. Everett K. Wilson (1971) offers the following as manifestations of this dynamic in terms of increases in population size:

1. A disproportionate increase in the number of social relationships.
2. An increased heterogeneity and/or diversification of social roles.
3. A significant increase in the proportion of coordinating roles (for example, administrative, supervisory, mediating).

Societal structures become increasingly more complex as populations increase in size. As a population grows arithmetically, the number and form of potential social relationships are vastly elaborated geometrically (see Chapter 9).

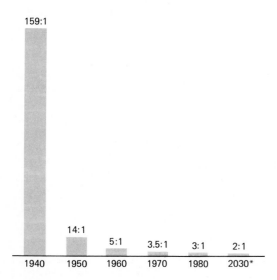

FIGURE 7-9 Ratio of Social Security Contributors to Beneficiaries.

* Other nations are experiencing the same problem. The current ratio of contributors to beneficiaries is 2:19 in West Germany and 1:41 in Italy (Anderson, 1983; Chickering, 1984).

Hence, it is not so much the sheer number of people that makes for an increase in the complexity of social structure, as it is the concomitant increase in the disproportionate number of role relationships, and the corresponding need for social regulation and social control. One example of this principle as it applies to societies is reflected in the per capita number of police found in different cities of various size. The larger the cities, the greater is the proportional size of its police force. The complexity of social structure, therefore, stems, in great part, from the disproportionate number of social relationships that parallel the simple increases in the number of people.

Even the very type of society, in terms of the sociocultural order, is dependent upon population size and composition. Georg Simmel (1908) concerned himself with how different social structures relate to the size of groups. Com-munal societies, argued Simmel, are possible only with very small populations, somewhere between 80 to 100 people. Social "experiments" in various types of modern communes, such as the well-known one of Twin Oaks in Virginia, have confirmed this principle. Similar affirmations can be had among the kibbutzim in Israel. Hence, the fundamental canon of communism—equality in terms of the distribution of production and rewards—can be realized rather easily in small societies. Such is not the case in large societies, or even those of moderate size, because of the inevitable social differentiation of its members that results from the heterogeneity of the population.

Related to this situation is another independent principle. Increases in population size usually result in a decrease in societal cohesion. Social solidarity and integration decrease in the measure to which numerical increases involve,

**313**

**Limited Utopias.** Communal and socialistic societies such as this Lama commune in New Mexico, which attempt to operate on the principle of social equality, are viable only with very small populations—usually not more than 100 people. (© Adam Woolfitt 1980)

▼ as they invariably do, the admission of heterogeneous elements in a social population. This principle can be demonstrated more easily on the microsociological level of family groups. Whenever there is an increase in size, there is usually an increase in the potential for social conflict because of a myriad of social differences in the family unit, not the least of which is the greater number of structural relationships and corresponding role interactions.

**314**

None of this discussion is intended to convey a negative judgment on numerically large societies. Rather, the message is that there is an inevitable correlation between population size and societal structure as well as social dynamics. To select one is to select the other. Such an understanding is fundamental at a time when people are expressing strong convictions about the ecological dimensions of population dynamics and the seemingly irreversible trend toward increasingly expansive populations and societies.

# Personality and Society

Are there significant variations among societal populations in the distribution of personality types or psychological characteristics? And, if so, how do these distinctive patterns affect the functioning of society? Scholars interested in these questions assume that a society is significantly affected by the particular types of personality or psychological characteristics that are present therein. The general thesis of this question is that particular types of society and their specific institutions are the result of certain types of personality and functionally require certain kinds of personalities.

## NATIONAL AND SOCIAL CHARACTER

Psychological differences among people from different societies is one of the most striking observations that anyone can make. The idea that members of various societies have different personalities or psychological patterns is probably as old as recorded history. We could mention, for example, that Thucydides, the ancient Greek historian, made note of the famous speech by Pericles on the characterological differences between Athenians and Spartans. Similar concerns, of course, can be cited in the writings of Plato and Aristotle. Plato, for instance, in his *Republic* dealt with the issue of developing in young people the qualities of character thought necessary for effective citizenship; and Aristotle in his *Politics* commented on the necessity of fitting the constitution of a city-state to the character of its people. The distinguished political thinker, Alexis de Tocqueville (1835), in much more recent history, remarked in his classic analysis of *Democracy in America* that:

> The manners [character] of the Americans of the United States are, then, the *real* cause which renders that people the only one of the American nations that is able to support a democratic government ... the physical circumstances are less efficient than the laws, and the laws very subordinate to the manners [character] of the American people.

Alex Inkeles (1978) has argued the case not only for a distinctively American national modal character, but one that has shown remarkable continuity over the past two centuries. Among the distinguishing traits of the American national modal character, Inkeles lists the following in first rank: self-reliance, independence, autonomy, voluntarism and communal action, interpersonal trust, a sense of efficacy, innovativeness (openness to new experience), antiauthoritarianism, and equality. Second-order traits include individualism, restless energy, pragmatism, tendency to boastfulness, this-worldliness, preference for the concrete, and discomfort in coping with aesthetic and emo-

**National Character.** These Italian men demonstrate how national character can be expressed in the gestures, spatial proximities, and physical intimacy that typify the people of a particular society. (Peter Menzel/Stock, Boston)

tional expression. While this description may be controversial in some respects, it nonetheless serves to demonstrate the objectives of this discussion. For other descriptions of the American social character, see Bellah (1985) and DiRenzo (1977a).

The existence of distinctive personality norms for relatively small, simple, and culturally homogeneous societies seem to be rather well established. Modern societies, however, invariably include a variety of subcultures, each with its own distinctive patterns, especially those involved with childrearing, the processes of social learning, and the various other experiences that relate to personality development, and which, as such, constitute the bases of social character. This situation makes the study of social character in large, modern, complex, and industrial societies more difficult but

not impossible—as many critics have contended.*

Many scholars (see, for example, Inkeles, 1961) share the view that the same approaches—with appropriate modifications in some techniques, and perhaps an acceptance of a lower level of generality or precision—can be applied just as effectively to the study of culturally heterogeneous societies in modern nations. The basic assumption is that for large, complex, and heterogeneous societies fewer elements of personality would normally be involved in the delineation of social character than would be the case in smaller, simpler, and more homogeneous societies.

* See DiRenzo (1977b) for a statement on the theoretical and methodological perspectives in the study of social character. A more exhaustive treatment on this question is offered by Terhune (1970).

▼

**316**

One of the fundamental problems in applying the perspectives of **social character** to relatively large, complex, and heterogeneous societies is the fallacy of hypothesizing the existence of a monolithic (singular or uniform) social character for all segments of the society in question. To speak of **national modal character** is not to imply that there is only, or may be only, one characterological type in any society. Nor is this to treat social character, as is frequently done, in terms of a uniqueness of psychological attributes. Any society, especially a socially and culturally complex one, may be characterized by several modal characters. It is unlikely, as Inkeles and Levinson (1969) state, that a particular personality or character type will be found in as much as 60 to 70 percent of any modern national population. Rather, they suggest, it is more likely that such a population, in order to accommodate its subcultural variations, will be marked by a limited number of modes, for example, five to six, some of which may apply to 10 percent or 15 percent, or even to as much as 30 percent of the total population. Hence, a multimodal conception of social character would seem, both theoretically and empirically, to be more realistic and more meaningful for modern, complex, industrial societies (see DiRenzo, 1977*b*).

Peabody (1985) has provided a large-scale, empirical study on the perceptions of national character, or what sometimes are called "national stereotypes." His study focused on six societies (Britain, West Germany, France, Italy, the Soviet Union, and the United States). Peabody compared his results with those from the social scientific accounts of national modal character and found that there is a surprising level of agreement between the two methods of assessment.

One classic contribution to the study of national and social character is the work of David Riesman (1950) and his collaborators in the well-known study of *The Lonely Crowd*. In this work, Riesman developed a typology of social character (inner-directed, other-directed, and tradition-directed) that represents different modes of social conformity and that was related to a number of structural features of a society, including its principal demographic patterns (see Box 7-5). Riesman claimed that each type is characteristic of a given society at a certain stage of development and that the three types together paralleled the hypothesis of demographic transition. The tradition-directed (for whom behavior is minutely controlled by traditional cultural standards, religion, kinship ties, and the etiquette of the community) was thought to be associated with *Gemeinschaft*, unchanging agricultural-type societies with great potential growth; and the other-directed with *Gesellschaft*, industrialized and capitalist societies that are marked by relatively stable populations. Inner-directed personalities were located midway on the continuum between these two polar types, and are associated with transitional kinds of society. These three ideal types of social character were described by Riesman as having many concrete varieties or manifestations.

According to Riesman the dominant type of social character in the metropolitan centers of the United States three decades ago was that of the other-directed personality—one for whom the chief source of direction, and the principal area of sensitivity, is located in other people. The other-directed character manifests the tendency to be extremely sensitive to what others think and feel, and to conform to their likes and wishes. Other-directed people are, in short, crowd followers. Riesman describes these individuals as wearing antennae tuned in to what everyone else is doing in order to be sure that they are doing the same thing. This type of social character is similar to that which the distinguished sociopsychoanalyst Erich Fromm (1947) described at about the same time as the "marketing orientation" in which the individual is seen as conforming his or her behavior to the buyer with the highest or most

# BOX 7-5. Riesman's Character Types ▼

David Riesman in his classic work on *The Lonely Crowd* describes three types of social character that are presumed to be modally associated with different kinds of societal organization.

*Tradition-Directed Character.* "... the conformity of the individual tends to reflect his membership in a particular age-grade, clan, or caste; he learns to understand and appreciate patterns which have endured for centuries, and are modified but slightly as the generations succeed each other. The important relationships of life may be controlled by careful and rigid etiquette, learned by the young during the years of intensive socialization that end with initiation into full adult membership. Moreover, the culture, in addition to its economic tasks, or as part of them, provides ritual, routine, and religion to occupy and to orient everyone. Little energy is directed toward finding new solutions of the age-old problems, let us say, of agricultural technique or medicine, the problems to which people are acculturated."

*Inner-Directed Character.* "... can manage to live socially without strict and self-evident tradition-direction ... the source of direction for the individual is "inner" in the sense that it is implanted early in life by the elders and directed toward generalized but nonetheless inescapably destined goals. ... The inner-directed person becomes capable of maintaining a delicate balance between the demands upon him of his life goal and the buffetings of his external environment."

*Other-Directed Character.* "... what is common to all the other-directed people is that their contemporaries are the source of direction for the individual—either those known to him or those with whom he is indirectly acquainted, through friends and through the mass media. This source is of course "internalized" in the sense that dependence on it for guidance in life is implanted early. The goals toward which the other-directed person strives shift with that guidance: it is only the process of striving itself and the process of paying close attention to the signals from others that remain unaltered throughout life. This mode of keeping in touch with others permits a close behavior conformity, not through drill in behavior itself, as in the tradition-directed character, but rather through an exceptional sensitivity to the actions and wishes of others."

Riesman argued that these three types of social character were associated, modally speaking, with different types of societal organization. Basic to both societal organization, and the corresponding types of social character, was the fundamental course of demographic dynamics, following the principle of the demographic transition (see p. 306). Peculiar to a given society on this basis, the tradition-directed character is associated with incipient population growth, the inner-directed character with transitional growth (high birth rates and low death rates), and the other-directed character with population decline. ▲

Source: David Riesman, Nathan Glazer, and Reuel Denny, *The Lonely Crowd.* New Haven, Conn.: Yale University Press, 1950, pp. 11–22.

▼

**318**

attractive bid in terms of social approval and social acceptance. The individual in this conception perceives himself or herself as a commodity to be marketed and holds a psychological orientation in which self-esteem depends primarily on the ability to impress others favorably rather than on one's own inner convictions. Many scholars (for example, Hsu, 1977) contend that basically the same type of social character—even in more ideal form—can be found as the modal pattern in the United States today. This issue, however, remains a controversial one. Inkeles (1978), for example, argues that Americans have become less other-directed as evidenced by a greater acceptance of a trend toward personal and deviant lifestyles. Bellah (1985), on the other hand, also makes the case that Americans today are heavily individualistic only in a materialistic and narcissistic sense. We shall consider this question in more detail, along with other trends in the American social character, in our discussion of social change in Chapter 14.

## SYMBIOTIC RELATIONSHIPS OF CHARACTER AND SOCIETY

Social character is not only the product of sociological and cultural processes and systems (as we saw in Chapter 5), but it is also one of their producers. Characterological dynamics play an instrumental role both in maintaining social equilibrium and in producing social change. Of relevance here is the consideration of the thesis of "social character" as developed quite specifically in the classic works of Erich Fromm (1941) and David Riesman (1950). "Social character" for these men refers, respectively, to the dimensions of functional requirements and of social conformity; and, in both instances, these phenomena are concerned with the strategic and logistic dynamics of society and various other types of social systems.

Among the tasks that need to be undertaken in the assessment of these questions is to distinguish the *actual* modal patterns of person-

ality structure that may be found in a given society, the *socially congenial* personality structures that may be assumed to perform optimally in a given society, and the *socially required* personality structures that are strategically necessary for the function of the corresponding society and its social systems (DiRenzo, 1977b). Such considerations of the symbiotic relationship between personality and society speak to the question of isomorphism—the degree of similarity or parallelism—between society and the personalities involved therein.

Laumann and Schumann (1967) related personality systems and social systems at the societal level of analysis in data taken from a study in the Detroit area by combining the sociological perspectives of Durkheim (mechanical versus organic solidarity) and Töennies (*Gemeinschaft* and *Gesellschaft*) with the psychological ones of Rokeach (1960) in his formulations of dogmatism or open- and closed-mindedness. They demonstrate the existence of a "structural isomorphism" between social systems and personality systems in terms of their degree of openness or closedness to the larger environment. Even the societal mode of subsistence appears to have a basis in the functional requirement of certain types of personality. On the basis of cross-cultural studies, McClelland (1976) has argued that capitalistic societies are dependent upon the presence of a substantial degree of achievement motive (nAch) or success drive in its members. Similarly, Inkeles (1960), relying on extensive cross-cultural studies, has described the "industrial man" thought to be both the psychological correlate and indispensable tool of industrialized societies (see Chapter 14).

The thesis implicit here is that the structure and organization of various types of societies (for example, democratic, authoritarian, militaristic, and so forth)—as well as those of distinctive ideological orientation (for example, democratic, fascistic, communistic)—not only produce particular types of social character, but, much more significantly, also require certain numbers of individuals with certain psychological or personality characteristics in order to achieve optimal, indeed even minimal, levels of function.*

Inkeles (1961:193–194) has posed the relevant question:

> Are the societies which have a long history of democracy peopled by a majority of individuals who possess a personality conducive to democracy? Alternatively, are societies which have experienced recurrent or prolonged authoritarian, dictatorial, or totalitarian government inhabited by proportionately large numbers of individuals with personality traits we have seen to be associated with extremism? Almost all the modern students of national character are convinced that the answer to this question is in the affirmative.

Conscious efforts at the formation of particular types of personality are inevitably the norm in totalitarian societies. Such indeed was the case in both fascist Germany and Italy earlier this century. Such is also the case today in the Soviet Union and China. The ideal personality structure in the Soviet and Chinese societies, notwithstanding differences in terms of cultural variations, has been one based on ideological principles of the Marxist-Leninist variety, and one that incorporates a totalitarian value orientation that emphasizes obedience and subjugation to authority, a sense of solidarity, commitment, industriousness in work, and honesty. Such an ideal personality profile was part and parcel of the early Communist regime in the Soviet Union up to about 1960, and in China from 1949 to 1978 under the regime of Mao Tse-Tung (Heiliger, 1980).

Inkeles and associates (1958) have shown the concrete relevance of this situation in their study of the modal personality patterns of Russians and their significance for functional adjustment to the Soviet sociopolitical system. This study reveals marked incongruence between the actual modal patterns of personality among the Russian people and the patterns desired and considered functionally necessary by the Communist (erstwhile Stalinist) regime. The desired patterns of personality in fact have been found to be characteristically modal among the higher socioeconomic levels of the U.S.S.R., such as in professional and other high-status occupational categories. This latter finding suggests that socioeconomic mobility within the Soviet society is correlated positively with a particular type of personality in terms of its congruent relationship with the structure of the Communist sociopolitical system.*

Dicks (1950), working with a sample of 1000 German prisoners during and after World War II, demonstrated the same points in a psychoanalytic perspective on the relationship between personality and orientations toward Nazism (see Figure 7-10). Dicks' findings show that, in terms of specific patterns of psychoanalytical variables, there is a distinct Nazi personality—a hard, fanatical type, holding Nazi beliefs and values with conviction—as opposed to the non-Nazi or the anti-Nazi German. It is this distinctive type of personality, Dicks contends, that constituted the Nazi elite during the Hitler regime. These findings and their interpretation provide an empirical substantiation for the thesis proposed by Fromm (1941), who argued that fascist institutions are strategically based on a specific type of personality, which he described as the "authoritarian character." Fromm explains the rise of Hitler and Nazism in Germany on the basis of a functional congruency between the ideological structure of Nazism and the psychological structure of the German national character. Presumably, the same thesis of functional congruence can be applied to Italy, Spain, Argentina, and other societies that have witnessed the rise of fascist governments in the past half-century.

**319**

---

* See DiRenzo (1974a) for detailed treatments of the relationship of personality to different types of political institutions, both in terms of their ideological basis and their particular variations in political methodology and strategy.

* For a followup study, see Kosa (1962).

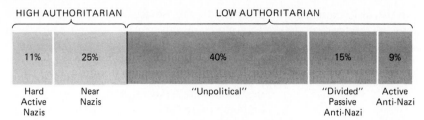

| HIGH AUTHORITARIAN | | LOW AUTHORITARIAN | | |
|---|---|---|---|---|
| 11% | 25% | 40% | 15% | 9% |
| Hard Active Nazis | Near Nazis | "Unpolitical" | "Divided" Passive Anti-Nazi | Active Anti-Nazi |

FIGURE 7-10   Distribution of Political Ideology and Personality Types. A study of one thousand German prisoners during World War II showed that individuals holding Nazi attitudes and beliefs were characterized by strong authoritarian personalities. Antithetical patterns of personality were found among individuals who maintained an opposing ideology or who were "unpolitical." Source: Henry V. Dicks, "Personality Traits and National Socialist Ideology," *Human Relations,* 1960, 3, pp. 111–153.

**320**

Consciously, or unconsciously, perhaps partly both, societies and cultures usually develop those types of personality that are not only compatible or congruent with the social and cultural lifestyles, but, indeed, even those that are necessary for strategic reasons. Fromm (1941) argues that the personality types in a given society serve either as a cement holding the system together or as an explosive tearing it apart, depending on the degree to which a given personality type fits the demands of the society and finds satisfaction within it. The fundamental proposition of this argument is that there is only a half-truth in the cliché, "It takes all kinds of people to make the world go around." Rather, for any "social world" or society to function properly and adequately, it takes certain kinds of people, who must be in certain positions and in certain proportions at certain times. Otherwise, there are likely to be dysfunctional consequences—for the society as well as for the individual personalities involved.

## Summary

Society is a relatively independent and self-sufficient social system, usually represented by a relatively large number of people, occupying a given territory, and interacting in terms of a commonly shared culture. Sociologists use several models in the analysis and understanding of society. Chief among these are evolutionary models, organismic models, and conflict models. No one model is sufficient in itself for a complete understanding of the complex dynamics of society.

Evolutionary models are predicated on the assumption that all societies automatically and inevitably go through specified stages of development from simple to complex forms. Organismic models analogize societal organizations to the structure and function of biological organisms and have as their fundamental concept that of homeostasis as it is applied to human physiology. Conflict models are premised on the position that conflict, instability, and change rather than order and equilibrium are the distinguishing features of social organization.

One principal method for the classification of societies is that based on their mode of subsistence—that is, the way in which they provide their members with fundamental biological needs, such as food, shelter, and clothing. Four basic types are recognized in this regard: hunting and gathering, horticultural, agrarian, and industrial. The more common type of societal classification, however, is in terms of the mode of social organization. Ideal-type conceptions of society are employed in this scheme. Several typologies have been developed; however, the most popular typology is that offered by Ferdinand Töennies, who differentiated between *Gemeinschaft* (community) and *Gesellschaft* (society) forms of social organization.

The principal and largest subunits of society are known as institutions. A social institution refers to all of the patterns of behavior, formal or informal, that are firmly or ideally established for the purposes of meeting a functional need of society. The number of institutions, as well as their individual complexity, varies from society to society. Several institutions can be found in all societies and are described as societal universals: family, education, government, economics, and religion.

Of these institutions, the family constitutes the core institution, which in many respects can be seen as a microcosm of society. The family is one of the most highly varied units of societal organization—particularly in terms of marital structures and dynamics. Among the principal functions of the family are those of sexual regulation, reproduction of children, socialization, emotional support, economic activities, and social placement.

Political institutions assume two basic forms: democracy and autocracy. Authoritarian and totalitarian governments, often in the form of oligarchies, military juntas, and fascistic states, assume total political control. The principal types of economic institutions that are prevalent in societies of the world today are those of capitalism, communism, socialism, and democratic socialism. Religious institutions are distinguished sociologically in terms of four major varieties: ecclesia, denomination, sect, and cult. Civil religion, a secular, nonsectarian form of religion, may be found in modern societies.

Human ecology is concerned with the relationship between people and their physical environment. Of special significance in the assessment of the ecological foundations of society is the concept of natural areas that develop

from the processes of ecological invasion and ecological segregation. The chief models for describing the development of urban spatial patterns in terms of these ecological processes are concentric zone theory, sector theory, and multiple nuclei theory. Social relations are in part a function of the spatial or geographical distributions of a societal population.

Demographic dynamics comprise another element that strongly influences the structure and function of society, as well as the nature and extent of interaction in a society. One major consideration is simply the sheer size of the population. Internal composition in terms of age and sex is also quite important in a number of respects, including in particular the dependency ratio. The population pyramid is one technique that is helpful in understanding the demographic foundation of a society. Of particular relevance to the growth and development of societies is the hypothesis of demographic transition.

Society is significantly affected in its structure and function by the specific types of personality or psychological character that are present therein. Particular types of society and their specific institutions are the result of certain types of personalities and functionally require certain kinds of personality. Significant in these central respects are the varieties of social character and national modal character that can be found in a given society.

# Key Concepts

agricultural society
associational society
autocracy
biosphere
capitalism
civil religion
communal society
communism
community
concentric zone theory

▼

322

conjugal family
consanguineal family
cult
democracy
demographic transition
demography
denomination
dependency ratio
ecclesia
ecological invasion
ecological segregation
economy
ecosystem
endogamy
exogamy
fascism
*Gemeinschaft*
*Gesellschaft*
group marriage
horticultural society
human ecology
hunting and gathering society
ideal type
incest taboo
industrial society
marriage

matriarchy
matrilineage
matrilocality
metropolitan statistical area
monogamy
multiple nuclei theory
national modal character
natural area
oligarchy
patriarchy
partrilineage
patrilocality
polity
polygamy
population pyramid
propinquity
sect
sector theory
sex ratio
social character
social institution
socialism
society
totalitarianism
urban gentrification
zero population growth

# 8  Complex and Formal Organizations

Complex organizations of all sizes and types can be found in every realm of modern society—government, business, religion, education, health, entertainment, and many others. Organizations exert an important influence in the life of every member of society. And, as a fundamental principle, it can be said that organizations beget organizations. Thus, no assessment of human social behavior can ignore an explanation of the nature, structure, and mode of functioning of complex organizations. What precisely is a complex organization? How do complex organizations differ from other kinds of social systems? What are the different types of complex organizations that exist? How do complex organizations function? What is the relationship between the individual and complex organizations? These are the type of questions that will be examined in this chapter. Our attention will focus in particular on the nature and dynamics of bureaucracies, a highly formal and complex type of organization that is found increasingly in modern society. ▲

## Outline

▼

▶ Many observers of the contemporary era have labeled it the age of complex organizations. Large organizations, however, are not new phenomena. Ancient societies also developed complex organizations in order to achieve a variety of goals. The Egyptian pyramids, for example, were the product of massive organizational efforts. The Roman Catholic Church that dominated medieval society was itself an excellent example of a highly bureaucratic organization. The same was true of extensive military forces that existed in centuries past. That the present period of civilization has been termed the age of complex organizations is not because they are new, but because they exist in larger numbers and greater complexity than ever before.

Complex and formal organizations permeate every aspect of human life. Many of an individual's most important activities occur within one type of organization or another. People are born in organizations called hospitals, and they may spend the latter period of their lives in organizations called nursing homes. In between, people spend a great deal of time in such organizations as schools, churches, corporations, governmental agencies, and the military—to name just a few. Even much of our leisure and recreational activity takes place within an organizational context. Hence, it is indeed quite true that social life in this modern era is virtually an organizational life.

# Nature of Complex and Formal Organizations

**Complex** and **formal organizations** consist of social systems that are characterized by an explicitly formulated set of goals, policies, procedures, and regulations that specify appropriate behavior for its many members. Much of the formality and complexity of these systems derive from the sheer size of organizations, which usually have such a large membership that close, personal, or informal relationships among all of its members are impossible.

To give examples of complex formal organizations is much easier than to define them. General Motors Corporation, the United Nations, the American Football League, the United States Navy, the Teamsters Union, the Church of England, and the University of Notre Dame are all quite well-known organizations. While each of these organizations can be distinguished by the nature of its individual enterprise or objectives (for example, economic profit, aggrandizement of political power, protection of the interests of members, and dissemination of values and knowledge), they nevertheless share the essential features of a complex or formal organization. Chief among these distinctive characteristics is the conscious and systematically coordinated behavior of a number of people for the purpose of obtaining a specific goal or set of goals.

Complex organizations are fundamentally distinguished from other kinds of social systems in that each constitutes an *enacted* type of social order. Complex organizations are not so much the product of spontaneous social forces, which as we shall see is more characteristic of social groups, as they are the product of planned activity and the considered action of individuals. Organizations are consciously formed by individuals who share common goals and realize that their goals can best be obtained if they get together and rationally coordinate their activities and pool their talents. Organizations are said to be rationally structured because their norms, procedures, and activities are explicitly designed to enable the organization to achieve its goals in an efficient manner.

## MAJOR CHARACTERISTICS OF COMPLEX ORGANIZATIONS

While there exists a great variety of complex organizations, all of them share certain characteristics which ideally distinguish them from

▼

**325**

▼

other kinds of social systems. These characteristics are the specification of goals, the specialization of tasks, a formal communication and authority structure, and a membership that is subject to change.

GOAL SPECIFICITY.   Organizations come into being in order to attain certain goals. The norms, procedures, communication networks, authority structures, and other components of organizations are created for the purpose of enabling the organization to achieve its goals. Many organizations have one clear-cut goal that is explicitly defined. The goal of the Exxon Corporation, for instance, is to make a profit. The earning statement of the corporation shows the extent to which it is successfully attaining its goal. It is an objective measure of its success. Other organizations may have several goals they wish to attain. A university has the goals of providing a general education to undergraduates, advanced training in specific fields for its graduate students, and a research setting for the faculty. Decisions often must be made as to which goal should be emphasized. Nonetheless, unlike the corporation which has an objective method of determining how well it is achieving its goals, the university lacks such a clear-cut method.

DIVISION OF LABOR.   Organizations are characterized by a division of labor. Each member is responsible for performing a particular, delimited job. Specialization of function is one method that serves to increase efficiency. An individual becomes expert in performing his or her task because it is relatively specific and only requires a limited range of skills. So, while all professors teach, they only teach those areas of their discipline in which they are most expert. Similarly, the administrative staff of the university is characterized by a division of labor. The dean of students has responsibilities and duties that are quite different from those of the dean for academic affairs.

FORMAL COMMUNICATION AND AUTHORITY STRUCTURES.   Relationships that exist among people occupying organizational positions are clearly specified, and often depicted in organizational charts, which show the chains of command and communication that exist within the organization. Organizations typically have hierarchical or pyramidal structures for both authority and communication. Interaction within organizations is determined essentially by the position that members occupy and their formal relationship to other positions and individuals.

CHANGING MEMBERSHIP.  Unlike other kinds of groups, such as the family, which has an irreplaceable, fixed membership, members of organizations are routinely replaced when they leave the organization. Hence, organizations typically exist longer than the lifetime or affiliation of any particular member. Even if an organization has a high rate of turnover, it will still survive as an entity so long as it finds adequate replacements for those who departed. As long as members who leave or die are replaced by others who can perform the duties associated with the various positions, the organization can continue to function as an ongoing concern.

## TYPES OF ORGANIZATIONS

While all organizations share certain essential features and are quite similar in terms of social structure, there are many significant differences among them. Mode of compliance is one distinguishing feature of particular significance. Etzioni (1975) has developed a useful typology of organizations based on the ways in which they get compliance from their members. He classifies organizations in terms of three basic types: voluntary, utilitarian, and coercive.

VOLUNTARY ORGANIZATIONS.   People become members of voluntary organiza-

326

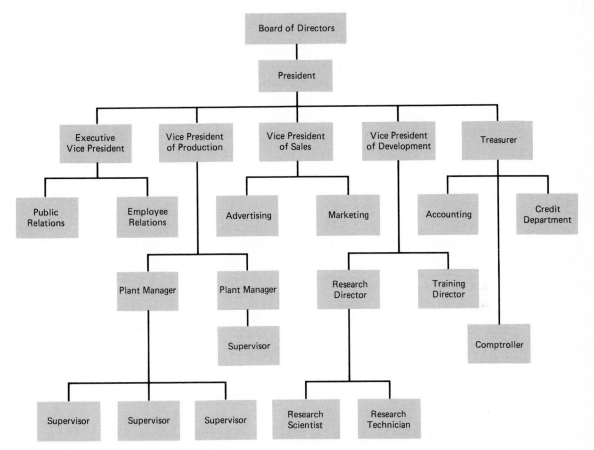

FIGURE 8-1   Typical Organizational Chart of a Complex Organization.

tions because they have certain common interests and goals. They share the basic values, ideals, and norms that constitute the essence of the organization. They comply with the norms and rules of the organization because they want to see the organization attain its goals, and thereby collectively fulfill their own shared interests. Thus, compliance comes about because there is a consensus among organizational members concerning goals and norms.

Voluntary organizations, sometimes called **voluntary associations,** may have many members who donate their time and talents to the organization. This type of organization has no real or formal control over its members. Mem-

bers may leave any time that they wish to do so without being subjected to negative sanctions. Examples of voluntary organizations would be the League of Women Voters, the National Rifle Association, and all types of professional, service, religious, fraternal, and charitable organizations. Individuals usually participate in voluntary organizations only on a part-time basis, often just to fill their leisure time.* Voluntary organizations have the broad

---

* Research shows that individuals who participate in voluntary organizations report higher levels of personal happiness, self-esteem, satisfaction, political effectiveness, and a sense of community (Hanks, 1981; Knoke, 1981; Litwak, 1961; Pollock, 1982).

▼

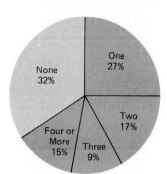

FIGURE 8-2 Membership in Voluntary Organizations. The vast majority of Americans belong to at least one voluntary organization. More than one-fourth belong to three or more organizations.
Source: General Social Surveys, 1972–1988. *Cumulative Codebook:* National Research Corporation, University of Chicago, 1987.

effect, nonetheless, of promoting participation in many aspects of social life, and fulfilling various functional needs of society. Interest in voluntary organizations depends in great part on the values of the particular society. Many societies do not permit their members the freedom of association that is the basis of voluntary organizations. The United States, on the other hand, is unique in the extent to which its members participate in voluntary organizations. Such a situation has been a long-standing characteristic of American society. As Alexis de Tocqueville (1835), the French political observer, noted more than a century and half ago: "Americans of all ages, all stations in life, and all types of disposition are forever forming associations." In 1984, 68 percent of Americans reported membership in one or more voluntary organizations (NORC, 1987). That number may be even somewhat higher now. Such indeed is all the more likely when one realizes that, in terms of nationwide operations alone, *The Encyclopedia of Associations* lists more than 23,000 voluntary organizations for the United States. Hence, we can see that a great portion of social life in many modern societies transpires in an organizational context.

**UTILITARIAN ORGANIZATIONS.** People join utilitarian organizations because they want to receive certain benefits or rewards from the organization. The best example of a utilitarian organization is the business corporation. People become employees of corporations in order to receive payment for their services. Thus, such organizations use money as the primary method of getting members to comply with their rules and procedures. If employees do not follow the politics of the corporation and help it to achieve its goals, they are likely to be dismissed. Members of utilitarian organizations are also free to leave them whenever they wish, but doing so will result in termination of material rewards that they have been receiving from the company. The necessity of these compensations usually makes for strong compliance.

**COERCIVE ORGANIZATIONS.** Unlike voluntary and utilitarian organizations, which people join of their own free will, individuals are forced to become members of coercive organizations. Schools, prisons, and the armed forces represent quite diverse examples of such organizations. Failure on the part of members to comply with the rules and regulations of the coercive organization results in the administration of particular forms of physical or psychological punishment. Members are free to leave coercive organizations only when an outside authority (for example, courts, officials) permits them to do so.

## INFORMAL STRUCTURES OF COMPLEX ORGANIZATIONS

Classical conceptions of complex organizations focused entirely on their formal and explicit dimensions. These dimensions, however, represent only one segment of complex organizations. The other segment consists of the informal relationships and patterns of interaction that emerge among the members of com-

▼

**Societal Obligations.** Medical examinations as part of a process of compulsory induction into the military exemplify the workings of a coercive organization. These people do not appear happy about the prospects of the kind of social life that awaits them. (The Bettman Archive)

plex organizations (Blau & Meyer, 1971). The informal structure cannot be discerned by examining the organizational chart. It can be known only by observing the unofficial relationships and interactions that develop among members of the organization.

As organizational members interact in formal relationships they come to know each other as individuals having unique personalities, not just as occupants of particular positions. Likes and dislikes develop among members, resulting in the emergence of friendships, cliques, and coalitions. Members become known as individuals possessing particular kinds of personality characteristics—some people being perceived as easy-going, friendly, and helpful; others are cranky, egotistical, and power-hungry.

Informal networks of communication develop which in many cases are quite different from the formal communication structure that is approved by organizational managers. As

one student of organizations notes, "It is also naive to believe that communication initiated at any level of authority will follow a perfect downward path commensurate with the organizational chart of the hierarchy of authority" (Champion, 1975:173). Information obtained via informal channels can at times be highly accurate; at other times, however, it may be grossly erroneous. There are instances when the informal communication structure transmits items of interest faster than the formal communication structure. It is not unusual, for example, for lower-echelon employees to learn of a change of company policy via the grapevine before they receive it through official notifications of the established communication network.

An integral part of the informal structure of an organization consists of the unofficial or informal norms that develop among members. These norms may contradict those that have

▼

**330**

been decreed by the managers of the organization. Informal norms or expectations may emerge which specify, for example, how much an employee should produce in a given time period. If workers exceed the limit, they are apt to be called "rate busters"; if they produce less than the informal norm specifies, they are likely to become known as "chiselers." In either case, they will be subject to one form of punishment or another for not adhering to the informal norm of production that was established by their fellow workers (Roethlisberger & Dickson, 1964). Thus, the formal standards of an organization may be upset by the emergence of highly informal, yet powerful and effective norms. Such situations present serious functional problems for both the organization and its members. Informal structures, however, are not necessarily counterproductive.

There are situations in which the existence of informal structures and mechanisms can serve to facilitate instead of impede the formal goals of a complex organization. An informal structure that prevents an effective circumventing of the formal organizational structure is one such instance. Formal structures, norms, and procedures may be so slow and cumbersome that they result in a delayed or ineffectual response to organizational problems or crises. Many employees realize that rigid adherence to formal rules and procedures can be highly dysfunctional, indeed even disastrous, for the organization. Consequently, they may bend or break the rules and thereby devise shortcuts that may facilitate their work by using unofficial procedures for handling problems. Often, for instance, employees may obtain informal permission to do something, do it, and only then, after they have completed the task, get official approval by completing the required forms and going through the formal channels of requisition.

The informal structure also serves the function of allowing members of the organization to express aspects of their personality which could not be done if they had to behave solely in terms of the formal structure.* The informal dimension of organizations allows members to "kid around" or "goof off," and engage in other forms of nonjob related behavior. These actions have a stress-releasing function that may result in better morale and job satisfaction. Such outcomes, along with opportunities to gratify personal needs, all contribute to the organizational ideals of efficiency and maximum productivity. We shall examine such aspects of the informal structure of organizations in more detail when we discuss different models of formal organizations in a subsequent section of this chapter.

# Bureaucracies

A major type of complex organization, one which represents an extreme pattern of formal structure, is the bureaucracy. The term "bureaucracy" usually evokes a series of negative images in the minds of most people. Individuals often think of petty officials (bureaucrats) who are more concerned with adhering to rules and procedures than with serving people. The image readily comes to mind of clerks who make people wait in endless lines, of being given the "runaround," and of having to contend with a seemingly perpetual chaos of "red tape." Such stereotypes are not without a firm basis in the realistic operation of bureaucracies.

Bureaucracy to the sociologist, however, has a quite technical meaning. Often "bureaucracy" in this context is used as just another term for complex organization. There are, nonetheless, some very important distinctions. Chief among the distinguishing elements of bureaucracy are its highly formal and rational character, as well as its emphasis on efficiency—both of which permeate its social structure and dynamics. **Bureaucracy,** quite technically, refers to "A formal,

---

* Erving Goffman (1961a) in his book on *Asylums* presents a description of the informal structure that exists among the patients in the complex organization of a mental hospital.

rationally organized social structure . . . [with] clearly defined patterns of activity in which, ideally, every series of actions is functionally related to the purpose of the organization" (Merton, 1957:195).

The classic study of bureaucracy was done by Max Weber. He was concerned with the principles of rational administration on a large scale and investigated primarily government bureaucracies. (The bureaucracy, however, is not just a governmental or political organization. However true this may have been at the time of their initiation, bureaucracies have become typical of all social agencies and institutions—universities, banks, corporations, hospitals, political parties, armies, and even churches.) Bureaucracies, according to Weber (1922), represent the most efficient way to organize people for the attainment of common goals. He argued that the bureaucratic form of organization is greatly superior to other forms and that, among various types of social systems, the bureaucracy alone is capable of attaining the highest degree of efficiency.

Weber contended that bureaucracies became widespread because of the increasing degree to which modern societies were becoming characterized by a process he called *rationalization*. A rationalized social order is one which has replaced tradition, custom, and mysticism with abstract rules and formal procedures. Bureaucracy was one of several consequences of the trend toward rationalization because it represented a social system that attempted to relate means to ends in a conscious and deliberate fashion. It had as its goal the reduction of uncertainty, arbitrariness, and illogical modes of organization. Procedures, rules, and activities were justified not on the basis of tradition or custom but because they would help to insure the most efficient attainment of goals. Weber also had a number of reservations about bureaucracies, specifically, their impersonal relationship to the individual. Nonetheless, he felt that, given the historical growth of societies and

their probable future, bureaucracies were an inevitable form of social organization, and one that would become quite pervasive. There is no doubt now about the validity of his expectations.

# MAJOR CHARACTERISTICS OF BUREAUCRACIES

Weber described and analyzed bureaucracies by developing an ideal type. He studied a large number of different bureaucracies and then abstracted the features that they had in common. The result is a pure or "ideal" conception of a bureaucracy. An **ideal type** is a nominal concept or mental construct (see Chapter 2) that emphasizes, indeed even exaggerates, the essential characteristics and distinctive features of a particular phenomenon.* Weber's ideal-type description of a bureaucracy does not constitute an evaluation of bureaucracy or a specification of its desirable elements; rather it consists of the principal or defining characteristics of any bureaucracy. Any actual or concrete bureaucracy is only an approximation of the ideal type, which according to Weber's (1947) formulation, possesses the following characteristics:

**TASK SPECIALIZATION.** Each unit or member of the bureaucracy is given a specialized task to perform. In order to accomplish its overall goal, the work of a bureaucracy is divided into a series of subgoals or activities with corresponding structural units or bureaus. The university library, for instance, may consist of several units or divisions within which individuals may be employed to do highly specific and delimited tasks. Within the acquisitions department, one employee may do nothing but

* As Weber (1949:90) stated, "In its conceptual purity, this mental construct (ideal type) cannot be found empirically anywhere in reality." This type of conception, however, is effectively used in many areas of sociological analysis besides that of bureaucratic organization.

331

▼ process book orders from faculty members, another person may be responsible only for cataloging books, and yet another for shelving them. It is believed that task specialization results in maximum efficiency. Hence, in these respects, all bureaucracies resemble the assembly-line type of operation.

HIERARCHICAL AUTHORITY. Bureaucracies are perhaps most commonly known for their clearly established system of super- and subordinate offices and positions. All members of bureaucratic organizations have varying degrees of authority over others depending on the particular office that they hold. Each office is under the control and supervision of a higher one. Those in supervisory positions are responsible for the performance of those that they supervise and are held responsible to their superiors for their own actions as well as those of their subordinates. This pattern assumes the structural shape of a pyramid as is commonly depicted in the organizational chart. The nature and scope of each person's authority is clearly

332

delineated. Authority and power, however, are attached to the position or office, not to the individual. Moreover, the authority that a person in the bureaucracy has is clearly circumscribed and strictly limited. A professor, for instance, can legitimately require students to purchase certain books, to attend classes, and to take examinations; he cannot legitimately demand, however, that students polish his car, discuss something with him during the weekend, or wear suits to class. Such demands are illegitimate because they are not part of the powers attached to the position of professor.

Another and parallel dimension of the authority structure consists of the formal channels of communication. Bureaucratic communication is also distinguished by its highly formal character, and it invariably assumes a written form. "Verbal orders don't go!" and "Put it in writing!" are bureaucratic directives that nearly everyone has received or experienced. Indeed, the memorandum (see Box 8-1) and the files that preserve them have become the epitome of bureaucratic artifacts!

## BOX 8-1. Formal Communication in Complex Organizations

### ILLINOIS DEPARTMENT OF LABOR
### BUREAU OF EMPLOYMENT SECURITY

#### MEMORANDUM

To:     David Gassman, Statistician                     Date: April 30, 1971
From:   Benjamin Greenstein, Chief
        Research and Statistics
Subject: Hazardous Use of Coffee Pot

The afternoon of April 29, while Mr. Arthur Haverly was on vacation, an electric coffee pot was plugged in his office and left unattended. It spread noxious fumes through the office and scorched a table belonging to the State.

You admitted that you plugged in that coffee pot and that you did it, although Mr. Haverly had told you that I had requested that it should not be done due to previous adverse experience. When I asked you why you plugged in that coffee pot, although I had requested that it should not be done, you stated that you did not take it that seriously. ▼

I may note also that Mr. Haverly informed me the previous day that he had not authorized you to connect the coffee pot in his office.

The following facts, therefore, emerge:

1. You had used your supervisor's office for cooking coffee without his authorization.
2. You did so, although you knew that I had requested that it should not be done.
3. You had left the coffee pot unattended. For that matter, there may have been a conflict between performing agency work and attending to the coffee pot.
4. You created a fire hazard for your fellow workers and subjected them to noxious fumes.
5. When I asked you why you plugged in the coffee pot in spite of my request to the contrary, you stated that you did not take it seriously. This is a rejection of supervision.
6. Your disregard of my authority has resulted in discomfort to your fellow workers and damage to State property.
7. On April 30, the day following the above actions and conversation, at 8:25 in the morning, I noted that you had again plugged in the coffee pot. When I pointed out that you were aware that I had asked you not to plug it in, you replied that it is not 8:30 yet. I then told you that I am in charge of the section, even though it is not 8:30 yet.

333

What should be done with respect to your actions, as specified above, is under consideration. In the meantime, you are emphatically requested not to repeat the hazard you created by plugging in the coffee pot. ▲

SEPARATION OF OFFICE FROM PERSON. People working in bureaucracies occupy an office or position that consists of a set of rights and duties. Authority and power, however, are attached to the position or office, not to the individual. Personal qualities or idiosyncratic characteristics that one may possess are irrelevant. Thus, what the dean of a college can or cannot legitimately do is determined by the rights and obligations attached to the Office of the Dean, not by his or her own whimsical notions. The authority and power, as well as the duties and obligations, that are associated with a given position are limited and clearly spelled out. The separation of office from person results in a condition in which no one is indispensable, and by which the organization can continue to operate when people leave. People

▼

**334**

in bureaucracies are much like interchangeable parts in a machine. The bureaucracy itself, then, consists of a number of interdependent offices or bureaus whose coordination and interaction are explicitly prescribed.

FORMAL RULES AND PROCEDURES. The norms that govern the operation of the bureaucracy are explicitly spelled out and codified in written form. The rules and procedures apply to specific circumstances and problem situations that are likely to emerge. Should a student, for example, accuse a professor of discriminating against him because of race or religion, there are formal mechanisms that exist for the purpose of determining the validity of the charges. Most bureaucracies have manuals which clearly specify the rights, responsibilities, and duties associated with each position or office, as well as the procedures that should be used to deal with a wide range of problems. "Going by the book" is a characteristic mode of operation in the bureaucracy which avoids subjective bias, inconsistency, and confusion. It also makes for personal detachment.

DETACHED ORIENTATION. Bureaucracies are goal-oriented structures. Thus, any activity or behavior that is not instrumental in achieving the stated goals is discouraged. Officials are not expected to express their emotions or multiple aspects of their personality.

An impersonal, detached orientation is encouraged because such an orientation will facilitate rational, objective decisions and actions. Personal feelings of a positive or negative kind toward others are discouraged lest they interfere with the efficient operation of the organization. There is little place in the ideal bureaucracy for joking, office romances, idle chatter, or conviviality. Conversation and interaction are to be restricted to job-related matters. Such impersonal relations obviously are intended to insure objectivity and rationality, as well as to promote equality of treatment and cooperation.

MERIT SELECTION. Individuals are usually attracted to bureaucracies because they anticipate being able to develop a professional career within them. The selection of people for employment, however, is based solely on their technical competence or personal qualifications (education and experience) and on how well they achieve on certain tests of aptitudes and skills. Similarly, whether an employee gets promoted depends on past performance, seniority, and test scores. Subjective, personal, nonjob-related factors are not supposed to have any bearing on whether a person gets hired or is promoted to a better position. Technical competence alone is the criterion for hiring, retaining, and promoting. It is "what you can do and have done," not "who you are" or "whom you

TABLE 8-1. Bureaucratic Organization

| Characteristics | Functions | Dysfunctions |
|---|---|---|
| Task specialization | Efficiency | Inflexibility |
| Hierarchical authority | Stability and order | Displacement of goals |
| Separation of office from person | Continuity | Impersonality |
| Formal rules and procedures | | Peter principle |
| Detached orientation | | Iron law of oligarchy |
| Merit selection | | |

know," that determine who gets employed and promoted. These impersonal, objective criteria supplant a set of procedures that existed in the past when the leader was "free to confer 'grace' on the basis of his personal pleasure or displeasure, personal likes or dislikes, quite arbitrarily, particularly in return for gifts which often became a source of regular income" (Weber, 1947:342).

Keep in mind that Weber's ideal-type formulation of bureaucracy is an analytical tool which is meant to be used for the comparative analysis of organizations. It is not intended to be a description of any empirically existing organization. No real organization completely conforms to the ideal-type characterization. Rather, different organizations possess most of these features in varying degrees.

# FUNCTIONS OF BUREAUCRACIES

Probably, few of us would like to be known as bureaucrats. Yet, that is precisely what the vast majority of us are at one time or another. Perhaps a brief consideration of the advantages or functions of bureaucracy may cast a different perspective on this dubious perception of self.

EFFICIENCY. In Weber's view, rational, efficient administration constitutes the principal criterion of an organization's function. He believed in this regard that the bureaucracy is the most rational type of structure that could be devised to coordinate the activities of individuals as they pursue the attainment of complex goals. The bureaucracy, with its division of labor, does not tax the abilities or energies of people. Furthermore, it enables people to become proficient in a specific task which, when combined with the "outputs" of others, contributes to the achievement of the organization's goal. The professor, for example, has to be concerned primarily with teaching and re-

search. He or she does not have to balance the university's budget, to see to it that the pipes do not freeze, or to order paper and chalk. In addition, by having a clearly delineated structure of authority, the person who works in the bureaucratic structure knows to whom he or she is responsible and to whom he or she can go for the purpose of rectifying any problem or grievance that may occur. Such objectivity avoids favoritism and personal biases, which ideally makes for equality of opportunity and treatment of members.

STABILITY AND ORDER. Perhaps more than anything else, the bureaucratic form of organization provides a high degree of stability and order that enables both officials and clients to predict each other's behavior. The professor knows that the people in the admissions office will do their best to recruit students, that the physical plant people will see to it that the buildings are open and functioning properly, and that the payroll office will have the salary checks available on payday. By the same token, students are able to predict that their professors will show up at the times their classes are scheduled, that the library will be open during certain hours, and that the bookstore will have the textbooks that they must buy. The bureaucratic form of organization, then, provides a high degree of certainty for both its members and the clients that it serves.

CONTINUITY. Bureaucracies exist independently of the people in them, and as such they provide incontrovertible evidence that there are no indispensable people. Popes and presidents come and go but their offices and organizations continue on. Indeed, no office or bureaucracy has had such an uninterrupted existence as that manifested in the nearly 2000-year continuity of the papacy and the highly formal and complex organization associated with it. Continuity and perpetuation of social existence can be assured by the bureaucracy.

**335**

## DYSFUNCTIONS OF BUREAUCRACIES

336

Up to this point we have stressed the positive consequences or functions of bureaucracies. The reader may have gotten the impression that the bureaucratic form of organization is without flaws or disadvantages. Such a situation is not the case at all. Surely everyone has experienced the dysfunctions of bureaucracy, and all of us have had to pay for whatever measure of inefficiency they have. Even Weber was aware of bureaucratic dysfunctions and for this reason had reservations about this form of social organization—however indispensable and inevitable it appeared to be in the modern era. There are a number of significant dysfunctions in bureaucracies. Paradoxically, in many instances, it is precisely those features of a bureaucracy which contribute to its functions that are also responsible for its dysfunctions. The following are some of the major problems that bureaucracies present in terms of organizational function.

INFLEXIBILITY.   The very set of rules, regulations, and procedures that enable the bureaucracy to handle many routine matters also inhibit it from dealing with unanticipated problems. Officials may get into a quandary when confronted with situations that are not covered by the formal set of rules that comprise the bureaucracy. Officials are trained to deal with a particular set of problem situations. Conditions change, however, and changing conditions may bring about new types of problems that require new responses. Actions based upon training and skills which have been successfully applied in the past may result in inappropriate responses under a different set of circumstances. Ironically, the more adequately officials have been trained to abide with the formal procedures, the more likely it is that they will exhibit what Thorstein Veblen (1933) called a "trained incapacity" whenever new conditions make the old procedures obsolete. This stifling of any initiative or imagination on the part of employees because of previous training which is implemented so ritualistically can be dysfunctional for both the individual and the organization.

DISPLACEMENT OF GOALS.   Bureaucrats at times may become so concerned with abiding by rules, regulations, and routines that they lose sight of the primary goals of the organization. Such a situation is known as an inversion of the means and ends of the organization. In short, the rules and procedures that were originally created to be the means by which organizational goals are to be attained become ends or goals in themselves. The hospital receptionist, for example, who insists that the seriously injured person fill out certain forms before being treated, has allowed the means to displace the goals of the hospital. The student who becomes more concerned with grades than with learning also illustrates this phenomenon.

Inflexible, perhaps even obsessive, adherence to rules, by following the letter of every word in "the book," regardless of circumstances, can significantly work against organizational goals. Such a case is dramatically portrayed in an account of the bombing of Pearl Harbor which triggered the entry of the United States into World War II:

> As enemy planes strafed military installations, personnel scrambled toward armories where weapons and ammunition were stored. As plane cannons barked overhead and bombs fell everywhere, some armory guards insisted on a formal requisition properly signed according to regulations and following proper channels before weapons would be issued (Champion, 1975:38).

Ritualistic conformity to rules makes it impossible to discern the goals which the means are intended to serve.

IMPERSONALITY. Bureaucratic officials are trained to deal with clients in impersonal terms. Clients are seen as examples of categories of problems for which certain ready-made solutions exist. Difficulties inevitably arise because clients, understandably, want to be treated as unique individuals, not as categories of problems. The impersonal treatment that clients receive may lead them to feel that officials "don't give a damn" about *their* problems and that, from the perspective of the bureaucrats, they are nothing but objects to be processed in a routine, dispassionate fashion. Students may develop this impression when they are waiting in long lines in order to get registered for courses or come to think of themselves "as just a number" in a heavily enrolled class or large university. The ever-expanding use of social security numbers brings home this message to all of us.

Alienation, a concept formulated by Karl Marx (1844), provides insight into this resulting state of depersonalization. **Alienation** is usually defined as a personal state in which one experiences feelings of meaninglessness, powerlessness, social isolation, and self-estrangement when confronted with social conditions the individual cannot control (Blauner, 1964). Alienated people may be described as those who are

in the organization, but not of it (see Chapter 10). In other words, alienated people are merely cogs in a wheel who have no control over their social world. Hence, while impersonality may contribute to organizational efficiency, it often results as well in a significant state of depersonalization and dehumanization. The paradox here is that a social system which is highly rational tends to lose sight of the rationality of its members.

THE PETER PRINCIPLE. Despite the ideal stress on competency as the criterion for assignment to positions and tasks, every bureaucracy contains a certain measure of incompetency, some more so than others. The sources of bureaucratic incompetency, of course, are many. One would be simple mistakes in the objective process of assessment, recruitment, and assignment. Another well-known, perhaps somewhat satirical, explanation for bureaucratic incompetence involves the **Peter principle:** "In any hierarchy every employee tends to rise to his level of incompetence."

This explanation, formulated by Lawrence Peter (Peter & Hull, 1969), asserts that bureaucrats—given the principles of career and advancement inherent in their system—are eventually promoted to their level of incompetence and usually remain there. This situation arises because bureaucrats are promoted to higher positions on the basis of their performance in the job from which they are being promoted. A professor who becomes dean, or a dean who becomes president, often offer striking examples of this phenomenon. The problematic situation here is that there is a totally different set of skills involved in the two jobs—research and/or teaching versus bureaucratic administration. It is for this reason that many universities hire presidents who possess degrees in business administration rather than academic credentials. Mention needs to be made, too, of the question of psychological requisites, and the need for personality congruency be-

IT'S REALLY KIND OF QUAINT WHEN YOU THINK ABOUT IT. THEY STILL GET TOGETHER EVERY 4 YEARS AND ELECT WHAT THEY CALL "A PRESIDENT!"

THE BUREAUCRACY

Miami News © 1981

**337**

▼

tween individual and position. The resulting dysfunctions, and confirmation of the Peter principle, are often all too clearly manifested when such academics relinquish their administrative positions and ostensibly "return to research and teaching."

The Peter principle, of course, is only a tendency inherent in bureaucracies. It does not operate all of the time, in every situation, in every organization. Bureaucracies are so large that a certain measure of incompetence can be absorbed. Work gets done because the vast majority of people either have not reached or do not reach their level of incompetence. The formulator of the Peter principle has humorously suggested that one way for individuals to avoid becoming victims of this bureaucratic dysfunction is to engage in "creative incompetency" or, in other words, to devise ways to make themselves look incompetent and thus prevent the fatal promotion!

**THE IRON LAW OF OLIGARCHY.** Another common, indeed almost inevitable, tendency found in bureaucracies is for control to become concentrated in the hands of a very small number of people. Roberto Michels (1915), an Italian-German social scientist who studied political parties, terms this principle the **iron law of oligarchy.** Hierarchy and bureaucracy inevitably produce oligarchy. Michels felt that over a period of time a small number of bureaucrats "at the top" become entrenched in office and, as their power and prestige increase, tend to perpetuate their influence, either openly or behind the scenes, in their own self-interests.

Michels argued that bureaucracies often are run by an elite who are skilled at acquiring and maintaining power, but who may not be technically competent to administer the organization. Hence, this elite is often the "power behind the power." Oligarchy, of course, becomes particularly problematic for democratic organi-

338

**Oligarchic Power.** The Board of directors of a business corporation often constitutes an oligarchy that, while perhaps technically incompetent to administer an organization, exercises virtually complete control of all significant decision-making. (Ellis Herwig/Stock, Boston)

zations. Yet, while an oligarchic structure may be a latent dysfunction of all complex organizations, at least potentially, there are mechanisms that can be instituted to curtail its emergence. One such mechanism is a time limit on years of service in positions of authority. Another check on the tendency toward oligarchy resides in the forces of competition for power that invariably are found in bureaucracies, especially political ones. Democratized structures in bureaucracies, thus, may not be the paradox that Michels had envisioned, and his law may not be so ironclad as he had proposed.

So complex has human society become, especially with its progressive growth in population, that the future of bureaucracies seems not only inevitable but indispensable. Moreover, the likelihood is quite strong that future bureaucracies will be even bigger and more complex than those that we have known thus far. Every segment of social life in modern societies has adopted the bureaucratic form of social organization; and, moreover, bureaucracies beget bureaucracies. This natural tendency for bureaucracies to expand has been satirically referred to as **Parkinson's law** (Parkinson, 1957). However, there are some social observers (for example, Bennis, 1966; Toffler, 1970) who feel that bureaucracies may not be inevitable— or, at least, not the tendency toward perpetual growth and internal expansion. One certain thing, nonetheless, is that steps are being taken throughout many segments of society to reduce the scope and dysfunctional aspects of bureaucracies—particularly their impersonal and alienating character. Only the future will tell us how successful these efforts can be.

# Theoretical Models of Complex Organizations

Social scientists have formulated several models of complex organizations and the relationship of the individual to them. These models or perspectives make certain assumptions about both the nature of organizations and the nature of human beings. Each model tends to emphasize certain types of variables and to de-emphasize, or even to exclude, others. Thus, no one model or theoretical perspective provides a total understanding of the nature of the structures and processes of complex organizations. This situation implies that the various models should be seen as complementing one another. Let us examine several models of complex organizations, indicating the basic assumptions that underlie them, and discuss their strengths and weaknesses.

## SCIENTIFIC MANAGEMENT MODEL

The **scientific management model** focuses on the formal and rational aspects of organization: organizational charts, the division of labor, authority relationships, and the flow of communication. This approach concentrates on the way in which a particular task can be performed in the most efficient manner. It is assumed that this objective can be accomplished through the use of time-and-motion studies. The idea here is to develop a set of instructions for performing a task which will enable workers to do it with the least expenditure of time and energy. This approach was developed primarily by Frederick W. Taylor (1911). He believed that through the careful observation and analysis of specific tasks, the one best way to do them could be determined. It was claimed that the workers, through repetition and practice, would become most proficient in performing a series of segmented, simple, and elementary operations.

Taylor also believed that workers were incapable of becoming self-motivated. The chief aim of the employee, according to the scientific management perspective, is to increase his or her wages. The economic motive is seen as overshadowing all others. Thus, the only way to develop a worker's motivation was through the use of pay-incentive systems. This assumption

**Management Strategy.** Formality and rationality, particularly in the formulation of a management strategy, are the essential foci in the scientific management model of complex organizations. (Aronson Photographics/ Stock, Boston)

led to the formulation of a bonus plan whereby workers who exceed the minimum standards of production are financially rewarded.

The scientific management approach conceives of the worker as a robotlike entity who will follow whatever instructions are given to it so long as the monetary incentive to do so exists. The employee is not credited with having feelings, motives (other than economic ones), or a creative capacity. Thus, the scientific management model does not take into account the psychological and social needs or wants of the worker.* The worker is viewed as a mere appendage of the machine that he or she operates. Another problem with this perspective is that it gives too much stress to the task-worker relationship. It does not give attention, for ex-

* This perspective is sometimes called a "physiological organization theory" (March & Simon, 1958) because of its stress on the influence of the capacities of the human organism on physical performance.

ample, to communication, coordination, conflict, and decision-making processes that occur within organizations. The scientific management approach to organization has given way to other perspectives, although several aspects of it still influence corporate managers and some elements of the model can be found in operation in a variety of organizations (Alvesson, 1982).

## HUMAN RELATIONS MODEL

The **human relations model** focuses on those elements of complex organizations that the bureaucratic and scientific management approaches neglect. Chief among the distinctions is its concern with the informal aspects of organizational behavior. Emphasis is given to the social and psychological variables that are involved in the worker-organization relationship. Unlike the scientific management per-

**Individual Needs.** Informal structures and processes play a major role in the human relations model of complex organizations, which stresses the personal needs of its members. (© Jerry Berndt, 1979/Stock, Boston)

spective, which views the worker as being concerned only with maximizing earnings, the human relations approach conceives of the worker as having a complex personality system consisting of a diverse set of motives, emotions, and predispositions.

This model stresses the types of satisfactions that workers obtain by interacting with others. Satisfying group relationships are viewed as leading to an increase in morale, job satisfaction, and performance. Work breaks, recreational activities, and worker participation in decisions that affect them are seen as helping to fulfill important noneconomic needs of individuals.

The human relations perspective emerged as the result of a series of experimental studies conducted between 1929 and 1932 at the Hawthorne plant of the Western Electric Company in Chicago. One of the studies that was developed sought to determine the relationship between such improved physical conditions as increased illumination and worker productivity. The investigation, undertaken in a scientific management perspective, had expected to find a positive relationship between improvements in physical working conditions and worker output. To the surprise of the investigators, the experiments did not show any consistent results. Worker productivity was found to increase when the lighting was increased and also when it was decreased. It seemed that no matter which change occurred in the working conditions of the employees, the results were the same—an increase in productivity. The researchers concluded that these outcomes (the increases in production) were due to the experiments themselves, which brought about

▼

**342**

greater feelings of satisfaction among the workers.* The fact that the employees who were part of the experiment were given special attention led to an increase in group cohesiveness, motivation, and morale (Roethlisberger & Dickson, 1964). It was the increase in the feelings of self-esteem and happiness among the workers, resulting from increased attention by management, that seemed to be responsible for greater productivity rather than any of the specific modifications that were made in their physical working conditions.

It also was concluded that the emergence of an informal social structure is itself instrumental in affecting the morale of employees. Workers obtained many social and psychological gratifications when they were able to interact with each other informally. During these episodes of informal interaction the workers developed their own norms which indicated what they expected of each other. Roethlisberger and Dickson (1964) cite the following set of normative expectations that emerged from the work group that they studied:

1. You must not produce too much; if you do, you are a "rate buster."
2. You must not produce too little; if you do, you are a "chiseler."
3. You must not squeal on a coworker to supervisory people.
4. You must not be a show-off or take advantage of anyone by flouting your authority.

The emergence of these and other types of informal norms, many of which may be in conflict with the norms established by management, give workers a feeling of control over their work situations. They do not feel as though they are at the absolute mercy of management and the formal rules of the organization.

---

* A situation in which dependent variables are produced by an experiment itself rather than by any of the manipulated variables in the experiment has come to be known as the "Hawthorne effect," after the name of the research site. The Hawthorne effect also refers to changes in the behavior of research subjects which result from their awareness and knowledge of the study.

These studies demonstrated that in order for organizations to achieve their goals, satisfied workers were fundamental. Hence, human relations theorists concentrate their attention on the **informal structure** of organizations, with particular emphasis given to the informal networks of communication and authority, and the way these organizational dimensions contribute to goal attainment through the satisfaction of members. The following points are also emphasized by the human relations model of the organization-worker relationship.

*Harmony and cooperation between workers and management.* Employers and employees are seen as sharing common goals. If the organization prospers, it is assumed, so will the worker. The workers and management people should not perceive themselves as pitted against each other; but rather, together they should direct their efforts and energies toward problems of mutual concern.

*A humanistic conception of the worker.* The worker is viewed as a total person having a complex set of needs and aspirations. Workers are not seen as motivated solely by the promise of material rewards. Rather, the importance of psychological and emotional satisfactions, in addition to economic ones, are acknowledged. Supervisors are trained to treat subordinates as human beings, not as robots or cogs in a machine. They are urged to be sensitive to the psychological and social needs of workers. Workers are to be treated with respect and dignity, regardless of their formal rank in the structure of the organization.

*Work conditions encouraging social interaction.* The physical environment of the workers should be such that it facilitates social interaction. The institution of rest periods, group discussions, and other mechanisms that promote interaction between employees and management should exist. Frequent interaction, it is believed, will prevent the development of feelings of resentment and work grievances. Such a harmonious situation, of course, is considered functional for both the organization and the individual.

The human relations approach provided a needed antidote or complement to scientific management. It offered very clear evidence that rationality, however basic and unique, is only one dimension of human behavior. The human relations model has been very influential in getting corporate managers to modify many of their policies toward employees. Nonetheless, both the human relations model and the scientific management model focus their attention on the social relations and interaction among workers and less so on the social character of the organization itself. Let us consider two other models that emphasize this latter dimension.

## SOCIAL SYSTEM MODEL

The **social system model** of complex organizations is based on the main tenets of system theory that we discussed in Chapter 6. Let us briefly highlight the chief aspects of this perspective as they pertain specifically to complex organizations. The social system model conceptualizes organizations as consisting, in part, of the totality of the patterned activities of a plurality of individuals interacting with one another. These activities are interdependent with one another, however, just as are the social positions that members of the organization occupy. The system approach views organizations as having subsystems that are related to one another and to the organization as a whole. These subsystems are functionally differentiated or specialized with respect to tasks and problems.

The organization as a whole is seen as engaging in exchanges with its environment which itself consists of other organizations. The organization draws upon its environment for labor, technology, and raw materials, which it

processes, and then sells its products and services to, or exchanges them with, other organizations in its environment. Many organizations receive money for their products or services. Money can be conceptualized as a form of energy that is used to perpetuate and to strengthen the organization (Katz & Kahn, 1978). Other organizations are not involved in the cycle of buying and selling. Some receive governmental appropriations or gifts. Still others, such as voluntary organizations, engage in activities which their members find intrinsically rewarding, and so they are not as dependent on resources from their environments.

Each component or subsystem of an organization contributes to the goal-attainment process. Every component must operate at a certain minimal level of efficiency if the organization is to function adequately and to be successful in achieving its goal. Thus, a college must have an adequate library and library staff if its educational goals are to be attained; it must also have a competent faculty, adequate physical facilities, a skillful administration, and an admissions department that is able to attract challenging students. If any of these or other components of the college perform inadequately, the college will experience difficulty in providing its students with a quality education.

Proponents of the system model focus on the interrelations that exist among the various subsystems of the organization and the degree of task specialization that exists within them. In addition, the social system model orients researchers to the exchanges that an organization has with the many other different kinds of systems within its environment. So, in studying a factory that manufactures furniture, attention would be given to the relationships that the factory has with other organizations, such as its suppliers and its advertising agency, as well as with its actual and potential customers. System theorists attempt to predict how changes in the subsystems or the environment of an organization may affect the functioning of the organization as a whole. What would happen,

▼

343

▼ for instance, if one of the suppliers of raw materials for the factory went on strike or went out of business? Would other suppliers be available; and, if so, would their prices be similar to those of the old supplier?

The social system model of organizations sensitizes people to the totality of structures and dynamics within the organization. It underscores the important relationships that organizations have both within their boundaries and within their environment. In addition, it attempts to show how changes in one component of the organization, or in one of the components of its environment, may affect the operation of the organization. The analysis of latent, as well as manifest, consequences constitutes a distinctive perspective of the social systems model in the assessment of organizational function.

## TECHNOLOGICAL MODEL

The **technological model** of formal organizations considers the type of technology that is used in organizations as the major determinant of the organizational structures and processes. Thus, in studying an oil refinery, for instance, those adhering to this approach would focus their attention on how the technology that is used to refine the oil requires particular types of communication, authority, and status structures.

Technology refers to the actions that an individual performs upon an object, with or without the aid of tools or mechanical devices, in order to make some change in that object (Perrow, 1972). That which is changed may be a human being or a particular type of inanimate material, as in the case of making buildings or bookcases. Hospitals, mental institutions, prisons, and schools are among the many complex organizations that use technology in order to bring about changes in people. Factories of various kinds would be examples of organizations that use technology to make changes in inanimate materials.

The technological perspective is based on the premise that different modes of technology produce variations in the status, authority, communication, and interpersonal structures of organizations. Different technologies are thought to require different types of organizational structures and processes. Organizational structures and processes must adjust to the type of technology being used in order to prevent various kinds of strains and problems from occurring. Research has shown that changes which develop in the social structure of hospitals are the direct consequences of shifts in medical technologies. Perrow (1972) explains this finding by observing that the growing complexity of medical technologies requires increasing interdependence of units, coordination of resources and personnel, and rationalization of the supportive structure. He believes that the determination of a variety of organizational structures and processes applies to all organizations, not just to hospitals. He would claim, for example, that a significant increase in the use of audiovisual equipment, together with the utilization of sophisticated information gathering and retrieval apparatus, in educational organizations will produce changes in the structures and patterns of these organizations. One needs to speculate at great length about how the expanding technology of electronics, computers, and robots will affect the fundamental structure and function of complex organizations in modern society.

The technological perspective implies that organizations that have the same functions may vary as much as those that have different functions. Some schools, hospitals, banks, and steel companies may have more in common, because of their customary character, than routine and nonroutine schools, routine and nonroutine hospitals, and so forth. Perrow (1972) argues that the technological differences among complex organizations that have the same purpose may be so drastic that some schools are like prisons, some prisons like churches, some churches like factories, some factories like uni-

344

versities, and so on. One appropriate example would be corporations that place a heavy stress on research and the development of new technology which thereby have much in common organizationally, and necessarily so, with universities that concentrate on research activity.

## THEORY Z MODEL

Of late, the growing concern about the dysfunctions of complex organizations has been addressed by attempts at constructing new forms of social organization. One of these is known as **Theory Z,** developed by William G. Ouchi (1981), a corporate specialist whose model is based on management practices that have been used chiefly in Japan with apparently significant success.

The focus of Theory Z is on the modification of bureaucracies in such a manner as to make for less hierarchy and formality, while at the same time enhancing the identification of members with the organization and its goals. Additional emphasis is placed on nonspecialized careers, collective decision making, relatively slow evaluation and promotion, and long-term planning. Basic to all of these objectives, however, is the development of an intense loyalty between workers and management. One central tactic in this latter goal that seems to work quite effectively in diminishing alienation is the mechanism of lifetime employment, with no fear of dismissals or layoffs.

Theory Z seems to make for both more effective productivity and greater work satisfaction. One indication of the latter is the strong sentiment against unionization on the part of workers. A number of major corporations in the United States have adopted elements of the Theory Z model. Among these are IBM, Hewlett-Packard, and Proctor and Gamble. Preliminary studies in the last few years reveal mixed

▼

**345**

**Japanese Techniques.** Daily calisthenics are one of the mechanisms often employed in Theory Z, a new model of organizational management that seeks to enhance productivity through increases in morale, team spirit, and loyalty among employees. (J. P. Laffont/SYGMA)

▼ success in applying the techniques of Theory Z in Western societies. Such results are due perhaps to cultural values and traditions in which the theory is strongly rooted. Nonetheless, the next few years, should provide a more significant test of Theory Z and other attempts to alter the organizational models that traditionally have been known in Western societies.

The various models or theoretical perspectives that we have examined should not be viewed in mutually exclusive terms. All of them contribute to our understanding of the nature, functions, and processes of complex organizations. No one of them is entirely adequate in itself for this task. Each focuses our attention on a different dimension of complex organizations. Together, however, they do provide a more comprehensive understanding of how organizations function.

# Personality and Complex Organizations

Personality, as we saw in Chapter 6, is a highly significant component of social systems. There we discussed at some length the relationship of personality to social organization in terms of status recruitment and role performance—and elaborated in those respects on the principle of functional congruence between personality and social systems. What, now, can be said about any particular relationships between personality and formal organizations?

## CONGRUENCY BETWEEN PERSONALITY AND ORGANIZATIONS

Complex organizations, quite apart from the specific statuses and roles within them, seem to require certain types of personality dynamics on the part of their members in order to achieve their goals in a relatively effective fashion. However compatible may be the interactional situation between personality and status-role, it does not follow that the same kind of congruence would exist in whichever organization the role may be exercised. To speak more concretely, an individual may find himself or herself quite psychologically compatible with a specific status, such as an occupation; however, this situation does not mean that the corresponding role or occupation can be exercised in any and all organizations with the same degree of efficiency.

To be a professor in one university with a certain measure of personal satisfaction is not to say that one could be as functional—both professionally and psychologically—in any other university. Such is true because of the variations in the social organization of different universities. The same can be said for functional congruence between personality and the status-role of student on the one hand, and that between personality and the status-role of student in a particular college or university. Many students who find themselves dissatisfied and unhappy, and rendering a poor performance at a particular college, transfer to another. Retaining the same academic major, they soon discover that both grades and spirits improve because they have been able to find "their kind of place"; that is, one in which their personality is relatively congruent with the organizational structure of the college or university.

Organizations, even those with the same objectives and engaged in the same activities, differ in a number of respects. One such dimension of variability is in terms of what may be called the culture of an organization. This organizational sphere includes such elements as traditions, values, ideologies, and philosophy. Another sphere of major variability is in terms of social structure. While organizations, as we have seen, are quite similar in these respects, there can be crucial differences in terms of the mode of governance or administration (democratic or authoritarian), distribution of authority and power, and the specificity of rules or norms regarding superordinate and subordinate relationships. Other variations are the "rhythm of work" (slow or fast, steady or pulsating), degree of formality or informality in personal relationships, formation of cliques and alliances, and the general emotional climate.

When an organization is able to attract or to recruit people whose personality systems are congruent with the needs and goals of the organization, the level of satisfaction and performance among its members will be high. Consequently, the organization is likely to function with a minimum of conflicts, hostility, and discord among its members, and correspondingly an optimal level of efficiency and productivity. DiRenzo (1967a), for example, in his study of professional politicians and the Italian parliament, has shown that such central dynamics of political organizations as coalitions and alliances appear to be, and indeed can be predicted, in terms of similarity or compatibility between the modal personality of the political parties in question—quite apart from ideological similarities or distinctions. Such a situation does not imply that all agents of a particular organization need to be of the modally congruent type. Only the active cooperation or functional support of a sufficient number of the appropriate type is required for any social organization to function as intended. In fact, it is quite possible that some of the variably diversified activities of highly complex organizations require different kinds of personalities at the specific status-role level.

Certain dynamics of individual behavior within formal organizations can also be understood more thoroughly in terms of the principle of reciprocal congruity between personality and organization—rather than as simple questions of aptitudes and motivations. One piece of empirical research quite effectively demonstrates this principle in terms of academic organizations.

Stern, Stein, and Bloom (1956) studied the personality and performance of college students in regard to the philosophy and organization of a particular college. Students were measured and classified in terms of stereopathy—a psychological dimension that is conceptually and dynamically similar to that of authoritarianism and dogmatism. Stereopaths tends to be authoritarian, rigid, extraceptive individuals who manifest a significant intolerance for ambiguity. Nonstereopaths, on the other hand, are individuals who possess an antithetical type of personality.

The college in question had an educational philosophy that stressed abstract analysis, relativity of values and judgment rather than fixed standards, and an intraceptive rather than an impersonal orientation. Its approach, in short, could be characterized as intellectually open, tolerant, and flexible. Clearly, the stereopaths possessed and manifested those psychological qualities which were highly incongruent with the values and ideology of the college, as well as its typical instructional or pedagogical approach. Eighty-four percent of the student body were assessed as nonstereopathic personalities, indicating a marked or substantial congruence between the student body and the pedagogical philosophy and organizational structure of the college. These figures show that the college did an effective job of recruitment from the perspective of its own interests and, as we shall see, in the interests of the students as well. The minority of stereopaths (16 percent) constituted a category whose personalities were markedly incongruent with the predominant values, ideology, and mode of operation of the college. What, then, can be said about the respective performance of these two categories of students?

Although the two types of personalities were matched in intelligence, the stereopaths received lower grades than the nonstereopaths. Stereopaths, moreover, withdrew from the college regardless of grade performance at twice the rate of nonstereopaths. Of all the withdrawals during the period under study, 38

347

▼

percent were stereopaths, only 1 percent were nonstereopaths, and the remaining 61 percent were middle-range scores.

These differential rates of two indicators of dysfunction seem to be related to the respective degree of congruence and incongruence between the two personality types and the college organization. As the investigators noted, if the college wished to reduce the number of students who either perform poorly or withdraw, they should admit only students who clearly possess a nonstereopathic personality.

Similar outcomes have been observed in organizations with a totally antithetical type of social structure. In a study of a mental institution that had a very restrictive, authoritarian, and custodial orientation toward its patients, researchers found that 35 percent of the least authoritarian and most humanistic aides resigned. On the other hand, only 6 percent of the most authoritarian and least humanistically oriented aides resigned (Berk & Goertzel, 1975). As a result, the aides that remained had personality systems that were congruent with the ideology and organizational structure of the hospital.

It is also possible that the personalities of people may change so that they will be compatible with the ideology and structure of the organization and the requirements of its roles. This possibility is supported by additional data from the study of mental hospital aides. Researchers measured the attitudes of aides after they had had 6 months of working in the wards and concluded that the overall direction of attitude change, as a consequence of regular role occupancy, was toward increased custodial orientations (Berk & Goertzel, 1975). This change was brought about primarily through the influence that the experienced staff members exerted upon the new aides. Those aides that worked with staff members who had a humanistic, treatment-oriented approach were likely to keep their humanistic perspective. On the other hand, if the aides were assigned to wards

348

whose staff had a custodial orientation, they would develop the same kind of perspective. The findings of this study may be interpreted to mean that organizations tend to generate a substantial degree of congruence between their goals and the attitudes of their members. As the authors of the mental hospital study observed, "Organizations shape, grind, or expand individuals to fit roles that are required of them to function adequately within the system" (p. 189). Congruency of organizational goals and philosophy with the personality systems of its members facilitates organizational effectiveness.

## THE BUREAUCRATIC PERSONALITY

What kind of personalities are typically found in bureaucracies? Apart from distinctive types of personality that may be associated with various types of complex organizations, is there a "bureaucratic personality" that cuts across the spectrum of large-scale organizations—one, perhaps, that corresponds to the fundamental or essential organizational structure of bureaucracies?

Many social scientists, beginning with Weber (1947), have raised the fundamental question of personality elements that are necessary for people to perform comfortably in the highly structured environments that are typical of bureaucracies. Several years ago, in a now classical article on the relationship of personality and bureaucracy, Merton (1940) argued that for reliable performance bureaucratic structures need an unusual degree of conformity with prescribed patterns of action, and, therefore, fundamentally require individuals who are highly disciplined. Merton conceived of the bureaucratic personality as being overly rigid, inflexible, conforming (cold, detached, impersonal), and domineering. He maintained that people who work in bureaucratic organizations would most likely develop these traits because they are congruent with the nature of bureaucracies, which characteristically value hierarchical authority, formality, rationality, efficiency, and impersonality.

Such indeed is the profile presented by William F. Whyte (1956) at mid-century in his well-known study of *The Organization Man*, in order to support his thesis that such individuals not only work for the organization; they "*belong* to it as well" (p. 3). Thirty years after the initial publication of his thesis, Whyte (1986:98) argued that "The people who staff [organizations today] are pretty much the same as those who did before." One change, argues Whyte, is that today, the organizational man may be less

**Bureaucratic Character.** Many social scientists maintain that bureaucracies mold people into a uniformly distinctive personality that is considered to be strategically functional but devoid of significant individuality. (Alan Carey/Image Works)

inclined to give his loyalty to only one organization. Rather now his allegiance is to organizations, pure and simple.

One aspect of this question of the bureaucratic personality relates to ascertaining an individual's orientation to at least three fundamental aspects of bureaucracy: (1) rules and regulations (the commonly known "red tape"), (2) hierarchical relationships (the "chain of command" type of authority), and (3) highly specialized task-type activities. One who is able or willing to exhibit self-restraint in these respects is more likely to show the strongest kinds of toleration for the demands of a highly structured or bureaucratic organization.

Baker and her colleagues (1973) identified and measured a dimension of personality that is related to an individual's performance in and personal response to work in highly structured or bureaucratic situations. They administered a test measuring tolerance of bureaucratic structure (TBS) to several samples of semi-skilled blue- and white-collar workers. TBS involved four related areas: attitudes toward rules and regulations, attitudes toward authority, orientation toward tasks, and attitudes toward delaying gratifications. Their data show that TBS correlates quite significantly with few changes of jobs and prolonged full-time employment. Also of related interest was the finding that workers who were retained by their employers after one year on the job had higher scores on the TBS test.

Rawls and Nelson (1975) similarly explored differences in personality manifestations in terms of preferences for particular kinds of managerial positions. Ninety-seven students enrolled in a graduate school of management expressed their preferences for ten different organizational or job categories: line versus staff, large versus small, ongoing operation versus new venture, producing products versus services, frequent versus infrequent travel, continual meeting of people versus working with a fixed set of individuals, group settings versus

**349**

▼ one-on-one situations, close supervision versus being left alone, and working with a large number of people versus working intimately with a few or working alone.

Results show that individuals having preferences for different types of organizations and managerial positions are really quite different kinds of people. All ten position categories showed individuals to differ significantly along a variety of personality and value dimensions. Rawls and Nelson conclude that subjects expressing preferences for different types of organizations and managerial positions are really very different kinds of individuals. Moreover, these findings show that the occupational values of today's potential managers are drastically different from those of a generation ago.

Are bureaucrats really social conformists, resistant to innovation and change, conventional in moralistic judgments, and inflexible in their thinking? Can they, in short, be modally characterized as essentially authoritarian and dogmatic? Does experience in a bureaucracy make automatons out of people?

Recent studies offer contradictory evidence that challenge the prevalent conception of the bureaucratic personality. Much of this inconsistency may be due to a monolithic conception of bureaucracies and a failure to appreciate their organizational differences—such as authoritarian and democratic structures. Another plausible explanation seems to be social change. Kohn (1971), for example, in a comprehensive study that compared the personalities of people working in bureaucratic settings and those employed in nonbureaucratic environments found that bureaucrats were more intellectually flexible, more open to new experience (innovation and change), more self-directed, and more personally responsible than those working in nonbureaucratic environments.

While Kohn argues that bureaucrats differ from nonbureaucrats in these respects primarily because they have experienced different conditions of occupational life, he does suggest that the observed findings may result in part from

**350**

the fact that bureaucracies recruit individuals who are more highly educated than those in the general population at large.

Kohn explains his findings on the differences in personality between bureaucratic and nonbureaucratic employees principally in terms of three structural factors that are characteristic of bureaucracies: job protection, task complexity, and job income.

*Job protection.* Bureaucrats usually have very good job security. It seems that people who are insulated from the uncertainties that the threat of being fired may produce are less fearful of new ideas and innovations. They are better suited to accept personal responsibility for their actions and make optimum use of their intellectual skills.

*Task complexity.* Bureaucrats tend to work at substantively more complex tasks than do other people with a similar educational level. This situation helps to explain the above-average amount of intellectual flexibility found to be characteristic of bureaucrats. It also shows why bureaucrats are most likely to spend their leisure time engaged in more intellectually demanding activities. Evidently, the experience of working at complex tasks influences how one will use free time during nonwork periods.

*Income.* Receiving a high income causes one to place a high value on self-direction and autonomy. Such people feel in control of their lives. They do not hesitate to set objectives for themselves and to make important decisions.

A controversial and highly complex question still surrounds these kinds of data on the bureaucratic personality. Is the bureaucratic personality essentially acquired "on the job," as Merton and Kohn argue, or do complex organizations select (attract and recruit) their particular types of personality? Much of the answer to this question depends, of course, on one's theoretical orientation toward the nature of personality and the question of personality development in terms of critical periods. We have stressed throughout much of our discussions on personality and social systems that individuals tend to be attracted to, and/or recruited into, social positions and social organizations in terms of preexisting and compatible personalities. Of course, a preexisting personality pattern is likely to be reinforced in a functionally congruent situation.

## THE CORPORATE CHARACTER

What about the elite of the bureaucratic world? The lingering stereotype of the autocratic and authoritarian executive seems to have given way to a new type of corporate character— even at the uppermost echelons—that is emerging not only in corporate-industrial America but even in other sectors of our society.

Michael Maccoby (1977) and his associates conducted a long-term study that sought to understand how modern corporations "select leaders and mold their character" or personality. He was interested in determining which kind of modal personality patterns could be discerned among high-level managers and executives of corporations, as well as the kinds of personality changes that such people may experience as a consequence of their administrative positions.

Over 250 corporate managers and executives were subjected to rather lengthy psychoanalytic interviews, including the administration of personality tests in many instances. Additionally, the wives and secretaries of many of these business leaders were also interviewed. The subjects were questioned in particular about their attitudes regarding their jobs, emotions, and personal goals. Maccoby's study generated three major findings:

The study discovered four major types of social character that dominate the corporate world today: the craftsman, the company man, the gamesman, and the jungle fighter. Most of the executives could be best described as blends of these character types with one kind comprising the focal or core psychological structure of the individual.

Each of the characterological types of executives can be distinguished by a somewhat different interpretation of a number of key concepts that pertain to dynamics within the corporation. Maccoby offers a focal example of these differences in terms of competition: ". . . all four described themselves as competitive, but for the craftsman, this meant competing against one's own performance or the materials to build a better product. For the company man, competition was defined as moving ahead to protect one's security, in order not to fall behind. For the jungle fighter, competition meant destroying one's rival or being destroyed by them. For the gamesman, competition was the thrill of the game, the goal of being the winner and avoiding becoming a loser" (1977:181).

The modal type of personality among corporate executives is the gamesman. Such may be the case because the gamesman seems most responsive to the leadership needs of corporations today in terms of the innovation of products and plans, interdependent teams of experts, fast-moving flexibility, and competition from every source. The gamesman may be psychologically profiled in the following manner: cooperative but competitive; detached and playful; compulsively driven to succeed; loves change and wants to influence it; likes to take calculated risks; fascinated by technique and new methods; perceives a developing project, human relations, and his own career in terms of options and possibilities, as in a game; a team player but a would-be superstar; a team leader, but often a rebel against the bureaucratic hierarchy; fair and unprejudiced; unsympathetic and contemptuous of weakness. "Unlike other

▼

## BOX 8-2. Modal Personalities in the Corporation

Michael Maccoby subjected over 250 corporate managers and executives from twelve major corporations in the United States to extensive psychological assessment. In his book, *The Gamesman,* Maccoby offers the following descriptions of the four modal types of corporate character that his work uncovered.

1. *The Craftsman.* The craftsman holds the traditional values of the productive-hoarding character—the work ethic, respect for people, concern for quality and thrift. When he talks about his work, his interest is in the *process* of making something; he enjoys building. He sees others, coworkers as well as superiors, in terms of whether they help or hinder him in doing a craftsman-like job. Most of the craftsmen whom we interviewed are quiet, sincere, modest, and practical, although there is a difference between those who are more receptive and democratic versus those who are more authoritarian and intolerant. Although his virtues are admired by everyone, his self-containment and perfectionism do not allow him to lead a complex and changing organization. Rather than engaging and trying to master the system with the cooperation of others who share his values, he tends to do his own thing and go along, sometimes reluctantly, toward goals he does not share, enjoying whatever opportunities he finds for interesting work.

2. *The Jungle Fighter.* The jungle fighter's goal is power. He experiences life and work as a jungle (not a game), where it is eat or be eaten, and the winners destroy the losers. A major part of his psychic resources is budgeted for his internal department of defense. Jungle fighters tend to see their peers in terms of accomplices or enemies and their subordinates as objects to be utilized. There are two subtypes of jungle fighters, lions and foxes. The lions are the conquerors who when successful may build an empire; the foxes make their nests in the corporate hierarchy and move ahead by stealth and politicking.

3. *The Company Man.* In the company man, we recognize the well-known organization man, or the functionary whose sense of identity is based on being part of the powerful, protective company. His strongest traits are his concern with the human side of the company, his interest in the feelings of the people around him and his commitment to maintain the organization's integrity. At his weakest, he is fearful and submissive, concerned with security even more than with success. The most creative company men sustain an atmosphere in their groups of cooperation, stimulation, and mutuality. The least creative find a little niche and satisfy themselves by feeling that somehow they share in the glory of the corporation.

4. *The Gamesman.* The gamesman is the new man, and, really, the leading character in this study. His main interest is in challenge, competitive activity where he can prove himself a winner. Impatient with others who are slower and more cautious, he likes to take risks and to motivate others to push themselves beyond their normal pace. He responds to work and life as a game. The contest hypes him up and he communicates his enthusiasm, thus energizing others. He enjoys new ideas, new techniques, fresh approaches and shortcuts. His talk and his thinking are terse, dynamic, sometimes playful and come in quick flashes. His main goal in life is to be a winner, and talking about himself

▼

invariably leads to discussion of his tactics and strategy in the corporate contest.

The new corporate top executive combines many gamesman traits with aspects of the company man. He is a team player whose center is the corporation. He feels himself responsible for the functioning of a system, and in his mind, his career goals have merged with those of the corporation. Thus he thinks in terms of what is good for the company, hardly separating that from what is good for himself. He tends to be a worrier, constantly on the lookout for something that might go wrong. He is self-protective and sees people in terms of their use for the larger organization. He even uses himself in this way, fine tuning his sensitivity. He has succeeded in submerging his ego and gaining strength from this exercise in self-control.

353

To function, the corporations need craftsmen, scientists, and company men (many could do without jungle fighters), but their future depends most of all on the gamesmen's capacity for mature development. ▲

Source: Michael Maccoby, *The Gamesman: The New Corporate Leaders.* New York: Simon and Schuster, 1976, pp. 42–45. Copyright © 1974 by Michael Maccoby. Reprinted by permission of Simon & Schuster, Inc.

business types, he is energized to compete not because he wants to build an empire or accumulate riches, but rather to attain fame and glory and to experience the exhilaration of running his team. His goal is to be known as a winner, and his deepest fear is to be labeled a loser" (1977:182).

The second main finding in the study was that the corporation can be conceived in terms of a "psychostructure" in which specific roles must be performed by individuals possessing particular types of personality. People having the "wrong" type of personality would not be able to perform their organizational roles adequately because their emotional attitudes would not be compatible with the work. Maccoby notes that this finding deals with the question of whether personality determines role or role determines personality. He argues that "role and character interact, but the psychostructure selects individuals for roles in terms of character" (1977:182).

Finally, the researchers also established that the personality of executives undergoes changes over time in order to respond to the particular demands of the corporation. Maccoby calls this dynamic "the process of internal selection; character traits adaptive to work are reinforced and strengthened, while unadaptive attitudes tend to wither away through disuse or suppression" (1977:182).

Maccoby's research highlights the mutual impact that personality and organizational roles have upon each other. He makes the interesting observation, a kind of social-psychological Peter principle, that in a corporation a person tends to rise to the level where his or her personality fits the organizational role. Regardless of degree of intellect, Maccoby argues, if the individual's personality conflicts with the requirements of the role, the person will not perform well because in such cases the person "will not *want* to do what *needs* to be done in order to keep the organization running smoothly" (1977:192).

Maccoby contends that similar types of corporate personalities along with their associated social dynamics are emerging in the field of politics as well. Some would claim that even the academic world, and other social institu-

▼ tions, to the extent that they have become increasingly more corporate and more political, are moving toward those kinds of organizations and psychosocial structures that Maccoby describes as recruiting and producing the corresponding corporate characters.

## PERSONALITY AND MODERN ORGANIZATIONS

Much concern has been expressed about the type of personality that is required in the modern type of organizations that exist today. Maccoby (1977) claims that the "social character" that is necessitated by the modern type of organization includes such characteristics as punctuality, accuracy, orderliness, efficiency, detachment, competitiveness, cooperativeness, and adherence to normative expectations. Other social scientists maintain that the functional requirements of highly structured organizations provide a "sympathetic environment" for individuals possessing an authoritarian or dogmatic type of personality system (Presthus, 1978). Sanford (1977), for example, argues that social organizations in today's society favor authoritarian modes of adjustment, and hence tend to capitalize on authoritarianism in the personality. Several values and attitudes that are associated with the authoritarian-dogmatic personality syndrome have been found to correlate with the personality profiles of samples of business executives (Presthus, 1978). Thus, individuals who have authoritarian-dogmatic personalities may be attracted to highly structured organizations because working within such an organization will enable them to satisfy deep-seated personality needs. Organizations, for their part, also find such personalities functional in terms of their own needs. These reciprocally strategic relationships represent a symbiotic relationship between individual and organization.

The broader significance of these findings on the relationship of personality to complex and bureaucratic organizations can be seen in that an increasing proportion of the world's labor force is participating in complex organizations, and much of the rest of the various segments of social life is becoming characterized by increasingly complex forms of social organization.

# Summary

Complex and formal organizations consist of social systems that are characterized by an explicity formulated set of goals, policies, procedures, and regulations that specify appropriate behavior for their many members. The major characteristics of complex organizations are goal specificity, division of labor, formal communication and authority structure, and changing membership. While all complex organizations share certain essential features and are quite similar in terms of social structure, there are many significant differences among them. One useful typology of complex organizations is based on the way in which they get compliance from their members. There are three basic types in this regard: voluntary, utilitarian, and coercive.

Classical conceptions of complex organizations focused entirely on their formal and explicit dimensions which represent only one segment of these social systems. Another highly integral segment consists of the informal relationships and patterns of interaction that emerge among the members of complex organizations.

A major type of complex organization is the bureaucracy, which represents an extreme pattern of formal structure. Weber described and analyzed bureaucracies by developing what he called ideal-type conceptions. Bureaucracies, according to Weber's formulations, possess the following characteristics: task specialization, hierarchical authority, separation of office from person, formal rules and procedures, detached orientations, and merit selection. The three primary functions of a bureaucracy are efficiency, stability or order, and continuity. Despite the stress on competency as the criterion for assignment to position and tasks, every bureaucracy contains a certain measure of incompetency. The chief dysfunctions of bureaucracy are inflexibility, displacement of goals, impersonality, status incompetency, and oligarchic control.

Social scientists have formulated several models of complex organizations and the relationship of the individual to them. Among the major models or theoretical perspectives are the scientific management model, the human relations model, the social system model, the technological model, and the Theory Z model.

Complex organizations, quite apart from the specific statuses and roles within them, seem to require certain types of personality dynamics on the part of their members in order to achieve their goals in a relatively effective fashion. However compatible may be the interactional situation between personality and status-role, it does not follow that the same kind of congruence exists in whichever organization the role may be exercised. One aspect of the question of the bureaucratic personality relates to an individual's orientation to at least three fundamental aspects of bureaucracy: rules and regulations, hierarchical relationships, and highly specialized task-type activities. One who is able to exhibit self-restraint in these respects is more likely to show the strongest kind of toleration for the demands of a highly structured or bureaucratic organization.

The broader significance of the relationship of personality to complex and bureaucratic organizations is that an increasing proportion of the world's labor force is participating in complex organizations, and many of the other segments of society are becoming characterized by increasingly complex forms of social organization.

**355**

# Key Concepts

alienation
bureaucracy
complex organization
Hawthorne effect
human relations model
ideal type
informal structure
iron law of oligarchy
Parkinson's law
Peter principle
scientific management model
social system model
technological model
Theory Z model
voluntary association

# 9 Social Groups

Our analysis of specific kinds of social organization concludes on the level of microsociology with the assessment of small groups. Social behavior that occurs in any social system is structured fundamentally within the various forms and processes of social groups. Yet, while social groups contain all of the essential elements of social organization—division of labor, values, norms, statuses, roles, and stratification—they also need to be understood in terms of their own unique structures and dynamics. Such is especially true of small groups, such as the family and the working group, which furnish the mediating links between society and the individual.

Our goals in this chapter will be to examine the nature and significance of social groups. We shall discuss the types of social groups that exist as well as the variety of structures and processes that characterize them. Within these contexts we shall explore the relevance that small groups have to other forms of social organization. Particular attention will be given to the significance of size on group dynamics, motivations for joining groups, group leadership, group decision making, and conformity and deviance in groups. Equally important from our particular perspective, of course, is the consideration of the relationships between social groups and the personality systems of individuals that participate in them. ▲

## Outline

▼

► Nearly all human activity—certainly the vast amount of social behavior—occurs within the context of social groups. If you stop to think about it for a moment, you will realize that many of the most significant and meaningful activities that you engage in occur within groups. Learning, working, worshipping, and playing take place, for the most part, within a group setting. Moreover, you will also recognize that the groups to which you belong provide you with many social and psychological satisfactions. Given the social nature of human beings, it would be very difficult for any person to be happy without having a reasonable number of group ties.

358

Each individual, it is estimated, belongs to an average of five or six social groups (Mills, 1967). Such a situation would mean that there are several billion social groups in the world at any given time. So much does human activity occur in social groups that the analysis of social groups could justifiably be called the sociology of everyday life.

# Nature and Significance of Social Groups

Social organization, as we have seen, consists of the complexity of positions, roles, norms, and values that structure the behavior of individuals and their relations with each other. The most elementary form of social organization is the social group. Indeed, social groups are the basis of every kind of social system—associations, institutions, complex organizations, bureaucracies, and, of course, societies. It is for this reason that the term "social group" is often applied indiscriminately to several different kinds of social collectivities, or pluralities of people. Technically, however, the term "social group" has a very precise meaning in the field of sociology.

# SOCIAL GROUPS AND SOCIAL COLLECTIVITIES

SOCIAL GROUPS. A **social group** refers to a plurality of people (two or more individuals) who share a common identity and who recurrently interact in respective status-role distinctions in the pursuit of a common goal.

Our definition specifies the distinctive features of a social group in contrast to other kinds of social collectivities or pluralities of people: (1) recurrent interaction, (2) social organization, (3) common identity, and (4) mutual objective. Groups, of course, vary in the degree to which they embody these distinguishing features. The classic example of a social group is that of the family. A football team or a college fraternity also exemplifies the social group.

The term "social group" applies technically to any structured collectivity regardless of size—from two people to an entire society. However, this designation is used more commonly to refer to small groupings (usually not much larger than fifty people) whose members know each other and are able to interact on a personal—though not necessarily informal—basis. Our considerations in this chapter will emphasize the structure and dynamics of small groups.

As our definition should make clear, not all collections of people constitute a social group. A social group is basically a social collectivity—that is, a collection or plurality of people—but one that is characterized by distinctive sociological features. Social groups in this regard need to be distinguished from other kinds of social collectivities, which we shall discuss in detail in Chapter 12. Particularly significant among these distinctions are those of the social aggregate and the social category.

SOCIAL AGGREGATES. A **social aggregate** is a collectivity of people that is distinguished by the fact that they share physical

**Social Aggregates.** Bus-riders, more or less conscious of each other, are fleeting collectivities of people who share physical proximity but manifest only minimal, if any, social interaction and no social organization. (George Gardner/Image Works)

proximity. People waiting on a particular street corner for a bus, or those in a stadium watching a baseball game, are two examples of social aggregates. Such individuals do not necessarily know each other and do not interact or communicate, except perhaps in a most superficial way. They lack both social organization and a common identity. All that these sets of people have in common is physical presence in a geographical locus.

SOCIAL CATEGORIES.   A **social category** consists of a plurality of people who share one or more common characteristics. All blondes, all tennis fans, all smokers, all Democrats, all widows, and all Blacks comprise respective social categories. Again, these particular sets of individuals do not know each other, do not

interact with each other, and hence are devoid of any social organization (although they may have a common identity in some cases). Neither do the members of a social category share a common physical presence. Such individuals constitute a social collectivity not by any action of their own, but by the analytical and classificatory schemes of the social scientist.

## FORMATION OF SOCIAL GROUPS

Social life without social organization would be very difficult, if not altogether impossible, on a continuous basis. Fortunately, as individuals interact over a period of time in pursuit of a shared goal, a variety of basic structures and processes inevitably emerge. We shall discuss

▼ TABLE 9-1. A Classification of Social Collectivities

| Type | Self-Awareness | Physical Contact | Social Interaction | Social Organization |
|---|---|---|---|---|
| Social category | No | No | None | No |
| Social aggregate | Yes | Yes | Minimal | No |
| Social group | Yes | Yes | Active | Yes |

360

the most important of these. Together they constitute the essential components in the formation of social groups.

SENSE OF GROUP IDENTITY. Given the mutuality of purpose and common experiences, members of social groups in time develop a strong emotional attachment to each other. The goals and values of the group become inseparable from those of the individual members. They are willing to make sacrifices and forego personal rewards for the sake of the group. This sense of belonging to the group or esprit de corps is essential if the group is to function effectively and attain its goals.

Such social cohesion was first recognized by Franklin H. Giddings (1896), one of the early social psychologists in the United States, who spoke of the "consciousness of kind" to designate the sense of identity and unity that characterizes social groups. This sense of mutual identity frequently is manifested by the possessive attitude that members adopt in reference to such things as "my bowling team" or "our gang." Of course, as with nearly all other characteristics of social organization, social groups vary in the degree to which their members manifest "consciousness of kind" or a mutual recognition of each other's interests and objectives. Often, it is this very dynamic of consciousness of kind—a personal similarity in terms of social background and common interests—that leads to the formation of social groups.

DEVELOPMENT OF GROUP BOUNDARIES. All groups have boundaries. Without a social demarcation of one sort or another there would be no way of distinguishing members from nonmembers. Some groups, such as families and neighborhoods, obviously can maintain boundaries more easily than others—such as the student population of a particular high school or college. As a general rule, the greater the sense of solidarity in a group, the sharper and more clear-cut will be its boundaries. The boundaries of a group, however, can take many different forms. Most boundaries are symbolic. Members of a particular street gang may wear a certain insignia on their jackets, members of a lodge may wear pins that stand for their group, and members of a college fraternity may use an idiosyncratic handshake to greet each other. Each of these groups most likely will adopt a distinctive name. Nearly anything can be used as a "boundary marker" or symbol of identification to distinguish members from nonmembers. Of course, there must be a consensus among group members concerning which symbols will differentiate their group from others. The mere existence of group symbols, however, serves to reinforce each member's sense of group identity.

EMERGENCE OF SOCIAL ORGANIZATION. When a number of individuals share a common set of goals and a mutual identity and engage in regular interaction with each other, social organization inevitably will emerge. First of all, a set of shared normative expectations develops. These norms will indicate which types of behavior are acceptable and which are prohibited. Those who deviate from the norms of the groups will be subjected to sanctions of one kind or another.

In addition to the emergence of norms, role differentiation or a division of labor will develop as well. Some members will specialize at, and be most successful in, solving the task problems of the group; others will be most skilled at maintaining harmony, peace, and solidarity among group members. These fundamental principles of social organization are as true of a set of neighbors or friends, as they are of people who unexpectedly find themselves trapped in an elevator for a prolonged period of time or confronted by a similar kind of emergency.

Groups also develop other elements of social organization. These include a sociometric structure, or patterns of attraction and repulsion among members; a status structure, or hierarchy of prestige and importance; and a leadership structure. These three particular structures will be examined in more detail further on in this chapter.

## SIGNIFICANCE OF SOCIAL GROUPS

It would be difficult indeed to overemphasize the significance of groups, especially small groups, to both the larger society and the individual. It is within social groups, as components of the larger society, that concrete human activities take place. Numerous events that occur on the society level are really the "aggregated products of individual events that either occur in or are directly influenced by small group associations" (Crosbie, 1975:2). For example, divorce rates are basically the result of events occurring in many families; likewise, the

gross national product of a society is the result of events transpiring in many industrial work groups throughout the nation. Thus, these and many other phenomena that are usually thought of as occurring at the societal level are an aggregation of numerous events taking place within a variety of social groups.

Small groups (such as the family, the peer group, the work group, the fraternity group, and the friendship group) furnish the mediating link between society and the individual. As we described in preceding chapters, it is principally within such small groups as the family, the peer group, and the classroom group that the individual develops a unique personality and learns how to become a member of society. Individuals develop their *human* nature and other characteristics that distinguish them from nonhumans within a group setting. Social groups thus play a crucial part in the process of socialization and human development.

Many of our values, standards, attributes, and opinions are determined by the groups to which we belong or aspire to join. So, for example, members of an adolescent peer group will share many ideas about dating, the use of drugs, styles of dress, and music. Similarly, members of a work group are likely to have the same views about their boss, working conditions, and politics. This is not to say, of course, that every person belonging to a particular group has identical attitudes and opinions. The point is that the groups to which we belong exert a strong influence on our life and opinions. Much of the present chapter is devoted to demonstrating this fundamental principle.

# Types of Groups

Even the neophyte observer can easily identify a vast variety of social groups. Some of the more common ones include families, friendship cliques, teenage gangs, work crews, intimate neighbors, athletic teams, fraternities, hobby clubs, parishes, and congregations. However

**361**

▼ much these various groups necessarily have in common, they nonetheless differ from each other in many significant respects.

Sociologists have developed a number of classificatory schemes that highlight the specific features that distinguish different types of groups. Among the principal criteria are size, function, cohesion, and duration. We shall describe the major types of groups in these respects.

362

## PRIMARY AND SECONDARY GROUPS

Perhaps the most significant distinction in the analysis of social groups is that based on the nature or quality of the social relations and interaction which exist among the members. Sociologists in this regard speak of primary groups and secondary groups. This distinction is not intended to be so much a discrete or absolute classification as it is a continuous one. Any particular group can be measured or described in terms of the degree to which it approximates the ideal of one type or the other.

PRIMARY GROUPS. A **primary group** is characterized by primary social relationships and consists of a relatively small number of people who interact on an intimate, personal, direct, informal, face-to-face basis. There is a strong emotional bond between the members which typically endures over a long period of time. Interaction in the primary group tends to

**Intimate Interaction.** Primary groups, such as the family, constitute goals in themselves. Such groups are characterized by informality, frequent interaction, strong cohesion, and a totality of personality involvement on the part of their members. (Alan Carey/Image Works)

be spontaneous, relatively unorganized, frequent, and intense.

Primary groups of necessity must be small, usually not larger than twenty to twenty-five people. Direct, personal, and intimate interaction is not possible in groups much larger than this. Not all small groups, however, are primary ones. Typical examples of a primary group are the family, a children's play group, and a clique of friends.

The concept of a primary group was originated by Charles H. Cooley (1902). For Cooley, the primary group was primary in a number of respects, but chiefly in that it is fundamental in forming the social nature and ideals of the individual. He described primary groups, in this respect, as the "nursery of human nature." It is within such groups that the individual experiences the basic developments of a self-concept and various other elements of personality. Primary groups, however, as our definition and description are intended to suggest, are primary not so much in a temporal or chronological sense as in terms of the intimate interaction, the sociopsychological quality, that characterizes their members. The essential features of a primary group in this respect are the following.

*Expressive orientation.* Interaction among members of primary groups is valued for its own sake rather than being seen as a means to an end. Such relationships are said to be expressive rather than instrumental ones. The interaction itself is experienced by members as being psychologically rewarding, and hence tends to be generally spontaneous and enduring.

*Face-to-face interaction.* Members of primary groups are usually in close physical proximity to one another. They perceive each other's reactions as shown through both verbal and nonverbal means. Facial expressions and other modes of body language are an important means of communication. Some primary relationships, families and close friends, may involve interaction at a distance, through communication. While face-to-face interaction is not essential, its prolonged absence does tend to result in the loss of the distinctive qualities that characterize the primary group. Conversely, face-to-face interaction that is recurring or prolonged tends to result in the formation of primary-group relationships.

*Emergence of emotional bonds.* People involved in primary relationships develop strong feelings and attachments toward one another. Feelings of love, loyalty, and admiration as well as of dislike, resentment, and jealousy are common in these relationships. As Cooley (1909:23) states, "The result of intimate association, psychologically, is a certain fusion of individualities in a common whole, so that one's very self, for many purposes at least, is the common life and purpose of the group. Perhaps the simplest way of describing this wholeness is by saying that it is a 'we'; it involves the sort of sympathy and mutual identification for which 'we' is the natural expression."

*Totality of personality involvement.* Interaction within primary groups, in terms of personality, is diffuse rather than specific or segmental. That is to say, individuals come to know each other quite intimately as unique individuals, rather than simply role players. Hence, many facets and dimensions of the personality of primary group members are involved in their relationships with each other.

*Enduring interaction.* Primary group members interact with one another over long periods of time. Chiefly responsible for this situation is the fact that primary groups are usually centered around people rather than around specific tasks. The perpetually recurrent interaction that characterizes family members and work-group participants exemplifies this element of primary relationships.

**363**

▼ *Irreplaceable membership.* Since members of primary groups are seen as unique individuals who are valued for their own sake, they cannot be replaced by anyone else. If you dislike the professor in a particular course, you may be able to switch to another section, or simply drop the course. Such a transfer of status-role interaction, however, is usually not possible, certainly not as easy, in the primary group. A father's daughter or son, for example, is irreplaceable. While other individuals could assume these roles, they would not constitute the same primary group. Relationships in primary groups are structured in great part in terms of unique individuals rather than simply in terms of the roles that are enacted.

SECONDARY GROUPS. Secondary groups have characteristics that are the opposite of those found in primary groups. They are distinguished by instrumental orientations, formal communications, nonemotional bonds, segmental personality involvements, transitory interactions, and replaceable memberships. Given these characteristics, such groups can be, and usually are, much larger than primary groups. However, even many small groups can consist essentially of secondary relationships.

A **secondary group** is one that is characterized by relatively formal, impersonal, limited, and goal-oriented interactions. Typical examples of a secondary group would be a college class, a professional soccer team, or perhaps a hobby club.

Communication among members of secondary groups is not face-to-face for the most part, but is indirect and mediated by formal mechanisms such as directives or memos. Many secondary relationships are relatively fleeting as opposed to being long-lasting. Secondary groups, moreover, tend to be short-lived. In most cases there are very few, if any, emotional bonds among members of secondary groups. Relationships among members are character-

ized by emotional detachment and neutrality. In contrast to primary relationships, where the total personality of individuals is manifested, in secondary relationships only certain aspects or segments of an individual's personality are involved in the interaction. People are enacting social roles that do not require them to reveal diverse aspects of their personalities. Thus, one does not usually know much about the personality of the professor in a particular course, the leader of a vacation tour, the bank teller who deposits your check, or the cashier at the supermarket who takes your money and bags your groceries.

Secondary relationships are essentially instrumental ones. The relationship with a person is not valued for its own sake as is the case with primary relationships; rather, it is seen as a means to a desired end. People join secondary groups or become involved in secondary relationships in order to achieve a highly specific objective. Thus, people join unions in the hope of obtaining higher pay and better working conditions. Similarly, a person interacts with a clothing salesperson for the purpose of buying clothes. Moreover, seldom do members of secondary groups interact with each other outside the goal-oriented activities of the group. Under these circumstances, members of secondary groups are replaceable and the turnover of personnel may be quite frequent. One does not really care which bus driver operates the bus as long as you get to your destination. Neither does one care which waiter is behind the counter in the diner, as long as you are served quickly.

The primary-secondary distinction should be viewed as constituting a continuum rather than a dichotomy. No real-life group or relationship is purely either primary or secondary. There are, for example, elements of secondary relationships in families. Much of the interaction occurring within families is of the instrumental nature. Parents want their children to take out the garbage, to go shopping, and to keep their

TABLE 9-2. Primary versus Secondary Groups ▼

|  | Primary Groups | Secondary Groups |
| --- | --- | --- |
| Size | Small | Large |
| Interaction | Frequent | Occasional |
| Relationships | Personal, intimate, diffuse | Impersonal, limited |
| Communication | Face-to-face | Indirect |
| Goals | General | Specific |
| Orientation | Expressive | Instrumental |
| Cohesion | Strong | Weak |
| Duration | Permanent | Temporary |
| Membership | Irreplaceable | Replaceable |
| Social structure | Informal | Formal |

**365**

rooms clean. Similarly, in certain cases, one or the other parent may not really know the total personality of their child, and vice versa. By the same token, secondary groups, especially the larger ones, usually contain primary relationships within them. Study groups within a college class exemplify this situation.

Many groups that begin as secondary ones may in time and through frequent interaction become primary ones. A worker may join a union to further his or her economic interests, but soon find enjoyment in associating with the union members as individuals. A person may also develop a strong relationship with other coworkers. The importance of the primary group was underscored in a series of studies aimed at determining why soldiers were motivated to remain in combat during World War II. It was found that both American and German soldiers were motivated to continue fighting mainly because of loyalty, trust, affection, and powerful emotional ties that emerged among them. Researchers (Stouffer, 1949) observed that values, ideals, and propaganda were relatively unimportant in maintaining a commitment to battle. Far more significant were the existence of strongly cohesive ties in terms

of such primary fighting units as platoons and squads (Van Creveld, 1982). Further substantiation for this position can be found in the Israeli military. Studies show that combat units which are hastily organized without providing their members with adequate time to establish personal bonds perform more poorly in battle and experience higher rates of psychiatric disorders than do combat units with cohesive bonds (Cordes, 1984). Many groups then contain elements that are associated with both primary and secondary relationships.

# MEMBERSHIP GROUPS VERSUS REFERENCE GROUPS

Much social behavior can be understood only in terms of the distinctions between membership groups and reference groups. The respective differences, however, do not apply exclusively to groups. Rather they serve to distinguish any kind of social collectivity. Perhaps "membership set" and "reference set" would be more appropriate in this situation because of the generic designation. Nonetheless, traditional usage has referred to membership groups and reference groups, so let us speak in these

▼ terms so long as the proper meaning is kept in mind.

MEMBERSHIP GROUPS. A **membership group** is simply a social group (or category) to which an individual belongs—one in which there is an actual membership. These groups may be primary or secondary groups. Individuals, especially in modern industrialized societies, may belong to many membership groups.

REFERENCE GROUPS. A **reference group** (or category) is one that individuals use as a frame of reference to guide their behavior and to evaluate themselves. It provides norms and standards by which individual behavior is regulated—and even understood in a given context. We are always evaluating ourselves in one respect or another—appearance, behavior, values, goals, lifestyles, and so forth. Such self-monitoring cannot take place without particular groups that are used as the standard of comparison. Peer groups serve as very important reference groups for children and adolescents.

Reference groups may be those to which one actually belongs (membership groups), or those in which one desires to hold membership. Even though an individual does not formally belong to a particular group, he or she may strongly identify with it and use it as a guide for behavior. Reference groups, then, imply a kind of psychological membership. Membership groups, on the other hand, are necessarily always reference groups, even when one rejects them. Such groups are said to be *negative reference groups*—those in which one does not desire membership or strives not to emulate. Sophomores often are admonished not to act like freshmen (negative reference group), but rather to emulate the lifestyle of seniors (positive reference group).

There are two types of reference groups: normative and comparative (Merton, 1968). A *normative reference group* is one that an individual utilizes as a source of values, attitudes, beliefs, norms, behavior, and expectations. A youngster who has a juvenile gang as a normative reference group will tend to behave in accordance with the norms and expectations of the gang. Accordingly, the youngster may engage in vandalism, petty robberies, and other forms of gang conduct. Even though he may not be an actual or formal member of the gang, his behavior will be similar to that of the actual gang members as long as he identifies with the gang, and perhaps aspires to membership within it.

Normative reference groups also function to influence a person's taste in food, art, music, and numerous other dimensions of a lifestyle. Members of the lower-middle class who are strongly status-conscious and upwardly mobile may have as their normative reference group members of the upper-middle class. Such individuals will attempt to develop an upper-middle-class lifestyle, or at least outwardly manifest aspects of one. The same dynamics are involved when freshmen emulate seniors rather than their own classmates.

A *comparative reference group* is one that individuals use to evaluate themselves and their behavior. The groups with which individuals compare themselves will be very influential in determining how they feel about themselves in terms of accomplishment and abilities. For instance, someone earning $20,000 who takes people earning $80,000 as a comparative reference group is likely to feel deprived and poor. On the other hand, if instead of comparing oneself to corporate executives, movie stars, and oil magnates, individuals compare their financial status to people with similar or lower incomes, they will not feel too bad about their economic situation. Similarly, the student who usually earns C's may develop feelings of inferiority if he compares himself to those who receive A's. On the other hand, if he instead begins to use students earning D's as his comparative reference group, he is apt to feel pretty good about his academic achievements.

As normative and comparative reference groups change, people are likely to experience changes in attitudes, beliefs, opinions, self-conceptions, and behavior—ones which often are relatively permanent. This phenomenon was demonstrated quite effectively several years ago in a long-term study of students at Bennington College in Vermont (Newcomb, 1943). The college had a liberal orientation, but the majority of its students came from wealthy, upper-class, conservative families. This situation presented a conflict between the political attitudes and philosophy of entering students and those of the faculty and other students. The majority of the students resolved the conflict by switching their reference groups from their families to the faculty and senior students. This situation was especially true of those students who became deeply involved in college activities and the college community. In fact, the switch in reference groups seemed to be facilitated by the frequency with which students interacted with their families. The longer students remained away from their parents, the more likely they were to adopt a liberal orientation. Subsequent data showed that these students did not revert to their former political beliefs after they graduated. Follow-up studies (Newcomb, 1967) revealed that women of the graduating class in question and their husbands were unusually liberal for people of their socioeconomic background. These data suggest the strong influence of reference groups in the alteration of highly significant behavior.

## IN-GROUPS AND OUT-GROUPS

Another set of groups that sociologists find analytically useful is that of in-groups and out-groups. Once again, distinctions involve both sociological and psychological characteristics.

IN-GROUPS.  An **in-group** is any group or social category with which a person has developed a strong sense of emotional and psychological attachment. There are feelings of pride, loyalty, and satisfaction in being a member. The person has an intense psychological identification with the group. There is a merging of the values, goals, and feelings of the group and those of the individual. There is a strong sense of "we-ness" and solidarity among its members. In-groups may be either primary or secondary groups, or simply social categories.

OUT-GROUPS.  An **out-group** is any group or social category of which one is not a member and toward which one feels a sense of indifference, avoidance, competition, conflict, or even disgust. The individual, obviously, does not share the values, norms, goals, or experiences of such a group. The out-group, then, represents the "they-group"—those who are outside the boundaries of the group.

In-groups and out-groups are reciprocal or correlative concepts. There cannot be an in-group without a corresponding out-group, and vice versa. These conceptual distinctions were developed by William G. Sumner (1906) as a means to explain the dynamics of ethnocentrism, which we discussed in Chapter 3. Israelis and Palestinians, as well as Catholics and Protestants of Northern Ireland, respectively constitute in-groups and out-groups for each other. In-groups usually serve as positive reference groups, while out-groups, of course, constitute negative reference groups—those one strives not to emulate.

Actual or perceived hostility between in-groups and out-groups often serves to reinforce the we-they feelings. In a series of classical experiments, Muzafer Sherif (1961) demonstrated that competition between groups leads to feelings of out-group hostility, and that an increase in hostility toward out-groups results in an increase of emotional attachment and solidarity among members of the in-group (see Box 9-1). On the other hand, when groups either need or are made to cooperate for the attainment of a common goal, or what Sherif called a superordinate goal, feelings of out-group hostility and

**367**

▼

## BOX 9-1. In-Group and Out-Group Dynamics

In-group and out-group dynamics have been documented in a series of experiments by Muzafer Sherif and his associates. In the well-known Robbers' Cave experiment, Sherif et al. (1961) utilized 11- and 12-year-old boys, unknown to each other, as subjects in the setting of a summer camp. These subjects were carefully selected in order to constitute a highly homogeneous sample on the basis of a number of social and personal characteristics. A few days after the boys were able to get to know each other and to form friendship cliques, they were randomly divided into two separate groups with a consequential disruption of the cliques that had already formed. Strong loyalties nonetheless soon developed within the new groups and each adopted a name—the Eagles and the Rattlers.

Sherif intentionally pitted the two groups against each other in a variety of competitive games and sports. What began as fun soon developed into a situation of rampant antagonism and hostility; name-calling, scuffling, and other modes of friction became quite commonplace. These developments were quite typical even among those boys who originally had formed friendships. Bringing the two groups together for pleasant social contact did not reduce the friction between them. Indeed, such contact only provided new opportunities for the manifestation of out-group hostility and intensification of in-group cohesion. Sherif and his associates then created a series of emergency situations, such as the destruction of the water supply, that challenged both groups to work together in a harmonious and teamlike fashion. Within a brief period both groups began to collaborate as a single group, and soon the intergroup frictions were virtually eliminated.

This experiment, and others like it, shows that mere social contact does not reduce hostility between rival groups. Such possibilities, however, are greatly enhanced when in-groups and out-groups are confronted with a common or superordinate goal that requires collaboration and positive interaction. ▲

animosity will be reduced, perhaps even annihilated, and harmony greatly enhanced. Moreover, the boundaries that seem to distinguish the two groups from one another will be weakened.

## The Significance of Group Size

The size of a group, perhaps more than any other variable, exerts the strongest influence in determining the nature of the quality and quantity of interaction that will take place among its members. Much of our understanding in this regard stems from the classic work of Georg Simmel, who observed that "a group upon reaching a certain size must develop forms and organs which serve its maintenance and promotion, but which a smaller group does not need. On the other hand, smaller groups have qualities, including types of interaction, among their members, which inevitably disappear when the groups grow larger" (1950:87).

### BASIC PRINCIPLES

Changes in group size invariably result in changes in the structure of social relationships. Group structure becomes increasingly complex and new properties emerge with increases in the size of a group. As a group grows arithmetically, the number and form of potential social relationships are vastly elaborated geometrically (at a rate far in excess of the sheer increase in numbers). The formula for this phenomenon is $R = n(n - 1)/2$, where $R$ equals the number of bilateral relationships and $n$ equals the number of people. For example, when two people comprise a group, only one relationship is possible. However, in a group of six people, 15 separate two-person relationships are possible, and 190 among 20 people. These principles and dynamics are illustrated in Figures 9-1 and 9-2.

Hence, it is not so much the sheer number of people that makes for the increase in the complexity of group structure as it is the concomitant increase in the disproportionate number of role relationships and the corresponding need for social regulations and social control. It is this principle that explains the multiplication of "chiefs" (administrators) in a social organization with the simple addition of "Indians." What an administrator administers or a supervisor supervises is not people but social relationships. Accordingly, as the number of social relationships increases, the number of supervisory tasks and corresponding roles increases as well. Complexity of social structure, therefore, stems in large part from a disproportionate number of social relationships that parallel simple increases in the number of people.

Increases in the size of a group also produce problems of communication and coordination. The amount of time that each member has for communication decreases, and there is a tendency for a handful of members to do most of the talking (Hare, 1976). Formal procedures must be developed that will coordinate the activities of the members. There is a tendency for the division of labor among group members to become more rigid and more sharply defined as the size of the group increases. The more people there are in a group, the less concerned the leader tends to be about the opinions and views of each individual. He or she is most likely to be interested in having the group reach a consensus about the matters under consideration. Groups of five people have been found

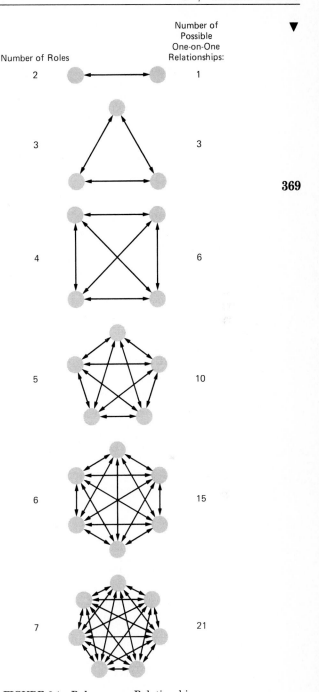

FIGURE 9-1   Roles versus Relationships.

**369**

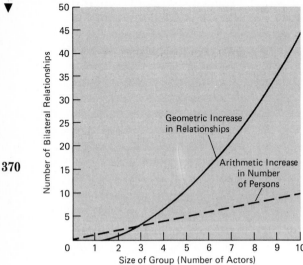

FIGURE 9-2 Group Size versus Social Relationships.

to be the optimal size for discussions (Bales, 1954; Slater, 1955).

Related to this situation is another independent principle. Increases in group size usually result in a decrease in social cohesion. Integration and social solidarity decrease in the measure to which numerical increases involve, as they invariably do, the admission of heterogeneous elements in a group. This principle is demonstrated quite commonly in family groups: an increase in size usually results in an increase in the potential for social conflict due to a myriad of personal and social differences in the family unit. The potential for conflict is also exacerbated by the larger number of structural relationships and corresponding role interactions.

The significant impact that size has on the nature of interaction in groups is shown most clearly in a discussion of dyads and triads.

## DYADS AND TRIADS

A **dyad** is the most elementary form of a social group. It consists of two people. Dyads are delicate and potentially very fragile groups. Unlike groups consisting of more than two people, the interaction of any one member is crucial for the dynamics and existence of the group. No communication or other type of interaction can take place within the dyad unless each individual assumes an active role. And the mere departure of one person from the dyad by definition means that the group has dissolved. Thus, in order to keep the group intact, members of a dyad must exhibit much greater involvement, effort, and mutual respect than members of larger groups. Emotions, both positive and negative, are apt to be more intense in a dyad than in larger groups. Members of dyads are especially apt to develop love-hate feelings toward each other. Similarly, there is a high exchange of information and a tendency to avoid disagreement in a dyad. Much of this situation may be necessary for the survival of the dyad. In comparison with larger groups, dyads are very fragile and vulnerable to dissolution.

When the dyad becomes a **triad** with the addition of another person, several significant changes occur. First of all, any one member can ignore the other two without threatening the existence of the group. More importantly, the formation of coalitions or alliances becomes a distinct possibility. Two members can conspire and pool their resources against the third. Indeed, according to Simmel (1950), the primary tendency in a threesome is segregation into a pair or another dyad. Think of a family consisting of a mother, father, and child. You may recall that often the child forms a coalition with one of the parents.

The triad group structure, unlike the dyad, also opens the possibility of one member playing the role of mediator when there is a conflict between the other two. In families, a child sometimes serves the function of holding the parents together (Nixon, 1979). The child can perform this function directly by actively mediating disputes between the parents. In most cases, moreover, the child represents a shared love object for the parents and as such may serve to in-

370

crease the affection that they have for one another while mitigating conflicts.

Compared to dyads, triads are less vulnerable to dissolution. There is less of a necessity for each member of a triad to be always involved in the interaction. One of the members of a triad can daydream or just make-believe that he or she is interested in the interaction, while the other two interact intensely. In addition, the emotions of the members of a triad can be diffused among them, resulting in a lower emotional tone than is the case with dyads. Hence, in comparison to dyads, for example, triads are likely to show less evidence of tension.

These various kinds of interaction continue to change as groups become larger. Simply by knowing the size of a group, one can make certain predictions about the nature and forms of interaction that are likely to occur.

# Why People Join Social Groups

What motivates people to join and participate in groups? Which kind of social and psychological functions does a group perform for its members? The basic propensity for group formation is the result of two basic motives—the affiliative and the instrumental—that are essential or imperative in the social person.

## THE AFFILIATIVE MOTIVE

Many people become members of groups because doing so helps to satisfy their need or desire for companionship, social interaction, recognition, and security. Involvement with groups is experienced as rewarding and enjoyable for its own sake. Georg Simmel (1950) referred to this point when he said that interaction in groups is accompanied by a feeling for, by a satisfaction in, the very fact that one is associated with others and that the solitariness

of the individual is resolved into togetherness, a union with others. Belonging to a group may provide an individual with an identity and a sense of meaning to life that one might not otherwise have.

Studies also suggest that affiliating with others helps to reduce feelings of anxiety and uneasiness (Schacter, 1959). One group of subjects was told that they would receive a series of painful shocks during an experiment; another group was told that no pain would be involved in the experiment. Subjects were then given the choice of either waiting alone in a room with magazines or with others in a vacant classroom. Those subjects who expected to receive painful shocks were most likely to prefer to wait with others.

Interacting with others in a group context also serves to reduce uncertainty and to give the individual an opportunity to compare his perception of a situation with that of others. When unexpected events occur, or when a person experiences difficulty in defining or making sense out of a situation, group interaction increases. When a massive power blackout occurred in New York City in 1965, strangers began interacting and communicating with one another. These individuals exchanged reasons or explanations for what was occurring. Small groups seemed to emerge spontaneously in order to help control traffic and provide other types of assistance. Thus, the need to clarify vague and unexpected situations intensifies the need for affiliation and thereby encourages group formation.

## THE INSTRUMENTAL MOTIVE

Many goals that a person desires to achieve can only be realized through cooperative group interaction. Such may be true whether the objective is to build a skyscraper or simply to have fun. Groups represent a pooling of a wide diversity of the resources of its members. Each

**371**

▼

member of the group brings to it special skills and talents that, when combined with those of the other members, enable the collective goal to be attained. It would be practically impossible, for example, for one person to construct a modern office building. Such an endeavor requires the combined talents of architects, electricians, plumbers, steelworkers, and many others. Similarly, if a person wants to improve his or her working conditions, receive a raise in pay, and obtain greater job security, he or she may join a labor union. Or perhaps the individual is concerned about the quality of an environment and the effects of pollution on the ecosystem; if so, he or she may become a member of an environmental protection group. People may be motivated to join a country club or a poker party in order to make business contacts. In all these examples, people join groups because they believe it will help them to achieve a particular goal. They believe that the group will be instrumental in enabling them to obtain their goals.

## INDISPENSABILITY OF PRIMARY GROUPS

Motivation for group formation and group participation is not an absolute. Much depends on the type of social group. Primary groups, in particular, are distinctive in the basis for their existence.

Primary groups are primary, as we have said, in a number of senses. They are especially primary in that they provide the initial, and most significant, experiences upon which socialization and human development occurs. They are primary also in that they are indispensable for the gratification of certain human needs, such as those of social response (affiliation), social recognition (identity and acceptance), and security (physical and psychological), which are necessary for human function. Primary groups provide in these respects a type of psychological expectation and gratification that only they can

provide given their particular nature, structure, and dynamics.

This significance of primary groups is dramatically evident to anyone whose primary-group relationships are severed by death, divorce, desertion, or even prolonged separation. The stronger and more exclusive the emotional bonds in such situations, the more painful the loss. Anyone who has experienced the loss of a parent or spouse, of even a broken love affair, knows all too well the pain that comes from such a fractured primary group. A similar realization of this significance of primary groups, perhaps a less painful one, occurs when primary groups are dissolved as individuals leave family and friends in order to marry, serve in the military, attend college, or move to a distant city. The pain that such situations produce stems not so much from the particular individuals for which there is genuine nostalgia as much as from the loss of the psychological experience and gratification of human needs that the breakup of primary groups involves, either temporarily or permanently. Fortunately, in the vast majority of cases, this loss is not a permanent one.

Sociologists have become concerned that in recent years primary-group relationships may be declining in modern societies. Social trends in physical mobility and urbanization have brought about—to a great extent unavoidably—a more formal and impersonal type of social life for growing numbers of people. Time was when whole communities, or at least neighborhoods, functioned essentially and quite effectively in terms of primary-group relationships. Even families, especially extended families, are becoming essentially secondary groups with the decreasing frequency of interaction and loosening of emotional bonds. One such indication is found in the increasing use of marriage contracts between spouses.

Primary groups in nearly all segments of social life today have been overshadowed by larger and more impersonal forms of social organization. Such a situation puts greater stress on those primary groups and primary-group relationships that do exist—and such a situation, as divorce rates suggest, may lead to further dissolution of primary groups, all of which generates a vicious cycle. All of this situation translates into fewer and fewer primary groups with which individuals can identify and from which they can derive the essential primary-group experience.

Some sociologists, however, contend that primary relationships and primary groups still play a vital part in modern industrialized society. The primary group has been "rediscovered" in the sense that many people are realizing "that primary groups could be found in important new forms, other than traditional family, play, or neighborhood groups, in secondary structures that were previously seen as destroying or replacing primary associations" (Nixon, 1979:17). In a study of over 1000 people living in fifty communities in northern California,

Fischer (1982) found that primary relationships continue to be quite important. The average person in his sample reported having fifteen to nineteen primary relationships.

Sociologists, nonetheless, now speak of quasi-primary groups or **surrogate primary groups** that, while ostensibly secondary groups organized around attainment of specific goals, emerge in modern societies for the fundamental purpose of providing the essential social and psychological experience of primary groups which is allegedly on the wane in modern society. The rather widespread establishment of communes among young adults during the 1960s, a situation that has not completely disappeared by any means, has been seen by many social observers as an attempt to create the primary-group experience. Athletic clubs, encounter groups, religious cults, interest groups, and neighborhood associations also fall into this category. Primary relationships and primary-group associations of a somewhat more

▼

**373**

**Surrogate Primary Groups.** Block parties often represent a "quasi-primary" group that emerges in modern society in an attempt to provide the essential social and psychological expression of primary relationships that many perceive to be diminishing in modern society. (Charles Gatewood/Image Works)

▼ genuine nature have been found to emerge and to exert much influence in such secondary groups as factories, prisons, corporations, and armies.

Other sociologists would argue that the trend away from primary-group relationships is not to be seen as completely negative. A lessening in primary-group relationships often means greater freedom in many ways for the individual, who can act more independently and make choices without the strong constraint and powerful sanctions usually associated with primary groups.

374

# Sociometric Structure: Liking and Disliking in Groups

As members of groups interact with one another over time, they begin to develop feelings of attraction and repulsion toward each other. After a while, these feelings tend to stabilize and we have the emergence of a sociometric structure. **Sociometric structure** refers to the patterns of interpersonal attraction and repulsion that exist among the members of a group. This phenomenon is an important type of group structure because it influences many other structures and processes. One social psychologist has observed that "when the role differentiation in a group is not too great, the category of likes and dislikes 'packages' most of the other determinants of interaction" (Tagiuri, 1958). Most particularly, sociometric structure can serve as a gauge for group cohesion and integration.

## MEASUREMENT OF INTERPERSONAL ATTRACTION

The method most frequently used to measure the likes and dislikes among members of a group is the sociometric test. This method was developed by J. L. Moreno (1953), a psychiatrist who was much interested in the nature of social dynamics. Basically, the sociometric test consists of a set of questions that are posed to group members. Each individual is asked to indicate with whom he or she would prefer to study, have dinner, share a room, go to a ball game, or engage in a variety of other activities. Once the questions are answered, it is possible to portray graphically the sociometric structure of the group by means of a sociogram. The **sociogram** is a kind of diagram that indicates attractions and rejections in the group and whether these feelings are shared (see Figure 9-3). The sociogram is able to indicate the cliques or subgroups that have emerged within the group as well, and serves further to identify the networks of communication, influence, and decision making of the group. In addition to this kind of paper-and-pencil test, sociologists may also assess sociometric structure by directly observing the patterns of interaction that transpire among group members. Ideally, both methods should be used. Sociometric techniques can be used to assess the simple patterns of friendships in groups, as well to determine quite specifically the more viable patterns of association for accomplishing particular tasks. Teachers, for example, can make use of sociometric analysis to arrange classroom seating that will both counteract unproductive cliques and integrate isolated and withdrawing students.

## DETERMINANTS OF INTERPERSONAL ATTRACTION

What are the factors that help to determine the sociometric structure of a group? Why do some members of a group become attracted to each other while others do not? Research suggests that propinquity or physical proximity is related to interpersonal attraction. The closer two people are to each other, the greater the chance

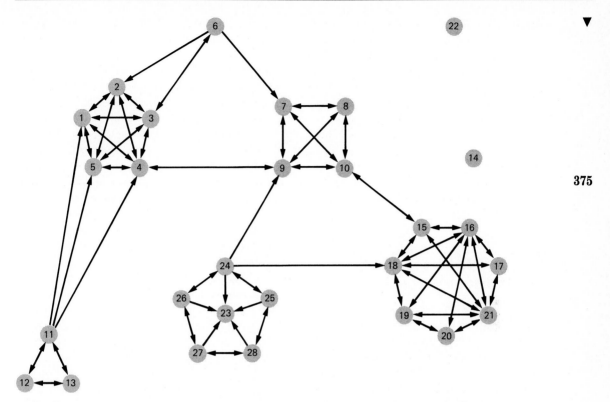

FIGURE 9-3 Sociometrics and Sociograms. Sociometric structure is measured by means of the socio-gram—a kind of diagram that indicates attractions and rejections of individuals in a group. This so-ciogram of a purely imaginary group reveals a number of cliques, as well as social "stars" and social isolates. Each circle represents one member. Arrows mark the direction of a choice of friendship. Double arrow marks on a line indicate a mutual choice. One indication of cohesion within a group can be had by measuring the number of mutual choices out of the total number of mutual choices that are possible. Another technique is to divide 1 by the number of isolates. Who do you think is the leader of the group? Can you identify any dyads or triads? Which clique, from your point of view, is the most desirable one?

that they will like one another (Crosbie, 1975). Investigators in one well-known study (Festinger et al., 1950) determined friendship patterns among people occupying two housing projects by asking: "Which three people in Westgate or Westgate West do you see most of socially?" Results showed that nearly half of the friendship selections by residents of one complex were for people living in adjacent apartments. Data from similar studies have shown consistently that the nearer people are to each other, the greater the probability that they will interact more, and perhaps become friends. Indeed, propinquity in

residence or the workplace has been consistently and highly related to the selection of marital partners.

Some social scientists account for this relationship by noting that it is easy for people who are closer to one another to initiate interaction than for people who are farther away from each other. For one thing, less costs are incurred. Many studies, moreover, indicate that people who have similar attitudes, beliefs, opinions, and other common characteristics are much more likely to be attracted to one another than those who differ in these respects (Byrne, 1967).

▼

The only way people can learn whether others share their attitudes and views is for them to communicate. Interaction and communication is facilitated when individuals who are seated close together learn that they have very different opinions and viewpoints; they are not likely to be attracted to each other. Being in close physical proximity provides people with the opportunity to find out how much they have in common. Accordingly, the variable of physical proximity may have only an indirect, but nonetheless instrumental, effect on interpersonal attraction.

## Cohesion and Solidarity in Groups

**Group cohesion** has been defined as "the resultant of all the forces acting on the members to remain in the group" (Festinger, 1950:274). Unlike the notion of sociometric structure, which refers to the patterns of attraction and rejection among specific members of the group, cohesion denotes the attraction that the group as a whole has for its members. It can be understood as the totality of the feelings of attraction to the group of all of the members of the group. To the extent that each member has a strong sense of identification with the group and equates its values and goals with his or her own, the group is cohesive. Hence, a sense of "weness" or esprit de corps is characteristic of highly cohesive groups. So are cooperation, frequent interaction, and a ready defense against external criticism.

The degree of cohesiveness in a group can be measured in several ways. One mathematical technique for assessing social cohesion is to divide the number of mutual choices or actions among group members by the total number of possible mutual choices. Correspondingly, an index of group integration can be found by dividing the number 1 by the number of isolates in a group, that is, individuals receiving no

choices. It is best, however, to use a set of questions and observations to determine cohesiveness because no one question or method can adequately measure it. For example, it was found that questions dealing with members' attraction to each other did not significantly relate to attitudes of attraction to the group as a whole (Peterson & Martens, 1973). Sociometric friendship choices among group members are only one aspect of cohesiveness. Other indicators or measures of group cohesiveness would be the extent to which members use the term "we" rather than "I," the degree to which they share norms, and the rate of absenteeism at group meetings and functions (Olmsted & Hare, 1978).

Cohesion is an extremely important element of group structure. Why are some groups more cohesive than others? What determines whether a group is highly cohesive? Olmsted and Hare (1978) state that the following factors have been found to produce group cohesiveness:

1. Stress on cooperation (instead of competition).
2. Democratic structure or climate (instead of an authoritarian or laissez faire one).
3. High-status group (instead of a low-status one).
4. Interest in the tasks and goals of the group.

The size and stability of groups, as well as the personal commitment that each person makes to the group, are also related to group cohesion. Evenly numbered groups, for example, tend to be characterized by more disagreements than do odd-numbered ones because of the potential formation of subgroups of equal size (Berelson & Steiner, 1964). Smaller groups and those that experience a low turnover in membership tend to have high levels of cohesion. Moskos (1970) offers a very interesting example of the role of stability in group cohesion. In a study of American soldiers in the Vietnam war, he suggests that the policy of rotating infantrymen once a year tended to make them "isolated and self-concerned." These soldiers became more preoccupied with making it through to the end of their tour when they were no longer a part of the combat group than they were with patriotism or dedication to a common effort. Similarly, group cohesion is related to the investment that each member makes in the group in terms of emotions, time, and other personal resources.

A classic study of group cohesion and its significance for group dynamics was undertaken by Emile Durkheim (1897). Working with data from several countries, Durkheim was able to establish intriguing relationships between degrees of social cohesion that characterized different kinds of social situations or collectivities and varying rates of suicide (see Chapter 13). The basic principle of Durkheim's theory can be applied to other forms of behavior, such as group function and productivity. Durkheim's analysis reveals, quite surprisingly, that the relationship between social cohesion and group function is not a logically expected unilinear one, but rather a curvilinear relationship. In other words, such dynamics as morale or esprit de corps and productivity or performance are not positively correlated, such that an increase in one results in an increase in the other; rather, the relationship is curvilinear, such that there is an optimal range for both factors (see Figure 9-4). Too much social cohesion, thus, can be as dysfunctional as too little.

What consequence does group cohesion have on the structure, activity, and functioning of groups? Do groups that score high on cohesiveness operate differently from those that score low on this dimension? After reviewing the relevant literature, Nixon (1979) has summarized some of the consequences of group cohesiveness. In comparison with low-cohesive groups, high-cohesive groups show:

1. Greater group influence over the attitudes and behavior of group members.
2. Greater membership consensus and acceptance of the group's values and norms.
3. Higher degree of social interaction and greater manifestation of friendliness.

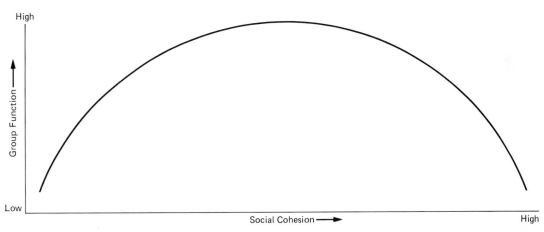

FIGURE 9-4 Group Function and Social Cohesion. Emile Durkheim (1897) intriguingly explained suicide as a social phenomenon that develops in situations that are characterized by extreme degrees of social cohesion. Hence, contrary to what may be popularly expected, the relationship between social order and social solidarity (morale, esprit de corps, commitment) is not unilinear, but curvilinear instead. Relatively too much or too little social cohesion produces essentially the same dysfunctional consequences. Fundamentally, similar relationships exist between social cohesion and many other kinds of behavior, such as economic productivity.

▼

4. Greater expressed satisfaction with the group and its products.
5. Increased goal attainment and efficiency.

In addition, it appears that members of highly cohesive groups are more receptive to change or influence and tend to cope better with frustration than do members of less cohesive groups (Olmsted & Hare, 1978). Hence, from the review of the research data, it is evident that group cohesiveness is a crucial factor that affects many aspects of group functioning.

# Conformity and Deviance in Groups

Norms are rules or expectations that specify socially acceptable and socially expected behavior. All groups have a normative structure that serves to give order and predictability to the actions of its members. Group norms are shared to varying degrees by its members. There must be a minimum amount of consensus regarding the normative structure if the group is to be able to function.

## CONFORMITY IN GROUPS

Pressure to conform to social expectations is quite strong throughout every area of social life. It seems to be especially powerful within the organization of social groups. Norms have a constraining influence on the members of a group. Each person feels pressured to conform to the norms of the group. Moreover, the more cohesive a group tends to be, the more likely it is that the group requires conformity from its members.

The significance of norms for groups is highlighted by Sherif and Sherif (1964) in a study of an adolescent group. These sociologists found that just because a youngster was able to engage in activities that the gang valued did not automatically ensure that he would be accepted as a member. For instance, merely because a boy was an excellent basketball player did not guarantee that he would be allowed to become a member of the group. He also had to conform to the special norms that the gang evolved concerning how its members were to play the game. Examples of these norms or expectations included the following:

1. When competing with other teams a gang member should not criticize the performance of a teammate.
2. Fouling is acceptable when the group is playing another gang, but it is unacceptable when the team is practicing among themselves.
3. The leader of the gang is allowed to foul his teammates.

These norms had been adhered to by the members of the gang. If they were consistently violated by a member, he would be subjected to various types of negative sanctions. These punishments could range in severity from a nasty look to physical abuse or expulsion from the gang. In addition to norms specifying what was acceptable and unacceptable behavior during the course of a basketball game, the Sherifs found that the gang also had norms dealing with such things as stealing, dating, parental interaction, police relationships, and interaction with rival gangs.

Once the norms of a group are accepted by a majority of its members, pressure is exerted upon other members to accept and behave in accordance with these rules. This situation is exemplified by the pressure exerted by workers on new employees to conform to the output norms set by the work group, as we saw in the last chapter in discussing the emergence of informal groups within formal organizations.

Asch (1952), in a series of classic experiments, clearly showed the import that even subtle group pressure has on members. A subject would be told that he would be a participant in an experiment dealing with visual perception. He would be led to a room where seven other "subjects" were present. (In reality, these seven individuals were confederates of the experimenter, and they were told beforehand which responses to give.) Everyone was shown a set of cards. There was one vertical line on one card; each of the other cards had a series of three vertical lines of significantly different lengths—one of which was exactly the same length as that on the single-line card (Figure 9-5). The subjects were asked to select from the series of three lines the one which most closely resembled the single line in length. Each member of the group was told to announce his answer out loud. The actual subject was instructed to give his answers last. On most of the trials the confederates deliberately gave incorrect answers. The purpose of the experiment was to determine whether the real subject would conform to the wrong responses given by the confederates. Asch found that in normal and solitary circumstances subjects would make errors less than 1 percent of the time. However, in the experimental situation when they heard the confederates deliberately giving incorrect

answers, the subjects, as if disbelieving their own eyes, made errors about 40 percent of the time. This experiment shows the power of group pressure. It is an especially revealing experiment because the confederates did not make any attempt to convince the subject of the "correctness" of their responses. A very large number of subjects gave erroneous answers (even though they thought they were wrong) because they did not want to appear to be different from the others in the group by giving the obviously correct answer.

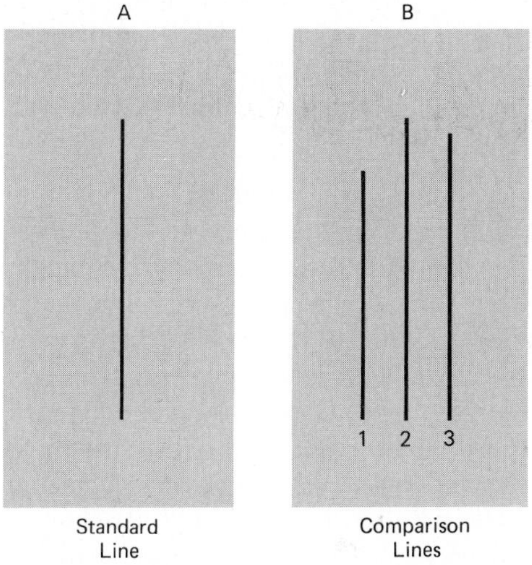

Group structure itself makes for social conformity and serves to counteract or to inhibit social deviation. The formation and change of attitudes, for example, are easier to accomplish in a group than when an individual is alone. Moreover, attitudes formed or changed in a group context tend to persist longer than is the case of those that develop in a solitary context.

FIGURE 9-5 Standard and Comparison Lines in the Asch Experiment. Source: Adapted from "Effects of Group Pressure upon the Modification and Distortion of Judgments" by Solomon E. Asch, Readings in Social Psychology. Englewood Cliffs, N.J.: Prentice-Hall, 1952, p. 452. Rev. Ed. by Swanson et al. and also in the 3rd Ed. by Maccoby et al.

## DEVIANCE IN GROUPS

In any group there will never be total conformity to its normative structure. Some members, for a variety of reasons, will behave in ways that are prohibited by the group. Why do members engage in deviant behavior? Several theories have been advanced to account for the existence of deviance in small groups. Let us briefly discuss two of them here.*

INTERNALIZATION THEORY. In the perspective of **internalization theory,** individuals violate group norms because they are incompatible with their internalized standards. Through the socialization process a person may have acquired norms that are inconsistent with those of the group. A youngster, for instance, may have strongly internalized a norm that says it is wrong to cheat. If the norms of one's school class encourage cheating behavior on the part

379

* A complete discussion of deviant behavior is given in Chapter 13.

▼ of its members, the youngster will be seen as a deviant if he or she does not cheat. Similarly, the norms of a college fraternity or sorority group may endorse premarital sexual relations. As a result, most of its members may engage in such behavior. Any member who does not, because he or she has internalized norms that define such behavior as "wrong" or "immoral," will be considered a deviant by the group.

380

SOCIAL COMPARISON THEORY. The tenets of **social comparison theory** explain deviance by claiming that those who violate the norms of a particular group are identifying themselves with another group. This other group has norms that are incompatible with those of the group to which the person objectively belongs. Thus, a youngster who is forced by his parents to join the Boy Scouts may identify with the neighborhood gang. By violating the norms of the scout group he is conforming to the expectations of the gang. The individual's reference group in this instance is different from his membership group. Moreover, it is psychologically more satisfying to him to behave in accordance with the norms of his reference group than with those of his membership group.

Apart from specific theories, it can be stated as a general principle that deviance in groups is most likely to occur when there is a low degree of consensus, task interdependence, and social solidarity (Crosbie, 1975). Moreover, research has shown that in groups which are in the process of formation and stabilization, high-status members will be most likely to conform to the group norms, while low-status ones are most apt to deviate from them. However, as the group structure solidifies and group interaction becomes routinized, high-status members are more likely to deviate from group norms (Crosbie, 1975). Consequently, medium-status members are the most likely to conform to group norms, while low- and high-status members are most apt to violate them.

## SOCIAL CONTROL IN GROUPS

Groups cannot tolerate too much deviance from their members. If a significant number of members consistently deviate from the norms of a group, the very existence of the group is threatened. Social control refers to the strategies that the group uses to deal with those members who violate group norms. How much deviance a group can tolerate before it resorts to harsh measures of social control depends in part on the nature and purpose of the group. Military groups, politically radical cadres, and street gangs, for example, are likely to have a low threshold for deviance, and thus utilize extreme measures to punish those who deviate (Nixon, 1979). On the other hand, clubs, sports teams, and friendship groups are apt to have a high threshold for deviance among their members and consequently use mild punishments.

When deviance does occur in groups, what are the social control mechanisms that may come into play to reduce the deviance? Crosbie (1975) has discussed four mechanisms that groups may use to deal with those who violate norms. They are rewarding conformity to norms, punishing violation of norms, activation of commitment, and normative redefinition.

REWARDING CONFORMITY. Groups reward members who conform to their norms by giving them esteem and status. These things are usually valued by members, and thus they will conform in order to receive them. In cases where these rewards are not enough to bring about conformity, greater ones may be offered. Examples would be allowing a member to have more decision-making power or become more actively involved in the group's activities.

**Cooptation** also may be used as a strategy to prevent or deal with deviance. This mechanism refers to the process of giving positions of leadership to members who are expected to deviate or who have deviated from the group rules. Similarly, articulate and assertive people, those

**Rewards and Punishments.** All groups functionally demand conformity to their norms and goals. Consistent violations of these requirements can result in various types of negative sanctions, including temporary or permanent exclusion. (Judy S. Gelles/Stock, Boston)

often seen as critics or wave makers, frequently are placed in positions of authority or leadership, with the intent of eliminating or stifling nonconformity on their part.

Each of these responses enable the norm-violator to have more influence over group activities, a situation which consequently, it is believed, will give the deviant greater satisfaction as a member of the group. As a result, he or she is likely to be more motivated to conform to the group's norms (Crosbie, 1975).

PUNISHMENT.   More likely than not, however, the group will punish those who deviate from its norms. Punishments run the gamut from nasty looks to the use of physical violence. Members may even be expelled from the group in some cases. The form of punishment given,

as we indicated, depends on the group's threshold for deviance, the nature of the deviance, and the status of the person who deviated from the norms.

The influence of the deviant's status in determining punishment was clearly shown in a naturalistic experiment conducted by Gerson (1967). The experimenter told members of a fraternity that a member was caught duplicating and selling the fraternity's exams. Some fraternity members were told that the culprit was a high-status member, others were informed that he was a medium-status member, and still others were given the name of someone who was of low status. When asked about the punishment which should be given to the offender, fraternity members who were led to believe that the offender was of high status

▼

# BOX 9-2. Research on Group Dynamics

**Much of the research on small groups involves sophisticated observation through two-way mirrors and video recordings by which every action (verbal or physical) on the part of any group may be classified and analyzed as a means of explaining the various structures and dynamics of social groups. One of the foremost social psychologists in this area of sociological research is Robert F. Bales of Harvard University. Figure 9-6 depicts one of the techniques, known as Interaction Process Analysis, that Bales (1979; 1950) has devised and employs in the observation and analysis of social groups. This method focuses on overt action in terms of both the expressive-integrative and instrumental-adaptive dimensions. Every overt act (for example, gesture, remark, statement) that occurs in a group is classified in one of twelve categories. Each of these categories is based on one of three basic functions that relate to the problem-solving and goal-attainment tasks of groups: communication (exchange of information), evaluation (more-or-less shared attitudes), and control (decision making). One fascinating application of this technique (Strodtbeck et al., 1957) involved the study of a jury in the course of its deliberations. ▲**

382

suggested minor forms of punishments, while those who thought that the norm-violator was of low status recommended severe sanctions.

High-status members are likely to be immune to harsh punishments because of their accumulation of **idiosyncrasy credit** (Hollander, 1958). These members have high status because they have made numerous and significant contributions to the group. They have been very instrumental in helping the group achieve its goals. As a result, group members will be more tolerant of high-status members when they deviate from the norms. The members feel indebted to such persons and are thus reluctant to punish them severely. On the other hand, high-status members may be more vulnerable to harsh sanctions than low-status members when they commit major violations of group norms (Crosbie, 1975).

ACTIVATION OF COMMITMENT. When people violate the norms of a group, other members may remind them that it is important to be loyal to the group and that they have a moral obligation to conform to the standards of the group. They may be told that the group has rewarded them with certain benefits and that it is their duty to behave in accordance with its expectations. An example of this mechanism occurs when a gang member refuses to participate in some caper and is reminded by other members that the group helped him or her out in the past or that he or she took an oath to go along with the members' decisions when granted admission to the gang. If the group can make the deviant member feel guilty for violating its norms, further acts of deviance by that member will be unlikely.

NORMATIVE REDEFINITION. If the above-cited mechanisms of social control are not successful in curbing an individual's deviant behavior, members may redefine the deviant behavior as acceptable. They may expand the realm of what constitutes acceptable behavior to include the behavior of that person. Such normative redefinition is especially likely to occur when the person violating the norms is of high status and has proved to be very valuable to the group in helping it to achieve its objectives. For example, the deviant may have some rare talents or skills that are useful to the group. Normative redefinition is also likely to occur when the deviance is fairly widespread among members. Let us suppose, for example, that the norms of a group prohibit smoking during meetings. If a high-status member smokes, or if many members do, the norms may be redefined to allow smoking but only in a certain part of the room. In the extreme case, smoking may be allowed in any section of the room.

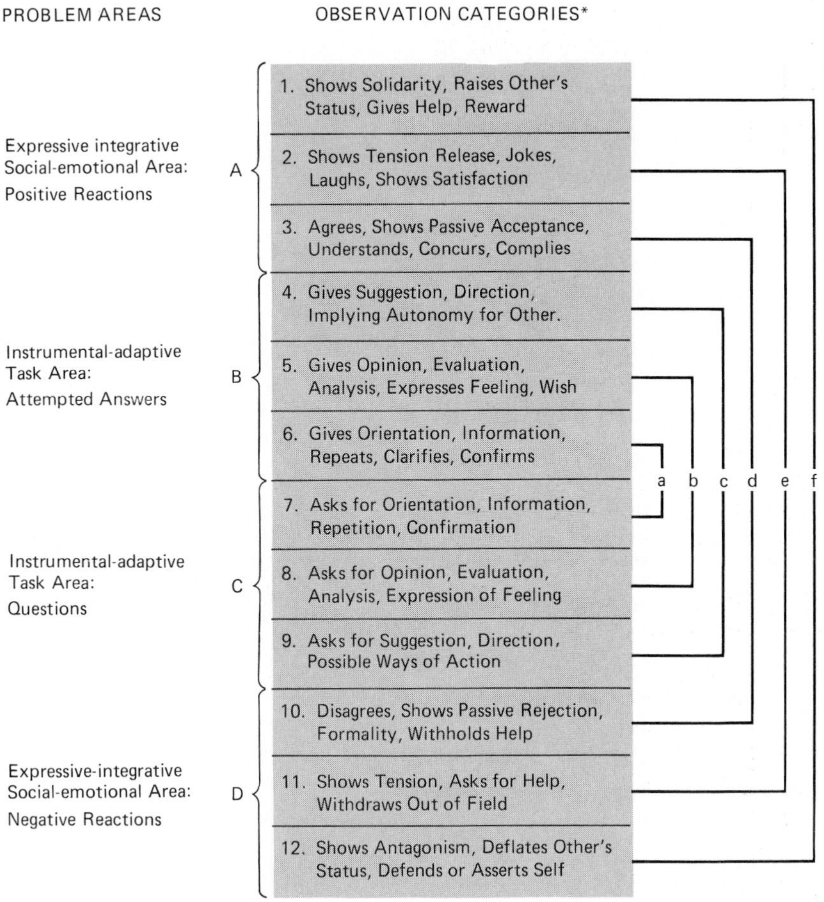

▼

PROBLEM AREAS                    OBSERVATION CATEGORIES*

| | | |
|---|---|---|
| Expressive integrative Social-emotional Area: Positive Reactions | A | 1. Shows Solidarity, Raises Other's Status, Gives Help, Reward |
| | | 2. Shows Tension Release, Jokes, Laughs, Shows Satisfaction |
| | | 3. Agrees, Shows Passive Acceptance, Understands, Concurs, Complies |
| Instrumental-adaptive Task Area: Attempted Answers | B | 4. Gives Suggestion, Direction, Implying Autonomy for Other. |
| | | 5. Gives Opinion, Evaluation, Analysis, Expresses Feeling, Wish |
| | | 6. Gives Orientation, Information, Repeats, Clarifies, Confirms |
| Instrumental-adaptive Task Area: Questions | C | 7. Asks for Orientation, Information, Repetition, Confirmation |
| | | 8. Asks for Opinion, Evaluation, Analysis, Expression of Feeling |
| | | 9. Asks for Suggestion, Direction, Possible Ways of Action |
| Expressive-integrative Social-emotional Area: Negative Reactions | D | 10. Disagrees, Shows Passive Rejection, Formality, Withholds Help |
| | | 11. Shows Tension, Asks for Help, Withdraws Out of Field |
| | | 12. Shows Antagonism, Deflates Other's Status, Defends or Asserts Self |

*A Subclassification of System Problems to Which Each Pair of Categories is Most Relevant:

a. Problems of Orientation.          d. Problems of Decision.
b. Problems of Evaluation.          e. Problems of Tension-management.
c. Problems of Control.               f. Problems of Integration.

FIGURE 9-6   Bales' Categories from the Analysis of Small Group Interaction. Source: Robert F. Bales, *Interaction Process Analysis: A Method for the Study of Small Groups.* Cambridge, MA: Addison-Wesley, 1950.

▼ # Leadership in Groups

When members of a group get together it is obvious that some members seem to have more influence than others. One or two persons will emerge who will take charge and either tell others what to do or strongly influence their behavior. They will define the goals of the group, suggest a means for achieving them, coordinate the activities of members, and try to maintain group harmony and solidarity. A person who does such things is called a **leader.** The functions that leaders provide are crucial; without them it is unlikely that groups would achieve their goals, or even be able to exist as going concerns for any significant period of time.

## TYPES OF GROUP LEADERSHIP

We usually speak in terms which suggest that a group has only one leader. However, Bales (1951) pointed out several years ago that in many groups two different types of leaders commonly emerge. One is called the task or instrumental leader, the other is the socio-emotional or expressive leader.

### THE INSTRUMENTAL LEADER. The **instrumental leader** is primarily concerned with having the group solve its problems and attain its goals. This leader will propose solutions for the consideration of the group, encourage others to offer solutions, coordinate the activities of the group, and engage in behavior that is apt to help the group attain its objectives. Such leaders have a no-nonsense, let's-get-down-to-work orientation.

### THE EXPRESSIVE LEADER. The individual who emerges as the **expressive leader** is concerned mainly with having the group function in a friendly, harmonious manner. He or she may crack jokes when things get too serious, attempt to arbitrate conflicts that develop among members, and in general do things that will create a positive and pleasant emotional climate. Such a person is most interested in elevating and maintaining the morale and spirits of the group.

According to Bales and Slater (1955), leadership differentiation occurs because the behavior required by the instrumental leader is incompatible with that demanded by the expressive leader. To get the group to complete its task successfully and rapidly demands actions that may create feelings of hostility among members. The instrumental leader, furthermore, might not have the time to joke around or be concerned with everyone's feelings as is the case for the expressive leader. Since both types of behavior are needed because they contribute to group functioning, leadership specialists emerge. This distinction is often found in the traditional American family, in which the husband-father-breadwinner performs the instrumental leadership, while the wife-mother-homemaker seves as the expressive leader.

Leadership differentiation, however, may not always emerge. Borgatta and his associates (1954) found that one person may make significant contributions to both the instrumental and the expressive functions. However, individuals who simultaneously and over a relatively long period of time are able to provide both instrumental and expressive leadership are very rare. Hence, nearly every group has at least two leaders and sometimes more. Usually, when a group is confronted with the problem of leadership, it selects only one leader and assigns both roles to the same person. More likely than not this individual is the most popular one. Leaders generally do not perform both roles for long, because individuals who direct group activities or engage primarily in instrumental behavior tend to lose popularity. In one experiment on small groups, Slater (1955) found

384

that in the first meeting most members gave top rating to the same individual for both expressive and instrumental leadership, but by the end of the fourth meeting, only 8 percent of the members still considered the leader likeable. Original leaders may retain the instrumental role, but usually another member of the group emerges to assume the expressive leadership role. It is not surprising, then, that when put to a choice, most leaders give up the instrumental role in favor of popularity (Bales, 1953).

## THEORIES OF LEADERSHIP

Why do some persons emerge as leaders while others do not? Which factors help determine who will be the leaders of the group? Are leaders born or made? We shall discuss three theories of leadership that attempt to deal with these and related questions. These theories are the personality, style, and situational explanations of leadership.

PERSONALITY THEORY OF LEADERSHIP.    The earliest theories of leadership were based on the assumption that leaders possess certain personality characteristics that distinguish them from nonleaders. Also known as the "great man" view of leadership (Borgatta et al., 1955), this approach maintains that leaders possess qualities and capacities that enable them to carry out leadership functions with great success. Numerous studies have been made to determine the distinctive personality characteristics of leaders. These studies indicated that, compared to nonleaders, leaders tend to be more intelligent, self-confident, healthy-minded, extroverted, assertive, energetic, verbose, and sensitive to the needs and feelings of people (Gibb, 1969). Bales (1958) more specifically found that in most groups different types of personality are associated with different types of roles, namely, those of the task-versus-maintenance variety.

The majority of studies attempting to discover distinctive personality characteristics that are related to leadership indicate that leaders have more positive traits than nonleaders. However, some psychohistorians (those who analyze the biographies of distinguished leaders) argue that many people may become leaders because of inferiority feelings. Such a thesis is advanced especially in the field of politics. In order to compensate psychologically for inferiority feelings and negative self-attitudes, political leaders, it is argued, often manifest a strong power motive (Lasswell, 1948). It is a drive for personal power, rather than altruistic objectives, that supposedly motivates them to become great leaders. There is some research evidence to confirm this thesis with appropriate qualifications in terms of such things as the method of leadership selection and the nature of the leadership role (see DiRenzo, 1974a). Power, however, may not be the only attraction for leadership. Any number of other motives, such as prestige, fame, popularity, or material gain, can also provide sufficient incentive for individuals to assume leadership roles.

The correlation, nonetheless, between the personality traits mentioned and leadership is low. In addition, while some evidence suggests that someone who is a leader in one group will also be a leader in another one, other data contradict this finding. One study, for example, revealed that a person who was a leader in a group working on a mechanical problem did not become the leader of a group trying to solve an intellectual problem (Carter & Nixon, 1949). It seems, then, that whether a leader in one group assumes that role in another group depends, at least in part, on the nature and goals of the group; one's personality is not in itself sufficient for leadership.

Another criticism of the personality trait theory is sometimes raised: Do particular psychological characteristics influence a person to become a leader, or does leadership itself result

385

▼

386

in the development of the traits? For example, being self-assured, assertive, and perceptive may help someone to become a leader. However, it is also plausible to argue that a person who becomes a leader will tend to develop these characteristics.

The resolution of these kinds of questions depends on a clear specification of which particular elements of personality constitute the subject of discourse. Some characteristics pertain to personality structure which, as we mentioned in Chapter 6, constitute functional requirements for particular social roles. Other personality characteristics may constitute only nonessential and quite variable elements of personality content. These latter aspects of personality may indeed be the consequences of role experience.

STYLE THEORY OF LEADERSHIP. This approach to leadership focuses on how leadership is exercised. It attempts to determine which methods, or styles, of leadership are most effective. There are three basic styles of leadership: autocratic, democratic, and laissez faire.

The *autocratic leader* is one who does not allow the group members to participate in the decision-making process. Such a leader rules with an iron hand, refuses to share power, and is quite inflexible.

The *democratic leader* allows members to be an integral part of the decision-making process. Decisions are made through the use of the vote or consensus. Such leaders are flexible, open-minded, and receptive to the suggestions of others.

The *laissez faire leader* does not provide any structure, guidance, or direction to the group. Such an individual maintains an extreme hands-off policy. The group is allowed to make all the decisions without any input from the leader.

An interesting study to determine the consequences that different styles of leadership have for the group was made by Lewin and his colleagues (1939). They manipulated the three different leadership styles in groups of 10-year-old boys who were working on hobby projects. The adult leaders were trained in all three styles of leadership and were switched from one group to another every few weeks. In this way no particular leadership style was associated with any specific person.

The autocratic leader set all goals, outlines, and policies. Members of his group were not allowed to have any influence on the activities of the group. Moreover, the boys in this group had no choice about which tasks they would be doing. They were assigned to different tasks by the leader. In contrast, the democratic leader allowed members to decide how to achieve the goals of the group. These boys could select their work partners and the type of task they wanted to do. The leader also participated actively in the group. The laissez faire leader permitted the group to do whatever they wanted. He did not give any direction or advice to it. The group was left alone most of the time.

Results clearly showed that the style of leadership has significant consequences for group interaction, productivity, and morale. Boys in the group that was subjected to an autocratic leader had many negative feelings, some of which were expressed and others repressed. Hostility, conflict, and property damage occurred in two of the autocratically led groups. In addition, boys in such groups tended to select scapegoats as targets for their aggressive feelings.

The democratic style of leadership resulted in a strong degree of group cohesion. The boys in this group completed their tasks and had fun doing so. Moreover, the quality of the work produced in the democratically led group was higher than in the other two groups. Boys in this group showed more maturity and motivation. For example, when the leader in the democratic group left the room, the boys continued to work; whereas when the leader of the autocratic group left, the members stopped working. The laissez faire group did very little work, and the work that was done was of poor quality. Much horseplay was characteristic of the laissez faire group.

Another interesting finding emerged from this experiment. When a group changed from an autocratic to a laissez faire leader, there was a significant increase in hostility and aggression among the members. Presumably, the accumulated frustration and anger that built up in the boys when they were in the autocratic group found expression under the laissez faire style of leadership. Autocratic leadership in this study was less effective than democratic leadership in maintaining group solidarity and achieving goals. Democratic leadership, on the other hand, was more effective with regard to the durability of the group, the satisfaction of its members, and their productivity tasks (Berelson & Steiner, 1964). Both democratic and autocratic leadership, however, may require different types of personality and psychological qualities (see DiRenzo, 1974a). Highly structured social groups, such as a police force or a military unit, would be quite ineffective with a democratic type of leadership. Correspondingly, democratic structures would be highly ineffective with authoritarian leadership.

SITUATIONAL THEORY OF LEADER-SHIP. A third approach to leadership contends that the nature of the specific group and the particular problems to be solved, as well as the expectations of the membership, are the most important factors that determine who will emerge as the leader of the group. This theory argues, for example, that just because a person may be a superb squad leader in combat does not necessarily mean that he will emerge as the leader of a group trying to raise funds for a political campaign. The objectives of the two groups, and most likely even the composition

of their membership, are different. The essence of the situational perspective of leadership is captured in a statement by Shaw (1981:331) that "a trait that is positively related to leadership in one situation may be unrelated or even negatively related in another." In order for a person to emerge as an effective leader in a particular group, he or she must have skills and knowledge that are relevant to the task with which the group is involved.

Some societies and cultures traditionally favor a particular type of leader. Autocratic leadership is often both expected and necessary in more traditional and primitive societies. Increasingly it is the case in the United States that democratic leadership is the desired mode. Autocratic leadership has become quite unpopular, however effective it might be in a given time and place. Thus, the situational view claims that leadership is not generalizable from one type of group or situation to another. Consequently, it disputes the notion that leaders have qualities that nonleaders lack. An individual who is highly effective in one type of situation may be very ineffective in another.

The three approaches to leadership that we have examined are not mutually exclusive. Leadership phenomena probably can be explained most thoroughly by using each of these theories in combination with one or two of the others. Leadership, like all other human behavior, is too complex to be reduced to an absolutely sociological or absolutely psychological set of circumstances.

# Group Problem Solving and Decision Making

Whenever a problem has to be solved, or a decision made, do you think that an effective solution or decision is more likely to come from an individual working alone or from a group

**387**

▼

effort? Are individuals or are groups most apt to make risky decisions? Does working within a group stifle or facilitate a person's creativity? Such questions are of more than academic interest. Many significant decisions, ones that affect the life of every person, are made by groups. Congressional committees and subcommittees formulate policies that may become the law of the land. Crucial domestic and foreign policy decisions are made by the President's inner circle of trusted advisers. Whether a corporation should market a new product, build another plant, or lay off some of its employees are questions that usually are decided by corporate officials interacting within a group. Such decisions, moreover, are becoming increasingly more typical even within families. Clearly, it seems that decisions made by a group are assumed to be superior to those made by a single individual, or several working alone. Is this a correct assumption?

Social psychologists have been concerned with this issue for a long time. Indeed, as early as 1897, one psychologist found that boys could ride on a bicycle and wind a fishing reel faster when others were present that when they were alone. The notion that an individual's performance on a task will improve if he or she is doing it in the presence of others is called **social facilitation.** Research indicates, however, that the social facilitation effect occurs only when the task a person is performing has been previously well-learned and is relatively simple (Zajonc, 1966). For tasks that require complex mental operations, or in cases in which people arrive at the solution via trial and error, the presence of others may interfere with performance. Moreover, research shows that when change is desired, it is typically more effective to influence people as members of groups than to do so in an isolated, individual-by-individual manner (Berelson & Steiner, 1964). Nonetheless, are two heads really better than one? Or do too many chefs spoil the soup? These are quite complex questions.

# WORKING TOGETHER OR ALONE

With respect to many types of physical work there is no question that individuals working together will be more efficient and do a better job than one person working alone. Imagine how long it would take one person to build a modern skyscraper or a housing complex. It would probably not be possible. With a clear-cut division of labor—each person doing a specialized task—buildings are constructed efficiently and rapidly. The same is true of a large number and variety of activities.

Does the same principle hold true, however, for intellectual tasks? The results of numerous studies designed to answer this question are conflicting. The answer depends on the type of intellectual or mental task being performed and the individual to whom the group is being compared. There are three basic kinds of mental tasks that have been used in experiments to determine whether the solutions arrived at by groups are better than those generated by individuals working alone. These are judgmental or observational tasks, problem-solving tasks, and creative tasks.

JUDGMENTAL TASKS. Would baseball be better off if it had several umpires assigned to each base to call the plays instead of just one? Would you be wise in having several of your friends help you estimate the number of gumdrops in a large jar, or should you make the estimate alone? In order to say that groups do better than individuals on judgmental tasks we would have to show that the responses of the group were more accurate than those of the most competent individual working alone. Studies indicate that, on the whole, group judgments are somewhat more correct than those made by individuals. After reviewing the literature in this area, Shaw (1981:59) states: "In general, it appears that group judgments are seldom less accurate than the average individ-

**Decision-Making.** Research suggests that group activity is more effective for judgmental and problem-solving tasks. Individuals working alone show a superiority in performance for tasks that require creativity. (© Bruce Davidson/Magnum)

ual judgment and are often superior." The adequacy of the group estimate, however, is clearly not always better than that of the most skilled individual.

PROBLEM-SOLVING TASKS.    In order to determine whether groups or individuals working alone are better problem-solvers, subjects are usually asked to solve a problem while they are in a group and then again when they are alone, or vice versa. Examples of the types of problems used in these experiments include making words from a given set of letters, puzzles, deciphering codes, and syllogistic reasoning exercises. Shaw (1981) sums up the findings of many studies by concluding that groups produce more and better solutions to problems

than do individuals, although the differences in overall time required for solution are not consistently better for individuals or groups. Evidence suggests that group decision making is likely to be more effective in complex problems that require specialized or technical knowledge because perhaps a broader range of expertise and skills can be used.

CREATIVE TASKS.    An advertising executive, A. F. Osborn (1957) developed a method called *brainstorming*, which he claimed could result in a greater number of more creative solutions to problems. A classical example of the type of problem the brainstorming technique was designed to solve would be, not so surprisingly, the creation of an advertising cam-

▼

paign to sell a particular product or type of service. Osborn contended that more and better ideas could be generated by a group as opposed to individuals working alone if the following rules were used:

1. Members of the group must freely convey any idea that comes to mind, regardless of whether they feel it has any merit.
2. Criticisms of the ideas generated are not allowed.
3. Ideas and suggestions which are elaborations or refinements of previously expressed notions are encouraged.

The evidence on brainstorming does not support Osborn's views. The majority of experiments that compared the creative output of individuals working alone (under brainstorming principles) with brainstorming groups indicated that the individuals generated more ideas (Lamm & Trommsdorf, 1973). Moreover, the view that groups produce higher-quality ideas than individuals also was not supported by the data. Creativity, it seems, tends to be a highly personal function.

## GROUPTHINK

When a group gets together for the purpose of making a decision, there is apt to be a strong tendency toward consensus. This pressure toward and desire for agreement is especially likely to be present if the group is very cohesive and does not have immediate access to information that will discredit its decision and if its leader supports the decision.

Irving L. Janis (1983), a social psychologist, coined the term **groupthink** to refer to a type of decision making that occurs in cohesive groups when the main concerns of its members are to perpetuate harmony, avoid conflict, and develop unanimity of opinion. In order to attain these goals, critical-analytical thought processes are suspended. Janis states that groupthink emerges when the members of a decision-making group desire to refrain from criticizing each other's ideas or those of their leader and assume a stance of self-censorship. As a consequence, they adopt a soft line of criticism, even in their own thinking. Members are amiable and seek complete concurrence on every important issue, with no bickering or conflict to spoil the cozy, we-feeling atmosphere.

Janis maintains that groupthink is not an inevitable consequence of group decision making. However, when members have similar values and philosophies, like each other, and find themselves in a crisis, chances are high that groupthink will occur. Even if groupthink does emerge, it does not automatically have to result in poor decisions. The probability that poor decisions will be reached, however, is high because critical and rational modes of thought are temporarily suspended. Such a situation is all the more likely to occur when the unanimity and cohesion of the group are combined with a sense of invulnerability.

Janis argues that groupthink was responsible for several major political fiascoes in recent decades. Among them are the American lack of preparedness for the attack on Pearl Harbor that effectively commenced World War II, the invasion of the Bay of Pigs in Cuba during the Kennedy administration, the escalation of the Vietnamese war in the Johnson presidency, the Watergate cover-up that led to the resignation of President Richard M. Nixon, the mission designed by the Carter cabinet to rescue the American hostages during the Iranian revolution, and the overwhelming defeat, by a unanimous veto in the Senate in the midst of enormous public protest, of legislation proposed by the Reagan administration to make drastic reductions in Social Security benefits.

390

Let us look more closely at one of these major significant events in American political history. After the invasion of Cuba in 1961 turned out to be a total failure, President John F. Kennedy asked, "How could we have been so stupid?" Clearly, Kennedy and such inner-circle advisers as Robert McNamara, the secretary of defense; Dean Rusk, the secretary of state; Arthur Schlesinger, Jr., the famed historian; and Robert Kennedy, the president's brother and attorney general, were not stupid people. They had the intellectual tools to discern the many flaws that the plan had. Why, then, did they support and order the plan implemented? They did so, according to Janis, because they were the victims of groupthink. Even the advisers who had doubts about the plan repressed them. The pressure toward uniformity of opinion and the desire not to "rock the boat" resulted in a need for some members to censor their own dissent. Schlesinger, for example, conveyed his misgivings about the invasion to the president via memoranda, but he was not able to voice his objections during meetings at the White House. Schlesinger (1965:225–259) writes:

> In the months after the Bay of Pigs I bitterly reproached myself for having kept so silent during those crucial discussions in the cabinet room. I can only explain my failure to do more than raise a few timid questions by reporting that one's impulse to blow the whistle on this nonsense was simply undone by the circumstances of the discussion. Our meetings were taking place in a curious atmosphere of assumed consensus. Had one senior adviser opposed the adventure, I believe that Kennedy would have cancelled it. Not one spoke against it.

Thus, while he was able to criticize the plan by communicating with the president directly, Schlesinger could not get himself to voice his disapproval within the group context because of the pressure exerted by others not to "upset the apple cart." Harmony, consensus, and uniformity of thought took priority over everything else, including the need to make good decisions.

Collective desires for consensus and harmonious relationships result in what Janis terms "an illusion of unanimity." The unanimity of opinion that existed was not real; it was an illusion. The group members did not convey their doubts and criticisms of the plan because each one thought that he was the only one who had any. Indeed, it is now clear that even Kennedy, Rusk, and McNamara held different premises about the invasion. Results of recent experiments (Hall, 1971) indicate that individuals can be trained to accept divergences of opinion and thus to avoid groupthink in the interest of achieving a more effective kind of decision making (see Box 9-3).

**391**

## THE RISKY SHIFT

A commonly held belief about group decisions is that they are considerably more conservative and cautious than decisions made by separate individuals alone. It is believed that the group context stifles creativity and innovative thought. Individuals may be reluctant to make bold and original suggestions for fear that they may be criticized or ridiculed by members of the group. As a consequence, group members, it is felt, will play it safe by offering comments and ideas that they feel will be acceptable to the group. This assumption has been challenged, however, by the results of a series of studies which show that decisions made in a group context were bolder and more daring than those made by the same individuals working alone (Stoner, 1961; Wallach et al., 1962). This finding has come to be known as the **risky shift** phenomenon.

In practically all of the studies designed to focus on this type of problem, the "choice dilemma" questionnaire has been used. Subjects in this procedure are asked to indicate how they would advise hypothetical individuals to deal

▼

## BOX 9-3.  Avoiding Groupthink

How can groupthink be avoided? What steps could be taken to lessen the chances of it arising during the decision-making process? Janis (1982) has offered several suggestions and strategies aimed at preventing groupthink. Among the more significant are the following:

1. At the onset of the meeting the group leader should alert group members to the causes and consequences of groupthink.
2. Members should be encouraged to evaluate critically all recommendations made. The leader also must show that he or she can and will accept criticism from members.
3. Those who ask a group to make a decision should not indicate their own preference or expectations as to the outcome.
4. An outside planning and evaluation group should be set up to work on the same question.
5. The group should ask outside experts to question each member about his or her views in a critical fashion.
6. Members should alternately play the role of devil's advocate, challenging those who support the majority opinion.
7. If the decision has to do with relations with other organizations, a significant portion of time should be devoted to studying their warning signals and intentions.
8. Group members should be invited to evaluate the merits of the group's decisions with trusted associates and to report their reactions.
9. From time to time the group should meet in subgroups with different leaders.
10. Once a decision is reached, the group should schedule another meeting for the purpose of allowing each member to communicate any doubts or second thoughts he or she may have developed about the decision.

These suggestions for avoiding groupthink have not been empirically tested. It is interesting to note, however, that President Kennedy incorporated several of these techniques in subsequent consultations with his advisers. Indeed, utilizing these techniques, the same group of advisers that had been involved in the Bay of Pigs fiasco subsequently resolved the Cuban missile crisis in a much more effective fashion in 1962. ▲

with certain imaginary dilemmas. Usually subjects must choose between several alternative decisions. Some of them are very attractive but also extremely risky. Others are less rewarding, yet much safer. For example, in one study subjects are told that an engineer must decide whether to leave a safe, secure job for one that will pay him considerably more money and give him an opportunity to become a part owner.

Job security at the new company, however, would be low since there was no way of knowing whether it could successfully compete against older, more financially secure, companies. Subjects are then asked individually to indicate the lowest odds of success they would want prior to suggesting that the hypothetical employee should take the new job. After that, the subjects collectively discuss the situation among themselves and again give suggestions. In the majority of cases subjects select the riskier alternative following their group discussion. Moreover, when a sample of the original subjects was asked to make the decision again, it was determined that they selected the riskier choice. The effects of the group discussion thus persisted over time. More recent research, however, has revealed that the risky shift is by no means absolute. Not all groups are more daring than their individual members.

Social psychologists were intrigued with the discovery of the risky shift phenomenon for two reasons. First, it was an unexpected and surprising finding. It went counter to a long-held belief that seemed to be very plausible. Social scientists become particularly excited when research yields unexpected findings. Secondly, the implications of the existence of the risky shift phenomenon were important. As we indicated at the beginning of this chapter, many of the most significant policies and decisions are those generated by groups. If it is true that decisions reached within a group context will tend to be more extreme and riskier than those made by individuals, then perhaps foreign policy decisions, and a host of similar types of decisions, are more likely to yield detrimental consequences for those concerned.

Once the risky shift phenomenon was firmly documented, several explanations were put forward to account for it. They include such hypotheses as the diffusion of responsibility, persuasion by leaders, and risk as a cultural value.

DIFFUSION OF RESPONSIBILITY. One explanation for the risky shift phenomenon may be the principle of the **diffusion of responsibility** (Clark, 1971). This principle states that when people are in groups they are more likely to make risky choices because if they turn out to be poor decisions each individual will have to bear only a portion of the responsibility. The blame for, and the negative conse-

quences of, a bad choice will be diffused among all of the members of the group.

PERSUASION BY LEADERS. This hypothesis claims that leaders of a group usually are more likely than other members to want to take risks and to choose the bolder alternative. They then use their position of leadership and authority to persuade other members to select the riskier alternative.

RISK AS A CULTURAL VALUE. Proponents of this explanation (Brown, 1965) maintain that individuals shift from a cautious to a risky choice whenever they are part of a group because riskiness is perceived by them as a group value. Since they do not wish to deviate from the values or norms of the group, individuals make bolder decisions because of social and cultural pressure. Moreover, the American culture places a high value on risk taking. People who take risks are admired and their activities are well-publicized. Thus, most of us would like to think of ourselves as risk-takers. We certainly would not want to give group members the impression that we are cowardly or overly cautious. Therefore, people will tend to opt for the riskier decision when they are part of a group that is involved in the decision-making process.

## GROUP POLARIZATION

As research on the risky shift phenomenon continued, it was discovered that while group decisions usually tended to be riskier than individual ones, this was not always the case. In fact, several studies showed that sometimes the group decision was more cautious than the one made on an individual basis (Deaux & Wrightsman, 1983). Thus, under certain conditions there was a group shift toward caution rather than toward risk.

In order to account for group shifts toward

**393**

▼

both risk and caution the group polarization hypothesis was developed (Moscovici & Doise, 1974). The hypothesis of **group polarization** contends that after discussion within a group, members' choices will be extreme versions of choices that were favored by the majority of people prior to the group discussion. Thus, for example, if most of the members were moderately inclined to a given course of action before the group discussion, they would be strongly in favor of it after the discussion. By the same token, if the majority of individuals were opposed to a particular policy before they discussed it in a group setting, they would strongly oppose it afterward. As long as group members have either a positive or negative opinion toward the issue being considered, group discussion will result in an intensification of the initially held attitudes.

Group polarization enables us to account for group shifts toward both risk and conservatism. A variety of studies have supported the group polarization explanation. One study, for example, reports that group discussion made initially prejudiced students more prejudiced, while the group consisting of unprejudiced students became even less prejudiced after discussion (Myers & Bishop, 1970).

## STAGES IN GROUP DECISION MAKING

Quite apart from the nature of decisions that are reached in group deliberation, research (Bales & Strodtbeck, 1951) has shown that much decision making in groups occurs in a four-step procedure that demonstrates the role of both instrumental and expressive behavior.

The first phase is *orientation* which consists of collecting information and analyzing the facts pertinent to the problem at hand. The second stage is *evaluation* during which members offer their assessments of the issues and also respond to the opinions of others. In the third phase of *decision making* emotional tensions may escalate as members form factions and coalitions. Hostility often develops, but eventually there emerges a majority that imposes its will on the minority. The fourth stage of *control*, achieving or reachieving group solidarity, develops once a final decision has been made. This final stage consists of a variety of behavior directed at restoring harmony within the group, and this objective requires a modicum of expressive or socioemotional behavior that is essentially positive. Members may engage in joking or horseplay which eases tensions and restores group solidarity.

# Personality and Groups

Insofar as personality represents a predisposition to behavior in a particular manner, one can obviously expect that the personality of group members significantly affects both the structure and the dynamics of social groups. Throughout this chapter we have cited some of the particular relationships that exist between the personality of group members and the functioning of groups. In this section we shall focus on several of these kinds of relationships regarding some of the patterns of personality that are present in groups and the significance that they have for both group structure and group dynamics.

## PERSONALITY AND GROUP DYNAMICS

There is good, though somewhat limited, evidence that behavior in groups is dependent in part on the personality attributes of the group members (Shaw, 1981). Various kinds of studies have documented several specific dimensions by which personality structures and personality dynamics are both facilitative and inhibitive of group processes. Personalities of leaders in particular exert a strong influence on group processes. Here are a few of the more significant dimensions of personality that influence group dynamics.

AUTHORITARIANISM. Behavior in group settings has been found to correlate significantly with measures of authoritarianism (see Chapter 5). Available evidence reveals that, consistent with theoretical expectations, the influence of personality in this regard is an interactive one that depends on the structure of the particular group. When authoritarians are in positions of authority, they exert power; they are demanding, directive, and controlling in their relationships with those who are less powerful than themselves. On the other hand, when authoritarians are in a subordinate position, they are submissive and compliant; they accept their subordinate role. Similarly, leaders that emerge in groups composed of highly authoritarian persons tend to behave more autocratically than leaders emerging in groups composed of highly nonauthoritarian individuals (Shaw, 1981).

Authoritarian personalities prefer status-laden leadership, accept strongly directive and

▼

395

**Authoritarian Personalities.** Adolf Hitler and his Nazi followers are the quintessential examples of the authoritarian personality. Depending on the social circumstances, such a personality is either aggressive and controlling or submissive and compliant. (UPI/Bettmann Newsphotos)

▼ goal-oriented leadership, and regard the authoritarian leader as more effective than a democratic counterpart. Equalitarian personalities, on the other hand, accept authoritarian leadership only as the circumstances may require it, such as in times of crisis (Gibbs, 1954). These kinds of personalities show preference for expressive-type leaders. Authoritarian individuals, however, tend to conform to the norms of a group more closely than do nonauthoritarians (Shaw, 1981).

**396**

APPROACH-AVOIDANCE TENDENCIES. Some people have personality characteristics that induce them to approach and interact with others. These individuals are more likely to be cooperative, trustful, and likeable. They prefer to be involved in situations that involve them with people rather than with things. Those having a social-avoidance orientation display behavior that is the opposite of that manifested by people who have social-approach tendencies. Shaw observes that the relevant research shows that people having approach tendencies enhance social interaction, cohesiveness, and morale in groups and suppress competitiveness. Avoidance tendencies suppress friendliness and cohesiveness in groups (1981:194).

SOCIAL SENSITIVITY. Some people have the ability to perceive, detect, and respond to the needs, emotions, and preferences of others. They are better able to detect what other people believe and feel, even without being told directly. People who have these empathic or role-taking abilities are more likely to be accepted by other group members, to participate more actively than the average person, and to occupy positions of leadership (Shaw, 1981).

MACHIAVELLIANISM. Manipulation is a frequently observed tactic in the dynamics of social groups. It occurs on the part of leaders as well as other members who wish to influence or control the behavior of groups. Social psychologists in recent years have been exploring the dynamics of this process under the label of Machiavellianism. The fundamental principle of **Machiavellianism,** a philosophy that has little regard for conventional morality and ethics, is that the end justifies the means. Christie (1970) has devised various versions of a so-called Mach Scale, based on the classic writings of Niccolo Macchiavelli (1469–1527), who advocated the use of manipulation and deceit as methods of securing and holding political and social power, for the purpose of analyzing the type of personalities that tend toward the control and manipulation of other people. Here are some representative examples of items from selective dimensions of the Mach scale.

**Tactics**
*High Mach:* The best way to handle people is to tell them what they want to hear.
*Low Mach:* Honesty is the best policy in all cases.

**Perceptions of human nature**
*High Mach:* It is safest to assume that all people have a vicious streak and it will come out when they are given a chance.
*Low Mach:* Barnum was very wrong when he said, "There's a sucker born every minute."

**Morality**
*High Mach:* The most important thing in life is winning.
*Low Mach:* All in all, it is better to be humble and honest than important and dishonest.

Extensive research (Christie & Geis, 1970) shows that individuals who endorse high-Mach statements more often than low-Mach statements are more likely to use exploitative and manipulative tactics when dealing with others. Moreover, the significance of these findings for group formation and dynamics is revealed in that only in ambiguous, emotion-arousing, and face-to-face situations do high-Machs exert greater influence. Under these circumstances, high-Mach subjects tend to assume leadership. High-Machs also seem to be less susceptible to the influence of others and more accurate in evaluating other people and situations. These findings suggest significant qualifications in our discussions above regarding the influence of group members on decision making. Such influence is more likely to occur on the part of certain types of individuals rather than others. The dimension of personality, then, offers a further specification—a sociopsychological specification—of some of the principles of group dynamics.

## PERSONALITY AND GROUP PERFORMANCE

Would a task or decision-making group be more efficient if its members had similar or different types of personalities? Available evidence suggests that groups consisting of people with heterogeneous or dissimilar personality profiles perform more effectively than groups whose members are homogeneous in this respect (Shaw, 1981). Most of the studies concerned with personality have found, for example, that group efficiency and achievement are enhanced if one member is more dominant and assertive than the others (Ghiselli & Lodahl, 1958). These findings seem quite plausible in one sense. If the majority of group members had dominant personalities, they would all want to rule, and there would be continual struggle for power. As a consequence, the task of the group would be neglected because the energy of its members would be diverted to engagement in power struggles. On the other hand, if most of the members possessed submissive or capitulating types of personalities, there would be no one to assume leadership and make the necessary decisions.

There are also data to suggest that groups whose members differ on a variety of other personality characteristics are likely to have more success in problem-solving tasks than groups whose members have homogeneous personalities. In one study, subjects were divided into two groups. One group consisted of individuals who had ten similar personality traits, the other group was comprised of people who possessed ten dissimilar characteristics. The group whose subjects had different personality traits was more successful in solving a variety of problems than the group whose members had similar traits (Hoffman, 1959; Hoffman & Maier, 1961). The researchers who conducted these studies explained the results by contending that people who have different personalities also may have different ways or strategies of solving problems. Consequently, they may put forth a larger variety of possible solutions than groups whose members use only one or two problem-solving methods. The larger the number of possible solutions that are offered, the greater is the probability that one or several combined may comprise the correct or most effective solution.

Another reason why groups composed of members having heterogeneous personalities may do better than those whose members have homogeneous ones concerns the need for task specialization in groups. As we have seen, a group must deal with two fundamental problems if it is to function adequately and to endure as an ongoing concern. These are the instrumental and expressive problems. The evidence suggests, as we have shown, that those members who make important contributions in helping the group to solve its instrumental problems are not the same ones who deal with the expressive problems. This is the situation in most cases because the solution to each set of problems requires skills and competencies that are most apt to be possessed by people having different personality systems. The person who is the expressive leader needs to have an easygoing, tolerant, flexible type of personality. He or she has to be someone who is able to get along well with a diverse range of people and who has the knack of defusing tense, hostile

**397**

▼

situations. The instrumental leader, on the other hand, must be achievement-oriented and able to instill a sense of dedication and discipline to members of the group. He or she must be able to delegate authority and to determine which members should be doing which kinds of work. The personality of the instrumental leader, then, is likely to be quite different in many respects from that of the expressive leader.

Our concern with personality here has dealt exclusively with personality content—beliefs, values, attitudes, traits, motives, capacities, and skills. In these terms, a heterogeneity of personality seems to be a more functional situation for group dynamics. Evidence relating to personality structure, however, suggests that a homogeneity of personality types comprises the most efficacious situation for group performance. Hence, the question of personality and group performance is not a simple one. Any answer requires, first of all, a specification of the principal dimensions of personality.

## NETWORK STRUCTURE OF PERSONALITY TYPES

Research during the past decade has sought to distinguish types of personality associated with particular modes of interaction in small groups. Bales (1979) has specified a multidimensional field into which members of small groups can be plotted on the basis of observed behavior, conversational imagery, or expressed values. This model, known as Symlog, focuses on three dimensions of group dynamics: (1) upward-downward, referring to the relative dominance or submissiveness of group members; (2) positive-negative, corresponding to friendly versus hostile orientations; and (3) forward-backward which relates to instrumental behavior as opposed to expressive orientations. These dimensions of analysis yield a classification of twenty-seven types of group roles, each of which is distinguished by a different kind of personality profile.

## COALITIONS AND ALLIANCES

Among the basic processes that occur in many groups, or actually take place between them, is the formation of coalitions and alliances. Obviously, as we already noted in this chapter, there are many bases for cleavage and consensus both within and between groups. Another dimension, one not explored as frequently, is that of the compatibility that exists among the personalities of group members and the significance that this matter has for decision making in groups. There is some evidence to suggest that coalitions and alliances, as specific manifestations of consensus and cleavage, are in part a function of significant similarities in the underlying personality structure of the respective groups.

DiRenzo (1967a) in a study of political groups in the Italian parliament has shown that those groups which enter into government coalitions, or form alliances among themselves, are characterized by significant similarities in the modal personality of their members. Correspondingly, those political groups that are not selected for these purposes reveal significant differences in modal personality. These data show, of course, that personality is not the sole determination upon which alliances and coalitions are formed. Some political groups revealing no significant differences in modal personality either were excluded or excluded themselves from many political alignments. Factors other than personality, particularly that of political ideology in this case, also are important in the formation of coalitions and alliances. Nonetheless, this study is important because it demonstrates that whether groups agree or differ in ideology, only those that share a basic and significant similarity in modal personality actually enter into coalitions and alliances.

One of the crucial questions that these data suggest for group dynamics concerns the degree of variation and difference that can be tolerated without consensus giving way to cleavage. What is the tolerable level of variation, or incongruence, within and between particular groups, on the basis of modal personality, that does not precipitate cleavage in the form of factions or defections; and similarly, between groups, what is the level of incongruence that can be tolerated without generating unstable or dysfunctional coalitions or alliances? Answers to these intriguing questions must await further sociopsychological research that requires more precision in both technology and theory. Presently available data, nonetheless, make it sufficiently clear that consensus and cleavage, both within and among groups, is in part a function of the composition of the total personality structures of respective groups and their modal personalities.

# Summary

The social group is the most elementary form of social organization. Social groups, as such, are the basis of every kind of social system—associations, institutions, complex organizations, bureaucracies, and, of course, societies.

A social group refers to a plurality of people (two or more) who share a common identity and who recurrently interact in respective status-role distinctions in the pursuit of a common goal. Social groups need to be distinguished from other kinds of social collectivities, and, in particular, those of the social aggregate and the social category.

The formation of social groups represents one of the fundamental sociological principles: As individuals interact over a period of time in pursuit of a shared goal, a variety of basic structures and processes inevitably emerge. The most important of these constitutes the essential components of a group: a sense of group identity, the development of group boundaries, and the emergence of social organization.

Sociologists have developed a number of classificatory schemes which highlight the specific features that distinguish different types of groups. Among the principal criteria are size, structure, function, cohesion, and duration. One of the most significant distinctions is that based on the nature or quality of the social relations and interaction that exist among the members: primary groups and secondary groups. A primary group consists of a relatively small number of people who interact on an intimate, personal, direct, informal, face-to-face basis and is characterized by strong emotional bonds that typically endure over a long period of time. A secondary group has characteristics that are the opposite of those found in primary groups. Another set of groups that sociologists find analytically useful is that of in-groups and out-groups.

Much social behavior can be understood only in terms of the distinctions between membership groups and reference groups. A membership group is one in which an individual holds an actual membership; a reference group is one that is used as a frame of reference to guide behavior and/or to evaluate oneself. These respective differences, however, do not apply exclusively to groups. Rather they may be used to distinguish any kind of social collectivity.

The size of a group, perhaps more than any other variable, exerts the strongest influence in determining the quantity and quality of the interaction that will take place among its members. Changes in group size invariably result in changes in the structure of social relationships. Group structure becomes increasingly more complex and new properties emerge with increases in the size of the group. As a group grows arithmetically, the number and form of potential social relationships are vastly elaborated geometrically.

The propensity for group formation resides

▼

**400**

in two basic motives—the affiliative and the instrumental—which are essential in the social person. As members of groups interact with one another over time, they begin to develop feelings of attraction and repulsion towards each other. Eventually, these feelings tend to stabilize, and a sociometric structure emerges. Sociometric structure refers to the patterns of interpersonal attraction and repulsion that exist among members of a group. Research shows that physical proximity (propinquity) is related to interpersonal attraction. Group cohesion has been defined as the result of all the forces acting on the members to remain in the group.

Group structure tends to make for social conformity. Internalization theory and social comparison theory are two explanations for deviance in social groups. Among the mechanisms for maintaining social control in groups are rewards, punishment, activation of commitment, and normative redefinition.

Two types of leaders commonly emerge in social groups: the instrumental leader and the expressive leader. The instrumental leader is primarily concerned with having the group solve its problems and obtain its goals. The expressive leader is concerned mainly with maintaining social cohesion and having the group function in a friendly and harmonious manner. Several theories attempt to explain why certain people become leaders: the personality theory of leadership, the style theory of leadership, and the situational theory of leadership.

Group problem solving and decision making occur in four stages—orientation, evaluation, decision making, and control—and involve such dynamics as social facilitation, groupthink, the risky shift, and group polarization.

There is good, though somewhat limited, evidence that behavior in groups is dependent in part on the personality attributes of the group members. A few of the more significant dimensions of personality that influence group

dynamics are authoritarianism, approach-avoidance tendencies, social sensitivity, and Machiavellianism. Similarities and differences in personality are important for group performance in terms of the particular tasks that are involved. Evidence relating to personality structure, however, suggests that a homogeneity of personality types comprises the most efficacious situation for group performance. Other data suggest that coalitions and alliances, as specific manifestations of consensus and cleavage, are in part a function of significant similarities in the underlying personality structures of the members of respective groups.

# Key Concepts

cooptation
diffusion of responsibility
dyad
expressive leader
group cohesion
groupthink
idiosyncrasy credit
in-group
instrumental leader
internalization theory
leader
Machiavellianism
membership group
out-group
primary group
reference group
risky shift
secondary group
social aggregate
social category
social comparison theory
social facilitation
social group
sociogram
sociometric structure
surrogate primary group
triad

# FOUR ▼ Social Differentiation

▼
▼
▼
▼

It is quite obvious that people are different from each other in a number of ways. Physical differences, especially gender and age, are the most apparent distinctions. Less obvious perhaps are differences ascribed to people by virtue of their being members of society. Many personal differences among people, whether inherited or socially acquired, often serve as the basis for differences in social behavior and relate quite importantly to the structure and function of society. Our concern in this section is how social differentiation—as a fundamental aspect of all societies—is accomplished, and its significance for both social and personal behavior in the dynamics of society. We shall discuss here two major types of social differentiation: social stratification and minority-majority relations. Each type represents a distinctive dimension of the differentiation of society into a number of various kinds of social space in which most social behavior takes place. Both in effect constitute the horizontal division of society in terms of differentially evaluated social levels, or strata, which in themselves comprise distinctive types of subcultures that provide the basis for understanding many of the dynamics of society. ▲

▶ Chapter 10 **SOCIAL STRATIFICATION**
▶ Chapter 11 **SOCIAL MINORITIES AND SOCIAL MAJORITIES**

# 10 ▼ Social Stratification

Social differentiation is a fundamental aspect of all societies. The principal example of this situation is the functional differentiation, or division of labor (different statuses and roles), that is the very essence of society. Social differentiation, however, given the unique ability of people as valuing beings, leads inevitably to rank differentiation. This phenomenon, known more generically as social stratification, consists of the ranking of people and groups in society into higher and lower social strata that, in effect, produces a hierarchy of social prestige and social influence.

We have referred to the phenomenon of social stratification throughout our discussions of social organization in the previous section. In this chapter we discuss social stratification in a more comprehensive manner, and consider this phenomenon within the broader context of society as a whole. Of course, as always, our discussion of social stratification will explore its significance for both individuals and society. Among specific issues to be examined are the nature and variety of systems of social stratification, methods of measurement, and a number of relevant processes, including in particular that of social mobility. We shall explore as well the behavioral correlates of social stratification in terms of various subcultures, lifestyles, and life chances. Finally, we shall assess the relationship of personality to social stratification and the dynamics of social mobility.

## Outline

► No casual observer of social behavior can escape noticing that some people (some types of people—those occupying certain statuses and performing certain social roles) are considered to be more important than others, or that at least what they do is considered more valuable. Some people have more influence, are shown more respect, and receive greater social rewards of various kinds. Behavior of this kind is a manifestation of social stratification, which refers to the process of according differential value and prestige to the many positions and activities that exist in any society. Such behavior can be found in every kind of social system, from small groups to highly complex societies. Why does such a situation exist—especially in societies wherein it is believed that all people are equal, or at least that they should be treated equally? Are these kinds of differential behavior inevitable, or are the people involved simply hypocritical? Why situations of differential treatment exist, and the significance they have for social organization and social behavior, are the central issues of this chapter.

# Nature of Social Stratification

Social organization, as we saw in previous chapters, is fundamentally a matter of statuses, or social positions, and their corresponding roles, which are intertwined into a matrix of recurring patterns. One of the most intrinsic and significant aspects of social statuses is the value attached to them—their importance to the objectives of a social system and its people. Each position in a social system actually occupies a hierarchical position relative to others—that is to say, it is more or less important. Consider, for example, the difference in value attached to the positions of a physician and an orderly in a hospital, of a professor and a janitor in a university, or of a vice president and a secretary in a business corporation. Each of these differentially valued social positions reflects the dynamics of social stratification.

## WHAT IS SOCIAL STRATIFICATION?

**Social stratification,** unlike mere social differentiation, refers to the process and system by which differential value and prestige are attached to the various statuses and roles—positions and activities—that are found in any society, as well as to the various social categories that can be distinguished in all societies. These relatively homogeneous ranks are known as social strata.

A **social stratum** consists of a category of people who share the same or similar social ranking in a particular community or society. In more common terminology, the term *social class* is used, although, as we shall see, this label often has a more specific meaning within the context of social stratification.

Social strata differ from other social categories by virtue of being hierarchically ranked on the basis of certain values. Much like physical strata in the field of stratigraphy or geology, social strata resemble a cross section of the earth's crust in which layers or strata of different kinds of soil and rock can be discerned.

Social strata essentially comprise a kind of social space, or subculture, in which most of a person's behavior takes place. Social stratification, however, has profound significance for social behavior and for many of the dynamics of society. Social stratification is important sociologically because it contributes to the ordering of social interaction—the structure of social relationships—and provides motivation for various kinds of social behavior, as is understood in the familiar process of "status seeking."

## HISTORICAL PERSPECTIVES

Social stratification has taken many different forms throughout history. One of the earliest

405

Reprinted by permission of UFS, Inc.

406

and oldest forms of social stratification is slavery. Its beginnings can be traced to ancient Greece and Rome, its endurance through the nineteenth century in the United States. Today there are an estimated 1 million slaves in the world, chiefly in African and Asian countries, usually involved in indentured labor (U.N. Commission on Human Rights). Slavery, wherever it exists, is a form of stratification that requires extensive repression and social control.

History has shown that social stratification has become a progressively more complex structure as societies evolved through different modes of production. In the early and most primitive, hunting and gathering, societies there was very little stratification—owing in great part to the fact that there was only a superficial division of labor in these societies. Agricultural societies, as we saw in Chapter 7, brought forth a greater division of labor and a larger number of people in the growth of cities. With these developments came more complex forms of social structure and social stratification.

One type of stratification associated with agrarian societies of the past was feudalism, or the estate system, which was found in its most elaborate form in Europe during the Middle Ages. Under the estate system, social status depended principally on a person's relationship to land. Peasants were required to work the land owned by nobles in exchange for military protection and other services. Four strata, or estates, usually were recognized under the feudal system: nobility, clergy, merchants, and peasants. Each **estate** had its own legally established sociopolitical set of rights and obligations. These distinctions among the four strata were quite sharp, and the system was characterized by very little mobility or movement from one status to another. Some forms of feudalism remain yet today in countries of South America that make use of the *hacienda* system of sharecropping.

Industrial societies continued and elaborated this progressively complex pattern of social structure with an even more highly diversified and specialized division of labor—one characterized by complex systems of social stratification. Modern societies are distinctively characterized by a very large variety of criteria for social differentiation, as well as a much greater degree of social mobility.

## UNIVERSALITY OF SOCIAL STRATIFICATION

Every known society, contemporary or historical, simple or complex, is characterized by social stratification in one form or another. There are two fundamental bases for social stratification. One is provided by the nature of society as essentially a systematic division of labor. The other basis inheres in the very nature of people as valuing beings—ones who can attach differential worth or importance to the phenomena in their world and express choices among them.*

Any valued differences among people, particularly if they are in short supply, can provide the basis for social stratification. Such is the case with differences in physical strength and intellectual ability. Academic grades—as marks of differentiation or distinction—have meaning only because of their value and limited supply. Among the fundamental differences that make for the universality of stratification, however, one can simply mention age and sex. People in every society are treated differently in terms of age, as can be easily seen in a contrast of the young and the elderly. Some societies, such as traditional Chinese society, accord greater prestige to its elder members; while in others, such as our own, it is the younger members who have higher social prestige.

Much the same is true in terms of sex. There are societies yet today, particularly in Asia, where gender is accorded highly differential treatment, and where one sex (usually male) is considered more important and desirable than the other. Female infanticide in situations of excess population or limited resources has been prevalent throughout history. Such a practice, as we mentioned in Chapter 7, is rather prevalent in China, where in some rural areas the male-female ratio is as high as five to one.

Usually, the most highly esteemed values of a society serve as a basis of its stratification. The criteria used for this purpose may differ from one society to another and can include

such factors as education, knowledge, money, ancestry, religion, power, race, ethnicity, and occupation. Attributes positively valued by one society may be negatively valued in another. Three criteria, nonetheless, have been found to be universal: wealth, power, and prestige. More fundamentally universal, however, is the basic action of differential evaluation—whatever the criteria.

**407**

## THE MYTH OF SOCIAL EQUALITY: IS CLASSLESS SOCIETY POSSIBLE?

Social stratification inherently and inevitably makes for social inequality in any society. Whenever tasks and positions come to be differentially evaluated in terms of social importance so that they are differentially rewarded, then social inequality exists. Differential evaluation on the basis of inescapable differences—as well as on the basis of differential contributions to the function of society—preclude any true social equality. Social stratification by its very nature divides society into strata of haves and have nots, or various levels thereof, with respect to highly valued criteria that exist in limited supply in every society.

Underlying our discussion to this point is the question: Is a classless society—one without social stratification—possible? Many people have wondered about the inevitability of social stratification, and the possibility of eradicating it. The goal of a classless society has been a longstanding aspiration for many throughout human history. However, as we have said, social stratification and social inequality are universal features of all societies. Both the nature of social organization and the nature of people as valuing beings strongly dictate the impossibility of a truly classless society. The universality of social stratification, like all universals, remains undisputed by the findings of social research, even by social experimentation. Attempts

---

* Social stratification is inherent in social organization; however, it is not limited to human societies. Stratification is found even among lower animals—social as well as nonsocial. The pecking order of hens is perhaps the most well known. However, stratified behavior is also found among other species of birds, many species of mammals, and even some species of insects, as evidenced by the status distinctions among queen bees, workers, and drones. These stratification systems, of course, are quite simple, rigid, and biologically determined. In human societies, social stratification is a more complex phenomenon and one that manifests considerable variability in many respects.

**408**

(© Jan Lukas/Photo Researchers)

**Classless Society.** Social inequality is inherent and inevitable in any society—even a communistic one. Differences in dress and clothing among women in the Soviet Union clearly reveal the existence of social strata and the variations that they offer in lifestyles. Policy changes in the Soviet Union during the past few years not only acknowledge these disparities, but indeed call for their expansion in order to provide incentives for increases in economic production.

(Neil Goldstein/Stock, Boston)

throughout history to establish classless societies, even in well-known communes and communistic societies, have failed.

That people are born equal is a prevalent belief in many societies. Perhaps even more prevalent is the belief that everyone should be treated equally. Politically and ideally such may be true. Socially and realistically, however, equality is never obtained in any society. Clearly, people are not equal—not even born equal—as gender variation and other physical differences pointedly demonstrate. Perhaps more significant is the fact that people at birth are ascribed a number of social distinctions, differences that have unequal value and lasting significance throughout the course of the life of every individual.

Utopias may be able to mute—indeed, annihilate—the effects of social stratification so that everyone, or nearly everyone, has a chance to achieve high rank or to be accorded equal treatment, evaluation, and appreciation, but utopias are "never-never lands" and have no realistic or empirical existence.

A society without social stratification—a classless society—is a sociological impossibility. Such a society is simply not possible, given the very nature of social organization as a division of labor coupled with the nature of people as valuing beings. Some societies, as we shall see in more detail in a subsequent section, are more extensively stratified than others. The degree of stratification, moreover, may be expanded or contracted. Similarly, visible symbols of stratification can be maximized or minimized, even removed in some cases, but history and the nature of stratification suggest that others will be invented. Quite simply, social stratification cannot be entirely eliminated from society. A more complete answer to this question of a classless society, however, requires a consideration of several of the other topics of this chapter, which describe the nature of social stratification in terms of its various forms and processes.

# Determinants of Social Stratification

▼

Determining a person's social rank, or that of a social category, is a far more complex matter than one might expect. For a long time in the field of sociology it was thought that social stratification consisted of a unidimensional structure. Such seems to have been the case in the early types of society. Even during the feudal period social ranking was a fairly simple matter, determined primarily in terms of economic considerations. Social stratification in modern societies, however, is a fairly complex phenomenon that has several, often inconsistent, dimensions.

**409**

## MULTIDIMENSIONAL ANALYSIS

Max Weber (1946a), the distinguished German sociologist to whom we have referred many times in other chapters, has offered a multidimensional analysis of social stratification that seems to be more consistent with the complex nature of modern society. Weber distinguished three basic components—or distinct dimensions—of social stratification: class, status, and power.* Each of these valued resources is available in limited supply in any society. Weber argued, quite persuasively for contemporary sociologists, that people are not ranked unidimensionally, but rather that a person's social rank is a synthesis of an evaluation of each of the three principal dimensions that he discerned. Weber maintained that modern societies actually are characterized by three distinct, yet related, systems of stratification. Extensive research shows, moreover, that these three dimensions of stratification are usually very much interrelated in real-life situations.

---

* Some sociologists nowadays prefer to use the respective terms *wealth, prestige, and power.*

▼

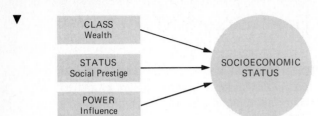

FIGURE 10-1 Dimensions of Social Stratification. Weber's model of social class consists of three dimensions frequently known as Socio-Economic Status (SES).

**410**

CLASS. **Class** refers to social ranking in terms of economic variables. It describes a category of people who share a similar access to wealth* or economic situation. Class retains this economic connotation for many people yet today—although often it is used generically to refer to a person's overall rank in the stratification system, and thus serves to denote both economic ranking and level of prestige.

Weber's distinctions have a highly justified meaning when one regards social stratification purely in economic terms. Such a consideration, however, provides an assessment of social stratification that many, social scientists and laypersons alike, would find highly distorted and inaccurate. Let us illustrate this situation with a brief description of income distribution in the United States.

The profile of income distribution in the United States has remained fairly stable since 1947. Hence, the severe inflation of recent years has not significantly affected the relative distribution of income. Median income and real purchasing power have increased enormously during the past forty years or so, but the levels of income distribution have not changed to any significant degree throughout this period. For each fifth of the American population, the following distribution in terms of income dispersion currently exists: 43 percent, 24 percent, 17

percent, 11 percent, 5 percent. See Figure 10-2 for some historical comparisons.*

Such a profile, which suggests that appreciably more than one-half of the population rank in the two uppermost strata of society and less than one-fifth in the two lowermost strata, is considerably distorted when compared to other data that are presented subsequently. Neither does such a picture square with the self-perception of the majority of Americans of their own class rank and the ranks of the rest of society.

STATUS. **Status** refers here to a social ranking in terms of social prestige or social honor conferred upon an individual by other members of society. Social status[†] in this sense includes the amount of respect, admiration, or deference that a person is accorded by others.

Status, or **social prestige,** must not be confused with social esteem, which refers to the appreciation a person receives for outstanding performance in a social role. Domestic servants, as was the case with slaves, are often highly esteemed by their employers because of their dedicated and loyal service, yet such people are obviously accorded little social prestige compared to that of the people whom they serve. Garbage collectors can be highly esteemed, yet they invariably rank extremely low in social prestige. Social esteem, thus, is a social invention that permits rewards to anyone showing good performance in a certain role. Unlike social prestige, social esteem is not a limited resource. One does not have to be selective regarding to whom or how much social esteem

---

* Wealth may be defined as the possession of any material asset that is deemed valuable—money, land, property, precious metals.

* Income in several other societies is either more equitably or more inequitably distributed. One measure of this difference is the wage ratio, which is the difference between the minimum and maximum salary. In the Soviet Union, for example, the wage ratio is about 50 to 1, versus about 300 to 1 in the United States.

† We can see here that social status has a dual meaning in sociology. It refers not only to social positions—as we have used the term up to this point—but also to the value or prestige attached to social positions.

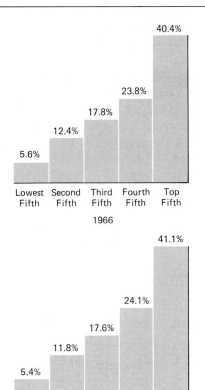

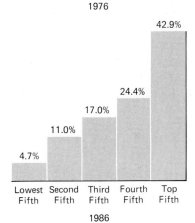

FIGURE 10-2 Distribution of Income among U.S. Families, 1966, 1976, and 1986. Source: U.S. Bureau of the Census, *Social Indicators* III. Washington, D.C.: U.S. Government Printing Office, 1980, Table 9/15; *Population Reports,* Series P-60. Washington D.C.: U.S. Government Printing Office, 1987.

is accorded. Social prestige, however, by its very nature, requires a differential application.

POWER. **Power** refers to social ranking in terms of the ability to control or to affect social events and activities. Power, as we discussed in Chapter 6, may assume different forms. Three somewhat ideal types are of importance here: (1) **influence,** the ability to induce others to act in a certain manner; (2) **authority,** or legitimate power; and (3) **coercion,** or illegitimate power. In agricultural and industrial societies, power rested chiefly in land ownership and capital, respectively. Much power in modern societies consists of access to information and knowledge.

**411**

## STATUS CONSISTENCY

Social rank in a stratification system, as we have seen, is multidimensional. **Status consistency** refers to how similarly a person ranks within the various dimensions of social stratification: wealth, prestige, and power. Heads of major corporations who, with high levels of education, earn enormous salaries (in some instances several hundred million dollars annually) have very high prestige and, by virtue of their economic position and social prestige, command unusual degrees of power. These people are clearly status consistent.

The three elements or dimensions of social stratification are usually highly correlated. Such is not always the case, however. Professors and clergymen are usually thought to be high in prestige, but low in wealth and power. Underworld criminals might be high in wealth, but low in prestige and power. Members of state legislatures or city councils may be high in power, but low in wealth and prestige. Businessmen may have high income, but low prestige. A situation in which an individual ranks high in one or two dimensions and low in another is known as **status inconsistency.**

▼    Status inconsistency has considerable significance for social dynamics. It can provide a catalyst for social mobility as well as social change. Conversely, social mobility may result in status inconsistency. Status inconsistency often leads as well to personal frustration and psychological insecurity. Such a situation is alleged to be owing to a person's uncertainty of what to expect in social interaction with others (Jackson, 1962).

**412**    Various studies have shown that status-inconsistent people act in many distinctive ways. Eitzen (1970), for example, found that they are more likely to be attracted to political extremism. Other studies have shown that status inconsistency tends to be related to psychological stress, physical disorders, social isolation, and prejudice toward social minorities. Physical disorders associated with psychological stress, such as weight loss, palpitations, dizziness, gastric complications, and trembling hands, were found more extensively among individuals reporting status discrepancy than those not so reporting (Jackson, 1962). There has also been evidence of greater frequency of suicide among people who experience status inconsistency than among those who do not (Gibbs & Martin, 1964).

Problems of personal frustration and psychological insecurity may result especially when a status-discrepant individual prefers to be treated in terms of his or her highest (most prestigious) status, yet finds that many people respond in terms of a less prestigious status. When this type of situation occurs, interaction is strained and may even become impossible.

# Theories of Social Stratification

Analysis of social stratification has constituted one of the major concerns of social thought from the beginnings of recorded history. Aristotle maintained that some people are by nature slaves, others free. Social contract theorists (see Chapter 1) asserted that people are born free and equal, but that inequalities are brought about by society. Among the principal questions that modern sociologists have sought to address are the following: Is social stratification truly inevitable? Can societies be created without social stratification? Can social stratification be altered or reduced in certain respects? What are the functions and dysfunctions of social stratification?

Answers to these questions are found in two principal sociological theories of social stratification: functionalist theory and conflict theory.

## STRUCTURAL-FUNCTIONAL THEORY

Functionalists maintain that social stratification is not only universal, but is so because it is a functional necessity of any society. No society, it is argued, can exist or function adequately without social stratification in one form or another. Social stratification, in brief, is endemic to social organization.

Every society, every social system, is confronted with a number of functional tasks—activities that need to be executed in order for society to function. These tasks, however, differ in importance, difficulty, and popularity. Hence, according to functionalist theory (Tumin, 1985), every society is confronted most basically by two fundamental problems that are directly related to social stratification: getting people to fill essential positions, and getting people to perform well within these positions.

Society resolves these problems by a system of differential rewards in the forms of income, power, and prestige. In so doing, society insures that vital, and hard-to-do, tasks are performed. Functionalist theory maintains that unequal rewards are necessary to induce people, especially the most qualified, to assume and to perform within important and necessary positions.

Moreover, once people are recruited to these social positions, differential rewards continue to be necessary in order to motivate them to put forth their maximum effort. Such is especially the case, it is argued, for positions that require a long and arduous preparation, such as that of a physician or professor. Positions like these inevitably involve deferred gratification, which in principle requires stronger motivation to compensate for the long periods of training and sacrifice during which people receive no rewards.

Functionalist theory asserts that important positions and tasks need not be the same in every society, since these are determined by the particular values of a given society. In some societies, for example, religious functions are among the most highly valued, while in others military positions are considered to be the most important. Of course, in terms of basic social organization, all societies share a common set of fundamental positions and tasks. Hence, according to functionalist theory, social stratification and a certain amount of inequality are both necessary and inevitable. Otherwise, it would be quite difficult, if not impossible, to meet the functional needs of society. As Davis and Moore (1945:243), the principal formulators of this theory, assert, "Social inequality is thus an unconsciously evolved device by which societies insure that the most important positions are conscientiously filled by the most qualified persons."

The functionalist perspectives have been extremely controversial. A frequent criticism is that the theory is simply a rationalization for social inequalities. It serves to perpetuate the privileged position of those already enjoying much social prestige and other perquisites of elevated social rank. Another major argument against the functionalist theory is that greater rewards do not always accrue to the more important positions/functions in society. Housewives and mothers, for example, receive neither the income nor the prestige that are commonly accorded to movie actresses. Moreover, it is alleged that it is not possible to distinguish objective importance between functional positions, such as garbage collector and physician, or teacher and janitor. Opponents of the functionalist view maintain that the differential evaluation of occupation is primarily subjective.

Another criticism of the functionalist approach contends that there are many occupations that command many rewards and a great deal of prestige even though the tasks performed do not seem necessary for the adequate operation of the society. Critics ask, for example, how the enormous salaries earned by some entertainers, novelists, and sports figures can be explained in terms of functionalist theory? Proponents of the functional approach respond that, obviously, many people in society highly value entertainment. Accordingly, entertainers and athletes satisfy an important personal need of many individuals. In addition, there is no question that the talents and skills of certain entertainers and athletes are very rare. Not many people, for instance, can hit a baseball more than four hundred feet, or be as consistently entertaining as the most popular comedians and singers.

One cannot deny that there are inconsistencies in systems of social stratification. They too, of course, need to be explained for a complete understanding of the phenomenon in question, and for the validation of any theory that attempts to explain it. Criticisms such as those mentioned, however, overlook one crucial point. In addition to sociocultural values of what is considered important or desirable, and even functionally necessary, it is the degree of training and skill required for a particular position that also determines social rank. Garbage collection is equally important as good medical care for the health and survival of society—but while the medical professional could perform the low-skill task of collecting garbage, the garbage collector is totally unqualified to perform

**413**

▼ the highly skilled task of delivering medical care.

Despite these criticisms, functionalist theory is the more popular of the two principal theories of social stratification. It remains, nonetheless, a controversial proposition for which empirical disconfirmation has not as yet been shown. The universal existence of social stratification in every society throughout the course of history—and the unsuccessful social experiments designed to establish societies and communities free of any rank differentiation or social stratification—indirectly provide confirmation of the functionalist perspective.

## CONFLICT THEORY

Quite in opposition to the functionalist perspective, conflict theory maintains that social stratification serves no useful purpose. Indeed, conflict theorists consider social stratification to be highly dysfunctional and the major source of human misery and suffering. From this perspective, it is not functional utility so much as power that creates social stratification. Social stratification results from a differential access to power, not from an uneven distribution of rewards. In substance, then, social stratification is essentially the result of a continuous conflict between the privileged and the disadvantaged—conflict between the power of the haves and the have nots. Social stratification, in the perspective of conflict theory, is neither necessary nor inevitable and, hence, need not be a universal feature of society. Society without social stratification is not only possible, but quite desirable in this theoretical perspective.

There are several conflict approaches to social stratification. The basic one is that formulated by Karl Marx (1848), and all other conflict theories incorporate its basic assumptions and tenets. For Marx, social inequality is the result of competition for scarce and desirable resources that leads to conflict, which in turn threatens society.

Social status in the Marxist perspective is determined by the relationship of one's position to the means of production: land, labor, and capital. There are two basic social classes in this respect:

1. **Bourgeoisie**/*Capitalists*, consisting of the owners and the controllers of the means of production, represent the dominant class of landowners or entrepreneurs.
2. **Proletariat**/*Workers*, consisting of peasants and industrial workers, represent the subordinate class who sell their labor for wages.

These two classes, according to Marx, are maintained by the differential use of power. The capitalist class, intent on maximizing its profits and position of dominance, engages in the unlimited manipulation and exploitation of workers. Capitalists allegedly impose poverty, ignorance, and powerlessness on workers through a combination of coercion and deception, all of which make for a false class consciousness among workers that obscures the objective realities of class structure and the inequities of social stratification.

Class struggle is inevitable because of the inequity and injustice in this two-class society. According to Marx, the proletariat eventually will become aware of their common economic interests (develop a true class consciousness) and will unite in overthrowing the bourgeoisie. In Marx's view, the dynamics involved are essentially of the following sort and sequence: Class consciousness promotes class conflict and an eventual revolution, which in turn ultimately brings about a truly classless society through the abolition of property or private ownership of the means of production, and the establishment of a communistic society.

Perhaps on first consideration, Marx's perspective seems plausible. So far, however, his predictions have not materialized. No industrial or capitalist society has witnessed a revolution on the part of its working class.

Wherever Communist revolutions have been successful, such as in Russia and China, there has always been an agricultural society involved. Moreover, there is much evidence that after a Marxist revolution takes place (again, China and the Soviet Union are suitable examples) and the traditional classes are abolished for the sake of equality, new class distinctions gradually reappear. In the Soviet Union today, for instance, one can find tremendous socioeconomic differences (see Herleman, 1986; Willis, 1985; and Voslensky, 1984).

Disparity between workers and managers alone is a highly striking example. In an automobile factory in Moscow, visited in 1979 by the author, the average monthly wage for an assembly worker was approximately the equivalent of $250, while the plant manager/director earned an admitted salary equivalent to approximately $800, plus additional benefits such as a chauffeured automobile.

On the same occasion mentioned above a reception given by the Soviet Academy of Sciences for visiting scholars consisted of endless supplies of vodka, wine, whiskey, champagne, caviar, and other exquisite foods, followed by rather lavish entertainment. The overwhelming majority of Soviet citizens perhaps know about such events only through descriptions alleged to be typical of the decay and demoralization of capitalistic societies. Quite relevant to this discussion is the policy proposed in 1987 by Premier Mikhail Gorbachev that wage differentials in the Soviet Union, between skilled and unskilled laborers, for example, be widened in order to provide incentives for increased production. Such a program is a fundamental manifestation of occupational and social stratification.

Political considerations are even more fundamental. Mere membership in the Communist Party—to say nothing of position within the party—confers a highly differential level of social prestige and influence (Kerbo, 1983). Some people, thus, are "more equal than others." (See Box 10-1 for another perspective on social inequality in the Soviet Union today.) Situations such as these are similarly true of social life in other Communist societies today (Matthews, 1978). Clearly, government ownership of the means of production can have, and indeed does have, the same social consequences as private ownership of the means of production, or capitalism.

It seems quite evident that the class struggle is not going as Marx had predicted. Increasing polarization between the bourgeoisie and proletariat has simply not materialized; on the contrary, the differences and gaps between social classes have diminished. The course of history in industrial societies has run directly counter to Marx's predictions. Workers have gained a stronger position in society during the past century, as witnessed by the development of potent labor movements and unionization in industrial societies. Particularly significant is the enormous extension of political and social rights to the masses (even during Marx's own lifetime) as more and more societies have become democratized and power has been increasingly redistributed throughout the class structure in a more—although not totally—equitable fashion. Witness world events in late 1989.

Today, the dominant thinking among conflict theorists is that Marx was only partially correct in his assessments and prediction of social stratification. Some conflict theorists even maintain that social stratification is inevitable (for example, Lenski, 1966; Dahrendorf, 1959). A classless society in terms of wealth, they argue, does not imply that the society would be unstratified. Stratification still would result in terms of prestige and power.

Marx's stress on economic factors as the primary determinant of social behavior was maintained at the expense of ignoring other dimensions of social unity, such as religion and nationality. One factor in particular that worked against Marx's predictions was the tremendous development of nationalism that took

▼

**415**

▼

## BOX 10-1. Social Stratification in the Soviet Union

416

Food shortages are among the most nagging problems of the Soviet economy. In many rural towns, meat is unavailable in the winter and it is often scarce even in the cities. The shortages of food—and the many other goods—have fostered a complex stratification of society in which membership in the elite is based less on monetary wealth than on access to consumer items and services in short supply. Money can be a factor, but often as not connections, in Russian called "blat," are more important in acquiring such coveted items as permission to reside in the big cities where shopping is comparatively abundant—and access to special stores with imported and other hard-to-get commodities. The result is a barter system in which people whose positions enable them to hold out rarities from public sale distribute them under the counter to friends who reciprocate with other scarcities. The goods and services bartered range from skilled surgery to ballet tickets to auto repairs.

Elitism is reinforced by policy as well as by inefficiency. Directors of research institutes, for example, receive 500 to 700 rubles a month ($690 to $966) while their junior researchers get 105 to 125 rubles ($145 to $172). The right of inheritance, abolished by a 1918 decree based on Marxist tenets, has been gradually reinstated over the years until now it is basically as uncontrolled as in the West.

Aside from cash, other benefits define class differences. Key officials are paid part of their salaries in so-called certificate rubles, which can be used in special stores carrying imported goods unavailable in regular shops and scarce Soviet-made items at as little as one-fifth the normal price. Travel abroad, highly prized and reserved for the select few, brings with it the privilege of special stores, because payment received in dollars or other hard currency may be converted to certificate rubles upon return home. Other stores exist only for those hand-picked officials and their families who hold special passes. Access to the better hospitals and clinics, restaurants, country dachas, apartment houses and vacation centers are similarly based on one's position in the party, the university or the factory.

Whatever this is, it is not Marxism. Yet it agrees with the traditions of Russian society, and therefore it seems to provoke no real domestic dissent from the left, no Chinese-style criticisms of the system. "Mao said we should reject material incentives and motivate our people with revolutionary ideas," Khrushchev declared in his memoirs. "But you can't make soup out of an idea." The remark says something about Soviet ideology today.... ▲

Source: Excerpted from David K. Shipler, "Social Stratification in Russia," *The New York Times,* November 6, 1977, 4, p. 5. Copyright © 1977 by The New York Times Company. Reprinted by permission.

TABLE 10-1. Two Perspectives on Social Stratification  ▼

| Structural-Functional Theory | Conflict Theory |
| --- | --- |
| 1. Stratification is universal, necessary, and inevitable. | 1. Stratification may be universal without being necessary or inevitable. |
| 2. Social organization shapes the stratification system. | 2. The stratification system shapes social organization. |
| 3. Stratification arises from society's need for integration, coordination, and cohesion. | 3. Stratification arises from group conquest, competition, and conflict. |
| 4. Stratification facilitates the optimal functioning of society and the individual. | 4. Stratification impedes the optimal functioning of society and the individual. |
| 5. Stratification is an expression of commonly shared social values. | 5. Stratification is an expression of the values of powerful groups. |
| 6. Tasks and rewards are equitably allocated. | 6. Tasks and rewards are inequitably allocated. |
| 7. The economic dimension is subordinate to other dimensions of society. | 7. The economic dimension is paramount in society. |
| 8. Stratification systems generally change through evolutionary processes. | 8. Stratification systems may change through revolutionary processes. |

Source: Arthur L. Stinchcombe, "Some Empirical Consequences of the Davis-Moore Theory of Stratification," *American Sociological Review,* 1963, 28:805–808.

place in many countries of Europe during the past century, especially in the decades before World War II. This spirit of nationalistic pride brought about a solidarity that transcended class distinctions. Such attitudes and values remain quite strong even today. Perhaps no better example than Poland can be offered.

That inequality and oppression exist in every society cannot be denied. That the powerful seek to maximize their advantages is quite apparent. That conflict occurs cannot be ignored. Yet, in the face of these circumstances, one cannot help but ask why class conflict and revolution do not take place in industrial societies. A number of reasons have been suggested to explain this dilemma. None of them is completely satisfactory. Perhaps together they make an otherwise inexplicable situation seem comprehensible. Let us look briefly at a few of these explanations.

Perhaps the most cogent explanation is that class conflict, however potential or real, has been institutionalized in labor-management negotiations. Labor unions and work contracts, along with supportive legislation, may in effect neutralize any dynamics of oppression and injustice to the satisfaction of all concerned. Recognition of the rights of workers, along with the power of labor to strike and to influence the system, has produced a situation that not only may be seen as more equitable and satisfactory, but is, in effect, one that offers the greatest return of rewards and an employment situation thought to be incomparable.

Related to this situation is the fact that workers in industrial societies have achieved unparalleled levels of socioeconomic success and unequaled standards of living—all the consequence of many different kinds of forces, but an outcome that in any event has produced

▼ relative satisfaction and contentment—devoid of any consciousness of exploitation or need to revolt. Equally significant is the relative ease and extent of social mobility.

Finally, we must consider the fact that many workers in industrial societies have themselves become capitalists of a kind. So many today are stockholders, that is proprietors and entrepreneurs, in major corporations, whether through profit-sharing, cooperatives, or outright ownership of stock. They are, in effect, the owners—owners of the means of production—and revolution would only be a revolt against themselves and their own interests.

All of these considerations suggest that acceptance of the myth of classless society, coupled with a belief in the American dream, may be much stronger than one might imagine.

## Occupational Prestige

**Occupational prestige** consists essentially of social rank accorded in terms of the value of a person's occupation. Like any other form of social evaluation, occupational prestige rests heavily on the dominant values of a particular society. Functional value and exclusivity (scarcity or limited supply), however, also play a crucial role.

Occupation, as research shows, is the single most powerful indicator of a person's position in the status hierarchy of any society. Many facets of social life are connected to occupation. Amount and kind of education, income, standard of living, and general lifestyle are the most important. Perfect correlation among these variables does not exist; however, occupation does serve as a focal factor in an individual's life. Notice how common it is that one of the first questions—indeed, often the very first question—asked of new acquaintances is, "What do you do?" or a variation thereof. The answer often reveals a wealth of unsolicited information about personal lifestyle, which in turn sets the tone for much of the social interaction that ensues—or perhaps does not!

Occupational prestige is measured by opinion surveys in which respondents are asked to evaluate or to rank various occupations. The most well-known of these kinds of studies are those conducted by the National Opinion Research Center (NORC) of the University of Chicago, which utilize cross-national samples to evaluate a selected set of occupations (see Table 10-2). Findings reveal remarkable similarity in the perceptions and evaluations of people from different social backgrounds (for example, people of different age, sex, income, race, and ethnicity).

Occupational rankings reveal high correlations with levels of education and income. Occupational prestige, however, is not always logical or explicable. Inconsistencies do exist, and one can perhaps detect instances of status inconsistency in any occupational prestige hierarchy in terms of the three principal dimensions of social status: wealth, prestige, and power.

One of the most significant findings in the study of occupational prestige is the consistency in ratings over time. A comparison of the three sets of data collected in 1947, 1963, and 1977 shows a remarkably high correlation (r = .99). These results suggest that occupational prestige has remained fairly constant for the past forty years or so.

The NORC data on occupational prestige further reveal that Americans use the same standard of evaluation as people in other industrial societies. Highly similar status profiles are found in most industrialized countries, and this situation suggests that there are gross uniformities in the social structure of similar types of societies, quite apart from their cultural differences (Treiman, 1977; Inkeles, 1968; Hodge, Treiman, & Rossi, 1966). In general, there is a tendency to accord high prestige to occupations

418

TABLE 10-2. Prestige Ranking of Selected Occupations

▼

| Occupation | Score | Occupation | Score |
|---|---|---|---|
| Physician | 82 | Bank teller | 50 |
| College teacher | 78 | Electrician | 49 |
| Lawyer | 76 | Police officer | 48 |
| Dentist | 74 | Insurance agent | 47 |
| Bank officer | 72 | Secretary | 46 |
| Airline pilot | 70 | Air traffic controller | 43 |
| Clergy | 69 | Mail carrier | 42 |
| Sociologist | 66 | Owner of a farm | 41 |
| Secondary school teacher | 63 | Restaurant manager | 39 |
| Registered nurse | 62 | Automobile mechanic | 37 |
| Pharmacist | 61 | Baker | 34 |
| Elementary school teacher | 60 | Sales clerk | 29 |
| Accountant | 56 | Gas station attendant | 22 |
| Painter | 56 | Waiter and waitress | 20 |
| Librarian | 55 | Laundry operator | 18 |
| Actor | 55 | Garbage collector | 17 |
| Funeral director | 52 | Janitor | 16 |
| Athlete | 51 | Usher | 15 |
| Reporter | 51 | Shoeshiner | 12 |

**419**

Source: *General Social Surveys, 1972–1987: Cumulative Codebook.* **Chicago: National Opinion Research Center, University of Chicago, 1987.**

that involve the use of authority or mental and verbal faculties, while low prestige is associated with occupations involving exclusively manual labor (Haller & Lewis, 1966).

Occupational prestige often involves an internal structure of stratification. Many occupations, from accountant to zoologist, are stratified in terms of specialized fields of interest as well as a person's professionally recognized credentials, often determined by examining or governing boards within the profession. The academic field, despite the extensive democracy within it, remains one of the most rigidly stratified professions, as witnessed by the traditional professorial ranks of assistant, associate, and full professor. Similar stratification can be found extensively within the medical field in terms of specialized areas of practice.

# Types of Stratification Systems

While stratification is found in all societies, its form is not universal. Stratification systems are differentiated by the method by which social positions are filled (whether by achievement or ascription), the extent to which various strata are clearly delineated, and the amount of mobility that is allowed or possible from one

▼ stratum to another. We can speak in these respects of two principal and ideal types of social stratification: open and closed, or class and caste, systems.

## THE CLASS SYSTEM

The **class system,** often called an "open-class" system, is one that is ideally characterized by the possibility of vertical mobility; an individual's position in the system is determined primarily by his or her own merits and achievements. Membership here is accorded on the basis of achieved status. Boundaries and criteria that differentiate social strata are neither rigid nor absolutely defined.

A person's initial status, or placement, in the class system of stratification is ascribed in terms of parental status. Any movement after the individual becomes socioeconomically independent is a result of his or her own accomplishments or lack thereof.

The United States provides a good example of the class system of stratification. Class distinctions are not very strong. Status consciousness is not very keen. Distinctive behavior and symbols for the various social strata are not so clear as in other types of stratification systems. There is relatively high mobility, or at least the potential for it.

## THE CASTE SYSTEM

The **caste system,** often called a "closed-class" system, is the ideal antithesis of the class system. In the caste system, the delineation of strata is quite clear and much sharper than in the class system. Status is ascribed and hereditary. Mobility in or out of a given caste is impossible or virtually nonexistent. Social life in the caste system is accordingly endogamous; marriage between people of different castes or strata is not allowed. Even much less intimate social relations are usually prohibited. Occupations, like caste membership itself, are lifelong and hereditary. Caste boundaries are usually maintained by legal and religious sanctions. Status consciousness is obviously very keen.

Caste systems seem to be viable only in rural environments. The more urbanized a society is, the more open the structure of its stratification system tends to be. Urbanization of a population affords individuals an opportunity for anonymity and unrestricted mobility. Also, the more education is widespread, the more likely that a stratification system is open. Caste and class systems, however, are related to cultural ideology and the degree of egalitarianism found in a given society. Visible differences such as skin color often facilitate caste systems.

Caste systems are rather rare today, although they are still found in parts of Africa and Asia. The prototypical example of the caste system is that which existed in India for thousands of years and endured into the middle of this century. Under this system, there were literally thousands of castes and subcastes based on occupation, race, tribe, and other social distinctions. However, these castes could be reduced to four principal ones, based on the degree of religious purity or "grades of being"* as prescribed by the Hindu religion:

1. *Brahman*—composed of Hindu priests and landowners.
2. *Kshatriya*—composed of the military and political aristocracy.
3. *Vaisya*—composed of merchants, artisans, and agriculturists.
4. *Sudra*—composed of laborers and unskilled workers.

Outside the entire caste system stood the *outcastes,* people considered to be "unclean" and "untouchable" by superior castes. People

---

* Each "grade of being" in the Hindu religion corresponds to one of the body parts of the mythical Purusa, whose dismemberment made possible the origin of the human species. Purusa's mouth produced priests (Brahmans); his arms, warriors (Kshatriyas); his thighs, artisans and merchants (Vaisyas); and his feet, laborers (Sudras).

▼

**Closed Class Systems.** Social strata in caste systems of stratification, such as that found in India, manifest rigidly drawn boundaries. Status-consciousness is keen, social life is endogamous, and social mobility is virtually nonexistent. (Ira Kirschenbaum/Stock, Boston)

in this lowest of all castes, known as *Harijans*, who constitute about 20 percent of the population, were those engaged in such "dirty" tasks as caring for animals, washing clothes, cleaning toilets, and sweeping floors. Even the breath and shadow of these outcastes were considered to be contaminating or polluting.

Castes were virtually segregated from each other in social interaction. One can imagine the elaborate and complex system of social norms that would be necessary to maintain the social isolation of thousands of castes from each other. Social pressure for caste maintenance was extremely acute, and violation or transgression of caste boundaries resulted in severe sanctions, usually expulsion or social ostracism.

The caste system in India, and a person's fate within it, was justified by the Hindu religion, which maintains that people are not born equal (Hutton, 1963). Part of this ideology involves a belief in reincarnation and the possibility thereby of being born into a higher or lower social caste, depending on how well a person remained faithful to his or her *varna*, or grade of being (Gould, 1971). Even those people in the lowest of castes accepted this religious ideology.

One can see in this example why conflict and revolt, as predicted by Marx and the conflict theorists, do not necessarily take place. Systems of stratification survive, in part, if people subscribe to beliefs that function to legitimate the differences involved.

The coming of industry to India, however, has undermined the caste system, at least in the urbanized regions of the country. Its peculiar

▼

type of social intercourse became difficult to maintain within a complex, bureaucratic, and modern society and was officially ended by law in the 1960s, at least in public contexts. Remnants abound in most rural areas of the country, and intermarriage between castes is still very rare (Schermerhorn, 1978). Indeed, the disappearance of the caste system in metropolitan areas involves only a minority of an enormous population, soon to be the world's largest at about a billion people. Recently, many Hindu untouchables have started large-scale conversions to other religions such as Buddhism, Christianity, and Islam in order to exchange oppression by higher castes for social equality.

## COMBINATION OR CASTE-LIKE SYSTEMS

Class and caste systems can co-exist in a society. Such a situation would be one in which classes exist within castes.

Today, caste-like systems are rare, but are not difficult to find. The Republic of South Africa maintains a caste-like system of stratification through the institution of apartheid, which physically and socially segregates Blacks and Whites (see Chapter 11 on Minority-Majority Relations). While there are different strata and the potential for social mobility in each segment of the society, the two segments are essentially closed from each other and remain totally endogamous or caste-like in many aspects of social activity.

Such a caste-like system also existed in the United States up to the mid-1960s. Many would argue that in some respects it is still operative today. In any event, a caste-like pattern of social relations between Blacks and Whites was unmistakable in several states of the United States, and indeed maintained by a legally sanctioned system of segregation. Classes could be distinguished among Blacks on the basis of the usual criteria of wealth, income, education, lifestyle,

and in this case even in terms of skin pigmentation. Yet each of these classes existed in tandem with, and virtually apart from, the class structure of Whites in American society. Physical segregation was maintained in housing and public accommodation; social discrimination was effected through the denial of legal and political rights, as well as an occupational caste system.

# Measuring Social Stratification

Distinguishing social strata has been a somewhat difficult, yet intriguing, challenge for sociologists. Such is the case because, at least in modern and complex societies, social classes have rather arbitrary boundaries, and hence are not easy to identify. Sociologists, however, through extensive research during the past forty years or so have turned this challenge into a highly sophisticated art. A number of techniques now exist that permit a rather simple, yet by no means perfect, measure of social class.

First of all, families, not individuals, are the usual units of measurement. Ordinarily, people in a single household share a lifestyle or standard of living. It is not typically the case that each family member has his or her own class standing. This is especially true of children and spouse who share in the social prestige of the husband/father, who basically determines the social class rank of the family, again primarily in terms of income, prestige, and influence associated with his occupation.

The various techniques for measuring social stratification may be classified into two major types—objective and subjective. Each has several variations. Subjective measurements were quite popular during the 1930s and 1940s, and these became the basis of more refined, objective techniques that are mainly used by sociologists today. Nonetheless, a discussion of the subjective measurements not only will tell us much about the objective measurements, but will also add significantly to a more complete understanding of social stratification.

## SUBJECTIVE MEASUREMENTS

Subjective measurements focus on a person's perception of his or her own position in the stratification structure. We have already looked at subjective measurements in the case of occupational prestige.

Subjective techniques for measuring social stratification are by far the most simple, at least in their administration. Their analysis is a much more complicated affair. Data collection consists fundamentally of simply asking people to identify the social class to which they feel they or others belong.

### SELF-CLASSIFICATION APPROACH.
The simplest of all subjective approaches is to ask people to identify the various social classes in society and to indicate the one to which they belong.

Americans usually respond overwhelmingly (90 percent) by saying that they are middle class.

However, if they are asked whether they regard themselves as upper, upper-middle, middle, working, or lower class, the vast majority usually split evenly into middle- and working-class identifications (Gilbert & Kahl, 1987). Two studies adequately illustrate this phenomenon.

In one study, Hodge and Treiman (1968) found that three-fourths of those in a national sample identified themselves as "middle class" in response to an open-ended query. Only 11 percent considered themselves to be "working class" or "lower class." When asked to select a given class on the basis of a forced-choice question, however, more than three-fourths of the respondents identified themselves as either middle class or working class. Jackman and Jackman (1983), in a more recent study, found virtually identical results (see Table 10-3).

Consistent results such as these suggest that Americans might not be very class conscious, or certainly much less so than people in many other societies. A number of factors undoubtedly account for this situation. One is the relative openness of the system of social stratification and the comparatively high mobility within it. Another is the relative similarity in many aspects of lifestyles among classes that

**423**

TABLE 10-3. Identification with Social Class

| 1968 | | 1975 | |
|---|---|---|---|
| Class | Percent | Class | Percent |
| Upper class | 2.2 | Upper class | 1.0 |
| Upper-middle class | 16.6 | Upper-middle class | 8.2 |
| Middle class | 44.0 | Middle class | 43.3 |
| Working class | 34.3 | Working class | 36.6 |
| Lower class | 2.3 | Poor | 7.6 |
| Don't believe in classes | 0.6 | No answer | 3.0 |

Source: Robert W. Hodge and Donald J. Treiman, "Class Identification in the United States," *American Journal of Sociology*, 1968, 73:535–547; Mary R. and Robert W. Jackman, *Class Awareness in the United States*. Berkeley, Calif.: University of California Press, 1983.

▼

have no rigid delimitations. Included too are many value orientations held in common by people in different social strata, not the least of which is equality. Finally, perhaps modesty and the need for respectability on various sides of the "middle class" produce the typical profile of these subjective classifications. At any rate, it is safe to say that results such as these reflect the aspirations of people more than the actualities of social stratification.

424

Self-identification and class-consciousness do not determine one's social class or social stratum. Social ranking, as we have said, is something accorded by others and not by oneself. Actual class distribution, as we shall see, is in significantly different proportions than those that result from self-classification.

REPUTATIONAL APPROACH. Another subjective, yet more sophisticated, measurement of social stratification employs various forms of the reputational approach. This consists essentially of using knowledgeable residents to report on their perspectives and understanding of the class structure of their particular communities. The reputational method is quite useful for studying small communities in which people are fairly well known to each other. It is not applicable to the analysis of large metropolitan areas or entire societies. A major advantage of this approach is that it provides an empirical basis for any hierarchical assessment in terms of the actual patterns of social interaction.

One of the first sociologists to employ the reputational approach in the study of social stratification was W. Lloyd Warner, who developed a technique known as "evaluative participation." Warner's best-known work utilizing this technique describes the class structure of a small New England community (Newburyport, Massachusetts), which he called "Yankee City," during the 1930s.

On the basis of his study, Warner and colleagues (1960) were able to identify a total of six social strata, which consisted of three principal strata, each with two subdivisions. His results showed that people are aware of different social strata and their respective rank, as well as their own relative positions within this system of stratification. What is even more interesting is that there is a high degree of consistency in these respects among the various social segments of local populations. Equally curious are the social perspectives that those in each of these social strata had of themselves and of those in other strata (see Table 10-4). Whether one looks up or down the social class hierarchy, self-respect and self-prestige are always relevant. Undoubtedly, these ad hoc labels would probably be somewhat different today, but there is little evidence to suggest that the pattern and structures of social stratification would be any different.

A. B. Hollingshead (1949) conducted a similar study during the 1940s in what he determined to be a fairly typical Midwestern town, which he called "Elmstown." His analysis also revealed that people are quite conscious of the system of social stratification in their local community, and understand rather well both their own position and that of other families within it. They also appeared to be quite knowledgeable about how the system works.

Hollingshead concluded from his analysis of these kinds of data that there were five social strata in Elmstown, which he labeled as follows: (1) the old upper class, (2) the upper-middle class, (3) the lower-middle class, (4) the respectable working class, and (5) the disreputable poor. Hollingshead subsequently found that a sample of local residents could accurately locate each family in Elmstown within the class structure he derived from the reputational technique.

Subjective measurement has been a very useful method for understanding the nature and significance of social stratification in many respects. It is especially useful, as we have suggested, in terms of class consciousness and the significance which this phenomenon, in turn, has for social behavior. Nonetheless, other

TABLE 10-4. Social Perceptions of Social Classes

| Upper-Upper Class | | Lower-Upper Class |
| --- | --- | --- |
| **"Old aristocracy"** | UU | "Old aristocracy" |
| "Aristocracy," but not "old" | LU | **"Aristocracy," but not "old"** |
| "Nice, respectable people" | UM | "Nice, respectable people" |
| "Good people, but 'nobody'" | LM | "Good people, but 'nobody'" |
| | UL | |
| "Po' whites" | LL | "Po' whites" |

| Upper-Middle Class | | Lower-Middle Class | |
| --- | --- | --- | --- |
| "Old families" | UU | | |
| "Society" but not "old families" | LU | "Old aristocracy" (older) | "Broken-down aristocracy" (younger) |
| **"People who should be upper class"** | UM | "People who think they are somebody" | |
| "People who don't have much money" | LM | **"We, poor folk"** | |
| | UL | "People poorer than us" | |
| "No 'count lot" | LL | "No 'count lot" | |

| Upper-Lower Class | | Lower-Lower Class |
| --- | --- | --- |
| | UU | |
| | LU | |
| "Society" or the "folks with money" | UM | "Society" or the "folks with money" |
| "People who are up because they have a little money" | LM | "Way-high-ups," but not "Society" |
| **"Poor but honest folk"** | UL | "Snobs trying to push up" |
| "Shiftless people" | LL | **"People just as good as anybody"** |

Source: W. Lloyd Warner et al., *Social Class in America*. New York: Harper and Row, 1960, p. 19.

425

kinds of sociological questions require both more reliable assessments of the structure of social stratification as well as more facile methods to accomplish them. Objective measurements provide assistance in this respect.

## OBJECTIVE MEASUREMENTS

Objective measurements of social stratification utilize single indicators or indices (combinations of indicators) that can be readily quantified and scored as a basis of assigning individuals to a particular social class category. Such measures provide an easy accessibility to relevant data, and they can be used to provide greater uniformity and standardization in the analysis of social stratification. Additionally, they are more appropriate, indeed indispensable, for such analyses involving societies at large, as opposed to studies on the local community level.

▼ The most frequently used indicators are occupation, income, and education. Education is usually measured in terms of the number of years of formal schooling, while income relies on median annual income. Differential weighting factors are assigned to each indicator on the basis of predetermined correlations and elaborate statistical analysis. Many social scientists, thus, commonly speak of **socioeconomic status** (SES) as a social class standing that combines these three elements. This trilogy constitutes a fairly standard index because of the empirical relationships between the three factors and the high statistical correlations they reveal. Education almost invariably determines occupation, which establishes income. Correlations, of course, are not perfect.

No single indicator is a highly reliable measure of social prestige or social class position. Such is especially the case with income. It is often not so much the amount of a person's income that affects his or her social class standing, as much as how the money/wealth was acquired. Inheritance and investments carry more weight than wages, welfare, or lottery winnings. Also, the "age" of one's wealth is invariably important to upper-upper class standing. The "newly rich" are considered to lack the appropriate aristocratic lifestyle of the upper-upper stratum, despite the extent of their wealth. Conversely, aristocrats may not in fact be very wealthy—perhaps just enough to maintain the appropriate lifestyle—yet their upper-upper class standing remains intact primarily because of respectable ancestry.

Education and income usually have a strong correlation. Indeed, the popular expectation is that they should, as is often reflected in the saying, "If you're so smart, why aren't you rich?" Clearly, status inconsistency is not expected in such cases, although in reality it does occur quite extensively. Education and income, nonetheless, frequently are combined as an index of social stratification.

One of the most powerful indicators of social class is occupation. Occupational prestige scales may be used in this regard (see Table 10-2). Occupation is commonly used by sociologists as a single measure of social stratification because it can be determined quite objectively and easily lends itself to quantification. Of course, its high level of correlation with education and income strengthens the reliability and predictive value of this indicator.

Two well-known objective measures of social class are those developed by W. Lloyd Warner and A. B. Hollingshead. See Box 10-2 on What Is Your Social Class Rank?

Until recently, families and not individuals have been the focus of social stratification and social mobility studies, primarily in terms of the male head of the household whose social characteristics as breadwinner determined the lifestyle for the family unit. The recent socioeconomic independence of women, as well as the greater prevalence of two-career families, have presented crucial challenges regarding the basis of social class evaluation. Research in these matters is just beginning. One of the more focal concerns is the manner of comparing one-career and two-career families, and how to combine both evaluations in terms of social rank for the principal dimensions of social stratification (power, wealth, prestige). A probable outcome is that wealth will become a more focal determinant of social rank. Total family income, or even lifestyle, may become more crucial than power or prestige as an indicator or measure of social class.

## CLASS CONSCIOUSNESS

**Class consciousness** refers to people's awareness of the system of social stratification, and their place or position within it. It often refers as well to an awareness of common interests with others of the same social stratum. One not uncommon manifestation of class consciousness is offered by people who express fears about the decline of property values should their neighborhood become populated by individuals of

# BOX 10-2.  What Is Your Social Class Rank?  ▼

Two rather quick methods for determining one's social class standing are the well-known objective measures developed by W. Lloyd Warner and A. B. Hollingshead. Utilizing your own or your parents' data in the following indices will provide a reasonable indication of your social class rank.

## WARNER'S INDEX OF STATUS CHARACTERISTICS.

427

Based on his "Evaluative Participation" technique, W. Lloyd Warner (1960) constructed an "Index of Status Characteristics." This measure consisted of four differentially weighted variables or indicators: occupation, source of income, type of house, and area of residence. These four indicators were weighted as follows: occupation × 4, income source × 3, house type × 3, and dwelling area × 2.

An index range of 12 to 84 was associated as follows with the six social classes that Warner derived from his work with the reputational approach (missing values represent intermediate ranks):

| | |
|---|---|
| upper-upper | 12 – 17 |
| lower-upper | 18 – 22 |
| upper-middle | 25 – 33 |
| lower-middle | 38 – 50 |
| upper-lower | 54 – 62 |
| lower-lower | 67 – 84 |

## HOLLINGSHEAD'S TWO-FACTOR INDEX.

Utilizing his study of social class in "Elmstown," A. B. Hollingshead developed a two-factor index of social class which relied on occupation and education (see Hollingshead & Redlich, 1958). Hollingshead subsequently developed a three-factor Index of Social Participation, based on a combination of occupation and education of the family head, and type of dwelling. These first two variables were differentially weighted as follows:

| Score | Occupation (Weight × 9) | Education (Weight × 5) |
|---|---|---|
| 1 | Executives of large corporations: major professionals, such as physicians. | Received a professional or graduate degree (beyond B. A.). |
| 2 | Managers of medium-sized businesses, lesser professionals. | Completed four years of college and received a degree. |
| 3 | Administrators in large concerns, owners of smaller businesses, semi-professionals. | Some college but did not complete four years. |

*(Continued)*

▼ BOX 10-2 *(Continued).*

| 4 | Owners of small businesses, clerical and sales workers. | Graduated from high school. |
| 5 | Skilled workers. | Some high school. |
| 6 | Semi-skilled workers. | Completed ninth grade. |
| 7 | Unskilled workers. | Less than seven years of school. |

The residence scale is the most subjective and perhaps the most difficult to use. It amounts to assigning a score value of 1 to 6 to all homes in a community. The finest homes in the best section of the city receive a value of 1; the poorest tenements or most run-down houses get a score of 6. Try to score your family's home. It may help, first, to determine whether it is about average (score 3 or 4), below average (score 5 or 6), or above average (score 1 or 2). Now, you should be able to narrow it down a little more. For example, if you rank the house about average, give it a score of 4; if you think most people in your community would consider it on the low side of average, but otherwise average, give it a 3 (Weight × 6).

The final step is to determine the social class that corresponds to the total score, using the following values:

| Range of Scores | Class |
|:---:|:---:|
| 20 – 31 | I |
| 32 – 55 | II |
| 56 – 86 | III |
| 87 – 115 | IV |
| 116 – 134 | V |

▲

particular racial, ethnic, or economic backgrounds. Class consciousness, or degree thereof, depends significantly on the type of system of social stratification (open or closed) that exists in a particular society and its specific cultural values, as well as a person's own class position within the system.

Class consciousness serves as an important reference process for people, and hence it can affect social behavior in many instances. It is very important in terms of the subjective determinants of social behavior. People often act, as we have stated repeatedly throughout these pages, on the basis of their definition of a social situation which—however accurate or distorted—provides a basis for real decisions and concrete actions. Eulau (1956), for example,

found that people who made the wrong class identification for themselves held political attitudes of the class with which they identified, rather than those of the class to which they actually belonged.

As revealed in the sociological studies previously mentioned, Americans are remarkably aware of the system of social stratification in their particular community, and understand quite well both their own position within it and how the system operates. In this sense, there seems to be considerable class consciousness in the United States today, in spite of the extensive inaccuracies involved in self-identification. In another sense, however, class consciousness is considerably absent. One such indication is that, with the exception of the country's upper class (Coleman & Rainwater, 1978), there is relatively little perception of extreme differences among the majority of American people. Several factors, particularly the strong similarities in the lifestyles of the various social strata and the relative ease of (or at least the belief in) social mobility, may account for this absence of class consciousness. Equally important are the American ideologies of the work ethic and rugged individualism, as well as an egalitarian value orientation.

Whatever their awareness of class distinctions, Americans do exhibit a rather low degree of class consciousness in comparison with people in many other countries. They do not perceive themselves primarily in terms of social class status. One explanation for this is that social class is only one of several possible bases for social identification and group loyalties in the United States. Ethnic, racial, religious, and regional similarities also serve as important sources of identifications and group loyalties in the highly heterogeneous American society. Such a situation has the effect of mitigating whatever class consciousness may exist.

## SOCIAL STRATIFICATION IN THE UNITED STATES

How many social classes are there in the United States today? There is no absolute answer to this question. The number of social classes depends on the particular community or region of the country. In certain parts of the Far West, for example, upper-upper classes probably are virtually nonexistent because the inhabitants have not lived in these areas for a long enough time to establish the "old family" criteria. Another particular consideration about social stratification in the United States is that the strata are neither sharply defined nor rigidly fixed, given the open structure and dynamics of mobility in this society.

All of the available data, nonetheless, suggest that there are not more than six social classes

in American society (Gilbert & Kahl, 1987). Sociologists frequently speak simply of three principal classes; however, research shows that such a discrimination is not a very precise one, and that each of these strata may be subdivided into two distinct substrata, all of which yields six rather distinct strata or social classes. The principal confirmation of this social reality is offered by Coleman and Rainwater (1978) in their comprehensive study of social stratification in two standard metropolitan statistical areas (Boston and Kansas City). The approximate distributions of the population on the basis of the six social classes that they were able to identify are depicted in Table 10-5 along with typical descriptions for the principal criteria of occupation, education, and income. One must be mindful that the data provided here are gross data for the American population as a whole. Distributions and profiles vary significantly for selected segments of the population, such as racial, ethnic, or regional categories.

Empirical findings such as these consistently show that most of the American population clearly falls in the lower-middle and upper-lower strata. These strata of the society comprise the well-known American "middle class." Despite a number of significant differences between these two strata—particularly in terms of wealth, prestige, and power—the class lines between them are neither rigid nor clear. Indeed, in terms of many aspects of social behavior and lifestyle, they are quite similar.

# Social Mobility

**Social mobility** refers to the movement of an individual or category from one social stratum to another or to movement within a given social stratum. More commonly, however, the term is used to refer to the former type of activity— movement of an individual between social classes. As we saw in our discussion on the types of social stratification, systems differ in the degree to which mobility is possible. They

▼ TABLE 10-5. The American Social Class Structure

| Class | Typical Occupation or Source of Income | Typical Education | Percent |
|---|---|---|---|
| **I. UPPER CLASS** | | | |
| Upper-Upper | Inherited wealth | Prestigious university | 2 |
| Lower-Upper | Top-level professionals, corporate executives | College, often postgraduate | 20 |
| **II. MIDDLE CLASS** | | | |
| Upper-Middle | Semi-professionals, low-level managers, small business executives | High school, often some college | 33 |
| Lower-Middle | Skilled laborers, craftsmen, clerical workers | High school | 37 |
| **III. LOWER CLASS** | | | |
| Upper-Lower | Unskilled laborers, service workers | Some high school | 4 |
| Lower-Lower | Unemployed or part-time, welfare recipients | Primary school | 4 |

**430**

Source: Richard P. Coleman and Lee Rainwater, *Social Standing in America: New Dimensions of Class.* New York: Basic Books, 1978; Dennis Gilbert and Joseph A. Kahl, *The American Class Structure: A New Synthesis,* Third edition. Chicago: Dorsey Press, 1987. Reprinted by permission of Wadsworth, Inc.

also differ in the amount of mobility that is characteristic or typical of them.

## TYPES OF MOBILITY

Sociologists distinguish different kinds of mobility. Among these distinctions are vertical and horizontal mobility in terms of direction, and individual or categorical mobility in terms of sources.

VERTICAL MOBILITY. **Vertical mobility** consists of movement up or down the social class hierarchy, that is, movement from one social stratum or class to another. Vertical mobility, in effect, is a change in social rank. People from the lower class who, by virtue of education and corresponding occupation, achieve mem-

bership in the middle class exemplify vertical mobility. Similarly, an industrial worker who becomes a foreman or an enlisted soldier who is promoted to the rank of an officer exemplifies vertical mobility.

Upward movement is more commonly intended when one speaks of vertical mobility; however, in open-class systems downward mobility is also possible. Indeed, downward mobility occurs with a fair degree of regularity and in considerable measure. People who, for whatever reason, lose their wealth or occupation are victims of downward mobility, as are those who become physically handicapped or permanently mentally disabled. People on skid row have also experienced downward mobility. Nobody is born on skid row. Its inhabitants invariably consist of older people, men and women, who have become derelicts and vagrants because of severe personal stress and psychological problems. Downward mobility is simply a result of a person's inability to maintain the standard of a particular lifestyle or social stratum, whether it be at the top or near the bottom of the class hierarchy.

HORIZONTAL MOBILITY. **Horizontal mobility** refers to changes in social positions that do not appreciably alter a person's social status or class rank. It is essentially a movement within the same social stratum or on the same social level. Typically, horizontal mobility involves nothing more than a change of occupation. A carpenter who becomes a painter, a janitor who becomes a gardener, or a soldier who becomes a police officer exemplifies horizontal mobility. Occupational mobility, as opposed to social mobility, does not typically involve vertical mobility.

INDIVIDUAL MOBILITY. **Individual mobility** refers to movement within the class structure on the part of a single person. Such mobility may assume any of the various forms described in this section.

CATEGORICAL MOBILITY. **Categorical mobility** is caused by large-scale structural changes in society and involves movement within the class structure of an entire set or category of individuals, such as those of a particular racial or ethnic background. Social mobility is chiefly of this type. The vast majority of individuals experience mobility simply by being a member of a particular social category.

Categorical mobility often stems from such dynamics as economic depression, war, immigration, and urbanization. The virtual end of segregation and many forms of discrimination directed against minorities in the United States, such as Blacks and women, also stimulated categorical mobility. Another major source of categorical mobility is technological innovation. The age of automation and electronics has

TABLE 10-6. Types of Social Mobility  ▼

| Horizontal | Movement within a given social stratum |
| Vertical | Upward or downward movement from one social stratum to another |
| Intragenerational | Vertical movement within one's lifetime |
| Intergenerational | Vertical movement within a family line over two or more generations |
| Individual | Movement within the class structure on the part of a single individual |
| Categorical | Movement of any type experienced by a category of people |

**431**

reduced the demand for unskilled and semi-skilled labor, while increasing the need for skilled and technical personnel. Concomitant to this development has been the expansion of "white-collar" administration and associated occupations caused by the increasing number of bureaucracies in the complex organizations of modern societies.

## MEASURES OF SOCIAL MOBILITY

Sociologists also distinguish between different kinds of measurement for social mobility. There are two principal types in this respect:

INTRAGENERATIONAL MOBILITY. **Intragenerational mobility** refers to vertical mobility within the stratification system during the course of an individual's lifetime. Sometimes this is called "career mobility," and is measured chiefly in terms of occupational mobility.

▼ INTERGENERATIONAL MOBILITY. **Intergenerational mobility** consists of vertical mobility within a particular family line over two or more generations. Usually it refers to the differences, or lack thereof, in the social class position of people and their parents. It is usually measured in terms of father-son comparisons. Occupation and income are again the most commonly used indicators for this kind of mobility. Intergenerational mobility provides the more reliable measurements and serves as a stronger indicator of the fluidity or rigidity of the stratification system in a particular society than does intragenerational mobility.

**432**

## DETERMINANTS OF SOCIAL MOBILITY

What affects mobility? Obviously, the fundamental answer is, Any change in the relative criteria that determine social rank. More spe-

## BOX 10-3. Dynamics of Social Mobility

**Social mobility is manifested in a number of different kinds of behavior. Among the more common of these are those known as status-seeking and conspicuous consumption.**

*Status-seeking* **refers to a variety of behavior designed to enhance one's social class standing. It invariably involves the accumulation of** *status symbols*—**material objects, titles, behavior, and other things that convey social rank or status. Such things have value only to the extent that they are visible and in limited supply. Fur coats, expensive automobiles, elegant houses, fashionable clothing, and jewelry are examples of status symbols. With some exceptions, the significance of status symbols is on the decline given the rise in income and their availability to all. A college degree, for example, is no longer as much a status symbol as it was a generation ago.**

*Conspicuous consumption* **(Veblen, 1899) refers to a form of behavior and pseudo-status by which people attempt to surround themselves with the external marks (status symbols) of a particular social class position in the hope that they will be treated accordingly. Buying expensive cars and clothes, dining in elegant restaurants, and partaking of luxurious vacations are among the more common forms of this behavior. Conspicuous consumption, thus, is essentially a matter of money—but, as we indicated above, money alone does not confer social status. Moreover, by itself, money is not a very strong indicator—and conspicuous consumers invariably betray themselves through inappropriate forms of social class behavior.**

**Conspicuous consumption may be used, however, by people who are trying to maintain—or, at least manifest—their true social status. It often takes the popularly known form of "keeping up with the Joneses" which refers to the phenomenon of** *relative deprivation*—**a sensitivity to others who are socially similar to oneself. Larger incomes and greater power, for example, do not in themselves bother people. It is only when they expect to have these possessions or rewards—judged against others with the same social status—that there is a problem.\* ▲**

---

\* Relative deprivation refers to a person's lack of goal attainments in terms of what he or she can rightly expect when compared with another individual or with another category that may be used as a point of reference.

cifically, however, one can ask, What are the situations, variables, factors, and dynamics that effect these changes?

Social mobility may be experienced on any of the three principal dimensions of social stratification (wealth, prestige, and power) or on all three. Hence, one can readily understand that social mobility may produce status inconsistency, as well as resolve it. On the other hand, as we have mentioned, it is status inconsistency itself that often provides the individual impetus for social mobility.

The dynamics of mobility, of course, are quite complicated. Various studies (for example, Jencks, 1979; Duncan & Featherman, 1972) have found that a host of factors influence the degree to which an individual may experience social mobility. Among these are family background (including father's occupation, number of siblings, parental education, family size, income), cognitive and intellectual abilities, educational attainment, and personality characteristics. On the basis of a comprehensive analysis of factors involved in mobility (defined primarily in economic terms), Jencks (1979) concluded that no one identifiable factor is able to account for an "enormous amount" of economic success. On the other hand, a combination of a number of relatively small advantages can significantly increase a person's chances of success. It is possible, however, to distinguish between individual and structural factors.

INDIVIDUAL FACTORS. Social mobility does not depend simply on a person's resolve, interest, determination, achievement-orientation, or aggression. Individuals with these characteristics often fail to experience upward mobility. Hence, talent and hard work, while certainly helpful, are no guarantee that a person will experience upward mobility. The desire to relocate, especially to urban areas, where high status positions are found, is important. Blau and Duncan (1967) found that men who remain

in their hometowns throughout their lifetimes have predominantly lower-status positions in contrast to those who relocate in their late teens.

The best routes to upward mobility are education and occupation, in that order. The greater the level of education, the greater the degree of social mobility. Marriage is not an uncommon route, but has generally worked up to now only for men. Women who marry someone in a class inferior to their own tend to be downwardly mobile. Early marriage for either men or women, however, like a lack of education, tends to influence downward mobility. Mobility also shows some relationship to family size, with a positive correlation between upward mobility and smaller families.

Another personal factor that undoubtedly affects social mobility is that of a person's "life-chances," which we shall explore in the next section. Suffice it to say here that the higher an individual's social rank, the stronger is the probability that he or she will experience social mobility. However, life-chances affect both downward and upward mobility. Individuals with better life-chances are less likely to experience downward mobility.

Deferred gratification often is a chief requirement for upward social mobility. This phenomenon is found predominantly in the middle and upper social classes. Those in the lower social strata cannot afford deferred gratification, given their immediate needs and limited resources, which in many cases require living on a day-to-day basis. Those in the upper social strata, on the whole, have no need for deferred gratification, since they can usually afford whatever they choose. Of course, even in these social strata, there is a certain degree of deferred gratification, such as through prolonged education.

We cannot discount the potential of personal factors such as intellectual capacity and ability in achieving upward social mobility. Intelligence, for example, influences the amount and kind of education a person may receive, and

▼ this in turn affects occupation and income. Personality, as we shall see, can also be instrumental. Certain types of occupations, especially those which are the most prestigious, often require particular kinds of personality characteristics. Moreover, having the right kind of personality can help a person's recruitment into certain occupations.

It is estimated that only about one-fifth of social mobility occurs as a result of individual factors. Hence, social mobility is chiefly a dynamic of the structure and processes of the social system.

**434**

STRUCTURAL FACTORS. There are a number of structural factors that produce or prevent social mobility, and they seem to play a more significant role in determining the rates of social mobility within any given society.

Certainly, social mobility is strongly dependent on the openness of the stratification system in question, as well as the sociocultural values of the society. Societies whose value orientations encourage and reward achievement and success are likely to have higher rates of upward mobility than those that maintain a neutral or negative view of such dynamics. The "American dream," for example, is the manifestation of the all-pervasive expectation that upward social mobility is a reality and a right for all Americans to enjoy. Quite dramatically, it is more than a right: it is a mandate. Making an effort to improve one's economic and social position often is considered to be obligatory, and those who remain satisfied with their achievements may be perceived by others as socially deviant. Belief in mobility, or at least in its possibility, affects the actual dynamics of mobility, especially the attempts of people to work for the mobility of both themselves and their children.

Apart from the ideology and values of a society, there are a number of other structural factors that affect social mobility. Among the more important of these are the following elements.

*Technological innovation.* Developments in technology tend to create a larger number of prestigious positions and brings about changes in the job market that may cause a reevaluation or new alignment of social statuses. Movement from agricultural to industrial society has typically caused people to move up to more highly valued manufacturing and service occupations. This situation can work both ways; automation often eliminates jobs and people are forced to find new work in less prestigious occupations.

*Differential fertility.* Differences in fertility rates on the part of various social classes influences both the size and the nature of the labor pool in any society. People in the upper social strata traditionally do not reproduce themselves, and this situation results in occupational openings at these levels, which are filled by individuals from the lower social strata.

*Migration,* whether within or from outside a society, often pushes many of the "locals" and "natives" into higher social classes. These dynamics affect the supply of personnel from which people are recruited to fill positions in the occupation hierarchy. This form of social mobility was a common phenomenon during the periods of great migration to the United States (1860–1920). Today, it is estimated that only 1 percent of social mobility is the result of migratory behavior.

*Industrialization.* Also related to the rate of mobility in a society is industrialization. As a society moves from an agricultural to an industrial economy, the ease and frequency of mobility increases, partly because of the changes in technology and their effect on the occupational structure of society, as well as the related dynamics of urbanization. The number and variety of medium- and high-status positions tend to remain relatively stable in agricultural societies. Industrial societies, on the other hand, have a larger number and variety of skilled and semi-skilled occupations than do agricultural societies.

*Urbanization.* Industrialization is invariably accompanied by urbanization. Urbanized societies and communities are characterized by a proliferation of occupations, especially those of high prestige.

*Two-career families.* A rather recent phenomenon that has occurred with the increased independence of women is that of two-career families. The more extensive employment and career orientation of women may make for increased mobility—especially through intergenerational mobility as these families acquire an increased capacity to produce better life-chances for their children.

*Political structure.* Rates of mobility are affected by the type of political structure in a particular society. Democratic political structures facilitate high mobility, whereas totalitarian ones tend to impede this process (Fox & Miller, 1965).

## EXTENT OF SOCIAL MOBILITY

One of the most distinctive aspects of the American stratification system, as we have stated, is the emphasis on upward mobility. The ideal of equality, an achievement orientation, the success ethic, and the striving for status are all focal aspects of an American value system that prizes social mobility. America has been known historically, and with ample justification, as the land of opportunity. Such beliefs and attitudes are still quite prevalent in the United States (Coleman & Rainwater, 1978). All of these factors have much to do with encouraging and enabling social mobility.

The extent of social mobility in American society, nonetheless, is not so great as one might expect. Most mobility is horizontal rather than vertical, occurring within the same social stratum rather than between strata; that is to say, occupational or career mobility is the principal

type of movement. The best estimates today say that about 50 percent of the American population remains stationary in social rank throughout life; in the other half of the population, 30 to 35 percent are upwardly mobile, and 10 to 20 percent downwardly mobile (Newman, 1988; Tumin, 1985; Grusky & Hauser, 1984). Quite interestingly, as depicted in Figure 10-3, the rates of total mobility seem to be fairly consistent in industrialized societies (Hope, 1982). Such a situation supports the contention that mobility is more a product of structural factors within society than of personal factors.

We can offer some specific findings on social mobility in the United States. Kahl (1957) analyzed the American occupational structure in 1920 and 1950. He assumed that the work force in 1950 was composed of the sons of people from the 1920 work force. On this basis, Kahl found that 67 percent of the work force was intergenerationally mobile (one or more class

**435**

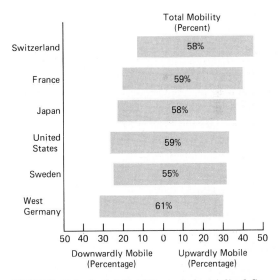

FIGURE 10-3 Social Mobility in Industrialized Societies. The data above compiled by Lipset and Bendix (1966) show that the rates of social mobility are fairly similar in the industrialized societies of the world. Such findings support the contention that mobility is more a product of structural factors within society than of personal factors.

▼

changes), mostly upward. While his basic assumption has been challenged, Kahl's findings are among the few that exist, and, furthermore, they are fairly consistent with other estimates, even though they may be a bit on the high side. Coleman and Rainwater (1978) in a more recent study, based on surveyed samples of people in metropolitan areas of Boston and Kansas City, determined that intergenerational mobility was experienced by 42 percent; 49 percent were immobile, remaining in the same social class as their parents; and 9 percent had undergone downward mobility. These figures are gross descriptions of the general population. For specific social categories, or segments of the population, such as females and Blacks, the findings varied somewhat.

436

As these data suggest, the general structure of social classes seems to remain fairly intact, the amounts of up and down movement tending to balance out. Although more common in the United States than in other industrial societies, "rags to riches" instances of social mobility are quite rare. Most mobility involves movement of only one-half social class up or down the social class ladder. The proportional distribution of the population within the social class structure, as well as the patterns of mobility, have remained fairly constant for the past several decades (McRoberts & Selbee, 1981). One such indication is the little change that has taken place in patterns of income distribution during this century (see Figure 10-2). The top two-fifths of the population claimed 68 percent of the available income in 1986, while the bottom two-fifths had only 16 percent. Such a situation is not much different than it was thirty to forty years ago. The social class structure in this respect, thus, tends to perpetuate itself.

Economic improvements, in income and standard of living, often are confused with changes in social prestige and social power. Enormous changes indeed have taken place in the American standard of living throughout the past several decades. The median income of the lowest one-fifth of the stratification hierarchy has more than doubled in constant dollars during the past thirty years. Working wives will probably increase this figure even more in the immediate future. Certainly, there is less poverty in the United States today, as in many other countries in the world, than there was two generations ago. Indeed, the percentage of people below the poverty line* has diminished. Today, less than 15 percent of the population lives in poverty, compared to twice that amount more than forty years ago. Hence, the general consensus among sociologists is that in many respects inequality among the various social strata in American society has been reduced over the past few decades. Such a situation, however, is often misleading in terms of actual increases in social mobility.

All in all, it seems that upward mobility is greater in the United States than in most other countries. It is clear that if the measure of upward mobility is movement into high-ranking white-collar occupational positions by manual workers, then there has been a much greater degree of social mobility in the United States than in other countries (Blau & Duncan, 1967). One study has shown that approximately 10 to 15 percent of Americans of working-class origin attain a top-echelon executive position. In contrast, the comparable percentages for other industrial societies are as follows: for Japan, 7 percent; Great Britain, less than 3 percent; for Denmark, West Germany, and France, less than 2 percent; and Italy, less than 1 percent (Miller, 1960). Another indicator of upward social mobility—the extent to which individuals from poor families become corporate executive officers—shows that this type of movement is greatest in the United States (Newcomer, 1955; Blau & Duncan, 1967). The United States, moreover, is one of the very few countries in

* The poverty level in 1988 was set at an annual income of $11,611 for a family of four. On the basis of this criterion, about 32 million people (about 14 percent of the American population) were classified as poor in 1988.

which upward mobility exceeds downward mobility (Hauser & Featherman, 1977).

Many social scientists expect that social mobility will remain fairly constant. Nevertheless, it is difficult to predict with much accuracy what societal changes, such as the coming of postindustrial society and a service-orientation among other things, will bring. Potentially most significant, however, is the mobility of women as their emphasis continues to shift from marital to occupational roles. Personal achievement, not ascription of spousal status, may indeed bring about significant consequences in social mobility and social stratification.

## CONSEQUENCES OF SOCIAL MOBILITY

Social mobility brings both advantages and disadvantages. These may be assessed as either personal or social consequences.

SOCIAL CONSEQUENCES.   High rates of social mobility, especially for social categories, can cause major social disorganization and social changes that require extensive personal and social adjustments. Among these changes could be a major impact on the gross national product of a society and a host of economic readjustments. Such developments in turn could have a significant effect on life-chances and lifestyles, which we shall discuss subsequently in more detail. A similar effect could be a reallocation of occupational prestige and its attendant influence on the power structures of society. High rates of social mobility, in short, could fundamentally alter the three principal structures of the stratification system: wealth, prestige, and power.

INDIVIDUAL CONSEQUENCES.   Considerable research indicates that significant changes in social status, whether upward or

downward, are likely to produce emotional disorders. Such a situation is especially apt to be true when status changes come about abruptly and unexpectedly, especially if status inconsistency is involved. Downward mobility, and its implications of failure in this upwardly mobile society, can be particularly stressful, producing feelings of worthlessness, shame, and despair. Suicide rates for downwardly mobile people are higher than for either upwardly or horizontally mobile individuals (Breed, 1963). While the downwardly mobile also have been found to be more susceptible to the more serious types of mental disorders, the upwardly mobile show above average rates for the less serious kinds of psychological problems. Upwardly mobile people, for example, have higher rates of neuroses and such psychosomatic disorders as high blood pressure and ulcers (Langer & Michael, 1963; Kessin, 1971).

While it is plausible that the downwardly mobile should experience psychological stress, it is less obvious why the upwardly mobile should also experience such stress. Upward mobility, however, can be just as similarly disturbing as downward mobility. There are, in fact, several factors associated with upward mobility that are stress-producing. In particular the need to demonstrate success in an achievement-oriented society can have serious psychological effects on a person. Here it is the fear of failure, rather than the reality, that is so upsetting. Moreover, being on the margin of the middle or upper-middle class is apt to produce anxiety, because the individual may feel uncomfortable in a new social environment and unsure how to interact with those who have always belonged to the higher class. The person may be self-consciously aware of certain identifiable traits of lower-class origins, which could include improper diction, a sparse vocabulary, or a lack of knowledge concerning the arts and world events. Upward mobility can also exert strong pressure on the lives of significant others, such as spouse, children, and parents.

437

▼

Upward mobility often requires the severance of personal and family ties, which may promote feelings of guilt. The person who finds him- or herself in a higher status must decide whether to disassociate from friends and relatives who have remained in the same socioeconomic position. The individual may not wish to be reminded of lower-class origins, and so may decide to terminate interaction with them. Such a decision, however, may generate feelings of guilt and anxiety. A study comparing the interactions of upwardly mobile couples with nonmobile couples showed that the upwardly mobile couples were much less likely even to speak of their relatives to friends and acquaintances than were the stable-status couples. The majority of people with whom the upwardly mobile people interacted socially were known to them for less than thirty years, while most of the friends of the stable-status couples were known to them for more than thirty years (Bruce, 1970). Upward mobility thus can upset existing patterns of family life and friendships in such a way as to produce highly significant consequences.

# Behavioral Consequences of Social Stratification

Social strata are not merely theoretical constructs. On the contrary, they constitute a type of distinct social reality. Social strata comprise a kind of social space within which people live. Within this social space, the greater portion of one's social life is spent—for many people, the entirety of one's social life. Nearly all facets of social life are affected, directly or indirectly, by the structure and dynamics of social stratification. Social class membership, in short, affects a great deal of what we do, and much of what happens to us in life.

The significance of social stratification is pervasive in the life of the individual and, of course, in the dynamics of society. Knowing a person's social class, or socioeconomic status, can tell us much about that individual's social behavior. Such things as family size, life expectancy, political orientation, and religion are just a few of the many aspects of social life that are related to a person's social stratum.

Let us look at some of the more significant behavioral consequences of social stratification. Much of our data and many of our examples are from the United States; however, basically the same patterns and dynamics exist in other societies, particularly in modern industrialized ones.

## SOCIAL STRATA AS SUBCULTURES

Every social stratum is in many respects a subculture with its own distinctive set of values and way of life. All of the aspects of culture (beliefs, values, norms, roles, language) may be found within social strata; they comprise, in short, a way of life for the people within them. Distinctive class cultures are especially likely to emerge in societies that have rigid boundaries separating their social strata and that, consequently, are characterized by relatively minimal degrees of social interaction. Societies whose stratification systems allow high rates of social mobility to occur (upward or downward) are less likely to have social strata characterized by distinctive subcultures.

This dynamic, however, is a bit complicated. Class culture also cuts across racial, religious, and ethnic as well as other types of subcultures. Therefore, one must be cautious in this kind of analysis. Many of the differences in racial, ethnic, and religious subcultures are to a considerable extent really class differences. Given the high correlations between many of these types of subcultures and social class, a great deal of the subcultural differences disappear when one allows for class in the analysis of the subcultures. One may speak in particular of the "cul-

438

ture of poverty" (Lewis, 1960) that allegedly is found among many of the people in the lowest social strata. Many of the poor are thought to form a distinctive subculture as a result of common social experiences. Hence, a culture of poverty cuts across ethnic, racial, religious, and regional boundaries. Among the distinctive features of this culture of poverty are apathy, insecurity, powerlessness, hopelessness, inability to plan for the future, cynicism, distrust of authority, fatalistic attitudes about the future, and a focus on immediate gratification—all of which work against mobility and perpetuate the status quo. These attitudes and behavioral patterns tend to be perpetuated from generation to generation.*

## LIFE-CHANCES

People who belong to the same socioeconomic class share the same life-chances, which can be described as an individual's access to "a supply of goods, external living conditions, and personal life experiences" (Warner, Meeker, & Eells, 1960:542).

**Life-chances,** then, refer to the differential access to social opportunities and social rewards that stem from an individual's position in the status hierarchy. A person's life-chances, in short, refer to the odds or probabilities of being either the beneficiary of an advantage or the victim of a disadvantage. The opportunities of life, as we shall see, are not equally or randomly distributed throughout the status hierarchy. Life-chances are, in general, positively correlated with the social class hierarchy. Let us look at some of the more important life-chances— those that are related to the major opportunities and the most significant events of life.

One very dramatic example of life-chances often mentioned in sociological literature con-

▼

**439**

**Social Opportunities.** Life-chances are not equally distributed in any society. The opportunity for upward mobility and socioeconomic success depends on one's place on the social class ladder. (Charles Gatewood/ Image Works)

cerns the survivors of the ill-fated *Titanic* that sank on its maiden voyage in 1912. According to Walter Lord in *A Night to Remember*, only 3 percent of the female passengers in first class drowned (and most of those that did remained behind voluntarily), versus 16 percent of those in second class and 45 percent in third class. Of course, one must remember that the higher social classes had cabins on the upper decks.

INCOME. That income is positively correlated with social class rank should be quite obvious from much of what we have said thus

---

* This subculture, of course, does not exist among all of the poor. The aged and the infirm poor are specific exceptions, since their poverty has a different source.

▼   TABLE 10-7.   Social Class and Life-Chances

| Life-Chances | Lower Class | Middle Class | Upper Class |
|---|---|---|---|
| Mortality ratio (mean, all classes = 1) | | | |
| White males 45–54 years old | 2.12 | 1.01 | 0.074 |
| Victims of heart disease | | | |
| Prevalence per 1,000 population | 114 | 40 | 35 |
| Obesity | 52% | 43% | 9% |
| Marital instability | | | |
| White males, 25–34, ever divorced | 23% | 10% | 6% |
| Victims of violent crime | | | |
| Per 1,000 population | 52 | 30 | 27 |
| Children who attend college | 26% | 37% | 58% |
| Describe themselves as "very happy" | 29% | 38% | 56% |

**Source: Dennis Gilbert and Joseph A. Kahl, _The American Class Structure_. Homewood, Ill.: Dorsey, 1987. Table 4-7, p. 111.**

440

far in this chapter. Let us consider, however, one specific point—the probability of lifetime earnings. The estimate of lifetime earnings (between the ages of eighteen and sixty-four) of a high school graduate is about $300,000 more than that of an elementary school graduate, while that of a college graduate is $350,000 more than a high school graduate.* In 1985, the ratio of median income for all college graduates compared with individuals with only a high school education was about 1.5.

EDUCATION.   There is considerable difference in the prestige of the schools and the quality of education available to people in different social classes. Differences in personal resources and family background often make for significant differences in the quantity and quality of education, which can have lifetime consequences (Bowles & Gintis, 1976). Upper classes can often afford private schools with a host of

extracurricular and cocurricular activities. The disadvantages of cultural deprivation, and the lag involved, become more and more significant as a person ages.

HEALTH.   Rates of morbidity and prevention of illness differ widely among the various social strata. The correlation of morbidity rates and social strata is an essentially negative one, while that for illness prevention is generally positive (Cockerham, 1986). Differential access to health care (nutrition, clothing, food, housing) is a fundamental explanation here. Significant too is the fact that dangerous occupations are disproportionately found among the lower social classes. Differences in the ability to pay for medical and dental care is an additional aspect of this situation (Califano, 1985; Krause, 1977). However, it is not simply a matter of cost, but also a matter of the quality and the availability of health care.

MENTAL HEALTH.   Severe psychological pathology does not appear to be uniformly dis-

* U.S. Bureau of the Census, _Statistical Abstract of the United States: 1985_. Washington, D.C.: U.S. Government Printing Office, 1985.

tributed throughout society. Various studies throughout the past half-century (see, for example, Faris & Dunham, 1939; Srole et al., 1962; Dohrenwend & Dohrenwend, 1974; Syme & Berkman, 1981; and Angermeyer, 1987) have shown that the lower social strata experience more mental illness than the others. In fact, there appears to be five times as much mental illness in the lowest social strata than in the highest. Suicide rates, moreover, are negatively correlated in terms of the social class hierarchy. Again, people in the lower social classes are less able to pay for care, hence the kind and extent of treatment to cope with the stresses of life show a differential association in terms of social class.

LONGEVITY.  Life expectancies for various social strata are considerably different. Longevity is obviously related to and is a reflection of a person's level of health and opportunities for health care. Even differences in infant mortality demonstrate this dimension of differential longevity in terms of social class. The infant death rate (per 1000 live births) for 1972 shows that the lower the family income, the less the chance that an infant will survive the first year of life. For families with an income under $3,000, the rate is 27.3 for Whites and 42.5 for Blacks; for families with an income over $10,000, the rate is 19.4 and 31.5 respectively.*

CRIMINAL JUSTICE.  Differences in terms of the frequency of arrests, as well as the kind and extent of punishment, are associated with social class (see, for example, Smith, 1987; Reiman, 1984; Thomson & Zingraff, 1981). Only a small percentage of all the people arrested and convicted of crime, or committed to prison, come from the upper social classes. People in the lower social classes are more likely than those in the higher social classes to be arrested, to be given stiffer fines and longer sentences, and even to be imprisoned or executed. Among the principal explanations for these differences is that lower-class people cannot afford bail costs or the fees of criminal lawyers, and their appearance (language, dress, and demeanor) often acts to their detriment while they are passing through the criminal justice system.

441

## LIFESTYLES

Social classes can be distinguished in terms of distinctive **lifestyles,** which refer to beliefs, values, attitudes, motivations, and actual patterns of behavior that typify or characterize a particular social stratum.

Lifestyles include the entire gamut of the elements of living, from tastes in food, clothing, music, and art to the organizations one prefers to join and the neighborhoods in which one chooses to reside. Lifestyles are commonly manifested by certain physical or tangible possessions (status symbols) that represent a particular social standing. Certain types of cars, clothes, jewelry, houses, and vacations are examples of status symbols that indicate variations in lifestyles. Such differences are reflected even in the choice of recreation. Tennis and golf, for example, have long been considered "upper class" sports, as witnessed by exclusive country clubs in which membership is reserved for "the right kind of people," even though in recent years these sports have experienced extensive popularity throughout many other social strata. Obviously, there are no hard-and-fast distinctions, for lifestyle does not refer to any one pattern of behavior. One frequently observes considerable imitation of one class (usually upper strata) by another.

Of increasing interest today is the sociological exploration of a new social phenomenon known as **embourgeoisement,** the tendency for lifestyles to become more homogeneous among

---

* From U.S. Department of Health, Education, and Welfare, *Infant Mortality Rates: Socio-Economic Factors, 1972,* Washington, D.C., U.S. Government Printing Office, 1973, p. 13.

▼

**442**

some of the social strata in society (see, for example, Wright, 1982; DeFronzo, 1974). Such a process seems to be more typical among working-class individuals who seek to adopt middle-class standards of social behavior. Rising levels of income and education within the working class are offered as one basis for this alleged change in lifestyle. Another is the expansion of white-collar "service jobs" among the working class. Other longitudinal research over the past half-century has shown that erstwhile differences in family life (for example, use of domestic help, frequency of working wives, educational aspirations of children) among the middle and working classes are reflecting patterns of partial convergence (Caplow & Chadwick, 1979).

A number of differences in behavior and lifestyle, nonetheless, do distinguish the various social strata, and it is unlikely that all of them will eventually disappear. It is safe to say, moreover, that the greater the distance between classes, the greater the differences in lifestyle. Let us look at some of the more common examples of variations in the lifestyles of social classes. Each of the following examples demonstrates differences in the fundamental values of the various social strata.

SOCIAL RELATIONS.  Social relations in all social classes tend to be endogamous—that is, undertaken between people in the same or adjacent social classes. People associate and interact on the basis of similar lifestyles. Social segregation tends to lead to physical segregation, which is perhaps evidenced most clearly in terms of residential segregation and housing styles—small apartments, comfortable bungalows, and cottages, as opposed to luxurious mansions, country estates, and summer houses, for example.

MARITAL AND FAMILY PATTERNS. Beginning with the selection of partners, marital and family patterns also tend to be endogamous. Matriarchy (female dominance) is a more likely form in the lower social strata. The number of children in a family, at least up to very recent years, has tended to be inversely correlated with social class rank. While these different patterns have been disappearing in the United States for a number of reasons during the past few years, they still obtain in many other societies.

SOCIALIZATION.  Patterns of childrearing show significant variations across social strata. There are significant differences, for example, in goals, techniques, and types of sanctions (physical or psychological), as well as in values and attitudes. Several studies have shown that the lower and upper classes are likely to distinguish themselves respectively in terms of the degree of emphasis on external and internal control of behavior. Erlanger (1974), for example, reports that working-class parents are likely to use spanking as a means of punishing children; middle-class parents, on the other hand, are more likely to use psychological means, such as threatening to withdraw affection.

Studies also show that socialization and educational experiences of the lower strata provide its people with fewer of the skills and social competencies considered necessary for coping with life (Kessler & Cleary, 1980). Differences such as these, of course, are reflected in turn in terms of life-chances, particularly in the matter of differential rates of mental health.

RELIGIOUS AFFILIATION.  Differential association of religious membership in terms of social class has been demonstrated repeatedly. Unitarians, Episcopalians, Presbyterians, and Jews draw their membership very heavily from the upper social classes; Lutherans, Methodists, and Catholics from the middle classes; while congregations in the Baptist, revivalist, and fundamentalist religions are comprised predominantly of people from the lower social strata. Each of the major religions, nonetheless, recruits its faithful from all social strata; hence there is not a simple homogeneity of class membership in any of them. Greater homogeneity is likely to be found, however, within specific congregations of a particular religion. Orthodox Jews, for example, are primarily from the lower social strata, while conservative and reformed believers reflect middle- and upper-class backgrounds.

POLITICAL ATTITUDES.   Although political parties in the United States are supported by people from all social classes, historical trends have shown that the lower social classes heavily favor the Democratic party, while the upper and middle classes strongly sustain the Republican party. However, there are subcategories within these social strata which are inconsistent with the dominant pattern. One such case is that of university and college professors, especially those in the humanities and social sciences, who in recent years have supported liberal and Democrat orientations (see Lipset & Ladd, 1972).

Because Americans are not very party- or issue-oriented, they tend to vote in terms of candidates rather than class interests. In general, the lower classes more often support radical candidates, who advocate drastic change, while the upper classes tend to endorse the more conservative candidates. Similar class differences are reflected in various political organizations such as the Ku Klux Klan and the American Civil Liberties Union.

VOLUNTARY ASSOCIATIONS.   People from the middle and upper social strata participate in voluntary organizations far more extensively than people in the lower social strata. Hausknecht (1962), for example, found that 29 percent of professionals, proprietors,

managers, and officials belong to two or more voluntary organizations, in contrast to only 5 percent of unskilled workers. There are also significant differences in the kinds of organizations with which members of different social classes affiliate. Individuals from the lower class are found predominantly in labor unions, religious groups, and fraternal organizations like the Elks or Moose. Those from the middle-class

443

**Spectator or Participant?** Individual sports frequently are part of the recreational lifestyle of upper social strata. Occupants of the lower strata more typically engage in team sports or participate as spectators. Differences in cost partly account for this variation. Here Jacqueline Kennedy Onassis and her son, John F. Kennedy, Jr., are shown participating in a fox hunt. (Wide World Photos)

▼

principally belong to service organizations such as the Kiwanis and Rotary Clubs. People in the upper class are members of social clubs, charitable organizations, country clubs, and professional organizations.

LEISURE AND RECREATION.   There are significant differences in the leisure and recreational activities of individuals in different social strata. Chief manifestations of these differences can be found in vacation styles and, as mentioned above, in preferences for sports activities—apart from the national pastimes of baseball, football, and basketball, which cut across class structure. Upper- and middle-class people are more likely to be involved in individual sports, and as active participants; while those in the lower- and working-classes tend to be engaged primarily in team sports, or as spectators and passive participants. Costs and the amount of leisure time available are among the factors that account for these differences.

# Personality and Social Stratification

Given that the dynamics of social stratification have such a pervasive influence on social life, one can readily expect that there also are significant relationships between personality and various dimensions of social stratification. Recent studies, for example, suggest that not more than about 50 percent of social mobility of individuals is due to identifiable social factors such as social background and education. This situation has led many social scientists (for example, Turner & Martinez, 1977; Jencks et al., 1972) to suspect that individual differences in personality may play a significant role in socioeconomic achievement. Let us consider a few of these questions in order to demonstrate the role of personality, as both a dependent and an independent variable, in the dynamics of social stratification.

## PERSONALITY DEVELOPMENT AND SOCIAL CLASS

A number of studies (for example, Kohn & Schooler, 1983; Lundberg, 1974) make it amply clear that social class background affects personality development. Such a situation should be quite evident, given our discussion above of social class as a distinct subculture and, more significant, the differential social learning that takes place in terms of social class. To the extent that individuals experience a similar socialization, we can expect to find similarities in personality as a product of this experience. Correspondingly, there will be relevant differences in personality to the extent that there are significantly different experiences in socialization. Of course, one must be cautious here. Variations in social class often overlap with or parallel other social variables, such as religious, racial, or ethnic backgrounds. Notwithstanding the specific and very significant influences of these factors, the reality and role of social class factors in and of themselves is quite clear. Kohn (1977), in a series of studies, found social class variables to be constant regardless of race, religion, national background, region of the country, or size of the community. One of the most dramatic examples in this regard can be seen in the dynamics of the "culture of poverty" and its influence on many facets of personality, which we shall discuss subsequently.

Consistent with the above findings, numerous studies have demonstrated the existence of modal patterns of personality among the various social classes. Lipset (1981), for example, has spoken in this regard of "working-class authoritarianism" and argues that the modal personality of the lower class can be described as more limited, more restricted, more closed, more dogmatic, and more authoritarian than that of the middle or upper classes. On the other hand, the multivalent, highly aggressive, strongly achievement-oriented personality (the "Type A" personality; see Box 10-4) that is well-known for intense status-seeking activity is

444

# Box 10-4. The "Type A" Personality ▼

American focal values of achievement and success are most keenly manifested perhaps in those individuals who possess what has come to be known as a "Type A" personality. This psychological syndrome, isolated by two cardiologists, Meyer Friedman and Ray Rosenman (1974), is found rather extensively among individuals who are highly achievement oriented and who exhibit a relatively intense drive for success.

There are three focal components of the Type A personality pattern:

1. Time urgency (a tendency to be impulsive and immediate in acting).
2. Chronic activation (a tendency to stay active or keyed up for most of the time).
3. Multiphasism (a tendency to do more than one thing at the same time).

445

Among the modes of behavior the Type A personality typically manifests are the following: hyperalertness, rapidity in movement (walking, talking, and eating), impatience with others in conversation and social interaction, forcefulness in speech (both in volume and content), simultaneous engagement in activities (for example, eating and reading, driving and shaving, watching television and reading), hostility, ease in developing anger, and obsessive-compulsive tendencies.

The "Type B" personality exhibits none of the patterns of behavior that characterize the Type A individual. Such people show no sense of urgency or impatience. They have no obsession or preoccupation with achievement and accomplishments, and are able to relax without a sense of guilt. Type B individuals participate in recreational activities for the sake of sheer enjoyment, rather than to exhibit ability or superiority.

Research using the *Jenkins Activity Survey* (Friedman & Ulmer, 1984) shows that the Type A personality is found to be much more prevalent among top-level administrators than among those in the lower levels of occupational rank. More specifically, this type of personality is particularly common in managerial and sales positions.

It seems that one has to pay a rather high price for ascribing to American values as well as for one's personality. People with a Type A personality are at greater risk of heart disease and myocardial infarction. Relevant data show that both the annual incidence of coronary disease and the percentage of recurrent myocardial infarctions are positively and significantly correlated with Type A personality scores. (Among men, such rates are nearly twice as high as among women.) For example, the annual rate for coronary heart disease among Type B men is 8.0 per 1000, versus 14.3 among Type A men. Here we have strong evidence of the interrelationships between personality, social behavior, and physiological functions. ▲

▼ found quite disproportionately in the middle and upper social strata.

Other research has shown that the incidence of dysfunctional self systems and abnormal patterns of personality are unevenly distributed in terms of social class backgrounds. Let us explore these questions in more detail.

## SELF-CONCEPT AND SOCIAL RANK

446

A person's self-evaluation is strongly influenced by class rank. As a general principle, people in the upper strata feel individually superior and have more positive feelings about themselves and their self-worth. The contrary seems to be true for those in the lower strata, especially the very lowest stratum. Lower-class people tend to have relatively low self-esteem and to be characterized by feelings of inefficacy, ineffectiveness, pessimism, and even downright fatalistic attitudes about life and their purpose in it. Skid row residents dramatically illustrate this principle.

One can imagine many of the consequences of the lack of self-esteem. The fact that the suicide rate and the rate of mental illness show an inverse correlation with social rank is thought to be reflective to a great extent of this sociopsychological situation. The same is true of such forms of deviant behavior as addiction to drugs and alcohol.

Lower-strata people who can look only up, and who perceive the chances for mobility as remote, often yield to a sense of fatalism and total failure. As Knupfer (1947), in a "Portrait of the Underdog," states: "Closely linked to economic underprivilege is psychological underprivilege: habits of submission, little access to sources of information, lack of verbal facility. These things appear to produce a lack of self-confidence which increases the unwillingness of the low-status person to participate in many phases of our predominantly middle-class culture."

**Personal Worth.** Social class position, reflecting differences in both achievements and opportunities, strongly influences one's self-concept and level of self-esteem. (© Joel Gordon 1974)

One study compared the self-image of college students in terms of social mobility (Cohen & Miller, 1969). There was a greater incidence of positive self-image among students who were socially mobile than among the nonmobile in these upper-middle-class students. The students who were mobile perceived themselves as more independent and productive, and had greater feelings of competence and adequacy, than did the stable-status students. Thus, during the adolescent stage of the life cycle, upward social mobility may generate positive rather than negative psychological feelings.

The interplay of stratification and self-concepts is most dramatic in the lower-lower class, where the "culture of poverty" is dominant. People who live in the culture of poverty are not only uncommonly poor, but, more often than not, emotionally and psychologically impoverished as well. Levels of positive affect and motivation found commonly in the dominant culture are significantly absent in the culture of poverty. Negative self-concept and low self-esteem, coupled with a pessimistic or near fatalistic outlook on life, have much to do with the production of a distinct type of personality that is characterized by passivity, unsociability, and low achievement orientation. The culture of poverty in many respects becomes a cycle of poverty that tends to reproduce itself and its distinctive types of personality.

## THE ALIENATED PERSONALITY

While one can speak of alienation in various contexts, this concept is associated in particular with Marx's theory of social stratification. It seems appropriate, therefore, to offer here a brief discussion of the alienated personality.

**Alienation** refers to a subjective condition, a feeling that society cannot, or will not, meet one's needs. The dynamics of alienation, according to Seeman (1959), include a sense of powerlessness (no control over one's efforts); social isolation (withdrawal from many aspects of life); meaninglessness (behavior devoid of personal significance), instrumentality (perceiving the self as a means rather than as a goal), and self-estrangement (treating the self as a commodity). Alienation, thus, is a nearly total emotional withdrawal and separation from society. The alienated individual may be described as one who is in society, but not of it—one with few group affiliations or institutional loyalties.

Marx's concern with alienation was in terms of the experiences of the industrial worker whom he saw as estranged from his work, as having no control over the work process or the product of his labor. The worker, in effect, was just a cog in the massive wheel of industrial production. Marx (1844/1962) argued that

> . . . in degrading labor—which should be man's free, spontaneous activity—to a mere means of physical subsistence, alienated labor degrades man's essential life to a mere means to an end. The awareness which man should have of his relationship to the rest of mankind is reduced to a state of detachment in which he and his fellows become simply unfeeling objects. Thus, alienated labor turns man's essential humanity into a non-human property. It estranges man from his own human body.

One important source of alienation in modern societies is the extreme division of labor which allegedly makes it impossible for the individual to use the totality of his capacities and skills, particularly those of an intellectual and emotional nature. The alienated personality, thus, in Marx's formulation, is one who is suffering from the lack of fulfillment or realization of basic human nature. Such people are allegedly found predominantly and overwhelmingly in the lower social strata and are the target victims of exploitation by the managerial and entrepreneurial classes.

## PERSONALITY AND SOCIAL MOBILITY

One of the most intriguing relationships between personality and social stratification involves the dynamics of social mobility. A number of studies have demonstrated that a wide range of personality variables have significant and systematic effects on status striving and socioeconomic achievement. This is reflected in the circulation of "survival guides" in the corporate world which stress the importance of personality in career attainment. Even stronger evidence that personality influences social mobility can be seen in the fact that certain social positions require specific

447

▼

personality characteristics—or types of personality—as shown by the extensive use of psychological testing in the personnel recruitment and selection processes of many organizations.

Several studies suggest that people who achieve higher social positions have distinguishing personality characteristics, as compared with those who do not. There is evidence, for example, that upwardly mobile people are more likely than nonmobile individuals to possess a Machiavellian personality (see Chapter 9). Machiavellianism, the ability to manage and to manipulate people, seems to have the strongest positive influence on upward occupational mobility in the realm of white-collar jobs (Turner & Martinez, 1977). The nature and characteristics of many of these jobs are allegedly such that Machiavellian individuals will be better able, under appropriate social circumstances, to achieve occupational advancement than people lacking such a personality structure.

Another relevant dimension of personality in this regard is that of achievement motivation. Crockett (1962) utilized the Thematic Apperception Test in a nationwide study to assess enduring personality dispositions to strive for tangibly evaluated success. He showed that the strength of achievement motivation is an important personality function contributing to intergenerational occupational mobility. The strength of achievement motivation, among persons sharing equal opportunity (for example, similar regional, occupational, and educational backgrounds), is positively associated with upward occupational mobility. Consequently, low achievement motivation was associated with downward occupational mobility for those reared in lower social strata.

Elder (1969) explored personality change as a consequence of occupational mobility in a longitudinal study to determine whether the personality features of upwardly mobile men differed from those of nonmobile ones. He compared sixty-nine men from working- and middle-class origins, some were upwardly mobile and others were not. The comparisons were made in three different time periods: junior high school, senior high school, and adulthood (between the ages of thirty-three and thirty-eight). Personality ratings and other measures indicated that the men who became upwardly mobile were brighter, more ambitious, and displayed a more integrative personality structure during adolescence than those men who did not go on to attain higher status. Elder (1969:322) observed that "The interplay between these attributes and occupational demands seemed to contribute to the increasing personality differences between mobility groups from adolescence to adulthood, with the upwardly mobile showing a considerable gain in productivity, dependability, self-control, and morale. Defeatist tendencies, withdrawal from frustration, opportunism, direct impulse expression, and heavy drinking were most prevalent among the nonmobile in adulthood."

Elder also found that approximately fourteen years after their graduation from high school, the self-concepts of the upwardly mobile men differed significantly from those of the nonmobile men. The upwardly mobile men scored higher on such dimensions as responsibility, well-being, and achievement through independence.

Another longitudinal study involved children who scored at least 140 on an I.Q. test. Those who went on to fulfill their potential were shown to be more emotionally stable and better able to adjust to a variety of social situations. They were also found to be more popular, more sensitive to the views of others, and freer from feelings of either superiority or inferiority in comparison with individuals of the same intelligence level who failed to realize their potential. Moreover, those who were successful as adults also demonstrated a greater degree of persistence in attaining their personal goals (Terman & Oden, 1947).

Research shows a broad range of pathology concentrated among the downwardly mobile; however, obsessive-compulsive disorders in particular are relatively more common among the upwardly mobile (see Langner & Michaels, 1963). The question is whether these psychological conditions precede and affect mobility, or are consequences of it and distinctive adaptations to social strata.

Some sociologists, nonetheless, maintain that while mobility or the lack of it may be one cause of mental illness, psychological dysfunctions and certain personality characteristics may facilitate either upward or downward mobility. These available data show that there is a reciprocal relationship between personality and upward mobility. Not only do certain personality characteristics facilitate upward mobility, but that the experience of being upwardly mobile also produces changes in the personality. As Elder (1969:321) puts it, there is "evidence of a circular reinforcing process in which early competencies are strengthened through the experiences and rewards of occupational success."

## ABNORMAL PERSONALITY AND SOCIAL CLASS

However much they may be considered deviant or abnormal, neurotic and psychotic individuals are distinctive types of personalities characterized by specific psychological syndromes. Considerable data demonstrate that the prevalence of distinctive types of psychiatric patients in the population is related significantly to social class. That is to say, apart from the differential prevalence of mental illness in terms of social class (inverse relationship between social class and mental illness), as we saw in our discussion of life-chances, here we can point to distinctive types of mental illness (including specific personality types) within various social classes. There is, in other words, a significant association between social class and specific psychiatric disorders.

Hollingshead and Redlich (1958) in a well-known study on social class and mental illness have shown that schizophrenic types of personality are found predominantly and dispro-

**449**

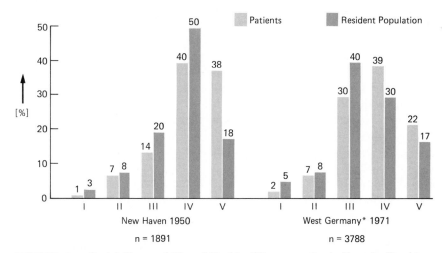

FIGURE 10-4 Social Class and Mental Health. *Three counties in Bavaria: Berchtesgaden, Rosenheim, Traunstein. Source: H. Dilling and S. Weyerer, "Social Class and Mental Disorders: Results from Upper Bavarian Studies." In M.C. Angermeyer (ed.), *From Social Class to Social Stress.* Berlin: Springer-Verlag, 1987.

▼

**450**

portionately in the lower social classes. These researchers found that the incidence of neurosis was fairly similar in all social classes, but that, as other studies have substantiated, psychosis, especially schizophrenia, occurs with much greater frequency in the lower social classes. Several other studies in various countries (see, for example, Angermeyer, 1987; Goodman et al., 1983; Straus, 1982; Dohrenwend, 1973; and Kohn, 1972) have also demonstrated a linear relationship between socioeconomic status and schizophrenia, as well as other forms of psychopathology, again with generally and unusually higher rates in the lowest socioeconomic strata of urban communities (see Figure 10-4).

The general conclusion to be drawn from these kinds of data is that they demonstrate the necessity for simultaneously considering the role of both personality factors and sociocultural factors in the analysis of social stratification and social mobility.

## Summary

Social stratification refers to the process and system by which differential value and prestige are attached to the different statuses and roles, as well as to the various social categories and social classifications, that can be distinguished in all societies.

A social stratum consists of a hierarchically ranked category of people who share the same or similar social ranking in a particular community or society. In more common terminology, the term "social class" is used, although this label often has a more specific meaning within the context of social stratification.

Every known society—contemporary or historical, simple or complex—is characterized by social stratification in one form or another. There are two fundamental bases for social stratification. One is provided by the nature of society as essentially a systematic division of labor. The other basis inheres in the very nature of people as valuing beings, ones who can attach differential worth or importance to the phenomena in their world and express choices among them. A society without social stratification—a classless society—is a sociological impossibility.

Weber distinguished three basic components of social stratification: class, status, and power. Class refers to social ranking in terms of economic variables. Status refers here to a social ranking in terms of social prestige or social honor that is conferred upon an individual by other members of society. Power refers to social ranking in terms of influence, or the ability to direct or to control others, to influence social events and activities. Status consistency refers to how similarly a person ranks in the various dimensions of social stratification: wealth, prestige, and power.

There are two principal sociological theories of social stratification: functional theory and conflict theory. Functionalists maintain that social stratification is not only universal, but is so because it is a functional necessity of any society. In the perspective of conflict theory, social stratification is neither necessary nor inevitable and, hence, need not be a universal feature of society. Conflict theorists, moreover, consider social stratification to be highly dysfunctional, as well as the major source of human misery and suffering. The basic conflict approach to social stratification is that formulated by Karl Marx, and all other conflict theories incorporate its basic assumptions and tenets.

Occupational prestige consists essentially of social rank accorded in terms of the value of a person's occupation. Like any other form of social evaluation, occupational prestige rests heavily on the dominant values of a particular society.

While stratification is found in all societies, its form is not universal. Stratification systems are differentiated by (1) the method by which social positions are filled—whether by achievement or ascription, (2) the extent to which various strata are clearly delineated, and (3) the degree of mobility that is allowed or possible from one stratum to another. One can speak in these respects of two principal and ideal types of social stratification: open and closed, or class and caste, systems.

The various techniques for measuring social stratification may be classified into two types, objective or subjective. Subjective measures focus on a person's own perception of his or her own or another's position in the stratification structure. Objective measures use single indicators and/or indices that can be readily quantified and scored as a basis of assigning individuals to a particular social class category. The most frequently used indicators are occupation, income, and education. Two well-known objective measures of social class are Warner's Index of Status Characteristics and Hollingshead's Two-Factor Index. All available data suggest that there are no more than six social classes in the American society.

Social mobility refers to the movement of an individual or category from one social stratum to another or to movement within a given social stratum. Sociologists distinguish between vertical and horizontal mobility in terms of direction, and individual or categorical mobility in terms of sources. Sociologists also differentiate between various kinds of measurements for social mobility; two principal types in this respect are intragenerational and intergenerational mobility. Sociologists also distinguish between individual and structural factors involved in determining mobility. Among the latter are technological innovation, differential fertility, migration, industrialization, urbanization, two-career families, and political structures.

Social strata are not merely theoretical constructs. On the contrary, they are a type of distinct social reality and comprise a kind of social space within which people live. People who belong to the same socioeconomic class share the same life-chances; they share the same access to social opportunities and social re-wards. Some of the more important components of life-chances are income, education, health, mental health, longevity, and criminal justice. Social classes can be distinguished as well in terms of distinctive lifestyles, which refer to beliefs, values, attitudes, motivations, and actual patterns of behavior that typify or characterize a particular social stratum. Variations in lifestyle often can be found in social relations, marital and family patterns, socialization, religious affiliation, political attitudes, voluntary associations, and leisure and recreation.

Personality is both a dependent and an independent variable in the dynamics of social stratification. Social class background affects personality development, and a person's self-evaluation is strongly influenced by class rank. Numerous studies have demonstrated the existence of modal patterns of personality among the various social classes. A wide range of personality variables have significant and systematic effects on status striving and socioeconomic achievement.

# Key Concepts

alienation
authority
bourgeoisie
caste system
categorical mobility
class
class consciousness
class system
coercion
conspicuous consumption
embourgeoisement
estate
horizontal mobility
individual mobility
influence
intergenerational mobility
intragenerational mobility
life-chances
lifestyles

451

▼    occupational prestige                    social stratum
     power                                    socioeconomic status
     proletariat                              status
     relative deprivation                     status seeking
     social mobility                          status symbol
     social prestige                          status consistency
     social stratification                    vertical mobility

452

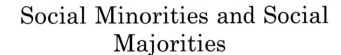

# 11    Social Minorities and Social Majorities

Our concerns with social differences in the last chapter dealt primarily with horizontal differentiation—ranked differentiation in society which in large part is the result of individual achievement. Here in this chapter we shall focus principally, but not exclusively, on vertical differentiation which rests upon social differences that are ascribed or attributed to individuals. Social differentiation in this regard is usually made in terms of the physical or cultural characteristics of the members of society. Chiefly involved are differences of a racial, ethnic, and religious nature, as well as those based on sex, age, physical capacities, and alternative lifestyles.

Ethnic and racial diversity, as we saw in Chapter 3, is the basis for an extensive variety of subcultures, which in themselves make for societal enrichment. Diversity of this kind, however, often constitutes a major source of social conflict, which manifests itself in a variety of forms. Our concerns in this chapter deal with minority-majority interactions, which refer to social patterns of subordination and superordination that characterize the organization and interaction of various racial and ethnic segments of society. Such dynamics, an integral part of the stratification systems that we discussed in the last chapter, present a host of sociologically significant consequences for human social behavior and for the structure and function of society.

We shall explore in this chapter the different forms and patterns that minority-majority relationships take, the dynamics of prejudice and discrimination central to these interactions, and the consequences of all these dynamics for the structure and function of society. These discussions will be concretized with descriptions of several of the major racial and ethnic minorities in the United States. Our considerations will include as well an assessment of the prejudiced personality, the personality correlates of minority status, and the patterns of modal personality that characterize minority categories. Each of these considerations will be described in terms of their significance for both social and personal dynamics. ▲

## Outline

NATURE OF MINORITIES AND
    MAJORITIES
Definitions
Universality

Basic Elements
  Differences
  Visibility
  Ideology

▶ Few societies in the world today are homogeneous in terms of the physical or cultural composition of their populations. Most societies consist of an amalgamation of people with a diversity of racial and ethnic, as well as religious, backgrounds. The United States, for example, has long been known as "the world's great ethnic melting pot"—a society whose population is comprised of people with a tremendous diversity of racial, ethnic, and religious backgrounds. The Soviet Union likewise consists of a large number of racially and ethnically diversified peoples, although in this case the variety is more a collection than an amalgamation of racial and ethnic differences. Even much smaller countries, such as Spain, Yugoslavia, France, and Switzerland, represent a diversity of ethnic subcultures. Such heterogeneous populations are usually the consequences of migration, war, and conquest which represent ancient patterns of human behavior. Other sociocultural factors, some of which we shall describe subsequently, also contribute to the presence of heterogeneous characteristics within societal populations. Whatever their origins, physical and cultural differences among people provide in many ways the basis for social interaction, but an interaction which may be described as consisting essentially of social conflict. Such is the case because of inequities in the prestige and power of the different segments of a society. Sociologists speak of this phenomenon in terms of minority-majority relationships.

# Nature of Minorities and Majorities

Minority-majority relationships pose enormous problems for many societies. This has been true especially for democratic societies, including in particular the United States. Throughout all its history, and even long before the nation began, American society has been preoccupied in many respects with interactional problems between Blacks and Whites. This situation has been heavily complicated by minority-majority relationships of a more strictly ethnic character that stem from the heavy immigration of foreigners to this country during the latter part of the last century and the first part of the current one. It is only during the past couple of decades that significant changes have occurred in these spheres of social life. Nonetheless, many problems still exist, and they have been exacerbated by the emergence of "new" minorities, such as Hispanics and Asians, as well as those comprised of women, the elderly, the physically handicapped, and those individuals who adopt certain types of alternative lifestyles.

## DEFINITIONS

Sociologists use the term "minority" to refer to a category of "people who, because of their physical or cultural characteristics, are singled out from the others in the society in which they live for differential and unequal treatment and who therefore regard themselves as objects of collective discrimination. The existence of a minority in society implies the existence of a corresponding dominant group with higher social status and greater privileges. Minority status carries with it the exclusion of full participation in the life of society" (Wirth, 1945:347).

The terms "minority" and "majority" refer to social statuses and not to demographic conditions. Hence, these terms have no essential reference to numbers or the respective size of the populations involved. Minorities, more specifically, are socially subordinate categories, not necessarily the smaller ones. Usually, however, a social minority is also a numerical minority. Perhaps the best example of the contrary can be found today in the Union of South Africa, where a White numerical minority socially dominates the native Black population. There 15 million Blacks, principally members of the Bantu tribe, comprise more than 80 percent of

455

▼

the population of the country; yet, it is the White population that dominates the society, controls its social institutions, and subordinates the Black Africans to a minority status.

A **minority,** then, refers to a category of people, distinguished by physical and/or sociocultural characteristics, which is the object of prejudice and/or discrimination, and which occupies a subordinate position in society. A **majority** refers correspondingly to a socially dominant category.

## UNIVERSALITY

Minority-majority relationships constitute a rather universal phenomenon. There are very few societies, past or present, that have not included one or more social minorities. Their absence is more likely to be the case in a relatively simple and highly homogeneous society. Few such societies exist today.

Our own limited experience with minorities in the United States may focus attention, often exclusively, on Black Americans and Hispanic Americans. Yet, while the particular categories that comprise minorities may vary, the dynamics involved are neither modern nor exclusively American. In Canada, for example, people of French-Catholic origins represent the largest minority, except in the province of Quebec where the social and political institutions are dominated by the Quebeçois, and French is the more prevalent, often exclusive, spoken language.

Historically, one can trace minorities in the form of slavery throughout the past twenty centuries. Slaves were maintained by the Greeks and the Romans and, more recently, slavery was an American institution in many of the southern states. Minority-majority relationships were continuously manifested throughout history in the perennial distinctions rigidly drawn between the nobility and the peasantry, and more especially in the abusive and cruel, often

subhuman, treatment to which peasants were subjected.

Minorities can be found in virtually every society today. Pygmies among Africans, Indians among South Americans, Catholics among Protestants in Northern Ireland, Asians and Africans in England and the Netherlands, Walloons in Belgium, Sicilians in Italy, Algerian Arabs in France, Turks in West Germany, Chinese in Mexico, African Jews in Israel, Asiatics in the Soviet Union, East Indians in Guyana, Croatians and Serbs in Yugoslavia, Arabs in Sudan, various castes in Tibet, India, Korea, and Japan, and the omnipresent Gypsies in just about any society, are but a few of the more well-known minorities that can be found in different countries of the world today.

## BASIC ELEMENTS

While the specific character of minorities may vary in many respects, the dynamics involved tend to be fundamentally the same. All minority-majority relationships include five basic elements: differences, visibility, ideology, power, and stratification.

DIFFERENCES. Minority-majority relationships are made possible by differences of one sort or another between people. Unless people are aware of differences between themselves and others, and unless these differences can be identified, minority-majority interactions cannot exist.

It is a common sociopsychological dynamic that the more homogeneous a population tends to be, the more significant its differences become, and the more they are emphasized. One common manifestation of this dynamic is, in terms of social-class differences, what could be called intraminority stratification. For a long time, Blacks in the United States discriminated against each other—and perhaps still do to a certain extent—on the basis of skin color, es-

456

pecially in the selection of marital partners. "Bronzeville," for example, referred to a section of the Black ghetto in the city of Chicago that was off-limits to dark-skinned Blacks. It was "reserved" exclusively for light-skinned Blacks by "directive" of light-skinned Blacks. Mexicans also rank themselves in terms of skin color and physiognomy (DeVos, 1977). At the pinnacle of the status hierarchy are the more Caucasoid, the more "Spanish-looking," individuals; while at the bottom are the most "Indian" or "Indio" people. In Israel, status distinctions are made between native-born Israelis (Sabras) and those of other national origins, such as the Sepharin (Jews from Spain and Portugal) and the Ashkenazin (Jews from western, central and eastern Europe).

VISIBILITY.   Differences among people are not in themselves sufficient for minority-majority relations. In order for differences to have behavioral significance, they need to be conspicuous ones. **Visibility,** then, is an important and fundamental element in all minority-majority relations. Quite specifically, the kind and extent of such fundamental dynamics as prejudice and discrimination are positively correlated with the kind and extent of visibility that a particular minority manifests.

Minorities often are described as "invisible" people. Such, however, is actually not true. It is only by being visible, in terms of their differences, that people can be maintained as minorities. No segment of a population can be treated as a minority unless it is distinguishable by identifiable characteristics. Indeed, members of the majority often are treated as minorities only because they manifest characteristics that are usually associated with a minority. Conversely, members of minorities who do not manifest their usually distinctive characteristics may escape minority treatment. One such example is that of albino Blacks who can "pass" as White by being physically indistinguishable from the latter.

Various physical signs and/or cultural symbols provide visibility for minorities—often unintentionally. Such things as skin color, hair texture, eye shape, language, accents, names, mannerisms, clothing, diet, decoration (for example, jewelry, medals, crosses), forms of behavior (for example, religious practices), and even styles of grooming are distinguishing marks that identify individuals as potential targets of differential and discriminatory treatment.

The importance of visibility in minority status was demonstrated quite clearly by the infamous Adolf Hitler in his persecution of Jewish people. The Nazis forced German and Polish Jews, during the 1930s and 1940s, to wear a yellow arm band or a yellow Star of David sewn on their clothing so that they could be visibly distinguished from other German and Polish people.

Minority status is often lost by simply shedding the visibility that makes it possible. Changing one's surname (for example, Bruno to Brown or Piccolo to Little) or shedding an accent may be sufficient for an individual to lose minority status. Even changing one's skin color, as has been done in a few experimental situations, can effect a loss of minority status.

IDEOLOGY. All minority-majority relations are maintained by a particular ideology—an integrated set of beliefs and values, including stereotypes and myths—that serves to justify the unequal treatment of different segments of a population. Among the principal ideologies that serve this function today are racism, ethnocentrism, sexism, and ageism. Each of these ideologies maintains the fundamental conviction that one or more segments of the population is innately superior to others.

**Racism*** provided, and still provides in some societies, the justification for such institutions

**457**

* The term *racism* is used more broadly nowadays to include beliefs and attitudes of superiority vis-à-vis ethnic minorities as well as racial ones.

**Passing.** Minority individuals who lack appropriate visibility, such as these modern gypsies in England, often escape victimization by prejudice and discrimination. (© Penny Tweedie 1979)

as slavery, colonialism, and segregation. It was racism that, during the 1930s and 1940s, permitted the German Nazis in their attempt to create a master Aryan race to justify the slaughter and extermination of 6 million Jews because of their "racial inferiority." Similarly, it was racism that historically legitimized the discriminatory immigration policies of the United States which, up to 1965, favored immigrants from certain countries in northern Europe over those from southern Europe and Asia. The practice of **apartheid** (segregation of the races) in the Union of South Africa is perhaps the most dramatic manifestation of racism today (see Box 11-1 on Race Relations).

Ideologies such as these inevitably involve the dynamics of the **self-fulfilling prophecy.** This phenomenon is a vicious circle of cause and effect. Once an incorrect assumption is accepted as true, then behavioral responses are adopted that produce the very situation that is deplored. People who are considered to be inferior are treated differently, particularly by being denied equal access to social opportunities; consequently, they soon develop and/or manifest a social inferiority in terms of unequal achievements and accomplishments, which in turn does indeed confirm the basic tenets of the ideology.

POWER.   Minority-majority relations do not exist unless various social segments of society possess unequal amounts of power—in what-

# BOX 11-1. Race Relations in the Union of South Africa

▼

It is unlawful for a White person and a non-White person to drink a cup of tea together in a tea room anywhere in South Africa, unless they have obtained a special permit to do so. . . .

Any policeman is entitled, without warrant, to enter and search, "at any reasonable time of the day or night," premises in a town in which he has reason to suspect that an African boy eighteen years of age is committing the criminal offense of residing with his father without having the necessary permission to do so.

A White person living in a town who employs an African to do any carpentry, bricklaying, electrical fitting or other skilled work in his home, commits a criminal offense unless special exemption has been granted by the Minister of Labour; so also does any African who performs such skilled work in a town elsewhere than in an area set aside for occupation by Africans. Each is liable to a fine not exceeding one hundred pounds, or to imprisonment for a period not exceeding one year, or to both such fine and such imprisonment. . . .

Any policeman may at any time call upon an African who has attained the age of sixteen years to produce his reference book. If a reference book has been issued to him but he fails to produce it because it is not in his possession at the time, he commits a criminal offence and is liable to a fine not exceeding ten pounds or imprisonment for a period not exceeding one month. . . .

If an Indian (or a Coloured or an African) sits on a bench in a public park, the bench being set apart for the exclusive use of White persons, by way of protest against the apartheid laws, he commits a criminal offense and is liable to a fine not exceeding three hundred pounds, or to imprisonment for a period not exceeding three years, or to a whipping not exceeding ten strokes, or to both such fine and such imprisonment, or to both such fine and such whipping, or to both such imprisonment and such whipping. . . .

If there is only one waiting-room in a railway station, it is lawful for the station master to reserve that waiting-room for the exclusive use of White persons, and any non-White person wilfully entering it commits a criminal offence and is liable to a fine not exceeding fifty pounds or to imprisonment for a period not exceeding three months or to both such fine and such imprisonment. . . .

Any policeman may, without warrant, enter premises in which a meeting is taking place, if he believes, on reasonable grounds, that the internal security of the Union is likely to be endangered as a result of the meeting, and that obtaining a warrant would cause serious delay. . . .

No African, lawfully residing in a town by virtue of a permit issued to him, is entitled, as of right, to have his wife and children residing with him. . . .

Any unmarried man who "in appearance obviously is or who by general acceptance and repute is a White person" and who attempts to have carnal intercourse with a woman who is not "obviously in appearance or by general acceptance and repute a white person," is guilty of an offense and liable on conviction to imprisonment with compulsory labour for a period not exceeding

*(Continued)*

459

▼        BOX 11-1   *(Continued).*

**seven years, unless he can prove to the satisfaction of the court that he had reasonable cause to believe, at the time when the alleged offence was committed, that she was "obviously in appearance or by general acceptance and repute a White person.". . . ▲**

Source: Leslie Rubin, *This is Apartheid.* London: Victor Gollancz, 1959, pp. 8–16. International Defense and Aid Fund for South Africa, 64 Essex Road, London N18 LR, United Kingdom.

460

ever form. To confine a minority to a subordinate position within the social structure requires that the majority have instruments and mechanisms for exercising the power that is necessary to sustain its dominant position. Such power usually takes the form of political and economic resources.

STRATIFICATION.   Minority-majority relations inevitably and essentially involve social stratification and all of its concomitant dynamics. Such patterns of stratification between minority and majority categories are manifested in terms of the usual disparities in life-chances and social mobility. More significantly, how-

ever, minorities often assume in many respects a caste-like structure vis-à-vis the majority category. Thus, while there is a hierarchy of social classes within both the majority and the minority segments of a society, a caste-like barrier separates the two in many spheres of social activity. Moreover, each stratum within the minority segment tends to look up, rather than across, to its class counterpart in the minority segment (see Figure 11-1).

## TYPES OF MINORITIES

Minorities, as our discussion above suggests, can be distinguished on the basis of different criteria and may assume several different forms. Any visible or known differences among people can serve as the basis for minority-majority relationships. Chiefly involved in this respect, however, are physical differences and cultural distinctions among people. Minorities are principally racial, ethnic, and religious in character. Other types of minorities that are becoming more common today are those based on age and sex statuses, as well as on physical handicaps and alternative lifestyles.

Race and ethnicity are terms that are frequently confused. They often are used interchangeably, yet incorrectly, in ordinary speech. These two terms, however, are technical ones, and quite distinct in their respective meanings. Race is defined in terms of physical criteria and relates to differences based on inherited characteristics. Ethnicity, on the other hand, is de-

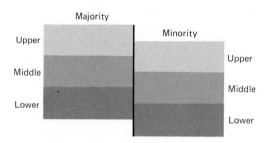

FIGURE 11-1   The Semi-Caste Structure of Minority Stratification. A Social class hierarchy characterizes both majority and minority segments of a population. The caste-like structure that separates minority and majority stratification, however, is such that many minority individuals look up rather than across to their corresponding class categories (counterparts) among the social majority. The uppermost class status, thus, is reserved for the majority, while the lowermost is accorded to members of the minority populations.

fined on the basis of cultural characteristics and relates to differences in socially acquired characteristics. Let us consider each of these sets of criteria in more detail.

# Racial Minorities

There are 5 billion people in the world today. These people, while exhibiting a variety of physical characteristics, constitute a single species* known as **Homo sapiens.** Physical differences among *Homo sapiens*, which are accidental rather than essential, have been traditionally distinguished in terms of race. Race, however, is a troublesome concept, frequently used loosely and incorrectly.

Popular usage of the term *race* often makes it synonymous with the human species, as in reference to the "human race." Race is also commonly confused in popular usage with nationality, as in references to the "Chinese race" or the "Italian race." Yet, people of identical nationality, such as Americans or Canadians, often include individuals from several different racial backgrounds. A similar error frequently is made in reference to cultural categories, such as those based on religion. Common examples in this regard include references to the "Jewish race" or the "Hindu race." Other principal misconceptions equate race with language, such as the "Arabic race" (people who speak arabic). Misconceptions about race, thus, are quite real, and they are most significant in terms of minority-majority interactions.

## RACE DEFINED

Race, technically, refers to physical distinctions of an innate nature that can be discerned in people. A **race,** then, is a classification (a subspecies) of people who can be distinguished by

---

* A biological classification of organisms that are capable of continuously interbreeding.

genetic characteristics. Chief among these are such phenotypic characteristics as skin color, hair texture, stature, and certain physical features such as the shape and size of eyes, lips, nose, and head.

There are no pure races. Race is a continuous rather than a discrete classification. Therefore, there are no absolute demarcations or separations of one category from another. Races, moreover, are arbitrary classifications; the physical criteria that are selected are not necessarily related to each other. Not so surprisingly then, scientists are not of one mind on precisely which characteristics, or combinations thereof, should constitute racial classifications.

Physical anthropologists and biologists have devised several schemes of racial classification consisting of a few to well over a hundred different races or subraces. The number of races that are delineated depends upon the particular criteria that are used and the specific purpose of the classification. Nonetheless, the conventional practice among biologists and physical anthropologists has been to speak principally of three racial classifications for the human species:

1. *Caucasoid* (white, fair skin; straight or wavy hair) exemplified by Europeans.
2. *Negroid* (black, dark skin, woolly hair) exemplified by Black Africans.
3. *Mongoloid* (yellow or brown skin) exemplified by Asiatics.

More than 95 percent of the human species can be racially categorized on the basis of this scheme. Millions of people, however, are not so classifiable, for the reasons given above as well as because of extensive interbreeding among the "races" throughout hundreds of thousands of years of human history. This is especially true, as Figure 11-2 shows, in the case of people of highly mixed ancestry, including Polynesian and Australian aborigines. The latter, for example, have dark, Negroid-type skin

▼

**461**

▼ along with wavy hair that often is blond. Similar difficulties are presented by the Ainu people of northern Japan who have Caucasian skin and hair characteristics along with Mongoloid facial features.

There are many variations within each of the principal racial classifications, and in this respect one may speak, with somewhat more precision, of subraces. Among the Caucasoid, for example, it has been customary to distin-

462

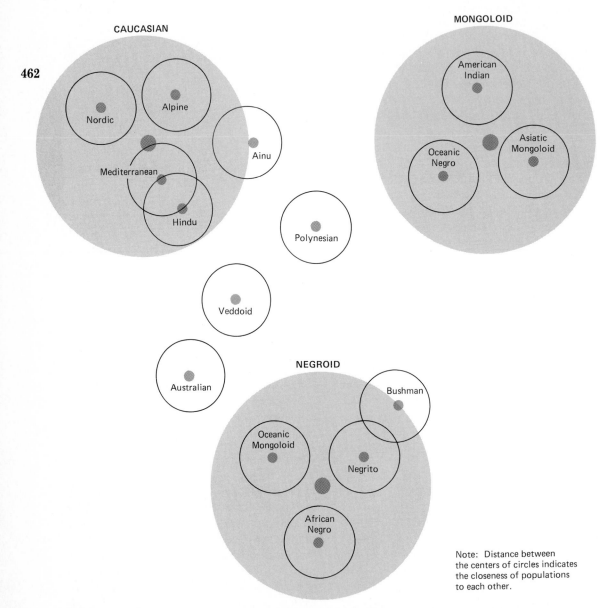

Note: Distance between the centers of circles indicates the closeness of populations to each other.

FIGURE 11-2 One Scheme of Racial Classification. Source: Alfred L. Kroeber, *Anthropology*. New York: Harcourt, Brace, 1948, p. 10.

guish four subtypes based on variations and similarities in anatomical features: Nordic, Alpine, Mediterranean, and Hindu. The physical differences involved vary quite extremely, from the tall, blue-eyed, white-complexioned blond (Nordic) to the short, brown-eyed, olive-complexioned, dark-haired individual (Mediterranean).

Today race has come to refer, with somewhat greater precision, simply to an interbreeding population among whom the incidence of specific genes varies significantly from that in other populations (Keeton & Gould, 1986). Specific genes can refer to any particular physical attribute, such as the gene for the sickle cell or the epicanthic eye fold, or perhaps more commonly for the chemicals (melanin and carotene) that determine skin color. A race, conceived as an interbreeding population, is essentially a statistical population—one without absolute demarcations.

## ORIGINS OF RACES

Racial differences among human beings inevitably raise questions about their origins.* Such a subject is highly complex, even controversial. Apart from the more basic question of the origin of humankind, which focuses on the theory of evolution and the hypothesis of direct creation, there are two hypotheses relative to the origin of races: **polygenesis** and **monogenesis.**

POLYGENESIS.  Polygenetic theory maintains that there were several independent origins of the human species, and that each race represents a separate beginning (creation or evolution). According to the folklore associated with this view, the Caucasoid race is the oldest

---

* Homo sapiens, on the basis of archaeological and anthropological evidence, appears to be more than 2 million years old. Racial differences that are observable today, however, are of relatively recent origin—perhaps no more than 500,000 years.

and most advanced and, as such, represents the most intelligent segment of the human species. The Negroid race is considered to be the youngest, the one closest to our subhuman or ape ancestors—a situation that allegedly is reflected in the simian-like characteristics of many Negroids, such as foreheads, jaws, and flat noses. The origin of Mongoloids, then, is placed at an intermediate point, between Caucasoids and Negroids. Biological and anthropological studies, however, show that a variety of phenotypic features (for example, lip form, lip color, body hair, jaw protrusion, head size, and nose shape) are neither exclusively nor consistently distributed among any one racial segment of the human species. Many phenotypic characteristics, in fact, tend to be normally distributed within each race.

MONOGENESIS.  Monogenetic theory, on the other hand, the dominant view, asserts a common or single origin for the human species. Such a position is supported by the fact that all races, being anatomically identical in general structure and function, are capable of continuous interbreeding and thus constitute a single species. The several races, according to monogenetic theory, are fundamentally the products of **genetic mutation**—changes in the structure of genes that determine physical features and physical development. Principally involved in these changes are three processes: natural selection, random genetic drift, and geographical isolation.

**Natural selection** refers to a tendency for the genetic characteristics most suitable to a particular physical environment to endure. The human species throughout its history has had to adapt to its physical environment. Certain physical characteristics have been historically more suitable than others to a particular environment. Natural selection, thus, involves evolutionary changes that occur whenever the environment favors the survival and reproduction of some specific, genetic characteristics

463

▼ over others. Skin color and body size seem to be two such examples.

Black skin among people in tropical and subtropical areas is thought to be a protection against hostile ultraviolet radiation, as well as from the overproduction of vitamin D which, like underproduction, can cause abnormalities in bone structure. Correspondingly, light skin is considered to be a biological adaptation to temperate environments that receive much less **464** sunlight.

People who inhabit high altitudes tend to have a large lung capacity, which facilitates breathing thin air that has a lower oxygen content. Similarly, populations in the Arctic regions tend to have small bodies with short limbs, which facilitate the conservation of body heat. Short bodies (stature) in the Arctic serve as conservers of body heat, just as tall bodies serve conversely to ventilate body heat. It is significant that over many, many generations, people with darker skin in the tropics have tended to be healthier, to have reproduced more, and to have lived longer than those with lighter skin. Correspondingly, lighter-skinned people have enjoyed the same advantages in areas where there was less sunlight.

**Random genetic drift** refers to processes by which a particular trait appears by chance and then becomes widespread within a given population, especially a population that is small and interbreeds. Variations in lip shape and the ability to taste certain chemicals are thought to be due to genetic drift.

**Geographical isolation** refers to the tendency, in the early history of the species, for certain segments to become isolated from one another. Migrations of small numbers of the species over the vast face of the earth accounted for this to a large extent. Such migration and isolation produced a restricted gene pool which, combined with natural selection and random genetic drift, produced physical characteristics that became more and more similar within a given population, and at the same time more

and more different from other populations. One such example is the American Indian as a Mongoloid. Modern examples of geographical isolation are epidemiological findings relative to the incidence of certain diseases, such as the high prevalence of hemophilia in certain areas of Appalachia.

It is important to understand that however true it may be that racial differences result from evolutionary processes and physical adaptation, they have very little significance in any functional sense today. People of all racial backgrounds, partly as a consequence of cultural adaptation, can function equally well in any physical environment. Eskimos can function in Africa, just as Blacks can in the Arctic.

## RACIAL DIFFERENCES

Racial differences, insofar as can be determined, are exclusively physical and, for the most part, virtually accidental, or insignificant so far as biological functions are concerned. Ample evidence has amassed to show that in terms of essential nature and human function there are no significant differences among the various biological classifications of humankind. While some racial differences are significant in terms of immunity or susceptibility to physical diseases,* they are of no significance in terms of psychological function. Many human characteristics, originally thought to be racial or genetic have proven to be cultural. This is especially clear in regard to emotions, motivation, and perceptive ability, as well as artistic talent and athletic or mechanical aptitudes.

That there are no systematic differences of

---

* Genetic populations are distinguished to some degree by varying susceptibility to certain diseases. Sickle cell anemia (a malformation of red blood cells) and lactose intolerance are predominant among Blacks. Thalassemia, also known as Cooley's anemia, is a form of blood disease found more extensively among White people, and their descendants, in the Mediterranean area. Tay-Sachs disease is a metabolic disorder involving mental retardation, which is peculiar to Jews of eastern European background.

an intellectual nature among the races is most significant. Indeed, such differences between individuals within any race greatly exceed whatever differences can be demonstrated between racial categories. The potential to learn certain forms of behavior or to develop complex culture, therefore, is not so much associated with biological capabilities as it is with cultural learning experiences. Occasionally, nonetheless, claims are advanced that there are intellectual and mental differences of a genetic nature between the races.

Arthur Jensen (1969; 1981), for example, has presented data to show that intelligence is determined primarily by genetic rather than environmental factors, and that on this basis, Blacks are generally inferior to Whites in intellectual and mental abilities. Jensen bases his contention on research that typically finds the average I.Q. scores of American Blacks to be about fifteen points lower than the average scores for Whites. He argues that genetic factors account for about 80 percent of such I.Q. differences between Blacks and Whites.

Jensen's thesis has been strongly rejected by other scientists (see, for example, Scarr, 1981; Taylor, 1980). Many have challenged the validity of Jensen's data with the argument that environmental factors were not adequately controlled in his research. Ample evidence exists that measurements of intelligence are strongly influenced by acquired knowledge and social experience. Merely to take an intelligence test— any of which is socially and culturally biased— presupposes some learning and, therefore, a particular sociocultural experience. Fundamental to any other prerequisite is a minimal mastery of the appropriate language and all its symbolic and sociocultural meanings.

It is difficult, of course, to separate biologically inherited behavior from sociocultural behavior. Accordingly, the evidence that intelligence is not primarily genetic is not absolutely conclusive, but the available data overwhelmingly support the contention that intellectual differences between the races, and between ethnic categories as well, are fundamentally environmental. Based on all of the available evidence, the National Academy of Sciences in 1967 took the position that no race can claim any genetic superiority over others.

That there are no essential differences— physical or intellectual—among the races and, moreover, that race itself is not a precise concept, does not mean that racial differences are totally insignificant. Race is of tremendous importance in a sociological sense. That such is the case is reflected in social and legal conceptions of race.

## SOCIAL AND LEGAL DEFINITIONS OF RACE

Quite apart from genetic or biological specifications, race may also be defined in terms of cultural criteria. Of principal significance in this regard are social and legal definitions of race, which are of crucial significance on the interactional level. Social and legal definitions need not be consistent with each other, nor need they be consistent from one society to another. Let us discuss each type of definition in more detail.

SOCIAL DEFINITIONS. Social conceptions of race refer to a category of people who are thought to comprise a physically or biologically distinct unit and who as such are treated accordingly. Visibility, of course, is again very important here.

Traditionally in South America, anyone with any White ancestry is considered White. In the United States, however, anyone with any Black ancestry is considered Black. Mulattoes, offsprings of Black-White miscegenation, are considered Black in the United States,* but White in South America. Skin color, then, is not as

---

* It has been estimated that about 21 percent of Americans classified as White have some Black ancestry, while nearly three-fourths of Blacks have some White ancestry (Burma, 1946; Stuckert, 1958).

**465**

▼ significant for racial distinctions in South America as are hair texture, eye color, and stature. Hence, in some countries of South America, many American Blacks would be considered and treated as Whites. Among other "social" races in the United States, one could mention the American Indians who, while technically members of the Mongoloid race, are considered Caucasian, both socially and legally. The same is true of more mixed types, such as Hawaiians, Filipinos, and Polynesians.

Social definitions of race often can play a fundamental role in the service of political objectives. One horrendous example is that of the Nazis who, under the leadership of Adolph Hitler during the 1930s and 1940s, sought to create a master race. For the Nazis, the "master race" was synonymous with what they called the "Ar-

466

## BOX 11-2. The Social and Legal Definitions of Race

JOHANNESBURG. South Africa, October 11, 1967 (AP)—Sandra Laing is a girl whom no schools want.

Her parents won an 18-month-long struggle to have her officially declared White, only to discover they can't find a school that wants her.

Parents in Sheepmoor, a tiny town in eastern Transvaal province, have threatened to remove their children from the local White primary school if 11-year-old Sandra is sent there as directed by the education department.

South African schools are strictly segregated along racial lines. Trouble occurs in borderline cases where a child is of dark appearance, as Sandra Laing is.

Sandra was going to boarding school in the country town of Piet Retief 18 months ago. Parents of other pupils objected to her presence, children taunted her, and eventually she was sent home by the school authorities.

Subsequently she was declared colored—that is, mulatto—by a government-appointed board, even though her parents are White. Then a change in the law provided that descent and not appearance is to be the deciding factor in borderline cases. She was reclassified White.

Sandra's storekeeper father, Abraham Laing, decided not to send her back to the same boarding school because of the scorn he felt she would meet.

He approached a number of convents, but they turned him down. Some said they had no vacancies. Others said that the Afrikaan-speaking girl would find the English-speaking situation in the convents difficult.

Then the education department notified Mr. Laing he must apply for Sandra to be admitted to the Sheepmoor school, the nearest their home.

Principal L. Dreyer said: "This is a terrible situation. I have my instructions from the education department to admit Sandra Laing. My hands are tied.

"However, I have reason to believe that, if this happens, most of the parents of the 53 other children at the school will remove their children."

Mrs. E. Van Tender, mother of two pupils at the school and a member of the school committee, commented: "The day Sandra Laing sets feet in the school, my children will be taken home. And they will stay home."

Abraham Laing doesn't know what to do about his daughter. ▲

yan race," idealized by individuals who were tall, blond, and blue-eyed. Hitler himself was of rather medium height and had black hair and brown eyes, as was true of a very large number of German people. Other paradoxes in this racist ideology can be seen in the case of the principal allies of the Nazis during World War II. The Mongoloid Japanese were declared "honorary" Aryans, and the Caucasoid Asian Indians were designated a subdivision of the Aryan race.

Another reflection of social definitions of "race" can be found in many of the immigration laws of the United States, which in the past favored the admission of northern Europeans (Alpine or Nordic racial stock) but restricted, by the use of quotas and other techniques, the admission of southern and eastern European migrants (Mediterranean racial stock). Justification for these laws and immigration policies was based on false notions regarding the consequences of the intermingling of "bad" and "good" racial stock and the eventual dilution of the latter.

LEGAL DEFINITIONS. Legal definitions of race constitute a more specific form of social definitions. Such definitions, which often merely codify social definitions, vary from country to country and even from state to state within the same country.

Legal definitions, as used not long ago in many of the states in our own country, were necessary to specify the criteria for segregation and other practices designed to prevent miscegenation and social intercourse. In most of the states in this country during the first half of this century, anyone with one-fourth or more Black ancestry (that is, anyone with one Black grandparent) was legally defined as Black. In some other states, however, it could be one-half (one parent) or one-eighth (one great-grandparent) Black ancestry that constituted the legal criteria for racial classification. The law in Louisiana, repealed only in 1983, stipulated that

anyone with 3 percent Black ancestry was officially Black.

Today the most stringent forms of the legal definition of race are found in the Union of South Africa. In that country, where segregation of the races is practiced with a high degree of institutionalization, four "races" have been distinguished: Black, White, Colored, and Asian. "Colored" consists of people of mixed ancestry, while "Asian" includes predominantly Indians and Chinese.

One interesting aspect of the legal definitions of race in the Union of South Africa can be seen in the case of Orientals. Japanese people there have been classified as "White," even though they are often indistinguishable in many respects from the Chinese, who are classified as "Asian." This paradoxical situation is explained expediently by favorable treaties that exist between Japan and the Union of South Africa.

Social and legal definitions of race, in summary, are very important sociologically. They are especially instrumental both in controlling social behavior and in furthering political objectives. It is difficult to comprehend fully many of the dynamics within the sphere of minority-majority interactions without a knowledge of the social and legal definitions of race on which these dynamics are based.

## Ethnic Minorities

Ethnic minorities consist of persecuted populations that can be distinguished in terms of culturally distinctive characteristics, such as national origins, customs, religions, languages, or distinctive lifestyles. Ethnic differences, unlike racial ones, are learned or acquired and not genetically inherited. Many ethnic categories, however, can also be distinguished by physical characteristics to a certain degree.

The United States is a highly ethnically heterogeneous society. With the exception of descendants of the British settlers to this coun-

467

▼ try—those who call themselves Yankees—every American, including descendants of the native Indians, is ethnic, or considered to be ethnic. Ethnicity, however, is not a simple matter of national origin or cultural characteristics. Rather, ethnicity refers as well to the dynamics of identification that people hold with respect to these kinds of subcultural distinctions. Ethnicity, in this perspective, needs to be seen not only as a social state, but also as a psychological state, consisting of a common identity or sense of belonging—a "consciousness of kind" or "we-feeling"—among a particular sociocultural segment of society.* **Ethnicity,** then, is a shared feeling or bond of peoplehood by which members of ethnic categories come to see themselves as being a distinct people—whether it be in terms of a common national origin, ancestry, language, religion, lifestyle, or even racial background—from the rest of the population. This cultural "we-feeling" represents a sense of social solidarity fundamental to many of the dynamics of minority-majority interactions.

468

Ethnic consciousness often transcends both cultural and racial backgrounds. Jews, for example, have a shared feeling of "Jewishness" despite the plurality of their cultures, national origins, and even racial backgrounds. Jews are perhaps most commonly thought of as people who share a fundamental set of religious beliefs. Many people who identify themselves as Jews, however, do not practice or believe in Judaism. Hence, it is not religion that accounts for the consciousness of kind among Jews. Neither do Jews, scattered throughout the world, share a common culture. Soviet Jews or German Jews are as culturally different from Syrian Jews or Moroccan Jews as they are from American or Italian Jews. Jewish people are of no one racial classification; therefore, they cannot be identified by physical characteristics. Although originally one genetic stock—sometimes called Semitic—and of common geographical origins, Jews dispersed over the entire face of the earth and interbred with many other peoples. While we may think of Jews as Caucasian, their ranks include individuals with both Negroid and Mongoloid racial backgrounds. Nor do they have any necessary allegiance or association with the state of Israel. Yet Jews represent one

**The Melting Pot.** Ethnic Americans largely comprise the millions of European and Asian immigrants to this country and their descendants, represented here by an Italian mother and her children after arrival in Ellis Island at the turn of the century. (The Bettmann Archive)

---

* Such feelings, of course, are not unique to minorities. Sentiments of this kind, however, often become intensified as a consequence of minority status and the prejudice/discrimination that it inevitably entails.

of the most socially cohesive ethnic peoples to be found in the world today. Jews, then, it seems, are simply people who think of themselves as Jews and/or are so regarded by others.

Ethnic consciousness is also reflected in the labels that minorities prefer for themselves. Lately, this involves shedding terms that are perceived to have stigmatizing, or essentially negative, connotations of subordinate status. Perhaps the foremost example of this development is the case of the term "Black" to replace "Negro,"* and, more especially, its demeaning corruption, "nigger." Such terms, according to Blacks, are associated, in their own minds and in the minds of many Whites, with slavery, segregation, and second-class citizenship.

Another term of interest, attractive among some Blacks today, is "Afro-American." Both new terms represent changes that are thought to be a positive declaration of identity and self-esteem. These changes, however, have a serious historical twist. Here is what Robert E. Park (1937:xxiv), a sociologist at the University of Chicago in the late 1930s, had to say in this regard:

> There is, finally, one small but insignificant change in the ritual of race relations that, it seems to me, needs to be specially noted. The great majority of Negroes now, after a good deal of discussion and differences of opinion, have adopted the term "Negro" as a racial designation in preference to another and more logical but less familiar expression like "Afro-American."

Other minorities have also created new labels for themselves in an effort to symbolize a positive sense of identity and to rally their members to action. One such case is that of French Canadians who communicate both a sense of pride and political activism in their choice of

the label "Quebeçois" which is even used to designate a political party in Canada. Mention should also be made of the new label "Chicano" (a word of obscure origin) that has been used in the past few decades to designate Mexican Americans.

Ethnic identity, of course, may be multifaceted. An individual's ethnic identity could be comprised of an amalgamation of several identities: nationality, race, religion, and regional residence. A common example of multifaceted ethnic identity, in this case that of a majority rather than a minority, is that of the WASP—White Anglo-Saxon Protestant.

Ethnicity is an important part of the personal identity of many people. In recent years, ethnic and racial identity has been increasingly flaunted in the American society. There has been an unprecedented interest and pride in ethnic and racial origins on the part of millions of Americans during the past two decades. Americans have become less interested in passing, which DeVos (1977:240) defines as "an act of social mobility in which the individual fabricates a past that will enhance his legitimacy to a higher form of social participation." A variety of factors help to explain this persistence of ethnicity. Among them are an interest in preserving cultural traditions, the desire to maintain family ties and continuity with the past, and continuing patterns of discrimination. Moreover, among other advantages, ethnicity provides many of the sociological and psychological benefits of social recognition without the negative implications of a hierarchical or inequitable stratification.

People vary, of course, in the extent to which they may be characterized by ethnic and/or racial consciousness and identity. For some people, ethnic identification is a salient and positive aspect of their self-concept and daily life. For others, ethnic identity is recognized only marginally, and perhaps only at family gatherings and relevant holidays. Still others view ethnic

▼

**469**

---

* *Negro* is Spanish for "black."

▼ identity negatively and suppress such consciousness, and any manifestation of it, to whatever extent possible. Such people, however, are in the minority. Recent surveys show that only one-fifth of the White-American population—about 40 million people—are unwilling to claim a specific ethnic heritage. Much of this reluctance, moreover, may be the consequence of their being offspring of ethnically mixed marriages rather than the generational distance from their immigratory ancestors.

**470**

Many social scientists not very long ago expected that urbanization and industrialization would erode traditional ethnic loyalties. In a surprising turn of events, however, we have witnessed a resurgence of ethnic consciousness during the past couple of decades (see Smith, 1981). This outcome was encouraged by the positive developments that emanated from the civil rights movement, beginning in the mid-1960s. Among the manifestations of this resurgence of ethnic and racial consciousness are the following:

1. Renewed interests in ethnicity.
2. Search for ancestral roots and the tracing of genealogies.
3. Visits to ancestral homes and lands.
4. Increased learning and use of one's ancestral language.
5. Increased exploration of one's ethnic history and culture.
6. Self-conscious examination of one's own cultural heritage.
7. Demands for proportional involvements in political and economic sectors.
8. Creation of new names and labels with positive or neutral connotations that convey a sense of pride.
9. Establishment of antidefamation organizations.
10. Increase in the number and percentage of people who voluntarily make an ethnic identification in population census surveys.
11. Decreased interest in passing.
12. Increased development of, and expansion of membership in, voluntary associations of ethnic interests.
13. Publication of ethnic newspapers and magazines.
14. Expansion of ethnic festivals and cultural fairs.
15. Establishment of holidays honoring ethnic heroes.

Each of these developments clearly suggests forceful resistance to an effective ethnic melting pot—the assimilation of all culturally diverse people into a homogeneous culture. On the contrary, these dynamics seem to constitute a powerful reassertion of the importance of ethnic pluralism in America. In any event, at the present time in American society, we are truly witnessing the "passing of passing" (DeVos, 1977).

Similar developments in ethnic nationalism have been occurring in Europe. Some examples of people who are reasserting their ethnic identity are the Bretons, Basques, Alsatians, and Corsicans in France; the Basques, Catalans, and Andalusians in Spain; the Scottish and Welsh in England; the Slovenes in Austria; the Madeirans and Azoreans in Portugal; the Greenlanders in Denmark; the Flemish and Walloons in Belgium; and the South Tyroleans in Italy.

The current increases in ethnic consciousness and identity are not just reactions to social discrimination, but rather actions that reflect the tenor of the times and the changing values of our society. Whether this revival of ethnic consciousness will endure is, of course, a difficult question to answer. Some sociologists are of the opinion that the resurgence of ethnic consciousness reached its peak about a decade ago, and now is on the wane. These developments, nonetheless, provide an argument against the Marxist thesis that workers in the various countries of the world would eventually realize their common class interests and unite in the cause of economic justice by eschewing social and ethnic differences within their society.

# Religious Minorities

Religious minorities consist of people who experience prejudice and discrimination, even persecution, simply because of their theological beliefs and practices. Differences in these respects often cause divisions, not only between religious minorities and majorities, but also among the minorities themselves. In either case, religious minorities tend to be characterized by shared values and relatively strong cohesion.

Religious discrimination can trace its origin to persecution of the Jews during biblical times. Its appearance in America, at least its effects, accompanied the first immigrants who came to these shores as passengers on the *Mayflower* in 1620. Much of the prejudice and discrimination expressed toward European migrants in the United States during the early part of this century, and the latter half of the last one, was directed specifically at religious minorities. The plight of Catholics is a particularly extensive example of religious discrimination, reflected quite clearly in their being denied the right to vote. Indeed, the Know-Nothing Party of the 1850s was organized for the most part in opposition to foreigners and Catholics. Even the Ku Klux Klan, usually associated with discrimination against Blacks and the commitment to maintaining the alleged supremacy of the Caucasian race, for a long time also directed its opposition toward Catholics and Jews. This anti-Catholic sentiment, with an associated fear of papal influence, was openly expressed as late as 1960, when many Americans questioned the loyalties of John F. Kennedy, a Catholic candidate for the presidency of the United States.

In the Soviet Union, officially an atheistic society like nearly all other Communist societies, the principal religious minority consists of members of the Russian Orthodox Church. Yet, in an officially atheistic society, all believers—regardless of their particular creed—constitute a religious minority. Religious minorities are also found extensively in many Eastern societies, such as Lebanon, Syria, Saudi Arabia, Iran, and India where Arabs, Moslems, Jews, Hindus, and Christians live among each other—none too harmoniously.

Perhaps the most well-known and oldest of all religious minorities is that of Jews whose status can be traced to their servitude during early Egyptian civilization. Jews have been the minority of minorities. No other people have had such a long history of being treated as a minority in so many different societies. The creation of the state of Israel, just about forty years ago, was motivated in great part by the desire to put an end to this situation by providing a kind of national and cultural unity for Jews. Yet, even in the Israeli society, many Jews have not escaped minority status. Sociological studies have shown that many Jews of European origin are prejudiced against "Oriental" Jews—those from Middle East and African countries—whom they consider to be culturally retarded (Eisenstadt, 1952).

Many religious minorities overlap membership with ethnic minorities. One example of this is provided by French Canadians who are nearly exclusively Catholic. Another case is that of Jews who, while primarily considered a religious category, are also perceived as an ethnic category. Many Jewish people, in fact, do not practice the Hebrew religion, and other Jews have religious beliefs and practices that vary widely; indeed, they may even be Christians* or atheists; yet, these people insist on identifying themselves as Jews and experience a strong sense of social cohesion, perhaps in great part on account of a religious and cultural past. Many Jewish people simply see themselves as descendants of those biblical exiles who, with Moses as their leader, endlessly searched for freedom in the Promised Land.

▼

**471**

---

* Many present-day Jews who have become Christians, as did the earliest adherents of Christianity, still celebrate Jewish holidays and identify themselves as "Jewish." These people prefer to be identified by such labels as "Jewish believer," "Messianic Jew," "Hebrew Christian," or "Jewish Christian."

▼ # The "New" Minorities

Up until very recent times, minorities have been defined and/or described nearly exclusively in racial, ethnic, or religious terms. Today, however, one can find references to a number of "new" minorities. While the recognition of these minorities may be new, their existence as victims of institutionalized patterns of discrimination has been of long-standing. Among the more important of these new minorities are those based on gender (sex) and age statuses, physical handicaps, and sexual orientations. Let us look briefly at each of these kinds of minorities.

## MINORITIES OF SEX STATUS: WOMEN

Women comprise slightly more than one-half the world's population, yet historically they have occupied a position categorically subordinate to men in nearly all fields of social life throughout the world. Traditionally and commonly, indeed nearly universally, men have been accorded much greater power, status, and privilege than have women. Second-class citizenship, in effect, has been the status accorded to women in the vast majority of societies. One example of the subordination of women is the denial of voting privileges, which have been enjoyed by women in the United States since only 1920 when the Nineteenth Amendment to the Constitution was ratified. Black men, on the other hand, were granted the right to vote in 1870.

Another long-standing example, commonly found in societies throughout the world, has been the double standard, implicit or explicit, in laws against adultery. Adultery has been defined as a crime more typically in the case of women than of men. Correspondingly, women invariably have been more severely punished for such deviant behavior. Women, much like slaves, have throughout history been widely perceived as male property. Such a sentiment is by no means nonexistent today, even in the American society. Indeed, until only the past decade, it has been legally impossible for a man to rape his wife. Such is no longer the case in many societies, including several states in our own country.

A third example is female infanticide which, as practiced yet today in some societies experiencing severe population pressures (see Chapter 7), represents the most extreme manifestation of **sexism**—the doctrine of natural inequality between the sexes.

Until very recent years, it was virtually a widespread belief in our society that women are naturally inferior to men, both intellectually and physically. Such a belief is still quite prevalent in many, perhaps in the vast majority, of the societies throughout the world. Indeed, in all societies of the world today women occupy a socially inferior position, however equal to men they may be considered in terms of political rights. Social scientists (for example, Myrdal, 1962; Hacker, 1974; Smith & Steward, 1983) have described a host of similarities between Blacks and women in terms of their social standing in our society (see Box 11-3 on Similarities between Blacks and Women). As we mentioned in the preceding chapter, the social status of a woman in American society has been determined traditionally by that of her father, and subsequently that of her husband. Any personally achieved status (for example, education, occupation, wealth) is by and large ignored or subordinated to that of the principal male figure of the household.

Public awareness of prolonged and systematic discrimination against women, particularly in terms of political subordination and economical exploitation, has come to the fore in many countries of the Western Hemisphere during the past decade. Throughout modern societies, the de facto status of women as a minority is now widely recognized. Sex dis-

472

BOX 11-3. Similarities between Blacks and Women as Minorities ▼

1. Both groups have high social visibility because of physical appearance or dress.
2. Both were originally forms of property, controlled by an absolute patriarch.
3. Women and Blacks were at one time unable to vote—the Fifteenth Amendment (permitting Black males to vote) came half a century before the Nineteenth (permitting women to vote).
4. Both have been believed to have an inferior mental endowment and limited educational opportunities have been provided for them.
5. Each was assigned a "place" in the social system and as long as they stayed in their subordinate status, they were approved; attempts to alter this scheme were disapproved.
6. Neither group, historically, had legal rights over property or guardianship of children.
7. Myths were created about the "contented woman" who did not want the vote or other civil rights and equal opportunities, just as myths were created about the "contented Black."
8. It has been hard for either to attain important public office.
9. Certain low-prestige, low-salary jobs were allotted for women and for Blacks.
10. It was thought "unnatural" for White men to work under Black supervisors or males to be supervised by women. ▲

473

Source: Gunnar Myrdal, *An American Dilemma*. New York: Harper and Brothers, 1962, pp. 1073–1078.

crimination, however, has differed in one very significant way from racial and ethnic discrimination. The differential treatment of women, historically imbued in our social institutions for centuries, has rested on general agreement, up to very recent times, of both men and women. Men and women have been socialized into accepting their different social roles and discriminatory treatment as a natural state of life (Wylie, 1979). Hence, one must not think that men have intentionally imposed a subjugation on women. While such indeed may have been true at one time in our history, and while many men would prefer the situation to stay as it is, so too would many women. And, correspondingly, efforts at change are coming from men as well as women.

Our social institutions have been imbued with sexism as evidenced by such common and long-standing clichés as "a woman's place is in the home," as well as common distinctions of "female jobs" or "woman's work," and the inequality of remuneration for equal work by males and females. Evidence for such discriminatory behavior can be found throughout the marketplace. Women, as a social category, are largely confined to occupations at the lower end of the economic and prestige scales, while occupations of higher status have been the nearly exclusive domain of men, except in very recent times. Women are not found, for example, in many professional or managerial occupations, or at least not in proportion to their numbers, while they are considerably overrepresented (in

▼

the approximate ratio of 6:1) in many other occupational fields, such as clerical and sales work. Women account for 99 percent of secretaries, 96 percent of nurses, 86 percent of librarians, 85 percent of elementary school teachers versus 20 percent of physicians, 7 percent of engineers, 20 percent of lawyers, and 37 percent of college professors (U.S. Bureau of the Census, *Statistical Abstract of the United States, 1989;* see Table 11-1). These figures assume an even more dramatic significance when one realizes that in 1984 the median number of years of education completed by people twenty-five years old and over was virtually the same for men and women: 12.7 years for men; 12.6 for women (U.S. Bureau of the Census, *Statistical Abstract of the United States, 1985*). Men, however, continue to exceed women in the levels of graduate and professional education.

Correspondingly, the median earnings of full-time employed women in recent years have been only about 65 percent of those of men (U.S. Bureau of the Census, *Statistical Abstract of the United States, 1989*). Even working women with college degrees earn only about two-thirds as much as their male counterparts. This disparity, of course, is not due solely to discrimination or unequal opportunities for women. Differences between male and female career styles and years of employment are reflected in these figures. However, when appropriate controls for seniority and the lack of comparable skills are introduced, women still do not achieve income parity with men (Treiman & Roos, 1983). All of these situations simply point to discrimination as the underlying factor: women do not get equal pay for equal work. The minority status of women in economic respects seems beyond dispute.

A number of justifications, often without substantiation, are offered for these patterns of economic discrimination against women. Such prejudices are not much different from those used in the case of racial and ethnic minority. Women are considered intellectually inferior to men as well as irresponsible, inconsistent, and

**474**

TABLE 11-1. Persons Employed in Selected Occupations, Percentage Female, 1987

| Occupation | Percentage Female |
|---|---|
| Secretaries | 99.1 |
| Child-care workers, except private household | 96.0 |
| Teacher's aides | 95.1 |
| Telephone operators | 92.2 |
| Bank tellers | 90.6 |
| Librarians, archivists, and curators | 85.6 |
| Elementary schoolteachers | 85.3 |
| Waitresses | 85.1 |
| Office clerks | 82.9 |
| File clerks | 82.5 |
| Social workers | 65.6 |
| Secondary schoolteachers | 54.3 |
| Real estate agents and brokers | 48.7 |
| Writers, artists, entertainers, and athletes | 45.9 |
| Financial managers | 43.8 |
| College and university teachers | 37.1 |
| Computer programmers | 36.6 |
| Marketing managers | 27.4 |
| Natural scientists | 24.1 |
| Lawyers and judges | 19.7 |
| Physicians | 19.5 |
| Farm operators and managers | 14.9 |
| Architects | 12.6 |
| Telephone installers | 11.7 |
| Police and detectives | 11.4 |
| Dentists | 8.9 |
| Engineers | 6.9 |
| Truck drivers | 4.2 |
| Carpenters | 1.2 |
| Automobile mechanics | .6 |

Source: Adapted from U.S. Bureau of the Census, *Statistical Abstract of the United States, 1989.* Washington, D.C.: Government Printing Office, 1989, pp. 376–377.

emotionally unstable. The social and economic gains women have made in the past decade refute this kind of prejudicial thinking and the patterns of discrimination that rest upon it.

Within the family, the economic provider role has been traditionally assigned to men. Domestic roles, child-rearing, and housework have long been considered the exclusive—and still, for the most part at least, the primary—province of women. Such sexism is crystallized in a quotation from Martin Luther: "Women should remain at home, sit still, keep house, and bear and bring up children" (*Table Talk*, 1569). Generically, these roles have come to be embodied in the euphemistic label "homemaker." In modern society throughout this century, however, an increasing number of wives and mothers are employed outside the home. The proportion of women, eighteen to sixty-four years old, who have jobs outside the home in the United States has changed from 20 percent in 1900 to more than 50 percent today. Similarly, within the church, ministerial roles have traditionally been reserved exclusively for males. Only very recently has this situation changed—and in only some religions.

Sexism is also reflected in many languages, including English, in which collective references are usually expressed in a masculine form. Nouns and adjectives in the English language do not have a gender, as is the case in several other languages, such as French, Italian, and Spanish. In English we use terms such as *work-man*, *freshman*, *policeman*, and *chairman*; and, in referring to both males and females, the pronouns *he* and *his* are usually used. Research shows, as mentioned in Chapter 3, that such "sexist language" does perpetuate the image of male domination of the social world (Schneider & Hacker, 1973).

We can understand now, rather clearly, that the old cliché "it's a man's world" has not been just an idle saying. Rather, it has rested on sound empirical evidence. While the situation has changed dramatically during the past few decades, complete equality for women has yet to become a social reality. Social differences between men and women are far greater and more extensive in many other societies of the world today, especially the less advanced ones.

Efforts to eliminate sexual discrimination involve many of the usual efforts. One major tactic is social activism for appropriate legislation. Most notable in this regard in the United States have been efforts during the past decade to enact a constitutional amendment, known as the Equal Rights Amendment (E.R.A.). Proposed as the Twenty-seventh Amendment to the Constitution, this simple amendment states: "Equality of rights under the law shall not be denied or abridged by the United States or by any state on account of sex." Passed by the House of Representatives in 1971, and by the Senate in 1972, the amendment failed to receive ratification by the necessary three-fourths of the states within the requisite period that ended in

▼

**475**

FRANK AND ERNEST by Bob Thaves

HOW CAN A WOMAN BE SUING US FOR SEX DISCRIMINATION?... WE'VE NEVER EVEN HAD ONE WORK HERE!

© 1981 by NEA, Inc., TM Reg. U.S. Pat. & TM Off.    THAVES 1-5-82

Reprinted by permission of NEA, Inc.

▼

**476**

1982. This failure need not be seen, however, as a sexist response, since historically amendments to the Constitution have not been easy to enact. Moreover, there is opposition on purely political and legal grounds. A primary concern is the possibility that women would be subject to military service in the same manner and to the same extent (for example, combat duty) as men. Many states in any event have enacted legislation that guarantees sexual equality in every sphere of life. Additionally, the federal government has enacted a series of civil rights laws which, together with judicial decisions, have effectively made sex discrimination illegal.

## MINORITIES OF AGE STATUS: THE ELDERLY

As people grow older in some societies, they tend to lose social prestige and power, and often are treated in many ways that are typical of the treatment of racial and ethnic minorities. Elderly people, at least in modern industrial society, are often accorded the status of unequal and unwanted members of society and are thus the victims of **ageism.**

One particularly offensive tactic is to infantilize the elderly—that is, to treat them as though they were babies (Arluke & Levin, 1984). Among the principal forms of this kind of treatment are the use of first names (as was previously done with Blacks) or terms of endearment for the elderly, and the habit of talking to them in a loud and slow manner. Such behavior may be necessary in interacting with some infirm elderly people, but the vast majority are not so infirm that they need to be treated in such a solicitous and overbearing manner that makes them feel helpless and dependent.

In our youth-oriented society, it is commonly the case that the wise advice of the elderly is rejected, and that their skills are not wanted.

Elderly people often are expected to play a sick or dependent role. They are made to feel that to be frail and/or helpless is a legitimate state of being. Retirement, unknown in primitive and less advanced societies, provides a convenient mechanism in the resolution of this "problem." Yet, retirement often results in isolation and loneliness, which in turn frequently become sources of depression for the elderly. High rates of suicide among older people, especially men, are common.

Ageism also has its own particular set of stereotypes, such as the conception of elderly people as useless and nuisances, as dependent and passive, or as senile and sick, as well as a number of distinctive myths such as the belief that sex is not for old people—often reflected in the labels "dirty old man" and "dirty old lady." The facts here, however, are quite devastating to these myths: only about 20 percent of people over sixty-five are incapable of managing for themselves, and less than 10 percent of people over seventy-five display symptoms of senility (Atchley, 1988). Yet, whether the myths or stereotypes that are part and parcel of ageism are accurate, they provide a necessary justification for denying the elderly an equal status in life, and a correspondingly equal access to positions of prestige and power. It is chiefly in the economic realm, however, that the elderly experience social discrimination. While discrimination on the basis of age is no longer legally permitted in the American society, the United States does have a legal age for permitting mandatory retirement—seventy years (it was sixty-five* up to 1978). Consequently, although many people are quite physically and mentally fit for full-time employment after age seventy, the elderly can categorically be denied employment,

---

* Age sixty-five was arbitrarily and whimsically selected as a retirement age by Prince Otto von Bismarck, the chancellor of Germany, where the first social security laws were introduced in 1889. American legislation simply imitated this German precedent, set without the benefit of any scientific evidence or empirical justification.

**Gray Power.** Many elderly Americans, experiencing the status of a social minority in various respects, have marshalled their collective strength into a militant stance of redress for "age discrimination." (Charles Gatewood/Image Works)

without consideration of individual skills, talents, or fitness.

Of course, the majority of people still retire quite willingly at sixty-five—a situation that has been made attractive by pension funds and other economic benefits. Nonetheless, many elderly individuals who do not wish to retire maintain that mandatory retirement constitutes blatant discrimination. Public opinion polls reveal that about one-third of retired people in our society would prefer to be working. One reason given is simply the desire to be active; another, the most common reason, is purely economic. Retirement invariably in-

volves a considerable decrease in income, modifications in lifestyle, and fear of being financially unprepared for the proverbial rainy day. For about 80 percent of retired Americans, Social Security is the only source of income—one that does not, in the vast majority of cases, maintain the standard of living that they have come to experience. No employment, of course, often means no credit. So a kind of vicious circle exists for the elderly, and the net result for millions of such people is a remaining life of poverty and fear. Yet the one common remedy for poverty, or poor economic status—employment—is the one thing denied to the elderly.

Our euphemistically called "senior citizens" are often the victims of unequal treatment in many other realms, including in particular the areas of health and medical care, at a time in life when services of these kinds are crucial. Chronic illness affects more than three-fourths of the people over sixty-five, who fill nearly one-third of all hospital beds in the country and use one-fourth of all the drugs sold, even though they represent only 11 percent of the population. Chiefly involved are the noncurable, often terminal, illnesses, such as arthritis, diabetes, glaucoma, cancer, heart disease, and senility. These health problems are especially compounded for the aged in terms of medical expenses, which are six times greater than those for young adults.

Medical expenses consume an increasingly large portion of the income of the elderly, invariably at the expense of other necessities, especially food and energy. Estimates are that about one-half of medical expenses of the aged are not covered by insurance—either private or government insurance such as Medicare. Thus, a disproportionately larger percentage of the fixed incomes (pensions, Social Security benefits) of many elderly people goes for medical and health expenses.

The social status of the elderly is of increasingly significant concern in modern societies. A sizable segment of the American population—

**477**

▼ TABLE 11-2. Growth of the Elderly Population, 1900–2050

| | 65 Years and Over | |
|---|---|---|
| Year | Number* | Percent |
| 1900 | 3,084 | 4.0 |
| 1910 | 3,950 | 4.3 |
| 1920 | 4,933 | 4.7 |
| 1930 | 6,634 | 5.4 |
| 1940 | 9,019 | 6.8 |
| 1950 | 12,270 | 8.1 |
| 1960 | 16,560 | 9.2 |
| 1970 | 19,980 | 9.8 |
| 1980 | 25,544 | 11.3 |
| 1990** | 31,799 | 12.7 |
| 2000** | 35,036 | 13.1 |
| 2010** | 39,269 | 13.9 |
| 2020** | 51,386 | 17.3 |
| 2030** | 64,345 | 21.1 |
| 2040** | 66,643 | 21.6 |
| 2050** | 67,061 | 21.7 |

\* In thousands
\*\* Projection
**Source: U.S. Bureau of the Census, *Current Population Reports,* Series P-23, No. 128, "America in Transition: An Aging Society" Washington, D.C.: U.S. Government Printing Office, 1983, p. 3.**

nearly 11 to 13 percent—is involved. This figure represents about 26 million people. Moreover, as we mentioned in Chapter 7, the populations of modern societies are growing older. It is expected that by the year 2030, the median age in the United States will be perhaps as high as thirty-seven, and that the aged will constitute 21 percent of our population or about 50 to 60 million (see Table 11-2). The vast majority of elderly people are women, given the sex differential in life expectancy, and so for many individuals there is a double minority status involved. The sex ratio for the elderly is 140:100; two-thirds of women over seventy-five are widows.

The growing numbers and percentages of elderly people in our society—a situation partly occasioned by expansion of the life span and changes in a number of demographic factors—have drawn more and more attention to this minority category in recent years. At the same time, and for the same reasons, more extensive efforts have been made to redress the grievances of our senior citizens through appropriate legislation and the reaffirmation of our fundamental values of social equality and justice. Older persons themselves have been organizing their collective power, under such labels as "Gray Panthers" and "Gray Power," in an effort to achieve the ideal goals of society and many of their own particular needs. The potential for political clout among the elderly can be seen in some of their already achieved gains: the increase of mandatory retirement age to seventy, the linking of Social Security pensions to the cost of living, and improvements in health care benefits.

## MINORITIES OF HANDICAPPED STATUS

Handicapped people represent another newly recognized minority in our society. Such a category consists in part of people who are disabled, physically or mentally, and who because of their disabilities are denied access to opportunities in many segments of society, especially in the economic and occupational realms. It is estimated that at the present time there are approximately 36 million disabled people in the United States.

Legislation enacted during the past decade, and reinforced by public protests and other collective actions, prohibits discrimination against the handicapped in nearly every segment of social life; moreover, there are laws that specifically mandate a number of provisions to ensure for them a fuller, more dignified, and more independent participation in social life. Such provisions include the installation of mechanical means and/or physical adaptations to permit the use of public transportation, automobiles, elevators, telephones, television, and computers, as well as to facilitate access to houses and buildings. Of significance too are provisions, particularly in the educational realm, for eliminating, wherever possible, the segregation of the handicapped from their peers, as well as for the development of programs for "mainstreaming" handicapped people as quickly as feasible. Of related value are special provisions designed to facilitate the employment of the handicapped in appropriate occupations.

Examples of these efforts are the Rehabilitation Act of 1973 and the Fair Housing Act of 1989. Among their provisions are the following: (1) newly constructed facilities must be readily accessible to handicapped persons; (2) colleges and universities must conduct their programs and activities in such a way that they are readily available to handicapped persons; (3) employers must eliminate bias against employees with handicaps; and (4) employers are required to make reasonable accommodations to the physical and mental handicaps of otherwise qualified people seeking employment, including the modification of work schedules and equipment. Provisions such as these should contribute immensely to affording more equitable opportunities to the millions of people in our society who suffer from a variety of physical and mental handicaps.

## MINORITIES OF SEXUAL ORIENTATION

Another basis of minority status, one especially manifest in recent years, consists of unorthodox sexual orientations. Prejudice and discrimination in this regard are directed chiefly at homosexuals who experience such behavior not only in the economic and employment areas but also in the political and military realms of society.

These concerns have been heightened during recent years with the discovery and spread of new forms of sexually transmitted disease. Fears have been particularly strong in regard to the fatal disease of acquired immune deficiency syndrome (AIDS), which has been found most prevalently among homosexual individuals.

It is estimated that approximately 10 percent of the population maintains a homosexual lifestyle, although not all of these people do so in an open or visible fashion. While many homosexuals do not personally experience prejudice and discrimination, they often suffer in silence by having to maintain a hidden identity.

Recently enacted legislation in the spirit of civil rights, as mentioned above, coupled with a changing moral ethic in our society, has resulted in a more open display of homosexual lifestyles. While such a situation in turn has exacerbated the discrimination against individuals with unorthodox sexual orientations, many victims of this minority treatment have militantly responded, using such terms as "gay rights" and "gay power." These actions have yielded a number of positive results, similar to those experienced by the elderly and handicapped minorities.

# Prejudice and Discrimination

The behavioral axis of minority-majority relations consists of the dynamics of prejudice and discrimination. These processes are the forces that create, maintain, and perpetuate the conflicts which constitute minority-majority relationships.

Prejudice and discrimination are frequently confused, but actually refer to distinct, though related, phenomena. These two phenomena, moreover, do not necessarily occur together nor even sequentially. Let us describe each and then discuss the ways in which they may be interrelated.

▼ PREJUDICE

Prejudice is an attitude. Like all attitudes, prejudice represents a predisposition to act—a predisposition for an individual to respond to an object in certain ways. Again like all attitudes, prejudice is a product of social learning.

Prejudice, as an attitudinal dynamic, consists of a system of beliefs, feelings, and action orientations. Like any other attitude, prejudice consists of three principal components:

1. A *cognitive element* which refers to the beliefs about what people are like (for example, inferior, jerky, lazy, stingy) without any judgment of these beliefs or ideas.
2. An *affective element* which concerns the way one feels about the object of prejudice—either liking or disliking an individual or members of a particular social category. This component involves an evaluation of the belief or cognitive element.
3. A *conative element* which involves a predisposition to act in a particular way, that is, to be drawn either toward or away from the object of prejudice. This component refers to the directionality of the attitude.

Prejudice, more specifically, involves both a prejudgment and a misjudgment. Such an attitude consists of preconceived ideas or beliefs that are not based on facts. Yet, more than merely a prejudgment, prejudice also involves biased and inflexible thinking, and as such constitutes a misjudgment as well. All prejudice, then, consists of categorical thinking that systematically misinterprets the facts.

Prejudice, however, has a much more limited meaning in the context of minority-majority relationships. In this respect, **prejudice** refers to negative beliefs and hostile feelings about people of a particular social category. Prejudice of this type is often a consequence of ethnocentrism—a set of beliefs and attitudes regarding the superiority of one's own culture or subculture (see Chapter 3). Conversely, once

prejudice exists, it tends to reinforce the relevant ethnocentrism, which produces mutual reinforcement.

## DISCRIMINATION

Discrimination, unlike prejudice, is an action concept and refers to overt behavior. As such, discrimination consists of the actual response of one person to another in a differential, usually negative or hostile, manner. It is discrimination, more than prejudice, that is the crux of minority status—the capacity of one individual to impose a differential treatment on another.

Discrimination—something we necessarily practice many times a day—means to discern, to distinguish, and/or to treat differently. Daily life requires us to discriminate between animals and people, between children and adults, and between food and poison. As used in the context of minority-majority relations, however, discrimination has a much more specific meaning. In this context, **discrimination** involves a differential treatment of certain individuals which consists of the unjust denial of opportunities granted to other individuals or members of society. Discrimination specifically involves the withholding of socially valued commodities, including especially respect, dignity, and the opportunity to achieve. Discrimination, then, excludes people from full participation in society and maintains a system of inequality.

## RELATIONSHIPS BETWEEN PREJUDICE AND DISCRIMINATION

Prejudice and discrimination, as we have indicated, do not necessarily occur together, nor even sequentially. While discrimination is usually an expression of prejudice, these two dynamics can vary independently of each other. Many examples of behavioral research show marked discrepancies between what people believe and say, and what they do. Such is often

480

# BOX 11-4. Justice Without Discrimination? ▼

## IN THE SUPERIOR COURT OF THE STATE OF CALIFORNIA
## IN AND FOR THE COUNTY OF SANTA CLARA JUVENILE DIVISION

HONORABLE GERALD S. CHARGIN, Judge.

In the Matter of PAUL PETE CASILLAS, JR., a minor.

### STATEMENTS OF THE COURT
San Jose, California September 2, 1969 10:25 a.m.

481

### APPEARANCES
For the Minor: FRED LUCERO, ESQ. Deputy Public Defender
For the Probation Department: WILLIAM TAPOGNA, ESQ. Court Probation Officer

*The Court:* There is some indication that you more or less didn't think that it was against the law or was improper. Haven't you had any moral training? Have you and your family gone to church?

*The Minor:* Yes, sir.

*The Court:* Don't you know that things like this are terribly wrong? This is one of the worst crimes that a person can commit. I just get so disgusted that I just figure what is the use? You are just an animal. You are lower than an animal. Even animals don't do that. You are pretty low.

I don't know why your parents haven't been able to teach you anything or train you. Mexican people, after 13 years of age, it's perfectly all right to go out and act like an animal. It's not even right to do that to a stranger, let alone a member of your own family. I don't have much hope for you. You will probably end up in State's Prison before you are 25, and that's where you belong, any how. There is nothing much you can do.

I think you haven't any moral principles. You won't acquire anything. Your parents won't teach you what is right or wrong and won't watch out.

Apparently, your sister is pregnant; is that right?

*The Minor's Father, Mr. Casillas:* Yes.

*The Court:* It's a fine situation. How old is she?

*The Minor's Mother, Mrs. Casillas:* Fifteen.

*The Court:* Well, probably she will have a half a dozen children and three or four marriages before she is 18.

The County will have to take care of you. You are no particular good to anybody. We ought to send you out of the country—send you back to Mexico. You belong in prison for the rest of your life for doing things of this kind. You ought to commit suicide. That's what I think of people of this kind. You are lower than animals and haven't the right to live in organized society—just miserable, lousy, rotten people.

There is nothing we can do with you. You expect the County to take care of you. Maybe Hitler was right. The animals in our society probably ought to be destroyed because they have no right to live among human

*(Continued)*

▼    BOX 11-4    *(Continued)*.

beings. If you refuse to act like a human being, then, you don't belong among the society of human beings.

*Mr. Lucero:* Your Honor, I don't think I can sit here and listen to that sort of thing.

*The Court:* You are going to have to listen to it because I consider this a very vulgar, rotten human being.

*Mr. Lucero:* The Court is indicting the whole Mexican group.

*The Court:* When they are 10 or 12 years of age, going out and having intercourse with anybody without any moral training—they don't even understand the Ten Commandments. That's all. Apparently, they don't want to.

So if you want to act like that, the County has a system of taking care of them. They don't care about that. They have no personal self-respect.

*Mr. Lucero:* The Court ought to look at this youngster and deal with this youngster's case.

*The Court:* All right. That's what I am going to do. The family should be able to control this boy and the young girl.

*Mr. Lucero:* What appalls me is that the Court is saying that Hitler was right in genocide.

*The Court:* What are we going to do with the mad dogs of our society? Either we have to kill them or send them to an institution or place them out of the hands of good people because that's the theory—one of the theories of punishment is if they get to the position that they want to act like mad dogs, then, we have to separate them from our society.

Well, I will go along with the recommendation. You will learn in time or else you will have to pay for the penalty with the law because the law grinds slowly but exceedingly well. If you are going to be a law violator—you have to make up your mind whether you are going to observe the law or not. If you can't observe the law, then, you have to be put away. ▲

482

the case for prejudice and discrimination. Merton (1949) has distinguished four possible relationships between prejudice and discrimination. They may be described in terms of the following types of individuals.

UNPREJUDICED NONDISCRIMINATOR. The *unprejudiced nondiscriminator* is one who adheres to the ideal of equality in both principle and practice. Such a person is not prejudiced and does not engage in discriminatory action against others. Merton labels these individuals "all-weather liberals," individuals who believe in the equal rights of all people and who practice their belief in all areas of social life, regardless of circumstance. Such people, in other words, live as they believe.

UNPREJUDICED DISCRIMINATOR. The *unprejudiced discriminator* is the individual who holds no personal prejudice, yet may discriminate whenever it is expedient to do so. Individuals like this discriminate only because it is to their personal advantage to do so, or they are fearful of doing otherwise. Merton describes such people as "fair-weather liberals," individuals who believe in equal rights in principle, but only so long as there is no potential for personal loss involved.

Often such persons are forced to behave in ways that are contrary to their beliefs and attitudes. Such a situation may exist when law, organizational policy, custom, or social pressure intervenes between an individual's personal attitudes and the relative freedom to act

TABLE 11-3. Merton's Typology of Prejudice and Discrimination

| | Discriminator | Non-Discriminator |
|---|---|---|
| **PREJUDICED** | Believes that not everyone should be treated equally and actively implements prejudicial beliefs. | The "timid bigot" who is prejudiced against others but is afraid of, or prevented from, manifesting prejudice. |
| **UNPREJUDICED** | Inadvertently discriminates or discriminates because it is convenient or because social pressures require discrimination. | Accepts the belief that everyone should be treated equally. |

Source: Robert K. Merton, "Discrimination and the American Creed," in Robert M. MacIver (ed.), *Discrimination and National Welfare,* New York: Harper and Brothers 1949, pp. 103–110.

accordingly. Examples of this kind of individual include the realtor who refuses to sell or to rent a house to a member of a minority, not because of dislike or hatred, but because of neighborhood pressure or out of fear that the property may be damaged or suffer a loss in value. Similarly, a merchant might discriminate against members of a minority not because of personal prejudice, but because doing so would be beneficial to business by not incurring a loss of trade from people who are prejudiced.

**PREJUDICED DISCRIMINATOR.** The *prejudiced discriminator* is an individual who does not believe in the ideology of equality, and correspondingly discriminates on the basis of prejudicial attitudes. Such an individual is both prejudiced and discriminating, regardless of cir-

cumstances. People like this practice what they believe, even though such a practice may not be open, and the relevant behavior may be justified by rationalization.

**PREJUDICED NONDISCRIMINATOR.** The *prejudiced nondiscriminator*, representing the converse situation, is the "timid bigot" who is prejudiced towards others, but who, because of legal restraints or social pressure, refuses to transform attitudes into action. Many prejudiced people today are inhibited from practicing discrimination toward various minorities in a host of circumstances by existing legislation and prevailing mores.

One must keep in mind that there is nothing definitive about Merton's classifications. While they help to explain the possible associations between prejudice and discrimination, the typology cannot be used as an absolute classification for all people. That is, individuals do not consistently represent any one social type. This is so because discrimination is a situation-specific phenomenon. As with all overt actions, social circumstances and other factors determine the kind of specific behavior that will take place in a given situation.

## MANIFESTATIONS OF PREJUDICE

Prejudice manifests itself in a number of ways other than discrimination. Three specific forms are of particular interest in minority-majority interactions. These are stereotypes, ethnopaulisms, and social distance.

**STEREOTYPES.** Prejudice virtually always involves **stereotypes,** which consist of exaggerated and rigid beliefs about a particular minority or social category. Stereotypes may be positive, neutral, or negative; in any case, they tend to be applied indiscriminately to all members of a particular social category or minority.

483

▼ Question: Since the beginning of our country people of many different religions, races, and nationalities have come here and settled. Here is a list of some different groups. (Card shown respondent.) Would you read down that list, and thinking both of what they have contributed to this country and have gotten from this country, for each one tell me whether you think on balance they've been a good thing or a bad thing for this country?

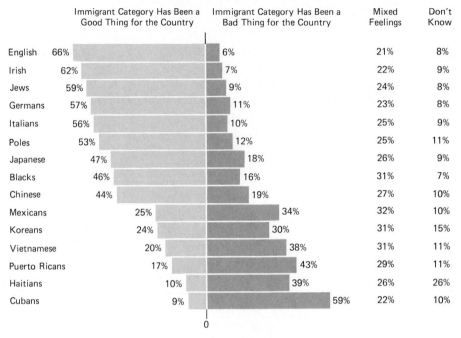

| | Immigrant Category Has Been a Good Thing for the Country | Immigrant Category Has Been a Bad Thing for the Country | Mixed Feelings | Don't Know |
|---|---|---|---|---|
| English | 66% | 6% | 21% | 8% |
| Irish | 62% | 7% | 22% | 9% |
| Jews | 59% | 9% | 24% | 8% |
| Germans | 57% | 11% | 23% | 8% |
| Italians | 56% | 10% | 25% | 9% |
| Poles | 53% | 12% | 25% | 11% |
| Japanese | 47% | 18% | 26% | 9% |
| Blacks | 46% | 16% | 31% | 7% |
| Chinese | 44% | 19% | 27% | 10% |
| Mexicans | 25% | 34% | 32% | 10% |
| Koreans | 24% | 30% | 31% | 15% |
| Vietnamese | 20% | 38% | 31% | 11% |
| Puerto Ricans | 17% | 43% | 29% | 11% |
| Haitians | 10% | 39% | 26% | 26% |
| Cubans | 9% | 59% | 22% | 10% |

0

FIGURE 11-3  American Attitudes toward Ethnic and Racial Immigrants. These data show that the categories of recent immigrants to the United States are less desirable than the older categories. While the number of social dynamics are operative in these attitudes of acceptance and rejection, actual social distance and achieved social mobility certainly account for some of the varying distributions. Source: Survey by the Roper Organization (Roper Report 82–4), March 20–27, 1982; *Public Opinion,* 5,3 (June–July 1982): 34. Reprinted with permission of the American Enterprise Institute for Public Policy Research.

They do not admit of any modifications of the general conception in terms of unique differences of an individual.

Stereotypical thinking, as a form of generalization and classification, is essential, of course, in order to comprehend and to interact with social reality. Responding to the general rather than to the unique character of nearly all phenomena encountered in daily life is not only necessary, but also provides a quick and easy guide to interaction. Hence, it is commonplace, as well as somewhat inevitable, to respond to people in terms of their categorical memberships (for example, professors, priests, and prostitutes), and one's personal knowledge or experience in these respects. Stereotypical thinking in the service of prejudice, however, involves beliefs and judgments that are basically neither rational nor verified against reality.

Common examples of stereotypes that have persisted over time in the American society are those of German people as "militaristic," Italians as "emotional, passionate, and irrational," Blacks as "lazy, child-like, superstitious, and promiscuous," Jews as "shrewd and mercenary," Chinese as "inscrutable and sly," Irish as "pugnacious and quick tempered," Poles as "stupid," Scotch as "stingy," women as "weak, fragile, and naive," and the elderly as "senile, cantankerous, and asexual" (Karlins et al., 1969; Berelson & Salter, 1946).

Stereotypes of "what people are like" are learned as part of normal enculturation and social experiences—indeed, even without personal contact, such as through the mass media. They usually are the result of limited and/or indirect experience. Moreover, once formed, stereotypes are quite resistant to change, even when one is faced with contradictory evidence. Hence, stereotypes tend to persist long after they no longer serve to justify prejudice and/or discrimination. Many racial and ethnic stereotypes, such as those mentioned above, can still be found today in textbooks, motion pictures, television programs, advertising/commercials, and various kinds of literature, despite efforts to eradicate them during the past two decades.

One dynamic that works to perpetuate stereotypes (and, consequently, prejudice) is differential perception. Stereotypes tend to highlight, to draw attention to, behavior that confirms or exemplifies them, rather than to behavior that is inconsistent with them.

ETHNOPAULISMS. Prejudice is commonly expressed in the form of verbal abuse. An **ethnopaulism** consists of various manifestations of prejudice through humor, jokes, caricatures, and name calling that uses derogatory terms such as wop, mick, jap, koon, kike, nigger, kraut, dago, gringo, frog, chink, polak, and spick. Ethnopaulistic behavior is one manifestation of prejudice that has decreased significantly in our society during the past couple of decades. Much of this decrease, however, may represent more a change in the form of prejudice than a decline in prejudice itself.

SOCIAL DISTANCE. Prejudice often is manifested in terms of the degree to which people are accepted or rejected in social relationships. **Social distance** is the degree of intimacy that an individual is willing to allow between himself or herself and members of a minority.

Social distance is implemented by spatial distance through such devices as segregation in housing, public facilities, schools, restaurants, places of employment, and other social contexts. Usually, the smaller the amount of social distance between two categories, the stronger is the assumption of equality between the categories, or the lack of prejudice between them. Maintaining social distance serves to keep minorities in their subordinate place, and to avoid thereby any competition that otherwise might occur. Various instruments have been devised to measure social distance in respect to various minorities. The most well-known of these techniques is the Bogardus Social Distance Scale (see Box 11-5).

# INSTITUTIONAL DISCRIMINATION

Long after discrimination and the ideologies which support it may be formally rejected in a society, as is currently the case in our own society, **institutional discrimination**—discrimination latently embedded within the institutional structure of society—may still linger on. Institutional discrimination* refers to prejudice and discrimination that endure within social structures long after conscious efforts have been made to eliminate such behavior. Many of the customs and social practices that originated in a context of genuine racism persist as consequences of passive efforts and resistance to social change. Foremost among such patterns of institutional discrimination is segregation

---

* Often called *institutional racism*.

485

▼

## BOX 11-5. Measuring Social Distance

Emory S. Bogardus (1933) devised an instrument to measure social distance with respect to particular minorities as a whole social category. This instrument consists of a hierarchy of social distances—from no distance (that is, willingness to have complete intimacy with members of a particular category) to complete isolation. Respondents are required to indicate the degree to which they would be willing to permit members of a particular minority or category to interact with them in terms of the following actions:

1. To close kinship by marriage.
2. To one's club as personal friends.
3. To one's street as neighbors.
4. To employment in one's occupation.
5. To citizenship in one's country.
6. To visitor's status in one's country.
7. To exclude from one's country.

This scheme permits a social distance score that is computed for each category, with 1.00 being the lowest possible score, and 7.00 being the highest possible score. Categories with the highest social distance scores are assumed to have the lowest prestige, and the most prejudice directed toward them. The Bogardus instrument is particularly useful for comparing the extent of prejudice between and among different minorities. In this latter respect, for example, racial minorities tend to experience greater social distance than ethnic minorities.

One application of the Bogardus instrument (Crull & Bruton, 1979), measuring social distance among 1000 college students in the mid-1970s, indicated that the subjects felt closest to Canadians, Germans, and Italians, while preferring to maintain the greatest social distance from Arabs, Russians, and Turks. The following data reveal the complete set of findings with the average scores for each nationality:

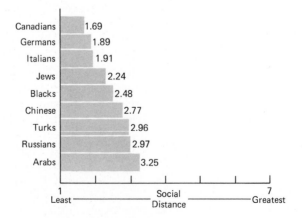

in housing, schools, churches, and various occupations.

Institutional discrimination, resulting from cultural lag in the day-to-day operations of society, is a particular kind of discrimination that is less overt and less identifiable, but nonetheless extremely damaging. The term describes situations in which a minority is indirectly, yet systematically, oppressed or exploited by the institutions of society. This form of discrimination, both impersonal and quite complex, can be said to be a latent dysfunction of societal structures and processes rather than a product of personal beliefs and attitudes.

Much racial and ethnic segregation in American schools during the past two decades is a result, as our courts have ruled, of discrimination in housing. Effectively segregated schools have resulted from virtually segregated neighborhoods. It is de facto segregation of this kind that brought about the forced busing of children to schools out of their neighborhoods as one conscious effort to alleviate discrimination and segregation. By this method, partial integration is achieved in neighborhood schools. Certain instances of the structural inequality that we referred to in Chapter 10 on Social Stratification may be taken as other manifestations of institutional discrimination. We can point, as we did there, to the life-chances and life expectancy of various minorities as examples of institutional discrimination. Other examples are reflected in the median family incomes of Whites and Blacks, as well as the differential employment rate for these two categories.

Blauner (1972) has described institutional racism within the American judicial system wherein jurors are drawn from voting lists. Black people, for example, are underrepresented on voting lists; accordingly, Blacks are less likely to be selected for jury duty. The method of drawing jurors from voting lists is not intended to exclude Blacks or any other minority; nonetheless, the net result, however

indirect, may indeed be a racist one. Similar patterns of institutional discrimination can be found in terms of ethnic, religious, and other types of minorities.

One of the most controversial interpretations of American race relations during the past decade contends that prejudice is no longer the major factor responsible for inequality in the economic and political spheres of social life (see, for example, Steinberg, 1981; Wilson, 1980). While not discounting the fact that racial discrimination is still pervasive in the American society, these social scientists claim that, in the economic sphere at least, it is institutional discrimination (not prejudice) that has become the primary source of continuing inequality for Black Americans and ethnic minorities. One sociologist specifically argues that "class has become more important than race in determining Black access to privilege and power" (Wilson, 1978:2). He attributes institutional discrimination to the growing use of industrial technology and to changes in the American economy. Many Blacks in the lower socioeconomic strata, argues Wilson (1978), are unable to compete in this modern economy because of the lack of required education and technical skills—itself a legacy of racial discrimination. Such a thesis implies that the removal of discrimination requires not only the elimination of minority-majority barriers, but also a restructuring of the American economy, quite a complex and intricate undertaking. These arguments, nonetheless, have been forcefully rebutted by other Black sociologists (see, for example, Pomer, 1986; Pinkney, 1984; Willie, 1979).

Among the more common forms of institutional discrimination is **gate-keeping** (that is, maintaining system boundaries), which refers to the decision-making process by which members of society are admitted to positions of privilege and power. Historically, it has been the White male power structure that controlled the critical gates of society in order to determine

▼

**487**

▼ who would be permitted to pass through the portals to good jobs, college, preferred housing, adequate health care, and a host of other desirable goals. Efforts have been made during recent years in both the public and private sectors to combat institutional discrimination through "affirmative action" programs (see Box 11-6).

## 488 Theories of Prejudice and Discrimination

Many theories have been advanced to explain prejudice and discrimination. All of them are perhaps valid, at least in some respects. Prejudice is much too complex a phenomenon to be understood in terms of a single explanation. Let us consider three of the principal types of explanations.

### SOCIALIZATION THEORIES

Many social scientists maintain that prejudice is most effectively explained as a product of the normal processes of social learning. Once prejudice and discrimination originate, they can become basic elements of culture and part of the normative order of society. As such, these attitudes and norms are transmitted by the various agencies of socialization in the usual course of life.

All types of learning theories* can be applied to the development and acquisition of prejudice. Behaviorists, for example, view prejudice and discrimination as responses that can be learned through classical or instrumental conditioning. Classical conditioning occurs when prejudice and/or discrimination become learned responses to social categories that have been associated with negative stimuli or experiences. Staats and Staats (1958) offer data

* See Chapter 4.

from an experiment involving classical conditioning in this regard.

Subjects were shown the names of different nationalities (for example, Dutch, Swedish) one at a time on a screen. As the subjects saw the name, the experimenter shouted out a word which the subjects were told to repeat. One set of the subjects heard only positive words (for example, *rich, good, beauty*), another set heard only negative words (for example, *ugly, bitter, vile*), and a third set heard only neutral words (for example, *key, chair*). When later asked how they felt about various nationalities, the subjects who were conditioned to respond negatively did so, while those who were conditioned to respond positively likewise did as they were conditioned.

Formulators of the theory of instrumental conditioning (operant reinforcement theory) provide a similar explanation for prejudice. The implications here are that people will become prejudiced and will engage in discrimination if such attitudes and/or behavior in the past resulted in rewards and/or the avoidance of punishment.

### THEORIES OF SOCIOECONOMIC GAIN

Another set of theories emphasizes the utilitarian or instrumental functions of prejudice and discrimination. Proponents of **socioeconomic theories** maintain that minorities are exploited for the purposes of providing cheap labor. Marxist theorists (for example, Cox, 1948) subscribe to this view, and maintain that racism is motivated essentially by economic exploitation. Moreover, racial and ethnic antagonism is encouraged, according to this view, in order to keep workers from uniting against the sources of their exploitation.

Competition is one of the fundamental social processes that takes place between individuals and groups in pursuit of socially valued and scarce resources such as wealth, prestige, power, employment, housing, education, and even mates. Prejudice and discrimination, in the context of competition, are seen as negative vehicles for achieving and maintaining socially valued goals. Competition, as a source of prejudice, involves the threat of personal loss because of rights and opportunities that may be given to or shared with minorities. People who are not in direct competition with members of minorities are less likely to be prejudiced toward them.

It is interesting to point out in this regard that there tends to be a negative correlation between prejudice and social-class status. Stronger prejudice toward minorities in general is found among the lower class. These people feel extremely threatened by the economic competition and social progress of minorities. Upper-class individuals, often having little or no contact with minorities, are not threatened by minorities, encounter no competition from them, and hence manifest little if any prejudice or discrimination toward them. Correspondingly, both education and status mobility have been found to be negatively correlated with prejudice and discrimination. Downwardly mobile persons, and those with lower levels of education, are the people more likely to be in competition with minority people in terms of jobs and housing, and are therefore the most prejudiced and discriminating.

Ample evidence supports the argument that competition is a central variable in all minority-majority relationships. American history, as well as that of other societies, reveals that much of the most severe discrimination and violence against minorities has occurred during periods of economic depression or hardship. One of the most blatant instances of this situation occurred when Chinese immigrants, who had come to the United States during the middle of the last century in order to work in the mining industry and in the construction of railroads, were viewed as unwanted competitors. This concern became massive fear, which eventually resulted in legislative enactments that for several decades excluded Chinese immigration and placed restrictive quotas on those from other lands as well.

## THEORIES OF PROJECTION

**Projection** is a psychological mechanism by which responsibility for one's behavior, or even the problems of society, are attributed to another individual or category, frequently one that is incapable of retaliation. It is quite common, it is argued, for people to take out their frustrations and hostilities on weak and helpless minorities.

Since hostility or aggression cannot always be directed toward the real source of frustration (for example, persons in authority), it is sometimes directed at another target called a **scapegoat.** Scapegoating usually occurs when individuals are powerless or unable to retaliate against the true source of the threat or frustration they are experiencing. Racial and ethnic minorities often provide socially convenient targets for scapegoating.

Southern Blacks, for example, in years past were frequently blamed for decreases in the price of cotton. Numerous lynchings of Blacks, from 1882 to 1920, were related quite directly to the marketability of cotton crops. Jews were faulted by the Nazis for the economic difficulties that seriously affected Germany after World War I, as they were during the great Depression of the 1930s. Today, unemployment and the high costs of welfare often are attributed to Mexican Americans.

**Displacement,** like projection, is a psychological device by which people also attribute to others characteristics that they reject, or are unwilling to recognize, in themselves. For example, the lynching and sadistic disemboweling of Blacks, which were rather common in the early decades of this century, are alleged to be

▼

**489**

▼

manifestations of guilt stemming from the sexual exploitation of Black females by White men. Prejudice, therefore, according to projection theories, can serve ego-defensive functions. People can protect themselves from threatening truths by displacing responsibility and/or hostility for their own personal failure onto socially targeted minorities.

One well-known version of projective theories is the frustration-aggression hypothesis that has been developed to explain various kinds of behavior. **Frustration-aggression theory** maintains that prejudice and discrimination, whatever their form, are always the unconscious expression of frustration—an interference with goal-directed behavior. This theory holds that "aggressive behavior always presupposes the existence of frustration, and contrariwise, that the existence of frustration always leads to some form of aggression" (Dollard et al., 1939: 1). Prejudice and discrimination thus may result from the ventilation of free-floating hostility that could have its basis in matters totally unrelated to minority-majority interactions. Many social scientists today do not believe that frustration is the only cause of aggression, nor that frustration necessarily must lead to aggression. Frustration-aggression theory, nonetheless, provides an explanation for certain forms of aggression that have been directed against minorities.

**490**

# Patterns of Minority-Majority Relations

Minority-majority relations assume many different forms, ranging from harmonious coexistence to outright warfare. Various patterns of adjustment are distinctive for both minorities and majorities. These patterns, however, are not mutually exclusive, either between the two categories or within each of them. Several patterns, moreover, may be used simultaneously within a particular society, some as official policies and others as informal patterns of interaction. Which specific patterns characterize a particular society depends in part upon the values and structure of that society, as well as the nature and size of the minorities present. Let us discuss first the principal patterns of majority reaction to minorities.

## EXTERMINATION

**Extermination** is the most brutal and vicious way to deal with minorities: their systematic annihilation. The elimination, or limitation, of a minority through sterilization, or the spreading of infectious diseases among them, could be other forms of extermination. Whatever its mode, extermination is assumed by the majority to be the ultimate solution—the complete destruction and elimination of minorities.

**Genocide** as one example of extermination is the deliberate and systematic killing of an entire people. Its most dramatic manifestation obtained at the hands of the German Nazis during the 1930s and 1940s in several European countries. Six million Jews, along with other "non-Aryan" people, such as Gypsies, were packed into cattle cars and taken to concentration camps where they were gassed to death. This heinous episode in modern history has come to be known as the Holocaust, which literally means "a burnt sacrificial offering."

Several other instances of minority extermination can be cited. During 1912, for example, one-half of the Armenian population was killed by the Turks. And, as recently as 1972, in Burundi, East Africa, the ruling Tutsi were accused of slaughtering an estimated 100,000 Hutus, a Bantu White people who traditionally had been accorded minority status.

## EXPULSION

**Expulsion** consists of the forcible removal of minorities from society. The basic objective of this pattern of reaction is usually to create a

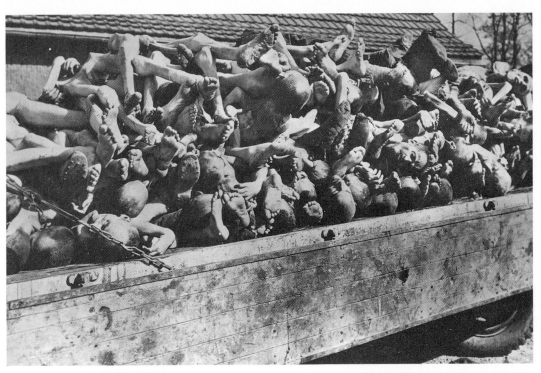

**The Final Solution.** Unburied victims of the Nazi concentration camp in Buchenwald, Germany, symbolize the massive attempt at eliminating the Jewish people through genocide. Six million Jews were exterminated in this unsuccessful effort. (The Bettmann Archive)

racially, ethnically, or religiously homogeneous society.

A biblical example, undoubtedly familiar to all, is that of the Hebrew people who were expelled many times into the African desert and who, under the guidance of their great leader, Moses, sought the Promised Land as a haven from their years of slavery in Egypt. Late in the nineteenth and early twentieth centuries, one-third of the Jewish population of eastern Europe fled their homelands during the pogroms (racial purges) of czarist Russia. Expulsion as a pattern of minority-majority interaction has been the historical fate of Jews throughout the centuries. Indeed, the state of Israel, established only in 1948, represents a long-sought homeland for Jewish people of every political and cultural background.

Other instances of expulsion as a pattern of minority-majority interaction are not difficult to find. Uganda, in 1972, deported East Indians from its territory. A more recent example of expulsion is that of many ethnic Chinese, the "boat people," who were driven from Vietnam during the late 1970s and sought refuge anywhere they could as they floated on the South China Sea.

One technique for effecting expulsion is that known as population transfer. **Population transfer** refers to the policy of physical separation of minorities from other segments of society by moving them from one geographical area to another, sometimes even forcing them into another society. Often such a policy can be indirectly enforced, such as when people leave "voluntarily" because of harassment. Such has

▼

been the case of many Jews who in recent years have left the Soviet Union. Population transfer was adopted as an official policy in this country during the nineteenth century when Indian tribes were relocated on reservations, many of which still exist in various parts of the nation. Cherokee Indians, for example, were forced by army troops to march from their native areas in Georgia to reservations in Oklahoma. Nearly 40 percent of the ten thousand people who made the trek died en route—a situation that itself contributed to the basic goal of expulsion.

The same objective was found in the policy of exclusion, as represented in legislation that established immigration quotas for southern and eastern Europeans between 1917 and 1965. Such legislation imposed on these people a total limit of 150,000 entrants per year and established specific quotas for each country. Immigrants from other, more desirable, countries—particularly those of northern Europe—were not subject to quotas. Great Britain, for example, was allowed 65,000 immigrants per year versus 6,000 for Italy and 1,000 for Hungary. These laws were repealed in 1965.

## SEGREGATION

**Segregation** refers to the stringent separation of a minority from the majority through the construction of social, and even physical, barriers. Often such an arrangement is intended, at least ideally, to be one of "separate, but equal" accommodation between the two categories in both physical and social respects. The model of segregation, as implied in this doctrine, however, seldom obtains. Segregation in reality is, more often than not, a means of keeping minorities subjugated to the majority in order to eliminate a significant amount of competition. Such a policy represents an economic and political advantage for the majority. Under such circumstances, there is usually no desire for segregation on the part of minorities, since they perceive themselves to be an exploitable asset.

Throughout much of their history, many states in this country adopted an official policy of segregation to regulate social intercourse between Blacks and Whites. The fundamental doctrine of "separate, but equal" accommodation upon which this policy officially rested was affirmed by the United States Supreme Court in 1896 in the *Plessy vs. Ferguson* case. This famous decision maintained that separate facilities for Blacks and Whites were not unconstitutional so long as the facilities were equal. This doctrine remained the law of the land until 1954, when the Supreme Court reversed itself in the case of *Brown vs. Board of Education of Topeka, Kansas* and ruled that physical separation with equal facilities was *inherently* unequal, that the mere fact of separation implied a differential treatment.

Legal segregation generally applies to both residential and public facilities, such as schools and churches. And, of course, marriage between minority and majority individuals is forbidden. In the Union of South Africa, the Immorality Act forbade Whites and non-Whites from interacting even socially. Accompanying segregation there is usually clearly detailed etiquette regarding the norms of social interaction between minority and majority individuals (see Doyle, 1937; Omond, 1986). During the era of legal segregation in the southern states, for example, adult Black men were usually addressed as "boy," or perhaps, if elderly, as "uncle." Deference to members of the White majority in a variety of appropriate ways, however, was always demanded of Blacks.

While legal, or de jure, segregation no longer exists in the United States, de facto segregation remains in many respects as a matter of chance, circumstances, or residues of institutional patterns that have been abandoned. One can speak, for example, of residential segregation as a latent function of zoning laws that require housing lots of a minimum size, and as the effect of physical mobility on the part of the majority (often known as "White flight") who may desert an ecological area rather than share it with

492

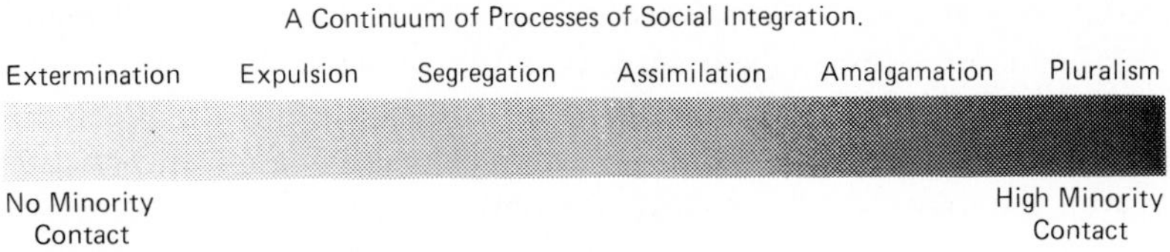

A Continuum of Processes of Social Integration.

Extermination    Expulsion    Segregation    Assimilation    Amalgamation    Pluralism

No Minority
  Contact

High Minority
  Contact

FIGURE 11-4   Majority Responses to Minorities.

members of racial or ethnic minorities. De facto segregation in instances such as these exemplifies institutionalized discrimination.

Although segregation is primarily involuntary, there are instances in which a minority may freely choose this pattern of accommodation. Such a situation often is found among religious minorities, such as the Mennonites and the Amish in our society. Another example of voluntary segregation is that of the Quebeçois of Canada. These people, representing a French-speaking Catholic segment of the Canadian population, have sought political separateness in recent years in the face of what they consider to be social discrimination and economic disadvantage.

Today, the most blatant instance of involuntary segregation as an official pattern of accommodation between majority and minorities can be found in the Union of South Africa. *Apartheid*, which means "apartness," is the name given to the official policy of segregation introduced in 1947 by the Dutch-dominated Afrikaner National Party.

**Partition** is a form of segregation that attempts to separate racial or ethnic peoples in terms of mutually acceptable political solutions. This type of segregation involves the political reorganization of a nation so that national boundaries correspond more closely to ethnic or racial ones. Several such examples can be found in the past half-century: the partitioning of Pakistan and India in 1947 after the end of British colonial rule was an attempt to segregate Moslems from Hindus respectively; Catholics and Protestants were similarly segregated in Ireland in 1912; Palestine was divided in 1948

by the British into separate areas for Arabs and Jews. History shows that such solutions are never permanent and, as the examples above have shown, often lead to continuous hostility.

## ASSIMILATION

**Assimilation** refers to the integrating processes by which a minority abandons its own cultural patterns and takes on those of the majority. Such a procedure, in effect, has as its objective the elimination of the minority as a minority through its absorption into the majority, and the creation of a culturally homogeneous society. Often assimilation is achieved through force when a minority is denied the right to practice its own culture.

The popular vision of the United States as "the world's great melting pot" (Zangwill, 1909) of racial and ethnic differences represents the ideal of assimilation. Such an ideal is also reflected in the motto of our country: *E pluribus unum* (one from many). These expectations, with considerable justification, have been the dream of millions of immigrants to these shores, despite the minority status that many of them encountered.

Assimilation in the United States, described traditionally as "Anglo conformity," has consisted by and large in the demand that immigrants and minorities absorb as quickly as possible the Anglo-Saxon cultural patterns of the majority. Such a mode of assimilation seeks to perpetuate the English institutions, traditions, and language upon which this country was founded. Nonetheless, for reasons that we shall make clear elsewhere in this chapter,

**493**

▼ assimilation in the United States has not been totally successful. For one thing, assimilation is usually difficult to achieve, since minorities invariably refuse to surrender their distinctive identities. And, sometimes, even the majority, for rather expedient reasons, wishes to retain the cultural differences.

American society, as DeVos (1977) contends, has been characterized more by political than social unification. Americans, he argues, are becoming less and less concerned with blending together, either biologically or culturally. On the other hand, the rate of assimilation through intermarriage increases with each generation. With the exception of Blacks, intermarriage rates for the various ethnic populations in the third generation range between 60 and 80 percent (see Alba, 1976).

Current trends in intergroup relations provide more evidence for assimilation as the chief pattern of minority-majority dynamics in the years ahead, at least in regard to the nonracial minorities (see, for example, Alba, 1985). Many social scientists are of the opinion that ethnicity will continue to play a significantly symbolic role for millions of Americans, especially for the "new" migrants, but that it will be a central identity and principal determinant of social behavior for relatively few people.

## AMALGAMATION

**Amalgamation,** in many ways similar to assimilation, refers to the blending of two or more culturally or physically distinct populations in order to produce a totally new synthesis or hybrid. Whereas assimilation refers to a minority's adopting the ways of the majority, amalgamation represents the fusion of minority and majority characteristics in such a way that a "new" type results.

Many people have had expectations that the United States throughout the course of its history would become a new society, a new amalgam, and the Americans a new people, through a synthesis, and loss, of the unique character and differences of each of the many subcultures which comprise our society.

Biological amalgamation occurs when two or more different races, or subraces, freely interbreed and produce thereby a blend of their physical types. Examples of biological amalgamation can be found in Polynesia where Caucasoids, Negroids, and Mongoloids have interbred so frequently that the three races have blended together and produced a relatively distinct offspring. Native Hawaiians, originally a mixture of Polynesians and Tahitians who over the years have interbred with Japanese, Chinese, Filipinos, and Europeans, represent another case of biological amalgamation.

Some observers (for example, DeVos, 1977) would argue that the American culture, despite its Anglo-Saxon dominance and heterogeneous character, is in many respects an amalgamation of its many ethnic subcultures. Moreover, consistently increasing rates of intermarriage among our minorities suggest that cultural amalgamation is becoming a more extensive pattern of response. Amalgamation has been enhanced as well by the slowly, but consistently, increasing number of interracial marriages in the American society.

## PLURALISM

**Pluralism,** the most tolerant of all policies pertaining to minority-majority relationships, represents a pattern of harmonious coexistence among people of diverse racial and ethnic backgrounds. No one segment of the population dominates the others, and each minority maintains its own identity and relative autonomy. Pluralism, thus, recognizes the social equality of all people and the superiority of none. A truly pluralistic society, in short, is one comprised of culturally and racially different people, all of whom are accorded equal rights and privileges.

Pluralism is not easy to achieve or maintain because societies generally stratify their cultur-

494

ally and racially diversified populations in the very nature of minority-majority interactions. Nonetheless, such a pattern of accommodation has been rather successful in several countries. Yugoslavia, a country of many ethnic popu- lations, has adopted official policies to protect the rights of all of its people. Among them are Croatians, Serbs, Montenegrins, Macedonians, Albanians, Muslims, and Slovenes. Included as well are lesser minorities, such as the Yugoslavs,

## BOX 11-6. Affirmative Action

A new pattern of response to minority-majority relationships, introduced by the U.S. Government during the 1970s, is that known as *affirmative action*. The intent of this essentially voluntary policy is to foster integration by increasing the number of individuals with minority backgrounds in the educational and occupational structures of the American society. Under this policy, preference in recruitment and placement for employment and college admissions is given to minority individuals whenever qualifications among applicants are thought to be virtually equal. Another dimension of affirmative action is the establishment of quotas for members of racial and ethnic minorities in various areas of occupational and educational activity.

495

Affirmative action programs are highly controversial. Some people within the majority ranks object quite strongly to affirmative action with the contention that such a practice constitutes "reverse discrimination." Such forms of preferential treatment, nonetheless, have been upheld by the courts, particularly as an effective way to compensate in part for past injustices towards minorities. These policies are intended to remain in force until the respective minorities are fairly represented in the workplace and the classroom.

Compliance with affirmative action policies is required for academic institutions that participate in federally funded programs and for employers, with fifty or more employees, who receive federal contracts. Relevant legislation not only makes it unlawful for these employers and institutions to discriminate against individuals on the basis of race, national origin, religion, or gender, but also requires them to ensure a sufficient number of applications from minority people. The same regulation applies to universities in terms of student recruitment.

The United States Supreme Court in 1978 rendered two historical decisions* relative to "reverse discrimination" and the "limits of affirmative action." It held, by a five-to-four margin, that quotas established for minorities or others were unconstitutional, but that minority status (specifically, racial) could be considered as one factor in the admissions policies of universities. The future of affirmative action, however, is somewhat problematic. Eventually, in 1984, the Civil Rights Commission of the United States, relying on the argument of reverse discrimination, voted strongly against the concept and practice of affirmative action. Much opposition ensued. The practice, nonetheless, has remained quite active on the local and state levels of government, as well as in the academic, corporate, and industrial sectors of society. ▲

* See *Regents of the University of California vs. Bakke.* The case involved Alan Bakke, a White man, twice denied admission by a California medical school, who argued successfully that less-qualified people had been granted admission through a special policy that reserved a number of positions for minorities.

▼ Hungarians, Bulgarians, Turks, Romanians, Ruthenians, Italians, Czechs, Vlachs, and Slovaks. Ethnic and religious prejudice, of course, still exists to a certain degree among the Yugoslavians, but, by and large, harmony pervades this highly ethnically diversified population. Other examples of pluralistic societies include Belgium (French and Flemish), Canada (French and English), and Switzerland (French, German, and Italian).

496 Our own nation has experienced renewed demands for pluralism as the preferred mode of majority-minority interaction. Such a policy has received support through civil rights legislation and various governmental programs instituted in the past two decades, as well as from the strong revival in ethnic consciousness among American people. Bilingualism, whether in education or government, seems to be a modern manifestation of cultural pluralism and may be itself an affirmation of the ineffectiveness of the American melting pot of ethnic and cultural diversity. The U.S. Office of Education, as of 1977 at least, has approved the use of twenty different languages in public schools for children who speak little or no English. Among these languages are Spanish, Greek, Japanese, Chinese, Vietnamese, French, Italian, Portuguese, and several native Indian languages. A parallel development of interest here is the extensively quasi-official use of Spanish as a second language in certain parts of the nation, especially in several southwestern states and in Florida on the East Coast. Miami, in fact, is officially a bilingual city. These instances are quite a reversal of the situation which obtained fifty to seventy years ago. During the peak of western European migration to the United States, children of foreign immigrants had to learn English—or suffer the consequences.

Some social scientists do not believe that pluralism will be an enduring pattern in the American society (see, for example, Stein & Hill, 1977). Pluralism, in any event, particularly for racial minorities, seems to be one of the most likely patterns for the immediate future. Such an eventuality is all the more probable, given the renewal of ethnic pride in America in recent decades.

# Minority Responses to Social Inequality

Contrary to what one might expect, minorities are not necessarily totally passive to the injustices that they experience. Minority response to social inequality can range from withdrawal and passivity to forms of aggression—both violent and nonviolent majority.

Reactions of minorities, of course, often are influenced by the official policies of the majority, as well as the characteristics of the minority itself. As with majority reactions, no one pattern of response is necessarily followed exclusively. Minority-majority relationships are usually too complex to permit any one pattern to prevail under all circumstances. One can note, nonetheless, that a particular pattern of response may be dominant or in vogue at a given time. Such seems to be the case in the United States, where at present the dominant pattern of response by several minorities appears to be that of militancy in search of both political and economic power. Usually, however, there is no unified or cohesive response on the part of minorities. Various types of responses are used by different minorities and by different members of any one minority.

There are four principal kinds of minority response, of which there may be many specific variations: acceptance, assimilation, avoidance, and aggression. The fundamental problem in minority response is whether the basic orientation should be directed toward integration or separation. Accordingly, as shown in Figure 11-5, there are four mixed reaction patterns. Let us discuss these four basic patterns of minority response.

## ACCEPTANCE

**Acceptance** refers to the process of acquiescence to the majority—that is, the acceptance by a minority of a disadvantaged and subordinate status in society. Minorities often come to internalize their stereotypes and believe that indeed they are innately inferior. Such a response may be necessary for survival, given the superior power of the majority; at the same time, passive acceptance supports the pattern of prejudice and discrimination, which in effect makes for a static situation.

Blacks in the American southern states for years generally responded in this fashion by simply manifesting various patterns of peaceful and obedient submission to the official and unofficial norms of minority-majority relationships. Among themselves, Black people who particularly manifested such behavior were known as "Uncle Toms" (a reference to the story of the obsequious Black servant in the well-known novel *Uncle Tom's Cabin* by Harriet Beecher Stowe). This label is still heard today with some frequency, particularly in reference to Blacks who prefer not to assume a militant role in the pursuit of political and civil rights.

One manifestation of acceptance involves various patterns of withdrawal of a minority into its own subculture. Such patterns may involve self-segregation, along with ghetto habitation, and a stress on ethnicity. Withdrawal behavior also includes such activities as dropping out of school, giving up on trying to find or to keep employment, and even resorting to such deviant action as alcohol and drug abuse in order to ease the psychological stress that may be produced by minority status.

## AVOIDANCE

Avoidance involves responses of a minority that can be classified as neither an acceptance nor a rejection of dominance by the majority. Its dynamics, however, may be directed principally toward one or the other mode. **Avoidance** may be described as a voluntary form of self-segregation. Such responses involve minimizing contact with the majority, and avoiding the occasions for being the victims of prejudice and discrimination.

Separation is the most extreme form of avoidance. Examples include attempts to set up totally independent societies, such as in the creation of the Jewish state of Israel by the partitioning of Palestine in 1948. Earlier in our own history, during the 1920s, Marcus Garvey advocated and implemented a "Back to Africa Movement" for the descendants of former Black slaves. A similar movement, in fact, nearly a century earlier, resulted in the colonization of the African state of Liberia. As recently as the 1970s, the Black Muslims, a militant organization based on the beliefs of Islam, opposed every effort at integration and sought the grant of a few states from the federal government in order to establish an all-Black nation. Today, many American Indian tribes advocate separatism. Less extreme forms of separation include the voluntary formation of racial and ethnic ghettos.* Middle-class as well as lower-class minorities that wish to remain in ghettos nowadays find a sense of security there.

## ASSIMILATION

**Assimilation** is a pattern by which a minority tries to blend into the dominant society by taking on its culture. Such a response includes attempts to learn the dominant language, styles of dress, patterns of behavior, and other cultural characteristics so that the minority becomes indistinguishable from the majority.

497

* The term *ghetto*, rather universally used today for any neighborhood occupied by a racial or ethnic minority, is of Italian origin. It derives from *borghetto*, the name given to the section of the city of Venice, in medieval times, where Jews were required to live. *Borghetto*, meaning "little borough," itself derives from *borgo*, meaning "borough," which refers to an outlying or fringe section of a city.

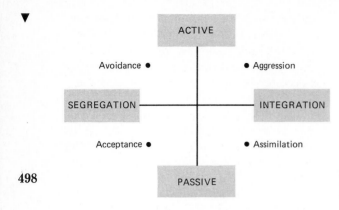

FIGURE 11-5  Patterns of Minority Response to Social Inequality.

Sometimes, when assimilation is not welcomed by the majority, it may be attempted surreptitiously. **Passing** is a clandestine form of assimilation that consists of various techniques by which an individual disguises his or her true identity, and attempts to be recognized as a member of a racial or ethnic majority to which the person does not belong. Many minority individuals who possess characteristics that are similar to those of the majority often abandon their racial or cultural heritage and "pass" themselves off as members of the majority, either totally and permanently, or simply partially and temporarily in only certain segments or spheres of the society, principally the economic.

Passing, of course, is an alternative more readily available to some minorities than others. People in ethnic minorities can usually pass more easily than those in racial minorities. Racial minorities, like those based on sex and age, have more difficulty in trying to hide their social status than do minorities based on nationality and religion. Among the techniques that have been used in this regard are name changes and skin changes. It is estimated that 40,000 to 50,000 American Blacks pass in the White community annually, while hundreds of thousands of ethnic Americans have Anglo-Saxonized their surnames in order to pass into the dominant society.

## AGGRESSION

**Aggression** as a pattern of response may take many forms, but in all cases consists essentially of striking out against subordinate status by seeking redress for social injustices.

Among the principal forms of aggression as a mode of minority response are boycotts, sit-ins, strikes, mass protests, civil disobedience, work slowdowns, legal actions, jokes, and political activity. Even serious forms of violence (such as sabotage and terrorism) may be used, as has been done in Northern Ireland by the Irish Republican Army, and by the Black Guerrilla Forces in South Africa and Rhodesia during the 1970s.

Aggression, both violent and nonviolent, has become a rather common reaction among American minorities, especially Blacks, since the 1960s. In 1963, for example, within a ten-week period, 758 riots and protest demonstrations took place in seventy-five cities. Nearly 14,000 arrests were involved in these actions. During this same period, a number of social movements of political protest were organized among American minorities. Examples of such militancy among American minorities include the organization of the following social movements:

1. The Southern Christian Leadership Conference (S.C.L.C.) organized by Martin Luther

King, Jr. constitutes a nonviolent protest movement that has sought a broad spectrum of redress and civil rights, including the elimination of segregation in public facilities and voting discrimination.

2. The American Indian Movement (A.I.M.) was inspired by the civil rights and Black movements. Under the label "red power," this organization has stressed identity, pride, and consciousness-raising, as well as demands for justice and the right of self-determination. Particularly in the forefront of the objectives of A.I.M. is a major struggle for the return of lands formerly occupied by various Indian tribes. More than one hundred lawsuits in this effort are presently pending, and many cash settlements already have been granted by the courts.

3. La Raza Unida, a Mexican-American organization under the leadership of Cesar Chavez, has focused its attention chiefly on the economic exploitation of farm laborers and migrant workers.

4. The National Organization for Women (N.O.W.), organized slightly more than a decade ago, constitutes an older branch of the women's liberation movement. Its efforts are channeled chiefly toward the cause of feminism and the elimination of all forms of discrimination directed at women. Among the principal concerns of N.O.W. have been those of an economic nature: equal pay for equal work, and access for women to traditionally male occupations and professions.

5. The American Association of Retired Persons (A.A.R.P.), presently numbering about 28 million members, is one of the political lobbies that have been particularly effective in promoting the interests and welfare of the elderly people in our society.

All of these organizations have achieved considerable success in the areas of voting rights, education, and the desegregation of public accommodations. Minority activity today focuses principally on achieving economic and political power which, as we have indicated, constitutes the crux of minority-majority relationships.

## TRENDS IN MINORITY-MAJORITY RELATIONS

Minority-majority relationships, on the whole, have improved significantly in the past two decades. Much of this progress is due to a host of legislated reforms that prohibit many forms of discriminatory and unequal treatment in the fields of housing, education, employment, public accommodation, and political rights. Greater tolerance and social equality are also expressions of changing values in America, and in many other societies of the world as well.

Occupational, educational, economic, and political attainments of American minorities, bolstered by more favorable attitudes and increased sensitivity on the part of other Americans, have been consistently diminishing the social inequities between the dominant and minority segments of our society. Such progress has been particularly true for ethnic minorities of European and Asian origins, but much less so for American Blacks, Indians, and Hispanics (Yetman, 1985).

The most dramatic changes have occurred in the field of education, where the gaps between minorities and the dominant segment are rapidly narrowing. The median number of school years completed is now nearly equal, in contrast to the gross inequalities that existed as late as the 1960s. Considerable disparity, however, still exists in the areas of occupation and income. The least change has occurred in housing, where many neighborhoods throughout the United States are still segregated. Much of the discrimination that remains can be described as institutional discrimination. Indeed, while quite controversial, several social scientists (see, for example, Steinberg, 1981; Wilson, 1980) argue that discrimination and other social obstacles

**499**

▼ encountered by minorities today, especially Blacks, are chiefly socioeconomic rather than racial. That is to say, discrimination is due more to structural factors inherent in the stratification system than to a person's own minority status.

No one, however, is so naive as to think that the many legislative reforms and numerous judicial decisions of the past few decades have completely eliminated all discrimination—let

**500** alone prejudice. Indeed, on the contrary, a substantial minority of Americans still hold segregationist attitudes (Kluegel & Smith, 1983). There is, nonetheless, a totally different kind of social context for minorities in the United States today.

Longitudinal analyses of public attitudes toward minorities since the 1940s have shown a significant decline in racial and ethnic prejudice—and indeed a notable increase in social equality. Such attitudes specifically reveal more tolerance toward minorities and a stronger belief in social integration, including equality of treatment in employment, education, public ac-

commodation, schools, and housing. For example, in 1942, 32 percent of Americans felt that Blacks and Whites should attend the same schools; by 1982, the figure was 90 percent (Schuman, Steeh, & Bobo, 1985).

## Minorities in American Society

Many of the general concepts and principles of minority-majority interaction that we have discussed thus far in this chapter can be concretized in a brief discussion of some of the racial and ethnic minorities that exist in the American society today.

Our country is primarily a nation of immigrants—a pattern that has continued unabated since the arrival of the Pilgrims in 1620. The heaviest period of immigration to the United States occurred between 1820 and 1920, a period of comparatively unrestricted immigration. Historians frequently distinguish between the "old" and the "new" immigration within

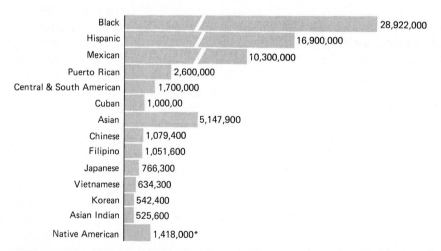

FIGURE 11-6 Racial and Ethnic Population of the United States, 1985. Sources: U.S. Bureau of the Census, *Statistical Abstract of the United States, 1986.* Washington, D.C.: U.S. Government Printing Office, 1985, p. 25.
* Data for Native Americans are for 1980.

this period. The "old" immigration, occurring before 1890, included peoples primarily from northern and western Europe; the "new" immigration, principally between 1890 and 1915, involved people from southern and eastern Europe.

Since 1917, a series of legislative enactments has controlled the flow of immigration to the United States, with quotas (and virtual exclusion) established for many nations in order to preserve the "cultural and social" composition of the American population. These effectively discriminatory laws were equitably revised in 1965. In recent years, the principal sources of immigrants to this country have consisted of Asian, Caribbean, and South American countries.

White Anglo-Saxon Protestants (WASPs), comprised primarily of the descendants of British settlers (native White Americans or Yankees as they are called), have been the dominant majority in the United States throughout its entire history. Today, WASPs account for about 35 percent of the American population, or approximately 80 million people. Immigrants from nearly all other countries, together with the truly native Americans (Indians), have occupied a minority status at one time or another. Such a situation still exists for many American people.

One curious pattern of minority status is that the more recent the arrival of a particular people, the more they encounter prejudice and discrimination from the "natives" who were, of course, the immigrants of a generation or two earlier. Therefore, one of the easiest ways to escape minority status for many people in our country, especially for ethnic minorities, has been to pass it along to newcomers!

While the experiences of minorities, especially within a single society, are quite similar in some ways, they are nevertheless quite different in other respects. Such is the case in terms of the historical conditions in which a specific minority originated, the socioeconomic circum-

stances through which it developed, and the degree to which it may have been compatible with, or easily assimilated into, the American culture. Moreover, the social experiences and life-chances of different minorities, as well as of individual members of any particular minority, are by no means identical. All minorities, however, simply by virtue of being minorities, are denied full and equal participation in the various aspects of society. Such is the case at the present for nearly two-thirds of the American people who in various ways experience social discrimination to a certain degree. Let us discuss some of the major racial and ethnic minorities in the United States.

# NATIVE AMERICANS

Native Americans represent the descendants of many Indian (as Christopher Columbus in search of India called them) tribes that existed in the United States when the first explorers and settlers came to these shores centuries ago. At that time, these Native Americans consisted of about one hundred different tribes that numbered approximately 1.5 million people. These numbers steadily decreased in the aftermath of European invasions, warfare, massacre, disease, starvation, and forced migration. The minority status of these people, however, is of much more recent origin, going back only to the nineteenth century.

The many Indian tribes that populated the continent became virtually a conquered people by the turn of the century through a series of "Indian Wars." White European settlers laid claim to nearly the entire territory in the Northern Hemisphere, and proceeded to colonize and to pioneer the land that had been systematically taken from these native peoples. So desperate were the American settlers to occupy the entire continent that genocide was an official policy in some parts of the land. There were even bounties paid for the capture and/or scalp of

▼

**501**

Indians. By 1850, only about 250,000 of these people remained—more than 80 percent had been annihilated. After 1871, Indians were made wards of the federal government, and the official policy became one of internment and segregation on reservations, about 250 of which yet exist.

Native Americans still comprise approximately 1.5 million people today, about 40 percent of whom live on reservations. There are among these people, who number less than 1 percent of the population, more than 170 Indian peoples with different cultures and histories. They are considered the most disadvantaged of American minorities, the poorest and most neglected of all. Holding such a marginal position in the American society, American Indians have a very high rate of unemployment (45–50 percent) and a very low average income (one-third subsisting below the poverty line). The life expectancy of Native Americans is far lower than the national average; their suicide rate is about double that of the national average, and their alcoholism rate is about five times as high. The life expectancy of Native Americans is only forty-six years, almost thirty years less than the rest of the American population. Similarly, Native Americans have a lower average level of education (8 years) than the national average of 12.1 years.

## BLACK AMERICANS

By far the largest, and most important, minority in the United States has been comprised of Blacks who trace their origins to the captured Africans brought to the shores of Jamestown and sold as slaves as early as 1619. Today, Blacks account for 12 percent of the population, or about 26 million people. In some regions and cities of the nation, however, the proportion of Blacks in the population is much greater, often as much as 30 percent.

After the founding of this nation, slavery continued to be the only legal status for Blacks (or

Negroes as they then were called) in many of the states. In 1863, the Emancipation Proclamation, issued by President Abraham Lincoln, gave Black slaves their freedom. Yet, even after that time, discrimination and segregation remained the lot of Blacks nearly everywhere in the United States. Indeed, segregation as an official policy was upheld by the U.S. Supreme Court in 1896 and remained the law of the land until 1954 when the Court reversed itself for the reasons mentioned in a previous section.

Only during the past twenty years have truly significant strides been made to eradicate the yoke of suppression and inequality that Black people have been forced to wear throughout American history. By 1975, nearly identical per-

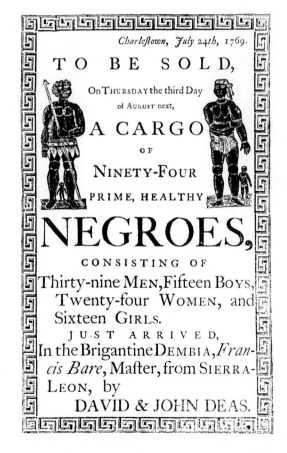

centages of Blacks and Whites (aged five to twenty) were enrolled in school (87 percent). While disparities still exist in many other areas of educational achievements, significant progress has been made to narrow the gap appreciably. There remains, however, considerable socioeconomic disparity between Blacks and the White majority. The median family income, as of 1988, for these two categories was respectively $18,098 and $32,274. Blacks earned only 56 percent of the income of Whites (U.S. Bureau of the Census, *Statistical Abstract of the United States, 1989*). Unemployment rates for Blacks are more than twice as high as for Whites, and while only 11 percent of White families subsist below the poverty line, more than 33 percent of Black families do so.

# HISPANIC AMERICANS

Spanish-speaking Americans number about 15 million people, or 7 percent of the population. Chiefly represented are Mexicans, Puerto Ricans, and Cubans. Only about one-fifth of Spanish-speaking Americans are comprised of migrants from Central or South America. While ethnically diverse in many ways, Hispanic Americans share a common language and religion (Roman Catholicism), as well as a history of Spanish colonialism. Moreover, a recent survey (Rangel, 1984) revealed a significant and growing feeling of unity among Hispanic Americans.

MEXICAN AMERICANS. Mexican Americans (Chicanos, as they are frequently called) represent the second largest and oldest minority in the United States. Many of these people trace their origin to Mexican territories that were annexed to the United States. About 8 million of them legally reside in our nation, nearly 90 percent in the Southwest (Texas, New Mexico, Colorado, Arizona, and California). The rest are aliens who have entered the country ille-

gally. More than 8,000 illegal migrants to the United States from Mexico are captured each year. It is estimated, however, that five times as many actually enter the country annually.

Mexican Americans are distinguished from other minorities in that for the most part they have been rural dwellers. Historically, Chicanos have been a source of cheap labor, and even today account for most of the migrant farm labor in the United States. The lower average income (about 56 percent of that of Whites), higher rates of unemployment, and lower levels of education among Mexican Americans offer ample evidence of the extensive discrimination that is uniformly directed at these people.

PUERTO RICANS. Puerto Rico has been a possession of the United States since the Spanish-American War, and its residents have enjoyed United States citizenship since 1917. Puerto Ricans are a people of mixed Spanish, Indian, and Negroid origins. Approximately 2.5 million of them presently live on the continent, chiefly in the New York City area, and about one-half of them are residents of lower-class ghettos. Mostly unskilled, Puerto Ricans on the continent represent one of the most impoverished ethnic populations in the United States. Forty percent of their numbers live below the poverty line.

CUBAN AMERICANS. Cubans, unlike other Hispanic Americans, consist of political refugees for the most part. Their migration to the United States occurred chiefly in 1959, when 500,000 fled the revolutionary establishment of a Marxist state under the dictatorship of Fidel Castro. A second major wave, numbering about 110,000, arrived on the Florida shores in 1980. This latter contingent consisted in large part of people of lower socioeconomic status, as well as criminals and other undesirables whom the Castro regime wanted to deport. Cuban Americans number about 1 million and are found principally in the greater Miami area. Unlike

▼

**503**

▼

other Hispanic Americans, they are drawn mainly from the middle and upper socioeconomic strata. About one-half of Cuban Americans tend to be skilled, to be well educated, hold prestigious occupations, and as a people constitute the most affluent of all Hispanics (Boswell & Curtis, 1983).

There is some speculation that Hispanic Americans, given their relative youth, numbers, and birth rate differentials, may soon become the largest minority in the United States. Such a probability is all the more likely, given their keen sense of ethnicity and their strong resistance to assimilation.

504

## ASIAN AMERICANS

Americans of Asiatic origins comprise about 1.5 percent of the total population, and number about 5 million people. Nearly two-thirds of these people reside in California and Hawaii. The largest categories are those of Chinese and Japanese origins; included in this minority as well are Filipinos, Hawaiians, Samoans, Guamanians, Koreans, and Vietnamese. Asian Americans represent the only racial minority that has achieved any significant degree of equality with the White majority.

CHINESE AMERICANS.   Chinese Americans trace their origins to the middle of the last century, when many people from China migrated to the United States in search of labor in the gold-mining industry on the West Coast and in the construction of railroads. Later these people were perceived by White workers as a social threat and economic competition. The extensive fear of the "yellow peril" provoked much harassment and mob violence, including many anti-Chinese riots, lynchings, and massacres.

As the consequence of so much hostility against Chinese immigrants, the Chinese Exclusion Act was passed in 1882 to prevent the immigration of Chinese laborers for ten years, and to declare those Chinese born in China as unacceptable for American citizenship. In 1904, Congress voted to prohibit Chinese immigration indefinitely, and this act was not repealed until 1943. Throughout this long period, the majority of the Chinese in the United States were confined to urban ghettos, still known at the present time as Chinatowns.

Today there are about 1 million Chinese Americans in the United States, still living primarily in densely populated communities. About 40 percent live in California, 20 percent in New York, and another 12 percent in Hawaii. Until recently, their assimilation has been greatly retarded, in large part because they have tended to remain voluntarily isolated from the American mainstream in order to preserve their cultural heritage. Nonetheless, Chinese Americans do quite well—on the average, better than the White majority—in the educational and economic realms.

JAPANESE AMERICANS.   The long history of discrimination against Japanese Americans is in many respects quite different from the experience of Chinese Americans. Japanese immigration to this country began in the 1880s. Yet, unlike the Chinese immigrants who were poor and unskilled, the Japanese people arrived in this country with a wealth of skills that made them economically mobile. Accordingly, they prospered and assimilated relatively well into the American culture. This happy situation changed drastically, however, when Japan attacked Pearl Harbor in 1941 and war was declared by the United States.

The most significant act of discrimination experienced by Japanese Americans during the hostilities of World War II, one resulting in severe economic destruction for many of the 120,000 people involved, was their relocation and internment in "security camps" (really concentration camps) because of widespread fear of their disloyalty to the United States. This action was taken without the exercise of due process as a consequence of Executive Order #9066 issued by President Franklin D. Roosevelt. Quite inexplicably the same action was not taken in the case of German Americans or Italian Americans, even though the United States was also at war with both Germany and Italy at that time.

Japanese Americans today account for more than three-quarters of a million people, about two-thirds of whom reside on the West Coast. They enjoy the largest per capita income, as well as the highest educational and occupational achievements, of any racial minority in the United States, and are the only minority that does not live mainly in neighborhood ghettos (Woodrum, 1981; Montero, 1981).

KOREAN AND VIETNAMESE AMERICANS. The ranks of Asian-American minorities have been expanded in recent decades by immigrants from Korea and Vietnam. This development is mainly a consequence of the wars in those nations since the 1950s. These migrations, however, have taken place during a time when the stigma and dynamics of minority status have been significantly lessened in our country, as a consequence of both effective legislation and a significant change in cultural values. Accordingly, while these people undoubtedly encounter prejudice and discrimination, their experiences in these respects have been less oppressive than those of other Asian Americans in a previous era. Like other Asian migrants, Korean and Vietnamese Americans, who together number more than 1 million people, show remarkable achievement in education and economic pursuits. About one-half of the Korean adult population are college graduates.

FILIPINO AMERICANS. The Philippine Islands became a possession of the United States in 1889 as a consequence of the Spanish-American War. Until 1935, Filipinos were considered to be American subjects, and thus were

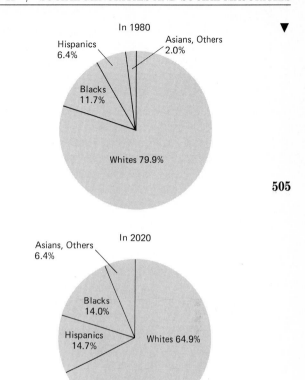

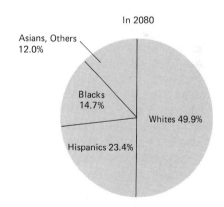

**505**

FIGURE 11-7  Projected Changes in U.S. Racial/Ethnic Composition. Assumes fertility remaining low and migration stabilizing at one million people. Source: Bouvier, Leon F. and Cary B. Davis, *The Future Racial Composition of the United States,* Washington, D.C.: Population Reference Bureau, 1982.

▼ not subject to immigration quotas. Stringent quotas were in force after that time, however, when the Philippines became a commonwealth of the United States. Filipinos encountered strong prejudice at that time, and became victims of legalized discrimination in many respects. Several states in the West, where Filipinos tended to concentrate, passed laws prohibiting intermarriage with Caucasians. Eventual changes in the immigration laws, coupled with civil rights legislation, reversed these patterns, and a sharp increase in Filipino immigration ensued. About a quarter of a million Filipinos entered the United States between 1966 and 1976, and by 1980 their population more than doubled and has reached about 1 million today. The vast majority of these individuals hold high levels of education and occupational training, giving them one of the nation's highest median family incomes. Demographic projections indicate that Filipino Americans should become the largest segment of the Asian American population within the next few decades.

**506**

## WHITE ETHNICS

White ethnics represent a generic minority of culturally different people. Among the principal nationalities represented among White ethnics are the Irish, Italian, Polish, Greek, and several eastern European peoples. Together White ethnics comprise about 30 percent of the nation's population (see Table 11-4). By and large, these people are Catholic—a commonality that on the one hand accounts for some degree of unity among them, yet, on the other hand, one that for a long time served as a basis for further discrimination.

The many ghettos that have segregated the different categories of White ethnics in the urban areas of America reflect both their cohesion and their status as minorities. Yet, despite whatever degree of political unity they may have,

TABLE 11-4. How Americans List Their Ancestry, White Ethnic Population, 1980

| | |
|---|---|
| English | 49,598,035 |
| German | 49,224,146 |
| Irish | 40,165,702 |
| French | 12,892,246 |
| Italian | 12,183,692 |
| Scottish | 10,048,816 |
| Polish | 8,228,037 |
| Dutch | 6,304,499 |
| Swedish | 4,345,392 |
| Norwegian | 3,453,839 |
| Russian | 2,781,432 |
| Spanish-Hispanic | 2,686,680 |
| Czech | 1,892,456 |
| Hungarian | 1,776,902 |
| Welsh | 1,664,598 |
| Danish | 1,518,273 |
| Portuguese | 1,024,351 |
| Swiss | 981,543 |
| Greek | 959,856 |
| Austrian | 948,558 |
| French-Canadian | 780,488 |
| Slovak | 776,806 |
| Lithuanian | 742,776 |
| Ukrainian | 730,056 |
| Finnish | 615,872 |
| Canadian | 456,212 |
| Belgian | 360,277 |
| Yugoslavian | 360,174 |
| Romanian | 315,258 |

Source: U.S. Bureau of the Census, *Statistical Abstract of the United States, 1980*. Washington, D.C.: U.S. Government Printing Office, 1981.

White ethnics reveal a stratification among themselves, and each nationality in many ways has assumed a specific type of minority status with respect to the others.

Each of these peoples encountered much hostility—sometimes open violence—when they first immigrated to this country. Many were able to assimilate effectively, often in part by shedding their ethnic and minority visibility through such actions as Anglo-Saxonizing their names and not permitting their children to speak the parental language. Many of these people, however, retain a strong ethnic identification, often a collective means to combat the discrimination they experience as a minority.

# Personality and Minority Relations

Personality, as we have shown in preceding chapters, can be both an independent and dependent variable of social processes. This situation is no less true in the sphere of minority-majority relations. Personality variables serve as both causes and effects of prejudice and discrimination. It is often difficult, because of the cyclical relationship of these kinds of variables, to make an absolute separation of one kind of personality dynamic from the other. Several patterns of each type, nonetheless, have been well documented by both sociological and psychological research.

## THE PREJUDICED PERSONALITY

Do some people have personality patterns or structures that predispose them to prejudice and/or to racist and similarly antihumanitarian ideologies? Extensive evidence suggests that such is indeed the case. It is now generally accepted that certain kinds of people are psychologically prone to prejudicial thinking and discriminatory behavior, that such dynamics for some people are part of their basic personality structure. Considerable data have been amassed to document the thesis that prejudice is often part of a general psychological syndrome, and that on this basis one can distinguish a distinctive type of personality.

The principal research in this regard was conducted initially in the early 1940s by a team of social and clinical psychologists at the University of California at Berkeley. Adorno (1950) and associates originally attempted to understand the dynamics of anti-Semitism, specifically the collective hatred that led to the persecution and extermination of millions of Jews by the German Nazis in the 1930s and 1940s. These researchers found, however, that subjects who scored high on projective tests measuring anti-Semitic attitudes also tended to score high on projective tests measuring racial and ethnic prejudice, as well as on those measuring receptivity to antidemocratic or fascist ideology. Further analyses revealed that the high-scoring subjects were characterized by a distinctive set of psychodynamics. This distinctive pattern of psychodynamics became known as the "authoritarian personality syndrome" which has been described in terms of nine subsets or components:

1. *Authoritarian aggression* (strong underlying hostility and aggression).
2. *Authoritarian submission* (uncritical submission to authority figures).
3. *Anti-intraception* (avoidance of inner examination or introspection).
4. *Power* (admiration of power and toughness).
5. *Conventionalism* (rigid adherence to conventional values).
6. *Projectivity* (tendency to project repressed psychodynamics onto others).
7. *Stereotypy* (tendency to think in rigid, oversimplified, and unambiguous terms).
8. *Cynicism* (suspicion and distrust of others).
9. *Sex* (strong, unconscious sexual drive and exaggerated sexual concerns).

The research on the **authoritarian personality** was the first of its kind to provide concrete

▼

507

▼ evidence that ethnic and racial prejudice is likely to be typical of individuals with certain types of personalities. Several other studies have offered further substantiation and elaboration for these findings. Chief among them is the work of Milton Rokeach (1960) who proposed an alternative approach to authoritarianism by utilizing cognitive theory rather than psychoanalytic theory as was the case in the Adorno study. Rokeach speaks in terms of dogmatism or open- and closed-mindedness, and deals primarily with modes of cognitive functioning rather than with unconscious dynamics and processes.

508

Rokeach (1954:195) defines **dogmatism** as a "relatively closed cognitive organization of beliefs and disbeliefs about reality, organized around a central set of beliefs and disbeliefs about absolute authority which, in turn, provide a framework for patterns of intolerance and qualified tolerance toward others." The intention here, therefore, is to delineate that personality structure which is associated with open and closed belief systems respectively; that is, the extent to which an individual's belief systems are prone to accept or to reject others (see Chapter 5). Rokeach describes the closed-minded individual as one who has a closed or dogmatic way of thinking about any ideology regardless of its content, is rigid in regard to opinions and beliefs, accepts authority uncritically, rejects those who disagree with him, and makes a qualified acceptance of those who do agree. Thus, it is not so much *what* one believes as *how* one believes that distinguishes the **dogmatic personality.**

The general personality profile that emerges from these major studies, and from literally hundreds of others that they have spawned, is that the prejudiced personality is characterized by the following personality structure and dynamics: a preference for strongly authoritarian leadership, a tendency to hold highly ethnocentric views of one's own values and lifestyle, a marked disposition to perceive the world in

a very rigid and stereotypical fashion, a conventionalized conformity to social norms, a puritanical conscience, a repressed hostility toward parents, a keen orientation to power, an advocacy of severe punishment, a high level of frustration, a rigidly dichotomous style of thinking, anti-intellectualism, intolerance of ambiguity, status anxiety, repressed sexuality, distrust of other people, a cynical view of the world as evil and dangerous, deep-seated insecurity, and displacement of aggression.

Research on the prejudiced personality helps to explain the rather common phenomenon that people who are prejudiced toward one mi-

**Prejudiced Personalities.** Members of the Ku Klux Klan openly attacked people marching in the town of Cummings in Forsyth County, Georgia, in January 1987 on the occasion of the birthday celebration for Martin Luther King, Jr., the Black civil rights leader who was assassinated in 1968. (Kelly Wilkinson/ SYGMA)

nority are likely to be prejudiced toward other minorities as well. Such people are likely to be prejudiced even toward minorities that they have never encountered or even previously heard about. A fascinating study by Eugene Hartley demonstrated this phenomenon. Hartley (1946) gave his subjects a list of thirty-five racial and ethnic minorities, and asked them to indicate their reactions to these people. Nearly three-fourths of the subjects who held negative attitudes toward Blacks and Jews also disliked such people as the Wallonians, Pireneans, and Danireans. Several of the subjects, in fact, recommended that members of these latter categories be expelled from the country. The curious thing here, however, is that the Wallonians, Pireneans, and Danireans are fictitious. These names were created by Hartley for the type of research in question. Prejudice, then, does not always stem from personal contact and experience with particular minorities. Rather, prejudice may be the product of personality dispositions which can be channeled to, or manifested toward, specific minorities in a given sociocultural context.

## PERSONALITY CORRELATES OF MINORITY STATUS

Minority status itself, it is widely believed, produces certain types of personality traits and patterns. These phenomena are not necessarily all what one might generally label as negative characteristics or dysfunctional patterns of personality. Nonetheless, some form of personality damage or psychological injury has been seen as a modal, although not universal, consequence of minority status and/or prolonged discrimination.

Much of the relevant research has emphasized low self-esteem (even self-hatred), false identity, repressed anger, and apathy, along with a lack of ambition and ego strength as constituting the major personality correlates

of minority status. Some observers, however, maintain that in many cases individuals among racial minorities develop a compulsion toward perfectionistic behavior (judged in terms of majority standards) in all that they do and, in the case of men, often exhibit a "masculine protest" through an exaggerated form of physical masculinity (Vontress, 1971).

Victims of prejudice and discrimination, it is generally argued, invariably develop negative self-images, which in turn are transmitted through the family and the minority subculture to each new generation. These images often result from the fact that in many instances minority individuals adopt the negative image held of them by the majority. Hence, a vicious circle is created through the dynamics of the self-fulfilling prophecy.

Studies of minority children have demonstrated that their life experiences generally give them negative and inferior self-conceptions. Relevant research shows, for example, that the drawings, stories, and dramas of young Black children often reveal a desire to be White and the belief that Black skin is ugly and inferior (Clinard, 1970).

Recent independent investigations among Black children in different cultures (United States and Trinidad) continue to confirm the existence of low levels of self-esteem among Blacks. Researchers asked both Black and White children to choose the Cabbage Patch doll that was the "nice doll," "pretty doll," or the "one they would like to play with." In virtually every study, about 65 percent of the Black children and 75 percent of the White children preferred the White doll (Barnes, 1987; McNichol, 1987).

Other pertinent findings have resulted from studies of anti-Semitism among Jews (see Simpson & Yinger, 1972), and from studies (for example, Dworkin, 1965; Ramirez, 1971) in which Black-American, Mexican-American, and Anglo-American schoolchildren significantly described themselves with negative adjectives

▼

**509**

▼

such as lazy, unfair, dull, and stubborn. Research has shown also that women score lower than men on self-esteem, especially on ability and character traits (Crain & Wiseman, 1972).

Apart from the various dimensions of negative self-esteem, there are three other patterns of personality that are particularly significant in minorities: authoritarianism, alienation, and achievement motivation. Each of these also seems to be essentially a consequence of minority status.

**510**

AUTHORITARIANISM. People low in power and prestige, as we saw in the preceding chapter, tend to manifest authoritarian behavior. On the basis of this principle, one might expect that minorities would manifest modal patterns of the authoritarian personality. Additionally, there is the more basic expectation that individuals who undergo an authoritarian life experience will develop a corresponding type of personality. Relevant research, indeed, reveals that Black Americans and Mexican Americans score relatively high on measures of authoritarianism (Simpson & Yinger, 1972). It is not surprising, then, that victims of prejudice and discrimination frequently develop and/or manifest prejudice toward others.

ALIENATION. Minority status has been found to correlate with alienation. Several studies have shown that, again, Black Americans typically score higher than White Americans on various measures of alienation (see Middleton, 1963; Guterman, 1972). American Indians and Mexican Americans also reveal high scores on measures of alienation and defeatism (Mason, 1971; Kamaroof, 1971). Black Americans have been found to be characterized by higher levels of various dimensions of alienation: powerlessness, meaninglessness, normlessness, social estrangement, and work estrangement. Manifestation of these modal patterns of personality is provided in the finding that minority people are more likely to agree with the following statements which exemplify the specific dimensions of alienation:

1. *Powerlessness:* "There is not much that I can do about most of the important problems that we face today."
2. *Meaninglessness:* "Things have become so complicated in the world that I really don't understand just what is going on."
3. *Normlessness:* "In order to get ahead in the world today, you are almost forced to do some things that are not right."
4. *Social Estrangement:* "I often feel lonely."
5. *Work Estrangement:* "I don't really enjoy most of the work that I do."

ACHIEVEMENT MOTIVATION. Various studies have found significant differences among racial and ethnic minorities in terms of achievement motivation. Several studies reveal that Blacks generally rank low in motivation to succeed (see Guterman, 1972), as do American Indians, Mexican Americans, and women (see, for example, Mason, 1971; Kamaroff, 1971). Other research reveals differences in "need achievement" between Mexican-American and Anglo-American children, the former typically ranking lower (McClintock, 1972; Anderson & Evans, 1976; Ramirez, 1971). Similar research shows that these minorities are characterized by a sense of impatience in civic affairs, as has been demonstrated (at least up to the present decade) by lethargy in voting and community participation.

# MODAL PERSONALITY OF MINORITIES

American society, as we saw in preceding chapters, does not have one unified social character. Rather, the American modal character is a complex and differentiated one. Much of this characterological diversity is rooted in the racial and ethnic composition of our society. Ample evidence shows that members of various minorities often can be distinguished by distinctive personality patterns, not all of which seem to be a psychological consequence of minority status.*

### ADAPTIVE AND TRADITIONAL CHARACTER.

Patterns of modal personality result principally from the socialization-enculturation process, and/or from other social experiences that are shared by a given population. It is helpful in these respects to distinguish between traditional social character and adaptive social character (Yinger, 1977). *Adaptive social character* represents a modal pattern of personality that results from similar attitudinal and behavioral responses to the experiences of minority status.

One focal dimension of personality that nicely illustrates adaptive social character concerns the factor of the *locus of control*, which refers to the perception of causality and the source of rewards for one's behavior (Rotter, 1966). The perception of an internal locus of control is defined as the belief that rewards are dependent upon individual behavior, while the perception of an external locus of control refers to the belief that rewards are controlled by forces outside the individual (for example, "the system," the power elite, or simply chance).

Much of the literature has assumed that an external locus of control can have only negative consequences for the individual. When associated with failure, however, an external orientation can protect self-esteem. A perception of external control, moreover, does not necessarily represent a belief in chance; it may indicate a realistic understanding of systematically constraining external forces, such as embedded patterns of discrimination. Thus, an external locus of control can have positive as well as negative effects upon the personality of minority persons.

Many studies have found that Black Americans and Mexican Americans are more likely than White Americans to perceive the locus of control as external (Coleman, et al., 1966; Crain & Wiseman, 1972; Gruen, Kort, & Baum, 1974; Jacobson, 1975). Crain and Wiseman (1972), for example, contend that the locus of control is causally related to the level of a person's achievement: Achievement correlates positively with an internal locus of control and negatively with an external locus. The interesting question here, then, is whether the external locus of control among racial and ethnic minorities is a result of their minority status and socioeconomic position, or whether their social-class standing is a result of their external locus of control.

### VARIATIONS IN MODAL PERSONALITY.

One must be cautious in speaking of modal personality in terms of minorities. However distinctive or characteristic any personality trait or pattern may be for a given minority, it is important to remember that such personality and psychological profiles are not unique to any particular racial or ethnic segment of the population. Moreover, variations in modal personality profiles exist in all minorities in terms of social class, age, sex, religion, region, and other elements of social background. In fact, it is often difficult to determine the extent to which differences in the modal personality of minorities may be related to their socioeconomic status, and to what extent they may be the result of socialization practices and social experiences that distinguish one subculture from another.

Class differences, for example, have been found in the amount of need achievement shown by Black children: upper-class Black children, unlike most other Black youngsters, reveal extremely high need achievement scores

▼

**511**

* Given that personality is a social product, it should be clear that whatever psychological differences exist among racial and ethnic populations, they are the product of social experiences, not genetic or biological differences. Such a statement is intended to refute in categorical terms the claims of any racist psychology which asserts that personality differences are essentially the product of genetic and/or biological characteristics.

▼ (Rosen, 1959). Another study (Grebler, Moore, & Guzman, 1970) that suggests the effects of socioeconomic class upon the modal personality of minorities found that Mexican Americans, as a whole, were not notably more passive than other populations, nor did they seem to value integration with relatives more than other populations; however, these characteristics were greater among the Mexican Americans with low socioeconomic backgrounds.

512 There is strong evidence that personality patterns of racial and ethnic minorities are also affected by the social conditions and subcultures of the regions in which these people live. Crain and Wiseman (1972) found that Blacks who were reared in the northern part of the United States were less inhibited than Blacks living in the South. Southern-born Blacks, especially those with dark skin whose parents socialized them to accept racial inequality, were more inhibited, unhappy adults with a low sense of internal control. Blacks who had attended integrated schools scored lower on anxiety and higher on security than Blacks who had attended segregated schools. Another study (Karon, 1975) found that northern Blacks differed from southern Blacks on the same characteristics, and in the same direction that distinguished northern Whites from southern Blacks. Thus, differences in social environment can result in distinguishable differences in the modal personality of both minorities and majorities.

MINORITY PERSONALITY AND SOCIAL CHANGE. Modal personality must be assessed in the context of cultural and structural factors that produce it. Earlier studies of this kind on various minorities were done within a context of widespread prejudice and discrimination, including legalized segregation. Today, however, the context is totally different for minorities in the United States, and the formation of personality among minority people of every kind must be seen in this new social context.

Beginning in the 1960s, there have been many collective efforts to build a new and positive self-image among minority people. Indeed, research evidence strongly suggests that the more pathological patterns of modal personality among minorities in the United States are changing significantly, both intensively and extensively, in the wake of decreasing social adversity for these people. An increasing number of studies shows that minorities are exhibiting higher levels of courage, assertiveness, poise, pride, and self-confidence (for example, Dworkin, 1965; Yinger, 1977). Relevant data reveal that the self-image of several minorities has been radically modified such that an unprece-

**Civil Rights.** Recent efforts to eradicate discrimination among American minorities have resulted in new levels of racial and ethnic pride, as well as the emergence of a heightened self-esteem that is more and more manifested in public displays. (Lionel J.-M. Delevingne/Stock, Boston)

dented level of self-esteem, with increased optimism and rising aspirations, characterizes minority people of every kind (see, for example, Porter & Washington, 1979).

On the other hand, Thomas and Hughes (1986) have marshalled various sets of data to show that whatever reduction in socioeconomic inequality between Whites and Blacks may have taken place in the past couple of decades, there has been little gain in the psychological well-being of Blacks. The evaluation of their own general happiness, life satisfaction, and sense of well-being has not shown significant improvement evidenced among Whites.

One of the most conspicuous changes in the modal personality profile of many minorities is the strong development of aggression and the externalization of hostility. Paralleling these developments is the manifestation of a higher level of political consciousness and increased feelings of stronger control over their environment; that is, an increased internal locus of control (Gutierrez & Hirch, 1971). Particularly evident is the stronger disposition to social activism and public protest. This new disposition even includes a greater readiness to use, or at least to consider to use, violent methods to correct felt injustices. Numerous incidents of riots among minorities during the past three decades testify to these changes in personality.

Of related significance have been the strong resurgence in ethnic and racial consciousness, and the associated pride, on the part of many American minorities. One manifestation of these developments was the emergence among Black Americans, a decade or so ago, of the notion of "soul." *Soul* epitomizes a sense of pride and achievement in the Black culture and social experience, along with a sense of empathy and cohesion with one's "brothers and sisters." Equally important here is the extensive consciousness-raising among other minorities, particularly women and homosexuals. DeVos (1977) argues that these developments, along with the "passing of passing," are part of a con-

temporary search for a new social identity among many minority Americans. Women have undergone similar personality changes as a consequence of their new modes of socialization and their typical social experiences, as well as changing attitudes and conceptions regarding sex-typed behavior and psychological characteristics.

We can expect significant changes in the modal personality of American minorities as new generations are reared and socialized in a social context of much less prejudice and discrimination than their parents and grandparents experienced. Such profound changes in the personality of millions of minority people could have a tremendously significant effect on the characterological profile of America, and on the structure and dynamics of our society.

## Summary

Sociologists use the term "minority" to refer to a category of people who, because of their physical and/or sociocultural characteristics, are singled out from others in the society in which they live for differential and unequal treatment, and who, therefore, regard themselves as objects of collective discrimination. A social minority, then, consists of a category of people, distinguished by physical and/or sociocultural characteristics, who are the objects of prejudice and/or discrimination, and who occupy a subordinate position in society. A sociological majority refers correspondingly to a socially dominant category.

Minority-majority relationships constitute a rather universal phenomenon. All minority-majority relationships involve five basic elements: differences, visibility, ideology, power, and stratification. Minorities can be distinguished on the basis of several different criteria and may assume many different forms. Most common among the various types are: racial minorities, ethnic minorities, religious minorities, and the

▼ "new" minorities. Among the more important of these "new" minorities are those based on gender/sex and age statuses, physical handicaps, and sexual orientation.

The behavioral axis of minority-majority relations consists of the dynamics of prejudice and discrimination. Prejudice is an attitude comprising a system of beliefs, feelings, and action orientations. Discrimination is an action concept and refers to overt behavior. It involves **514** a differential treatment of individuals that includes the denial of the opportunities granted to other individuals or members of society. Merton has distinguished four possible relationships between prejudice and discrimination, described in terms of the following individuals: unprejudiced nondiscriminator, unprejudiced discriminator, prejudiced discriminator, and prejudiced nondiscriminator. Prejudice manifests itself in a number of ways other than discrimination. These include stereotypes, ethnopaulisms, and social distances.

Institutional discrimination refers to prejudice and discrimination that persist within social structures long after conscious efforts have been made to eliminate such behavior. Discrimination of this kind, resulting from cultural lag, tends not to be overt or readily identifiable, but primarily latent and impersonal. One of the more common forms of institutional discrimination is that of gate-keeping, which refers to the decision-making process by which members of society are admitted to positions of privilege and power.

Many theories have been advanced to explain prejudice and discrimination. Chief among these are socialization theories, theories of socioeconomic gain, and theories of projection.

Minority-majority relationships assume many different forms, ranging from harmonious coexistence to outright warfare. The principal patterns of majority reactions to minorities include expulsion, extermination, segregation, assimilation, amalgamation, and pluralism.

Minority responses to social inequality include acceptance, assimilation, avoidance, and aggression.

Personality can be both an independent and a dependent variable of social processes in the sphere of minority-majority relationships. Considerable data have been amassed to document the thesis that prejudice and receptivity to antihumanitarian ideologies are often part of a general psychological syndrome of authoritarianism and/or dogmatism.

Minority status itself, it is widely believed, produces certain types of personality traits and patterns. Apart from the various dimensions of negative self-esteem, there are three other patterns of personality that are particularly significant in minorities: authoritarianism, alienation, and achievement motivation. Each seems to be essentially a consequence of minority status. Ample evidence shows further that members of various minorities often can be distinguished by distinctive psychological and/or personality patterns, not all of which seem to be a psychological consequence of minority status.

# Key Concepts

acceptance
affirmative action
ageism
amalgamation
apartheid
assimilation
authoritarian personality
avoidance
discrimination
displacement
dogmatic personality
dogmatism
ethnicity
ethnopaulism
expulsion
extermination

frustration-aggression theory
gate-keeping
genetic mutation
genocide
geographical isolation
Homo sapiens
institutional discrimination
majority
minority
monogenesis
natural selection
partition
passing
pluralism
polygenesis

population transfer ▼
prejudice
projection
race
racism
random genetic drift
scapegoat
segregation
self-fulfilling prophecy
sexism
social distance **515**
socioeconomic gain theory
stereotype
visibility

# FIVE ▼ Social Dynamics

Here in this section we explore a vast variety of social behavior. Our focus is in part on those kinds of social action that are known as *collective behavior* and *deviant behavior*. Collective behavior usually involves social situations which are unanticipated and for which there are no clearly established social norms, while deviant behavior essentially consists of the violation of social norms. Both kinds of dynamics can be quite significant for social change, which we shall discuss rather thoroughly in the concluding chapter of this volume.

Much of the social action which falls under the designation of collective behavior consists of social activity that tends to be unstructured and episodic, such as that involved in riots and panic. Also included, however, are the phenomena of social movements which tend to be quite structured and long-enduring. Collective behavior, whatever its duration, often involves social deviance—the violation of conventional norms of behavior. Deviant behavior, despite its essentially problematic nature, can have both functional as well as dysfunctional consequences for society. Social deviance, nonetheless, invariably elicits the forces of social control which themselves can assume many different kinds of structures and dynamics.

Our concerns in the next two chapters will involve an analysis of the several forms of social dynamics that constitute both collective behavior and deviant behavior. We shall explore a number of theories for each of these classes of behavior, as well as many explanations that apply to only specific varieties of each type of social action. Our discussions also will include considerations of the types of personalities that tend to be associated with these very significant social dynamics.

Collective behavior and deviant behavior are important because, among other reasons, they represent vehicles by which people continually influence the formation and reformation of society. These considerations speak directly to the phenomenon of social change—a process consisting of the continuous transformation of society. Our sociological analysis of human

▼    social behavior concludes with an extended treatment, in Chapter 14, on the all-encompassing dynamics of social change. ▲

▶ Chapter 12 **COLLECTIVE BEHAVIOR AND SOCIAL MOVEMENTS**

▶ Chapter 13 **DEVIANT BEHAVIOR AND SOCIAL CONTROL**

▶ Chapter 14 **SOCIAL CHANGE**

# 12 ▽ Collective Behavior and Social Movements

Our primary concern to this point has been to account for behavior that is relatively stable and routinized—behavior that is guided by institutionalized values, norms, and expectations. This chapter, however, focuses on social phenomena that, initially at least, seem to defy explanation. We have in mind such episodic and unstructured phenomena as crowds, mobs, riots, fads, fashions, panics, rumors, mass hysteria, and social movements. All these forms of social action fall under the heading of collective behavior. However episodic, collective behavior is nonetheless quite common in modern societies, so much so in fact that, in one form or another, it can be said to constitute a recurrent or perpetual form of social action. Hence, collective behavior, in its many varieties, is a very definite part of the fundamental dynamics of society today, and it constitutes a most important element in the process of social change.

How do we account for the existence of collective behavior? In which ways are its various forms distinguished from one another? What are the major theories that have been developed by social scientists to explain the origins and dynamics of the different kinds of collective behavior? What is the relationship between various kinds of collective behavior and the personalities of those individuals who are involved in such episodes? What function does collective behavior serve in society? These and similar questions constitute the focus of this chapter. ▲

## Outline

▶ Social life is, for the most part, quite orderly and fairly predictable. Nearly all social activity, as we have seen throughout the preceding chapters, is regulated by norms. Social behavior in many instances, nonetheless, does not follow a patterned and predictable course. Every individual sooner or later confronts a social situation for which there are no established norms—or, at least, one for which a norm may be very poorly defined. Fires, explosions, natural disasters, and automobile accidents are rather common cases in point. Similarly, people in all societies occasionally, and not too infrequently, engage in various kinds of seemingly unorganized—indeed, at times, even quite chaotic—behavior. Dramatic examples of such behavior can be observed in panics, riots, mobs, and mass hysteria. Others are evident in crowds, fads, fashions, and social movements. These various forms of unanticipated and extraordinary behavior which develop in relatively unstructured situations, and for which usually there are no established norms, are known as collective behavior.

Collective behavior is essentially a phenomenon of modern, advanced society, although many of its forms can be found in any type of society. It is important because, among other things, the various forms of collective behavior represent mechanisms of social change, and ways in which individuals continually influence the formation of society.

# Nature of Collective Behavior

Sociology, in a very fundamental sense, is the study of all collective or shared behavior. The term **collective behavior,** however, is used technically to refer to only certain kinds of social behavior. This label is reserved for various forms of social behavior that develop rather spontaneously in unstructured situations on the part of large numbers of people, and which, as

such, are not regulated by the conventional norms of conduct. Such activity, often unpredictably, includes a wide range or variety of behavior from that of a simple audience to a major social movement. Social behavior in these kinds of situations is more characteristically parallel or common, rather than reciprocal or complementary.

Collective behavior as a specific category of social activity is ideally or typically distinguished further by the following set of distinctive features:

1. Relatively spontaneous and unplanned.
2. Relatively unstructured and not governed by institutionalized norms or expectations.
3. Relatively transitory and short-lived.
4. Enacted by people who, at least initially, are strangers to each other.
5. Dependent on mutual stimulation among its participants.
6. Parallel or common (nonreciprocal) rather than interactional.

Mobs, panics, riots, fads, reactions to disasters, and certain types of social movements all share these features to varying degrees. These social phenomena all involve a plurality of people who find themselves behaving in response to a particular set of circumstances that have arisen rather spontaneously. The situation in which they find themselves, however, is not culturally or socially institutionalized. Prescribed patterns of behavior for defining or responding to such situations do not usually exist. The resulting social behavior, in any event, tends to be quite brief in most situations.

People involved in episodes of collective behavior usually have a shared focus of attention, and they may come to desire mutual goals. These objectives, however, are not planned or set before the collective behavior develops, nor are there any socially or culturally prescribed means for attainment. Accordingly, people who are in a crowded theater when a fire breaks out would all share the goal of escaping, even

▼ though there may not be any culturally or socially established norms to help them achieve their objective. Similarly, people caught up in a disaster of one kind or another would share a set of common concerns. Their initial reactions, however, are likely to be unorganized and haphazard.

**522** However unorganized and unstructured collective behavior may be in comparison with conventional forms of behavior, it is not entirely without pattern and structure. Once an episode of collective behavior develops, norms may emerge which provide some structure for the ensuing behavior. The main point is that in contrast to most forms of conventional behavior, which is influenced by preexisting norms, the norms that may emerge during episodes of collective behavior do not exist prior to the episode. During a riot, for example, a norm may emerge that prohibits the rioters from damaging specific business establishments. Similarly, during a disaster, a norm may emerge which indicates that able-bodied individuals should help rescue others instead of remaining with their families.

Our definition and description of collective behavior must be given with some reservations. So diverse is the wide range of behavior within this category that perhaps no unqualified explanation can be made for it. To complete our definition and description of collective behavior we need to look in some detail at its many diverse forms. Such a consideration should give us a better understanding of the nature of collective behavior.

# Types of Collective Behavior

Collective behavior refers to action on the part of either social aggregates or social categories (see Chapter 9). A **social aggregate** represents a plurality of people who share physical proximity (are spatially proximate), such as a crowd and an audience. A **social category,** on the other hand, consists of a spatially diffuse collectivity or plurality of people, such as a mass or a public. Within these two principal types, there is a rather wide variety of collective behavior. Let us look in detail at several of the forms that collective behavior may assume.

## CROWDS

The simplest example of collective behavior is a crowd. A **crowd** may be defined as a temporary aggregate of people who have assembled for a specific purpose, or who are responding to a common stimulus. It is the shared focus of attention that holds a crowd together and distinguishes it from a mere aggregate of individuals. Most members of a crowd do not know each other. Initially, at least, crowds do not have any organization or leadership. As the crowd continues to exist, however, a certain degree of organization and leadership may emerge. All crowds, in any event, are relatively short-lived.

Many different kinds of social gatherings constitute a crowd—from a small congregation at church to a mass of people fleeing from a fire or explosion. The degree of social structure and interpersonal contact, however, varies significantly among the various types of crowds. Blumer (1951), in this respect, has constructed a useful typology of crowds, distinguishing four basic types: casual, conventional, expressive, and acting.

THE CASUAL CROWD.   The *casual crowd*, the simplest type of crowd, consists of a passive collection of people that exhibits very little, if any, social organization. It is the least structured type of crowd. Its occurrence is entirely unplanned, and it is most likely to disband after a very short period of time. Examples of the casual crowd are an aggregate of people watching workers erect a building, individuals listening to the sales pitch of a sidewalk vendor, or people attracted by an unusual occurrence in the street, such as an accident.

THE CONVENTIONAL CROWD. A *conventional crowd*, sometimes called an audience, consists of an aggregate of individuals who have deliberately planned to attend a particular event. The behavior of people in a conventional crowd is under the limited influence of conventional norms and manifests a certain degree of regularity or predictability. Interaction, nonetheless, is quite minimal. An audience at a theater, spectators watching a sporting event, and people attending a church service are examples of conventional crowds.

THE EXPRESSIVE CROWD. The *expressive crowd* is one that is highly emotionally charged, and provides occasions for the release and manifestation of feelings and sentiments. Such a crowd does not usually have an external object of focus, but rather concentrates its attention on a free-floating ventilation of emotions. Expressive crowds may be characterized by singing, dancing, drinking, shouting, and other forms of behavior that in themselves and under other circumstances are considered to be deviant. The expressive crowd is exemplified by those aggregates found at carnivals, county fairs, street festivals, rock concerts, and revival meetings. Some forms of the protest crowd, those that engage in such peaceful and orderly activities as picketing and sit-ins, also provide examples of the expressive crowd. Among the well-known expressive crowds that appear annually in the United States are those found at

▼

**523**

**Mass Rock.** "Live Aid," billed as the "Concert of the Century," with appearances throughout the world, attracted an expressive crowd of 72,000 people for a two-hour performance in Wembley Stadium in England in 1985. (Jacques Langevin/SYGMA)

▼

the New Year's Eve celebration in New York City, the Mardi Gras carnival in New Orleans, and the Fourth of July celebrations in many other cities and towns.

THE ACTING CROWD.   The *acting crowd* is distinguished by the desire of its members to take a form of action against someone or something. Unlike the casual or conventional crowd, the acting crowd exhibits intense emotional involvement. In addition, the behavior of its participants is not apt to be restrained in any way by conventional norms or standards. Acting crowds are typically angry or hostile, and may engage in violence. Their actions invariably are guided by one or more leaders who either have incited people to form the crowd initially, or may have emerged once the crowd already had formed.

There are two major forms of an acting crowd—the mob and the riot. Each represents a quite dramatic and volatile form of behavior.

The **mob** is a form of acting crowd with immediate and limited objectives. Its members are highly emotionally aroused and wish to vent their anger and hostility upon a specific object or person. Its target may be real or symbolic; however, mobs act with a single-minded purpose to inflict harm on a particular victim or set of victims, or to damage property. Often it is a trivial matter that converts a milling crowd into a mob. Its violence and destructiveness are, nevertheless, real. Typically, there is one or several individuals in a mob who function as leaders by trying to focus the attention and the emotions of people on a particular target or goal. Slogans or emotionally laden phrases may be used to incite the members of a mob. They function to justify both the mob's feelings and its contemplated actions. Once a mob obtains its objectives, it usually disbands quickly.

Perhaps the most dramatic illustrations of a mob are the lynch mobs and vigilantes that emerged, quite distinctively, in the American South and West during the past century. These

524

mobs consisted of highly emotionally aroused people who wanted to "see justice done" or who acted in "the interest of preserving tradition." They illegally attacked, or killed, individuals who they felt either had committed a particularly offensive act or were responsible for certain undesirable conditions, such as the state of the economy. More than 3,000 people were reportedly lynched in the United States between 1900 and 1950 alone.

The **riot** is a type of diffuse mob—one with less focus, organization, and leadership—whose acts of violence are randomly directed. Less discrimination, if any, is shown in regard to the persons or things that are attacked in a riot. In fact, the specific objectives of the rioting crowd often are not easy to discern. Other than to create disorder or chaos, riots seem to have few specific objectives. Riots invariably are spontaneous in their formation. Immediate or proximate causes of riots, however, often can be easily identified, but the latent causes are not so readily discerned. Indeed, each individual may be rioting for a different reason. Moreover, the actual behavior of people in a riot may take many diverse forms, although invariably it is of an essentially violent and destructive nature.

Examples of major riots in the United States include those in the Black ghettos of Los Angeles, Detroit, New York, and other cities in the mid-1960s; a somewhat more unusual one (a police riot) that occurred at the 1968 National Convention of the Democratic Party in Chicago; and several others that took place in conjunction with blackouts in New York City in July 1977. In the 1965 riot in the Watts section of Los Angeles, which focused on race relations, researchers were able to identify at least 1878 incidents of riotous behavior. These violent acts were classified into five categories: 926 reported fires, 555 lootings, 174 rock throwings, 138 false alarms, and 185 crowd-gathering incidents. More recently, and more tragically, in May 1980, a three-day riot occurred in the

Black neighborhoods of Miami, following the acquittal by an all-White jury of five White police officers who were accused of manslaughter in the death of a Black insurance executive. Thirteen people, including five Blacks, were beaten, stoned, stabbed, or burned to death by the Black rioters (Porter & Dunn, 1984).

Rioting has become rather common in conjunction with spectator sports in recent years. One of the most serious of such riots occurred in Belgium in May 1985 during a European championship soccer match between England and Italy, which resulted in the deaths of 38 people, with another 450 injured. No riot in recent history, however, has had such tragic consequences as that which took place in Mecca, Saudi Arabia, in July 1987 in conjunction with Islamic religious celebrations. This event resulted in the deaths of 402 people, and injuries for another 609. Nearly three-fourths of the victims were Iranian pilgrims. News of these deaths and injuries provoked mob attacks on four foreign embassies in Tehran, the capital city of Iran, the next day.

Journalistic conceptions of riots usually portray them as being perpetuated by an emotionally influential aggregate of rowdies who have nothing else to do but "cause trouble." The behavior of rioters, moreover, is seen as being motivated by simple selfishness. The evidence, however, does not support such a view of rioters as "riffraff." A report issued by the National Advisory Committee on Civil Disorders which investigated the urban riots during the 1960s portrayed a conception of the Black rioter that contradicts the lay conception. The average rioter was described by the commission as male, better educated than most Blacks, and either unemployed or underemployed. The rioters believed that racial discrimination was the primary reason for their not having jobs or being underemployed. Research by Caplan & Paige (1968) showed that rioters perceived their behavior as a form of protest against racial discrimination, rather than violence and destruction for their own sake. Blacks who rioted were most apt to blame White society for their problems. Moreover, they felt that socially approved mechanisms for bringing about positive change were not available. Consequently, they believed their only hope for an improvement in their position was through illegitimate methods.

Not all riots, however, are the result of felt injustices. Individual greed and avarice also help to account for riots. Some evidence indicates that whether looting occurs in a riot area is partly dependent on the attractiveness the available store merchandise may have to the rioters (Berk & Aldrich, 1972). Clothing, sporting goods, and home appliance stores, for instance, are more likely to be looted than pet or hardware stores. Riots, then, may have a multiplicity of causes and cannot be explained by attributing a single motivational pattern to those who engage in them.

Demarcations between these principal types of crowds are often quite arbitrary. This is especially true because one type often develops into another. Let us describe how this may happen, in a hypothetical example.

People entering, or waiting to enter, a baseball park constitute a casual crowd. Once seated in the park, with their attention on the activity of the game, this aggregate would constitute a conventional crowd. Should the aggregate become emotionally aroused by the action of the umpires, one call perceived to be wrong could trigger a mob's descent from the stands onto the field in pursuit of any or all officials. Restraint by police, or an eventual defeat of the favorite team, could precipitate a riot, with wanton destruction and widespread violence directed randomly at any suitable target. Once order is restored, many of the individuals involved might adjourn to another place for a postgame celebration that permits a more legitimate expression of their emotions. It is difficult to predict whether the gathering will eventually disperse at this point or again

▼

**525**

▼ take on any one or more versions of the crowd. In any event, crowds of whatever type are a temporary and unstable form of collective behavior.

## PANIC BEHAVIOR

**Panic** is a sudden, highly emotional, somewhat irrational, and chaotic response on the part of a plurality of people who fear that they face an immediate and severe threat from which there is no escape. Panic may be the reaction of an entire crowd or merely that of a number of people acting in an individual, yet parallel, fashion. In either case, people are collectively seeking rapid exit or relief from a situation perceived to be severely threatening and for which the means of escape appear to be blocked or nonexistent. Behavior of this kind occasionally occurs in cases of fires, combat, earthquakes, and other such life-threatening situations, but usually only immediately before or during the first moments of such threatening events—not afterward—since panic, involving such a highly emotional state, cannot be sustained for a long period of time. Such was the situation during the tragic fire that occurred at the Iroquois Theater in Chicago in 1903 and at the Coconut Grove nightclub in Boston in 1942. Five hundred people perished in each of these tragedies. A similar situation occurred during 1977 in a supper club in Southgate, Kentucky, in which 164 people died. We shall never know how many of these lives could have been saved had the crowds remained rational and orderly.

Another form of panic behavior, one in response to a truly inescapable crisis, manifested itself during the crash of the American stock market in 1929. Panic behavior in this unfortunate situation facilitated the collapse of the American economy, which in turn resulted in an extensive period of misery.

It is primarily harm to individuals that usually results from panic behavior. While 500 people were killed during the Iroquois Theater fire

in less than ten minutes, the physical damage to the theater was minimal. When the theatergoers became aware of the fire, they fearfully rushed to the exits all at once, causing the doors to be blocked, and only a few escaped to safety. Fire inspectors found the majority of the bodies lumped together at the doors. During episodes of panic people become most concerned with their own safety and do not stop to consider the consequences of their actions. Communication between people usually falters during panics. What ensues is the actualization of the self-fulfilling prophecy: People's expectations actually produce a situation which otherwise would not occur.

There are many instances when, although conditions exist for a panic to develop, nothing happens; or, at least, nothing happens for *all* the people involved. During the sinking of the *Titanic*, many people calmly resigned themselves to death. We still do not know why panic ensues in one situation but not in another that is quite similar. Some social scientists contend that a panic is most likely to occur in a crisis situation when there is no leader present. Panic, nonetheless, is especially apt to develop when people feel that organized and cooperative actions will be of no help. Consequently, each person behaves in an individualistic manner. A leader, however, can attempt to organize the crowd by shouting very specific directions to them. The leader can also serve as a positive role model for the crowd by remaining calm and rational.

## MASS HYSTERIA

**Mass hysteria** occurs when an unfounded or irrational belief diffuses widely among people and causes them to behave in a compulsive or frenzied manner. Emotions and reactions produced by this belief take on a contagious quality. Many times the particular belief implies that the safety and well-being of people are threatened. Hence, in this respect, hysteria is similar to panic. The principal difference, however, is that the threat which serves as the basis of hysteria tends to be relatively distant rather than immediate. Moreover, mass hysteria does not occur in a crowd, although it may result in the formation of crowds.

Episodes of mass hysteria are rather rare. (See Box 12-1 for a classic example.) Two of the more interesting ones that have occurred in this country during the past few decades, and which have been of particular interest to social scientists, are the Seattle Windshield Pitting Incident of 1954 (Medalia & Larsen, 1958) and the June Bug Epidemic of 1962 (Kerckhoff & Back, 1968).

THE SEATTLE WINDSHIELD INCIDENT. This incident was presumed to have been related to occasional reports in the Seattle newspapers of damage to automobile wind-

shields in cities in northwestern Washington. The latest report of such damage appeared in the newspapers of April 14, 1954. Between that day and the next, more than 15,000 people called the Seattle police department to complain of damage to the windshields of their automobiles.

The damage generally consisted of small pitting marks—usually less than the size of a penny. The same fate allegedly was experienced even by individuals who had covered their windshields or garaged their cars. Obviously, in these cases, vandals could not be blamed. The principal cause was presumed to be the H-bomb, which a short time earlier had been tested in the Pacific. Interestingly enough, for about two months before this episode, Seattle newspapers had been publishing ominous reports about H-bomb testing and the disastrous consequences of radioactive fallout.

▼

**527**

# BOX 12-1. Invasion from Mars

A classic instance of mass hysteria occurred in the United States during the first half of this century. It involved the science-fiction account of aliens landing from outer space in Grovers Mill, New Jersey.

On the evening of October 30, 1938, the late movie actor and director Orson Welles produced a radio dramatization of H. G. Wells' *War of the Worlds,* which focused on a fictitious invasion from Mars (see Koch, 1970). It is estimated that more than 1 million people, including many (42 percent based on one poll) who had tuned in while the broadcast was in progress, mistook the highly realistic dramatization for an authentic news report, and became terrified that hostile beings from outer space actually had landed on earth and were attacking people. These fears were confirmed by reporters "on the scene" who vividly described the mass destruction caused by the death rays of the Martians.

Switchboards of police departments and military installations were inundated with frantic calls. Many people hid in cellars. Others tried to escape by automobile, which resulted in clogged highways. And still others prepared for their inevitable death. Crowds formed throughout the broadcast area, and a host of ensuing rumors continually provided fuel for these irrational responses. Welles' prankish Halloween entertainment was obviously much more successful in frightening people than had been intended. That such bizarre behavior could take place needs to be understood partially in terms of the media technology of the times, and the ominous rumors of impending worldwide war, as well as the limited fund of knowledge in the pre-space era. ▲

▼ The mayor sought help from both the governor and the president of the United States, but the epidemic ended almost as quickly as it had begun. On April 16, local newspapers suggested that mass hysteria, not radioactive fallout, was the cause of the problem. Only forty-six complaints were received by the police on that day, a mere ten on the next day, and none at all thereafter.

528 Careful analysis of the pitted windshields showed that the amount of pitting increased with the age and mileage of the car. There was no evidence of any pitting that could not be explained by ordinary road damage. It seems that the motorists of Seattle had begun to look *at* their windshields as well as merely *through* them.

THE JUNE BUG EPIDEMIC.   In the case of the June Bug Epidemic, which took place in a southern mill town, there was a mysterious epidemic of alleged insect bites. Within a ten-day period, sixty-two people (fifty-nine of whom were women) sought medical treatment for such complaints. Fifty-nine of these people worked on the same shift, and fifty-eight in the same department of the same plant. Fifty of these cases occurred within two days, and all reported the same symptoms: skin eruptions all over the body, accompanied by nausea. The plant in question was closed in the interest of addressing what appeared to be a major health hazard.

The mysterious sickness was blamed on bites from an insect, presumed to have arrived with a shipment of foreign goods, although there was no evidence for such a claim. These reports of illness were apparently the result of suggestibility and widespread anxiety. The episode, typical of cases of mass hysteria, ended abruptly.

## BEHAVIOR IN DISASTERS

Human behavior in response to various types of disasters is usually categorized as a form of collective behavior. Recent research has shown that the popular conception of how people act immediately after a disaster has occurred is erroneous. The popular view is that there is a complete breakdown of norms and rational patterns of behavior (Raphael, 1985). It is thought that people flee in panic and engage in irrational, intensively emotional behavior. The popular conception also assumes that disaster victims are incapable of helping themselves or each other, and thus become completely dependent on aid from governmental or private agencies. Moreover, the conventional view presupposes that after the initial impact of the disaster, people become psychologically paralyzed and suffer from what has been termed "disaster syndrome."

Disaster syndrome is described as an interrelated set of feelings and actions that includes indecisiveness, lack of emotion, docility, and trance-like patterns of behavior. Undoubtedly, many people do have this traumatic experience. Erikson (1976) speaks of such an occurrence, especially in terms of the loss of communality, by which he means a state of mind shared among a particular people. In *Everything in Its Path*, Erikson (1976) describes the personal and social consequences of the destruction of a mining company's makeshift dam in the hills of West Virginia. A flood of water swept down Buffalo Creek and destroyed several communities. One hundred twenty-five people were killed in this disaster in February 1972. Erikson argues that the disaster turned a tightly knit community into a collection of people with no sense of "we-feeling" or social cohesion.

Quarantelli and Dynes (1977) and their associates at the Disaster Research Center based at the University of Delaware have studied human responses to a variety of disasters and conclude that the popular beliefs are erroneous. These researchers maintain that disaster situations are characterized by far stronger degrees of order and cohesion. They contend, for example, that many people learning about an im-

▼

529

**Pro-Social Behavior.** Contrary to widely held beliefs, victims of mass disaster often respond with altruistic behavior—providing assistance in the rescue and care of others, as well as seeking remedies for the causes and consequences of these conditions. The mammoth earthquake that killed nearly 30,000 people in Armenia in 1988 reaffirmed this principle. (T. Orban/SYGMA)

pending disaster do not flee, and that those who leave do so in an orderly fashion. Moreover, the majority of those choosing to leave the area depart with their families. Such reactions were documented in the Three Mile Island nuclear accident in Pennsylvania during 1979, as well as in the volcanic eruption of Mount Saint Helens in 1980.

Research also shows that disaster victims are much more independent, self-reliant, and competent than had been previously believed. They are able to cope with the aftermath of disaster in a generally effective way, and they are not entirely dependent on outside agencies for help. A case in point is the aftermath of a tornado that struck Worcester, Massachusetts in 1953. About 10,000 people became homeless, yet only

about 50 were sheltered by public agencies. Most of them moved in with other family members, neighbors, and friends. Primary-group relationships, thus, play an important part in helping people to cope with the effects of disasters.

These observations support earlier studies. Killian (1952) studied disaster behavior in a Texas city that was the site of a severe explosion and in three towns in Oklahoma that were hit by tornadoes. The people in these places did not resort to disorganized, chaotic, or counterproductive behavior when the disaster struck. Established cultural and normative patterns did not become entirely inoperative. Past experiences, previously learned role patterns, and internalized expectations did not become

▼

530

completely overshadowed by the crisis situation. Role conflict, however, was found to be quite extensive in the aftermath of disasters. To whom does one manifest primary allegiance at such a time—family, community, or occupation? Many men, for example, were torn between their conflicting love for and responsibilities to family, community, and occupation. Such was especially the case when a person's occupation involved a vital service (police, fire, health jobs). Role abandonment, however, did not occur; on the contrary, the assumption of pro-social roles was much in evidence.

Victims of disaster seem to be able to deal with most problems produced by tragedy, with the exception of those that require complex equipment or skilled behavior. In support of this contention, Quarantelli and Dynes (1972) describe the situation in a tornado disaster that struck a Michigan town in 1953. Between two-thirds to three-fourths of the 927 casualties were rescued and taken to hospitals within three to four hours of the tornado with practically no aid from formal organizations. Research also belies the belief that people who experience a disaster will suffer from severe psychological problems—the disaster syndrome. In a study on the psychological effects of a tornado that hit Xenia, Ohio, in 1974, killing 33 people and injuring another 1200, it was found that the amount of postdisaster psychological problems experienced by the people was relatively low (Taylor, 1977). Survivors handled the crisis well; moreover, they showed an increase in self-esteem over the long term.

Quarantelli (1977) summarizes the results of his research by stating that "disasters do not create situations of total anomie. Only some of the customary large-scale behavior patterns are rendered ineffective, and this usually only in relatively extensive and devastating crises. And in such situations new social patterns quickly emerge after the impact to restore a social equilibrium." Further research in this relatively new area of sociological investigation should provide valuable knowledge for coping with disasters.

## RUMOR

A **rumor** consists of an unverified communication that occurs in an ambiguous situation for the purpose of providing a meaningful interpretation. Rumors may be true, partially true, or false. Whatever their substance, rumors constitute a pervasive ingredient of many types of collective behavior. Indeed, rumors may actually serve to produce certain types of collective behavior. Mobs and riots, for example, often develop on the basis of a rumor.

Rumors are most likely to emerge in situations that are ambiguous, stressful, and threatening to people. Moreover, at times when the regular or formal means of communication are blocked or perceived to be unreliable, rumors also tend to develop (Rosnow & Fine, 1976). People are desperate for information under such circumstances. Accordingly, rumors emerge to satisfy their need, and can be used to control an ambiguous and/or anxiety-producing situation.

All of the necessary and sufficient conditions for the emergence of rumors were present one evening in 1964 when a complete failure of electrical power occurred in New York City. Some people claimed that the Russians were responsible for the blackout and that an attack from them was imminent. Others suggested that the power failure was the work of aliens from another planet. Similarly, many adverse rumors developed immediately after the assassination of President John F. Kennedy in 1963. Chief among them were the allegations that other government officials would be killed, that the assassination was a prelude to an attack upon the government, and that a major domestic overthrow was in process. Rumors tend to arise in situations of cognitive ambiguity. People have a fundamentally human need to understand their circumstances.

The commercial rumor became the dominant form of rumor in the late 1970s (Koenig, 1985). Several of this type involved well-known food products. One story claimed that McDonald's restaurants added worms to their hamburgers as a way of strengthening the protein content. Another maintained that drinking soda while eating Pop Rocks candy caused one's stomach to explode. Neither of these two tales, of course, was true. McDonald's and General Foods (the makers of Pop Rocks), nonetheless, were forced to spend hundreds of thousands of dollars on advertising and other public relations activities in order to squelch these damaging stories. Another rumor during this period involved the shortage of toilet paper (see Box 12-2).

## BOX 12-2. The "Shortage" of Bathroom Tissue: A Classic Study in Rumor

531

Chester, Pa., Feb. 2—"You know, we've got all sorts of shortages these days," Johnny Carson told his faithful late-night audience. "But have you heard the latest? I'm not kidding. I saw it in the paper. There's a shortage of toilet paper."

Thus began, on the night of Dec. 19, the second chapter in what may go down in history as one of the nation's most unusual crises—The Toilet Paper Shortage— a phenomenon that saw millions of Americans strip every roll of bathroom tissue from thousands of grocery shelves.

It was a shortage full of humor, misunderstanding and fear. It was a shortage involving government officials, a TV personality, a well-meaning Wisconsin Congressman, eager reporters, industrial executives and ordinary consumers.

And it was a shortage that need never have been. For the toilet paper shortage was a rumor run wild in a nation that has recently become geared to expect shortages in items considered absolute necessities.

Fears of a possible bathroom tissue shortage, which continue in some areas as the result of abnormal buying and hoarding, seem to have sprouted last November, when news agencies carried articles about a shortage in Japan.

Meanwhile, in Washington, Representative Harold V. Froehlich, a 41-year-old Republican from Wisconsin's heavily forested Eighth District, was getting considerable complaints from his constituents of a shortage of pulp paper, allegedly caused by companies that increased paper exports to avoid Federal price controls.

On Nov. 16, Mr. Froehlich issued a news release that began, "The Government Printing Office is facing a serious shortage of paper." Like most other news releases from such sources, it was virtually ignored.

Then Mr. Froehlich discovered that the Federal Government's National Buying Center had fallen 50 percent short in obtaining bids to provide 182,050 boxes of toilet tissue, a four-month's supply for the country's bureaucrats and soldiers.

On Dec. 11, a day now etched in the minds of Mr. Froehlich's staff, he issued another news release. It began:

"The United States may face a serious shortage of toilet paper within a few months. . . . I hope we don't have to ration toilet tissue. . . . A toilet paper shortage is no laughing matter. It is a problem that will touch every American."

"It got more attention than we ever dreamed of," one aide said of the release. The wire services picked it up. So did television networks. Radio stations called

*(Continued)*

▼     BOX 12-2   *(Continued).*

to talk. German and Japanese correspondents lined up for interviews. In some reports, however, qualifying words like "potential" somehow disappeared.

In Philadelphia, reporters called the headquarters of the Scott Paper Company, one of the nation's 10 largest paper manufacturers. Television crews then filmed supermarkets and toilet paper streaming from machines in Scott's suburban plant here.

Company officers went on television to urge calm, saying there was no shortage if people bought normally.

532

## MANY CREDIBILITY GAPS

Some consumers may have believed those remarks—until they saw other shoppers wheeling cases of toilet tissue from some stores or signs rationing each buyer to two rolls each. "There are so many credibility gaps today," said one paper executive, "and we fell into one."

Wire service reporters and broadcast newsmen passed the self-fulfilling shortage reports on to their readers and audiences, one of whom included Johnny Carson, a television talk show host whose nightly program is often geared to current events.

On Dec. 20, the day after his comments, the toilet-paper-buying binge began nationally.

In the Bronx, Jimmy Detrain, manager of the Food Cart Store on Lydig Avenue, watched customers check out with $20 in toilet paper purchases.

"I heard about it on the news," said Mrs. Paul McCoy of Houston, "so I bought an extra 15 rolls."

In Seattle, one store owner ordered an extra 21 cases of toilet paper. When he received only three cases, he became worried and rationed his supply. That prompted more buying, even at increased prices.

When Mrs. Clare Clark of Jenkintown, Pa., gave a party, guests asked what they could bring. "I told them toilet paper," she said.

Here in Chester, at Scott's plant, the world's largest such facility (capable of producing 7,500 miles of tissue every day), production continued at full capacity.

Although paper industry officials say The Toilet Paper Shortage was hard to believe, Steuart Henderson Britt, a professor of marketing at Northwestern University, regards the shortage as a classic study in rumor.

"Everybody likes to be the first to know something," he said. "It's the 'did-you-hear-that' syndrome. In the old days, a rumor took a long time to spread, enough time to let people discover its validity. Now all it takes is one TV personality to joke about it and instantly the rumor is in all 50 states."

Professor Britt said the rumor had all the necessary elements. "It could affect everyone intimately," he said. "There was a Congressman, presumably an authority, talking about it. He says there could be a problem. The next person says there probably is a problem. The next person says there is a problem."

Mr. Britt expects the shortage rumor to die as soon as shoppers discover that tissue paper supplies have been replenished.

And things are returning to normal. Congressman Froehlich issued another

▼

release last week; it was largely ignored. At least one Chicago store is advertising that there is no shortage of record players, apparently hoping that this will prompt a run on record players. And Johnny Carson has apologized on his show.

"I don't want to be remembered as the man who created a false toilet paper scare," he said. "I just picked up the item from the paper and enlarged on it somewhat and made some jokes as to what they could do about it. There's no shortage."

### More Shortages Feared

But even as they spread the word about the end of the toilet paper shortage, dozens of consumers are already expressing concern over other shortages.

Rumor in the supermarket aisles has it that there are new shortages in mustard, chile sauce, vegetable oil, cheese, catfood, salmon, birdseed, raisins, toilet seats and yellow tennis balls.

**533**

"Everyone agrees consumers created the toilet paper shortage," says Mrs. Kathy Pittenger of Paoli, Pa. "I wonder how many other shortages are created this way. You know, I can't stand to pass a gas station any more without filling up."▲

---

Rumors tend to become progressively distorted as they are communicated from one person to another (Allport & Postman, 1947). The original message is changed in three ways: leveling, sharpening, and assimilation.

*Leveling* is a process by which the story becomes more concise, shorter, and easier to understand. Details typically fade quite dramatically as rumors spread.

*Sharpening* occurs when certain elements of the story are emphasized while others are either underplayed or entirely ignored. People tend to change aspects of the story to make it more plausible and compatible with their own pet theories and prejudices.

*Assimilation* is the process by which the story becomes consistent with motives, interests, and concerns of the communicator. The changes made in the report tend to reinforce the communicator's definition of the situation or perception of reality. Racial prejudice, for instance, appeared to be at work in one laboratory experiment. White subjects unconsciously modified an original story which said that a White

person had a knife in his hand, to one that claimed a Black person was holding a razor.

These findings on rumor distortion are based on laboratory experiments. Some sociologists have criticized such studies on the grounds that contrived experiments cannot adequately reflect behavior that occurs in natural settings. They also cite studies of rumor transmission in the armed forces as being contrary to the laboratory findings. These studies found that accuracy in rumor transmission was very high (Lang & Lang, 1961). Whether a rumor is distorted during transmission, however, depends on the characteristics of those transmitting the rumor, the nature of the situation, and the content of the rumor (Buckner, 1969).

Some people have a critical mental set and apply it to determine the truth of any rumor. Others have an uncritical, passive orientation, in which case they will not try to ascertain the veracity of a rumor. The social structure of the group that hears a rumor also helps to determine whether it will be transmitted accurately. Groups that are cohesive and well disciplined

▼ are apt to maintain a critical stance toward rumors. Perhaps this explains why members of the armed forces were found not to distort rumors. Moreover, military personnel, especially those in combat, are likely to have a critical mind-set toward rumors precisely because the situation in which they interact breeds them at a rapid rate.

534

## PUBLICS AND PUBLIC OPINION

Other basic forms of collective behavior are represented by publics and public opinion. These two varieties of collective behavior, in many respects, are fundamental to several of the other types that are discussed in this chapter.

PUBLICS.   A **public** refers to large numbers or a category of people who share an interest and concern about a particular issue. Members of publics, unlike participants in crowds, are usually dispersed over a large geographic area and do not have much, if any, face-to-face interaction with one another. When they do so, it is the result of an organized effort. Publics, therefore, constitute another form of spatially diffuse collective behavior. Examples of publics would be all of those people who in recent years have been described as "the silent majority" or "the moral majority."

While many use the term "public" to denote the entire population of a country, such usage does not have much value. It is more accurate to speak of "publics" because there is a public for each issue that exists and is of concern to a significant number of people. Thus, each collectivity of individuals who are concerned about and have opinions on such issues as pollution, gun control, abortion, ecology, capital punishment, and the plight of migrant farm workers, for example, represents a public. We can say that there are as many publics as there are public issues. Not every member of a society will be part of every public. If an individual is not interested in a particular issue and does not have an opinion about it, he or she is not part of the public for that issue. Whether people are even aware of an issue depends on how the issue affects them personally, as well as the amount of coverage given to it by the mass media.

PUBLIC OPINION.   **Public opinion** refers to the beliefs and attitudes that a particular public has about an issue. Public opinion is not unanimous or monolithic, but rather is usually divided or fragmented into several opinions. This situation is especially the case in modern societies that have many subcultures and socially diverse segments.

Generally, the greater the heterogeneity of a society, the more likely is there to be a variety of opinions on different issues. Even if there is consensus about the existence and importance of an issue, as well as the need for its resolution, there is apt to be disagreement on how the problem should be handled. Some people believe that the solution to the energy problem lies in decontrolling the price of oil so that the producing companies will have more money to use for exploration. Others, arguing that decontrol will hurt only the poor through higher fuel costs, feel that the emphasis should be on enforced conservation and the development of new sources of energy such as solar power. Still others contend that the solution to the energy problem lies in nationalizing the oil industry. This situation notwithstanding, the term "public opinion" often is used to refer to the dominant opinion among a particular population.

Public opinion is not static. Rather, in most cases, it is fluid and quite changeable. As a public is exposed to new information by the mass media, its opinions are likely to be modified. Also, personal involvement with an issue may produce a change in opinion. Many nuclear plant workers who always had felt that nuclear power was a safe source of energy have changed their opinions since being involved in the accident at the Three Mile Island plant in Pennsylvania in 1979. By the same token, some people who were initially opposed to gun control legislation have altered their views after they themselves or their loved ones become victims of a crime in which a gun was used.

Public opinion is also heavily influenced by social background factors. Chief among such variables are age, sex, race, ethnicity, religion, socioeconomic status, and area of residence. The degree of influence of any one of these factors depends on the particular issue under consideration, as well as the competing and interactional influence of the others. Individuals with the same social backgrounds, however, tend to have highly similar opinions on many issues.

What people think is important, regardless of whether it is consistent with the reality of the situation in question. One such example is the **self-fulfilling prophecy,** a dynamic according to which people hold a mistaken belief, and by acting as if it were so, cause the erroneous belief to come true. Teachers, for example, who perceive their students to be either low or high achievers, could actually fulfill their expectations by treating the students accordingly. Such a situation has come to be known as the *teacher-expectancy effect* (see Rosenthal & Jacobson, 1968). The same dynamic, obviously with more pervasive and forceful consequences, can occur on the part of publics and public opinion. If people think that there is a food shortage and hoard food, their very action could bring about a shortage of food. The *self-defeating prophecy* has a similar dynamic: people who stay away from the polls because they believe their favorite candidate is assured of victory can by their actions bring about his or her defeat. Both of these situations exemplify the "Thomas theorem," a principle espoused by the early American social

psychologist, William I. Thomas (1928): "If men define situations as real, they are real in their consequences."

FORMATION OF PUBLIC OPINION. One of the most intriguing questions about public opinion concerns the process of its formation. Much public opinion rests on basic values; but, unlike values, which remain relatively constant throughout life, public opinion typically changes quite easily and quite frequently. Again unlike basic values, public opinion is greatly affected by the realities of specific situations.

The formation of public opinion, nevertheless, is not as simple as one may be led to believe. It is, first of all, a highly social process, one that involves more than exposure to the mass media. Furthermore, while the mass media exert a significant influence on the formation of public opinion, their impact is not direct. The notion that people automatically absorb, accept, and then act upon whatever the media communicate to them is simplistic. Several theories have been developed to specify the nature of the formation process for public opinion. We shall discuss two of the more important of them.

According to the **two-step flow theory of communication** (Katz & Lazarsfeld, 1955), the transmission of information and news proceeds directly from the mass media to opinion leaders, and in turn to the majority of citizens through networks of social interaction. *Opinion leaders* are those prominent individuals whose ideas and views are given much weight by others. They are able to influence the attitudes and decisions of other people in a variety of circumstances. Opinion leaders are likely to be more competent and intelligent than the average citizen. They also are apt to have a broader range of acquaintances and contacts, especially with the media, than the ordinary citizen (Katz, 1957). It is significant too that opinion leaders are likely to be of the same or

▼

**535**

▼

higher socioeconomic class than those whom they influence. Opinion leaders also exemplify the values and outlooks of the groups to which they belong. Accordingly, people who are members of an opinion leader's group are likely to identify with and look up to the opinion leader.

Opinion leaders function to alleviate or to modify the effects of the mass media on the population. Katz and Lazarsfeld (1955), for example, found that personal interaction with others was more influential than the mass media in determining voting behavior in a presidential election. They found also that the personal influence of opinion leaders had a greater impact than the media in determining such things as the shopping behavior of women, fashions in clothing, and attendance at movies.

**536**

At first it was thought that opinion leaders were highly specialized. So, for example, a person who was an opinion leader in the realm of politics would not necessarily be one in the realm of sports or the arts. Research, however, has indicated that people who may be opinion leaders in one realm are also likely to have influence in related areas.

While the two-step flow theory of the opinion formation process is an improvement over earlier theories, it may be somewhat of an oversimplification. Opinion leaders, argue Secord and Bachman (1974), are not a necessary link between the mass media and their respondents. Under certain circumstances, the role of the opinion leader is minimal, or even nonexistent. Further research is required to refine the specifications of this theory.

Perhaps a more accurate conception of the process of opinion formation is presented in the **circular-flow theory of communication** (Oskamp, 1977). The circular flow model depicts a process of much alternation between media sources and personal sources. Events of a shocking nature tend to be communicated more through personal communication than through the mass media. Once people learn about the occurrence of such an event, however, they are apt to turn to the media for confirmation and additional details (Greenberg, 1964). Such was the case with the assassination of President John F. Kennedy and other similarly shocking tragedies. In other instances, people may initially learn about an event or issue via the media, then become stimulated to discuss it with others in order to determine how their friends and acquaintances perceive the situation (Oskamp, 1977).

INFLUENCING PUBLIC OPINION. Many segments of society have a vested interest in wanting the population to hold certain attitudes and opinions and behave in terms of them. Corporations which produce goods and services, for example, want people to feel that they have a need for the products and services they offer. In addition, companies which produce the same product or offer the same service attempt to convince people that their product or service is better than that of their competitors. As a consequence, they launch large-scale and costly advertising campaigns. Similarly, politicians try to persuade citizens that they are the best candidates and solely worthy of the people's vote. Lobbyists representing different industries and public interest organizations attempt to get both politicians and the people to accept the validity of their points of view. Billions of dollars are spent every year on public opinion polls, market surveys, and media campaigns to assess and to influence public opinion in desired directions. Public opinion, thus, is a very valuable commodity in any democratic society. To control public opinion is to control behavior in many respects. Testimony to this principle is offered by the many societies in which public opinion is subject to censor.

Corporations, government officials, politicians, and interest groups that attempt to mold or to create public opinion often make use of propaganda. **Propaganda** is any deliberate attempt to persuade people to adopt a particular set of beliefs, attitudes, or opinions. Propaganda may consist of truths, incomplete truths, or falsehoods. Whereas education trains individuals to think for themselves and to reach their own conclusions after a careful consideration of the facts, propaganda is based on emotional appeal and gives only a one-sided interpretation of a given situation. The distinction between propaganda and education, however, is not always clear-cut. Propaganda is often disguised as education. A variety of subtle techniques, usually playing on the fears and anxieties of the people, are employed. See Figure 12-1 for a description of some of the fundamental tricks of the art.

An excellent example of how some interest groups attempt to disguise their propaganda, as well as some of the psychological tactics they use to persuade the public, is provided by a letter sent to American mothers by Frank Nicholas, president of the Beech-Nut Nutrition Company. In this letter Nicholas wrote that home-prepared baby food was a potential health hazard to babies. At the same time, he praised the virtues of commercial baby food, especially food prepared by Beech-Nut. The letter was said to have been sent as a "public service" according to a Beech-Nut official. It should be noted that the May 1976 issue of *Consumer Reports* magazine concluded that, generally, home-made baby foods are more nutritious and healthful than the commercial kind. Social scientists (Zimbardo et al., 1977) analyzed the Beech-Nut letter in order to determine the type of tactics that were used to convince mothers that home-prepared baby foods were potentially dangerous. They note that the letter contains a strong fear appeal, which is made to appear to come from a reliable source. Also, the letter depicts a threat to the loved ones of the audience to whom it is directed. Finally, the

▼

**537**

 **Name calling**—giving an idea a bad label—is used to make us reject and condemn the idea without examining the evidence. Symbolized by the ancient sign of condemnation used by the Vestal Virgins in the Roman Coliseum, a thumb turned down.

 **Glittering generality**—associating an idea with a "virtue" word—is used to make us accept and approve the idea without examining the evidence. Symbolized by a glittering gem that may or may not have much intrinsic value.

 **Transfer**—associating an idea with a person, image, or symbol which is respected and revered making us accept or reject the idea not on its own merit, but on the basis of the authority and prestige that has been transferred to it. Symbolized by the theatrical mask.

 **Testimonial**—having some loved or hated person approve or condemn a given idea. Symbolized by a seal and ribbons, the "stamp of authority."

 **Plain folks**—attempting to convince one's public that one's ideas are good because they are those "of the people." Symbolized by the traditional analogue for an old friend, an old shoe.

 **Card-stacking**—the use of only such highly selected material, whether true or false, as supports one's case. Symbolized by the ace of spades, the card traditionally used to signify treachery.

 **Band wagon**—"Everybody's doing it," with the implication that we must therefore "jump on the band wagon." Symbolized by a bandmaster's hat and baton, used on old-fashioned band wagons.

FIGURE 12-1   Propaganda: The Tricks of the Trade. Source: Reprinted by permission from *The Fine Art of Propaganda* by Alfred McClung Lee and Elizabeth Briant Lee. Copyright by the authors 1939, 1967. New York: Octagon Books, 1972, and San Francisco: International Society for General Semantics, 1979. Octagon Books: A division of Hippocrene Books, Inc. The propaganda symbols were designed by Lee and Lee.

▼ letter deals with a topic that the lay person is not familiar with and which requires the knowledge of an expert.

## MASS BEHAVIOR

**538**

Not all collective behavior takes place in crowds. Much also occurs in widely dispersed collectivities of people, or what at times are called "diffuse crowds." Collective behavior in diffuse crowds is commonly referred to as mass behavior. Every football season, millions of people separately, or perhaps in very small groups, sit in front of a television set and watch the same game. This too is collective behavior.

**Mass behavior,** then, represents that behavior performed by many people acting individually in the same way or for the same purpose. Under these circumstances, people have little or no contact with each other, but in general are aware of one another's existence and their mutual interests or common objectives. Mass behavior, as a form of collective behavior, is a distinctly parallel activity, rather than one based on social interaction.

Mass behavior, unlike crowd behavior, is not particularly brief or episodic. It tends to be more enduring as it arises from, and is perpetuated by, the totality of many individual actions occurring over a relatively long period of time. Moreover, mass behavior is not considered essential to the basic functions of society. Yet, while the various forms of mass behavior are quite innocuous in themselves, often they play an important role in the dynamics of social change. Hence, much of today's unstructured social action may become tomorrow's normative behavior in terms of the fundamental aspects of culture and social institutions.

There are many types of mass behavior. Chief among them are fads, fashions, and crazes.

FASHIONS.   A **fashion** refers to a currently accepted and temporary style or model of behavior. While "fashion" usually connotes a par-ticular style of dress, it may apply also to the arts, child-rearing, grooming, and many other realms of human behavior. As such, fashions constitute continually changing patterns of behavior in any area of cultural activity. Jazz in the 1950s, miniskirts in the 1960s, long hair in the 1970s, and disco-rock music and preppy clothes in the 1980s are illustrative of fashions through the past few decades. Whatever is popular or in vogue at a given time is fashionable. Fashions, then, constitute a relatively long-enduring part of a continuous process. Indeed, fashions are typically cyclical in nature, especially since there are limits to innovation in certain realms of life. The options, in other words, are limited; and to a great extent, they are manipulated by manufacturers and advertisers who seek to induce consumer response in the interests of profit making. It is for this reason that we see particular types of grooming and dress reoccurring every so many years.

FADS.   A **fad** consists of an enthusiastically pursued, but short-lived and frivolous, form of behavior engaged in by large numbers of people. Usually, they represent the appearance of a new activity or object of interest.

Fads develop primarily in the realms of dress, speech, or amusements, but they are quite common in many other areas of daily life as well. Intense, but short-lived, fascination with hula hoops, skateboards, water beds, panty raids, streaking (running nude in public), Pac-Man computer games, Cabbage Patch dolls, the Rubic cube, leg warmers, and goldfish swallowing are examples of fads that have seen their day. Fads that are more common today include designer jeans, slogan T-shirts, bumper stickers, video games, disposable cameras, and trivia games.

The desire to gain or to maintain social recognition or social prestige by being different is often the basic motive for faddish behavior on the part of many people. Teenagers and young adults are especially likely to invent and to engage in faddish behavior because, initially at least, it provides them with a much sought-after and distinctive identity. One can easily understand on this basis why fads quickly lose their appeal as they become extensively popular, and new ones are continuously being invented.

CRAZES.    A **craze** represents an extremely intense and obsessive preoccupation with something for the purpose of economic gain or personal satisfaction. Resembling fads in some respects, crazes may be relatively superficial or serious. They are distinguished chiefly, however, by their compulsive character. Additionally, crazes represent a form of the self-fulfilling prophecy, but one that survives only temporarily, since they eventually defeat themselves.

Regardless of their specific nature, crazes engage people in extreme forms of behavior that otherwise would be considered quite foolish or irrational.

Crazes may develop in practically any realm of life. Typically, they consist of behavior that is perceived by individuals as a quick way to an economic reward without much effort. The tulip craze that occurred in Holland in 1634 is a case in point. So intense was the desire to own tulip bulbs, which produce a flower highly desired for its beauty and previously found only in the Middle East, that they were bid up to fantastic prices. In time, tulips lost their appeal and their market value tumbled. A less remote example, one quite atypical because of its more positive consequences, is provided by the gold

▼

**539**

**Price No Object.** So strong was the craze that customers stood in line for hours in the hope of buying a Cabbage Patch Doll in 1984. Usually, only one person in twenty was successful. Such greedy behavior merely inflated the price and spread the contagion. (Bill Tiernzn/SYGMA)

▼ rushes that dominated the Western frontiers of America during the nineteenth century.

Craze behavior in recent years has centered on the obsession of many individuals to establish officially recognized records for all kinds of specific activities, both serious and trivial. Even more recent has been the mania surrounding videotapes of the film *E.T.* and the multimillion dollar state lotteries.

**540**

# Theories of Collective Behavior

Studying collective behavior is one of the most difficult tasks in the field of sociology. Its frequently spontaneous and short-lived character does not permit the kind of planning and design that form the basis of empirical research. Many episodes of collective behavior are over and done with before social scientists can design and implement a research strategy. Moreover, collective behavior does not lend itself to simulation or re-creation in the laboratory. Despite these methodological handicaps, however, much is known about the dynamics of collective behavior. Sociologists and psychologists have developed several theories to account for the socially unconventional and seemingly elusive phenomena that constitute the field of collective behavior. Some of these theories attempt to account for many forms of collective behavior, while others concentrate on explaining only one or two specific types. A discussion of several of the major theories of collective behavior can provide a rather comprehensive understanding of these diverse phenomena (see also Table 12-1).

## CONTAGION THEORY

In one of the earliest attempts to account for collective behavior, Gustav LeBon, a French social scientist, argued that crowds develop a reality independent of their members. The characteristics of crowds are more than, and different from, the sum of characteristics of its participants. As LeBon (1896) put it, "under certain given conditions . . . an agglomeration of men presents new characteristics very different from those of individuals composing it." The crowd develops, in short, what LeBon called a "collective mind," which is manifested

TABLE 12-1. Theories of Collective Behavior

| | |
|---|---|
| Contagion Theory | Irrational behavior spreads among crowd participants because of anonymity, suggestibility, and emotional contagion. |
| De-individuation Theory | Individuals in a crowd lose a sense of personal identity and psychological restraints that inhibit socially unacceptable behavior. |
| Convergence Theory | Crowds are composed of like-minded people brought together by common interests. |
| Emergent Norm Theory | Norms emerge in unstructured situations through crowd interaction and shared expectations. |
| Game Theory | People in crowds are motivated to maximize rewards and minimize costs. |
| Value-Added Theory | Collective behavior and social movements develop through a specific sequence of stages that are related to social conditions in a particular situation. |

in the form of highly emotional and irrational behavior. This notion of psychic unity is thought to be reflected in references to such expressions as the "roar of the crowd" and the "frenzy of the mob."

LeBon claimed that crowds, regardless of the characteristics of their members, have the following qualities: impulsiveness, irritability, inability to reason or to think critically, and an intensified set of emotions. The "collective mind" of a crowd, LeBon claimed, is unified, purposeful, and impervious to normative regulations. Once in and under the influence of a crowd, individuals become dominated by a single idea or purpose. They tend to act virtually identically and temporarily lose their ability to think in a critical and logical fashion. Under circumstances of this nature, people are apt to accept and act upon ideas that they would reject under other conditions.

Why does such a situation occur? According to LeBon, there are three factors that transform an aggregate into a crowd: anonymity, suggestibility, and emotional contagion.

ANONYMITY.   People lose their sense of individual identity when they are part of a crowd. Each one's identity as a particular person with a unique set of personality characteristics becomes overshadowed by the collective and homogeneous identity of the crowd. Individuals lose their inhibitions and sense of responsibility. Norms that function to restrain behavior under conventional conditions lose their power. There often develops, moreover, a belief in the strength of sheer numbers, and a feeling of invincibility. In a crowd, people may believe that they are insulated from any negative sanctions for disorderly conduct. As a result, individuals are prone to engage in behavior that they would not think of undertaking outside a crowd situation.

Experimental evidence supports these contentions regarding anonymity and disorderly or deviant conduct. Subjects in one experiment

(Festinger et al., 1952) were asked to make negative statements about their parents. When the discussion occurred in a dark room, with subjects wearing shapeless coats over their attire, there were a greater number of hostile remarks made than when the discussion took place in a conventional setting where the identities of the subjects were known.

Gergen and his associates (1973) report on another interesting experiment in which 90 percent of the subjects placed in totally dark rooms with strangers engaged nearly half the time in purposeful and intimate touching. Behavior of this kind was not observed when all the factors were the same except that the lights were on. Personal identity and social surveillance contribute significantly to normative behavior.

SUGGESTIBILITY.   Suggestibility involves the nonconscious states of human activity. The emotional intensity that characterizes a crowd situation tends to make people very vulnerable to the suggestion. Individuals crave certainty and order, elements that are absent in a crowd. Thus, in such a situation, they are prone to accept suggestions made by others, especially when they are made in a decisive and authoritative manner.

EMOTIONAL CONTAGION. Here we have a situation that is analogous to an epidemic. **Emotional contagion** occurs when beliefs, feelings, and actions are transmitted from one person to another in a crowd, as members stimulate and respond to one another. Unconscious imitation is the fundamental dynamic. Infectious applause or a standing ovation are commonly experienced examples of emotional and behavioral contagion. Often such actions are intentionally stimulated by claques who are hired by theatrical producers to achieve favorable public response and reviews.

Contagion helps to explain the higher degree of emotionality that is a feature of many crowds.

▼

**541**

▼

**542**

Blumer (1951) observes that under normal circumstances, before responding, people first interpret and evaluate each other's statements and actions. However, under conditions of unrest, uncertainty, and frustration, people engage in "circular reactions," whereby they uncritically imitate one another's emotions and behavior. Consequently, their emotions and actions become highly intensified by a series of mutual stimulations. A person who shouts, "Fire!" will go on shouting, "Fire!" Surges of emotion are rapidly transmitted among members of a crowd, as though the excitement were literally contagious. Perhaps you have both experienced and contributed to a circular reaction when you were part of a boisterous crowd or were caught up in the collective excitement of a football or baseball game.

This ongoing process of reciprocal emotional stimulation may lead to actions that were not initially intended by participants. Such a situation occurs when the emotions of the crowd become so intense that they must be transformed into action. It is at this point that crowd members are most vulnerable to suggestions. When there is heightened emotionality in a crowd, and when there are strong feelings of uncertainty and frustration, people are most likely to accept without criticism the statements made by others, and to act on them accordingly. Their analytical and evaluative faculties become temporarily inoperative. In addition, emotional and behavioral contagion is facilitated when people in a crowd believe that the other crowd members have similar beliefs and feelings. Such a perception functions to reinforce further the "collective mind" dimension of the crowd.

Little doubt exists that some types of behavior are contagious. Indeed, people are more suggestible in crowds as they look to others for a definition of the situation or other relevant cues for understanding the unusual circumstances in which they find themselves. Nonetheless, social scientists today by and large have abandoned the specific notion of a "collective mind" to explain collective behavior. The general idea, however, remains popular, as evidenced by common references to people who "act like irrational animals" or "follow the crowd." Crowds, however, are not homogeneous in their reactions, and people in them vary in the degree of their participation. Contagion theory, thus, is unable to explain why all people in a crowd do not react uniformly. Nonetheless, there is still widespread belief that anonymity, suggestibility, and emotional contagion—individually and jointly—operate quite fundamentally in the dynamics of collective behavior.

## DE-INDIVIDUATION THEORY

Another explanation, somewhat similar to that of emotional contagion, is de-individuation theory (Festinger et al., 1952). **De-individuation** is the process by which an individual loses his sense of personal identity as a result of being part of a crowd or group, and thereby engages in nonconventional or deviant behavior. The sociological and psychological restraints that inhibit a person from behaving in socially acceptable ways are weakened in the process of de-individuation and behavioral contagion comes into play.

Philip Zimbardo (1970) has done extensive research on de-individuation. He explains the influence of de-individuation on antisocial behavior in the following way. First, people in a large group or crowd are prone to develop feelings of anonymity. They will feel that they have become constituents of the crowd and will not be judged as unique individuals. These individuals thus begin to lose their sense of identity. As a consequence, they become less and less concerned about how others are apt to judge their actions. They feel that as long as they are part of the crowd they will escape any negative sanctions for antisocial behavior. Second, being part of a crowd or a large group results in their feeling less responsible for any deviant behavior they may commit. Blame and responsibility are diffused rather than focused on each of them. Finally, the presence of others who engage in deviant action provides models for the individuals to emulate. All of these mechanisms increase the chances that these persons will engage in antisocial behavior.

Both laboratory and naturalistic studies have supported the theory of de-individuation and its effects on behavior. In one laboratory study, for example, subjects who were nameless and made to feel de-individuated gave helpless people stronger and longer (what they believed to be) electric shocks, in comparison with those subjects who knew that they were easily identifiable (Milgram, 1974). In another study, automobiles were abandoned on streets in the metropolis of New York City and in the small city of Palo Alto, California. Within a relatively short time, a New York car had been robbed of its battery, air cleaner, windshield wipers, and other parts. The looters were clean-cut and dressed in middle-class fashion. The car that was left in Palo Alto, however, remained intact during its seven days on the street (Zimbardo, 1970).

Many of the cruelest actions that people subject one another to occur under conditions that facilitate feelings of de-individuation. Appropriate examples are riots, mob violence, lynchings, and wars. Much gang violence also occurs in contexts that are conducive to de-individuation. Soldiers' uniforms, the hooded masks and baggy robes of the Ku Klux Klan, and the leather jackets that gang members are prone to wear give the members of these groups feelings of de-individuation. These people feel anonymous and an intimate part of their group. They do not experience themselves as unique individuals but as elements of a larger, amorphous mass. The strong feelings of group identity that such garb generates within members serve to diffuse any emotions of guilt or shame that may result from engaging in antisocial actions. The intense emotions generated by the speeches and cross burnings that occur at Klan rallies reinforce a state of de-individuation among its members. Similarly, insignia, names, and slogans serve to bring about a loss of individual identity and responsibility among members of youth gangs. Aggressive behavior is further encouraged and facilitated in these organizations through the processes of modeling and behavioral contagion. Hence, in anonymous situations, individuals who initially may be reluctant to engage in antisocial behavior are more likely to do so as they see others perform such actions.

▼

**543**

**Lost Identity.** De-individuation, making for anonymity as well as the loss of social and psychological restraints, is thought to facilitate both the occurrence and the diffusion of some of the most severe forms of deviant behavior. (Donald Dietz/Stock, Boston)

## CONVERGENCE THEORY

**Convergence theory** focuses on the dynamics by which a crowd releases the latent personal tendencies of its members. It emphasizes the shared

▼

characteristics—social, cultural, or psychological—of people who chance to come together in crowd formations (Miller, 1985). These mutual characteristics, representing a latent homogeneity or "consciousness of kind" in the gathering together of like-minded people, leads to collective behavior as the consequence of a particular incident or precipitating factor, such as a speech or slogan.

**544**

Convergence theory maintains more specifically that people have latent hostile and aggressive impulses that yearn for expression. Usually held in check by a person's internalized norms and the fear of punishment, these predispositions express themselves when the norms are inoperative (Turner & Killian, 1987). This theory claims that the "veneer of civilization" is indeed thin and that the crowd provides the milieu that enables these deep-seated aspirations to be manifested. Convergence theory, thus, views crowd behavior as the sum of the behavior of its participants. It assumes also that the same social stimulus will evoke similar latent behavioral tendencies in members of different crowds.

Contagion, de-individuation, and the convergence explanations of collective behavior emphasize the part that anonymity and the diffusion of responsibility play in producing crowd reactions by weakening the effect of internalized norms and fear of negative sanctions. Other theories focus more attention on the conscious and rational forces operative in collective behavior. Let us now discuss three such explanations: emergent norm theory, game theory, and value-added theory.

## EMERGENT NORM THEORY

Emergent norm theory questions the assumption, held by both contagion theory and convergence theory, that there is a uniformity of attitudes, feelings, and actions in a crowd. Proponents of emergent norm theory hold that the appearance of homogeneity in crowds is more illusory than real (Turner & Killian, 1987). In most crowds, the theory maintains, only a relatively small number of people are active participants. The majority are simply passive onlookers, and some may even be opposed to the sentiments and actions of the highly visible members. This silence and passivity are deceptive, creating an illusion of a collective mentality. Unanimity of emotions and conduct appears to exist because the most visible behavior is perceived as being characteristic of the whole crowd.

Unlike the previously discussed theories which stress the nonrational nature of crowds, **emergent norm theory** argues that many aspects of crowd behavior are under normative control. Proponents of this theory argue that not all norms disintegrate into episodes of collective behavior. Rather, as people interact in such situations, new norms—suggested by the actions of one person or a small number of highly visible and assertive participants—usually emerge and become the determinants of the appropriate behavior in the particular situation. People in crowds, when confronted with an unusual problem or situation, simply look to each other for definitions of appropriate behavior.

Since the crowd situation is ambiguous and most people are uncertain as to how they should behave, they are especially likely to accept and to follow the definitions of the situation set by the few active and assertive participants. These emergent norms, as a way of responding to unstructured conditions, both encourage appropriate behavior as well as inhibit inappropriate conduct. Once the newly established norms become known, members of the crowd may feel constrained to act in accordance with them, or at least not to behave in ways that are incompatible with them. For instance, if some crowd participants are looting, others who may condemn such actions may refrain from expressing their feelings because of the fear of negative sanctions. Those not showing opposition to crowd actions are perceived as approving its conduct. This explanation, thus, is able to account for distinctive forms of behavior among crowd participants. Such otherwise uncouth behavior as yelling, hissing, or stone throwing now becomes sanctioned.

Accordingly, the emergent norm theory explains collective behavior in much the same way that all other social behavior is explained: by the social norms existing in the social situation. The only difference is that the norms for collective behavior are made up on the spot—in order to fit the particular situation—and, furthermore, they apply only to the particular situation.

## GAME THEORY

The **game theory** of collective behavior offers a highly rational explanation. It is based on the premise that each person in a crowd is motivated to maximize rewards and to minimize costs. This theory maintains that people, before engaging in a particular behavior, rationally calculate whether their actions are likely to result in greater rewards or greater costs for themselves (Berk, 1974). If the individual concludes that the probable rewards will exceed the potential costs, he or she will engage in the calculated behavior. Thus, according to this perspective, a person who is angry at a boxing referee will rationally consider whether the satisfaction to be gained by throwing a beer can at the official will outweigh the potential cost of being caught and punished. Similarly, workers contemplating a strike will assess whether the loss in wages will be more than compensated by the eventual winning of their demands. The gains to be achieved by participating in a protest demonstration, by the same token, may be weighed against the likelihood of personal injury. The fundamental consideration then, in more popular terms, is this: Is it worth it?

Game theorists contend that the crowd situation is such that it has the effect of making

the individual believe that the probability of being caught and punished for engaging in such actions is small. The assumptions of game theory are the opposite of those upon which contagion theory is based. While contagion theory claims that people are swept up by emotional excitement and lose their ability to think critically and rationally, game theory argues that people in crowds do behave rationally, carefully weighing the pros and cons associated with a particular behavior before deciding to perform it.

## VALUE-ADDED THEORY

**Value-added theory** is a comprehensive model that can be used to account for a wide variety of collective behavior. This theory, which attempts to synthesize many of the elements of the other theories already discussed, has been used to provide a framework for analyzing and explaining nearly all of the many forms of collective behavior. Smelser (1962) argues that any form of collective behavior is essentially an attempt by people to alter their environment when facing conditions of threat, uncertainty, or strain. A particularly noteworthy aspect of his theory is that it integrates the sociological and psychological dimensions of social behavior.

Smelser identifies six essential elements of collective behavior: structural conduciveness, structural strain, generalized belief, precipitating factors, mobilization for action, and operation of social control mechanisms. These determinants, or preconditions, appear in a regular order, each building on the other, and together they influence the particular type of collective behavior that occurs. Smelser uses the "value-added" approach to order these factors in a sequence that goes from the general to the particular.

The value-added notion was borrowed from economics, where it refers to the different stages involved in the manufacture of a product. Let

**545**

▼

us take the production of automobiles for an illustration of this concept. First, iron ore is mined and processed, then it is combined with other metals. Next it is shaped in a particular way, and finally it is painted. The material in question has additional value after the completion of each stage of the production process. Moreover, the completion of each stage serves to limit the number of things that can be done with the "raw" material. Hence, central to the value-added approach is the sequence of events that influences the particular type of collective behavior which takes place. Let us look in more detail at each of the elements of this essential set of preconditions.

STRUCTURAL CONDUCIVENESS. Structural conduciveness is the most general determinant of collective behavior. It refers to the preconditions and organizational context that must exist in order for collective behavior to occur. Small, traditional societies, for example, are not structurally conducive to many kinds of collective behavior, but large numbers of people in a modern society are. Similarly, there could never be a panic in a theater if only two or three people were present, nor could there ever be a race riot if all the members of a society were of the same race. Even such a physical matter as inclement weather may prohibit the emergence of collective behavior. The banking system, for example, that prevailed in the United States in the 1920s was responsible in part for the economic disaster that occurred during that period. Structural conduciveness, then, denotes the entire set of objective conditions that must be present in order that a particular type of collective behavior have any chance of developing. The existence of structural conduciveness, however, does not by any means guarantee that an episode of collective behavior will take place.

STRUCTURAL STRAIN. The second factor refers to feelings of frustration, anxiety, and fear that individuals may experience because of the existence of any undesirable social condition. Structural strain often develops as a consequence of discrepancy between social values and social practices. Discrimination, poverty, war, economic depression, unemployment, injustice, and rapid social change are examples of conditions that may produce structural strain. More concrete examples include the overcrowding, poor food, and inadequate medical treatment that frequently contribute to prison riots.

GENERALIZED BELIEF. While structural conduciveness and structural strain are necessary conditions for any type of collective behavior to occur, they are not by themselves sufficient to produce collective behavior. People also must develop a particular generalized belief relative to the cause or source of strain and its alleviation. It is this generalized belief that justifies the collective behavior. Whether such beliefs are correct is irrelevant. Reform movements, for example, develop in response to the belief that norms can be changed. If people in a depressed economy believe that food or fuel supplies are about to be exhausted, chances are good that panic buying and hoarding will occur. Similarly, if members of a minority believe that the use of overt violence is the only way to reduce discrimination, riots may take place. By the same token, mass hysteria may develop in a situation where a significant number of townspeople believe that a nearby nuclear power plant is spewing forth radioactive waste.

PRECIPITATING FACTORS. The first three determinants, when present together, set the stage for a particular form of collective behavior to happen. What now is needed is an observable incident that provides a confirmation of the generalized belief. Such an event constitutes the spark that sets off or triggers a particular episode of collective behavior. A precipitating event could take the form of some-

▼

**Fear and Hopelessness.** Widespread poverty, such as that found in Haiti, is an example of those kinds of social situations that often produce the structural strain that value-added theory incorporates as one of the essential elements for many kinds of collective behavior, such as prison riots and revolutions. (© Eddie Adams/Woodfin Camp & Associates, Inc.)

one yelling out "Fire!" in a crowded theater; a White police officer hitting a Black person in a racially tense neighborhood; or the announced evacuation of a nuclear power plant. Given the existence of the first three conditions, even a trivial factor, such as a mere rumor, may serve as the spark, or objective confirmation, that sets off the episode of collective behavior.

MOBILIZATION FOR ACTION. Once the precipitating event occurs and becomes widely known, chances are good that people will join together and engage in a particular type of collective behavior. Mere physical closeness in a milling crowd sets the stage for social interaction and social cohesion. Loud complaining is typical. At this point, leaders are apt to emerge who arouse people and urge them to take some action. These self-appointed leaders

may exhort the crowd to "go to the police station" or to "get some action" after learning that a member of his minority category was subjected to "police brutality." Similarly, neighborhood leaders may urge people to leave town immediately if a nuclear power plant is evacuated. Mobilization for action, in short, consists of rallying to the cause.

OPERATION OF SOCIAL CONTROL MECHANISMS. Social control mechanisms refer to actions taken by the authorities which have the purpose of either preventing an occurrence of collective behavior, or squelching it once the activity gets under way. Hence, the outcome of any episode of collective behavior depends on the success or failure of social control. Authorities may squelch rumors that claim a member of a social minority was abused by

▼

548

the police, or that radiation is leaking from a nuclear power plant. Often in a crisis situation a "rumor control center" may be established for the purpose of enabling people to determine whether there is any truth to a particular rumor. On the other hand, social control mechanisms and responsible officials may be incapable of preventing collective behavior. Smelser notes that at times the conduct of social control agents may have the unintended effect of exacerbating the episode of collective behavior. Such a condition is most likely to occur when harsh and rigid actions are alternated with obvious weakness. Displays of harshness and inflexibility may furnish the participants with evidence of the authorities' unreasonable character. This kind of perception serves to justify the militant behavior of participants. Displays of weakness or timidity on the part of control agents may be interpreted as evidence that the participants' extreme actions are effective and may lend some degree of credence to their feelings of omnipotence.

Value-added theory is merely a scheme for understanding collective behavior in general. It does not explain why collective behavior occurs, nor does it have any predictive power. The collective behavior that develops depends on what specifically happens at each stage and how the particular situation therein is defined. Smelser contends, nonetheless, that the six basic factors together provide the "necessary and sufficient" conditions for any form of collective behavior to occur. Still under constant analysis and refinement, value-added theory is today the most widely used theoretical approach for the explanation of collective behavior.

# Psychological Dimensions of Collective Behavior

Much of the study of collective behavior today concentrates on the visible or overt behavior of crowd members. However, the subjective factors involved in the many seemingly bizarre types of collective behavior also need to be explored for a proper understanding of these social phenomena. Indeed, without such information, these kinds of social behavior often remain inexplicable.

Institutional behavior is based heavily on social factors. Theories of collective behavior that deal with only social determinants make the questionable assumption that everyone perceives, interprets, and reacts to a given social condition in the same way. This is hardly the case. The way in which a person responds to a particular social condition is determined to a great extent by his or her personality system and unique life experience. A person who has a strong, stable, and positive self-concept is not apt to "go to pieces" when he or she loses a job or faces a similar crisis. Indeed, the individual may be spurred on to find a better job. On the other hand, the experience of being unemployed might lead to feelings of inferiority, depression, and despair in a person who has a negative self-image. Smelser (1962) argues that if "we ignore this diversity of psychological meanings of the same event for different individuals, we are guilty of presenting an unwarranted psychological generalization about human reactions to economic deprivation."

Theorists of collective behavior usually stress the impulsive, emotional, and irrational actions of participants. Such an emphasis, while useful, ignores the fact that an individual's conduct is continuously being monitored by internalized controls. Some people's internalized controls may be weak and apt to lose their efficacy under certain conditions. When a person, for example, is in the midst of an acting crowd that is emotionally aroused, personal controls may prove to be ineffective. Consequently, the individual may be swept up by the intensity of the situation and behave in a disorderly fashion. On the other hand, people who have strongly internalized norms that prohibit such actions will not be likely to engage in an episode of collective behavior. An awareness of the differential strength and nature of an individual's personal controls helps us to understand why some people engage in collective behavior while others do not in the face of the same social conditions.

Personality variables also help to sensitize us to the fact that people engage in collective outbursts for different reasons. Smelser observes that most people assume that racial hostility is what motivates individuals to participate in a race riot. While such motivation may exist for some, others become involved in the episode only after the police or other authorities have arrived. This suggests that their hostility is directed more toward the police (who may symbolize authority) than toward people of another race. Similarly, others may participate in the riot because of the opportunity it gives them to loot. Thus, the motivations of the participants are likely to differ and cannot be inferred by the simple observation of the general features of the episode of collective behavior.

Personality variables also help to explain the different types of participation that individuals manifest during episodes of collective behavior. Contrary to some conventional notions of collective behavior, all participants do not behave in the same manner. As Smelser (1962) observes, "Some participants become involved as leaders; others as activist followers; others as passive followers; others as sympathizers who do not actually engage in any overt behavior; and so on." People having certain types of personality systems may be predisposed to participate in one way; those having other types of personalities will be inclined to participate in another way. An individual who is typically timid, reserved, and shy is not likely to take on the role of leader during an episode of collective behavior. A person will be most apt to participate in ways that are congruent with his or her personality characteristics. We shall have more to say about personality factors in collective behavior in our discussion of social movements in the section that follows.

# Social Movements ▼

Another type of collective behavior is represented by social movements. So different are social movements, however, that they deserve particular treatment. Unlike the forms of collective behavior that we have discussed already, social movements represent a relatively more structured, more purposive, and more enduring type of social phenomenon. More specifically, social movements differ from crowds and other elementary types of collective behavior, such as a protest crowd. Social movements, in certain respects, share features of both collective and organized (unstructured and normative) social phenomena. A number of more specific characteristics, however, distinguish the social movement as a distinctive type of collective behavior.

**549**

## NATURE OF SOCIAL MOVEMENTS

A **social movement** is a relatively sustained or long-lasting collective effort by widely dispersed and large numbers of people either to achieve or to prevent social change. More specifically, social movements attempt to alter the existing social order, either by correcting a situation considered problematic or undesirable, or by establishing a new way of life. Fundamentally, in either case, social movements are directed at changing the way people think and behave, at preserving the values and norms within society, or establishing new ones. Usually these activities are socially and geographically widespread, rather than confined to a relatively local situation, as is the case with many other types of collective behavior.

Unlike other forms of collective behavior, social movements are sustained by an identifiable ideology (shared values and goals), long-term objectives, a considerable degree of social organization, a continuity of action (long-lasting),

▼

and relatively strong cohesion. Moreover, they are comparatively quite slow in developing, and hence are not spontaneous responses to particular situations. Correspondingly, they have longer life spans, often stretching over decades, than do the many other types of collective behavior. There is an indefinite and shifting membership in social movements.

**550**

Like other forms of collective behavior, social movements arise out of conditions of societal unrest and social strain or dissatisfaction with current social situations. Many nations, including our own, emerged as the successful outcome of a social movement. Since the colonial era, the United States has witnessed hundreds of social movements for a variety of causes (see Ash, 1972; Gamson, 1975). Recent examples of social movements, particularly those that have brought about profound and lasting changes in the American society, include the civil rights movement and the women's liberation movement. Contemporary movements include those that focus on the causes of antinuclear energy and the enactment of legislation regarding abortion (see Box 12-3). Social movements often have one or more complex organizations associated with them. The Congress of Racial Equality (C.O.R.E.) and the National Organization of Women (N.O.W.) are representative examples of organizations that have been associated respectively with the civil rights movement and the women's liberation movement.

Social movements represent a phenomenon that is peculiar to modern society, in which they perform a number of important functions. First of all, social movements provide a means for active participation in society, and thereby generate a dynamism and vitality that in many ways are wholesome and beneficial for both society and the individuals who participate in them. Personal involvement in the dynamics of society can serve as a counterbalance to the alienating forces of mass society. Social movements, more than many other forms of collective behavior, are powerful and enduring

vehicles for social change. Out of social movements come new social orders and many of the social institutions of the future. New social movements are continually in the process of development.

## EMERGENCE OF SOCIAL MOVEMENTS

Certain kinds of social conditions must be present for social movements to emerge. These conditions focus on the dynamics of personal insecurity or discontent and their societal sources. The existence of these conditions, however, does not automatically ensure that a social movement will occur. Rather, they simply increase its probability. Equally important are social organization and the necessary resources. The following are the major conditions that encourage the formation of social movements.

SENSE OF DISCONTENT.   If everyone in a society were happy and satisfied with the existing social order, there would be no reason for social movements to emerge. Thus, one necessary, but insufficient, condition for the emergence of a social movement is that a significant number of people have a sense of discontent about the way things are. Feelings of dissatisfaction and constraint may be engendered by the existence of such problems as poverty, discrimination, and unemployment, or from a general feeling that the society is basically unjust or corrupt. More fundamentally, and perhaps with much less general awareness, social discontent and frustration are likely to develop when individuals experience alienation or estrangement from society.

COMMUNICATION OF DISCONTENT. For a social movement to emerge, it is important that those experiencing social discontent communicate this attitude to others who also feel that way. This communication of discontent helps to produce a collective sense of identity among the people. Individuals then realize that they are not the only ones being affected by the problem. They may begin to discuss among themselves the possible causes and solutions to the problem. Such a process can constitute the beginning of a social movement.

## SOCIAL ATTRIBUTION OF DISCONTENT.

People are not likely to join a social movement if they believe that their sense of strain and frustration is due to their own personal defects or inadequacy. However, when people feel that their problems stem from societal conditions, then the probability is high that people will engage in a collective form of action. There needs to be a social attribution of discontent. People must perceive their frustration and suffering as being produced by a particular set of social arrangements in order to be motivated to form a social movement. If Blacks, for instance, had felt that their low status and income were due to personal inadequacies, rather than a consequence of widespread and systematic discrimination, it is unlikely that the civil rights movement would have emerged.

## PROBABILITY OF RESOLUTION OF DISCONTENT.

Those who are affected by undesirable social conditions must have some hope that their collective efforts can relieve the problem. Otherwise, there would be no point in organizing or participating in a social movement. There must be a belief in a different, and improved, state of affairs if a social movement is to emerge.

Social movements, especially in their initial stages, are quite fluid and subject to dissolution. Moreover, social movements do not usually enjoy much public support at the onset of their development. This is particularly true of those movements that advocate changes which may be perceived as threatening to the status quo. The labor movement in America was viewed initially as a threat to the capitalistic system by many corporate officials. Similarly, the current women's liberation movement has been seen in many quarters as constituting a jeopardy to the traditional nuclear family.

## RESOURCE MOBILIZATION.

One of the latest attempts to understand the emergence of social movements focuses on organizational structure and resource mobilization. Proponents of this view (Jenkins, 1983; McCarthy & Zald, 1977) maintain that social movements constitute rational and purposive activity which, much like any significant activity of political organizations or other interest groups, is based on leadership, membership support, financial assets, professional talent, access to media, appropriate equipment, physical quarters, and other kinds of resources. In this perspective, deprivation or discontent usually is taken to be a given or only a secondary component. Collective action, however, successfully depends on the mobilization of discontent through the effective deployment of resources. Advocates of the resource mobilization perspective argue that much discontent is never expressed in a social movement because of a lack of the proper resources.

# IDEOLOGY AND SOCIAL MOVEMENTS

The ideology of a social movement consists of its doctrines, which state the nature, causes, and solutions to a social problem. Herein are formulated the justification for the programs and practices that a social movement undertakes. It is characteristic of ideologies that they distort or simplify the issues and problems involved in order to make the social movement more accessible and attractive to others.

Ideology performs several crucial functions in the dynamics of a social movement. First, it serves to legitimate the existence of the social

▼

551

▼

movement. It does this by delineating a particular problem and by stating which societal conditions are responsible for it. Depending on the specific issue and the particular leaders, the analysis of a problem can be very abstract and philosophical or quite concrete and down-to-earth. Some social movements, for example, may adopt a Marxist framework for analyzing and proposing solutions to a problem. Others may not make use of any particular social or political philosophy.

Second, an ideology specifies what must be changed for the problem to be eliminated. Specific, focused proposals may be offered, or the perceived solutions may be somewhat general and vague. One popular criticism made of many social movements is that they do not propose solutions or recommendations, but merely criticize "the establishment" or the existing social order. The ideology of such movements may not be as revolutionary or reformistic as one is given to believe.

Third, ideology functions to justify the actions of social movements. Hence, in certain cases, ideology may be used to legitimate the use of violence or other socially unacceptable methods. Finally, an ideology furnishes its movement with a distinct identity. Not only does it distinguish members from nonmembers, but it also serves to reinforce feelings of cohesiveness and morale within the movement. This latter contribution is indispensable to the success of any social movement.

## TYPES OF SOCIAL MOVEMENTS

There are many ways in which social movements can be classified. Basically, they are categorized according to their specific objectives or their principal tactics. Many utilize peaceful means and work through the existing social system; others espouse violence and have highly diffuse goals. One of the more popular schemes of classification employed by sociologists, how-

552

ever, focuses on the relationship of social movements to the existing social order. We can speak in this regard of four basic types of social movement: reform, revolutionary, reactionary, and expressive.

REFORM MOVEMENTS. Reform movements are concerned with changing specific features of society. This type of movement accepts the existing social order and wishes to preserve it. It seeks only to correct the particular injustice or problematic situation by espousing specific changes in certain institutions or prevailing policies. Often such objectives consist simply of bringing social practices in line with social ideas. At other times, an emphasis on social progress may require more extensive or profound modifications of society.

Examples of reform movements are the environmentalist, gay rights, and feminist movements. The concerns of these movements are relatively limited in scope. They aim to correct abuses or injustices that their followers believe exist in society. Reform movements work within the system rather than against the system. Such movements are quite common in democratic society, quite rare in societies in which social dissent is repressed.

REVOLUTIONARY MOVEMENTS. Unlike reform movements which advocate specific and limited modifications and which work within the system, revolutionary movements espouse widespread and radical changes in societal values, institutions, and practices. The goal of the revolutionary movement is the fundamental reconstruction of the entire society—replacing the existing social order with a totally new one. Proponents of such movements believe that the prevailing societal institutions and organizations constitute the cause of all the ills society is experiencing.

Revolutionary movements are most likely to occur in societies in which reform movements are prohibited. Under such conditions, a rev-

## BOX 12-3. Social Movements: The Abortion Question

▼

An ongoing, and rather long-standing, social movement in our society is that involving the issue of abortion. This movement is somewhat unique and complex because there are really two major movements associated with the abortion issue. One, usually known as Freedom of Choice, seeks to establish a national policy that guarantees abortion on demand for any woman. The other, known as Right to Life, has an antithetical objective in seeking to repeal laws that permit abortion and to effect a constitutional amendment that would ban the practice in nearly every respect.

553

Basic to both sides of the abortion question is a judgment about the human status of the fetus. Right to Life exponents argue that a human fetus is a human being, and that an abortion is tantamount to murder. Proponents of Freedom of Choice usually maintain that a human fetus is only a potential human being—and not even that, in cases where the fetus may be severely and permanently defective. Hence, under these circumstances, abortion is viewed merely as a surgical procedure without any inherently ethical or moral implications.

Except under very limited circumstances—primarily when the health of the mother or the unborn child was endangered—abortion was illegal in the United States, although rather commonly practiced, until 1973. In that year, the Supreme Court affirmed, in *Roe vs. Wade,* that abortion is a legal right of any woman, available on demand, so long as it is performed during the first trimester of the pregnancy. In the second trimester, this right is subject to regulation by each state. Abortions on demand are illegal in the third trimester.

Since this decision, the Pro-Choice and Pro-Life forces have assumed a strongly militant stance. Any resolution of the abortion question, however, promises to be most difficult, since a host of complex issues—medical, ethical, and legal—are involved. Among the latter are such considerations as whether abortion is a purely personal matter, or one involving other people; whether a woman has the right to control her own body, as well as that of another being; and whether the father also has a claim to the fetus.

The American population is evenly divided on the abortion issue. While the large majority of Americans support abortion in cases of rape, incest, or a threat to the mother's health, only about one-half of the people support abortion on demand. The question in any event, is likely to remain controversial for a long time to come. One reason is the existence of another, highly similar, "life" issue—that of euthanasia or "mercy killing." Many people perceive these practices as presenting identical questions on the opposite ends of the life cycle. Such a situation is likely to precipitate another set of social movements. ▲

olutionary movement is the only alternative for those desiring any type of social change. Members of revolutionary movements, moreover, do not hesitate to utilize any means at their disposal in order to further their cause. Many re-

volutionaries believe that the end justifies the means. Consequently, the use of violence often is typical of revolutionary movements.

Numerous nations in existence today originated through revolutionary movements.

▼ Among them in particular are France, the United States, and the Soviet Union. A more contemporary example of such a movement is the Chinese Communist revolution that led to the establishment of the People's Republic of China in 1949. Other revolutionary movements of major concern during the past half-century include the Cuban revolution (the 26th of July movement) of the late 1950s in which the regime of Fulgencio Battista was overthrown by Fidel Castro and his followers; the Iranian revolution under the leadership of the Ayatollah Khomeini, which deposed the Shah in 1979; and the Nicaraguan revolution in 1980, during which the Sandinista National Liberation Front overthrew the dictatorship of Anastasio Somoza.

**554**

REACTIONARY MOVEMENTS. The goal of a reactionary movement is to eradicate certain changes that already have occurred or to prevent particular changes from taking place. Hence, it often assumes the role of a counter-movement. This type of movement is most likely to emerge during periods of radical social change. During such times, many people experience feelings of ambiguity, anxiety, and uncertainty. As a consequence, they seek to maintain the status quo or to return to the way things were.

Nearly every significant social change generates a reactionary movement. The civil rights movement, for example, has produced a number of backlash movements among people whose goals are to abolish or to retard integration, fair employment, and other types of social policies achieved by the civil rights movement. One specific example in this regard is the recent rebirth of the Ku Klux Klan and other similarly oriented organizations. Other examples of reactionary movements include the var-

**Counter-Movements.** The antinuclear forces represent a reactionary type of social movement, which seeks either to prevent social change or to eradicate change that already has occurred. (© Joel Gordon 1982)

ious campaigns against the Equal Rights Amendment advocated by the feminist movement; the Right-to-Life movement seeking the repeal of legalized abortion; the Moral Majority which advocates a return to fundamental principles of Christian religion; and, in more recent years, the anti-nuclear movement.

EXPRESSIVE MOVEMENTS.  Expressive movements have their focus on the individual rather than on society. Unlike reform, revolutionary, and reactionary movements, which attempt to promote or to resist sociocultural change, and which typically are political in nature, expressive movements are oriented toward psychological change. They seek to bring about a sense of emotional satisfaction and well-being in people through the development of a new identity or lifestyle.

People join expressive movements in many cases in the hope of finding an effective way to cope with feelings of frustration caused by oppressive social conditions. Rather than attempting to change society, or any particular aspect of it, these individuals seek to change their relationship or reaction to society by adopting a new philosophy of life or a revised system of beliefs and values. Recent examples of expressive movements in the United States include the counterculture movements of the 1960s, the Pentecostal and Jesus movements of the 1970s, and the conscious-raising efforts promoted in conjunction with the gay liberation movement and the women's liberation movement.

Demarcations between the different kinds of social movements are never absolute. Most social movements incorporate elements of each of the four types we have discussed. These distinctions, nonetheless, facilitate the analysis and the explanation of a complex phenomenon that is becoming evermore common in modern society. Social movements of all kinds no doubt will increase as democratization and mass communication spread throughout the world in the years ahead.

# LIFE CYCLES OF SOCIAL MOVEMENTS ▼

Nearly all social movements, regardless of their type, exhibit similar dynamics and patterns in terms of their longitudinal development. Sociologists have sought to identify typical stages in the life cycle of social movements. Ryan (1969) has identified four stages, although not all social movements actually go through an entire cycle. This formulation is simply an ideal pattern that helps to show how many of the dynamics and processes of social movements are related to one another over the course of time.

**555**

INCIPIENT STAGE.  In the life cycle of a social movement, there must be initially a type of structured strain, or unsatisfactory social condition, experienced by a large number of people. A certain amount of discontent, excitement, and unrest needs to center on a specific issue, such as discrimination or unemployment. Such a situation of malaise, advanced alienation, mass uneasiness, and restlessness is typically characterized by confusion and a readiness for action.

POPULAR STAGE.  The next stage, the popular stage in the cycle, develops as large numbers of people begin to recognize that their feelings are shared by others. Identification with the movement increases rapidly as discontent becomes popularized. Leaders, or agitators, emerge at this stage and provide rallying points by dramatizing the situation and attracting followers. Principal activities here involve the clarification of issues and goals, along with the maintenance of the diverse activities of the membership focused on the goals of the movement.

ORGANIZATIONAL STAGE.  During the organizational stage there is a further clarification of goals and mobilization for action.

▼ Formal groups and complex organizations become established. It is during this third stage that the more typically unconventional kinds of collective behavior give way to structured behavior. Clearly defined leadership roles emerge, formal leaders are identified, task assignments are developed, specific policies and programs for action are prepared, definite goals are established, and strategies for their achievement are implemented. Factions may develop in this phase, depending on the size of the movement, based on differences of opinion about the issues and the methods proposed for their resolution. Such developments could terminate the movement at this point.

**556**

INSTITUTIONAL STAGE.    The final stage, the institutional stage, develops when a successful movement is integrated into the broader social structure of society. Once this situation is achieved, the social movement is no longer a phenomenon of collective behavior. Its organization becomes part of the permanent social organization and the institutional structure of society. Bureaucratic professionals replace volunteers. And, like most complex and bureaucratic organizations, there is a tendency for expansion and self-perpetuation. Most social movements never reach this final stage. Among those that have done so are the Protestant Reformation and the American labor movement. The League of Women Voters, despite a somewhat different emphasis today, is a remnant of the women's suffrage movement of the mid-1800s.

# LEADERSHIP OF SOCIAL MOVEMENTS

The internal differentiation of social movements into leaders and followers is both the most visible and the most important role specialization occurring within a movement. Indeed, many times a movement is associated with the name of a leader who is seen as embodying the ideology of the movement. Killian (1964) notes that most social movements usually have several leaders arranged in a hierarchy, who direct the movement: "Even the most dynamic, dedicated single 'messiah' must first gather around him a small group of devoted lieutenants to serve as a nucleus around which the larger, more dispersed body of followers may cluster." All leaders seek to establish rapport and gain trust with their followers. Not all, however, operate in the same way or achieve the same degree of success. Let us discuss briefly the functions and types of leaders.

FUNCTIONS OF LEADERS.    Leaders of social movements perform several crucial functions. It is the leader who articulates, both to the general public and to other members, the ideology of a movement. In doing so, the leader hopes to attract new members to the movement and to sustain the enthusiasm of current ones. The leader also helps to arbitrate conflicts that may emerge among members of the movement. Many times there is agreement among members on the causes and solutions to the problem, but there may be disagreement in regard to the methods to be used to achieve the goals of the movement. Some members of social movements demand the use of violent methods; others want to adopt only lawful and peaceful tactics. Unless the leader can reconcile conflicts among factions, the movement may become splintered. One of the factions may leave the movement and form a new movement. Such a competitive situation is usually problematic in terms of the success or failure of the common goal.

TYPES OF LEADERS.    Leaders of social movements can be classified into three major types: charismatic, administrative, and intellectual. These differ both in task and in style.

The **charismatic leader** is one who holds power primarily because of personal qualities and, usually, the ability to inspire a certain degree of hero worship. Killian (1964) describes such a leader in the following way.

> He tends to be bold, even impulsive, given to the dramatic gesture and the stirring appeal to emotions. He is both prophet and agitator. He states the movement's values in absolute terms often through slogans. He exudes confidence and may propose novel, dramatic tactics which promise success for the movement against all odds. . . . This type of leader may appear impractical, idealistic and even fanatical to the outsider. But he quickly assumes heroic proportions in the eyes of people already committed, and to many who are dissatisfied with the status quo but not yet committed to a specific program of change.

The charismatic leader is especially likely to prevail during the initial stages of a social movement. Examples of charismatic leaders who have been associated with social movements during this century include Adolph Hitler, Martin Luther King, Jr., and the Ayatollah Khomeini.

The **administrative leader** is most concerned with the day-to-day operation of a social movement. He or she is oriented to practical issues that require immediate solutions. Problems such as where to acquire office equipment, which lecture hall to rent, and which members will hand out leaflets at the next rally, are dealt with by the administrative leader. Leaders of this type are concerned also with uniting warring factions and weighing the costs and benefits of particular tactics.

The **intellectual leader** is most interested in developing and elaborating the ideology of the movement. He or she functions best when legitimating the existence of a movement and its tactics. Many intellectual leaders have the task of responding to criticisms of their movements. This type of leader may be well-schooled in a particular philosophical respect. Karl Marx and Vladimir Lenin exemplified the intellectual leader in the cause of socialism.

Most leaders of social movements possess some of the qualities associated with these three different types. It is quite unusual, however, for one leader to be highly charismatic, a superb administrator, and a great theoretician. The most typical situation is for a leader to excel in only one of the three areas. Obviously, then, the vast majority of social movements—especially those that achieve any significant measure of success—have a number of leaders of various kinds.

**557**

## SUCCESS OR FAILURE IN SOCIAL MOVEMENTS

What are the factors that contribute to the success or failure of a social movement? Why are some social movements able to recruit many members and gain public support while others are not?

Public perception of a social movement is one factor that helps to determine whether it will be successful. If the U.S. public views a social movement as a threat to its interest, inspired and led by "foreigners" who hold "un-American" ideas, chances are slight that the movement will flourish. On the other hand, if leaders can convince the public that a social movement represents a more effective effort to implement basic values into public practices, it stands a good chance of winning public support. The public also must approve of the methods of a social movement. Movements that advocate and use violence are less likely to gain public support than those that use nonviolent tactics. Moreover, reform-oriented movements are more likely to obtain public approval than revolutionary movements.

Once a social movement has gained public support and is successful in attracting new members, how are political officials likely to respond? In many cases, the government may adopt and make into law some of the very policies that the movement advocates. This is especially likely to occur if, again, the movement

▼

**558**

is reform-oriented. Many of the programs advocated by the Democratic party, such as social security, minimum wage laws, fair employment practices, and child labor laws, were originally proposed by leftist-oriented social movements. Legislation, thus, is a very effective way to diffuse a social movement. If government implements many of the proposed reforms of a particular movement, what reason would the movement have to justify its continued existence? In a certain sense, then, we can say that a movement has been successful when government adopts many of its programs. On the other hand, government is not apt to adopt the more "radical" proposals of a movement. As a result, the social movement will be unsuccessful in bringing about fundamental changes in the structure of the society. Governments, for example, often implement many reforms that are advocated by the Socialist party, but do not do away with the private enterprise economic system.

If a government is very much opposed to the policies espoused by a social movement, it may attempt to discredit it in the eyes of the public. The American government, for instance, claimed that the anti-Vietnam War movement in the 1960s was led, inspired, and supported by Communists. The government may also claim that much harm would result if the demands of a social movement were to be put into practice. Right now, for example, we are being told by both the government and the utility companies that power failures would occur and that the cost of electricity would increase enormously if all the nuclear power plants in the country were to be shut down. Should the government or other organizations be successful in discrediting social movements that incorporate an antinuclear campaign, the movement is not likely to gain public support.

Whether a social movement achieves its goals is dependent also on several internal variables. Perhaps the greatest internal danger to a movement is the emergence of factions. Disagreement over policies and tactics may result in a bitter struggle for leadership. Such conflicts are a drain on the resources of a movement and they dilute its effectiveness. If the struggle cannot be resolved, the movement may splinter leaving both the old and the new movements in a weakened position. Such a situation occurred when one faction of the Students for a Democratic Society, the Weathermen, formed their own movement.

Even if a social movement does not become fragmented, it may still lose some of its effectiveness with the passage of time. There is a tendency for movements to become formalized as they mature. New leaders tend to be less charismatic than those who initiated the movement. Instead, they are more administrative and task-oriented, and invariably have less contact with the lower echelon members. Accordingly, the enthusiasm and idealism that characterized a movement during its early stages usually diminishes as the movement becomes more and more bureaucratized.

# Personality and Social Movements

What kinds of people participate in social movements? In order to survive and to be effective, a social movement must attract and retain members who are willing to make personal sacrifices for the cause. Moreover, the larger the membership of a social movement, the more likely are the chances of its success. For their part, members must be willing to dedicate their time, energy, and resources to the movement. They must be ready to take criticism and abuse from friends and associates who may not sympathize with their cause. Indeed, even the severance of ties with family and friends who may be much opposed to one's involvement with a particular social movement is often the price one has to pay for participation in a social movement. Why would anyone be willing to make these and similar sacrifices?

It is a rather popular assumption that people who become involved in social movements are somewhat "abnormal" compared with the majority of people in society. Such a view maintains that the followers of social movements are either motivated by deviant tendencies or experience a variety of psychological problems. That such may indeed be the case for some people does not rule out the position that "normal" people may rationally come to the conclusion that something may be wrong with society, and not with the people who wish to change it.

Notwithstanding these prefatory comments, the assumption that certain kinds of people are susceptible to the appeal of social movements cannot be denied. Such a view, however, must not be a simplistic one. Social movements, like any other form of social behavior, constitute highly complex phenomena. Such is particularly the case given merely the different types and variety of social movements. What needs to be stressed, therefore, is that different kinds of people may participate in social movements for a variety of reasons or motivations, including the gratification of psychological needs.

## PERSONALITY NEEDS AND SOCIAL MOVEMENTS

**559**

Psychological attraction to a social movement would seem to depend not only on its particular nature and specific goals, but also on its particular dynamics at a given stage. What may stimulate recruitment to social movements at

КУРСОМ ОКТЯБРЯ

**Personalities in Action.** Participants and nonparticipants in social movements can be distinguished by distinctive types of personality. Similar differences obtain in terms of the modes of social protest, such as violence or nonviolence, and the specific techniques that people choose to employ in these efforts. (B. Bisson, T. Orban/ SYGMA)

▼

a certain stage with a given set of dynamics, such as protests and demonstrations, may lose its attractiveness at another stage, such as that of institutionalization. Bureaucracy and formal organization, as we saw in Chapter 8, may present in their turn a totally different kind of psychological attraction to the same individuals or to even quite different people.

Notwithstanding these cautions, the literature in social science offers ample speculation on the personal motives of people for joining social movements. Some argue that in becoming members of a social movement, people hope to find meaning and purpose for their lives. These individuals, it is said, suffer from "psychic deprivation" or a general malaise of meaninglessness (Glock, 1968). Eric Hoffer (1951:39), for example, states that "A rising mass movement attracts and holds a following not by its doctrine and promises but by the refuge it offers from anxieties, barrenness and meaninglessness of an individual's existence." Furthermore, Hoffer claims that for many people the purpose and ideology of a movement are not instrumental factors in convincing them to join. As he says, "When people are ripe for a mass movement they are usually ripe for any effective movement, and not solely for one with a particular doctrine or program." Those who agree with Hoffer's position deny that people join social movements in order to rectify certain wrongs they believe exist. Rather, their reasons for joining are seen as the desire to satisfy deep-seated personality needs. Among these psychological motivations in particular is thought to be the desire to avoid the stresses of alienation which themselves emanate from the social order.

Erich Fromm (1941) claimed that some people are attracted to social movements because they need an authoritarian figure or structure to tell them what to value, what to believe, and what to think. Such people, according to Fromm, cannot tolerate freedom or intellectual ambiguity. They want to be told what is right or wrong, good or bad, desirable or undesirable.

Their fundamental motivation, then, is to escape from social and psychological situations that are stress-producing or anxiety-producing and behaviorally paralytic. Fromm developed this thesis in his attempt to account for the rise and appeal of Nazism in the 1930s and the 1940s. It has served as a theoretical basis for the psychological syndrome of authoritarianism and represents some of the fundamental dynamics of the authoritarian personality (see Chapters 5 and 11).

Erik Erikson (1968) has developed the view that the ideology of a social movement may provide certain people with a personal identity. This notion helps to explain why the youth in a society are especially vulnerable to the appeals made by social movements. Many young people have not formed a stable identity or sense of self. They are searching for a worldview or philosophy that will give meaning to their lives. Erikson states that "Ideologies offer the members of this age-group overly simplified and yet determined answers to exactly those vague inner states and those urgent positions which arise in consequence of identity conflict."

Other, more recent, studies (Davies, 1962; Gurr, 1970) have developed the argument that the emergence of many social movements, especially revolutionary movements, is rooted in the dynamics of relative deprivation* which is a sense or feeling of having less than what one could have or might have in comparison to others. Lichter and Rothman (1982), reporting on the analyses of projective tests administered to large samples of American university students during the early 1970s, concluded that radicals were significantly distinguished by power motivations, narcissism, a self-assertive psychosocial orientation, and a lack of affiliative motivation. Individuals characterized by this syndrome also revealed perceptions of protests and militancy as sources of power.

* See definition in Chapter 9.

560

That people may be attracted to and join social movements because doing so will satisfy their personality needs is difficult to deny. Many others, however, become members out of a sincere desire to help change social situations and to ameliorate their own personal circumstances. These people simply share the perceptions and goals of the movement in question. Participation in a social movement, then, may be seen as a rational response to undesirable conditions. Kenniston (1968) observes in this regard that many students who became involved in the political movements of the latter 1960s and early 1970s were motivated to do so because they saw a wide gap between American ideals and the social conditions actually existent at that time. Many who did not want to be drafted became members of the anti-Vietnam War movements of the period. Not all victims of social oppression or social stress, however, resort to the formation of social movements, or even participate in them. Some people just resign themselves, whatever the social and personal consequences may be. An obvious question, then, is whether those who become active or remain passive can be distinguished in terms of personality.

## PERSONALITY TYPES AND SOCIAL MOVEMENTS

Several recent studies have reported distinctive personality profiles among participants in a diverse set of social movements (for example, Candee, 1974; Edwards, 1970; Haan, 1968). These many studies substantiate the thesis that certain personality characteristics have a high degree of incidence among individuals who find themselves attracted to various kinds of social movements, and, moreover, that it is these personality characteristics that cause the attraction. Markle and his associates (1978), for example, in a study on the importance of attitudinal orientation that predisposes individuals to join different kinds of movements, suggest that the precise content of the protest (or social movement) to which individuals are attracted is less critical than the protest behavior itself. The hypothesis advanced here is that the same or similar populations of individuals, in terms of personality profiles, would be attracted to the same types of social movement, regardless of their specific objectives.

DiRenzo (1978), in a study of participants in student movements in Italy, has shown that individuals can be distinguished on the basis of personality structure in terms of their participation in movements of social reform, and the degree thereof. His study of a sample of 1,000 students drawn at the University of Rome in May 1969—at the height of the worldwide student protest of that decade—found that the more students participated in social movements (the greater the degree of their involvement), the more they were characterized by modal patterns of the democratic or antiauthoritarian personality. Students distinguished by dogmatic personality structures tended not to participate in social movements, or to do so only to minimal degrees (see Table 12-2). Even more interesting, perhaps, is the finding that significant differences in personality structure were found among individuals utilizing or advocating different modes of social protest and social reform.

DiRenzo found that nondogmatic personalities were likely to utilize or advocate violence and other radical forms of social protest and social reform. Dogmatic personalities, on the other hand, were more likely to advocate and to use less extreme and nonviolent modes of social protest, such as passive boycotts and democratic negotiations. These findings counter the popular belief that all radicals and revolutionaries have a fascistic mentality and character.

The role of personality in social movements can be explained in two basic dimensions: (1) personality as an independent variable in the

▼

561

▼ TABLE 12-2. Personality Structure and Participation in Specific Techniques of Social Protest

| Form of Protest** | Non-Dogmatic | | Dogmatic | | Total |
|---|---|---|---|---|---|
| | n | % | n | % | n |
| University Demonstrations* | | | | | |
| Minimal participation | 82 | 75 | 156 | 89 | 238 |
| Maximal participation | 27 | 25 | 21 | 11 | 48 |
| Totals | 109 | (39) | 177 | (61) | 286 |
| Occupation of University Buildings† | | | | | |
| Minimal participation | 42 | 61 | 156 | 89 | 198 |
| Maximal participation | 26 | 39 | 21 | 11 | 47 |
| Totals | 68 | (28) | 177 | (72) | 245 |

**562**

* $\chi^2 = 8.03$; $df = 1$; $p < 0.01$. † $\chi^2 = 22.03$; $df = 1$; $p < 0.001$.

** Subjects self-rated the degree of their participation on a five-point Likert-type scale, polarized from "very low" to "very high." These data represent a contrast of only the polar extremes.

Source: Gordon J. DiRenzo, "Personality Typologies and Modes of Social Change," *Social Behavior and Personality,* 1978, 6: 11–16.

dynamics of social movements, and (2) the effects that social movements have on the personalities of their participants as dependent variables. Often it is the latter situation that constitutes the very objective of social movements. Hence, such considerations are important for society when they have extensive consequences, as many social movements do. Our concern here, however, is more sociological than psychological. We have focused primarily on the ways in which personality, as an independent variable, may contribute to the origin and dynamics of social movements.

## Summary

The term *collective behavior* is used to refer to various forms of social behavior that develop rather spontaneously in unstructured situations on the part of a large number of people, and which as such are not regulated by conventional norms. Collective behavior as a specific category of social activity is ideally or typically distinguished further by the following set of distinctive features:

1. Spontaneity and lack of planning.
2. Lack of structure and governance by institutional norms or expectations.
3. Transitory and short-lived behavior.
4. Enactment by people who, at least initially, are strangers to each other.
5. Mutual stimulation among its participants.
6. Parallel or common (nonreciprocal) rather than interactional behavior.

Crowds, mobs, panics, riots, fads, reactions to disasters, mass hysteria, rumor, public opinion, and certain types of social movements all share these features to varying degrees.

Sociologists and psychologists have developed several theories to account specifically for the socially unconventional and seemingly elusive phenomena that constitute the field of collective behavior. Many of these theories focus on the dynamics by which a crowd tends to release the latent personal tendencies of its members. Contagion theory postulates that three factors transform an aggregate into a crowd: anonymity, suggestibility, and emotional contagion. De-individuation theory refers to the process whereby an individual loses his or her sense of personal identity as a result of being part of a crowd or group, and thereby engages in nonconventional or deviant behavior. Convergence theory emphasizes the shared characteristics—social, cultural, or psychological—of people who chance to come together in crowd formations and experience a "consciousness of kind" or like-mindedness. Unlike other theories that stress the nonrational nature of crowds, emergent norm theory argues that many aspects of crowd behavior are under normative control and that new norms emerge as people interact in such situations. The game theory of collective behavior offers a highly rational explanation: each person in a crowd is motivated to maximize rewards and to minimize costs. Before engaging in a certain behavior, people are likely to calculate whether their actions are likely to result in greater rewards or costs for themselves.

A comprehensive theory that can be used to account for a wide variety of collective behavior is value-added theory. This formulation attempts to synthesize many of the elements of other theories already discussed. A particularly worthy aspect of the theory is that it integrates the social and psychological dimensions of social behavior. The value-added model identifies six essential elements that constitute a sequential set of preconditions for collective behavior: structural conduciveness, structural strain, generalized belief, precipitating factors, mobilization for action, and operation of social control mechanisms.

Another type of collective behavior is represented by social movements. A social movement is a relatively sustained or long-lasting collective effort by widely dispersed and large numbers of people, either to achieve or to prevent change. Social movements are directed at changing the way people think and behave, at preserving the values and norms of a society, or at establishing new ones. Certain kinds of conditions must be present for a social movement to emerge. The following are the conditions that provide fertile soil for the formation of a social movement: sense of discontent, communication of discontent, social attribution of discontent, probability of resolution of discontent, and resource mobilization.

Social movements are categorized according to their specific objectives or the principal tactics that are employed. Sociologists speak in this regard of four basic types: reform, revolutionary, reactionary, and expressive movements. Nearly all social movements, regardless of their type, exhibit similar dynamics and patterns in terms of their longitudinal development. Typical in the life cycle of social movements are the following four stages: incipient, popular, organizational, and institutional. Leaders of movements can be classified into three major types: charismatic, administrative, and intellectual.

The role of personality in social movements can be explained in two basic dimensions: (1) as an independent variable in the emergence and dynamics of social movements, and (2) as a dependent variable in terms of the effects that social movements have on the personality of their participants.

**563**

# Key Concepts

collective behavior
convergence theory
craze
crowd
de-individuation
emergent norm theory
emotional contagion
fad

▼

fashion
game theory
mass behavior
mass hysteria
mob
panic
propaganda
public

public opinion
riot
rumor
self-fulfilling prophecy
social aggregate
social category
social movement
value-added theory

# 13

## Deviant Behavior and Social Control

Our discussions throughout most of this text have centered on the organization of society and the structured or normative behavior that takes place in society. In the last chapter, our analysis of collective behavior dealt with behavior that, for the most part, is unstructured. Each of those many kinds of behavior, nonetheless, falls in the category of socially acceptable, if not always necessarily socially approved, behavior. In this chapter, however, our deliberations focus on behavior that is considered—at least by some elements of society, usually the majority—to be undesirable. We speak of deviant behavior—behavior that, in one way or another, violates socially established norms of expected or acceptable conduct.

Why do people violate social norms? What consequences does deviant behavior have for society? What are the functions and dysfunctions of deviant behavior? Is it possible to distinguish deviants from nondeviants on the basis of social and personality profiles? These are the principal questions that our discussion will address. Additionally, we shall explore in this chapter the topic of social control—the means and processes by which society responds to deviant behavior and attempts to prevent its occurrence. ▲

## Outline

▶ Society is predicated on social order. That human behavior in society is not only orderly but predictable is the basis of social organization. Social order, nonetheless, is to a great extent an ideal. While most people do respect the norms of society and those of its many organizations and groups, some people—perhaps even all people at one time or another—break the rules. Whatever the reasons or circumstances, deviant behavior, or the violation of social norms, is as much a part of social life as are the ideal patterns that provide its foundations. Understanding social deviance, therefore, is as important as understanding social organization.

# What Is Deviant Behavior?

Deviant behavior, to the minds of most people, no doubt suggests a world of criminals, weirdos, troublemakers, and other people engaged in illegal, immoral, or unethical behavior. Such a view, however, is all too simplistic. That criminal and delinquent behavior are deviant is indisputable. Considerable disagreement, however, often exists about many other forms of behavior, such as homosexuality, transvestism, mental illness, drug addiction, and bohemian lifestyles—just to mention a few of the more controversial varieties. Social deviance, like other forms of social behavior, is nevertheless a very complex phenomenon. Its proper understanding requires an exploration of the various conceptions and misconceptions about it.

## CONCEPTIONS OF SOCIAL DEVIANCE

Technically speaking, any behavior that violates a norm or standard, be it social or otherwise, is deviant. More commonly in sociological usage, however, deviance refers primarily, if not exclusively, to behavior that violates only social norms—the required or expected patterns of behavior. It should be helpful for our purposes here in understanding the nature of deviant behavior to explore briefly the principal conceptions of social deviance, as well as a few of the major misconceptions.

DEVIANCE AS STATISTICALLY INFREQUENT BEHAVIOR. Deviance in one sense may be defined as anything that is not typical, anything that is abnormal or atypical. Any behavior or attribute that is statistically infrequent in a society can be viewed as deviant (see Figure 13-1). In terms of this general conception of deviance, behavior or attributes that are not modal or typical are considered to be deviant. People who are left-handed, have blonde hair, have an I.Q. of 70 or 170, can run the mile under four minutes, are less than five or more than seven feet tall, or enjoy swimming in the Arctic Ocean during the wintertime could be considered deviant.

Each of the above attributes or types of behavior is atypical or nonmodal. The quality or

**567**

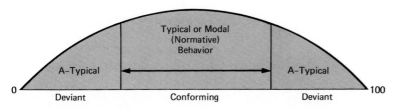

FIGURE 13-1 Statistical Normality and Statistically Deviant Behavior.

▼

action in question may be socially disapproved and hence sometimes referred to as negative deviance; on the other hand, it may be socially approved, and accordingly defined as positive deviance; in other instances, no value judgment or moral evaluation at all may be evoked. The conception of deviance in terms of statistical normality, however, does not necessarily encompass the kinds of conduct that are particularly significant from a sociological perspective: violations of social norms.

DEVIANCE AS NORM VIOLATION. **Deviance** in its more specifically sociological usage refers to social behavior that violates any societal or group norm—any violation of required or expected behavior. All violations of the prescribed or proscribed norms of behavior are thought to be detrimental in some way to society and its members. Deviance in this conception, however, does not necessarily imply a judgment of behavior in terms of its moral or ethical basis, beyond what may be implied in the respective norm.

Sociologists, thus, focus on behavior that is considered to be socially deviant, or behavior that at least is so defined. Such an approach, however, is not an easy one today, because of the increasing lack of consensus as to the norms or standards of behavior in a great number of social situations. Rapid social change, coupled with an unsurpassed level of personal freedom, has created a relatively high level of confusion regarding appropriate kinds of behavior in a number of social situations. Such is especially the case concerning moral and ethical situations. Hence, where there is a plurality of definitions of what is desirable behavior, deviance as norm violation is difficult to measure.

One must keep in mind that the concept of social norm (as explained in Chapter 3) denotes a range of permissible behavior. While norms are relatively precise in specifying which kinds of action are acceptable and which are not, they seldom prescribe how an individual should behave down to the last detail. Many norms are only abstract standards that offer guidelines for action. People are expected only to approximate the ideal behavior in their daily activities. No person could ever conform completely to all of the norms of society in every detail. It is expected, however, that an individual's behavior will fall within the limits circumscribed by the relevant norms.

Deviance as norm violation, moreover, does not depend on the frequency of a given behavior. The fact that "everybody does it"—a great number, or even a majority, being involved—does not make a particular behavior any less deviant. In fact, even some kinds of behavior in which a great number of people allegedly engage—such as cheating on income taxes—may still be defined as deviant behavior by the very people involved. Nonetheless, since most people conform to the norms of society, prescribed social behavior invariably assumes a statistical normality. Socially "normal" behavior, that is to say, becomes statistically normal or modal behavior.

## MISCONCEPTIONS OF SOCIAL DEVIANCE

Deviance must not be confused in particular with two other social phenomena: social disorganization and social problems. These terms were commonly used as synonyms for deviant behavior during the first half of this century. The practice has not died out completely, but even these labels now have acquired quite distinctive meanings.

SOCIAL DISORGANIZATION.  **Social disorganization,** sometimes called **social pathology,** refers to a social situation that is dysfunctional, a type of social disease or illness, as it were. We shall elaborate in a subsequent section on the contention that, however dysfunctional, social deviance can also be functional in many respects.

Social disorganization results when a social system lacks any significant margin of social order or social control. A breakdown of the institutionalized structures of a social system, such as war, or social or political revolution, indeed even a cultural upheaval of sufficient magnitude, or massive change in population composition, can produce social disorganization. Yet, while social disorganization may encourage some forms of deviant behavior, much deviance is highly organized. Such is the case in the operations of organized crime and social revolution. Societies, moreover, can usually tolerate a considerable amount of deviance without incurring social disorganization. Massive or prolonged deviance, however, can produce a state of social disorganization.

SOCIAL PROBLEMS.   **Social problems** refer to undesirable social situations that affect a significant number of people. Several forms of deviant behavior, as we shall explain, are not so perceived. Certainly, many of the people engaged in deviant behavior would not view their actions in this way. On the other hand, many forms of deviance never reach such sufficient magnitude, either in terms of their extent or their gravity, to be considered social problems.

Deviant behavior becomes a social problem only when it affects, or includes, a significant number of people—however vague "significant" must be in this context. Marijuana has been used in this country since the early years of the century. Only in quite recent years, when its use involved massive numbers of people, especially young people, has marijuana consumption been deemed a social problem. The same can be said about the excessive use of alcohol and, even more recently, smoking and other uses of tobacco. Finally, it needs to be understood that not all social problems involve deviance or the violation of social norms. Mental illness and poverty are two major social problems that exist in American society, but neither one involves any violations of social norms in the course of their generation.

# RELATIVITY OF SOCIAL DEVIANCE

▼

Insofar as deviance is defined as the violation of social norms, it has an essentially relevant character. Social norms, as discussed in Chapter 3, vary widely both among and within cultures. Accordingly, all deviant behavior, by definition, is relative in terms of the particular social norms to which it refers. Moreover, insofar as social norms themselves vary in a number of respects, so too does deviant behavior. Killing another human being does not necessarily constitute deviant behavior. Under certain circumstances, such as in war, killing is not defined as murder, nor are other instances of justifiable homicide. The same is true of many other forms of deviant behavior.

The relativity of deviance is of three basic types: cultural, temporal, and circumstantial. Let us look at each of these types in more detail.

RELATIVITY OF CULTURE. Social norms vary widely from culture to culture. While there are some universal *types* of deviant behavior, there are no universal *acts* of deviant behavior. Murder and incest are two types of behavior that are universally considered deviant, but what constitutes murder and incest in terms of specific acts varies both culturally and socially. Incest in the American culture, for example, includes sexual relations among members of the same nuclear family; yet, in other cultures, incest may be defined only as sexual relations between parents and children.

Even within a given culture, deviance may be subjected to the specific norms of a particular subculture. Some kinds of behavior that are considered culturally deviant may be defined as normative within certain subcultures, while other culturally normative kinds of behavior are defined as deviant by the same subcultures. Perhaps the best illustrations of this situation are the crimes that are perpetrated by the criminal underworld. Religious subcultures often permit, and are permitted, certain types of

**569**

▼ behavior that would otherwise be considered highly deviant by the dominant culture. The use of narcotics and hallucinogenic substances as a religous practice among certain American Indian tribes in one such example.

Crime, as one form of deviant behavior, offers a very special example of cultural relativity. Behavior that is considered to be criminal or delinquent varies significantly from society to society (see Table 13-1). Included in this category of relative deviance is criminal behavior that varies from state to state in our own country. Gambling is considered a crime in most states, yet in Nevada and New Jersey there are legalized forms of gambling. Indeed, most states permit gambling of certain kinds or at certain times, such as that which takes place for fundraising and charitable events. Not even prostitution, which is legal in Nevada and in many other societies, can be considered a universal crime.

RELATIVITY OF TIME. For a host of reasons, but especially because of change in the dominant values of society, any kind of behavior may take on a different meaning or purpose.

Hence, deviant behavior, or what is defined as deviant behavior, may vary with the passage of time. Abortion and homosexuality would be fairly close to the top of any such list of historical relativity at the present time in American society, and in much of the Western world as well. Up to the 1970s these kinds of behavior were considered among the most deviant and criminal of all social actions. Such is not necessarily the case today, even though millions of people have not altered their views about these two practices. Abortion is now permitted in all states and homosexuality in some. Similar situations exist in many other societies of the world.

Not long ago, smoking on the part of women was viewed as quite deviant, although not illegal. The same could be said of men wearing long hair and using cosmetics. Even wearing jeans in school or in white-collar jobs was considered deviant behavior not many years ago. Many parts of the United States have witnessed the legal age for the consumption of alcoholic beverages undergo significant changes during the past decade; indeed, the mere consumption of alcohol, while controlled in many respects

**570**

TABLE 13-1. Cultural Relativity of Deviance

| Type of Act | Percentage Who Think Act Should Be Prohibited By Law | | | | |
|---|---|---|---|---|---|
| | India | Iran | Italy (Sardinia) | U.S. | Yugoslavia |
| Homosexuality | 74 | 90 | 87 | 18 | 72 |
| Public protest, nonviolent | 33 | 77 | 35 | 6 | 46 |
| Abortion | 41 | 84 | 77 | 22 | 25 |
| Failure to help another person in danger | 45 | 56 | 80 | 28 | 77 |
| Use of drugs | 75 | 90 | 92 | 90 | 89 |
| Incest | 94 | 98 | 98 | 71 | 95 |
| Air pollution by a factory | 99 | 98 | 96 | 96 | 92 |
| Robbery | 97 | 98 | 100 | 100 | 98 |

Source: Reproduced with permission of Graeme Newman from *Comparative Deviance: Perception and Law in Six Cultures*. New York: Elsevier, 1976, p. 116, Table 4. © 1976.

**Timely Deviance.** Time often literally determines whether behavior is deviant. Seventeen seconds remained for these teenagers before a change in Massachusetts law reversed the legality of drinking for people between the ages of 18 and 20 and made it a criminal offense. (The Bettmann Archive)

today, was totally illegal during the Prohibition period from 1920 to 1933. Another example is that of adultery, which only in the past few years has been decriminalized in many states, after being defined for centuries as a most serious form of deviant behavior. Adultery now is commonly regarded as a personal matter. Hence, actions that at one time were deemed deviant, even criminal, may not be seen as such at the present time; conversely, behavior once considered proper and legal may now be deemed deviant or illegal. Littering is one such example.

Public smoking in many respects is slowly joining the categories of both deviant and criminal behavior.

In modern societies certain segments of the population are always likely to urge that specific illegal acts should be decriminalized, or that other actions not currently defined as crimes should be made illegal. Public pressure has been exerted by certain groups in our society to have prostitution, gambling, and the possession or use of certain drugs decriminalized. Other segments of the population at the same time are urging that the manufacture and sale of toxic products, industrial practices that cause pollution, pornography, the possession of guns, and public smoking should be illegal. In a complex, heterogeneous society that represents a plurality of value systems, any form of social behavior is always subject to differential and changing definitions in terms of its permissibility or desirability.

RELATIVITY OF SOCIAL CIRCUMSTANCES. Social behavior may be defined as deviant in one situation, but not in another. This is due to the situational specificity of special norms. Nudity, or simply wearing a bikini, is a form of behavior that may be allowed on the beach, but not in the office. Similarly, conduct that is thought to be perfectly appropriate at a party may be perceived as quite inappropriate in other situations, such as at a funeral or in the classroom.

Many acts of deviance can be performed only by individuals occupying certain social positions. Such an act of deviance has come to be known more technically as a **status offense.** Perhaps the most well-known examples of status offenses, and status offenders, are the criminal acts of individuals in a certain age category, such as minors who may engage in behavior that would not be considered deviant on the part of other people. These acts include truancy, waywardness, incorrigibility, and violations of curfew. By the same token, many forms of behavior enacted by juveniles may not be

571

▼ considered deviant or criminal because there is a lack of either criminal intent (*mens rea*) or of sufficient comprehension of the nature of the act to justify responsibility.

Other examples of status offenses may be those committed by individuals of a particular sex. Quite recently, prostitution was considered to be a form of deviant behavior limited to women; however, in the past decade it has not been uncommon to speak of male prostitution. Perhaps even more common of late has been the arrest of males who patronize prostitutes.

**572**

## UNIVERSALITY OF SOCIAL DEVIANCE

While deviance may be relative—to place, time, and circumstances—the question may still be asked about whether there is any universally deviant behavior. The answer to this question is yes and no. Again, while there are universal *types* of deviance, there are no universal *acts* of deviance.

Deviance, thus, is a universal phenomenon. All societies have strong prohibitions against certain types of activity. Some types of behavior are universally condemned, irrespective of culture, era, or circumstance. Such actions are viewed as being intrinsically wrong, and there is a great deal of consensus among people in different societies on this matter. Among the principal types of such behavior are incest, murder, assault, property damage, and theft. Nonetheless, there is no universal consensus on precisely which acts constitute incest, murder, assault, malicious property damage, or theft.

# Varieties of Deviant Behavior

Given the definition of deviance as norm violation, a list of deviant behavior would be virtually without end. Nonetheless, it is helpful to distinguish several of the principal types of deviance.

Our discussion excludes minor forms of social deviance as violations of custom, manners, or etiquette. We concentrate instead on the more strongly disapproved or controversial forms of deviant behavior that invite relatively severe sanctions and warrant major societal efforts to control them. The categories that follow are by no means absolute. Cross-listing, the same behavior being classifiable in more than one category, is possible in several instances.

## CRIME AND DELINQUENCY

Crime is invariably the first type of deviance that comes to mind. It is this form of deviance that receives the greatest amount of attention. Nonetheless, we must not lose sight of the fact that crime is only one form of deviant behavior, indeed one that perhaps accounts for only a modest amount of deviance. Hence, while all criminal acts are deviant, not all deviant acts are criminal.

**Crime** consists specifically of any intentional behavior that violates the legal codes of society. Legal codes consist of a set of laws, or institutionalized norms, whose violations result in the punishment of the violator. Norms become institutionalized and enacted into law through the political and judicial processes of society. Laws are intended to apply generally to all its members, and they are enforced through judiciary procedures or, more broadly, through what has come to be known in recent years as the criminal justice system.

Crime and delinquency are among the most serious forms of social deviance. Some crimes, however, like other forms of deviant behavior, are considered more serious than others. Legally, in this respect, a basic distinction is made between misdemeanors and felonies.

MISDEMEANORS. A **misdemeanor** is a relatively minor offense against the law that is usually punishable by a small fine or a prison sentence of less than one year. Traffic violations, petty thefts, public intoxication, and prostitution are misdemeanors. Many misdemeanors do not carry the stigma of crime, and hence are not regarded as very serious by many segments of society.

FELONIES. A **felony,** on the other hand, consists of a much more serious crime that is punishable by heavy fines and/or prolonged periods of incarceration, or even execution. Armed robbery, rape, and murder are rather common examples of felonious behavior.

Useful distinctions are also made between crimes committed against people, which are essentially crimes of violence (for example, rape and murder) and crimes against property (for example, arson and theft). Most common in the former category is physical assault, followed by rape and homicide. Crimes against property are far more common. Motor vehicle theft is the most frequent type of property crime. Others include burglary, larceny, and arson.

DELINQUENCY. A subdivision of crime consists of delinquent behavior. **Delinquency** refers to criminal offenses that are committed by individuals below the age of criminal responsibility, usually sixteen. However, like many other aspects of the criminal law, the technicalities of delinquent action differ from one jurisdiction to another; hence, there is a fair measure of variation among the states in our own country, and others, regarding criminal responsibility on the part of minors.

Also included in this category of delinquency are offenses that can be committed only by juveniles. Among these forms of deviant behavior are truancy, waywardness, incorrigibility, curfew violations, and underage drinking. Delinquency also represents a distinctive form of deviant behavior in that the sanctions applied to deviants in this category are on the whole primarily reformative and rehabilitative in nature, rather than punitive as in the case of adult criminals.

WHITE-COLLAR CRIME. One generally thinks of crime as a form of deviant behavior associated with the poor, illiterate, uneducated, pathological, unrefined, and unfortunate people from the lowest ranks of society. Actually, crime is a phenomenon found at every level of society, although in different form and measure. Wealth and civility can breed crime just as much as, and perhaps in some cases even more than, poverty and illiteracy.

One such type of crime that is associated more commonly with the middle and upper strata of society is that known as "white-collar crime." **White-collar crime** may be defined as "crime committed by a person of respectability and high social standards [usually] in the course of his occupation" (Sutherland, 1949). Fraud, pilfering, embezzlement, and bribery are common examples of white-collar crime. White-collar crime consists of a host of illegal activities that essentially involve an abuse or violation of trust. Such activities include the behavior of lawyers who cheat clients, physicians who overbill patients, and corporate executives who steal goods from their employers. Any type of political corruption can also be classified as a form of white-collar crime. Among new terms for white-collar crime and other forms of deviance performed by the rich and powerful segments of society is that of **elite deviance** (see Coleman, 1985; Simon & Eitzen, 1986).

White-collar crime is not widely regarded as a serious form of crime or deviant behavior, even though it constitutes a major economic loss to society and to those individuals who have to pay for it. With respect to fraud, for example, it is estimated that at least $20 billion change hands each year by way of such things as kickbacks and commercial bribery.

CORPORATE CRIME. One variation of white-collar crime is **corporate crime.** Deviant behavior of this kind consists of crimes committed technically by corporations, rather than

**573**

▼ by the individuals who may be personally responsible for them. Any activity that gives a company an unfair advantage in the marketplace, at the expense of consumers, competitors, or the government, can be termed corporate crime. False advertising, restraint of trade, price-fixing, stock manipulation, and patent infringement are examples of corporate crime. Environmental pollution by industrial corporations has been a rather common example of corporate crime during the past few years.

Corporate crime is by no means rare and appears to be consistently increasing in modern societies. Research shows that about one-half of the major corporations in the country have been guilty of at least one major crime or other forms of illegal behavior (Clinard & Yeager, 1980; Ermann & Lundman, 1987). In the years

574

## BOX 13-1. Fake Juice Costs Firm $2 Million

New York—Beech-Nut Nutrition Corp., the nation's second-largest baby food producer, pleaded guilty Friday to 215 felony counts of intentionally shipping millions of jars of bogus apple juice for babies.

According to the government, Beech-Nut knew the jars were filled with a cheaper mix of other juices and sugar syrups.

U.S. District Judge Thomas C. Platt in Brooklyn imposed a $2 million fine, the largest "by at least sixfold" ever paid under the Food, Drug & Cosmetic Act of 1938, said Assistant Attorney General Richard K. Willard.

"We hope that such prosecutions send a strong message that consumer fraud will not be tolerated by the government."

Beech-Nut counsel John S. Martin told Platt that an "extensive investigation" by his law firm had confirmed government charges that tests by the company's own chemists over the years had led some employees "to seriously question the authenticity" of Beech-Nut's claim that it was using pure concentrates of apple juice.

Beech-Nut, of Fort Washington, Pa., is second only to Gerber Products Co. in the $1.8 billion baby-food industry, and has been wholly-owned by Nesfood Inc., a subsidiary of Nestle S.A. of Switzerland, since November 1979.

In addition to Beech-Nut, the indictment named in all but 20 of its 470 counts Niels L. Hoyvald, Beech-Nut's president and chief executive officer, and John F. Lavery, the company's vice president for manufacturing in Canajoharie, N.Y., where what was sold as "pure apple juice concentrate" was heavily diluted with beet sugar, corn syrup and other ingredients.

Hoyvald and Lavery are to go to trial Monday.

The indictment said the adulterated products—mostly apple juice, but including apple-cherry and other juices—were shipped over five years, ending in March 1983.

The wholesalers and food chains that bought the phony products were in 20 states, Puerto Rico, the Virgin Islands, the Bahamas, the Dominican Republic, Japan, Saudi Arabia and Taiwan. ▲

Source: "Beech-Nut Guilty in Juice Fraud: $2 Million Fine Set by U.S. Judge After Firm Admits Liability," by Morton Mintz, *Washington Post*, November 14, 1987.

1975 to 1984, 62 percent of America's Fortune 500 corporations were cited for one or more illegal activities by courts or government agencies. Forty-two percent of these corporations were involved in two or more illegal activities, and 15 percent in five or more. A recent well-known case of corporate crime in the United States occurred a few years ago involving the prestigious General Motors Corporation, which was found guilty of mounting (allegedly less expensive) Chevrolet engines on the chassis of more expensive Oldsmobiles. The manufacturer was severely fined and ordered to make compensation to the buyers in question. Now all General Motors cars have engines that simply indicate that they were manufactured in a General Motors plant, without specification of any particular brand or line of automobile. Another recent case of corporate crime is that of the Beech-Nut Nutrition Corporation (see Box 13-1).

A new type of corporate crime that began to emerge during the 1980s is computer crime, which involves breaking into the access codes and computerized data banks of commercial and governmental organizations. A 1984 survey of 283 companies and governmental agencies found that one-fourth of them experienced financial losses as a result of computer crime (*Science Digest*, 1984). These losses ranged from $2 million to $10 million.

VICTIMLESS CRIME.    A newly introduced classification of deviant behavior among sociologists is that known as "victimless crime" (Schur, 1965; Schur & Bedau, 1974). The specific types of behavior involved, however, are not new. Deviant behavior under the classification of **victimless crime,** sometimes referred to as moral crime, includes a number of different acts undertaken in private, either by single individuals or consenting adults acting in concert, and allegedly to the detriment of neither society nor any of its members. Included here are many forms of crime mentioned above as types of

either personal or collective deviance: prostitution, homosexuality, drug abuse, gambling, and vagrancy.

Victimless crime is perhaps very widely undertaken. Table 13-2 offers an estimate of the number of arrests for different types of victimless crime. It is estimated, for example, that 10 percent of the American population engages regularly in homosexual behavior. Gambling and drug abuse are even much more widespread, engaged in by perhaps as much as 25 percent of the population. Such extensive practice is frequently offered as one argument for the decriminalization of victimless crime. Moreover, in the absence of formal complaints, and given its private nature, it is difficult to control such deviance. Laws against these types of behavior are virtually impossible to enforce.

It is questionable, however, whether these types of behavior are really victimless. Some would argue that the well-being of society is the victim, if not the deviants or criminals themselves. There is, thus, the question of social harm, if not personal harm, that cannot be easily dismissed. "Victimless" crimes often threaten

**575**

TABLE 13-2.   Arrests for Crimes Without Victims, 1987

| Crime | Estimated Number of Arrests |
| --- | --- |
| Drug Abuse Violations | 811,000 |
| Drunkenness | 701,000 |
| Runaways (Juveniles) | 136,000 |
| Prostitution and Commercialized Vice | 101,000 |
| Curfew, Loitering (Juveniles) | 76,000 |
| Illegal Gambling | 23,000 |

**Source: U.S. Bureau of the Census, *Statistical Abstract of the United States, 1989.* Washington, D.C.: U.S. Department of Commerce, 1988, p. 173.**

▼

the physical and psychological well-being of the perpetrators. Venereal disease and drug abuse are cases in point. Such situations, when reaching significant proportions, can represent major threats to the well-being and function of society—the social order—as well. Moreover, what cannot be overlooked is the variety of other kinds of criminal activity that are associated with victimless crimes.

**576**

Some have suggested that this category of deviant behavior should be known more appropriately as "crimes without complainants." Nonetheless, for the reasons given above, decriminalization of much behavior in this category is quite likely in the near future.

## TORTS OR CIVIL DEVIANCE

Crime and delinquency, however harmful to individuals, are technically considered to be illegal acts against society. A **tort,** on the other hand, represents a category of wrong or harmful acts that victimize individuals rather than society. While illegal in character, torts are based on civil law rather than criminal law. Technically, torts are defined as acts that are simply forbidden rather than acts that are considered to be intrinsically wrong as is the case with crime.

Violations of the civil law do not necessarily result in punishment. Tort actions primarily seek redress of personal injury of whatever nature—physical, psychological, or economic. An individual victim may seek legal redress and compensation for injuries and damages incurred as a result of another's deviant behavior, such as negligence in an automobile accident, or those which stem from malpractice in occupational services rendered by a physician, psychologist, attorney, or other professional. While such acts are not necessarily criminal, crime may be involved as well, and societal sanctions could be imposed on the deviants.

## DEVIANT LIFESTYLES

Much behavior in society is considered deviant simply because it is perceived to be immoral, sinful, or unnatural. Included in this category are deviant lifestyles and personal deviance (Lowney et al., 1981). Personal deviance includes behavior that is considered to be a violation of customs and morality, or conduct that is simply "disturbing to people." Some forms of deviance in this category may also be considered crimes, including alcoholism, drug addiction, homosexuality, prostitution, transvestism, vagrancy. Included here as well are various violations of civility, propriety, manners, and etiquette—or, simply put, folkways.

Many forms of personal deviance today have become quite controversial in our society and several others. This situation is due, in large part, to the extensive democratization and liberalization of the respective social orders. Social changes such as these have made for a greater heterogeneity of social behavior, as well as unprecedented levels of toleration for it. Perhaps the strongest polemics surround the issue of homosexual behavior. Nearly one-third of the people in any public opinion poll, when asked to describe or give an example of deviance, mention homosexuality immediately. In a study from the 1960s (Simmons, 1969), in which people were asked to list things or types of persons regarded as deviant, more than 60 percent mentioned homosexuality. Yet, while the largest number of people view homosexuality as a pathological condition, many—lay people and professionals alike—are changing their views on this question. The American Psychiatric Association in 1974 voted to remove homosexuality from its taxonomy of mental illness. On the other hand, a poll of 2,500 psychiatrists conducted in 1977 found that 69 percent considered homosexuality to be a pathological adaptation, not merely an alternative but

**Personal Deviance.** Alternative lifestyles that are considered immoral or unnatural typically present a challenge to any social order. Homosexuality, however increasingly tolerated, is widely considered to be one of the principal forms of deviant behavior in our society. (J. P. Laffont/SYGMA)

wholesome lifestyle.* Many societies, such as England, do not regard homosexual behavior between consenting adults and in a private setting to be a criminal offense. American attitudes seem to be shifting more and more toward a similar point of view. One rather recent study in the United States found that 67 percent of the respondents opposed any legal prohibition of homosexuality (Newman, 1976). Not all sectors of American society, of course, share this perspective. Recently (1980), the U.S. Department of Defense adopted a policy of barring homosexuals from the military. Nevertheless, whatever the distribution of opinion and practice, homosexual behavior remains officially a crime in most jurisdictions of the United

* *Behavior Today*, December 5, 1977.

States—not to mention that throughout our society such behavior is also subject to social sanctions.

Modern societies by their very complex and heterogeneous nature, as well as the dynamics of social change that they typically generate, are always likely to produce a number of alternative lifestyles that present a challenge to the existing social order. Deviance in this respect would seem to be inevitable.

## COLLECTIVE DEVIANCE

Not all deviance consists of individual acts. It is possible to speak of collective deviance undertaken by large numbers of people working more or less in concert. Much deviance assumes

▼

**578**

the form of countercultures—subcultures that are neither congruent nor integrated with the dominant culture (see Chapter 3). Included here are such activities as the criminal underworld, delinquent gangs, drug syndicates, religious cults, communes, and revolutionary organizations. Organized crime, one particular form of collective deviance, is alleged to be so extensive that in terms of causing economic loss to society alone, it vastly exceeds all other forms of crime combined. Added to this loss are other kinds of "costs" in terms of personal and psychological injury to victims of these activities.

Much personal deviance takes place within the ambience of subcultures where individuals find a significant measure of social rapport and psychological reinforcement, and in which they accordingly can assume a posture of social conformity. Apart from offering an environment in which to practice various forms of deviance without the stress of concealment and stigmatization, countercultures usually provide a means of continuing education in the forms and techniques of deviant behavior.

# Extent and Distribution of Deviance

It is difficult to know the complete extent of deviance in any society, particularly in a modern society. Social deviance, for the most part, consists of covert activity. Such is especially the case, of course, in the matter of deviant behavior that takes place within the private environment of individuals. The very undesirable nature of deviance, and the corresponding sanctions that are risked, keep it from public observation. Moreover, much deviance consists of eccentric behavior that is limited to certain social situations, and which by and large is considered fairly harmless. All available estimates, in any event, suggest that deviance is far more extensive than one might suspect.

# NORMALITY OF SOCIAL DEVIANCE

Deviance is so pervasive in our society—indeed, in many others as well—that one can easily speak of the "normality" of deviance. Several studies have shown that the vast majority of people, at one time or another, engage in behavior that is considered to be seriously deviant, even serious enough to warrant imprisonment in many cases. A study of residents in New York, for example, revealed that 91 percent of the sample reported that, as adults, they had violated at least one law for which fines or imprisonment could have been imposed (Wallerstein & Wylie, 1947).

Everyone no doubt is deviant in some respects at one time or another. Here again we need to recall the distinction that we made above, and in Chapter 3, between the ideal and the real norms of behavior. Probably everyone has engaged in an act—even on a regular basis—that technically is criminal. Among such types of behavior that are most frequently overlooked as deviant or criminal are speeding, jaywalking, sampling food in stores, cheating on income taxes, or petty theft at work. Kinsey (1948) maintained, based on his findings in the area of sexual activity, that one-half of adult Americans could be imprisoned for engaging in forms of sexual behavior defined as illegal in most states. In many respects, however, these norms have changed during the past thirty-five years or so.

That crime and other forms of deviance are prevalent in our society is reflected in the extensive measures that are taken for their control and deterrence. Security systems, alarms for houses and buildings, double- and triple-bolt locks, antitheft chains for bicycles and automobiles, tear gas, firearms owned by private citizens, proctors at examinations, chaperone and escort services for women on college campuses and elsewhere, contracts that prescribe damages for noncompliance, and government checks and balances are among the many kinds of protection which people in today's society use to escape the consequences of being victimized by crime and other forms of deviant behavior. (One recent survey reported that 44 percent of the American people have dogs and 48 percent possess firearms, primarily as forms of protection against criminals.) Nonetheless, most forms of deviance, however widespread they may be, are still considered to be the undertaking of only a minority of people in society.

## CRIME STATISTICS

Crime, being only one type of deviance, can provide only a modest measure of the extent of deviant behavior. In advanced societies, such as our own, records are kept on criminal activity, but even these are considered to be grossly inaccurate. The Federal Bureau of Investigation annually issues a *Uniform Crime Report* that provides statistics on several major types of crime. These data, despite their value in many respects, are widely considered not to be very reflective of the actual extent of criminal deviance in the United States. First of all, these data represent only "crimes known and reported to the police." Much crime—perhaps the greater portion—simply goes unreported, or even undetected. Various reasons for this situation include fear, embarrassment, a sense of futility, and official incompetence. Indeed, even all of the "crimes known to the police" do not get officially listed in the crime statistics. Many police agencies throughout the country do not submit annual statistics to the Federal Bureau of Investigation.

Moreover, as suggested above, only major types of crime are reported by the *Uniform Crime Reports*. Statistics are available for twenty-nine categories of crime. There is con-

centration, however, on eight offenses, known as index crimes: murder, rape, robbery, aggravated assault, burglary, larceny, auto theft, and arson. No provision is made here for corporate crime. Similarly, very little data are available for white-collar crime, including fairly common violations such as tax evasion, bribery, fraud, and embezzlement. (The Internal Revenue Service in 1984 estimated that government losses as a result of tax evasion exceed $100 billion each year.) Inclusion of these additional forms of crime in the official statistics would significantly alter the common perspectives on both the extent of crime and the social profile of criminals.

In 1965–1966, the National Opinion Research Council (NORC) at the University of Chicago conducted a national survey of 10,000 households for the President's Crime Commission in order to determine the accuracy of official crime statistics. Pollsters inquired whether any family member had been a victim of crime during the preceding year. Results of this poll (Wilson, 1967) suggested crime rates that would at least double those based on the FBI/UCR statistics. Indeed, the poll revealed that four times as many rapes, three times as many burglaries, and twice as many assaults occurred as were reported by the FBI. The rates for murder and motor vehicle theft, on the other hand, appeared to be quite accurate. Accordingly, from these data it appears that three-fourths of the rapes, two-thirds of the burglaries, and one-half of the assaults that probably occurred were never reported.

A National Crime Survey (NCS), involving 46,000 housing units and about 100,000 individuals, estimates that in 1987 about 34.7 million persons (aged 12 or older) were victims of criminal offenses (both actual and attempted). Only about 37 percent of all the crimes recorded by the NCS were reported to police (see Figure 13-2). Such a pattern has been fairly consistent in these surveys for at least the past decade.

▼

**579**

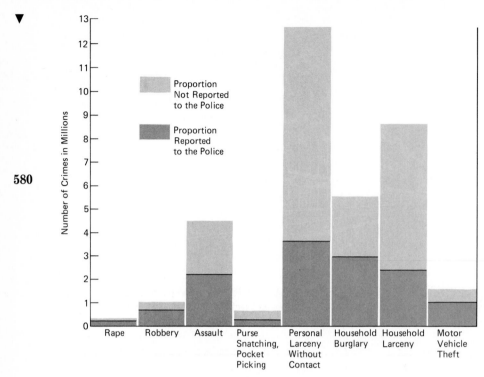

FIGURE 13-2   Criminal Victimization in the United States, 1987. Source: *National Crime Survey*, U.S. Department of Justice Statistics. Washington, D.C.: Government Printing Office, 1988.

The rate of reporting, of course, varies with the particular crime and its degree of gravity. These data, nonetheless, once again offer a sharp contrast to the much lower extent of crime presented in the *Uniform Crime Reports*.

Despite the unreliability of crime statistics, the mere number of reported crimes in the United States is overwhelming. For 1987, the FBI/UCR listed a total of 13,508,708 index crimes alone (see Table 13-3). This figure represents a rate of 5550 crimes per 100,000 inhabitants (UCR, 1980:41). These statistics assume a more dramatic perspective when illustrated in Figure 13-3 in terms of the frequency of their occurrence in seconds and minutes. There is approximately one violent crime every twenty-one seconds and one

TABLE 13-3.   Criminal Offenses in the United States Known to the Police: 1987

| Crime | Number | Percent |
|---|---|---|
| Murder | 20,096 | 0.2 |
| Forcible Rape | 91,111 | 0.7 |
| Robbery | 517,704 | 3.8 |
| Aggravated Assault | 855,088 | 6.3 |
| Auto Theft | 1,288,674 | 9.5 |
| Burglary | 3,236,184 | 24.0 |
| Larceny | 7,449,851 | 55.5 |
| Total | 13,508,708 | 100.0 |

Source: U.S. Bureau of the Census, *Statistical Abstract of the United States, 1989*. Washington, D.C.: U.S. Government Printing Office, 1989, p. 166.

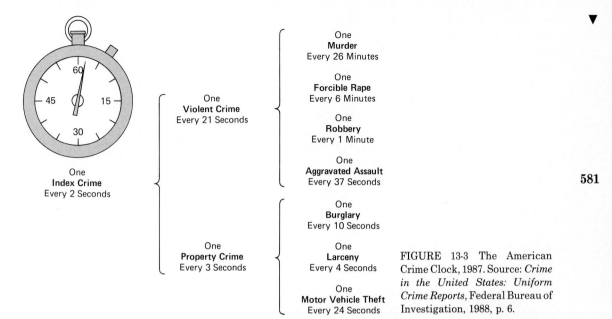

One
**Index Crime**
Every 2 Seconds

One
**Violent Crime**
Every 21 Seconds

One
**Property Crime**
Every 3 Seconds

One
**Murder**
Every 26 Minutes

One
**Forcible Rape**
Every 6 Minutes

One
**Robbery**
Every 1 Minute

One
**Aggravated Assault**
Every 37 Seconds

One
**Burglary**
Every 10 Seconds

One
**Larceny**
Every 4 Seconds

One
**Motor Vehicle Theft**
Every 24 Seconds

581

FIGURE 13-3 The American Crime Clock, 1987. Source: *Crime in the United States: Uniform Crime Reports*, Federal Bureau of Investigation, 1988, p. 6.

property crime every three seconds, so that in a typical day the number of crimes in the United States would be approximately 32,914. Once again, this enormous figure represents only seven major crimes.

Perhaps another valuable indicator of the extent of crime is its cost. The U.S. Department of Justice estimates that the price tag in 1985 for only personal and household crime in this country was $13 billion. Seventy-five percent, or $9.7 billion, was a result of burglary, motor vehicle theft, and household larceny. The remaining "cost" came from personal crimes of rape, robbery, assault, and personal larceny. The total cost of crime to society, of course, is extremely difficult to measure and, in all probability, can never be fully ascertained. Most impossible to determine, particularly in dollars and cents, is the extent of the suffering and emotional trauma experienced by the victims of crime.

American society frequently has been described as a violent society. That an enormous amount of violence exists in this country cannot be denied. What concerns criminologists is the reasons for the apparently greater amount of violent forms of deviance in the United States than in many other societies of the world. There is no general consensus for why this is so. Some allege that this relatively high crime rate is a function of the relatively youthful American population. Others attribute it to the particular set of values in the American society. Extensive violence may be a function, however, not so much of the specific values of the American culture as of its type of society—a postindustrial one that, among other distinctive characteristics, is experiencing tremendous social change. Crime rates in many other countries seem to be escalating as they too move into highly modern and industrialized types of structures. Nonetheless, without adequate and comparable data for other societies, it is difficult to determine just how normal and extensive deviance is in any society.

Numerous sociological studies reveal that the frequency and specific kinds of crime and other forms of deviance vary in terms of sex, age, race,

▼

ethnicity, religion, socioeconomics, occupation, and regional backgrounds of people. In the United States, it appears that the crime rate is highest among males (nearly four times higher than among women), Blacks, members of the lower classes, and city dwellers. These rates, however, may reflect, at least in part, differential reporting, arrest, and prosecution procedures.

582

Among the major forms of deviance in American society today that have been of particular concern are organized crime and drug abuse. These two forms of deviance are by no means unrelated.

## ORGANIZED CRIME

**Organized crime** includes a number of illegal activities that are undertaken on a massive scale as business enterprises. Organized crime consists nearly exclusively of crimes against public safety and public morals, such as gambling, prostitution, drug traffic, loan sharking, labor racketeering, and extortion. Such crimes are the work of highly organized syndicates (known by such popular names as the "Syndicate," the "Mafia," the "Camorra," the "Cosa Nostra," or simply the "Mob") that masquerade as legitimate business activities or "fronts," as they are known in the criminal world. Organized crime syndicates, moreover, have a virtual monopoly in many areas of legitimate businesses.

The profits from organized crime make this activity one of the largest businesses in the United States today. It was estimated in 1983 that organized crime "earns" approximately $150 billion annually (Mannheim, 1983). Such a figure is several times greater than that which is spent for the maintenance of the entire criminal justice system (police, courts, corrections) in the United States. Government spending for law enforcement in 1985 amounted to more than $46 billion. The success of organized crime as a commercial enterprise testifies to both the extent, as well as the apparent need, of certain forms of deviant behavior in the United States.

The extensive operation of organized crime obviously requires enormous patronage and support by millions of people. One may wonder whether such extensive deviance suggests a significant lack of legitimate outlets for the social and personal needs of people.

## DRUG AND ALCOHOL ABUSE

Once again, there are no adequate statistics on the extent of drug abuse in the United States. About one-half million people seek treatment each year for drug addiction, but this figure is thought to represent only a small portion of the problem. It is estimated that nearly one-fourth of the population between the ages of eighteen and twenty-five uses drugs on a regular basis. Moreover, it appears that drug abuse has been on the increase during the past few decades.

Forms of drug abuse (nowadays often called substance abuse) are not always recognized as deviant behavior. Examples include the misuse of medical prescriptions and the illegal use of stimulants such as amphetamines (known in street slang as "speed" or "uppers") which are used as energy boosters, or of sedative-hypnotics such as barbiturates ("downers") which induce relaxation and sleep. Major forms of drug abuse and addiction involve much more potent narcotics, such as heroin (an analgesic and tranquillizing type of drug) and a variety of hallucinogenic or "mind-altering" substances, such as lysergic acid (LSD).

Quite controversial in many societies at the present time is the widespread use of marijuana and cocaine. While alleged not to be physically addictive, these drugs remain illegal, nonetheless, in many countries. The decriminalization of these drugs, at least in some respects, has been advocated in recent years by the American Medical Association and American Bar Association. In some jurisdictions possession of less than one ounce of marijuana is now only a misdemeanor. Even if decriminalization of marijuana should come about many people would undoubtedly still classify its use as deviant behavior because of moralistic beliefs.

Related to drug addiction is the use of alcohol. While the consumption of alcohol is widely prevalent, it has not been given much attention as a form of drug abuse until recent years. Such a situation has come about because of the expanded use, and abuse, of alcohol by minors. The easy access to alcohol, its relatively low cost, and the fact that its consumption is legal for many, have exacerbated both the extent of and concern about problems associated with alcohol abuse. The growing dimension of the problem is reflected dramatically in the estimate that in the United States alone 9 million people are addicted to alcohol. Such a figure does not reflect the far greater number of people who engage in various forms of deviant behavior while under its influence.

# Theories of Social Deviance

Why do people engage in deviant behavior? Why are some people "always in trouble with the law" or typically nonconformists? Why are other people paragons of virtue, civility, and conformity? Are some people destined to be one way, and the rest of us another? These are a few of the principal questions about deviant behavior that sociologists and other scientists have tried to answer for the past several decades.

It is, first of all, very difficult to talk about explanations of deviant behavior, given its many different forms and its characteristic relativity. "Deviance," as we saw above, encompasses a wide variety of social behavior. Nonetheless, its pervasiveness and seriousness have stimulated scientists in many fields to seek explanations, however partial, for social deviance. These explanations for the most part are concerned not so much with single acts of deviance as they are with constant patterns of deviant lifestyles. Principal varieties of explanations for deviant behavior include biological, psychological, sociopsychological, and sociological theories. We shall discuss each of these types. Our emphasis, of course, will be on the sociological and sociopsychological varieties.

## BIOLOGICAL THEORIES

583

There have been many attempts to link deviant behavior, especially crime and mental illness, to biological factors (see, for example, Mednick et al., 1987). Several of these explanations have focused on genetic or physiological abnormalities, while others have concentrated on normal anatomical structures and neurophysiological processes. All such theories have suffered from methodological deficiencies, and, more specifically, from a lack of any substantial evidence to support their tenability. Let us discuss some of the more popular examples of biological theories of social deviance.

THEORY OF THE "BORN CRIMINAL." The first "scientific" attempt to formulate a biological theory of deviant behavior was made by Cesare Lombroso (1836–1909), an Italian physician. Lombroso maintained that criminals had distinctive biological structures that were essentially atavistic, or "throwbacks" to early and primitive forms of human beings (Lombroso-Ferrero, 1911). These "born criminals" could be visibly identified by a series of "criminal stigmata" which included slanted foreheads, huge jaws, high cheekbones, flat noses, big ears, unusually long arms, and red hair.

Lombroso's work lacked the scientific controls that would be demanded in this day and age. He studied only prison populations, in limited numbers, to confirm his theory. Subsequent studies, however, by Charles Goring (1913), a British physician, who utilized large samples of noncriminal populations—using methods and

▼ measurements similar to those employed by Lombroso—revealed that these people were not physically different from Lombroso's criminal subjects. Goring, nonetheless, reaffirmed the belief that criminals could be distinguished from noncriminals in terms of anatomical and physiological criteria. Lombroso's theory has been virtually discredited today; however, the basic tenets occasionally are resurrected in one form or another.

584

CONSTITUTIONAL TYPES. The idea that certain body types or anatomical structures (somatypes) are predisposed to certain kinds of behavior originated in ancient times. The Greek physician Hippocrates (460–360 B.C.) proposed that individual styles of behavior were related to variations in the biological organism. One of the latest formulations of this type of theory was made by William H. Sheldon (1942) in his theory of constitutional psychology. Sheldon argued that temperament was inherited and varied in terms of a person's anatomical structure. His typology consisted of three basic body types, or somatypes:

1. *Endomorph*, marked by viscerotonia (soft, short, and round physique) with tendencies toward gregariousness, physical comfort, and relaxation.

2. *Ectomorph*, marked by cerebrotonia (fragile, slender, tall, and flat-chested) with tendencies toward social inhibition, restraint, and introversion.

3. *Mesomorph*, marked by somatotonia (firm, muscular, and upright physique) with tendencies toward assertiveness, physical courage, and risk taking.

Sheldon argued that delinquents and alcoholics tend to be mesomorphs. Some support was given to this contention by subsequent sociological studies. Eleanor and Sheldon Glueck (1950) in *Unravelling Juvenile Delinquency* reported that in a sample of 500 delinquents who were matched against 500 alleged "nondelinquents," 60 percent were classified as mesomorphic. Their work, however, has been heavily criticized for statistical inadequacy and other methodological deficiencies. The basic thesis, nonetheless, has been presented anew quite recently by James Q. Wilson and Richard Herrnstein (1985), two contemporary professors at Harvard University. These researchers argue that, on the average, criminals differ from noncriminals not only in mesomorphic physique, but also in being characterized by lower levels of intelligence and impulsive personalities.

Aside from the lack of significant empirical confirmation of any association between de-

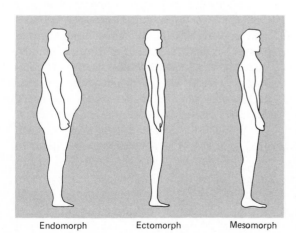

Endomorph        Ectomorph        Mesomorph

FIGURE 13-4 Somatypes and Deviant Behavior. Constitutional or morphological explanations represent one type of biological theory for deviant behavior. William H. Sheldon (1942) identified three basic body types: endomorph, ectomorph, and mesomorph. Proponents of the theory of constitutional type maintain that criminals and delinquents are more likely to be mesomorphic in anatomical structure.

viance and anatomical structure, Sheldon's typology, like all forms of constitutional psychology, has been virtually discredited.

THEORIES OF CHROMOSOMAL ABNORMALITY. During the past couple of decades interest in biological theories has been generated by research on chromosomal abnormalities (see Mednick & Volavaka, 1980). Theories of deviant behavior in this regard have been applied exclusively to males for whom the normal sex-chromosomal pattern is XY (versus XX for women). Laboratory investigations have focused on irregularities in this regard.

Amir and Berman (1970) found in laboratory testing that a high percentage of people who had committed violent crimes had abnormal chromosomal patterns. Chief among these irregularities was what came to be known as the "criminal chromosome," which consisted of an XYY pattern (a double male chromosome matched with a single female chromosome). Such individuals were thought to be taller, more aggressive, and decidedly more antisocial than those possessing the typical male chromosomal pattern.

This line of interesting and provocative analysis was prompted by the discovery that Richard Speck, who murdered seven nursing students at Northwestern University in Chicago in 1966, had the genetic abnormality of the "criminal chromosome." Again, however, the problem of selective and faulty sampling was present. Subsequent research has shown that the genetic abnormality of the XYY chromosome pattern can be found in fairly equal proportions among noncriminal as well as criminal segments. Moreover, many criminals, even the most hardened and the most violent, are not characterized by this chromosomal pattern (Sarbin & Miller, 1970).

SOCIOBIOLOGICAL THEORIES. Of some relevance for the explanation of deviance in re-

cent years has been the work of sociobiologists. Sociobiological theories (see Chapter 3) maintain that human behavior and certain kinds of deviance are the result of genetic and/or psychological programming that is characteristic of the human species. Principal examples of these kinds of explanations include the work of Konrad Lorenz (1966), an ethologist (one who studies the behavior of animals in their natural habitat), and E. O. Wilson (1975), who has concentrated on altruistic behavior in nonhuman animals. Their theories are somewhat contradictory. Lorenz advocates a theory of the innate aggression of human beings, while Wilson argues more fundamentally that prosocial behavior is genetically and evolutionarily based.

Sociobiological theories, nevertheless, have been criticized on several grounds. First of all, most explanations of this kind are based on the observations of animals that are at the lower end of the phylogenetic or evolutionary hierarchy. Propositions about human behavior that are based on culture-free animals, whose activity is totally determined by genetic principles, do not set well with social scientists who are concerned with the essential relativity and variability of deviance. Second, sociobiological theories are unable to account for the marked discrepancies in the rates of different forms of social deviance, both among human societies and among various social segments within them.

Biological theories, whatever their specific nature and postulation, tend to exonerate individuals of personal responsibility. If biological theories are correct, then it is pointless to have a system of criminal justice. Individuals can neither be held responsible, nor punished, for actions that are beyond their control.*

---

* Much of the same argument would apply to theories of psychological determination, or at least to psychological processes and personality systems that develop beyond the control or responsibility of the individual.

585

# ▼ PSYCHOLOGICAL THEORIES

Psychological theories, like biological theories, locate the cause of deviant behavior within the individual and see the deviant individual as essentially pathological, one who is unable to cope with both internal and external pressures.* Three theories in particular have been used to provide psychological explanations for deviant behavior: psychoanalytical theory, frustration-aggression theory, and personality theory.

PSYCHOANALYTICAL THEORY. In psychoanalytical theory (Freud, 1947), the deviant is characterized by an inadequate formation of personality, and/or as one who experiences an inadequate resolution of unconscious conflict between the principal components of personality (id, ego, and superego).

Deviance can result also from psychological conflict in the adequate or mature personality. According to the principles of psychoanalytic theory, individuals frequently experience psychological desires that are incompatible with their internalized standards. Unresolved conflict (between a person's psychological desires and internalized standards) produces feelings of anxiety and guilt. Deviant behavior is viewed by psychoanalytic theorists as "a device contrived by the personality to protect itself from this anxiety and guilt" (Cohen, 1966:33). These devices, assuming the form of any one of several dynamics, are referred to as defense mechanisms, which conceal the unacceptable or conflicting desire from the individual. Deviants, consequently, are psychologically incapable of knowing the real motive for their antisocial behavior.

A weak and/or undeveloped conscience (superego) is frequently associated with the deviant who suffers from an inadequate formation of personality. Psychopaths, now more commonly called sociopaths, are the extreme manifestation of this personality deficiency.

Psychoanalytical theory, as we saw in Chapter 5, has been criticized first and foremost because it does not lend itself to empirical confirmation. While the tenets of this theory may make logical sense, even psychological sense, it is difficult, if not totally impossible in many respects, to submit psychoanalytic concepts and principles to scientific validation. One can always, and quite easily, make ex post facto postulations of intra-psychic causes of deviant behavior. Furthermore, operating in this mode, one can substitute various explanations at will when trying to relate unconscious dynamics to overt behavior. Of serious concern too is the lack of attention given by psychoanalytical theory to cultural and situational factors. Psychoanalytic theory, thus, is essentially reductionistic in terms of intrapsychic phenomena and ignores the great degree of variability in human social behavior.

FRUSTRATION-AGGRESSION THEORY. Frustration-aggression theory (Dollard et al., 1939) maintains that certain kinds of deviance are forms of aggression—directed toward other people or toward the society—which stem from the frustration or nonsatisfaction of particular needs or wishes. Aggressive behavior is a release of the psychic energy that has been utilized by the particular motives in question, and thus serves as a ventilation of the frustration. The kind and degree of aggression depends on the amount of frustration, which in turn is based on the strength of the obstructed need or wish.

This theoretical formulation is unable to explain why frustration does not invariably lead to aggression. Alternatively, in some instances of frustration, aggression is turned inward toward the self. Suicide and other forms of self-assault exemplify this situation. Additionally, many forms of deviance involve neither frustration nor aggression.

---

* See Chapter 5 for a more detailed discussion of psychological theories.

PERSONALITY THEORY. A third variety of "psychological" theory often consists of various approaches that focus on personality traits or typologies of personality. Given the particular perspective of this volume, personality needs to be seen as an integral part of psychosocial types of explanations. Hence, it is difficult to classify personality explanations here as purely psychological explanations. We devote an entire section to personality and social deviance in a subsequent section of this chapter.

Psychological theories attempt to explain the behavior of the individual deviant. Hence, they do not usually shed much light on why the incidence of deviance seems to correlate with social categories or situations (for example, age, sex, social class, ethnic status, and residential area). Nonetheless, while psychological explanations are of little help in explaining the incidence of certain forms of deviance, such a situation does not mean that deviants may not be characterized by distinctive psychological processes, characteristics, and typologies, or personality types. If such associations can be shown in reference to "normal" behavior—as much of the data presented in several of the preceding chapters suggests—it should be possible to do the same in regard to social deviance, especially given its arbitrary nature. Berkowitz (1978) and Toch (1969), for examples, found that men who repeatedly committed physical assault were distinguished by very low degrees of self-esteem. Theoretical perspectives of this kind, used in conjunction with other scientific dimensions, have the potential of providing a more comprehensive explanation of social deviance. We shall pursue these considerations in a subsequent section of this chapter.

# SOCIOPSYCHOLOGICAL THEORIES

One variety of sociological theories in the field of deviance are those that may be distinguished as sociopsychological. These particular kinds of theories focus on interactional variables and their significance in the production of deviant behavior. There are two such theories that have been especially popular in sociology: differential association theory and labeling theory.

DIFFERENTIAL ASSOCIATION THEORY. One of the first sociological theories created specifically to explain deviant behavior is that known as differential association theory, which emphasized the role of social interaction and communication in the production of deviance. Proposed by Edwin Sutherland (1934), primarily as an explanation for crime, **differential association theory** maintains that deviant behavior, like all behavior, is learned through differential exposure to situations that influence a person's definition of appropriate and inappropriate behavior. Socialization to deviance, in short, is stronger than socialization to conformity. As Sutherland and Cressey (1978:5) state:

> Criminal behavior is learned in interaction with other persons in a process of communication. . . . The principal part of the learning of criminal behavior occurs within intimate personal groups. . . . When criminal behavior is learned, the learning includes (a) techniques of committing the crime, which are sometimes very complicated, sometimes very simple; (b) the specific direction of motives, drives, rationalization, and attitudes. . . . The specific direction of motives and drives is learned from definition of the legal codes as favorable or unfavorable. . . . A person becomes delinquent because of an excess of definitions favorable to violations of law over definitions unfavorable to the law. This is the principle of differential association.

Exposure to deviant patterns of behavior and isolation from antideviant patterns is the essence of the differential association theory. Sutherland maintained that an individual engages in criminal behavior when he "acquires an excess of definitions favorable to violations of law over definitions unfavorable to violations

587

▼

(© F.B. Grunzweig/Photo Researchers)

(Robert Kalman/Image Bank)

**Companionships.** The theory of differential association maintains that delinquent behavior and other forms of deviance are the learned products of interaction with different sets of social influences and experiences. Whether an individual pursues a career as a criminal or as a criminal lawyer depends much on the particular kinds of company that one keeps.

of law." That is, there is more association and closer interaction with people who favor deviance than with those who oppose it. The deviant individual also learns from others the specific techniques associated with particular crimes (for example, how to pick a lock, crack a safe, steal a car), as well as the rationalizations, justifications, or excuses that alleviate any guilt or shame the individual may develop as a consequence of his or her deviant behavior.

Attempts have been made in recent years to extend differential association theory and to make it more comprehensive by combining it with certain principles of behavioristic psychology and operant-reinforcement theory (Akers, 1985; Jeffrey, 1965). Such efforts have served to specify the mechanisms by which deviant attitudes and actions are learned and sustained. One of the basic premises for these theoretical modifications is that individuals will continue to engage in deviant behavior if in the past such behavior has resulted in more positive reinforcement than has conventional behavior.

Differential association has been criticized primarily in that it provides an explanation for conformity as much as it does for deviance. Others argue, for example, that since the same environment at times produces both deviance and nondeviance, differential association theory is unable to account for the antithetical responses that supposedly are due to differential perceptions of the same situation. These objections suggest that factors other than differential association and social learning may be involved in deviant behavior.

Another principal criticism of differential association theory is that it does not provide an explanation for primary deviance, that is, for the development of deviant subcultures or the deviant definitions that are learned. Rather, it offers chiefly an explanation for the perpetuation of deviant values and attitudes. Differential association, therefore, is seen as a sort of after-the-fact explanation. As such, the theory lacks any predictive value.

Differential association theory has been faulted as well for not being able to explain those forms of deviance that may be learned in isolation, or in association with a conforming culture. Embezzlement and fraud often are offered as examples in this regard. Similarly, the theory is unable to account for episodic deviance, such as crimes that are committed on impulse. Differential association theory is seen by many as representing only a partial explanation of deviant behavior at best.

**LABELING THEORY.** A somewhat novel theory that emerged with great popularity in the early 1960s is labeling theory. Labeling theory, also known as the societal reaction theory, employs a symbolic interaction approach in the explanation of deviant behavior. Chief protagonists of this view are Allen Liska (1981), Howard Becker (1963), and Erving Goffman (1963).

Labeling theory focuses on how society reacts to norm violators and the effects of that action. In the perspectives of **labeling theory,** then, deviant action itself is subordinated and emphasis is put on the labels that are placed on deviants—the processes and consequences of labeling. As Becker states, "From this point of view, deviance is *not* a quality of the act that a person commits, but rather a consequence of the application by others of the rules and sanctions to an offender. The deviant is one to whom that label has successfully been applied; deviant behavior is behavior people so label" (1963:9).

Labeling theorists, thus, assume that all deviance is created by society. Somewhat of a paradox is involved here, because labeling theory puts society in the position of producing the very behavior it seeks to eliminate. The criminal justice system (police, courts, corrections), in particular, is seen as contributing significantly to the perpetuation of crime and delinquency. At any rate, labeling theorists maintain that no act is inherently criminal or noncriminal. Rather, people react to behavior by formulating definitions, meanings, images, evaluations, designations, or—in short— labels. The "deviant" labels carry pejorative meanings. Such common examples are "pervert," "queer," "whore," "nut," "junkie," "rapist," "faggot," "criminal," "ex-con," "psychotic," "schizo," "bum," and even "bad boy." Many of these labels are indelible. People become stigmatized for life, such as in the case of the "ex-con."

Labeling theorists seek to explain how people get labeled as deviant and the consequences of that labeling. Liska (1981) has identified three principal ways in which labels can predispose

589

▼

people to engage in deviant behavior: (1) a deviant label often precludes one's engaging in legitimate economic and occupational undertakings; (2) a deviant label limits one's interpersonal relations; and (3) a deviant label can affect one's self-confidence.

Not all people who commit deviant acts are treated as deviants—or labeled as such. Common examples are people who are not given tickets for traffic violations, or perhaps those who can get such tickets fixed. Whether a person becomes labeled as deviant or not frequently depends in part on his or her social background—socioeconomic or minority status. Lower-class deviants may be labeled delinquent, whereas middle- and upper-class individuals who commit the same offenses may be called simply "pranksters." Labeling, then, is seen as more of a function of who people are rather than what they do.

Deviance, thus, in the perspective of labeling theory is not so much the quality of a person's act as much as a consequence of the application by others of roles and sanctions to an "offender." An interesting study by Rosenhan (1973), "On Being Sane in Insane Places," provides dramatic confirmation that the labels placed on people can make a very significant difference in the way they are treated. Rosenhan, a psychologist, and seven colleagues contrived to have themselves admitted as patients to several mental hospitals. None of these people had a history of mental disturbance or psychiatric treatment. They gained admission to the hospitals by claiming to be hearing voices. Upon being admitted to the hospitals, they no longer feigned any mental disorders, but acted normally. Their deception was not detected by physicians, nurses, or other hospital staff. On the contrary, seven of these researchers were diagnosed as schizophrenic, and one as manic-depressive. Throughout their hospital stays, which ranged from seven to fifty-two days, these people were treated as though they were irrational, just like all the other patients. It is quite curious, nonetheless, that 35 of the 118 real patients on the ward of one hospital were of the opinion that the pseudopatients were not sick at all.

Of crucial importance in labeling theory are the personal and social consequences of being labeled deviant. Labeling often leads to an alienation from family and friends, as well as from society. Certainly, deviants encounter differential treatment and various forms of discrimination. Difficulties that known deviants encounter in holding offices, jobs, professional practices, and certain social positions are well known. Such a situation implies a curtailment of an individual's normal life-chances. Labeling may also lead to an altered self-concept and to further deviance.

**Secondary deviance** (Lemert, 1972) is a term used to describe behavior that deviants develop as a result of being labeled deviant and their internalization of being so labeled. As Goffman (1963) points out, "One response to being labeled deviant is to embrace the label and its referent lifestyle or behavior." Deviants may accept the label, and so identify themselves, and develop a compatible lifestyle. The more they define themselves as deviant, the more they are so treated, and the more they engage in further deviance. A kind of self-fulfilling prophecy is involved here: "Once a deviant, always a deviant." People come to act as they are expected to act.

Another factor that contributes to secondary deviance involves the reactions of other people, once a deviant label has been applied. According to Becker (1963), the deviant label becomes a "master status." It tends to overshadow all the other identities a person may have. People respond to the deviant primarily in terms of his or her deviant status. Relatively little weight is given to the individual's other attributes, many of which may be positive. Moreover, once the public attributes a deviant status to an individual, it tends to impute other negative qualities to him or her as well. One consequence of this is that nondeviants tend to avoid interaction with those who have been labeled deviant. As a result, the stigmatized individual is left to interact with others who have been accorded the same deviant label. This process encourages the formation of deviant subcultures, which serve to stabilize, strengthen, and reinforce deviant lifestyles.

Many of the basic assumptions of labeling theory have not been supported by empirical evidence, while others have received inconsistent support. Critics generally take the position that labeling theory is an oversimplified explanation of deviant behavior. Labeling theory may offer a potential explanation for some types of "career" deviance, such as drug addiction and homosexuality, but not for many other types. There is widespread contention, however, that it is not the labels of society that make the deviant. Rather, it is the deviant's own behavior that leads to his or her being labeled. People are mentally ill, for example, not because of labels, but in the vast majority of cases because of dysfunctions in psychological or physiological processes. It does not make sense to assume that if there were no labeling, there would be no deviance.

Another principal criticism is that labeling does not necessarily lead to secondary deviance. The label itself, as empirical evidence suggests (Tittle, 1975), may be enough to terminate any pattern or potential pattern of deviance. Critics argue that many deviants, particularly alcoholics and drug addicts, do rehabilitate or reform themselves, and cease to follow a deviant lifestyle. Moreover, many other deviants, such as those who commit a crime of passion, are only one-time offenders, label or no label.

Perhaps the major criticism of labeling theory is that it does not explain primary deviance—the original cause of labeling. One of the problems here is that many people, perhaps the majority, who engage in primary deviance never get labeled, yet their behavior and its consequences require explanation too. As we have indicated in earlier sections of this chapter, probably everyone in his or her life commits several, even serious, deviant acts; yet, they remain personal secrets—all to the social advantage of the individual who escapes the public stigmatization of a deviant label.

# SOCIOLOGICAL THEORIES

Purely sociological theories of deviant behavior stress the roles of social structure and social situations in the generation of social deviance. Many of these explanations are variations or applications of major sociological theories that we discussed initially in Chapter 1, and have explored more specifically in subsequent chapters. They too, like sociopsychological theories, seek to explain the variation and frequency of deviant behavior among societies and within their subdivisions. We shall consider three of the more important of these kinds of theories: deviant subculture theory, anomie theory, and conflict theory.

DEVIANT SUBCULTURE THEORY. Here we have a family of theories rather than just one. Representative samples of deviant subculture theory are those developed by Miller (1958) and Cohen (1966). While each of these theories is different in certain respects, the fundamental principle of deviant subculture theory is that individuals inevitably assimilate their own specific culture or subculture.

Subcultures, as we saw in Chapter 3, represent distinct lifestyles or sociocultural worlds that pertain to particular segments of society. They generally represent, and share, the dominant culture. Deviant subcultures, on the other hand, consist of subcultures whose values and norms contradict or are in conflict with the dominant culture. Not all deviant subcultures represent countercultures as such, but their norms and values are sufficiently different in

591

▼ some respects as to require a different mode of behavior—and, obviously, one that is deviant in terms of the dominant cultural patterns.

Deviant subculture theories focus on the nature and characteristics of deviant groups—their shared values, beliefs, attitudes, norms, and lifestyles that guide behavior—and how they relate to, and subsist within, the dominant culture. Of special interest are the patterns of deviant behavior that members of deviant subcultures share and how they are acquired and reinforced. Also of concern is the generation of subcultures, the kinds of social situations and factors that facilitate the development of subcultures. Examples of deviant subcultures are delinquent youth gangs and the Pagans and Hell's Angels motorcycle gangs. Others include hustlers who frequent pool halls and various types of beatniks (see Polsky, 1985).

**592**

Deviant subculture theories hold that it is countercultures that transmit and perpetuate deviance within society. People who are members of deviant subcultures, or associate with those who are, come to learn values and norms of the counterculture in much the same way that any set of cultural values and norms are learned. This learning may be intentional or unintentional, direct or indirect, and usually it involves all forms. Such learning may involve a variety of groups and social situations. The deviant subcultures not only socialize or teach individuals how to be deviant and the occasions for such behavior, but also provide emotional support and reinforcement for deviant behavior. Deviance meets with approval within the deviant subculture. Such behavior is no longer considered deviant, but rather "normal" and conformist. Social support and psychological

**Countercultures.** "The New Jersey Breed," a motorcycle "outlaw" gang modeled after the Hell's Angels, represents a deviant subculture that provides its members with both emotional support and reinforcement for deviant behavior. (© G. Arvid Peterson/Photo Researchers)

reinforcement of this kind contribute significantly to the perpetuation of deviant behavior and lifestyles.

Deviant subculture theories are unable to specify whether an individual's membership in a deviant group is the cause or consequence of deviant behavior. Hence, the problem of unexplained primary deviance exists in these theories as well. These explanations are criticized also for being unable to account for deviance that occurs, both on a regular as well as an irregular basis, within the many segments of the dominant cultures whose values, norms, and lifestyles are essentially conformist.

ANOMIE THEORY.   Anomie is a concept introduced by Emile Durkheim (1897), the influential French sociologist, in conjunction with his classic analysis of suicide. Technically, **anomie** refers to a social order without norms or values—a normless state existing within a society, or perhaps within a group. Of course, by definition, there is no normless society or group, but it is possible to speak of the degree to which a society or group has a normative structure. Hence, for sociologists, anomie refers to a society that is characterized either by a relative state of normlessness or by conflict in social norms. Anomic situations, then, are defined as those in which there is a relative absence or ambiguity of social norms, which in turn lose their regulating and controlling powers. People in anomic situations are subject to confusion and ambivalence that often are incapacitating, and which may lead to psychological strain and frustration.

Durkheim (1897) showed that the rates of suicide in many European countries, over a period of several years, were linked to varying levels of anomie in different social situations. Suicide rates were high, for example, in times of economic and political crises, as well as in periods of rapid social change. Similar associations were observed on the basis of variations in the degree of social cohesion or integration

that characterized different kinds of social situations (see Figure 13-5). Durkheim's data revealed, for example, that suicide rates were lowest among large families (of generation), Catholics, and married people; highest among small families, Protestants, and divorced people. The former situations were described by Durkheim as strongly cohesive, while the latter as poorly integrated.

Contemporary research supports Durkheim's thesis on the relationship of deviance and anomie. Crutchfield (1983) has shown that crime rates in several major cities of the United States are correlated with social integration as measured in terms of population turnovers (the percentage of people who are recent newcomers or who recently have moved to a new neighborhood within the same city). Similar confirmation for social cohesion was presented by Stack (1983) who examined the relationship between religiosity (as measured by church attendance) and suicide rates in the United States. His data revealed an inverse relationship between church attendance and suicide rates. Stack argues, as Durkheim did, that religion integrates people into a moral community that is by nature strongly cohesive and thereby provides strength and security.

Modern and complex societies are usually described as being typically anomic because of the heterogeneity of their cultures and the diverse, often competing, groups of which they are comprised. Conflict about appropriate norms and values—about what is right and wrong, valuable or nonvaluable, important or unimportant—is thought to be a characteristic pattern. Hence, individuals who function in these kinds of sociocultural situations are likely to experience an overwhelming and bewildering array of different and conflicting norms. The "generation gap" often is cited as a rather common example of anomie in today's rapidly changing society. One of the more prevalent examples of this situation is the extensive confusion among young people and their parents

▼

593

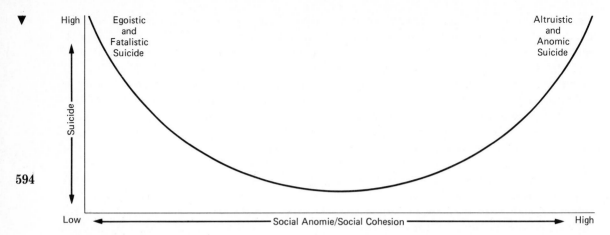

FIGURE 13-5  Suicide as Social Deviance. Emile Durkheim (1897) explained suicide as a phenomenon that develops in situations that are characterized by extreme degrees of either social anomie (regulation) or social cohesion (integration). Relatively too much or too little social anomie/social cohesion produces essentially the same dysfunctional consequences. Durkheim's data revealed, for example, that suicide rates were lowest among large families (of generation), Catholics, and married people; highest among small families, Protestants, and divorced people. The former situations were described by Durkheim as strongly cohesive, while the latter as poorly integrated. Thus, as shown in the figure above, the relationship between suicide rates and social anomie/social cohesion is curvilinear rather than unilinear.

regarding the norms of morality. Several works on stress and anomie have shown the deleterious consequences of such states in terms of physical and mental health (see, for example, Dohrenwend, 1969, 1975; House, 1974; Levine & Scotch, 1970).

Building on Durkheim's work, Robert Merton (1938, 1968) has utilized the concept of anomie, with certain modifications, to explain the cause of social deviance and the different rates of deviance that are found among various segments of the population. For Merton, anomie refers more specifically to disjuncture between culture and social structure, particularly between cultural goals and the institutionalized means for their attainment. The former represent those things which are defined by society as valuable and worth striving for (for example, health, justice, success). The latter, on the other hand, refers to the ways a society prescribes as legitimate for achieving its specified goals (for

example, hard work, occupational advancement, employment, education). Anomie, in Merton's theme, develops when individuals are denied access to the prescribed means for achieving culturally sanctioned goals. The consequence of this situation is often deviant behavior, which as such involves the use of illegitimate means to achieve legitimate goals. Merton (1949:103) says such deviant behavior "is in a sense 'called forth' by certain conventional values of the culture *and* by the class structure involving differential access to the approved opportunities for legitimate, prestige-bearing pursuit of the culture goals."

People, then, are predisposed to deviance when they have internalized the culturally prescribed goals of society but, for whatever reasons, do not have access to, or are incapable of utilizing, the socially acceptable means to achieve them. Not all segments of the population have equal access to socially prescribed means (for example, education and employ-ment) for the attainment of culturally pre-scribed goals. Lower-class, poor, handicapped, and minority people are decidedly at a disad-vantage in this regard, as we saw in our dis-cussions of life-chances in Chapter 10.

American culture, perhaps more than others, and certainly unlike many, places a strong value on economic and material or worldly success. The inability to achieve these cultural goals, which are not equally available to all in a land of ideal equality and unlimited opportunity, is seen as a personal failure or shortcoming. In other cultures, the lack of emphasis on such values may not reflect so unfavorably on the individual. Hence, it is the cultural motivation to succeed, or not to fail, rather than a social condition of poverty itself that provides the stimulation for deviant behavior. Under these kinds of circumstances, one may experience tre-mendous pressure to search for alternative means—illegitimate or deviant means—to achieve cultural success. As Merton (1957:146–169) states:

> It is only when a system of cultural values ex-tols, virtually above all else, certain common suc-cess goals for the population at large while the social structure rigorously restricts or completely closes access to approved modes of reaching these goals for a considerable part of the same popu-lation, that deviant behavior ensues on a large scale. . . . The moral mandate to achieve success thus exerts pressure to succeed, by fair means if possible and by foul means if necessary.

Merton (1957) has formulated a typology of adaptation to cultural values and institution-alized means. His scheme consists of five pos-sible ways in which one can reconcile the interaction of these two dimensions of the so-ciocultural system and deal with whatever kind of anomie may be involved. Four of these re-actions consist essentially of illegitimate modes of adaptation, and as such represent the basis of social deviance. Merton's typology is rep-resented in Table 13-4. The following are brief descriptions of each of the five modes of adap-tation.

1. *Conformity*, the dominant mode of adapta-tion, involves an acceptance of both cultur-ally prescribed goals and institutionalized means for their attainment. There is, of course, no deviant behavior in this mode of adaptation. Even those individuals who may not experience cultural success persist in the search of the respective goals through the use of legitimate means.

2. *Innovation* involves an acceptance of cultur-ally sanctioned goals, but a rejection of the institutionalized means for their attainment. Underworld crime and organized vice (pros-titution, gambling, racketeering) provide ex-amples. This mode of adaptation represents the most prevalent source of deviance. In-novation, thus, involves the development of new, but illegitimate or deviant means, for attaining culturally approved norms. Theft, fraud, embezzlement, rape, and cheating on examinations are all examples of innovation.

**595**

TABLE 13-4. A Typology of Modes of Individual Adaptation

| Modes of Adaptation | Cultural Goals | Institutionalized Means |
|---|---|---|
| I. Conformity | + | + |
| II. Innovation | + | − |
| III. Ritualism | − | + |
| IV. Retreatism | − | − |
| V. Rebellion | ± | ± |

▼

596

3. *Ritualism* is the repudiation of recognized goals, while retaining the established means for achieving them. This mode of adaptation consists essentially of a rigid adherence to norms with a simultaneous rejection of goals. Even though ritualists realize that the attainment of goals is unlikely, or even impossible, they routinely, even compulsively, continue to uphold and to enforce the established means. A classic example of ritualism is the bureaucrat who as the ideal-typical "rule stickler" follows all regulations meticulously and unquestionably; that is, one who does everything "by the book." People who attend church out of habit, yet no longer believe in the respective faith, are also examples of ritualistic adaptation. Deviance in this situation consists of a social conformity that is both superficial and artificial.

4. *Retreatism* involves a rejection of both the culturally prescribed goals and the institutionalized means for their attainment. This form of adaptation is exemplified by various kinds of societal "drop-outs" who no longer believe in the cultural goals and reject as well the established means for their attainment. Retreatists are exemplified by hippies, hobos, skid-rowers, alcoholics, drug addicts, vagrants, hermits, members of communes, and some people with certain types of mental illness. Even academic drop-outs often manifest retreatism. Retreatists have lost faith in both the ends and the means. They are people who may be described as *in* society but not *of* it, and their mode of adaptation is essentially a mechanism of escape.

5. *Rebellion*, the fifth mode of adaptation, is quite different from the others, and more complex. It basically involves efforts to change the existing order rather than to act within it. In addition to rejecting both goals and means, rebels at the same time actively try to replace them with substitute goals and the utilization of new means. Rebels or revolutionaries, in effect, attempt to overthrow the existing social order and to replace it with another. During the turbulent 1960s, several radical sociopolitical movements, such as the Weathermen, the Black Panthers, and the Minutemen exemplified rebellious forms of adaptation.

Despite the strong attention that anomie theory has received in sociological circles in the past few decades, it is not without criticism. One principal objection focuses on the fundamental assumption of anomie theory that cultural goals are universal and uniformly shared (Hyman, 1953). Some critics argue that members of different socioeconomic classes actually have different values and goals, and that deviance needs to be explained in these terms. Hence, the criticism here attacks the assumption that people in the lower social classes and other social segments really internalize the dominant cultural goals and norms—or, at least, that they do so to the same extent that might be true in other segments of society. One specific objection in this regard is that crime rates are higher for men than women throughout the various strata of society, yet it has not been demonstrated that men experience anomie more than women do. Such a situation, of course, may indeed be the case in a heavily male-dominant society where up to the past few years success and achievement have been predominantly a responsibility of males.

Anomie theory, like all purely sociological theory, is insufficient to account for deviance in yet another respect. Not all people in anomic situations engage in deviant behavior, whatever its form. The theory, therefore, cannot explain why some people adapt via conformity and others by deviant action. And, by extension, anomie theory does not explain why among deviants one form of adaptation is chosen rather than another. Such explanations are particularly needed to account for the differences between deviance in goals and deviance in means. Cloward and Ohlin (1960) have attempted to refine Merton's theory somewhat. They argue that the kind of adaptation made by people who are denied access to legitimate means for pursuing cultural goals depends on the "opportunity structure" in their environment. Individuals with ready access to illegal and violent means are more likely to become deviant.

Apart from these principal objections, anomie theory has been faulted for not being able to explain all kinds of deviance. Chief examples in this regard are such things as sex crimes and vandalism. Deviance that springs from irrational and spontaneous responses, such as crimes of passion, is another example. Moreover, there is a problem with anomie theory in trying to explain white-collar crime. Corporate executives who embezzle, or well-paid politicians who accept bribes, cannot be viewed as being disadvantaged or lacking in the skills that would enable them to attain wealth via socially acceptable means. Indeed, many of them are quite wealthy. Thus, anomie theory cannot explain why people who have not been shackled with various kinds of disadvantages engage in deviant behavior. Anomie theory seems more useful, therefore, in accounting for deviance among members of the lower social strata. Indeed, that the greatest amount of conventional crime—or at least, reported crime—occurs in the lower classes often is offered as a confirmation of anomie theory. There is considerable difficulty, however, in using anomie theory to explain deviance that occurs on the part of people in the middle and upper classes of society.

CONFLICT THEORY. A popular explanation for social deviance during the past decade or so has focused on an application of the basic principles of conflict theory. Essentially, as in all perspectives of conflict theory, social deviance is deemed to be the result of the exploitation of people by those who own the means of production (the capitalists or the bourgeoisie). It is these same people who also establish the norms of society, and who control all other social institutions in the service of their own aims and objectives.

In the perspectives of conflict theory, the criminal justice system (police, courts, corrections) exists to secure and to perpetuate the capitalistic goals of the ruling class. The criminal law, according to Marxist theory, is simply a device made and used by the ruling classes to preserve the existing order and power structure that favor their own interests (Chambliss & Seidman, 1982; Quinney, 1980). Under such a system, the criminal law is just another mechanism for perpetuating social inequality. Deviance, in effect, becomes the inescapable lot of the poor and the disadvantaged. Marxist and other conflict perspectives of deviance have received particular attention in very recent years.

Unlike labeling theory, conflict theory focuses on the labelers and not the labels. Crime and deviance, nonetheless, are seen as functions of society, and not of individuals. Essentially, deviance is an element in the alienating processes that constitute the prevalent and perennial struggle between the various social classes of society.

Not all conflict theorists, however, utilize an essentially Marxist perspective. Others simply assert that deviance is fundamentally a conflict between various groups or segments of society that are characterized by an incompatibility of social values and social objectives. The stronger and the more powerful segments that are responsible for establishing the social norms become conformists, and those with opposing beliefs and values assume the subordinate role of deviants.

Conflict theorists are criticized for holding a rather simplistic view of the legal system. While certain laws may serve the interest of the rich and powerful, and many have come into existence as a result of their influence, many other laws are of interest to all members of the society, regardless of their socioeconomic status. Clearly, it is in the interest of poor people as

**597**

▼ well as wealthy ones to have laws against rape, assault, kidnapping, and homicide.

## THEORIES OF DEVIANCE
## IN PERSPECTIVE

598

Social deviance, as should be clear by now, is a highly diversified and complex phenomenon. Given the enormous variety of deviant behavior, as well as its socially and culturally arbitrary nature, no one theory can account—or can be expected to account—for all social deviance. Much more than in other forms of social behavior, there is no room for monistic (single-cause) explanations for deviance. The motives of individuals who engage in deviance are too diverse, and the occasions too varied, as are the nature and kinds of deviants themselves.

While no one theory can explain all forms of social deviance, many of them do make a significant contribution to the understanding of this highly diversified and complex phenomenon. Similarly, no one theory provides a thorough explanation of any one type of deviance. Taken together or in combination, however, these theories offer a more complete understanding of social deviance. Despite their highly different approaches and perspectives, several of these theories are not incompatible with each other. Indeed, in many respects, the sociological and sociopsychological theories in particular can be integrated into a more complex and comprehensive explanation of social deviance.

Each of these theories, moreover, contributes to our understanding of human behavior not only in terms of deviance, but also in terms of social conformity. Indeed, some would argue that since deviance is a nominal rather than a real concept, we can expect to explain only the reality of behavior and not the arbitrariness of our social and cultural definitions of it. Given the sociocultural relativity of social deviance, the causes or motives for deviant behavior— what is labeled as such—may be identical for

behavior that is not so labeled. Accordingly, we need to give considerable reflection to the possibility of explaining social deviance as "normal" or conformist behavior. At any rate, social behavior, at all times, must be explained consistently. It is not the case that social behavior can be explained one way when defined as deviance, and in another way when defined as conformity. Such an approach would violate the fundamental tenets of any logic of scientific inquiry.

Purely sociological theories, as we have seen, attempt to explain deviant behavior in terms of social states and statistical frequencies. Each fundamentally seeks to explain why different social states have varying rates of deviance. These theories, however, remain essentially incomplete. What the theories do not explain is why some people in particular social situations engage in deviant behavior and others do not. Sociological theories of deviant behavior, we believe, need to account for the occurrence as well as the absence of deviance, that is, for conformity. Much variance is left unaccounted for by sociological theories that fail to address this problem. Our discussion on the role of personality in social deviance in the next section attempts to provide a dimension for the resolution, however partial, of this theoretical issue. Such an approach is directed at a more complete and comprehensive understanding of deviant behavior.

# Personality and Social Deviance

One may tend to think of deviant or abnormal personalities as a psychological contradiction. Yet, insofar as personality is the product of social processes and social situations, one should quickly see the significance that deviant personalities and the personalities of deviants have for sociology and its concern with social deviance. We shall consider two dimensions of the relationship of personality to social deviance: pathological personalities that constitute a specific form of deviant behavior, and the personalities of deviants that play a role in many specific kinds of deviant behavior.

## THE DEVIANT PERSONALITY

Much social deviance takes the form of personality dysfunction. Moderate and severe dysfunction usually make it difficult or impossible for people to perform their various social roles within the limits of normative expectations. Consequences of this abnormal social interaction are felt in all segments of society. Such a form of social deviance is undoubtedly far more extensive than one might suspect.

NORMAL VERSUS ABNORMAL PERSONALITY.   What, then, is the deviant personality? To answer this sometimes highly controversial question, we need to come back to our consideration of how one distinguishes normality or normal behavior. With regard to the specific question at hand, there are at least three kinds of bases for "normality" or the "normal personality." These are: (1) statistically modal behavior—what most people do; (2) sociocultural normality—normal personalities, like any normal behavior, are always defined in part by the sociocultural context; and (3) clinical normality, which essentially has an objective and universally determinable, or cross-cultural, basis. Abnormalities in this third category are usually quite clear in that they can be determined by empirical analysis. Dysfunctions of an organic nature with a biological, physiological, or neurological basis, such as mental retardation and other forms of brain damage, are relatively simple to verify. Deviant personality patterns that have no demonstrably organic basis are not so easy to reconcile in terms of normal-abnormal distinctions.

▼

599

**Street Life.** Homeless individuals, whether or not they manifest signs of clinical dysfunction, often are labelled as abnormal personalities in that their behavior and lifestyle deviate from the statistical and sociocultural standards of "normal" behavior. (© E. B. Grunzweig/Photo Researchers)

▼

**600**

Reconciling these three criteria for the determination of deviant personality is no easy matter. A deviant personality, like any other form of social deviance, is always determined in part by the values of the sociocultural context. Kwakiutl Indians, living off the coast of the state of Washington, are fiercely competitive people to whom the label of megalomania is usually applied. Italians in general are very loud and boisterous people. Both of these peoples no doubt would view Americans, in whom these respective cultural patterns are modally absent, as somewhat pathological or at least wanting in psychological maturity. Again, one must expect to find a high correlation between normal personalities that are defined in terms of sociocultural norms, and those so defined on the basis of statistical frequency. Hence, sociocultural normality in large part becomes statistical normality.

Whichever criteria one chooses to use, we need to keep in mind that the difference between "normal" and "abnormal" personality is always a matter of degree and not one of kind or absolute distinction. That is to say, abnormal personalities are not distinguished so much by kinds of behavior as by the exaggerated manifestation of "normal" kinds of behavior. Delusions and hallucinations, phobias and manias, depressions and agitations, which typically distinguish or are used to distinguish abnormal or deviant personalities, can be found most assuredly, yet in a much less pronounced and dysfunctional manner, in the "normal" types of personality.

Deviation in personality may have several sources. Many of those outside the organic (biological, physiological, or neurological) sphere are considered to be directly or indirectly the products of social interaction. Chief among these, of course, is an improper personality development that can be related to the socialization process. Equally significant in this regard are interpersonal relations and the interdependent dynamics of the individual and the society.

Psychological stress produced in this latter regard by incongruent expectations can be the source of severe incapacitation for many people.

One of the prevalent and paradoxical notions in society is that people should be held individually responsible for their personalities—functional or dysfunctional—even though it is simultaneously maintained that personality is essentially a social product. The idea here seems to be that while people are victims of physical illness, psychological abnormality or dysfunction is of a person's own doing. Such a position is not easy to reconcile with the widespread admission that psychological stress, stemming from such social dynamics as alienation and anomie, is sociologically produced in most cases.

Social deviance in the form of personality abnormality or mental illness, nonetheless, is no doubt far more extensive than one might suspect. A survey of mental health in midtown Manhattan (Srole et al., 1978) in the late 1950s revealed that only 2 percent of the population sampled showed no symptoms of psychiatrically defined abnormalities, such as neurosis or psychosis.* On the basis of this well-received study, it has been estimated that one out of fifty people in the American population is severely mentally disturbed. Undoubtedly, using less extreme criteria for determining mental illness, the

---

* "Neurosis" and "psychosis" represent traditional psychiatric terms that are still used extensively in the behavioral and medical sciences for broadly descriptive purposes. *Neurosis* usually refers to less serious forms of mental illness in which the individual is in touch with reality and able to function adequately in society. Examples of neurotic behavior include phobias, anxiety reactions, and psychosomatic disorders. *Psychosis*, a most serious form of mental disorder, usually involves a loss of contact with reality and requires hospitalization. Often impairment of brain function is involved in psychotic behavior. Major types of psychosis include schizophrenic, affective, and paranoid disorders. More recently, in an attempt to achieve greater clinical precision, the American Psychiatric Association has developed a new system for the classification of mental disorders: *The Diagnostic and Statistical Manual of Mental Disorders*, revised 1987. This system of classification closely corresponds to the international one formulated by the World Heath Organization.

projected figures would be much higher. For the past few decades it has been routinely estimated that one out of every ten people would probably spend some time in a mental hospital during his or her lifetime. Far greater numbers will require other, less extreme, forms of treatment. A comprehensive survey undertaken by the National Institute of Mental Health in 1984 suggests that at any given time nearly one in five adults in the United States suffers from a psychiatric disorder, ranging from mildly disabling anxiety or depression to severe psychosis such as schizophrenia.

No matter which figure and projections one chooses to use, there is little escaping the fact that deviant personalities exist in large numbers in modern, complex societies. It would not be unjustified to assume that much social deviance is related to this extensive pattern of deviant personality. Indeed, the many individuals who are judged and incarcerated as "criminally insane" offer ample evidence of this assumption.

PSYCHOPATHS AND SOCIOPATHS. Deviant personalities that are involved in social deviance manifest a variety of personality disorders. One type of abnormal personality, however, has had particular significance for many serious forms of deviant behavior. This is that type of personality which for a long time has been known as the **psychopath.** In more recent years, the designation for this personality has become "sociopath"—a matter of curious significance for sociology and the relationship of deviant personalities to this field.

The **sociopath** is a personality type that results from inadequate, ineffective, or inappropriate socialization. In more psychological terms, particularly when the label "psychopath" was prevalent, such a personality was said to lack a conscience or superego. Of course, such is not the case at all. These individuals, being quite normal in a psychological or clinical sense, are able to distinguish right from wrong. Moreover, sociopaths are quite aware of the

sanctions that are likely to be imposed for the violation of various social norms. Their abnormality lies in their nearly total lack of internalization of the values and norms of society. Hence, lacking this internal control, they experience no guilt or shame in the commission of deviant behavior. The individual who can kill another person "in cold blood" without batting an eyelash, or with no emotional concern, provides an extreme example of the sociopath. See Box 13-2 for a psychological profile of the sociopath.

Behavioral manifestations of the sociopath before the end of his or her teens include truancy, delinquency, lying, substance abuse,

## BOX 13-2. The Sociopathic Personality

**Among the principal characteristics of the sociopathic/psychopathic personality are the following:**

1. **Superficial charm, poise, rationality, and verbal facility.**
2. **Average or above average intelligence.**
3. **Lack of personal responsibility and reliability.**
4. **Untruthfulness, insincerity, callousness, manipulativeness.**
5. **Anti-social behavior without remorse, regret, or shame.**
6. **Pathological egocentricity and incapacity for love.**
7. **Unresponsiveness in interpersonal relations.**
8. **Lack of insight into personal motivations.**
9. **Ingratitude.**
10. **General poverty in major affective relations.** ▲

Source: Hervey M. Cleckley, *The Mask of Sanity.* St. Louis: C. V. Mosby, 1976.

▼ theft, and vandalism. Sociopaths, as adults, typically manifest an inability to maintain a satisfactory job performance, inability to function as a responsible parent, unlawful behavior, failure to honor financial obligations, impulsivity, lying, and recklessness. Sociopaths are widely considered to be essentially impossible to reform.

## 602 PERSONALITY OF DEVIANTS

There is sufficient evidence to warrant the contention that significant relationships exist between particular types of personality ("normal" or "abnormal") and specific forms of deviant behavior. While it may not be possible to say that deviants are categorically distinguishable from nondeviants in terms of distinctive personality profiles, it seems valid to contend that people with certain types of personality, in terms of traits or structures, are more likely to engage in deviance or certain forms of deviance (see Case & Glaser, 1974). Without allowing for methodological evaluations, research data that attempt to discern distinctive personality characteristics among deviants are rather impressive. A review of 113 studies that addressed this question showed that 42 percent were able to differentiate delinquents and criminals from nonoffenders on the basis of personality characteristics (Schuessler & Cressy, 1950). Similarly, Waldo and Dinitz (1967) found that 81 percent of 94 studies published between 1950 and 1965 discriminated significantly between delinquents or criminals and presumed nonoffenders on the basis of personality variables.

Let us consider a few types of deviants in terms of distinctive personality structures and dynamics: the criminal, the rapist, the addict, and the suicidal victim.

THE CRIMINAL PERSONALITY. Extensive data, not without controversy and criticism, have been compiled during the past several years that suggest a variety of both distinctive and significantly different personality profiles among criminals. Among studies of this type are the following that may be mentioned as illustrations.

Yochelson and Samenow (1976) have produced a highly detailed study of the criminal personality which they distinguished in terms of distinctive patterns of thought as well as patterns of action. These researchers identified fifty-two "errors of thinking" that were present in all of the offenders whom they studied. Most prominent among these deviant patterns of thought were extreme fearfulness, extreme and persistent anger, fatalism or despair, criminal pride, and a superoptimism about the outcome of their criminal acts. The habitual criminal, moreover, is described as a liar and a deceiver, and one who has little capacity for love, friendship, or companionship. He wants trust and respect, yet is himself both untrustworthy and disrespectful. An individual with this profile may be described essentially as a psychopath or sociopath.

Megargee and Bohn (1979), in an extensive study of criminals based on the Minnesota Multiphasic Personality Inventory (MMPI), have formulated a taxonomic classification of ten types of criminals. Their research found that 96 percent of the inmates at the Federal Correctional Institute in Tallahassee, Florida, could be assigned to one of these personality types. Research of this kind has been reported to be quite helpful in the clinical classification of inmates for rehabilitative purposes.

Of interest here too is the work of H. Warren Dunham (1959) in his *Sociological Theory and Mental Disorder*. On the basis of extensive research in the field of social psychiatry, Dunham concluded that criminals who are psychotic are more likely to suffer from schizophrenia than from any other form of psychosis. Moreover, catatonic and paranoid types of schizophrenia show a higher incidence of crime than do other categories. Crimes committed by psychotics are more likely to be against people than against property.

**THE RAPIST PERSONALITY.** Rape traditionally has been viewed as a crime of sexual passion. Undoubtedly, many crimes of rape are so motivated. Considerable evidence, however, exists to demonstrate that rape is overwhelmingly an act of violence and aggression in which the sexual dynamics and motivations do not play a predominant role. Such a conclusion appears even more understandable when one thinks of the children, the unattractive—even ugly—individuals, the very aged, and the infirm people who comprise a fair number of the victims of rape.

An interesting study (Groth & Birnbaum, 1979), based on over 15 years of extensive clinical experience with more than five hundred sexual offenders, examined the psychological and emotional factors that predisposed a person to react to situational and life events with sexual violence. This work provides a framework for the development histories, lifestyles, and motivations of men who rape; and it offers guidelines for the identification, diagnostic assessment, and treatment of such offenders.

Analyses of these data reveal rape to be chiefly the sexual expression of power and anger. It is a pseudosexual act, complex and multidetermined, but addressing issues of hostility (anger) and control (power), more than passion (sexuality). The study differentiates patterns of assault among such offenders and examines clinical aspects of their rape behavior, such as the selection of the victim, the determination of the sexual act, the offender's subjective reaction during the assault, the role of alcohol, sexual dysfunction, and other related issues.

**THE ADDICTIVE PERSONALITY. Addiction** constitutes physical or psychological dependency on a drug or an activity—even a positive activity, such as shopping, bicycling, eating, working, television viewing, or meditation. The source of pleasure, whatever it may be, becomes an addictive habit—one characterized by excessive, compulsive or repetitive, and impulsive or immediate gratification. Our concern here with the addictive personality is primarily in terms of psychological addiction that constitutes a characteristic way of dealing with life. Psychological addiction exists when a person is so attracted to a substance, activity, or sensation that he or she loses an appreciation for other aspects of the environment or the self. The addict typically views the world from a negative perspective and lacks confidence to face life independently.

Not all addicts, of course, are alike. Such is true in part because of the variety of addictions and the situations in which they are used. It is important, nonetheless, to distinguish casual and nonaddictive behavior from the compulsive and excessive variety. Perhaps the stereotype of the drug addict, and alcoholic as well, is the compulsive individual who craves the abused substance and has little or no control over his or her addiction. On the other hand, there are millions of people who are able to consume alcohol and some other types of drugs without any loss of control over their use. Such nonmedical use of drugs and alcohol is not considered deviant in most situations. Rather, it is the abuse and compulsive use that constitutes deviance.

We believe, nonetheless, that it is possible to speak quite cogently about a modal personality in regard to drug addicts, as well as alcoholics and other types of addicts. In the case of drug addiction, moreover, given the variety of substance abuse, not present in the mere consumption of alcohol whatever its form may be, we can distinguish specific types of personality. The fact that many drug addicts are concentrated in certain social environments (for example, crowded, poverty-ridden inner cities) and adopt distinctive lifestyles, facilitates a psychosocial profile of addictive personalities; but,

▼

**603**

▼

again, one must remember that lifestyles and patterns of drug use are by no means homogeneous among addicts, and that one needs to allow for a possible diversity of personality types among a diversity of addicts.

Empirical typological studies of personality among drug addicts have emerged recently. Many of them center on the concept of psychopathy (sociopathy) which is commonly used as a means to understand the addict. Stein and Rozynko (1974) reported on one study involving a random sample of 201 male voluntary admissions to the detoxification ward of a state hospital. Ninety-one percent had been using heroin regularly on a daily basis, and 70 percent used other drugs as well, mostly marijuana and barbiturates. These individuals were administered structured interviews, including a series of personal inventories, which focused on four general areas: emotional disturbance, cognitive-intellectual functioning, expressiveness, and socialization. Data analysis, utilizing a system of computer derivation, yielded a typology of ten personality types or patterns, each of which can be distinguished by distinct social and psychological profiles.

Most forms of physical and psychological dependencies are thought to be caused by unfulfilled emotional needs. Research, for example, on the "placebo effect" (the effect produced by the fake administration of narcotics) demonstrates that the addict's belief in receiving or taking a narcotic often produces an effect stronger than the actual physical impact of the addicting substance. There is considerable consensus that the drug-addictive personality is characterized by low frustration tolerance and chronic feelings of inferiority, boredom, fearfulness, powerlessness, and dependency. The same personality profile is thought to be characteristic of other types of addicts, such as the alcoholic and the compulsive gambler. These psychological profiles are considered to be *a priori* personality patterns, that is to say, preexisting ones that lead to the respective forms of

**604**

deviant behavior, rather than psychological profiles that result from addiction.

THE SUICIDAL PERSONALITY. Suicide, while not a major problem compared to many other types of deviance, has been a form of behavior of particular interest to sociologists. Perhaps the major reason for this is that sociological interests in suicide can be traced back to a classic study of suicide in 1897 by Emile Durkheim, itself one of the first major empirical investigations in the field of sociology—which we have mentioned already.

Durkheim spoke of four "types" of suicide (egoistic, altruistic, anomic, and fatalistic) that can be distinguished by the social circumstances in which this form of deviant behavior takes place. Egoistic suicide results from social situations characterized by relatively low degrees of either social solidarity or social cohesion—situations that, in other terms, are distinguished by strong degrees of alienation and/or extreme individualism. The customary social restraints in these types of situations are either loosened or absent. Suicide by a lonely and despondent, or estranged, person exemplifies egoistic suicide. Altruistic suicide, on the other hand, is the product of antithetical forces of social structure-situations that are characterized by high degrees of social cohesion and extreme integration. Herein one finds social restraints of an extremely strong nature. Altruistic suicide may be exemplified by the Japanese kamikaze pilots during World War II. Many of the more than nine hundred suicides that took place one day in 1978 at the People's Temple, a religious cult located in what became known as Jonestown in Guyana, also exemplify altruistic suicide (see Wooden, 1981). Anomic suicide occurs in social situations that tend to be characterized by relatively low levels of social regulation and social organization—situations in which social norms and expectations are either absent or grossly ambiguous. Such situations are commonly found in periods of rapid social change or in times of political and economic crises. Fatalistic suicide is the antithesis of the anomic variety, and occurs in social situations that are so highly regulated or controlled that the individual feels a strong sense of powerlessness.

Durkheim's theory is essentially valid yet today (see Danigelis & Pope, 1979; Gibbs, 1982), and the basic principles of the relationship between social cohesion or social regulation and social dysfunction can be applied to other forms of behavior, deviant as well as nondeviant. His formulation, nonetheless, is fundamentally a state-rate (S-R) explanation. That is, in what has become a traditional and typical sociological perspective, it proposes to explain varying rates of behavior in terms of variations in social states. More specifically, this theoretical model attempts to account for the existence of a certain incidence of suicide in terms of a certain degree of social integration or social regulation. What the theory cannot do, however, is to explain why only certain individuals are the victims of suicidal structures and others are not.

Henry and Short (1954), attempting a refinement of Durkheim's theory, analyzed sui-

cidal and homicidal behavior by means of a more complex theoretical paradigm that combined the sociological theory with a psychological one, namely, the frustration-aggression hypothesis (see section above, "Theories of Deviance"). This psychological theory maintains that aggressive behavior presupposes psychological frustration. Assuming that frustration must be vented, the generated aggression may be expressed either inwardly (turned on the self) or outwardly (turned on others) in a variety of specific behavioral forms. The typical direction of ventilation is a function of an individual's personality structure. However, such ventilation may itself be frustrated by the social structure of a particular society. What happens when different kinds of personalities, in terms of their typical patterns of ventilation, find themselves in social situations characterized by different types of social regulation (anomie) and/or social integration (cohesion) which can be assessed in terms of their tolerance for outwardly vented aggression? Projections are shown in Figure 13-6.

Henry and Short's paradigm treats personality as an intervening variable, and offers a

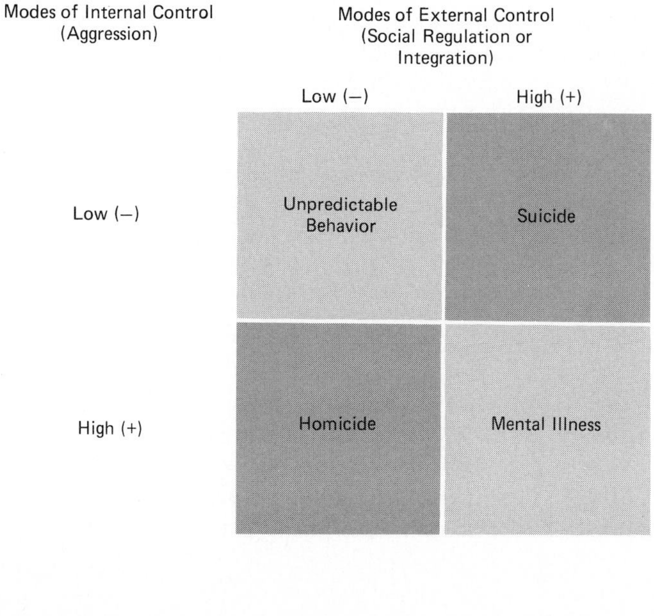

▼

**605**

| Modes of Internal Control (Aggression) | Modes of External Control (Social Regulation or Integration) | |
| --- | --- | --- |
| | Low (−) | High (+) |
| Low (−) | Unpredictable Behavior | Suicide |
| High (+) | Homicide | Mental Illness |

FIGURE 13-6 Personality and Suicide. Modes of internal control refer to the inability of the individual to vent aggression inwardly or toward the self. Modes of external control refer to the inability of the individual to vent aggression outwardly or toward others. The chart shows, according to the thesis of Henry and Short (1954), the likely kinds of behavior, in extreme situations, when internal and external restraints are juxtaposed.

▼

more complex theoretical model: state-person-ality-rate (S-P-R). This theory, providing a more precise explanation of suicide, as well as of homicide, shows that these forms of deviant behavior are the products of only certain kinds of people who find themselves in certain kinds of social situations. Suicide is more likely the product of individuals characterized by low modes of internal control within social situations characterized by high modes of external control; while homocide is more likely to occur under psychological and sociological conditions that are antithetical.

The S-P-R model dramatically demonstrates the significant interaction of personality and social systems. No attempt, of course, is made to apply this explanation to any single case of deviance. As a more refined and complex theory of social behavior, however, it constitutes a more comprehensive *sociological* theory that can account for a greater amount of the phenomena in question, and serve much more effectively as a predictor of such behavior.

Attempts at constructing these types of complex and multifocal theories continue to be made yet today in the area of deviant behavior. One can expect them to be the theories or models of the future, as we look for comprehensive explanations that are able to explain all, or at least much more, of the phenomena (or variance) in question.

## Functions and Dysfunctions of Social Deviance

While deviance is fundamentally an undesirable phenomenon in any society, this is not to say that it is totally dysfunctional. As we saw in our discussion of functional analysis in Chapter 6, any mechanism, or any given behavior, is most likely to have both functional and dysfunctional consequences. Such is thought to be

no less the case with deviance. Deviant behavior, thus, may be considered to be functional as well as dysfunctional.

Durkheim (1964) was one of the first to speculate on the functional consequences of deviant behavior. He drew attention to the existence of crime in all societies, and speculated on the positive functions it could have for society. Durkheim argued that deviance both promotes and reaffirms stability and social solidarity because it accentuates the shared normative patterns which serve to unify and to hold the society together. Kai Erikson (1966) illustrates Durkheim's thesis in a study of deviant behavior among the colonial settlers in New England. He argues that the puritanical emphasis on harsh punishment for offenders reinforced a sense of community solidarity.

Durkheim believed that societal expressions of outrage and indignation against deviant behavior reaffirm and underscore the normative structure of society. Morally condemning certain acts confirms the validity of the violated norms and declares once again where the boundaries of social norms are located. Deviance, thus, functions to increase solidarity and cohesiveness among members of a society with respect to its normative structure. When an especially outrageous action occurs, people tend to intermingle and to exchange expressions of moral indignation. As Durkheim (1964:102) noted:

> We have only to notice what happens, particularly in a small town, when some moral scandal has just been committed. [Citizens] stop each other on the street, they visit each other, they seek to come together to talk of the event and wax indignant in common. From all the similar impressions which are exchanged . . . there emerges a unique temper . . . which is everybody's without being anybody's in particular.

The following, primarily latent, dynamics are thought to be among the principal functional consequences of social deviance.

606

1. Social norms are clarified insofar as deviance indicates or establishes the tolerable limits of behavior.
2. Punishment of deviant behavior, in whatever form, reaffirms social norms which in turn makes for social cohesion and solidarity among those who conform to them.
3. Tensions and stress are released that otherwise might be highly dysfunctional for both society and the individual, and which preserve both social order and personal well-being. Prostitution, gambling, and the use of alcohol and drugs are relevant examples of this dysfunctional consequence. Kingsley Davis (1932) offered a classic analysis of the functions of deviance in his study "The Sociology of Prostitution." He argued that prostitution exists so widely, and in some instances is allowed to exist—legally and otherwise—because it meets needs that for some kinds of people cannot be satisfied by legitimate social institutions. Davis had in mind unmarried, familially estranged, and physically deformed people, as well as those who may be interested in unconventional forms of sexual expression.

   Indeed, many forms of deviant behavior are permitted on certain occassions, such as Halloween, Mardi Gras, national holidays, and at certain sporting events. The destruction of goal posts at the conclusion of a football game is quite likely to be looked upon with amusement, but at any other time those involved in such behavior would risk very severe sanctions. Many colleges, and high schools as well, permit "Hell Week" or some sort of event during which dress codes and other forms of obligatory conduct are significantly relaxed.
4. Deviance may serve also as a mechanism of social control. Often one kind of deviant behavior is permitted in order to effect the control of another kind. Prisoners frequently are allowed to engage in certain forms of deviant behavior so long as they agree to serve as informants on other deviance thought to be more serious, thereby assisting in the control and repression of other kinds of deviant behavior considered to be more dysfunctional.
5. Deviance may signal dysfunctions of society, especially in terms of the nonsatisfaction of individual needs. Deviant behavior often draws public attention to the existence of certain injustices in society. Black Americans who participated in widespread sit-ins in the South through the 1960s undertook a form of deviant behavior in violating the norms of their communities regarding seating arrangements and the use of segregated facilities. Such deviant activity helped to promote changes in the law and in social arrangements regarding public accommodation.
6. Deviance may serve as a source of social change in that extensive or widespread forms of "deviant" behavior frequently become legitimized by society. The widespread effects of civil disobedience during the past two decades are dramatic examples of such a situation. Other social changes brought about by deviance and violations of social norms include the repeal of Prohibition laws against the consumption of alcohol and the "blue laws" that in many states prohibited commercial transactions on Sundays. Another, more timely, example can be seen in current efforts being made for the decriminalization of the personal use of marijuana.
7. Not all new behavior or new norms are the result of consensus or legislative enactment. Often it is through social deviance found in various types of collective behavior that new forms of behavior and new norms emerge. Hence, if many of yesterday's deviants are today's conformists, one can expect that some of today's deviants may become tomorrow's conformists.
8. Excessive deviance on the organizational level may serve as a warning signal that the existing arrangements or social policies are

▼

607

▼

608

in need of change. Cohen (1966:10) observes that evidence such as "increases in absenteeism from work, truancy from school, AWOL's from the Army, runaways and other disturbances in correction institutions, surly and sullen compliance with orders, and deliberate defects in workmanship" can promote a reexamination of existing procedures, which could reveal unsuspected causes of discontent. Out of this analysis could come suggestions for change designed to enhance efficiency and raise morale in social groups.

The dysfunctional consequences of deviant behavior, of course, are the more obvious ones. Basically, the dysfunctional aspects of deviance lie in the fact that deviant behavior is fundamentally a threat to society, an aberration in the social order upon which any social system rests. Deviance challenges social norms and the functions they serve. Effective social interaction presupposes a relatively orderly and stable society. Excessive deviance can undermine the very basic structure of society. Deviance, thus, is a fundamental threat to the stability and predictability of society. The weakening of social norms, in turn, produces a situation of cognitive ambiguity that can present a variety of dysfunctional consequences on the personal level.

Since we have spoken for the most part in this chapter of the dysfunctions of social deviance, it should be sufficient for our purposes here merely to restate the more significant and generic ones in very brief form. Social deviance:

1. Threatens order and stability necessary for social life.
2. Endangers physical and psychological well-being of individuals.
3. Makes social life unpredictable.
4. Necessitates costs for social control.
5. Leads to more deviance when uncontrolled.

The incompatibility between the dysfunctions and functions of social deviance raises the obvious question of how much deviance can be allowed without upsetting a seemingly tolerable balance between these two types of consequences. The question, then, is this: At what point does deviance become predominantly, or for all intents and purposes even totally, dysfunctional? This matter is difficult to determine, particularly because we do not know the extent of deviance in society.

While any social system can tolerate a certain amount of deviance, it does seem logical to assume that there is a point beyond which the order (stability and predictability), and indeed the very existence, of society is jeopardized. It is at this hypothetical point, which of course depends on the particular social system, that deviance can give way to social disorganization or the collapse of institutionalized structures. Unfortunately, the sociological analysis and explanation of deviance is not yet so sophisticated as to permit a precise determination of this "point of diminishing returns."

# Social Control of Deviance

**Social control** consists essentially of the processes and mechanisms by which society encourages and/or enforces conformity to social norms that have been designed for the effective operation of the social order. There are two principal kinds of methods by which social control is achieved: (1) internalization of social values and norms, which rests on the processes and mechanisms of socialization, and (2) external social pressure, which involves the application of social sanctions. We already have discussed each of these processes in Chapter 3, but they need to be explored here in terms of their particular significance for social deviance.

## NORMATIVE INTERNALIZATION

One of the fundamental objectives of socialization, as we discussed in Chapter 4, is essentially the internalization of social norms; that is, accepting them as one's own and incorporating them into one's own self system. Internalized control of social deviance makes effective use of one's conscience, the violation of which may lead to feelings of remorse or guilt, which in turn could become a source of severe psychological pain or stress. The avoidance of this internal pain, if conscience is sufficiently developed, serves ideally to ensure conformity in the absence of external vigilance. When **normative internalization** exists, people obey the norms of society because they believe it is the proper thing to do—that a given law or norm is just. In such situations individuals conform to societal norms because they want to and not because they fear negative sanctions. Since police and other norm-enforcing agents cannot be everywhere at every moment, normative internalization obviously can be both a necessary and effective method of social control. Honor codes in schools and colleges, such as those used at West Point and the Naval and Air Force Academies, exemplify social control by means of normative internalization.

Deviance in the perspective of normative internalization is seen as failure of the socialization system. Such a situation may involve an inadequacy, inappropriateness, or ambivalence of socialization. **Inadequate socialization** consists of an insufficient amount of either teaching or learning, as well as the deprivation of a suitable social or psychological environment and the resources for these processes. **Inappropriate socialization** involves the internalization of values and norms that are incompatible with the particular culture and specific social situations. Socialization that takes place in deviant subcultures is an illustration of inappropriate socialization. However adequate such socialization may be for the deviant subculture, it is inappropriate and dysfunctional for the dominant culture. **Ambivalent socialization** occurs when an individual has internalized both conventional and deviant norms or values. Such situations invariably generate cognitive ambiguity and social conflict. Behav-

ior choices in such situations of cognitive ambiguity often automatically involve social deviance. Socialization, of course, is seldom totally effective, given the susceptibility to change in social norms, as well as their sheer quantity and differential importance. Moreover, external pressures often outweigh any measure of self-control of which a person may be capable.

## EXTERNAL PROCESSES OF SOCIAL CONTROL

External control refers to the processes and mechanisms by which other people exert pressure upon the individual to conform to societal norms. Within this mode of social control, one can distinguish between mechanisms of blockage that make deviance difficult or costly, and mechanisms that essentially involve punishment of one kind or another.

Abiding by the norms of society, as surely all of us know, is often difficult, painful, and even costly. Social conformity frequently involves personal sacrifice, which most people endure in the interest of the common good—namely, order and predictability in social interaction. People who deviate, therefore, usually encounter negative, often quite hostile, responses to their apparent self-centeredness and lack of social consciousness.

Not all norm violations, of course, are looked upon by society with equal alarm. Generally, to the extent that deviant behavior is seen as threatening the existence of society, there will be little toleration of the deviance, and sanctions for such behavior will be severe. Murder, assault, rape, and theft are examples of deviance that, if allowed to go unchecked, would severely endanger the very existence of society. Deviant behavior such as speeding, littering, and jaywalking, however, is tolerated to a much greater degree, and the penalties are correspondingly mild. Based on the relative seriousness of deviant behavior, sociologists distinguish between types of social control in terms of informal and formal sanctions.

▼ INFORMAL SANCTIONS.   Informal sanctions, often vague, variable, and inconsistent, include such methods or techniques as gossip, ridicule, laughter, ostracism, shunning, and social rejection. Informal methods are quite effective—often the only effective ones—in primary-group structures, or *Gemeinschaft*-type societies characterized by a high degree of social cohesion, social stability, and face-to-face interaction. Disapproval of one's behavior by family, friends, and close acquaintances or associates does indeed have considerable influence on behavior. The effect of group pressure in small-group situations has been demonstrated in a host of studies on the dynamics of social conformity. Mention can be made in particular of the well-known research by Asch (1952) and Sherif (1966) that was discussed in Chapter 9.

While informal modes of social control can be very instrumental in preventing deviance, there are two drawbacks to these methods. First, people may not have a clear understanding of the type and degree of punishment they are likely to incur should they engage in deviant behavior. As a result, the punishment will have less of a deterrent effect. Second, feelings of personal esteem, loyalty, and sympathy may impede or interfere with the administration of negative sanctions. A person usually has mixed emotions about applying negative sanctions to family and friends who are involved in social deviance, of whatever kind or degree. Nonetheless, on the whole, informal methods are the more effective ones.

FORMAL SANCTIONS.   Formal sanctions involve fines and imprisonment, as well as physical punishments such as isolation, whipping, torture, mutilation, and even execution. These methods are usually applied by specifically established or designated social agencies. They are utilized more commonly in *Gesellschaft*-type societies. The size, mobility, heterogeneity, and anonymity of large complex societies require methods that are correspondingly more formal and impersonal in character. Informal methods of social control are by and large either impossible or ineffective in large, complex, heterogeneous, and anonymous societies.

## CRIMINAL JUSTICE SYSTEMS

Particular mention, in regard to formal structures for the social control of deviance, needs to be made of what lately has come to be widely known as the *criminal justice system*. Essentially involved in this designation are three separate, yet related, institutions of modern societies: po-

**610**

**FRANK AND ERNEST ®by Bob Thaves**

Reprinted by permission of NEA, Inc.

lice, courts, and corrections. The division of responsibility for social control in this interlocking network may be described briefly in the following terms: Police comprise an agency responsible for the surveillance, apprehension, and detention of deviants. Courts hold responsibility for adjudicating the guilt or innocence of individuals charged with social deviance, and administering appropriate sanctions for the transgressions of social norms. Corrections consist of those agencies that are delegated the authority to execute sanctions as well as to provide for the rehabilitation of deviant offenders.

Social scientists often prefer to describe the criminal justice system as a funnel, in which the number of crimes decreases as they are processed from commission through the various stages of disposition. The process, as depicted in Figure 13-7, is quite selective. First of all, as indicated in our discussion on the extent of crime, about one-half of all crimes committed are never brought to the attention of the police. Only a small fraction of all reported crime, for a variety of legal, political, and social reasons, ever results in conviction or punishment for its perpetrators. The funneling effect varies significantly for different types of crime. There is, for example, less "dropout" for crimes against people than there is for crimes against property. Nonetheless, this funneling effect of the criminal justice system, as we indicated in Chapter 10, operates inequitably for the different socioeconomic segments of the population.

▼

# SOCIETAL REACTIONS TO SOCIAL DEVIANCE

Societal response to deviance involves three basic objectives: punishment, deterrence, and rehabilitation. The execution of these functions often overlaps among the various institutions and agencies that comprise the criminal justice system.

611

PUNISHMENT. Nearly all societies respond to deviance with a form of punishment. These responses can range from such mild and innocuous forms as fines and ostracism to torture and execution. As Sykes points out, "When one examines the punishments inflicted on wrongdoers in different societies in different historical periods, one must be struck by the brutality and cruelty so commonly exhibited. Burning, branding, flogging, impaling, beheading, exiling, caging—these are but some of the long list of social sanctions, often imposed for crime that today would be considered trivial" (1978:458).

Punishment often involves incarceration. Sanctions of this type are imposed particularly

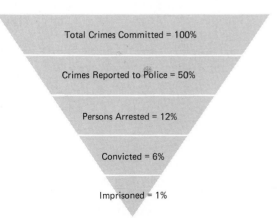

FIGURE 13-7 The Criminal Justice Funnel. Source: Figure from J. A. Humphrey and M. E. Milakovich, *The Administration of Justice*. New York: Human Sciences Press, 1981, p. 129. Reprinted with permission of Human Sciences Press.

▼

**Societal Responses.** Confinement in today's prisons and jails attempts to meet three basic objectives: punishment, deterrence, and rehabilitation. High rates for criminal recidivism, however, suggest that these goals more often are not fully achieved. (R. Benyas/Black Star)

for the more serious offenses, although incarceration is used quite commonly as well as a mild form of punishment for offenses that are not considered to be very serious. Many authorities argue that segregation, apart from its function as punishment through the deprivation of liberty and autonomy, provides a necessary form of deterrence and prevention until rehabilitation is accomplished.

While punishment may have various functions with respect to social deviance, retribution is usually considered to be the most fundamental. Retribution has been defined as "the infliction of pain or deprivation for reasons of vengeance or satisfaction of the sense of justice" (Cohen & Short, 1958). The rationale behind the concept of retribution is encapsulated in the saying "An eye for an eye, a tooth for a tooth." Retribution is also thought to serve the purpose of sustaining the morale of nonoffenders. Many people who abide by societal norms feel that even though doing so involves sacrifice and self-discipline, it should be the responsibility of all members of society. Those who violate the social norms should not be privileged to "get away with it" but instead should be obliged to pay for their deviance.

DETERRENCE. Various forms of punishment, including capital punishment, are thought by some to be effective in inhibiting deviance, especially secondary deviance. It is argued that punishing offenders also has the effect of discouraging potential deviants from violating social norms. Many penologists, however, are of the opinion that formal punishments, even capital punishments, are not very effective deterrents. Their position seems well founded when one considers that the overall rate for **recidivism** (repeat offenses) in the United States is about 65 percent. Even more astonishing statistics can be had in the rates of recidivism for specific types of crime (see Figure 13-8). Recidivism for most major offenses in 1987, measured in terms of re-arrests after six years of release from prison, averaged 69 percent, with an average rate of 53 percent for reconvictions. One should not conclude from these figures that punishment has no deterrent effect. It might in fact have a very strong effect. All that can be said is that the extent of the deterrent effects of punishment are unknown.

Quite controversial is the question of whether the deterrence of crime is related to the severity of punishment. Especially controversial in this regard is capital punishment which, after being suspended for a period in the 1960s and 1970s, has had renewed application in this country during the past few years. Critics argue that states which permit and utilize capital punishment, whatever its form, do not necessarily have lower crime rates for respective offenses and, moreover, that in many such states these crime rates are much higher than in states that do not permit capital punishment. Proponents of capital punishment argue that despite these findings and the rates of recidivism, an effective function of any punishment as a form of deterrence is the social reaffirmation of the importance and strength of social norms.

▼

**613**

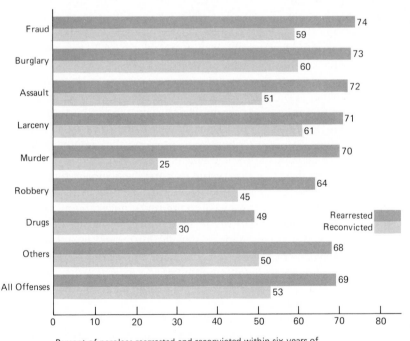

Percent of parolees rearrested and reconvicted within six years of release in terms of most serious offense for which paroled.

FIGURE 13-8   Percent of Recidivism by Type of Crime. Source: U.S. Department of Justice, Bureau of Justice Statistics: *Special Report: Recidivism of Young Parolees, 1987.* Washington, D.C.: U.S. Government Printing Office, 1987.

▼ REHABILITATION. Rehabilitation refers to any effort to "resocialize" social deviants in order to prevent the continuation of norm violation. All such programs incorporate the basic method of normative internalization. The fundamental assumption is that nearly all deviants are the victims of inadequate, inappropriate, or ambiguous socialization, and hence are in need of "resocialization" in one form or another. Rehabilitation programs, however, are not found in all correctional systems. One reason for this is the matter of expense. Nearly all modern systems of criminal justice, however, incorporate rehabilitation programs.

**614**

Specific methods used for rehabilitation take a rather wide variety of forms. Nearly all of these techniques and methods, however, fall into three principal types: psychotherapy, behavior modification, and vocational training. These procedures, of course, are not mutually exclusive, and often are used in one combination or another.

**Psychotherapy,** whether in the individual or group mode, aims to change the personality system of deviants in such a manner that they will not be motivated to engage in further norm violations. These efforts focus on the alteration of one's beliefs, values, and attitudes. Psychotherapy is widely practiced by a diversity of practitioners and for a variety of behavior. Nearly all such programs, however, have been severely criticized, and their efficiency in the control of social deviance is really unknown. Martinson (1974) reviewed over two hundred studies designed to measure the effects of psychotherapy, and concluded that the majority of the studies suggested that psychotherapy had no positive effects and, moreover, that in some cases it appeared to have harmful consequences.

**Behavior modification** focuses on changing the overt behavior of deviants directly. The many techniques of behavior modification essentially involve an application of the principles of either classical conditioning theory or operant reinforcement theory (see Chapter 5). One form of behavior modification consists of aversion therapy, used in the treatment of alcoholism. The procedure requires the individual to ingest drugs (for example, Antabuse) in conjunction with alcohol, which induces such negative reactions as vomiting, cramps, and loss of voluntary muscle control. The intention is to produce a conditioned association between the deviant behavior and the violent physical effect. Methods such as these are not without criticism. One objection in particular is that the induced association is only temporary and, furthermore, that it presupposes a commitment on the part of the deviant, which itself may need to be developed first of all.

**Vocational rehabilitation** is perhaps the most widely used form of rehabilitation. Unfortunately, the type of training given to deviants is not always related to the kinds of jobs or occupations that may be available to them after release from any detention that might be involved. Nonetheless, it appears that work-training programs that lead to successful employment are related to lower rates of recidivism (Glaser, 1964).

Prisons themselves seem to be a formidable obstacle in any effective type of rehabilitation program. The chief reason for this is that nearly all prisons and reformatories have been described as institutions that remove offenders from practically all contact with the general society and its norms and subject them instead to almost continual contact with individuals who have committed crimes ranging from petty larceny to murder, and homosexual rape and fraud. Prisons in this respect have been called "schools for crime" in which the motivation to commit criminal acts as well as the knowledge required to perform them are learned and reinforced.

Prison subcultures, in most cases, work against rehabilitation efforts. Indeed, the very social structure of prisons and reformatories facilitates the emergence of attitudes and behavior that the authorities seek to eliminate. Consequences such as this are evidenced in a simulation study done by Zimbardo (1972) on social interaction in prisons. College students were assigned randomly to two groups: one group consisted of subjects who were to play the role of prisoners; the other group was composed of students who were to enact the role of prison guards. All subjects were outfitted in appropriate uniforms, and they enacted their respective roles in a realistic setting with appropriate props. After a few days the experiment had to be terminated because of serious, and potentially harmful, behavioral changes that took place in both groups. The "guards" became sadistic and insensitive, and took on many other characteristics and actions that seemed to be typical of real-life prison guards. Correspondingly, the students playing the role of prisoners seemed to feel and to behave like real prisoners. They engaged in protests and hunger strikes; moreover, when their attempt to escape failed, they fell into deep depression.

One must keep in mind that the subjects who played the roles of guards and prisoners were law-abiding, above average in intelligence, and psychologically sound college students. Yet, when they became enmeshed in their assigned roles, they took on the feelings and actions of those whom they were asked to characterize. They became so engulfed in their roles that they forgot their real identities, and acted as though they were not involved in a psychological study but rather in a real-life episode. Zimbardo's studies suggest that the behavior of guards and prisoners is more a function of the structure of the situation in which they find themselves, and the normative expectations linked to their roles, rather than a function of specific personality abnormalities. Prison subcultures, thus, are severely criticized for the pathological effects produced by the structural and interactive relationships that exist among prisoners, guards, and administrators. Rehabilitation under such circumstances is thought to be ineffective.

It is not surprising that under such circumstances, many criminologists and other sociologists, as well as lawyers, judges, and politicians, claim that rehabilitation efforts are not only ineffective, but indeed impossible. As further proof of this contention, critics point to the high rates of recidivism that exist in fairly equal proportion among deviants who have been the subject of rehabilitative efforts, as well as among those who have not (see, for example, Greenberg, 1977; Van den Haag, 1975). Nonetheless, in the past decades, a tremendous amount of money has been spent by the federal government to underwrite a variety of experiments and other kinds of research programs designed to modernize the criminal justice system, as well as to develop effective methods for the rehabilitation of deviants and the deterrence of all forms of social deviance.

Nearly all societal response to deviant behavior is influenced by the social position or the identity of the deviant. As we have indicated, children do not usually incur the same strong sanctions that adults would elicit by identical or similar violations. Sex also has been a basis of differential treatment in that women traditionally have not been treated as severely as men in terms of social sanctions. Capital punishment in the case of women has been extremely rare in this country, as well as in nearly all others. Socioeconomic status also plays a highly significant role in societal response. A wealthy White corporate executive is likely to receive a much milder penalty for certain types of deviant behavior than a Black male living on welfare. Some critics argue that it is this differential application of criminal justice that accounts in great part for the preponderance of reported crime among certain segments of the population, particularly those of minority and lower-class backgrounds.

Another source of difficulty is that different people have different conceptions of what the criminal justice system should accomplish. Many expect a number of things to be accomplished at the same time: that no criminal should go free; that no innocent person should be punished; that the wicked should be made to suffer for their sins; that deviants should be humanely and compassionately transformed

▼

615

▼ into upright citizens who deplore wrongdoing. The problem is that those methods likely to promote one objective are also likely to prevent the accomplishment of another.

## SOCIETAL MODIFICATION

It would be appropriate to conclude this section on social control with the suggestion that much deviance may not fundamentally involve inadequate, inappropriate, or ambiguous socialization. This is to say, deviance may not be so much the responsibility of the individual as of society, and it may not be so much "resocialization" as "societal restructuring" that is needed. Etzioni (1977) has suggested that the dominant belief in society seems to be that whenever there is social deviance, it is always the individual that has malfunctioned. Seldom is the position taken that perhaps society needs to be modified in terms of individual functions. Etzioni's position, fundamentally, is that a society may be making behavioral demands of people that are beyond an individual's human or personal capacity. Attempts to cope with such conflicting and disturbing situations may involve various forms of deviance. Especially relevant here would be unresponsive (that is, alienating and/or inauthentic) societies that are, by their very structure, incapable of satisfying the basic *human* needs of its members (see Chapter 14), such as those for social response, social recognition, autonomy, and self-esteem, as well as for physical and social security. Attention, too, should be given to social institutions and social systems that foster deviance. Perhaps some thought, with appropriate research efforts, needs to be given to this potential dimension of social control.

## Summary

Deviance, in one sense, may be defined as anything that is not typical—anything that is abnormal or atypical. Deviance in its more specifically sociological usage refers to social behavior that violates any societal or group norm, any violation of required or expected behavior. Deviance must not be confused in particular with two other social phenomena, social disorganization and social problems.

Social disorganization refers to a social situation that is dysfunctional. Social problems are social situations that affect a significant number of people and that are considered undesirable. Not all social problems involve deviance or violation of social norms. Insofar as deviance is defined as the violation of social norms, it has an essentially relevant character. All deviant behavior, by definition, is relative in terms of the particular social norms to which it refers. More specifically, in terms of the relativity of deviant behavior, we speak of relativity of place (cultural relativity), relativity of time, and relativity of circumstances.

Deviance is a universal phenomenon. Yet, while there are universal types of deviance (for example, murder, incest, assault, property damage, and theft), there are no universal acts of deviance.

It is helpful to distinguish several of the principal types of deviance. The following categories are helpful in this respect: crime (misdemeanors, felonies), delinquency, torts or civil deviance, deviant lifestyles, and collective deviance (for example, organized crime).

It is difficult to know the true extent of deviance in any society, particularly in a modern society. Social deviance, for the most part, consists ideally of covert activity. Yet, deviance is so pervasive in our society, and in many others as well, that one can easily speak of the "normality" of deviance.

Varieties of explanations for deviant behavior include biological, psychological, sociopsychological, and sociological theories. Biological explanations include the theory of the "born criminal," constitutional types, theories of chromosomal abnormality, and sociobiological theories. Psychological theories locate the cause of deviant behavior within the individual, and view the deviant individual as essentially pathological—one who is unable to cope with internal and external pressures. Three theories in particular among the psychological explanations for deviant behavior have received major attention: psychoanalytical theory, frustration-aggression theory, and personality theory. Sociopsychological theories focus on interactional variables and their significance in the production of deviant behavior. There are two such theories that have been especially popular in sociology: differential association theory and labeling theory.

Purely sociological theories of deviant behavior stress the role of social structure and social situations in the generation of social deviance. Three of the more important of these theories are deviant subculture theory, anomie theory, and conflict theory.

Personality is related to social deviance in terms of (1) pathological personalities that constitute a specific form of deviant behavior, such as sociopaths, and (2) the personalities of deviants that play a role in many specific kinds of deviant behavior. There is sufficient evidence to warrant the contention that significant relationships exist between particular types of personality ("normal" or "abnormal") and specific forms of deviant behavior.

Social control consists essentially of the processes and mechanisms by which society encourages and/or enforces conformity to its norms and expectations. Social control promotes compliance with the social norms that have been designed for the effective operation of the social order. There are two principal kinds of methods by which social control is achieved: (1) internalization of social values and norms, and (2) external social pressure, which involves the application of social sanctions. External processes of social control include informal sanctions, formal sanctions, and the use of criminal justice systems. Societal response to social deviance involves three basic objectives: punishment, deterrence, and rehabilitation.

Social deviance may not be so much the responsibility of the individual as of society, and it may not be so much "resocialization" as "societal restructuring" that is required for its control and elimination.

617

# Key Concepts

addiction
ambivalent socialization
anomie
corporate crime
crime
delinquency
deviance
differential association theory
elite deviance
felony
inadequate socialization
inappropriate socialization
labeling theory
misdemeanor
normative internalization
organized crime
psychopath
recidivism
secondary deviance
social control
social disorganization
sociopath
social pathology
social problem
status offense
tort
victimless crime
white-collar crime

# Social Change

This volume began with the statement that sociology attempts to provide some answers to fundamental questions of human life. One of the questions we asked was, "Where is man going?" Is humankind headed in any particular social direction—toward any particular end or goal? Is there a universal pattern to the development and life of human societies? Some people say that societal life is just a vicious circle. Others, in the majority, contend that mankind is in a continuous state of evolution and progress. Nearly all agree, however, that society is essentially a dynamic phenomenon out of which inevitably comes the continually diversified and modified forms of social life. It is to these issues, and that of social change more generally, that we turn our attention in this concluding chapter. We shall address such questions as the following: How does social change occur? Why does social change occur? Are there particular patterns to social change? What are the consequences of social change? And, is personality related to social change? These are the kinds of questions—mainly attempts to understand the continual transformation of society—that captured the attention of many pioneer sociologists in the middle of the nineteenth century. That sociologists are still much preoccupied by the same questions is testimony to the fact that the study of social change holds a central place in the discipline today. ▲

## Outline

▼    ► Social life is, by its very definition, a dynamic phenomenon. Society does not stand still. Change is a continuous event inherent in the very essence of society. Throughout several of the preceding chapters, we have talked about social change in one respect or another. Such processes as social learning, social mobility, and social movements are all aspects of social change. Here, in this final chapter, we wish to talk in considerable detail about the very phenomenon of social change. We shall explore the nature and dynamics of social change, some of the theories that attempt to explain it, and look more concretely at several ways in which human societies are presently changing, as well as the probable consequences of these dynamics—both for society and for the individual.

**620**

## Nature of Social Change

Social systems are characterized by two basic types of processes: (1) those that maintain, or tend to maintain, the system, such as social learning and social control; and (2) those that tend to alter or to modify the system, such as social movements. Often the line between these two types of dynamics is a nebulous one. For example, change in the form of societal adaptation to the physical environment is directed essentially at maintaining the system. Other types of change often have a contrary effect or purpose in bringing about social disorganization. Change, in either case, is as important as equilibrium to studying and explaining social systems and human behavior.

### DEFINITION
### AND DESCRIPTION
### OF SOCIAL CHANGE

**Social change** refers to any relatively enduring modification in the established or existing structure or function of a social system. The qualification "relatively enduring" is intended to distinguish social change from the myriad kinds of temporary innovations or alterations, such as fads and fashions, that do not usually involve any significant or substantial modification in the established patterns of social and cultural dynamics. The same is true of social disorganization and social deviance, which refer to dysfunction within the existing, and usually continuing, structure of society rather than to modifications of relative permanence. Of course, social deviance and social disorganization may be directed at effecting social change, as indeed may be the case with collective behavior such as fashions and fads; but, in themselves, these processes do not necessarily constitute social change. "Change," as Nisbet (1970:302) contends, "is a succession of differences in time in a persisting identity."

Social scientists frequently make an analytical distinction between "social change" and "cultural change." The latter refers technically, and more specifically, to changes in the realm of culture, such as values, beliefs, norms, customs, knowledge, ideologies, attitudes, arts, and technology; the former is restricted to modifications in the structure (size, composition, and organization) of society or other social systems, and hence focuses more specifically on the relationships between individuals and groups. While such an analytical distinction may be technically correct and often helpful in attempts to describe and to explain social change, it is also quite academic for all intents and purposes. Society and culture, as we saw particularly in Chapter 3 and Chapter 7, are two dimensions of the same phenomenon. One cannot exist without the other, thus social change and cultural change are invariably linked. Social change, then, in this generic sense, frequently goes under the label *sociocultural change* and refers to any alteration in the social and cultural organization of a society or its subdivisions, and includes, but is not limited to, changes in institutions, groups, statuses, roles, norms, values, beliefs, relationships, and patterns of behavior. Among the many specific types of social change that are included in this generic classification are the following: technological change (discoveries and inventions), demographic change (modifications in size and composition of populations), ecological change (alterations in the physical environment), and characterological change (the introduction of new personnel or the psychological alteration of existing personnel).

Some societies experience more change than others, but none can escape this naturally inevitable phenomenon. Even those recently discovered societies that are referred to as "Stone Age" civilizations (for example, the Tasaday in the Philippines) have undergone social change in one form or another. Change, then, is a universal and constant process, but one that occurs in different ways and at different rates.

Most readers of this book may not have lived long enough yet (and they need not be in any hurry!) to grasp, in a fully personal and subjective sense, the nature, as well as the implications, of social change. Indeed, many of the really recent changes—those of the past quarter-century—that will be described in this chapter probably seem to the students of today to be either historical or perennial events. Yet, people in their parents' generation would not see these same phenomena quite that way, however realistically much of the behavior involved may have become "old-fashioned."

Some singular examples of social change that the American society, and many other societies in the Western world, have witnessed in the past decade or two include attitudes and practices regarding divorce, abortion, church attendance, sexual behavior, morality, gender and marital roles, work roles, family size, forms of worship, legal ages for voting, consumption of alcohol and drugs, styles of living, dress, grooming, music and art, and in literally thousands of other areas. Given the speed and the extent of social change in industrial societies such as our own, the "generation gap" may indeed be-

come a permanent or persistent characteristic of modern life.

Human species, it is estimated, have been around for about a million years—and Homo sapiens for at least several thousand. Human societies, however, are notoriously much shorter-lived. Few have lasted the approximately 900 years that the early Roman civilization did. Even our own society, which probably seems ancient to many of us, is barely more than 200 years old—or even 400 years old, if one wishes to include the colonial beginnings. There are, then, two specific questions here that are basic to the phenomenon of social change: Why is it that societies are so relatively short-lived? And, second, how is it that certain levels of civilization are achieved in some societies, but not in others?

## DIMENSIONS OF SOCIAL CHANGE

Not all societies experience the universal phenomenon of social change in the same way. Among the dimensions of social change that vary are those of magnitude, rate, force, and direction. The novelty of social change today lies in some of these dimensions—and not in the phenomenon itself. Some segments of our society, for example the Taos Indians and other tribes of New Mexico and the Amish and other religious sects, experience very limited change and at a drastically slower pace. Why some societies, or segments and aspects of them, do not change, especially in the larger context of social change, is as important to explain as is change itself. To answer this question, however, it is necessary to understand something of the various dimensions and qualities of social change.

1. *Magnitude* of social change refers to the number and different kinds of things or elements that either undergo or are affected by it.

621

▼

2. *Rate* of social change refers to how quickly change takes place, or to how long a given aspect of the structure or content of society and culture endures. Hence, the speed of change refers to the relative permanency of an existing pattern of social organization.

3. *Force* of social change refers to the extent or profundity of its effects on society and culture, and their many components.

**622**

4. *Direction* of social change refers to the subjective consideration of whether it is moving toward or against the desired objectives of society and its members. Implied here is the notion of social progress, to which we shall return in a subsequent section of this chapter.

Each of these dimensions of social change is interrelated, and each in turn is both cause and effect of the exponential factor: the more elements that change or exist as potentials for change, the greater will be the change. Social change, then, has a fundamentally geometric character.

## SOCIAL CHANGE VERSUS SOCIAL PROGRESS

Not all social change is social progress, despite the pervasive notion in Western society, and indeed much of the world, that change is "for the better." The extensive confusion that surrounds this very basic distinction is one that cannot be ignored without further clarification and comment, especially in this day and age when so much human energy is being directed at both social change and social progress.

**Social progress** refers to the *quality* of social change, which rests fundamentally on the subjective consideration of whether it is good or bad, better or worse, desirable or undesirable. Some people consider social change in any form as being progressive and, therefore, good for all in one way or another. The perceptive student by now should realize immediately that such a conception of social change involves a judg-

**Progress or Change?** Elements of Western culture, such as dress and grooming, are considered morally decadent in many segments of Iranian society. This young woman, valuing both historical tradition and modern norms, experiences the ambiguity and uncertainty that often accompany social change. (© David Burnett 1979/Woodfin Camp & Associates, Inc.)

ment of values. Social change can be observed and measured objectively and, as such, would be perceived and defined by all in highly similar, if not identical, terms. Social progress, on the other hand, can be defined and measured only subjectively, according to the relative standards and highly variable frames of reference that an observer may choose to use. Hence, nearly everyone who has lived long enough can identify social change in one respect or another, but not everyone would care to place the label "social progress" on all of these observable or observed changes.

Many people presently view the likely course and trends of social change with much cynicism, even downright pessimism (see, for example, Berger et al., 1973; Heilbroner, 1980; Lasch, 1984; and Marris, 1974), and often they express a preference for "the good old days" or doing things "like we used to do in the past" as opposed to some of the social standards and social practices that characterize the societies and social systems of today. Usually, these observers talk only of the "negative" aspects of social change, even though it is quite probable that none of them would really want to go back to a primitive or earlier state—perhaps not even to a time less than a half- or quarter-century ago.

There are few societies in the world today that are not openly and actively committed to social change and modernization. Nonetheless, without suggesting that these processes are either progressive or regressive, we can describe some of the usual effects of social change, and assess their implications for both society and the individual.

## TYPES OF SOCIAL CHANGE: SPONTANEOUS VERSUS PLANNED CHANGE

Some social change, as we have seen, is of the type that occurs, or at least seems to occur, by itself. Such *spontaneous* or *evolutionary change* is in the nature of a latent function: it is unrecognized and frequently undesired. Examples of spontaneous change are the modifications in the social organization of the family as a consequence of technological development, and changes in the realm of religious behavior as a consequence of the growth of science. These examples of spontaneous change do not overlook the fact that in the manifest realm of reality, there may be a concomitant and auxiliary force, perhaps in the form of social movements, directed at the respective goal. Spontaneous change, however, seems to be the result of the very dynamics of social interaction and the

functions of society. We say "seems to be" because, unfortunately, as we shall see, there is no complete explanation for social change.

*Planned change* (social planning), more in the nature of a manifest function, is that change which is intentionally sought by members of society. It refers to the conscious attempts or efforts to control the nature and dimensions (magnitude, rate, force, and direction) of social change. One example of planned change, as we saw in Chapter 12, is that of social movements.

Is it really possible to plan social change? The extreme evolutionist, of course, would argue in the negative. Most social scientists, including the neo-evolutionists, however, rejecting any form of determinism, contend that social change can be effected and controlled within certain limits. Indeed, today a great number of sociologists, along with other social scientists, are engaged in various forms and processes of social activism. They seek to bring about, as some of the founding fathers of sociology tried to do, a "better" society—and, alas, even at the risk of inevitable failure—a utopia. The resolution of this question can be seen in part in an evaluation of the degree to which social movements experience or achieve success.

Given the state of our knowledge about social change, it is difficult to draw a sharp line between "spontaneous" and "planned" change. Indeed, such a distinction may be a false one. It seems useful for our analytical purposes, nonetheless, to keep in mind the distinctions between spontaneous and planned change.

# Theories of Social Change

Why does social change seem to affect some societies and not others? Why do some societies experience social change in one way and others in another way? Why do some societies undergo more change than others? Precisely how do societies change? Is there a pattern, or a fixed

**623**

▼

**624**

process, to the dynamics of society? All of these questions, in short, can be reduced to a simple one: Can social change be explained?

There are no known laws of social change. Many attempts have been made, however, since the beginnings of social science in fact, to discover a scientific explanation for social change. Preoccupation with the dynamics of social change among social thinkers began in the early nineteenth century. It was in this context, as we saw in Chapter 1, that sociology emerged as a scientific discipline. Today, we have several, somewhat competing, theories that have been formulated to explain the omnipresent phenomenon of social change, but no empirically validated explanations for it. Such a situation should not be surprising, given the fact that neither are there definitive explanations of social stability. Social change and social stability are believed to be integral parts of the same phenomenon. To explain one requires an explanation of the other. Indeed, many of our theories and explanations for social change are the same as those for the origin, development, and function of societies and cultures. Social statics and social dynamics are essential parts of all social systems. Consequently, given the assumption of social scientists that the explanation of these social phenomena is possible, the search goes on with an explicit emphasis on one aspect or the other.

A number of general theories of social change have been formulated by sociologists and anthropologists, as well as by historians who, understandably, have a genuine interest in this question. Some theories have tried to identify universal processes of social change. Others have sought to determine the causes and dynamics of social change in specific kinds of circumstances and social situations. The various theories that have been formulated to explain social change may be categorized into four principal classifications: evolutionary, cyclical, monistic, and modern. Let us describe some of the principal varieties of each kind.

# EVOLUTIONARY THEORY

The category of **evolutionary theory** refers to several formulations which essentially assert that social change is both inevitable and progressive: societies change naturally and gradually from simple forms to the more complex. Many of these evolutionary theories often take the more advanced Western civilizations as models of social change. Such a position is somewhat contradictory, since ideally these advanced societies should merely represent the current stage of social evolution.

The idea that change is omnipresent and continuous can be traced back to ancient Greek philosophers, especially to Heraclitus (ca. 535– ca. 475 B.C.) who spoke of the phenomenon of constant flux that characterizes all of reality. Evolutionary theory, however, had its principal origin in the nineteenth century during a time when social thought was dominated by the idea and value of social progress—the development of bigger and better societies. This period was an era of optimism emerging from the rapid technological development of political and industrial revolution in Europe and America, which lasted until World War I and the subsequent worldwide depression. We should recall that it was in this very context that the discipline of sociology had its formal beginning, and that some of the principal figures in the development of sociology were among the early formulators of evolutionary theory. Let us describe briefly the major kinds of evolutionary theories of social change.

UNILINEAR EVOLUTION. The initial form of evolutionary theory postulated unilinear change and development or progress as essential characteristics of societal dynamics. Unilinear evolutionists assert that every society develops in the same pattern of a fixed set of stages, and that change is not only inevitable but irreversible. Two principal varieties of **unilinear evolution** are those of positivistic philosophy and social Darwinism which we discussed in Chapter 1.

August Comte was the first to introduce an evolutionary theory of social change in his *Course of Positive Philosophy* (1842). Social progress, for Comte, was a natural state of being, and every society developed by passing through three fixed stages of increasing complexity, which he identified and described as follows:

1. *Theological*—phenomena explained in terms of gods and magic; fate controls all; no human intervention is possible.
2. *Metaphysical*—phenomena explained by reason and logic; rejection of supernatural control.
3. *Positivistic* or *scientific*—phenomena explained on the basis of sensible or empirical knowledge; control of human events possible in this stage.

The perfect society is realized in the third stage. Comte contended that Western civilization during his time had entered into this final stage of evolution in terms of its physical environment, and was working toward control of

*"Evolution's been good to you, Sid."*

Drawing by Lorenz; © 1980 The New Yorker Magazine, Inc.

the social environment. Despite a combination of faulty and sketchy data, evolutionary theory gained considerable following and popularity in its time.

Comte's theory was elaborated in the late nineteenth century by the sociologist Herbert Spencer (1862) and anthropologists Edward B. Tylor (1871), Lewis H. Morgan (1877), and William G. Sumner (1906). These theorists developed the thesis that came to be known as **social Darwinism** because it was based on the perspectives of Charles Darwin, expressed in his well-known treatise *On the Origin of the Species* (1859), which proposed that biological evolution is a continuous process that is characterized by the selective adaptation of organisms to the physical environment. Social Darwinism assumes that social evolution follows the same principles and dynamics as biological evolution and, consequently, that the growth and development of societies are determined by the principle of "the survival of the fittest"—a term coined, incidentally, by Spencer.

Evolution in this view is automatic and inevitable—the natural course of events—which, in the case of society, means that it moves from a primitive state to a civilized state. Morgan (1877) identified three stages in this process: savagery, barbarism, and civilization. Today's empirical evidence offers little substantiation for the universal stages of development of societies. In quite recent times, highly primitive societies have been transformed into rather advanced civilizations in a matter of just a few decades. Several nations of the Third World, in Africa, Asia, and South America, are dramatic examples of this phenomenon.

In the social Darwinian conception of social change, all that transpires in society, whatever change takes place—even war, famine, and disaster—is part of evolution, which is essentially progressive and therefore good. Moreover, evolutionary theory maintains not only that change is good and irreversible, but also that any attempt to interfere with this natural proc-

625

▼

ess is apt to be detrimental. The laws of evolution are considered to be superior to human intuition and manipulation, and all social phenomena are perceived to be inexorably moving toward naturally positive and beneficial goals for humankind.

Social Darwinism was used to support social and political conservatism, and in particular the philosophical doctrine of laissez faire (free enterprise and competition) that serves as the basis of capitalism (see Hofstader, 1955). Until its effective demise in the worldwide depression following World War I, social Darwinism was a highly influential theory and philosophy, both in the social sciences and in several other fields, notably business, economics, and government.

MULTILINEAR EVOLUTION: THE MODERN VIEW. Evolutionary theory commands a substantial allegiance still today. The modern version, however, is that of **multilinear evolution** (often referred to as neo-evolution or general evolution), which does not incorporate the notions of progress and fixed stages as essential elements. Evolution in this conception is merely a "process of cumulative change" (Lenski & Lenski, 1987).

Evolution in the multilinear perspective is conceived of as a general or basic tendency rather than as a universal law, on the assumption that there are many different ways by which societies may develop from simple to complex forms. Change, then, is not seen as similarly patterned, or moving in the same direction, in all societies. Neither is change conceived as an inevitable or irreversible experience of all societies. Rather, in this conception of social change, it is human society or the culture of humankind as a whole that evolves, and not individual societies or cultures.

Multilinear evolutionary theory has been developed most extensively by cultural anthropologists, chief among whom have been Ralph

626

Linton (1936), Leslie A. White (1949), and Marshall Sahlins and Elman Service (1960). Says White, perhaps the leading exponent of the "universal theory" of evolution: "The whole development is focusing on a single distant point toward which we are inexorably moving. The future promises for all mankind inexorably higher levels of integration . . . greater concentrations of political power and control . . . a single political organization that will embrace the entire planet and the whole human race" (1949: 388ff.).

The history of human societies has shown an unsteady progression in the rise and fall of several major civilizations, such as those of the Romans, Greeks, Byzantines, Chinese, Egyptians, Mayas, and Incas. Multilinear evolutionary theory seems to fit the empirical evidence and has become a more widely accepted position in the social sciences today. Moreover, unlike unilinear evolutionary theory that merely offers a description for the process of social change but not an explanation for why it does or should occur, multilinear evolution is more successful in explaining evolution in these latter respects. Multilinear theory holds, for example, that the more elaborate and complex a culture, the greater is the probability of invention and discovery; and, the more efficient the mode of production, the greater is the use made of the environment, such as population growth, industrialization, and urbanization. Yet, even in these respects, multilinear evolution still explains only some, but not all, social change. War and revolution remain among the unexplained phenomena of social change.

## CYCLICAL THEORIES

Somewhat antithetical to the evolutionary explanations are cyclical theories of social change, which contend that societies move toward inevitable extinction rather than progress. Focusing on the "rise and fall" or "growth and decline" of civilizations, **cyclical theories** of social change assert that history repeats itself as all societies move through a life cycle of birth, growth, maturation, decline or decay, and extinction. Several varieties of cyclical theories of social change, some of which incorporate an evolutionary perspective, have been developed by a number of individuals.

Oswald Spengler, a German schoolteacher, wrote *The Decline of the West* (1918) in which he describes the destiny of all societies as inevitable decay and extinction. In this view, societies emerge, develop rapidly to a "golden age" of maturity, and then decline slowly to an eventual disintegration. Spengler argued that—like the great civilizations of Egypt, Greece, and Rome—Western society had reached its "golden age" during the Enlightenment of the eighteenth century and was in its period of decline and extinction.

Spengler derived his organic analogy from the study of only eight major civilizations, and concluded that the average life span of most societies is fifty years. His data obviously were highly selective, and perhaps even quite faulty. Whatever their eventual fate, history records numerous societies that have survived for hundreds of years. Spengler's theory, presented at the end of World War I, received strong popular and political, though not scholarly, support.

Arnold Toynbee, a British historian, in the multivolume work *A Study of History* (1934–1961), based on data from twenty civilizations, was more optimistic. He argued that decay and extinction are not the inevitable fate of societies and, moreover, that a perfect civilization is possible. The advance or decline of society, as well as the level of civilization that it attains, is a function of its "response" to the inescapable and reoccurring "challenges" presented by the physical and social environments.

Such challenges, maintained Toynbee, provide the impetus for social progress. Social progress results from successfully conquering the environment, an apparently never-ending task of all enduring societies.

Pitirim A. Sorokin, the Russian-American sociologist, who established the Department of Sociology at Harvard University, presented a pendulum model of the cyclical theory of social change, one that pictures society as swinging back and forth between different eras. Sorokin, in his multivolume work *Social and Cultural Dynamics* (1937–1941), described two kinds of society: the *sensate*, which, dominated by individual self-interests and emphasizing what can be perceived directly by the senses, is practical, hedonistic, sensual, and materialistic; and the *ideational*, which, placing the common welfare above the well-being of the individual, emphasizes what can be perceived by the mind, such as religion and spiritual values. These societal phases are recognizable by the symbolic products of a culture, for instance, art and technology. The medieval period of Western civilization exemplified a strongly ideational form of society, while contemporary Western society, Sorokin felt, is moving in a highly sensate phase. All societies, operating on the principle of self-directed impulse, continuously oscillate between these two polar extremes—neither of which, as an ideal type, is ever fully developed or attained. Sorokin also described a third societal form, the *idealistic* society, a combination of the two primary types.

Cyclical theories of social change, in addition to being criticized as too subjective and too speculative, are widely faulted for offering neither an adequate description nor an adequate explanation of social change. Neither the how nor the why is addressed in any satisfactory manner. More crucial in this evaluation is that these theories never explain why cycles themselves should exist as part of the essential process of social change.

▼

**627**

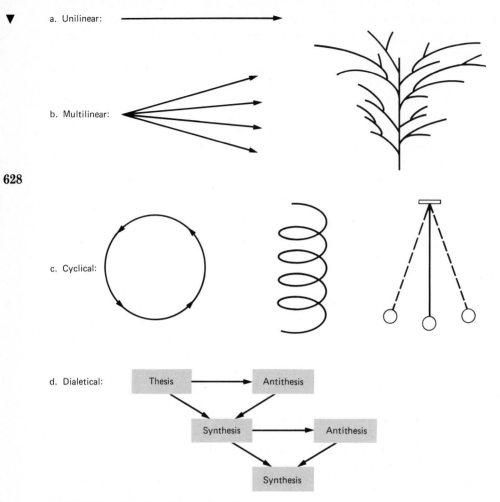

FIGURE 14-1   Models of Social Evolution.

## MONISTIC THEORIES

A number of theories that posit a single cause or factor to explain social change have been offered throughout the history of social science, and even dating back long before this relatively short period. Several of these explanations, known as **monistic theories,** are substantially similar to those for cultural development and growth that we looked at in Chapter 3. All of the monistic explanations are deterministic in

nature, leaving little or no room for any variation or other explanation. Let us mention briefly some representative examples.

CULTURAL DETERMINISM.   Change, in the perspective of cultural determinism, results from the spread and transfer of cultural elements from one society to another, either by borrowing or imposition. As a new cultural element enters society, it brings about changes in many respects. This principle cannot be denied in the face of strong empirical evidence: The extent of intercultural contact throughout the world today has resulted in very rapid and widespread cultural diffusion. Yet, while quite important as a factor in the dynamics of social change, theories of cultural diffusion have not been very successful in explaining why, when, or precisely how diffusion occurs, or, more specifically, why different rates of diffusion occur in different societies and for different kinds of sociocultural phenomena.

GEOGRAPHICAL DETERMINISM. The principle of geographical determinism is really quite simple: sociocultural development, growth, and change are exclusively the product of geographical factors such as terrain, climate, and physical resources (see, for example, Buckle, 1987; Huntington, 1972). As changes of a geographical nature occur, corresponding modifications take place in the social and cultural adaptations that people must make to the physical environment.

ECOLOGICAL DETERMINISM. Social change is at times explained in terms of social ecology. Ecological determinism maintains essentially that social change flows from the symbiotic relationships between people and their sociophysical environments. Chiefly involved are the dynamics of ecological invasion and segregation (see, for example, Park, 1984). These propositions were discussed at length in our consideration of the ecological foundations of society in Chapter 7.

BIOLOGICAL DETERMINISM. In an essentially similar manner, biological determinism maintains that the development and change of societies are absolute and exclusive functions of the genetic quality, or racial purity, of a societal population. Observable differences among societies, and the various changes that

take place therein, are due to qualitative differences in the biological and genetic composition of particular populations (see, for example, Chamberlain, 1977; de Gobineau, 1984). It follows, then, that proper inbreeding and improvement of biological stock can bring about social and cultural progress. The underlying fallacy of this theory is that there are no pure races, and the genetic principles of hybridization counter its claims: miscegenation tends to improve, strengthen rather than weaken, a gene pool or biological population. Hence, this theory, like any other deterministic theory, is in much disrepute today because of its simplistic approach as well as its lack of empirical verification; yet, occasionally, an advocate emerges to restate the case anew, usually with claims of new "evidence."

Other monistic explanations, with essentially the same or similarly deterministic perspectives, are those of the technological, economic, and theological variety. Each of these monistic explanations for social change falls quite short of the explanatory mark. In addition to being overly simple and somewhat contradictory, they are absolutistic and reductionistic. Ample evidence, nonetheless, supports the position that the focal element of each of these theories can and does play a contributory role in social change. Accordingly, it is more appropriate and valid to treat these theories as factors or sources of social change. We shall say more about some of them in these respects in a subsequent section of this chapter.

## MODERN THEORIES

Two competing theories of social change are of major interest in the social sciences today. These modern or contemporary approaches to social change are those embodied in the somewhat opposed, sociological orientations of structural-functional analysis and conflict theory.

▼ FUNCTIONAL OR EQUILIBRIUM THE-ORY. Functionalism, in a technical sense, is essentially not a theory of social change—at least it did not originate as such; however, no treatment of the theories of social change can neglect an appropriate discussion of **functionalism** for reasons which will become evident in a moment.

630

Functional or equilibrium theories (Merton, 1957; Parsons, 1951) have been concerned primarily with social statics rather than social dynamics, and, as such, they emphasize the integrating and stabilizing processes found in society. Society for the functionalist is a balanced, well-integrated entity that consists of interdependent parts or units, each of which contributes to the maintenance of order and stability in the system as a whole. The various changes within the many parts of society are so coordinated and integrated that the total system is relatively the same from one day to the next.

Society, according to functionalists, absorbs destructive forces in such a fashion as to maintain overall stability in its constant search for equilibrium. Changes that occur in one part of society are counterbalanced by adjustments in other parts. This position is severely criticized as extremely conservative and one which itself works to stifle social change and social progress. Some functionalists respond that conservatism is not a condition inherent in the structural-functional model which, adopting a basically evolutionary approach, is quite well able to handle most problems of change. Indeed, certain kinds of change are considered necessary and functional for the system. No society, by its very nature, is absolutely static. Neither is it ever fully integrated. Equilibrium, therefore, must be conceived as essentially dynamic, and integration as always partial.

CONFLICT THEORY. Totally in contrast to functionalism, **conflict theory** stresses social dynamics and emphasizes the forces that pro-duce instability and disorganization. Conflict, in fact, is perceived to be the essence of social interaction. Dissensus rather than consensus is assumed to be the fundamental dynamic of society. Every society, thus, is in a process of continuous conflict and inevitable change, and all the elements of society contribute to this dynamism as a permanent characteristic and substantial feature of society (Simmel, 1908). Conflict, then, is seen as a normal rather than an abnormal dynamic of society.

The foremost proponent of conflict theory was Karl Marx, who can also be described as a basically evolutionary theorist, since he saw social conflict as resulting in social progress and, eventually, in a more perfect society in the form of communism. "All history," argued Marx and Engels (1848), "is the history of class conflict." Change, then, is the result of tensions between competing interests in society, chief among which today are those of the owners of the means of production (the bourgeoisie) and the working class (the proletariat). Each class competes for preserving or changing the status quo in terms of its respective interests.

Contemporary advocates of conflict theory (for example, Dahrendorf, 1959; Mills, 1956) contend that functionalism is basically adequate to account for the forces of integration, but inadequate when it tries to account for the forces of disruption. Conflict theorists argue that the mechanisms of integration are never totally effective and, therefore, that conflict is present at least potentially in all societies at all times. Social change is inherent in any attempt to resolve, through modifications of the existing situation, the inevitable conflict that can be found in every social system.

Virtually all social scientists today accept conflict as a basic social process, and as one among many elements of social change. Conflict theory, however, as a comprehensive explanation of social change, is not so widely accepted. There are many types of social change—such as that within social institutions, the familial in particular—for which it cannot account, nor can it provide an adequate explanation of the future course of social change.

These contemporary theories of social change, functionalism and conflict theory, appear on the surface to be quite contradictory. Indeed, the strongly critical stance which each takes toward the other often connotes an element of irreconcilable competition. It seems fair to say, however, that each theory emphasizes different aspects of society at the expense, rather than the denial, of others (see Table 14-1). Each of these theories, moreover, is still quite incom-

TABLE 14-1.   Assumptions of Functional and Conflict Theories of Social Change

| Functional Theory | Conflict Theory |
| --- | --- |
| 1. Every society is a relatively persisting configuration of elements. | 1. Every society is subject at every moment to social change: social change is ubiquitous. |
| 2. Every society is a well-integrated configuration of elements. | 2. Every society experiences at every moment social conflict: social conflict is ubiquitous. |
| 3. Every element in a society contributes to its functioning. | 3. Every element in a society contributes to its change. |
| 4. Every society rests on the consensus of its members. | 4. Every society rests on the constraint of some of its members by others. |

Source: Ralf Dahrendorf, "Towards a Theory of Social Conflict," in Amitai Etzioni and Eva Etzioni (eds.), *Social Change,* New York: Basic Books, 1964, p. 103.

plete. Neither model can fully explain social change. We need to know much more about why and how society maintains itself, as well as why and how it changes. Attempts to provide answers to one set of these questions most likely will provide answers to the other.

There is no logical reason that both of these theories cannot be integrated into a more comprehensive, perhaps more valid, explanation of social change. Such attempts indeed have been made by protagonists in each camp. Coser (1956), van den Berghe (1963), Smelser (1968*b*), and Gouldner (1970) speak of the "functions" of social conflict, and Merton (1957) has introduced the concepts of "strain" and "tension" into functionalist theory. Multilinear evolutionary theory is compatible, as we have implied, with both functionalist theory and conflict theory. Such a complex combination or integration of these three approaches appears to be directed toward the construction of a highly viable theory of social change. Indeed, Marx's conflict theory of social change, as we mentioned, may be viewed as evolutionary theory, especially with regard to the notion of sequential stages of social organization; correspondingly, many of the functionalist theorists assume the principles of evolution in their formulations. Nonetheless, agreement on any such integrated theory of social change is not imminent.

A viable theory of social change would seem to be one that is not only capable of describing elements of change, and the processes by which it occurs, but can also explain its essential direction and why the very phenomenon takes place. To reiterate a previous statement, any adequate theory of social change (social dynamics) seems to require an adequate theory of social stability (social statics). No general theory of society or social systems can be considered complete unless it is able to explain both order and change. Such an accomplishment awaits the sociological imagination and the expertise of all social scientists.

▼

**631**

▼ # Factors in Social Change

Apart from the theories of social change that attempt to explain why it occurs and how it occurs, there are a number of interacting factors that enter into this highly complex process. Extensive research on the dynamics of social change has yielded a set of general principles that provide a further understanding of several of the dimensions of the phenomenon: magnitude, rate, extent, and direction. Let us look at some of these factors and principles of social change.

632

## SOURCES AND CONSEQUENCES OF SOCIAL CHANGE

Today, we can point to a number of variables that serve as sources, perhaps in the nature of efficient causes, as well as consequences of social change. Here we have one of the "chicken-or-the-egg" type of dilemmas that often characterize explanation in sociology and the other social sciences.

So highly interrelated are the causes and the effects of social change that often it is exceedingly difficult, at the present stage of our knowledge, to distinguish one set of factors from another. More often than not, the same factor can serve as both a cause and an effect—although in significantly different respects—and in a "vicious circle" kind of phenomenon. For example, a growth in a given social population usually brings about ecological change that is invariably followed by modifications in social relations, which in turn result in population changes, and so on through the cause-and-effect process of social change. Hence, any one factor can, and usually does, serve as both an independent and dependent variable in the highly complex process of social change. Many factors in social change, in fact, are the same ones that influence the nature and development of culture, which we looked at in Chapter 3.

Let us examine the factors that comprise the fundamental sources (and sometimes consequences) of social change.

INNOVATION. **Innovation** refers to the emergence of new phenomena, usually of a cultural and/or technological nature, within a particular society. There are two principal forms of innovation: discovery and invention.

**Discovery** may be defined as the perception of a reality that previously had been unknown. Electricity and the chemical element uranium, for example, are discoveries, as is the social nature of human beings and other animals. Creative elements of culture, such as democracy and capitalism as political and economic institutions, are also considered to be discoveries.

**Invention** is a recombination of existing social or cultural elements in order to form a significantly new element. The automobile, airplane, and television are examples of material inventions. A constitutional monarchy represents a social invention.

Distinctions between a discovery and an invention are often subtle ones, especially when they are interrelated. Here are a couple of examples of these differences. Electricity represents a discovery; the electric light bulb is an invention. Uranium was discovered; the atomic bomb was invented.

CULTURAL BASE. **Cultural base** consists of the accumulation or fund of knowledge and technology available for further inventions. The greater the cultural base, the greater is the likely number of innovations and, in exponential fashion, the greater the amount of social change that is likely to occur. Similarly, the more discoveries and inventions there are in a given society, the larger the number that will be developed and lend themselves, in turn, to even more social change. One specific aspect of this phenomenon of cultural base is that the more advanced the technology of a society is, the more rapid social change is likely to be.

**CULTURAL DIFFUSION.** **Cultural diffusion** refers to the spread of culture, which usually takes place by way of borrowing from one society or culture by another. Diffusion, in part a function of cultural contact and isolation, is perhaps the largest single source of social change. Murdock (1934) estimated that 90 percent of the contents of every culture is acquired from other societies. Perhaps the most outstanding examples of contemporary social change is the diffusion of industrialization and the consequential processes of modernization that are thought to comprise a nearly universal phenomenon in the world today, and about which we shall have much more to say later.

Generally, culture diffuses outwardly from the point of origin along the most extensively used lines of communication, transportation, and other types of contact. Among the many factors that are instrumental in cultural diffusion are trade, mass communication, tourism, intermarriage, religious mission, diplomacy, cultural exchange, and migration. Selectivity, however, plays a significant role in cultural diffusion. Technology and material traits are more likely than ideology (beliefs or values) to be the objects of diffusion. Often the latter becomes a source of cultural conflict within the receiving society. Aside from considerations of congeniality and compatibility, those cultural traits that are objectively demonstrable to be functionally superior or that come from more powerful or prestigious sources are especially likely to be adopted.

**CULTURAL LAG.** **Cultural lag,** a hypothesis formulated by William F. Ogburn (1922), states that the "material" and "nonmaterial" aspects of culture develop or change at different rates, and that the resulting lag between the two becomes the basis of social problems and, essentially, of further social change. Usually, it is the material phase that lags behind the nonmaterial. Technological development, either as discovery or invention, invariably brings about a disruption in the social system through consequent attempts at social adaptation to the material innovations.

Normative changes in social relations and in the organization of society are usually required in such situations of cultural lag. Social change, then, always follows technological change. Yet, however real cultural lag is as a phenomenon, it does not explain the origin or direction of sociocultural change, since technological change, which is alleged to be the source of change, is itself an aspect of social change.

**IDEOLOGY AND VALUES.** A liberal and future-oriented society is likely to facilitate change, in contrast to one that is conservative and tradition-bound. The United States is an example of the former. As we saw in Chapter 3, the dominant ideologies and values in the American culture emphasize youth and the future. A most poignant example of the role of ideology in social change can be seen in the classic argument (see Weber, 1958) of the indispensable role of the Protestant ethic, with its focal values on hard work and worldly asceticism, in the emergence and expansion of capitalism and the industrial revolution.

Another reason that the United States may be relatively less tradition-oriented and less change-resistant is that its cultural past has been a very short one in contrast to countries such as Italy and Greece, where one finds stronger appreciation for the past and, consequently, a slower rate of change in many respects. More extreme examples of this situation can be found in the case of primitive societies in various parts of the world.

**DEMOGRAPHY AND ECOLOGY.** Changes in the size and composition of a societal population, as we saw in Chapter 7, inevitably result in fundamental changes in social organization, as well as in the nature and extent of social interaction. The same is true regarding the ecological structure of society. Ecological

**633**

▼ dynamics, such as invasion and segregation, are essentially and inescapably change producing.

SOCIAL MOVEMENTS. Social movements clearly demonstrate both the sources and the consequences of social change. The former are obvious, in that social movements are usually thought of as activistic efforts at social planning, and one form of initiative for social change. The role of social movements as consequences of social change is seen when collective action is organized to prevent or to forestall change. Examples of the latter situation can be found in movements to repeal progressive or liberal legislation, such as the anti-abortion movement, and those organized to oppose technological development that may alter the ecology, such as the effort mounted by the foes of nuclear energy.

REVOLUTION. A major source of social change—one that often essentially involves the structure and dynamics of a social movement—is revolution. A **revolution** consists of a profound and relatively rapid change in the political and economic system of a society, as well as in its dominant ideology. Such radical transformation of an existing social and political order fundamentally involves a form of social conflict, frequently manifested in severe and extensive violence, between different social classes or the various elements of political organization within a society. These dynamics often are given impetus by an intense competition for power.

Each revolution differs, of course, in terms of its particular set of causes and specific origins. Social scientists, however, have sought to identify several common patterns or structures in the revolutionary process (see Jenkins, 1982; Taylor, 1984). Goldstone (1981) speaks of the "natural history" of revolutions and has summarized a number of common characteristics and a similar sequence of stages in their unfolding. Skocpol (1979), on the other hand, has taken a structural approach and argues that each revolution needs to be understood in its own economic, political, and international context. These approaches appear to be complementary in several respects. One curious finding, however, is that revolution tends to be a phenomenon of preindustrial societies that are based on an agricultural economy. Such a revelation is inconsistent with the classical Marxist assertion that revolutions are products of decaying capitalist-industrialist societies.

Major revolutions that have been responsible for profound and extensive social change in the past few centuries are the French revolution of 1789 and the Russian revolution of 1917, as well as the American revolution of 1776 that led to the creation of these United States. Notable examples of major revolutions in the past few decades that brought about significant social change, with ramifications throughout the world, are those that have occurred in China, Cuba, and Iran.

SOCIAL CONFLICT. Social conflict is an intrinsic part of any social system. The more heterogeneous and complex a social system tends to be—either in its structure or in its content—the greater is the likelihood and inevitability of conflict. We need not elaborate any further on the nature or extent of social conflict, having done so already in preceding chapters as well as in the previous section of this one. The message here is simply that attempts to resolve such conflict, particularly in the power and authority structures of society, often involve changes or modifications in the existing content and patterns of sociocultural organization.

TRAUMATIC EVENTS. Singular or episodic events such as natural disasters (for example, floods, earthquakes, famines) or manmade ones (for example, revolutions and wars) can initiate extensive social change. Indeed, in the case of revolution and war, change is usually their very objective.

634

PERSONALITY.   Both as independent and as dependent variables, the dynamics of personality exert a substantial, and indeed even indispensable or inevitable, role in social change. We shall elaborate on these aspects of social change in a subsequent section of this chapter.

Each of these several factors plays a differential as well as an interdependent role in social change. The various dimensions of social change—magnitude, rate, force, and direction—are in part a function of these factors and their interaction.

## EMPIRICALLY DERIVED PRINCIPLES OF SOCIAL CHANGE

To supplement this discussion of factors in social change, we should like to mention a brief list of principles of social change which have emerged from the vast accumulation of relevant research findings. These principles can serve as well to describe some of the dynamics of the specific factors that were discussed above.

The list* that follows is only a partial one and, in any event, should be considered quite tentative. All knowledge, even in sociology, is subject to revision upon the discovery of new evidence that is itself a form of social change. The usual caveat "all other things being equal" applies to each principle.

1. Social change is more likely to occur in heterogeneous than in homogeneous societies.
2. The more integrated a society is in terms of values and institutions, the more successfully it is likely to respond to change in any of several ways, such as resistance, facilitation, incorporation, or adjustment.
3. Change that is externally imposed is less likely to be accepted. Forced choice from

* Bernard Berelson and Gary A. Steiner, *Human Behavior: An Inventory of Scientific Findings*, New York: Harcourt, Brace and World, 1964, pp. 613–619.

▼

the outside tends to result in overt compliance, and tends to generate covert resistance as well.
4. The more change threatens, or appears to threaten, traditional values, the greater the resistance is likely to be.
5. Change is more likely to occur in the "material" aspects of culture (for example, technology) than in values or beliefs.
6. Change is more likely to occur in the focal rather than in the peripheral elements of culture.
7. Change is more likely to occur in the less fundamental, less emotionally charged, less sacred, and more instrumental or technical aspects of culture and society (for example, tactics, tools, impersonal means) than in the antithetical situations (for example, territorial stability, primary-group relations, patterns of religious worship, systems of prestige).
8. Change is more likely to occur in the simple elements of society rather than in the complex elements.
9. Change is more likely to occur in the non-symbolic elements of society rather than in the symbolic elements.
10. Change is more likely to occur in form than in substance.
11. Change is more likely to occur in elements for which roughly equivalent substitutes are available or provided in the society.
12. Change is more likely to occur in elements that are compatible rather than alien to a given culture or society.
13. Change is more likely to occur in periods of crisis and stress than in normal or quiescent periods.
14. The larger the cultural base of society, the more likely it is that change will occur.
15. Change is more likely to occur in and through urban areas than rural areas.
16. The more slowly changes are introduced, the less resistance and disruption there is likely to be.

**635**

▼ # Effects of Social Change

Discerning the consequences of social change, as we mentioned in the preceding section, is not an easy task because the seeming consequences of social change often *are* the social change. A given phenomenon or situation, to repeat, can be both cause and effect of social change—although, of course, in quite different respects. Social change, for example, often has a profound impact on the individual in a number of psychosocial respects which, in turn, are themselves instrumental in effecting social change. Such is the cyclical nature of social change in terms of its interaction between society and the individual.

**636**

Social change affects virtually every dimension of society. Many specific examples of social change and its effects have been mentioned in preceding chapters devoted to particular aspects of society or social organization. Here we wish to discuss some of the fundamental or general consequences of social change—in terms of both their sociological and psychological dimensions—which themselves often provide the context for further social change.

## SOCIAL AND PERSONAL DISORGANIZATION

Social change and social disorganization often are inseparable. Any major change in society inevitably produces a number of social problems—situations causing conflict, stress, tension, dysfunction, and other undesirable consequences that affect significantly large numbers of people in society. Either the changing situations themselves (for example, changes in the size and composition of population) are problems, or they produce a number of problems by way of social and personal disorganization. One of the more common, and perhaps more extensive, illustrations is found in generational conflict (the "generation gap") which itself appears to be exacerbated by rapid social change.

Social disorganization is most acute in traditional and developing countries. Social transformation often involves a much more radical, much more stressful, type of social change for these societies. Such a situation is particularly critical as these societies seek to narrow the gap between themselves and those societies that constitute the prototypes of modern civilization. Modern societies, on the other hand, however much they experience a more extensive and rapid type of social change, are to a considerable extent structured to expect and accept social change to a much greater degree than are more traditional societies. An example of this is manifested in the principle of technological obsolescence that holds such a pivotal, even indispensable, position in the economy of highly industrialized and rapidly changing societies. People in such societies are enculturated to be change-oriented—to look forward to innovation and to value the future.

Mass disorientation, nonetheless, is often the result of a constant bombardment of new sociocultural elements that render obsolete the learned and engrained patterns of social behavior. Personal disorganization in some portions of the population is usually inevitable to a certain degree when social disorganization is rapid or continuous. Indeed, under some circumstances, there is a substantially positive correlation between social and personal disorganization. Toffler (1970), in *Future Shock*, elaborates on the personal stresses and anxieties of the rapid social change that characterizes contemporary societies throughout much of the world. Inkeles and Smith (1974*b*), however, in their cross-cultural studies of industrialization, conclude that contact with modern sources of social change (for example, education, urban residence, factory employment, and mass media) does not in itself produce deleterious effects on the individual. Similarly, Suzman (1977), utilizing data from American studies of social change, shows a positive correlation between personal contact with modernity and the level of psychosocial development. Neither of these studies, however, denies that urbanization and industrialization may generate social disorganization, which in turn may produce psychic stress. The contention is only that personal disorganization is not inherent in, and therefore not a universal accompaniment of, industrialization, urbanization, and social change. Psychic strain may arise from the mere failure to adapt to such conditions. Again, the ability to tolerate social change and social disorganization, as we shall discuss subsequently, is related to one's personality structure.

Much of the effect of social change depends on the personal meanings it has for people in terms of their own particular social conditions. Laurer (1974) provides evidence that psychological stress and personality disintegration are linked to perceived, if not to actual, rates of social change. Here again, in terms of the psychological consequences of social processes, we need to recall the well-known dictum of W. I. Thomas (1928) to the effect that if people define situations as real, they are real in their consequences. Still other research (Laurer & Thomas, 1976) has presented a well-documented case that the incidence of mental illness increases as a function of the rapidity of sociocultural change. That personal disorganization can be a consequence of social change seems clear. Its precise relationship in this regard, however, is in need of further specification.

## CULTURAL LAG

The phenomenon of cultural lag, which was mentioned in the preceding section on contributing factors, offers an excellent example of a factor that can serve simultaneously as cause and effect of social change. **Cultural lag** refers to unequal rates of change in the different aspects of society or culture, and the social disorganization or social problems that are left in the wake of this disjuncture. Usually, cultural lag refers to the hiatus between the "material" and the "nonmaterial" segments or aspects of culture. Technological development that appreciably exceeds appropriate adjustment in social norms demonstrates the principle of cultural lag. One example is the existence and enforcement of archaic laws that are no longer compatible with the modern technology and social dynamics to which they are applied. Laws regarding the definition of life and death that are inconsistent with modern technology in biology and medicine (for example, "heart death" versus "brain death") demonstrate this situation. Other situations of cultural lag involve the absence of social policy (see Box 14-1). Such is the case of technological development in the areas of artificial insemination, in-utero surgery, surrogate parenting, brain tissue transplants, and cryogenics (research involving frozen bodies). Another timely, and much more pervasive, example of cultural lag involves the ever-expanding technology of the electronic computer that continuously outpaces the capability of society to absorb the social consequences of its seemingly endless applications.

When social change occurs slowly, there is usually ample opportunity to adjust the various dimensions of culture and society to each other. Rapid social change, however, does not permit this fundamental adjustment, especially as it concerns human psychological factors. Moreover, for a host of social and psychological reasons, social change is not always as easily inducible in one segment of society or culture as it may be in another. In any event, social change nowadays seems to have a geometric character to its movement and acceleration. Such a situation tends to exacerbate the dynamics of cultural lag.

## COGNITIVE AMBIGUITY

Social change, primarily in the context of the two effects described above, often produces **cognitive ambiguity,** a psychological state of confusion about the status of social reality, both

**637**

▼

## BOX 14-1. Cultural Lag

Cultural lag occurs when technological developments outpace the nontechnological dimensions of society and culture, such as norms and values. The lag or gap between the "material" and "nonmaterial" components often raises social questions and produces social problems of a most serious dimension.

Social situations that involve cultural lag seem to be occuring much more frequently nowadays as technological change reveals an inevitable, and much more rapid, path of complex development. Among such situations are the following representative episodes:

638

1. Washington, D.C., 1988. Scientists are considering the use of aborted fetuses as a source of brain cells which could be transplanted to genetically related individuals suffering from brain diseases, such as Parkinson's disease. Consider the moral and legal issues that are likely to develop if people were to engage in conceptive practices, natural or artificial, in order to produce a fetus for such purposes. What problems might exist were a man's sperm to be used to impregnate his daughter's or granddaughter's ova for this purpose?

2. California, 1987. The head was removed from the body of an 83-year-old woman suffering from severe arthritis, and frozen in the hope that medical technology one day will advance to the point where the woman can be "brought back to life." The objective is to replace her body with one free of arthritis and other crippling diseases. Would such a person, from a legal perspective, be the same person or a totally different one? What kind of culture shock might such a person experience in encountering society after a total absence of twenty-five or fifty years.

3. New York, 1986. A woman was unable to sustain a pregnancy. She and her husband conceived a child through "test-tube" fertilization. The embryo was implanted in the womb of another woman, who had contracted to serve as the child's surrogate mother. After the child's birth, however, the surrogate mother decided not to surrender the child to its "original" parents—the biological father and his wife. Who are the legal parents of the child? Which biological parent should have custody of the child?

4. Australia, 1981. A couple conceived three embryos through "test-tube" fertilization. One embryo was implanted successfully in the woman's uterus, although she miscarried ten days later. The other two embryos were frozen. Two years later, the couple was killed in an airplane crash. They left an estate valued at several million dollars. To whom do the frozen embryos belong? Are these embryos heirs to the deceased couple's estate? ▲

real and ideal, which in an extreme degree people find quite intolerable. The level at which cognitive ambiguity can be tolerated is a basic function of the structure of one's personality (Frenkel-Brunswik, 1949). Some types of personality, especially the highly dogmatic and authoritarian varieties, are most intolerant of cognitive ambiguity. We shall have more to say on this matter in a subsequent section on the relationship of personality to social change.

The inability to cope with cognitive ambiguity in rather extreme situations can lead to personal and social paralysis—an abstention from appropriate and relevant behavior or deviation from one's expected obligations and socially relevant norms. One example of such a situation is that of parents who, in dealing with the phenomenon of the "generation gap," often become uncertain about the propriety of changing norms of social behavior in regard to such things as personal relationships and lifestyles. Wishing to be neither hypocritical nor "old-fashioned" in the face of social change, yet grossly confused in any case, many of these people abstain from making, or are unable to make, parental decisions or rules for their children. Doing nothing but "ride the fence" in such a situation constitutes a paralytic reaction that may be seen as a violation of the norms of parental responsibility. In more extreme situations, unsuccessful attempts to cope properly with cognitive ambiguity can lead to serious forms of personal dysfunction, such as mental illness or substance abuse. Reactions such as these on a large scale can constitute major problems for society.

## ANOMIE

Social change under the set of circumstances described above often leads to **anomie,** a state of relative normlessness and social instability. Changing and conflicting definitions of values and norms are the two principal elements of anomie which, in turn, aggravate many of the other effects of social change, such as cognitive ambiguity and personal disorganization.

Anomie is thought to have its psychological counterpart in **anomia,** the subjective state in which an individual experiences a distressing lack of purpose, direction, and social integration (see Srole, 1956). These dynamics, in relatively extreme situations, are thought to lead to both personal and social forms of deviant behavior, which in turn can provide the source of further social disorganization and social

change. One must not conclude from this interpretation, however, that chaos or change without stability is the basic order of society. Social change is only one of the many dynamics in the complex functioning of society. Its effects are as much a part of the natural order of society as is its generation.

## SOCIAL INSTITUTIONS: CHANGE AND SURVIVAL

Chief among the effects of social change are those that relate to social institutions. Social institutions, as we noted in Chapter 7, have undergone considerable change throughout the recorded history of humankind. All are affected, some more than others, because social institutions are so highly interconnected as subsystems of society that the dynamics in any one necessarily influence the dynamics in another.

New forms and practices of the basic social institutions (religion, education, family, government, and economy) occasionally lead people to fear that social institutions and, hence, society itself are fading away. Of greatest concern is the family, and perhaps religion as well. Many people today wonder about the fate of the family and the church—whether they are on the way to extinction—given the extensive and rapid changes that these institutions have undergone in very recent years. Let us look at these questions in more detail.

THE FAMILIAL INSTITUTION. Alterations in the familial institutions of modern societies constitute one of the more dramatic examples of social change during the past three to four decades. Nearly every facet of family life has been affected by social change, although its manifestations are perhaps greatest in terms of new values regarding the married state and family size, as well as the corresponding roles of family members (see Table 14-2). During the 1970s, for example, the number of households in the United States containing married couples

▼    TABLE 14-2.   Changes in the American Family, 1965–1985

|                                                                                      | 1965 | 1985   |
| ------------------------------------------------------------------------------------ | ---- | ------ |
| Median Age at First Marriage                                                         |      |        |
|    Men                                                                 | 22.8 | 25.5   |
|    Women                                                               | 20.6 | 23.3   |
| Fertility Rate (Number of Children the Typical Woman Will Have During Her Childbearing Years) | 2.9  | 1.8    |
| Marriage Rate (per 1000 population)                                                  | 9.3  | 10.2*  |
| Divorce Rate (per 1000 population)                                                   | 2.5  | 5.0    |
| Working Women (Percent 16 years and over)                                            | 36.7 | 54.7   |
| Single-Parent Families (Percent of all Families with Children Under 18)              | 10.1 | 26.3   |
| Premarital Births (Percent of all Births)                                            | 7.7  | 21.5   |
| Single-Person Households                                                             | 15.0 | 23.7   |

**\* New marriages account for one-third of this figure.**
**Source: U.S. Bureau of Census, National Center for Health Statistics, U.S. Department of Labor.**

and children declined by 1 million; single-parent households, however, nearly doubled percentagewise.* These figures simply reflect an increase in the divorce rate and the fact that fewer people today are getting married or are doing so at a later age. Involved too is an apparent increase in widowhood as a result of the expansion of our life span. Single people accounted for 16 percent of our population in 1970, whereas in 1985, the figure was 24 percent. The figures for married people were, respectively, 72 percent and 64 percent. Family size is also reflected in trends in the fertility rate— the number of children per women of childbearing age. This rate, consistent with a worldwide trend, has decreased from 2.9 in 1965 to 1.8 in 1985. (A rate of 2.2 is required for the natural replacement of the population.)

The disappearance or decline of many functions traditionally associated with the family, and the consequential weakening of its solidarity or social cohesion, also constitute highly significant changes. The extended family is becoming more and more limited in its functions, in great part because of the geographical and social mobility that has become increasingly characteristic of highly industrialized and urbanized societies. With the loosening and severing of kinship ties, the nuclear family has assumed a more central role in many respects. The stability of the nuclear family is also of paramount concern. Nearly 28 percent of all households in the United States today consist of only one person. Similarly, single-parent families now account for 26 percent of all families— an increase from 13 percent in 1970—89 percent of which are headed by women. Increases in this familial form are due less to the death

* The following statistics, taken from the *Harvard University Gazette*, not only point up the change in family size in the United States, but perhaps say more about the impact of social change on the American family than would an elaborate discussion. Of the Radcliffe (women's college) class of 1952, 127 or about one-half of the graduates were married within five years after graduation and during those five years produced a total of 154 children. Of the Radcliffe class of 1961, 109 or about one-third of the grads were married within five years after graduation and during that time produced a total of only four children. Marital and familial change has continued in these directions.

of spouses, and much more to the increasing prevalence of separation and divorce, as well as the popularity of cohabitation* on the part of unmarried individuals (about 70 percent), as well as the increase in out-of-wedlock births (about 22 percent). The marriage/divorce ratio is currently 2:1, versus 4:1 about 25 years ago.† This trend does not appear to have reached its peak. It is estimated that about 40 percent of new marriages today will terminate in divorce, with the average duration of these marriages having been less than seven years (U.S. Bureau of the Census, 1980).

Such a situation does not mean that marriage and the family are doomed to extinction. Rather, it is likely that new forms (or an expansion thereof) of marriage and the family may appear. Among these new types are serial monogamy (a continual cycle of marriage and divorce) and the binuclear or reconstituted family (an integration of children from a present and previous marriage) (see Masnick & Bane, 1980). The fact of the matter is that three-fourths of the people between the ages of twenty-five and sixty-five are married, and about 90 percent expect to marry at some time (Walsh, 1986). Thus, even though the divorce rate has tripled in the past sixty years, the divorced do remarry—and overwhelmingly so: 80 percent of men, and 75 percent of women.

The family as an institution, regardless of its type, provides personal and social functions that not only are indispensable, but indeed cannot be adequately or as effectively fulfilled, at least so it seems, by other institutions or social mechanisms.* Thus, as Lasch (1977) has argued so well, the family is a "haven in a heartless world" in that it is uniquely able to provide a private refuge of intimate companionship and emotional support which, it is appropriate to say, are indispensable for human function.

Another major change in the American familial institution is that of work roles, particularly in terms of the sharp increase in the number of women in the work force. Today, over 55 percent of adult women are engaged in gainful employment outside the home, in contrast to only 27 percent in 1940. Correspondingly, the educational institution has taken on more and more functions from other institutions, particularly the socialization functions of the family. Education, moreover, is no longer a privilege of the elite segments of society. More and more education in all forms and at all levels has become available for the masses, and with this development have come tremendous changes in both educational organizations and educational technology.

**641**

THE RELIGIOUS INSTITUTION.  Much change has occurred as well in the religious institutions of the world, especially those within the realm of Christianity. Numerous modifications have been made in the various liturgical forms of worship, and in the roles of religious functionaries, along with the recruitment of women as priests. While tenets of faith have remained greatly unchanged, new interpretations of morality have been quite prevalent in

---

* Cohabitation represents more a modern version of "going steady" and/or trial marriage than a new marital form, since it is not officially recognized. While some observers think that cohabitation may become an institutionalized stage in the courtship process, given its four-fold increase in the past couple of decades, it presently accounts for only about four million people (4% of the American households).

† During the 1970's, single-parent families maintained by divorced women increased from 29% to 38%; and by never-married women from 7% to 15%; while those headed by widows dropped from 20% to 12%.

* It is interesting to point out that extensive, yet unsuccessful, attempts were made by the Bolsheviks (the Communist Party) to eliminate many functions of the family in the Soviet Union in the 1920's. Such efforts were in the ideological interests of equality, and would have been consistent with Socialist and Communist doctrine by eliminating inherited property and male dominance, as well as the parental responsibility for children and their responsibility in turn for elderly parents (Geiger, 1968). One unexpected development was the emergence of literally thousands of homeless juvenile delinquents who in turn became an overwhelming burden for the Soviet government. The failure of this experiment shows how difficult it is not only to eliminate the basic functions of the family, but even to alter its structure.

▼

recent years, and these revisions have significantly altered social behavior in just about every realm of social intercourse. Formal religions, moreover, to a considerable extent have been removed from the hub of social institutions. Secular beliefs have become quite common, and they have greatly replaced traditional religion as the central element in the belief system of much of society (Stark & Bainbridge, 1985).

642

There seems to be a widespread impression that religion is on the decline in the United States. Yet, our society is more religious today than it was fifty to sixty years ago. Sociological studies show that nowadays there are proportionately more churches, more people attending religious services, and more money being donated to churches (Caplow et al., 1983). Moreover, many people respond "none" to questions of religious affiliation, when in fact they believe in new forms of religion, such as astrology, reincarnation, psychic phenomenon, mysticism, and scientology.

A rather peculiarly American phenomenon among the contemporary forms of religion and church membership has been the emergence and prosperous diffusion of televangelism (Hadden & Swann, 1981). As of 1988, there were over 1600 televangelistic ministers in this country, and one-quarter of the American population report watching religious television programs on a weekly basis.* So while formal religious worship may have decreased somewhat in the past few decades, the belief in God and the importance of religion seem just as strong today as in the past several decades. In fact, people in the United States, it turns out, attach greater importance to religion than do those in perhaps any other major society except India. While figures vary, public opinion polls have shown that as many as 95 percent of Americans believe in "God or a universal spirit," and about 60 to 70 percent report belonging to a specific religion (see Jacquet, 1987). Trends in

* Gallup Opinion Poll, 1987.

other societies, of course, may not be the same, but many do show similar patterns.

Social institutions today, as throughout human history, are not dissolving, but rather evolving. Social change has been as endemic to social institutions as it has been to society itself. The functions served by the basic institutions of society, especially the familial, the religious, and the educational, have clearly undergone continuous change throughout recorded history, but the institutions themselves continue on in modified form. One may question the efficiency of any particular institutional form as compared with another—in terms of meeting functional or societal goals—but this is quite a different question, however much related. It is important to understand that, at least as regards basic institutions, social change has been taking place *within* the existing institutions and has not involved their replacement or annihilation. One relevant study is a fifty-year follow-up on a classic inquiry (Lynd & Lynd, 1929) of life in Muncie, Indiana, which in 1925 had been selected by a team of sociologists for intensive investigation as a typical American community. The modern investigation (Caplow et al., 1982) reports that the many precipitous changes that have taken place in American society in recent decades have failed to erode either the nuclear family or religion. The modern investigators, in fact, suggest that these long-established traditions may have gained strength over the past half-century. To annihilate basic institutions is to annihilate society—and, consequently, the individual, given the dependent relationship. Hence, whether institutions endure, especially the basic ones, is a question that is inextricably tied to the survival of society and the people whom it serves.

## FORMAL ORGANIZATIONS AND THE FUTURE

Complex organizations and large-scale bureaucracies have become a more extensive and integral part of human society. Their continued expansion in both number and size, given the sheer growth of societal populations, seems to be even more likely throughout many underdeveloped parts of the world, particularly as they become industrialized and urbanized.

Just how gargantuan and complex formal organizations can become is an unanswerable question. Many social scientists argue that, as in any social system, there are functional limits beyond which bureaucracies cannot operate effectively. Their characteristic rationality and efficiency, they argue, reach a point of diminishing returns. They simply become unmanageable.

Several social scientists, nonetheless, foresee the eventual demise of bureaucracies and the emergence of alternative types of social organization. Chiefly under attack in these various perceptions are the formalization, routinization, and impersonality of the bureaucracy. Social systems with these characteristics are alleged to be unresponsive to the social trends (for example, humanism, democracy) and organizational challenges of the modern and postindustrial era, including especially the need for highly organized skills. Rapidly changing or temporary conditions, it is believed, require a more fluid organization, a special-purpose unit that is dissolved when its task is completed. Toffler (1970) speaks in this regard of the "adhocracy" that will consist of temporary work groups composed of highly skilled workers who are utilized to confront specific, nonroutine problems. Bennis (1970) similarly foresees the replacement of bureaucracies by the end of this century with organizations that will be adaptive, temporary, and rapidly changing systems with the distinctive ability to utilize what he calls "task forces."

Just how formal organizations will change, of course, is not completely clear. Yet, lest this discussion seem completely negative, regarding change as dysfunctional, let us conclude by mentioning once again that social change for many, even under the very circumstances and effects that have been described, is seen as social progress. Social change in such a view inevitably provides new opportunities for human growth and creativity on both the societal and individual levels.

# Patterns and Trends of Sociocultural Change

Human societies, on the whole, have been changing for thousands and thousands of years, apparently since they first came into existence. Anthropological evidence is sufficient to demonstrate that changes have been continuous in many dimensions of human social life. The most basic change has occurred in terms of societal modes of subsistence, from hunting and gathering types to industrial types. Correspondingly, another fundamental type of societal change has been the development of structurally and culturally simple forms of social organization into highly complex ones. Many of the patterns of social change responsible for these trends remain at work yet today. The following are among the more important of these patterns and trends of sociocultural change.

## URBANIZATION

One of the basic trends in terms of human ecology is the unabated convergence of rural and urban patterns of societal organization and social life. About 45 percent of the world's population today is urbanized. It is estimated that by the year 2020, more than 60 percent of the people in the world will be living in an urban environment (see Figure 14-2). Some countries, such as our own and most of those in Western Europe, already are considerably highly urbanized. (In 1987, about 77 percent of the American population lived in metropolitan statistical areas alone.) The reason for this is not so much that cities are expanding as that suburban and

643

▼

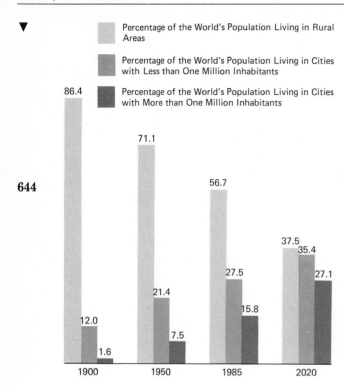

Percentage of the World's Population Living in Rural Areas

Percentage of the World's Population Living in Cities with Less than One Million Inhabitants

Percentage of the World's Population Living in Cities with More than One Million Inhabitants

**644**

FIGURE 14-2 Patterns of World Urbanization 1900–2020. Source: Population Reference Bureau.

rural areas are developing into larger and larger metropolitan areas.

One dimension of the pattern of rural-urban convergence in our society is reflected in the concept of the **megalopolis,** a term applied to an enormous and continuously expanding urban region that may lead to ever-more complex structures of societal and social organization. One such feature of the megalopolis, known more technically as a consolidated metropolitan statistical area (CMSA),* is seen in the suggested centralization of government of local, county, and state levels into regional ones. Another, more realistic, aspect is that of economic development on a regional basis, such as in

* A CMSA is a metropolitan area with a population of one million or more people that consists of two or more smaller metropolitan areas. More than one-third of the American population resides in the nation's twenty-two CMSA's.

terms of transportation centers (airports and railroads), sports and cultural complexes, and the distribution of electrical energy. So too could education and other institutional aspects of society be absorbed into the megalopolistic structure. An omen of such developments may be the county-wide school districts that have emerged in metropolitan and urban areas during the past few years.

The prototype of the megalopolis is the urban strip on the East Coast, known as "Boswash," that stretches from north of Boston to south of Washington, D.C., and contains nearly 20 percent of the population of the United States. This "strip city," about 500 miles long and 150 miles wide, has a population of more than 36 million people. Other megalopolises are "Chipitts" in the Midwest, spreading from Chicago to Pittsburgh, and "SanSan" in the far West, running from San Francisco to San Diego. Some de-

1.  Metropolitan Belt
1A  Atlantic Seaboard
1B  Lower Great Lakes
2.  California Region
3.  Florida Peninsula
4.  Gulf Coast
5.  East Central Texas –
    Red River

6.  Southern Piedmont
7.  North Georgia –
    South East Tennessee
8.  Puget Sound
9.  Twin Cities Region
10. Colorado Piedmont
11. St. Louis
12. Metropolitan Arizona

13. Willamette Valley
14. Central Oklahoma –
    Arkansas Valley
15. Missouri – Kaw Valley
16. North Alabama
17. Blue Grass
18. Southern Coastal Plain
19. Salt Lake Valley

20. Central Illinois
21. Nashville Region
22. East Tennessee
23. Memphis
24. El Paso –
    Ciudad Juarez

Numbered in Order of Population Size.

FIGURE 14-3  Megalopolises Projected in the United States for the Year 2000. Source: Presidential Commission on Population Growth and the American Future. Adapted from *Population Growth and the American Future.* Washington, D.C.: U.S. Government Printing Office, 1972, p. 33.

mographers (Eells & Walton, 1969) have projected that these three megalopolises alone will include one-half of the nation's population by the year 2000 (see Figure 14-3).

## INDUSTRIALIZATION

The transition from agricultural to industrial types of society has been perhaps the most rad-

ical juncture in the course of sociocultural evolution. Up until two centuries ago, the vast majority of the human population lived in localized and isolated societies whose economies were based on hunting, gathering, horticulture, pastoralism, fishing, or agriculture.

The industrial revolution brought an entirely new type of society, one that, as we saw in Chapter 7, is based on massive technological development, mechanization, and manufacture.

▼ Nearly all types of societies have been transformed by the industrial model, even though there are many instances of other types still existing. Yet, so quickly are nonindustrial societies vanishing that they can be labeled an endangered species.

**646**

While the industrial revolution made its debut about two centuries ago, this process is still occurring in many societies of the world, either in an expanded or an incipient stage. Many other societies are even still looking forward to it, despite the major social problems that industrialization inevitably will bring with it. In the more advanced and highly industrialized societies (United States, England, Canada, Sweden, West Germany, Italy, France, Japan), nonetheless, one question that gets much attention today concerns the next step in societal evolution and change.

## THE COMING OF POST-INDUSTRIAL SOCIETY

Advanced industrial society cannot be the end of social evolution—if evolution there be. Futurists, a new variety of social scientists, foresee the emergence of yet another type of society, one marked by a significant change in the chief mode of economic production as well as in the structure of the sociocultural system and the nature of social relations. A number of different labels (futuristic, postindustrial, superindustrial, technocratic, technological, informational, leisure, service, mass, and postmodern) have been proposed for the next stage of social development, but the descriptions of these new forms of society are highly similar.

The most common term, first popularized by Bell (1973), that has been used to characterize highly modernized societies, such as the United States, is "postindustrial society." Other metaphors suggested in more recent years, however, also appropriately describe the forces of mod-

ernization. Toffler (1980) in this respect has spoken of the "third wave" of human civilization, and Naisbitt (1982) has used the label "megatrends" to characterize the thrust and dynamics of social change beyond the industrial level of society. Postindustrial society in these various depictions is perceived to be one with an economy that pivots on extensive automation and a work force that is highly specialized, the bulk of which is far removed from production. It is a society characterized by a significant expansion of service-oriented employment and leisure activities, all resulting in an unparalleled level of economic affluence and personal fulfillment (see Box 14-2).

The problem of production has been solved with the attainment of a phenomenal rate of economic growth. It is consumption that now becomes the problematic feature of the economy—consumption of all kinds. One facet of the consuming society is reflected today in the extensive choices that our society offers to the consumer. A decade ago, for example, the average supermarket stocked 9000 items. Today our supermarkets carry about 22,000 items. This wealth of choice is not without appreciable difficulty. Imagine having to choose between 23 flavors of *9 Lives* cat food or 157 shades of lipstick offered by one company alone!

An integral part of the consuming society is the expanded role of leisure, recreation, and other nonproductive activity (see Box 14-2). The movement toward more leisure and less work is reflected in one simple statistic: The average workweek today is about thirty-five hours, compared to sixty hours in 1890. A drop of this magnitude represents an average decrease in the workweek of about 2.5 hours per decade (see Figure 14-4).

Paralleling these economic changes more fundamentally is the emergence of service activities—not only those associated with leisure and recreational enterprises, but also those increasingly associated with information and

# BOX 14-2. The Leisure Society ▼

Among the more interesting, undoubtedly even quite appealing, characterizations that have been made of the emerging form of societal organization in the post-industrial era is that of the leisure society (see Seabrook, 1988; Kando, 1975). Such a development has come about because an increasing portion of daily activity for many people in the modern and technologically advanced society is being devoted to nongainful enterprises.

Statistics show that the workweek in the United States has been decreasing from an average of sixty hours in 1890 to about thirty-five hours today. And, in some industries, the workweek is considerably below the average. Added to this situation are the increases in the number of holidays and paid vacation time. Moreover, early retirement, and thus a reduction in the number of years one spends in the labor force, is more and more commonplace. While the mandatory retirement age has been increased to seventy, a steadily increasing number of people, chiefly in the professional and semiprofessional ranks, are retiring in their fifties.

The figures reflecting a decrease in the workweek and in the years spent on the job, however, are not fully revealing. Today, much more time has also been made available for leisure activities as a consequence of time-saving domestic appliances (for example, dishwashers, disposals, microwave ovens) and other automated equipment commonly found in many households. The relative abundance of free time and the emergence of the leisure society are reflected further in the number and proportion of people, as well as the share of the gross national product, involved in recreation, entertainment, travel, and other leisure activities.

All of these developments have brought about profound and extensive changes not only in the economic sector of society, but throughout many of its other basic institutions as well, including in particular the family. ▲

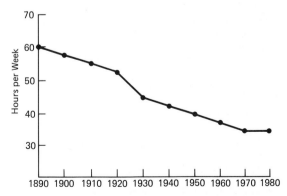

FIGURE 14-4   Average Work Week in the United States Since 1890.

647

▼

data processing—as the dominant mode of subsistence in the postindustrial society. By 1985, 68 percent of the American labor force was in the field of services, 26 percent in industry, and less than 3 percent in agriculture (see Figure 14-5). Futurists predict that by the year 2000 manufacturing will account for only 11 percent of American jobs, while 89 percent will be in the service sector of the economy.

648

Changes of these kinds would seem to be a welcomed state of affairs, ones that promise more and more of "the good life" for more and more people. On the other hand, some futurists are much less optimistic. Indeed, they are downright pessimistic and even foresee the extinction of industrial society, insofar as postindustrial society requires the perpetuation, and undoubtedly the expansion, of resource depletion—all of which is aggravated by a continuation of population growth. Ophuls

(1977), for example, describes a "scarcity society" in which the depletion of resources leads to a lower standard of living and a strong authoritarian state, a situation we have seen many times in several of the Communist countries of the world, and to a limited degree have experienced on occasion in our own society in recent years in terms of energy resources.

## TECHNOLOGICAL SOCIETY

So much has the age of automation entered into the culture and structure of highly industrialized societies that some observers have begun to speak of, and even to fear, the emergence of a technocratic society—one that places an emphasis on the development and diffusion of mass technology and mechanization, chiefly into previously untouched segments of social

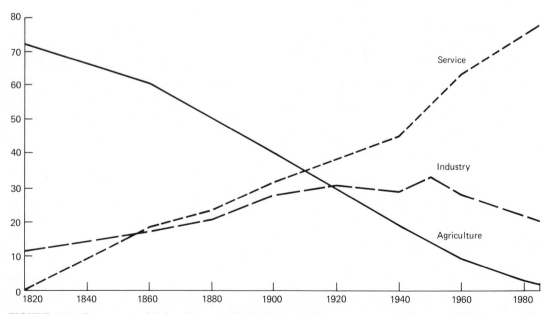

FIGURE 14-5 Percentage of Labor Force in Major Economic Sectors, 1820–1985. Source: U.S. Bureau of the census, *Historical Statistics of the United States: Colonial Times to 1970,* Washington, D.C.: U.S. Government Printing Office. 1975; U.S. Bureau of the Census, *Statistical Abstracts of the United States,* Washington, D.C.: U.S. Government Printing Office, 1985.

life (see Borgmann, 1984; Ellul, 1964; Teich, 1986).

The reason for this concern is that as technology becomes increasingly more complex, the fewer are the individuals who are able to comprehend it; hence technological specialists assume ever-increasing responsibilities and power, which could set the stage for an eventual technocracy: government by an elite corps of technological experts. Taken as one indicator of the trend toward technocratic society is the increasing proliferation of job titles. The U.S. Department of Labor has distinguished more than 30,000 occupational specialties. That is

almost a 30,000 percent increase in comparison with the very simple economic role in hunting and gathering societies!

Technology will undoubtedly become ever more sophisticated and complex. Indeed, to predict the future of technological change would seem to be frolicking in science fiction. Such surely was the case only a few decades ago when one spoke, tongue-in-cheek, of "going to the moon." So extensive have been the scientific and technical advances during the past quarter-century that seldom does the more perceptive individual doubt the technological possibilities of the future. Test-tube conceptions,

▼

649

NASA-S-71-4297 V

**Futuristic Societies.** Communities of the future most likely will include lunar colonies consisting of relatively self-contained cities. Undepicted in this artistic rendition are the new modes of social interaction and social structure that may be necessary. (NASA/Image Works)

▼ artificial heart implants, laser-beam technology, robots, satellite communications, and outer-space travel—once mere fiction—have now become commonplace.

Some people perhaps would welcome these technological developments as human progress—or, at least, view them as the mere evolution of humankind (see Pascarella, 1979). Others, again making a value judgment, perceive such situations—indeed, even the very reality of today's technology—with dismay and alarm. This reaction is reflected in a report on technology by the National Academy of Sciences (1967):

> Whether rightly or wrongly, the belief is now widely held that the continuation of certain technological trends would pose grave dangers for the future of man, and, indeed, the ill-considered exploitation of technology has already contributed to some of the most urgent of our contemporary problems: the specter of thermonuclear destruction; the tensions of congested cities; the hazards of a polluted and despoiled biosphere; the expanding arsenal of techniques for the surveillance and manipulation of private thoughts and behavior; the alienation of those who feel excluded from power in an increasingly technical civilization.

One needs to be mindful as well of the technological possibilities in the behavioral and social sciences which could involve extensive behavior modification, including behavior control. Such eventualities, undoubtedly, are even more mind-boggling than technological advances in the physical realm.

## INFORMATIONAL SOCIETY

One of the most distinctive elements of the technological society is the extensive development of electronic data processing. The chief tool, of course, is the computer, along with all of its ancillary equipment. Continuous expansion of this technology has given birth, since the late 1950s, to what has lately become known as the "information society." Indeed, the major forms of technological innovation in postindustrial society are those that are associated with the enormous and increasing activity involved in the gathering, processing, storing, and dissemination of information (see, for example, Naisbitt, 1982). More than 50 percent of the labor force in the United States today is composed of workers in the field of information services. By the year 2000, it is expected that over two-thirds of the labor force will be working in this field.

The communications and information revolution, perhaps the most dramatic social change taking place at the present time, has yet to reach its peak. It is possible, nonetheless, to predict somewhat how revolutionary this new

**The Computer Culture.** A microcomputer chip, smaller than an aspirin and containing more information than could be stored in hundreds of filing cabinets, is the core element of the electronic technology that promises to revolutionize decision making and social behavior in the modern society. (© Charles M. Falco/Photo Researchers)

650

technology will be. Home computers in the not-too-distant future will be nearly as ordinary as telephones and television sets—and perhaps may even replace these modern conveniences. Similarly, personal computers in the classroom will be nearly as commonplace as pencils and ballpoint pens. Many facets of social life already are being altered significantly by the emergence of the "computer culture" (see, for example, Turkle, 1984). Consider such things as tele-conferencing, electronic mail, computerized shopping and banking, robotic machinery, video-interactive schooling, telecommuting (working at home via computer networks), and computerized domestics for house maintenance, all of which are either already here or soon to be part of daily life. A computerized society undoubtedly will require new modes of social interaction. Perhaps even more significant is that such an electronic society, increasingly based on the structure and dynamics of artificial intelligence, will revolutionize the fundamental process of decision making in just about every sector and dimension of human life.

The computerized society, like all other types, will bring its own set of societal problems (see Lyon, 1989). Chief among these concerns are likely to be questions of privacy and the differential access to information with its implications for power, prestige, and other aspects of social stratification. Whereas in agricultural and industrial societies the sources of power are rooted respectively in land and capital, it is information, or access to information, that is likely to distinguish the power elite and those who command high social prestige. Indeed, even today some social scientists speak of the "informational poor" (those individuals lacking, or lacking access to, information). Representing about 20 percent of the population, these individuals are seen in many ways as quite low in social rank.

Unknown are the limits of a computerized technology. One rather startling indication is that while there are 5 billion people in the world today, the existing number of computers can do the work of trillions of people. It is likely that the effect of the computer revolution will surpass the tremendous impact of the industrial revolution on human society.

## MASS SOCIETY

*Mass society* is another of the more commonly used terms to describe the current directions in which societal organization is moving. The characteristic mark of nearly every aspect of societal function is coming to be that of massive social organization. Massive governments, massive businesses, and massive schools (at the secondary and college levels) have resulted in what appears to many to be an inevitably greater powerlessness, insignificance, and alienation for individual members of society. These trends, somewhat paradoxically it may seem, have been exacerbated by the structural modification of such typically primary-group organizations as the family and the church.

The growing expansion of urban structures and industrial development, of course, has not meant the end of *Gemeinschaft* or community-type societies. The unmistakable trend in social organization, however, is in the direction of a *Gesellschaft*, or an associational type of societal structure, one in which secondary-group associations and orientations increasingly replace primary groups, for the most part, and dominate all forms of social relations and social organization. Anonymity, impersonality, mobility, formality, specialization of social roles, aemotional relations, and, of course, rapid social change are becoming more prevalent in every area of human life as the character of society becomes more bureaucratic and complex in nearly all aspects. America today is increasingly a "drive-thru" society, and this development can be witnessed in all kinds of social activities that do not require one to leave

651

**Mass Alienation.** The development of massive forms of social organization, even in academia, eventually result in a loss of individuality, as well as a greater sense of powerlessness and insignificance. (Ralph Schuyler/Stock, Boston)

the automobile: transactions at stores, restaurants, banks, service stations, car washes, and even funeral homes. Mass society, in short, is one in which the ideal-type conception of the *Gesellschaft* is concretized to a much greater degree.

What are the effects of the emergence of mass society on personal and social character? Is "mass man" significantly different from "folk man"? Yes, say futurists and other observers. One effect of mass society, they argue, is a homogenization of individuals in terms of psychological qualities or personality. More and more, in a society of this type, the individual becomes or resembles the "typical" or "average" or modal person. Distinctions in social character erode to their minimum. We shall say

more about this in the next section of this chapter.

Social scientists (Kerr et al., 1960; Lerner, 1968) who have formulated the **convergence thesis** of social change argue that industrialization leads to common forms of organization in societies of widely different cultures (based on the supposition that demands of efficiency and technology will necessitate the development of roughly similar forms of industrial organization). Moreover, these modern organizations will consist of forceful environments that in turn produce common patterns of values, attitudes, beliefs, perceptions, and thought in the personalities of their participants. Hence, the general hypothesis that derives from this assertion is that societies with similar institutions and environments—tend to exert standard or uniform influences on individuals within them, and thereby mold a uniform psychological structure of common values and attitudes that cuts across national and cultural boundaries. This intriguing idea is not a completely new one. Marx and Engels, in writing on the conditions of the proletariat in *The Communist Manifesto*, noted that "modern industrial labor, modern subjection to capital the same in England as in France, in America as in Germany, has stripped [the worker] of every trace of national character." Empirical evidence now offers some substantiation for certain aspects of this long-standing thesis.

Inkeles (1960) in his paper "Industrial Man" offers evidence supporting the thesis that the standard institutional environments of industrial society induce standard patterns of response in perceptions, attitudes, and values that relate to a wide range of situations—despite the countervailing effects of persisting traditional patterns of culture. Inkeles speculates that although it may seem far off, or even far-fetched, it could very well be that we shall come to have a fairly uniform culture—one in which subgroups and even nations will have lost their distinctive cultures. Accordingly, despite differences in language, people will come to share a uniform, homogeneous culture, and hence become indistinguishable in perceptual tendency, opinion, and belief not only from their fellow citizens but from all people everywhere.* Marcuse (1964), in his formulation of "one-dimensional man," also advances the hypothesis of a monolithic society—one essentially without opposition or alternative forms—in which people are the products of a common sociological and psychological mold.

In a similar fashion, Inglehart (1976), reporting on cross-cultural studies conducted in a longitudinal perspective of the past decade, has shown that highly similar values and attitudes have become increasingly modal among young people in societies that have undergone similar industrial and postindustrial development. Inglehart observes a clear pattern from country to country, which he has labeled a "postbourgeoise" trend of values among people born during the past thirty-five to forty years. These trends in societal convergence cannot be denied. Still there exists a wide range of cultural diversity that probably will last for another half-century at least.

## MULTINATIONAL SOCIETY

One feature of the postindustrial and modern era seems to be the emergence of the international community. So far, in a formal sense, such seems to be the case only in the political and economic spheres. Examples of this movement include not only the well-known attempts at worldwide political entities such as the former League of Nations and, currently, the United Nations in the political sphere; and NATO, SEATO, and the Baltic Pact on the military level; but also, more recently, the emergence on the economic level of Benelux (Belgium, Netherlands, and Luxembourg) and similar economic alliances among Scandinavian nations, Arab states, and the several Communist countries. Most impressive of all is the European Economic Community which, along with a European Parliament, is envisioned as a more complete outgrowth of the European Common Market. It is designed to comprise not only the latter's economic dimensions, but to extend as well to the political and educational sectors, including even a common language as a further development of a common culture. Indeed, the European Parliament, presently representing nine nations, is already a reality—having held it inaugural meeting in July 1977—and has even debated this very

653

---

* An extreme argument on this position is offered by Roderick Seidenberg in *Post-Historic Man: An Inquiry* (1957).

▼

**654**

question of a common language.* Similar kinds of societal and cultural convergence are taking place in other parts of the world, such as in Africa, Asia, and South America.

The revolution in rapid communication by means of radio, picture telephone, television, electronic computer, and satellite has made possible not only instantaneous sociocultural diffusion, but also an increasing cultural and societal standardization throughout the world. Equally significant in this regard has been the massive expansion of worldwide travel. These developments are seen by many people as the basis of social organization on a world or multisocietal level and the beginning of an international society. Sociologists and other social scientists in recent years have begun to analyze the entire world as a single social system (Boulding, 1985). They are turning their attention now to problems that require assessment on a global scale, including questions on such subjects as world trade, multinational corporations, energy, and even nuclear defense.†

One theoretical perspective along these lines which has gained considerable attention in recent years is that of **world-system theory,** also known as dependence theory (see Chirot & Hall, 1982; Wallerstein, 1988, 1980, 1974). Proponents of this view, working within the context of conflict theory and focusing on economic structures, maintain that modernization is neither an inevitable nor a convergent course of action for societies. Rather, the argument here is that the patterns of development in a given society may be divergent and are affected in any event by the position and role of a society in a world system, as well as by its own cultural and social heritage.

The world system—a global economic and political community—is conceived as consisting of three principal components: core, peripheral, and semiperipheral societies. These major elements are dynamically linked in an international division of labor. The core societies, such as the United States, are independent, dominate the world economy, and allegedly exploit the other social and economic units. It is the role of the peripheral societies, as exemplified by those of the Third World, to contribute raw materials and other resources. Falling between the exploited and the exploiting segments of the world economy are the semiperipheral societies. Both the rate of social change and the level of cultural development vary significantly among these three segments of the world system. The path to modernization, thus, is neither uniform nor absolute.

Much of what we have said, and will say, about the future directions of social change is, of course, speculation—given the absence of any general or substantive theory from which to make predictions. To be sure, some societies that are evolving from agricultural to industrial society, from the structurally simple to the complex, can see a great deal of their future reflected in the history of those societies (United States, France, Italy, West Germany, England, and Japan) that have had this experience. A perfect replication cannot be expected, of course, because many of the crucial variables are not the same. There does appear, nonetheless, to be some universal or constant elements in the processes of social change. To predict the course of future change for the more advanced and modern societies is much more difficult. The accumulated evidence on the nature and dynamics of society can serve only to make highly tentative projections, not reliable predictions. For these reasons, the development of a comprehensive theory of social change is of high priority for sociology and other social sciences (see Smelser, 1968*b*). Such a task is a formidable challenge to which a successful response will not only facilitate the adaptation of humankind to its future world, but also undoubtedly unlock

---

* One tangible indication of greater unity within the ECC was its decision in 1985 to offer a European passport as an option for citizens of the member nations.

† For discussions on these questions, see Inkeles (1979) and Bergesen (1980).

many of the mysteries about the fundamental principles of human social life.

# Social Change and Personality

Contemporary explanations of social change have devoted but little attention to the role of personality and the psychological dimensions of these processes. Personality, however, is highly instrumental in social change as both an independent and a dependent variable—as cause and as effect. Changes in social character, for example, are not simply the effects of changes in society and culture, but are also, in part, the causes of social change. The relationship between social character and social change, in fact, is a mutually dependent one. Changes in one will bring about changes in the other. Let us discuss personality and its relationship to social change as both an independent and a dependent variable.

## PERSONALITY AS INDEPENDENT VARIABLE

Social change, like all social behavior, is in a number of ways dependent upon those individuals who are its agents. Research suggests that all kinds of personalities are actively involved in social change, although in significantly different ways and in substantially different proportions. Some personalities are receptive to social change; others are not. Similarly, some personalities are receptive to only certain kinds of social change, or to only certain techniques for its achievement; others are not. Empirical data (DiRenzo, 1978) show that individuals can be distinguished, in terms of modal patterns of personality structure, in regard to (1) differential orientations to social change, (2) differential participation in movements of social reform, (3) the utilization or advocacy of different modes of social protest

and social reform, and (4) differential activity in specific forms of social protest and social reform. It is these varied patterns which perhaps account, at least in part, for the fact that the occurrence of social change is not uniform in the various segments of society, nor even within all societies.

Markus (1969), for example, in a study of staff members in five large social welfare agencies, found that workers with certain personality traits (greater disposition to self-actualization and greater perception of ambiguity or conflict in organizational goals) assume social-change roles to a greater degree than do individuals who lack these psychological qualities. DiRenzo (1967b), in research on changes in liturgical reforms in the Roman Catholic Church, has shown that, in terms of significant differences in personality structure, individuals vary in the degree of their predisposition to, and their acceptance or rejection of, change in social norms and social roles.

Several theories have addressed the thesis that social change, particularly certain types of social change, and the manner and extent to which it occurs, is related to the extent to which certain types or elements of personality are present within the population of a given society. Among the more important of these explanations are the following.

THE ACHIEVEMENT-ORIENTED PERSONALITY. David C. McClelland (1985, 1976) has attempted to explain economic growth and development as a particular form of social change in his lifetime work on the achievement motive (nAch). McClelland's thesis is that differences in the economic development of nations result from differences in the frequency with which national populations produce individuals with high nAch, who are most likely to undertake the entrepreneurial activity that leads to economic development.

By means of various techniques of content analysis and personality testing, McClelland

▼ has traced the presence or absence of nAch in many different societies. He shows that those societies that have experienced the greatest industrial and economic growth (for example, the United States and Canada) are also those that reveal the highest levels of nAch. Such societies, moreover, develop and change at a much faster rate than do others whose members do not possess these psychological dispositions.

**656** THE CREATIVE PERSONALITY. Seeking to extend the work of McClelland, Everett C. Hagen (1962) has offered a somewhat similar theory, connecting personality with economic development and sociocultural change more broadly. Hagen's theory is an explanation for the phenomenon of self-sustaining growth. He argues that a major causative factor in economic growth is the influence of creative or innovative personalities. The structure of traditional society endures in many cases, in his view, because of a lack of these kinds of personalities.

Conventionalism as a psychological attribute is not a chance quality of traditional society, but rather an intrinsic attribute and part of such societies. Hagen argues that a change in the typical and modal profile of personality from the conventional type (which tends to enforce traditional patterns of behavior) to the innovative type (which tends to seek new and better ways of doing things) must take place before a society can accept and/or encourage social change.

THE AUTHORITARIAN/DOGMATIC PERSONALITY. Nonreceptivity to social change, more basically, is a particular attribute of the authoritarian and dogmatic types of personality, which we have discussed in preceding chapters. Authoritarian/dogmatic individuals tend to be traditionalists who oppose change and actively seek to avoid and prevent it. The antithetical types (democratic and nondogmatic, or tolerant, individuals) tend to be innovators who not only are pro-change but actively seek change, often comprising the avante-garde of social reform movements. That authoritarian/dogmatic personalities are less psychologically able than their counterparts to change old beliefs or patterns of behavior does not imply that such personalities do not change, rather only that they are resistant to change and relatively intolerant of innovation in the social order.

Research data (DiRenzo, 1978) show that dogmatic or authoritarian individuals, to the extent that they participate in reformistic or revolutionary movements of social change (as discussed in Chapter 12), are likely to do so less intensely and less actively than individuals who are nondogmatic and nonauthoritarian in personality structure or type, and that when authoritarian or dogmatic individuals engage in such movements of social change, they are less likely to advocate or to utilize the more extreme or violent modes. As Frenkel-Brunswik (1952) has stated: "He [the authoritarian personality] is not adapted to change and thus lacks one of the most important requirements in all modern societies." Authoritarian personalities, however, as history has shown so well, often do engage quite actively in regressive change. Such change is invariably atavistic, conservative-oriented, or "changing back," as Hitler, Khomeini, and other dictatorial leaders have demonstrated.

THE INDIVIDUAL MODERNITY SYNDROME. Alex Inkeles (1983, 1975), in extensive cross-cultural research, has isolated a personality syndrome that is thought to be both producer and product of social change—a correlate of industrial, and even postindustrial, types of society.

Inkeles has labeled the observed set of reliably coherent personality and psychological attributes as the **individual modernity syndrome** (see Box 14-3). Its principal components are efficacy, control over nature, ability to plan

# BOX 14-3. Individual Modernity Syndrome

▼

The individual modernity syndrome, discovered by Alex Inkeles (1966) in cross-cultural research, has been suggested as both product and producer of social change. This syndrome consists, in part, of the following psychological elements and behavioral manifestations.

1. Orientation toward present and future activities.
2. Openness to new experience and social change.
3. Assertion of increasing independence from the authority of traditional figures, such as parents and priests, and the shift of allegiance to leaders of government, public affairs, trade unions, co-ops, and so forth.
4. Belief in the efficacy of science and technology, and a general abandonment of passivity and fatalism in the face of the difficulties of life.
5. Ambition for oneself and one's children to achieve high occupational and educational goals.
6. Belief in the dignity of self and others.
7. Punctuality and interest in carefully planning and organizing one's affairs in advance.
8. Commitment to distributive justice—rewards according to contributions.
9. Taking an active part in civic and community affairs and local politics.
10. Striving energetically to keep up with the news, and within this effort to prefer news of national and international import over items dealing with sports, religion, and purely local affairs. ▲

Source: Alex Inkeles, "The Modernization of Man" in Myron Weiner (ed.), *Modernization: The Dynamics of Growth,* New York: Basic Books, 1966.

657

ahead, aspiration, active citizenship, secularism, openness to new experience, support for women's rights, and tolerance for diversity.

The individual modernity syndrome does not refer to a merely contemporary profile, but more significantly to a type of personality thought to be indispensable to the function of industrialized society. Such a thesis has not been without criticism (Armer & Isaac, 1978), but it is one that empirical evidence has neither substantially refuted nor confirmed. This is an undertaking that can be accomplished only by longitudinal data from a substantial number of cross-national studies. We shall have much more to say about the individual modernity syndrome in a subsequent section of this chapter.

THE GREAT MAN THEORY: PERSONALITY OF LEADERS. Something should be said about those rare individuals and charismatic personalities who, because of intellectual and/or other psychological qualities, are thought to be able to effect social change on a grand scale. One can easily mention in this regard such political and religious figures as Jesus Christ, Julius Caesar, Martin Luther, Napoleon Bonaparte, Vladimir Lenin, Mahatma Gandhi, Adolph Hitler, Martin Luther King, Jr., Pope John XXIII, and John F. Kennedy, among a number of other individuals who have left their personal marks on the course of human history.

Individual personalities often trigger processes that eventuate in radical change.

▼

**658**

Whether the role that charismatic leadership plays in social change, however, is dependent upon other factors—psychological as well as sociological—is a perplexing question that has not been adequately addressed (see DiRenzo, 1974*a*). Suffice it to say that effective social movements, as we saw in Chapter 12, require a tremendous amount of collective energy as well as psychological compatibility on the part of a significant number of involved people. The complexities of social phenomena belie the simplistic implications of the "great man theory" of social change.

## PERSONALITY AS DEPENDENT VARIABLE

Personality, as a product of social experiences, often undergoes a number of significant changes as a consequence of social change. The formation of new values and attitudes, as well as various modifications in the social character of a society, are examples of these consequential changes. Changes in modal patterns of personality, however, are likely to be less frequent, less rapid, and less extensive than sociocultural changes (Inkeles, 1971).

New types of personality can emerge in a society as a consequence of endemic strains that have themselves led to extensive social change. One such instance, many social scientists contend, can be seen in the youth rebellion of the late 1960s. Almond (1977), for example, has argued that while the process of social development for young people had sharply increased in both scale and difficulty during this period the social institution (family, church, and school) normally performing socializing functions were losing some of their authority and indoctrinative capacity. The overall consequence of these changes was a significant change in the modal personality patterns of youth in America and other Western societies.

Another such example of personality change,

as we discussed in Chapter 11, can be seen in the case of Black Americans and other minorities as a consequence of social changes connected with the massive movements of social integration in the past few decades (see Clinard, 1970; Yinger, 1977). The expansion of a mass educational system and new employment opportunities, coupled with the extensions and guarantees of civil rights, are sources of dramatic alterations in the motivational systems and self-concepts of millions of minority people. These personality changes, in turn, have themselves had a profound impact on the processes of social change.

A third illustration of the relationship of social change to modal patterns of personality is provided, more concretely, by Inkeles (1975, 1983) who has worked on a major cross-cultural project, related to his earlier formulation of "Industrial Man" (Inkeles, 1960). He investigated the effects of social change, especially through industrial experiences, on the individual. Working with a sample of more than six thousand men drawn from six countries (Argentina, Chile, India, Israel, Nigeria, and East Pakistan), Inkeles claims to have discerned a type of personality that is quite similar in each of these culturally different countries.

Inkeles alleges that the individual modernity syndrome (see Box 14-4) represents a characterological prototype of personality in postindustrial society, one that emerges from the complex dynamics of industrialization, urbanization, and attendant social processes, regardless of national and cultural boundaries. Work, especially factory work, and school experience are the main agents of this psychological modernity. On the basis of his extensive research, Inkeles has concluded that the same "structural mechanisms" underlie the sociopsychic function of individuals whenever and wherever the basic processes of social change are similar (see Inkeles & Smith, 1974*b*).

That institutions with similar structures tend to induce common psychic structures and contents in the personalities of their participants—

even though the ideological bases of the polity and economy, as well as other cultural dimensions, may be substantially different—is an intriguing hypothesis and one of profound implication for the future of social change throughout the world. Research on this controversial question, however, is all quite recent. Such propositions must await further methodological refinements in the measurements of social change, as well as more extensive cross-cultural analysis. That social change produces personality change is, nonetheless, abundantly clear, as we shall see in our next consideration of the directions of social character in America.

## SOCIAL CHANGE AND SOCIAL CHARACTER

Attempts to document changes in the American social character during the past few decades have been many. Much of the evidence, however, may not be strongly manifest, since modifications in social character do not appear to be as dramatic in terms of magnitude and rate as those in society and its institutions. Many of the answers to the relevant questions, therefore, are quite speculative and tentative at this time.

Among the more pertinent studies are those of Marcuse (1964) who has formulated the conception of "one-dimensional man" as the product of a culturally homogeneous and mass society; Lifton (1970) who, with his concept of "protean man," and Toffler (1970) who, with that of "modular man," discuss the multiple identities of the modern person; Yablonsky (1972) who describes the "robopath"; Kando (1975) who discusses the emerging leisure consciousness; Sanford (1977) who speaks of nonmorality and decay in American life; Gergen (1977) who assesses the changing and increasingly complex structure of the self; Sennett (1977) who speaks of the emergence of "privatized man," whom he describes as one moving out of the public domain into his own private world; Etzioni (1982) who talks of an "ego-centered mentality" that is damaging our social institutions; Lasch (1978, 1984) who describes the ascendancy of self-centeredness and the dominance of the supernarcissistic individual; and Bellah (1985) and associates who speak of the focal role of both materialistic and narcissistic values.*

These many observers have concerned themselves with different aspects and dimensions of personality (for example, values, self-images, beliefs, attitudes, motives). One of the chief themes of several of these assessments, however, is that dehumanization and alienation are emerging as distinctive marks of American character, as well as of people in other Western societies. Americans are perceived to have become less individualistic, less autonomous, less inner-oriented, and less innovative; correspondingly, they are more other-directed, conforming, sheepish, and essentially chameleon-like (changing appearances at will and taking on the coloring of a variety of social atmospheres as needed). Such tendencies are deplored by their many observers, who maintain essentially that the American ethic of individualism and self-sufficiency is vulnerable to large-scale social change over which the individual has little, if any, control.

Characterological change, nonetheless, may have an even more fundamental dimension. Social scientists from various disciplines have independently advanced the provocative thesis that the American social character is moving rapidly toward an increasing focus on self-gratification, with a concomitant loss of commitment to community and society. Americans, argues Slater (1976) in *The Pursuit of Loneliness*, have become emotionally detached from society in "the belief that everyone should pursue

---

* Other relevant analyses, both of actual and probable changes in the American social character, are those of Reich (1970); Zijderveld (1971); Wheelis (1973a); Berger et al. (1973); DiRenzo (1977a); Varenne (1977); Toffler (1980); and Veroff et al. (1981).

▼

**660**

his own destiny." Proponents of the view that there is developing a dominant egocentric disposition in the American social character (for example, Bell, 1976; Harris, 1981; Lasch, 1984; Yankelovich, 1981) maintain that, beginning effectively in the 1960s, the traditional values of hard work, frugality, self-denial, and moderation (the Protestant ethic and the Puritan spirit) have increasingly given way to a new ethic of self-fulfillment and self-indulgence. Its focal values are those of leisure, hedonism, and indulgence (for example, "Fly now; pay later!" "You deserve a break today!" and "You can have it all!"), which allegedly are the consequences of the economic dynamics of mass production and mass consumption in the postindustrial era. One indication of this apparent transition in the fundamental ethic of America is reflected in the changing values of college students (see Figure 14-6).

Many analysts view this pattern of alleged characterological change as negative and dysfunctional, and even as a pathological development. Bell (1976), for example, argues that self-expression and self-indulgence, along with anti-intellectual ways of knowing and experiencing the world, contradict the fundamental values and needs of a capitalistic society, namely, those of rationality, hierarchy, bureaucracy, efficiency, and work. Bellah and his associates (1985) similarly perceive this strong individualism and its associated materialism as rampantly eroding the very foundations of the American society. It is the emergence of the mass society, as well as the expansion of bureaucratic forms of social organization, that are considered to be at the root of an extended pathology of alienation and the shrinkage of true individualism in the American social character (see Lasch, 1984). Such a thesis has been reaffirmed by Gans (1988)—with particular reference to "Middle Americans" (working-class and lower middle-class people)—who sees the future of truly representative democracy jeopardized by the increasing avoidance of, and

alienation from, the mass sectors of our political and economic institutions.

One principal exception to these negative perceptions is taken by Yankelovich (1981) who hails the emergence of the new ethic of self-fulfillment as a positive development. Yankelovich, claims that nearly 80 percent of all adult Americans today could be described as "self-fulfillers" and interprets this self-fulfillment as self-improvement or self-actualization, not as self-indulgence or selfishness. Relying on data from public opinion surveys, he optimistically assesses the expanded individualism as the emergence of a new ethic of social commitment, one with a renewed and expanded concern for community and lasting relationships.

Many of the other alleged developments in the American social character too are not viewed as totally negative by all social scientists. Fromm (1947), for example, concedes that some of these traits (other-directedness and sensitivity to others) may be functional, in that rapid social change in technological societies requires a high degree of flexibility. He sees sensitivity to others as permitting or facilitating necessary change. Others would argue that the complexities of social life today do not permit the degree of independence and freedom that may have characterized earlier times.

The conformist character as a modal expression of Americans, in any event, is not a novel development when seen against such earlier formulations of "the marketing orientation" by Fromm (1947), "the other-directed" type by Riesman (1950), and "the organization man" by Whyte (1956), among others, which we discussed in earlier chapters. The consensus, however, is that conformist tendencies and behavior seem to be on the increase—notwithstanding the expansion of personal and civic freedoms; indeed, some would argue, because of them in great part. Americans, in this paradoxical perspective, overconform in order to compensate for the lack of self-esteem that an excessive individualism is alleged to create (see Hsu, 1977;

▼

**Supernarcissism.** An expanding preoccupation with self-gratification, such as through suntanning, has caused many social scientists to perceive the emergence and dominance of the supernarcissistic individual, and the parallel loss of commitment to community, in modern society. (Michael Gordon Edrington/Image Works)

Lasch, 1984; Slater, 1976). Such an alleged trend is quite significant, given the individualism that has served—if only ideally—as a traditional hallmark of social character in America.

Other observers, on the contrary, speak in more positive terms of the emergence of a new type of social character in America. Spindler (1977), for example, while believing in the endurance of many of the traditional aspects of American social character, speaks of the appearance of a new type of "other-directedness" that is an end instead of a means—not sheer external conformity but rather conformity with profound internal commitment. Individualism, Spindler maintains, has been significantly reinterpreted during the past couple of decades, and it has given way, in the traditional and somewhat egocentric sense, to a more socialistic or communal variety of individualism. Similarly, Toffler (1980), describing the characterological change that is expected to be associated with postindustrial society, speaks of the likely expansion of individuality and psychological diversity.

Suzman (1977), focusing on personality development in a psychoanalytic dimension, also describes an expanding, if not a basically new, type of social character in America—one represented essentially by the individual modernity syndrome. He contends that this "new" modernity syndrome is a synthesis of the "inner-directed" and the "other-directed" structures described by Riesman (1950) and seems to represent a characterological prototype of personality in postindustrial society that will cut across national, cultural, and social boundaries.

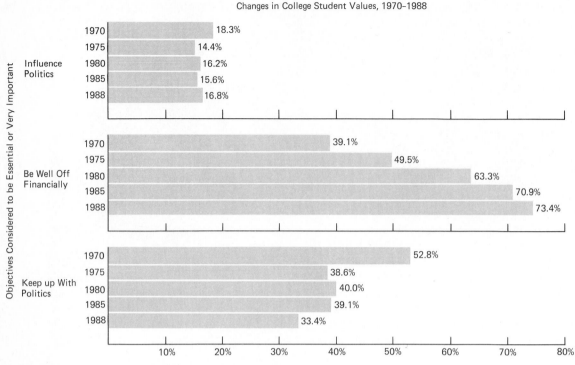

FIGURE 14-6   Changes in College Student Values, 1970–1988. Each year a sample of freshman at nearly 500 colleges and universities completes a questionnaire about their values. More than 20,000 students were involved in this latest study. The interests and priorities of students show considerable change during the past two decades. College students today, compared to their counterparts of the early 1970s, have much less interest in the political sphere and are much more concerned about being well-off financially. Source: American Council on Education, *National Norms for Entering Freshman, Fall 1970,* ACE Research Reports, pp. 42–43; and (with the University of California Graduate School of Education, Los Angeles) *The American Freshman: National Norms for Fall 1975; The American Freshman: National Norms for Fall 1980; The American Freshman: National Norms for Fall 1985,* and *The American Freshman: National Norms for Fall 1988.* Data were collected by the Higher Education Research Institute, University of California, Los Angeles.

Suzman sees the pivotal dimension of this new genre of social character as consisting of a service orientation, its emphasis on such values as humanitarianism, altruism, civic-mindedness, political awareness, and political involvement.

Many of the characterological changes in the American society are thought, by most social scientists, to be the product of changes in the structure of society, chiefly those in the economic realm. Yet, surely, the profound modifications in the political sector, and the emphasis on and expansion of equality and democracy, are also quite relevant for whatever changes there may be in the American social character. Almond (1977), for example, has maintained that because of the rapid diffusion of a new political culture among young people, the expectation for the American character is a more open, change-oriented, and complex personality, with greater analytical and problem-solving capacity than the relatively closed, rigid, and parochial type prevalent in recent years. Rothman and Lichter (1978*a*, 1978*b*, 1982), however, marshal quantities of empirical data to challenge the thesis (see Keniston, 1968; Marcuse, 1964; Reich, 1970) that the radical students of the 1960s were the vanguard of a "liberated" generation and a new type of "protean man" or multifaceted individual, one characterized by warmth, openness, humanitarianism, social motivation, advanced morality, and psychological health. Quite to the contrary, they perceive the radical movement and its protagonists as authoritarian, self-interested, and pragmatic—a view shared in great part by Sanford (1977) in his observations on the decline of morality and the endurance of authoritarianism in the American character.

Inkeles (1978), while documenting a persistent and remarkable continuity in the American national character for the past two centuries, similarly argues that it appears to be becoming more inner-directed, as manifested in the emergence of allegedly strong values for the tolerance of deviant lifestyles and social equality. He describes the distinctive American social character (as mentioned in Chapter 7) in the following principal terms: self-reliance, independence, autonomy, voluntarism (communal action, cooperation with neighbors), interpersonal trust, sense of efficacy (versus fatalism), optimism, innovativeness (openness to new experience), antiauthoritarianism, and equality. A second-level set of characteristics includes the following attributes: individualism, restless energy, pragmatism, tendency to brashness or boastfulness, this-worldliness, preference for the concrete, and a certain discomfort in coping with aesthetic and emotional expression.

Another focal dimension of this question of characterological change in America is the consideration of the alleged changes in the self system. Gergen (1977), among others, has spoken in this regard of "multiple identities" to describe the structure of the kind of self that, in his view, is associated with highly pluralistic, heterogeneous, and complex modern societies. He argues that the lack of strong and consistent experiences in contemporary childhood is producing a modal type of individual who is marked by a multiplicity of self conceptions. This is a situation that contrasts to the unitary and well-integrated self-image which, in Gergen's view, characterized a bygone era of our society. Individuals in modern societies, he states, must play an increasing number of roles each day, and most of these roles demand a performance that is convincing, both to others and to themselves. Hence, in such perspectives, perhaps the alleged American "identity crisis" can be expected to persist into the future, with social life dominated by the standard query: "Will the real me please stand up?"

This conception of the "multiple self" is consistent with the formulation of "protean man" by Lifton (1976), as well as that of the "modular man" proposed by Toffler (1970), whom he describes as one capable of only temporary interpersonal relationships. Says Toffler, "We have created the disposable man.... Rather than entangling ourselves with the whole man, we plug into a module of his personality." Gergen, however, contends that the new psychosocial development of what he calls a "repertory culture" and its "multiple-identity individual" is a positive one, since it will create a more flexible and more adaptive individual who thereby will be able to respond effectively to the problems of contemporary society (see also Turner, 1976; Zurcher, 1977).

As our society has become more complex and more differentiated, so too American social character appears to have become more pluralistic in some respects—which is not to deny that in other respects it has become more monolithic. A variety of modal types, in some dimensions of personality at least, has arisen in the American social character in recent years, matched by a corresponding multiplication of lifestyles in various sociocultural segments of our population—racial, ethnic, sex, age, and occupational categories, among others. The

▼

**663**

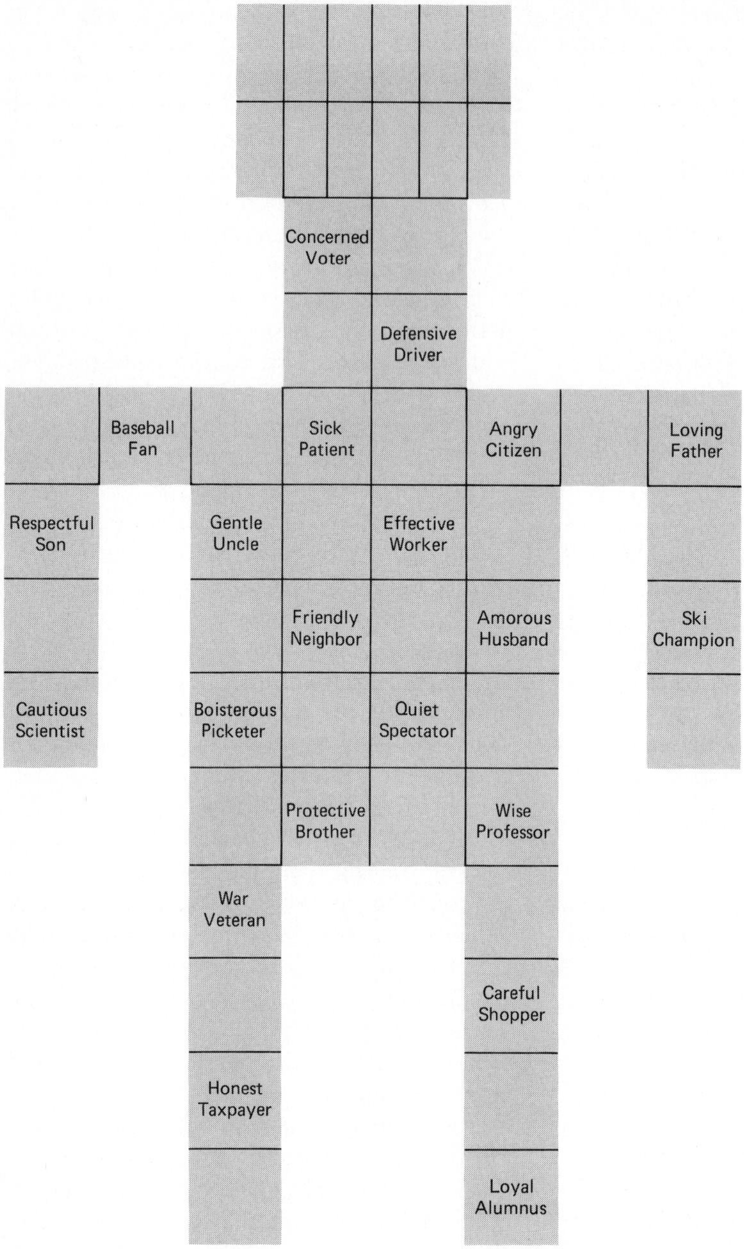

▼

Concerned Voter

Defensive Driver

Baseball Fan

Sick Patient

Angry Citizen

Loving Father

Respectful Son

Gentle Uncle

Effective Worker

Friendly Neighbor

Amorous Husband

Ski Champion

Cautious Scientist

Boisterous Picketer

Quiet Spectator

Protective Brother

Wise Professor

War Veteran

Careful Shopper

Honest Taxpayer

Loyal Alumnus

FIGURE 14-7   Modular Man—The Robopath. An increasingly popular conception of the modern individual is one consisting of a system of sociopsychological modules, each of which can be selectively adapted to a complexity of social publics.

diversification of personality types, that is, the number of modal types, can be expected to increase so long as sociocultural systems increase in internal differentiation, role specialization, and institutional complexity (Inkeles, 1971; Toffler, 1980). One can imagine the social and personal implication of what Riesman (1950) has called "the characterological struggle," the mixing and interaction of different types of personality and social characters. Such a consideration is of central importance to the continued acceleration of physical mobility that has become a principal facet of social change throughout much of the world.

What about the future of social character in America? Any answer is obviously quite speculative, given the lack of consensus as described here. Many futurists speak of a continuity of existing patterns; others (for example, Toffler, 1980) foresee volcanic changes in personality as a parallel to the expected patterns of extensive social change in postindustrial society. Most observers of this phenomenon, however, are essentially optimistic: The American characterological profile will become even more healthy and more socially productive than it has been during the past two hundred years.* Much depends, however, on the direction of social change as well as the nature of society in the future and, in particular, its ability to respond to *human* needs.

## CONGRUENT AND INCONGRUENT CHANGE

Personality is a dynamic element that not only facilitates social change, but may also serve to impede it. Research results (DiRenzo, 1978) suggest that social change, in its various dimensions and dynamics, may be functionally dependent (1) more generally upon change-

oriented individuals, and (2) more specifically upon individuals who are congruent with particular modes (structures and methods) of social change.

It appears that stability and change within societies and other social systems are to an extent a function of the congruity and incongruity that they share with the personality systems therein: the greater the congruity, the more minimal the change. Where there is incongruence between personality systems and social systems, one likely consequence is change in either the social system, or in the personalities within the social system—or even in both. Just which system is likely to undergo change as a consequence of incongruence depends on a number of sociological factors, not the least of which includes the initial sources of innovation— whether they are sociological or psychological. Hence, if incongruence is due to modifications in the personality composition of a population, it is likely that the social system will in turn undergo change; correspondingly, where incongruence is brought about because of modifications in the social system, then the personalities involved are likely to undergo change or, more likely, replacement (see Inkeles & Levinson, 1969).

Congruent change, in both personality systems and social systems, appears to be much more easily produced than incongruent change—that is, change which is not conducive, compatible, or consistent with the preexisting values, norms, and structures of either the individual or society. People tend not to accept new institutional and organizational structures or new forms of behavior that are incongruent with their personality structures. Imagine, for example, the implicit difficulties in trying to effect a type of social change in which highly liberal-minded individuals are placed in a situation demanding (incongruent) change to a much more conservative position than one to which they are accustomed. The individual modernity syndrome, which we discussed above,

665

* For a message of unrelieved negativism regarding modernity and the future, see Lasch (1984).

▼

666

refers to that type of personality allegedly necessary for a person to function effectively in modern society; it is not a psychological modality of mere contemporaneity.

Individuals are more likely to accept new behavioral forms and modes that are congruent, or at least not incongruent, with their personality structures. Each personality, moreover, appears to be receptive to only a limited number of available modes or mechanisms of social change, specifically those that have the greatest value in meeting its functional requirements. Personality facilitates the acceptance and/or the creation of those mechanisms and social structures that are personally meaningful, and the rejection of those choices which are similarly incompatible (Levinson, 1959).

It is perhaps this situation which accounts, at least in part, for the fact that the occurrence of social change is not uniform within the various segments of society, nor even within all societies. To the extent that the quality of social change (differences in such things as the amount, direction, speed, and rate) is dependent on the kind of social structures and processes used to produce it (Moore, 1963), then it follows that the quality of social change is dependent likewise upon the kind of individuals who are recruited as change-agents for the particular social structures and social processes.

Some social scientists have foreseen, and in the company of many laymen have even promoted, the "active society" (Etzioni, 1968b), one in which the members of society are actively in control of their social destiny. It seems that initially much attention in this respect needs to be given to developing personalities that are change-oriented and change-congruent, in terms of both objectives and methods.

Successful attempts at social change require the right kind of social structure and social processes, as well as the right kind and the right number of individuals. Whether movements of social protest and social reform, for example,

can become viable forces of social change is contingent upon a sufficient number of individuals among the ranks, who are both change-oriented and appropriately change-congruent with the particular modes of social change, either involved or advocated, for ideological and/or practical purposes. The necessary number, of course, depends upon the interplay of sociological structure and particular sets of sociological variables. For example, a small minority with the right type of personality, in the absence of opposition, or even in the face of silent opposition, can be much more successful in achieving its goal than if it faced open opposition. Further research is needed to refine the precise interaction of the various sociological dimensions of social change and the particular relationship of personality to them.

# Responsive and Unresponsive Social Systems

Social change, so it appears, has always existed and, undoubtedly, will always be with us. Social systems are highly dynamic, rather than merely static entities. Change in itself, therefore, is not necessarily a problem. The significant concern about social change, rather, refers to the question of whether new societal and institutional structures that are emerging, or may emerge in the future, can provide—as effectively as in the past, indeed even more effectively than in the past—their proper and necessary functions. If not, then, what is the significance, both sociologically and psychologically, for the individual as well as for society?

Bell (1976), for example, perceives a profound cultural lag in the disjuncture between role demands that are set by our increasingly technological society, and the emerging psychological patterns and modal personalities. Toffler (1970) similarly has spoken of society as remaining in a permanent state of "future shock" as a result of the acceleration of technological and social change at such rates of speed that it is beyond the ability of people to adjust. We have here, if such theses are correct, the makings of a crucial and widespread situation of **unresponsive social systems,** societies and social organizations that by their very contents and structure are unable to respond effectively to the basic human needs of individuals (Etzioni, 1968a, 1977; Israel, 1971) as well as to external challenges such as economic crises or resource depletion. An unresponsive society often is tantamount to an inauthentic or an alienating society.

One question that seems to be grossly overlooked—in planned social change, at least—is whether the individual is psychologically capable of adapting to and functioning within whatever new forms of social systems and cultural technology we may be able to develop, or which may even emerge spontaneously in the evolutionary process (see DiRenzo, 1990). The implicit belief prevalent in this respect is that human beings are infinitely malleable in terms of their psychological nature. All that needs to be done, it is assumed, is to teach or to train individuals to adapt and to function within these new societal and cultural forms. Yet, the contrary thesis is just as plausible and, indeed, there is evidence to support it: There is a fixed human nature that cannot be ignored or transgressed except at the cost of extensive social dysfunction and serious personal harm to the people involved.

It seems more logical, given our knowledge of many other entities and—as a consequence of social and behavioral research—even more empirically justified, to assume that there may be, at any given point in the evolutionary process, a fixed and delimited nature for the human psychological system, one with its own inherent structure, laws, functional requisites, and dynamism. The available data in support of the thesis of a specific and limited human nature, as opposed to a highly malleable one, are not conclusive; but the thesis has gained in plausibility as a result of numerous studies which, contrary to popularly held beliefs, show that attempts to remold people in terms of significant personality dimensions, as in psychotherapy, criminal rehabilitation, and brainwashing, have little effect (Etzioni, 1977). The fact, moreover, that human beings in many instances do not adapt effectively to social change and different social structures is itself compelling evidence that they may not be automatically and infinitely malleable. Otherwise, the frustration and anxiety, as well as other personal and social problems, that allegedly stem from such situations would not occur. The point is that human nature has not necessarily changed; human society and its technology, however, have undergone radical transformations.

On the assumption, then, that the human being, like society itself, has certain functional requisites—**basic human needs** (see Chapter 5)—that must be fulfilled for the individual to function at an adequate or optimal level, the inevitable question follows: Are societies, given their particular social organization, responsive to these needs? It is conceivable that we may develop societies, such as those envisioned in the postindustrial models, which, because of their structure and content, are unable to gratify the functional needs of people. Such a situation on a large scale can be, in turn, severely dysfunctional for society.

The concept of "basic human needs" rests fundamentally on human nature. It asserts that there is a universal set of human needs that are determined by the general processes of social learning rather than specific social structures or cultural patterns. Some sociologists (DiRenzo, 1977a; Etzioni, 1968a, 1977) speak in this regard of "inherent human needs." Others speak in various ways of "immanent human

▼

▼ requirements" (Berger et al., 1973; Marris, 1974; Shibutani, 1961) and "psychosocial homeostasis" (Hsu, 1977). Included in the category of basic human needs are such things as the need for relatedness to others (social response and social recognition), the need for freedom and autonomy (self-actualization and new adventure), and the need for cognitive clarity. These various formulations assume that since these human needs are universal, whereas societies differ in their cultural patterns, then societies must differ also in the extent to which they are able to satisfy the essential needs of their members.

**668**

Some social scientists (see Etzioni, 1968a) have argued that unresponsive social systems are a major source of much social disorganization, as manifested in social and personal deviance in the forms of mental illness, crime, drug abuse, alcohol addiction, and marital conflict, among other societal problems. The implication of this argument is that society itself may be responsible—or, at least, equally responsible—for its problems, rather than their resulting from merely inadequate socialization or personal deviation. No society, of course, can be expected to be fully responsive. Such a society would comprise a utopia which, by definition, is beyond the limits of reality. The very dynamics of society and social life will continually pose new problems; accordingly, the task of reforming or transforming society is never-ending, as is that of achieving functional congruity with the individuals involved.

**Human Requirements.** A haunting question for many social scientists is whether, in the future, the increasingly massive structures of social organization and the complex technology associated with them will be capable of fulfilling the basic human needs of all of the members of society. (© 1981 Hazel Hankin)

Many sociologists have expressed grave reservations about the infinite or unlimited movement of human society toward an ever-expanding *Gesellschaft*-type social structure. Is such a society viable? The assumption in this doubt, one gaining more and more attention, is that it is not possible to build society on an absolutely, or even predominantly, secondary-group type of structure. Such an attempt is considered to be dysfunctional, if not totally fatalistic for society. Basic to this argument is the position that individuals are psychologically structured to need, as a functional requisite, the psychosocial experience that can be had only in and from primary-group structures. Assuming this position to be correct, what is not known is the point of no return, that point on the *Gemeinschaft* to *Gesellschaft* (primary-group to secondary-group) continuum at which societal disaster or serious social and personal disorganization would occur.

It is not difficult, however, to find social scientists who argue that in many respects our society has reached, and even has gone beyond, a point of no return. Berger (1973) and his colleagues, for example, in their book *The Homeless Mind* decry the rampant alienation and dehumanization they perceive to be the omnipresent consequence of technological modernization. It is in the modern technocracy, say these authors, that people suffer the most profound loss of meaning and identity. While contemporary Americans long to belong more desperately than ever, they belong nowhere anymore—they are homeless. Lasch (1984), Hsu (1977) and Zijderveld (1971), among others, have expressed similar observations on the trends of characterological change in America. The argument in all cases is that we need to recognize more keenly the basic human needs of individuals, and to design our social systems so that they are capable of being responsive to these needs. One of the basic problems facing all contemporary societies in this regard, as they evolve from more traditional and authoritarian

structures into those of a more modern and democratic variety, is that of the need of personal freedom versus institutional authority.

Of prevalent concern in this regard are the sociopsychological dynamics of alienation, which refers to social situations beyond the control of the individual and therefore unresponsive to his or her needs. At the core of this situation, some would argue, is the institution of the family. Lasch (1977), for example, has argued that the more the modern family has come to be needed as a haven of nurturance and support in an alienating society, the less capable it has become of providing these comforts. Also related is what Fromm (1944) has called "moral aloneness" or lack of relatedness to values, symbols, and social patterns. Large segments of people throughout the world feel increasingly excluded from, and powerless and insignificant in the face of, the evolutionary and structural dynamics of contemporary society. Various countercultural and cultist manifestations that have appeared in the past several years are considered to be reactions to this situation. The emergence of religious movements, communes, and many other creations of alternative lifestyles is seen in great part as a demonstrable consequence of unresponsive social systems and as a defense against alienation and dehumanization.

Some social scientists (as we mentioned in Chapter 9) have argued in similar terms that there have arisen in modern, *Gesellschaft*-type societies a myriad of "quasi-primary groups," or "surrogate primary groups," particularly in the nature of voluntary associations. While devoted to specific goals on the level of manifest function, these groups principally provide on the latent level the psychological essentials of primary-group experience—however limited their success may be. For example, the formation of neighborhood organizations or block associations devoted to such things as leisure and recreational activities, and even the extensive development of encounter groups and

▼

**669**

▼

other forms of group therapy, are seen in great part as stemming from the pursuit of primary-group experience and the gratification of basic human needs.

Arguing for what he has termed "psycho-social homeostasis," Hsu (1977) perceives modern Western society as experiencing an increasing "shrinkage of affect" (loss of emotional involvement), which in great measure is "the most widespread and unforeseen result of the drive for individualist ambitions." The separation of affect from social roles that have increased in both number and proficiency with the industrialization and modernization of society has resulted in a search for effective outlets elsewhere, in secondary and transitory relationships, such as those provided by a variety of voluntary organizations, and even abstract causes. Another consequence of this phenomenon, according to Hsu, is the lavishing of affect on the totally controllable, such as pets or inanimate objects.

Other social scientists take a more sanguine view of the present and the future. Gergen (1977), for example, maintains that, rather than becoming diminished, affect has taken on a new meaning and a new mode of expression in modern American society. His argument is that while the more complex and pluralistic nature of modern society has caused human relationships to become less permanent and more transitory, they remain as real as ever. The new meanings and functions of human relationships, in this view, are accidental and external, not essential or absolute, changes. Inkeles (1978) contends that the persistent elements of American national character, as mentioned above, are the most effective for a modern democracy within a massive or large-scale industrialized and technological society that is likely to expand in the immediate future. Still others argue that the very functional dependency between the sociological and psychological systems, barring any catastrophic dysfunction in the normal course of interaction, serves to impose correc-

**670**

tive mechanisms on each other, so that a viable state of equilibrium—one that does not preclude change—exists for both society and the personality system. Only the future will provide a definitive answer to these fateful questions.

# Summary

Social change refers to any relatively enduring modification in the established or existing structure or function of a social system. Social change is a continuous, or constant, and universal phenomenon. Not all societies, however, experience social change in the same way. Among the varying dimensions of social change are magnitude, rate, force, and direction. Social progress refers to the quality of social change and rests fundamentally on the subjective consideration of whether it is good or bad, better or worse, desirable or undesirable.

Spontaneous or evolutionary change is in the nature of a latent function: unrecognized and frequently undesired social change. Planned change, more in the nature of a manifest function, is that change which is intentionally sought by members of society.

The various theories that have been formulated to explain social change may be categorized into four principal classifications: evolutionary, cyclical, monistic, and modern.

Evolutionary theories may be either unilinear or multilinear. Cyclical theories typically focus on the "rise and fall" of civilizations, although some may incorporate an evolutionary perspective. Monistic theories include cultural determinism, geographical determinism, ecological determinism, and biological determinism. Modern theories consist principally of functional, or equilibrium, theories and conflict theories.

Apart from the theories of social change that attempt to explain why it occurs, and how it occurs, there are a number of factors that enter into this highly complex phenomenon. Chief among the factors that comprise the fundamental sources of social change are innovation, cultural base, cultural diffusion, cultural lag, ideology and values, demography and ecology, social movements, revolution, social conflict, traumatic events, and personality.

Some of the fundamental or general consequences of social change include social and personal disorganization, cultural lag, cognitive ambiguity, anomie, and new forms and practices of social institutions.

Social change is seen by some as inevitably providing new opportunities for human growth and creativity on both the societal and individual levels. Patterns and trends of sociocultural change include urbanization, industrialization, postindustrial society, technological society, informational society, leisure society, mass society, and multinational society.

Personality is highly instrumental in social change as both an independent and a dependent variable—as cause and as effect—and may serve not only to facilitate social change, but also to impede it. Several theories have addressed the thesis that social change, particularly certain types of social change, how it occurs, and the extent to which it occurs, are related to the extent to which certain types or elements of personality are present within the population of a given society. Among the more important of these explanations are the following: the achievement-oriented personality, the creative personality, the authoritarian/dogmatic personality, the individual modernity syndrome, and the "great man" theory.

Personality, as a product of social experiences, often undergoes a number of significant changes as a consequence of social change. The formation of new values and attitudes, as well as various modifications in the social character of a society, are examples of the sociopsychological consequences of social change.

Stability and change within societies and other social systems are to an extent the function of the congruity or incongruity they share with the personality systems therein. It appears that social change, in its various dimensions and dynamics, may be functionally dependent (1) more generally upon change-oriented individuals, and (2) more specifically upon individuals who are congruent with particular modes (structures and methods) of social change.

One underlying concern about social change is whether new societal and institutional structures that may emerge will be responsive to their fundamental and intended function of fulfilling basic human needs.

**671**

# Key Concepts

anomia
anomie
basic human need
cognitive ambiguity
conflict theory
convergence thesis
cultural base
cultural diffusion
cultural lag
cyclical theory
discovery
evolutionary theory
functionalism
individual modernity syndrome
innovation
invention
megalopolis
monistic theory
multilinear evolution
revolution
social change
social Darwinism
social progress
unilinear evolution
unresponsive social system
world-system theory

# Glossary

▼

**acceptance**  The process of acquiescence on the part of a social minority to its subordinate status in society.

**acculturation**  The transmission/acquisition of culture after human development has been completed; also, the process by which a social minority adopts the dominant culture of a society.

**achieved status**  A social position that one holds by virtue of his or her own choice or efforts.

**acting crowd**  An aggregate of individuals who desire to take action against someone or something.

**activity theory**  A perspective which maintains that elderly people have the same social and psychological needs as other people.

**addiction**  A physical and/or psychological dependency on a substance or an activity.

**adequate sample**  One that is of an appropriate and sufficient size to permit the kind of analysis and projections that the researcher desires to perform.

**affective system**  Emotional dimensions of the personality, and the patterns or modes of their arousal and discharge.

**affirmative action**  A policy by which preference in occupational recruitment and placement is given to minority individuals.

**ageism**  A doctrine which advocates the social inferiority of elderly people.

**agency of socialization**  An individual, group, or organization that has either a primary responsibility or a particularly strong influence in the socialization and enculturation process.

**aggression**  Any pattern of response by which a social minority seeks redress for social injustices and its subordinate status.

**AGIL paradigm**  A model for the functional requisites of a social system which includes adaptation, goal attainment, integration, and latent pattern maintenance.

**agrarian society**  One whose mode of subsistence involves the production of goods on a large scale through mechanical means of cultivation.

**agricultural society**  See *agrarian society*.

**alienation**  A subjective state in which one experiences feelings of meaninglessness, powerlessness, instrumentalization, social isolation, and self-estrangement.

**amalgamation**  The blending of two or more physically or culturally distinct populations in order to form a hybrid.

**ambivalent socialization**  Socialization which involves the internalization of both conventional and deviant norms or values.

**anomia**  A subjective state in which the individual experiences a distressing lack of purpose, direction, and social integration.

**anomie**  A social situation relatively devoid of clearly articulated norms and/or values.

▼

**anomie theory**   An explanation for deviant behavior that postulates a lack of correspondence between socially articulated goals and socially approved means.

**anthropology**   The science of the origin and development of the human species. See *cultural anthropology* and *physical anthropology*.

**anticipatory socialization**   The process of learning about and rehearsing social roles corresponding to positions that one will occupy in the future.

**674**

**apartheid**   The practice of racial segregation in the Union of South Africa.

**area sampling**   Sampling which selects individuals from particular physical or geographical areas.

**artifact**   A concrete, physical object that is an expression of culture.

**ascribed status**   A social position that is accorded an individual through no personal efforts, but rather which is usually the result of birth, inheritance, or circumstances beyond one's control.

**assimilation**   The process by which a social minority loses its cultural identity through absorption of the dominant culture in a society.

**associational society**   One which tends to be relatively large, formal, bureaucratic, and heterogeneous in social organization, with an extensive division of labor, low degree of social cohesion or integration, and only partial personal involvement or commitment.

**authoritarianism**   A political doctrine which asserts subjection to authority as opposed to individual freedom. Also, a personality syndrome that focuses on the elements of power and authority as its central dynamics. See *authoritarian personality*.

**authoritarian personality**   A personality syndrome which manifests ambivalence to authority, anti-intraception, admiration of

power, conventionalism, projectivity, stereotypy, cynicism, and exaggerated sexual concerns. See *dogmatic personality*.

**authority**   Legitimate power.

**autocracy**   A form of government in which political power is exercised supremely by a single person.

**availability sampling**   Sampling that utilizes whichever individuals are available in a particular place at a given time.

**avoidance**   A pattern of self-segregation adopted voluntarily by a social minority.

**basic human need**   A universal motive neither innate nor present at birth, but acquired through the humanization processes of socialization and enculturation.

**basic personality structure**   Similarities in the core of personality that derive primarily from common enculturation experiences and sharing in the fundamental aspects of culture.

**bilineal descent**   Family lineage in which the official or formal lines of descent are maintained through both parents.

**biogenic motive**   An innate, physiological drive that is considered imperative for the homeostatic function or life of an organism.

**biogram**   A document describing events in which one personally participates.

**biosociology**   A branch of sociology concerned with explaining the biological dimensions of human social behavior.

**biosphere**   That locus or environment of soil, water, and air which is located at or near the surface of the earth where organic life exists.

**bourgeoisie**   Owners and controllers of the means of production; landowners; entrepreneurs; capitalists.

**bureaucracy**   A formal, rationally organized social system with clearly defined patterns of activity in which every series of actions is functionally related to the purpose of the organization.

**capitalism**   An economic system based on

comparatively free and individualistic enterprise.

**case-study technique** An in-depth assessment of one or a small number of selected cases or observations.

**caste** A social stratum which is ascribed and from which vertical mobility is not possible.

**caste system** Stratification that precludes vertical mobility.

**casual crowd** A passive aggregate of individuals exhibiting little emotion and little, if any, social organization.

**categorical mobility** Movement within the stratification structure on the part of an entire set or category of individuals.

**cause** A necessary and sufficient condition for the occurrence of a given phenomenon.

**charisma** Personal qualities that serve as a source of authority.

**charismatic authority** Authority rooted in the personal qualities of an individual.

**civil religion** A set of theistic beliefs, values, symbols, and practices that provide a type of ideological cohesion for a particular society.

**class** Social rank in terms of economic variables.

**class consciousness** The awareness of social stratification and one's position within the system.

**class system** Stratification characterized by the possibility of vertical mobility.

**classical conditioning** The process whereby an initially neutral stimulus, by being associated with a stimulus that produces a specific response, also becomes capable of producing that response.

**closed system** One that does not have connection to its environment and does not engage in exchanging relations with it.

**coding** The process by which qualitative data are reduced to manageable categories for statistical and theoretical analyses.

**coefficient of correlation** A statistical measure of correlation. Also known as *Pearson's r.*

**coercion** Arbitrary and illegitimate power.

**cognitive ambiguity** A psychological state of confusion about the status, both real and ideal, of social reality.

**cognitive system** Beliefs, values, attitudes, opinions and other conceptual variables which constitute the thought processes and intellectual functions of the personality.

**cohort** A social category comprised of people of approximately the same age.

**collective behavior** Social behavior that develops spontaneously in unstructured situations on the part of large numbers of people, and which is not regulated by conventional norms of conduct.

**communal society** One which tends to have the following characteristics: small in size, primary-group based, informal and homogeneous in social organization, a minimal division of labor, a high degree of social cohesion, and total personal involvement or commitment.

**communication** Transference of messages (intentions or meanings) from one individual to another.

**communism** An economic system based on collective activity and mutual ownership of wealth and other means of production.

**community** A subunit of society that operates within a limited geographical area, such as a village, town, city, or suburb, and within which a comprehensive social life is enacted.

**complex organization** A social system that is characterized by an explicitly formulated set of goals, policies, procedures, and regulations that specify appropriate behavior for its members.

**concentric zone theory** An ecological model in which cities develop outwardly in a series of concentric circles that are characterized by differences in land usage.

▼ **concept**   A symbolic representation of universal application which comprehends the characteristics of a category of phenomena.

**conflict theory**   A theoretical orientation based on the processes and forms of conflict in human behavior and which focuses on the elements of change and revolution.

**conjugal family**   A family that consists of spouses (man and woman) and their children living within one household.

676

**consanguineal family**   A family that consists of the nuclear family and other relatives.

**consolidated metropolitan statistical area (CMSA)**   A metropolitan area with a population of one million or more that consists of two or more smaller metropolitan areas.

**conspicuous consumption**   A form of behavior by which people attempt to surround themselves with the status symbols of a particular social class position in the expectation that they will be treated accordingly.

**contagion theory**   An explanation for collective behavior based on the dynamics of emotion, irrationality, and reciprocal stimulation.

**content analysis**   A form of data collection which consists of the assessment of themes in written documents.

**conventional crowd**   An aggregate of individuals who have deliberately planned to attend a particular event.

**convergence theory**   An explanation for collective behavior based on similar characteristics and needs of people.

**convergence thesis**   The hypothesis that industrialization leads to common forms of organization in culturally different societies.

**co-optation**   The process of giving positions of leadership to group members who are expected to deviate or who have deviated from group rules.

**core cultural value**   A value that forms the foundation upon which a society functions.

**corporate crime**   Illegal actions committed by commercial and industrial companies in the course of business.

**counterculture**   A subculture which is characterized by lifestyles that are both significantly different from, and in conflict with, the dominant culture.

**craze**   An extremely intense and obsessive preoccupation with something for the purpose of economic gain or personal satisfaction.

**crescive social organization**   One which develops spontaneously as a product of social relationships that reoccur among people over a prolonged period of time.

**crime**   Any intentional behavior that violates the legal codes of society.

**criminal justice system**   Institutions of social control consisting of police, courts, and corrections.

**critical period**   A specific time-period in the maturational cycle during which exposure to certain cues is imperative for a particular learning experience.

**cross-sectional research**   An investigation consisting of a single set of observations and analyses of data at a given point in time.

**crowd**   A temporary aggregate of people who have assembled for a specific purpose or who are responding to a common stimulus.

**cult**   A type of religion represented by a small, highly informal, organized group of individuals without a coherent body of beliefs, liturgy, or trained ministry.

**cultural alternative**   An element of culture which offers people within a particular culture a choice of mechanisms in meeting personal and social needs or wishes.

**cultural anthropology**   A division of anthropology concerned with the development and organization of human societies, and the sociocultural life of human beings.

**cultural base**   The fund of knowledge and techniques that is available for further inventions.

**cultural change** See *social change.*

**cultural diffusion** The dynamics by which elements of one culture are transmitted to other cultures.

**cultural ethic** See *ethos.*

**cultural institution** A set of culture complexes that are thought of as being functionally related to any basic social need of human beings or to functional needs of society.

**cultural integration** The degree of consistency and cohesion among the elements of a culture.

**cultural lag** The phenomenon in which the "material" and "non-material" aspects of culture develop or change at different rates.

**cultural relativism** A doctrine which maintains that in order to understand a culture and social facts meaningfully, one must perceive such phenomena in terms of the particular culture and society of which they are a part.

**cultural specialty** An element of culture which is shared by people of certain social categories, but not by the total population of a particular society.

**cultural universal** An element of culture which is common to people everywhere.

**culturation** The transmission of culture from one generation to another.

**culture** The entirety of knowledge and habitual patterns of behavior which are shared and perpetuated by the members of a particular society or group.

**culture complex** A set of functionally interrelated culture traits.

**culture trait** An irreducible, smallest possible unit or simplest element of culture.

**cyclical theory** An explanation of social change which postulates that all societies pass through alternating phases of development and decay.

**de facto discrimination** Discriminating behavior that is based on social custom; see *institutional discrimination.*

**de-individuation theory** An explanation for collective behavior that focuses on the process by which individuals lose their sense of personal identity and engage in nonconventional or deviant actions.

**de jure discrimination** Officially or legally sanctioned discriminatory behavior.

**delinquency** A criminal offense that is committed by an individual below the age of criminal responsibility.

**democracy** A form of government that allocates authority to the individual members of society who in turn may delegate it to their representatives.

**democratic socialism** A mixed type of economy that combines principles of democracy and socialism. Also known as the *welfare state.*

**demographic transition** The process by which a population becomes stabilized as a society moves from an agrarian type to a completely industrialized one.

**demography** A branch of sociology concerned with population composition and dynamics.

**denomination** A religion that is independent of the state and usually one among many in a given society.

**dependency ratio** The number or percentage of dependents in a population divided by the number or percentage of producers.

**dependent variable** The phenomenon under investigation; the effect factor in a cause-and-effect relationship.

**descriptive analysis** An investigation that seeks to provide answers to the question "what?" concerning the occurrence of phenomena.

**descriptive statistics** Methods for organizing and summarizing quantitative data.

677

▼ **determinism** The doctrine that phenomena are not uncaused, but rather the result of antecedent events, such as economic, geographical, and biological.

**deviance** Social behavior that violates any societal or group norm; any violation of required or expected behavior.

**dialectic materialism** Marxist theory of social change as the product of contradictions and conflicts in society.

**678**

**dialectic process** An approach to logical reasoning which maintains that an idea (thesis) generates its opposite (antithesis), with the ensuing conflict resulting in a reconciliation (synthesis) that in turn becomes a new thesis.

**differential association theory** A theory which maintains that deviant behavior is learned through differential exposure to situations that influence one's definition of appropriate and inappropriate behavior.

**diffusion of responsibility** A sociopsychological principle which states that people acting in groups are more likely to make risky choices because each individual will have to bear only a portion of the responsibility. Also, the principle by which any individual in a group or other collectivity tends not to assume responsibility for action on the assumption that others will.

**discovery** The perception of reality that previously had been unknown.

**discrimination** The differential treatment of an individual through the denial of rights and privileges normally accorded to members of society.

**disengagement theory** A perspective that views the later stages of the life cycle as ones in which the individual gradually and steadily withdraws from the statuses that had been occupied during adulthood.

**displacement** See *projection*.

**dogmatic personality** A personality syndrome which manifests a cognitive organization that is relatively closed and rigid, as well as being intolerant of opposing beliefs. See *authoritarian personality*.

**dogmatism** A closed-minded system of beliefs, associated with an intolerance of opposing beliefs.

**dominant value** A value that is shared by the largest number of people in a society.

**dramaturgy** A variation on the symbolic interactionist perspective which focuses on impression management and the way that individuals play roles in order to create and to control particular reactions.

**dyad** The most elementary form of social group which consists of two people.

**dynamic equilibrium** The tendency of units that comprise a system to maintain the relationship which they have with one another.

**dynamic unconscious** A system of personality which consists of a number of mental mechanisms whose function is to resolve psychological conflict.

**dysfunction** A mechanism that has the effect of impeding the functioning of a system and the attainment of its goals.

**ecclesia** A large, formally organized, and highly complex religion with an explicit creed, liturgy, and ordained ministry.

**ecological invasion** The entrance of a particular social category or activity into a specified ecological area.

**ecological segregation** The voluntary or compulsory process by which geographical areas come to be socially differentiated and maintained.

**economics** A science that studies aspects of human social life which involve the production, distribution, and consumption of material goods and services.

**economy** An economic institution.

**ecosystem** A self-sustaining system of mutual interdependence between human societies and the physical environment.

**ego** In psychoanalytic theory, a partly unconscious dimension of personality which is reality-oriented and which develops through social learning.

**ego psychology** A brand of psychodynamic theory of personality that focuses on the psychosocial stages of the life cycle.

**elite deviance** Crime committed by the rich and powerful segments of society.

**embourgeoisement** The tendency for lifestyle to become more homogeneous among different social classes.

**emergent norm theory** A perspective which maintains that in situations of collective behavior new norms emerge and become determinants of appropriate action.

**emotion** A feeling or affect that is social and cultural in its development and expression.

**emotional contagion** Process by which beliefs, feelings, and actions are transmitted from one person to another in a crowd as members stimulate and respond to one another.

**empirical generalization** A descriptive, but factual, statement concerning phenomena under analysis.

**empirical method** A set of procedures and techniques which consists of the controlled, sensory observations of reality.

**enacted social organization** One which is the result of deliberate and formally planned action.

**enculturation** The culturation of the neonate or culture-free organism.

**endocrine system** A series of ductless glands which produce hormones that regulate the rhythm and intensity of the physiological processes of the organism.

**endogamy** A marital structure which permits marriage only between individuals who are members of the same group, be it a kin, tribe, community, village, or society.

**epistemology** The philosophical study of the principles of knowledge.

**estate** A stratum of society with its own set of legally defined sociopolitical rights and obligations.

**ethnic category** A people who share a common racial and/or cultural heritage.

**ethnicity** A shared feeling of peoplehood among members of cultural or racial categories.

**ethnocentrism** An attitude of superiority regarding one's own culture or subculture.

**ethnomethodology** A sociological perspective that seeks to understand the unspecified guidelines, or "folk rules" by which people construct social reality and engage in social activity.

**ethnopaulism** A manifestation of prejudice through humor, jokes, caricatures, or derogatory name-calling.

**ethos** A set of guiding principles that give a people a distinctive character in both a sociological as well as a psychological sense. Also known as *cultural ethic*.

**eufunction** A mechanism that has the effect of promoting the operation and survival of a social system.

**evolutionary theory** An analytical perspective which maintains that social change is inevitable, orderly, and progressive: societies change naturally and gradually from more simple forms to more complex forms.

**existentialism** A theoretical perspective that focuses on conscious events, one's unique experiences, and the meaning and purpose of existence.

**exogamy** A marital structure which requires that individuals select a partner from outside a designated group, usually a kin group.

**experimentation** A form of observation which involves the manipulation of social phenomena or social situations in order to measure their effect in selected respects.

**explanatory analysis** An investigation that seeks to provide answers to the question of

▼

**679**

▼ "why?" concerning the occurrence of phenomena.

**explanatory research** Descriptive or experimental research that seeks to provide substantive answers to a research problem.

**exploratory research** A preliminary and basically descriptive type of research that seeks to refine various elements of a research problem and research design.

**680**

**expressive crowd** One whose members are highly emotionally charged, and which provides an occasion for the release and manifestation of feelings and sentiments.

**expressive leader** One concerned primarily with the development and maintenance of the morale and cohesion of a group. Also known as *socioemotional leader*.

**extant self** That conception of self which the individual actually perceives when engaged in self-reflection.

**extended family** See *consanguineal family*.

**extermination** See *genocide*.

**factor analysis** A statistical method for identifying specific traits of personality and determining the trait structure of a personality system.

**factor analytic theory** A trait theory of personality which utilizes statistical techniques of measurement for the core traits of personality.

**fad** An enthusiastically pursued, but short-lived and frivolous, form of behavior engaged in by large numbers of people.

**family of orientation** The family into which an individual is born or adopted.

**family of procreation** The family which an individual and spouse produce biologically and/or socially.

**fascism** A form of government that allocates supreme authority to the state.

**fashion** A currently accepted and temporary style or mode of behavior.

**feedback** That part of the informational output being produced by a system which is sent back into the system in order to motivate and to guide its component parts and processes.

**felony** A serious crime that is punishable by heavy fines and/or prolonged periods of incarceration and even execution.

**feral people** Individuals allegedly reared by animals.

**field research** Research conducted in the true context of the behavior under study.

**folkway** A norm that is reinforced by mild or moderate degrees of sanction.

**formal organization** See *complex organization*.

**frustration-aggression theory** A theoretical perspective which maintains that prejudice, discrimination, and deviance are unconscious expressions of frustration.

**function** See *eufunction*.

**functionalism** See *structural-functional analysis*.

**functional differentiation** The specialized tasks performed by the units that comprise a system.

**functional equivalent** A mechanism which produces the same set of eufunctions and dysfunctions as another.

**functional requisite** A task and/or mechanism essential for developing and maintaining dynamic equilibrium in a social system.

**game theory** A perspective of collective behavior which maintains that people in such situations calculate whether their actions are likely to result in greater rewards or costs for themselves.

**gate-keeping** The decision-making process by which members of society are admitted to positions of privilege and power.

*Gemeinschaft* See *communal society*.

**generalized other** A conception of the beliefs, values, norms, attitudes, and expectations held by the members of a community or society.

**genetic mutation** An alteration in genetic structure.

**genocide** The systematic extermination of a racially or culturally distinct category of people.

**geographical isolation** The tendency for certain segments of a genetic population to become isolated from others.

**geography** A science concerned with the relationships of people and social dynamics to the physical environment.

*Gesellschaft* See *associational society.*

**ghetto** A neighborhood inhabited chiefly by a racial or ethnic minority.

**group cohesion** The totality of feelings of attraction to a group on the part of all of its members.

**group marriage** A practice by which two or more men are all married simultaneously to each of two or more women.

**group polarization** A hypothesis which asserts that initially held attitudes and opinions become intensified as a consequence of group discussion.

**group think** A type of decision-making that occurs in cohesive groups when the main concerns of its members are to perpetuate harmony, avoid conflict, and develop unanimity of opinion.

**Hawthorne effect** A situation in which dependent variables are produced by an experiment itself rather than by any of the manipulated variables in the experiment; also refers to changes in the behavior of research subjects which result from their awareness and knowledge of the study.

**hermaphrodite** A person who possesses the genitals of both sexes.

**Homo sapiens** The current species of mankind.

**horizontal mobility** Movement within the same social stratum or on the same social level.

**horticultural society** One whose primary mode of subsistence consists of limited food production through cultivation by hand tools.

**human ecology** A branch of sociology which is concerned with the relations between people and their physical environment.

**human relations model** A theoretical perspective for complex organizations which focuses more on the informal rather than the formal aspects of organizational behavior.

**humanistic method** An investigative method that relies primarily on subjective analysis, including intuition, speculation, impression, insight, and common sense as the principal elements.

**humanistic theory** A type of personality theory which stresses the holistic and integrative nature of personality, with an emphasis on rationality and free will.

**hunting and gathering society** One in which the only mode of subsistence consists of the constant search for food through hunting or fishing.

**hypothesis** A statement of assumed relationship between two or more phenomena (rational hypothesis) or simply of the occurrence of phenomena (descriptive hypothesis).

**id** In psychoanalytic theory, the unconscious dimension of personality which is sensually pleasure-oriented.

**idealized self** That conception of personality one would like to perceive upon self-reflection.

**ideal type** A mental construct which emphasizes, often exaggerates, distinctive qualities of a phenomenon.

**identification** See *modeling.* In psychoanalytic theory, the process by which the norms and

681

▼ values of society become incorporated or internalized, largely unconsciously, within the individual.

**ideology** A system of beliefs and values.

**idiographic theory** A trait theory of personality which focuses on unique and individual psychological phenomena.

**idiosyncrasy credit** Special privilege accorded to individuals because of their social prestige within a social group.

682

**imprinting** A genetically based process of learning through imitation and which is characterized by critical periods, the primacy effect, and irreversibility.

**inadequate socialization** An insufficient amount of teaching or learning, as well as the deprivation of a suitable social or psychological environment and the resources for these processes.

**inappropriate socialization** The internalization of values and norms that are incompatible with a particular culture and specific social situations.

**incest taboo** A social norm which prohibits sexual relations (and/or marriage) between any member of a nuclear family and designated members of extended families.

**independent variable** The causal factor in a cause-and-effect relationship; or the given and invariant factor.

**individual mobility** Movement within the class structure on the part of a single person.

**individual modernity syndrome** A system of personality characteristics thought to be associated with and required for effective participation in modern industrial society.

**industrial society** One whose mode of subsistence is distinguished by massive mechanization and automation.

**inferential statistics** Statistical analysis concerned with causal associations between independent and dependent variables.

**influence** The power to persuade or to induce another individual to act in a certain way.

**informal structure** An official network of personal relationships that forms within a complex or formal organization.

**informed consent** The principle of voluntary participation, with full disclosure of objectives and risks, afforded to subjects in scientific research.

**in-group** Any group or social category with which a person has developed a strong sense of emotional and psychological attachment.

**innovation** The emergence of a new phenomenon, usually of a cultural nature, within a particular society.

**instinct** A genetically transmitted behavior that is universal to the species, directed toward a highly specific goal, and unalterable by the individual animal.

**institutional discrimination** Discrimination latently embedded within the institutional structure of society.

**institutional racism** See *institutional discrimination.*

**instrumental conditioning** See *operant reinforcement theory.*

**instrumental leader** One concerned primarily with the resolution of problems and the attainment of group goals. Also known as *task leader.*

**intergenerational mobility** Vertical mobility within a stratification system on the part of a particular family over two or more generations.

**internalization** Process by which one accepts the beliefs, values, and norms of society and incorporates them into the self system.

**internalization theory** A theory of social deviance which maintains that an individual violates group norms because they are incompatible with one's internalized standards.

**intervening variable** A test factor or experimental element that is introduced into an experiment in order to determine its ability to produce a dependent variable as a consequence of its interaction with an independent factor.

**interview** A highly structured conversation aimed at revealing one's attitudes, opinions, values, beliefs, and modes of behavior relevant to a particular topic.

**interview guide** An enumeration of topics to be covered in an interview.

**interview schedule** A tool for the systematization of questions posed in an interview.

**intragenerational mobility** Vertical mobility within a stratification system during the course of one's lifetime.

**invention** A recombination of existing social and cultural elements in order to form a significantly new element.

**iron law of oligarchy** The common, almost inevitable, tendency found in bureaucracies for control to become concentrated in the hands of a very small number of people.

**labeling theory** An explanation of social deviance which focuses on the significance that names given to specific kinds of behavior and their agents have for the continued production of the behavior itself.

**laboratory research** An investigation conducted under simulated conditions in the artificial confines of a laboratory.

**laissez faire** A doctrine that opposes all forms of government control of social life.

**language** A system of signs (written or oral) with particular, but arbitrary, meanings attached to them, along with conventional rules that govern the use of these symbols.

**latent function** A consequence of a social mechanism which is neither intended nor recognized by the participants in a social system.

**latent property space** The hidden, nonphysical reality that is the true locus of sociological explanation.

**law** A statement of invariant relationship between phenomena.

**leader** One who defines the goals of a group, suggests means for achieving them, coordinates activities of members, and tries to maintain group harmony and solidarity.

**learning** The process by which behavior, or the potentiality for behavior, is modified as the result of experience.

**libido** In psychoanalytic theory, the reservoir of unconscious biological and psychological energy consisting basically of sexual and aggressive drives.

**life-chances** The differential access to rewards and opportunities that stem from one's social class position.

**lifestyle** Beliefs, values, attitudes, motivations, and actual patterns of behavior which characterize a particular individual or social category.

**linguistic relativity hypothesis** The contention that reality is known through the particular language which people use, and therefore, through one's culture.

**locus of control** The perception of causality and the source of rewards for one's behavior.

**longitudinal research** An investigation consisting of repeated sets of observations and analyses over a given period of time.

**looking-glass self** A conception of the self which derives from a "social mirror," or as a reflection of how one believes others see and evaluate the individual.

**Machiavellianism** A philosophy that has little regard for conventional morality and ethics, and whose fundamental principle is that the end justifies the means.

**macrosociology** That facet of sociology which studies society as a whole and is concerned with grand-scale analysis.

**majority** The socially and politically dominant category in society.

**mania** See *craze*.

683

▼ **manifest function**  A consequence of a social mechanism which is intended and recognized by participants in a social system.

**manifest property space**  The physical and accessible phenomena that are the focus of direct observation.

**marriage**  The process by which families are formed.

684

**mass behavior**  Behavior performed by many people acting individually in the same way or for the same purpose.

**mass hysteria**  Compulsive or frenzied behavior which results from an unfounded or irrational belief that is widely diffused among people.

**mass media**  A variety of modes of communication in which there is no personal interaction between the senders and the recipients of messages.

**material culture**  Artifacts or physical objects that are expressions of culture.

**matriarchy**  A marital and family form in which the wife or mother serves as the principal authority figure.

**matrilineal descent**  Family lineage that is traced via the mother's family or kin.

**matrilocality**  The situation in which a newly created family establishes its residence in the household or locale of the wife or her kin group.

**maturation**  The physiological and biological development of the human organism.

**mean**  A measure of central tendency which is arithmetically derived.

**measure of central tendency**  A statistic that summarizes a set of measurements.

**measure of correlation**  A statistic that indicates the degree to which two variables covary.

**median**  A measure of central tendency which represents the midpoint in a distribution of values.

**megalopolis**  An enormous and continually expanding urban region.

**membership group**  A social group or category to which an individual belongs—one in which there is an actual membership.

**metropolitan statistical area (MSA)**  Any county or group of counties containing a city of at least 50,000 people.

**microsociology**  That facet of sociology which is concerned with the analysis of the elementary forms and processes of social behavior, as well as behavior which takes place in the context of small groups.

**minority**  A social category which holds a subordinate place in society and which is the object of prejudice and discrimination.

**misdemeanor**  A relatively minor offense of the law which is usually punishable by a small fine or a prison sentence of less than one year.

**mob**  A form of acting crowd with immediate and limited objectives, and whose highly emotionally aroused members seek to vent hostility on a specific person or thing.

**modal personality**  The central tendency of personality typology within a given society or segment thereof.

**mode**  A measure of central tendency which represents the most frequently occurring value in a distribution.

**model**  The reproduction, in another form or medium, of any phenomenon or behavior that is to be explained.

**modeling**  Process of picking up cues from a significant person in one's environment and imitating the relevant actions of that individual.

**monarchy**  A form of government which allocates authority to a single individual or supreme ruler.

**monistic theory**  An explanation of cultural development and social change which postulates a single cause.

**monogamy** A form of marriage which permits only one spouse of the opposite sex for each partner at a time.

**monogenesis** A theory which maintains that the human species has evolved from a single origin.

**mores** Norms that are reinforced by strong sanctions.

**motivational system** Aspects of personality which are responsible for the initiation and maintenance of behavior.

**motive** The mobilization of energy within an individual and the selection of a goal for its dissipation.

**multilinear evolution** An evolutionary theory which postulates that social change takes place in different forms and at different rates in different societies.

**multiple nuclei theory** An ecological model in which cities develop around a number of focal areas, each with a distinct function.

**national modal character** Relatively enduring personality characteristics that are modal among the adult members of a society.

**natural area** A geographical sector of an urban community which is clearly distinguished by a specific kind of social activity, such as industry, commerce, transportation, or housing.

**natural selection** The tendency for genetic characteristics that are most suitable to a particular physical environment to endure.

**neolocality** A situation in which newlyweds establish an independent household.

**neurosis** A less serious form of mental illness involving no loss of contact with reality.

**nominal concept** A mental construct or symbolic representation whose definition represents a resolution concerning the use of verbal symbols.

**nonparticipant observation** A method by which the observer takes a totally passive and noninvolved part in the behavior under investigation.

**norm** A rule of behavior which specifies the kinds of action that are expected or required, as well as the kinds that are forbidden, among a particular people.

**normative internalization** See *internalization*.

**nuclear family** See *conjugal family*.

**observation** Use of one's senses to record information: seeing, feeling, tasting, touching, and smelling.

**685**

**occupational prestige** Social rank accorded to a person in terms of the value of one's occupation.

**oligarchy** An authoritarian form of government in which political power is exercised by an elite or small number of people.

**open system** One that engages in active interchange (input-output relations) with other systems or with aspects of its environment.

**operant reinforcement theory** The process by which behavior that is positively or negatively reinforced tends to be learned and repeated, while actions that are followed by punishment are not likely to occur again; also known as *instrumental conditioning*.

**operational definition** A type of nominal concept which is defined by the procedures or operations that one undertakes in order to measure a given phenomenon.

**organized crime** Illegal activity undertaken on a massive scale as a form of business enterprise.

**out-group** Any group or social category of which the individual is not a member and toward which one feels a sense of indifference, avoidance, competition, or conflict.

**panic** A sudden, highly emotional, somewhat irrational, and chaotic response on the part of a plurality of people who fear that they face an immediate and severe threat from which there is no escape.

▼ **Parkinson's law** A satirical reference to the tendency of bureaucracies to expand and to become ever more complex.

**participant observation** A method by which the observer plays an active role in the behavior under investigation.

**partition** A form of segregation which attempts to separate racial or ethnic peoples in terms of mutually acceptable political solutions.

686

**passing** A clandestine form of assimilation consisting of any technique by which an individual disguises one's social or cultural identity and attempts to be recognized as a member of the social majority.

**patriarchy** A marital and family form in which primary authority is vested in the husband or father.

**patrilineal descent** Family lineage which is traced via the father's family or kin.

**patrilocality** The situation in which a newly created family establishes its residence in the household of the husband or his kin group.

**peer** A person of roughly one's own age, who shares the same status or interests.

**perceived self** One's image of how others view and evaluate the individual.

**personality** The acquired, unique, relatively enduring, yet dynamic, system of predispositions to behavior which is localized within the individual.

**personality content** The specific elements or units that comprise the personality system: beliefs, motivations, values, attitudes, ideologies, emotions, psychological traits, cognitions, and self-conceptions.

**personality development** The inner, psychological formation of the individual in terms of unique or individuating qualities and/or attributes.

**personality inventory** An instrument that assesses psychological and personality variables.

**personality structure** The coordinated arrangement and dynamic relationships among the components of personality content, manifested through such dimensions as complexity, integration, isolation, and cohesion.

**personality trait** A relatively enduring psychological characteristic that has a fairly generalized effect on behavior in diverse settings.

**Peter principle** The tendency for every individual in any hierarchy to rise to the level of his or her incompetency.

**phenomenology** A theoretical perspective that focuses on consciousness and the subjective experiences of reality.

**physical anthropology** A division of anthropology concerned with the evolution and development of the human species.

**planned change** Social change that is intentionally sought by members of society.

**pluralism** The harmonious coexistence of several racial and ethnic categories in a society.

**pluralist model** A democratic perspective of the political process which maintains that a variety of interests compete for and have access to political and economic powers.

**political science** A science concerned with theories and systems of government and political behavior.

**polity** A political institution.

**polyandry** A form of marriage in which females may have several husbands simultaneously.

**polygamy** A form of marriage which provides for multiple spouses of the opposite sex for one of the partners at the same time.

**polygenesis** A theory which maintains that the human species has evolved from several independent origins.

**polygyny** A form of marriage which permits males to have more than one wife at the same time.

**population** See *universe*.

**population pyramid** An instrument for graphically illustrating the distribution of a population in terms of age and sex categories.

**population transfer** A form of segregation which involves moving people from one geographical area to another.

**positivistic philosophy** A brand of philosophy developed by Auguste Comte, which advocated the use of systematic observation and experimentation in order to understand social phenomena.

**postindustrial society** One in which the dominant mode of economic activity involves the production and distribution of services, as well as that characterized by extensive automation and mass consumption.

**power** The ability to control or to influence the actions of others.

**power elite** A perspective of the political process which maintains that power is held and exercised primarily by an interlocking set of leaders in the fields of politics, business, and the military.

**prejudice** Negative beliefs and hostile feelings about people of a particular social category.

**primary group** A relatively small number of people who interact on an intimate, personal, direct, informal, face-to-face basis and who are characterized by strong emotional bonds that typically endure over a long period of time.

**probabilistic relationship** A statement that specifies the tendency for two or more variables to be related in one way or another.

**projection** A psychological mechanism by which responsibility for one's behavior and/or shortcomings are attributed to another individual or social category.

**projective test** An instrument for the assessment of personality and psychological variables which is constructed in such a manner that its objective is disguised.

**proletariat** Peasants; workers.

**propaganda** A deliberate attempt to persuade people to adopt a particular set of beliefs, attitudes, and opinions.

**propinquity** The sociological phenomenon by which people in close physical proximity tend to develop social contacts that frequently lead to lasting and intimate relationships.

**psychoanalysis** A theory of personality and form of therapy developed by Sigmund Freud.

**psychodynamic theory** A type of personality theory which focuses on unconscious dynamics as well as the social and psychological experiences of early life.

**psychology** A science concerned with the individual behavior of the human being, especially mental phenomena, including sensation, perception, cognition, motivation, and affect.

**psychopath** See *sociopath*.

**psychosis** A serious form of mental illness, usually involving a loss of contact with reality.

**public** A large number or category of people who share an interest or concern about a particular issue.

**public opinion** The beliefs and attitudes that a particular public has about an issue.

**qualitative analysis** The logical ordering of data including such processes as conceptual specification and theoretical interpretation.

**quantitative analysis** The reduction of data through such methods as coding and statistical analysis.

**questionnaire** An instrument for securing answers to questions which is self-administered by the respondent.

**quota sampling** Sampling which establishes a fixed number of individuals with particular characteristics.

**race** A division of the human species on the basis of genetic and/or physical characteristics.

▼ **racism**  A doctrine which advocates the innate inferiority of one race or genetic category.

**random genetic drift**  The process by which a genetic trait appears by chance and then becomes widespread in a given population.

**random sampling**  Sampling which affords an equal probability of selection to each individual in the population under investigation.

**rational-legal authority**  Authority based on the legitimacy of laws and formally defined rights and obligations.

**real concept**  A symbolic representation of the essential attributes and/or substance of a given phenomenon.

**recidivism**  Repeated offenses of deviant behavior.

**reference group**  A social group or category that an individual uses as a frame of reference to guide one's behavior and to evaluate oneself.

**regulatory mechanism**  A unit of a system which provides feedback or relays data about the state and efficiency of the system to other units.

**relative deprivation**  The lack of goal attainment in terms of one's expectations when compared to the achievements of others who are used as a reference group.

**reliability**  The degree to which a scientific investigation, or its research tools, is not influenced by irrelevant and extraneous factors.

**representative sample**  One that, being free of bias and distortion, truly represents the characteristics of the population from which it is drawn.

**research design**  The comprehensive plan for conducting a research study.

**resocialization**  The process of unlearning existing beliefs, values, and norms, and substituting them with new ones acquired in a new social context.

**respondent conditioning**  See *classical conditioning*.

**revolution**  A profound and relatively rapid change in the political and economic system of a society as well as in its dominant ideology.

**riot**  A type of diffuse mob characterized by relatively little focus, organization, and leadership and that manifests randomly directed violence.

**risky shift**  The principle that decisions within a group context tend to be more extreme and riskier than those made by individuals.

**rite of passage**  A public ceremony that formally marks an individual's transition from one status to another.

**role behavior**  The actual behavior of a person enacting a role.

**role conflict**  Strain or tension resulting from incompatible conceptions of how one should enact a given role.

**role deviation**  Concrete action, or role behavior, that is inconsistent with the prescriptions and/or proscriptions of a role.

**role distancing behavior**  An action which indicates that one does not hold a commitment to a particular role.

**role set**  The totality of status-role relationships which a person has with other people occupying statuses that are related to a given status.

**role strain**  Difficulty in coping with the demands of a social role.

**ruling class model**  A perspective which views the power structure of modern society as composed of a small and dominant class of entrepreneurs.

**rumor**  An unverified communication that occurs in ambiguous situations for the purpose of providing a meaningful interpretation.

**sample**  The set of particular individuals selected to represent the total population or universe under investigation.

**sampling** The process by which a portion of a population is selected as representative of that population.

**sanction** An action that rewards conformity and/or punishes non-conformity.

**Sapir-Whorf hypothesis** See *linguistic relativity hypothesis.*

**scapegoat** A substitute target for venting hostility or frustration.

**scientific management model** A theoretical perspective for complex organizations which focuses on the formal and rational aspects of organization.

**scientific method** A method of objective and empirical analysis, including observation and experimentation.

**secondary deviance** Behavior that deviants develop as a result of being labeled deviant and their internalization of such labels.

**secondary group** A group that is characterized by relatively formal, impersonal, and goal-oriented interactions.

**sect** A religion that is a dissenting version of a larger denomination.

**sector theory** An ecological model in which cities develop in terms of distinctive sectors that are distinguished by differences in land usage.

**segregation** The physical separation of one social category from another.

**self-concept** See *self system.*

**self-fulfilling prophecy** A dynamic by which a false belief or prediction starts a chain of behavioral events which make the belief or prediction come true.

**self system** The segment of personality which consists of the total constellation and configuration of cognitions, affects, and motivations that pertain directly to the individual as an object.

**sex-associated behavior** A behavioral disposition or action which through differential social learning is typically found in a particular sex.

**sexism** A doctrine which advocates the innate and/or social inferiority of one sex, usually female.

**sex-linked behavior** A behavioral disposition or action which through genetic determination is found exclusively in a particular sex.

**sex ratio** The number of males per 100 females in a given population.

**sex-role socialization** The process by which children learn behavior and personal characteristics that are deemed appropriate or preferred by their respective culture for males and females.

**sex-typed behavior** An action that is rewarded or punished depending upon the gender to which it is assigned.

**significant other** An individual whose judgment and social approval are valued.

**simple observation** An informal type of observation that involves no standardization of techniques, and no control over pertinent variables.

**social aggregate** A collectivity of people who are distinguished by the fact that they share physical proximity.

**social category** A plurality of people who share one or more common characteristics.

**social change** Any relatively enduring modification in the established or existing structure or function of a social system.

**social character** See *national modal character.*

**social cohesion** See *group cohesion.*

**social comparison theory** A perspective which explains social deviance by claiming that people who violate the norms of a particular group are identifying themselves with another group.

**social content** The established beliefs, knowledge, values, norms, and roles that comprise the element of social organization.

**689**

▼

**690**

**social contract theory**  A thesis which asserts that individuals, originally existing in a "state of nature," voluntarily surrendered their independent rights and personal freedom in order to form an absolute government for their own mutual harmony and collective protection against a social order motivated only by self-interests and characterized by perpetual conflict.

**social control**  All of the processes and mechanisms whereby society encourages and/or enforces social conformity.

**social Darwinism**  A theoretical perspective which postulates that societies, like physical organisms, develop according to the principles and processes of evolution.

**social disorganization**  A social situation that is dysfunctional.

**social distance**  The degree of social intimacy that an individual is willing to allow between oneself and members of a social minority.

**social engineering**  An applied field concerned with the construction and/or improvement of society and the social environment.

**social evolution**  A doctrine asserting the law of progress, or the natural development of societies in progressive states.

**social exchange theory**  A theoretical orientation, based on the principles of behavioristic psychology, which focuses on the elementary forms of social behavior, including the goals and motives of participants in social interaction.

**social facilitation**  The thesis that an individual's performance of a task will improve if he or she is doing it in the presence of others.

**social group**  A plurality of people (two or more individuals) who share a common identity, and who recurrently interact in respective status-role distinctions in the pursuit of a common goal.

**social indicator**  A measure of the quality of life in a society.

**social institution**  All of the patterns of behavior, formal or informal, which are formally or ideally established for the purpose of meeting a functional need or goal of society.

**social learning theory**  An approach to socialization and individual development that stresses observation, modeling, internalization, and cognition.

**social mobility**  The movement of an individual or social category from one social stratum to another, or movement within a given social stratum.

**social movement**  A relatively sustained or long-lasting collective effort by widely dispersed and large numbers of people either to achieve or to prevent social change.

**social pathology**  See *social disorganization*.

**social philosophy**  Knowledge of social behavior which is derived principally from the methods of inductive and deductive reasoning.

**social prestige**  Social recognition accorded to an individual in terms of achievement or rank.

**social problem**  A social situation that affects a significant number of people and which is considered to be undesirable.

**social progress**  Social change defined as desirable.

**social psychology**  A field of sociology concerned with the psychological dimensions of human social behavior; also, a field of psychology concerned with the social dimensions of human individual behavior.

**social role**  A set of interrelated norms which indicate how individuals occupying a particular position, in a given social organization, are expected to act.

**social self**  The person one seeks to implant in the minds of others.

**social status**  A specific, socially designated or identifiable position within a system of social relationships.

**social stratification**  The process and system by which differential value and prestige are attached to the various statuses and roles that are found in society, as well as to the various social categories that can be distinguished in society.

**social stratum**  A category of people who share the same or similar ranking in a particular community or society.

**social structure**  The integral arrangement or configuration of all interrelationships within a social system.

**social system**  The total configuration of established patterns of social activity which are proper to a given number of people functioning independently as a unit.

**social system model**  A theoretical perspective for complex organizations which views organizations as having subsystems that are functionally related to one another and to the organization as a whole.

**social work**  A field of endeavor concerned with providing assistance and therapy to individuals in undesirable or unfortunate social circumstances.

**socialism**  A political and economic philosophy that advocates the vesting of social control and the means of production in the community or society as a whole.

**socialization**  The process of humanization through the acquisition of culture and symbolic reasoning.

**society**  A relatively independent and self-sufficient social system, usually represented by a relatively large number of people occupying a given territory, and interacting in terms of a commonly shared culture.

**sociobiology**  A field of biology concerned with the social behavior of non-human species.

**socioeconomic gain theory**  A theoretical perspective that emphasizes the utilitarian or instrumental functions of prejudice and discrimination.

**socioeconomic status**  A position of social rank based on a combination of wealth, power, and prestige.

**socioemotional leader**  See *expressive leader*.

**sociogenic motive**  A socially and/or culturally acquired drive which is neither universal nor essential for human function

**sociogram**  An instrument that indicates attractions and rejections in a particular group and whether these feelings are shared.

**sociological ambivalence**  An incompatibility in the normative expectations of a single status or set of statuses.

**sociological problem**  A situation which involves the explanation of the nature and dynamics of social behavior.

**sociology**  The science of human social behavior.

**sociometric structure**  The patterns of interpersonal attraction and repulsion which exist among the members of a group.

**sociopath**  A personality type that results from inadequate, ineffective, or inappropriate socialization, and experiences no guilt or shame in the commission of deviant behavior.

**statistical analysis**  A method for reducing quantitative data in order to represent them in a more orderly and/or meaningful way.

**status**  Social ranking in terms of social prestige.

**status conflict**  Strain or tension resulting from the incompatible demands of two or more different statuses that are occupied simultaneously.

**status consistency**  The similarity of social rank within different dimensions of social stratification.

**status hierarchy**  The arrangement of social positions within a social system on the basis of prestige and power.

**status offense**  An act of deviance that can be performed only by an individual occupying a certain social position.

691

▼ **status seeking**   Behavior designed to enhance one's social class standing.

**status set**   The complex totality of statuses which one occupies at a given time.

**status symbol**   A material object, title, behavior, or other thing that conveys social rank or status.

**stereotype**   A set of ideas, based on distortion and exaggeration, which is applied to all members of a particular category without consideration of individual differences.

**stratified sampling**   Sampling which utilizes the principles of random selection within the various sub-categories of a particular universe.

**structural alternative**   A mechanism that has the same purpose as another, and thus is intended to achieve the same objective.

**structural-functional analysis**   A theoretical orientation which assumes that order, regularity, and balance are the principal forces of social activity.

**subculture**   A distinctive culture that is wholly contained within a larger culture.

**superego**   In psychoanalytical theory, the moral component of the personality which serves as a behavioral censor or mechanism of social control.

**surrogate primary group**   A secondary group that may be used to provide the essential social and psychological experience of a primary group.

**survey research**   Research which assesses the behavior of people in terms of the systematic analysis of such things as attitudes, values, opinions, beliefs, and customary practices.

**symbol**   Any object or event used to represent something else.

**symbolate**   A category of phenomena which includes objects that for their existence are dependent upon the act of symboling.

**symbolic interactionism**   A theoretical perspective in sociology which focuses on the symbols and meanings that serve as the media of social behavior.

**system**   A plurality of parts that function as a unit, with the implication that the whole is greater than the mere sum of the parts.

**systematic observation**   A formal type of observation that places controls on both the observer and the observed phenomenon, usually involving highly refined procedures and various types of instruments.

**systemic content**   The specific units or elements which constitute a system.

**systemic structure**   The coordinated arrangement or relationships that exist among the components of a system.

**taboo**   A strongly proscribed or prohibited behavior.

**task leader**   See *instrumental leader*.

**technological model**   A theoretical perspective for formal organizations which considers the type of technology that is used in organizations as the major determinant of organizational structures and processes.

**technology**   A set of knowledge and tools used to manipulate an environment for practical ends.

**temperament**   The major affective dispositions and typical moods, which are physiological and genetic in nature, of an individual.

**theory**   A set of logically interrelated concepts of empirical reference that purport to explain reality.

**Theory Z model**   A theoretical perspective for formal organizations which de-emphasizes hierarchy and formality, while enhancing the identification of members.

**tort**   An illegal action that victimizes individuals rather than society.

**total institution**   A segment of society which is relatively isolated from all other sectors, and which constitutes an all-encompassing environment for the fulfillment of the needs of its members.

**totalitarianism**  An authoritarian form of government in which rulers recognize no limits to their authority in any sphere of social life.

**traditional authority**  Authority based on ancient custom or long-standing practices.

**trait theory**  A type of personality theory which focuses on psychological characteristics.

**triad**  A social group which consists of three people.

**unilinear evolution**  A theory which asserts that every society develops in the same pattern through a series of fixed stages.

**universe**  The set of individuals comprising the subject of analysis.

**unobtrusive measures**  Techniques of data collection which are disguised or in other ways do not intrude on the behavior under study.

**unresponsive social system**  One which is incapable of effectively fulfilling the basic human needs of its members.

**urban gentrification**  The renovation of urban slums and the replacement of their dwellers by affluent suburbanites.

**validity**  The correspondence between that which a scientific investigation or research instrument intends to assess and that which it actually assesses.

**value**  A conception of that which is good, important, or desirable.

**value-added theory**  An explanation for collective behavior and social movements which postulates a specific sequence of stages: structural conduciveness, structural strain, generalized beliefs, precipitating factors, mobilization for action, and social control.

**value judgment**  An expression of the desirability or preference of phenomena and events.

**variable**  A phenomenon or condition whose properties or values may vary rather than being fixed.

**variant value**  A value that is an alternative conception of a given phenomenon and which is shared by a minority of people within a particular society.

*Verstehen*  A method of sociological analysis that calls for "sympathetic understanding" of the mind of social actors.

**693**

**vertical mobility**  Movement up or down the social class hierarchy; movement from one social stratum to another.

**victimless crime**  Crime undertaken in privacy, either by single individuals or consenting adults acting in concert, and allegedly to the detriment of neither society nor any of its members.

**visibility**  Physical or cultural characteristics which serve to identify members of a social minority.

**voluntary association**  A complex organization for which an individual volunteers or pays to be a member.

**welfare state**  See *democratic socialism.*

**white-collar crime**  Crime committed by a person of respectability and high social standards, usually in the course of one's occupation.

**world-system theory**  A mode of sociological analysis which focuses on the structure of interdependent and exploitative relationships among societies on a global scale.

**zero population growth (ZPG)**  A demographic policy which advocates no net increase in a societal population.

# Bibliography

Aberle, D. F., A. K. Cohen, A. K. Davis, M. J. Levy, and F. X. Sutton: "The Functional Prerequisites of Society," *Ethics*, 1950, vol. 60, pp. 100–111.

Adler, Alfred: *The Practice and Theory of Individual Psychology*. New York: Harcourt, Brace, and World, 1929.

Adorno, T. N., E. Frenkel-Brunswik, D. J. Levinson, and R. Nevitt Sanford: *The Authoritarian Personality*. New York: Harper and Row, 1950.

Akers, Ronald L.: *Deviant Behavior: A Social Learning Approach*. 3d ed. Belmont, Calif.: Wadsworth, 1985.

Alba, Richard D.: "Social Assimilation Among American Catholics," *American Sociological Review*, 1976, vol. 41, pp. 1036–1039.

Alba, Richard D.: *Italian Americans: Into the Twilight of Ethnicity*. Englewood Cliffs, N.J.: Prentice-Hall, 1985.

Alexander, Jeffrey C., and Paul Colomy (eds.): *Differentiation Theory: Problems and Prospects*. New York: Columbia University Press, 1990.

Allport, Gordon W.: *Personality: A Psychological Interpretation*. New York: Holt, 1937.

Allport, Gordon W.: *Pattern and Growth in Personality*. New York: Holt, 1961.

Allport, Gordon W., and H. S. Odbert: "Trait-Names: A Psycho-Lexical Study," *Psychological Monographs*, 1936, vol. 47.

Allport, Gordon, and Leo Postman: *The Psychology of Rumors*. New York: Holt, Rinehart and Winston, 1947.

Almond, Gabriel A.: "Youth Character and Changing Political Culture," in Gordon J. DiRenzo (ed.) *We, The People: American Character and Social Change*. Westport, Conn.: Greenwood Press, 1977.

Alvesson, Mats: "The Limits and Shortcomings of Humanistic Organization Theory," *Acta Sociologica*, 1982, vol. 25, pp. 117–131.

American Council on Education: *National Norms for Entering Freshmen, Fall, 1970*. Washington, D.C.: American Council on Education, 1970.

American Psychiatric Association: *Diagnostic and Statistical Manual of Mental Disorders*. Washington, D.C., 1987.

Amir, Menachem, and Yitzchak Berman: "Chromosomal Deviation and Crime," *Federal Probation*, 1970, vol. 34, pp. 55–62.

Anastasi, Anne: *Psychological Testing*. 6th ed. New York: Macmillan Publishing Co., 1988.

Anderson, J. G., and F. B. Evans: "Socialization and Achievement in Two Cultures," *Sociometry*, 1976, vol. 39, pp. 209–222.

Angermeyer, Matthias C. (ed.): *From Social Class to Social Stress*. New York: Springer Verlag, 1987.

Argyle, Michael: *The Social Psychology of Work*. New York: Taplinger Publishing Company, 1972.

Aristotle: *Politics*. 384–322 B.C.

Arluke, Arnold, and Jack Levin: "Another Stereotype: Old Age as a Second Childhood," *Aging*, August–September 1984, No. 346, pp. 7–11.

Armer, Michael, and L. Isaac: "Determinants and Behavioral Consequences of Psychological Modernity: Empirical Evidence from Costa Rica," *American Sociological Review*, 1978, vol. 43, pp. 316–334.

Asch, Solomon E.: *Social Psychology*. Englewood Cliffs, N.J.: Prentice-Hall, 1952.

Asch, Solomon: "Opinions and Social Pressure," *Scientific American*, 1955, vol. 193, pp. 31–35.

Ash, Roberta: *Social Movements in America*. Chicago: Markham, 1972.

Ashford, Douglas E.: *The Emergence of the Welfare States*. New York: Basil Blackwell, Inc., 1988.

Atchley, Robert C.: *Social Forces and Aging: An Introduction to Social Gerontology*. 5th ed. Belmont, Calif.: Wadsworth, 1988.

▼ Atchley, Robert C., and S. J. Miller: "Types of Elderly Couples," in Timothy H. Brubaker (ed.) *Family Relationships in Later Life.* Beverly Hills, Calif.: Sage, 1983.

Atkinson, Rita L., Richard C. Atkinson, and Ernest R. Hilgard: *Introduction to Psychology.* 8th ed. New York: Harcourt, Brace and Company, 1983.

Aurelius, Marcus: *Meditations.* 121–180 A.D.

Bacon, Francis: *New Atlantis.* 1624.

Baker, Sally H., Amitai Etzioni, Richard Hansen, and Marvin Sontag: "Tolerance for Bureaucratic Structure: Theory and Measurement," *Human Relations*, 1973, vol. 26, pp. 775–786.

Bales, Robert F.: *Interaction Process Analysis: A Method for the Study of Small Groups.* Cambridge, Mass.: Addison-Wesley, 1950.

Bales, Robert F.: "The Equilibrium Problem in Small Groups," in Talcott Parsons, Robert F. Bales, and Edward A. Shils: *Working Papers in the Theory of Action.* Glencoe, Ill.: The Free Press, 1953.

Bales, Robert F.: *Family Socialization and Interaction Process.* Glencoe, Ill.: Free Press, 1954.

Bales, Robert F.: "Task Roles and Social Roles in Problem Solving Groups," in E. E. Maccoby, Theodore M. Newcomb, and Eugene L. Hartley (eds.) *Readings in Social Psychology.* New York: Holt, Rinehart and Winston, 1958.

Bales, Robert F., and Stephen P. Cohen: *Symlog: A System of Multiple Level Observation of Groups.* New York: The Free Press, 1979.

Bales, Robert F., and Fred L. Strodtbeck: "Phases in Group Problem Solving," *Journal of Abnormal and Social Psychology*, 1951, vol. 46, pp. 485–495.

Ball, Samuel, and G. Bogatz: *The First Year of Sesame Street: An Evaluation.* Princeton, N.J.: Educational Testing Service, 1970.

Baltes, P. B., and O. G. Brim (eds.): *Life-Span Development and Behavior: Research and Theory*, New York: Academic Press, 1979.

Bandura, Albert: *Social Learning Theory.* Englewood Cliffs, N.J.: Prentice Hall, 1977.

Barash, David P.: *Sociobiology and Behavior.* 2d ed. New York: Elsevier, 1982.

Barker, Eileen: *The Making of a Moonie.* New York: Basil Blackwell, Inc., 1986.

Barnes, Michael J.: "Studies of Young Black and Latino Children." Paper presented at annual meeting of the American Psychological Association, New York, September 1987.

Baron, Jonathan: *Rationality and Intelligence.* New York: Cambridge University Press, 1985.

Becker, Howard S.: "Processes of Secularization," *Sociological Review*, 1932, vol. 24, pp. 138–154; 266–286.

Becker, Howard S.: *Boys in White.* Chicago: University of Chicago Press, 1961.

Becker, Howard S.: *Outsiders: Studies in the Sociology of Deviance.* New York: Free Press, 1963.

Bell, Daniel: *The Coming of Post-Industrial Society.* New York: Basic Books, 1973.

Bell, Daniel: *The Cultural Contradictions of Capitalism.* New York: Basic Books, 1976.

Bell, Daniel: "Talcott Parsons: Nobody's Theories Were Bigger." *New York Times,* May 13, 1979.

Bellah, Robert N.: "Civil Religion in America," *Daedalus*, Winter 1967, vol. 96, pp. 1–21.

Bellah, Robert N., and Phillip E. Hammond: *Varieties of Civil Religion.* San Francisco: Harper and Row, 1986.

Bellah, Robert N., Richard Madsen, William M. Sullivan, Ann Swidler, and Steven M. Tipton: *Habits of the Heart: Individualism and Commitment in American Life.* Berkeley, Calif.: University of California Press, 1985.

Belsky, Jay, and Lawrence D. Steinberg: "The Effects of Day Care: A Critical Review," *Child Development*, 1978, vol. 49, pp. 929–949.

Belson, W. A.: *Television and the Adolescent Boy.* London: Saxon House, 1978.

Bem, Sandra L.: "The Measurement of Psychological Androgyny," *Journal of Consulting and Clinical Psychology*, 1974, vol. 42, pp. 155–162.

Benedict, Ruth: *Patterns of Culture.* New York: Houghton Mifflin, 1961. Originally published 1934.

Benedict, Ruth: *The Chrysanthemum and the Sword.* Boston: Houghton Mifflin, 1946.

Bennett, John W.: *The Ecological Transition: Cultural Anthropology and Human Adaptation.* New York: Pergamon, 1976.

Bennis, Warren G.: *Changing Organizations.* New York: McGraw-Hill, 1966.

Bennis, Warren G. (ed.): *American Bureaucracy.* Chicago: Transaction Books, 1970.

Berelson, Bernard, and Patricia Salter: "Majority and Minority Americans: An Analysis of Magazine Fiction," *Public Opinion Quarterly*, 1946, vol. 10, pp. 168–190.

**696**

Berelson, Bernard, and Gary A. Steiner: *Human Behavior: An Inventory of Scientific Findings.* New York: Harcourt, Brace, and World, 1964.

Berger, Peter L.: *Invitation to Sociology: A Humanistic Perspective.* Garden City, N.Y.: Doubleday, 1963.

Berger, Peter L.: *The Capitalist Revolution.* New York: Basic Books, 1986.

Berger, Peter L., Brigette Berger, and Hansfried Kellner: *The Homeless Mind.* New York: Vintage, 1973.

Bergesen, Albert: *Studies of the Modern World-System.* New York: Academic Press, 1980.

Berk, Richard A.: "A Gaming Approach to Crowd Behavior," *American Journal of Sociology,* 1974, vol. 79, pp. 355–73.

Berk, Richard A., and Howard E. Aldrich: "Patterns of Vandalism During Civil Disorders as an Indicator of Selection of Targets," *American Sociological Review,* 1972, vol. 37, pp. 533–547.

Berk, Bernard B., and Victor Goertzel: "Selection versus Role Occupancy as Determinants of Role-Related Attitudes Among Psychiatric Aides," *Journal of Health and Social Behavior,* 1975, vol. 16, pp. 183–191.

Berkowitz, Leonard: "Is Criminal Violence Normative Behavior?" *Journal of Research in Crime and Delinquency,* 1978, vol. 15, pp. 148–161.

Berlin, Brent, and P. Kay: *Basic Color Terms: Their Universality and Evolution.* Berkeley, Calif.: University of California Press, 1969.

Bernard, Jessie: *The Female World.* New York: The Free Press, 1981.

Berrien, F. K.: *General and Social Systems.* New Brunswick, N.J.: Rutgers University Press, 1968.

Bertalanffy, Ludwig: *General System Theory.* New York: George Braziller, 1968.

Bettleheim, Bruno: "Individual and Mass Behavior in Extreme Situations," *Journal of Abnormal and Social Psychology,* 1943, vol. 38, pp. 417–452.

Bettleheim, Bruno: "Feral Children and Autistic Children," *American Journal of Sociology,* 1959, vol. 64, pp. 455–467.

Bierstedt, Robert: *The Social Order.* New York: McGraw-Hill, 1963. Rev. ed. 1974.

Black, Max: *The Social Theories of Talcott Parsons.* Englewood Cliffs, N.J.: Prentice-Hall, 1961.

Blau, Peter M.: *Exchange and Power in Social Life.* New York: Wiley, 1964.

Blau, Peter M.: "Theories of Organizations," *Encyclopedia of the Social Sciences.* New York: Macmillan, 1968.

Blau, Peter M., and Otis D. Duncan: *The American Occupational Structure.* New York: Wiley, 1967.

Blau, Peter M., and Marshall W. Meyer: *Bureaucracy in Modern Society.* 2d ed. New York: Random House, 1971.

Blauner, Robert: *Alienation and Freedom.* Chicago: University of Chicago Press, 1964.

Blauner, Robert: *Racial Oppression in America.* New York: Harper, 1972.

Block, Jack: "Some Enduring and Consequential Structures of Personality," in A. I. Rabin, Joel Aronoff, Andrew M. Barclay, and Robert A. Zucker (eds.). *Further Explorations in Personality.* New York: Wiley Interscience, 1981.

Blumberg, Abraham S.: *Criminal Justice: Issues and Ironics.* 2d ed. New York: New Viewpoints, 1979.

Blumer, Herbert: "Social Psychology," in Emerson P. Schmidt (ed.) *Man and Society.* New York: Prentice-Hall, 1939.

Blumer, Herbert: "Collective Behavior," in A. M. Lee (ed.) *Principles of Sociology,* New York: Barnes and Noble, 1951.

Blumer, Herbert: *Symbolic Interactionism: Perspective and Method.* Englewood Cliffs, N.J.: Prentice-Hall, 1969.

Bogardus, Emory S.: "A Social Distance Scale," *Sociology and Social Research,* 1933, vol. 17, pp. 265–271.

Bogardus, Emory S.: *Social Distance.* Yellow Springs, Ohio: Antioch Press, 1959.

Bogoras, Waldemar: *The Chukchee.* New York: AMS Press, 1975.

Booth, A., and S. Welch: "Crowding and Urban Crime Rates." Paper presented at the annual meeting of the Midwest Sociological Society, Omaha, Neb., 1974.

Borgatta, Edgar F., Arthur S. Couch, and Robert F. Bales: "Some Findings Relevant to the Great Man Theory of Leadership," in A. Paul Hare, Edgar F. Borgatta, and Robert F. Bales (eds.) *Small Groups: Studies in Social Interaction.* New York: Alfred Knopf, 1955.

Borgmann, Albert: *Technology and the Character of Contemporary Life.* Chicago: University of Chicago Press, 1984.

Bornstein, Marc H. (ed.): *Sensitive Periods in*

▼     *Development: Interdisciplinary Perspectives.* Hillsdale, N.J.: Lawrence Erlbaum Associates, 1987.

Boswell, Thomas D., and J. R. Curtis: *The Cuban-American Experience: Culture, Images, and Perspectives.* Totowa, N.J.: Rowman and Allanheld, 1983.

Bouchard, T. J., and M. McGue: "Familial Studies of Intelligence: A Review," *Science,* 1981, vol. 212, pp. 1055–59.

Boulding, Kenneth: *The World as a Total System.* Beverly Hills, Calif.: Sage Publications, 1985.

**698**    Bowlby, John: *Attachment and Loss.* New York: Basic Books, 1969.

Bowles, Samuel, and Herbert Gintis: *Schooling in Capitalist America: Educational Reform and the Contradictions of Economic Life.* New York: Basic Books, 1976.

Breed, Warren: "Occupational Mobility and Suicide Among White Males," *American Sociological Review,* 1963, vol. 28, pp. 179–188.

Brim, Orville G., Jr., and Jerome Kagan (eds.): *Constancy and Change in Human Development.* Cambridge, Mass.: Harvard University Press, 1980.

Bronfenbrenner, Urie: *Two Worlds of Childhood: U.S. and U.S.S.R.* New York: Russell Sage Foundation, 1970.

Bronfenbrenner, Urie. "The Origins of Alienation," *Scientific American,* 1974, vol. 21, pp. 53–61.

Brown, Roger: *Social Psychology.* New York: Free Press, 1965.

Bryce, James: *The American Commonwealth.* New York: Macmillan, 1910.

Buckle, Henry T.: *History of Civilization in England.* Fort Worth, Tex.: William S. Davis, 1987. Originally published 1857.

Buckner, H. Taylor: "A Theory of Rumor Transition," in Robert R. Evans (ed.) *Readings in Collective Behavior.* Chicago: Rand McNally, 1969.

Bulmer, Martin: *The Chicago School of Sociology.* Chicago: University of Chicago Press, 1984.

Burgess, Ernest W.: "The Growth of the City," in R. E. Park, E. W. Burgess, R. D. McKenzie, and L. Wirth (eds.) *The City.* Chicago: University of Chicago Press, 1925.

Burgess, R. L., and D. Bushell: *Behavioral Sociology.* New York: Columbia University Press, 1969.

Burma, John H.: "The Measurement of Negro Passing," *American Journal of Sociology,* 1946, vol. 52, pp. 18–22.

Byrne, Donn, William Grifft, and Daniel Stefaniak: "Attraction and Similarity of Personality Characteristics," *Journal of Personality and Social Psychology,* 1967, vol. 5, pp. 82–90.

Califano, Joseph A.: *America's Health Care Revolution.* New York: Random House, 1985.

Campbell, Ernest Q.: "Adolescent Socialization," in D. A. Goslin (ed.) *Handbook of Socialization Theory and Research.* Chicago: Rand McNally, 1969.

Candee, Dan: "Ego Developmental Aspects of New Left Ideology," *Journal of Personality and Social Psychology,* 1974, vol. 30, pp. 620–30.

Caplan, Arthur L. (ed.): *The Sociobiology Debate.* New York: Harper and Row, 1979.

Caplan, Nathan, and Jeffrey Paige: "A Study of Ghetto Rioters," *Scientific American,* 1968, vol. 219, pp. 15–21.

Caplow, Theodore, and Bruce A. Chadwick: "Inequality and Life-Styles in Middletown, 1920–1978," *Social Science Quarterly,* 1979, vol. 60, pp. 367–386.

Caplow, Theodore, Howard M. Bahr, Bruce A. Chadwick, Reuben Hill, and Margaret H. Williamson: *Middletown Families: Fifty Years of Change and Continuity.* Minneapolis: University of Minnesota Press, 1982.

Caplow, Theodore, Howard M. Bahr, and Bruce A. Chadwick: *All Faithful People: Change and Continuity in Middletown's Religion.* Minneapolis: University of Minnesota Press, 1983.

Carroll, John B., (ed.): *Language, Thought, and Reality: Selected Writings of Benjamin Lee Whorf.* Cambridge, Mass.: Massachusetts Institute of Technology Press, 1956.

Cattell, Raymond B.: "Personality and Motivation Theory Based on Structural Measurement," in J. L. McCary (ed.) *Psychology of Personality.* New York: Logos Press, 1956.

Cattell, Raymond W.: *Personality and Learning Theory.* New York: Springer, 1979.

Chamberlain, Houston Stuart: *The Foundations of the Nineteenth Century.* New York: H. Fertig, Inc., 1977. Originally published 1910.

Chambliss, William J., and Robert Seidman: *Law, Order and Power,* 2d ed.: Reading, Mass.: Addison-Wesley, 1982.

Champion, Dean J.: *The Sociology of Organizations.* New York: McGraw-Hill, 1975.

Chapin, F. Stuart: *Contemporary American Institutions.* New York: Harper and Row, Publishers, Inc., 1935.

Chirot, Daniel, and Thomas D. Hall: "World-System Theory," in Ralth H. Turner and James H. Short, Jr. (eds.) *Annual Review of Sociology.* Vol. 8. Palo Alto, Calif.: Annual Reviews, Inc., 1982.

Christie, Richard: "Scale Construction," in R. Christie and F. Geis (eds.): *Studies in Machiavellianism.* New York: Academic Press, 1970.

Christie, Richard, and Florence Geis (eds.): *Studies in Machivellianism.* New York: Academic Press, 1970.

Christie, Richard, and Marie Jahoda (eds.): *Studies in the Scope and Method of "The Authoritarian Personality."* Glencoe, Ill.: The Free Press, 1954.

Cicero: *De Republica.* 106–43 B.C.

Cicero: *De Legibus.* 106–43 B.C.

Clark, H. H., and E. V. Clark: *Psychology and Language: An Introduction to Psycholinguistics.* New York: Harcourt Brace Jovanovich, 1977.

Clark, R. D.: "Group-Induced Shift Toward Risk: A Critical Appraisal," *Psychological Bulletin,* 1971, vol. 76, pp. 251–270.

Clausen, John A.: "Perspectives on Childhood Socialization," in his *Socialization and Society,* Boston: Little Brown, 1968.

Clausen, John A.: *The Life Course: A Sociological Perspective.* Englewood Cliffs, N.J.: Prentice-Hall, 1986.

Cleckley, Hervey M.: *The Mask of Sanity.* St. Louis, Mo.: C. V. Mosby Co., 1976.

Clinard, Marshall: "The Role of Motivation and Self-Image in Social Change in Slum Areas," in Vernon L. Allen (ed.). *Psychological Factors in Poverty.* New York: Markham Publishing Company, 1970.

Clinard, Marshall B., and Peter C. Yeager: *Corporate Crime.* New York: Free Press, 1980.

Cloward, Richard A., and Lloyd E. Ohlin: *Delinquency and Opportunity.* New York: Free Press, 1960.

Coburn, David: "Job-Worker Incongruence: Consequences for Health," *Journal of Health and Social Behavior,* 1975, vol. 16, pp. 198–212.

Cochran, Moncrieff M., and Lars Gunnarson: "A Follow-Up Study of Group Day Care and Family-Based Childrearing Patterns," *Journal of Marriage and the Family,* 1985, vol. 47, pp. 297–309.

Cockerham, William C.: *Medical Sociology.* 3d ed. Englewood Cliffs, N.J.: Prentice-Hall, 1986.

Cohen, Albert K.: *Deviance and Control.* Englewood Cliffs, N.J.: Prentice-Hall, 1966.

Cohen, Albert K., and James F. Short: "Research in Delinquent Subcultures," *Journal of Social Issues,* 1958, vol. 14, pp. 20–37.

Cohen, Helen A., and Rivka Miller: "Mobility as a Factor in Adolescent Identity Problems," *Psychological Reports,* 1969, vol. 25, pp. 775–778.

Cohen, Morris R., and Ernest Nagel: *An Introduction to Logic and Scientific Method.* New York: Harcourt, Brace and Company, 1934.

Cole, Michael D.: *The Maya.* 3d ed. New York: Thames and Hudson, 1984.

Coleman, David, and Roger Schofield (eds.): *The State of Population Theory.* New York: Basil Blackwell, Inc., 1988.

Coleman, James: *The Adolescent Society.* New York: The Free Press, 1961.

Coleman, J., E. Campbell, J. McPartland, A. Mood, F. Weinfeld, and R. York: *Equality of Educational Opportunity.* Washington, D.C.: Government Printing Office, 1966.

Coleman, James W.: *The Criminal Elite: The Sociology of White Collar Crime.* New York: St. Martin's Press, 1985.

Coleman, Richard P., and Lee Rainwater: *Social Standing in America: New Dimensions of Class.* New York: Basic Books, 1978.

Collins, Randall: *Conflict Sociology.* New York: Academic Press, 1975.

Comstock, George, Steven Chaffee, Natan Katzman, Maxwell McCombs, and Donald Roberts: *Television and Human Behavior.* New York: Columbia University Press, 1978.

Comte, Auguste: *The Positive Philosophy.* New York: C. Blanchard Company, 1855. Originally published 1830–42.

Comte, Auguste: *System of Positive Polity.* London: Longmans, Green and Company, 1875–77. Originally published 1851–54.

Converse, Jean M.: *Survey Research in the United States.* Berkeley, Calif.: University of California Press, 1987.

Cooley, Charles H.: *Human Nature and the Social Order.* New York: Charles Scribner's Sons, 1902.

Cooley, Charles H.: *Social Organization.* New York: Charles Scribner's Sons, 1909.

▼ Cooley, Charles H.: *Social Process*. New York: Charles Scribner's Sons, 1918.

Coombs, C. H., L. C. Coombs, and G. H. McClelland: "Preference Scales for Number and Sex of Children," *Population Studies*, 1975, vol. 29, pp. 273–298.

Coopersmith, S.: *The Antecedents of Self-Esteem*. San Francisco: Freeman, 1967.

Cordes, Colleen: "Behavior Therapists Examine How Emotion, Cognition Relate," *Monitor*, February 1984, p. 18.

**700** Coser, Lewis A.: *The Functions of Social Conflict*. New York: Free Press, 1956.

Coser, Lewis A.: *Continuities in the Study of Social Conflict*. New York: Free Press, 1967.

Cox, Oliver: *Caste, Class, and Race: A Study in Social Dynamics*. Garden City, N. Y.: Doubleday, 1948.

Craig, Maude, and Selma Glick: *A Manual of Procedures for Application of the Glueck Prediction Table*. New York: Youth Board Research Institute, 1964.

Craik, Kenneth H., and George E. McKechnie (eds.): *Personality and the Environment*. Beverly Hills, Calif.: Sage, 1977.

Crain, Robert L., and Carol S. Wiseman: *Discrimination, Personality, and Achievement*. New York: Seminar Press, 1972.

Crano, William D., and Phyllis M. Mellon: "Causal Influence of Teachers' Expectancies on Children's Academic Performance: A Cross-Lagged Panel Analysis," *Journal of Educational Psychology*, 1978, vol. 70, pp. 39–49.

Crockett, Harry J.: "The Achievement Motive and Differential Mobility in the United States," *American Sociological Review*, 1962, vol. 27, pp. 191–204.

Crosbie, Paul V., (ed.): *Interaction in Small Groups*. New York: Macmillan, 1975.

Crull, Sue R., and Brent T. Bruton: "Bogardus Social Distance in the 1970s," *Sociology and Social Research*, 1979, vol. 63, pp. 771–783.

Crutchfield, Robert, Michael Geerken, and Walter R. Gove: "Crime Rates and Social Integration," *Criminology*, 1983, vol. 20, pp. 467–478.

Cumming, Elaine, and William Henry: *Growing Old: The Process of Disengagement*. New York: Basic Books, 1961.

Cunningham, Susan: "Chimps Use Sign Language to Talk to Each Other," American Psychological Association, *Monitor*, 1985, vol. 16, p. 11.

Curtiss, S.: *Genie: A Psycholinguistic Study of a Modern World "Wild Child."* New York: Academic Press, 1977.

Dahl, Robert: *Who Governs?* New Haven, Conn.: Yale University Press, 1961.

Dahl, Robert A.: *Democracy in the United States: Promise and Performance*. 4th ed. Boston: Houghton Mifflin, 1981.

Dahrendorf, Ralf: *Class and Class Conflict in Industrial Society*. Stanford, Calif.: Stanford University Press, 1959.

Dahrendorf, Ralf: "Towards a Theory of Social Conflict," in Amitai Etzioni and Eva Etzioni (eds.) *Social Change*. New York: Basic Books, Inc., 1964.

Danielson, Bengt: *Love in the South Seas*. New York: Renal and Co., 1956.

Danigelis, Nick, and Whitney Pope: "Durkheim's Theory of Suicide as Applied to a Family: An Empirical Test," *Social Forces*, 1979, vol. 57, pp. 1081–1103.

Darwin, Charles R.: *On the Origin of Species by Means of Natural Selection, or the Preservation of Favoured Races in the Struggle for Life*. London: Murray, 1859.

Datan, N., and L. H. Ginsberg (eds.): *Life Span Development Psychology: Normative Life Crises*. New York: Academic Press, 1975.

Davies, James C.: "Toward a Theory of Revolution," *American Sociological Review*, 1962, vol. 27, pp. 5–18.

Davis, Kingsley: "The Sociology of Prostitution," *American Sociological Review*, 1932, vol. 2, pp. 744–755.

Davis, Kingsley: "Final Note on a Case of Extreme Isolation," *American Journal of Sociology*, 1947, vol. 52, pp. 432–437.

Davis, Kingsley, and Wilbert Moore: "Some Principles of Stratification," *American Sociological Review*, 1945, vol. 10, pp. 242–249.

Deaux, Kay, and Lawrence S. Wrightsman: *Social Psychology in the 80's*, 4th ed. Monterey, Calif.: Brooks/Cole, 1983.

DeFronzo, James: "Embourgoisement in Indianapolis," *Social Problems*, 1974, vol. 21, pp. 269–283.

de Gobineau, Joseph A.: *Essay on the Inequality of Human Races*. New York: Garland Press, 1984. Originally published 1853–55.

de Luce, Judith, and Hugh T. Wilder: *Language in Primates*. New York: Springer-Verlag, 1983.

Descartes, Rene: *Discourse on Method.* 1637.

Despelder, Lynne Ann, and Albert Lee Strickland: *The Last Dance: Encountering Death and Dying.* Palo Alto, Calif.: Mayfield, 1983.

Deutscher, Irwin: "Socialization for Post-Parental Life," in Arnold M. Rose (ed.) *Human Behavior and Social Processes.* Boston: Houghton Mifflin, 1962.

DeVos, George A.: "The Passing of Passing: Ethnic Pluralism and the New Ideal in American Society," in Gordon J. DiRenzo (ed.) *We, the People: American Character and Social Change.* Westport, Conn.: Greenwood Press, 1977.

Dicks, Henry V.: "Personality Traits and National Socialist Ideology," *Human Relations,* 1950, vol. 3, pp. 111–154.

Dilling, H., and S. Weyerer: "Social Class and Mental Disorders: Results from Upper Bavaria Studies," in M. C. Angermeyer (ed.) *From Social Class to Social Stress.* Berlin: Springer-Verlag, 1987.

DiRenzo, Gordon J.: "Conceptual Definition in the Behavioral Sciences," in Gordon J. DiRenzo (ed.) *Concepts, Theory, and Explanation in the Behavioral Sciences.* New York: Random House, 1966a.

DiRenzo, Gordon J.: "Toward Explanation in the Behavioral Sciences," in Gordon J. DiRenzo (ed.) *Concepts, Theory, and Explanation in the Behavioral Sciences.* New York: Random House, 1966b.

DiRenzo, Gordon J.: *Personality, Power and Politics.* Notre Dame, Ind: University of Notre Dame Press, 1967a.

DiRenzo, Gordon J.: "The Role of Personality in Liturgical Change," *Worship,* 1967b, vol. 41, pp. 348–363.

DiRenzo, Gordon J. (ed.): *Personality and Politics.* New York: Doubleday, 1974a.

DiRenzo, Gordon J.: "Congruences in Personality Structure and Academic Curricula as Determinants of Occupational Careers," *Psychological Reports,* 1974b, vol. 34, pp. 1295–1298.

DiRenzo, Gordon J. (ed.): *We, The People: American Character and Social Change.* Westport, Conn: Greenwood Press, 1977a.

DiRenzo, Gordon J.: "Theoretical and Methodological Perspectives on the Study of Social Character," in Gordon J. DiRenzo (ed.) *We, The People: American Character and Social Change.* Westport, Conn.: Greenwood Press, 1977b.

DiRenzo, Gordon J.: "Politicians and Personality: A Cross-Cultural Perspective," in Margaret G. Hermann (ed.) *A Psychological Examination of Political Leaders.* New York: Free Press, 1977c.

DiRenzo, Gordon J.: "Socialization, Personality, and Social Systems," *Annual Review of Sociology,* 1977d, vol. 3, pp. 261–95.

DiRenzo, Gordon J.: "Personality Typologies and Modes of Social Change," *Social Behavior and Personality,* 1978, vol. 6, pp. 11–16.

DiRenzo, Gordon J.: "Probability and Law in Sociological Explanation," *Sociological Theory,* 1987, vol. 5, pp. 26–28.

DiRenzo, Gordon J.: "Socialization for Citizenship in Modern Democratic Society," in O. Ichilov (ed.) *Political Socialization for Democracy.* New York: Teachers College Press, Columbia University, 1990.

Dohrenwend, Bruce P.: "Social Status and Stressful Life Events," *Journal of Personality and Social Psychology,* 1973, vol. 28, pp. 225–35.

Dohrenwend, Bruce P.: "Socio-Cultural and Social-Psychological Factors in the Genesis of Mental Disorders," *Journal of Health and Social Behavior,* 1975, vol. 16, pp. 365–392.

Dohrenwend, Bruce P., and Barbara S. Dohrenwend: *Social Status and Psychological Disorder.* New York: Wiley, 1969.

Dohrenwend, Bruce P., and Barbara S. Dohrenwend: "Social and Cultural Differences on Psychopathology," *Annual Review of Psychology,* 1974, vol. 25, pp. 417–452.

Dollard, John, and Neal E. Miller: *Frustration and Aggression.* New Haven: Yale University Press, 1947.

Dollard, J., N. E. Miller, O. H. Doob, O. H. Mowrer, and R. R. Seers: *Frustration and Aggression.* New Haven, Conn.: Yale University Press, 1939.

Domhoff, G. William: *Who Rules America Now?* Englewood Cliffs, N.J.: Prentice-Hall, 1983.

Donne, John: "Meditation XVIII," from *Devotions upon Emergent Occasions.* 1624.

Doyle, Bertram W.: *The Etiquette of Race Relations in the South.* Chicago: University of Chicago Press, 1937.

DuBois, Cora: *The People of Alor.* Minneapolis: University of Minnesota Press, 1944.

Duijker, H. C. J., and N. H. Frijda: *National Character and National Stereotypes: A Trend Report Prepared for the International Union of Scientific Psychology.* Amsterdam: North Holland Publishing Company, 1960.

▼ Duncan, Otis, Beverly Otis, and D. L. Featherman: *Socio-Economic Background and Achievement.* New York: Seminar Press, 1972.

Dunham, Warren H.: *Sociological Theory and Mental Disorder.* Detroit: Wayne State University Press, 1959.

Durkheim, Emile: *The Division of Labor in Society.* New York: The Free Press, 1947. Originally published 1893.

Durkheim, Emile: *The Rules of Sociological Method.* New York: The Free Press, 1938. Originally published 1895.

Durkheim, Emile: *Suicide.* New York: The Free Press, 1964. Originally published 1897.

Dusek, Jerome B., (ed.): *Teacher Expectancies.* Hillsdale, N. J.: Erlbaum, 1985.

Dworkin, Anthony G.: "Stereotypes and Self Images Held by Native-Born and Foreign-Born Mexican Americans," *Sociology and Social Research*, 1965, vol. 49, pp. 214–224.

Eberstein, William: *Today's Isms.* Englewood Cliffs, N. J.: Prentice-Hall, 1980.

Edwards, A. L.: "Social Desirability and the Description of Others," *Journal of Abnormal and Social Psychology*, 1959, vol. 59, pp. 434–436.

Edwards, Harry: *Black Students.* New York: Free Press, 1970.

Eells, Richard, and Clarence Walton (eds.): *Man in the City of the Future.* New York: Macmillan, 1969.

Ehrlich, Paul R.: *The Population Bomb.* New York: Ballantine Books, 1968.

Ehrlich, Paul R.: "The Population Explosion," in Gerald Sicard and Philip Weinberger (eds.) *Sociology for Our Times.* Glenview, Ill.: Scott, Foresman, 1977.

Eisenstadt, S. N.: "The Process of Absorption of New Immigrants in Israel," *Human Relations*, 1952, vol. 5, pp. 223–246.

Eisenstadt, S. N., and H. J. Helle: *Perspectives on Sociological Theory.* Vols. 1 and 2. Newbury Park, Calif.: Sage Publications, 1985.

Einstein, Albert: "On the Electrodynamics of Moving Bodies," *Annalen der Physik*, 1905, vol. 17, p. 891ff.

Einstein, Albert: "Albert Einstein: Philosopher-Scientist," in Paul A. Schlipp (ed.): *The Library of Living Philosophers.* Evanston, Ill.: Northwestern University Press, 1949.

Eitzen, D. Stanley: "Status Inconsistency and Wallace Supporters in Midwestern City," *Social Forces*, 1970, vol. 48, pp. 493–498.

Elder, Glen H.: "Occupational Mobility, Life Patterns and Personality," *Journal of Health and Social Behavior*, 1969, vol. 10, pp. 308–322.

Elder, Glen H.: *Children of the Great Depression.* Chicago: University of Chicago Press, 1974.

Elder, Glen H.: *Life Course Dynamics: Trajectories and Transitions, 1968–1980.* Ithaca, N. Y.: Cornell University Press, 1985.

Elkin, Frederick, and Gerald Handel: *The Child and Society: The Process of Socialization.* 4th ed. New York: Random House, 1984.

Elkind, David: *All Grown Up and No Place to Go: Teenagers in Crisis.* Reading, Mass.: Addison-Wesley, 1984.

Ellis, Albert: "Rational-Emotive Theory," in A. Burton (ed.) *Operational Theories of Personality.* New York: Brunner/Mazel, 1974.

Ellis, Godfrey J., Gary R. Lee, and Larry R. Petersen: "Supervision and Conformity: A Cross-Cultural Analysis of Parental Socialization Values," *American Journal of Sociology*, 1978, vol. 84, pp. 386–403.

Ellul, J.: *The Technological Society.* New York: Alfred A. Knopf, 1964.

Ellwood Charles A.: *Sociology in Its Psychological Aspects.* New York: Appleton, 1912.

Elster, John (ed.): *The Multiple Self.* New York: Cambridge University Press, 1988.

Encyclopaedia Britannica: *Britannica Book of the Year, 1989.* Chicago: Encyclopaedia Britannica, Inc., 1989.

Erikson, Erik H.: *Childhood and Society.* New York: W. W. Norton, 1950. Rev. ed., 1964.

Erikson, Erik H.: *Identity, Youth, and Crisis.* New York: W. W. Norton, 1968.

Erikson, Erik H.: *The Life Cycle Completed: A Review.* New York: W. W. Norton and Company, 1982.

Erikson, Kai: *Wayward Puritans.* New York: Wiley, 1966.

Erikson, Kai: *Everything in Its Path.* New York: Simon and Schuster, 1976.

Erlanger, Howard S.: "Social Class and Corporal Punishment in Child Rearing: A Reassessment," *American Sociological Review*, 1974, vol. 39, pp. 68–85.

Ermann, David M., and Richard J. Lundman: *Corporate and Governmental Deviance: Problems of Organizational Behavior in Contemporary Society. 3d ed. New York: Oxford University Press, 1987.

Etzioni, Amitai: "Basic Human Needs, Alienation, and Inauthenticity," *American Sociological Review*, 1968a, vol. 32, pp. 870–885.

Etzioni, Amitai: *The Active Society*. New York: Macmillan, 1968b.

Etzioni, Amitai: *A Comparative Analysis of Complex Organizations*. Rev. ed. New York: Free Press, 1975.

Etzioni, Amitai: "Basic Characterological Needs and Changing Social Systems," in Gordon J. DiRenzo (ed.) *We, The People: American Character and Social Change*. Westport, Conn.: Greenwood Press, 1977.

Etzioni, Amitai: *An Immodest Agenda: Rebuilding America Before the Twenty-First Century*. New York: McGraw-Hill, 1982.

Eulau, Hans: "Identification with Class and Political Role Behavior," *Public Opinion Quarterly*, 1956, vol. 20, pp. 515–529.

Evans, Bergen: *The Natural History of Nonsense*. New York: Alfred A. Knopf, 1946.

Evans, Sue L., John B. Rinehart, and Ruth A. Succop: "Failure to Thrive: A Study of 45 Children and their Families," *Journal of Child Psychiatry*, 1972, vol. 11, pp. 440–457.

Eysenck, Hans J.: *Dimensions of Personality*. London: Kegan Paul, 1947.

Eysenck, Hans J.: *The Biological Basis of Personality*. Springfield, Ill.: Charles C. Thomas, 1967.

Fagot, Beverly I., and Gerald R. Patterson: "An In-Vivo Analysis of Reinforcing Contingencies for Sex-Role Behaviors in the Preschool Child," *Developmental Psychology*, 1969, vol. 1, pp. 563–568.

Farb, Peter: *Word Play*. New York: Alfred Knopf, 1973.

Faris, Robert E. L., and H. Warren Dunham: *Mental Disorders in Urban Areas*. Chicago: University of Chicago Press, 1939.

Farley, Reynolds: "Trends in Racial Inequalities: Have the Gains of the 1960s Disappeared in the 1970s?" *American Sociological Review*, 1977, vol. 42, pp. 189–208.

Feagin, Joe R., and Clairece Booker Feagin: *Discrimination American Style: Institutional Racism and Sexism*. Englewood Cliffs, N. J.: Prentice-Hall, 1978.

Festinger, Leon: *A Theory of Cognitive Dissonance*. New York: Harper and Row, 1957.

Festinger, L., A. Pepitone, and T. Newcomb: "Some Consequences of De-Individuation in a Group," *Journal of Abnormal and Social Psychology*, 1952, vol. 47, pp. 382–389.

Festinger, Leon, Stanley Schachter, and Kurt Back: *Social Pressures in Informal Groups*. New York: Harper, 1950.

Fine, Gary A.: *With the Boys: Little League Baseball and Preadolescent Culture*. Chicago: University of Chicago Press, 1987.

Fischer, Claude S.: *To Dwell Among Friends: Personal Networks in Town and City*. Chicago: University of Chicago Press, 1982.

Fischer, Claude S.: *The Urban Experience: A Social Psychological View*. 2d. ed. New York: Harcourt Brace Jovanovich, 1984.

Fisher, Seymour, and Roger P. Greenberg: *The Scientific Credibility of Freud's Theories and Therapy*. New York: Basic Books, 1977.

Fox, Thomas G., and S. M. Miller: "Economic, Political, and Social Determinants of Mobility," *Acta Sociologica*, 1965, vol. 9, pp. 76–93.

Freedman, Jonathan L.: *Crowding and Behavior*. San Francisco: W. H. Freeman and Company, 1975.

Freedman, R., and B. Berelson: "The Human Population," *Scientific American*, 1974, vol. 231, pp. 22, 30–39.

Freeman, Derek: *Margaret Mead and Samoa: The Making and Unmaking of an Anthropological Myth*. Cambridge, Mass.: Harvard University Press, 1983.

Frenkel-Brunswik, Else: "Intolerance of Ambiguity as an Emotional and Personality Variable," *Journal of Personality*, 1949, vol. 18, pp. 108–143.

Frenkel-Brunswik, Else: "Interaction of Psychological and Sociological Factors in Political Behavior," *American Political Science Review*, 1952, vol. 46, pp. 44–56.

Freud, Sigmund: *The Ego and the Id*. Vol. 19. London: Hogarth, 1947. Originally published 1923.

Freud, Sigmund: *The Basic Writings of Sigmund Freud*. Edited by A. A. Brill. New York: Random House, 1938.

Friedman, Meyer, and Ray Rosenman: *Type A Behavior and Your Heart*. New York: Alfred A. Knopf, 1974.

▼ Friedman, Meyer, and Diane Ulmer: *Treating Type A Behavior and Your Heart*. New York: Alfred A. Knopf, 1984.

Friedrich, Carl J., and Zbigniew Brzezinski: *Totalitarian Dictatorships and Autocracy*. Cambridge, Mass.: Harvard University Press, 1965.

Frith, Simon: *Sound Effects: Youth, Leisure, and the Politics of Rock 'n' Roll*. New York: Pantheon, 1982.

Fritz, Jan: *The Clinical Sociology Handbook*. New York: Garland, 1985.

**704** Fromkin, V., S. Krashen, S. Curtiss, D. Rigler, and M. Rigler: "The Development of Language in Genie: A Case of Language Acquisition Beyond the Critical Period," *Brain and Language*, 1974, vol. 1, pp. 81–107.

Fromm, Erich: "A Social-Psychological Approach to 'Authority and Family'," in M. Horkheimer (ed.) *Studien über Authorität und Familie*. Paris: Librarie Felix Alcan, 1936.

Fromm, Erich: *Escape from Freedom*. New York: Holt, Rinehart and Winston, 1941.

Fromm, Erich: "The Individual and Social Origins of Neurosis," *American Sociological Review*, 1944, vol. 9, pp. 380–384.

Fromm, Erich: *Man for Himself: An Inquiry into the Psychology of Ethics*. New York: Rinehart and Company, 1947.

Furfey, Paul H.: *The Method and Scope of Sociology*. New York: Harper and Brothers, 1953.

Furth, Hans: *Piaget and Knowledge*. Englewood Cliffs, N. J.: Prentice-Hall, 1969.

Gagnon, John, and William Simon: *Sexual Conduct: The Social Sources of Human Sexuality*. Chicago: Aldine, 1973.

Gale Research Company: "National Organizations of the United States," *The Encyclopedia of Associations*. Vol. 1, 21st ed. Detroit, 1987.

Gallup, Gordon G.: "Self-Awareness in Primates," *American Scientist*, 1979, vol. 67, no. 4, pp. 417–421.

Gamson, William A.: *The Strategy of Social Protest*. Homewood, Ill.: Dorsey Press, 1975.

Gans, Herbert: *The Urban Villagers*. New York: Free Press, 1982. Originally published 1962.

Gans, Herbert J.: *Middle American Individualism*. New York: The Free Press, 1988.

Garfinkel, Harold: *Studies in Ethnomethodology*. Englewood Cliffs, N. J.: Prentice-Hall, 1967.

Geiger, H. Kent: *The Family in the Soviet Union*. Cambridge, Mass.: Harvard University Press, 1968.

Gergen, Kenneth J.: "The Decline of Character: Socialization and Self-Consistency," in Gordon J. DiRenzo (ed.) *We, The People: American Character and Social Change*. Westport, Conn.: Greenwood Press, 1977.

Gergen, Kenneth J., Mary M. Gergen, and William Barton: "Deviance in the Dark," *Psychology Today*, 1973, vol. 7, no. 5, pp. 129–131.

Gerson, Lowell W.: "Punishment and Position: The Sanctioning of Deviants in Small Groups," *Case Western Reserve Journal of Sociology*, 1967, vol. 1, pp. 54–62.

Ghiselli, E. E., and T. M. Lodahl: "Patterns of Managerial Traits and Group Effectiveness," *Journal of Abnormal and Social Psychology*, 1958, vol. 57, pp. 61–66.

Gibb, Cecil A.: "Leadership," in Gardner Lindzey and E. Aronson (eds.) *Handbook of Social Psychology*. Reading, Mass.: Addison-Wesley, 1969.

Gibbs, Jack P.: "Status Integration and Suicide Rates," *American Sociological Review*, 1982, vol. 47, pp. 227–237.

Gibbs, Jack P., and W. T. Martin: "A Theory of Status Integration and Its Relationship to Suicide," *American Sociological Review*, 1962, vol. 27, pp. 469–80.

Gibbs, Jack P., and Walter T. Martin: *Status Integration and Suicide*. Eugene: University of Oregon Books, 1964.

Giddings, Franklin H.: *Principles of Sociology*. New York: The Macmillan Co., 1896.

Giddings, Franklin H.: *Elements of Sociology*. New York: The Macmillan Co., 1898.

Gilbert, Dennis, and Joseph A. Kahl: *The American Class Structure*. 3d ed. Chicago: The Dorsey Press, 1987.

Gilbert, Doris C., and Daniel J. Levinson: "Ideology, Personality, and Institutional Policy in the Mental Hospital," *Journal of Abnormal and Social Psychology*, 1950, vol. 53, pp. 263–271.

Glaser, Daniel: *The Effectiveness of a Prison and Parole System*. New York: Bobbs-Merrill, 1964.

Glaser, Daniel: "The Classification of Offenses and Offenders," in D. Glaser (ed.) *Handbook of Criminology*. Chicago: Rand McNally College Publishing Co., 1974.

Glaser, Daniel: *Crime in Our Changing Society.* New York: Holt, Rinehart and Winston, 1978.

Gleitman, L. R., and H. Gleitman: "Language," in H. Gleitman (ed.) *Psychology.* New York: Norton, 1981.

Glock, Charles Y.: "The Role of Deprivation in the Origin and Evolution of Religious Groups," in Robert Lee and Martin Marty (eds.) *Religions and Social Conflict.* New York: Oxford University Press, 1964.

Glueck, Eleanor, and Sheldon Glueck: *Unravelling Juvenile Delinquency.* Cambridge, Mass.: Harvard University Press, 1950.

Goffman, Erving: *The Presentation of Self in Everyday Life.* New York: Doubleday, 1959.

Goffman, Erving: *Asylums.* Garden City, N. Y.: Doubleday/Anchor, 1961a.

Goffman, Erving: *Encounters: Two Studies in the Sociology of Interaction.* Indianapolis, Ind.: Bobbs-Merrill, 1961b.

Goffman, Erving: *Stigma.* Englewood Cliffs, N. J.: Prentice-Hall, 1963.

Goffman, Erving: *Interaction Ritual: Essays on Face-to-Face Behavior.* Garden City and New York: Doubleday/Anchor, 1967.

Goffman, Erving: *Relations in Public.* New York: Basic Books, 1971.

Goldfarb, William: "Psychological Privation in Infancy and Subsequent Adjustment," *American Journal of Orthopsychiatry,* 1945, vol. 15, pp. 247–255.

Goldstone, Jack A.: "The Comparative and Historical Study of Revolutions," in J. A. Goldstone (ed.) *Revolution.* San Diego: Harcourt Brace Jovanovich, 1986.

Good, Thomas L., and Jere E. Brophy: *Looking in Classrooms.* New York: Harper and Row, 1973.

Goode, William J.: "A Theory of Role Strain," *American Sociological Review,* 1960, vol. 25, pp. 483–496.

Goodman, Ann B., Carole Siegel, Thomas J. Craig, and Shang P. Lin: "The Relationship between Socioeconomic Class and Prevalence of Schizophrenia, Alcoholism, and Affective Disorders Treated by Inpatient Care in a Suburban Area," *American Journal of Sociology,* 1983, vol. 140, pp. 166–170.

Gordon, C. Wayne: *The Social System of the High School.* New York: The Free Press, 1957.

Gordon, David M.: "Capitalism and the Roots of Urban Crisis," in Roger A. Alcaly and David Mermelstein (eds.) *The Fiscal Crisis of American Cities.* New York: Vintage Press, 1977.

Gordon, Steven L.: "The Sociology of Sentiments and Emotions," in Morris Rosenberg and Ralph H. Turner (eds.) *Social Psychology: Sociological Perspectives.* New York: Basic Books, 1981.

Gorer, Geoffrey: *The American People: A Study in National Character.* New York: W. W. Norton Co., 1948.

Goring, Charles: *The English Convict.* London: His Majesty's Stationery Office, 1913.

Gould, H.: "Caste and Class: A Comparative View," *Module,* 1971, vol. 11, pp. 1–24.

Gouldner, Alvin: *The Coming Crisis of Western Sociology.* New York: Basic Books, 1970.

Gove, Walter R., (ed.): *The Labelling of Deviance: Evaluating a Perspective.* 2d ed. Beverly Hills, Calif.: Sage Publications, 1980.

Grebler, Leo, Joan Moore, and Ralph Guzman: *The Mexican-American People.* New York: Free Press, 1970.

Greeley, Andrew: *Unsecular Man.* New York: Schocken Books, 1972.

Greeley, Andrew M.: *Religious Change in America.* Cambridge, Mass.: Harvard University Press, 1989.

Greenberg, Bradley S.: "Person-to-Person Communication in the Diffusion of News Events," *Journalism Quarterly,* 1964, vol. 41, pp. 489–494.

Greenberg, B.S., and B. Dervin: *Uses of Mass Media by the Poor.* New York: Praeger, 1970.

Greenberg, David F.: "The Correctional Effects of Corrections: A Survey of Evaluations," in David F. Greenberg (ed.) *Corrections and Punishment.* Beverly Hills, Calif.: Sage, 1977.

Groth, A. Nicholas, and H. Jean Birnbaum: *Men Who Rape: The Psychology of the Offender.* New York, Plenum Press, 1979.

Gruen, G., J. Korte, and J. Baum: "Group Measure of Locus of Control," *Developmental Psychology,* 1974, vol. 10, pp. 683–686.

Grusky, David B., and Robert M. Hauser: "Comparative Social Mobility Revisited: Models of Convergence and Divergence in Sixteen Countries," *American Sociological Review,* 1984, vol. 49, pp. 19–38.

Guilford, J. P.: *The Nature of Human Intelligence.* New York: McGraw-Hill, 1967.

▼

**705**

▼ Guilford, J. P., and Ralph Hoepfner: *The Analysis of Intelligence.* New York: McGraw-Hill, 1971.

Gumplowicz, Ludwig: *The Outlines of Sociology.* Philadelphia: American Academy of Political and Social Science, 1899.

Gurr, Ted R.: *Why Men Rebel.* Princeton N. J.: Princeton University Press, 1970.

Guterman, Stanley S., (ed.): *Black Psyche: The Modal Personality Patterns of Black Americans.* Berkeley, Calif.: Glendessary Press, 1972.

**706** Gutierrez, Armando, and Herbert Hirsch: "The Militant Challenge to the American Ethos: 'Chicanos' and 'Mexican Americans'," in C. A. Hernandez, M. J. Haug, and N. N. Wagner (eds.) *Chicanos: Social and Psychological Perspectives.* St Louis, Mo.: C. V. Mosby, 1971.

Guttentag, Marcia, and Paul F. Secord: *Too Many Women? The Sex Ratio Question.* Beverly Hills, Calif.: Sage, 1983.

Haan, Norma, M. Brewster Smith, and Jeanne Block: "Moral Reasoning of Young Adults: Political and Social Behavior, Family Background and Personality Correlates," *Journal of Personality and Social Psychology,* 1968, vol. 10, pp. 183–201.

Haas, Jack: "The Stages of the High-Steel Ironworker Apprentice Career," *The Sociological Quarterly,* 1974, vol. 15, pp. 93–107.

Hacker, Helen M.: "Women as a Minority Group: Twenty Years Later," in Florence Denmark (ed.) *Who Discriminates Against Women?* Beverly Hills, Calif.: Sage, 1974.

Hadden, Jeffrey K., and C. E. Swann: *Prime Time Preachers: The Rising Power of Televangelism.* Reading, Mass.: Addison-Wesley, 1981.

Hagen, Everett C.: *On the Theory of Social Change.* Homewood, Ill.: Dorsey Press, 1962.

Hall, Calvin S., and Gardner Lindzey: *Theories of Personality.* New York: John Wiley and Sons, 1978.

Hall, Elizabeth: "China's Only Child," *Psychology Today,* 1987, vol. 21, pp. 45–47.

Hall, J.: "Decisions, Decisions, Decisions," *Psychology Today,* 1971, vol. 5, pp. 51–54ff.

Haller, A. Q.: "A Correlation Analysis of the Relationship between Status and Personality." Ph.D. diss., University of Wisconsin, 1954.

Haller, Archibald, and David Lewis: "The Hypothesis of International Similarity in Occupational Prestige Hierarchies," *American Journal of Sociology,* 1966, vol. 72, pp. 210–216.

Hamblin, Robert (ed.): *The Humanization Process: A Social, Behavioral Analysis of Children's Problems.* New York: Wiley, 1971.

Handel, Warren: *Ethnomethodology: How People Make Sense.* Englewood Cliffs, N. J.: Prentice-Hall, 1982.

Handlin, Oscar: *The Uprooted.* Boston: Little, Brown, 1951.

Hanks, Michael: "Youth, Voluntary Associations and Political Socialization," *Social Forces,* 1981, vol. 60, pp. 211–223.

Hardesty, Donald L.: *Ecological Anthropology.* New York: Wiley, 1977.

Hare, A. Paul: *Handbook of Small Group Research.* 2d ed. New York: Free Press, 1976.

Harris, Chauncey D., and Edward L. Ullman: "The Nature of Cities," *Annals of the American Academy of Political and Social Sciences,* 1945, vol. 242, pp. 7–17.

Harris, Dona, and Paul Ebbert: "Personality Types of Family Practice Residents as Measured by the Myers-Briggs Type Indicator," *Family Medicine,* 1985, vol. 27, pp. 8–10.

Harris, Marvin: *Cannibals and Kings: The Origins of Culture.* New York: Random House, 1977.

Harris, Marvin: *Cultural Materialism.* New York: Random House, 1979.

Harris, Marvin: *America Now: The Anthropology of a Changing Culture.* New York: Simon and Schuster, 1981.

Harris, Marvin: *Good to Eat: Riddles of Food and Culture.* New York: Simon and Schuster, 1985.

Hartley, Eugene L.: *Problems in Prejudice.* New York: Columbia University Press, 1946.

Hauser, Robert M., and David L. Featherman: *The Process of Stratification: Trends and Analysis.* New York: Academic Press, 1977.

Hauskinecht, Murray: *The Joiners: A Sociological Description of Voluntary Association Membership in the United States.* New York: Bedminister Press, 1962.

Hawley, Amos: *Urban Society: An Ecological Approach.* 2d ed. New York: Wiley, 1981.

Hawley, Amos H.: *Human Ecology: A Theoretical Essay.* Chicago: University of Chicago Press, 1986.

Hegel, Georg: *Philosophy of Right*. London: Bell, 1896. Originally published 1821.

Hegel, Georg: *Philosophy of History*. New York: P. F. Collier, 1900. Originally published 1837.

Heilbroner, Robert: *An Inquiry into the Human Prospect*. New York: Norton, 1980.

Heiliger, Wilhelm S.: *Soviet and Chinese Personalities*. Lanham, Md.: University Press of America, 1980.

Heisenberg, Werner: *Nuclear Physics*. New York: Philosophical Library, 1953.

Henry, Andrew F., and James F. Short: *Suicide and Homicide*. New York: Free Press, 1954.

Herlemann, Horst G.: *The Quality of Life in the Soviet Union*. Boulder, Colo.: Westview Press, 1986.

Hermann, Margaret G.: "Assessing the Personalities of Soviet Politburo Members," *Personality and Social Psychology Bulletin*, 1980, vol. 6, pp. 332–352.

Hernandez, Carol A., Marsha J. Haug, and Nathaniel N. Wagner (eds.): *Chicanos: Social and Psychological Perspectives*. St Louis, Mo.: C. V. Mosby Company, 1971.

Hill, Jane H.: "Apes and Language," *Annual Review of Anthropology*. Vol. 7. Palo Alto, Calif.: Annual Reviews Inc., 1978.

Hitt, William D.: "Two Models of Man," *American Psychologist*, 1969, vol. 24, pp. 651–658.

Hobbes, Thomas: *The Leviathan*. London: Royston, 1651.

Hodge, Robert W., and Donald J. Treiman: "Class Identification in the United States," *American Journal of Sociology*, 1968, vol. 73, pp. 535–547.

Hodge, Robert, D. Treiman, and P. Rossi: "A Comparative Study of Occupational Prestige," in R. Bendix and S. Lipset (eds.) *Class, Status, and Power*. New York: The Free Press, 1966.

Hoffer, Eric: *The True Believer: Thoughts on the Nature of Mass Movements*. New York: Harper and Brothers, 1951.

Hoffman, L. R.: "Homogeneity of Member Personality and Its Effect on Group Problem-Solving," *Journal of Abnormal and Social Psychology*, 1959, vol. 58, pp. 27–32.

Hoffman, L. R., and N. R. F. Maier: "Quality and Acceptance of Problem Solutions by Members of Homogeneous and Heterogeneous Groups," *Journal of Abnormal and Social Psychology*, 1961, vol. 62, pp. 401–407.

Hofstadter, Richard: *Social Darwinism in American Thought*. Rev. ed. New York: George Braziller, Inc., 1955.

Hoijer, Harry: *A Navajo Lexicon*. Berkeley, Calif.: University of California, 1974.

Hollander, Edwin P.: "Conformity, Status, and Idiosyncrasy Credit," *Psychological Review*, 1958, vol. 65, pp. 117–127.

Hollander, Paul: "Research on Marxist Societies: The Relationship Between Theory and Practice," *Annual Review of Sociology*. Vol. 8. Palo Alto, Calif.: Annual Reviews, Inc., 1982.

Hollingshead, A. B.: *Elmtown's Youth*. New York: Wiley, 1949.

Hollingshead, A. B., and F. Redlich: *Social Class and Mental Illness*. New York: Wiley, 1958.

Holtzman, W. H., R. Diaz-Guerrero, and J. D. Swartz: *Personality Development in Two Cultures*. Austin, Tex.: University of Texas Press, 1975.

Homans, George C.: *The Human Group*. New York: Harcourt, Brace, and World, 1950.

Homans, George C.: *Social Behavior: Its Elementary Forms*. 2d ed. New York: Harcourt, Brace, and World, 1974.

Honigman, John J.: *Understanding Culture*. New York: Harper and Row, 1963.

Hope, Keith: "Vertical and Nonvertical Class Mobility in Three Countries," *American Sociological Review*, 1982, vol. 47, pp. 99–113.

Horn, Gabriel: *Memory, Imprinting, and the Brain: An Inquiry into Mechanisms*. New York: Oxford University Press, 1985.

Horney, Karen: *The Neurotic Personality of Our Time*. New York: W. W. Norton, 1937.

Hostetler, John A.: *Amish Society*. Baltimore: Johns Hopkins University Press, 1980.

House, James S.: "Occupational Stress and Coronary Heart Disease: A Review and Theoretical Integration," *Journal of Health and Social Behavior*, 1974, vol. 15, pp. 12–27.

House, James S.: "Social Structure and Personality," in Morris Rosenberg and Ralph H. Turner (eds.) *Social Psychology: Sociological Perspectives*. New York: Basic Books, Inc., 1981.

Hoyt, Homer: *The Structure and Growth of Residential Neighborhoods in American Cities*. Washington: Federal Housing Administration, 1939.

Hsu, Francis L. K.: "Individual Fulfillment, Social

▼ Stability, and Cultural Progress," in Gordon J. DiRenzo (ed.) *We, The People: American Character and Social Change*. Westport, Conn.: Greenwood Press, 1977.

Hughes, Everett C.: "Personality Types and the Division of Labor," *American Journal of Sociology*, 1928, vol. 33, pp. 754–768.

Hughes, Everett C.: "Work and Self," in J. H. Rohrer and Musafer Sherif (eds.) *Social Psychology at the Crossroads*. New York, Harper and Row, Publishers, Inc., 1951.

**708**  Hume, David: *Treatise of Human Nature*. London: Noon, 1739.

Humphrey, J. A., and M. E. Milakovich: *The Administration of Justice*. New York: Human Sciences Press, 1981.

Humphreys, Laud: *Tearoom Trade: Impersonal Sex in Public Places*. Chicago: Aldine, 1975.

Hunter, Floyd: *Community Power Structure*. Chapel Hill, N. C.: University of North Carolina Press, 1953.

Huntington, Ellsworth: *Mainsprings of Civilization*. New York: Arno Press, 1972. Originally published 1945.

Hutton, J. H.: *Caste in India: Its Nature, Functions and Origins*. New York: Oxford University Press, 1963.

Hyman, Herbert H.: "The Value Systems of Different Classes: A Social-Psychological Contribution to the Analysis of Stratification," in R. Bendix and S. M. Lipset (eds.) *Class, Status, and Power*. New York: Free Press, 1953.

Inglehart, Ronald: *The Silent Revolution*. Princeton: N. J.: Princeton University Press, 1976.

Inkeles, Alex: "Industrial Man: The Relation of Status to Experience, Perception, and Value," *American Journal of Sociology*, 1960, vol. 66, pp. 1–31.

Inkeles, Alex: "National Character and Modern Political Systems," in Francis L. K. Hsu (ed.) *Psychological Anthropology*. Homewood, Ill.: Dorsey Press, 1961.

Inkeles, Alex: "The Modernization of Man," in Myron Weiner (ed.) *Modernization: The Dynamics of Growth*. New York: Basic Books, 1966.

Inkeles, Alex: "Social Stratification and Mobility in the Soviet Union," in Reinhard Bendix and Seymour Martin Lipset (eds.) *Class, Status, and Power*. Glencoe, Ill.: The Free Press, 1968.

Inkeles, Alex: "Continuity and Change in the Interaction of the Personal and the Sociocultural Systems," in Bernard Barber and Alex Inkeles, *Stability and Social Change*. Boston: Little, Brown, and Company, 1971.

Inkeles, Alex: "Becoming Modern: Individual Change in Six Developing Countries," *Ethos*, 1975, vol. 3, pp. 323–42.

Inkeles, Alex: "Continuity and Change in the American National Character," in S. M. Lipset (ed.) *The Third Century: America as a Post-Industrial Society*. Stanford, Calif.: Hoover Institution Press, 1978.

Inkeles, Alex: "Studying the World System," *Bulletin of the American Academy of Arts and Sciences*, 1979, vol. 23, pp. 30–31.

Inkeles, Alex: *Exploring Individual Modernity*. New York: Columbia University Press, 1983.

Inkeles, Alex, E. Hanfmann, and H. Beier: "Modal Personality and Adjustment to the Soviet Socio-Political System," *Human Relations*, 1958, vol. 11, pp. 3–22.

Inkeles, Alex, and Daniel J. Levinson: "National Character: The Study of Modal Personality and Socio-Cultural Systems," in Gardner Lindzey and Elliott Aronson (eds.) *Handbook of Social Psychology*. Reading, Mass.: Addison-Wesley, 1969.

Inkeles, Alex, and David H. Smith: "The Fate of Personal Adjustment in the Process of Modernization," *International Journal of Comparative Sociology*, 1974a, vol. 15, pp. 81–114.

Inkeles, Alex and David H. Smith: *Becoming Modern: Individual Change in Six Developing Countries*. Cambridge, Mass.: Harvard University Press, 1974b.

Ismael, J.S., and T.Y. Ismael: "Social Change in Islamic Society: The Political Thought of the Ayatollah Khomeini," *Social Problems*, 1980, vol. 64, pp. 714–732.

Israel, Joachim: *Alienation: From Marx to Modern Society*. Boston: Allyn and Bacon, 1971.

Jackman, Mary R., and Robert W. Jackman: *Class Awareness in the United States*. Berkeley, Calif.: University of California Press, 1983.

Jackson, Elton F.: "Status Consistency and Symptoms of Stress," *American Sociological Review*, 1962, vol. 27, pp. 469–480.

Jacobson, C. K.: "The Saliency of Personal Control and Racial Separatism for Black and White Southern Students," *Psychological Record*, 1975, vol. 25, pp. 243–253.

Jacquet, Constant H.: *Yearbook of American and Canadian Churches*. Nashville, Tenn.: Abingdon Press, 1987.

James, William: *Principles of Psychology*. New York: Holt, 1890.

Janis, Irving L.: "Counteracting the Adverse Effects of Concurrence-Seeking in Policy-Planning Groups: Theory and Research Perspectives," in I. H. Brandstatter, J. H. Davis, and G. Stocker-Kreichgauer (eds.) *Group Decision Making*. New York: Academic Press, 1982.

Janis, Irving L.: *Groupthink: Psychological Studies of Policy Decisions and Fiascoes*. 2d ed. Boston: Houghton Mifflin Co., 1983.

Jeffrey, C. R.: "Criminal Behavior and Learning Theory," *Journal of Criminal Law, Criminology, and Police Science*, 1965, vol. 56, pp. 294–300.

Jencks, Christopher: *Who Gets Ahead: The Determinants of Economic Success in America*. New York: Basic Books, 1979.

Jencks, Christopher, M. Smith, H. Aeland, M. Bane, D. Cohen, H. Gintis, B. Heyns, and S. Michaelson: *Inequality: A Reassessment of the Effect of Family and Schooling in America*. New York: Basic Books, 1972.

Jenkins, Craig J.: "Resource Mobilization Theory and the Study of Social Movements," in Ralph H. Turner and James F. Short, Jr. (eds.) *Annual Review of Sociology*. Palo Alto, Calif.: Annual Reviews, Inc., 1983, vol. 9, pp. 527–553.

Jensen, Arthur: "How Much Can We Boost I.Q. and Scholastic Achievement?" *Harvard Educational Review*, 1969, vol. 39, pp. 1–123.

Jensen, Arthur R.: *Straight Talk About Mental Tests*. New York, Free Press, 1981.

Johnson, Harry M.: *Sociology*. New York: Harcourt, Brace and Company, 1960.

Jones, Brian J., Bernard J. Gallahger, and Joseph A. McFalls: *Social Problems*. New York: McGraw-Hill Book Company, 1988.

Josephy, Alvin M., Jr.: *Now That the Buffalo's Gone: A Study of Today's American Indians*. New York: Alfred A. Knopf, 1982.

Jourard, Sidney M.: *The Transparent Self*. New York: Van Nostrand Reinhold, 1971.

Jung, Carl: *Psychological Types*. New York: Harcourt, Brace, 1938.

Jung, Carl: *Psychological Types*. Vol. 6, Complete works. Princeton, N. J.: Bollinger Press, 1972.

Kagan, Jerome: "The Child in the Family," *Daedalus*, Spring 1977, vol. 106, pp. 33–56.

Kagan, Jerome: *Emotions, Cognitions, and Behavior*. New York: Cambridge University Press, 1984.

Kahl, Joseph A.: *The American Class Structure*. New York: Holt, Rinehart and Winston, 1957. Rev. ed. 1961.

Kammeyer, Kenneth C.W., and Helen L. Ginn: *An Introduction to Population*. Chicago: The Dorsey Press, 1986.

Kando, Thomas M.: *Leisure and Popular Culture in Transition*. St. Louis: C. V. Mosby, 1975.

Kant, Immanuel: *Critique of Pure Reason*. 1781.

Kaplan, Howard B. (ed.): *Psychosocial Stress: Trends in Theory and Research*. New York: Academic Press, 1983.

Kardiner, Abram: *The Individual and His Society: The Psychodynamics of Primitive Social Organization*. New York: Columbia University Press, 1939.

Kardiner, Abram: *The Psychological Frontiers of Society*. New York: Columbia University Press, 1945.

Karlins, M., T. Coffman, and G. Walters: "On the Fading of Social Stereotypes: Studies in Three Generations of College Students," *Journal of Personality and Social Psychology*, 1969, vol. 20, pp. 1–16.

Karon, Bertram P.: *Black Scars*. New York: Springer Publishing Company, 1975.

Katz, Daniel, and Robert L. Kahn: *The Social Psychology of Organizations*. New York: Wiley, 1978.

Katz, Elihu: "The Two-Step Flow of Communication: An Up-to-Date Report on an Hypothesis," *Public Opinion Quarterly*, 1957, vol. 21, pp. 61–78.

Katz, E., and P. F. Lazarsfeld: *Personal Influence*. Glencoe, Ill.: Free Press, 1955.

Katz, Gregory: "It's a Crime: Only 1 of 3 Are Reported," *USA Today*, December 2, 1985.

Kaufman, Felix: *Methodology of the Social Sciences*. New York: Oxford University Press, 1944.

Kay, Paul, and Willett Kempton: "What Is the Sapir-Whorf Hypothesis?" *American Anthropologist*, 1984, vol. 86, pp. 65–79.

Keeton, William T., and James Gould: *Biological Science*, 4th ed. New York: W.W. Norton, 1986.

Keller, Helen: *The Story of My Life*. Garden City, N. Y.: Doubleday, 1954.

▼ Kellogg, W. N., and L. A. Kellogg: *The Ape and the Child.* New York: McGraw-Hill, 1933.

Kelly, George A.: *The Psychology of Personal Constructs.* New York: Norton, 1955.

Kenniston, Kenneth: *Young Radicals.* New York: Harcourt, Brace and Jovanovich, 1968.

Kerbo, Harold R.: *Social Stratification and Inequality.* New York: McGraw-Hill, 1983.

Kerckhoff, Alan C., and Kurt W. Back: *The June Bug: A Study of Hysterical Contagion.* New York: Appleton-Century-Crofts, 1968.

**710** Kerr, Clark, John T. Dunlop, Frederick H. Harbison, and Charles A. Myers: *Industrialism and Industrial Man.* Cambridge, Mass.: Harvard University Press, 1960.

Kessin, Kenneth: "Social and Psychological Consequences of Intergenerational Occupational Mobility," *American Journal of Sociology,* 1971, vol. 77, pp. 1–18.

Kessler, Ronald, and Paul Cleary: "Social Class and Psychological Distress," *American Sociological Review,* 1980, vol. 45, pp. 463–78.

Khaldun, Ibn: *Prologomena (Muqaddimah).* 1377.

Killian, Lewis: "The Significance of Group Membership in Disasters," *American Journal of Sociology,* 1952, vol. 57, pp. 309–314.

Killian, Lewis: "Social Movements," in R. E. L. Faris (ed.) *Handbook of Modern Sociology.* Chicago: Rand McNally, 1964.

Kinsey, Alfred C., Wardell B. Pomeroy, and Clyde E. Martin: *Sexual Behavior in the Human Male.* Philadelphia: Saunders, 1948.

Klaus, Marshall H., and John H. Kennell: *Parent-Infant Bonding.* 2d ed. St. Louis: C. V. Mosby, 1982.

Kluckhohn, Clyde: *Mirror for Man.* New York: McGraw-Hill, 1949.

Kluckhohn, Clyde, and Henry A. Murray: *Personality in Nature, Society, and Culture.* New York: Alfred A. Knopf, 1953.

Kluckhohn, Florence R.: "Dominant and Variant Value Orientations," in C. Kluckhohn, H. A. Murray, and D. M. Schneider (eds.) *Personality in Nature, Society, and Culture.* New York: Alfred Knopf, 1953.

Kluegel, James R., and Eliot R. Smith: "Affirmative Action Attitudes: Effects of Self Interest, Racial Affect, and Stratification Beliefs on Whites' Views," *Social Forces,* 1983, vol. 61, pp. 797–822.

Knoke, David: "Commitment and Detachment in Voluntary Associations," *American Sociological Review,* 1981, vol. 46, pp. 141–158.

Knupfer, Genevieve: "Portrait of the Underdog," *Public Opinion Quarterly,* 1947, vol. 11, pp. 103–114.

Koch, Howard: *The Panic Broadcast: Portrait of an Event.* Boston: Little, Brown and Company, 1970.

Koenig, Fredrick: *Rumor in the Marketplace: The Social Psychology of Commercial Hearsay.* Dover, Mass.: Auburn House Publishing Co., 1985.

Kohlberg, Lawrence: "A Cognitive-Developmental Analysis of Children's Sex Role Concepts and Attitudes," in Eleanor E. Maccoby (ed.) *The Development of Sex Differences.* Palo Alto, Calif.: Stanford University Press, 1966.

Kohlberg, Lawrence: "Stage and Sequence: The Cognitive Developmental Approach to Socialization," in David A. Goslin (ed.) *Handbook of Socialization Theory and Research.* Chicago: Rand McNally and Company, 1969.

Kohlberg, Lawrence: *The Philosophy of Moral Development.* New York: Harper and Row, 1981.

Kohlberg, Lawrence: *Child Psychology and Childhood Education: A Cognitive-Developmental View.* New York: Longman, 1987.

Kohlberg, L., and C. Gilligan: "The Adolescent as a Philosopher: The Discovery of the Self in a Post Conventional World," *Daedalus,* Fall 1971, pp. 1051–1086.

Kohn, Melvin L.: *Class and Conformity: A Study in Values.* Homewood, Ill.: Dorsey Press, 1969. 2d ed. 1977.

Kohn, Melvin L.: "Bureaucratic Man: A Portrait and an Interpretation," *American Sociological Review,* 1971, vol. 36, pp. 461–474.

Kohn, Melvin L.: "Social Class and Schizophrenia: A Critical Review," in David R. Heise (ed.) *Personality and Socialization.* Chicago: Rand McNally, 1972.

Kohn, Melvin, and Carmi Schooler: "Occupational Experience and Psychological Functioning: An Assessment of Reciprocal Effects," *American Sociological Review,* 1973, vol. 8, pp. 97–118.

Kohn, Melvin L., and Carmi Schooler: "Job Conditions and Personality: A Longitudinal Assessment of Their Reciprocal Effects," *American Journal of Sociology,* 1982, vol. 87, pp. 1257–1286.

Kohn, Melvin, and Carmi Schooler: *Work and Personality. An Inquiry into the Impact of Social Strat-*

*ification.* Norwood, N. J.: Ablex Publishing Corporation, 1983.

Kosa, John: *Two Generations of Soviet Man.* Chapel Hill, N.C.: University of North Carolina Press, 1962.

Krause, Elliot A.: *Power and Illness: The Political Sociology of Health and Medical Care.* New York: Elsevier, 1977.

Kretschmer, Ernest: *Physique and Character.* London: Routledge and Kegan Paul, 1925.

Kroeber, Alfred L.: *Anthropology: Biology and Race.* New York: Harcourt, Brace and World, 1948.

Kroeber, Alfred L., and Clyde Kluckhohn: "Culture: A Critical Review of Concepts and Definitions," Papers of the Peabody Museum of American Archaeology and Ethnology, Harvard University, vol. 47, no. 1. Cambridge, Mass.: The Museum, 1952.

Kronholz, June: "Saga of 'Lost' Tribe in Philippines Shows Marcos Era's Dark Side," *Wall Street Journal,* September 15, 1985, p. 1ff.

Kübler-Ross, Elizabeth: *Living with Death and Dying.* New York: Macmillan, 1981.

Kuhn, D., J. Langer, L. Kohlberg, and N. Haan: "The Development of Formal Operations in Logical and Moral Judgment," *Genetic Psychology Monographs,* 1977, vol. 95, pp. 97–188.

Kuhn, Manford H.: "Major Trends in Symbolic Interaction Theory in the Past Twenty-Five Years," *Sociological Quarterly,* 1964, vol. 5, pp. 61–84.

Kuhn, M. H., and T. McPartland: "An Empirical Investigation of Self-Attitudes," *American Sociological Review,* 1954, vol. 19, pp. 68–76.

Lackey, Pat N.: *Invitation to Talcott Parsons' Theory.* Houston, Tex.: Cap and Gown Press, Inc., 1987.

Laing, Ronald David: *The Divided Self: An Existential Study in Sanity and Madness.* Baltimore: Penguin Books, 1969.

Lamberth, John, Herbert Rappaport, and Margaret Rappaport: *Personality: An Introduction.* New York: Alfred A. Knopf, 1978.

Lamm, Helmut, Gisela Trommsdorf, and Edith Rost-Schaude: "Group-Induced Extremization: Review of Evidence and a Minority-Change Explanation," *Psychological Reports,* 1973, vol. 33, pp. 471–484.

Lang, Kurt, and Gladys Engel Lang: *Collective Dynamics.* New York: Crowell, 1961.

Langner, Thomas A., and Stanley T. Michael: *Life Stress and Mental Health.* New York: The Free Press, 1963.

Lasch, Christopher: *Haven in a Heartless World: The Family Beseiged.* New York: Basic Books, 1977.

Lasch, Christopher: *The Culture of Narcissism.* New York: Warner Books, 1978.

Lasch, Christopher: *The Minimal Self.* New York: W. W. Norton, 1984.

Lasswell, Harold D.: *Power and Personality.* New York: W. W. Norton, 1948.

Latane, Bibb, and John M. Darley: *The Unresponsive Bystander: Why Doesn't He Help?* New York: Appleton, Century, Crofts, 1970.

Laumann, E. O., and H. Schumann: "Open and Closed Structures." Paper presented at the annual meeting of the American Sociological Association. San Francisco, 1967.

Laurer, Robert H.: "Rate of Change and Stress: A Test of the Future Shock Thesis," *Social Forces,* 1974, vol. 52, pp. 510–526.

Laurer, Robert H., and Rance Thomas: "A Comparable Analysis of the Psychological Consequences of Change," *Human Relations,* 1976, vol. 29, pp. 239–248.

Lazar, I.: "Longitudinal Data in Child Development Programs (I)." Paper presented at the Office of Child Development Conference: Parents, Children, Continuity. El Paso, Tex., 1977.

Lazarsfeld, Paul F.: "The American Soldier," *Public Opinion Quarterly,* 1949, vol. 13, pp. 379–380.

Lazarsfeld, Paul F.: "Concept Formation and Measurement in the Behavioral Sciences: Some Historical Observations," in Gordon J. DiRenzo (ed.) *Concepts, Theory, and Explanation in the Behavioral Sciences.* New York: Random House, 1966.

LeBon, Gustav: *The Crowd.* London: T. Fisher Unwin, 1896.

Lee, Alfred McClung: *Toward Humanist Sociology.* New York: Prentice-Hall, 1973.

Lee, Alfred McClung, and Elizabeth Briant Lee: *The Fine Art of Propaganda.* New York: Octagon Books, 1972.

Leiter, Kenneth C.: *A Primer on Ethnomethodology.* New York: Oxford University Press, 1980.

Lemert, Edwin M.: *Human Deviance, Social Problems and Social Control.* Rev. ed. Englewood Cliffs, N. J.: Prentice-Hall, 1972.

▼ Lennenberg, Eric H.: *Biological Foundations of Language*. New York: Wiley, 1984.

Lenski, Gerhard: *Human Societies*. New York: McGraw-Hill, 1970.

Lenski, Gerhard, and Jean Lenski: *Power and Privilege: A Theory of Social Stratification*. New York: Macmillan, 1966.

Lenski, Gerhard, and Jean Lenski: *Human Societies: An Introduction to Macrosociology*. 5th ed. New York: McGraw-Hill, 1987.

**712** Lerner, Daniel: "Modernization: Social Aspects," in D. L. Sills (ed.) *International Encyclopedia of the Social Sciences*. Vol. 10. New York: Free Press, 1968.

Levine, S., and N. A. Scotch: *Social Stress*. Chicago: Aldine Publishing Company, 1970.

Levinson, Daniel J.: "Role, Personality, and Social Structure in the Organizational Setting," *Journal of Abnormal and Social Psychology*, 1959, vol. 58, pp. 170–180.

Levinson, Daniel J.: "The Changing Character of Middle Adulthood in American Society," in Gordon J. DiRenzo (ed.) *We, The People: American Character and Social Change*. Westport, Conn.: Greenwood Press, 1977a.

Levinson, Daniel J.: *The Seasons of a Man's Life*. New York: Alfred A. Knopf, 1977b.

Levinson, Daniel J.: "A Conception of Adult Development," *American Psychologist*, 1986, vol. 41, pp. 3–13.

Lewin, Kurt: *A Dynamic Theory of Personality*. New York: McGraw-Hill, 1935.

Lewin, R., R. Lippitt, and R. White: "Patterns of Aggressive Behavior in Experimentally Created 'Social Climates'," *Journal of Social Psychology*, 1939, vol. 10, pp. 271–299.

Lewis, Michael: "Culture and Gender Roles: There's No Unisex in the Nursery," *Psychology Today*, 1972, vol. 5, pp. 54–57.

Lewis, Oscar: "The Culture of Poverty," *Scientific American*, 1960, vol. 4, pp. 19–25.

Lewontin, R. C., Rose Steven, and Leon J. Kamin: *Not in Our Genes: Biology, Ideology, and Human Nature*. New York: Pantheon, 1984.

Lichter, S. Robert, and Stanley Rothman: "The Radical Personality: Social Psychological Correlates of New Left Ideology," *Political Behavior*, 1982, vol. 4, pp. 207–235.

Lieberman, S.: "The Effects of Changes in Roles on the Attitudes of Role Occupants," *Human Relations*, 1950, vol. 9, pp. 385–403.

Liebert, Robert M., and Rita W. Poulos: "TV for Kiddies: Truth, Goodness, Beauty—and a Little Bit of Brainwash," *Psychology Today*, November 1972, vol. 6, pp. 122–128.

Liebow, Elliot: *Tally's Corner*. Boston: Little, Brown, 1967.

Lifton, Robert J.: *History and Human Survival*. New York: Random House, 1970.

Lifton, Robert J.: *The Life of the Self*. New York: Simon and Schuster, 1976.

Lindesmith, Alfred R., and Anselm L. Strauss: *Social Psychology*. New York: Holt, Rinehart and Winston, 1968.

Linton, Ralph: *The Study of Man*. New York: Appleton-Century-Crofts, 1936.

Linton, Ralph: "The One Hundred Percent American," *The American Mercury*, 1937, vol. 40, pp. 427–429.

Linton, Ralph: *The Cultural Background of Personality*. New York: Appleton, 1945.

Lipset, Seymour M.: *Political Man*. New York: Doubleday, 1960.

Lipset, Seymour M.: *Political Man: The Social Bases of Politics*. Exp. ed. Baltimore: Johns Hopkins University Press, 1981.

Lipset, Seymour M., and Reinhard Bendix: *Social Mobility in Industrial Society*. Berkeley, Calif.: University of California Press, 1966.

Lipset, Seymour M., and Everett C. Ladd: "The Politics of American Sociologists," *American Journal of Sociology*, 1972, vol. 78, pp. 67–104.

Lipton, Douglas, Robert Martinson, and Judith Wilks: *The Effectiveness of Correctional Treatment Evaluation Studies: A Survey of Treatment*. New York: Praeger, 1975.

Liska, Allen E.: *Perspectives on Deviance*. Englewood Cliffs, N. J.: Prentice-Hall, 1981.

Litwak, Eugene: "Voluntary Association and Neighborhood Cohesion," *American Sociological Review*, 1961, vol. 26, pp. 266–271.

Lloyd, Jean: *Sociology and Social Life*. New York: D. Van Nostrand Company, 1979.

Loevinger, Jane: "The Meaning and Measurement of Ego Development," *American Psychologist*, 1966, vol. 21, pp. 195–206.

Loevinger, Jane: *Ego Development*. San Francisco: Jossey Bass, 1976.

Locke, John: *Two Treatises of Government*. London: Churchill, 1690.

Lombroso, Cesare: *Crime: Its Causes and Remedies*. Boston: Little, Brown, 1911.

Lombroso-Ferrero, Gina: *Criminal Man*. Montclair, N. J.: Patterson-Smith, 1911.

Long, Theodore, and Jeffrey Hadden: "Religious Conversion and the Concept of Socialization: Integrating the Brainwashing and Draft Models," *Journal for the Scientific Study of Religion*, 1983, vol. 22, pp. 1–14.

Lopreato, Joseph: *Human Nature and Biocultural Evolution*. Winchester, Mass.: Allen and Unwin, 1984.

Lord, Walter: *A Night to Remember*. New York: Holt, 1955.

Lorenz, Konrad: *On Aggression*. New York: Harcourt, Brace and World, 1966.

Lorenz, Konrad: *The Foundation of Ethology*. New York: Springer Verlag, 1981.

Lumsden, Charles J., and E. O. Wilson: *Promethean Fire*. Cambridge, Mass.: Harvard University Press, 1983.

Lundberg, George A., Clarence C. Schrag, Otto N. Larson, William R. Catton, Jr.: *Sociology*. New York: Harper and Row, 1968.

Lundberg, M. J.: *The Incomplete Adult: Social Class Constraints on Personality Development*. Westport, Conn.: Greenwood Press, 1974.

Luther, Martin: *Table Talk*. 1569.

Lynd, Robert S., and Helen M. Lynd: *Middletown: A Study in American Culture*. New York: Harcourt, 1929.

Lyon, David: *Information Society*. New York: Basil Blackwell, Inc., 1989.

Maccoby, Eleanor E., and Carol N. Jacklin: *The Psychology of Sex Differences*. Stanford, Calif.: Stanford University Press, 1974.

Maccoby, Eleanor E., and Carol N. Jacklin: "Sex Differences in Aggression: A Rejoinder and Reprise," *Child Development*, 1980, vol. 51, pp. 964–980.

Maccoby, Michael: *The Gamesman: The New Corporate Leaders*. New York: Simon and Schuster, 1976.

Maccoby, Michael: "The Changing Corporate Character," in Gordon J. DiRenzo (ed.) *We, The People: American Character and Social Change*. Westport, Conn.: Greenwood Press, 1977.

MacDonald, K. B. (ed.): *Sociobiological Perspectives on Human Development*. New York: Springer-Verlag, 1987.

Maine, Henry J.: *Ancient Law*. London: Hazell, Watson and Viney, 1861.

Malson, Lucien: *Wolf Children and the Problem of Human Nature*. New York: Monthly Review Press, 1972.

Manis, Jerome G., and Bernard Meltzer (eds.): *Symbolic Interaction*. London: Routledge and Kegan Paul, 1975.

Mannheim, H.: "Organized Crime," *Encyclopaedia Britannica*. Vol. 7. Chicago: Encyclopaedia Britannica, Inc., 1983.

March, James G., and Herbert A. Simon: *Organizations*. New York: John Wiley, 1958.

Marcuse, Herbert: *One Dimensional Man: Studies in the Ideology of Advanced Industrial Society*. Boston: Beacon Press, 1964.

Markle, Gerald, James C. Peterson, and Morton O. Wagenfeld: "Notes from the Cancer Underground: Participating in the Laetrile Movement," *Social Science and Medicine*, 1978, vol. 12, pp. 31–37.

Markus, Nathan: "Staff Participation in Organizational Change: A Study of the Participation of Staff Members of Social Service Organizations in Activities Aimed at Influencing Changes in the Services and Functions of the Employing Agencies." Ph.D. diss., School of Social Work, University of Toronto, 1969.

Marris, Peter: *Loss and Change*. New York: Pantheon Books, 1974.

Marshall, Victor W.: "Socialization for Impending Death in a Retirement Village," *American Journal of Sociology*, 1975, vol. 80, pp. 1124–1144.

Marshall, Victor W.: *Last Chances: A Sociology of Aging and Dying*. Monterey, Calif.: Brooks/Cole, 1980.

Martin, David G.: *Personality: Effective and Ineffective*. Monterey, Calif.: Brooks/Cole Publishing Company, 1976.

Martinson, R.: "What Works? Questions and Answers About Prison Reform," *The Public Interest*, 1974, vol. 35, pp. 22–54.

Marx, Gary: *Protest and Prejudice: A Study of Belief*

▼ in the Black Community. New York: Harper and Row, 1969.

Marx, Karl: "Alienated Labor," in Eric and Mary Josephson (eds.) Man Alone: Alienation in Modern Society. New York: Dell, 1962. Originally published 1844.

Marx, Karl: Capital: A Critique of Political Economy. New York: Vintage Books, 1977. Originally published 1867.

Marx, Karl, and Friedrich Engels: The Communist Manifesto. Chicago: Regnery, 1954. Originally published 1848.

**714**

Maslow, Abram H.: Motivation and Personality. New York: Harper, 1954.

Masnick, George, and Mary Jo Bane: The Nation's Families: 1960–1990. Cambridge, Mass.: Joint Center for Urban Studies of Massachusetts Institute of Technology and Harvard University, 1980.

Mason, Evelyn P.: "Cross-Validation Study of Personality Characteristics of Junior High Students from American Indian, Mexican, and Caucasian Ethnic Backgrounds," in C. Hernandez, Nathaniel N. Wagner, and Marsha J. Haug (eds.) Chicanos: Social and Psychological Perspectives. St. Louis, Mo.: C. V. Mosby Company, 1971.

Matthews, Mervyn: Privilege in the Soviet Union: A Study of Elite Life-Styles Under Communism. London: George Allen and Unwin, 1978.

Matthiessen, Peter: In the Spirit of Crazy Horse. New York: Viking, 1983.

May, Rollo R.: The Discovery of Being: Writings in Existential Psychology. New York: W. W. Norton, 1983.

McArthur, Leslie Zebrowitz: "Television and Sex Role Stereotyping: Are Children Being Programmed?" The Brandeis Quarterly, 1982, vol. 2, pp. 12–13.

McCarthy, John D., and Mayer N. Zald: "Resource Mobilization and Social Movements: A Partial Theory," American Journal of Sociology, 1977, vol. 82, pp. 1212–1241.

McCaulley, Mary H.: "Jung's Theory of Psychological Types and the Myers-Briggs Type Indicator," in Paul McReynolds (ed.) Advances in Psychological Assessment V. San Francisco, Calif.: Jossey-Bass, 1981.

McClelland, David C.: The Achieving Society. New York: Irvington Publishers, 1976.

McClelland, David C.: Human Motivation. Glenview, Ill.: Scott, Foresman, 1985.

McClintock, C. G.: "Social Motivation—A Set of Propositions," Behavioral Science, 1972, vol. 17, pp. 438–454.

McGiffert, Michael (ed.): The Character of Americans. Homewood, Ill.: Dorsey Press, 1970.

McLean, Charles: The Wolf Children. New York: Hill and Wang, 1978.

McManus, I.C., and C. G. N. Taylor: "Biosocial Correlates of Cognitive Abilities," Journal of Biosocial Sciences, 1983, vol. 15, pp. 289–306.

McNichol, Sharon: "A Cross-Cultural Study of the Effects of Modeling Reinforcement and Color Meaning Word Association on Doll Color Preferences of Black Preschool Children and White Preschool Children in New York and Trinidad." Paper presented at the annual meeting of the American Psychological Association, New York, September 1987.

McRoberts, Hugh A., and Kevin Selbee: "Trends in Occupational Mobility in Canada and the United States: A Comparison," American Sociological Review, 1981, vol. 46, pp. 406–421.

Mead, George H.: Mind, Self, and Society. Chicago: University of Chicago Press, 1967. Originally published 1934.

Mead, Margaret: Coming of Age in Samoa. New York: Blue Ribbon Books, 1928.

Mead, Margaret: Growing Up in New Guinea. New York: William Morrow and Company, 1930.

Mead, Margaret: And Keep Your Powder Dry. New York: William Morrow and Company, 1943.

Mead, Margaret: Sex and Temperament in Three Primitive Societies. New York: Morrow Quill Paperbacks, 1980. Originally published 1950.

Mead, Margaret: "Cultural Determinants of Behavior," in A. Roe and George G. Simpson (eds.) Behavior and Evaluation. New Haven, Conn.: Yale University Press, 1958.

Medalia, Nehum A., and Otto N. Larsen: "Diffusion and Belief in a Collective Delusion: The Seattle Windshield Pitting Epidemic," American Sociological Review, 1958, vol. 23, pp. 221–232.

Mednick, Sarnoff A., and J. Volavaka: "Biology and Crime," in N. Morris and M. Tonry (eds.) Crime and Justice: An Annual Review of Research. Vol. 2. Chicago: University of Chicago Press, 1980.

Mednick, Sarnoff A., Terrie E. Moffitt, and Susan

Stack: *The Causes of Crime*. New York: Cambridge University Press, 1987.

Megargee, Edwin I., and Martin J. Bohn: *Classifying Criminal Offenders*. San Francisco: Sage Publications, 1979.

Melton, J. Gordon: *The Encyclopedia of American Religions*. 2d ed. Detroit, Mich.: Gale Research Company, 1987.

Merton, Robert K.: "Social Structure and Anomie," *American Sociological Review*, 1938, vol. 3, pp. 672–682.

Merton, Robert K.: "Bureacratic Structure and Personality," *Social Forces*, 1940, vol. 18, pp. 560–568.

Merton, Robert K.: "Discrimination and the American Creed," in Robert M. MacIver (ed.) *Discrimination and National Welfare*. New York: Harper and Brothers, 1949.

Merton, Robert K.: *Social Theory and Social Structure*. Glencoe, Ill.: The Free Press, 1957. Rev. ed. 1968.

Merton, Robert K.: "The Mosaic of the Behavioral Sciences," in Bernard Berelson (ed.) *The Behavioral Sciences Today*. New York: Harper, 1963.

Merton, Robert K.: *Sociological Ambivalence and Other Essays*. New York: Free Press, 1976.

Michels, Roberto: *Political Parties*. New York: The Free Press, 1967. Originally published 1915.

Middleton, Russell: "Alienation, Race, and Education," *American Sociological Review*, 1963, vol. 28, pp. 973–977.

Milbrath, Lester: *Environmentalists: Vanguard for a New Society*. Albany, N. Y.: State University of New York Press, 1984.

Milgram, Stanley: *Obedience to Authority*. New York: Harper and Row, 1974.

Mill, John Stuart: *A System of Logic, Ratiocinative and Inductive*. London: Parker, 1843.

Miller, David L.: *Introduction to Collective Behavior*. Belmont, Calif.: Wadsworth Publishing Company, 1985.

Miller, Delbert C.: *Handbook of Research Design and Social Measurement*. 4th ed. New York: David McKay, 1983.

Miller, S. M.: "Comparative Social Mobility," *Current Sociology*, 1960, vol. 9, pp. 1–89.

Miller, Walter B.: "Lower Class Culture as a Generating Milieu of Gang Delinquency," *Journal of Social Issues*, 1958, vol. 14, pp. 5–19.

Mills, C. Wright: *The Power Elite*. London: Oxford University Press, 1956.

Mills, C. Wright: *The Sociological Imagination*. New York: Oxford University Press, 1959.

Mills, Theodore M.: *The Sociology of Small Groups*. Englewood Cliffs, N. J.: Prentice-Hall, 1967.

Mischel, W., and H. Mischel: "A Cognitive Social-Learning Approach to Morality and Self-Regulation," in T. Lickona (ed.) *Moral Development and Behavior*. New York: Holt, Rinehart and Winston, 1976.

Mitchell, James V.: *Tests in Print*. 9th ed. Highland Park, N. J.: Gryphon, 1985.

Miyamoto, S. Frank, and Sanford M. Dornbusch: "A Test of Interactionist Hypotheses of Self-Conception," *American Journal of Sociology*, 1956, vol. 61, pp. 399–403.

Mohan, Raj P., and Don Martindale (eds.): *Handbook of Contemporary Developments in World Sociology*. Westport, Conn.: Greenwood Press, 1975.

Molitor, Graham T. T.: "The Information Society: The Path to Post-Industrial Growth," *The Futurist*, April, 1981.

Money, John, and A. Ehrhardt: *Man and Woman, Boy and Girl*. Baltimore: Johns Hopkins University Press, 1972.

Money, John, and Patricia Tucker: *Sexual Signatures*. Boston: Little, Brown, 1975.

Montagu, Ashley (ed.): *Sociobiology Examined*. New York: Oxford University Press, 1980.

Montero, Darrel: "The Japanese Americans: Changing Patterns of Assimilation over Three Generations," *American Sociological Review*, 1981, vol. 46, pp. 829–839.

Montesquieu, Charles: *The Spirit of the Laws*. 1748.

Moore, Wilbert E.: *Social Change*. Englewood Cliffs, N. J.: Prentice-Hall, 1963.

More, Thomas: *Utopia*. 1516.

Moreno, Jacob L.: *Who Shall Survive?* Beacon, N. Y.: Beacon House, 1953.

Morgan, Lewis H.: *Ancient Society*. New York: H. Holt, 1877.

Mortimer, Jeylan T., and Roberta G. Simmons: "Adult Socialization," in Ralph H. Turner, James Coleman, and Renee C. Fox (eds.) *Annual Review of Sociology*. Palo Alto, Calif.: Annual Reviews, 1978, vol. 4, pp. 421–454.

Mosca, Gaetano: *The Ruling Class*. New York: McGraw-Hill, 1939. Originally published 1896.

▼ Moscovici, Serge, and Willem Doise: "Decision Making in Groups," in C. Nemeth (ed.) *Social Psychology: Classic and Contemporary Integrations.* Chicago: Rand McNally, 1974.

Moskos, Charles C.: *The Enlisted Man.* New York: Russell Sage Foundation, 1970.

Mounin, Georges: "Chimpanzees, Language, and Communication," *Current Anthropology*, 1976, vol. 17, pp. 1–22.

Murdock, George P.: *Our Primitive Contemporaries.* New York: Macmillan, 1934.

**716** Murdock, George P.: "The Common Denominator in Cultures," in Ralph Linton (ed.) *The Science of Man in the World Crisis.* New York: Columbia University Press, 1945.

Murdock, George P.: *Social Structure.* New York: Macmillan, 1949.

Murray, Henry A.: *Explorations in Personality.* New York: Oxford University Press, 1938.

Mussen, Paul H.: "Early Sex-Role Development," in David Goslin (ed.) *Handbook of Socialization Theory and Research.* Chicago: Rand McNally, 1969.

Mussen, Paul H., John J. Conger, Jerome Kagan, and Aletha Carol Huston: *Child Development and Personality.* 6th ed. New York: Harper and Row, 1984.

Myers, D. G., and G. D. Bishop: "Discussion Effects on Racial Attitudes," *Science*, 1970, vol. 169, pp. 778–789.

Myers, Isabel Briggs: *Manual of the Myers-Briggs Type Indicator.* Palo Alto, Calif.: Consulting Psychologists Press, 1985.

Myers, Isabel Briggs: *Introduction to Type: A Description of the Theory and Application of the Myers-Briggs Type Indicator.* 4th ed. Palo Alto, Calif.: Consulting Psychologists Press, 1987.

Myrdal, Gunnar: *An American Dilemma.* New York: Harper and Brothers, 1962. Originally published 1944.

Nadel, Siegried F.: *The Nuba: An Anthropological Study of the Hill Tribes in Kordofan.* London: Oxford University Press, 1947.

Naisbitt, John: *Megatrends.* New York: Warner Books, 1982.

Nance, John: *The Gentle Tasaday.* New York: Harcourt Brace Jovanovich, 1975.

National Institute of Mental Health: *Television and Behavior: Ten Years of Scientific Progress and Im-*plications for the Eighties. Washington, D.C.: U.S. Government Printing Office, 1982.

National Opinion Research Center: *General Social Surveys, 1972–1987: Cumulative Codebook.* Chicago: University of Chicago, 1987.

Neugarten, Bernice L.: "Personality Change in Later Life: A Developmental Perspective," in C. Eisdorfer and M. P. Lawton (eds.) *The Psychology of Adult Development.* Washington, D.C.: American Psychological Association, 1973.

Newcomb, Theodore M.: *Personality and Social Change.* New York: Dryden Press, 1943.

Newcomb, T. M., K. E. Koenig, R. Flacks, and D. P. Warwick: *Persistence and Change.* New York: Wiley, 1967.

Newcombe, Nora, Mary M. Bandura, and Dawn G. Taylor: "Sex Differences in Spatial Ability and Spatial Activities," *Social Roles*, 1983, vol. 9, pp. 377–386.

Newcomer, M.: *The Big Business Executive: The Factors That Made Him.* New York: Columbia University Press, 1955.

Newman, Graeme: *Comparative Deviance: Perception and Law in Six Cultures.* New York: Elsevier, 1976.

Newman, Katherine S.: *Falling from Grace.* New York: The Free Press, 1988.

Nisbet, Robert A.: *The Sociological Tradition.* New York: Basic Books, 1966.

Nisbet, Robert A.: *The Social Bond.* New York: Alfred A. Knopf, 1970.

Nisbet, Robert, and Robert Perrin: *The Social Bond: An Introduction to the Study of Society.* 2d ed. New York: Alfred A. Knopf, 1977.

Nixon, Howard L.: *The Small Group.* Englewood Cliffs, N. J.: Prentice-Hall, 1979.

Ogburn, William F.: *Social Change.* New York: B. W. Huebsch, 1922.

Olmsted, Michael S., and A. Paul Hare: *The Small Group.* 2d ed. New York: Random House, 1978.

Omond, Roger: *The Apartheid Handbook.* Harmondsworth, Middlesex, England: Penguin, 1986.

Ophuls, William: *Ecology and the Politics of Scarcity.* San Francisco: W. H. Freeman, 1977.

Osborn, A. F.: *Applied Imagination.* New York: Scribner, 1957.

Oskamp, Stuart: *Attitudes and Opinions.* Englewood Cliffs, N. J.: Prentice-Hall, 1977.

Ouchi, William: *Theory Z: How American Business*

*Can Meet the Japanese Challenge.* Reading, Mass.: Addison-Wesley, 1981.

Palen, John J.: *The Urban World.* 3d ed. New York: McGraw-Hill Book Company, 1986.

Palmer, F. H.: "The Effects of Early Intervention on Subsequent I.Q. Scores and Reading Achievement." Final Report to the Educational Commission of the States Contract 13-76-068-461. Stony Brook, N. Y.: State University of New York, 1976.

Pareto, Vilfredo: *Treatise on General Sociology.* New York: Harcourt Brace, 1935. Originally published 1916.

Park, Robert E.: 'Introduction' to *The Etiquette of Race Relations in the South,* by Bertram W. Doyle. Chicago: University of Chicago Press, 1937.

Park, Robert E., Ernest W. Burgess, and Roderick D. McKenzie (eds.): *The City.* Chicago: University of Chicago Press, 1984. Originally published 1925.

Parkinson, C. Northcote: *Parkinson's Law.* Boston: Houghton, Mifflin, 1957.

Parsons, Talcott: *The Structure of Social Action.* New York: The Free Press, 1937.

Parsons, Talcott: *The Social System.* Glencoe, Ill.: The Free Press, 1951.

Parsons, Talcott, and Edward A. Shils: *Toward a General Theory of Action.* Cambridge, Mass.: Harvard University Press, 1951.

Pascarella, Perry: *Technology: Fire in a Dark World.* New York: Van Nostrand Reinhold, 1979.

Pavlov, Ivan P.: *Conditioned Reflexes.* London: Oxford University Press, 1927.

Pebley, Anne R., and Charles F. Westoff: "Women's Sex Preferences in the United States: 1970 to 1975," *Demography,* 1982, vol. 19, no. 2, pp. 177–190.

Perrow, Charles: *Complex Organizations: A Critical Essay.* Glenview, Ill.: Scott, Foresman, 1972.

Perry, David C., and Alfred J. Watkins: "Regional Change and the Impact of Uneven Urban Development," in David C. Perry and Alfred J. Watkins (eds.) *The Rise of the Sunbelt Cities.* Beverly Hills, Calif.: Sage Publications, 1978.

Perry, David C., and Alfred J. Watkins (eds.): *The Rise of the Sunbelt Cities.* Beverly Hills, Calif.: Sage Publications, 1978.

Perry, John, and Erna Perry: *The Social Web.* San Francisco: The Canfield Press, 1976.

Persell, Caroline H.: *Understanding Society: An Introduction to Sociology.* New York: Harper and Row, 1984.

Peter, Lawrence J., and R. Hull: *The Peter Principle.* New York: Morrow and Company, 1969.

Peterson, James A., and Rainer Martens: "Success and Residential Affiliation as Determinants of Team Cohesiveness," *Research Quarterly,* 1972, vol. 43, pp. 62–76.

Piaget, Jean: *The Moral Judgment of the Child.* New York: Harcourt, Brace, World, 1932.

Piaget, Jean: *The Psychology of Intelligence.* London: Routledge, Kegan Paul, 1950.

Piaget, Jean, and Barbel Inhelder: *The Psychology of the Child.* New York: Basic Books, 1969.

Pierson, George W.: "The M-Factor in American History," *American Quarterly,* 1962, vol. 14, pp. 275–289.

Piliavin, I. M., J. Rodin, and J. A. Piliavin: "Good Samaritanism: An Underground Phenomenon?" *Journal of Personality and Social Psychology,* 1969, vol. 13, pp. 289–299.

Pines, Maya: "The Civilizing of Genie," *Psychology Today,* September 1981, vol. 14, pp. 28–34.

Pinkney, Alphonso: *The Myth of Black Progress.* New York: Cambridge University Press, 1984.

Plato: *Apology.* 427–347 B.C.

Plato: *Republic.* 427–347 B.C.

Pollock, Philip H.: "Organizations and Alienation: The Mediation Hypothesis Revisited," *The Sociological Quarterly,* 1982, vol. 23, pp. 143–155.

Polsky, Ned.: *Hustlers, Beats, and Others.* 2d ed. Chicago: University of Chicago Press, 1985.

Pomer, Marshall I.: "Labor Market Structure, Intragenerational Mobility, and Discrimination: Black Male Advancement Out of Low-Paying Occupations, 1962–73," *American Sociological Review,* 1986, vol. 51, pp. 650–659.

Population Reference Bureau: *World Population Fundamentals of Growth.* Washington, D.C.: Population Reference Bureau, 1987.

Porter, Bruce, and Marvin Dunn: *The Miami Riot of 1980.* Lexington, Mass.: Lexington Books, 1984.

Porter, Judith R., and Robert E. Washington: "Black Identity and Self-Esteem: A Review of Studies of Black Self-Concept, 1968–1978," *Annual Review of Sociology,* 1979, vol. 5, pp. 53–74.

Potter, David: *People of Plenty: Economic Abundance and the American Character.* Chicago: University of Chicago Press, 1954.

717

▼ Premack, David, and Ann J. Premack: *The Mind of an Ape.* New York: Norton, 1983.

Presidential Commission on Population Growth and the American Future: *Population Growth and the American Future.* Washington, D.C.: U.S. Government Printing Office, 1972.

Presthus, Robert: *The Organizational Society.* Rev. ed. New York: St. Martin's Press, 1978.

Provence, S., and R. C. Lipton: *Infants in Institutions.* New York: International Universities Press, 1962.

Quarantelli, Enrico L. (ed.): *Disasters: Theory and Research.* London: Sage Publications, 1977.

**718** Quarantelli, Enrico L., and Russell R. Dynes: "When Disaster Strikes: It Isn't Much Like What You've Heard and Read About," *Psychology Today,* 1972, vol. 5, pp. 66–70.

Quarantelli, Enrico L., and Russell R. Dynes: "Community Conflict: Its Absence and Its Presence in Natural Disasters," *Mass Emergencies,* 1976, vol. 1, pp. 139–152.

Quarantelli, Enrico L., and Russell R. Dynes: "Response to Social Crisis and Disaster," in Alex Inkeles, James Coleman, and Neil Smelser (eds.) *Annual Review of Sociology.* Vol. 3. Palo Alto, Calif.: Annual Reviews, Inc., 1977.

Quenk, Naomi, and Warren A. Heffron: "Types of Family Practice—Teachers and Residents: A Comparative Study," *Journal of Family Practice,* 1975, vol. 2, pp. 195–200.

Quetelet, Adolphe: *On Man and the Development of Human Faculties: An Essay on Social Physics.* Brussels: C. Muquardt, 1869. Originally published 1835.

Quinney, Richard: *Critique of Legal Order: Crime Control in Capitalist Society.* Boston: Little, Brown, 1974.

Quinney, Richard: *Class, State, and Crime.* 2d ed. New York: Longman, 1980.

Ramirez, Manuel: "Cognitive Styles and Cultural Democracy in Education," in C. Hernandez, N. N. Wagner, and M. J. Haug (eds.) *Chicanos: Social and Psychological Perspectives.* St. Louis, Mo.: C. V. Mosby and Company, 1971.

Rangel, Jesus: "Survey Finds Hispanic Groups More Unified," *New York Times,* September 8, 1984.

Raphael, Beverly: *When Disaster Strikes: How Communities and Individuals Cope with Disasters.* New York: Basic Books, 1985.

Rawls, James R., and Oscar T. Nelson: "Characteristics Associated with Preferences for Certain Managerial Positions," *Psychological Reports,* 1975, vol. 36, pp. 911–918.

Redfield, Robert: "The Folk Society," *American Journal of Sociology,* 1947, vol. 52, pp. 293–308.

Reich, Charles A.: *The Greening of America.* New York: Random House, 1970.

Reich, Wilhelm: *The Mass Psychology of Fascism.* New York: Orgone Institute Press, 1946.

Reiman, Jeffrey H.: *The Rich Get Richer and the Poor Get Prison.* 2d ed. New York: John Wiley and Sons, 1984.

Riesman, David: *The Lonely Crowd.* New Haven: Yale University Press, 1950.

Riesman, David: "From 'Inner-Directed' to 'Other-Directed'," in Amitai Etzioni and Eva Etzioni-Halevy (eds.) *Social Change: Sources, Patterns, and Consequences.* New York: Basic Books, 1973.

Rivlin, Alice M., and P. Michael Timpane (eds.): *Ethical and Legal Issues of Social Experimentation.* Washington, D.C.: Brookings Institution, 1975.

Roethlisberger, Fritz J., and William J. Dickinson: *Management and the Worker.* Cambridge, Mass.: Harvard University Press, 1964.

Rogers, Carl R.: *Client-Centered Therapy: Its Practice, Implications, and Theory.* Boston: Houghton Mifflin, 1951.

Rohrer, J. H., and Muzafer Sherif (eds.): *Social Psychology at the Crossroads,* New York: Harper and Row Publishers, Inc., 1951.

Rokeach, Milton: "The Nature and Meaning of Dogmatism," *Psychological Review,* 1954, vol. 61, pp. 194–204.

Rokeach, Milton: "Political and Religious Dogmatism: An Alternative to the Authoritarian Personality," *Psychological Monographs,* 1956, vol. 70, no. 18.

Rokeach, Milton: *The Open and Closed Mind.* New York: Basic Books, 1960.

Rosch, E.: "Linguistic Relativity," in A. Silverstein (ed.) *Human Communication: Theoretical Perspectives.* New York: Halstead Press, 1974.

Rosen, Bernard C.: "Race, Ethnicity and the Achievement Syndrome," *American Sociological Review,* 1959, vol. 24, pp. 47–60.

Rosenberg, Morris: "Which Significant Other?" *American Behavioral Scientist,* 1973, vol. 16, pp. 829–860.

Rosenberg, Morris: *Conceiving the Self.* New York: Basic Books, 1979.

Rosenberg, Morris, and Howard B. Kaplan (eds.):

*Social Psychology of the Self-Concept.* Arlington Heights, Ill.: Harlan Davidson, 1982.

Rosenhan, D. L.: "On Being Sane in Insane Places," *Science*, 1973, vol. 179, pp. 250–258.

Rosenthal, R., and L. Jacobson: *Pygmalion in the Classroom: Teacher Expectations and Pupils' Intellectual Development.* New York: Holt, Rinehart and Winston, 1968.

Rosnow, Ralph L., and Gary Alan Fine: *Rumor and Gossip: The Social Psychology of Hearsay.* New York: Elsevier, 1976.

Rosow, Irving: *Socialization to Old Age.* Berkeley, Calif.: University of California Press, 1974.

Ross, Ellsworth A.: *Social Psychology.* New York: Macmillan, 1908.

Ross, James B., and Mary M. McLaughlin (eds.): *The Portable Medieval Reader.* New York: Viking Press, 1949.

Ross, Ralph: *Symbols and Civilization.* New York: Harcourt, 1957.

Rothman, Stanley, and Robert S. Lichter: "The Case of the Student Left," *Social Research*, 1978a, vol. 45, pp. 535–609.

Rothman, Stanley, and Robert S. Lichter: "Power, Politics, and Personality in Post-Industrial Society," *Journal of Politics*, 1978b, vol. 40, pp. 675–707.

Rotter, Julian B.: "Generalized Expectations for Internal versus External Control of Reinforcement," *Psychological Monographs*, 1966, vol. 80, no. 609.

Rousseau, Jean Jacques: *Discourse on the Origin of Inequality.* Amsterdam: Chez Marc-Michel Rey, 1755.

Rousseau, Jean Jacques: *Contrat Social.* Amsterdam: Chez Marc-Michel Rey, 1762.

Rubin, J. Z., F. J. Provenzano, and Z. L. Luria: "The Eye of the Beholder: Parents' Views on Sex of Newborns," *American Journal of Orthopsychiatry*, 1974, vol. 44, pp. 512–519.

Rubin, Leslie: *This Is Apartheid.* London: Victor Gollancz, 1959.

Rubin, Zick: "Does Personality Really Change After 20?" *Psychology Today*, May, 1981, vol. 15, no. 5, p. 18ff.

Rubin, Zick: *Liking and Loving: An Invitation to Social Psychology.* New York: Holt, Rinehart and Winston, 1973.

Ryan, Bryce F.: *Social and Cultural Change.* New York: Ronald Press, 1969.

St. Augustine: *The Confessions.* 399 A.D.

Sahlins, Marshall D., and Elman R. Service: *Evolution and Culture.* Ann Arbor, Mich.: University of Michigan Press, 1960.

Saint-Simon, Claude Henri de: *The Political Thought of Saint-Simon.* Edited by Ghita Ionescu. London: Oxford University Press, 1976.

Sanford, Nevitt: "The Loss and Rediscovery of Moral Character," in Gordon J. DiRenzo (ed.) *We, The People: American Character and Social Change.* Westport, Conn.: Greenwood Press, 1977.

Sapir, Edward: "The Status of Linguistics as a Science," *Language*, 1929, vol. 5, pp. 207–214.

Sarbin, Theodore and Jeffrey E. Miller: "Demonism Revisited: The Chromosomal Abnormality," *Issues in Criminology*, 1970, vol. 6, pp. 195–207.

Scarr, Sandra: *Race, Social Class, and Individual Differences in I.Q.* Hillsdale, N. J.: Erlbaum, 1981.

Schermerhorn, Richard A.: *Ethnic Plurality in India.* Tucson: University of Arizona Press, 1978.

Schuessler, Karl F. and Donald R. Cressey: "Personality Characteristics of Criminals," *American Journal of Sociology*, 1950, vol. 55, pp. 476–484.

Schlesinger, Arthur M., Jr.: *A Thousand Days.* Boston: Houghton Mifflin, 1965.

Schneider, Joseph W., and Sally H. Hacker: "Sex-Role Imagery and Use of the Generic 'Man' in Introductory Texts: A Case in the Sociology of Sociology," *The American Sociologist*, 1973, vol. 8, pp. 12–18.

Schramm, W., J. Lyle, and E. B. Parker: *Television in the Lives of Our Children.* Stanford, Calif.: Stanford University Press, 1961.

Schulze, Rolf: "A Shortened Version of the Rokeach Dogmatism Scale," *Journal of Psychological Studies*, 1961, vol. 13, pp. 93–97.

Schuman, Howard, Charlotte Steeh, and Lawrence Bobo: *Racial Attitudes in America: Trends and Interpretations.* Cambridge, Mass.: Harvard University Press, 1985.

Schur, Edwin M.: *Crimes Without Victims.* Englewood Cliffs, N. J.: Prentice-Hall, 1965.

Schur, Edwin M., and H. A. Bedau: *Victimless Crimes: Two Sides of a Controversy.* Englewood Cliffs, N. J.: Prentice-Hall, 1974.

Schwartz, Shalom H., and Ari Gottlieb: "Bystander Anonymity and Reaction to Emergencies," *Journal of Personality and Social Psychology*, 1980, vol. 39, pp. 418–440.

Scott, John Paul (ed.): *Critical Periods.* New York: Scientific and Academic Editions, 1978.

**719**

▼ Scott, W. Richard: *Organizations: Rational, Natural, and Open Systems*. 2d ed. Englewood Cliffs, N. J.: Prentice-Hall, 1987.

Seabrook, Jeremy: *The Leisure Society*. New York: Basil Blackwell, 1988.

Sears, R. R., J. W. M. Whiting, V. Nowlis, and P. S. Sears: "Some Child-Rearing Antecedents of Aggression and Dependency in Young Children," *Genetic Psychological Monographs*, 1953, vol. 47, pp. 135–136.

**720** Secord, Paul F., and Carl W. Backman: *Social Psychology*. New York: McGraw-Hill, 1974.

Seeman, Melvin: "On the Meaning of Alienation," *American Sociological Review*, 1959, vol. 24, pp. 783–791.

Seidenberg, Roderick: *Post-Historic Man: An Inquiry*. Boston: Beacon Press, 1957.

Sennett, Richard: *The Fall of Public Man*. New York: Alfred A. Knopf, 1977.

Sewell, William H.: "Infant Training and the Personality of the Child," *American Journal of Sociology*, 1952, vol. 58, pp. 150–159.

Sharrock, Wes, and B. Anderson: *The Ethnomethodologists*. Chichester, England: Ellis Horwood, 1986.

Shaver, P., and J. L. Freedman: "Your Pursuit of Happiness," *Psychology Today*, 1976, vol. 10, pp. 26–32.

Shaw, Marvin E.: *Group Dynamics: The Psychology of Small Group Behavior*. 3d ed. New York: McGraw-Hill, 1981.

Sheldon, William H.: *The Varieties of Temperament: A Psychology of Constitutional Differences*. New York: Harper and Row, 1942.

Sheldon, William H.: *An Introduction to Constitutional Psychiatry*. New York: Harper and Brothers, 1949.

Shepher, Joseph: *Incest: A Biosocial View*. New York: Academic Press, 1983.

Sherif, Muzafer: *The Psychology of Social Norms*. New York: Harper and Brothers, 1966.

Sherif, M., O. J. Harvey, B. J. White, W. R. Hood, and C. Sherif: *Intergroup Conflict and Cooperation: The Robbers Cave Experiment*. Norman, Okla.: University of Oklahoma Book Exchange, 1961.

Sherif, Muzafer, and C. W. Sherif: *Reference Groups*. New York: Harper and Row, 1964.

Shibutani, Tamotsu: *Society and Personality*. New York: Prentice-Hall, 1961.

Shipler, David K.: "Social Stratification in Russia," *The New York Times*, November 6, 1977, section 4, p. 5.

Silberman, Charles E.: *Crisis in Black and White*. New York: Random House, 1964.

Simmel, Georg: "The Sociology of Conflict," *American Journal of Sociology*, 1904, vol. 9, p. 490ff.

Simmel, Georg: *Soziologie*. Leipzig: Duncker and Humblot, 1908.

Simmel, Georg: *The Sociology of Georg Simmel*. Edited and translated by Kurt H. Wolff. Glencoe, Ill.: Free Press, 1950.

Simmons, J. L.: *Deviants*. Berkeley, Calif.: Glendessary Press, 1969.

Simon, David R., and D. Stanley Eitzen: *Elite Deviance*. 2d ed. Boston: Allyn and Bacon, 1986.

Simon, Julian L.: *The Ultimate Resource*. Princeton, N. J.: Princeton University Press, 1981.

Simpson, George E., and Milton J. Yinger: *Racial and Cultural Minorities: An Analysis of Prejudice*. New York: Harper and Row, 1972.

Singer, Jerome L., and Dorothy G. Singer: *Television, Imagination, and Aggression: A Study of Preschoolers*. Hillsdale, N. J.: Erlbaum, 1981.

Singh, J. A. L., and Robert M. Zingg: *Wolf Children and Feral Man*. New York: Harper and Row, 1942.

Sjoberg, Gideon: *The Preindustrial City*. New York: The Free Press, 1960.

Sjoberg, Gideon, (ed.): *Ethics, Politics and Social Research*. Cambridge, Mass.: Schenkman, 1967.

Skinner, Buros F.: *Walden Two*. New York: Macmillan Company, 1948.

Skinner, Buros F.: *Science and Human Behavior*. New York: Macmillan, 1953.

Skinner, Buros F.: *Beyond Freedom and Dignity*. New York: Alfred Knopf, 1971.

Skinner, Buros F.: *About Behaviorism*. New York: Random House, 1976.

Skocpol, Theda: *States and Social Revolutions*. New York: Cambridge University Press, 1979.

Slater, Philip E.: "Role Differentiation in Small Groups," *American Sociological Review*, 1955, vol. 20, pp. 300–310.

Slater, Philip E.: *The Pursuit of Loneliness*. Rev. ed. Boston: Beacon Press, 1976.

Slobin, D. I.: *Psycholinguistics*. 2d ed. Glenview, Ill.: Scott, Foresman, 1979.

Small, Albion W.: *General Sociology*. Chicago: University of Chicago Press, 1905.

Smelser, Neil J.: *Theory of Collective Behavior.* New York: The Free Press, 1962.

Smelser, Neil J.: "Sociological and Psychological Dimensions of Collective Behavior," in his *Essays in Sociological Explanation.* Englewood Cliffs, N. J.: Prentice-Hall, 1968a.

Smelser, Neil J.: *Essays in Sociological Explanation.* Englewood Cliffs, N. J.: Prentice-Hall, 1968b.

Smith, Althea, and Abigail J. Steward: "Approaches to Studying Racism and Sexism in Black Women's Lives," *Journal of Social Issues,* 1983, vol. 39, pp. 1–15.

Smith, Anthony D.: *The Ethnic Revival.* New York: Cambridge University Press, 1981.

Smith, Douglas: "Police Response to Interpersonal Violence: Defining the Parameters of Legal Control," *Social Forces,* 1987, vol. 65, pp. 767–782.

Snow, David A., and Cynthia L. Phillips: "The Changing Self-Orientations of College Students: From Institutions to Impulse," *Social Science Quarterly,* 1982, vol. 63, pp. 462–476.

Sorokin, Pitirim A.: *Social and Cultural Dynamics.* Totawa, N. J.: Bedminster Press, 1937–1941.

Spencer, Herbert: *Principles of Sociology.* New York: Appleton, 1898. Originally published 1876–1896.

Spengler, Oswald: *The Decline of the West.* New York: Alfred Knopf, 1926. Originally published 1918.

Spindler, George D.: "Change in Continuity in American Core Cultural Values: An Anthropological Perspective," in Gordon J. DiRenzo (ed.) *We, The People: American Character and Social Change.* Westport, Conn.: Greenwood Press, 1977.

Spindler, George D., and Louise Spindler: "Anthropologists View American Culture," *Annual Review of Anthropology.* Vol. 12. Palo Alto, Calif.: Annual Reviews, Inc., 1983.

Spitz, Rene A.: "Hospitalism: An Inquiry into the Genesis of Psychiatric Conditions in Early Childhood," *The Psychoanalytic Study of the Child.* 1945, vol. 1, pp. 53–74.

Spitz, Rene A.: "Hospitalism: A Follow-up Report," *The Psychoanalytic Study of the Child.* 1946, vol. 2, pp. 113–117.

Srole, Leo: "Social Integration and Certain Correlates: An Exploratory Study," *American Sociological Review,* 1956, vol. 21, pp. 709–716.

Srole, Leo, Thomas S. Langner, Stanley T. Michael, Marvin K. Opler, and Thomas A. C. Rennie: *Mental Health in the Metropolis.* New York: McGraw-Hill, 1962.

Srole, Leo, and Anita Kassen Fischer (eds.): *Mental Health in the Metropolis: The Midtown Manhattan Study.* New York: New York University Press, 1978.

Staats, Arthur W., and Carolyn K. Staats: "Attitudes Established by Classical Conditioning," *Journal of Abnormal and Social Psychology,* 1958, vol. 57, pp. 437–440.

Stack, Steven: "Religion and Suicide," *Journal for the Scientific Study of Religion,* 1983, vol. 22, pp. 239–252.

Stark, Rodney, and William S. Bainbridge: "American Born Sects: Initial Findings," *Journal for the Scientific Study of Religion,* 1981, vol. 18, pp. 117–133.

Stark, Rodney, and William S. Bainbridge: *The Future of Religion: Secularization, Revival, and Cult Formation.* Berkeley, Calif.: University of California Press, 1985.

Stein, Howard F., and Robert F. Hill: *The Ethnic Imperative: Examining the New White Ethnic Movement.* University Park, Pa.: Pennsylvania State University Press, 1977.

Stein, Kenneth B., and V. Rozynko: "Psychological and Social Variables and Personality Patterns of Drug Abusers," *International Journal of the Addictions,* 1974, vol. 9, pp. 431–446.

Steinberg, Stephen: *The Ethnic Myth: Race, Ethnicity and Class in America.* New York: Atheneum, 1981.

Stern, G. G., M. I. Stein, and B. S. Bloom: *Methods of Personality Assessment: Trauma Behavior in Complex Social Situations.* Glencoe, Ill.: Free Press, 1956.

Sternberg, Robert J., and William Salter: "Conceptions of Intelligence," in Robert Sternberg, (ed.) *Handbook of Human Intelligence.* New York: Cambridge University Press, 1982.

Sternglanz, S. H., and Lisa A. Serbin: "Sex Role Stereotyping in Children's Television Programs," *Developmental Psychology,* 1974, vol. 10, pp. 710–715.

Stinchcombe, Arthur L.: "Some Empirical Consequences of the Davis-Moore Theory of Stratification," *American Sociological Review,* 1963, vol. 28, pp. 805–808.

Stith, Sandra M., and Albert J. Davis: "Employed Mothers and Family Day-Care Substitute Care-

▼ givers: A Comparative Analysis of Infant Care," *Child Development*, 1984, vol. 55, pp. 1340–1348.

Stone, Marvin: "Bring Back the Melting Pot," *U.S. News and World Report*, (December 5, 1977), vol. 12, p. 92ff.

Stoner, J. A. F.: "A Comparison of Individual and Group Decisions Involving Risk." Master's thesis, Massachusetts Institute of Technology, Cambridge, 1961.

Stouffer, Samuel A., Edward A. Suchman, Leland C. DeVinney, Shirley A. Star, and Robin W. Williams, Jr.: *The American Soldier*. Princeton, N. J.: University Press, 1949.

Strauss, J. S.: "Behavioral Aspects of Being Disadvantaged and Risk for Schizophrenia," in D. L. Parron, F. Solomon, and C. D. Jenkins (eds.) *Behavior, Health Risks, and Social Disadvantage*. Washington, D.C.: National Academy Press, 1982.

Strodtbeck, Fred L., Rita M. James, and C. Hawkins: "Social Status in Jury Deliberations," *American Sociological Review*, 1957, vol. 22, pp. 713–719.

Struckert, Robert P.: "African Ancestry of the White American Population," *Ohio Journal of Science*, 1958, vol. 58, pp. 155–160.

Stryker, Sheldon: "Developments in 'Two Social Psychologies': Toward an Appreciation of Mutual Relevance," *Sociometry*, 1977, vol. 40, pp. 145–160.

Stryker, Sheldon: *Symbolic Interactionism: A Social Structural Version*. Menlo Park, Calif.: Benjamin/Cummings, 1980.

Sullivan, Harry Stack: *The Interpersonal Theory of Psychiatry*. New York: W. W. Norton and Company, 1953.

Sumner, William G.: *Folkways*. New York: New American Library, 1960. Originally published 1906.

Suransky, Valerie Polakow: *The Erosion of Childhood*. Chicago: University of Chicago Press, 1982.

Suter, Larry E., and Herman P. Miller: "Income Differences Between Men and Career Women," *American Journal of Sociology*, 1973, vol. 78, pp. 962–974.

Sutherland, Edwin H.: *Principles of Criminology*. Philadelphia: J. B. Lippincott, 1934.

Sutherland, Edwin H.: *White Collar Crime*. New York: Dryden, 1949.

Sutherland, Edwin H., and Donald R. Cressey: *Criminology*. 10th ed. Philadelphia: J. B. Lippincott, 1978.

Suzman, Richard M.: "The Modernization of Personality," in Gordon J. DiRenzo (ed.) *We, The People: American Character and Social Change*. Westport, Conn.: Greenwood Press, 1977.

Swift, Jonathan: *Gulliver's Travels*. 1726.

Sykes, Gresham M.: *Criminology*. New York: Harcourt Brace Jovanovich, 1978.

Syme, S. Leonard, and Lisa F. Berkman: "Social Class, Susceptibility, and Sickness," in Peter Conrad and Rochelle Kern (eds.) *The Sociology of Health and Illness*. New York: St. Martin's Press, 1981.

Taeuber, Conrad and Irene: *The Changing Population of the United States*. New York: Wiley, 1958.

Tagiuri, R.: "Social Preference and Its Perception," in R. Tagiuri and L. Petrullo (eds.) *Person Perception and Interpersonal Behavior*. Stanford, Calif.: Stanford University Press, 1958.

Tangey, June P., and Seymour Feshbach: "Children's Television-Viewing Frequency: Individual Differences and Demographic Correlates," *Personality and Social Psychology Bulletin*, 1988, vol. 14, pp. 145–158.

Tarde, Gabriel: *Laws of Imitation*. New York: Holt and Company, 1903. Originally published 1890.

Tavris, Carol, and Carole Offir: *The Longest War: Sex Differences in Perspective*. 2d ed. New York: Harcourt Brace Javonovich, 1984.

Taylor, Frederick W.: *Scientific Management*. New York: Harper, 1911.

Taylor, Howard: *The I.Q. Game*. New Brunswick, N. J.: Rutgers University Press, 1980.

Taylor, Stan: *Social Science and Revolutions*. New York: St. Martin's Press, 1984.

Taylor, V. A.: "Delivery of Emergency Medical Services in Disasters." Ph.D. diss., Ohio State University, 1977.

Teich, Albert H. (ed.): *Technology and the Future*. 4th ed. New York: St. Martin's Press, 1986.

Terhune, Kenneth W.: "From National Character to National Behavior: A Reformation," *Journal of Conflict Resolution*, 1970, vol. 14, pp. 203–263.

Terman, Lewis M., and Melita H. Oden: *The Gifted Child Grows Up*. Stanford, Calif.: Stanford University Press, 1947.

Terrace, H. S.: *Nim*. New York: Knopf/Random House, 1979.

Tetlock, Philip E.: "Cognitive Style and Political Belief Systems in the British House of Commons,"

722

*Journal of Personality and Social Psychology*, 1984, vol. 46, pp. 365–375.

Thernstrom, Stephan (ed.): *Harvard Encyclopedia of American Ethnic Groups*. Cambridge, Mass.: Harvard University Press, 1980.

Thomas, Melvin E., and Michael Hughes: "The Continuing Significance of Race: A Study of Race, Class, and Quality of Life in America, 1972–1985," *American Sociological Review*, 1986, vol. 51, pp. 830–841.

Thomas, William I.: *Source Book of Social Origins*. Boston: R. G. Badger, 1909.

Thomas, William I.: *The Unadjusted Girl*. Boston: Little, Brown, 1923.

Thomas, William I.: *Primitive Behavior*. New York: McGraw-Hill, 1937.

Thomas, William I., and Dorothy S. Thomas: *The Child in America*. New York: Alfred Knopf, 1928.

Thomas, William I., and Florian Znaniecki: *The Polish Peasant in Europe and America*. Chicago: University of Chicago Press, 1918.

Thompson, Warren S.: "Recent Trends in World Population," *American Journal of Sociology*, 1929, vol. 34, pp. 959–975.

Thompson, Warren S., and David T. Lewis: *Population Problems*. New York: McGraw-Hill, 1965.

Thomson, Randall J., and Matthew T. Zingraff: "Detecting Sentencing Disparity: Some Problems and Evidence," *American Journal of Sociology*, 1981, vol. 86, pp. 869–880.

Tittle, Charles R.: "Deterrents of Labeling," *Social Forces*, 1975, vol. 53, pp. 394–410.

Toch, Hans: *Violent Man: An Inquiry into the Psychology of Violence*. Chicago: Aldine, 1969.

Tocqueville, Alexis de: *Democracy in America*. Garden City, N. Y.: Doubleday, 1969. Originally published 1835.

Töennies, Ferdinand: *Community and Society*. East Lansing, Mich.: Michigan State University, 1957. Originally published as *Gemeinschaft und Gesellschaft*, 1877.

Toffler, Alvin: *Future Shock*. New York: Random House, 1970.

Toffler, Alvin: *The Third Wave*. New York: William Morrow and Company, 1980.

Toynbee, Arnold: *A Study of History*. London: Oxford University Press, 1972. Originally published in 12 volumes, 1934–1961.

Treiman, Donald J.: *Occupational Prestige in Comparative Perspective*. New York: Academic Press, 1977.

Treiman, Donald J., and Patricia A. Roos: "Sex and Earnings in Industrial Society: A Nine-Nation Comparison," *American Journal of Sociology*, 1983, vol. 89, pp. 612–650.

Tuddenham, R. D.: "Jean Piaget and the World of the Child," *American Psychologist*, 1966, vol. 21, pp. 207–217.

Tumin, Melvin: "Some Principles of Stratification: A Critical Review," *American Sociological Review*, 1953, vol. 18, pp. 387–394.

Tumin, Melvin M.: *Social Stratification: The Forms and Functions of Social Inequality*. 2d ed. Englewood Cliffs, N. J.: Prentice-Hall, 1985.

Turkle, Sherry: *The Second Self: Computers and the Human Spirit*. New York: Simon and Schuster, Inc., 1984.

Turner, Charles F., and Daniel C. Martinez: "Socioeconomic Achievement and the Machiavellian Personality," *Sociometry*, 1977, vol. 40, pp. 325–336.

Turner, Ralph H.: "The Real Self: From Institution to Impulse." *American Journal of Sociology*, 1975, vol. 81, pp. 989–1016.

Turner, Ralph H.: "Personality in Society: Social Psychology's Contribution to Sociology," *Social Psychological Quarterly*, 1988, vol. 51, pp. 1–10.

Turner, Ralph H., and Lewis Killian: *Collective Behavior*. Englewood Cliffs, N. J.: Prentice-Hall, 1987.

Tylor, Edward B.: *Primitive Culture*. London: John Murray, 1871.

University of California Graduate School of Education: *The American Freshman: National Norms for Fall 1975*. Los Angeles, Calif. University of California Graduate School of Education, 1975.

University of California Graduate School of Education: *The American Freshman: National Norms for Fall 1980*. Los Angeles, Calif. University of California Graduate School of Education, 1980.

University of California Graduate School of Education: *The American Freshman: National Norms for Fall 1985*. Los Angeles, Calif. University of California Graduate School of Education, 1985.

University of California Graduate School of Education: *The American Freshman: National Norms for Fall 1988*. Los Angeles, Calif. University of California Graduate School of Education, 1988.

▼ U.S. Department of Health, Education, and Welfare, *Infant Mortality Rates: Socio-Economic Factors, 1972*. Washington, D.C.: U.S. Government Printing Office, 1973.

U.S. Bureau of the Census, Table #227, "Life-time and Mean Income of Males in Current and Constant (1972) Dollars, by Years of School Completed: 1967–1972," *Statistical Abstract of the United States: 1977*. Washington, D.C.: U.S. Government Printing Office, 1977.

U.S. Bureau of the Census, *Historical Statistics of the United States. Colonial Times to 1970*. Washington, D.C.: U.S. Government Printing Office, 1975.

U.S. Bureau of the Census, *Social Indicators, III*. Washington, D.C.: U.S. Government Printing Office, 1980.

U.S. Bureau of the Census, *Statistical Abstract of the United States: 1981*. Washington, D.C.: U.S. Government Printing Office, 1981.

U.S. Bureau of the Census, *Current Population Reports*, Series P-23. "America in Transition: An Aging Society," Washington, D.C.: U.S. Government Printing Office, 1983.

U.S. Bureau of the Census, *Estimates of the Population of the United States by Age, Sex, and Race, 1980–84*. Washington, D.C.: U.S. Government Printing Office, 1985.

U.S. Bureau of the Census, *Statistical Abstract of the United States, 1985*. Washington, D.C.: U.S. Government Printing Office, 1985.

U.S. Bureau of the Census, *Statistical Abstract of the United States, 1987*. Washington, D.C.: U.S. Government Printing Office, 1987.

U.S. Bureau of Census, *Population Reports*, Series P-60, U.S. Government Printing Office, 1987.

U.S. Bureau of the Census, *Statistical Abstract of the United States, 1988*. Washington, D.C.: U.S. Government Printing Office, 1988.

U.S. Bureau of Census, *Current Population Reports*, Series P-25. Washington, D.C.: U.S: Government Printing Office, November 1971, December 1972, September 1982, May 1988.

U.S. Bureau of the Census, *Statistical Abstract of the United States, 1989*. Washington, D.C.: U.S. Government Printing Office, 1989.

U.S. Department of Justice, Bureau of Statistics, *National Crime Survey*. Washington, D.C.: U.S. Government Printing Office, 1988.

U.S. Department of Justice, Bureau of Statistics. *Special Report: Recidivism of Young Parolees*, Washington, D.C.: U.S. Government Printing Office, 1988.

U.S. Department of Justice, Federal Bureau of Investigation, *Crime in the United States. Uniform Crime Reports*. Washington, D.C.: Federal Bureau of Investigation, 1987.

Van Creveld, Martin: *Fighting Power: German and U. S. Army Performance, 1939–1945*. Westport, Conn.: Greenwood Press, 1982.

van den Berghe, Pierre L.: "Dialectic and Functionalism: Toward a Theoretical Synthesis," *American Sociological Review*, 1963, vol. 28, pp. 695–705.

van den Berghe, Pierre L.: *Man in Society: A Biosocial View*. New York: Elsevier North-Holland, 1978.

Van den Haag, Ernest: *On Punishing Criminals: Concerning an Old and Very Painful Question*. New York: Basic Books, 1975.

Vander Zanden, James: *American Minority Relations*. New York: Ronald Press, 1972.

Varenne, Hervé: *Americans Together: Structured Diversity in a Midwestern Town*. New York: Teachers College Press, 1977.

Vaughn, Ted R.: "Governmental Intervention in Social Research: Political and Ethical Dimensions in the Wichita Jury Recordings," in Gideon Sjoberg (ed.) *Ethics, Politics, and Social Research*. Cambridge, Mass.: Schenkman, 1967.

Veblen, Thorstein: *The Theory of the Leisure Class*. New York: Macmillan, 1899. Reprinted, New York: Mentor Books, 1963.

Veblen, Thorstein: *The Engineers and the Price System*. New York: Viking, 1933.

Ventimiglia, Joseph C., and Gordon J. DiRenzo: "Sociological Conceptions of Personality," *Social Behavior and Personality*, 1982, vol. 10, pp. 25–37.

Vernon, Glenn M.: *Sociology of Religion*. New York: McGraw-Hill Book Company, 1962.

Veroff, Joseph, Elizabeth Douvan, and Richard A. Kulka: *The Inner American*. New York: Basic Books, 1981.

Vontress, Clemmont E.: "The Black Male Personality," *The Black Scholar*, 1971, vol. 2, pp. 10–16.

Voslensky, Michael: *Nomenklatura: The Soviet Ruling Class*. New York: Doubleday, 1984.

Waldo, Gordon P., and Simon Dinitz: "Personality Attributes of the Criminal: An Analysis of Research Studies, 1950–1965," *Journal of Research in Crime and Delinquency*, 1967, vol. 4, pp. 185–202.

Wallach, M. A., N. Kogan, and D. J. Bem: "Group Influence on Individual Risk Taking," *Journal of Abnormal and Social Psychology*, 1962, vol. 65, pp. 75–86.

Wallerstein, Immanuel: *The Modern World-System: Capitalist Agriculture and the Origins of the European World Economy in the Sixteenth Century.* New York: Academic Press, 1974.

Wallerstein, Immanuel: *The Modern World-System II: Mercantilism and the Consolidation of the European World Economy, 1600–1750.* New York: Academic Press, 1980.

Wallerstein, Immanuel: *The Modern World-System III.* New York: Academic Press, 1988.

Wallerstein, James S., and Clement J. Wylie: "Our Law-Abiding Law-Breakers," *Probation,* 1947, vol. 25, pp. 107–112.

Walum, Laurel R.: *The Dynamics of Sex and Gender: A Sociological Perspective.* Chicago: Rand McNally, 1977.

Walsh, Doris L.: "What Women Want," *American Demographics*, 1986, vol. 8, no. 6, p. 60.

Ward, Lester F.: *Dynamic Sociology.* New York: D. Appleton and Company, 1897.

Warner, W. Lloyd, and P. S. Lunt: *The Social Life of a Modern Community.* New Haven: Yale University Press, 1941.

Warner, W. L., J. O. Low, P. S. Lunt, and L. Srole: *Yankee City.* New Haven, Conn.: Yale University Press, 1941.

Warner, W. Lloyd, Marchia Meeker, and Kenneth Eells: *Social Class in America.* New York: Harper and Row, 1960.

Watson, J. B., and R. Raynor: "Conditioned Emotional Reactions," *Journal of Experimental Psychology*, 1920, vol. 3, pp. 1–14.

Webb, Eugene J.: *Non-Reactive Measures in the Social Sciences.* Chicago: Rand McNally, 1981.

Weber, Max: *Economy and Society.* Berkeley, Calif.: University of California Press, 1978. Originally published 1922.

Weber, Max: *From Max Weber: Essays in Sociology.* H. H. Gerth and C. W. Mills (eds.) New York: Oxford University Press, 1946a.

Weber, Max: "Politics as a Vocation," in Hans H. Gerth and C. Wright Mills (eds.) *From Max Weber: Essays in Sociology.* New York: Oxford University Press, 1946b. Originally published 1919.

Weber, Max: *The Methodology of the Social Sciences.* New York: The Free Press, 1949.

Weber, Max: *The Theory of Social and Economic Organization.* New York: The Free Press, 1947. Originally published 1922.

Weber, Max: *The Protestant Ethic and the Spirit of Capitalism.* New York: Charles Scribner's Sons, 1958. Originally published 1905.

Weitzman, Lenore J., Deborah Eifler, Elizabeth Hokada, and Catherine Ross: "Sex-Role Socialization in Picture Books for Preschool Children," *American Journal of Sociology*, 1972, vol. 77, pp. 1125.

Wells, H. G.: *War of the Worlds.* New York: Harper and Brothers, 1898.

Westie, Frank: "A Technique for the Measurement of Race Attitudes," *American Sociological Review*, 1953, vol. 18, pp. 73–78.

Westoff, Charles: "Some Speculations on Marriage and Fertility," *Family Planning Perspective*, 1978, vol. 10, pp. 79–83.

Wheelis, Allen: *The Quest for Identity.* New York: W. W. Norton, 1958.

Wheelis, Allen: *How People Change.* New York: Harper, 1973a.

Wheelis, Allen: *The Moralist.* Baltimore: Penguin Books, 1973b.

White, Burton: "An Experimental Approach to the Effects of Experience on Human Behavior," in J. P. Hill (ed.) *Minnesota Symposium on Child Psychology.* Minneapolis: University of Minnesota Press, 1967.

White, Leslie A.: *The Science of Culture.* New York: Farrar, Strauss and Cudahy, 1949.

White, Leslie A.: "Definitions and Conceptions of Culture," in Gordon J. DiRenzo (ed.) *Concepts, Theory, and Explanation in the Behavioral Sciences.* New York: Random House, 1966.

Whitehead, Alfred N.: *Modes of Thought.* New York: The Macmillan Company, 1938.

Whyte, William F.: *Street Corner Society: The Social Structure of an Italian Slum.* 3d ed. Chicago: University of Chicago Press, 1981. Originally published 1943.

Whyte, William H.: *The Organization Man.* New York: Simon and Schuster, 1956.

Whyte, William H.: "The Organization Man: A

725

▼ Rejoinder," *The New York Times Magazine*, December 7, 1986, *Business World*, p. 98.

Wilder, Gita, Diane Mackie, and Joel Cooper: "Gender and Computers: Two Surveys of Computer-Related Attitudes," *Sex Roles*, 1985, vol. 13, pp. 215–228.

Wiley, Norbert: *The Marx-Weber Debate*. Newbury Park, Calif.: Sage Publications, 1987.

Williams, John E., and Deborah L. Best: *Measuring Sex Stereotypes*. Beverly Hills, Calif.: Sage Publications, 1982.

**726**  Williams, Robin M.: *American Society: A Sociological Interpretation*. 3d ed. New York: Alfred A. Knopf, 1970.

Williams, Terry, and Ted Major: *The Secret Language of Snow*. New York: Pantheon Books, 1984.

Williamson, Nancy E.: "Boys or Girls? Preferences and Sex Control," *Population Bulletin*, 33. Washington: Population Reference Bureau, 1978.

Willie, Charles V.: *The Caste and Class Controversy*. Bayside, N.Y.: General Hall, 1979.

Willis, David K.: *How Russians Really Live*. New York: St. Martin's Press, 1985.

Wilson, Edward O.: *Sociobiology: The New Synthesis*. Cambridge, Mass.: Harvard University Press, 1975.

Wilson, Edward O.: *On Human Nature*. Cambridge, Mass.: Harvard University Press, 1978.

Wilson, Edward O.: *Promethean Fire*. Cambridge, Mass.: Harvard University Press, 1983.

Wilson, Edward O.: *Biophilia: The Human Bond to Other Species*. Cambridge, Mass.: Harvard University Press, 1984.

Wilson, Everett K.: *Sociology: Rules, Roles, Relationships*. The Dorsey Press, 1971.

Wilson, James Q.: "Crime in the Streets," *The Public Interest*, Fall 1966, no. 5, pp. 26–35.

Wilson, James Q., and Richard J. Herrnstein: *Crime and Human Nature*. New York: Simon and Schuster, 1985.

Wilson, William Julius: *The Declining Significance of Race: Blacks and Changing American Institutions*. Chicago: University of Chicago Press, 1978. 2d ed., 1980.

Winn, Marie: *Children Without Childhood*. New York: Pantheon, 1983.

Wirth, Louis: "The Problem of Minority Groups," in Ralph Linton (ed.) *The Science of Man in the World Crisis*. New York: Columbia University Press, 1945.

Wooden, Kenneth: *The Children of Jonestown*. New York: McGraw-Hill Book Company, 1981.

Woodrum, Eric: "An Assessment of Japanese American Assimilation, Pluralism and Subordination," *American Journal of Sociology*, 1981, vol. 87, pp. 157–169.

*The World Factbook*. Washington, D.C.: U.S. Government Printing Office, 1988.

Wright, Erik C., David Hachen, Cynthia Costello, and Joey Sprague: "The American Class Structure," *American Sociological Review*, 1982, vol. 47, pp. 709–726.

Wrong, Dennis: "The Oversocialized Conception of Man in Modern Sociology," *American Sociological Review*, 1961, vol. 26, pp. 183–193.

Wundt, Wilhelm: *Elements of Folk Psychology*. New York: Macmillan, 1916.

Wylie, Ruth C., Erik O. Wright, David Hachen, Cynthia Costello, and Joey Sprague: *The Self Concept*. Lincoln, Neb.: University of Nebraska Press, 1979.

Yablonsky, Lewis: *The Hippie Trip*. New York: Pegasus, 1968.

Yablonsky, Lewis: *Robopaths: People as Machines*. Indianapolis: Bobbs-Merrill, 1972.

Yankelovich, Daniel: *New Rules: Searching for Self-Fulfillment in a World Turned Upside Down*. New York: Random House, 1981.

Yetman, Norman R. (ed.): *Majority and Minority: The Dynamics of Race and Ethnicity in American Life*. 4th ed. Boston: Allyn and Bacon, 1985.

Yinger, J. Milton: *Toward a Field Theory of Behavior*. New York: McGraw-Hill, 1965.

Yinger, J. Milton: *Religion, Society, and the Individual*. New York: Macmillan, 1970.

Yinger, J. Milton: "Characterological Change Among Black Americans: A Contextual Interpretation," in Gordon J. DiRenzo (ed.) *We, The People: American Character and Social Change*. Westport, Conn.: Greenwood Press, 1977.

Yinger, J. Milton: *Countercultures: The Promise and the Peril of a World Turned Upside Down*. New York: The Free Press, 1982.

Yochelson, Samuel, and Stanton E. Samenow: *The Criminal Personality*. New York: Jason Aronson, 1976.

Young, W. R., R. Goy, and C. Phoenix: "Hormones and Sexual Behavior," *Science*, 1964, vol. 143, pp. 212–218.

Zajonc, Robert B.: *Social Psychology: An Experimental Approach.* Belmont, Calif.: Wadsworth Publishing Company, 1966.

Zangwill, Israel: *The Melting Pot.* New York: Jewish Publishing Society, 1909.

Zigler, E. F., M. E. Lamb, and I. L. Child: *Socialization and Personality Development.* New York: Oxford University Press, 1982.

Zijderveld, Anton C.: *A Cultural Analysis of Our Time.* New York: Anchor Books, 1971.

Zimbardo, Philip G.: "The Human Choice: Individuation, Reason, and Order versus Deindividuation, Impulse, and Chaos," *Nebraska Symposium on Motivation*, 1970, vol. 17, pp. 237–307.

Zimbardo, Philip G.: "Pathology of Imprisonment," *Society*, 1972, vol. 9, pp. 4–8.

Zimbardo, Philip G., W. Curtis Banks, Craig Haney, and David Jaffee: "A Pirandellian Prison: The Mind is a Formidable Jailer," *The New York Times Magazine*, April 8, 1973, pp. 39–60.

Zimbardo, P. G., E. B. Ebbesen, and C. Maslach: *Influencing Attitudes and Changing Behavior.* Reading, Mass.: Addison-Wesley, 1977.

Zurcher, Louis A.: *The Mutable Self: A Self-Concept for Social Change.* Beverly Hills, Calif.: Sage Publications, 1977.

▼

**727**

# Name Index

**731**

# Subject Index

**737**

▼

743